The Dictionary of
BIRDS
in colour

BRUCE CAMPBELL

Photographs from
ARDEA PHOTOGRAPHICS
London
and Aquila Photographics
David Attenborough
Biofotos
Bruce Coleman Ltd
Nicole Duplaix-Hall
Robert Harding Associates
Bobby Tulloch

MICHAEL JOSEPH LIMITED
LONDON

First published in Great Britain by
Michael Joseph Ltd
52 Bedford Square, London WC1
1974

ISBN 0 7181 1257 1

This book was designed and produced by
Rainbird Reference Books Ltd
Marble Arch House, 44 Edgware Road
London W2, England

Assistant editor: Rachel Dunham
Designers: George Sharp and Margaret Thomas
Illustrations: Annabel Milne
Cartographer: Tom Stalker Miller

Filmset by Jolly & Barber Limited
Rugby, England

Printed in the Netherlands by
de Lange/van Leer b.v. Deventer

The Dictionary of Birds in colour

Contents

Introduction

Birds, it can be argued, might have become the highest form of life upon earth. But to defy gravity so effortlessly demanded too drastic a stream-lining and jettisoning of cerebral ballast. It was left to a small group of terrestrial mammals to evolve the only reasoning species so far capable of observing and recording all other animals and plants. But civilised man's view remains largely subjective, conceivably at fault in many respects. When an ornithological expedition was seeking a very rare bird somewhere in Africa, its leader showed a village headman the most realistic representation of the sought-for species by a western artist. After looking at it for a time in puzzlement, the headman turned the drawing upside down.

By relying on the camera's rather than the human eye, this dictionary attempts to show as objective a representation as possible of a thousand species of birds; a further number are described in text alone. Between them they constitute about an eighth of the known kinds of living birds, believed to total about 8,650, out of some 51,000 species in the subphylum of vertebrate animals, which also includes the jawless (e.g. lampreys), cartilaginous (e.g. sharks and rays) and bony fishes (e.g. herring), the amphibia (e.g. frogs and newts), reptiles (e.g. snakes, lizards, turtles, crocodiles) and mammals, of which there are only about 4,250 species. The world total of insects is about a million, with many species being discovered every year, while no one would dare compute the number of other invertebrate animals.

Birds and mammals are the only two classes of warm-blooded vertebrates, able therefore to survive in greater climatic extremes than the reptiles and amphibians; but each has evolved a numerically dominant order of species generally small in size and most successful in dense vegetation: the passerine (sparrow-like) or perching birds, numbering over 5,000 species; and the rodents with over 1,700. At the top of the numerical pyramid each class has a comparatively few large predators living on land; both have relatively few fish-eating, sea-living species; but some of these, until man's fatal influence intervened, numbered millions of individuals; the reader can amuse himself by drawing other parallels, for example between the palatable waterfowl and game-birds and the ungulate mammals.

The few thousand kinds of bird that surround us today are the relics of a vast array of predecessors, estimated at anywhere between half a million and a million and a half species. Indeed, some authorities insist that the heyday of the birds was in Pleistocene times, down to 250,000 years ago, before the Ice Ages wreaked their havoc, and that we are now witnesses of their slow decline, at least in terms of species.

All the same, birds manage to occupy or visit every part of the biosphere except the depths of ocean. An alpine chough has been recorded at 8,200 metres (nearly 27,000 feet) on Everest, and migrant birds commonly fly at up to 7,000 metres or 21,000 feet. At the other extreme, the divers or loons and the Long-tailed Duck or Oldsquaw are credited with dives down to 60 metres (200 feet) and the ability to stay under water for up to three minutes. Some seabirds spend almost their whole lives outside the breeding season in the air; indeed, frigate birds only exceptionally settle on the water. Other seabirds spend most of their time miles offshore, while the Emperor Penguin, which nests on the antarctic ice, never touches land. Few birds burrow vertically downward more than a metre or so, but laterally they may inhabit tunnels up to 4 metres in length, like those artificially made to protect the rare Bermuda Cahow from its Tropicbird nest-rival.

A geographical consideration of bird distribution might start with areas having extreme conditions, like the great mountain ranges of south-central Asia, where a variety of beautiful pheasants and allied species are found to the limits of tree growth; higher up are their more distant relatives the Snowcocks and the unique Snow Partridge, *Lerwa*. The altitudinal level of bird life falls with latitude, but another group of game birds, the ptarmigan, with their feathered feet and snow-burrowing adaptations, can survive as residents in the arctic in a quite different way to the penguins on their southern ice floes.

The deserts also support some birds, especially larks and sand-grouse, though the Sahara can be the graveyard of some of the millions of migrants that annually overfly it. Another sort of desert, the man-scape of megalopolis, has its bird inhabitants, though the disappearance of horse traffic has probably reduced the number of House or English Sparrows in city centres, and many civic bodies look askance at the Feral Pigeons which see in tall and ornamented buildings replicas of the sea cliffs and mountain crags from which their remote ancestors came.

Bird life increases progressively from the polar regions, the great deserts of the world and the huge conurbations. Sometimes it is transient, a brief but multitudinous occupation during the short northern summer of perpetual daylight when there is a chance to raise a brood quickly on the suddenly abundant plant and small animal life. The rains bring a similar situation to tropical desert fringes and savannahs, but the suburbs of temperate zone cities tend to have a more stable and resident population, rich in individuals if not in species and sure of commensal food supply from man. Perhaps one of the loudest dawn choruses, competing with the perpetual traffic, is that of many Blackbirds and fewer Song Thrushes in the parks of inner London. Central Park, New York, on the other hand, is famous for its visitors on passage.

The land masses of the world were first divided in 1858 into zoo-geographical regions by P. L. Sclater, a leading British ornithologist; today we recognise six main regions, each with a distinctive fauna of breeding birds, though receiving large numbers of winter and passage visitors from other regions. The *Palaearctic* region (sometimes regarded as a sub-region of an *Holarctic* region) covers all Europe, Mediterranean Africa and most of Asia down to the great mountain chains; in Alaska it meets the other component of the Holarctic, the *Nearctic* region, which stretches down North America to Mexico. There is a zone of blending between the Palaearctic and the *Oriental* region, which latter covers the Indian sub-continent, south-east Asia and many of its islands, to meet the *Australasian* region in another blending zone round the Celebes. Here is the famous Wallace's Line, called after the co-discoverer of natural selection, A. R. Wallace, which passes between the islands of Bali and Lombok, noted for their distinct faunas. New Zealand constitutes a sub-region of the Australian region. The *Ethiopian*, with a Madagascan sub-region, meets the Palaearctic in a broad blending zone across the Saharan and Arabian deserts. Finally, the *Neotropical* region marches with the Nearctic region in Mexico. The Antarctic and the oceanic island groups are often regarded as outside the regions.

In terms of 'richness' the regions may be placed in this order: Neotropical (with 25 indigenous families and nearly 3,000 breeding species), Ethiopian, Australasian, Oriental and Holarctic (Palaearctic and Nearctic). The last, containing the north temperate zone, is where the scientific study of nature began, with the fewest species on which to work. Paradoxically, therefore, we know at present most about the few hundred breeding birds of this great region and least about the teeming bird life of South America.

Each of these major faunal regions contains a variety of terrains, and the novice bird-watcher, in whatever part of the world he finds himself, may well prefer an ecological to a purely systematic approach when getting on terms with the birds. The two are often related: woodpeckers are found in forests or on their edges, ducks in the wetlands, and bustards on open plains or their equivalent. There is also the fascination of seeing how the different 'niches' are filled in each habitat. In woodland, for example, there is a series of horizontal layers or zones: the field, herb or ground layer; the shrub layer (sometimes more than one); the trunks and lower parts of the main branches; and the canopy or crowns of the trees. Each presents certain opportunities for birds to exploit for food, as song or display perches, roosting places, nesting sites, or the source of nest materials. In the course of time each species has claimed the niches it needs, and competition will occur only if there is, say, a

shortage of nest-sites for birds with similar requirements, or if there is only one drinking or bathing place in a pool or stream. The species in each community may be drawn from quite different groups or there may be several close relatives, like the titmice in European forests. The result is a mosaic of bird life in a mosaic of vegetation.

The Faunal Regions

1. PALAEARCTIC (with acknowledgements to R. Meinertzhagen and K. H. Voous)

The region covers that part of the Old World subjected to arctic conditions during the ice ages which ended about 10,000 years ago. Not all of it, however, was under ice and there were many centres whence bird life could recolonise as the climate improved. Today, working southward from the polar ice-cap, the main habitats are the tundra, a frozen or, in summer, largely waterlogged swamp or bog with a short season of arctic flora among the mosses and lichens; the taiga or coniferous forest zone, studded with lakes often of great size; the mixed and deciduous or broadleaved forest, originally dominating the lowlands but giving way to areas of moor and heath, to alpine mountain zones running usually from east to west; and to the savannah or steppe, now largely cultivated in western Europe and merging into desert in central Asia and elsewhere; round the Mediterranean there is the much denuded zone of aromatic scrub (macchia or maquis). The whole region is traversed by river valleys, often as in China highly cultivated, but also with riverine forest, marshes and wet grass-

Map of zoogeographical regions

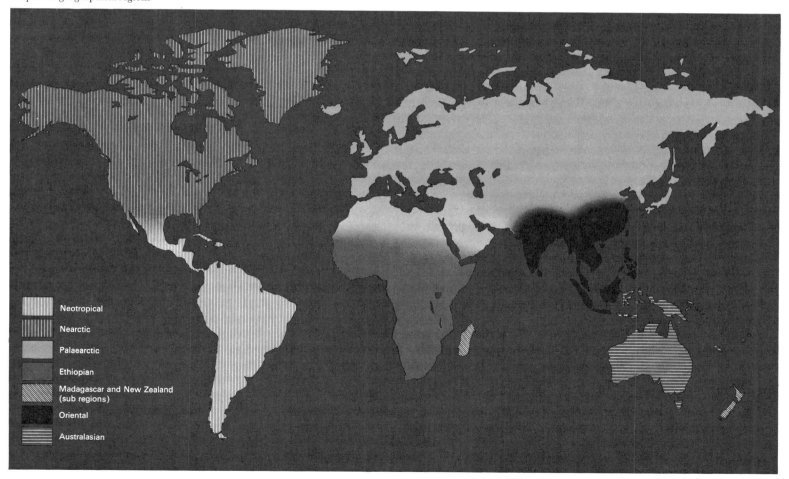

- Neotropical
- Nearctic
- Palaearctic
- Ethiopian
- Madagascar and New Zealand (sub regions)
- Oriental
- Australasian

land. The northern and western coasts are noted for their rocky islands and headlands.

The characteristic bird-life of the *tundra* is a mixture of hardy residents, ptarmigan and a few birds of prey, and an abundant temporary breeding population of waterfowl, waders, gulls and terns, a few passerine birds associated with open country like the pipits and buntings,[1] and an élite of predators. The *taiga*, on the other hand, is dominated by perching birds: seed-eating finches like the crossbills and grosbeaks, insect-eating tits and woodpeckers, and predators like the Ural and Hawk Owls. It is from the taiga, with high numbers and no food, irruptions of Crossbills, Waxwings and other species spread southward in late summer.

Transitional between tundra and taiga are zones of birch and bog where hardy warblers and other northern passerines breed alongside the waders. Southward the taiga shades into the main broadleaved forest of which oak is the characteristic tree and the acorn-eating Jay the typical bird. The bird communities are dominated by perching species, mostly song-birds *(Oscines)*, but including woodpeckers, owls, hawks and pigeons. It is this group which has spread out into the cultivated landscape of so much of the western Palaearctic, especially the great lowland stretching from France to the Urals; this is a form of steppe with its own birds, of which the Rook is a good example. Another vaster area of broad-leaved woodland once covered south-east Asia, parts of China and Japan; laughing thrushes and a variety of pheasants are typical inhabitants.

The mountain ranges rise out of the forests, with rather a sparse bird life in the west (Wallcreeper and Alpine Accentor are examples), but the great mountainous areas centred on Tibet carry a much richer fauna, typified by monal pheasants and partridges, passerines like rosefinches, redstarts, rock thrushes and choughs, and an aberrant avocet, the Ibisbill of high level lakes. At sea level the scrub woods round the Mediterranean have suffered from centuries of browsing, but are still the habitat of elusive warblers; they give way to arid areas and deserts stretching north-east to Mongolia, characterised by rock partridges, chats and wheatears, and by some penetration from the Ethiopian region.

But it is the cliffs and offshore islands of the Palaearctic with their wealth of seabirds – auks, gulls, terns, petrels and shearwaters, gannet and cormorants – that are one of the chief glories of the region, posing great problems of conservation in face of increasing pollution of the ocean.

2. NEARCTIC (with acknowledgements to Ernst Mayr)
The habitats of this region are comparable to those of the Palaearctic, with the geographical difference that the mountain ranges of North America run north and south, while those of Eurasia run mainly east and west. They therefore constitute a barrier to the advance of both plants and animals, while the American configuration allows the penetration of tongues of habitat with associated birds. Thus both tundra and taiga extend southward along the mountain ranges while the Rufous Hummingbird actually breeds northward to Alaska.

The taiga or 'Canadian conifer forest' is gradually replaced by a deciduous forest belt in areas of high rainfall, with species of oak prominent as in the Palaearctic. But the mid-west of the continent is characterised by its prairies, stretching north into Canada and merging southward with increasingly arid areas until the true desert is reached in the south-west of the region, where Mexico is substantially the broad frontier belt with the Neotropical region. The habitat pattern is variegated by the Great Lakes, by many great river systems with their associated wetlands, and by coastal cliffs and islands, especially in the far north-east and along the north-western coast.

The bird life of each major zone is characteristic, with relatively little overlap. The tundra and far northern species closely resemble those of the Palaearctic, but some, like the Snow Goose, and Canada Goose (now introduced to Europe) and several waders, are exclusively Nearctic. Three species, Great Northern Diver or Common Loon, Barrow's Goldeneye and Harlequin Duck, are found in Palaearctic Iceland and the diver, a regular winter visitor to Europe, has now bred in Scotland. Outstanding in the muskeg zone, where conifers and tundra meet, is the Whooping Crane, one of the world's rarest birds; at the other end of the size scale, many species of New World wood warblers breed in the forests. Summer visitors like the cranes and most of the breeding species, provide much excitement in spring and autumn on their passage through the bird-watching belt of the USA.

Found in a variety of habitats, the wrens are considered to be of Nearctic origin, though the Winter Wren of North America is also the Common Wren of Eurasia. Other indigenous families of the mixed or broadleaved forest belt, which as in the Palaearctic is now much diversified by cultivations and buildings, are the mocking birds or mimic thrushes, vireos and bunting-like American sparrows, which include a number of open country and even prairie and desert species. Several kinds of grouse are typical prairie birds and so are the meadowlarks, which are icterids and not larks in the Old World sense. The Roadrunner, related to the cuckoos, is an obvious inhabitant of the arid country in the south of the region.

The great ranges of the North American continent, of which the Rocky Mountains and Sierra Nevada are the most notable, and the intervening deserts and semi-deserts confine a number of species to the coastal areas of California. In the mountains to the south of the state the last remnant of the California Condor just survives; at the other extreme of size several hummingbirds occur as breeding species at high altitudes, where they may meet the all-brown Dipper that haunts the fast-flowing streams like its Old World counterpart.

The islands of the north-east Atlantic coast have much the same wealth of seabirds as throng the cliffs on the European side; but the Pacific coast boasts some distinctive auks; the nest of one, Kittlitz's Murrelet, has only quite recently been discovered high in the mountains of Alaska.

3. NEOTROPICAL (with acknowledgements to Ernst Mayr and C. C. Olrog)
Alfred Russel Wallace, quoted by Professor Mayr, described this region as 'distinguished from all the other great Zoological divisions of the globe by the small proportion of its surface covered by deserts, by the large proportion of its lowlands, and by the altogether unequalled extent and luxuriance of its tropical forests'. How long the last claim can stand, with the rapid and ruthless felling of this priceless resource, is open to question. Mayr also points out that the Andes, extending through 80° of latitude, are the greatest mountain range in the world, and the Amazon its greatest river.

These factors are reflected in a very rich but surprisingly uniform bird fauna; the lack of latitudinal barriers east of the Andes has allowed colonisation almost throughout the continent by tropical and sub-tropical species. On the other hand, the temperate zone is small in area, though it has some characteristic birds, like the little family of seedsnipe. Unique elements in South American bird life are the Hoatzin, Sun Bittern and Oilbird, and there are several very small endemic families, like the rheas and trumpeters. In contrast are the numerous hummingbirds (320 species) and such typical groups as the tinamous, puff birds, jacamars and toucans. Overshadowing these numerically are three large groupings of passerines, some 800 species strong, which dominate the sub-order Clamatores or Tyranni. This abundance reflects niches in the diversity of the tropical and sub-tropical forests, as compared with coniferous or temperate broad-leaved woodland.

But Mayr points out that few Neotropical birds have ventured into the Nearctic although, even before the Panama land bridge appeared, there were convenient island 'stepping stones'. Northern species, however, have not been slow to move south, some a very a very long time ago, like the tanagers, cardinals, honeycreepers and troupials. Then came the guans, quails, pigeons, jays and thrushes, followed by wrens, vireos, wood warblers and motmots. Most surprising are the arrivals of the holarctic Shorelark (Horned Lark) and Short-eared Owl, presumably along the Rockies and the Andes, and Mayr's view is that parrots made their way to the Nearctic by means of the Bering Straits.

Some water birds, in which the region as in all else is rich, have colonised it quite recently; other widespread groups have been established long enough to have evolved native species like the Andean torrent ducks and the peculiar Coscoroba Swan.

Most of the West Indian birds come from Central America, which has a very mixed bird fauna, but have been in the islands long enough for unique types to appear such as the family of todies and the Palm Chat. The majority of the Caribbean wild life is very much at risk today due to injudicious introductions like the mongoose, and to property development regardless of nature and amenity.

The seabird colonies of the Neotropical include the famous islands off the Peruvian coast where centuries of droppings (guano) from Guanay Cormorants produced most valuable deposits of fertiliser; there are other islands of great ornithological interest and their fauna is immortalised in R. C. Murphy's massive *Oceanic Birds of South America*, 1936. The Falkland Islands with their kelp geese also fall in the region but most important of all is the Galapagos group, some 600 miles west of Ecuador in the Pacific, where an invasion of supposedly South American finches has led to the classic model of species formation, an inspiration to every generation of zoologists since Charles Darwin first pondered their origins. The islands have other unique birds, like the Flightless Cormorant, Swallow-tailed Gull, Galapagos Albatross, and the most northerly breeding colony of penguins.

Central and South America, like Africa south of the Sahara, form a great reception area, in their case for birds breeding in the Nearctic. These include many water birds – some ducks and herons but many more almost cosmopolitan waders or shorebirds, gulls and terns – birds of prey, and millions of passerines, so that, during the northern winter, over half the bird species in the world will be represented in the Neotropical region. Nor are all its secrets given up; native species new to science are still being discovered at the rate of about one a year.

4. ETHIOPIAN (with acknowledgements to J. P. Chapin and R. E. Moreau)

The region covers Africa south of the Sahara, which forms a broad zone of blending with the Palaearctic; it includes the very important sub-regional fauna of Madagascar and the Mascarene Islands. The Ethiopian total of about 1,500 breeding species is only about half that of the Neotropical but contains great diversity and several endemic families.

R. E. Moreau emphasises a distinction within the region between the bird life of the evergreen rain forest, which covers much of Africa along the Equator, and all other habitats. There is also a considerable difference between the lowland and montane areas in both major ecological divisions of the region.

As the rain is of Atlantic origin, the equatorial forest declines eastward across the Continent. In its virgin state, with tall trunks limbless for perhaps 50 metres, it is not as hospitable a habitat as man creates by his cultivations or nature by the fall of a giant tree or the passage of a stream with consequent multiplying of the vegetation layers. The main birds of the forest floor are relatives of the game birds, thrushes and babblers; the curious 'bald crows' or rockfowl of West Africa are now considered to be 'way-out' babblers. Moreau lists many more groups in the upper layers of the forest: cuckoos, touracos, trogons, hornbills, barbets, starlings and weavers of the same family *Ploceidae* that embraces the House Sparrow. Flycatchers and warblers occur at all levels, and bulbuls in the undergrowth.

The rain forest is sandwiched between two zones characterised by a varying admixture of perennial grasses and deciduous trees, the products of a long dry season and a short wet period. Large areas of sparse leguminous *Brachystegia* woodland are found in the southern belt; at the other extreme is the savannah with only scattered trees, adapted to survive frequent burning in the dry season. The trees may form 'gallery forest' along drainage channels and, as many of them bear fruit, they are important to bird life. On the other hand the dense grass in the wet season makes penetration by birds difficult and it is not surprising that the very small *Cisticola* warblers are typical inhabitants, with seed-eating weavers of the ploceid and estrildid families. In what Moreau calls semi-arid zones the vegetation is reduced to thorny scrub and annual herbs. These zones are along the southern fringe of the Sahara, in the north-east of the region and in South-West Africa. Typical ground birds are coursers, bustards and larks.

Above about 1,700 metres or 5,000 feet there is a pronounced change in both plants and animals in what Moreau calls montane areas. These include the Cameroon Mountain in West Africa, the Abyssinian plateau and Kenya highlands, isolated peaks like Kilimanjaro (over 6,000 metres or nearly 20,000 feet high), and the central ranges of Ruwenzori and Kivu. Remarkably, several of these widely-separated mountains have many species of bird in common, even with 1,000 miles of the Congo basin between them, and must have been linked during the last ice age. (The whole question is discussed in detail in Moreau's *The Bird Faunas of Africa and its Islands*, 1966).

Although few families of birds seem to have originated in the Ethiopian region, it is notable for the unique Secretary Bird, Hamerkop, and Ostrich (since its extinction in Asia), and for the guineafowl, mousebirds or colies, touracos and wood hoopoes, while other not exclusively African groups such as barbets, shrikes and helmet shrikes are strongly represented. Though perhaps not so remarkable as in some other regions, the seabird colonies of Africa include the much studied (and threatened) Ascension Island.

Like the Neotropical region, the Ethiopian receives millions of birds during the northern winter. Moreau has calculated that about a third of all Palaearctic species, including some from north-east Asia, are winter residents and may, like the European Swallow, reach the southernmost parts of the continent.

Madagascar and the Mascarene Islands, sometimes called the Malagasy region, are full of evolutionary interest and problems. Most of Madagascar's 240,000 square miles are covered by wooded savannah, with a block of wet evergreen forest in the east and an arid south-western area; but there is little truly montane habitat. The distinctive mammals like the lemurs are well-known, but Madagascar is also the home of several small endemic bird groups: the mesites, rather like the rails or crakes, the asities, primitive perching birds, the vanga shrikes, the cuckoo rollers and the ground roller; indeed, a third of all the island's bird species are found nowhere else. Madagascar was also the home of the extinct giant Elephant Bird, while the Mascarene islands have suffered many extinctions, demonstrably at man's hands: the Dodo and the solitaires are the most famous. The Seychelles, to which much attention has been given in recent years, have not only important seabird colonies but several of the world's rarest land birds: a kestrel, *Falco area;* owl, *Otus insularis;* paradise fly-catcher, *Terpsiphone corvina;* magpie robin, *Copsychus sechellarum;* warbler, *Bebrornis sechellensis* and fody (weaver bird), *Foudia sechellarum.*

5. ORIENTAL (with acknowledgements to Salim Ali)
Much of the boundary between this and the Palaearctic is provided by the great east-west mountain chains from the Hindu Kush to the Himalaya and its eastern extensions. In the south-west the valley of the Indus and to the east the Yangtze Kiang mark the approximate limits. The large islands of Taiwan and Hainan are included and most of the groups to the south-east: Indonesia, the Philippines and Borneo. The boundary with Australasia was first defined by Wallace's line between Bali and Lombok, Borneo and Celebes. Huxley altered this to put the Philippines in Australasia, but the present line, modified from that first suggested by Weber in 1902, is farther east again. More strikingly than other inter-regional frontiers this one shows how abruptly the range of some groups can end, for example the barbets on Bali and the Australian honeyeaters and cockatoos on Lombok.

Salim Ali favours three sub-regional divisions. The 'Indo-Chinese' and 'Indo-Malayan' are predominantly areas of humid tropical and sub-tropical forest, but the first inclines both for plants and animals to the Palaearctic, the second to the Australasian. 'Indo-China' then includes the southern slopes of the Himalaya up to 3,000-4,000 metres (9,000 to 12,000 feet), grading into a montane habitat, as well as the richly vegetated mainland countries and islands to the east. 'Indo-Malaya', lying mainly 10° on either side of the equator, is almost entirely tropical and lacks both the Palaearctic links of 'Indo-China' and the Ethiopian association of the 'Indian' sub-region, which is roughly the same as the geographical sub-continent (including Ceylon), south of the Himalayan foothills. But within it Salim Ali distinguishes a 'south-western province', which is a tropical zone with resemblances to the other two sub-regions, possessing the Crimson-backed Wood-pecker, Great Hornbill and other sedentary species also found in Malaya, Burma and the eastern Himalaya 1,000 to 1,500 miles away. It has been suggested that the Himalaya was once connected by way of the Satpura Mountains and Western Ghats with Kerala and Ceylon, which has not received as many species as the mainland; vultures of the genus *Gyps* are also absent from the island.

In the larger division of the Indian sub-region are arid and near-desert areas, where species with Ethiopian connections, like the apparently extinct courser *Rhinoptilus bitorquatus,* are to be found.

The Oriental region as a whole is noted for the strong representation of the pheasant family, 42 out of 48 species; and no less than eight genera are endemic to it. These include the peacocks and argus pheasants as well as the Jungle Fowl, ancestor of all domestic breeds. Other groups like the tragopans and monals are found at higher altitudes. The Western, Blyth's and Cabot's Tragopans, Sclater's and the Chinese Monals are now great rarities, Swinhoe's and the Mikado Pheasants are confined to Taiwan; the first has been bred in captivity in Britain and birds have been released in its native habitat. Several genera of smaller birds are peculiar to the region; Salim Ali lists the *Harpactes* trogons, *Nyctiornis* bee-eaters, *Psittacus* and *Loriculus* parrots, *Acridotheres* and *Gracula* starlings and the *Pericrocotes* cuckoo-shrikes.

The Philippines have some remarkable indigenous birds, including the very rare Monkey-eating Eagle, the Great Scops Owl and several pigeons and doves. The various smaller island groups attract colonies of seabirds, with some terns of cosmopolitan range, but the region is not so noted in this respect as the other five.

Like the Neotropical and Ethiopian, the Oriental is the home of many species during the northern winter. Then the jheels of India fill with water fowl and their banks are thronged with waders. The small passerine visitors are less obvious, but leaf warblers *Phylloscopus* of which many species occur, pose field problems for the growing number of Indian ornithologists.

6. AUSTRALASIAN (with acknowledgements to D. L. Serventy and B. B. Roberts)
This region, with its far-flung sub-regions of New Zealand and Antarctica (which some authorities consider should be treated separately outwith the 'classical' six regions of Sclater), has many curious features, due to its relatively long separation geologically from the rest of the world's land masses. Also partly due to this and unlike the other three regions wholly or mainly within the southern hemisphere, it is visited by comparatively few wintering species, except by waders, from the north.

The Australian and Asian land-masses have probably been apart since the early Tertiary 60 or 70 million years ago and New Zealand from Australia even longer, if indeed they were ever connected. This means, as Dr Serventy points out, a terrestrial separation since before the evolution of modern birds. But, according to Mayr, all the indications from a study of the bird life of both regions is that the Australasian derived from the Oriental. Infiltration evidently took place over a long period by way of island links, so that the present day birds of the region show many differences from their assumed ancestors. 'The later immigrants,' writes Serventy, 'show progressively closer relationship with Palaeo-tropical (Old World Tropical) and Palaearctic forms, and most of the widespread families are represented. The process of colonisation is still going on'. But Hawaiian birds, as might be expected, appear to be both Neotropical and Australasian in origins.

Continental Australia is geographically and climatically distinct from the other main land-masses of the region. Both New Guinea and New Zealand are mountainous and forest-covered, one with tropical and the other with sub-tropical and temperate vegetation. In contrast, Australia is like a huge shallow saucer with some of the world's most extreme desert conditions at the centre, becoming progressively more benign towards the rim, where there are even some humid areas with associated forest, for example in north Queensland.

Although some have not reached Australia and others, like the flamingos, died out, most Old World groups arrived and are now fitted to the diverse habitats. Secondary differentiation has meant the emergence of some endemic families showing little trace of their affinities; among them Serventy lists the Emu and cassowaries in open country, and woodland or scrub dwellers such as the mega-podes, many parrots (including, of course, the 'budgie'), frog-mouths, lyrebirds, scrub birds, wood swallows, honeyeaters (some of which have invaded extra-regional Hawaii), bower birds, magpie larks and 'magpies'; names which typify Australia to laymen as well as to ornithologists. More recent arrivals show their relationships clearly: quails, rails, grebes, cranes, *Accipiter* hawks, king-fishers, white-eyes, crows; even the Clamorous Reed Warbler and Richard's Pipit (known locally as the Australian or New Zealand Pipit) unaltered as to species. The Cattle Egret is the newest arrival as part of a remarkable expansion that has taken it also across the Atlantic from Africa.

In spite of its notable lack of fresh water compared with other land-masses, Australia is well off for water birds, with some unusual species like the Brolga crane, Magpie Goose (which has no webs between its toes), very rare Cape Barren Goose, and the philatelic Black Swan.

New Guinea is so famous as the main home of birds of paradise that its other specialities like the cassowaries and the crowned pigeons, giants of their order, are less regarded. This is one of the few areas of the world where new discoveries are still likely.

New Zealand has suffered enormous changes in habitat during the short period of European domination, though the last moas vanished in Maori times. Much of the primeval forest has been replaced by northern hemisphere conifers and, considering the size of the country, introductions both of mammals and birds – mostly European 'garden' species – has been on a scale unequalled elsewhere in the world. Nevertheless some remarkable natives survive, of which the rediscovered flightless rail, the Takahe, is mainly known to ornithologists while the Kiwi has become the national emblem. The Kakapo or Owl Parrot is now very rare and the Huia, in which the bills of male and female were differently shaped and had different functions, is presumed extinct. It was one of the wattlebirds; these include the Saddleback and Kokako and are considered by C. A. Fleming to show the nearest approach to that adaptive radiation which makes the Galapagos finches and Hawaiian honeycreepers of outstanding evolutionary interest.

Hawaii, an oceanic group outside the region, is also the home of the Nene, another goose with poorly developed webs to its feet, and one of the very few examples of a species successfully reinforced, in its native crater habitat, by stock bred in captivity thousands of miles away.

The South Island of New Zealand is the home of great seabird colonies, including both penguins and albatrosses; so are many of the archipelagoes and small islands, which may be regarded as extra-regional. As W. H. Drury has pointed out, in contrast to the land-masses of the north temperate and arctic zones, the south temperate and subantarctic are characterised by scattered island groups, populated by relatively few species of seabird but often in enormous numbers. B. B. Roberts can claim only forty breeding species for the whole antarctic zone, all seabirds: penguins, petrels; skuas, gulls and terns; shags; and sheathbills.

Origins and Species

The sections on the great zoogeographical regions of the world have indicated summarily that certain groups of birds are believed to have originated in one region rather than another. But what does 'originate' imply and what were the ancestors of these birds? Unfortunately the avian skeleton does not survive well and the fossil record is most imperfect; but it is generally accepted that the first birds evolved from reptiles; that is to say, through many generations over vast periods of time and by the process of natural selection, transition from a scale-covered four-footed reptile to a two-footed winged and feathered bird was achieved.

The spur to evolution was the appearance of a niche or ecological place for this new creature to occupy most efficiently, and progress towards it was made by the action of minute variations in the inheritance of each generation which conferred equally minute advantages.

Fortunately, there is the vital testimony of the magpie-sized *Archaeopteryx*, which lived about 140 million years ago and of which three individual remains have been found in Jurassic limestone in Germany, one as recently as 1956. Unequivocally a bird, it yet exemplifies a sort of half way stage in the long sequence of changes. It had a long tail with twenty free vertebrae, a short sacrum with only six vertebrae, free metacarpal bones in the hand,

Archaeopteryx. An artist's reconstruction
By courtesy of the American Museum of Natural History.

with claws on the fingers, teeth with alternative socket replacement and a simple brain with a small cerebellum, control centre for muscular co-ordination. Its bird-like features were a covering of true feathers, and their arrangement as primary and secondary flight feathers or remiges on the hand and the ulna; fusion of the collar bones into a wishbone; fusion of certain small bones in the foot, which had an opposable big toe for gripping branches.

Archaeopteryx's ancestor is considered to have been one of the small Pseudosuchian group of reptiles, which flourished about 200 million years ago and whose fossils have been found in the Lower Trias both in Europe and South Africa. The suggestion is that these animals took to living in trees, feeding on insects; so sight became more important, the sense of smell less so, and this gave advantage to bigger-eyed, larger brained variations. They then began to jump from branch to branch, and this developed into gliding with the consequent evolution of wings to replace the forelegs; but *Archaeopteryx* still had to climb upwards by means of its clawed fingers, vestiges of which are found in some existing birds, notably the young of the South American Hoatzin.

Remains of some dozens of kinds of bird are claimed from the Cretaceous or Chalk system, 70 to 135 million years ago. Almost all of them are water birds, whose skeletons stood a better chance of surviving in layers of sediment. *Icthyornis*, a tern-like bird, had a fully developed keel to the breastbone, so between its appearance and that of *Archaeopteryx* the full power of flight had been evolved, though the intermediate fossil evidence may never be found. The other remarkable feature of these Cretaceous birds is that some, like *Hesperornis*, the often illustrated six-foot long diver-like bird, had already lost the power of flight again and with it the carina or keel to the sternum.

For a long time it was believed that the existing or recently extinct ratite or flat-breasted birds, like the Ostrich, Emu, moas and elephant birds, were descended from forms that never had functional wings. But there are now strong anatomical grounds for thinking that all flightless birds show a secondary evolution, having surrendered the advantages of flight for increased size and great mobility over the ground – Ostriches are in effect two-legged plains game – or because, as on many islands, even as large as New Zealand's components, there were no enemies from whom escape by flight was necessary. They had yet to reckon with man and his 'best friends'! Incidentally, loss of flight for this reason confirms the importance which modern behaviour students attach to the influence of the predator in determining the actions and even the anatomy of potential prey animals.

The Eocene or early part of the Tertiary, 40 to 70 million years ago, saw a great proliferation of new bird fossils, including the first representatives of modern families. So it is appropriate to leave the palaeological scene and discuss both how birds came to be distributed over the earth and how species, the truest biological units in nature, came to be formed.

All animals must respond to the opportunities for living (or niches) offered by an environment or face extinction; so it seems probable that the first birds evolved in an age of forests and made themselves at home in the trees, and the example of this adaptation has been given the status of a species, *Archaeopteryx lithographica*. This successful animal would then multiply and spread through the forests accessible to it as a gliding but not a flying creature. Gradually populations would become separated from each other, by mountains, plains or water and, given much time and many generations, which is essential for the operation of natural selection, these discrete populations would, through slight variations occurring in the genetic material or genes, develop different features of structure or habit. When in time they again met their now distant relatives, they would or could no longer interbreed and had become, in fact, separate species. But were the features that would turn *Archaeopteryx* from a primitive into a modern bird – the fusing of the tail vertebrae into a pygostyle which carries the tail feathers, the development of a keeled breastbone and the powerful pectoral muscles needed for flight, an increase in the size of the cerebellum – evolved by several descendent species simultaneously, or did the dispersal and species-formation just described take place later, when *Archaeopteryx* itself had evolved further? Or were there other prototypes contemporary with it, of which no fossils have come to light? Whatever the pattern, by Cretaceous times there were at least a number of contrasting kinds of bird in the world and some of them found new niches in the water and became adapted to a different way of life.

Once birds attained full flight or could swim long distances, the sort of geographical isolation needed for the evolution of new species becomes easy to envisage; the current view is that this is the only way in which bird speciation takes place and it was one of the most recent examples of this – the diversification of *Geospiza* finches in the Galapagos – that put Darwin on the track of natural selection. It is assumed that a single population of finches found its way to the archipelago and that the groups which landed on each island evolved characteristics sufficiently different for them to be ecologically and specifically distinct when they met again. Although the importance of time in evolutionary change has been stressed, small birds with a new generation each year may begin to show changes, as have the House Sparrows introduced to North America, in a little more than a century. These are at present only sub-specific, but at that rate not many millenia would be needed to see specific differences appear in the Galapagos finches.

'Darwin's finches' and the Hawaiian honeycreepers are examples of adaptive radiation from one original species. The opposite process is convergence, when species of quite different origins occupy the same niches in other parts of the world. The Old World and New World vultures and warblers are examples on the family scale. A most striking example of plumage convergence is that between the taxonomically distinct meadowlarks of American prairies and the longclaws of African near-deserts.

There are several criteria to be used when discussing how birds came to be distributed world-wide. There may be fossils which show that closely related forms have occupied the same area for millions of years. The adaptations of a group may be strongly suggestive; for example the sedentary ptarmigan with their feathered legs indicate a sub-arctic origin, just as their distant relatives, the brilliant plumaged, short-flighted pheasants, seem long adapted

to life in the forests of southern Asia. In general the occurrence of a number of closely allied species is taken to indicate the 'home' area; for example the wrens in North America, even though one has successfully invaded Eurasia. But invasions and large scale movements are constantly in progress and must have been more pronounced at periods of stress like the ice ages. On the other hand, it is clear that flightless species in general have evolved in the limited range in which each is now found, and this applies also to very small or monotypic (single species) families with no near relatives anywhere else. Conversely the origins of highly mobile groups like some of the seabirds must be largely conjectural.

Since Cretaceous times, when birds first began to flourish as a class, it is estimated that anywhere between half a million and $1\frac{1}{2}$ million species have been evolved and become extinct. The span of a species's existence seems to have become much shorter in recent times and the ice ages may have hastened the depletion of the world's birds. Today's 8,650 species are a mere handful by comparison, but they pose enough problems to keep generations of ornithologists occupied.

The Bird's Anatomy

There are a few superficial reminders that the birds of today are descended remotely from reptiles. The scales on their legs are the most obvious; their bills carry a hint of reptilian jaws and their eyes of saurian impersonality. They lay eggs, but only the megapodes show a complete lack of parental care; the young, especially of pelicans and their relatives, have an ancestral look; a few species can become torpid and at least one can hibernate.

On the other hand the many qualities which have made birds the most popular animals to study and admire in the wild are, literally and metaphorically, warm-blooded: flight, plumage, song, the devotion of a mother to her brood, the high metabolic rate which makes them normally so active and their lethargy when cold or ill so distressing. Many of these qualities depend on the evolution of feathers, the character that distinguishes the whole class from all other animals. Feathers, made entirely of keratin, are generally supposed to have evolved from scales, though no clinching connection between the two has yet been found.

Flight came with feathers and with flight came modifications of the skeleton from the reptilian and mammalian quadruped form. The body became concentrated so that its centre of gravity lies close both to the shoulder girdle, which connects the wings, and the hip girdle from which the legs depend. The pelvic bones have fused for strength, those of the shoulder have not, except the collarbones which are combined in the furcula, better known as the wishbone or merrythought.

But fusion has taken place in the vertebrae of the breast region; the breastbone or sternum, which connects the ribs in front, is now in the vast majority of birds a deep, keeled plate, protecting the lungs and providing a surface to which are attached the great pectoralis muscles that power the downbeat of the wings. Ratites like the Ostrich have lost the keel but evidence suggests that they were once able to fly, while penguins still need strong muscles to work their flippers when swimming.

The transformation of the forelimbs into wings meant that the bird's bill had to take on part of their role. To achieve this the neck has become extremely mobile and often very long compared to almost all mammals, who have only seven vertebrae in the neck against 11 to 25 among birds. The bill can therefore reach all parts of the body.

When a bird's bill is preening its other extremity, it meets a

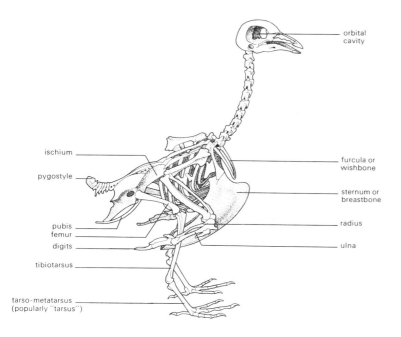

orbital
cavity

ischium

pygostyle

furcula or
wishbone

sternum or
breastbone

pubis
femur

radius

digits

ulna

tibiotarsus

tarso-metatarsus
(popularly "tarsus")

Skeleton of a pigeon

further adaptation for flight. The vertebrae in the middle of the spinal column are fused to the synsacrum, which is firmly attached to the hip girdle. But beyond it are movable tail vertebrae. These end in another fused structure, the pygostyle, which bears the tail feathers or rectrices; as their scientific name suggests, they are vital to the aerial manoeuvres of most flying birds.

A reptilian feature of the bill is that the attachment of the upper jaw or mandible to the skull allows some movement; this hinge-like character is most noticeable in parrots and ducks. Other modifications of the skull are the development of the sockets to hold the large eyes of an animal that relies on sight rather than smell. Birds that hunt other vertebrates can focus their eyes together in front as can hunting mammals like cats, dogs and man. Prey species, such as the thrushes and many small song-birds, have eyes on opposite sides of the head, like rabbits, to get the widest view of possible enemies. Birds' brains, while they do not compare in relative size or complexity with the higher mammals and have become a slang term for witlessness, are larger than those of reptiles and are housed with the eyes and ears in a very light skull. Inside the bill, which has taken many forms to suit the feeding niches occupied by birds, lies the tongue, with a bony or cartilaginous skeleton of rods. Sunbirds, hummingbirds and woodpeckers are noted for their very long tongues; some species of the last group house the supporting hyoid bones in a curve round the back of the skull, the horns even entering a nostril and travelling down it to the tip of the bill. No modern birds have teeth, though their mandibles may have serrated edges, for example to grip slippery fish. Food is broken up by the powerful muscles of the gizzard wall; seed-eaters swallow grit which assists in the crushing process.

Nostrils are normally sited in the upper mandible but are carried externally along it by one group of seabirds. Except for the ducks and the kiwis, whose nostrils open at the tip of the sensitive bill, birds are not credited with much sense of smell. Their hearing, like their eyesight, is acute.

The modified forelimb that is the wing articulates with the shoulder girdle at a ball and socket joint; the upper arm bone (humerus) is short and strong because of the flight muscles attached to it. The ulna of the forearm carries the secondary flight feathers; then comes the 'wrist', angle or carpal joint beyond which a combination of two fused 'fingers' carries the primaries. The third re-

maining digit carries the bastard wing or alula, prototype of the aeroplane's slot.

The larger bones of the wing are often 'pneumatised' or hollow and filled with air from the lungs by way of the air sacs in the body cavity. This adaptation, particularly helpful to slow-flying species, is widespread among birds. But those that dive tend to have more solid bones, and the skulls of woodpeckers, which hammer or drum on tree trunks, are also not pneumatised.

Birds, unlike flat-footed man, stand on their toes; the little metatarsal bones of the foot are fused to form the tarsus or shank and the tibiotarsus above the 'ankle joint'. The thigh bone (femur) is hidden in the body. The ankle is a strong joint simplified for walking, hopping, running and, above all, taking off into flight. Although the normal cover of the legs and feet is scales, separate or fused, a number of species are feathered down to the claws, which are similar structures to our nails. Typically birds have the first toe (hallux or thumb) directed backwards and numbers 2 to 4 in front; there is no fifth toe. Species that habitually run tend to have the hallux raised off the ground, reduced to a vestige or even absent. There are various arrangements of the toes to suit different ways of life, and this applies to the legs as a whole; swifts, divers and many seabirds cannot stand, but crouch on their shanks. At the other extreme are the cranes and storks with their elongated legs and springing dances.

The final structures to be considered in this survey of special features of the avian anatomy are the feathers. Most birds appear to be covered with them, but a number of groups have part or all of the head and neck bare. This may be an adaptation to a particular diet as with vultures and the marabou storks, or for display as with the game birds, in which the bare skin may grow colourful warty caruncles and wattles or even hanging lappets. But only a few groups have an even growth of feathers all over the body: the flightless ratites, the penguins and the toucans are the chief examples of what may be a primitive condition, though obviously of advantage to the penguins in their antarctic sea life. The normal arrangement, however, is for the feathers to grow in some eight defined tracts, leaving bare areas of skin or 'apteries' of which the brood patches used when incubating eggs are the most obvious.

Feathers grow out of the outer skin layer or epidermis and many chicks are hatched with a downy covering. This is replaced by plumage feathers which may be of several types. The vane or contour feathers make up the visible plumage; song-birds have between 1,500 and 3,000 of these, a hummingbird as few as a thousand of all types, a swan in winter, when protected by down as well, as many as 25,000. A vane feather consists of a central shaft, a continuation of the quill lodged in the skin, from which a row of barbs extends on either side, usually asymmetrically. The barbules of the barbs interlock to give the normally smooth surface. If the web is ruffled, the bird has only to run the barbs through its bill for them to join up again. Such feathers are 'pennaceous', but there are others on which the barbules do not interlock or only towards the tip and these are, like down, 'plumaceous'. True down ('plumulae'), which is abundant on ducks, geese and swans and used for nest lining, is not normally visible. Filoplumes are the curious hair-like, vaneless feathers that remain when a bird has been plucked. They too are not usually visible, except on the napes of certain song-birds, for example the bulbuls.

Bristles or vibrissae are found round the bill and gape particularly of species which hunt insects on the wing, like nightjars and flycatchers; a few birds sport them as eyelashes, notably the Ostrich, giving it a feminine aura among cartoonists, hornbills, some cuckoos and the eagle owls *Bubo*. Finally there is powder-down, found in patches and perpetually growing and breaking off into dust, which is used to clean the plumage by those birds,

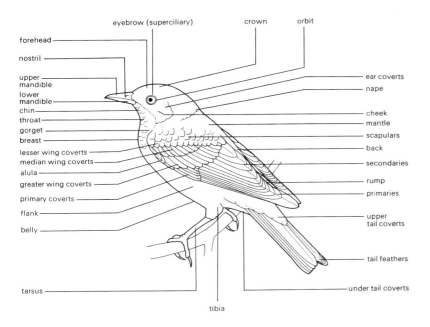

forehead
nostril
upper mandible
lower mandible
chin
throat
gorget
breast
lesser wing coverts
median wing coverts
alula
greater wing coverts
primary coverts
flank
belly
tarsus
tibia

eyebrow (superciliary) crown orbit

ear coverts
nape
cheek
mantle
scapulars
back
secondaries
rump
primaries
upper tail coverts
tail feathers
under tail coverts

External features of bird

for example, herons, toucans, parrots and wood swallows, that possess it.

It is the plumage as a whole which is the most helpful single character in recognition, not only by bird-watchers but by the members of each species; it has evolved into a remarkable complexity in which the lengths and shapes of feathers as well as their colours play a part in establishing specific identity. Feathers derive their colours either from pigment cells within their structure or by the reflection of light off their surfaces. There are two types of pigment cell, providing light and dark colours, while blues and iridescence are the results of reflected light. Well-pigmented feathers last better than others, which is suggested to be the reason for black tails and black wing-tips.

Feathers are normally changed by regular moults. Juveniles may go through a succession of immature plumages and many large birds do not attain full adult dress for five years or longer. Adults usually moult completely only once a year, after breeding, when ducks and some other groups actually become flightless (drakes, in fact, have a double moult at this time of 'eclipse'). Some changes from winter to summer plumage are effected simply by abrasion of the tips of the feathers. Feathers also bleach; this accounts for the disappearance of the delicate pink flush on the breasts of some gulls and terns. A change of diet, secretions (hormones) from glands, age, illness or injury may all cause plumage change. Variations may also be caused by excess of pigment, for example 'melanistic' (black) mutants. Complete albinism is a hereditary condition, usually eliminated in the wild by natural selection; but pied birds seem to be hardier and not only survive but transmit their condition. There are also dilute or 'leucistic' forms, where the typical plumage pattern is seen faintly beneath a creamy or sandy tint, apparently because of failure of pigmentation. Some species regularly show different colour phases, such as the light and dark plumages of the skuas which are evidently hereditary.

Birds maintain their feathers by preening with the bill, after rubbing in the preen gland above the tail. This assists in keeping the plumage waterproof and warm: it is probable that feathers were evolved first for protection rather than flight. Pockets of trapped air also help preserve the high body temperature in cold climates. Birds do not sweat; sweat would affect the set of their feathers which is so important for their survival. They cope with high temperatures by rapid panting, rather like a dog, and with cold by fluffing out their feathers to increase the volume of air trapped by them, on the principle of the string vests recommended for polar explorers.

Classification

To the layman the classification of plants and animals, though described as scientific, often appears bewildering, and enlightenment is not assisted by constant changes, both in the names of species and in the ways in which they are grouped. Taxonomy, as the science of classification is called, grew like most departments of human knowledge from small and slow beginnings; it was not until the seventeenth century that bats, grouped among the unclean fowls in Leviticus and Deuteronomy, were finally recognised as interlopers and assigned to the class of mammals.

First attempts to describe species accurately in Latin led to long phrases, for example *Lanius minor cinerascens cum macula in scapulis alba*. The great contribution of Linnaeus, the Swedish naturalist, to the biological sciences was the introduction of a binominal system under which the genus and the species became the units, and each species was identified by generic and specific names in that order. The generic name is unique in the animal kingdom, but specific names may be used many times over, though not, of course, in the same genus. Thus, in the scientific name of the Starling, the generic *Sturnus* is used for no other group of animals, but the specific *vulgaris* recurs constantly.

The species is the only 'taxon' or taxonomic unit with real biological meaning: the individuals within it recognise each other and normally interbreed; though interspecific or cross breeding does occur, it is comparatively rare and often due to unusual circumstances, the most common being captivity by man.

Species have been defined by Ernst Mayr as 'groups of actually or potentially interbreeding populations which are reproductively isolated from other such groups'. The means by which speciation is believed to be achieved among birds have already been discussed under origins and species. That the results are not always easily appreciated by man is illustrated by the Eurasian Marsh and Willow Tits, which were only realised to be distinct species in Germany in the nineteenth century; the first British Willow Tit was not identified until 1900. In spite of their close physical resemblance, they have a number of distinguishing characteristics of voice and habit; they frequently occur in the same habitats but are not known to interbreed; they are 'sympatric' species, which, after presumed separation, now occur together in the same area.

On the other hand the Carrion and Hooded Crows of Eurasia have more or less distinct geographical ranges, with only a narrow zone of overlap, in which they interbreed freely, producing fertile hybrids. A. J. Cain regards the persistence of these zones as evidence that the hybrids are not as successful as the parent stocks and that, while the two forms are now generally regarded as races of one species, they may be in process of evolving into two.

A further problem arises when two populations, similar in anatomy, appearance and habits, remain 'allopatric' and do not meet at all. Should they be regarded as distinct species? The Willow Tit again furnishes an example; for about half a century it was regarded as one species with the North American Black-capped Chickadee, until convincing evidence of differing characteristics was produced.

But the genus, equally important in the binominal system, is even more a matter of scientific opinion, which is basically subjective, than the definition of species. It was clear to Linnaeus, as it is to us, that the Fieldfare, Mistle Thrush, Redwing, Song Thrush, Ring Ousel, Blackbird and its counterpart the American Robin are closely related and merit inclusion in the same genus *Turdus*; but very many other relationships are not so obvious and so genera go on being redefined, with consequent changes to scientific names and a swinging pendulum between 'lumpers' and 'splitters'.

Controversy has also arisen over the order in which the members of a genus should be listed, another handicap of the human need to compress into linear form the three dimensional world of nature. Some authorities favour working out an order which they consider to represent the evolutionary relationship of the species; others maintain that this is usually quite arbitrary and that the only solution is to be completely so and list the birds in alphabetic order of the specific names within the genus, a system which naturally commends itself to a dictionary such as this.

The genus was Linnaeus's own invention. The ranks in his classification, which applied to both plant and animal kingdoms, were *Classis* (class), *Ordo* (order), *Genus, Species* and *Varietas* (variety), which is not the same as the subspecies or geographical race and is not used in bird nomenclature. The missing rank, now considered of great importance, is the *Familia* (family): to some extent Linnaeus's wide concept of the genus covered it.

A great deal has happened, including acceptance of the theory of evolution by natural selection, since the founding date of the binominal system, which is taken as 1st January 1758, the publication year of the tenth edition of Linnaeus's *Systema Naturae*. Less than a century later came the trinominal system which allowed the addition of a third, sub-specific or racial name to that of genus and species. The subspecies concept became very popular and not wholly for good scientific reasons. Publication of a new race gave the author immortality, since his name became attached to it; subspecies also swelled the number of bird forms which a country could claim. *The Handbook of British Birds,* published between 1938 and 1941 with H. F. Witherby as chief editor, is based on the trinominal system and has a check-list of 520 forms or about a hundred more than the bimominal or species total.

Zoological scientific names are now governed by an International Code, which lays down firm rules. Names, whatever their origins, must be in Latin form and may not contain hyphens, accents or apostrophes. The generic name has an initial capital letter; the specific name has a small (lower case) initial letter (even if derived from a proper name) and must be either an adjective agreeing in gender with the generic name, another noun in apposition, or a noun in the genitive case. Both names are normally printed in italic type.

So in the genus *Sterna* of the terns there are *Sterna sandvicensis* (adjective) the Sandwich Tern; *Sterna hirundo* (noun *hirundo* = Swallow in apposition) the Common Tern; and *Sterna dougallii* (genitive *dougallii* = of Macdougall) the Roseate Tern. Although *Hirundo* is the generic name of the Swallow, it can be properly used as the specific name of another bird. In fact, among the owls we find both *Asio otus* and *Otus asio*.

A full citation carries, after the generic and specific names, the name, often abbreviated, of the author who first conferred the specific, and sometimes the year of the publication in which he did so. If the author's name is in brackets, it means that the genus of the species has been changed since he first named it.

A specific name may be a tautonym, for example, *Troglodytes troglodytes,* the Common Wren of Eurasia, Winter Wren in North America. The type subspecies is *Troglodytes troglodytes troglodytes* (Linnaeus), which can be slightly abbreviated *Troglodytes t. troglodytes.* The subspecies the St Kilda Wren is *Troglodytes trog-*

lodytes hirtensis Seebohm, commemorating the authority who first defined it.

The Wren is a good example of the divergence between the type concept in classification and evolutionary reality. *T.t. troglodytes* is the type species of the genus, although, as has already been mentioned, the wrens almost certainly originated in America. But the European 'invader' was best known to Linnaeus, who actually called it *Motacilla troglodytes*, putting it surprisingly in the same genus as the wagtails.

There could be an enjoyable digression on the origins and meanings of the scientific names applied to birds. The vertebrates as a whole started with the advantage that a fair number of Eurasian and African animals already had classical names. But when it was clear that the ancients had lumped two species together, problems arose. Greek as well as Latin mythology was ransacked for suitable words and there was even recourse to anagrams like *Lacedo* and *Dacela* both from *Alcedo*, a kingfisher. Some specific names are aptly descriptive, like *Pernis apivorus* which records the bee-eating propensities of the Honey Buzzard, or *Numenius arquata,* referring to the bow-shaped bill of the Curlew. *Apus,* both generic and specific for the (Greek: a-pous) Swift, expresses its apparent footlessness; so does *Paradisaea apoda* for the Greater Bird of Paradise: the first skins traded to Europeans had the feet removed. But others may be wide of the mark; the Tree Sparrow *Passer montanus* is hardly a mountain bird, while *Parus palustris* for the Marsh Tit is as misleading as the English name, the bird having no particular associations with marshes.

For a long time scientific names were recognised on a supposedly strict system of priority of publication, and it became a favourite activity of desk-bound zoologists to ferret out almost forgotten authors and claim for the names they bestowed precedence over well-established ones. This involved proving that the earlier author was referring to the right species which, at a time it was quite possible for the dissimilar sexes of the same bird to be given different names, was by no means always easy to establish. Since 1961, however, it has been ruled that a name not in use for half a century or more may be 'forgotten', and it is hoped that one irritating source of name changes has been dried up.

But changes, especially in generic and higher categories, continue as views on the relationships of birds change. Originally identity and relationship rested on the morphological characters of anatomy and plumage. Now, as the study of bird behaviour develops, kinship may also emerge from related displays and habits; for example, the taxonomic connection between the sandgrouse and the doves rests largely on their common habit of sucking up water rather than sipping it. Biochemistry may also be used as evidence; the structure of protein molecules is genetically determined in the same way as anatomical structure. Therefore if a relationship between the molecules of two species can be shown, it is an argument for their evolutionary kinship. Methods of ascertaining this are complicated: the proteins in egg-white have been extensively used by C. G. Sibley, who pioneered such analyses, and his colleagues. In most cases their results have strikingly confirmed relationships based on morphology and behaviour, which makes any exceptions worth investigating further.

As a whole the class of birds is less diverse than some others, especially the mammals. To observe the fundamental relationship between an Ostrich, a duck, an owl and a thrush needs no great percipience. But for thousands of years man failed to realise that whales, deer and bats were all mammals. The effect of this on bird classification is to make for somewhat exaggerated attention to details, with the result that, as well as the basic taxa recognised under the International Code – family, genus and species – a whole hierarchy of subdivisions has been argued into existence:

Class, sub-class, super-order, order, sub-order, super-family, family, sub-family, tribe, genus, sub-genus, super-species, species and subspecies.

The sub-generic name is sometimes put in brackets between the generic and specific names, but not in this book. Hybrids between species are usually indicated thus: *Aythya ferina* × *fuligula*. Although no nominal differences are recognised below the subspecies or geographical race, there may be a gradation of populations over the distributional range; this is called a cline.

In the annotated classification of living birds which follows, the sequence of orders and families is that used by Sir Landsborough Thomson in *A New Dictionary of Birds* and is essentially that of the *Check-List of Birds of the World* by J. L. Peters and his successors. As far as any linear arrangement can, it accords with present thinking about the evolutionary relationship of birds, starting from the

most 'primitive' orders and ending with the most 'advanced' families of the huge passerine order – though the two quoted adjectives beg many questions.

The main text of the dictionary follows the alphabetical order of scientific generic names. The photographs, on the other hand, are arranged for comparative purposes in the systematic order of families; in alphabetical order of scientific generic names within each family and in alphabetical order of specific names within each genus.

All living birds fall into the sub-class Neornithes and super-order Neognathae, though some authorities separate the penguins into the super-order Impennes. This arrangement is not adopted here, so the review of orders begins with that containing the largest living bird, and one that is completely monotypic: that is, it consists of only one family, one genus and one species.

Order STRUTHIONIFORMES
(the first of the four flightless ratite Orders represented by living species; named from the flat, raft-like breast-bone)
Family 1 *Struthionidae* OSTRICHES Sexes differ
Today the family consists of a single species, divided into 5 races, which were once regarded as separate species; five fossil species are known, the oldest about 50 to 60 million years ago (early Tertiary).

Order RHEIFORMES
Family 2 *Rheidae* RHEAS Sexes alike
The family consists of 2 species, the Common Rhea or 'American Ostrich', *Rhea americana,* which is the largest American bird, and the smaller Darwin's Rhea, *Pterocnemia pennata,* with a more restricted distribution, from Patagonia to high altitudes in southern Peru. Superficially like the African Ostrich, the Rhea is smaller, has softer plumage, no tail feathers, is feathered over head, neck and thighs, has 3 toes, and relatively larger but equally useless wings, which form a mantle over the rump. Rheas live in flocks, sometimes associating with deer, in open 'campo' with patches of taller vegetation. White Common Rheas are not unusual; Darwin's Rhea has white spots on a generally brown plumage.

Order CASUARIIFORMES
Family 3 *Casuariidae* CASSOWARIES Sexes alike
Unlike the two previous ratite families, cassowaries are primarily forest dwellers, in north-eastern Australia, New Guinea, New Britain and neighbouring island groups. They are now reduced to 3 species, with numerous races: the Australian *Casuarius casuarius,* which has two colourful wattles, the One Wattled *C. unappendiculatus* and the small, wattle-less Bennett's Cassowary *C. bennettii,* both found in New Guinea. All have rough, spiky plumage, with flight feathers reduced to spines. These, with the characteristic casque (helmet), provide protection when in thick cover. Unlike ostriches and rheas, cassowaries are monogamous and the females are larger than the males.

Family 4 *Dromaiidae* EMUS Sexes alike
The only living species, *Dromadius novaehollandiae,* confined to the Australian continent, is second only to the Ostrich in size. The 3 allopatric species (i.e. evolved in isolation), on Tasmania, King Island and Kangaroo Island, were exterminated by man in the nineteenth century, and there are 3 fossil species from the Pleistocene, 15,000 to 100,000 years ago. The Emu is still widespread in open country, especially in Western Australia, running in small flocks. Emus have a similar 'hairy' plumage of two-shafted feathers to the cassowaries, but lack the spiny wing quills and casque; the head is feathered except for 2 spots.

Order APTERYGIFORMES
Family 5 *Apterygidae* KIWIS Sexes alike
Although considered by some to be related to the ex-

tinct moas, the 3 species of kiwi, also confined to New Zealand, differ from other ratites in many respects, not only in their small size and long curved bills with nostrils at the end, which suggest that, unlike most other birds, they have a developed sense of smell. There exists today 3 races of the Common or Brown Kiwi: *Apteryx australis mantelli* in North Island, *A. a. australis* in South and *A. a. lawryi* on Stewart Island. The Great Spotted *A. haasti* and Little Spotted Kiwis *A. oweni* are found in the west and south of South Island; two more species are known from Pleistocene deposits.

Order TINAMIFORMES
Family 6 *Tinamidae* TINAMOUS Sexes alike
This first 'carinate' family consists of 9 genera and up to 50 species, found in a variety of South American habitats from the pampas and lowland forest to plateaux over 10,000 ft up in the Andes. Tinamous have the same size range as game-birds (Family 35) but are not related to them; their affinities, in spite of the keeled breastbone and other features, including the possession of powder down, may be closest to the rheas; some authorities regard them as the most primitive of living birds. All species are sedentary and most of them solitary, though some form small coveys. Their flight, in spite of appropriate muscular development, is surprisingly weak; this may be connected with the relatively small heart and lungs. Shaped superficially like guineafowl (Family 36) tinamous are cryptically plumaged in browns and greys, often striped and spotted.

Order SPHENISCIFORMES
Family 7 *Spheniscidae* PENGUINS Sexes alike
The unique black and white penguins are the only carinate birds without flight feathers, but embryonic quills show that they once possessed the power of flight. Now the wing is a stiff flipper, movable only from the shoulder. Feathers cover the penguin's body like a mat, not in definite tracts, one of its many adaptations to a life at sea and often under water. The name, from the Welsh *pen gwyn* (white head) was apparently transferred from the extinct Great Auk, *Pinguinus impennis,* by seamen many years ago. But penguins are all birds of the southern hemisphere (though not necessarily of the antarctic), only one species reaching the equator at the Galapagos. The 6 genera now recognised, with the number of species in each, are: *Aptenodytes* (2 – Emperor and King Penguins); *Eudyptes* (5); *Eudyptula* (2); *Megadyptes* (1); *Pygoscelis* (3) and *Spheniscus* (4).

Order GAVIIFORMES
Family 8 *Gaviidae* DIVERS or LOONS Sexes alike
This small family of 4 species is of Holarctic distribution, nesting in the north of Eurasia and America and wintering, usually at sea, farther south. Well adapted like the penguins to an aquatic life, they have, however, retained the power of flight, though it takes an

effort to become airborne, partly because their bones are solid and not pneumatic as in most birds. Another adaptation is the housing of the legs within the body as far down as the ankle joint. This makes divers cumbersome on land, but they use their feet for swimming, unlike penguins which depend on their flippers. All the species are of 1 genus *Gavia* and are alike in their strikingly patterned summer plumages and drabber dark and white winter dress. They are noted for their wild and eerie calls.

Order PODICIPEDIFORMES
Family 9 *Podicipedidae* GREBES Sexes alike
Although alike in some respects because of their aquatic adaptations, grebes are unrelated to divers. The legs are partly housed within the body but the toes are not webbed: each has a distinct flap or lobe, as is found also in the coots, finfoots and phalaropes. The tight plumage, satiny on the breast, was once sought after by milliners. About 20 species are recognised, either in the major genus *Podiceps* or in mainly monotypic genera, mostly confined to the New World, where at least one, the Short-winged Grebe, *Centropelma micropterum* is flightless and others are not much better endowed. But some *Podiceps* grebes make migratory flights, and are found in all continents except Antarctica; some species have an almost cosmopolitan distribution. Grebes are noted for their elaborate mutual displays and for their habit of eating their own feathers (and feeding them to their young) apparently as an aid to digestion.

Order PROCELLARIIFORMES
Family 10 *Diomedeidae* ALBATROSSES
Sexes usually alike
The 'tube-noses' form an order of sea-birds, mainly inhabiting the southern oceans, and without close relatives. Their nostrils are carried in external tubes along the top or sides of the upper mandible, suggesting a well-developed sense of smell. The name 'albatross' is a corruption of the Portuguese 'alcatraz' or big sea-bird, originally applied to the pelican, and albatrosses are mostly gannet-sized birds with black and white or brown and white plumage, renowned for their mastery of gliding flight as they follow ships against the strong winds south of the Tropic of Capricorn. They seldom land on the water, though they dive to feed. They make open nests in colonies on dry land where remarkable mutual and communal displays take place. The 12 species are usually divided into the genera *Diomedea* (10) and *Phoebetria* (2 species).

Family 11 *Procellariidae* SHEARWATERS, FULMARS, LARGER PETRELS Sexes usually alike
This family of medium-sized tube-noses may be divided into some 9 genera and nearly 50 species; the majority found in the southern hemisphere but some range far to the north, of which the Atlantic Fulmar, *Fulmarus glacialis,* is the most notable, largely because of its enormous increase in the twentieth cen-

tury. Shearwaters get their names from their wave-cutting actions and they use both fast flapping and gliding flight. They come ashore only to nest, most species using burrows which they excavate, and visit mainly by night. The family may be divided into the 'true' shearwaters, the fulmars, the medium-sized *Bulweria* and *Pterodroma* petrels, the elegant prions and the monotypic Snow (*Pelagodroma*) and Cape (*Daption*) Petrels.

Family 12 *Hydrobatidae* STORM PETRELS
Sexes alike
This family, which contains the smallest sea-birds, has 22 species, divided, according to different authorities, into 2-8 genera. They are found in both hemispheres, but the 3 frigate petrels, with white on their undersides, are confined to the south. Storm petrels are active throughout 24 hours, seldom resting on the water, but picking food off it with pattering feet, or diving shallowly. They only visit their breeding colonies by night; like shearwaters, they excavate their burrows, a remarkable feat for such apparently feeble bills and legs, or nest under stones. Traditionally storm petrels follow ships, hunting zooplankton disturbed by the propellers or taking fragments of offal; seamen are believed to have given them the names petrels (little St Peters) and Mother Carey's chickens, from *Mater cara,* the divine guardian of sailors.

Family 13 *Pelecanoididae* DIVING PETRELS
Sexes alike
This small family of southern hemisphere tube-noses is quite distinct from the others because its members have adopted an underwater feeding regime like that of the auks of the northern hemisphere, and they resemble auks (Family 66) with their stout bodies, short wings and rapid, whirring flight. Five species have been described in the single genus *Pelecanoides,* of which *P. georgicus* is the most southerly, while *P. garnottii* is found up the western coast of S. America as far as northern Peru.

Order PELECANIFORMES

Family 14 *Phaethontidae* TROPICBIRDS Sexes alike
The first of 6 families in one of the oldest bird orders, probably most closely related to the tube-noses. All the families have the unique feature of webbing between all 4 toes, the hind toe moving forward to be linked with the innermost front toe. The 3 tropicbirds, found in southern waters, are the most pelagic (sea-going) in the order, spending most of their time in the air over the sea, though they swim well and habitually dive for fish close to the surface. All are distinguished by the two central tail streamers, a foot longer than the rest and supposedly the origin of the name bo'sun bird, from the bo'sun's marlinspike. The Red-tailed, *Phaethon rubricauda,* is the largest, the Red-billed, *P. aethereus,* has bars on its white plumage, and the smallest, the Yellow-billed, *P. lepturus,* has a bright orange-pink plumaged race, *P.l. fulvus,* on the Indian Ocean Christmas Island.

Family 15 *Pelecanidae* PELICANS Sexes alike
The type family of the order is characterised by the enormous gular (throat) pouch, holding more than twice the stomach capacity. All seven species (5 in the Old, 2 in the New World) are social at all seasons, nesting in large colonies in trees or on the ground; some species hunt together on the water in a crescent which closes like a splash net round the frightened fish. The Brown Pelican, however, fishes with a bent-wing dive. The Dalmatian, *Pelecanus crispus,* is primarily Eurasian; the White, *P. onocrotalus,* rare in Europe, is found in Asia and in Africa, where the Pink-backed, *P. rufescens,* is the common species. The Grey, *P. philippensis,* is the Asian pelican; *P. conspicillatus* is the Australian, while *P. erythrorhynchus,* also called 'White', and the Brown, *P. occidentalis,* are the American representatives.

Family 16 *Sulidae* GANNETS and BOOBIES
Sexes alike
This wholly marine family divides into the 3 white, black wing-tipped gannets (sometimes regarded as 1 species, or as a separate genus *Morus)* found in temperate waters, and 6 smaller *Sula* boobies, some of them predominantly brown, inhabiting the tropics. But juvenile and immature plumages are all brownish. Gannets and boobies are powerful, streamlined flying machines additionally adapted to plunge from a height on their prey which they grip between mandibles. All are colonial, nesting on rocks or in trees, and spend much of the year socially; the 'true' gannets are migratory, young birds travelling farther than adults. Gannets have no brood patches; those species laying a single egg incubate it by spreading their webbed feet over it.

Family 17 *Phalacrocoracidae* CORMORANTS and SHAGS Sexes alike
Apart from inland areas of N. America and northern Asia and the central Pacific, the 30 kinds of cormorant (shag is purely an alternative name, perhaps derived from the 'shaggy' breeding season crests; cormorant = sea crow) are found on fresh or salt water all over the world. Slightly more species inhabit the southern hemisphere and are distinguished by white undersides contrasting with dark, sheeny uppersides; the northern species tend to be dark all over. Although competent on the wing, except for the flightless *Nannopterum harrisi* of the Galapagos, cormorants are most at home in the water, jump-diving to pursue fish with such skill that they are tamed and trained for this purpose in China and Japan. Yet apparently their waterproofing is less effective than in other sea-birds, which accounts for their 'heraldic' wing-spread posture on land, though it has been suggested that this aids balance and even digestion.

Family 18 *Anhingidae* DARTERS Sexes differ
These fresh or brackish-water relatives of the cormorants (some authorities put them in the same family) may be regarded according to taxonomic taste as 1, 2 or 4 species with *Anhinga afra* inhabiting southern Africa and Madagascar; *A. melanogaster* in south-east Asia; *A. novaehollandiae* in Australia and New Guinea; and *A. anhinga,* the New World. Darters are known as anhingas (the Amazonian Indian name), snake-birds and even, in America, as water turkeys. They spend more time on land than their relatives, though they can fly well and swim with great skill to spear or grip their prey.

Family 19 *Fregatidae* FRIGATEBIRDS Sexes differ
The Frigatebirds or Man-o'-War birds are sea-birds that 'hate the sea', adapted to an almost entirely aerial existence; though they have webbed feet, their sharp claws are used to anchor them to the branches of the low trees in which they prefer to nest. Their slender, light bodies and wing spans of up to 7 ft give them the 'greatest plane surface in proportion to weight of any bird' (O. L. Austin). They feed by catching flying fish, by snapping objects off the water or young birds from sea-bird colonies, even of their own kind, and by pirating laden birds in the air like skuas (Family 63); but their waterproofing is poor and they cannot stay on the sea for long. The males are distinguished by red throat pouches which they inflate in display to attract the less spectacular females; juveniles of all species are white-headed. The 5 species, all in the genus *Fregata,* are scattered round the tropical and subtropical oceans, usually not going far from their island breeding colonies.

Order CICONIIFORMES

Family 20 *Ardeidae* HERONS, EGRETS and BITTERNS
Sexes mainly alike
This important family of long-legged wading birds consists of some 63 species in 15 genera and of worldwide distribution. Unlike other families in the order, all species have feathered heads except for the lores (area between bill and eye), vertebrae of unequal length (an adaptation for quick striking with the powerful pointed bill) causing them to fly with necks bent, and a comb-like claw to the middle toe. This is connected with the patches of powder-down, perpetually growing and disintegrating feathers; the 'powder' is used after a fishy meal to clean the plumage, which is then combed with the claw. The typical herons and egrets are notable for their long plumes in the breeding season, once commercially sought by milliners; they are mainly diurnal, but other groups, especially the night herons, are nocturnal or crepuscular. Most herons are colonial but the 2 genera of bitterns are solitary, cryptically coloured and escape attention by 'freezing' in thick vegetation; the larger species utter a 'boom' or far-carrying call in spring. The peculiar Boat-billed Heron, *Cochlearius cochlearius,* of Central and South America is put by some authorities in a separate family.

Family 21 *Balaenicipitidae* SHOEBILL Sexes alike
The single species, known as the Shoebill or Whale-headed Stork, *Balaeniceps rex,* has disputed affinities, one authority even suggesting that it belongs in the Pelecaniformes. It flies with neck bent like a heron, has a slight comb on the central claw and a pair of powder-down patches. Its distribution today is limited to parts of tropical East Africa where it is found in lakeside or riparian papyrus swamps.

Family 22 *Scopidae* HAMERKOP Sexes alike
Another monotypic African family whose only member, the Hamerkop or Hammerhead, *Scopus umbretta,* has a much wider distribution than the Shoebill, reaching from the south-west of Arabia to Madagascar, and to West Africa, where there is a dwarf race. The Hamerkop flies like a heron and has a comb-claw but no powder-down patches. It is usually considered a bird of ill-omen, which has contributed to its safety.

Family 23 *Ciconiidae* STORKS Sexes alike
The 17 species are divided into 10 or 11 genera, distributed throughout the warmer regions of the world, reaching Australia but not New Zealand. They fly with legs and neck extended, flapping and soaring; their plumage is predominantly black and white with varying areas of head and neck bare and often colourful; legs and bills are also brightly coloured. Storks lack the herons' powder-down patches and comb-claw; their rather short toes are partially webbed. Their voice-box lacks muscles and they can only produce muted calls, apart from the loud bill-rattling in the displays of some species. Although adapted to wade after fish and frogs, some storks feed largely on dry land and others eat carrion. The Palaearctic White and Black Storks, *Ciconia* species, migrate to Africa where 5 more species are found, including the largest, the Marabou, *Leptoptilus crumeniferus.* The Woolly-necked Stork, *Dissoura episcopus,* extends into Asia, where there are 4 more species, one of which reaches Australia. There are two straight-billed storks in tropical America, and the Wood Stork, *Mycteria americana,* with a curved bill; to its genus are now added 3 Old World species, formerly and confusingly in a genus *Ibis.*

Family 24 *Threskiornithidae* IBISES and SPOONBILLS
Sexes alike
There are some 25 species of ibis in about 17 genera, and 6 species of spoonbill in 2 genera. They have features in common: freshwater habitat, colonial nesting, extended legs and neck in flight, bare or partly feathered heads and necks, and partly webbed toes. The ibises have slender curved bills, while those of spoonbills are straight with uniquely spatulate tips. The curlew-sized Glossy Ibis, *Plegadis falcinellus,* is cosmopolitan in range; species of the genus *Threskiornis* are found from Africa through Asia to Australia, home of the Straw-necked Ibis, *T. spinicollis.* Five species of other genera are found in Africa, the very local Waldrapp, *Geronticus eremita,* in North Africa and the Middle East, and 4 more species in Asia. There are 7 mainly tropical New World species. The 5 Old World spoonbills form the genus *Platalea;* the only American is the beautiful and rare Roseate Spoonbill, *Ajaia ajaja.*

Family 25 *Phoenicopteridae* FLAMINGOS Sexes alike
Although placed in the stork order, flamingos may be more closely connected to the geese; sometimes they are given an order of their own. They have proportionally the longest legs and necks of any birds and stretch them in flight. Their filter mechanism is also unique: the large bent bill is held upsidedown in the water, which is strained between platelets on the lower mandible and the large tongue. Present classification allows 1 world-wide species, the Greater Flamingo, *Phoenicopterus ruber,* with 3 races: in the Old World, the West Indies (and the Galapagos) and in South America; the Lesser, *Phoeniconaias minor,* which num-

bers millions in Africa and 2 *Phoenicoparrus* species confined to high-level Andes lakes.

Order ANSERIFORMES

Family 26 *Anhimidae* SCREAMERS
Sexes more or less alike

Although superficially like game birds and soaring like birds of prey, this South American family of 3 species has closer affinities with the waterfowl, and the unique features of 2 spurs on each wing, hollow bones extending to those of the toes and wings, and an intricate system of air-sacs between skin and body. Screamers, found in pairs or small flocks, are vegetarian; they frequently perch in trees above their wet habitats and their name expresses their most obvious trait: noisiness at all seasons, night and day.

Family 27 *Anatidae* DUCKS, GEESE and SWANS
Sexes alike or very dissimilar

This large, world-wide family is subdivided into 10 tribes, 43 genera, 147 species and 247 races. The tribes are the monotypic Magpie Goose, *Anseranas*; whistling or tree ducks; swans and true geese; shelducks; dabbling ducks, e.g. genus *Anas*; pochards e.g. *Aythya*; perching ducks and geese; eiders, scoters, goldeneyes and mergansers; stiff tails. Their common features are adaptation to life in the water, relatively long necks and broad bills, body-down used to line the nest, unspotted eggs and a flightless period during moult (a few species are totally flightless). Contrasting are the swans and geese whose males and females have similar plumage and who show strong family ties, and the ducks with brightly plumaged drakes, who usually take no part in rearing the young. Owing to their amenable behaviour in captivity and high sporting value, waterfowl have been studied more thoroughly than any other non-passerine family.

Order FALCONIFORMES

Family 28 *Cathartidae* NEW WORLD VULTURES
Sexes alike

The 6 species are split between 5 genera, distributed over South and North America up to southern Canada. Superficially very like the Old World vultures in the next family, they are anatomically distinct with affinities to the storks and Pelecaniformes. Their rather weak bills are only able to tackle rotten meat, their long claws are not hooked for gripping and are partially webbed. Lacking a voice-box, they can only hiss. The 2 condors, Andean, *Vultur gryphus*, and very rare Californian, *Gymnogyps*, are about the largest living birds that fly; their extinct relative *Teratornis incredibilis* had a wingspan up to 17 ft. The most strikingly plumaged is the black and white King Vulture, *Sarcorhamphus*; the 3 smaller species include the widespread 'Turkey Buzzard', correctly Turkey Vulture.

Family 29 *Accipitridae* OLD WORLD VULTURES, EAGLES, BUZZARDS, HAWKS, KITES, HARRIERS, OSPREY
Sexes generally alike, sizes may differ

Divided into 10 subfamilies, 65 genera and over 200 species, this large family covers most of the diurnal birds of prey except the falcons, ranging from the huge soaring vultures and eagles to the swift sparrowhawks hunting by surprise, and the elegant ground-quartering harriers. Members are found throughout the world except Antarctica and in habitats of all types, though principally in forests or at least tree-clad savannahs. They are generally distinguished from the falcons by their unnotched upper mandibles and broader wings; the majority make substantial nests. There is a tendency, especially in the genus *Accipiter*, for females to be larger than males, indicating a division of duty between covering the brood and doing most of the hunting. Many have specialised habits, and the fish-eating Osprey, *Pandion haliaetus*, is often given monotypic family status.

Family 30 *Falconidae* FALCONS and CARACARAS
Sexes often differ

Three subfamilies are united by the notched upper mandible and other anatomical features. The true falcons include the large world-wide genus *Falco* and 3 tropical genera, *Spiziapteryx* (monotypic), *Poliohierax* and *Microhierax*, the smallest of all birds of prey: the

insect-eating *M. erythrogenys* is just over 6 ins long. The forest falcons *Herpetotherinae* of South America include the long-legged, rather harrier-like genus *Micrastur* and the monotypic *Herpetotheres*. The *Daptriinae* or caracaras of Central and South America consists of 4 genera of long-legged, carrion-eating and piratical buzzard-sized birds, which build their own nests, whereas the true falcons only make scrapes. Falcons are noted for their aerial mastery, striking down their prey with their talons after a lightning stoop from a height; males (tiercels) are usually smaller than females (falcons) and often show plumage differences.

Family 31 *Sagittariidae* SECRETARY BIRD
Sexes alike

This monotypic family is sometimes put in a sub-order of its own. The single species is now confined to Africa south of the Sahara, though fossils have been found in France. It is distinguished by very long legs, by a web joining the 3 front toes and by a very small hind toe.

Order GALLIFORMES

Family 32 *Megapodidae* MEGAPODES or MOUND BUILDERS Sexes alike

This curious family of 'game birds', confined to Australia and neighbouring islands to the north-east, is unique in not warming eggs or young by means of parental body heat. The 12 species now recognised are in 7 genera; the 'junglefowl' *Megacephalon* (1 species), *Eulipoa* (1) and *Megapodius* (3); the brush turkeys *Alectura* (1), *Aepypodius* (2), and *Talegalla* (3); and the monotypic Mallee Fowl, *Leipoa ocellata*. Ranging in size from small chickens to turkeys, all species have short, strong, slightly curved bills and strong legs with long toes. They fly reluctantly but some can cover long distances. Their distinguishing habit is that they lay either in warm soil or in specially built mounds of rotting vegetation, the temperature of which is controlled by the males during the long incubation period. The birds are not present when the eggs hatch at intervals, and the young, able to run in a few hours and fly within a day, look after themselves like young reptiles.

Family 33 *Cracidae* CURASSOWS, GUANS and CHACHALACAS Sexes alike or differ

This Central and South American family of tree-haunting, rather pheasant-like birds contains about 40 species in 11 genera, all sharing the characteristics of long tails, short, rounded wings and strong feet with large hind toes like the megapodes. Unlike other game birds most species build relatively small nests of sticks in trees and lay only 2 to 3 eggs. The young, fed by the parents, can fly in a few days. The curassows are the most impressive group, the males in black and white plumage with adornments to their orange or yellow bills; both sexes have erectile crests. The sexes of the smaller guans are alike; they are distinguished by bare faces. They flock outside the breeding season. The chachalacas, mostly in the genus *Ortalus*, are the smallest in size, with brownish or olive-green plumage and bare patches on the face. They are also gregarious and noisy.

Family 34 *Tetraonidae* GROUSE and PTARMIGAN
Sexes differ or alike

This North Temperate family is divided into 11 genera (4 Palaearctic, 6 Nearctic and 1, the ptarmigans *Lagopus*, Holarctic) but only 12 species. They are distinguished from other game birds by their feathered nostrils and legs feathered down to the toes in some species, others developing comb-like fringes to the toes in winter. The hind toe is raised but there is no spur. Bills are short and curved; there is a bare patch above the eyes with erectile wattles. Some species have spectacular male plumages (Capercaillie, *Tetrao urogallus*, Prairie Chicken, *Tympanuchus cupido*) associated with remarkable solitary or communal displays (e.g. the lek of the Black Grouse, *Lyrurus tetrix*) and are polygamous, the males taking no part in family life. But cock and hen ptarmigan look very much alike and are monogamous (compare ducks, swans and geese in this respect).

Family 35 *Phasianidae* PHEASANTS, PEACOCKS, PARTRIDGES, QUAIL, FRANCOLINS Sexes mainly differ

This large, predominantly Eurasian family contains about 50 genera and 170 species, showing broadly the same division as in the grouse between species with conspicuous male plumages, linked with their displays, and polygamous habits, and the duller monogamous species in which the cocks help rear the family. Males of many species carry spurs on their shanks. The only native New World group is the subfamily of American quails with 36 species. Apart from some Eurasian quails, the family is sedentary and many species, with heavy bodies and short, rounded wings, have very limited powers of flight. On the whole the Old World quails, partridges and francolins are gregarious, short-tailed and dull plumaged and inhabit open country from near desert to cultivated western Europe, whereas the pheasants (including monals and tragopans) and peacocks live in the jungles and forests of Asia, home of the Jungle Fowl, *Gallus gallus*, ancestor of all domestic chickens. The Pheasant, *Phasianus colchicus*, has been introduced for sport all over the world. The Congo Peacock, *Afropavus congensis*, only discovered in 1936, is the solitary African 'pheasant'.

Family 36 *Numididae* GUINEAFOWL Sexes alike

Seven species split between 5 genera inhabit Africa, including Madagascar and the Comoro Islands, and just extend into Arabia. They are all rather similar (except for the gay-plumaged Vulturine, *Acryllium vulturinum*), hump-backed and grey, spotted with white, with various adornments to the partially bare head, from crests to the horny helmet of *Numida meleagris* from which the domestic stock is descended. Some species carry small spurs. They normally run to avoid danger but are good fliers and roost in trees, though foraging, often gregariously, in open country. Little is known about the forest species of West Africa, the White-breasted, *Agelastes meleagrides*, and Black, *A. niger*, smallest of all guineafowl.

Family 37 *Meleagridae* TURKEYS Sexes differ

There are only 2 generically monotypic species in this exclusively American family of very large woodland game birds. The name 'turkey' seems to have arisen from confusion with the guineafowl which came to Europe from a Mohammedan ('Turkish') region. The turkeys are distinguished anatomically by a straight, slender wishbone, externally by their fanned, square-ended tail feathers and bare, carunculated (warty) heads. The Wild Turkey, *Meleagris gallopavo*, ancestor of the domestic stock, is much commoner than the Ocellated, *Agriocharis ocellata*, found in parts of Central America and has been introduced into Germany.

Family 38 *Opisthocomidae* HOATZIN Sexes alike

The monotypic Hoatzin, *Opisthocomus hoatzin* (some authorities give it an order to itself) is a primitive game bird confined to flooded riverine forests in northern South America. It has many peculiarities: food is digested not in the gizzard but in a large convoluted crop, which may be why the pectoral girdle is poorly developed and the bird is a weak flier. The bill is strongly muscled and the upper mandible articulates with the skull as in parrots. Most remarkable of all, the young carry well-developed claws on the first and second wing digits and do not fly precociously like other game birds; the claws disappear with maturity.

Order GRUIFORMES

Family 39 *Mesitornithidae* MESITES or ROATELOS
Sexes differ or alike

Remarkably little is known about this family of 3 species, confined to Madagascar; their affinities appear to be closest to the heterogeneous order which includes cranes, rails and bustards, though they are given sub-ordinal status. Mesites are about a foot long, with rather long tails, slender bills, short wings and generally brownish plumage. They prefer to run or walk on feet with the normal arrangements of toes, and at least one species may be flightless. Their unique feature is the possession of 5 powder-down patches. *Mesites unicolor* lives in rain forest to the east of Madagascar, *M. variegata* in the dry forest of the north-west, and *Monias benschi* in the dry brushlands of the south-west; it may be polyandrous, with the males incubating the eggs and rearing the young.

Family 40 *Turnicidae* HEMIPODES or BUTTONQUAILS
Sexes differ somewhat
Another curious family, with strong superficial and habit resemblances to the true quails (Family 35) and some affinities to sandgrouse and pigeons (Family 68). All are small (4 to 8 ins long), very short-tailed and round-winged, with only 3 toes and a slenderer bill than a quail's. They have no crop. The 13 or 14 species of genus *Turnix* are distributed from south-west Europe through Africa and Asia to the islands of the Far East and Australia; one migratory species is found in China and Korea. In general females are brighter than males and polyandrous; one may lay several clutches for her mates to incubate. The eggs hatch remarkably quickly and the nidifugous young are fed by the male; they go through two moults in about 10 weeks and are mature at three to four months. The Lark Quail, *Ortyxeles meiffrenii*, of tropical East African grassland comprises the other, monotypic, genus of the family.

Family 41 *Pedionomidae* PLAINS WANDERER
Sexes differ
Also called the Collared Hemipode, *Pedionomus torquatus,* is placed in a separate family from the buttonquails because it has a hind toe and lays wader-like pyriform instead of oval eggs. It also differs in habits, standing up rather then crouching in its grassland habitat in south-eastern Australia, though it will freeze rather than fly from danger. In the brighter female plumage and polyandrous habits it resembles the buttonquails.

Plains Wanderer (*Pedionomus torquatus*) ♀

Family 42 *Gruidae* CRANES Sexes alike
In contrast to the 3 preceding families are the magnificent cranes, of which 14 species, most of them threatened by extinction, are found in North America, Eurasia, Africa and Australia. Their great size (some are 5 ft tall), long legs, necks and bills, striking plumages and colourful, often partly bare heads are equalled by their fantastic courtship and group displays, for most species congregate outside the breeding season. Internally the convoluted windpipe, entering a space in the keel of the breastbone behind the collarbones, is an anatomical feature which allows cranes, especially the males, to utter loud and penetrating calls, characteristically on migration. Ten species are in the genus *Grus*: among them the 2 North Americans and the Brolga or Native Companion of Australia, *G. rubicunda*; most of the others inhabit Asia. Three species sometimes placed in monotypic genera *Tetrapteryx, Bugeranus* and *Balearica* are found in Africa; the

Demoiselle, *Anthropoides virgo*, breeds in eastern Europe and Asia.

Family 43 *Aramidae* LIMPKIN Sexes alike
Another monotypic family and genus is represented by the anatomically crane-like Limpkin, *Aramus guarauna*, though its digestive system and appearance suggest a large rail. Four races are recognised in the wide range from the south-eastern USA to central Argentina.

Family 44 *Psophiidae* TRUMPETERS Sexes alike
The 3 species, *Psophia crepitans, P. viridis* and *P. leucoptera*, are confined to South American tropical rain forests, where they live in flocks on the ground, roosting in trees. They are about the size of a domestic hen but longer-legged, with a rather chicken-like head and bill, and a pronounced hump-backed appearance due to rounded wings over a short tail. Plumage tends to be rich purplish black. The call, which gives the English name, is uttered by the males of groups of birds and is long drawn-out and far carrying.

Family 45 *Rallidae* RAILS, CRAKES, COOTS and GALLINULES Sexes may differ
The largest and most diverse family in the order is divided into 45 genera and about 120 species, an ever-reducing total due to extinctions among the largely monotypic flightless genera. Members are, however, found all over the world except in polar regions, usually in swampy habitats, and range from the small to medium-sized long-billed rails and short-billed crakes, with thin bodies, long legs and toes, generally brown plumage and unobtrusive habits but loud voices, to the conspicuous coots and gallinules, blackish or purple in colour. Gallinules or moorhens have narrow flanges of skin along their toes to assist in swimming, while coots have lobes between the joints like finfoots, grebes and phalaropes. Both groups have frontal shields extending from the bills. Short tails, soft plumage and generally weak, leg-trailing flight (though some species are migratory) are family characteristics; so is flightlessness, an adaptation to life on islands with no predators. Most species lay large clutches of eggs in substantial nests.

Family 46 *Heliornithidae* FINFOOTS or SUN GREBES
Sexes differ
Although showing affinities to several other orders, this small family of 3 monotypic genera is now considered nearest to the rails; they are distinguished by lobed toes, long thin necks and a tail pronouncedly graduated. They are aquatic, ungainly on land and reluctant to fly, feeding in riparian habitats usually surrounded by forests. The smallest, *Heliornis fulica,* is a Central and South American species and its olive-brown plumage resembles that of the Asian *Heliopais personata.* The largest, *Podica senegalensis,* with 4 races in southern and West Africa, is the most colourful. The females of each species tend to be brighter than the males.

Family 47 *Rhynochetidae* KAGU Sexes alike
The Kagu, *Rhynochetes jubatus,* represents yet another peculiar monotypic family in this diverse order; it is considered to be closest to the Sun Bittern. Confined to the mountains of New Caledonia, and nocturnal in habits, comparatively little is known about it except that its numbers give cause for anxiety.

Family 48 *Eurypygidae* SUN BITTERN Sexes alike
Another monotypic family, represented by the Sun

Bittern, *Eurypyga helias,* of Central and South America, gets its English name from its appearance in display with wings spread like an Aztec totem. It is divided into 3 races, found along the courses of rivers and in swamps among the forests.

Family 49 *Cariamidae* SERIEMAS Sexes alike
A relict South American family with 2 monotypic genera related to the large extinct carnivorous *Mesembriornis* and *Brontornis*, which may have stood 8 or 9 ft high; fossils of the massive *Diatryma*, as big as the largest moas, have been found in North America and Europe. The modern seriemas *Cariama cristata* and Burmeister's, *Chunga burmeisteri,* are about 1½ ft long, rather like small cranes with long necks, legs and bodies, but with long tails and short bills. They have rounded wings and curious tufted crests.

Family 50 *Otididae* BUSTARDS Sexes differ
This is a relatively homogeneous Old World family of 22 species in 10 to 14 genera, highly adapted to open habitats, from grassland to deserts, and ranging in size from a chicken to some of the largest flying birds, over 4 ft long and nearly 40 lbs in weight. Most species are found in Africa, but there are 6 in Eurasia and 1 in Australia. Bustards have strong legs with only 3 toes and relatively broad soles. The rather long, thick neck carries the flattened head and straight bill. The broad wings are capable of sustained flight but most species prefer to walk or run. Plumage is generally attuned to arid conditions, a medley of browns, greys and whites, but the males sport bright plumes for use in their dramatic displays. Some species are monogamous, others promiscuous.

Order CHARADRIIFORMES
Family 51 *Jacanidae* JACANAS or LILY-TROTTERS
Sexes alike, differ in size
Superficially the 7 species resemble gallinules with even longer legs and toes (the hind claw is longer than its toe), frontal shields above rather short bills and rather dark plumage. But the spurs or spikes at the bend of their wings occur also in some plovers. Females are usually larger than males, who generally look after the nidifugous young. Superbly adapted to life on the surface of tropical and subtropical waters, 3 species, *Actophilornis africana, A. albinucha* (Madagascar) and *Microparra capensis* are found in Africa, the strikingly long-tailed *Hydrophasianus chirurgus* and Bronze-winged, *Metopidius indicus* in southern Asia, the Lotus Bird, *Irediparra gallinacea* in Australia, and the variable *Jacana spinosa* in Central and South America.

Family 52 *Rostratulidae* PAINTED SNIPE
Sexes alike or differ
A curious family of 2 monotypic genera, living in marshy areas of the tropics or subtropics up to a considerable altitude. Resemblance to the true snipe is superficial; the breast bone has 2 notches on its posterior border as in the jacanas and cranes. The nostrils of the Old World *Rostratula benghalensis* lie in deep grooves on either side of the long, slightly curved upper mandible; the bill of the smaller South American *Nycticryphes semicollaris* is more curved, and flattened at the tip.

Family 53 *Oystercatchers* HAEMATOPODIDAE
Sexes alike
A world-wide family of 1 genus with from 4 to 7 species according to different views. Oystercatchers are large pied or black wading birds with brightly coloured legs, bills and eyes. The powerful, laterally compressed bill has been evolved to strike or prise open molluscs; the three-toed feet are slightly webbed, the wings long and pointed. The most widespread *Haematopus ostralegus,* with several races and black mutant forms, breeds all over Europe from Iceland to the Caspian, in the Canary Islands and South Africa, and across Asia to Australia and New Zealand, where several pied and sooty forms have been given specific status. The black *H. bachmani* and pied *H. palliatus* are North American; *H. ater* and *H. leucopodus* are South American.

Family 54 *Charadriidae* PLOVERS and LAPWINGS
Sexes mainly alike
This world-wide family of some 60 species, occupying

open habitats of all types, may be divided into the typical plovers of the genera *Pluvialis* and *Charadrius*, the lapwings *Vanellus*, and several rather aberrant and mainly monotypic genera. The true plovers are stout-bodied, short-billed rather cryptically coloured waders with long pointed wings and the hind toe absent or vestigial. A number of species have showy spring and duller winter plumages. They tend to nest in the arctic and north temperate zones and migrate far south in winter. The lapwings are based on tropical Africa but extend throughout the Old World, with 3 species in South America. They are boldly patterned, broad-winged birds, several characterised by spurs or hard knobs on their wings. The dotterels *Eudromias* are much like *Charadrius* plovers; more aberrant are *Pluvianellus socialis* of Tierra del Fuego, another South American, the sandpiper-like *Phegornis mitchellii*, which lives by high level streams and lakes, and the Wrybilled Plover, *Anarhynchus frontalis*, of New Zealand, unique among birds in having its lower bill bent to the right.

Family 55 *Scolopacidae* LONG-BILLED WADERS, SANDPIPERS Sexes usually alike

This important family of waders, nearly all breeding in the north temperate or arctic and performing long migrations, contains species from 5 ins to 2 ft long, with legs and bills of varying length and shape, but generally rather cryptic brownish plumage, paler below, though a number have a richer spring and duller winter dress. Most spend their lives, including nesting, on the ground in open habitats, and form flocks, sometimes of enormous size and remarkable co-ordination, after breeding when they move to the shoreline. The 24 genera and 70 species are grouped in 4 sub-families. The *Tringinae* include the largest waders, the curlews (8 species), and the most graceful *Tringa* sandpipers and 'shanks'. *Scolopacinae* include woodcock and snipe, which tend to be solitary and have distinctive aerial displays involving mechanical sounds. *Calidritinae* include compact, gregarious waders like the knots and dunlins, as well as the large godwits and dowitchers. *Arenariinae* contain the 2 turnstones and the Surfbird, *Aphriza virgata*, which nests in Alaska; they are sometimes put in *Charadriidae*.

Family 56 *Recurvirostridae* STILTS and AVOCETS Sexes more or less alike

A small family of distinctive long-legged, long-billed waders. The 4, predominantly pied, avocets are the Eurasian *Recurvirostra avosetta*, wintering in Africa and southern Asia, *R. americana* breeding from Texas and S. California up to southern Canada, *R. andina* con-fined to salt lakes in the Andes, and the Australian *R. novaehollandiae*. All frequent shallow, usually brackish lagoons and nest by them. So does the Stilt, *H. himantopus*, whose five races (sometimes given specific status) are more or less world-wide. The Banded Stilt, *Cladorhynchus leucocephala*, is Australian, while the aberrant Ibisbill, *Ibidorhyncha struthersii*, with short legs and decurved red bill, breeds by rivers in the plateaux of central Asia.

Family 57 *Phalaropodidae* PHALAROPES Sexes more or less alike

A group of 3 specialised waders with lobed toes and swimming habits, two making long oceanic migrations and all changing from a bright summer to a grey and white winter plumage. Some authorities put them in monotypic genera. The Red-necked, *Phalaropus* or *Lobipes lobatus*, and Grey (or Red), *P. fulicarius*, are holarctic breeders; Wilson's Phalarope, *Phalaropus* or *Steganopus tricolor*, is North American with a more southerly breeding distribution.

Family 58 *Dromadidae* CRAB PLOVER Sexes alike

A monotypic family whose only representative *Dromas ardeola* is found along the east coast of Africa and in south-west Asia. Anatomically it resembles a plover with long legs, and has partially webbed feet like an avocet but well developed hind toes.

Family 59 *Burhinidae* THICK-KNEES or STONE CURLEWS Sexes alike

Thick-knees are anatomically close to the plovers but superficially resemble bustards whose bare habitats they frequently share. Special features are the enlarged intertarsal joints, the broad head in which are set enormous yellow eyes associated with nocturnal habits, and the short, plover-like bill. Plumage is generally cryptic, though black and white wing bars show in flight. The family is split into one monotypic genus and *Burhinus* with 7 species, of which *B. oedicnemus* is the most northerly and only long-distance migrant. The African *B. vermiculatus* and *B. senegalensis* are associated with water, but *B. capensis* with dry scrub. The South American *B. bistriatus* and *B. superciliosus* and the large Australian *B. magnirostris* are grassland birds. *Esacus magnirostris*, of Asia and Australasia, is riparian and littoral in different parts of its range.

Family 60 *Glareolidae* COURSERS and PRATINCOLES Sexes alike

A family of aberrant Old World waders, anatomically alike, gregarious and with their base in Africa and

Ibisbill (*Ibidorhyncha struthersii*)

southern Asia. The subfamily *Cursoriinae* contains 9 species, alike in long legs, thin curved bills and a sandy plumage adapted to arid habitats, in which they search the distance by stretching upward on tiptoe; but they tend to crouch when alarmed and run rather than fly. There are 9 or 10 species of the genera *Cursorius* and *Rhinoptilus* in Africa and Asia, with the monotypic Australian Dotterel, *Peltohyas australis*. The Egyptian Plover, *Pluvianus aegyptius*, differs in many respects and is the bird reputed to enter the crocodile's mouth. The 7 pratincoles are well described as 'swallow plovers'; the genera *Glareolus* and *Galachrysia* have 3 species each in Eurasia and Africa, with the monotypic courser-like *Stiltia isabella* in Australia.

Family 61 *Thinocoridae* SEEDSNIPE Sexes alike

Superficially like a mixture between a bunting and a partridge, the 4 South American seedsnipe show their wader affinities in their tails, pointed wings and erratic snipe-like flight. A unique feature is the flaps covering the nostrils, possibly as a protection against flying sand. Gay's Seedsnipe, *Attagis gayi*, is migratory from its high level (up to 18,000 ft) nesting places, while the White-bellied, *A. malouinus*, is coastal, reaching the Falkland Islands. D'Orbigny's, *Thinocoris orbignyianus*, has a wide distribution and the Piping Seedsnipe, *T. rumicivorus*, is found both on the coast and inland.

Family 62 *Chionididae* SHEATHBILLS Sexes alike

The 2 species, found in South America and some subantarctic islands, are considered to be a link between waders and gulls. They are rather stout birds with short necks, bills and legs, which have vestigial webs between the front toes and a well developed hind toe. There is a spur at the bend of the wing as in some plovers, and they can swim well when necessary. The face is wattled and the name comes from the horny sheath at the base of the powerful scavenging bill; the plumage is white. *Chionis alba*, with a yellow or pinkish bill, is found in the south-west Atlantic area; the black-billed *C. minor* inhabits the Crozets, Kerguelen and other island groups.

Family 63 *Stercorariidae* SKUAS or JAEGERS Sexes alike

The 4 'pirate gulls' breed in the Holarctic and migrate far to the south, but the Great Skua, *Stercorarius* or *Catharacta skua* uniquely has a breeding population in the Antarctic as well. The Arctic, *S. parasiticus*, and Pomarine, *S. pomarinus*, have light and dark colour phases with intermediate plumages; the Long-tailed, *S. longicaudus*, smallest and most graceful of the group, is light-phased. The 3 smaller species are streamlined, with long pointed wings, short legs, webbed feet and short powerful bills, and are distinguished by the varying elongation of the central tail feathers.

Family 64 *Laridae* GULLS and TERNS Sexes alike

The 78 species have been rationalised into 4 genera of which *Larus* contains most of the gulls and *Sterna* the terns. Gulls are medium to large seabirds with shortish, often squared tails, long pointed wings, strong necks and powerful bills characterised by a projection on the lower mandible, the gonys. The 3 front toes are webbed, the hind toe small or vestigial. Adult plumage is predominantly white with grey or darker mantles and upper sides of the wings; a number of species have brown or black hoods in spring and a few are dark all over. Legs are black, yellow, red or pink, eyes brown or fiercely yellow. Gulls are coastal rather than oceanic, except for the cliff-breeding Kittiwake, *Rissa tridactyla*, and may live all or part of their lives inland; they are world-wide in littoral or fresh water habitats. Terns are 'sea swallows', elegant miniatures of the gulls, often with forked tails, narrow pointed wings and a lazy syncopated flight, as against the forceful flaps and glides of the gulls. Many species have black caps in spring and some are dark brown or grey all over. The short web-footed legs are red, yellow or black, as are the bills. Terns, summer visitors to the north temperate and arctic perform some of the longest migrations; they are also found in similar habitats to the gulls, all over the world.

Family 65 *Rynchopidae* SKIMMERS Sexes alike

These aberrant gull-terns form a single genus of 3 species, very long-winged, black and white, and are the only birds with longer lower than upper mandibles, adapted to their surface-skimming fishing: the outer part of the lower mandible has a sharp edge which fits into a groove on the upper to grasp the prey. The neck muscles and attachment of skull to neck are also specially strengthened. Skimmers live gregariously and hunt in parties at dusk or by night, resting on shores or river banks by day. The Black, *Rynchops nigra*, is American, *R. flavirostris* is African and *R. albicollis* Indian. There is some seasonal plumage change.

Family 66 *Alcidae* AUKS, GUILLEMOTS or MURRES, PUFFINS Sexes alike
The 'penguins' of the northern oceans, 3 species being holarctic, 16 confined to the North Pacific and 3 (with the recently extinct Great Auk, *Pinguinus impennis*) to the North Atlantic. Although superficially the black and white plumage and upright stance of many species and the use of the wings under water are penguin-like, these are convergent features and the auks are not so distantly related to the gulls. All surviving species propel their stout bodies in fast whirring flight and are broadly migratory over the oceans, nesting in sometimes huge colonies on cliffs and rocky islands. The bill shape varies from the stub of the Little Auk, *Plautus alle*, with its distensible pouch, to the daggers of the guillemots, the compressed razor of the Razorbill, *Alca torda*, and the ornamented parrot noses of the puffins, assumed, as are colourful head adornments, in spring. The 22 existing species are split into no less than 7 tribes and 10 to 14 genera.

Order COLUMBIFORMES
Family 67 *Pteroclidae* SANDGROUSE
Sexes differ slightly
Sandgrouse, superficially like long-tailed partridges, are closely related to the pigeons but lack the fleshy cere at the base of the bill, and have thicker skins. They are also completely terrestrial, with very short feathered legs, and are unable to run. Once on the wing they fly well, some going tens of miles to find water which they drink like pigeons with bill immersed. The family is divided into the genera *Pterocles* (14 species) and *Syrrhaptes* (2). All are gregarious and cryptically coloured (males brighter than females) and live in open, often desert country in southern Europe, Asia and Africa. Some are migratory, others irruptive like Pallas's Sandgrouse, *Syrrhaptes paradoxus*, which invaded Britain three times within half a century.

Family 68 *Columbidae* PIGEONS and DOVES
Sexes usually alike
Pigeon and dove are interchangeable names for these stout-bodied, soft-plumaged, short-legged, small-headed birds with a very strong general resemblance. The feathers are remarkably loose. The nostrils are lodged in the fleshy cere. The pointed wings are often angled in flight; some species are migratory, most are gregarious. The helpless young, hatched from usually two white eggs, are fed by regurgitation on 'pigeon's milk' made in the crop. Pigeons do not sip but suck up water when drinking. Some 255 species in 40 genera are distributed round the world in temperate and tropical zones with their centre in south-east Asia and Australia. The genera range in size from 50 species of *Columba* 'typical pigeons' and *Ptilinopus* fruit doves to a monotypic dozen. Size ranges from the little ground doves *Columbina* of America to the almost turkey-sized crested *Goura* of New Guinea.

Order PSITTACIFORMES
Family 69 *Psittacidae* PARROTS Sexes usually alike
The parrots, not closely related to any other order, are remarkably homogeneous, although ranging in size from *Micropsitta* less than 4 in long to the 40 in macaws of Central and South America. Tails vary in length and shape, but the round head and rounded hooked bill with fleshy, often feathered cere and slightly mobile upper mandible are characteristic. So is the 2 forward, 2 backward (zygodactylous) arrangement of the toes with their powerful hooked claws: alone of bird groups parrots hold up food in one foot to eat it. The plumage, often brilliant in colour, is composed of rather few, stiff feathers, with powder-down scattered among them. Their voices are loud, often raucous, but some species become celebrated mimics in captivity. Many species are tree-living but some spend most of their time on the ground and 2 are almost flightless. Parrots are primarily vegetarian and hole nesting, though the S. American Quaker Parakeet, *Myiopsitta monachus*, builds large communal nests of sticks. The 315 species are divided into about 80 genera and 6 subfamilies, of which the *Psittacinae* is by far the largest. Parrots are found all round the world in the tropics and subtropics, a few extending into the temperate zones.

Order CUCULIFORMES
Family 70 *Musophagidae* TOURACOS Sexes alike
Confined to Africa south of the Sahara, touracos are now considered most closely related to the cuckoos, though generally more brightly coloured, with long tails, rounded rather ineffective wings, mop-like or narrow crests and short, blunt bills. The outer toe can be directed either forward or backward. The nostrils vary in shape and position even in closely related species; the plumage of the head and breast lacks barbules, giving a 'hairy' appearance. But their most remarkable feature is the green turacoverdin and red turacin pigments of *Tauraco* and *Musophaga* species. Turacin, found in feathers of the head and wing, is unique to these birds and readily soluble in alkali. The 18 or 19 species of touracos, also called plantain-eaters, louries and go-away-birds, are all tree-living and their young are born with wing-claws, enabling them to clamber about the branches.

Family 71 *Cuculidae* CUCKOOS, COUCALS, ROADRUNNERS Sexes usually alike
The parasitic breeding habits for which the 47 typical cuckoos *Cuculinae* are famous are only shared by 3 South American ground cuckoos. On the whole cuckoos are slimmer than turacos, but usually with long tails and fairly powerful, slightly curved bills. Legs are short, except in the terrestrial species, and the outer toe is reversible. Wings range in length and effectiveness: some fly long migrations, and several parasitic species resemble birds of prey or their hosts. There are about 130 species in the family, in 38 genera and 6 sub-families; they are found in all continents, but the typical cuckoos, though confined to the Old World, reach New Zealand whence the migration of the Shining Cuckoo, *Chalcites lucidus*, 2,000 miles over the sea to the Solomons is one of the most remarkable undertaken by a land-bird. The non-parasitic sub-families are *Phaenicophaeinae* in Asia (including the malkohas), Africa and the Americas, the anis and guiras *Crotophaginae* in the Americas, the couas *Couinae* of Madagascar and the coucals *Centropodinae* in Africa, Asia and Australasia. The *Neomorphinae*, with 3 parasitic species, include the 2 long-legged reptile-hunting roadrunners of southern North America.

Order STRIGIFORMES
Family 72 *Tytonidae* BARN OWLS Sexes alike
Ten species are separated from the other owls on rather minor points, including the heart-shaped facial disc and long feathered legs. There is also a comb-claw on the middle toe, as in the herons and some nightjars. The Barn Owl, *Tyto alba*, is one of the most cosmopolitan birds, with 32 subspecies. The other 9 are found in Africa and Madagascar, south-east Asia and Australia, but not New Zealand; several inhabit open country and are called grass owls.

Family 73 *Strigidae* TYPICAL OWLS
Sexes usually alike
Owls range in size from that of a sparrow *(Glaucidium passerinum* is the name of the Eurasian Pygmy Owl) to the 'eagle' and horned owls *Bubo*. Superficially like diurnal birds of prey, owls are most nearly related to nightjars, but form a distinctive group with their rounded facial discs, acting like parabolic reflectors in channelling sound, and often asymmetrical ears, apparently adapted to locate sounds in all planes. The hawk-like bill with fleshy cere is sunk between the halves of the facial disc; the claws are often powerfully hooked and the legs feathered. Eyes are very large and effective in daylight, but are not capable of independent movement; instead, the neck is very flexible. The soft, subfusc plumage allows almost soundless flight, on usually broad, rounded wings, but owls are vocally masters of a wide variety of shrieks, hoots and gobbling calls. The 125 typical owls, in 25 genera, are worldwide in distribution and mostly sedentary. Principally tree-living, they include species adapted to the arctic tundra and tropical grasslands, and to hunt anything from rabbits to fish and insects.

Order CAPRIMULGIFORMES
Family 74 *Steatornithidae* OILBIRD Sexes alike
Given not only a family but a sub-order *(Steatornithes)* to itself, the Oilbird, *Steatornis caripensis*, of

Trinidad and northern South America is a unique aberrant member of the nightjar order (on present views) but with affinities to the owls. Its well-developed olfactory organ suggests that, unlike most birds, it has an active sense of smell.

Family 75 *Podargidae* FROGMOUTHS Sexes alike
These large nightjars with flattened bills and huge gapes, inhabiting southern Asia from India eastwards to New Guinea and Australia (but not New Zealand), are divided into the genera *Podargus* (3 species) and *Batrachostomus* (9). They differ from typical nightjars in many small points of anatomy and have a pair of powder-down patches on either side of the tail; *Podargus* has no oil gland, *Batrachostomus* only a small one. Frogmouths catch most of their prey in trees or on the ground after a short pouncing flight. In daytime their blending plumage and upright stance with bill pointing upward gives a remarkable illusion of a broken branch.

Family 76 *Nyctibiidae* POTOOS Sexes alike
Like the frogmouths, the 5 species of Central and South American potoos are 'broken branch' counterfeiters, not only on day perches but when incubating their single egg lodged in a crevice. They do not have the facial bristles of typical nightjars or the central comb-claw. Partly because of their nocturnal habits, little is known about most of the species, but they hunt their insect prey like traditional flycatchers, returning to a look-out perch after each sally.

Family 77 *Aegothelidae* OWLET FROGMOUTHS
Sexes alike
This single-genus family has 7 or 8 species, mostly in New Guinea but represented in the Moluccas, New Caledonia and by the 'moth owl' *Aegotheles cristata* in Australia. Only 6 to 12 ins long, owlet frogmouths are 'like tiny long-tailed owls' (O.L.Austin). Anatomically they resemble the frogmouths in several respects, but they have no powder-down and their little bills are almost hidden by stiff filoplumous feathers. They sit upright and across not along branches, and hunt nocturnally both on the wing and on the ground.

Family 78 *Caprimulgidae* NIGHTJARS and NIGHTHAWKS
Sexes differ slightly
The 70 species are divided into 18 genera and 2 sub-families, of which the *Caprimulginae*, of almost world-wide distribution, includes the typical nightjars *Caprimulgus*, mostly highly adapted to a crepuscular life, catching insects on the wing in their wide gapes fringed with bristles. Their bills are small and so are their feet, on which the middle toe has a well developed comb-claw, apparently for cleaning the rictal bristles round the gape. Plumages are soft in texture and range of colours, though males tend to have white spots on their pointed wings and long tails. During the day nightjars rest either on the ground or along branches. The males' reeling and other curious calls have given rise to names like Whip-poor-will for *Caprimulgus vociferus* and Chuck-will's-widow for *C. carolinensis*. Remarkable elongation of a flight feather on each wing is shown by the Standard-winged, *Macrodipteryx longipennis*, and Pennant-winged Nightjar *Macrodipteryx vexillarius*, of Africa; other species have long tail-feathers. The American Poor-will, *Phalaenoptilus nuttalli*, is the only bird proved to hibernate in the wild. The subfamily *Chordeilinae* is confined to the Americas; its members have no rictal bristles. They include the Common Nighthawk, *Chordeiles minor*, which has adapted in part to city life on flat roofs.

Family 79 *Apodidae* SWIFTS Sexes alike
The birds most highly adapted to a high-speed aerial life, the generally dark-coloured swifts have short, thick bones in the upper 'arm' but a long wrist with ten primary flight feathers. Their bodies are streamlined, the forked tails short and the feet small and weak, though able to grip vertical surfaces; in some species all four toes point forward. Swifts can rise off the ground unaided, move one wing slightly faster than the other, collect nest material, mate and sleep in the air, though some roost on cliffs or trees. Both adults and young become torpid in unfavourable weather when the flying insect food, which they collect in a pouch below the wide gape, is hard to get. The subfamily

Apodinae of some 17 species includes both Old and New World genera with varied nesting habits; the *Chaeturinae* contains some 48 species in Asia, Africa and America, including the spinetails *Chaetura*, whose larger species are reputed to exceed 100 mph in flight. The *Collocalia* cave swiftlets use echo-location and build the famous edible nests of saliva, which all swifts use in nest construction.

Family 80 *Hemiprocnidae* CRESTED SWIFTS
Sexes differ
The small family consists of 3 species in the genus *Hemiprocne*, ranging from India to the Solomon Islands. They are less specialised than the typical swifts, can perch on trees, and the males have patches of bright colour. They are most active at dawn and dusk. Their tiny nests, holding a single egg, are attached to the side of a branch.

Indian Crested Swift (*Hemiprocne longipennis*)

Family 81 *Trochilidae* HUMMINGBIRDS
Sexes usually differ
The 320 species, split into some 80 genera, of this New World family show an astonishing diversity of form in their bills, tongues and tails, yet in many respects are closely similar. Their inclusion with the swifts in one order is questionable, but they do show comparable features in the wings with a very short, strong upper 'arm' and long wrist and 'fingers'. The keel of the breastbone is relatively very deep and the attached muscles which drive the wings make up nearly a third of the total body weight. This power accounts for the family's mastery of controlled flight forward, hovering and even backwards. The feet are only used for perching. All this adaptation is directed towards the hummingbirds' dependence on flowers for their nectar and for the insects trapped in them, a niche shared by other insects rather than birds. The development of the skull is related to that of the woodpeckers which also have very long tongues, but those of hummingbirds are tubular at the tip. The brilliant iridescence of the plumage results from diffraction of light through feathers coloured by the basic black and rufous pigments. The greatest diversity of hummingbirds occurs in northern South America but individual species reach the tip of the Argentine and southern Alaska as summer visitors, performing a migration which seems impossible for such minute creatures.

Order COLIIFORMES
Family 82 *Coliidae* COLIES or MOUSEBIRDS
Sexes alike
This family with a single genus of 6 very similar species, confined to Ethiopian Africa (south of Sahara) is given ordinal status because of lack of close resemblance to any other group. Colies are sparrow-sized but with tapering tails sometimes twice as long as their bodies; all have crests. The short legs have a reversible outer

toe and powerful claws; the bill is short and rather finch-like; the soft, loose plumage grows all over the body not in tracts and this – together with their movements in foliage or on the ground – suggests the name 'mousebird'. Except when nesting, colies are gregarious, often flying pellmell into cover, to emerge in rapid succession. They roost together and some species hang upsidedown. They are primarily vegetarian and may do much damage to crops.

Order TROGONIFORMES
Family 83 *Trogonidae* TROGONS
Sexes usually differ
Another order with a single family and no close affinities, but with 35 to 40 species in a number of genera, some of them monotypic. Fossil remains from France, ascribed to *Archaeotrogon*, suggest that trogons were once widespread forest birds in warm climates. This would account for their present relict distribution in Central and South America (about 20 species in five genera), Ethiopian Africa (3 species) and southern Asia (11 species in one genus *Harpactes*). Essentially perching birds of rather uniform appearance, trogons are unique in being zygodactylous with the inner (second) toe pointing backwards; the forward-pointing toes are joined at the base. Bills are short and broad, with rictal bristles, adapted to take insects (and pick off fruit) on the wing. The skin holding the colourful plumage is remarkable thin. Tails are long, wings rounded and not very powerful. American and African species tend to be metallic green above with brightly coloured underparts; the Asian species, though only one is metallic, are also eye-catching, and females, though duller above, often match the males below.

Order CORACIIFORMES
Family 84 *Alcedinidae* KINGFISHERS
Sexes usually alike
Another mainly tropical and world-wide family with some 60 of its 84 species (in about 12 genera) distributed throughout south-east Asia to Australasia, including New Zealand (1 species). The subfamily *Cerylinae* includes the New World genus *Chloroceryle*; single species also nest well into the Palaearctic and Nearctic. Kingfishers, like trogons, are fairly uniform in appearance, 4 to 18 ins in length, stout-bodied, round-winged birds, usually with short tails and very long, straight, laterally compressed or sometimes broad bills, which may have been evolved first to catch insects and small vertebrates on land, the traditional plunge-fishing being a secondary adaptation. Legs are small and weak; the 2nd and 3rd toes are joined at the base, the 3rd and 4th more extensively; the first toe points backward when perching. Colours are brilliant, with iridescent greens and blues on the back of many species and females often as bright as males. Voices are loud. The majority of the family live in wooded habitats, some far from water.

Family 85 *Todidae* TODIES Sexes alike
The only family confined to the West Indies. The 5 species in the one genus *Todus* are remarkably alike, only about 4 ins long, with relatively long and broad serrated bills and rictal bristles, short tails, plumage green above and white below, with a red throat. Four inhabit lowland wet and dry forest, where they are hard to see at rest but, when catching insects in flight, their wings whirr, apparently due to an attenuated outer primary feather.

Family 86 *Momotidae* MOTMOTS Sexes alike
Another New World family, the 6 genera (4 monotypic) and 8 species being confined to the mainland of tropical Central and South America. Ranging from about 6 to 20 ins in total length, motmots are notable for their broad, curved and serrated bills, beautiful variegated plumage and long graduated tails. The two central feathers of several species lose their barbs for part of their length, leaving racquet-shaped tips, which are swung from side to side when perching. Their toes are arranged like those of kingfishers. Primarily forest birds, they take large insects, small reptiles, snails and even fruit, beating their bigger victims on the perch before swallowing them.

Family 87 *Meropidae* BEE-EATERS
Sexes much alike
An Old World family of 24 species, divided into 7 genera, 3 of them monotypic. Although related to the kingfishers and having similar rather small legs and feet with syndactylous (joined) toes, which are also effective for burrowing nest-holes (like kingfishers and motmots), their wings are relatively longer and adapted for flight after aerial insects; tails are long, sometimes with elongated central feathers and sometimes forked. Their colours are among the most brilliant of all birds, with greens predominating, and their gregarious habits create beautiful mass effects. Four genera and 18 species are found only in Africa, 2 genera and 6 species only in Asia. The Rainbow Bird, *Merops ornatus*, is native to Australia; its genus of 9 species is the most widespread, including *M. apiaster* which has nested in Britain.

Cuckoo Roller
(*Leptosomus discolor*) ♂

Family 88 *Leptosomatidae* CUCKOO ROLLER
Sexes differ
A monotypic family and genus, the only species, *Leptosomus discolor*, being confined to the forests and bush of Madagascar and the Comoro Islands. Uniquely among coraciids it has a pair of powder-down patches on the rump. In most respects its habits, as far as known, resemble those of the true and ground rollers.

Family 89 *Coraciidae* ROLLERS and GROUND ROLLERS
Sexes alike
This Old World family gets its name from the aerial antics during courtship of males in the genus *Coracias*, which has 7 species, mainly in Africa, but including the European, *C. garrulus*, and Indian 'Blue Jay', *C. benghalensis*. Rollers are jay-sized, mainly blue, green and chestnut in colour, with large heads, strong legs (toes syndactylous), bills and wings. On the ground they hop, but spend most of their hunting time perched, watching for prey to drop on. The 4 *Eurystomus* species are broad-billed and do not roll but swoop in display. They are found in Africa (2 species) and Madagascar (1), while the Broad-mouthed Dollarbird, *E. orientalis*, ranges over Asia to Manchuria, the Solomon Islands and Australia. The 5 aberrant ground rollers of the subfamily *Brachypteraciinae* are found in Madagascar, divided into 3 genera. They are brightly coloured and stout-bodied birds about a foot to 1½ ft long, notable for larger heads, eyes and bills; 4 species inhabit rain forest, the 5th, the monotypic *Uratelornis chimaera*, is a desert bird.

Family 90 *Upupidae* HOOPOE Sexes alike
Now regarded as monotypic, *Upupa epops*, the 'lapwing' of the Old Testament, is found in the Palaearctic, much of Africa including Madagascar, India and the larger islands of south-east Asia. The northern population is migratory. The long, curved bill contains rather a short tongue; the shank is short, but the toes long, the

3rd and 4th being joined at the base. The scientific and English names are onomatopaeic, from the male's whooping call in spring.

Family 91 *Phoeniculidae* WOOD HOOPOES
Sexes alike
The 6 species are divided into 3 genera, all confined to Ethiopian Africa. They are slimmer than the typical Hoopoe and crestless. The bill is shortest and least curved in the genus *Scoptelus,* largest and gently curved in *Phoeniculus,* sharply curved in *Rhinopomastes,* apparently all adaptations for probing tree trunks. The long graduated tail of 10 feathers is notable; wings are rounded, some with a conspicuous white bar and mainly blue and green plumage is attractive though not brilliant. Wood Hoopoes are found in savannah country or in clearings, rather than in continuous forest.

Family 92 *Bucerotidae* HORNBILLS
Sexes generally alike
The largest birds of the order are found in this remarkable family, which may be divided into the *Bucoracinae,* containing only the 2 species of African ground hornbills *Bucorus,* and the *Bucerotinae* with the other 43 species, found in Ethiopian Africa, India and south-east Asia as far as New Guinea (but not Australia). Hornbills show the coraciiform united 2nd, 3rd and 4th toes, with a free hind toe on their broad-soled feet, but in many other respects they are unique. Most remarkable is the cumbrous, varyingly shaped casque or helmet (usually hollow or 'spongy' with small cells) which surmounts the curved, serrated and often grooved bill. The eyelashes are also an unusual feature. Plumages are mostly in shades of black, brown and white; the wings of the larger species make a loud noise in flight because the bases of the flight feathers are not overlaid by wing-coverts. Hornbills have a range of loud and even frightening calls. But their outstanding trait (not shown by the ground hornbills) is the walling up in her tree-hole of the nesting female, during incubation and part of the nestling period. She is fed through a small aperture by the male. After she breaks out, the young may wall themselves in again until ready to fly.

Order PICIFORMES

Family 93 *Galbulidae* JACAMARS
Sexes differ slightly
A tropical American family of some 15 species in 5 genera, ranging up to a foot in length, with long tails, slender bodies, very long curved bills, the whole suggesting an outsize hummingbird or Old World bee-eater: they prey on insects up to large butterflies in size. Four-toed species are zygodactylous but the genus *Jacamaralcyon* has only 3, the inner hind toes being absent. Jacamars are noisy, and conspicuous as they sally out from their perches. They are found mainly at the forest edge and, like many birds in this and related orders, they excavate nest-holes in the ground. Alone among picarian birds, the young are not naked when hatched but clad in long down.

Family 94 *Bucconidae* PUFFBIRDS Sexes alike
Another tropical American family of forest habitats, in spite of appearances closely related to the jacamars. Some 30 species are split into 10 genera. Puffbirds are small ($5\frac{1}{2}$ to $10\frac{1}{2}$ ins long) rather short-tailed and big-headed with full, usually rather dull-coloured plumage which is fluffed out to earn the English name. Toes are zygodactylous and bills shortish and stout, slightly curved to a hooked tip. Puffbirds sally like jacamars from a perch after insects, taking on the whole smaller types. They are notably silent for forest birds, flicking their tails laterally when uttering their rather feeble calls. Most are therefore inconspicuous, but the Swallow-wing, *Chelidoptera tenebrosa,* has longer wings than its relatives and makes long flights after insects from the tops of riverside trees, according to A. F. Skutch, one of the few ornithologists who have studied the family.

Family 95 *Capitonidae* BARBETS
Sexes alike or differ
The distribution of this essentially tropical forest family resembles that of the trogons (Family 83). Nearly 40 out of the 72 to 76 species are found in Africa, 23 are Asian and about 12 inhabit tropical America. Ranging in size from $3\frac{1}{2}$ ins to a foot, barbets are stout-bodied, large-headed little birds with the zygodactylous toe arrangement of the order, and strong conical bills surrounded by rictal bristles or feathers, giving a bearded appearance, hence the English name. Tails are not accentuated, the rounded wings are used only for short flights: all species are sedentary. Plumage is often variegated and in some Asian barbets brilliant. Barbets are noted for their monotonous songs, often uttered for long spells from one perch; the Asian *Megalaima haemacephala* is called the coppersmith and the very small species of the genus *Pogoniulus* are tinkerbirds. Some barbets climb and feed like woodpeckers; others are vegetarian. Some are solitary, others form small flocks.

Family 96 *Indicatoridae* HONEYGUIDES Sexes alike
The 11 or 12 species of this Old World, mainly tropical family are mostly in the genus *Indicator;* the others are *Prodotiscus, Melignomon* and the monotypic *Melichneutes,* whose sole member is the Lyre-tailed Honeyguide, *M. robustus,* of Guinean rain forests, believed to produce a non-vocal sound in its aerial display like a snipe. Other honeyguides are generally brown or grey above, pale below, showing white on the graduated tail in flight; length 5 to 8 ins. They are zygodactylous and their bills are usually stubby. All honeyguides are parasitic either on open or hole-nesting birds, and two African species have evolved the remarkable behaviour that gives the family name: by their obtrusive presence they lead either honey badgers (ratels) or men (coincidentally the two most aggressive mammals!) to bees' nests. When the nest has been broken into, the honeyguides feed principally on the wax, a unique taste among birds. But they also eat bees, wasps, their larvae and other insects. Two species of *Indicator* inhabit Asia, one in the Himilayan foothills, the other in the south-east; all the rest are African.

Family 97 *Ramphastidae* TOUCANS
Sexes mostly alike
This is probably the best known of tropical American bird families, with some 37 species in 5 genera. Toucans are forest birds, 1-2 ft long, with strong feet and zygodactylous toes, long tails, short rounded wings allowing short undulating flights, and the outsize bill which distinguishes both the large *Ramphastos* species and the little toucanets; yet its evolution and true function remain mysterious. The bill is a honeycomb of cells, strutted with bone and therefore quite light. A toucan's tongue may be 6 ins long, flat and thin, notched at the sides and bristly at the tip. Toucans are the most gregarious of the picarians, the habit being best developed in the 11 araçaris, *Pteroglossus.* The hill toucans *Andigena* move seasonally up and down the Andean slopes, while the toucanets *Aulacorhynchus* live in the high forests about 10,000 ft up. The family is primarily fruit-eating, in which the huge bill may be of use, and all are cavity-nesters.

Family 98 *Picidae* WOODPECKERS
Sexes mostly alike
By far the largest family in the order and divided into 3 subfamilies, of which the typical *Picinae* number 179 species spread over all the great zoogeographical regions except Australia and Madagascar. Woodpeckers are typically zygodactylous, though the small genus *Picoides* has only 3 toes, and hold themselves vertically on tree trunks with 2 toes forward and the others held sideways; further support is given by the stiff tail feathers. Other important adaptations concern the straight chiselling bill with strong neck muscles to power it, and the remarkably long tongue, which projects far beyond the bill and has various forms at the tip – bristles or barbs – with which grubs can be extracted from their holes or ants picked off the ground. At rest the tongue is coiled in complicated routes round the skull and eyesockets. Plumages are principally mixtures of black, white, green and brown, with red, often indicating the male, on head and nape. Loud, ringing, repeated calls are characteristic, while some species drum on wood or even metal. Most species have a looping flight of several wingbeats followed by a glide and terminal swoop up to perch. Woodpeckers, found largely in tropical or subtropical forests, are generally sedentary, but some temperate zone nesters are migratory. A few species live and even nest on the ground (in burrows); the vast majority bore holes in trunks and sink shafts to the nest chamber. There are 2 species of soft-plumaged wrynecks *Jynx* in the subfamily *Jynginae,* and 8 in the *Picumninae* piculets, of which 5 belong to the Neotropical genus *Picumnus; Nesoctites* (Haiti), *Verreauxia* (Africa) and *Sasia* (south-east Asia) are monotypic. These tiny birds fall between the supposedly primitive wrynecks and the typical woodpeckers.

Order PASSERIFORMES

The species in this great order, which includes well over half the existing birds in the world, are united in the possession of 3 forward toes and 1 well developed hind toe, which is not reversible, this being a general adaptation to perching. They have certain anatomical features in common, e.g. 14 cervical vertebrae, are generally small in size in relation to non-passerines, and their young are helpless and usually naked when hatched.

Family 99 *Eurylaimidae* BROADBILLS Sexes alike
The only family in the Old World *Eurylaimi,* the first suborder into which the 'suboscine' passerines are divided, as distinct from the *Oscines* or songbirds. Suboscines have four or fewer pairs of muscles controlling the voice box or syrinx, and are considered to be more primitive. Broadbills are stout-bodied, brightly coloured, sedentary forest birds, closest to the *Pittidae* (Family 105) but differing in anatomical details; alone of passerine groups they have 15 cervical vertebrae. They have rounded or graduated tails, round wings, strong feet and a flattish bill with a wide gape; hence the name; head and eyes are large. The 14 species are usually divided on bill shape into 8 genera, 5 of which are monotypic. Their headquarters are the islands of south-east Asia, but they extend to India and have African representatives in the genera *Smithornis* and the monotypic *Pseudocalyptomena,* discovered quite recently in the mountains of the eastern Congo. Broadbills are gregarious, noisy, mainly insectivorous and build complex pear-shaped nests.

Family 100 *Dencrocolaptidae* WOODCREEPERS
Sexes alike
The first of 12 families in the suboscine *Tyranni,* this, like several others, is confined to central and South America and consists of 48 species, from under 6 ins to over a foot in length, in 13 genera. There is strong convergence with the treecreepers *Certhiidae* (Family 131) and, in respect of the stiff tail-feathers, the woodpeckers. In fact, woodcreepers are closely related to the ovenbirds *Furnariidae,* having the front toes joined at the base, but round instead of slit nostrils. Most species get their food by working spirally up trees, probing crevices; also like treecreepers they are predominantly brown plumaged, paler below, sedentary in habits and apt to associate with parties of mixed species. Their legs are short, with sharp claws, and their bills show great diversity, from short straight ones in several genera to the Scythebill, *Campylorhynchus falcularius,* whose organ is between $\frac{1}{4}$ and $\frac{1}{3}$ of its total length.

Family 101 *Furnariidae* OVENBIRDS
Sexes usually alike
One of the largest bird families, some 220 species in nearly 60 genera, and one of the least well-known, as most of its members are forest species, ranging from Mexico to the south of Argentina. Ovenbirds get their name from the prominent mud nests of the genus *Furnarius* but display an enormous variety of adaptation in appearance and ecology, though all are small and the predominant plumage colour is brown. Some are very like woodcreepers without their stiff tails, but others have moved into open country or mountain areas, where the genus *Cinclodes* behaves like dippers *Cinclidae* (Family 124); one even feeds on floating seaweed offshore like a Rock Pipit, *Anthus spinoletta.* Five subfamilies have been recognised: *Furnariinae,* embracing 'miners', 'plainrunners', 'earthcreepers' and 'shaketails'; *Synallaxinae* 'spinetails', which build huge stick nests; *Philydorinae,* covering 'treerunners', 'tree-

hunters', cachalotes and 'foliage gleaners'; the wood-creeper-like *Margarornithinae;* and the *Sclerurinae,* including only *Sclererus* 'leaf-scrapers' and the Sharp-tailed Streamcreeper, *Lochmias nematura.*

Family 102 *Formicariidae* ANTBIRDS
Sexes usually distinct

Another very large (220 species in over 50 genera) Neotropical family of small, rather subfusc birds, inhabiting forest or secondary woodland and about which, except for a few species, very little is known. Antbirds are closely related to ovenbirds but differ in having a hooked and notched tip to the upper mandible and in showing distinct male and female plumages (sexual dimorphism). Males are more strikingly coloured in darker shades with stripes and bars, of which females sport brown copies. Some species do follow columns of ants, but the habit is not universal, though all species are insectivorous. Many genera have been given somewhat inappropriate English names referring to other groups, e.g. ant-thrush, ant-wren, ant-shrike, ant-vireo, ant-pitta, but, on the whole antbirds seem to have diversified very much less than ovenbirds.

Family 103 *Conopophagidae* ANTPIPITS or
GNATEATERS Sexes alike or differ

In contrast to the two preceding families, to which it is closely related, this third Neotropical family has only 2 genera. The 9 *Conopophaga* species are small (about 6 ins), relatively long-legged but short-tailed, round-winged birds with thick plumage. A 'post-ocular stripe' or tuft of silky, usually white feathers is a characteristic feature. They are ground birds in woodland habitats. The 2 *Corythopus* species, with long tails and no sexual dimorphism, are more pipit-like, walking and not hopping, but they are also forest dwellers. As the alternative name suggests, the family is insectivorous.

Family 104 *Rhinocryptidae* TAPACULOS
Sexes usually alike

Another New World family of small brown birds, but found in the temperate and montane regions of Central and South America. The 27 tapaculos are divided into 12 genera, half of them monotypic. Their peculiarity, which the present scientific name expresses, is the operculum or movable covering of the nostrils, apparently a protection against dust (see *Thinocoridae* Family 61). They and the antpipits are the only passerines to have four notches to the back edge of the breastbone. Tapaculos have long legs and weak rounded wings which they use very little. They scratch like miniature chickens and the habit of cocking the tail upward has earned some species the name Gallito. Others are seldom seen in the thick undergrowth they favour, but a number are adapted to the open pampas; all are insectivorous. They are remarkably vocal for suboscines and both sexes may sing.

Family 105 *Pittidae* PITTAS Sexes alike or differ
A remarkably compact family and single genus of 23 Old World tropical forest species, with their base in south-east Asia, and 3 species reaching Australia and 2 confined to Africa. Pittas have no clear affinities: the musculature of the voice box lands them in the Tyranni; they have a distinct form of shank or tarsus, which is always long. Very stout bodies, thrush-sized or larger, short, even degenerate tails, rounded wings on which they can fly fast for short distances, and erectile crests are common to all species; where they vary is in their brilliant plumages, though these are seldom in evidence in their chosen habitat, the densely shaded forest floor. Pittas are solitary or live in pairs, hopping among the leaves after their mainly insect prey. They build large domed nests near the ground, but roost higher up.

Family 106 *Philepittidae* ASITIES Sexes alike
Another relict passerine family assigned to the *Tyranni;* the 2 genera, each with 2 species, are confined to the forests of Madagascar. In the east of the island lives the Velvet Asity, *Philepitta castanea,* 6 ins long and rather like a tree-living fruit-eating pitta; in the west is found the little-known Schlegel's Asity, *P. schlegeli.* The False Sunbird, *Neodrepanis coruscans,* (4 ins long) is brilliantly coloured and convergent in habits with the

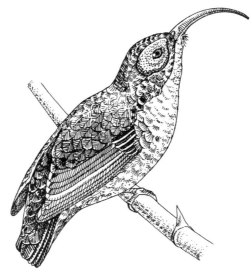

False Sunbird (*Neodrepanis coruscans*)

true sunbirds, with which it was long confused. Very little is known about the other species *N. hypoxantha* of the western forests, but both are solitary and keep to dense cover.

Family 107 *Xenicidae* NEW ZEALAND WRENS
Sexes alike or differ

Also known as *Acanthisittidae,* this tiny New Zealand family of tiny birds has only 3 living species, the Rifleman, *Acanthisitta chloris,* and Bush Wren, *Xenicus longipes,* found on both main islands, (but the wren is very rare); and the Rock Wren, *X. gilviventris,* of South Island. The Stephen Island Wren, *X. lyalli,* was discovered in 1894, reported to be flightless and almost at once wiped out by a cat. The family is supposed to be related to the pittas, but has probably no close affinities. Human activity has obscured the original ecology, but the two widespread species are insectivorous forest birds.

Family 108 *Tyrannidae* TYRANT FLYCATCHERS
Sexes mainly alike

Considered by one authority to have over 360 species in 115 genera, many of them monotypic, this is the dominant tyrannid family in numbers, ecology and behaviour, found all over the Americas (the temperate breeding species being migratory), and mainly in woodland or forest habitats, though some species are adapted to open country. Tyrants, ranging from 4 to 16 ins in length and with 2 front toes joined as in the cotingas and manakins, have the general suboscine features, with hook-tipped bills, but a recurring characteristic is a bright, usually yellow or orange crest, only exposed in moments of excitement, in otherwise rather sober plumages with greys and greens predominating. Only a few species are brightly coloured all over. Tails are usually moderate, with some exceptions like the Scissor-tailed, *Muscivora forficata,* and Swallow-tailed Flycatcher, *M. tyrannus.* Wings are pointed but flight among the sedentary majority of species is weak. The genus *Tyrannus* and others, with their upright stance and dashing sallies, show close convergence with the Old World flycatchers (Family 128, subfamily *Muscicapinae*); some are notoriously aggressive, attacking birds of prey and feeding on small birds and other animals, though most species are insectivorous and some vegetarian. Nesting habits vary enormously: open and domed structures, cavity and crevice sites are all found. The Sharpbill, *Oxyruncus cristatus,* is sometimes accorded monotypic family status on the strength of the character implied by its name.

Family 109 *Pipridae* MANAKINS
Sexes usually differ

Another Neotropical forest family of some 59 species in 20 genera, closely related to the cotingas, less so to the tyrants. They are nearly all under 6 ins long though a few have elongated tails, with rounded wings and short, straight, slightly hooked bills. The males of

some species have evolved modifications of the flight feathers which produce mechanical noises; typically males are brilliantly coloured and females dull, though some, possibly primitive genera, e.g. *Schiffornis,* show no dimorphism. Manakins feed largely by picking fruit off trees in flight. They are most notable for the unique displays of the males, differing in different genera. Some *Manacus* species clear a patch on the forest floor with a small tree as display perch; *Pipra* species perform on branches 30 ft up, while *Chiroxiphia* males dance up and down. Remarkable vocal and mechanical noises are produced, and mating often takes place on the perches.

Family 110 *Cotingidae* COTINGAS
Sexes alike or differ

The most diverse and bizarre-looking of the Neotropical tyrannid families, the 90 species of cotingas, becards, tityras and bellbirds, in size from sparrows to crows, have a similar anatomy, with short legs, rounded wings and slightly hooked bills. They are tropical forest birds, but two becards *Platypsaris* reach the southern USA and Jamaica. Best known of the family are the 2 ground-living but ledge-nesting cocks-of-the-rock *Rupicola,* which have communal 'lek' displays (see *Lyrurus tetrix*). The Umbrellabird, *Cephalopterus ornatus,* spreads its crest while emitting a rumbling sound; the function of head adornments of other species is unknown because their tree-top displays have not been described; but a remarkable range of calls are produced. Cotingas are both insectivorous and fruit-eating; little is known about the nesting of many of them.

Family 111 *Phytotomidae* PLANTCUTTERS
Sexes differ somewhat

There are 3 species in the single genus of this temperate South American family: the Chilean *Phytotoma rara,* Red-breasted, *P. rutila,* and the least widespread Peruvian Plantcutter, *P. raimondii.* The size of a large finch, with sparrow-like upperparts and brighter underparts, stout conical bills and slight crests, their true affinities are not apparent. They are birds of open woodland, scrub and prairie and their destructive feeding habits are indicated by the name. The Chilean species is migratory, nesting in the Andean foothills, and forms small parties in winter.

Chilean Plantcutter (*Phytotoma rara*) ♂

Family 112 *Menuridae* LYREBIRDS Sexes differ
One of 2 families in the 3rd suboscine sub-order *Menurae*, this consists of two species found in south-eastern Australia. The Superb Lyrebird, *Menura superba,* the country's national bird, has somewhat over-shadowed the rarer and less obtrusive Albert's Lyrebird, *M. alberti.* Superficially like pheasants with which, as with birds of paradise, they were at times confused, lyrebirds are the largest suboscine passerines, having several anatomical peculiarities connected with the voice box and breastbone. They belong to sub-tropical forest, feeding on the ground on small animal life and nesting in winter when it is most abundant. The remarkable tail is the male adornment; with this and an astonishing repertoire of specific and mimicked notes, he conducts his displays on up to ten clearings in his large territory, taking no part in hatching and rearing the single chick.

Family 113 *Atrichornithidae* SCRUB BIRDS
Sexes differ
Most nearly related to the lyrebirds and therefore placed in the same sub-order are the 2 scrub birds, the 6½ ins Rufous, *Atrichornis rufescens,* of south-eastern Australia, and the 8 ins Noisy, *A. clamosus,* believed extinct and rediscovered in 1961 in one small area of Western Australia. Alone among passerines, their collarbones are not fused to form a wishbone and scrub birds are therefore very poor fliers. Their name indicates their habitat, in which observation is very difficult, but they appear to behave like miniature lyrebirds, fleet-footed and with a surprising and loud repertoire.

Family 114 *Alaudidae* LARKS
Sexes usually alike
Appropriately the oscine or song-bird sub-order is headed by a family renowned for beautiful voices. Some 75 species in 15 genera are recognised, 50 of them occurring in Africa and only 1, the holarctic Horned or Shore Lark, *Eremophila alpestris,* in America; 1 also reaches Australia and 1, New Guinea, but there are a number in both Europe and Asia. The larks are a remarkably uniform family, distinguished by the scaled and rounded back to the shank and by the very long hind claw, a sign of their running gait; the voice box also has special, rather primitive features. Larks are the passerines of open habits, from beaches and deserts to cultivated land, showing neat plumage adaptations to different backgrounds. But the predominantly African bush larks of the large genus *Mirafra* regularly perch. Some of these build domed nests instead of the typical simple open cup. The diet is varied, both vegetable and animal, and the famous songs are delivered most effectively in flight.

Family 115 *Hirundinidae* SWALLOWS and MARTINS
Sexes usually alike
One of the best known and relatively uniform passerine families, found almost all over the world except New Zealand (stragglers only), Antarctica and some other large islands. Nearly 80 species, from 5 to 9 ins long, are divided into 19 genera, some of doubtful validity. The anatomical feature of complete bronchial rings is not obvious; but the forked tails, pointed 9-primaried wings, small bills with wide bristle-edged gapes, evolved as aerial bagnets for insects, and usually glossy upper plumage can cause confusion only with the even more aerially adapted swifts (Family 79). Swallows and martins are summer visitors to the temperate zones, performing their long and well publicised migrations by day and feeding on the wing. Although swallows can perch, their weak feet having strong claws, they only land to collect material for their mud nests. Other species take over cavities or burrow in banks, but the Swallow, *Hirundo rustica,* and its near relatives now site their nests almost entirely on human artefacts. The large, monotypic African River Martin, *Pseudochelidon eurystomina,* is put in a separate subfamily because of its peculiar bronchial structure; it is extremely gregarious.

Family 116 *Motacillidae* PIPITS and WAGTAILS
Sexes alike (pipits), differ (wagtails)
Although with 9 instead of 10 primaries and cosmopolitan in range, the 50 odd species (in 4 to 6 genera) of this family are about as different in appearance and habits from the previous one as is possible among passerines. But they show superficial resemblances to the larks, being also adapted to open habitats, where they run, walk or fly after insect prey. They are mostly about sparrow size. The pipits, over 30 of them in the genus *Anthus,* have generally streaked plumages and their longish tails show white outer feathers. They have sharp straight bills and strong legs with notably long hind claws, most developed in the African longclaws *Macronyx,* whose bright yellow underparts and black necklace shows classic convergence with the American meadowlarks (Family 141). The wagtails, all in *Motacilla* except for the rather aberrant Asian Forest Wagtail, *Dendromanthus indicus,* are brighter than most pipits, often associated with water and include one species, the 'Yellow' *M. flava,* with most striking subspecific differentiation, indicated by the ♂ head plumage. One race nests in extreme north-western North America, where 2 pipits have also penetrated. At the other extreme Richard's Pipit, *Anthus novaeseelandiae,* reaches New Zealand, but the heartlands of the family are Eurasia, to which some members are summer visitors, and Africa. Like larks they build open nests, and pipits have well developed songs, often uttered in flight.

Family 117 *Campephagidae* CUCKOO SHRIKES and MINIVETS Sexes generally differ
Superficial characteristics govern the twofold English name of one group in this family of 70 species, now divided into 9 genera, and distributed primarily in the forests of the Old World tropics, extending to Australia. Size ranges from sparrow to pigeon; tails and pointed wings are longish; the rather broad bills are sometimes covered by bristles but the interesting feature of most species is the dense, loose plumage of feathers with stiff-pointed shafts on the lower back and rump: these are easily shed, possibly as a protective device. The cuckoo shrikes, typical genus *Campephaga,* are generally rather dull-coloured; some larger species have a distinctive wing-lifting display accompanied by loud calls. The 10 minivets *Pericrocotus* are sparrow-sized, with graduated rails and bright male plumages of red and black. The family as a whole is insectivorous, tree-living and open-nesting; the aberrant Ground Cuckoo Shrike of Australia, *Pteropodocys maxima,* is a bird of open country, but nests high in trees.

Family 118 *Pycnonotidae* BULBULS
Sexes alike, females sometimes smaller
Another Old World, primarily tropical family, its eastward range ending at Wallace's Line, only bridged by recent introductions to Australia. The 120 species are split into 15 genera, of which 10 are endemic to Africa and Madagascar and 2 to Asia. The widely distributed type genus *Pycnonotus* contains 50 species. Bulbuls, sparrow to thrush sized, are generally dull-plumaged except for bright patches, e.g. on cheek or vent, with rather long tails and short ineffective wings. Feet also are weak, bills straight and bristle-based; the dense back plumage recalls the cuckoo shrikes. Many species are crested, but the most distinctive feature is the patch of hair-like feathers at the nape. Originally forest birds, some bulbuls have spread into secondary and cultivated habitats close to man, enjoyed for their songs, as by Omar Khayyam, and active behaviour; others remain very secretive. They are primarily fruit-eaters and build open nests.

Family 119 *Irenidae* LEAFBIRDS Sexes differ
An Oriental Asian forest family, brightly coloured relatives of the bulbuls, with which they share many features, including the 'hairy' patch on the nape. The 8 leafbirds *Chloropsis* are about 8 ins long, generally greenish, with rather curved pointed bills and fruit-eating habits. The 4 little ioras *Aegithina* are more insectivorous, with relatively longer legs and bills; the males have rather striking aerial displays and a non-breeding plumage. The 2 fairy bluebirds *Irena* are starling-sized; 1 species is endemic to the Philippines, the other more widely distributed in south-east Asia, where the small, fruit-eating flocks are often conspicuous.

Family 120 *Laniidae* SHRIKES
Sexes usually alike
One classification of these predatory passerines defines 74 species in 4 subfamilies. Shrikes are primarily Old World birds of open woodland and scrub; they do not occur in Australia or the Pacific islands, and only 2 species (1 endemic) inhabit North America. In general they are from 7 ins to a foot long, with longish round or graduated tails, rather pointed wings, strong legs and claws, and powerful hooked and notched bills with which they do their killing. The type subfamily *Laniinae,* with 25 members, includes the migratory North Temperate species, characterised by black, white and grey in the plumage and often with a mask, and by the habit of building up larders of prey, from insects to small mammals. They are both conspicuous and secretive, with rudimentary songs, and build open nests. As well as *Lanius* the monotypic *Corvinella* and *Urolestes* are included. The bush shrikes *Malaconotinae* are all African and include 'duetting' species like the Brubru, *Nilaus afer,* the curious puffbacks *Dryoscopus,* and a possible interloper, *Lanioturdus torquatus.* The helmet shrikes *Prionopinae* – also African – have black and white plumages and are distinguished by the caruncles of skin round their eyes and by their striking crests. Finally, the monotypic *Pityriasinae,* whose sole representative is the Borneo Bristlehead, *Pityriasis gymnocephala,* which may not be a shrike at all, partly because of the uncharacteristic bill.

Family 121 *Vangidae* VANGA SHRIKES
Sexes alike or differ
A Madagascan family of rather brightly coloured forest birds, 5 ins to a foot long, presumed to be descended from an immigrant shrike ancestor, but now diversified into 12 species in 8 genera, 6 of them monotypic. They resemble true shrikes in many anatomical respects, but their bills show modifications, especially the enormous proboscis of the Helmetbird, *Aerocharis prevostii.* Vangas are gregarious and insectivorous rather than solitary and predatory, and are noisy on the move. They build open nests but little is known of their breeding biology.

Family 122 *Bombycillidae* WAXWINGS, SILKY FLYCATCHERS, HYPOCOLIUS Sexes alike or differ
A composite family of Northern Hemisphere, gregarious, medium-sized, fruit-eating passerines, whose relationship is somewhat tenuous, though the three subfamilies have similar anatomy, soft plumage, a tendency to crests and a tree-living habit. The (Bohemian) Waxwing, *Bombycilla garrulus,* is a holarctic conifer bird and classic irruption species; the Cedar, *B. cedrorum,* is North American and the Japanese, *B. japonica,* is confined to eastern Asia. The 4 Central American silky flycatchers are *Phainopepla nitens, Phainoptila melanoxantha* and 2 species of *Ptilogonys,* all about 7½ ins long; they are so little known as to have no English names and range from Panama to central California. The Grey Hypocolius, *Hypocolius ampelinus,* sole member of its subfamily and genus, is found in the valleys of the Tigris and Euphrates, irrupting like the Waxwing to north-western India and occasionally to north-east Africa.

Family 123 *Dulidae* PALM CHAT Sexes alike
Sometimes regarded as another monotypic subfamily in the *Bombycillidae* the Palm Chat, *Dulus dominicus,* of Hispaniola is a gregarious, fruit-eating species with communal nesting habits.

Family 124 *Cinclidae* DIPPERS Sexes alike
The 4 similar species in the single genus are the Dipper, *Cinclus cinclus,* of Europe, western Asia (including high levels in the Himalayas) and North Africa; the Brown, *C. pallasii,* of northern Asia and Japan, the western North American, *C. mexicanus,* also brown all over, and the White-headed, *C. leucocephalus,* of the Andes. Dippers look like thrush-sized wrens, with their strong legs, short uptilted tails and round bodies and are probably closely related, even sharing a musty smell. They are the only truly aquatic passerines, yet have no webbed feet or obvious specialisation except for an operculum to the nostrils and effective eyelids. But they can swim, dive and move about under water in all directions, using wings and feet. They are all insectivorous, sedentary and solitary (except perhaps for

roosting), with attractive warbling songs; they build domed nests like wrens.

Family 125 *Troglodytidae* WRENS Sexes alike
The 60 species are divided into 12 to 14 genera and range in distribution from the Zapata Wren, *Ferminia cerverai*, confined to one marsh in Cuba, to the holarctic (Winter) Wren, *Troglodytes troglodytes*, found over much of Eurasia and into North Africa as well as North America. All other wrens are American, with most genera and species in the tropics. Wrens are remarkably uniform, 4 to 8 ins long, with brown, black-streaked plumage, tails usually short and uptilted, rather long-shanked strong legs and thin, slightly curved probing bills. Both sexes may sing and some tropical species are duettists. They are insectivorous, and build external domed nests or occupy cavities; several species are polygamous, the males building a number of 'cock's nests'. Solitary by day, wrens may collect in large numbers to roost. They are found in habitats of all kinds, from tropical forests to marshes (*Cistothorus* species), coasts, mountains and deserts, like the large Cactus Wren, *Campylorhynchus bruneicapillus*.

Family 126 *Mimidae* MOCKINGBIRDS OR MIMIC THRUSHES Sexes alike
The 34 species of this all-American family of wooded country and scrub are divided into 13 genera, 9 of them monotypic. They appear to be intermediate between the wrens and the true thrushes in size and characteristics. Some have long tails but carry them uptilted like wrens; most of them have curved probing bills. But they build open thrush-like nests. Plumages, with few exceptions, e.g. the colourful Blue and Blue and White Mockingbirds, *Melanotis caerulescens* and *M. hypoleucus*, are shades of brown and grey. So the birds make up for it by their loud songs, containing mimic phrases or notes. The type genus *Mimus* has 9 species, distributed over the whole range of the family from Canada to Argentina, though the Galapagos super-species is put in its own genus as *Nesomimus trifasciatus*. Another islander is the Thrasher, *Mimodes graysoni*, of Socorro off the west coast of Mexico. There are 10 species of typical thrashers *Toxostoma* in North America; some appear to be evolving towards a totally ground-living habit.

Family 127 *Prunellidae* ACCENTORS Sexes alike
This family of a single genus *Prunella* and 12 species is almost exclusively Palaearctic, associated with conifer forests, secondary growth, mountain scrub and higher slopes, up to 17,000 ft in the Himalayas. Accentors are sparrow-sized or larger, rather inconspicuously plumaged in browns streaked with black or grey, have strong legs, pointed insectivorous bills but the crop and muscular gizzard of seedeaters; in fact, they feed mainly on insects in summer, on fruits and seeds in winter, all taken on or near the ground. They have simple, melodious songs, and build cup nests with blue eggs.

Family 128 *Muscicapidae*
This huge agglomeration of formerly separate families, totalling between them about 1,000 species, is best treated under the subfamilies as now recognised.

Turdinae THRUSHES, CHATS, ROBINS
Sexes alike or differ
Over 300 species in 45 genera are distributed all over the world, reaching New Zealand by introduction. They are rather unspecialised, small to medium-sized song birds, with 10 primary flight feathers (as throughout the whole family), tails short to long, straight bills and rictal bristles (usually the sign of an insect diet) and strong legs and feet for a life spent much on the ground. They build mainly open nests though some use holes. Above all they include some of the world's best songsters. The type genus *Turdus* (about 60 species) has the largest kinds, with its centre in Eurasia and Africa but members also in both Americas; several have colonised remote islands. Other genera are the Nearctic bluebirds, *Sialis* and thrushes, *Hylocichlas*, the mainly Neotropical *Catharus* and *Myadestes* (solitaires, best of tropical songsters) and the monotypic Wren Thrush, *Zeledonia coronata*. Genera of smaller birds include *Oenanthe* wheatears, several chats (e.g. *Saxicola*), *Luscinia* nightingales and bluethroats, *Phoenicurus* redstarts, and the Robin, *Erithacus rubecula*, whose name has caused confusion all over the world, applied to all sorts of red-breasted birds.

Timaliinae BABBLERS, WREN TIT
Sexes alike or differ slightly
A very large Old World (including Australia) grouping, to which the monotypic North American Wren Tit, *Chaemia fasciata*, is attached. Babblers have relatively longer tails than thrushes and brighter plumages, but feebler, rounded wings and spend most of their time in cover on or near the ground; they unite in small flocks or parties with other species outside the breeding season. They are both insectivorous and vegetarian, build both open and covered nests and their young do not have a spotted first plumage. They include some fine song birds. The 5 tribes (in addition to the *Chamaeini* above) are the jungle babblers of the Ethiopian and Oriental regions, of dull plumage and secretive habits, divided into 5 genera. The scimitar and wren babblers are insectivorous, ground-living birds with 11 genera and 28 species, extending to New Guinea and Australia. The tit babblers are 6 genera and 35 species of small birds with a Madagascan genus *Neomixis* the jerys. The 140 song babblers in 17 genera are the largest tribe, distributed throughout Africa and southern Asia and including the brighter plumaged, tree-living forms. The Arrow-marked Babbler, *Turdoides jardineii*, is one of the 26 species in its genus, whereas the laughing thrushes *Garrulax* number 50, with some fine songsters. Finally there are the 2 large West African rockfowl, the Grey-necked *Picathartes gymnocephalus* and White-necked *P. oreas*, with bare heads and other aberrant characters.

Cinclosomatinae RAIL BABBLERS Sexes alike or differ
The bird giving its name to this composite group, the Rail Babbler, *Eupetes macrocerus*, is the only species occurring in Malaysia, the rest being found in Australia and New Guinea, primarily living on or near the ground in forest or scrub. They have long shanks, broad tails, densely feathered backs and rather small heads and bills. But they vary a great deal between some 10 small genera, of which the scrub robins, *Drymodes*, and quail thrushes, *Cinclosoma*, are rather thrush-like. The New Guinea logrunners, *Orthonyx*, are characterised by very large feet.

Paradoxornithinae PARROTBILLS
Sexes alike or differ
This subfamily contains about 20 species in the type genus *Paradoxornis* and the monotypic *Conostoma* (the Himalayan *C. oemodium* is about a foot long) and *Panurus*, represented by the Bearded Tit or Reedling *P. biarmicus*, which is Palaearctic. Most of the *Paradoxornis* species are found in the Oriental region, excluding Malaya, and are notable for their short, compressed, convex, usually yellowish bills; they are mostly robust, thick plumaged forest and woodland birds, insectivorous and vegetarian, frequently seen in small flocks. The smaller species tend to be the more brightly coloured. They build open nests but not much is known about the breeding biology of most of them.

Polioptilinae GNATCATCHERS Sexes differ slightly
A dozen species of small New World (Canada to Mexico and Bahamas) insect-eating birds, most closely related to the Old World warblers, grey above and pale below, with long, constantly moving tails, found mostly in or near wetlands. There are 8 *Polioptilina* species and 4 in the genera *Microbates* and *Ramphocaenus*, known as 'gnat wrens'.

Sylviinae OLD WORLD WARBLERS
Sexes alike or differ
Some 300 species in about 30 genera are contained in this subfamily; they are overwhelmingly Eurasian or African, the northern members being migratory. Two kinglets, *Regulus*, and 1 leaf warbler, *Phylloscopus*, reach North America; about 20 species breed in Australia and the Fernbird, *Bowdleria punctata*, of New Zealand is also included. Warblers are typically slim, dull plumaged above, lighter below, rather elegant long-tailed little birds, insectivorous and fruit-eating, working their way through thick vegetation in canopy, scrub or grassland and building dainty cups or substantial domed nests. Many have fine songs, often delivered in flight, as by the 70 members of the largest genus *Cisticola*, the primarily African grass warblers. Other important genera are *Sylvia*, 'true' warblers, *Phylloscopus*, the often puzzling little green leaf warblers, *Acrocephalus*, reed warblers, *Locustella*, grasshopper warblers, and *Cettia* including the tuneful Japanese Bush Warbler, *C. diphone*. The several tropical genera include the tailor birds, *Orthotomus*, which sew leaves together to hold their nests, and the wren warblers, *Prinia*. The kinglets, and 2 Asian tit warblers *Leptopoecile* are also included.

Malurinae AUSTRALIAN WREN WARBLERS
Sexes alike or differ
Another 'assemblage' of some 80 species in over 20 genera, found in Australia, New Guinea and New Zealand. They are generally small insectivorous birds resembling the *Sylviinae* but *Malurus* includes some brilliantly coloured species, hence the names 'superb warbler' and 'fairy wren'. Most species are tree-living, building domed nests which are frequently parasitised by cuckoos. Aberrant in various respects are the emu wrens, *Stipiturus*, with only 6 modified tail feathers, the Spinifex Bird, *Eremiornis carteri*, the *Ephthianura* 'chats' and the pipit-like song larks, *Cinclorhamphus*.

Muscicapinae FLYCATCHERS Sexes alike or differ
A very large Old World subfamily, extending to Australia and New Zealand (the fantails *Rhipidura*) in distribution and convergent in habits with the tyrant flycatchers of America (Family 108). Several hundred species are divided into tens of genera. The typical Palaearctic genera *Muscicapa* and *Ficedula* are small, weak-footed, essentially perching birds whose broad bills and rictal bristles proclaim their 'trade'. They are migratory, cavity-nesting and have spotted juveniles like the thrushes. Very different are the strikingly plumaged, very long-tailed paradise flycatchers, *Terpsiphone*, with their neat open nests. These and the puffbacks, *Batis*, wattle eyes, *Platysteira* and *Diaphorophyia* of Asia, *Arses* of New Guinea and *Zeocephus* of the Philippines have colourful fleshy eye rings. *Bradornis* of Africa contains the largest species, shrike-like in hunting habits; *Abrornis* is no larger than a kinglet. Most flycatchers are solitary but the *Newtonia* species of Madagascar form flocks to search the foliage. The diversity within the subfamily is almost as wide as in the whole order.

Pachycephalinae THICKHEADS OR WHISTLERS
Sexes usually alike
A subfamily of robust flycatchers from Australia, New Guinea and the islands of south-east Asia; they have a number of popular Australian names. In size from sparrow to jay, whistlers are often yellow and green. mixed with black and reddish; wattles are exceptional, but some species are crested. Juveniles are sometimes spotted. *Pachycephala* is by far the largest of the genera. Nests may be open or well-hidden; the Australian Crested Bellbird, *Oreica gutturalis*, garnishes the rim with paralysed caterpillars. Most species have pleasant call notes and the pairs of some sing duets; hence apparently the name whistler.

Family 129 *Paridae* TITMICE
Sexes may differ slightly
The family may be considered in 3 subfamilies, of which the typical *Parinae* contains 43 of the 65 species; its main strength lies in the Palaearctic, but some are found in Africa to the very south and in North America. Tits are small (3 to 8 ins long) very active, tree-living birds, with moderately long tails, round bodies, rather rounded wings and powerful, somewhat conical bills with which they break nuts and penetrate bark. Yellow, blue and grey-green on the body, with black caps and white cheeks, are plumage characteristics. Most species nest in holes and form communal flocks after breeding, searching the foliage for insects and nuts, which several northern species store. The *Aegithalinae* or long-tailed tits consist of 8 species, counting the 2 tiny North American bush tits *Psaltriparus*. This group builds elaborate domed nests. *Remizinae*, the penduline tits, have finer bills and are found more in open wooded country than the forest-loving Parus tits, and the Penduline Tit, *R. pendulinus*. is associated with water. There are 6 *Anthoscopus* species in Africa and in North America the monotypic Verdin, *Auriparus flaviceps*, inhabiting sem-desert. The subfamily is noted for its durable penduline nests.

Family 130 *Sittidae* NUTHATCHES
Sexes alike or differ
Closely related to the tits are the typically Holarctic nuthatches *Sitta*, 18 species out of 31 in the family. They are stout-bodied birds from tit to woodpecker size (*S. magna*, the Giant Nuthatch of mountainous southern Asia) with strong legs and claws and rather long straight bills with which to probe bark, chip wood and hammer nuts. They do not use their tails, which are short and soft, to support themselves against trunks, but rely on their claws; they also climb head downwards. The Eurasian species use mud to reduce the entrance to the hole nest and the 2 rock-haunting species build mud frontages to their chosen cavities. Only the Nuthatch, *S. europaea*, enters North Africa; there are 4 species in North America. The Wallcreeper, *Tichodroma muraria*, is an aberrant Eurasian monotype, to which the Afro-Asian Spotted Creeper, *Salpornis spilonotus*, may be related. The two creepers, *Rhabdornis*, live in the Philippines, several treerunners, *Sitella*, more colourful than *Sitta*, in Australia and New Guinea, also the home of the Wonder Treerunner, *Daphoenositta miranda*. But Madagascar has the most aberrant species, *Hypositta corallirostris*, which may be not a nuthatch at all.

Family 131 *Certhiidae* TREECREEPERS Sexes alike
This Old World family of 5 species reverses the position of the wrens, 1 having penetrated America as far south as Nicaragua, where it meets the convergent woodcreepers (Family 100). Treecreepers are slender little birds, mottled brown above and white below, with long claws and thin, curved probing bills. Like woodpeckers they support themselves against tree trunks on stiff tail feathers, which are moulted from the outermost inwards. They hunt by spiralling round a trunk, then fly down to the base of the next; sometimes they 'back-pedal' with fluttering wings or even move head downwards; their prey is almost entirely invertebrate and they often link up with tit flocks when foraging. They nest in crevices. The Treecreeper or Brown Creeper, *Certhia familiaris*, is the Holarctic species. In Eurasian deciduous woodland it is replaced by the Short-toed, *C. brachydactyla*, which also penetrates north-west Africa. The distribution of the other 3 species, *C. himalayana*, *C. discors* and *C. nipalensis* is primarily the Himalayan foothills.

Family 132 *Climacteridae* AUSTRALIAN TREECREEPERS Sexes differ slightly
This small group of 6 or 9 mainly east Australian species has been placed in both the 2 previous families, but has claims to be considered on its own. About 6 ins long, these birds are more strikingly plumaged than the Eurasian treecreepers, with a coloured wing bar and striped underparts. They have longer legs and toes, prominent curved claws and a long curved bill, but their tail feathers are soft, not adapted as supports. They live in a variety of wooded habitats, haunting tree trunks like *Certhia* but do not join mixed flocks. They nest in tree holes.

Family 133 *Dicaeidae* FLOWERPECKERS
Sexes alike or differ
The majority of the 55 species in this Oriental and Australian family are in the genera *Prionochilus* and *Dicaeum*. They are small birds with short, stumpy tails and partially serrated, variably shaped bills, some rather tit-like, some long and curved; the tip of the tongue is semi-tubular. Plumages range from the drab (with sexes alike) to species with brightly coloured males. Two *Dicaeum* species reach the Palaearctic; but the Philippines have 13, of which 11 are endemic and New Guinea has 11 endemics, including 3 monotypic genera *Oreocharis*, *Paramythia* and *Rhamphocharis*. The 7 small, 'snub-nosed' pardalotes *Pardalotus* range from New Guinea to Tasmania; the name refers to the generally spotted plumage pattern. Flowerpeckers inhabit forests and secondary growth, including bamboo clumps and gardens. They feed on fruit, nectar and insects; several species, e.g. *Dicaeum hirundinaceum*, concentrate on mistle-toe berries and are responsible for their dissemination, some birds scraping the seeds off their bills and on to fresh hosts, and others evacuating them fairly rapidly through a specially adapted stomach.

Family 134 *Nectariniidae* SUNBIRDS
Sexes differ in sunbirds, alike in spiderhunters
This large Old World family, counterpart to the hummingbirds, has been variously arranged but now numbers over 100 species in relatively few genera, of which the more important are *Nectarinia*, *Cinnyris*, *Aethopyga* and *Anthreptes*. While over half the species live in Africa, the range extends via Palestine to India, south-east Asia, the Pacific islands and (1 species) to Australia. In size from about 3 to 8 ins long, sunbirds are generally larger than hummingbirds and much less diversified as to tails and bills. They drink nectar both directly and by piercing the tubular corollas of large flowers, and usually perch to do so, though they can hover. They have specialised tongues, partly tubular and forked at the tip. In striking metallic colours male sunbirds can match the hummingbirds; they also have a duller non-breeding plumage and females are usually, though not always, much drabber. They are generally solitary but several, of different species, may visit the same flowers. They are also mainly sedentary, but some show quite extensive seasonal movements. The domed or purse nests of plant fibres and cobwebs are often conspicuous; some species of *Cinnyris* and *Chalcomitra* associate with social insects (Hymenoptera) and spiders when nesting. The 9 spiderhunters *Arachnothera* of the Oriental region form rather a distinct group, generally larger with duller plumages alike in both sexes; most of them feed only on invertebrates.

Family 135 *Zosteropidae* WHITE-EYES Sexes alike
A family noted for uniform plumages in which yellow-green, grey, brown and white are predominant. Some authorities would put all 85 species in the genus *Zosterops*; others allot 62, with 23 in 11 other genera. White-eyes are found throughout the Ethiopian, Oriental and Australasian regions, mainly in the tropics and inhabiting wooded country of all kinds, including gardens, but not dense forest. Most are about 4 ins long and nearly all show the white orbital ring of feathers that gives the name. They have 9 functional primaries on their rounded wings, and short rather curved bills with which they pierce fruit, removing the inside with bristle-tipped tongues; they also feed on nectar and insects. Their songs are not notable. They are highly gregarious and this is believed to account for their success, though apparently weak fliers, in colonising remote islands not reached by other passerines. They reached New Zealand naturally about 1850 but were introduced to Hawaii and elsewhere. They build open nests and have a remarkably short ($10\frac{1}{2}$ days) incubation period; the young may leave the nest with part of the head still featherless.

Family 136 *Meliphagidae* HONEYEATERS, SUGARBIRDS Sexes alike or differ
Unlike the white-eyes, this is a very diverse family of 167 species divided into 38 genera, 14 of them monotypic, and primarily Australasian in distribution, though 1 or 2 species have penetrated the Oriental and even to the Palaearctic region. Size and structure show enormous diversity, but all species have long semi-tubular, cleft, bristle-tipped tongues adapted to nectar-feeding. Bills are of diverse lengths and shapes. Plumages are on the whole dull, with a tendency to bare patches, lobes and wattles on the head; some dimorphic *Myzomela* species are brilliantly coloured. Habits are also very variable, though all species are tree-living and nearly all build their nests off the ground. Honeyeaters are gregarious, nomadic and have a looping flight. Besides nectar, they take insects and fruit, but they have an important role as pollinators of many Australian trees and shrubs, which are adapted for bird visitors, just as the honeyeaters' tongues and digestive systems have been reciprocally evolved. Some species have good songs, sometimes uttered in flight, while those of the New Zealand Tui, *Prosthemadera novaeseelandiae*, and Bellbird, *Anthornis melonura*, are famous. The 2 sugarbirds *Promerops* are found in South Africa and attached to the family by virtue of similar tongue and intestinal structure; they are long-tailed with long curved bills.

Family 137 *Emberizidae* BUNTINGS, TANAGERS, HONEYCREEPERS Sexes alike or differ
This is a somewhat controversial grouping, best treated in its 5 subfamilies.

Emberizinae: a subfamily of New World origin, with about 160 species in 50 genera. Predominantly small (sparrow-sized – hence the American name for many species) brown birds with streaked plumages above and a tendency to white outer tail feathers, but with exceptions like the Towhees, *Pipilo* and Juncos, *Junco*. Some 37 *Emberiza* buntings have colonised the Old World (Palaearctic and Ethiopian) while the Crested Bunting, *Melophus lathami*, is found in the Oriental. The Snow, *Plectrophenax nivalis*, and Lapland Bunting or Longspur, *Calcarius lapponicus*, are Holarctic. Buntings are open country birds with strong feet and generally blunt seed-eating bills; migratory species have longer wings than sedentary forms. They build mainly on the ground. The head patterns of the males are often diagnostic.

Pyrrhuloxiinae: 'Cardinal-Grosbeaks': a New World group with 11 genera. Primarily tropical with some migratory North American breeding species. Most species nest in trees. The subfamily includes some of the most colourful species, e.g. the Indigo, *Passerina cyanea*, and Painted Bunting, *P. ciris*.

Thraupinae: the tanagers are another New World group of some 200 species, smallish (4 to 8 ins) birds of woodland but not dense forest. Some are brilliantly plumaged, but poor songsters. They feed mainly on fruits and some insects. The small euphonia, *Tanagra*, species disseminate mistle-toe by their partiality to its berries. The South American Plush-capped Finch, *Catamblyrhynchus diadema*, is one aberrant; another is the Swallow Tanager, *Tersina viridis*, which is given its own subfamily – *Tersinae;* it nests in burrows.

Coerebinae: the Honeycreepers do not look much like the other subfamilies and their modified tongues approach those of the *Meliphagidae* (Family 136). They are another Neotropical nectar-feeding group, with which are included the flowerpeckers *Diglossa* and the Bananaquit, *Coereba flaveola*. They are generally rather small birds with long thin curved bills and brilliantly coloured males, though the flowerpeckers are dull. They are sedentary, gregarious, forest-edge birds, working the canopy; the Bananaquit has become closely associated with man. Most build open nests in forks of trees or bushes.

Family 138 *Parulidae* AMERICAN OR WOOD WARBLERS Sexes usually differ
The taxonomic position of this important New World family has varied, but it is generally agreed to be somewhere close to the tanagers (Family 137, subfamily *Thraupinae*), certainly nowhere near the Old World warblers (Family 128, subfamily *Sylviinae*), unless the aberrant Olive Warbler, *Peucedramus taeniatus*, really belongs there. Few of the 113 species, arranged in 26 genera, are more than 6 ins long; about half of them breed only in North America and the West Indies; the rest are tropical or widely distributed. They are found in a variety of habitats but are primarily tree-living. The northern breeding species are migratory and, while recognisable in their spring plumages, pose problems of identification when they return south drably feathered in autumn. Yellow, orange, black and white are favourite colours, but some species, especially in the tropics, show red. Many are insectivorous, with rictal bristles and bills appropriately flattened for aerial capture; others are fruit and berry eaters. They build nests, usually open, from ground level to 60 ft in trees; the Ovenbird, *Seiurus aurocapillus*, makes a large domed structure on the ground.

Family 139 *Drepanididae* HAWAIIAN HONEYCREEPERS Sexes alike or differ
A small family of 22 species (9 of them recently extinct) in 9 genera, 4 of them monotypic, and one of the classic examples of adaptive radiation from a common ancestor into species with, for example, specialised bills ranging from the short, cross-bill of the Akepa, *Loxops coccinea*, to the very long curved probe of the Kauai Akialoa, *Hemignathus wilsoni*, or the stubby, parrot or finch-like organ of the Palila, *Psittirostra bailleui*. Honeycreepers are 4 to 8 ins long, males usually bigger

than females. Plumages are very varied: green, yellow, red and black. The crested, *Palmeria dolei*, is grey and red. Habits are solitary or gregarious, songs not remarkable and nests open. All members of the family have a musky smell, one indication of their common ancestor. Their survival under modern conditions is one of the serious problems of conservation.

Family 140 *Vireonidae* VIREOS, SHRIKE VIREOS, PEPPERSHRIKES Sexes alike

Another New World family with 1 vestigial and 9 functional primary feathers. Considered by some to be most closely related to the previous family, the 40 odd species in the subfamily *Vireoninae* are much more uniform in plumage, grey-green above, yellow and white below. They are 4 to 7 ins long, with typical perching feet and claws and short rather hooked bills. They live mainly in open woodland, sometimes in the tree canopy and build delicate nests slung between twigs. About 20 species in the genus *Vireo* include those nesting in North America – and therefore migratory – of which the Red-eyed, *V. olivaceus*, Yellow-throated, *V. flavifrons* and White-eyed, *V. griseus,* are very well known, the first for its persistent, monotonous summerlong song. The neotropical genus *Hylophilus* consists of 15 greenlets, smaller and even more uniform than the typical vireos; 3 species are found north of Panama. The Neotropical subfamily *Vireolaniinae* contains the Chestnut-sided Shrike Vireo, *Vireolanius melitophrys,* larger than the vireos and a hunter of big insects, and 2 or 3 species of *Smaragdolanius* which are smaller and little known, living high in the forest canopy. The *Cyclarhinae* consists of the 2 strongly-built pepper shrikes, *Cyclarhis gujanensis* and *C. nigrirostris,* predators on large insects and living in the middle storeys of the forest.

Family 141 *Icteridae* ICTERIDS Sexes usually differ

About 90 species are included in this heterogeneous family of 9 primaried New World passerines, related to the *Emberizidae* (Family 137). They have conical, usually straight, unnotched bills, and lack rictal bristles; there is also a propensity to black plumage. Apart from these points, there is great diversity in size (6 to 21 ins), plumage, length of tail and habits. Diet varies through a range of plants and small animals. The strength of the family is in tropical forest but members are found in all sorts of habitats and latitudes: the Rusty Blackbird, *Euphagus carolinus,* breeds within the Arctic Circle and another 'northerner', the Bobolink, *Dolichonyx oryzivorus,* migrates in winter to the south of Argentina. The tropical species, on the other hand, are mainly sedentary. The meadowlarks *Sturnella* are scattered and solitary; the grackles *Cassidex* and some blackbirds *Agelaius* are immensely social, not only for nesting, but form huge multi-specific roosts. The nests of Bobolink and meadowlarks are simple cups in the grass, whereas the orioles, of the genus *Icterus,* among others, build elaborate hanging nests, often in colonies. The cowbirds, especially the Brown-headed, *Molothrus ater,* are brood parasites on a range of species, including their own relatives.

Family 142 *Fringillidae* FINCHES Sexes usually differ

There has been much taxonomic debate about the relationship of the seed-eating passerines (see *Emberizidae* Family 137). Three subfamilies are included here, united by 12 tail feathers, 9 primaries and normally a stout conical bill suited for breaking seeds or even nuts. The *Fringillinae* consist only of the Chaffinch, *Fringilla coelebs,* the very restricted Canary Islands Chaffinch, *F. teydea,* and the Brambling, *F. montifringilla,* all Palaearctic. They lack a crop, have for seed-eaters relatively fine bills and feed insects to their young in open nests. To the *Carduelinae* are ascribed 122 species in a number of genera, many monotypic and including the little-known Asian Przevalski's Rosefinch *Urocynchramus pylzowi,* which has a functional tenth primary. The strength of the group (68 species in 21 genera) lies in the Palaearctic, but there are 30 species in 9 genera in the Ethiopian region and 25 species in 8 genera are recorded in the New World, where 2 genera are endemic. Included in the subfamily are the whole range of finches from the large (and very large-billed) grosbeaks (*Coccothraustes, Eophona, Hes-*

periphona, Mycerobas), crossbills (*Loxia*), rosefinches (*Carpodacus,* 20 species) and goldfinches (*Acanthis, Carduelis, Spinus*). The third subfamily is the remarkable Darwin's finches *Geospizinae,* 13 species in 3 genera in the Galapagos and one monotypic genus in the Cocos. They show classic adaptive radiation from a finch ancestor. There are minor differences, e.g. in plumage and size, but it is the specialisation of the bills to take different foods which is so striking.

Family 143 *Estrildidae* WEAVER FINCHES and VIDUINE WHYDAHS Sexes differ

Another family of seed-eaters with taxonomic problems. The waxbills, grassfinches and mannikins comprise some 108 species in 15 genera, all in southern parts of the Old World, including Australasia They are mostly very small and differ from the ploceid weavers (Family 144) in their untidy nests, white eggs and remarkable patterning of palate and tongue in the young. These mature very quickly and may breed at a few months, much more precociously than the ploceids. They have a great variety of courtship displays. The waxbills, tribe *Estrildini,* have about 10 genera confined to Africa, 2 Oriental avadavats and the Sydney Waxbill, *Estrilda temporalis,* which may not be closely related. There is a good deal of adaptive radiation in the tribe, as reflected in bill shapes. The grassfinches *Erythurini* are mostly Australian; they show some beautiful plumages and include some well-known cagebirds. The mannikins *Amadini* show less plumage variation but are geographically spread over south-east Asia, including India and Ceylon, Australasia and Africa, where the genus *Lonchura* occurs. Although the relationship is doubtful, the 11 species of whydahs or widow birds in the genus *Vidua* are included here. They are all Ethiopian, living socially on the savannahs in mixed flocks and laying their eggs in waxbills' nests. Their young counterfeit the mouth pattern of their hosts and their juvenile plumages. Male whydahs in breeding plumage are noted for their elongated central tail feathers.

Family 144 *Ploceidae* WEAVERS and SPARROWS Sexes alike or differ

The last of these complicated families of mainly Old World seed-eaters may be divided into 3 subfamilies. In general they are larger than estrildids (size range linnet to thrush) with 12 tail-feathers, a reduced tenth primary and the expected strong bills. They build covered nests, sometimes communally, and their young do not have coloured mouth patterns. There are only 2 buffalo weavers *Bubalornithinae,* the largest (10 ins long) members of the family, the Black, *Bubalornis albirostris,* and White-headed, *Dinemellia dinemelli,* the first being polygamous. Both forage on the ground in parties for a varied diet. The 'true' weavers *Ploceinae* comprise about 90 species, predominantly African, with 5 in south-east Asia and India. Red and yellow are characteristic plumage tints, especially in the genus *Ploceus* (57 species) and *Malimbus* (10 species), which are tree-living groups, noted for their complex nests with protective devices e.g. tunnels, sites over water, association with wasps, and exceptionally variable egg colours. The diochs *Quelea,* fodies *Foudia,* and bishops (with the 'non-viduine' whydahs) *Euplectes* are distinguished by brilliant male plumages and, frequently, long tails. There are also the monotypic genera *Amblyospiza, Neospiza* (only 2 specimens known) and parasitic *Anomalospiza.* The diochs and bishops build in grass and the fodies in trees; their nests are not so well protected as the ploceines' and their eggs are more uniform. Male bishops and whydahs are noted for their long tails, the most extreme being that of the Sakabula, *Euplectes progne,* which is 20 ins long. These birds of open habitats tend to be strongly territorial, with remarkable displays. The Old World sparrows *Passerinae* include the 8 African sparrow weavers in 4 genera of generally brown-plumaged open country birds, of which the Black-billed, *Plocepasser mahali,* is the most widespread; the Sociable Weaver, *Philetarius socius,* builds the most remarkable communal nest. There are 2 African scaly weavers *Sporopipes frontalis* and *S. squamifrons,* dry-country colonial birds. The northern groups of the *Passerinae* include the 7 snow finches *Montifringilla,* 6 confined to Asia where they are some of the highest breeding

species. The 4 rock sparrows *Petronia* have 1 African and 1 species found in India; of the other 2 southern Palaearctic species, one reaches Europe. Finally there are the *Passer* sparrows which include the almost ubiquitous (partly due to introductions) House Sparrow, *P. domesticus;* at least 8 species are more or less commensal with man.

Family 145 *Sturnidae* STARLINGS, MYNAHS, OXPECKERS Sexes more or less alike

The 110 species of this Old World family are split into 25 genera and are most numerous in India and southeast Asia, though also well represented in Africa. Only 1 species reaches Australia though the genus *Aplonis* is well-known in Polynesia. There are a few Palaearctic species, of which the Starling, *Sturnus vulgaris,* (a too successful colonist of North America after introduction) and irruptive Rosy Pastor, *S. roseus,* are the best known. Starlings are medium to large (7 to 17 ins) strongly built, long-legged, long-billed highly gregarious passerines, with poor songs but some excellent mimics; black predominates in the plumage, which may also be iridescent. Some species have wattles, lappets or bristly feathers as head ornaments. Starlings tend to be omnivorous and the Wattled, *Creatophora cinerea,* is a considerable predator on locust swarms in Africa. Starlings build open or cavity nests and the Celebes Starling, *Scissirostrum dubium,* excavates a hole, having a woodpecker-like bill and stiff tail-feathers. The 2 African oxpeckers *Buphagus,* with their specialised ecology dependent on large mammals, are included in the family.

Family 146 *Oriolidae* OLD WORLD ORIOLES Sexes differ

A homogeneous family of some 30 mainly tropical Old World species, in size from starling to jay, with long pointed wings, longish tails, curved bills and a tendency to black and gold in male plumages. They are tree-living, feeding on invertebrates and fruit, usually in evergreen forest, and build hammock nests in forked branches. The beautiful fluting song is well developed in the Golden, *Oriolus oriolus,* which, like the E Asian Black-naped, *O. chinensis,* penetrates the Palaearctic as a summer visitor. Several species have evolved on small islands, e.g. Sao Tomé (Guinea) and the Moluccas, while the Kinkimavo, *Tylas,* of Madagascar may be an aberrant oriole. The 4 fig birds *Sphecotheres* are primarily Australasian; they have bare skin around their eyes and build flimsier nests than *Oriolus.*

Family 147 *Dicruridae* DRONGOS Sexes differ somewhat

Another family of Old World tropical passerines, starling to jay sized excluding the long variable tail of 10 to 12 feathers, most spectacularly developed in the Asian Giant Racket-tailed Drongo, *Dicrurus paradiseus,* also an accomplished mimic. Apart from the monotypic Mountain Drongo, *Chaetorhynchus papuensis,* of New Guinea, all other species are *Dicrurus,* with generally metallic black plumages. A number sport crests of various shapes, rictal bristles are prominent and the iris is often red. Most variation is shown by the Asian species, several of which penetrate to the Palaearctic. The long-winged, strong-billed drongos are solitary and notably aggressive; the King Crow, *D. macrocercus,* of India recalls the Kingbird of North America (Family 108). Drongos attack birds of prey fiercely, but they allow other species to nest in their vicinity; their own nests are rather shallow hanging cradles. They feed primarily on insects and small vertebrates.

Family 148 *Callaeidae* WATTLEBIRDS Sexes more or less alike

A small New Zealand family of 2 living and 1 recently extinct species, for which various relationships have been suggested. All three have paired wattles of unknown function drooping from their gapes; their long tails show projecting feather shafts, they have long first primaries on their rounded wings, strong feet with long hind claws, and generally black plumage except for the bright wattles. They live in the primitive forest, in pairs or flocks, feeding on the ground or travelling from branch to branch without sustained flight. The Huia, *Heteralocha acutirostris,* largest of the three (19 to 21 ins) and last seen in 1907, was famous for the difference between the male and female bills. The male's shorter organ picked out grubs from decayed trees while the female's long flexible probe entered borings in harder wood. The starling-sized Saddleback, *Creadon carunculatus*, has separate races on North and South Islands, as has the Kokako or Wattled Crow, *Callaeus cinerea*, 17 to 18 ins, said to be the finest native song bird.

Family 149 *Grallinidae* MAGPIE LARKS or MUDNEST BUILDERS Sexes alike or differ

A small Australian family of 4 rather diverse species, having in common their habit of building mud cup-nests on trees near water. The strikingly black and white Magpie Lark or Mudlark, *Grallina cyanoleuca*, starling-sized, hunts invertebrate food on the ground, is pugnacious against passing birds of prey and pairs for life, though large flocks have been reported outside the breeding season. Little is known about the smaller *G. bruijni* of New Guinea. The Apostlebird, *Struthidea cinerea*, gets its name from its small flocks of about 12. The larger White-winged Chough, *Corcorax melanorhamphus*, is also a bird of south-east Australian open woodland. Both species nest communally in groups of up to 20, each female contributing probably 2 eggs.

Family 150 *Artamidae* WOOD SWALLOWS or SHRIKES Sexes usually alike

A principally Australian family with a single genus *Artamus* of 10 to 15 species, from 5 to 8 ins long, the only passerines with powder-down patches. The species radiate from Australia to the islands of south-west Asia, one reaching India and western China. Wood swallows are rather stocky, short-tailed birds with long pointed wings; their slightly curved pointed bills have wide gapes. The soft plumage is predominantly of grey, brown, black and white. They fly rather like slow-beating swallows but can also glide, the larger species spiralling in up-currents, for they are birds of open country rather than dense woods and dart after insects like flycatchers. They will attack passing predators, uttering harsh calls, and may be found in small parties, huddled on a branch, or roosting in much larger numbers. They build shallow cup nests high up on the base of a branch or other projection.

Family 151 *Cracticidae* SONG SHRIKES Sexes alike

Another small but diverse Australian family, fairly closely related to the crows; they have been given a number of English names. Ranging from 10 ins to 2 ft in length, these are strongly built birds with large heads and powerful, usually hooked bills; legs are strong and shanks rather long; plumages are often black or black and white. All species fly well and most are noisy, gregarious and tree-living. Only two currawongs, the Pied, *Strepera graculina*, and Grey, *S. versicolor*, are now recognised, both having several rather variable races. They have a mixed diet, including small vertebrates, flock in winter but breed separately, building open nests in trees, as do the other two genera. There are 2 (or 3) species of bell magpie, *Gymnorhina*, covering most of Australia between them. Both black- and white-backed forms of *G. tibicen* have been introduced to New Zealand. The Western, *G. dorsalis*, lives, apparently promiscuously, in groups of varying sex composition on communally defended territories. The 6 or 7 butcherbirds *Cracticus* show convergence with the shrikes (*Laniidae* Family 120), even to the extent of establishing larders of prey. The Pied, *C. nigrogularis*, is considered to be one of the world's best song birds. Two species are confined to New Guinea.

Family 152 *Ptilinorhynchidae* BOWER BIRDS Sexes generally differ

Another and very famous Australasian family, confined to New Guinea and northern Australia. The 19 species range from thrush to crow size; they are forest birds with short shanks and strong perching feet, short, sometimes curved or even hooked bills. Wings and tails are also short but they fly strongly and spend little time on the ground except when displaying; nests are built often high in trees. The catbirds, subfamily *Ailuroedinae*, do not build bowers. The Green, *Ailuroedus crassirostris*, and White-throated, *A. buccoides*, have 'normal' passerine displays. The male Stagemaker or Tooth-billed Catbird, *Scenopoeetes dentirostris*, of Queensland, however, clears a space on the forest floor and covers it each morning with fresh leaves, cut with its specialised bill. He then perches above and advertises his stage. There are three groups of typical bower birds *Ptilinorhynchinae* according to their constructions: the platform builders *Archboldia*; the maypole builders, *Prionodura* and *Amblyornis*; and the avenue makers *Ptilinorhynchus*, *Chlamydera* and *Sericulus*. The members of the first two groups, except for the Golden or Newton's Bower Bird, *Prionodura newtoniana*, are confined to the New Guinea rain forests and little is known about their displays. The avenue makers are also found in Australia and their behaviour has been watched. The function of the bower, built early in the season, is apparently to attract the female to the already sexually advanced male. The male, whose plumage is often brilliant, displays to the female but without approaching her until she is ready to mate, a state coinciding with the onset of insect life needed to rear the brood which she does by herself. The painting activities of the Regent, *Sericulus chrysocephalus*, and Satin Bower Birds, *Ptilinorhynchus violaceous*, using respectively bark and leaves to apply the mixture of charcoal, fruit pulp, wood and saliva to the bower are two more proved examples of tool-using by birds like the probe used by the Galapagos Woodpecker Finch, *Camarhynchus pallidus*.

Family 153 *Paradisaeidae* BIRDS OF PARADISE Sexes alike or differ widely

Some 40 species are recognised in this, perhaps the most spectacular bird family of all, with its centre in New Guinea and adjacent islands, e.g. the Arus; there are a few – the most studied – species in northern Australia and 2 in the Moluccas, the large Paradise Crow, *Lycocorax pyrrhopterus*, silky black and brown-winged, and the smaller Standardwing, *Semioptera wallacei*, with long plumes at the 'wrists' of the wings. The occurrence of natural hybrids even across generic boundaries is believed to indicate the origin of the fantastic male plumages and displays for which the family is famous: they are a device to prevent too much interbreeding between promiscuous and polygamous birds. But some species do not show sexual dimorphism and are not polygamous, the males assisting in rearing the brood, e.g. the large, wattled Moluccan Bird of Paradise, *Macgregoria pulchra*, and the glossy manucodes *Manucodia* and *Phonygammus*. Those species with most bizarre plumages and displays are the polygamous ones. Displays may be solitary or communal, on the ground or in trees, where, for example, the Emperor Bird of Paradise, *Paradisaea guilielmi*, hangs upside-down on his perch. The bulky nest built of sticks is placed in a tree, but the clutch is relatively small, being of only one or two eggs.

Family 154 *Corvidae* CROWS, MAGPIES, JAYS Sexes alike

The last and perhaps 'most evolved' of all bird families is 100 species strong, nearly world-wide and contains the largest of all passerines, the Holarctic Raven, *Corvus corax*, over 2 ft long. The smallest jays are about a foot long, but all the family is characterised by stout bodies, strong feet and legs, the shanks scaled in front and smooth behind, powerful slightly hooked bills with bristles covering the nostrils, and rather broad unspecialised but effective wings for flapping and soaring. Many species are omnivorous and all build stick nests on trees, rocks or in holes. Crows have colonised some islands but not New Zealand and others in the Pacific. Jays are strongly represented in northern South America but not in its temperate zone, while only typical crows have crossed the Sahara. Remarkable distribution patterns are shown by the Azure-winged Magpie, *Cyanopica cyanus*, (Spain and north-east Asia, but nowhere between) and the Scrub Jay, *Aphelocoma coerulescens*, found on the west coasts of North America and in Florida. Crows may be solitary or gregarious, or a mixture of both; they are found in all types of habitat, including the 'manscape' and the success of many of them as human commensals is considered by our conceited species to be proof of their intelligence.

Glossary

Parts of the plumage are named on the illustration on page 14. Some other terms used in the descriptions are:

cere: bare area at base of upper mandible
culmen: central longitudinal ridge of upper mandible
distal: furthest from the body as opposed to basal or nearest
'eyebrow': stripe above the eye
eyestripe: stripe through the eye
flight feathers: primary and secondary wing feathers
gonys: projection on lower mandible, as in larger gulls
gorget: rounded area, including chin, throat, part of upper breast
isabelline: light sandy brown or yellowish grey
lappet: hanging folds of skin on head or neck
legs: shanks (tarsus) and feet taken together

mesquite: a common name of *Prospis* species
ocelli: eye-like spots on plumage
orbit: skin round eye
rictal bristles: stiff bristles at gape of bill
sclerophyll: hard leaved (as holly)
shoulders: area less defined than scapulars
underparts: whole area from chin to under tail coverts
undertail: area less defined than under tail coverts
underwing: whole underside of wing
upperparts: whole area from forehead to tail including upper sides of wings
vermiculated: close wavy, wormlike barring as back of Mallard drake *Anas platyrhinchos*
wrist: area round carpal joint of wing

Abbreviations and notes

The 1200 specific accounts which follow are arranged in alphabetical order of scientific generic names. A second scientific name is given where still current. One or more English names follow, and the approximate length in inches of the bird from bill-tip to tail-tip, unless otherwise particularised.

Each account normally begins with the zoogeographical region where the species breeds. The usual order thereafter is: breeding and wintering distribution and breeding habitat; colours refer to adults of both sexes unless otherwise stated; some remarks on habits and behaviour, including displays, voice and principal foods; breeding season and details of nest, eggs, incubation and fledging where available.

The descriptions of plumage for species which have several or many subspecies or races have been made as general as possible. Sometimes colours in the photographs may appear to be different to those given in the text. This is because the use of artificial lighting inevitably affects the colour values. But, without it, it would not be possible to photograph many shy, nocturnal or rare species; in cases of doubt the text description should be followed.

Initial letters are used for the points of the compass unless liable to cause confusion. ♂ (plural ♂♂) for male; ♀ (plural ♀♀) for female; and *c.* for about.

'Race' is used as equivalent to 'subspecies' in the summary of distribution; the 'nominate race' is that which bears the specific name, e.g. *Troglodytes troglodytes troglodytes*; it has no biological significance.

Technical terms describing behaviour have been avoided as far as possible. 'Injury-feigning' covers the display at the nest or with young designed to lure an enemy away. 'Precocious' describes young who leave the nest soon after hatching. 'Successive polygamy' occurs when a male

transfers his attentions to a second mate after the first has begun to incubate her clutch.

As far as possible modern names are used for countries; 'East Africa' = Kenya, Tanzania and Uganda; 'Central Africa' = Malawi, Zambia and Rhodesia; 'Southern Africa' lies south of the Cunene and Zambesi rivers; 'Congo' is used for an area larger than the modern state of Zaire. All these areas, being political, are subject to changes of name. However, we have used Ceylon instead of Sri Lanka.

Symbols used in Plates	
♂	male
♀	female
♂	juvenile or immature
○	summer or breeding plumage
⊕	winter or non-breeding plumage

Acknowledgements

My most important debt is to Sir Landsborough Thomson, firstly for editing *A New Dictionary of Birds* (1964), secondly for reading through and commenting on the introduction to this work, which in its classification and nomenclature follows his Dictionary. Its numerous expert articles have also been of great value in compiling the accounts of families and species. *Birds of the World* (1961) by Oliver L. Austin Jr, illustrated by Arthur Singer, and the nine volume part-book of the same name, edited by John Gooders, have also been constant standbys.

The main sources in English for the different zoogeographical regions have been: Palaearctic: K. H. Voous's *Atlas of European Birds* (1960), the evergreen *Handbook of British Birds* (1938-41), the translation of *The Birds of the USSR* by G. P. Dementriev and others, and the numerous European field guides of recent years, especially that by Hermann Heinzel, Richard Fitter and John Parslow (1972) with its additional cover of North Africa and the Middle East.

Oriental: *Handbook of the Birds of India and Pakistan* (1968-) by Salim Ali and S. Dillon Ripon, and the senior author's many other works on the birds of the Indian subcontinent; B. E. Smythies's twin volumes on the birds of Burma (revised 1953) and Borneo (1960) and C. A. Gibson-Hill's *An Annotated List of the Birds of Malaya* (1949).

Australasia: N. W. Cayley's *What Bird is That?* (revised 1955) and *Birds in the Australian High Country*, edited by H. J. Frith (1969); A. L. Rand and E. T. Gilliard's *Handbook of New Guinea Birds* (1967); and the modern field guides covering Australia by Peter Slater, and New Zealand by R. A. Falla, R. B. Sibson and E. G. Turbott.

Ethiopian: the six volumes comprising the *African Handbook of Birds* (1952-73) by C. W. Mackworth-Praed and the late C. H. B. Grant; G. R. MacLachlan and R. Liversidge's revision (1970) of *Robert's Birds of South Africa*; and the modern field guides by O. P. M. Prozesky and J. G. Williams.

Nearctic: A. C. Bent's *Life Histories of North American Birds* are still pre-eminent, supported by numerous modern field guides, especially those written for the National Audubon Society by Richard H. Pough.

Neotropical: R. Meyer de Schauensee's *A Guide to the Birds of South America* (1970), A. W. Johnson's *The Birds of Chile* (1967) and the remarkable field studies by A. F. Skutch, Fr Haverschmidt and D. W. Snow.

Monographs on different groups which were consulted include those on Waterfowl and Pheasants (Jean Delacour), Birds of Prey (L. H. Brown and Dean Amadon), Pigeons and Doves (Derek Goodwin), Owls (edited by John A. Burton), Australian Parrots (J. M. Forshaw), Australian Honeyeaters (H. R. Officer), Bowerbirds and Birds of Paradise (A. J. Marshall, E. T. Gilliard) and Seabirds (R. C. Murphy).

In addition a great number of other books and papers in journals provided information and I am most grateful to Christopher Perrins of The Edward Grey Institute (Oxford University Department of Zoology) for unfailing advice, and to Dorothy Vincent, Librarian of the Institute's Alexander Library, for her ready help.

The specific texts for a number of groups were prepared by a strong team of helpers: John White (African species of touracos, kingfishers, bee-eaters, hornbills, barbets, honeyguides and woodpeckers); Peter Lack (larks, swallows, Old World warblers); Robert Gibson (babblers, rail babblers, parrotbills, gnatcatchers, Old World warblers); Christopher Taylor (shrikes); my son Robert Campbell (waterfowl, gulls and terns, pigeons, Australian wren warblers, starlings, bowerbirds, crows), while my wife Margaret knocked into shape my drafts on some birds of prey and cranes. Finally, Professor Richard Holmes of Dartford College, Hanover, New Hampshire, USA, read through the entire text, making a number of most valuable suggestions; but any residual errors must be laid at my door. Anne Bell and Susan Digby Firth shared the arduous task of typing out the whole text and preparing the accompanying card index of species.

John and Su Gooders of Ardea Photographics spent many hours with me choosing the illustrations; Annabel Milne has supplied the line drawings in the Introduction, while Tom Wellsted, Rachel Dunham and George Sharp (Design) have done all and more than an author has a right to expect of his house editors.

BRUCE CAMPBELL

AQUILA PHOTOGRAPHICS:

R. J. C. Blewitt – Plates 743, 805

S. C. Brown – Plates 278, 296, 744

Horace Kinloch – Plates 16, 916

C. Linford – Plate 998

J. V. Tranter – Plate 106

M. Wilks – Plate 632

ARDEA PHOTOGRAPHICS:

Plates: 202, 225, 391, 392, 396, 639, 641, 659, 660, 712, 714, 721, 833, 853, 855, 856, 868, 870, 871, 919, 923, 931, 936, 943, 946, 949, 962.

Peter Alden – Plates 27, 49, 53, 142, 154, 381, 424, 428, 456, 471, 534, 550, 562, 580, 581, 582, 584, 619, 664, 665, 693, 891, 914.

S. S. Bainbridge – Plate 31.

I. & L. Beames – Plates 93, 104, 196.

Uno Berggren – Plate 803.

Hans & Judy Beste – Plates 3, 4, 10, 33, 35, 65, 88, 100, 151, 153, 177, 195, 213, 222, 243, 259, 294, 393, 394, 395, 398, 399, 400, 402, 409, 444, 455, 462, 487, 504, 597, 715, 756, 760, 765, 771, 835, 840, 981, 987, 988.

Brian Bevan – Plates 389, 436, 450, 545, 633, 651, 725, 749, 808, 922, 928.

P. Blasdale – Plates 47, 123, 125, 141, 158, 348, 379, 413, 418, 485, 499, 501, 503, 505, 515, 539, 605, 624, 634, 703, 734, 736, 774, 807.

R. J. C. Blewitt – Plates 54, 204, 332, 357, 358, 378, 627, 681, 698, 801, 813, 1005.

R. M. Bloomfield – Plates 137, 144, 161, 164, 166, 200, 210, 214, 260, 261, 268, 269, 307, 309, 328, 437, 459, 498, 509, 510, 519, 526, 529, 532, 636, 640, 649, 655, 656, 678, 679, 683, 689, 702, 738, 781, 822, 832, 970.

J. B. & S. Bottomley – Plates 18, 28, 103, 188, 189, 205, 266, 267, 276, 281, 286, 289, 300, 316, 329, 375, 453, 599, 607, 699, 754, 857, 954, 999, 1000.

A. D. Brewer – Plates 179, 431, 460, 522, 551, 577, 579, 620, 622, 748, 811, 925, 1006.

G. J. Broekhuysen – Plates 122, 145, 226, 253, 284, 319, 355, 410, 440, 486, 548, 604, 611, 612, 614, 615, 621, 625, 629, 638, 647, 676, 682, 696, 708, 713, 727, 728, 729, 737, 782, 797, 821, 826, 929, 937, 950, 955.

D. Bromhall – Plate 81.

Leslie Brown – Plates 41, 79, 91, 420.

Donald D. Burgess – Plates 63, 233, 262, 427, 542, 543, 585, 670, 672, 673, 684, 873, 893, 910, 920, 927, 932.

Elizabeth Burgess – Plates 61, 131, 170, 291, 345, 383, 541, 547, 669, 700, 707, 994.

Kevin Carlson – Plates 183, 308, 311, 434, 502, 600, 616, 654, 694, 704, 709, 752, 957.

Graeme Chapman – Plates 51, 59, 124, 249, 318, 330, 336, 339, 370, 371, 372, 386, 388, 389, 426, 463, 726, 735, 758, 777, 789, 793, 794, 796, 818, 836, 839, 845, 848, 939, 982.

F. Collet – Plates 39, 102, 109, 114, 869, 935, 940, 941, 942.

Werner Curth – Plates 19, 299, 337, 464, 484, 553, 617, 662, 921, 975, 1007.

John Dunning – Plates 7, 171, 194, 250, 352, 359, 364, 470, 472, 473, 474, 477, 482, 483, 523, 524, 525, 536, 552, 558-561, 563-571, 583, 587, 588, 589, 592, 593, 596, 666, 675, 680, 722, 723, 851, 874-882, 884-890, 894, 895, 897, 898, 900, 904, 905, 906, 908, 909, 913, 917, 933.

M. D. England – Plates 55, 56, 64, 70, 71, 73, 76, 83, 85, 87, 94, 98, 115, 149, 152, 155, 159, 163, 175, 216, 217, 219, 221, 231, 240, 242, 245, 246, 252, 271, 279, 298, 347, 374, 404, 405, 419, 488, 491, 495, 497, 500, 508, 516, 530, 572, 573, 606, 613, 653, 677, 691, 692, 701, 731, 732, 739, 751, 753, 778, 810, 811, 819, 854, 872, 938, 959, 960, 963, 973, 977, 985, 1004.

K. W. Fink – Plates 6, 20, 40, 52, 58, 60, 62, 74, 80, 92, 97, 99, 110, 117, 127, 128, 132, 134, 135, 140, 165, 167, 169, 176, 180, 181, 182, 184, 187, 190, 192, 193, 197, 201, 206, 207, 208, 223, 232, 236, 237, 256, 283, 286, 306, 313, 323, 324, 326, 340, 350, 360, 367, 373, 390, 401, 412, 416, 417, 439, 443, 446, 449, 451, 452, 461, 465, 467, 468, 469, 512, 513, 554, 556, 574, 590, 591, 595, 643, 710, 847, 883, 968, 971, 997, 1001, 1002.

Jim Flegg – Plate 608.

P. Germain – Plates 25, 32, 43.

John Gooders – Plates 42, 90, 108, 111, 113, 118, 120, 121, 220, 241, 594.

Su Gooders – Plates 2, 101, 105, 178, 203, 385.

D. W. Greenslade – Plates 406, 711, 824, 967, 974, 995.

Don Hadden – Plates 228, 234, 397, 761, 831.

Edgar T. Jones – Plates 441, 476, 578, 586, 746, 861, 862, 892, 896, 901, 902, 903.

Gary R. Jones – Plates 24, 265, 280, 288, 303, 341, 432, 445, 475, 667, 865, 866.

Chris Knights – Plates 918, 926.

M. Krishnan – Plate 67.

Andrew Lack – Plate 496.

Peter Laub – Plates 274, 287, 327, 344, 609, 674, 706, 724, 750, 780.

Ake Lindau – Plates 69, 292, 549, 686, 745.

Eric Lindgren – Plates 36, 235, 273, 314, 361, 407, 430, 511, 992.

Trevor Marshall – Plates 282, 285, 62, 852, 864.

E. McNamara – Plates 257, 363, 365, 366, 598, 717, 718, 719, 720, 764, 766-770, 788, 791, 800, 816, 841, 846, 945.

P. R. Messent – Plate 317.

Edwin Mickleburgh – Plates 8, 48.

P. Morris – Plates 5, 77, 78, 333, 353, 415, 438, 454, 457, 531, 944.

Chris Mylne – Plates 160, 224, 806.

Irene Neufeldt – Plates 458, 485, 690, 733, 740, 741, 776, 784, 859, 934.

New Zealand Wildlife Service – Plate 230, 980.

R. F. Porter – Plates 50, 84, 506, 695.

Ralf Richter – Plates 21, 258, 263, 297, 320, 603, 650, 697, 804, 915.

Betty Risden – Plate 238.

S. Roberts – Plates 14, 95, 107, 129, 186, 227, 293, 304, 325, 335, 343, 425, 742.

W. Roberts – Plates 989, 990, 991.

Brian Sage – Plate 185.

Robert T. Smith – Plates 133, 429, 435, 546, 626, 668, 747, 780, 785, 809, 860, 956.

Bruce Sorrie – Plates 423, 494, 688, 907, 912.

Peter Steyn – Plates 12, 82, 136, 162, 168, 174, 248, 310, 369, 377, 403, 414, 433, 442, 447, 479, 527, 537, 538, 557, 642, 645, 705, 930, 958, 972, 976, 996.

Bernard Stonehouse – Plates 11, 13, 38, 322.

W. Stribling – Plates 15, 290, 338.

W. R. Taylor – Plates 45, 143, 264, 362, 368, 387, 489, 637, 757, 759, 762, 763, 772, 779, 783, 786, 787, 790, 795, 814, 815, 817, 834, 838, 842, 843, 844, 978, 983, 984, 986.

Richard Vaughan – Plates 68, 126, 254, 275, 277, 302, 334, 687.

J. P. Voisin – Plates 9, 22, 26, 29.

Richard Waller – Plate 961.

John Warham – Plate 37

Adrian Warren – Plates 23, 44, 46, 72, 139, 212, 321, 382, 466, 493, 671, 924.

A. J. S. Weaving – Plates 66, 75, 89, 218, 251, 270, 301, 380, 448, 507, 517, 520, 521, 630, 657, 716, 755, 792, 799, 969.

John Wightman – Plates 1, 112, 116, 119, 130, 146, 147, 148, 156, 157, 172, 199, 209, 215, 229, 243, 244, 247, 272, 312, 342, 346, 349, 354, 376, 384, 411, 421, 422, 518, 528, 540, 544, 555, 602, 610, 618, 628, 631, 635, 646, 648, 652, 773, 812, 820, 823, 825, 827, 828, 830, 859, 947, 948, 951, 953, 964, 965, 966, 1008.

Tom Willock – Plates 96, 211, 331, 601, 663, 993, 1003.

DAVID ATTENBOROUGH – Plate 658.

BIOFOTOS – 798, 952.

BRUCE COLEMAN LTD/INC. – Plate 351.

Des & Jan Bartlett – Plates 17, 514, 661.

E. Breeze-Jones – Plate 34.

Jane Burton – Plates 138, 480, 979.

L. R. Dawson – Plate 295, 356.

A. J. Deane – Plates 492, 533, 829.

Jack Dermid – Plate 899.

Francisco Erize – Plates 315, 535, 849.

Cyril Laubscher – Plates 198, 490.

Leonard Lee Rue – Plate 802.

John Markham – Plates 191, 644.

Oxford Scientific Films – Plate 478.

H. Rivarola – Plate 173.

M. F. Soper – Plates 30, 255, 408, 575, 576, 730, 837, 850.

Norman Tomalin – Plates 57, 481.

Joseph Van Wormer – Plates 863, 867.

NICOLE DUPLAIX-HALL – Plate 239.

ROBERT HARDING ASSOCIATES – Plate 86.

Sassoon – Plate 775.

BOBBY TULLOCH – Plate 150.

ERRATUM

Illustration **693** is of the extremely restricted Sooty Robin, *Turdus nigrescens*, and was only identified as such when the book was printing. The photograph was first misidentified as of the Sooty Chat, *Myrmecocichla nigra*, a more familiar African species. The Sooty Robin is therefore printed slightly out of place and apologies are tendered for this error. The Sooty Robin has not been described in the Dictionary section but the entry is now offered here.

Turdus nigrescens *Muscicapidae : Turdinae*
SOOTY ROBIN OR THRUSH
A very local Central American bird, confined to high mountain tops, not below 7,000 ft and mostly at 9,000 ft, in Costa Rica and W Panama. Habits and song very similar to the American Robin, *Turdus migratorius*. Breeds early April, nest largely grass and mud in tree fork about 25 ft up. Eggs pale blue like American Robin. **693**

STRUTHIONIFORMES

1
Struthio camelus ♂ ♀ ♂

RHEIFORMES

2
Rhea americana ♂

CASUARIIFORMES

3
Casuarius casuarius

4
Dromius novaehollandiae

APTERYGIFORMES
5
Apteryx australis

TINAMIFORMES
6
Nothoprocta perdicaria

7
Tinamus guttatus

SPHENISCIFORMES
8
Aptenodytes forsteri

9
Eudyptes chrysolophus

10
Eudyptes minor

11
Pygoscelis adeliae

12
Spheniscus demersus

13
Spheniscus humboldti

GAVIIFORMES

14
Gavia arctica ○

15
Gavia immer ○

16
Gavia stellata ○

35

PODICIPEDIFORMES

17
Aechmophorus occidentalis ○

18
Podiceps auritus ○

19
Podiceps cristatus ○

20
Podilymbus podiceps ○

21
Tachybaptus ruficollis ○

PROCELLARIIFORMES

22
Diomedea exulans ♂

23
Diomedea irrorata ♀♂

24
Diomedea melanophris

25
Diomedea nigripes

26
Phoebetria palpebrata ♂ ♀

27
Daption capensis

28
Fulmarus glacialis

29
Macronectes giganteus

30
Pachyptila desolata

31
Pterodroma cahow

32
Puffinus gravis

33
Puffinus pacificus

34
Puffinus puffinus

35
Puffinus tenuirostris

36
Pelagodroma marina

37
Pelecanoides urinatrix exsul

PELECANIFORMES

38
Phaethon lepturus

39
Pelecanus conspicillatus

40
Pelecanus occidentalis

41
Pelecanus onocrotalus

42
Sula bassana

43
Sula leucogaster

44
Sula nebouxii

45
Sula sula

46
Nannopterum harrisi ♂

47
Phalacrocorax africanus ⬚

48
Phalacrocorax atriceps

49
Phalacrocorax bougainvillii

54
Ardea cinerea

55
Ardea goliath

56
Bubulcus ibis

57
Cochlearius cochlearius

58
Egretta alba

59
Egretta sacra

60
Egretta thula

61
Florida caerulea

62
Hydranassa tricolor

63
Nyctanassa violacea

64
Nycticorax nycticorax

65
Notophoyx novaehollandiae

66
Scopus umbretta

67
Anastomus oscitans

68
Ciconia alba

69
Ciconia nigra

70
Dissoura episcopus

71
Ephippiorhynchus senegalensis

72
Jabiru mycteria

73
Leptoptilus crumeniferus

74
Mycteria americana

75
Mycteria ibis

76
Mycteria leucocephala

77
Balaeniceps rex

78
Ajaia ajaja

79
Bostrychia carunculata

47

80
Eudocimus albus

81
Eudocimus ruber

82
Geronticus calvus

83
Hagedashia hagedash

84
Platalea leucorodia

85
Plegadis falcinellus

86
Pseudibis papillosa

87
Threskiornis aethiopicus

88
Threskiornis spinicollis

89
Phoeniconaias minor

90
Phoenicoparrus andinus

91
Phoenicopterus ruber

ANSERIFORMES

92
Anhima cornuta

93
Aix galericulata ♀♂

94
Alopochen aegyptiaca ♂♀

95
Anas acuta ♀ ♂

96
Anas clypeata ♂

97
Anas platyrhynchos ♀ ♂ ♀

98
Anseranas semipalmata

99
Anser anser ♀

100
Anser caerulescens

101
Aythya fuligula ♂

102
Biziura lobata ♂

103
Branta canadensis

104
Branta leucopsis

105
Branta sandvicensis

106
Bucephala islandica ♂

107
Cairina moschata

108
Calonetta leucophrys ♀♂

109
Cereopsis novaehollandiae

110
Chloephaga hybrida hybrida ♂♀

111
Chloephaga picta♂

112
Clangula hyemalis♂ ○

113
Coscoroba coscoroba

114
Cygnus atratus

115
Dendrocygna viduata

116
Histrionicus histrionicus♂♂

117
Lophonetta specularoides alticola ○

118
Marmaronetta angustirostris ○

53

124
Oxyura australis ♂ ♀

125
Plectopterus gambiensis ♂ ○

126
Polysticta stelleri

127
Sarkidiornis melanotos ♂

128
Tachyeres pteneres

129
Tadorna tadorna ♂

FALCONIFORMES

130
Cathartes aura

131
Coragyps atratus

132
Sarcorhamphus papa

133
Accipiter nisus ♀

134
Aquila audax

135
Aquila chrysaetos

136
Aquila rapax

55

137
Aquila verreauxi

138
Aquila wahlbergi ♂

139
Buteo galapagoensis

140
Buteo lineatus

141
Chelictinia riocourii

142
Circaetus cinereus

143
Circus approximans ♂

144
Circus ranivorus

145
Elanus caeruleus

146
Gypaetus barbatus

147
Gypohierax angolensis

148
Gyps africanus

149
Gyps bengalensis

150
Haliaeetus albicilla

151
Haliaeetus leucogaster

152
Haliaeetus vocifer

153
Haliastur sphenorus

154
Heterospizias meridionalis

155
Hieratus pennatus

156
Lophoaetus occipitalis

157
Melierax canorus

158
Milvus migrans aegyptius

59

159
Neophron percnopterus

160
Pandion haliaetus

161
Polemaetus bellicosus ♀ ♂

162
Polyboroides typus

163
Sarcogyps calvus

164
Stephanoetus coronatus

165
Terathopius ecaudatus

166
Trigonoceps occipitalis

167
Falco berigora

168
Falco biarmicus ♀

169
Falco peregrinus ♀

174
Sagittarius serpentarius

GALLIFORMES

175
Leipoa ocellata

176
Megacephalon maleo

177
Megapodius freycinet ♀

178
Crax daubentoni ♂

179
Ortalis ruficauda

180
Ortalis vetula ⊕

181
Centrocercus urophasianus ♂

182
Dendragapus obscurus ♀

183
Lagopus lagopus ♀ ○

184
Lagopus leucurus ♂ ○

185
Lagopus mutus ♀ ○

186
Lyrurus tetrix ♂

187
Pedioecetes phasianellus ♂ ○

188
Tetrao urogallus ♀ ○

189
Tetrastes bonasus ♀ ○

190
Tympanuchus cupido ♂ ○

191
Alectoris rufa

192
Chrysolophus amherstiae ♂

193
Chrysolophus pictus ♂

194
Colinus virginianus ♂

195
Coturnix pectoralis ♂

196
Crossoptilon crossoptilon ♂

197
Dendrortyx leucophrys

68

198
Francolinus coqui ♂

199
Francolinus jacksoni ♀ ♂

200
Francolinus swainsoni

201
Gallus gallus ♂

202
Lophortyx californicus ♂

203
Pavo cristatus ♂

204
Phasianus colchicus ♂

205
Perdix perdix ♀

206
Polyplectron emphanum ♂

207
Rollulus roulroul ♂

208
Tragopan satyra ♂

209
Acryllium vulturinum ♀♂

210
Numida meleagris ♀

211
Meleagris gallopavo ♂

212
Opisthocomus hoatzin

71

213
Turnix varia ♂

214
Anthropoides paradisaea

215
Anthropoides virgo

216
Balearica pavonina

217
Grus antigone ♀♂

218
Grus carunculatus

219
Grus grus

220
Grus japonensis

221
Grus leucogeranus ♀♂

222
Grus rubicundus

223
Aramus guarauna

224
Crex crex

225
Fulica atra

226
Fulica cristata

227
Gallinula chloropus

228
Gallirallus australis greyi

229
Limnocorax flavirostra

74

237
Rallus owstoni

238
Psophia leucoptera

239
Rhynochetus jubatus

240
Eurypyga helias

241
Cariama cristata

242
Choriotis kori

243
Eupodotis australis

244
Eupodotis senegalensis ♂

245
Lissotis melanogaster ♂

246
Otis tarda ♀

248
Actophilornis africana

249
Irediparra gallinacea ♀♂

250
Jacana spinosa

251
Microparra capensis

252
Rostratula benghalensis ♀

253
Haematopus moquini

254
Haematopus ostralegus

255
Anarhynchus frontalis

256
Charadrius alexandrinus

257
Charadrius cucullatus

Charadrius hiaticula ♂ ○ **258**

264
Lobibyx novaehollandiae

265
Pluvialis apricaria ○

266
Pluvialis dominica fulva ◍

267
Pluvialis squatarola ◍

268
Vanellus armatus

269
Vanellus coronatus

270
Vanellus senegallus

271
Vanellus spinosus

272
Vanellus tectus

273
Vanellus tricolor

274
Vanellus vanellus

275
Arenaria interpres ⊕

276
Calidris alba ♂

277
Calidris alpina ◯

278
Calidris canutus ◍

279
Calidris ferruginea ◯

280
Calidris fuscicollis ♀ ◯

281
Calidris maritima ◍

282
Calidris temminckii ◯

85

283
Catoptrophorus semipalmatus ○

284
Gallinago nigripennis ○

285
Limicola falcinellus ○

286
Limnodromus scolopaceus ◍

287
Limosa limosa ○

288
Micropalma himantopus ○

289
Numenius arquata ○

290
Numenius phaeopus ○

291
Philohela minor ♀ ○

292
Philomachus pugnax ♂ ○

293
Scolopax rusticola ♀ ○

294
Tringa brevipes ♂

295
Tringa erythropus ♂

296
Tringa glareola ♂

297
Tringa hypoleucos ○

298
Tringa stagnatilis ◉

299
Tringa totanus ○

300
Tringytes subruficollis

309
Cursorius temminckii

310
Galachrysia nuchalis

311
Glareola pratincola

312
Hemerodromus africanus

313
Pluvianus aegyptius

314
Stiltia isabella ○

315
Chionis alba

316
Stercorarius longicauda ○

317
Stercorarius skua

318
Anous stolidus

319
Chlidonias hybrida ○

320
Chlidonias niger ○

321
Creagrus furcatus ○

322
Gygis alba

323
Hydroprogne caspia ○

324
Larosterna inca ○

325
Larus argentatus ♀♂ ○

326
Larus californicus ○

327
Larus canus ○

328
Larus cirrocephalus ○

329
Larus minutus ♂

330
Larus pacificus ○

331
Larus pipixcan ○

332
Larus ridibundus ○

333
Rissa tridactyla ○

93

334
Sterna albifrons ○

335
Sterna dougallii ○

336
Sterna fuscata ○

337
Sterna hirundo ○

338
Sterna paradisaea ○

339
Sterna sumatrana ○

340
Thalasseus elegans ○

341
Xema sabini ○

342
Rynchops nigra ○

343
Alca torda ○

344
Cepphus grylle ○

345
Fratercula arctica ○

346
Uria aalge

347
Eremialector decoratus♂

348
Eremialector quadricinctus ♀ ♂

349
Pterocles exustus ♂

350
Caloenas nicobarica ♂

351
Chalcophaps indica ♂

352
Claravis pretiosa ♂

353
Columba albitorques ○

354
Columba aquatrix

355
Columba guinea ○

356
Columba livia

362
Geopelia humeralis

363
Geopelia striata ○

364
Geotrygon montana ♂

365
Leucosarcia melanoleuca

366
Lopholaimus antarcticus

367
Macropygia phasianella

368
Ocyphaps lophotes

369
Oena capensis ♂

370
Petrophassa albipennis

371
Petrophassa scripta

372
Phaps histrionica ♂

373
Ptilinopus melanospila ♂

374
Streptopelia chinensis

375
Streptopelia decaocto

376
Streptopelia semitorquata

377
Streptopelia senegalensis

378
Streptopelia turtur

379
Turtur abyssinicus

380
Turtur chalcospilos

381
Zenaida auriculata

382
Zenaida galapagoensis ♂

383
Zenaida macroura

384
Agapornis personata

385
Anodorhynchus hyacinthinus

386
Aprosmictus scapularis ♂

387
Barnardius barnardi

388
Cacatua roseicapilla

389
Callocephalon fimbriatum ♂

390
Cyanoramphus novaezelandiae

391
Domicella domicella

392
Eos squamata

393
Glossopsitta pusilla

394
Lathamus discolor

395
Melopsittacus undulatus ♀

396
Neophemia elegans

397
Nestor meridionalis

398
Nymphicus hollandicus ♀

399
Opopsitta leadbeateri

400
Pezoporus wallicus

401
Pionus sordidus

402
Platycercus elegans

107

403
Poicephalus meyeri

404
Psephotus haematodus ♂

405
Psittacula krameri ♂

406
Psittacus erithacus

407
Psitteuteles goldiei

408
Strigops habroptilus

409
Trichoglossus haematodus

CUCULIFORMES

410
Corythaeola cristata

411
Corythaixodes concolor

412
Corythaixodes leucogaster

413
Crinifer zonurus

414
Gallirex porphyreolophus

421
Chrysococcyx caprius♂

422
Clamator glandarius

423
Crotophaga ani

424
Crotophaga major

425
Cuculus canorus♂

426
Cuculus pallidus♂

427
Geococcyx californianus

428
Piaya cayana

STRIGIFORMES

429
Tyto alba ♀♂

430
Tyto tenebricosa

431
Aegolius acadicus

432
Aegolius funereus

433
Asio capensis

434
Asio flammeus

435
Asio otus

436
Athene noctua

437
Bubo africanus

438
Bubo bubo

439
Bubo ketupu

440
Bubo lacteus

441
Bubo virginianus

442
Ciccaba woodfordii

443
Micrathene whitneyi

444
Ninox novaeseelandiae

445
Nyctaea scandiaca ♀

446
Otus asio

447
Otus leucotis

448
Otus scops

449
Speotyto cunicularia

450
Strix aluco

451
Strix nebulosa

452
Strix varia

453
Surnia ulula

454
Steatornis caripensis

455
Podargus strigoides

456
Nyctibius grandis

457
Nyctibius griseus

458
Aegotheles cristata

459
Caprimulgus indicus ♀

460
Caprimulgus pectoralis

461
Caprimulgus vociferus ♀

462
Chordeiles minor

463
Eurostopodus guttatus

APODIFORMES

464
Apus apus

465
Aglaiocercus kingi ♂

466
Archilochus colubris ♂♂

467
Calypte anna ♀

468
Calypte costae ♂

469
Chlorostilbon maugaeus ♀

123

478
Trochilus polytmus ♂

COLIIFORMES

479
Colius indicus

480
Colius striatus

TROGONIFORMES

481
Pharomachrus mocinno ♂

482
Trogon collaris ♂

483
Trogon rufus ♂

484
Alcedo athis

485
Ceryle rudis

486
Corythornis cristata

487
Dacelo gigas

488
Halcyon leucocephala

489
Halcyon sancta

490
Halcyon senegalensis

491
Halcyon smyrnensis

492
Ispidina picta

493
Megaceryle maxima ♂

494
Todus mexicanus

495
Baryphthengus ruficapillus

496
Momotus momota

497
Aerops albicollis

498
Melittophagus bullockoides

499
Melittophagus bulocki

500
Melittophagus oreobates

501
Melittophagus pusillus

502
Merops apiaster

503
Merops orientalis

504
Merops ornatus

505
Coracias abyssinica

506
Coracias benghalensis

507
Coracias caudata

508
Coracias garrulus

509
Upupa epops africana

510
Phoeniculus purpureus

511
Aceros plicatus

512
Anthracoceros malabaricus

513
Berenicornis comatus ♂

514
Buceros bicornis ♀

515
Bucorvus abyssinicus ♂

516
Bucorvus leadbeateri ♂

517
Tockus alboterminatus

518
Tockus deckeni ♂

519
Tockus erythrorhynchus

520
Tockus flavirostris

521
Tockus nasutus ♂

PICIFORMES

522
Galbula ruficauda

523
Bucco macrodactylus

524
Malacoptila panamensis

525
Eubucco bourcierii ♀

526
Lybius leucomelas

527
Lybius torquatus

528
Pogoniulus bilineatus

529
Pogoniulus chrysoconus

530
Trachyphonus darnaudii

531
Trachyphonus erythrocephalus

532
Trachyphonus vaillantii

533
Indicator minor

534
Aulacorhynchus caeruleogularis

535
Aulacorhynchus prasinus

536
Pteroglossus pluricinctus

537
Campethera abingoni

538
Campethera bennettii ♂

539
Campethera punctuligera ♀

540
Centurus carolinus ♂

541
Centurus uropygialis ♀

542
Colaptes auratus ♀

543
Colaptes chrysoides ♀

544
Dendrocopos major ♂

545
Dendrocopos minor ♂

546
Dendrocopos syriacus ♂

547
Dendrocopos villosus ♀

137

548
Geocolaptes olivaceus

549
Jynx torquilla

550
Melanerpes pucherani ♂

551
Melanerpes rubricapillus ♂

552
Picumnus squamulatus

553
Picus canus ♂

554
Sphyrapicus varius ♂

555
Thripias namaquus ♂

556
Calyptomena viridis ♂

557
Smithornis capensis ♂

558
Campylorhamphus falcularius

559
Glyphorynchus spirurus

560
Xiphorhynchus guttatus

561
Automolus leucophthalmus

562
Cinclodes fuscus

563
Margarornis squamiger

564
Thripadectes virgaticeps

565
Xenops minutus

566
Cymbilaimus lineatus ♀

567
Formicarius analis

568
Grallaricula ferrugineipectus

569
Phlegopsis nigromaculata

570
Pithys albifrons

571
Conopophaga lineata

572
Pitta brachyura

573
Pitta guajana♂

574
Pitta gurneyi♂

575
Acanthisitta chloris ♀

576
Xenicus gilviventris

577
Contopus virens

578
Empidonax flavirostris

579
Empidonax minimus

580
Muscivora tyrannus ♂

581
Myiodynastes maculatus

582
Myiozetetes similis

583
Oxyruncus cristatus

584
Tyrannus melancholicus

144

585
Tyrannus tyrannus ♀♂

586
Tyrannus verticalis ♂

587
Chiroxiphia linearis ♂

145

588
Machaeropterus regulus ♂

589
Manacus manacus ♂

590
Cephalopterus ornatus penduliger ♂

591
Cotinga cayana ♂

592
Pachyrhamphus marginatus ♀♂

593
Pipreola riefferii ♂

594
Procnias nudicollis♂

595
Rupicola peruviana♂

596
Tityra cayana♂

597
Menura novaehollandiae♂

598
Atrichornis rufescens

599
Alauda arvensis

147

600
Calandrella cinerea ♂

601
Eremophila alpestris ♂

602
Eremophila bilopha ♂

603
Galerida cristata

604
Galerida magnirostris

605
Galerida modesta

606
Galerida theklae ♀

607
Lullula arborea

608
Mirafra africana

609
Delichon urbica

610
Hirundo abyssinica

611
Hirundo albigularis

612
Hirundo cucullata

613
Hirundo daurica

614
Hirundo dimidiata

615
Hirundo fuligula

616
Hirundo rupestris

617
Hirundo rustica

618
Hirundo senegalensis

619
Hirundo smithii ♂

620
Progne subis ♀

621
Riparia paludicola

622
Tachycineta bicolor

623
Anthus cervinus ♀

624
Anthus leucophrys

625
Anthus novaeseelandiae

626
Anthus pratensis + ♂ *Cuculus canorus*

627
Anthus trivialis ♂ ♀

628
Macronyx ameliae ♂

629
Macronyx capensis ♂

630
Macronyx croceus

631
Motacilla aguimp

632
Motacilla alba ♀

633
Motacilla cinerea ♀

634
Motacilla flava flava♂

635
Tmetothylacus tenellus♂

636
Campephaga sulphurata♀

637
Coracina novaehollandiae

638
Andropadus importunus

639
Hypsipetes flavalus

640
Pycnonotus barbatus

641
Pycnonotus cafer

642
Pycnonotus nigricans

643
Chloropsis aurifrons

644
Irena puella ♂

645
Dryoscopus cubla ♀

646
Eurocephalus anguitimens

647
Laniarius aethiopicus

648
Lanius cabanisi

649
Lanius collaris ♂

650
Lanius collurio ♂

651
Lanius excubitor ♂

652
Lanius minor

653
Lanius schach

654
Lanius senator ♂ ♀

655
Malaconotus zeylonus

656
Prionops plumata

657
Tchagra senegala

658
Xenopirostris xenopirostris

659
Bombycilla cedrorum

660
Bombycilla garrulus ♀

661
Phainopepla nitens ♀

662
Cinclus cinclus

663
Cinclus mexicanus ♂

664
Campylorhynchus bruneicapillus

665
Campylorhynchus griseus

666
Cyphorinus thoracicus

667
Telmatodytes palustris

668
Troglodytes troglodytes

669
Dumetella carolinensis

670
Mimus polyglottos

160

671
Nesomimus trifasciatus

672
Toxostoma curvirostre

673
Toxostoma rufum

674
Prunella modularis ♀♂

675
Catharus fuscater

676
Cercomela familiaris

677
Cercotrichas galactotes ♀♂

678
Cossypha caffra

679
Cossypha humeralis

680
Entomodestes coracinus

681
Erithacus rubecula

682
Erythropygia coryphaeus

683
Erythropygia zambesiana

684
Hylocichla mustelina

685
Luscinia calliope ♂

686
Luscinia luscinia

687
Luscinia svecica ♂

688
Mimocichla plumbea

689
Monticola angolensis ♂ ♀

690
Monticola cinclorhynchus gularis ♂

691
Monticola saxatilis ♂

692
Monticola solitarius ♂

693
Turdus nigrescens

694
Oenanthe hispanica ♂

695
Oenanthe monacha ♀

696
Oenanthe monticola ♀

697
Oenanthe oenanthe ♂

698
Phoenicurus phoenicurus ♂

699
Saxicola torquata ♂

700
Sialia sialis ♂

701
Tarsiger cyanurus ♂

Thamnolaea cinnamomeiventris ♂

703
Thamnolaea coronata ♂

704
Turdus iliacus

705
Turdus libonyanus

706
Turdus merula ♂

707
Turdus migratorius ♂

708
Turdus olivaceus

167

709
Turdus viscivorus

710
Garrulax caerulatus

711
Leiothrix argentauris ♀

712
Leiothrix lutea

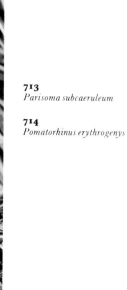

713
Parisoma subcaeruleum

714
Pomatorhinus erythrogenys

715
Pomatostomus superciliosus

716
Turdoides jardinei

717
Cinclosoma castanotum

718
Cinclosoma cinnamomeum ♂

719
Orthonyx spaldingi ♀

720
Psophodes olivaceus

721
Panurus biarmicus ♀

722
Polioptila caerulea

723
Ramphocaenus melanurus

724
Acrocephalus palustris

725
Acrocephalus schoenobaenus ♀ ♂

726
Acrocephalus stentoreus

727
Apalis thoracica

728
Bradypterus baboecalus

729
Bradypterus sylvaticus

730
Bowdleria punctata

731
Camaroptera brevicaudata

732
Cettia cetti

733
Cettia squameiceps

734
Cisticola aridula

735
Cisticola exilis ♂ ○

736
Cisticola galactotes ⬚

737
Cisticola subruficapilla

738
Eremomela icteropygialis

739
Hippolais polyglotta

740
Leptopoecile sophiae ♀

741
Locustella fasciolata

742
Locustella naevia

743
Phylloscopus collybita

744
Phylloscopus sibilatrix ♀ ♂

745
Phylloscopus trochilus

746
Regulus calendula

747
Regulus regulus

748
Regulus satrapa

749
Sylvia atricapilla ♂

750
Sylvia borin

751
Sylvia cantillans ♀

75²
Sylvia hortensis

753
Sylvia melanocephala ♂

754
Sylvia nisoria ♀

755
Sylvietta rufescens

75⁶
Acanthiza auropygialis

757
Acanthiza chrysorrhoa

758
Chthonicola sagittata

759
Cinclorhamphus mathewsi

760
Ephthianura aurifrons ♂

761
Gerygone igata ♀

762
Gerygone olivacea

763
Malurus assimilis ♂

764
Malurus callainus ♂

765
Malurus cyaneus ♂

766
Malurus cyanotus ♂

767
Malurus lamberti ♂

768
Malurus melanocephalus ♂

769
Malurus melanotus ♂

770
Pycnoptilus floccosus

771
Sericornis frontalis

772
Smicrornis brevirostris

773
Alseonax adustus

774
Alseonax aquaticus

775
Bradornis pallidus ♂

776
Cyanoptila cyanomelana ♂

179

777
Dryomodus brunneipygia

778
Diptrornis fischeri

779
Eopsaltria australis

780
Ficedula hypoleuca ♂

781
Melaenornis pammelaina

782
Melaenornis silens ♂

783
Microeca fascinans

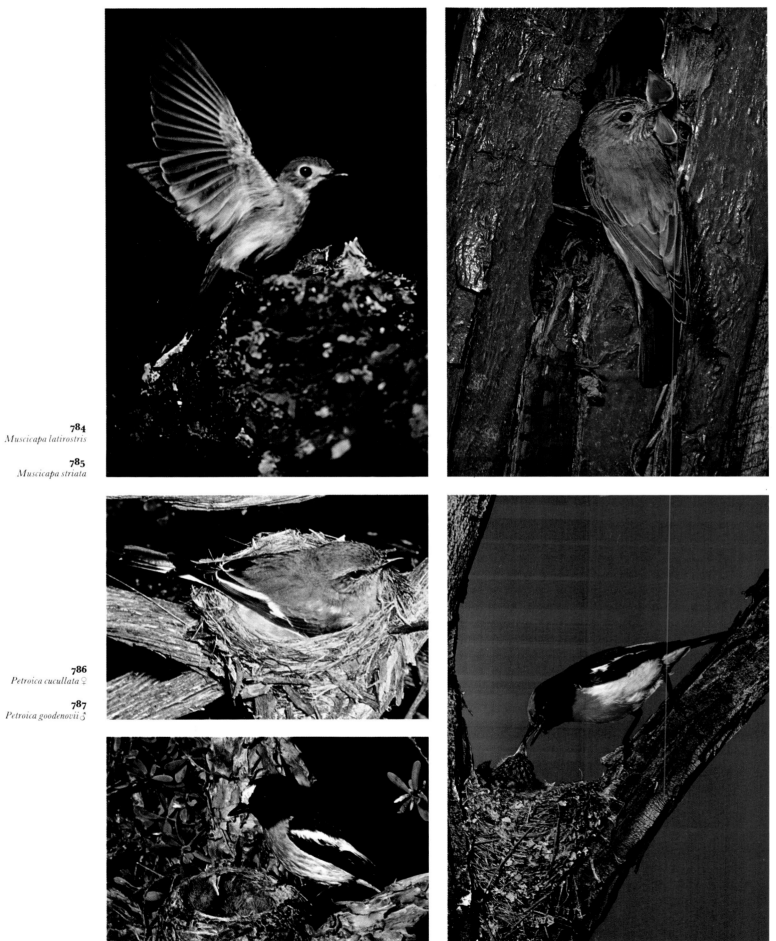

784
Muscicapa latirostris

785
Muscicapa striata

786
Petroica cucullata ♀

787
Petroica goodenovii ♂

788
Petroica multicolor ♂

789
Petroica rodinogaster ♂

790
Rhipidura fuliginosa

791
Rhipidura rufifrons

792
Batis molitor ♂

793
Monarcha melanopsis

794
Myiagra cyanoleuca ♂

795
Myiagra inquieta ♂

796
Myiagra rubecula ♂

797
Stenostira scita

798
Terpsiphone corvina ♀

806
Parus montanus

807
Parus niger ♂

808
Parus palustris

809
Remiz pendulinus

810
Sitta canadensis ♂

811
Sitta europaea

812
Sitta neumayer

813
Certhia familiaris

814
Climacteris picumnus

815
Dicaeum hirundinaceum ♀

816
Pardalotus melanocephalus

817
Pardalotus punctatus♂

818
Pardalotus striatus

819
Arachnothera magna

820
Chalcomitra senegalensis♂

821
Cinnyris chalybeus ♂

822
Cinnyris talatala ♀

823
Cinnyris venustus ♂

824
Cyanomitra verticalis ♂

825
Drepanorhynchus reichenowi ♂

826
Nectarinia famosa ♀

827
Nectarinia kilimensis ♂

828
Nectarinia pulchella ♂

829
Nectarinia tacazze ♂

830
Zosterops kikuyuensis

831
Zosterops lateralis ♀

832
Zosterops pallida

833
Zosterops palpebrosa

834
Acanthogenys rufogularis

835
Acanthorhynchus tenuirostris ♂

836
Anthochaera chrysoptera

837
Anthornis melanura ♂

838
Entomyzon cyanotus

839
Gliciphila albifrons ♀

840
Gliciphila melanops

841
Meliornis niger

842
Meliphaga chrysops

843
Meliphaga leucotis

844
Meliphaga melanops

845
Myzomela nigra ♂

846
Philemon corniculatus

847
Philemon yorki

848
Plectorhyncha lanceolata

849
Promerops cafer ♂

850
Prosthemadera novaeseelandiae ♂

851
Arremon schlegeli

852
Calcarius lapponicus ♂

853
Emberiza calandra

854
Emberiza cia ♀ ♂

855
Emberiza citrinella

856
Emberiza flaviventris ♂

857
Emberiza hortulana

858
Emberiza leucocephala ♂

859
Emberiza melanocephalus ♂

860
Emberiza schoeniclus ♂

861
Melospiza melodia

862
Passerella iliaca

863
Pipilo erythrophthalmus ♀

864
Plectrophenax nivalis ♂ ○

865
Spizella arborea

866
Zonotrichia albicollis ♀

867
Zonotrichia leucophrys ♂

868
Gubernatrix cristata ♂

869
Paroaria cucullata

870
Passerina amoena ♂

199

871
Passerina ciris ♂

872
Passerina leclancheri ♂

873
Pyrrhuloxia cardinalis ♂

874
Saltator atripennis

875
Chlorochrysa phoenicotis

876
Iridosornis rufivertex

877
Piranga rubra ♂

878
Ramphocelus icteronotus ♂

879
Ramphocelus nigrogularis ♂

880
Tanagra laniirostris ♂

881
Tangara cyanoptera ♂

882
Tangara gyrola

883
Tangara nigroviridis

884
Thraupis episcopus ♂

885
Tersina viridis ♂

886
Coereba flaveola

887
Cyanerpes caeruleus ♀♂

888
Dacnis lineata ♂

889
Diglossa caerulescens ♂

890
Basileuterus rufifrons

891
Dendroica dominica ♂

892
Dendroica magnoliae ⊕

893
Dendroica petechia ♂

894
Helmitheros vermivorus

895
Icteria virens

896
Mniotilta varia ♂

897
Myioborus miniatus

898
Myioborus ornatus

899
Seiurus auricapillus

900
Setophaga ruticilla ♂

901
Vermivora celata

902
Wilsonia canadensis ♂

903
Wilsonia pusilla ♂

904
Cyclarhis gujanensis

905
Hylophilus ochraceiceps

906
Vireo griseus

907
Agelaius xanthomus

908
Cacicus cela

909
Gymnomystax mexicanus

910
Icterus galbula ♀

911
Molothrus ater ♂ ♀

912
Quiscalus niger ♂

913
Quiscalus quiscala ♂

914
Sturnella magna ♂

915
Acanthis cannabina ♂

916
Acanthis flammea ♀

917
Atlapetes semirufus

918
Carduelis carduelis

919
Carduelis chloris ♂

920
Carpodacus mexicanus ♂

921
Coccothraustes coccothraustes

922
Fringilla coelebs ♂

923
Fringilla montifringilla ♂ ◫

924
Geospiza fortis ♀

925
Hesperiphona vespertina ♂ ◫

926
Loxia curvirostra ♀

927
Pheucticus melanocephalus ♂

928
Pyrrhula pyrrhula ♂ ♀

929
Serinus alario ♂

930
Serinus flaviventris ♂

931
Serinus serinus ♀

932
Spinus tristis ♂ ○

933
Sporophila americana ♂

934
Uragus sibiricus ♂

935
Aidemosyne modesta ♂ ♀

936
Amadina erythrocephala

937
Estrilda astrild

938
Lagonisticta rubricata ♂

939
Lonchura castaneothorax♂ ♀

940
Neochmia phaeton ♂

941
Padda oryzivora

942
Poephila gouldiae ♂

943
Pytilia phoenicoptera ♂

944
Steganura paradisaea ♂ ○

945
Taenopygia castanotis ♂

946
Uraeginthus bengalus ♂ ♀

947
Vidua macroura ♂ ○

948
Dinemellia dinemelli

949
Euplectes macrourus ♂ ○

950
Euplectes orix ♂ ○

951
Euplectes progne ♂ ○

952
Foudia sechellarum

953
Montifringilla nivalis ♂

954
Passer domesticus ♂

955
Passer melanurus ♂

956
Passer montanus

963
Acridotheres tristis

964
Buphagus africanus

965
Buphagus erythrorhynchus ♀♂

966
Cosmopsarus regius ♂

967
Creatophora cinerea ♀

968
Gracula religiosa

969
Lamprocolius chalybeus

970
Lamprotornis australis

971
Leucopsar rothschildi ♀♂

972
Onychognathus nabouroup

973
Spreo superbus

974
Sturnus vulgaris ♀ ○

975
Temenuchus pagodarum

976
Oriolus larvatus

977 ↓
Oriolus oriolus ♂

978
Oriolus sagittatus

979
Dicrurus adsimilis

980
Creadion carunculatus

981
Grallina cyanoleuca♂

982
Artamus leucorhynchus

983
Cracticus torquatus ♂

984
Gymnorhina tibicen ♂♂

985
Strepera graculina

986
Chlamydera maculata ♂

987
Prionodura newtoniana ♂

988
Ptilinorhynchus violaceus ♂

989
Astrapia stephaniae ♀

990
Cicinnurus regius ♂

991
Epimachus meyeri ♀

992
Paradisaea raggiana ♂

993
Aphelocoma caerulescens

994
Aphelocoma ultramarina

995
Cissa chinensis

996
Corvultur albicollis

997
Corvus corax

998
Corvus corone cornix

999
Corvus frugilegus

1000
Corvus monedula

1001
Corvus ossifragus

1002
Cyanocitta stelleri

1003
Cyanocorax yncas

1004
Cyanopica cyanus

1005
Garrulus glandarius

1006
Nucifraga columbiana

1007
Pica pica

1008
Pyrrhocorax graculus

Acanthis hornemanni see under **A. flammea**

ABYSSINIAN

GROUND HORNBILL see **Bucorvus abyssinicus**
ROLLER see **Coracias abyssinicus**

ACADIAN FLYCATCHER see *Empidonax virescens* under **Empidonax traillii**

Acanthis cannabina or Carduelis cannabina
Fringillidae

LINNET   5¼ ins

Palaearctic: Europe to *c.* 60°N (S Scandinavia), extending E to head waters River Ob, SE through Asia Minor to Palestine, Iran; isolated population Turkestan; local N African coasts, Canary Is. Resident and migrant, northern birds wintering Mediterranean area, Iraq, Iran; also large wandering flocks with other finches. Habitat forest edge, wooded and cultivated areas with trees, hedges, habitations; heaths and dunes; in mountains to tree limit; farmland and fallows in winter. ♂: back chestnut; white edges to brownish-black wings, tail; head, neck greyish; cap and breast crimson; throat spotted black; belly greyish white, flanks buff-chestnut. Winter ♂ loses most of crimson, resembles ♀ with streaked buff underparts. Juvenile even more striated. Legs dark brown, bill grey (♂ spring) or horn; eyes very dark brown. Hops on ground; favours low perches. Winter flocks in wavering, undulating flight, calling *chichichichit;* also *tsooeet* of anxiety and rather formless but attractive twittering song. ♂ vibrates spread tail, drooping wings in display. Diet mainly weed seeds; some insects and larvae in summer, especially for young. Breeds April to September, solitary or in groups. ♀. attended ♂, builds nest of stalks, grass, moss, rootlets, softly lined, in variety of bushes up to 12 ft, often gorse *Ulex* in Britain and Ireland; also in grass tufts, banks, walls, young conifers. 4 to 6 pale blue or bluish-white eggs, spotted and streaked dark brown, incubated mainly ♀ 11-12 days; both parents feed young from throat; they fly 11-13 days. 2, sometimes 3 broods. **915**

Acanthis flammea or Carduelis flammea
Fringillidae

REDPOLL   *c.* 5 ins

Holarctic: combined breeding range with Arctic Redpoll *A. hornemanni*, often regarded as conspecific, round N Hemisphere, between 60° and 70°N, extending farther N in Siberia, Baffin Land, Greenland, S to Britain, Ireland, isolated populations European mountains; also Labrador, Newfoundland; introduced New Zealand. Resident with dispersal movements, some southward migration. Habitat open coniferous and broadleaved woodlands (birch, willow, alder) on riverbanks, round lakes, swamps; through larch to dwarf pine in Alps; conifer plantations, heaths, commons, cultivated land in Britain, Ireland; birchwoods, riparian alders in winter. Upperparts, including head, throat, flanks, varying browns (according to race), streaked darker brown, with red cap, black bib, white belly, 2 pale or white wingbars. Breast, rump of spring ♂ suffused crimson in British 'Lesser' and Eurasian 'Mealy' races, hardly at all in much paler Arctic Redpoll. Juvenile lacks cap, only traces of bib. Legs, eyes dark brown, bill mainly yellow. Hops on ground. Very pronounced bouncing flight with metallic *chuch-uch-uch* note; *tsooeet* of anxiety. Song develops from flight call with added *errr*, often in display of loops and circles, several ♂♂ together. Takes seeds alder, birch, conifers, extracting them from cones with tweezer action of bill; also weed seeds; small insects in summer when feeding young. Breeds mid April to August, solitary or in groups. ♀, attended ♂, builds foundation of twigs, rootlets, cup of moss, bark, lichens, softly lined, 3 to 15 ft or more in variety of bushes, small trees, especially birch, sallow, young conifers in wilder habitats. 4 to 6 blue eggs, streaked, spotted red-brown often in zone, incubated ♀ *c.* 11 days; ♀ and ♂ feed young from throat; they fly *c.* 12 days. Sometimes 2 broods. **916**

Acanthisitta chloris *Xenicidae*

RIFLEMAN   3 ins

Confined to New Zealand (absent northern third North Island) and some offshore islands; resident native forest remnants, e.g. mountainous *Nothofagus* beech woods, also introduced trees, even hedgerows and gorse bushes. ♂: upperparts bright yellow-green; yellow bar and white spot on wing; rump, flanks yellow; very short black tail tipped buff; dark eyestripe, white 'eyebrow'; underparts white, tinged buff; legs blackish, bill black, slightly uptilted, eyes dark brown. ♀ has upperparts striped dark and light brown, otherwise as ♂. Juvenile as ♀. Characteristic rapid flicking of wings when perched, but habits like treecreeper, searching bark, mosses, lichens on tree trunks and branches, even to twigs and at all heights, for insects and spiders; rarely on ground. Call: sharp, high-pitched *zipt*, often rapidly repeated, several birds calling together. Breeds August to January, building substantial domed nest of plant debris, loosely woven and lined feathers, in hollow branch or crevice, ground level to 60 ft m, generally 10 to 20 ft up; also in stone walls and other artefacts. 4 or 5 white eggs incubated ♀ and ♂, who also feed young. 2 broods, young of first sometimes feeding second; many ♂♂ polygamous (M. F. Soper). **575**

Acanthiza auropygialis *Muscicapidae : Malurinae*

CHESTNUT-TAILED THORNBILL   *c.* 3¾ ins

Australia: mainly S of Tropic of Capricorn; frequents dry inland scrub country. Upperparts greyish brown; whitish freckles on forehead and ear coverts; wings dusky brown; rump rich chestnut; tail black, tipped white; underparts dully greyish white. Legs blackish, bill dark brown, eyes white. Gregarious, especially when not breeding; usually on ground or in lower levels of scrub; feeds on insects. Voice: long, animated song; steady twittering in flocks. Breeds August to December; domed nest with side entrance, of grass and bark strips bound cobwebs, thickly lined fur, hair or feathers; often in hollow spout of dead tree, also behind loose bark, generally 3 to 18 ft up; 2 to 4 eggs white with reddish brown spots, and commonly 2 broods. **756**

Acanthiza chrysorrhoa *Muscicapidae : Malurinae*

YELLOW-BILLED THORNBILL   *c.* 4¾ ins

Australia S of Tropic of Capricorn. Habitat: open woodland; parties may visit suburbs. Upperparts: olive-brown; flight feathers dark brown; forehead blackish with white spots, pale line over eye; rump deep yellow, tail dark with black terminal band; underparts dirty white, throat white. Legs and bill blackish, eyes grey. Feeds on insects taken from ground and lower parts of trees and bushes. Call: short *zip* in flight; song: attractive run of notes. Breeds second half of year; domed nest usually *c.* 6 ft up in dense outer foliage of tree or shrub, chamber and hooded side entrance low down, below false open nest, made of grass and other plant debris, lined finer grasses, feathers, wool or fur. ♀ alone incubates 3 pale, flesh coloured eggs, 18-20 days; both parents tend young who fly 17-19 days; members of earlier broods may assist. Up to 4 broods. **757**

Acanthogenys rufogularis *Meliphagidae*

SPINY-CHEEKED HONEYEATER   10 ins

Australasian: interior continental Australia; mainly resident, scrub and lightly timbered country; mangroves. Upperparts grey and brown, streaked dark brown, rump lighter brown; wings, white-tipped tail brown; eyestripe black, ear coverts white, spiny cheek yellowish white, dark moustachial stripe; chin, throat, upper breast rich buff, rest underparts yellowish, streaked brown; legs slate grey, bill black-tipped, pink at base extending under blue eyes. 'Bold and quarrelsome' like its relatives. Calls: clear *quock*, quiet *click* when feeding, plaintive musical trill. ♂ has soaring flight, calling on descent. Diet: insects, nectar, fruit, e.g. mistletoe berries. Breeds August to end November; nest of grass, rootlets bound cobwebs, cocoons, lined hair, other soft stuff; usually suspended from fork of tree, mistletoe clump, up to 50 ft. 2 or 3 very

pale olive green eggs, marked umber over purplish grey, incubated ♀; both ♀ and ♂ tend young. **834**

Acanthorhynchus tenuirostris *Meliphagidae*

EASTERN SPINEBILL   5½-6 (bill 1) ins

Australasian: continental from N Queensland to S Australia, Kangaroo I, Tasmania, Bass Strait Is. Resident open forest, scrub, heathlands, gardens, usually near water. ♂: crown, wings, tail grey; back of neck rufous; lower back olive grey; cheeks black, white moustachial stripe joins broken crescent on breast; underparts: light rufous buff with white central streak; pale throat has wine-brown patch; legs, bill blackish, eyes red. ♀ duller. Usually in pairs, flitting from flower to flower, probing with long spine-like bill; wings make clapping sound. Call: succession of 4 musical notes, last one prolonged. Diet: insects, nectar taken while hovering (assists pollination), *Banksia, Grevillea* flowers in winter. Breeds August to December; ♀ (mainly) builds deep cup bark, grasses, moss, lined fine grass, feathers; suspended from thin lateral fork, 4 to 20 ft up or more. 2 or 3 pale buff eggs, spotted chestnut over purplish grey at big end, incubated ♀, ♂ guarding territory; ♀ and ♂ feed young. Often 2 broods. **835**

ACCENTOR,

ALPINE see **Prunella collaris**
HEDGE see **Prunella modularis**

Accipiter nisus *Accipitridae*

SPARROWHAWK   11-15 ins (♀ much larger)

Palaearctic: resident right across N temperate zone from Spain to Japan, also to N Africa and Burma, in well-wooded, usually cultivated country, with some preference for coniferous areas. ♂: slate grey upperparts, tail and wings browner, with dark bars, underparts closely barred rufous. ♀: upperparts much browner, white stripe over eye; underparts whitish, flanks rufous. Much variation and immatures browner. Legs, cere and eyes yellow, bill dark. Flight usually fast and low with 3-4 wingbeats then long glide; also zigzags through trees. Surprises prey, mainly small birds, or outflies them; also takes insects, small mammals. Soaring, especially in spring display, with tail widespread. Alarm call repeated *kek kek kek;* whistles in display, other notes at nest. Breeds from end April in N temperate, building platform of sticks in conifer or hardwood at varying heights. 4 to 6 pale blue eggs, marked red brown, incubated by ♀ *c.* 35 days; ♂ brings food to her for young, which fly in 24-30 days. **133**

Aceros plicatus or Rhyticeros plicatus *Bucerotidae*

PAPUAN or BLYTH'S HORNBILL   ♀: 30, ♂: 36 ins

Oriental and Australasian: Burma, Malaysia, New Guinea, Bismarck and Solomon Is; resident lowland forests up to 4,000 ft. ♂: black with white tail and golden or buff ochre head and neck; legs greyish black, bill dusty white, base brownish red, 4 to 8 folds in casque; eyes red brown, facial skin pale bluish green. ♀ black except for white tail; bill shorter than ♂, 4 to 6 folds on casque. Immature ♀ resembles adult ♂. Parties seen flying over tree tops or at considerable heights, sometimes in hundreds when going to roost; loud swishing from wings. Rather silent but horn-like *hoo-ha* or *hoo* repeated frequently at times. Feeds on fruit from tips of forest trees; apparently collects earth for walling up nests from plains. Breeds February Burma, using hole in tree 60 to 100 ft up. Clutch 1 to 3 white eggs; nesting habits as relatives, see *Buceros bicornis*. **511**

ACORN WOODPECKER see **Melanerpes formicivorus**

Acridotheres tristis *Sturnidae*

COMMON MYNAH   *c.* 9 ins

Oriental, Palaearctic: Indian subcontinent; Turkestan, Afghanistan, S E Iran, Baluchistan, Nepal, Sikkim, Bhutan, Burma, Thailand and Indochina; introduced S Africa, Seychelles, Mauritius, Australia, Tasmania and New Zealand. Habitat: open populated country, near man, cultivated areas to towns and cities; up to *c.* 9,000 ft Himalayas, descending in winter. Head, neck and upper breast glossy black; rest rich vinous-brown, belly paler; large white patch at base of dark brown primaries; tail brownish black with white tip. Legs and bill yellowish, bare patch below and behind eye bright yellow, eyes brown or reddish brown mottled white. Scavenger, tame, sociable, usually in small parties, roosts communally, larger flocks in winter; strongly territorial when breeding, attacking any intruder. Call: varies from squeaks and chattering to harsh, grating cries; mimics. Omnivorous, feeding in trees but mainly on ground, taking chiefly fruit, grain and insects. Usually breeds April to July but peaks vary; suitable nest sites fought over and used repeatedly, hole in tree, bank, building 6 to 20 ft up; untidy nest of twigs, roots and rubbish, sometimes 2 or 3 nests one above the other in same hole; 4 or 5, sometimes 3 or 6, pale blue eggs, incubated mainly ♀ 14-18 days; young fledge 22-24 days. **963**

Acrocephalus arundinaceus *Muscicapidae: Sylviinae*
GREAT REED WARBLER $7\frac{1}{2}$ ins
Palaearctic: N Africa, Europe except Britain N to Baltic, through Turkey to 95°E, where replaced by similar species. Winters in tropical African marshes, woodland, savannah; breeds reed marshes beside fresh or brackish water. Upperparts warm olive brown, more tawny on rump; narrow pale 'eyebrow'; throat white merging with creamy buff underparts; brown streaks on upper throat more conspicuous in winter; legs pale brownish grey; long straight bill: upper brown, lower pinkish; eyes yellowish brown. Less skulking than other reed warblers; perches on bushes, telegraph wires. Flies jerkily with spread tail, low over water. Loud calls include harsh *tack,* churring croak, shrike-like alarm chatter. Very loud, harsh, prolonged song, based on repeated *karekiet,* audible at long range; uttered from cover or exposed perch; also in winter quarters. Insectivorous. Breeds mid May onwards, socially in reed beds. ♀ builds deep cup of sedge, reed leaves, lined reed 'flowers', suspended from 3 or 4 reed stems or *Salix* twigs. 4 to 6 bluish or greenish eggs, blotched dark brown, black. Both sexes incubate 14-15 days, feed young, who leave nest after 12 days, fledging 4 days later. Occasionally 2 broods.

Acrocephalus palustris *Muscicapidae: Sylviinae*
MARSH WARBLER 5 ins
W Palaearctic: Central and E Europe, from E France, S England to Caspian Sea, N to S Sweden, Finland, range expanded since 1900; winters in savannah regions of E Africa S to Cape Province. Breeding habitat willows, other bushes, nettles and tall plants, beside river, lake or reed bed; also in cornfields, rank vegetation away from water. Upperparts olive brown, rump paler; 'eyebrow', underparts buffish white; throat paler; legs brownish-flesh; bill, upper: dark brown, lower: flesh; eyes olive brown. Reed Warbler, *A. scirpaceus,* is more rufous above, less white below. Rather skulking, but shows itself at times, especially when ♂ sings loud musical song, including mimicry and characteristic 'canary trill', nasal *za-wee,* from top of tall plant or tree; other calls: loud repeated *tchuc,* quiet *tuc.* Feeds on insects, spiders picked from leaves; berries in autumn. Breeds June in England; untidy nest of dry grass, lined rootlets, hair, attached to vegetation by 'basket handles'; to nettles, incorporating dead stem, riparian plants, willow bushes, corn. 4 to 5 bluish or greenish white eggs with few bold olive brown spots, fine black specks. Both parents incubate *c.* 12 days and feed young, who fly 10-14 days. **724**

Acrocephalus schoenobaenus *Muscicapidae: Sylviinae*
SEDGE WARBLER 5 ins
Palaearctic: Europe, except Spain, N to Arctic Ocean in Scandinavia and E to 85°; winters tropical Africa S to Natal. Habitat: all types riparian vegetation, marshes, bogs, usually with low bushes; also in drier areas with similar cover. Crown brown, streaked black; mantle duller, less heavily streaked; rump unstreaked tawny; wings, rather pointed tail blackish-brown edged paler; prominent 'eyebrow', underparts creamy white; flanks yellower; legs pale grey; bill: upper black, lower yellowish; eyes brown. Creeps amongst vegetation, descending to ground in thick cover. Flies low with tail spread, depressed. Calls: scolding, explosive *tucc,* often running into trill; grating *chirr.* Loud varied song lasting about a minute, delivered from cover, exposed perch or in short, vertical display flight. Diet mainly insects, larvae, spiders; also berries in autumn. Breeding season: May to July. Untidy cup nest of dead grass lined down, feathers built by ♀ in rank vegetation; up to 2 ft or more from ground; occasionally suspended from reeds. 5 or 6 dark brown eggs, thickly speckled ochre, incubated mainly ♀ 13-14 days. Young, fed by both parents, leave nest 13-14 days. 2 broods in S. **725**

Acrocephalus scirpaceus see under **A. palustris**

Acrocephalus stentoreus *Muscicapidae: Sylviinae*
CLAMOROUS REED WARBLER 7 ins
S Palaearctic (Egypt) through Iran, Afghanistan, Oriental, Australasian, continental and regions, partly migratory. Breeds in dense reed beds; also introduced willows overhanging water. Upperparts brown tinged olive; rump pale fawn; pale whitish 'eyebrow'; buffy white underparts, darker on flanks, legs grey; long bill horn; eyes dark brown. Habits generally as other reed warblers. Breeds November to June in S New South Wales, September to February farther N. Nest: deep cup of dead reeds and decaying plant material, lined fibres, feathers, woven around several reed stems. 3 or 4 eggs, bluish white to yellowish brown, spotted red brown: incubation and fledging much as *A. arundinaceus.* **726**

Acryllium vulturinum *Numididae*
VULTURINE GUINEAFOWL 22-26 ins
Ethiopian: Somalia to Tanzania; resident desert thorn scrub, sometimes in dense forest. Generally black, streaked and spotted white; cape of long black, white and cobalt blue feathers with chestnut tuft at nape; underparts cobalt blue; secondaries edged pink; central tail feathers elongated; legs blackish, bill bluish-white, eyes red, facial skin grey-blue. Parties rove veld, drinking at same spot each evening, then roosting in trees. Shrill cackle of alarm and when going to roost; clucks when feeding. Otherwise silent. Food dug up: seeds, bulbs, roots, also reptiles, amphibians, molluscs and insects. Breeding variable, from April in N to February in S of range. Lined scrape in grass among rocks or bushes holds up to 13 or 14 pale cream eggs with pitted shells, incubated by ♀ 30-32 days; young soon join flock. **209**

Actitis hypoleucos see **Tringa hypoleucos**

Actophilornis africana *Jacanidae*
AFRICAN JACANA or LILY TROTTER 12 ins
Ethiopian: almost entire region, with local migrations: swamps and pools of still water, slow-flowing rivers, up to 8,000 ft in E Africa. Body, wings (except black primaries) and tail dark chestnut brown; crown and back of neck black; cheeks, front of neck white, upper breast golden yellow; legs slate, bill grey, frontal shield pale blue, eyes dark brown. Juvenile's upperparts washed yellow-green. Usually singly or in pairs, stepping delicately over floating plants; sometimes in larger numbers. Flies well, legs stretched behind, toes turned up or bent downward. Sharp coot-like call and high-pitched *kruk*; rattling screech in flight; also calls in duets. Food: water insects and their larvae; seeds of water plants. Breeds all year round in some part of range, making small nest of local plants and debris at water's edge. 2 to 5 glossy, pear-shaped light brown eggs, scribbled all over dark brown, incubated by ♀ and ♂ 22-24 days. Parents tend young; ♀ known to carry them, also said to hold eggs under wings, when nest partially submerged. **248**

ADELIE PENGUIN see **Pygoscelis adeliae**

Aechmophorus occidentalis *Podicipedidae*
WESTERN GREBE 22-29 (body 18) ins
Nearctic: W North America, moving to coast and southward in winter, when may form large flocks. Black and slate-grey above, white below, with very long, largely white neck and long, pointed, mainly yellow bill; legs olive-green, eyes red. Remarkable courtship displays in spring on breeding lakes: swimming side by side with head movements, 'walking on water' and presenting billful of weed. Carries young on back like other grebes. Shows long neck, slender body, white wing-bar, in flight. Calls trilling, double-toned *creeerree,* also piping whistle and subdued growl. Dives after fish, apparently spearing them with bill: also other aquatic animals, some vegetable matter and swallows feathers like other grebes. Breeds colonially May-July, building floating mass of and in aquatic vegetation; eggs usually 3 or 4, buff to bluish green, soon stained though not usually covered; incubated for 23 days by ♀ and ♂; young, not striped, swim at once. **17**

Aegithalos caudatus *Paridae*
LONG-TAILED TIT *c.* $5\frac{1}{2}$ (tail *c.* 3) ins
Palaearctic: Europe (except extreme NE and SE Russia); also Asia Minor, Caucasus, Iran, extending between 50° and 60°N to Pacific coast, Kamtchatka, Sakhalin, Japan, and S into China, where population sometimes regarded as separate *A. glaucogularis.* Resident broadleaved woodland with dense or little undergrowth, up to montane forests at 9,000 ft Yunnan, largely of spruce; pine (Japan); riverine strips, cultivated country, parks, gardens. Upperparts blackish mixed pink; scapulars, rump mainly pink, very round wings (secondaries white-edged), tail (white on outer feathers) blackish; head off-white with blackish band through eye to mantle (nominate northern race white-headed, whiter underparts, secondaries); underparts off-white shading pinkish; legs black-brown, very small bill black, eyes dark hazel. Bobbing, undulating flight as parties flit between cover, often with other tits and 'allies'; flicks wings and tail. Seldom on ground. Roosts clustered together, up to 50. Calls abrupt *tupp,* penetrating *zee zee zee,* trilling *tsirrrp;* short bubbling song of repeated calls. Butterfly flight of ♂ in display; also chases ♀. Food small insects, spiders, their eggs, from twigs; some seeds and leaf buds. Breeds end February to early June Britain; ♀ and ♂ building celebrated oval ball of moss, cobwebs, hair, covered grey lichen, lined up to 2,000 feathers; entrance in side usually near top; from 3 to 6 ft in low bushes, creepers, up to high tree forks. 7 to 12 white eggs finely speckled reddish in zone, incubated mainly by ♀ 14-18 days; ♀, served by ♂, feeds young, who fly 15-16 days. **801**

Aegithalos glaucogularis see under **A. caudatus**

Aegithina aurifrons see **Chloropsis aurifrons**

Aegolius acadicus *Strigidae*
SAW-WHET OWL $7\text{-}8\frac{1}{2}$ ins
Nearctic: SE Alaska to Nova Scotia, S to Mexico and Guatemala; northern birds winter S to Louisiana, Georgia, S California. Habitat: woodland, especially conifers, in mountainous country in S of range. Upperparts brown with pale stripes from feather edges; facial disc whitish, lightly streaked; underparts heavily streaked dark brown; feathered legs white, feet and bill dark, eyes yellow. Juvenile chocolate brown, including much of facial disc, with white 'eyebrows'. Very tame; usual call a mellow whistle, repeated up to 130 times a minute: *too too too;* also weak rasping call of two syllables. Food: small rodents, especially wood mice, up to rats and small squirrels. Breeds from February or April according to latitude, laying 3 to 6 white eggs in tree-holes, often made by woodpeckers; also old crows' nests, nestboxes. Incubation and fledging periods much as *A. funereus.* **431**

Aegolius funereus *Strigidae* *c.* 10 ins
TENGMALM'S, BOREAL or RICHARDSON'S OWL
Holarctic: band round world, broad in Eurasia, on either side of 60°N, narrow in N America, from S Alaska SE to Newfoundland; isolated areas Central Europe, Crimea, Caucasus; Kansu, Tien-Shan, Tarbagatai in mountains of Asia; resident but irrupts S in very cold winters. Habitat typically dense coniferous forests of taiga and subalpine zone, also mixed woodland with birch, poplar, even pine-clad heaths. Rather like *A. acadicus:* upperparts chocolate brown,

spotted white, densely on relatively large head; underparts less strongly marked; legs feathered white down to brown-black claws, bill and eyes yellow. Juvenile much like *A. acadicus*, chocolate-brown all over. Rests during day in dense conifers, enters houses, even igloos in cold weather. Hunts in daylight of arctic summer. Wing-clapping by ♂ in display flight over trees, uttering 'song', repetition of soft, liquid *poo* with varying stress; or may be trilled *oolooloolooo*. Takes small mammals: lemmings, voles, mice, shrews; also birds, frogs, occasionally insects. Breeds from June in taiga, earlier in Central Europe, mainly in small tree holes, especially old woodpecker nests. 3 to 6 white eggs incubated by ♀ at least 25 days; young fledge 30-32 days; occasionally 2 broods. **432**

Aegotheles cristata *Aegothelidae*
OWLET FROGMOUTH 8-9 ins
Australasian: New Guinea, New Caledonia, continental Australia, Tasmania; resident in forests and open woodlands. Upperparts mottled greyish with white on head, cheeks, base of neck and tail, barred darker; underparts pale, barred brown; filoplumes on head, bill obscured by feathering. Usually solitary or in pairs. Nocturnal, resting in hollow trees during day. Perches upright on branches. Call a loud churring. Hunts mainly from ground, on terrestrial invertebrates, but rises as well to hawk after flying insects, chiefly moths and beetles. Breeds September-December in Australia, lining hole in tree with leaves, sometimes using tunnel in bark. 3 or 4 rounded eggs, usually white, sometimes spotted. Often 2 broods. **458**

Aerocharis prevostii or Euryceros prevostii *Vangidae*
HELMETBIRD *c.* 12 ins
Madagascar: forests of humid east, sea level to *c.* 5,500 ft. Mainly black, with rufous back and scapulars; remarkably large blue bill with convex upper mandible and hooked tip. Moves through canopy in parties of 5 to 10, often with other species; occasionally perches low down. Call: tremulous whistle. Food: large to medium insects and other invertebrates from trees; small treefrogs, lizards.

Aerops albicollis *Meropidae*
WHITE-THROATED
BEE-EATER 12 (central tail feathers 6) ins
Ethiopian: resident coast-to-coast belt Senegal to Ethiopia as far S as Uganda; in non-breeding season migrates S to Ghana, Angola, Tanzania, E to SW Arabia, Somalia; large flocks fly over high, calling *quilp quilp*. Found anywhere with trees except solid rain forest or land above 5,000 ft. Generally pale green shading to blue (rump, tail) brown (neck, wings) or white (forehead, chin, belly), with contrasting black crown, stripe through eye, upper breast; long curved bill. Continuously gregarious, parties hawk insects from tree or wire, periodically circle round with fast wing beats, short glides; drink on the wing like swallows, a beautiful sight as setting sun lights up their coppery wings. Colonial breeders, usually late summer, 3-5 glossy white eggs in long tunnel in bank. **497**

Afribyx senegallus see **Vanellus senegallus**

AFRICAN
BLACK CRAKE see **Limnocorax flavirostra**
BLACK-HEADED ORIOLE see **Oriolus larvatus**
BLACK OYSTERCATCHER see **Haematopus moquini**
BROADBILL see **Smithornis capensis**
FINFOOT see **Podica senegalensis**
FIREFINCH see **Lagonisticta rubricata**
FISH EAGLE see **Haliaeetus vocifer**
GREY PARROT see **Psittacus erithacus**
HARRIER HAWK see **Polyboroides typus**
JACANA see **Actophilornis africanus**
MARSH HARRIER see **Circus ranivorus**
MARSH OWL see **Asio capensis**
PARADISE FLYCATCHER see **Terpsiphone viridis**
PEAFOWL see **Afropavo congensis**
PENDULINE TIT see under **Eremomela icteropygialis**
PIED WAGTAIL see **Motacilla aguimp**

PITTA see under **Pitta brachyura**
POCHARD see **Netta erythrophthalma**
PYGMY FALCON see **Poliohierax semitorquatus**
RIVER MARTIN see **Pseudochelidon eurystomina**
ROCK MARTIN see **Hirundo fuligula**
SAND MARTIN see **Riparia paludicola**
SEDGE WARBLER see **Bradypterus baboecala**
SNIPE see **Gallinago nigripennis**
WHITE-BACKED VULTURE see **Gyps africanus**
WOOD OWL see **Ciccaba woodfordii**

Afropavo congensis *Phasianidae*
AFRICAN PEAFOWL 24-27 ins
Ethiopian: confined to area of Zaire (Congo); dense lowland forests between 2°N and 5°S. ♂: generally blackish, glossed green and bronze on back, rump; violet sheen on hindneck, breast; underparts glossed dark green; crown has vertical white and black tufts; bare neck patch orange-red, bare face blue; ♀: reddish brown and black, upperparts glossed green, bronze; crown has short brown crest; bare orange-red neck patch, bare blue face. Legs blackish-grey, spur whitish, bill slaty, eyes light brown. ♂'s upper tail coverts as long as tail and used in display. Said to live in pairs; flies heavily, roosting in trees and taking refuge in them when disturbed. Call: loud duet *zowe-zowah*, ♂ leading, usually in evening; also clucking. Food largely fallen fruits. Breeding season in wild unknown; captive nests of sticks built off ground. 2 or 3 brownish eggs incubated ♀ 30-32 days. Young leave nest at once, can flutter 3-4 days.

Agapornis personata *Psittacidae*
YELLOW-COLLARED LOVEBIRD 6 ins
Ethiopian: confined to Central Tanzania; introduced Dar es Salaam; resident in acacia bush. Upperparts green with black bar across outer tail feathers, which also have yellow-brown bars; head blackish brown, hind neck round to breast lemon yellow; underparts, including under wing coverts, green; legs grey, bill red, white circle round black eyes. Little known of habits; forms small flocks after breeding. Call 'squeaking twitter'. Food: mainly seeds of acacia. May visit shallow water to drink 4 times a day. Breeds March to April Tanzania; July to August in Dar es Salaam where occupies holes in buildings and old swifts' nests; usually in tree hole, especially baobab (sometimes old barbet holes), partly blocked with thorns and crude domed nest inside. Clutch 3 to 9 white eggs. **385**

Agelaius
humeralis see under **A. xanthomus**
phoeniceus see under **Quiscalus quiscala**

Agelaius xanthomus *Icteridae*
YELLOW-SHOULDERED BLACKBIRD 8-9 ins
Neotropical: Puerto Rico and Mona I. Resident lowlands, especially near lagoons, coastal swamps; also open country but rare woodlands and not hills; restricted to limestone plateau Mona. Uniformly black except for yellow shoulder patches. Gregarious like relations; call short *chic* like Tawny-shouldered Blackbird, *A. humeralis;* song also similar: 'strange, wheezy notes'. Food: insects and seeds. Breeds socially, ♀ building cup-shaped nest of local plant materials in tree, palm, tall cactus. 3 or 4 greyish-white eggs, spotted brown and grey, incubated ♀ 12 days; fledging period the same. **907**

Aglaiocercus kingi *Trochilidae*
LONG-TAILED SYLPH ♀: 3¾, ♂: 7 (bill ½) ins
Neotropical: Venezuela, Colombia to Ecuador, E Peru and Bolivia; forest and scrub up mountains to *c.* 7,500 ft. ♂: upperparts dark glossy green, underparts duller, shaded olive; crown patch iridescent green, throat iridescent violet blue; tail graduated with very short inner feathers, outermost to 4¾ ins, basally blue black, exposed parts iridescent purple, undertail blackish. ♀: upperparts much as ♂; throat buffish white with green crescents; underparts cinnamon brown; tail forked, not elongated: central short feathers glossy green, outer ones green outer web and tip, inner web dark blue; outermost feathers dark blue

with white tips. For general hummingbird habits and behaviour, see *Archilochus colubris, Calypte anna, C. costae, Selasphorus sasin.* **465**

Aidemosyne modesta *Estrildidae*
PLUM-HEADED FINCH 4-4½ ins
Australia: Queensland (River Nogoa, Port Denison) to S and Central W New South Wales; nomadic, dependent on water. Habitat: grasslands and reeds along watercourses; open country with eucalypts and bushes; orchards, gardens. ♂: generally olive-brown, upperparts closely barred; 2 white bars on dark brown wings; white crescents on coverts above black tail; cap 'plum'-coloured, bib deep claret, nearly black, cheeks white; underparts off-white scaled brown; legs flesh-brown, broad bill black, eyes dark brown. ♀ similar but less 'plum' on forehead, chin; throat whitish, underparts less scaly. Immature deep olive-brown above, underparts greyish white. Tame in field, in pairs or flocks up to 300, sometimes with other species. Flight strong, slightly undulating. Various calls, usually *tlip* and identifying *tyiit;* low 'voiceless' song. ♂ carries green grass in courtship, singing and bobbing on perch, drops grass, shows off plumage. Feeds on or near ground, climbing stems: seeds of grasses and herbs; drinks every hour. Breeds September to June; small bottle-shaped nest of green grasses, lined feathers, tiny entrance; in tall grass, thistles, low bush (raspberries and blackberries, N New South Wales) within 3 ft of ground; living stems woven into fabric. 4 to 7 white eggs incubated ♀ and ♂ 12-13 days; both feed young, who fly *c.* 3 weeks. **935**

Aix galericulata *Anatidae*
MANDARIN 18 ins
E Palaearctic, but introduced widely as 'ornamental': E Asia from Amur and Ussuri, S through Korea, E China, Japan to Formosa; some movement S for winter. Habitat: ponds or waterways with heavily wooded edges. ♂ unmistakable, ♀ less coloured but similar characteristic facial pattern with white circle round eye giving off-white curving streak down side of neck. ♂ eclipse like ♀ but latter has 2 white wing bars and ♂ only one. Legs: ♂ dull orange, ♀ yellowish brown; bill: ♂ vermillion, ♀ greyish brown but pink in Korean ♀. Flight swift and straight, gregarious especially in autumn, feeds usually on land on acorns, nuts and similar plant matter. ♂'s call nasal *pfrrreuib* (J. Delacour); ♀ utters squawks and squeaks. Solitary nester in tree-holes often as high as 45 ft, and several hundred yards from water; lines nest with plant material, particularly bits of rotten wood, and white down. 9 to 12 or more glossy, pale buff eggs, incubated by ♀ 28 to 30 days. Despite height of nest, ducklings jump to ground almost immediately after hatching; tended by ♀ and fly *c.* 6 weeks. **93**

Ajaia ajaja *Threskiornithidae*
ROSEATE SPOONBILL 30-34 ins
Nearctic and Neotropical: extreme southern USA through Central America, W Indies, much of N and E South America to Argentina and (very locally) Chile; local movements mainly within range. Habitat usually coastal: marshes, lagoons and mudflats. Adults pink to carmine all over, but areas of white on neck, back and breast of younger birds; tail orange-buff; naked head greenish, legs ruby-magenta, bill, with excrescences, variable, eyes red. Usually in small flocks, sometimes with other species. Strong, direct flight. Courtship and threat displays at colonies. Alarm call low, rapid *huh huh huh huh;* other notes when feeding and at nest, uttered with head raised and bill open. Sweeps bill from side to side, sometimes with head immersed, to catch small fish and water animals, also takes some vegetable matter. Breeding season varies within range; colonies on dry coastal islands, usually in bushes and trees, reeds or even on ground. Rather bulky nest of sticks with finer lining holds usually 2 or 3 white eggs, spotted brown, incubated 23-24 days by ♀ and ♂, who also tend young. They leave nest 5-6 weeks, independent *c.* 8 weeks. **78**

Alaemon alaudipes *Alaudidae*
BIFASCIATED or HOOPOE LARK 8 ins
Palaearctic, marginally Ethiopian and Oriental: 4

races; mainly resident, breeding Cape Verdes, Sahara from Morocco to the Nile, down Red Sea coast to Somaliland, Arabia, Iraq to Afghanistan and NW Indian subcontinent. Habitat: open arid desert plains. Upperparts uniform sandy-buff to grey-brown; distinct white 'eyebrow'; underparts white with prominent dark spots on breast; wings darker with 2 broad white bars; long legs whitish; legs greenish horn, long heavy decurved bill dark horn, eyes dark brown. Rarely flies except for very high song flight. Displays round nest during egg-laying, churning up sand into regular dancing channels. Territory up to 1 sq. mile of desert. Call long-drawn and melodious; song a series of pipes and whistles. Feeds on grubs, locust pupae and seeds, frequently digging up to 2 inches into soil. Breeds February to April Red Sea; nest vestigial or substantial, on ground except in hottest areas where a few inches up in shade of bush. 2 (usually) white eggs, marked with rufous and lilac.

Alauda arvensis *Alaudidae*
SKYLARK   7 ins
Palaearctic; 10 races; breeds in band between about 45°N and 70°N from Britain to Japan, also small part of N Africa east coast and band round S of Caspian E to W Sinkiang. Southern races resident but northern ones winter south to N Africa and NW India. Habitat: moors, arable and pasture fields, marshes, sand-dunes. Upperparts brown with dark streaks, underparts buffish-white with boldly streaked breast; short but quite prominent crest; wings dark, fringed white; longish tail with white outer feathers; legs yellowish brown, bill horn, eyes brown. Gregarious outside breeding season. Call, often given when flushed and in flight, liquid *chirrup;* song sustained, most usually uttered in flight from very early in morning. Feeds on seeds and invertebrates. Breeding season April to July; grass nest on ground, sometimes open, often very well concealed, built by ♀. 3 to 5 dull greyish eggs, thickly spotted brown over grey. Incubation by ♀ 11 days. Young, fed by both sexes, 9-10 days in nest, fly 10 days later. 2 or 3 broods. **599**

ALBATROSS,
   BLACK-BROWED see **Diomedea melanophris**
   BLACK-FOOTED see **Diomedea nigripes**
   GALAPAGOS see **Diomedea irrorata**
   LAYSAN see under **Diomedea nigripes**
   LIGHT-MANTLED SOOTY see **Phoebetria palpebrata**
   WANDERING see **Diomedea exulans**

Alca torda *Alcidae*
RAZORBILL   c. 16 ins
Holarctic (N Atlantic): Britain and Ireland, Scandinavia and Baltic, Iceland, W Greenland, Newfoundland and adjacent coasts N America. Northern birds move S in winter, remaining fairly near shore; some enter W Mediterranean. Breeds sea cliffs and rocky islands; inland only on Lake Ladoga. Summer: upperparts from head to pointed tail black, with white trailing edge to wing and underparts; legs black, deep narrow 'razor' bill black circled narrow white line in middle; eyes dark brown. Upperparts duller in winter, throat and cheeks white. Usually seen in parties on sea, flying low over it in wavering lines or sitting penguin-like on rocks. Wings used underwater to help propulsion. Call a grating *kaarrr*. Mutual displays, e.g. bills raised vertically and rattled. Food: fish, crustaceans, worms, other marine animals. Breeds from early May Britain in scattered colonies often among Guillemots, *Uria aalge,* and other cliff birds; single egg, white to chocolate, variously marked rich dark brown, laid in crevice, under boulders, sometimes on open ledge; incubation by ♀ and ♂ 26 to 30 days; parents feed young c. 2 weeks; then it descends to sea and they continue to tend it. **343**

Alcedo atthis *Alcedinidae*
KINGFISHER   c. 6½ (bill 1½) ins
Palaearctic, Oriental: European race, *ispida,* mid Sweden S to N Italy, E to central Russia; other races farther S to NW Africa, E to S Russia and SE over Asia to India, China, Japan and Malay Archipelago. Habitat: fresh waters and, particularly in winter, tidal

estuaries and rocky sea shores. Upperparts, including short tail, glossy cobalt blue or emerald green depending on light; underparts and cheeks orange chestnut; white throat and patch on sides of neck. Legs bright red, long strong tapering bill black with reddish base to lower mandible, eyes dark brown. Flight very fast and usually low over water. Call: loud shrill repeated *chee.* Plunges straight into water to take fish; sometimes insects and other small aquatic animals. Breeds April to August; makes tunnel 1½ to 3 ft, ending in circular chamber, in steep banks of rivers and streams or sometimes suitable banks away from water. 6 or 7 glossy white eggs, incubated by ♀ and ♂ 19-21 days. They both tend young, who fly 23-27 days. Usually 2 broods. **484**

ALDER FLYCATCHER see **Empidonax traillii**

Alectoris
   barbara see under **A. rufa**
   graeca see under **A. rufa**

Alectoris rufa *Phasianidae*
RED-LEGGED PARTRIDGE   c. 13½ ins
W Palaearctic: SW Europe, mainly France, Iberia; introduced Britain, Azores, Madeira, Canary Is. Closely related to Chukor *A. graeca,* which has similar habits and ranges E from Mediterranean through S Palaearctic to Pacific at c. 40°N. Barbary Partridge *A. barbara* is confined to Mediterranean N Africa. Resident lowland scrub, sunny hillsides, vineyards, heaths; in England on drier cultivated land and dunes. Upperparts uniform mouse brown shading to grey on forehead; cheeks and throat white, bordered black, making distinctive gorget of black streaks and spots; white stripe over eye; short tail rufous; flanks grey, barred black, white, chestnut; belly buff; legs, bill and orbits red, eyes brown. Looks less humpbacked than Common Partridge *P. perdix,* runs rather than fly and coveys scatter if put to flight. Often perches at some height. Display call of ♂ *chik-chikar,* softer from ♀; *kuk kuk* when running or about to fly. Food mainly vegetable: stems, leaves, buds, berries and grass seeds; also insects and spiders. Breeds from mid-April, lining well-hidden scrape with grass and leaves. Eggs 10 to 16, pale yellow brown, spotted dull red and ashy; ♀ often lays 2 clutches, each parent incubating one 23-24 days. Young, attended by one or both parents, fly 3 weeks, fully grown 16 weeks. Sometimes lays in nests of other birds. **191**

Alisterus scapularis see **Aprosmictus scapularis**

ALLEN'S HUMMINGBIRD see **Selasphorus sasin**

Alopochen aegyptiaca *Anatidae*
EGYPTIAN GOOSE   24 ins
Ethiopian, S. Palaearctic: S Palestine, Nile Valley and Africa S of Sahara. Common anywhere except deep forest and desert, usually near water, sometimes on open plains. ♂: buff, wing coverts white with black primaries, green secondaries and brown tertiaries, belly paler, mantle darker; back, rump and tail black; chestnut patch round eyes, ring round neck and patch on breast. 2 colour phases, one with greyer back. ♀: similar but slightly smaller. Long legs pink, bill pink, with black tip and base, eyes dark yellow. Perches and roosts in trees often using same branch each night; dives freely in moult; wary, in small groups or very large flocks; noisy, often fighting. Call: loud *kak-kak,* hissing when annoyed. Feeds on crops and young grass. Breeds all months, nest site varies: on ground, in holes in trees or cliffs, deserted tree nests, up to mile from water. Nest grass, reeds down lined: 6 to 10 yellowish white eggs, incubated 28-30 days. **94**

ALPINE
   ACCENTOR see **Prunella collaris**
   CHOUGH see **Pyrrhocorax graculus**
   SWIFT see **Apus melba**

Alseonax adustus or Muscicapa adusta
Muscicapidae: Muscicapinae
DUSKY FLYCATCHER   4½-5 ins
Ethiopian: several races cover much of region except

Somalia, parts of W Africa. Resident, usually open forest and edges; evergreen and *Brachystegia* in Central Africa; now in gardens E Africa, where becomes tame; often near water. Upperparts grey-brown; throat, belly off-white; breast, flanks, ashy brown, streaked whitish; legs, bill, eyes dark. Juvenile umber-brown. Races vary in degree of greyness or brown. In pairs, behaving much as Spotted Flycatcher, *Muscicapa striata,* e.g. wing flicking, but takes insects on ground and foliage as well as in air, hawking from low perch, though Kenyan race *A. a. marsabit* perches treetops. Call quiet *tsirit tsit tsirit;* trilling alarm note. Breeds throughout year in different parts range, building nest of grass, fibres, rootlets, often bound cobwebs and lined plant down; well-hidden at varying heights on lichen-covered bough, stump, creeper, rock ledge or building. 2 or 3 pale blue, green or dull white eggs, marked brown or red brown over purple. Breeding details much as *Muscicapa* species. **773**

Alseonax aquaticus *Muscicapidae: Muscicapinae*
SWAMP FLYCATCHER   5½ ins
Ethiopian: E from Gambia to Sudan, then S to NE Zambia; resident mainly elephant grass, papyrus, reed beds by lakes or rivers. Upperparts dark sooty brown (race *A. a. infulatus*), ash brown (nominate race); underparts white with ashy breast band and flanks. Legs, bill, eyes dark. Juvenile spotted buff above, dark streaks on breast. Behaves as other flycatchers, but runs over water lily leaves picking off insects. Sharp alarm call *pzitt;* song distinctive *tweet a weet tit weet a weet* (H. F. I. Elliott). Breeds January to June in different parts of range, usually taking over old weaver nests, with or without spouts, also crevices in bark; adds lining of fine grass, feathers. Usually 2 pale blue eggs, thickly spotted red-brown, especially at big end. **774**

Amadina erythrocephala *Estrildidae*
RED-HEADED FINCH   5¾ ins
Ethiopian: Central and NW Southern Africa, Angola; resident dry open savannah. ♂: upperparts pale brown, variously barred, flecked black and white, e.g. outer tail feathers; head, nape, chin red; upper breast grey, faintly barred; lower breast, flanks chestnut, flecked black and white; rest underparts whitish. ♀ lacks all red; underparts pale grey, barred. Immature as ♀. Legs flesh, bill horn, eyes brown. Pairs or small flocks feed on ground, perch trees, gather at drinking places. Call: *chuk chuk:* song distinctive, ♂ puffs throat feathers out. Diet mainly seeds. Breeds March to September, taking over nest-holes of other species in trees or buildings, especially sparrows and weavers. 4 to 6 white eggs, incubated ♀ and ♂, who also feed young. **936**

AMAKIHI see **Loxops virens**

Amazonetta brasiliensis *Anatidae*
BRAZILIAN TEAL   15 ins
Neotropical: Guyana, E Venezuela, Colombia E of Andes; Brazil, N and E Bolivia, Paraguay, Uruguay, Argentina S to Cordoba and Buenos Aires; open lagoons and swamps in mainly tropical woodland. Two colour phases, light and dark. ♂: generally brown, more rufous on breast; crown, nape, lower back, rump, tail, inner wing coverts black; primaries blackish green, greater coverts, outer secondaries bright metallic green, becoming purple on inner secondaries which show broad white band; underparts variously spotted. No special eclipse plumage; legs red, bill orange, eyes brown. ♀ much as ♂ but white spots in front of and above eye, and at base of olive bill. Immature as ♀ but duller. In small family parties or flocks; rather aggressive. Often perches trees; swims well, but seldom dives. Food mainly vegetable. ♂ utters strong, squeaking whistle; ♀ has loud, deep quack. ♂'s display of simple head and neck movements. Nest of plant debris and down on ground near water or in old nests of other birds, e.g. Quaker Parakeet, *Myiopsitta monacha.* 6 to 8 round glossy white eggs incubated ♀ 25 days; both sexes share care of brood.

Amazonia brasiliensis *Psittacidae*   14 ins
BLUE-HEADED OR BLUE-CHEEKED AMAZON PARROT
Neotropical: one distinctive race Guyanas; another in parts of Venezuela and Brazil; resident in tropical forest. Mainly green; crown red in front, yellow behind, feathers edged green; cheeks purplish blue; base of tail crimson. Guyana race: forehead and lores orange-yellow, crown yellowish, cheeks cornflower blue; orange on inner webs of tail feathers; 'Venezuelan' race: lores yellow, cheeks blue; speculum orange; red patch on inner webs of outer tail feathers. Remains in pairs. Noisy in flight, uttering piercing calls, especially before roosting. Nests in tree hole, especially in palms, laying 2 to 4 white eggs.

Amazonia ventralis *Psittacidae*
HISPANIOLA PARROT   11-12 ins
Neotropical: confined to Hispaniola and neighbouring small islands. Resident in forests. Predominantly green, darker above, lighter below with dark blue flight feathers; white forehead surrounded by blue band, black spot behind eye; maroon patch on belly. upper part of undertail red; legs light brown, bill pale horn, eyes dark with white orbits. Usually in pairs or flocks, particularly active at dawn or late afternoon, flying with rapid, shallow wing beats to feed on fruit, sometimes damaging cultivated fruit crops. Nest in tree hole contains 2 to 4 white eggs.

AMAZON
    PARROT, BLUE-CHEEKED see **Amazonia brasiliensis**
    PARROT, BLUE-HEADED see **Amazonia brasiliensis**

AMERICAN
    DIPPER see **Cinclus mexicanus**
    GOLDFINCH see **Spinus tristis**
    KESTREL see **Falco sparverius**
    PURPLE GALLINULE see **Porphyrula martinica**
    PYGMY KINGFISHER see **Chloroceryle aenea**
    REDSTART see **Setophaga ruticilla**
    ROBIN see **Turdus migratorius**
    SKIMMER see **Rynchops nigra**
    SPARROWHAWK see **Falco sparverius**
    TREE SPARROW see **Spizella arborea**
    WOODCOCK see **Philohela minor**

Amytornis housei *Muscicapidae: Malurinae*
BLACK GRASS WREN   *c.* 8 ins
Rediscovered (1968) at Manning Creek, Kimberley Division, Western Australia in area of tumbled rock, spinifex and trees; habitat probably savannah woodland. ♂: mainly black with white shaft-streaks to feathers; rump dark brown. ♀: similar but lower breast and belly chestnut with buff shaft-streaks. Juvenile uniformly black with faint white striations. Small party hopping amongst rocks ran into cover 'like mice' when alarmed. Call: loud ticking interspersed with grating sounds when alarmed, otherwise calls similar to Blue Wren, *Malurus cyaneus*, but harsher and more continuous. Feeds on insects, also some grass and sedge seeds.

Anarhynchus frontalis *Charadriidae*
WRYBILL PLOVER   8 ins
New Zealand: breeding confined to South Island (Canterbury, N Otago), on larger river beds; winters sea shores North Island (Firth of Thames, Manukau, Kaipara). Upperparts grey, underparts white; in breeding dress well defined black breast band, white forehead (thin black line above) extends into 'eyebrows'; bill (*c.* 1 in.) has tip turned to right, unique feature; eyes dark brown. Runs fast with head tucked in; often rests one leg and hops about; in winter shelters from wind behind shore plants. Complicated flock aerobatics before southward spring migration. Call: high-pitched whistle; also shrill *peep* like ringed plovers *Charadrius;* chattering note from flock; trilling courtship song. Feeds on small invertebrates, supposedly using wry bill to prise up stones. Breeds September onwards, laying 2 grey eggs, tinged blue or green and densely speckled, scrawled, dark and paler markings; usual site a scrape in bare shingle not far from water.

Anas acuta *Anatidae*
PINTAIL   22 (body 14) ins
Holarctic: broad band across region from 70° to 50°N and farther S in W North America; winters from N Africa across to S China, W Indies and Panama; on coasts and estuaries as well as fresh waters. Breeds lakes, river valleys and marshes. ♂: grey with chocolate head and neck; white stripe extends up side of neck from white breast and belly; flanks vermiculated grey, wing and tail pattern black, white and buff with elongated central tail feathers; legs blue-grey, eyes brown. ♀: similar to Mallard ♀, *A. platyrhynchos*, but greyer, with shorter tail than ♂; both have dark speculum, glossed green or bronze. Flies rapidly in loose formation, when long neck, tail and light trailing edge to wings distinctive. Walks well on land, usually feeding on vegetation by night, in pairs or small groups, associating with other species. Rather silent; ♀ quacks and ♂ has musical *quuck quuck*. Display resembles Mallard. Breeds from late April often on islands or riparian grassland, making scrape, lined down, sometimes in very low cover. 7 to 9 yellowish-green eggs incubated by ♀ 23 days. Young, tended mainly by ♀, fly 6-7 weeks. **95**

Anas angustirostris see **Marmaronetta angustirostris**

Anas clypeata *Anatidae*
SHOVELER   20 (neck 8) ins
Holarctic: broad band between 70° and 40°N, fairly common W North America; winters to tropical Africa, SE Asia, Central and N South America; mainly on fresh water. Breeds near still waters and slow rivers. ♂'s white breast and chestnut flanks stand out from glossy dark green head and dark brown back; tail pattern black and white. ♀ and eclipse ♂ mottled dark and light brown. Both sexes show pale blue forewing, green speculum in flight. Legs orange, large flattened bill brown to black, eyes light brown to gold. Works shallow, muddy waters, often with reed fringes, running bill along surface, also snaps insects in air and upends. Poor walker, but flies readily; several ♂♂ may chase ♀ in spring; flocks in winter on open water. ♀ quacks, ♂ has low double quack; *tuk tuk* in flight. Food mainly small water animals, insects, some plant material. Breeds from April in bogs, swamps, grassland, sometimes long way from water, laying 8 to 12 greenish or buffish white eggs in scrape lined with down; incubation by ♀ 3½ weeks. She usually rears brood without ♂'s help in *c.* 6 weeks. **96**

Anas leucophrys see **Calonetta leucophrys**

Anas platyrhynchos *Anatidae*
MALLARD   23 (body 15) ins
Holarctic: almost throughout region except arctic zone; winters southern half of breeding range down to N Africa, SE Asia and S Mexico; coastal as well as fresh waters. Breeds general neighbourhood of water: lakes, ponds, river valleys, estuaries and sheltered coasts, often in town parks. ♂: dark green head, white collar, vermiculated grey body and chestnut breast, black and white tail pattern. ♀: mottled brown (eclipse ♂ darker) and black; both sexes show black-edged violet-purple speculum bordered white. Legs orange-red, bill: ♂ greenish yellow, ♀ dark olive, eyes brown. Easy walker and swift flight with vertical take-off. Groups of ♂♂ gather when ♀♀ nesting, but generally gregarious, resting on open water by day, flying in shapeless flocks to feed at dusk, taking various plants, seeds and grain; also upends after water weeds. ♀ quacks loudly, ♂ quieter and higher-pitched. Complicated courtship by ♀ by ♂♂ with head movements prominent. Breeds March onwards, making down-lined scrape in variety of thick cover, often up trees and in old nests. 7 to 16 greyish-green to buff eggs incubated by ♀ 28 days; she tends precocious young who fly *c.* 7½ weeks; ♂ occasionally assists. **97**

Anastomus oscitans *Ciconiidae*
ASIAN OPEN-BILLED STORK   32 ins
Oriental: Indian subcontinent, Nepal, Ceylon, SE Asia. Resident inland waters and marshes, moving locally with water level. Mainly white with glossy black mantle, wings and tail. Legs dark flesh, bill greenish to dull red with diagnostic arched mandible; facial skin black, eyes white to pale brown. Non-breeding and juvenile upperparts smoky grey. Singly, small parties and flocks. Soars for hours, with spectacular hurtling descent. Silent except at nest, where clatters bill in display. Specialised bill helps extract bodies of molluscs, especially snails, *Pila globosa*. Breeds colonially various months throughout range. Usually in water-side trees, building stick nest, lined leaves. 2-5 whitish eggs incubated ♀ and ♂ *c.* 3½ weeks. Both parents feed young, from throat. **67**

ANDEAN
    CONDOR see **Vultur gryphus**
    CRESTED DUCK see **Lophonetta specularoides alticola**
    FLAMINGO see **Phoenicoparrus andinus**
    TAPACULO see **Scytalopus magelianicus**

Andropadus importunus *Pycnonotidae*   8 ins
SOMBRE BULBUL OR ZANZIBAR SOMBRE GREENBUL
Ethiopian: locally distributed, mainly near E coast, Somalia to S Africa; resident dense forest and coastal bush; cultivated areas. Upperparts olive-green; underparts variable, pale olive-green to yellowish-brown; under wing coverts lemon-yellow; legs, bill grey, eyes almost white. Juvenile duller. Solitary and skulking though shows up when singing, a warbling twitter ending in metallic click; loud, whistling *villi*, used also for alarm, followed by soft *chuke-achuke-achuke* and ending in a drawn-out *pheeooo*, described from S Africa. Searches scrub foliage and dead leaves for insects; also takes berries. Breeding season varies within range; builds rather flimsy nest of twigs and creepers, lined fine fibres and seed heads. 2 dull white or cream eggs, marked red-brown and purple over ash-grey, often in zone. **638**

ANGOLA
    KINGFISHER see **Halcyon senegalensis**
    ROCK THRUSH see **Monticola angolensis**

Anhima cornuta *Anhimidae*
HORNED SCREAMER   35 ins
Neotropical: Guyanas, Venezuela N of Orinoco and N Colombia to E Peru, Brazil, Bolivia and probably NW Argentina; resident in open lowlands: grasslands and marshes. Black with green sheen, belly white and white mottling on head and neck; hornlike quill on crown; thick legs, feet and bill grey, eyes yellow; spur on forward edge of wing. Swims and wades, walking over mat vegetation on long toes; rises with heavy, audible wing-beats to soar efficiently, assisted by many air sacs in body. Flocks of up to 100 outside breeding season, calling by night, loud clanging *mo-hoo-ca*, giving Indian name Mahooka; perch on trees. Feeds on ground, mainly vegetarian but some insects. Breeding season variable; builds nest of sticks and reeds usually in marshy ground; 2 white eggs incubated by ♀ and ♂ *c.* 6 weeks; young leave nest on hatching and follow parents. **92**

ANHINGA see **Anhinga anhinga**

Anhinga anhinga *Anhingidae*
ANHINGA OR DARTER
Nearctic, Neotropical: USA to Galapagos and Argentina, on inland and tidal waters with well-wooded swampy surrounds; some movement southwards after breeding. Mainly black or very dark brown with silvery patches on forewings; ♀ has buff-brown throat and breast; legs and very pointed bill yellowish, eyes red. Behaves much as cormorant, perching upright on branches or waterlogged trunks, often holding wings open. Excellent in air after clumsy take-off, soaring with neck stretched, tail fanned. Hunts fish and other water animals, sometimes spearing them, but bringing them to surface between mandibles, to be thrown in air and swallowed. Call a rapid clicking; also harsh croaks and whistlings at nest of sticks in colony, often with other species, in trees or bushes usually over water. Breeding season varies with latitude; 3 to 6 chalky pale blue or green eggs incubated 25-28 days by ♀ and ♂, who tend young for 6-8 weeks. **52**

ANI,
GREATER see **Crotophaga major**
SMOOTH-BILLED see **Crotophaga ani**

ANNA'S HUMMINGBIRD see **Calypte anna**

Anodorhynchus hyacinthinus *Psittacidae*
HYACINTHINE MACAW 37 ins
Neotropical: E Brazil; resident tropical forest, palm groves, swamps; almost uniform deep hyacinth blue; facial skin yellow, legs, very large bill, eyes all black. Generally in small parties in flight, uttering only loud, raucous monosyllabic calls. Diet (captive) mainly fruits but bill appears capable of cracking nuts. Breeds in tree cavities, laying *c.* 4 round white eggs, incubated by ♀ and ♂ who care for the slow-growing young; family parties keep together for several months. **385**

Anous alba see **Gygis alba**

Anous stolidus *Laridae*
COMMON NODDY *c.* $15\frac{1}{2}$ (tail *c.* 6) ins
S Hemisphere: nominate race, coast of tropical S America, Bahamas S to Tristan da Cunha; *A. s. plumbeigularis*, Red Sea and Gulf of Aden; other races Madagascar, India across to Philippines. Habitat: rocky islets and cliffs in warm ocean areas. Sooty brown, flight feathers blacker, forehead and crown greyish white washed with lavender; throat and sides of head grey; rounded fan-shaped tail. Head and throat sooty brown when not breeding. Immature paler, grey-brown crown and white 'eyebrow'. Legs and bill grey, eyes dark brown. Slow flyer, does not dive for fish like other terns but settles on water and feeds like gull or hovers just above surface snatching prey; usually rests on exposed rocks or driftwood rather than in water. Elaborate nodding display whenever paired birds meet. Calls: deep croaking *karr-karr* and shrill *pay-ee*. Breeds in colonies on islands any month; single greyish stone coloured egg, sparsely blotched reddish brown, lavender undermarkings, laid on rocky shelf or in nest of sticks and seaweed on grass clumps, in shrubs or sometimes trees. Both sexes incubate *c.* 32-35 days; young leave nest *c.* 2 months, fed by both parents. **318**

Anseranas semipalmata *Anatidae*
MAGPIE GOOSE ♀: *c.* 30, ♂: *c.* 33 ins
Australasian: breeds S New Guinea and N Australia between Fitzroy River in Western Australia and Bowen in Queensland, generally within 50 miles of coast; otherwise slightly wider ranging, sometimes reaching SW Australia. Habitat: swamps, mangrove flats, estuaries, lakes, rivers and edges of lagoons. Head, neck, wings, rump and tail black; upper wing coverts, mantle, flanks and belly white; cranial knob larger in ♂. Legs yellow, hooked bill and bare skin of face flesh coloured, eyes brown. Slow flight, easy walker, fairly tame, usually in large flocks, sometimes perches in trees. Call: loud resonant honk, higher in ♂. Visits dry plains to feed on grass, otherwise feeds shallow water filtering mud with bill or up-ending. Breeds in colonies depending on rainfall but usually January to March; builds large unlined nest of rushes and herbage on trampled-down tussock of reeds, often sited in swamp. 3 to 11 creamy white eggs, may be laid by 2 ♀'s; all parents whether pair or trio incubate *c.* 24 days and tend young who fly *c.* 11 weeks. **98**

Anser anser *Anatidae*
GREYLAG GOOSE 29-35 (body 19-20) ins
Palaearctic: western race *A. a. anser* breeds Iceland, W Palaearctic, winters Britain, Netherlands, France, Spain, N Africa; eastern *rubirostris* breeds Asia, winters from E Mediterranean across to China; intermediate form in W Russia, Balkans. Habitat: hilly country or lakes in river valleys, sometimes remote islands in sea; winters on marshes, usually near estuaries or low coastline, and larger rivers. Grey-brown head and body with pale grey forewing, black blotches on breast, white upper and lower tail coverts; legs pinkish-grey, heavy bill bright orange (*anser*), pink (*rubirostris*), eyes brown, orbits coral red. Wary like most geese and gregarious when not breeding, but family parties within flock; takes up V formation on longer flights, honking on wing like domesticated descendant. Grazes grassland, marshes, sometimes cultivated land, also shallow water. Breeds April onwards in loose colonies, commonly on islands or reedbeds. 4 to 6 creamy white eggs laid in nest of down and plant debris, incubated by ♀ 28 days; ♂ guards and helps tend brood, which fly *c.* 8 weeks. **99**

Anser caerulescens *Anatidae*
SNOW GOOSE 25-28 (body 17-18) ins
Nearctic: Greater Snow Goose, *A. atlanticus*, breeds coast of NW Greenland, Ellesmere Land and nearby islands, wintering S to coast of USA from Chesapeake Bay to N Carolina; Lesser Snow Goose, *A. caerulescens*, breeds Baffin and Southampton Is, wintering S to coast of N America from Hudson Bay westward and NE Siberia with the grey phase, or Blue Goose, favouring coast of Gulf of Mexico. Habitat outside breeding season: marshes or cultivated land near sea or estuaries, and open shore. Almost pure white with black primaries, reddish legs and pink bill, eyes dark brown; grey phase has white head, neck and rump but rest dark, slightly blue grey. Not too shy, mixes with other species; flies in bent line or V formation; feeds on vegetable matter and some small aquatic animals. High pitched monosyllabic call or low gabbling. Breeds mid June onwards in large colonies on open tundra; 4 to 7 white, slightly creamy or bluish eggs in hollow amongst grass or similar cover well lined with grass, moss, feathers and down. ♀ incubates 24-26 days with ♂ nearby; young tended by both parents. **100**

ANTARCTIC PRION see **Pachyptila desolata**

ANTBIRD, WHITE-PLUMED see **Pithys albifrons**

Anthochaera chrysoptera *Meliphagidae*
LTTLE WATTLEBIRD 11 ins.
Australasian: continental coasts S Queensland to Victoria, S and SW Australia; Kangaroo I, Tasmania; mainly on heaths, also forests, gardens. Upperparts grey-brown, long white streaks down back; pale edges dark wing feathers, chestnut patch shows in flight; white tips outer feathers long graduated tail; cheeks, sides of neck greyish, with small red wattle; bib black, underparts greyish, streaked like back; legs slate black, curved bill dark brown, eyes chestnut. ♀ duller. Pairs or small parties, active and noisy, often in *Banksia* areas; other species attacked. Various harsh, coughing calls, e.g. *cookaycock;* subdued chuckling; rattling call with head, tail raised, bill pointed upwards. Diet chiefly insects, nectar, fruit. Breeds August to December, building loose nest of small twigs, lined soft grasses, bark, in fork of bush or tree, 5 to 25 ft up. Single to 3 pinkish buff eggs, marked reddish-brown, purplish grey at big end, incubated ♀. May have 'several' broods in same nest. **836**

Anthornis melanura *Meliphagidae*
BELLBIRD ♀: $7\frac{1}{2}$, ♂: 8 ins
Confined New Zealand and neighbouring islands; separate race Three Kings (*obscura*); resident all types wooded areas from primary forest to gardens, including 'exotic' plantations. ♂: generally olive-green, variably glossed purple on head; flight and slightly forked tail feathers brownish-black; belly, sides yellowish; under tail coverts pale yellow; tuft of yellow feathers on side near angle of closed wing. ♀ much drabber, olive brown above, yellowish brown tinged olive below; little gloss on head; side tufts, under tail coverts yellowish-white; narrow white moustachial stripe. Legs blue-grey, slightly curved bill black; eyes ♂ dark red, ♀ brown. Three Kings race larger, less yellow. Active forest bird, feeding insects, fruits and nectar from variety of native trees, also honeydew from aphids. Usually located by bell-like liquid song, phrases varying locally (B. J. Marples); ♀ has weaker song of shorter phrases. Harsh, repeated alarm calls: *pek pek pek*. Breeds September to January, rather untidy twig and fibre nest lined fine grass, feathers, often well hidden in tree fork 4 to 40 ft up. 3 or 4 pinkish eggs, marked reddish brown, especially at big end, incubated ♀, probably fed ♂, 14 days. Young, fed insects by parents (perhaps nectar at first), fly 14 days, tended further 10. 2 broods. **837**

Anthoscopus caroli see under **Eremomela icteropygialis**

Anthracoceros coronatus, see under **A. malabaricus**

Anthracoceros malabaricus *Bucerotidae*
INDIAN PIED HORNBILL 26-30 ins
Oriental region: widespread resident on forest edge with paddyfields and cultivations. Generally black with deep blue and green sheen; wingtips, tail tip (except central feathers), belly white, giving pied appearance in flight; legs grey, bill and casque creamy yellow with black markings; facial skin white, eyes, with prominent lashes, brown. Replaced in some areas by closely allied *A. coronatus*, in which outer tail feathers are all white; habits more or less identical. Form flocks of *c.* 12, sometimes many more. Flight alternate flap and glide, birds following each other in line. Voice high-pitched and strident. Fond of dust-bathing. Diet: insects e.g. large grasshoppers; catches flying termites rather clumsily but efficiently at nests; also nestlings, lizards, snakes; figs, berries. Breeds early March Burma, April to May Indian subcontinent, laying 2 or 3 white eggs in hollow tree or branch, in which ♀ is walled in by ♂, coming out when young a few days old and walling them in; excreta voided through narrow slit. **512**

Anthropoides paradisaea or Tetrapteryx paradisaea *Gruidae*
BLUE OR STANLEY'S CRANE 43 ins
Ethiopian: parts of Southern Africa; migrant locally. Inhabits open grassland and cultivations, riversides, sometimes far from water. Predominantly slate-grey, but head pale blue-grey; flight feathers, including elongated secondaries, black; legs black, bill pinkish-yellow, eyes brown. Immature lacks long secondaries. In pairs before breeding, afterwards in flocks; often roosts in shallow water. Duet of croaks between lower-pitched ♂ and higher-pitched ♀. Feeds mainly on large insects, reptiles, sometimes fish; also seeds and grain. Breeding season October to December. Lays 2 buffish brown eggs, marked olive-brown, in scrape in ground. Both parents incubate for *c.* 4 weeks and feed young. **214**

Anthropoides virgo *Gruidae*
DEMOISELLE CRANE 38 ins
Palaearctic: very local NW Africa; from Black Sea, Caspian areas E into southern Siberia; winters NE Africa, Palestine, Persian Gulf, Indian subcontinent, Burma. Habitat: marshy river valleys in grass and shrub steppes; winters cultivated land, e.g. stubbles, paddyfields; riversides and jheels (lakes). Upperparts generally grey; flight feathers black; underparts from head, face, black, with black plumes breast, tail; white stripe back from eyes becomes plumed on nape; crown greyish; legs dull horn grey, bill pinkish, eyes light brown. Deliberate walk; neck, legs stretched in flight. Very large winter flocks India, often with Common Crane, *G. grus*. Communal displays especially mornings and evenings: bouncing and leaping, extending breast plumes. Food mainly vegetable but small animals fed to young. Breeds late spring Siberia, collecting pile plant stems on islet or bank of river. 2 green or grey eggs, marked reddish brown, incubated 25-30 days. **215**

Anthus australis see **A. novaeseelandiae**

Anthus cervinus *Motacillidae*
RED-THROATED PIPIT *c.* $5\frac{3}{4}$ ins
Palaearctic, marginally Nearctic: narrow zone more or less following N Eurasian coastline round about 70°N, reaching Seward Peninsula, Alaska; winters tropical S and SE Asia and Africa; also tropical W Africa. Breeds shrub and moss tundra beyond tree-line, especially marshy areas, also sea and freshwater shores; birch and willow in Scandinavia; wet areas in winter. Pipit pattern of brown upperparts with blackish-brown feather centres, especially on rump, lighter underparts and streaked breast and flanks; white outer tail feathers; pale red throat and breast in summer. Legs yellowish-flesh, bill mainly dark brown, eyes dark brown. Closely resembles Tree Pipit,

A. trivialis, perching on buildings, fences, wires, trees. Flocks in winter. Call 'full, musical, rather abrupt *chüp*' (B. W. Tucker); song in three parts delivered in full display flight, also from perch. Food principally insects and their larvae, also worms, molluscs, grass seeds in winter. Breeds mid-June to early July, building nest of local plant material in side of hummock or tussock, or sheltered by low shrub. 5 to 6 eggs, varying in ground colour and markings, incubated by ♀, fed by ♂, *c.* 14 days; young, fed by ♀ and ♂, fly probably 12-13 days. **623**

Anthus leucophrys *Motacillidae*
PLAIN-BACKED PIPIT   6 ins
Ethiopian: several races cover most of region in suitable habitats: open short-grass country, often in mountains. Upperparts dark or rufous brown without streaks; 'eyebrow' and outer tail feathers pale buff; underparts rufous or buff brown with faint dark streaks and spots on breast. Ground-living, presumably insectivorous. Forms small flocks outside breeding season. Builds well-hidden grass nest, laying 3 off-white eggs, speckled brown and grey; other details much as relatives, but confusion exists with very similar but paler Sandy Plain-backed Pipit, *A. vaalensis*, also fairly widely distributed in region. It has song flight consisting of upward climb *c.* 30 ft, then planing descent. **624**

Anthus novaeseelandiae *or A. australis Motacillidae*
RICHARD'S, AUSTRALIAN or
NEW ZEALAND PIPIT   *c.* 7 ins
E Palaearctic, Oriental, Australasian: several races from Siberia SE through Indian subcontinent, Malaysia to Australia, Tasmania, New Zealand; also most of Ethiopian region; northern populations mingle with southern races in winter. Habitats vary through enormous range, but predominantly rough grassland and meadows not far from water; in winter marshes and ricefields. Upperparts brown, feathers with darker centres giving streaked effect; whitish 'eyebrow'; breast buff, streaked dark brown, shading to white belly; outer tail feathers white. Legs pale flesh, upper bill dark brown, lower paler; eyes dark brown. Noticeably erect carriage; walks and runs swiftly; strong, undulating flight. Variously described harsh call and softer two-syllabled chirp; song, rendered *chichi chee-chee-chee*, delivered from perch or in descending flight. Mainly insectivorous throughout year; some seeds in winter. Breeding season varies with range, e.g. August to March New Zealand, June to July Siberia. Nest of local plant material, hidden by tussock. 3 to 6 greenish-grey to pink eggs, mottled olive or reddish-brown and grey, incubated mainly by ♀ *c.* 14 days; young fed by ♀ and ♂, fly 14-16 days. 2 or 3 broods. **625**

Anthus pratensis *Motacillidae*
MEADOW PIPIT   *c.* 5¾ ins
Palaearctic, marginally Nearctic: NW Eurasia, N of line from SW France to River Ob; also Italian Abruzzi, Iceland (where reputed to be commonest bird), E Greenland; winters W Europe, Mediterranean area. Breeds rough, often wet, grasslands, heaths, moors, dunes; wooded and shrub tundra; open woodland, alpine meadows: winters on cultivated land, sea shores. Pipit pattern with white outer tail feathers, tends to be more olive brown than relatives, with heavier streaking upperparts: but very variable. Legs pale brown, bill mainly dark brown, eyes black-brown. Typical small passerine of open country in summer, rising to dog observer with persistent *tsip* calls in undulating flight. Uses high perches, e.g. wires, when available but mainly on ground. Forms flocks or loose parties after breeding. Display flight upward from ground, then sails down, wings spread, tail lifted, with series of calls making up simple song. Insectivorous: flies and mosquitos in summer, but great variety taken, also worms, spiders, some seeds. Breeds mid-April to August Britain; nest of grasses with fine lining typically hidden in grass or heather-grass tussock, but in many kinds of cover, often on slope. 4 to 5 off-white eggs, heavily freckled brown and grey, incubated by ♀ 13-14 days; young, fed by ♀ and ♂, fly 13-14 days. 2 broods. **626**

Anthus trivialis *Motacillidae*
TREE PIPIT   *c.* 6 ins
Palaearctic: Europe (except Iberia, Ireland) E into Asia N of Lat 60° with extension S to Himalayas; also S of Black Sea to Caucasus; winters Oriental and Ethiopian regions. Breeds dry or wet grassland, heaths and moors with scattered trees, also open woodlands and wooded steppes; winters in savannah and park-like habitats. Pipit pattern, but browns rather brighter, more buff, especially on breast than Meadow Pipit, *A. pratensis*; white outer tail feathers. Legs brownish-flesh, bill tip and upper mandible dark brown, rest pale flesh, eyes black-brown. Stands more erect than Meadow Pipit, usually walks, but can run fast. Rather jerky flight. Less active than Meadow Pipit and very shy in winter quarters, where usually solitary. Perches in trees, sings from them, takes off from one in 'paper dart' song flight, uttering sustained burst, ending *seea seea seea*. Food mainly insects of several orders; also spiders, some seeds. Breeds end April to July Britain; grass nest usually very well hidden under variety of low cover, often on bank. 4 to 6 extremely variable eggs, both in ground colour and markings: grey, brown, green, red, incubated by ♀ 13-14 days; young, fed by ♀ and ♂, fly 12-13 days. Sometimes 2 broods in S of range. **627**

Anthus vaalensis see under **A. leucophrys**

ANTILLEAN GRACKLE, GREATER see **Quiscalus niger**

ANTPITTA, RUSTY-BREASTED see **Grallaricula ferrugineipectus**

ANTSHRIKE, FASCIATED see **Cymbilaimus lineatus**

ANTTHRUSH, BLACK-FACED see **Formicarius analis**

APALIS, BAR-THROATED see **Apalis thoracica**

Apalis murina see **A. thoracica**

Apalis thoracica *or A. murina Muscicapidae: Sylviinae*
BAR-THROATED APALIS   5 ins
Ethiopian: Southern and E Africa S of Equator, except E coast. Resident in forest, from shrub to canopy layer; also along wooded streams. Upperparts greyish or greenish; outer tail white; breast band and around eye black; underparts white, washed pale yellow on belly; legs pink, bill black, eyes pale yellow. Behaviour restless and inquisitive. Song varies over range, usually whistled trill; ♂'s call, loud penetrating *pil pil* answered by softer note of ♀. Insectivorous. Breeding season variable: August to February in Rhodesia, September to December Cape Province. Ball nest of moss, lichens, built among thick leaves or sewn on to hanging leaf; nest lined fibrous material, ornamented mosses, lichens. 2 or 3 white eggs, freckled reddish, lilac. **727**

Aphelocoma coerulescens *Corvidae*
SCRUB JAY   11½-12 ins
Nearctic, marginally Neotropical: Florida peninsula, then 1,000 mile gap to western range: S Wyoming, S Washington to S Mexico; W Nebraska, Central Texas W to Pacific. Florida race resident dense scrub of oaks, myrtle, sand pines, palmettos; western race resident from riparian willow thickets to montane woodlands with chaparral; also juniper thickets in piñon country. Back grey; wings blue, primaries tipped dark grey; rump, tail bright blue; head, nape blue, earcoverts dark blue, white 'eyebrow'; throat white bordered blue gorget; underparts grey-white; legs bill, blackish, eyes dark brown. Florida race smaller, duller than western birds. Juvenile grey or brown where adult blue. Keeps much to cover, but sometimes on exposed perch, tail hanging straight down; bows deeply on alighting and strikes perch with bill when anxious. Harsh 1 and 2 note calls; soft musical song. Diet: variety of insects, occasional lizards; molluscs and crustaceans on shore, Florida; pine nuts in piñon country. Breeds April to May, building nest of twigs

and stems, lined rootlets, in dense bush or small tree 2 to 12 ft up; 3 to 5 dull bluish green eggs, marked olive or umber brown over lilac. **993**

Aphelocoma ultramarina *Corvidae*
MEXICAN JAY   *c.* 13 ins
Nearctic, marginally Neotropical: resident evergreen oak regions of central and S Arizona, S New Mexico, W Texas, Mexico. Upperparts light blue, brownish on back, purplish and greenish gloss on wings, sides of head blackish; underparts pale grey. Legs, bill and eyes blackish. Gregarious, 3 or more birds may work on one nest, member of flock may feed another's young. Call: range of squawks. Omnivorous; catches flies, pulls off acorns from branches, steals from campers, robs other birds. Breeds socially, early April to mid May; bulky nest of oak twigs lined with rootlets and hairs, usually in crotch of oak branch. Lays 4 to 5 greenish eggs, unmarked, incubated ♀ only *c.* 16 days. **994**

Aphriza virgata *Scolopacidae*
SURFBIRD   9-9½ ins
Nearctic: breeds mountains of Alaska on rocky ridges of tundra with creeping willow, other low-growing plants; winters all down Pacific coast America to Tierra del Fuego, on rocky shores. Plump; winter plumage: upperparts, breast, flanks greyish-brown streaked dusky black; underparts from throat white; small white patch above eye. Summer: generally mottled brown, black and white; underparts spotted black; crown, scapulars rusty brown, feathers black-tipped; white wing-bar; rump, tail white with black triangular patch at tip; legs yellow; short grey bill, base of lower mandible yellow; eyes dark brown with white orbits. Call: shrill whistling *ke-week* or *key-we-ah*; *throi-dee* on breeding grounds. Feeds close to tideline in winter on molluscs, especially barnacles, crustacea; occasionally picks food off sandy shores; insects when breeding. Lays early June in sparingly lined scrape often quite exposed. 4 buffish eggs, brown spots usually concentrated big end, incubated ♂. Young feed themselves, parents leave them July for long migration.

APOSTLEBIRD see **Struthidea cinerea**

Aprosmictus erythropterus see under **A. scapularis**

Aprosmictus scapularis *or Alisterus scapularis Psittacidae*
KING PARROT   16 ins
Australia E coast: in montane rain forest to 5,200 ft or dense riverine scrub; less often savannah woodland; seasonal movements to lowlands in winter, including farmlands, even city suburbs. Variable; ♂: upperparts green; head, underparts red; rump blue, long broad tail, blue black; legs light grey, bill red, tipped black, eyes yellow. ♀ differs in green head and breast, wings, tail darker, under tail coverts barred black; bill grey, eyes white. Awkward on ground; heavy but powerful flight. Pairs, families or groups of 20-30 immatures feed outermost branches of eucalypts and acacias on fruits, berries and nectar; attack green and fruit crops. Scratches with foot over wing. Call on wing shrill *crassack crassack*. ♂ has soft double note and courts ♀ with elaborate puffing of feathers, wing-flicking; ♀ bobs head. Breeds September to January; nest chamber often far down in hollow trunk or branch, usually of eucalypt. 3 to 6 white eggs incubated by ♀ 20 days, ♂ near; young fledge *c.* 5 weeks. May hybridise with Crimson-winged Parrot, *A. erythropterus*. **386**

Aptenodytes forsteri *Spheniscidae*
EMPEROR PENGUIN   4 ft tall
Antarctic distribution, making trips of up to 60 miles to breeding stations, from which young move north in October to November. Penguin pattern of black and white with orange yellow patches on side of neck. Legs black; bill black with orange streak; eyes dark. Normal stance upright but toboggans, using legs and flippers, when alarmed; masterly in water, fishing in open spaces among pack ice. Long breeding season (June to February) colonially on sea ice; no nest, ♂ taking over single egg, holding it on feet, warmed by fold of skin,

while ♀ goes many miles to feed, returning towards end of *c.* 60 day incubation period to relieve ♂ and feed chick, reared during winter, latterly in anti-predator crêches, ready to migrate to ice floes when moult complete. **8**

Apteryx australis *Apterygidae*
BROWN KIWI 18-22 ins
Three races resident in North, South and Stewart Islands of New Zealand; introduced to offshore islands. Original habitat forest, now in scrub and other modified woodland. ♀ larger than ♂, flightless; streaked reddish-brown to black except on greyish head, legs pale to dark brown, bill (longer in ♀) pale brown, eyes dark. Nocturnal, probing debris of forest floor for insect larvae and worms; sight weak but bill sensitive with nostrils at tip; can run quite well. ♂ whistles *kiwi* shrilly; ♀ has deep hoarse cry, but voice varies between races. Usually one (2 in N Island race) heavy, glazed white or greenish egg laid July to February in scrape, sometimes excavated, in vegetation, tree roots or hollow log; incubated 75-80 days by ♂, who helps young to feed after 6 days in nest; fledging period unknown. **5**

Apus apus *Apodidae*
COMMON SWIFT *c.* 6½ ins
Palaearctic and Oriental: breeds arctic Europe and Siberia, S to Mediterranean and NW Africa, E to Transcaucasia; winters W and S Africa, also Madagascar. Eastern race, *pekinensis*, breeds Iran across to India and China, winters S Africa and Andamans. Almost always aerial, often very high, even roosting on wing. Sooty brown (*pekinensis* browner) with long narrow wings and forked tail, white throat. Legs and bill blackish, eyes dark brown. Flight rapid, wheeling and dashing; can perch on vertical surface of rock or masonry, but takes off from ground with difficulty. Call: shrill screaming. Food: takes insects on wing. Breeds late May to early June, colonial; uses saliva to stick together plant debris and feathers to make low cup in crevices, caves, eaves of houses and sometimes fissures in cliff faces, holes in trees, old nests of House Martin, *Delichon urbica*, or nestboxes. 2 or 3 white eggs incubated *c.* 18-20 days by both parents; both also tend young, who fly *c.* 6 weeks. **464**

Apus melba *Apodidae*
ALPINE SWIFT *c.* 8¼ ins
Palaearctic, Ethiopian: breeds S Europe down to N Morocco, E to Turkestan; winters Africa, S Arabia and S India. Almost exclusively aerial, over mountains, about sea cliffs and sometimes old buildings. Paler brown upperparts, larger white throat patch and white on belly. Main African race, *A. m. africanus*, found Uganda, Ethiopia and Kenya S to S Africa, darker with smaller white throat patch. Legs dark brown, bill black, eyes dark brown. Usually in small flocks, flight similar to Common Swift, *Apus apus*, but faster; feeds on insects taken in flight. Call: loud, descending and ascending trill. Colonial breeder, late May to early June; glues feathers and plant debris together to make cup-shaped nest in crevices or caves in rocky, mountainous areas, sea-cliffs, old buildings, occassionally tree holes. 2 or 3 white eggs, incubated *c.* 20 days by both parents; both tend young, who fly *c.* 7 weeks.

Aquila audax or Uroaetus audax *Accipitridae*
WEDGE-TAILED EAGLE 30-36 ins
Australia and Tasmania, sedentary. In forests to near-deserts but prefers open country. Glossy brownish black with rufous feathers on nape, rufous edging to wing coverts and undertail; legs and cere yellow, bill dark, eyes brown. Immature lighter coloured, with white rump. Spends day either on wing or perched in tree, on ant hill or ground. Attacks prey with slanting stoop. Prefers rabbits and hares but takes variety of vertebrates and is persecuted for supposed lamb-killing; also takes carrion, feeding on it in large parties. Aerial displays take place well in advance of breeding season which begins in July. Variety of calls, including shrill *pee-ya pee-ya*, mainly uttered in breeding season. Nests usually 20 to 40 ft up in tree, huge structure of sticks, built over years. Usually lays 2 buff or white eggs marked brown. Incubated by ♀, who feeds young on food brought by ♂. Fledging period *c.* 10 weeks. **134**

Aquila chrysaetos *Accipitridae*
GOLDEN EAGLE 30-35 ins (♀ larger)
Holarctic: Eurasia S to N Africa, Arabia and Nearctic S to Mexico; resident in mountainous and moorland areas, also montane forests, occasionally sea cliffs and plains. Almost uniform dark tawny to chocolate brown, lighter on body and with 'golden' crown and nape; young has pale 'mirror' under wing, white tail with black terminal band. Legs feathered, toes and cere yellow, bill dark, eyes hazel. Usually solitary; leisurely flapping and gliding flight; soars with primaries spread; perches on tree or rock for long periods. Beats low over ground to hunt, dropping on prey: hares, rabbits, ptarmigan and variety of birds; also fish and carrion; accused of lamb-killing. Usually silent, but yelps, barks and whistles in alarm. Breeds March onwards, building huge nest of sticks and heather with finer lining on cliff ledge, tree, even ground. Usually 2 white eggs, marked red brown and grey, incubated mainly by ♀ 43-45 days. Young fed by ♀ and ♂, fly 65-70 days, one eaglet of two may kill other. **135**

Aquila rapax *Accipitridae*
TAWNY EAGLE 26-31 ins
Palaearctic, Ethiopian and Oriental: Rumania east to Mongolia, S to almost all Africa, Arabia and Indian subcontinent. Northern populations migrate S in flocks; local movements in tropics. Wide habitat range, though avoiding forests. Variable in shades of very dark to light rufous brown, with pale bars on wings; flight feathers and tail dark; rump pale; legs feathered, feet and cere yellow, bill dark-tipped, eyes brown. Rather silent except in display or aggression, uttering crow-like *kowk kowk*. Gregarious outside breeding season, when may perform display flights. Catholic taste in food, from carrion to mammals and ground birds; robs other predators after aerial chase and scavenges round habitations. Breeding season varies throughout vast range. Usually nests in tree at 10 to 100 ft, also on low elevations on ground. Rather small nest of sticks, with finer lining, holds 1 to 3 white eggs with variable brown markings. Incubated apparently only by ♀ *c.* 45 days. Both parents feed young which fly *c.* 10 weeks. **136**

Aquila verreauxi *Accipitridae*
VERREAUX'S EAGLE 30-32 ins
Ethiopian: S from Sudan and Somalia, in rocky hills of dry country, breeding up to 13,000 ft. Black except for large white V on shoulders; white wing bar in flight, legs feathered, feet and cere yellow, bill dark, eyes brown. Immature a mixture of dark and light brown. Spends hours on wing without hunting, with striking undulating display flight; will "buzz" leopards and humans visiting nest. Usually silent, but clucks, barks (alarm) and whistles (display). Catches prey by quick twist and plunge; staple diet hyraxes (small mammals) *Procaria* and *Heterohyrax*, but takes larger, and many birds. Breeding season from April (South Africa) to December (Sudan). Usually nests on crags, sometimes trees. Builds flat nest of sticks, lays usually 2 white eggs, occasionally marked brown. Incubation largely by ♀ for 43-46 days. Chicks fed by both parents. One eaglet usually kills other, flies in about 14 weeks. **137**

Aquila wahlbergi *Accipitridae*
WAHLBERG'S EAGLE 22 ins
Ethiopian: from line between Gambia and Eritrea S to Cape Province; well wooded savannah and thorny bushveld: frequently cultivated land. Partially migratory in wet season. Dark brown, with paler areas on wings, head and belly, flight feathers blackish; distinct crest; lighter phases occur, one with head and body creamy white; legs feathered, feet and cere yellow, bill dark, eyes brown. Normally silent but variety of calls include high pitched repeated *kyip*. Hunts small vertebrates, largely reptiles, by 'tree hopping' and pouncing, especially in grass fires. Also soars up to 400 ft and displays, often singly, over nest site, in tree from 25 to 100 ft. Lays single (occasionally 2) white egg, usually marked brown, in September or October. Normally incubated by ♀ only for 46 days. Eaglet fed by both parents, flies in 10-11 weeks. **138**

Ara ararauna *Psittacidae*
BLUE AND YELLOW MACAW 33-36 (tail 21) ins
Neotropical: E Panama and Trinidad S to SE Brazil, NW Argentina; resident in forests, 'inaccessible swamp' on Trinidad. Upperparts blue, darker on flight feathers and tail; forehead green-blue; underparts from side of neck yellow but under tail coverts dull turquoise; black throat border to white facial skin; legs grey-horn, bill black, eyes yellowish-white. Facial skin 'blushes' pink when excited. Parties of from 4 to 15 birds fly screeching over trees, feeding on palm nuts; also take various fruits and seeds; but numbers on evening flights run into hundreds, pairs keeping together within the flock. Breeds April and May in Trinidad, in holes of dead trees, e.g. *Maurita* and *Oreodoxa* palms. 2 to 4 white eggs incubated by ♀ 24-26 days; young, fed by parents, remain in nest *c.* 13 weeks, when they resemble adults with shorter tails.

ARAÇARI, MANY-BANDED see **Pteroglossus pluricinctus**

Arachnothera longirostris *Nectariniidae*
LTTLE SPIDERHUNTER 6 ins
Oriental: widespread resident in region; forests up to 5,000 ft. Upperparts plain olive green (head spotted in race *A. l. buttikoferi*); chin, throat, greyish; underparts yellow; legs blackish, long curved bill black above, grey below; eyes brown. Restless and noisy, with direct flight. Calls: single bleat on wing (B. E. Smythies); repeated *chet* while feeding. Hangs upside-down, clinging to bracts of plantains, while bill poked inside for nectar from inflorescence; also takes spiders, locusts and other soft-bodied insects (T. H. Harrisson). Breeds between March and September; ♀ and ♂ build nest of dead leaves 'sewn to underside of large leaf, which forms one side of pocket'. 2 or 3 pinkish-white eggs, spotted bright red, mainly in zone at big end. Incubation and feeding of young by both parents.

Arachnothera magna *Nectariniidae*
STREAKED SPIDERHUNTER 8½ (bill 2) ins
Oriental: Lower Himalayas, Chittagong, Sikkim, Assam, Yunnan, Burma, Thailand, N Indochina; resident tropical and wet evergreen forests, *c.* 1,500 to 5,000 ft Sikkim, where closely associated with wild banana *Musa* (Salim Ali); also clearings, tea plantations, gardens. Upperparts generally olive yellow, heavily streaked black; short tail olive yellow with pale yellowish tips; and broad black subterminal bands; underparts pale yellow streaked blackish; legs yellow, long curved bill horn-brown or black, orange edge to lower mandible; eyes brown. Tree-living, in pairs or singly, visiting many flowering trees, shrubs and mistletoes for nectar and insects; may hover to take spider out of web. Call: sharp metallic *kikiki* on wing and when feeding. Breeds April-May Himalayan area; neat nest of skeleton leaves held together by cobwebs and softly lined, sewn with vegetable down to underside of large drooping leaf, e.g. banana, leaving small entrance at top. 2 or 3 eggs in variable shades of brown, darker zone at big end, incubated ♀ and ♂, who also feed young. In spite of tiny nest hole, some parasitism by cuckoos. **819**

Aramus guarauna *Aramidae*
LIMPKIN 23-28 ins
Nearctic fringe, Neotropical: extreme SE USA, Greater Antilles, Central America, then E of Andes to Central Argentina, W of Andes to W Ecuador; resident wooded swamps, often mangroves; less often marshes, even arid areas in W Indies. Dark brown, each feather on body with large white crescent, giving streaked effect; tail short and broad, wings broad and rounded; legs blackish brown, curved bill light base, dark tip, eyes dark. Long neck held erect, extended in heavy, reluctant flight with legs dangling. Stands or perches at any height, swims well without webbed feet. Call a carrying *krr-oww* by night; also screams

and clucks. Diet: mainly large *Pomacea* snails taken from water, extracted on shore where shells accumulate; also bivalves, reptiles, many water animals and worms. Breeds August to October in S of range, building flimsy nest of sticks and dead stems on ground, in bush or tree. 4 to 8 pale buff eggs, marked light brown, incubated by ♀ and ♂. Young leave nest early but continue to be fed even after fledging. **223**

Archilochus colubris *Trochilidae*

RUBY-THROATED HUMMINGBIRD   3½ ins
Nearctic: breeds E North America from Great Lakes to Gulf of Florida, winters Mexico, Central America, W Indies, involving 500 mile flights. Habitat: woodlands, orchards, gardens; forest in winter. ♂: upperparts iridescent green from head to slightly forked, blackish tail; cheeks and throat ruby red; underparts white, undertail blackish. ♀ has white throat, spotted black, white tips to tail feathers. Legs, long straightish bill, eyes dark. Usually solitary or in pairs; aggressive on territory, attacking other birds up to eagles. ♂ in display swings in wide arc 3 to 40 ft radius, humming on each of 15 to 20 swings; also chases ♀. Wingbeats 55 to 75 per second. Voice 'high-pitched, mouselike, petulant' (R. T. Peterson). Bathes frequently in dew off leaves. Takes tiny insects and nectar from corollas of flowers, also insects on wing. Breeds May to June, building lichen-covered little cup of plant materials, bound with spider web, saddled on horizontal branch of c. 1 inch diameter, usually more than 6 ft up. 2 elliptical white eggs incubated by ♀ (who also builds nest) for c. 16 days; she rears young, 'discharging' food from gullet or carrying insects in bill, until they fledge 22-24 days. This account of breeding applies generally to the family. **466**

ARCTIC
REDPOLL see under **Acanthis flammea**
TERN see **Sterna paradisaea**

Ardea cinerea *Ardeidae*

GREY HERON   36 (body 16) ins
Palaearctic, Ethiopian and Oriental: across temperate Eurasia to Japan, but also India and SE China; very local Africa and W Madagascar. Generally grey, but white on head and neck with black eyestripe extending to plumes on nape; black streaks on neck, underwing black. Legs brown, bill yellowish, eyes yellow, bare facial skin yellowish to green. Usually solitary, standing motionless beside shallow water, head sunk in plumage or raised in S-bend, but also stalks prey deliberately then stabs fish, frogs, small mammals, young birds; also molluscs, crustaceans and insects. Flies with neck bent, legs stretched, sometimes giving *kaark* call. Breeds January to August in Europe, in colonies of large stick nests in trees, sometimes bushes, cliffs, reedbeds or ground. Both sexes incubate 3 to 5 chalky blue eggs for 3½ weeks, then tend brood which fledges in 8 weeks; in nest they chatter noisily. **54**

Ardea goliath *Ardeidae*

GOLIATH HERON   55-60 ins
Ethiopian and S Palaearctic: Senegal and Egypt to Madagascar and S Africa; Red Sea area. Habitat coastal mudflats to swamps and shores of E African lakes and rivers. Upperparts grey; head, neck and underparts chestnut; chin and throat white; juvenile browner; legs blackish, bill grey with darker tip, eyes yellow. Solitary or in pairs; in flight slow and measured, with legs tending to sag. Takes fish and other water animals. Deep, loud *aarrrk* call like baying hound; young call *cack cack cack*. Breeding varies with latitude; young in April and September at Lake Rudolph. Nest platform of sticks in tree, reedbed or among large boulders at L. Rudolph; often solitary in colony of other herons. Both sexes incubate usually 3 pale blue eggs and tend the young, who fly in 5-6 weeks. **55**

Ardea novaehollandiae see **Notophoyx novaehollandiae**

Ardeotis kori see **Choriotis kori**

Arenaria interpres *Scolopacidae*

TURNSTONE   c. 9 ins
Holarctic: temperate (Baltic, Scandinavia), otherwise circumpolar arctic coasts; cosmopolitan in winter from N temperate S to Argentina, S Africa, New Zealand; rocky coasts and harbours, coral reefs, sandy beaches. Breeds rocky or stony shores, locally inland on moss and lichen tundra. Summer: upperparts mottled rufous and black; crown white, streaked black; black and white pattern on cheeks and neck; wing blackish-brown with white bar; white patch on rump, tail white with black subterminal band; black band on breast, underparts white; short legs orange, shortish straight bill black, eyes brown. Winter: upperparts, including head and neck, mottled dark brown. Usually in small parties, busily lifting seaweed or stones, then flying on with twittering *kititit*. This preceded in spring by *quitta quitta quitta* as 'song', when ♂ chases ♀ in courtship. Food: small marine animals from under stones or seaweed; seeds of tundra plants, insects. Breeds from mid May in S of range, making scrape among stones, splash zone vegetation; on moss and lichen of tundra, sometimes sheltered or well hidden. 4 greyish-green eggs, marked brown and ash-grey, incubated by ♀ and ♂; ♂ takes chief share tending brood. **275**

ARGUS PHEASANT, GREAT see **Argusianus argus**

Argusianus argus *Phasianidae*

GREAT ARGUS PHEASANT   ♀: 27-30
♂ (including tail 49-52): 70-73 ins
Oriental: S Burma, Malaysia, Indo-China, Sumatra, Borneo; resident lowland but not lowlying evergreen forests up to c. 4,000 ft. ♂: generally mottled chestnut, yellow and black, lighter on upperparts, richer brown underparts; very broad, ocellated secondaries twice as long as finely mottled primaries; 2 central tail feathers, dark grey and brown, spotted white, very broad, immensely elongated; head, neck mainly bare blue skin, but nape and crown to small crest blackish; legs red, bill very pale yellow; eyes red. ♀: duller, secondaries little longer than primaries, lacks long tail feathers. Solitary, ♀ wandering in jungle, only visiting ♂ to mate. He clears dancing area 6 to 8 yards square, with escape alley, and remains in vicinity. Three stage display: ♂ fidgets round ♀, then spreads wings, raises tail, sinks head to become vertical concave fan of feathers; finally bows to ♀. ♂'s call repeated *how how*; ♀: *how-owoo*, repeated at increasing tempo; audible up to mile or more, prompted by gunshots or other loud noises. Diet: fallen fruit swallowed whole, nuts, seeds, leaves; slugs, ants and other insects. Breeding irregular but not at height of rains. 2 creamy white eggs laid in scrape under thick cover, incubated ♀, who also tends chicks.

Arremon aurantiirostris see under **A. schlegeli**

Arremon schlegeli *Emberizidae: Emberizinae*

GOLDEN-WINGED SPARROW   6¼ ins
Neotropical: N Venezuela, Colombia W slope E Andes; semi-arid forests and thickets, sea level to c. 4,000 ft. ♂: back grey, becoming more or less tinged olive towards dusky tail, wings olive with yellow at shoulder; head black, underparts white, black patch each side breast; flanks grey; bill lemon yellow with black ridge. ♀: flanks clay-coloured. Closely related Pectoral Sparrow, *A. taciturnus*, with somewhat similar distribution, has repeated high thin call: *tsn*. Breeds during rainy season, building bulky domed nest in thick forest cover, laying 2 white eggs, spotted brown. Incubation of Central American Orange-billed Sparrow, *A. aurantiirostris*, is by ♀, 14-17 days. **851**

Arremon taciturnus see under **A. schlegeli**

ARROW-MARKED BABBLER see **Turdoides jardinei**

Artamus cyanopterus see under **A. superciliosus**

Artamus leucorhynchus *Artamidae*

WHITE-BREASTED WOOD SWALLOW   7 ins
Oriental, Australasian: Andamans, Indonesia, Borneo, Philippines, New Guinea and islands to New

Hebrides, Fiji; N coastal Australia from Shark's Bay in W to Manning and Murray Rivers (New South Wales) in E, where extends far inland. Resident open wooded country, especially near coast, e.g. casuarina trees Borneo, mangroves tropical Australia, inland along watercourses and up to c. 4,000 ft Borneo; round habitations N Queensland. Upperparts grey-brown; flight feathers, tail blackish; head to throat grey-black; rump, underparts, underwing white; legs leaden grey, bill light blue, eyes dark brown. Very social, characteristically huddling together on bare branches, whence attacks other passing birds, even pecking birds of prey, crows and kingfishers on the head, uttering almost continuous twittering or chattering calls. Graceful gliding and soaring flight takes birds out over estuaries and open sea; insect prey hawked in air. Breeds October in April Borneo, August to January Australia, in loose colonies; ♀ and ♂ build nest of fine twigs lined grasses, sometimes in old nest of Magpie Lark, *Grallina cyanoleuca*, more usually in high fork or snag end of tree branch. 2 to 4 buffish white eggs, marked rich dark brown and purplish over grey, incubated ♀ and ♂, probably c. 14 days; fledging c. 12 days. **982**

Artamus personatus see under **A. superciliosus**

Artamus superciliosus *Artamidae*

WHITE-BROWED WOOD SWALLOW   c. 8 ins
Australian; breeds mainly two areas: in SE, and in SE Queensland; winters locally throughout continent, moving nomadically often in flocks with Masked Wood Swallow, *A. personatus*. Habitat principally arid scrub and grassy savannah. Upperparts dark grey with white 'eyebrow' above black lores; outer tail feathers tipped white; underparts rich dark chestnut. ♀ duller; juvenile mottled. Legs leaden grey, bill light blue, tipped black; eyes black brown. Flocks up to 200, aggressive like relatives, with harsh mobbing call. Twittering similar to but distinct from Dusky Wood Swallow, *A. cyanopterus*; also mimics neighbour species. Insectivorous, following caterpillar and locust plagues. Breeds socially August to December, ♀ and ♂ building nest of thin twigs, roots, stems, lined rootlets, fine grass, usually in fork of branch, projecting bark, snag end, occasionally old nest Magpie Lark, *Grallina cyanoleuca*, c. 10 ft up. 2 to 3 greenish-grey to buffish white eggs, marked rich dark brown over slate grey, incubated by night ♀ and ♂ 16 days in SE range; fledging 15 days, less inland.

ASIAN
KING VULTURE see **Sarcogyps calvus**
WHITE-CRESTED HORNBILL see **Berenicornis comatus**
SPICE FINCH see under **Lonchura castaneothorax**

Asio capensis *Strigidae*

AFRICAN MARSH OWL   14½ ins
SW Palaearctic (W North Africa); Ethiopian: most of region except extreme E; habitat: grassy swamps and watercourses. Upperparts, including breast, sepia; underparts paler, both flecked and mottled lighter or darker; tail barred dark and light brown; dark-rimmed facial disc pale with blackish patches round brown eyes; very short ear tufts; legs feathered, feet and bill black. Usually in small parties; may begin to hunt before dusk, perching on post before quartering ground with rather erratic flight. Inquisitive at humans; settles, sometimes fatally, on roads. Call: frog-like croak, uttered on wing at dusk. Food: large insects; scorpions, frogs, lizards. Breeding variable throughout range; nest a pad of grass, usually 'roofed over' in long grass or rushes, with 2 to 4 white eggs. Incubation and fledging probably much as *A. flammeus*. **433**

Asio flammeus *Strigidae*

SHORT-EARED OWL   14½-15 ins
Holarctic and Neotropical: most of Palaearctic Eurasia, including Iceland, but except Mediterranean area, NE Siberia; most N America to 71° N in Alaska, elsewhere at high latitudes; isolated 'colonies' W Indies, especially Hispaniola, and northern S America; from 25° S in Peru to Patagonia and Falkland Is; also

Hawaii, Carolines, Galapagos; northern and southern populations migrate, sedentary in tropics; also irregular dispersal. Habitat: open bogs and marshes, moorland, grassland, steppes and savannahs, wet clearings in forests, river banks, salt marshes, dunes, wet tundra; in scrub to 1,000 ft in S America; in winter on cultivated land. Variable: upperparts richly marbled buff and dark brown, wings and tail barred; underparts buff, streaked dark brown; well defined facial disc, darker round golden-yellow eyes, ear tufts hardly show; legs feathered, feet black, bill dark brown, tip paler. Winters far N if food sufficient, also collects in numbers during vole plagues. Largely diurnal and terrestrial, but perches posts, stumps, trees at times. Harrier-like with relatively long wings as it quarters ground after small rodents; also birds, some insects: beetles. Generally silent but has harsh flight note and barks when nest approached. Song in display flight, low pitched, hollow, repeated *boo boo boo boo*; ♂ circles with spread wings, also claps them rapidly beneath body. Breeding season variable; nest scrape on ground in thick cover holds 4 to 7 (more in vole or lemming years) white eggs. ♀ incubates 24-28 days; ♂ brings her food for young, who fly *c.* 3½ weeks; 2 broods in vole years. **434**

Asio otus *Strigidae*
LONG-EARED OWL   *c.* 13½ ins
Holarctic: across Eurasia from Ireland, Iberia, NW Africa to Japan, mostly between 40° and 60°N; isolated area S China; N America mainly between 40° and 50°N with extensions N in Central Canada, S to Lower California; northern birds migrate S, especially when food short. Habitat: broadleaved and coniferous forest, riverine tree belts, isolated clumps in cultivated land, parks and large gardens. Upperparts mottled and vermiculated greyish-buff and dark brown; underparts buff streaked dark brown, with rather faint barrings; wings, tail barred; facial disc as *A. flammeus* but ear tufts prominent; legs feathered, claws blackish-horn, bill dark horn, tip pale grey, eyes golden orange. Nocturnal, rests in daytime elongated against tree trunk. Display flight among trees or above them, clapping wings. Arched posture in defence if injured. ♂'s 'song' low, cooing *oo oo oo*, ending abruptly; ♀ may duet with slurred, higher-pitched *shoo-oogh*; *woof woof* when nest approached. Hunger call of young like unoiled hinge (C. Oldham). Food: variety of small mammals, birds up to Jay-size, insects: (e.g. beetles). Breeds from February in Europe, usually in old nest of other bird up to 50 ft, also scrape on ground under cover. 3 to 6 white eggs incubated mainly by ♀ 27-28 days; young, fed by both parents, fly *c.* 3½ weeks. **435**

ASITY see **Neodrepanis coruscans**

ASITY, VELVET see **Philepitta castanea**

Astrapia mayeri see under **A. stephaniae**

Astrapia stephaniae *Paradisaeidae*
PRINCESS STEPHANIE'S
BIRD OF PARADISE   ♂ 30-33 (tail 13-15) ins
Australasian: SE New Guinea; resident montane forests, 5,500 ft to 9,500 ft and higher. ♂: upperparts black, glossed green; wings, tail black, broad central tail feathers iridescent, much elongated but graduated with rest of tail, white shafts at base; crown, nape iridescent green, tinged violet; cheeks, hindneck glossed purple; orbital area, throat, neck, upper breast iridescent yellow green, tinged blue; broad black breast band, glossed bronze, above reddish copper band; underparts dark copper brown, indistinctly barred green; flanks, under tail coverts black; legs bluish-grey, bill black (gape green), eyes dark brown. ♀: upperparts black to dusky brown; head, upper breast black glossed green; wings, tail blackish brown; underparts buffish, barred black; legs dark grey, bill black, eyes brownish grey. Immature ♂ at first much as ♀. ♀♀, young ♂♂ singly or small parties; adult ♂♂ probably live apart. Call: (captive) ♂: shrill *quee quee*; ♀: catlike *meow*. ♂'s wings rustle in flight. ♂ seen to work epiphytic moss in canopy, presumably for insects; also takes small fruits. Display by holding

primaries at right angles to body, 'wrists' touching over back, head pulled down. Breeds October (egg found); nestlings May, June. Shallow nest of large leaves, creeper stems, lined rootlets. Single, glossy light brown egg, streaked longitudinally, incubated presumably ♀, as ♂ polygamous. Hybridises with *A. mayeri* in one area. **989**

Athene noctua *Strigidae*
LITTLE OWL   *c.* 8½-9 ins
Palaearctic and Ethiopian: across Europe from Britain (introduced) and Iberia to Manchuria and Gulf of Chi-li, largely between 40° and 50°N, also Mediterranean area, Arabia and down African side of Red Sea; resident in wooded country or cultivated savannah, orchards, palm groves, rocky semi-desert and steppes, e.g. in Tibet, but not in mountains. Generally grey-brown, darker on upperparts, barred, mottled and spotted white, boldly on underparts; facial disc pale round edges; legs feathered, claws dark horn, bill greenish yellow, eyes lemon yellow. Mainly crepuscular but also seen by day, perched on tree, building, post, wires, or in undulating woodpecker-like flight; also hovers. Walks awkwardly. Bobs up and down in display. Call: *kiew kiew*, with variations, used as 'song'; also hoarse *shah* repeated at short intervals; duets in spring between ♂ and ♀. Food varied: small mammals, birds, but nearly half insects, mainly beetles; some other invertebrates and plant material. Breeds from March in Britain, making scrape in tree hole, buildings, rabbit hole, quarries and low cliffs, ricks. 3 to 5 white eggs incubated by ♀ 24-25 days; young fed by both parents, fly *c.* 3½ weeks. **436**

Atlapetes semirufus *Fringillidae*
OCHRE-BREASTED BRUSH FINCH   6½ ins
Neotropical: Venezuela N of Orinoco (separate race in Tachira); Colombia both slopes of E Andes, S to Boyaca; resident forest and scrub, 4,000 ft upwards. Upperparts, including wings, tail, olive; head, throat, breast orange rufous (centre throat white in Tachira race); centre belly yellow, flanks olive. Legs, bill horn-brown, eyes brown. **917**

Atrichornis clamosus see under **A. rufescens**

Atrichornis rufescens *Atrichornithidae*
RUFOUS SCRUB BIRD   7 ins
Australasian: SE Queensland and NE New South Wales; resident in undergrowth of big scrubs. Upperparts generally barred, flecked, vermiculated dark rufous and light brown; underparts similar but paler, especially on throat; long graduated tail; ♂ has black patch on breast; legs, bill horn brown, eyes brown. Very shy, moving silently in litter of undergrowth, usually in pairs; flies feebly if disturbed. Call deafening *chipchipchip* repeated with crescendo; also ventriloquial mimicking. Scratches ground for insects, crustaceans, molluscs, worms, occasional seeds. Breeds September to December, nest taking month to build: domed, of dead leaves, fern fronds, twigs, grass stems, smooth lining of wood pulp applied when wet; in clump of grass or ferns only 6 ins above ground. 2 pinkish white or buff eggs, spotted and blotched pinkish-red, red-brown, purplish at big end, incubated by ♀, who also rears young. Larger (8½ ins) Noisy Scrub Bird, *A. clamosus*, confined to very small area SW Australia, where rediscovered 1960; named for its very loud call, producing effect of 'shrill whistle blown in small room'; habits much as *A. rufescens*. **598**

Attagis malouinus *Thinocoridae*
WHITE-BELLIED SEEDSNIPE   11 ins
Neotropical: from Rio Negro, Argentina, and Magellanes, Chile, S to Staten Is, Tierra del Fuego, Falkland Is; bare heaths, usually at some altitude, descending at first snowfall. ♂: upperparts sandy rufous, feathers edged black and mottled arrow-shaped black markings; outer wing coverts black, bordered white; cheeks, throat pale ash-grey spotted black, rest underparts white. ♀: upperparts blackish, feathers mottled and edged cinnamon; breast cinnamon-buff, feathers edged black; throat, rest underparts white. Short legs, short conical bill yellow, eyes dark brown. Crouches, then suddenly flies off with snipe-like jinking, uttering

short, rasping alarm call. Feeds almost entirely on seeds. Breeds January S Chile, building nest of moss, lichen, heather twiglets on low hummock in peaty heath. 4 dark olive-green eggs, heavily marked dark brown, black, blend with surroundings.

Aulacorhynchus caeruleogularis *Ramphastidae*
BLUE-THROATED TOUCANET   *c.* 11 ins
Neotropical: Costa Rica and W Panama; 'vertical migrant' in mountainous areas, up to 10,000 ft. Generally rather dull green; cheeks, chin, throat dark blue; under tail coverts chestnut; bill predominantly yellow, with red, white and black. Behaviour and habits much as *A. prasinus*. Food: berries and small fruits; insects, including winged termites taken in air; spiders; eggs and young of other birds. Nests in hole of tree, laying 2 to 4 white eggs, incubated by ♀ and ♂, who both tend young for long fledging period of 43-46 days. **534**

Aulacorhynchus prasinus *Ramphastidae*
EMERALD TOUCANET   12 (bill 3) ins
Neotropical: Mexico to N Venezuela, Colombia, E Ecuador and E Peru; 'vertical migrant' in forests between 3,000 and 10,000 ft. Predominantly shades of green, bronzed on head and neck, bright on underparts; throat white, grey, blue or black according to race; under tail coverts and tips of tail feathers chestnut; bill mainly black, ridge of culmen yellow, base of lower mandible red or black, sharply outlined white. Usually in straggling parties of *c.* 8, working tree canopy, seldom coming low. Food: berries, fruits; insects; eggs and young of small birds. Groups break up before breeding. ♀♀ leaving first. Nest-site in tree hole, often hidden by creepers and sometimes taken from another bird; 7 to 90 ft up. 3 or 4 white eggs, incubated in short spells by ♀ and ♂ *c.* 16 days. Young blind for 16 days, fly *c.* 40, both parents feeding them and keeping nest clean. **535**

Auriparus flavus *Paridae*
VERDIN   4¼ ins
Nearctic: resident from S Texas, SE New Mexico, SW Utah, S California to N Mexico; dense thickets to arid country with scattered thorns and cacti. ♂: upperparts light brown, darker on primaries, longish tail; chestnut shoulder patch; crown, face, throat lemon yellow; underparts white. ♀: duller and greyer, less yellow on head. Legs, bill greyish; eyes dark brown. Juvenile uniform brownish-grey above, paler below. Apparently does without water either for bathing or drinking, taking insects and berries. Several tit-like calls and loud contact note *slip* between feeding pair; far-carrying song of 3 or 4 clear, whistled notes on same pitch. Breeds May (Texas), building globular nest of thorny twigs woven round fork near end of branch, 2 to 20 ft up, lined leaves, grasses, then feathers. 4 or 5 pale bluish-greenish-blue eggs, marked red-brown. Individuals build smaller winter roosting nests.

AURORA FINCH see **Pytilia phoenicoptera**

AUSTRALIAN
   BROWN FLYCATCHER see **Microeca fascinans**
   BROWN TREECREEPER see **Climacteris picumnus**
   BUSTARD see **Eupodotis australis**
   CRESTED BELLBIRD see **Oreoica gutturalis**
   GANNET see under **Sula bassana**
   JACANA see **Irediparra gallinacea**
   MAGPIE see **Gymnorhina tibicen**
   PELICAN see **Pelecanus conspicillatus**
   PIPIT see **Anthus novaeseelandiae**
   PRATINCOLE see **Stiltia isabella**
   SPUR-WINGED PLOVER see **Lobibyx novaehollandiae**

Automolus leucophthalmus *Furnariidae*
WHITE-EYED FOLIAGE GLEANER   7¼-7¾ ins
Neotropical: Brazil to NE Paraguay and NE Argentina; resident in bamboo thickets. Upperparts, including crested crown, reddish brown; rump and tail cinnamon rufous; lores and throat white, rest of underparts pale ochre, becoming light brown on

belly; large Brazilian race has darker upperparts and tail; eyes white. Usually keeps to cover, venturing into open only in poor light; searches dead leaves caught in branches for small insects and their larvae. Closely related Chestnut-tailed or Buff-throated Foliage Gleaner, *A. ochrolaemus,* has loud rattling call, excavates short tunnel in bank, laying 2 or 3 white eggs in substantial nest at end. Incubation *c.* 19 days and feeding of young (fledge 18 days) by both parents.

Automolus ochrolaemus see under **A. leucophthalmus**

Aythya fuligula *Anatidae*
TUFTED DUCK   17 (body 11) ins
N and central Palaearctic from Iceland to Commander Is in Pacific, wintering S to Nile Valley, Persian Gulf, India, S China and Phillipines. Frequents reservoirs, lakes and large ponds and, especially when breeding, those surrounded by cover; also marshes. Pure white flanks in contrast with dark glossy blue-black plumage distinguishes ♂ along with drooping tuft. ♀ dark brown with stubby tail and white base to bill; in winter often white on sides and below tail; both show narrow white wing-bar in flight. Legs and bill grey; eyes yellow. Easily becomes tame; particularly gregarious in winter; feeds (by diving) mainly on animals from frogs to small insects and some plant matter. Call: ♀ typical croak of diving ducks; ♂ low whistle in breeding season. Lays 6 to 14 greenish grey eggs in May or June, nesting close to water in cover, using grasses, rushes and much down; sometimes semi-colonial. ♀ incubates *c.* 24 days and tends young, who fly after 6 - 7 weeks. **101**

Balaeniceps rex *Balaenicipitidae*
SHOEBILL or WHALEHEAD   5 ft
Ethiopian: Sudan, Uganda and Zaire to Katanga; sedentary in papyrus swamps along rivers and by lakes. Generally grey, back with green sheen; plumes on breast blackish-centred; legs black, huge bill mottled green and olive brown, eyes yellow. Solitary or in pairs, skulking by day in papyrus and feeding by night. Stance with bill on breast; flies with neck bent like herons and first few primaries separated; occasionally soars, when may call. Clatters bill when annoyed. Takes fish, especially *Protopterus,* frogs, reptiles and small mammals. Breeding season December to June in Nile Valley and Uganda; nest a flattened area in tall grasses on dry ground; eggs 1 or 2 dull chalky white, soon stained. **77**

Balearica pavonina *Gruidae*
CROWNED CRANE   43 ins
Ethiopian: widespread in region; the southern population has been regarded as a distinct species, *Balearica regulorum.* Inhabits open plains, riversides, cultivated land. Slate-grey with white upper and under wing coverts, black primaries and chestnut secondaries; black down on head and 'crown' of stiff golden bristles; golden-brown plumes on inner wing coverts; legs and bill black, eyes light grey, facial skin white and red, throat lappet scarlet. Immature mottled brown. Pairs or family parties, building up to flocks of over 100; stamp as they walk, disturbing insects; also take reptiles, seeds, grain. 'Slow motion' dances with wing

flapping; heavy flight with feet hanging down. Gregarious roosts in riverbeds and trees. A trumpeting call *u-wang u-wang;* also guttural grunt. Breeding season varies throughout range. Lays 2 or 3 glossy, dirty white eggs with small brown spots, becoming stained, in heap of dry grasses in trampled area of swamp. Both parents incubate *c.* 4 weeks and feed young who soon leave nest. **216**

Balearica regulorum see under **B. pavonina**

Barnardius barnardi *Psittacidae*
RING-NECKED PARROT or BULN BULN   13 ins
Australasian: coastal areas Australia, from SW Queensland to NW New South Wales; isolated race Cloncurry Parrot, *B. b. macgillivrayi,* in W Queensland, adjacent Northern Teritory; resident in mallee (eucalypt) scrub, savannah, riverine woodland; Cloncurry Parrot favours tall riverside eucalypts. Upperparts, flight feathers dark blue-green, also distal part of long tail, rest of body shades of green, pale on rump and upper wing, with red frontal band (Cloncurry has no red, and other distinctions), dark eyestripe, narrow yellow collar; buff-brown band on breast; legs dark grey, bill light grey, eyes dark. ♀ duller; juvenile paler than ♀. Undulating flap-glide flight, but spends much time on ground in pairs or small groups; drinks soon after dawn. Call ringing *twink twink twink.* Food: grass and other seeds; buds, blossoms, fruits of mallee and other eucalypts. ♂ displays to ♀ with fanned tail. Breeds August to January in favourable seasons, in hole of trunk or branch, often in coolabah tree on savannah or along streams. 4 to 6 white eggs laid on wood dust, incubated by ♀ *c.* 3 weeks; ♂ near. Young fly *c.* 30 days; sometimes two broods. **387**

Baryphthengus ruficapillus *Momotidae*
RUFOUS MOTMOT   18 (bill 1½) ins
Neotropical: Central America from Nicaragua S into Colombia and E of Andes to Paraguay and Argentina; resident in forests sea level to *c.* 4,500 ft. Largest member of family; upperparts and under tail coverts green, long tail green to bluish green with or without racquet tips; head and underparts rufous (in one race underparts olive with rufous band across belly); mask and small spot on breast black. Habits resemble *Momotus momota,* but has hollow hooting call and nest entrance not usually so well concealed. **495**

Basileuterus rufifrons *Parulidae*
RUFOUS-CAPPED WARBLER   4¾ ins
Neotropical: Mexico, Central America to N Colombia, W Venezuela; scrubby lowlands to 7,000 ft. Upperparts, including wings, tail olive; crown, ear-coverts chestnut, lores dusky, 'eyebrow' white, nape greyish olive; underparts bright yellow (belly white in northern races), insectivorous. ♂ helps ♀ build domed nest on or near ground. Usually 2 or 3 eggs, incubated ♀ 16-19 days; young, fed ♀ and ♂, fly 12-14 days. **890**

Batis molitor *Muscicapidae: Muscicapinae*
CHIN-SPOT PUFFBACK or WHITE-FLANKED FLYCATCHER   4½ ins
Ethiopian: from E Cape (S Africa) N to S Sudan, S Ethiopia; to S edge Congo Forest in W. Rather distinct race *soror* coastal Kenya, Tanzania, Mozambique. Resident open acacia woodland, forest edge, cultivated areas, gardens. ♂: upperparts from crown dark grey; sides of face, neck, ear coverts, wings, tail black; edges of secondaries white, small white tips to tail feathers. Underparts white, broad black band across breast, rufous in ♀, who also has rufous chin spot. Legs, bill black, eyes red. Fluffs up rump feathers when excited, hence 'puff-back'. Searches trees like tit, aerial sallies like flycatcher, hovers close to leaves. Usually in pairs but joins mixed parties in S of range in winter; food almost entirely insects. Call clear double squeak; lower, sharper double alarm note; ♂'s song 3 whistles on descending scale. Display flight with whirring or clapping wings, but some evidence ♀ dominant in courtship. Breeds beginning of rains in N, in summer in S, building small cup moss, fibres, bound cobwebs, lined hair, decorated lichens, neatly blended in fork of tree, bush. Usually 2 greyish or greenish white eggs, zoned small brown or black spots, incubated mainly ♀. **792**

Batrachostomus stellatus *Podargidae*
GOULD'S FROGMOUTH   8½ ins
Oriental: Malaysia and Indonesia, but not Java; resident in primary lowland forest. Upperparts bright russet brown (or dark rufous brown) with darker mantle and cream and black half collar at back of neck; 2 pale bars and V-shaped patch on closed wing; tail faintly barred; belly creamy white with narrow red-brown margins to feathers. Feet: ♂ pinkish, ♀ very pale yellow; bill brown with prominent bristles; eyes: ♂ golden, ♀ dark brown with pale yellow orbits. Nocturnal: silent at all times. Picks insects, especially locusts, off branches and variety of invertebrates off ground. Breeds end April Borneo, laying single white egg in small cup of own down, spiders' webs and lichen, woven on to horizontal branch. Incubation by ♀ *c.* 30 days; both parents feed chick for *c.* 30 days.

BEARDED
TIT see **Panurus biarmicus**
WOODPECKER see **Thripias namaquus**

BEAUTIFUL SUNBIRD see **Nectarinia pulchella**

Bebrornis sechellensis or Nesillas sechellensis
Muscicapidae: Sylviinae
SEYCHELLES BRUSH WARBLER
Seychelles (Indian Ocean): confined to Cousin Island, in mangrove swamps, undergrowth by shore, palm groves. Upperparts olive green, underparts pale yellow-grey; legs, bill mainly slaty blue. Juvenile darker, breast spotted (R. Gaymer, M. Penny). Singly or in pairs. Weak, fluttering flight. Sweet mellow song: *saw see see*, repeated three times, gives local name *petit merle*. Hawks insects in air, also takes them and their larvae from trees, bushes, ground. Breeds mainly October to March, building cup nest of dry grass, other plant material, usually in vertical fork of tree or bush, e.g. mangroves, bamboos, 5 to 15 ft up. Usually single white egg, heavily marked brown, incubated *c*. 15 days. Young soon mobile and fledging period hard to determine, 20-28 days (M. Penny, D. Lloyd).

BECARD,
BLACK-CAPPED see **Pachyrhamphus marginatus**
WHITE-WINGED see under **Pachyrhamphus marginatus**

BEE-EATER,
BLUE-CHEEKED see **Merops superciliosus**
CARMINE see **Merops nubicus**
CINNAMON-CHESTED see **Melittophagus oreobates**
EUROPEAN see **Merops apiaster**
LITTLE see **Melittophagus pusillus**
LITTLE GREEN see **Merops orientalis**
RED-THROATED see **Melittophagus bulocki**
WHITE-FRONTED see **Melittophagus bullockoides**
WHITE-THROATED see **Aerops albicollis**

BEE HUMMINGBIRD see **Mellisuga helenae**

BELL BIRD see **Anthornis melanura**

BELLBIRD,
AUSTRALIAN CRESTED see **Oreoica gutturalis**
BARE-THROATED see **Procnias nudicollis**
BEARDED see under **Procnias nudicollis**
WHITE see under **Procnias nudicollis**

BELTED KINGFISHER see **Megaceryle alcyon**

BENNETT'S WOODPECKER see **Campethera bennettii**

Berenicornis comatus *Bucerotidae*
ASIAN WHITE-CRESTED HORNBILL   30-40 ins
Oriental: Annam, Burma, Malaysia; resident in lowland evergreen forest. ♂: head, 'fluffy' crest, neck, breast, wingtips and tail white, rest of plumage black; ♀ has sides of neck and whole underparts black. Legs, bill and small casque, facial skin black, gape sky blue, eyes orange. Flight almost noiseless, flapping continuously; but keeps much to undergrowth in small parties. Call: soft *hoo* when taking wing, repeated when feed on ground. Takes fruit, lizards, small birds, even cave swiftlets snapped up on wing. Breeding much as other hornbills (see *Buceros bicornis*).
513

BERMUDA PETREL see **Pterodroma cahow**

BICOLOURED WREN see **Campylorhynchus griseus**

BIFASCIATED LARK see **Alaemon alaudipes**

BIRD OF PARADISE,
COUNT RAGGI's see **Paradisaea raggiana**
EMPEROR see **Paradisaea guilielmi**
GREATER see **Paradisaea apoda**
KING see **Cicinnurus regius**
LESSER see under **Paradisaea guilielmi**
MOLUCCAN see **Macgregoria pulchra**
PRINCESS STEPHANIE's see **Astrapia stephaniae**
SICKLE-BILLED see **Epimachus meyeri**

BITTERN see **Botaurus stellaris**

BITTERN, SUN see **Eurypyga helias**

Biziura lobata *Anatidae*
MUSK DUCK   ♀: *c*. 22, ♂: *c*. 26 ins
Australasian: SW and SE Australia as far N as Rockhampton, Queensland; also Tasmania. Breeds in deep permanent water with dense vegetation, otherwise found in more open waters, estuaries and coastal bays. Blackish brown, crossed with fine lines of lighter brown; lower breast whitish brown, primaries and erect tail almost black; legs dark grey, bill black with large pendulous lobe underneath (smaller in ♀), eyes dark brown. Fairly solitary, occasionally in small flocks; completely aquatic and helpless on land; sinks slowly below surface up to eyes and nostrils when alarmed; when flying, requires open water for long take-off. Call: ♂ shrill whistle, also uses feet to make deep *plonk* and noisy splashing; ♀ occasional soft quack. Dives in deep water for aquatic animals, chiefly insects, and some plant matter. Breeds usually August to December; builds bulky cup-shaped nest by beating down and interlacing stems, lined thinly with grass and down, sited in reeds, often small clumps. 1 to 3, sometimes up to 10, pale green eggs, incubated by ♀, who also tends young alone, sometimes carrying them on her back. **102**

BLACK
CHAT, WHITE-HEADED see under **Myrmecocichla nigra**
CRAKE, AFRICAN see **Limnocorax flavirostra**
CUCKOO SHRIKE see **Campephaga sulphurata**
DRONGO see under **Dicrurus annectans**
FLYCATCHER, SOUTH AFRICAN see **Melaenornis pammelaina**
FLYCATCHER, WEST AFRICAN see under **Melaenornis pammelaina**
GRASS WREN see **Amytornis housei**
GROUSE see **Lyrurus tetrix**
GUILLEMOT see **Cepphus grylle**
HONEY-EATER see **Myzomela nigra**
IBIS see **Pseudibis papillosa**
KITE see **Milvus migrans**
OYSTERCATCHER, AFRICAN see **Haematopus moquini**
PUFF-BACKED SHRIKE see **Dryoscopus cubla**
REDSTART see under **Phoenicurus phoenicurus**
SCOTER see **Melanitta nigra**
SOLITAIRE see **Entomodestes coracinus**
STORK see **Ciconia nigra**
SWAN see **Cygnus atratus**
TERN see **Chlidonias niger**
TIT see under **Parus niger**
TIT, SOUTHERN see **Parus niger**
VULTURE see **Coragyps atratus**

BLACK AND GREEN TANAGER see **Tangara nigroviridis**

BLACK AND WHITE
WARBLER see **Mniotilta varia**
WOODPECKER see **Phloceastes melanoleucos**
WREN see **Malurus leucopterus**

BLACK AND YELLOW SILKY FLYCATCHER see **Phainoptila melanoxantha**

BLACK-BACKED
BRUBRU see under **Nilaus afer**
GULL, LESSER see under **Larus argentatus**
WREN see **Malurus melanotus**

BLACK-BANDED PETCHARY see under **Cacicus cela**

BLACK-BELLIED
BUSTARD see **Lissotis melanogaster**
PLOVER see **Pluvialis squatarola**

BLACK-BILLED
BLUE-SPOTTED WOOD DOVE see **Turtur abyssinicus**
SCYTHEBILL see **Campylorhamphus falcularius**
TOURACO see under **Tauraco livingstonii**

BLACKBIRD see **Turdus merula**

BLACKBIRD,
ORIOLE see **Gymnomystax mexicanus**
RED-WINGED see under **Quiscalus quiscala**
RUSTY see **Euphagus carolinus**
TAWNY-SHOULDERED see under **Agelaius xanthomus**
YELLOW-SHOULDERED see **Agelaius xanthomus**

BLACK-BROWED ALBATROSS see **Diomedea melanophris**

BLACKCAP
see **Sylvia atricapilla**
BUSH SHRIKE see **Tchagra minuta**

BLACK-CAPPED
BECARD see **Pachyrhamphus marginatus**
CHICKADEE see **Parus atricapillus**

BLACK-CHEEKED WOODPECKER see **Melanerpes pucherani**

BLACK-COLLARED BARBET see **Pybius torquatus**

BLACK-EARED
CUCKOO see under **Chthonicola sagittata**
WHEATEAR see **Oenanthe hispanica**

BLACK-EYED BULBUL see **Pycnonotus barbatus**

BLACK-FACED
ANT THRUSH see **Formicarius analis**
CUCKOO SHRIKE see **Coracina novaehollandiae**
DACNIS see **Dacnis lineata**
MONARCH see **Monarcha melanopsis**
SAND GROUSE see **Eremialector decoratus**

BLACK-FOOTED
ALBATROSS see **Diomedea nigripes**
DOTTEREL see **Charadrius melanops**

BLACK-HEADED
BUNTING see **Emberiza melanocephalus**
BUSH SHRIKE see **Tchagra senegala**
CANARY see **Serinus alario**
FOREST ORIOLE see under **Oriolus larvatus**
GULL see **Larus ridibundus**
GULL, PATAGONIAN see under **Larus ridibundus**
ORIOLE, WESTERN see under **Oriolus larvatus**
PARDALOTE see **Pardalotus melanocephalus**
SHRIKE see **Lanius schach**
TANAGER see **Tangara cyanoptera**
WEAVER see **Ploceus cucullatus**

BLACKHEAD PLOVER see **Vanellus tectus**

BLACK-NAPED TERN see **Sterna sumatrana**

BLACK-NECKED SCREAMER see **Chauna chavaria**

BLACKPOLL WARBLER see under **Mniotilta varia**

BLACK-SHOULDERED KITE see **Elanus caeruleus**

BLACKSMITH PLOVER see **Vanellus armatus**

BLACK-SPOTTED
BARBET see **Capito niger**
BARE-EYE see **Phlegopsis migromaculata**

BLACK-TAILED
GODWIT see **Limosa limosa**
TITYRA see **Tityra cayana**

BLACK-THROATED
  DIVER see **Gavia arctica**
  TROGON see **Trogon rufus**

BLACK-WINGED
  ORIOLE see under **Oriolus larvatus**
  PRATINCOLE see under **Glareola pratincola**
  RED BISHOP see under **Euplectes orix**
  SALTATOR see **Saltator atripennis**
  STILT see **Himantopus himantopus**

BLEEDING HEART, LUZON see **Gallicolumba luzonica**

BLUE
  CHAFFINCH see under **Fringilla coelebs**
  CRANE see **Anthropoides paradisaea**
  GROUND DOVE see **Claravis pretiosa**
  GROUSE see **Dendragapus obscurus**
  HERON, LITTLE see **Florida caerulea**
  PENGUIN, LITTLE see **Eudyptes minor**
  ROCK THRUSH see **Monticola solitarius**
  TIT see **Parus caeruleus**
  TOURACO, GREAT see **Corythaeola cristata**
  WREN see **Malurus cyaneus**
  WREN, BANDED see under **Malurus callainus**

BLUE AND WHITE FLYCATCHER see **Cyanoptila cyanomelana**

BLUE AND YELLOW MACAW see **Ara ararauna**

BLUE-BILLED DUCK see **Oxyura australis**

BLUEBIRD,
  EASTERN see **Sialia sialis**
  FAIRY see **Irena puella**
  WESTERN see under **Peucedramus taeniatus**

BLUE-CHEEKED
  AMAZON PARROT see **Amazonia brasiliensis**
  BEE-EATER see **Merops superciliosus**

BLUE-CROWNED MOTMOT see **Momotus momota**

BLUE-EARED GLOSSY STARLING see **Lamprocolius chalybeus**

BLUE-EYED SHAG see **Phalacrocorax atriceps**

BLUE-FACED HONEY-EATER see **Entomyzon cyanotus**

BLUE-FOOTED BOOBY see **Sula nebouxii**

BLUE-GREY
  GNATCATCHER see **Polioptila caerulea**
  TANAGER see **Thraupis episcopus**

BLUE-HEADED AMAZON PARROT see **Amazonia brasiliensis**

BLUE-NAPED
  FRUIT DOVE see **Ptilinopus melanospila**
  MOUSEBIRD see **Colius macrouros**

BLUE-SPOTTED WOOD DOVE see under **Turtur abyssinicus**

BLUE-SPOTTED WOOD DOVE BLACK-BILLED see **Turtur abyssinicus**

BLUE-TAILED PITTA see **Pitta guajana**

BLUETAIL, RED-FLANKED see **Tarsiger cyanurus**

BLUETHROAT see **Luscinia svecica**

BLUE-THROATED
  HUMMINGBIRD see **Lampornis clemenciae**
  SYLPH see **Lampornis clemenciae**
  TOUCANET see **Aulacorhynchus caeruleogularis**

BLUE-WINGED PITTA see **Pitta brachyura**

BLUISH FLOWERPECKER see **Diglossa caerulescens**

BOATBILL see **Cochlearius cochlearius**

BOBOLINK see **Dolichonyx oryzivorus**

BOBWHITE see **Colinus virginianus**

Bocagia minuta see **Tchagra minuta**

BOKMAKIERIE see **Malaconotus zeylonus**

BOHEMIAN WAXWING see **Bombycilla garrulus**

Bombycilla cedrorum *Bombycillidae*
CEDAR WAXWING   7¼ ins
Nearctic: breeds from Cape Breton Is, Quebec, Ontario, British Columbia S to Georgia, New Mexico, California; winters S to W Indies, Panama. Habitat open, scattered trees, e.g. in swamps, orchards, rather than continuous woodland like *B. garrulus*. Very similar to *B. garrulus* but under tail coverts white, no white and yellow wing markings, white round black mask more pronounced. Juvenile resembles *B. garrulus* with prominent pale 'eyebrow'. Habits, voice, feeding also similar, flocks staying together most of year. Breeds variably, late June into August, building relatively large nest of plant material 6 to 35 ft up on lateral branch of broadleaved or coniferous tree. 4 to 6 grey-blue eggs, spotted black and brown. **659**

Bombycilla garrulus *Bombycillidae*
(BOHEMIAN) WAXWING   8 ins
Holarctic: across northern Eurasia from 20°E in Scandinavia, mainly between 60° and 70°N to Sea of Okhotsk; Kamtchatka; replaced N Manchuria, Sakhalin, Japan by very similar *B. japonica*. Breeds N America mainly down W side from Alaska to N Idaho; irregular migrant usually into temperate zone to about 35°N, e.g. Asia Minor, S California. Habitat: often dense coniferous and mixed woodland and their edges, wintering woodland parks, gardens, even into cities. Upperparts, including prominent crest, vinaceous brown; rump, short tail grey with subterminal black, yellow tip; flight feathers greyish-black to black with white and yellow tips; shafts of tail feathers and secondaries may have red 'waxy' tips; eyestripe, bib black; underparts pale vinaceous shading to deep sienna under tail coverts; legs black, bill mainly black, eyes dark brown. ♀ greyer, wing and tail markings less bright and no waxy red; juvenile duller, underparts streaked. Often perches high, but quite tame. Flight strong with long undulations; wings rattle when rising and descending. Gregarious in winter. Rather silent, usual call high, trilling *sirrr*, from which rather jumbled song develops. Agile in trees when feeding on berries; also hawks insects in air and feeds on ground; drinks freely. Breeds from mid June Lapland, ♀ and ♂ building nest of twigs, lichens *Cladonia*, *Usnea*, some grass or softer lining. 4 to 6 ashy-grey or pale blue eggs, spotted black or blackish brown over grey, incubated mainly ♀, fed by ♂, c. 14 days. **660**

Bombycilla japonica see under **B. garrulus**

BONAPARTE'S GULL see **Larus philadelphia**

BOOBOOK OWL see **Ninox novaeseelandiae**

BOOBY,
  BLUE-FOOTED see **Sula nebouxii**
  BROWN see **Sula leucogaster**
  RED-FOOTED see **Sula sula**

BOOTED EAGLE see **Hieraetus pennatus**

BOREAL OWL see **Aegolius funereus**

BORNEO BRISTLEHEAD see **Pityriasis gymnocephala**

Bostrychia carunculata *Threskiornithidae*
WATTLED IBIS   c. 32 ins
Ethiopia and Eritrea; resident in swamps and high moorland. Upperparts dull iridescent green, underparts brown, washed green; white wing-bar distinguishes from other ibises. Face feathered but wattle hangs from throat. Usually in flocks of 50 to 100, roosting in ravines. Harsh call *haa*, with loud raucous roars as flock takes off. Diet: snakes, frogs, mice, insects. Breeds April or July in Ethiopia; nest of sticks with finer lining of grass and bark, in trees, or bushes on cliffs. 2 rough shelled white eggs, other details much as Hadada Ibis, *Hagedashia hagedash*. **79**

BOUBOU see **Laniarius ferrugineus**

Bowdleria punctata *Muscicapidae: Sylviinae*
FERNBIRD   7 ins
Confined to New Zealand and neighbouring islands; separate races Stewart (*B. p. stewartiana*), Codfish (*wilsoni*) and Snares Islands (*caudata*); now mainly in swamps, undeveloped land (*pakihi*) and ferny scrub. Upperparts, flanks warm brown, streaked darker; forehead, forecrown chestnut; feathers of longish tail look spiny due to disconnected barbs; underparts white, spotted dark brown throat, breast. Flies with trailing tail seldom more than 50 yds, remaining hidden in foliage, though Snares race often in open, feeding in penguin colonies and floor of *Olearia* forest. Insectivorous: variety taken to young. Call: low note followed by sharp metallic one; also soft *click*; contact calls between pair: *plik* and *coot*. Breeds September to February; nest deep in vegetation from ground level to c. 4 ft above water, neatly woven cup of plant stems, lined feathers, built ♀ and ♂. 2 or 3 white or pinkish eggs heavily marked brown and purplish, usually at big end, incubated by ♀ and ♂ 12½ days. Young, fed both parents, fly 12-13 days (M. F. Soper). 2 broods on Snares I (E. F. Stead).

BOWER BIRD,
  GOLDEN see **Prionodura newtoniana**
  NEWTON'S see **Prionodura newtoniana**
  SATIN see **Ptilinorhynchus violaceus**
  SPOTTED see **Chlamydera maculata**

Brachyrhamphus brevirostris *Alcidae*
KITTLITZ'S MURRELET   9 ins
Holarctic: from arctic E Siberia, Kamtchatka to Aleutians and Alaska (Cape Lisburne, Glacier Bay); winters Aleutians, Kamtchatka to Japan. Habitat: breeds rocky mountain slopes above tree line; otherwise coastal waters. Upperparts slaty grey, streaked buff; flight feathers very dark grey; outer tail feathers white; throat, breast, flanks mottled buff and grey; belly white, feathers edged sooty grey; very short legs and bill dark; eyes very dark brown. Winter; crown, upperparts dark slate; underparts, cheeks, white; white bar between wing and back. Short bill and nearly complete dark band on breast help distinguish from Marbled Murrelet, *B. marmoratus*. Habits little studied; feeds small crustaceans, other invertebrates. Breeds bare lichened rock, blending with plumage; single yellowish or light olive green egg, evenly marked brown.

Brachyrhamphus marmoratus see under **B. brevirostris**

Bradornis pallidus *Muscicapidae: Muscicapinae*
PALE FLYCATCHER   6-7 ins
Ethiopian: several races cover most of region; resident savanna woodland, acacia bush, coastal scrub, grazed pastures, maize fields, gardens. Upperparts, including cheeks, breast, grey-brown, wings darker; underparts pale brown shading to white on throat, centre belly, flanks tinged buff. Legs, bill black, eyes very dark brown. Juvenile streaked and spotted. Larger, stouter than Spotted Flycatcher, *Muscicapa striata*, and less conspicuous than most flycatchers, taking much of food from ground: spiders, termites, flies, moths. Often perches motionless on low boughs. Calls: *chirp* or *churr*; rasping *tsek* of alarm; occasional warbling twitter of 6 to 7 notes as song. Breeds at or just before beginning of wet season, building neat but slight cup nest of rootlets in fork of tree or

bush. Usually 3 pale green eggs, marked reddish brown over violet. Family parties stay together a long time; some evidence that 'auxiliary adults' help parents rear brood. **775**

Bradypterus baboecalus *Muscicapidae: Sylviinae*
AFRICAN SEDGE or LITTLE RUSH WARBLER   6 ins
Ethiopian: throughout region, wherever suitable habitat (reedbeds, long swampy grass) occurs. Upperparts warm dusky brown; flight feathers edged paler; broad graduated tail; 'eyebrow', underparts pale buff with dusky streaks on side neck; legs grey, bill brown, eyes brown. Behaviour inquisitive, often perches at top of reeds. Flies with whirring or snapping wings. Song: jerky, unmelodious, like stick on revolving spokes; other calls include ventriloquial *thri*, croaking *crack, crack* . . . Feeds on insects, small molluscs. Breeding season varies over range; deep cup nest of coarse grass, lined fibres, built low in reeds. 2 to 4 green to pinkish white eggs, marked grey and variably spotted. **728**

Bradypterus sylvaticus *Muscicapidae: Sylviinae*
KNYSNA SCRUB WARBLER   5½-6 ins
Ethiopian; very local S Africa around Table Mountain and E Cape Province to coastal Natal. Resident in dense tangled scrub, e.g. bramble thickets on SE slopes Table Mountain, at forest edge. Upperparts, including wings, tail, light olivaceous brown; tail short, rounded; underparts paler, chin and throat whitish, mottled and streaked brown; belly whitish. Legs olive brown, bill pinkish brown, eyes dark hazel. Very skulking, identified mainly by fine song (August to December): series of high-pitched notes, followed by rapid lower notes merging into 'blurred trill' and ending in 'bubbling trill' (McLachlan and Liversidge). Breeds September, building bowl-shaped nest of dry leaves, grasses, with finer lining, off ground and below leaf canopy in thicket. 3 pinky-white eggs, finely marked red, incubated 19 days; young fly 13-14 days. **729**

BRAMBLING see **Fringilla montifringilla**

Branta canadensis *Anatidae*
CANADA GOOSE   36-40 (body 21-24) ins
Nearctic: 10 races spread across Alaska, Canada and northern USA, wintering S to coast of Gulf of Mexico; introduced in Europe. Habitat: swamps and around lakes and ponds with tree cover, also more open cultivated country; in winter greater tendency to frequent seashore. All races have black neck and head with white patch from chin to behind eyes; legs and bill dark, eyes dark brown. Body colour varies from dark brown of Vancouver Canada Goose, *B. c. occidentalis* to light brown-grey, with pale front, of Eastern Canada Goose *canadensis,* race now well established Britain. Flies in V formation on longer passages, gregarious outside breeding season, normally feeds by day on grass, with some animal food in summer, but may feed on water when breeding, upending like ducks; can dive when moulting or injured. Call: trumpeting honk. Nests, often in small colonies, in April on islands or sometimes sheltered marshes, making hollow in ground lined with grasses, reeds, down and feathers. Usually 5 or 6 near white eggs, incubated 28-29 days by ♀ guarded by ♂; young, flying at 6 weeks, are tended by ♀ with ♂ nearby. **103**

Branta leucopsis *Anatidae*
BARNACLE GOOSE   23-27 ins
W Palaearctic: breeds NE Greenland, Spitzbergen and Novaya Zemlya; winters Scotland, Ireland and coasts of Denmark, Germany and Netherlands. Mainly terrestrial, grazing at night on pastures and marshes near shore and sometimes on tidal flats; occasionally rests at sea. Shining black breast; neck and crown with creamy white face and forehead; upper body dark grey with black and white bars, underneath pale grey; tail, legs and small bill black, eyes dark chestnut. Flock, punctuated with squabbles between individuals, keeps to itself but less shy than other geese, feeds on vegetable matter such as leaves, seeds and grass; flies in V formation on longer passages. Call: repeated

shrill short barks. Nests late May to mid June in colonies often on face of cliff or sometimes on islands, laying 3 to 5 greyish white eggs in hollow, often used repeatedly, lined with down, droppings and a little moss. ♀ incubates, guarded by ♂, for 24-25 days; young fly after 7 weeks, tended by both parents. **104**

Branta sandvicensis *Anatidae*
NENE or HAWAIIAN GOOSE   23-26 ins
Confined to Hawaiian Is: Hawaii, Maui (reintroduced). Habitat: dry lava slopes and craters, only watered by rain pools; descends to *c.* 1,200 ft in winter. Body mottled brown, black and white; head, face, chin, back of neck black; cheeks, front of neck buff, feathers furrowed. Powerful, black legs, feet, toenails, only partially webbed; bill black; eyes very dark brown with white orbits. Aggressive in breeding season, vibrating furrowed neck feathers. Head-dipping in courtship, mates on land. In flocks after breeding, flighting between feeding and roosting places. Call: low moaning, hence *ne-ne*; raucous noises in courtship. Diet: plant leaves and stems, flowers, berries; 'plucks' seeds from grass, sedges (P. H. Baldwin). Breeds late October to February, ♀ building nest of plant debris, lined down, among rocks, and incubating 3 to 6 white to greenish eggs, *c.* 30 days. Young, attended both parents, fledge 10-12 weeks Hawaii. Classic example of 'dying' species revived by liberation of captive-bred stock in native habitat. **105**

BRAZILIAN TEAL see **Amazonetta brasiliensis**

BRISTLEHEAD, BORNEA see **Pityriasis gymnocephala**

BROADBILL, AFRICAN see **Smithornis capensis**

BROAD-BILLED
    HUMMINGBIRD see **Cynanthus latirostris**
    PRION see under **Pachyptila desolata**
    SANDPIPER see **Limicola falcinellus**

BROADBILL,
    GRAUER'S see **Pseudocalyptomena graueri**
    GREEN see **Calyptomena viridis**

BROAD-TAILED PARADISE WHYDAH see under **Steganura paradisaea**

BROLGA see **Grus rubicundus**

BRONZE CUCKOO, HORSFIELD see under **Malurus leucopterus**

BRONZY SUNBIRD see **Nectarinia kilimensis**

BROWN
    BOOBY see **Sula leucogaster**
    CREEPER see **Certhia familiaris**
    CUCKOO DOVE, LARGE see **Macropygia phasianella**
    FLYCATCHER, AUSTRALIAN see **Microeca fascinans**
    FLYCATCHER, EURASIAN see **Muscicapa latirostris**
    HARRIER see **Circaetus cinereus**
    HAWK see **Falco berigora**
    KIWI see **Apteryx australis**
    MESITE see **Mesitornis unicolor**
    PARROT see **Poicephalus meyeri**
    PELICAN see **Pelecanus occidentalis**
    PIGEON see **Macropygia phasianella**
    SONGLARK see **Cinclorhamphus cruralis**
    THRASHER see **Toxostoma rufum**
    TREECREEPER, AUSTRALIAN see **Climacteris picumnus**
    WEEBILL see **Smicrornis brevirostris**
    WOOD OWL, JAVAN see **Strix leptogrammica**
    WOOD OWL, MALAYSIAN see **Strix leptogrammica**

BROWN-EARED
    BULBUL see **Hypsipetes flavala**
    PHEASANT see **Crossoptilon mantchuricum**

BROWN-HEADED
    BUSH SHRIKE see **Tchagra australis**
    COWBIRD see **Molothrus ater**

BRUBRU see **Nilaus afer**

BRUBRU, BLACK-BACKED see under **Nilaus afer**

BRUSH FINCH, OCHRE-BREASTED see **Atlapetes semirufus**

BRUSH WARBLER, SEYCHELLES see **Bebrornis sechellensis**

Bubo africanus *Strigidae*
SPOTTED EAGLE OWL   18½ ins
SE Palaearctic: S Arabia; Ethiopian: 2 races cover almost whole region; northern race *B. a. cinerascens* resident in variety of habitats; southern *africanus* in rocky country with steep, bush-clad ravines. Upperparts mottled grey, black and white, with white spots on mantle; flight feathers and tail broadly barred; ear tufts prominent; underparts from breast barred and flecked grey-brown; feathered legs barred dark and white; bill blackish horn, eyes yellow. Brownish phase also occurs; *cinerascens* has fine vermiculations on upperparts. Nocturnal; sleeping on ground during day; seen early morning on elevated perches. Hooting duets, ♂'s mournful-sounding *hu hu*, answered by ♀'s *hu hu hu*; clicking alarm 'call' probably with bill. Diet: mainly beetles, but some small birds, mammals and reptiles. Breeding season variable throughout range; makes scrape on overhung rock ledge, among roots of trees, occasionally large tree hole; sometimes old nest of other bird, head of *Borassus* palm; lays usually 2 white eggs. Incubation and fledging much as *B. bubo.* **437**

Bubo bubo *Strigidae*
EAGLE OWL   *c.* 25-28 ins, ♀ larger than ♂
Palaearctic, Oriental, marginally Ethiopian: across Eurasia from Scandinavia and Iberia to Pacific, mainly between 30° and 60°N; also Indian subcontinent; N Africa into Sahara; resident in coniferous taiga, lowland and montane forests farther S; steep rocks in ravines, rocky islands, cliffs in sandy and stony deserts, ruins, sometimes reedbeds. Upperparts mottled blackish and tawny; wings and tail barred; underparts buff with fine wavy bars and bold streaks on breast; facial disc not marked but erectile ear tufts prominent; legs feathered, claws and bill black, eyes orange. Upright stance when perched, close to trunk. Noiseless flight, usually low and wavering but sometimes rises high; hunts in dusk, and in daylight in northern summer. Roosts in rocks or thick foliage. Calls: rather feeble *oo oo oo* and low *kreak kreak*; spits and snaps bill when alarmed; song loud, deep *boo hoo*, repeated at longish intervals and audible far; ♀ higher-pitched, duets with ♂. Wing-claps in display. Takes variety of mammals up to roe deer fawns, birds up to buzzards; reptiles, amphibians, even beetles. Breeds from March in Europe, in cavities and clefts, overhung ledges, old nests of other birds; pyramids in Egypt. 2 or 3 white eggs incubated by ♀ 34-36 days; ♂ brings food to her for young, who leave nest *c.* 5 weeks, before fledging. **438**

Bubo ketupu *Strigidae*
MALAYSIAN FISH OWL   18 ins
Oriental: Indo-China, Malaysia; resident in paddy field areas, river banks in primary forest, casuarina trees on shore (Borneo). Upperparts dark brown, mottled light brown with buff feather edges; light and dark bars on wings and tail; facial disc brown, finely streaked; ear tufts prominent; underparts buff, rather delicately streaked red-brown; bare legs greyish-white; bill black, yellower at cere, eyes lemon-yellow. Very much at home in water, taking fish, frogs, crustaceans and large water bugs. Call a melancholy repeated trill or whistle. Breeding season: young nearly full grown mid-February in Borneo. **439**

Bubo lacteus *Strigidae*
GIANT EAGLE OWL   25 ins
Ethiopian: almost whole region, except Congo Forests, SW tip S Africa. Resident in country with tall timber but not continuous forest, e.g. acacia savannah. Generally blackish grey, but dark colour phases occur; underparts from head finely vermiculated grey-brown and white; facial disc black-fringed, long ear tufts very dark brown; legs feathered to claws, strong bill white, eyes brown. Juvenile largely barred smoky grey. Nocturnal; hooting 'song' a string of notes in ascending scale, of mournful quality to human ears. Clicks bill when alarmed. Food: snakes, lizards, caterpillars; birds up to guinea-fowl size; may attack poultry. Breeding season variable throughout region; lays usually 2 white eggs on decayed wood in hollow trees, on platform of sticks in large fork, occasionally in old nests, even old petrol drum. Incubation and fledging much as *B. bubo*. **440**

Bubo virginianus *Strigidae*
GREAT HORNED OWL   18-23 ins
Nearctic and Neotropical: from arctic tree limit to Straits of Magellan; not W Indies. Resident in wooded country from dense forests to coastal mangrove swamps; not common in tropical lowlands. Upperparts generally mottled brown, black and white; facial disc chestnut, dark fringed above white half-collar with vertical streaks; underparts barred dark and light. Subarctic race may be almost white, western race very pale, Labrador race very dark. Feathered legs white, bill dark horn, eyes yellow. Nocturnal; deep resonant hoot usually *hoo hoohoo hoo hoo* (R. T. Peterson); also frightening shriek. ♂'s courtship includes nodding, head rotation, bowing, wing-clapping. Food: variety of mammals and birds up to rabbits, grouse, poultry, quite often skunks; has killed geese, turkeys. Breeds from January in USA, in old nests of other birds, holes in large trees, rock crevices. 2 to 4 white eggs incubated by ♀ *c.* 5 weeks; young leave nest *c.* 30 days, before fledging. **441**

Bubulcus ibis *Ardeidae*
CATTLE EGRET   20 (of which neck and legs 9) ins
SW Palaearctic, Ethiopian, Oriental, quite recently Australasian (partly introduced), Neotropical and Nearctic. Plumage generally white with seasonal pale buff plumes on head and mantle. Legs mainly dark brown; bill and eyes yellow – all variable seasonally. Breeds in riparian and riverine woods and reedbeds; otherwise in open, not necessarily wet, country where parties accompany large wild or domestic mammals, snapping up disturbed insects; also perch on backs to remove parasites, and take frogs and lizards from ground. Mutual displays at nest with croaking and guttural notes; gregarious roosts in trees. Breeding season varies with latitude: April to July in N. Forms colonies often with other species in trees, bushes, reeds or rocky islets; 4 to 6 pale blue eggs laid in nest of local plant material and incubated for 21-24 days by ♀ and ♂, who also feed brood; young fly in *c.* 7 weeks. Two broods in tropics. **56**

Bucco macrodactylus *Bucconidae*
CHESTNUT-CAPPED PUFFBIRD   5½ ins
Neotropical: S Venezuela W to Colombian Andes; S to E Peru, W Amazonian Brazil, N Bolivia; resident in forests. Upperparts to tail brown, speckled white and golden-brown; crown chestnut, cheeks black, white stripe below ear coverts; collar orange rufous; white throat and upper breast traversed by broad black underparts buffish, lightly barred dusky grey; thick hooked bill. Solitary and difficult to observe: habits generally as *Malacoptila panamensis*; largely insectivorous, excavating tunnel and nest chamber in ground for 2 or 3 white eggs. **523**

Bucephala clangula see under **B. islandica**

Bucephala islandica *Anatidae*
BARROW'S GOLDENEYE   *c.* 18 ins
Nearctic, marginally Palaearctic: breeds Iceland, SW Greenland, Labrador and mountains of W North America S to central California; residents of Iceland and Greenland winter S to coast, N American birds go

S as far as Long Island on Atlantic and San Francisco on Pacific coast. Habitat: lakes and streams in mountains when breeding. ♂: head purplish blue, upperparts black with large white patches on scapular and wing coverts (but less white than Common Goldeneye, *B. clangula*); underparts, neck and crescent markings on face white. ♀: head brown, lower neck and underparts white with grey breast, flanks, thighs and vent; upperparts mottled blackish and grey with white patches on wing coverts. Legs, ♂ orange-yellow, ♀ brownish yellow; bill (shorter and higher than in *B. clangula*), ♂ black, ♀ black with yellow patch, extensive in N American birds; eyes, ♂ yellow, ♀ pale yellow. Strong flyer, wings whistle in flight, usually in small flocks, fairly tame; feeds on small aquatic animals and sometimes pondweeds, may dive for up to 50 seconds to turn over stones on bottom to expose food. Call: hoarse croak and a vibrant mew. Semi-colonial, nests in tree-holes, sometimes up to ½ mile from water; in treeless regions such as Iceland uses cavities in or under rocks, in stream banks or even walls. 8 to 12 pale green eggs, incubated by ♀ *c.* 30 days. **106**

Buceros bicornis *Bucerotidae*
GREAT or GREAT PIED HORNBILL   *c.* 52 ins
Oriental: Western Ghats (India) from about Kandala to S Travancore; Himalayas, up to *c.* 5,000 ft, from Kumaon to Assam; Burma and through Malaysia to Sumatra. Resident heavy evergreen forest. ♂: face, back, underparts and wings (with double white bars) black; neck, belly and tail coverts white; tail white with broad black sub-terminal band; huge horn-shaped bill under U-shaped casque. Legs greenish, bill yellow with reddish tip and black on ridge below casque (yellow with black front and back), eyes blood-red. ♀: smaller, especially bill and casque; back of casque red, eyes pearly white. Usually in pairs or small parties; noisy laboured flight. Calls: deep, harsh roars and croaks; characteristic loud reverberating *tok*. Food: fruit, chiefly wild figs; also reptiles, rodents, nestlings, large insects. Breeds March-April onwards, earlier in S. 2 (sometimes 1) white eggs in large unlined tree hollow, usually 60 ft or more up. ♀ walls up entrance from inside, using own faeces; fed by ♂ through narrow slit; incubates *c.* 31 days, breaks out when young *c.* 2 weeks old and usually rebuilds wall. Both parents feed young. **514**

Bucorvus abyssinicus *Bucerotidae*
ABYSSINIAN GROUND HORNBILL   42 ins
Ethiopian: from Somalia down to Equator in Kenya, E across to Guinea coast, keeping N of Congo forest belt, in any kind of open country, bush, savannah, thin woodland. All black except white primaries (conspicuous only in flight); bare skin round eye, upper throat blue; lower throat, neck, red in ♂, blue in ♀; bill has some red, casque open in front. Walk along like stately turkeys in small parties picking up insects, small reptiles, covering considerable distances, rarely fly. Voice a deep grunting *oomp, oomp, oomp*. Nest in holes in trees, rocks, not mudded up, eggs 1 to 3 dirty white. Stick nests up trees have been recorded. **515**

Bucorvus leadbeateri *Bucerotidae*
GROUND HORNBILL   42 ins
Ethiopian: replaces preceding species to S, i.e. from Equator in Kenya down to E Cape Province, W to Angola, skirting Congo forests to NW Kalahari to SW. Resembles *B. abyssinicus* in all respects except ♂ has all red face and upper neck; bill blackish, casque closed. **516**

BUDGERIGAR see **Melopsittacus undulatus**

BUFFALO WEAVER, WHITE-HEADED see **Dinemellia dinemelli**

BUFF-BREASTED SANDPIPER see **Tryngites subruficollis**

BUFF-CROWNED WOOD PARTRIDGE see **Dendrortyx leucophrys**

BUFF-THROATED
   FOLIAGE GLEANER see under **Automolus leucophthalmus**
   WOODCREEPER see **Xiphorhynchus guttatus**

Bugeranus carunculatus see **Grus carunculatus**

BULBUL,
   ASHY see **Hypsipetes flavala**
   BLACK-EYED see **Pycnonotus barbatus**
   BROWN-EARED see **Hypsipetes flavala**
   CAPE see under **Pycnonotus nigricans**
   RED-EYED see **Pycnonotus nigricans**
   RED-VENTED see **Pycnonotus cafer**
   SOMBRE see **Andropadus importunus**
   WHITE-CHEEKED see under **Pycnonotus cafer**
   WHITE-VENTED see **Pycnonotus barbatus**

BULLFINCH see **Pyrrhula pyrrhula**

BULLY CANARY see under **Serinus albogularis**

BULN BULN see **Barnardius barnardi**

BUNTING,
   BLACK-HEADED see **Emberiza melanocephalus**
   CIRL see under **Emberiza cia**
   CORN see **Emberiza calandra**
   CRESTED see **Melophus lathami**
   GOLDEN-BREASTED see **Emberiza flaviventris**
   GREY-NECKED see under **Emberiza hortulana**
   LAPLAND see **Calcarius lapponicus**
   LAZULI see **Passerina amoena**
   PAINTED see **Passerina ciris**
   PINE see **Emberiza leucocephala**
   RAINBOW see **Passerina leclancheri**
   RED-HEADED see under **Emberiza melanocephalus**
   REED see **Emberiza schoeniclus**
   ROCK see **Emberiza cia**
   SNOW see **Plectrophenax nivalis**
   STRIOLATED see under **Melophus lathami**

Buphagus africanus *Sturnidae*
YELLOW-BILLED OXPECKER   *c.* 8½ ins
Ethiopian: Eritrea S (but not E Kenya, E Tanzania) to S Africa (Zululand, Ovamboland); Angola. Resident in habitats of host animals; in Zambia: buffalo; eland, kudu, roan antelopes; rhinoceros (R. I. G. Attwell). Upperparts, including wings, tail, dark earth brown; rump, upper tail coverts buff-brown; throat, neck as upperparts; breast dusky, rest underparts buff-brown; legs black; bill, with broad base lower mandible, yellow, tip red; eyes orange. Juvenile's bill yellow. Usually near game or large domestic animals; perching on them in upright posture or sidling all over them by means of sharp claws, searching for ticks; even displays and mates on host. Hides on opposite side from observer. Several may collect on one animal before flying off with rattling call; distinct from hissing *kriss kriss*. May enlarge wounds on host; also takes flies. Breeds during rains, e.g. October-November S Africa, May-June Sudan; nest of straw, grasses, lined fine grass, hair, feathers, in tree holes, rock crevices, under eaves. 2 or 3 white or very pale blue eggs, sometimes spotted chestnut, brown over violet. Incubation, fledging probably as *B. erythrorhynchus*; young fed by 4 adults at one nest (R. J. Dowsett). **964**

Buphagus erythrorhynchus *Sturnidae*
RED-BILLED OXPECKER   8-8½ ins
Ethiopian: E side of continent from Eritrea, Ethiopia, southward to Botswana, S Africa (Transvaal, Natal); resident savannah, forest edge, 4,600 to 8,500 ft Kenya; favourite hosts Zambia: eland, kudu, roan, sable antelopes; hippopotamus; rhinoceros (Attwell), also buffalo, warthog. Closely resembles *B. africanus* but upperparts pale ashy brown, uniform with rump; bare facial area; legs blackish, bill red; eyes yellow to red, orbits yellow. Juvenile sooty brown above. Habits much as *B. africanus*; reputed to return to same animal; defaecates clear of host (V. D. van Someren).

Chattering display usually on host's back. Roosts reedbeds, sometimes tree holes. Various calls: hissing *tsee*; *churrr*; *tzik tzik*; warning rattle; shrill twittering in flight. Fond of dustbathing. Food mainly ticks (*c.* 2,300 in 55 stomachs – R. E. Moreau); also flies and wound tissue of host. Occasionally seen to drink. Breeding variable within range: mainly during rains. Nest in crevice, tree hole, wall, under eaves; of plant debris, lined hair from living host. 3 to 5 bluish white to off-white eggs, rough shelled, marked shades of brown. Incubation 11-12 days; fledging 28-29 days. **965**

BURCHELL'S GLOSSY STARLING, see **Lamprotornis australis**

Burhinus bistriatus *Burhinidae*
DOUBLE-STRIPED STONE CURLEW   18 ins
Neotropical: Mexico, Costa Rica, Hispaniola S to NE Columbia, Venezuela, Guyana, N Brazil; resident in savannahs and open cultivated country. Resembles *B. oedicnemus*: upperparts streaked tawny and dark brown; broad white wing bar and bars on tail; black and white bands over eye; throat and underparts white; breast streaked buff; legs olive-green, bill black, eyes yellow. Habits and behaviour much as relatives; utters 'loud cackling notes'. Clutch 2 eggs and breeding details probably as relatives. **306**

Burhinus capensis *Burhinidae*
SPOTTED THICK-KNEE   *c.* 17 ins
Ethiopian: several races almost throughout region, except SW, in suitable habitat: dry open or bush veld, usually near water, e.g. rocky river beds; some local migration. Resembles Stone Curlew, *B. oedicnemus*; upperparts pale brown spotted and streaked black; wings show black tip with small white square and spot on coverts; neck, breast, flanks buff streaked black; legs yellow, bill black, large eyes yellow. Immature more heavily marked black. Crepuscular habits and behaviour much as Stone Curlew. Calls plaintive *tche-uuuu*; of Stone Curlew's call; also excited *pi pi pi pi*. Food largely insects. Breeding season variable throughout range. Lays 2 pale brown eggs marked dark brown and grey on flat ground or bare scrape; nesting details much as Stone Curlew, *B. bistriatus*. **307**

Burhinus magnirostris see under **Esacus magnirostris**

Burhinus oedicnemus *Burhinidae*
STONE CURLEW   *c.* 16 ins
Palaearctic, Oriental: broad band from SE England, Iberia and NW Africa (including Canary Islands) to Lake Balkash, Burma, Ceylon and Arabia. Northern birds migrate mainly to N Africa in winter. Habitat: open shingle, riverbeds, sand dunes and deserts, heaths, dry salt marshes, even cultivated land. Fairly uniform light brown, streaked and flecked dark brown, with paler throat and underparts; much of flight feathers black with white marks and two white bars across coverts; tail shows white crescent between black borders; legs pale yellow, bill blackish, base yellow, eyes yellow. Crepuscular, performing evening flights in flocks with eerie *cur-lew* calls. Usually runs with short steps, stopping to stand upright, sometimes bobbing head down, hind part up; frequently squats on tarsus. Feeds mainly by night on small land animals up to lizards and mice. Breeds from first half April in S Europe, making large, usually unlined scrape on bare ground. 2 rounded eggs, pale buff with dark brown and grey streaks, spots and scrawls, incubated by ♀ and ♂ 25-27 days; both tend young *c.* 6 weeks; sometimes a second brood. **308**

Burhinus vermiculatus *Burhinidae*
WATER DIKKOP OR THICK-KNEE   15 ins
Ethiopian: several races S throughout region from Kenya; resident in neighbourhood of water: river beaches, banks and islets. Resembles Stone Curlew, *B. oedicnemus*: upperparts tone grey, barred and vermiculated black; black and white bars on shoulder of closed wing; primaries dark grey, coverts grey; underparts white but neck and breast streaked black, under tail coverts buff; legs greenish slate, bill black, base yellow, eyes pale green. More approachable than

relatives; associates locally with crocodiles, e.g. Murchison Falls, Uganda. Often in small parties, roosts in shade by day. Call rendered plaintive *kwa-lee-vee* cf Stone Curlew. Food largely insects. Breeding season variable throughout range. 2 buff eggs, heavily marked rich brown, chocolate and purple, laid in scrape on sandy shore or rocky islet. Incubation and fledging much as Stone Curlew. **309**

BURROWING OWL see **Speotyto cunicularia**

BUSH
      CHAT, RUFOUS see **Cercotrichas galactotes**
      LARK see **Mirafra africana**
      SHRIKE, BLACKCAP see **Tchagra minuta**
      SHRIKE, BLACK-HEADED see **Tchagra senegala**
      SHRIKE, FASCIATED see **Cymbilaimus lineatus**
      WARBLER, CHINESE see **Cettia diphone**
      WARBLER, SEYCHELLES see **Bebrornis sechellensis**
      WARBLER, SHORT-TAILED see **Cettia squameiceps**

BUSTARD,
      AUSTRALIAN see **Eupodotis australis**
      BLACK-BELLIED see **Lissotis melanogaster**
      DENHAM'S see **Neotis denhami**
      GREAT see **Otis tarda**
      HARTLAUB'S see **Lissotis hartlaubii**
      KORI see **Choriotis kori**
      LITTLE see **Otis tetrax**
      WHITE-BELLIED see **Eupodotis senegalensis**

BUTCHERBIRD,
      GREY see **Cracticus torquatus**
      PIED see under **Cracticus torquatus**
      SILVER-BACKED see under **Cracticus torquatus**

Buteo galapagoensis *Accipitridae*
GALAPAGOS HAWK   ♂: 18, ♀: 21 ins
Confined to Galapagos where sedentary but ranges over nine islands. Variable brown with crown darker than back; mantle feathers pale edged; tail silvery grey, barred black; under wing coverts black, but flight feathers with pale bars; underparts light, spotted brown, legs yellow, bill blackish, cere yellow, eyes brown. Immature variegated buff, white and black. Very noisy in breeding season, uttering series of short screams. Usually solitary or in pairs and family groups, perching on tree or lava ledge, then soaring up for display flights. Hunts varied prey, including young marine iguanas; takes edible human leavings and has little fear of man. Breeding season irregular. Nest, on ledge, low tree or ground, built up year after year, of sticks with finer linings. Lays 1 to 3 white eggs, incubated ♀ and ♂ 37-38 days. Young, fed at first mainly by ♂, fledged 50-60 days. Both periods longer than for other buzzards. ♀ often has two mates (Tjitte de Vries). **139**

Buteo lineatus *Accipitridae*
RED-SHOULDERED HAWK   20-22 ins
Nearctic: S Canada to S Florida and Central Mexico; northern birds migratory. Habitat moist or swampy woodlands, e.g. along river bottoms. Blackish brown above, streaked rufous, especially shoulders; tail black with white bars and tip; wings dark brown flecked white; throat white, flecked dark brown; breast rufous, becoming barred lighter brown on belly; whitish 'mirror' under wings in flight. Legs greenish yellow, cere yellow, bill black, eyes brown. Unobtrusive and sedentary in winter, becoming conspicuous in breeding season, uttering triple whistling scream and displaying in air. Food varied: small vertebrates and large insects, e.g. grasshoppers. Breeds from late January (Florida) to April (New England), building nest of sticks and debris in tall tree. 2 to 4 white eggs, marked shades of brown, incubated by ♀ and ♂ *c.* 4 weeks. Young, fed by ♀ and ♂, fly 5-6 weeks. **140**

BUZZARD,
      CRESTED HONEY see under **Pernis apivorus**
      HONEY see **Pernis apivorus**

Bycanistes subcylindricus *Bucerotidae*
BLACK AND WHITE CASQUED HORNBILL   30 ins
Ethiopian: W African rain-forest zone as far E as W Kenya, NW Tanzania. Genus contains some half dozen species of similar appearance, habits with overlapping ranges in heavily forested parts of region. All are heavily built black and white birds with very large casqued bills, feeding mainly on fruit, also insects and sometimes eggs and young of small birds. *B. subcylindricus* distinguishable by large white wing patch; lower belly, under tail coverts, ends of outer tail feathers all white, otherwise all black. Flight cumbersome, noisy, several rapid beats followed by long glide, often above canopy. Loud raucous voice, *rark rark rark*. Hole-nester, usually in high tree, sometimes rocks; entrance reduced to small slit by mud-plastering, through which ♀ fed by ♂ while incubating. Eggs 1 to 3, white.

CABOT'S TERN see **Sterna sandvicensis**

Cacatua roseicapilla or Kakatoe roseicapilla *Psittacidae*.
GALAH   14 ins
Continental Australia, except E and W coastal areas; open country, wooded savannah, dry plains, crop fields, up to 5,000 ft; local movements according to food supply. Variable: upperparts, wings, under tail coverts grey; scapulars and rump paler; forehead and crown pale pink; face, nape, underparts deep pink; tail light grey above, very dark underneath; legs grey, bill brown, eyes dark brown, facial skin red. Wheeling flight of flaps and glides; flocks of hundreds manoeuvre at dawn, dusk or during rain; rests during day, often biting off green twigs, chewing bark and rotten wood. Call: loud whistling screech of two syllables. Ground feeder on grass, clover and other seeds, locally damages crops; also roots, bulbs, shoots; tree seeds in drought; insects and their larvae. Gulps when drinking. ♂ displays to ♀ with crest raised and head movements. Breeds variably, mainly July to December in S, February to June in N following rains. Lines tree hole, locally rock crevice, near water with eucalypt leaves. 2 to 5 white eggs incubated by ♀ and ♂ *c.* 4 weeks; both feed young who fly 5-6 weeks; 2 broods in good seasons. **388**

Cacicus cela *Icteridae*
YELLOW-RUMPED CACIQUE   ♀: 9½: ♂: 11 (bill 1½) ins
Neotropical: Central and E Panama, Trinidad, Guyanas, Venezuela, E Colombia S to N Bolivia; Amazonian and E Brazil S to Bahia; Central and N Colombia; W Ecuador, NW Peru; resident open woodland, edge mangrove swamps, riverbanks, sea level to *c.* 4,500 ft; lowlands in Trinidad. Generally glossy black with narrow crest, but lower back, inner wing coverts, upper and under tail coverts bright golden or orange yellow according to race; basal half tail yellow, rest black; legs black, bill dusky green or yellowish to ivory according to race, eyes pale cobalt blue. Outstanding songster (both sexes), noisy in breeding colonies, often in solitary tree near house or in village or town. Food: insects, fruit. Breeds January to June Trinidad; ♀ builds tubular nest 1½ to 2 ft long, of grass, plant fibres, round chamber lined leaves, suspended from branch of tree. 2 elongated white, cream or greenish eggs variably marked dark umber over pale brown, lilac, incubated ♀ *c.* 12 days; fledging period similar. Sometimes evicted by tyrannid, Black-banded Petchary, *Legatus leucophaius*. **908**

CACIQUE, YELLOW-RUMPED see **Cacicus cela**

CACTUS WREN see **Campylorhynchus bruneicapillus**

Cairina moschata *Anatidae*
MUSCOVY DUCK   ♀: 26, ♂: 33 ins
Neotropical: Mexico, Central America, S America S to Peru and Uruguay. Ancestor of farmyard Muscovy Duck. Habitat: forest streams, ponds and marshes surrounded by woodlands. ♂: head, crest, neck and underparts brownish black; upperparts black with green gloss, wing coverts and axillaries white; bare black skin surrounded by small caruncles from bill to

eyes. ♀: smaller with much reduced bare face patch. Legs black, bill black with pale pink band near tip, eyes yellow-brown. Roosts and spends much of day perched in large trees; heavy slow flight; congregates in small flocks in dry season, feeds dawn and dusk on aquatic vegetation and small animals. ♂♂ polygamous and fight fiercely. Call: usually silent, ♂ hisses, ♀ gives weak quack. Nests in hollows of trees, old nests and large forks; lays 8 to 15 white eggs with greenish sheen, incubated *c*. 35 days. The domestic form is illustrated. **107**

Calamanthus campestris *Muscicapidae: Malurinae*
RUFOUS FIELD WREN   *c*. 4¾ ins
Australia: W New South Wales, NW Victoria and southern S Australia W to Eyre Peninsula. Habitat: low scrub on open plains. Upperparts rufous-brown streaked black; crown, cheeks and rump more rufous; 'eyebrow' white; underparts whitish streaked dark brown; dark brownish tail with white tip. Legs and bill brown, eyes very pale yellow. Smaller and more rufous plumage than closely related Striated Field Wren, *C. fuliginosus*. Usually in pairs or small parties; shy, scuttles over ground; insectivorous. Call: lark-like, uttered from top of bush. Breeds after heavy rain in all seasons; globular nest with side entrance, in tuft of grass, underneath low bush or on bare patch of ground; of grass with feather lining; 3, sometimes 4, light brown eggs, darker and richer at larger end.

Calamanthus fuliginosus see under **C. campestris**

Calandrella cinerea *Alaudidae*
SHORT-TOED LARK   5½ ins
Palaearctic, Ethiopian; *c*. 14 races; breeds in belt 30°N to 45°N, Mongolia to Spain and N Africa; also S Africa up E side to Uganda, Ethiopia and SW Arabia; winters southern breeding range S to Sahara, Sudan and Central India. Habitat: open sandy or stony fields usually with very little vegetation. Upperparts pale brownish with broad dark streaks, less so on rump; underparts white with sandy-buff band across upper breast and dark mark on sides of breast. Some races more reddish. Legs pale brownish flesh, bill horn, eyes brown. Call: hard *chichirrp* recalling House Martin, *Delichon urbica*. Song stereotyped *tee-tsit-si-wee*, *tsi-wichoo*, especially in flight. Song-flight prolonged and undulates at *c*. 50 feet. Outside breeding season in large flocks. Food mainly seeds but also takes insects. Breeding season varies with race (Europe mid April to July). Nests on ground in deep cup rather sheltered. 3 to 5 usually yellowish finely freckled eggs, incubated by ♀ 11-13 days. Young leave nest *c*. 9 days and fly 7-10 days later. Usually 2 broods. **600**

Calcarius lapponicus *Emberizidae: Emberizinae*
LAPLAND BUNTING or LONGSPUR   *c*. 6 ins
Holarctic: N coasts Eurasia from Norway to Arctic America and Greenland (not Iceland, Spitsbergen); migrates S to temperate zone for winter: NW Europe; SE Russia and across Asia. Breeds above or beyond tree line on high 'fjeld' (Norway) and moss tundra with creeping birch and crowberry *Empetrum;* winters steppes, rough grassland, stubbles near coast in Europe. ♂: upperparts brown streaked black, outer tail feathers white; crown to throat black, partly framed narrow white stripe which curves round to eye; nape chestnut; underparts whitish, flanks streaked black. Head pattern much obscured brown in winter, as ♀ all seasons. Legs, eyes dark brown, bill yellow tipped black. Normally runs but can hop. Perches hummocks in tundra, trees where available. Flight undulating. Joins winter flocks of other seed-eaters, Skylarks, *Alauda arvensis*, but generally rather wild. Breeding season calls: *teeleu* (anxiety), *teeuu*, *ticky-tick* (also on passage); sharp *zit*, explosive *peet-teu*. Song in display flight 'lively outpouring' (B. W. Tucker) like beginning of Skylark. ♂ flutters up to 40 ft, planes round, wings stretched, then sinks downward. Food: seeds of grasses and other plants, insects and their larvae in summer. Breeds end May onwards, ♀ building nest of grasses, moss, lined fine bents, hair, feathers, in hollow in ground or side of tussock. 4 to 6 greenish grey to olive brown eggs, heavily marked

reddish brown and blackish, incubated mainly ♀, 13-14 days; both parents feed young, who leave nest 8-10 days. **852**

Calendula magnirostris see **Galerida magnirostris**

Calidris alba or *Crocethia alba Scolopacidae*
SANDERLING   *c*. 8 ins
Holarctic: local on arctic coasts and islands; summer visitor for only 2 months, cosmopolitan in winter on sandy beaches to Argentina, S. Africa (rare), New Zealand, probably also inland Central Asia. Breeds stony lichen tundra with low vegetation, e.g. creeping willow. Summer: upperparts, including head, neck, upper breast, mottled light chestnut and black; wing pattern black with white wing bar; tail brown and blackish, edged white; underparts white; legs and bill black, eyes brown. Winter: upperparts pale grey, head whitish; black shoulder patch; underparts white. Juvenile mottled black and buff above with pale buff face and breast. Usually seen in parties, stout little birds running fast after retreating surge; fly with *twick twick* call. Churring note by ♂ on song flight. Eats mainly small insects in summer, otherwise small crustaceans, molluscs, gasteropods, beach insects. Breeds from mid or late June, making scrape on dry, rocky tundra. 4 dull greenish-olive eggs, sparsely marked brown and grey, incubated by ♀ and ♂ 23-24 days; ♀ and ♂ tend young, who fly in *c*. 2 weeks. **276**

Calidris alpina *Scolopacidae*
DUNLIN or RED-BACKED SANDPIPER   6¾-7½ ins
Holarctic: more or less circumpolar in temperate to arctic zones, farthest S in Britain, Ireland and Baltic; wintering mainly N temperate, not crossing Equator; coastal, estuarine and muddy lake shores. Breeds well vegetated damp areas, usually near pools, in low level or mountain tundra; coastal marshes and river valleys in temperate, moorland up to 3,000 ft in Britain. Summer: upperparts mottled chestnut and black; head brown, chin white, throat streaked; black patch on lower breast; wings brown and blackish with white bar; tail dark, white edged, black tipped; underparts white; legs dark olive; long, slightly curved bill black, eyes brown. Winter: upperparts and head grey-brown with black streaks; underparts white with dark patch on breast. Singly, in parties or huge flocks in winter, often mixing with other small waders and indulging in massed aerial evolutions. Usual call short nasal *tshripp*, expanded in spring to musical reeling mainly by ♂, who hovers lark-like in display flight; also *kwot kwot* of alarm when with young. Takes mainly small insects, their larvae and crustaceans when breeding; in winter also worms and snails. Breed from early May in S of range, making usually well hidden scrape in grass, moss, other low but thick cover. 4 bluish-green to buff eggs, spotted and spirally streaked red-brown and grey, incubated by ♀ and ♂ 21-22 days; both tend young, who fly *c*. 4 weeks. **277**

Calidris canutus *Scolopacidae*
KNOT   *c*. 10 ins
Holarctic: discontinuous in arctic zone; summer visitor *c*. 2 months, wintering mainly N temperate muddy estuaries and coasts, but reaches Argentina, S Africa, New Zealand, exceptionally Macquarie 55°S. Breeds dry level stony tundra. Summer: upperparts black and chestnut, crown streaked black; head and underparts chestnut; wings with black tips, white bar; tail dark brown; legs olive brown, straight bill black, eyes brown. Winter: upperparts grey, underparts white, faintly streaked. Juvenile has grey-brown upperparts, breast buff. Flocks in winter like Dunlin, *C. alpina*, packing even closer. Winter call *knut* (hence name?) and whistling *twit-wit;* fluty 'song' by ♂ in display flight; *quee quee quee* of alarm with young. Food in summer insects, spiders, crustaceans, parts of tundra plants; mainly small marine animals in winter. Breeds from mid June Siberia, making scrape on rocky or stony tundra. 4 greenish to buff eggs, with small brown and grey spots, incubated by ♀ and ♂ 20-25 days. ♂ takes main share tending young, who fly *c*. 3 weeks. **278**

Calidris ferruginea *Scolopacidae*
CURLEW SANDPIPER   *c*. 7½ ins
Palaearctic: arctic Siberia from Yenisei to Kolynin; summer visitor, wintering Mediterranean area, Ethiopian, Oriental and Australasian regions; sandy and muddy shores and creeks. Breeds low ground near rivers, tundra slopes. Summer (♂ brighter): upperparts mottled chestnut and black; face, neck underparts rich chestnut like Knot, *C. canutus;* wings grey-brown, white bar and black tips; rump white, tail blackish; under tail coverts white; legs olive-brown, long finely curved bill black, eyes black brown. Winter: upperparts dark grey-brown, face and underparts much as Dunlin, from which bill and white rump distinguish it. Juvenile has buff breast. Associates with Dunlin, *C. alpina*, on shore, looking taller and slimmer. Call soft chirrup; trilling song on breeding ground, where pairs or small parties chase each other; *wick wick wick* of alarm with young. Takes insects and their larvae in summer; otherwise small crustaceans, molluscs and worms. Breeds from *c*. 20 June semi-socially, making scrapes often on southerly slopes of tundra. ♀ and ♂ incubate 4 greenish to buff eggs, heavily marked dark brown and grey, and tend young, whole cycle taking *c*. 6 weeks. **279**

Calidris fuscicollis or *Erolia fuscicollis Scolopacidae*
WHITE-RUMPED SANDPIPER   *c*. 7 ins
Nearctic: N coasts and islands of Alaska and Canada to S Baffin Is; summer visitor, migrating to S Argentina and Falkland Islands; winters mud flats, shores of fresh and salt lagoons, marshes. Breeds boggy tundra, shores of lakes and rivers. Summer: upperparts mottled rich brown and black; pale grey breast streaked and spotted black; wings pale with dark tips; rump white above black terminal bar to tail; underparts white, legs and bill dark, eyes black brown. Winter: upperparts grey-brown. Juvenile as summer adult. Resembles Dunlin, *C. alpina*, in habits. Sometimes crouches rather than flies. Call a squeaky *jeet;* also faint squeaky spring song in flight up to 60 ft. Diet mainly animal: worms, molluscs, insects, also crustaceans and leeches; some plant seeds. Breeds from second half June, making scrape, usually lined grass and willow leaves, in hummock on wet tundra. ♀ incubates 4 greenish or buff eggs, spotted and speckled tawny brown and grey and tends brood; ♂♂ collect in parties. **280**

Calidris maritima *Scolopacidae*
PURPLE SANDPIPER   *c*. 8 ins
Holarctic: discontinuous in subarctic and arctic zones, but S to Kuriles in N Pacific, where regarded by some as separate species, Rock Sandpiper *C. ptilocnemus* Resident ice-free N Pacific, others winter temperate zone to 45°N; rocky coasts, frequently in harbours. Breeds often in cloud or mist cover on swampy tundra, bare mountain tops, islands off coast. Summer: upperparts dark brown with rufous margins to feathers on back, which has purplish sheen; wings dark with white bar; tail centrally dark with light edges; breast mottled brown extending to white underparts with dark flank marks; legs yellow, bill black-brown, base yellow, eyes brown. Upperparts much greyer in winter, legs duller. Associates with Turnstones, *Arenaria interpres*, in winter, allowing close approach before flying off silently or with low *weet-wit*. Other notes on breeding ground, where flight becomes erratic; 'song' loud trill in gliding flight; also raises and lowers wings in display on ground. Takes insects and their larvae, tundra herbage, including seeds and moss spores; crustaceans and gasteropods in winter. Breeds from mid-June, making scrape, lined with leaves, in moss and tundra plants. 4 eggs, greenish when fresh and marked dark brown and purple, incubated mainly by ♂ 21-22 days; he tends young who fly *c*. 3 weeks. **281**

Calidris
    minuta see under **C. temminckii**
    ptilocnemus see under **C. maritima**

Calidris temminckii *Scolopacidae*
TEMMINCK'S STINT   *c*. 5½ ins
Palaearctic: subarctic (breeds sporadically Britain)

and arctic zones from Scandinavia to Bering Straits; summer visitor, wintering freshwater margins, mainly Ethiopian and Oriental regions. Breeds swampy areas of scrub and birch zone, often near grassy valleys. Summer: upperparts grey-brown with black-brown marks and rufous feather edges; wings with dark trailing edge and tips and narrow white bar; tail centrally dark with white edges; underparts from throat white; legs variable, bill and eyes very dark brown. Winter and juvenile greyer with grey-brown patch on breast. Haunts cover much more than Little Stint, *C. minuta*, towering into erratic flight like miniature snipe. Call high-pitched trilling titter; sings in moth-like display flight and on ground with wings raised. Takes mainly small insects and their larvae, picked off vegetation and mud. Breeds early June onwards, making well hidden scrape in moss and low cover. ♀ sometimes lays two clutches of 4 greenish-grey eggs, spotted evenly liver brown, incubating one herself, ♂ the other, 21-22 days. Each tends own brood, which fledge 2-2½ weeks. **282**

CALIFORNIA
GULL see **Larus californicus**
QUAIL see **Lophortyx californicus**

CALIFORNIAN CONDOR see **Gymnogyps californicus**

Callaeas cinerea *Callaeidae*
KOKAKO 15 ins
Confined to New Zealand; N Island race *C. c. wilsoni* quite widespread; S Island *cinerea* barely survives. Resident native forest. Generally dark bluish-grey, tinged olive brown from lower back and belly downward; flight and tail feathers blackish brown, tinged slaty; velvety black band over bill encircles dark brown eyes; wattles blue (*wilsoni*) or orange (*cinerea*); legs, bill black. Immature more generally tinged brown, wattles smaller, paler. Progresses by hopping up limbs and trunks, then gliding on to next tree, seldom flies far. Pairs remain together all year, taking mainly or entirely vegetable food: leaves, flowers, fruits, from outer branches of native trees; use feet like parrot when feeding. Calls various: quiet, repeated *took*, probably of alarm; low mewing; bell-like note followed by sharp *kik;* full song, audible at distance, 'two long rich organ notes' (Maning) followed by 3 short *pips*. Breeds November to March, ♀ and ♂ building platform of twigs, with finer material, rotten wood on top; cup of moss lined softly, e.g. tree-fern scales. Usually 3 pale brownish grey eggs, marked brown and purplish brown, incubated ♀ *c.* 25 days. ♂ helps feed young on fruit and leaves; they fly 27-28 days.

Callocephalon fimbriatum *Psittacidae*
GANG-GANG COCKATOO 13½ ins
Confined to SE Australia; habitat spring and summer dense montane forest up to 7,000 ft; comes into open, often round habitations, autumn and winter. ♂: dark grey with pale feather edges, head scarlet with large crest of separated brush-like feathers. ♀ has underparts barred brick-red and white, dark grey head with small dark crest. Legs grey, bill horn-grey, eyes dark brown. Juvenile like ♀ but crest red-tipped. Small flocks outside breeding season sit preening in tree-tops, calling wheezily, as also in silent, owl-like flight. Often takes off in short playful flight and returns to trees; but makes long flights over hills. Lands only to drink. Alarm call, prolonged rasping screech. Food: green seeds of wattle, acacia, eucalypts; berries in winter, e.g. of introduced hawthorn, pyracantha; holds food in left foot, standing on right. Breeds October to January, 60 to 70 ft up in tree hole enlarged by birds, usually near water. 2 or 3 white eggs incubated by ♀ and ♂ *c.* 28 days; young fly *c.* 7 weeks, fed by ♀ and ♂ further 4-6 weeks. **389**

Caloenas nicobarica *Columbidae*
NICOBAR DOVE *c.* 16 ins
Oriental, Australasian: smaller wooded islands and islets off larger land masses from Nicobars and Mergui Archipelago E to Philippines, New Guinea and Solomon Is; moves between islands. ♂: dark slate grey with glossy metallic blue-green and copper-bronze upperparts and short white tail; short feathers on head contrasting with long hair-like feathers that hang down from neck. ♀: slightly smaller, shorter neck hackles and greyer head, neck and breast. Legs purplish red with yellow-brown claws, fairly heavy bill and cere (smaller in ♀) dark grey, eyes pale brown. Adapted to poor light of forest floor where it feeds by flicking aside leaves with bill to expose seeds, fruits and small animals. Walks with wings drooping low at sides; flight swift and powerful. Call: occasionally short, deep but soft cooing. Breeds in colonies on islands, often several nests in a tree; single white egg on untidy twig platform in thick cover. **350**

Calonetta leucophrys or Anas leucophrys *Anatidae*
RINGED TEAL 14 ins
Neotropical: S Brazil, Uruguay, Paraguay, S Bolivia and NE Argentina. Habitat: open pools and lagoons in marshes, often near woodland. ♂: fairly decorative, top of head and hind neck black, breast pink with black spots, flanks grey; face, sides of head and throat creamy, mantle olive grey, scapulars chestnut-red, back, rump and tail black; wings black with white patch, secondaries green, tertiaries olive brown. ♀: pale with dark brown back and wings, top of head and hind neck, sides of head and throat white with brown markings; irregular brown spots on breast. Legs lilac pink, slender bill lead blue (duller in ♀), eyes brown. Flies and swims well, perches easily. Call: ♂, soft long whistle; ♀, short harsh quack. Nests late summer in tree holes; lays 5 to 8 white eggs, incubated *c.* 23 days. **108**

Caloperdix oculea *Phasianidae*
FERRUGINOUS WOOD PARTRIDGE 9-10½ ins
Oriental: SE Asia, SW Siam, Malaysia, Sumatra, Borneo. Sedentary in lowland bamboo jungle and secondary forest up to 3,000 ft; usually near streams. Back and tail black spotted and barred chestnut; wings olive brown marked black; head, neck, underparts reddish chestnut, crown darker, face and throat paler, short blackish stripe behind eye; mantle and sides black, barred white, belly whitish, flanks spotted black; legs dull greenish yellow, bill black-brown, eyes brown. Usually in bevies of 4 or 5. Duets: ♂ calls 8 or 9 times, accelerating up scale, breaking into *E-terang* 2 to 4 times; ♀ replies with long series of faster notes (T. H. Harrisson). Diet: insects, especially termites and beetles; berries, seeds, grasses. Breeding variable within range; December and January in Borneo. Nest a lined scrape or domed with hole at side (Borneo) sheltered by bush. 8 to 10 white eggs incubated probably by ♀.

Calypte anna *Trochilidae*
ANNA'S HUMMINGBIRD 4 ins
Nearctic: California, partly resident or moving locally to mountains in summer, coast in winter. Habitat: canyons, foothills, riverine woodland with oaks, scarcer in deserts and chaparral; now frequent in gardens and parks. ♂: upperparts iridescent dark green from nape to slightly forked tail; underparts white, flanks washed green; crown, face, throat rose red with lobes at sides of neck. ♀ has green head, white throat spotted dark green, often with traces rose red. Legs, bill, eyes dark. ♂ in display flies backward 'like helicopter', sings briefly, then rises *c.* 100 ft, dives down and up again in narrow U, with sharp *peek* from vibration of spread tail feathers. Feeding and alarm call *chick;* rattling *ztikl ztikl ztikl* when ♂ chases ♀; jumbled song from perch. Takes nectar and insects from flowers, insects and small spiders off leaves or in air; drinks tree sap and comes to sugar solutions; punctures soft fruits. Becomes torpid at night. Breeds from late December, ♀ building nest of plant materials, decorated lichens, often lined feathers, on twig, typically of oak, 3 to 30 ft. 2 white eggs incubated by ♀ 16 days; she feeds young who fly 21 days. 2 broods. **467**

Calypte costae *Trochilidae*
COSTA'S HUMMINGBIRD 3¼ ins
Nearctic: breeds from S Central California, S Nevada, SW Utah, to SW New Mexico, SE Arizona, S Lower California; winters mainly Lower California, W Sonora (Mexico). Habitat: dry foothills and desert slopes with sages, cacti, yuccas, mesquite and other shrubs; marginally into chaparral and canyon woodlands. ♂ as Anna's Hummingbird, *C. anna*, but purple (looking black in dull light) replaces rose red on head, gorget and side lobes; ♀ and immature lack this colour or have only traces. In display ♂ swoops down from up to 200 ft, passing close to tops of shrubs and climbing again slowly to complete U some 75-100 ft across; successive dives may be from different angles. Also dances in front of ♀ with spread gorget, throwing tail from side to side. Soft *chick* when feeding, and rattling calls in chases. Song 2 or 3 hissing *tss-tss-see;* drawn-out version of this in display flight one of highest bird sounds audible to man. Feeds on nectar and insects from tubular flowers; also catches insects and spiders in air or off leaves. Nest of mixed plant materials like other species but looser in texture than *C. anna;* outside decorated dry leaves or lichens; from 1 to 9 ft in shrub, often exposed to sun. ♀ incubates 2 white eggs 16 days, feeds young, who fledge 22 days. **468**

Calyptomena viridis *Eurylaimidae*
GREEN BROADBILL 6 ins.
Oriental: Burma, Malaysia, Indonesia to Borneo; resident in evergreen forest, sometimes thinner cover and near or distant from water. ♂: iridescent grass-green with black patches on head and three bars on wing; ♀ dull green without markings, green ring round eye; feet dull green with yellowish soles, deep bill, largely concealed by tight crest of feathers, black above, greenish below and at tip, edges yellow; eyes dark brown. Described as 'sluggish', remaining in tops of tall trees. Calls: *chai* repeated fast, and soft pleasant whistle (B. E. Smythies). Throat-fluffing, bill raising and gaping display by ♂. Feeds on fruit. Breeds February to April Burma, ♂ and ♀ building gourd-shaped nest of coarse vegetable fibres or dead bamboo leaves, hung by narrow neck from branch and with tail of material hanging down; entrance at side. Clutch: 2 or 3 creamy white eggs, tinged pale brown. Both parents incubate eggs and feed young. **556**

Camaroptera brevicaudata *Muscicapidae:Sylviinae*
GREY-BACKED CAMAROPTERA 4½ ins
Ethiopian: almost whole region, except Cape Province. Resident in varied habitats, from secondary forest growth to arid sandy country with few bushes. Upperparts dark grey, except 'panel' formed by golden green edges to wing feathers; paler greyish buff below; 'thighs' yellow; long legs yellowish brown; long bill horn; eyes brown. Some south-eastern races have green rump, tail. Feeds on ground, carrying short tail upright. In arid areas spends much time in deep shade. Nicknamed 'Bush goat' from low buzzing call; other calls include explosive alarm note, loud ringing *plick, plick*. Eats insects, spiders. Breeding season varies: October to April in Zaire; shorter in S. Domed nest of fine grass, spider webs built in bag of *c.* 6 leaves sewn together; probably mimics tailor-ant nest. 2 white eggs, spotted lilac, reddish brown. **731**

CAMAROPTERA, GREY-BACKED see **Camaroptera brevicaudata**

Campephaga sulphurata *Campephagidae*
BLACK CUCKOO SHRIKE 9 ins
Ethiopian: Sudan, Ethiopia, Somalia, to Angola, S Africa; resident wooded country from lowland scrub to forests. ♂: black all over, glossed bluish green, sometimes yellow shoulders; yellow gape wattles distinguish from drongos with which often associates. ♀: upperparts olive-brown with dusky bars; wings, tail edged yellow and white; underparts white barred black and yellow. Legs, bill black, eyes light brown. Juvenile resembles ♀. Usually in pairs in parties of other species, hunting through canopy, whence takes insects and larvae from foliage; also fruits and tree seeds; sometimes feeds on ground. Usually silent but has soft, low trill and *chup* call. Breeding season varies within range. Builds very small nest for its size, of plant materials in moss or lichen on bough or in fork. 2 pale greyish or yellowish green eggs, heavily marked shades of brown over lilac. **636**

Campethera abingoni *Picidae*
GOLDEN-TAILED WOODPECKER 7 ins
Ethiopian: one race in Senegal, across to Sudan, others in E and Central Africa from Somalia down to Natal, in most kinds of woodland at all altitudes. Olive-green above with paler green spots, bars; forehead to nape and sides of throat crimson; pale yellow below with black streaks; golden yellow tail. Usual woodpecker behaviour, hopping up trees supported on stumpy tail, undulating flight, loud laughing call. Feeds on ants, grubs; lays 2 or 3 round white eggs in tree-hole. **537**

Campethera bennettii *Picidae*
BENNETT'S WOODPECKER 7 ins
Ethiopian: S Zaire across to Tanzania, S to Natal, in dry thorn bush country. ♂: upperparts including wings dark green, barred and spotted lighter green and whitish; head to nape and moustachial stripe crimson; earcoverts, chin, throat white; rest of underparts pale yellow, spotted black on neck, breast, flanks; lower flanks sometimes barred; tail dusky yellow, barred darker and usually black-tipped. ♀'s forehead and crown black, spotted white; earcoverts, throat chocolate brown; moustachial stripe white, speckled black. Legs, bill dark grey, eyes red. Juvenile like ♀ but more spotted. Fast undulating flight. Deep, bell-like call unusual for woodpecker. Feeds on insects, especially ants. Breeds September to January, boring hole in dead tree, laying 3 white eggs. Habits very little studied. **538**

Campethera punctuligera *Picidae*
FINE SPOTTED WOODPECKER 7 ins
Ethiopian: Senegal, NE Zaire, S Sudan in well-wooded open country. Very similar to *C. abingoni*, but much more finely barred above and spotted below. Usual woodpecker habits, feeding on ground as well as in trees. Call a kestrel-like *kweeyu*. **539**

Campylopterus falcatus *Trochilidae*
LAZULINE SABREWING 4½ (bill nearly 1) ins
Neotropical: N Venezuela, Colombia; E Ecuador; resident forest and scrub from *c.* 4,500 to *c.* 9,500 ft. ♂: upperparts iridescent green, blue on crown; outer primaries with thickened bent shafts, resembling sabres; tail feathers chestnut, central pair with broad bronze-green tips; throat and breast iridescent dark violet blue shading to blue green on underparts. ♀ has upperparts and tail like ♂, throat iridescent blue, underparts grey. See *Aglaiocercus kingi* for general hummingbird habits and behaviour.

Campylorhamphus falcularius *Dendrocolaptidae*
BLACK-BILLED SCYTHEBILL 10 (bill 3) ins
Neotropical: Brazil, E Paraguay and Argentina; resident in forests. Mainly olivaceous brown, wings and tail rufous chestnut; underparts pale brown; yellow-brown streaks on sides of neck, upper mantle, breast; throat whitish; long curved bill dusky grey. Behaves like giant treecreeper, extracting insects, their larvae and eggs from tree trunks, also probing among clustered palm fruits and between stems of vines. Nests in tree hole, laying probably 2 or 3 eggs. **558**

Campylorhynchus bruneicapillus *Troglodytidae*
CACTUS WREN 8 ins
Nearctic, marginally Neotropical: Central Texas, S Utah, S California to Central Mexico; resident cactus desert, mesquite, arid scrublands. Back brown flecked black and white, long tail greyish brown, barred darker, white spots outer edge; wings grey-brown heavily barred; crown chestnut, prominent white 'eyebrow' stretching to nape; cheeks, chin mainly white, underparts pale, upper breast densely spotted black, thinning out on belly. Legs flesh-brown, slightly curved bill horn-coloured, eyes brown. Tail not usually cocked up as shorter-tailed wrens. Flies low over ground. Call monotonous, 'unbirdlike' (R. T. Peterson) *chuh chuh chuh chuh* on one pitch, but gaining in rapidity. Mainly insectivorous. Breeds April onwards, building large purse-shaped nest of grasses and twigs, lined feathers, fur, in cactus or thorny bush, usually quite low. 4 or 5 creamy white eggs, thickly spotted pale reddish brown. 2 or 3 broods. **664**

Campylorhynchus griseus *Troglodytidae*
SPOTTED OR BICOLOURED WREN 7-8½ ins
Neotropical: W Guyana, Venezuela S of Orinoco and adjacent Brazil, lowlands of Colombia; Magdalena Valley; resident forest edge, clearings, semi-arid scrub, savannah, sea level to 4,500 ft. Black rufous; unbarred wings blackish, also tail with outer feathers more or less barred and tipped white; crown, nape, ear coverts dark brown; 'eyebrow' and underparts white. Large Magdalena Valley race has back brownish black, wings edged rufous, all but central tail feathers white towards ends, with narrow black tips. Habits generally as other wrens; mainly insectivorous; both sexes sing. 2 or 3 eggs, fledging period up to 18 days. **665**

CANADA
  GOOSE see **Branta canadensis**
  WARBLER see **Wilsonia canadensis**

CANARY see **Serinus albogularis**

CANARY
  BLACK-HEADED see **Serinus alario**
  BULLY see under **Serinus albogularis**
  WHITE-THROATED see **Serinus albogularis**
  YELLOW see **Serinus flaviventris**

CAPE
  BARREN GOOSE see **Cereopsis novaehollandiae**
  BULBUL see under **Pycnonotus nigricans**
  GANNET see under **Sula bassana**
  PIGEON see **Daption capensis**
  ROBIN CHAT see **Cossypha caffra**
  SPARROW see **Passer melanurus**
  SUGARBIRD see **Promerops cafer**

CAPERCAILLIE see **Tetrao urogallus**

Capito niger *Capitonidae*
BLACK-SPOTTED BARBET 6½ ins
Neotropical: Venezuela S of Orinoco, Colombia E of Andes to Peru, Bolivia; W Amazonian Brazil; resident tropical rain forest, swampy woodlands, secondary growth. ♂: upperparts to tail black with yellow bar across wing coverts and yellow suffusion of crown; forehead and large patch on throat red; underparts bright yellow with dark crescents on flanks and lower belly; legs, powerful bill black, eyes dark brown. ♀ has throat, breast, flanks heavily spotted dark brown; underwings and undertail brown. Keeps high in trees, sometimes clinging to bark like nuthatch; flight straight, not undulating. Diet: berries and other fruits; large insects. Excavates nest hole in tree, also taking woodpecker holes, up to 20 ft. 2 white eggs incubated by ♀ and ♂, who both tend young.

CAPPED PETREL see under **Pterodroma cahow**

Caprimulgus indicus *Caprimulgidae*
MIGRATORY OR JUNGLE NIGHTJAR 11 ins
E Palaearctic and Oriental: breeds E Siberia, Japan, southward to Burma, Indian subcontinent and Ceylon; winters S E Asia. Habitat in S of range higher afforested hills. Upperparts marbled and mottled with browns and blacks and grey vermiculations; oval white throat patch, breast grey; belly buff, barred brown. ♂ has white patches on first 4 primaries (rufous in ♀) and subterminal white bands on first 4 outer tail feathers. Feet flesh-brown, bill pinkish brown with black bristles, eyes dark brown. Nocturnal, taking flying ants and termites, grasshoppers, locusts, beetles, small wasps. Can run for short distances. Call: *tuc tuc tuc* repeated rapidly; less rapid *chuckoo chuckoo chuckoo*, repeated 3 to 14 times, fading into expiring whistle. Indian race also calls *uk-krukroo*, repeated every 2 seconds. Breeds February onwards in subcontinent, laying 2 eggs on ground, usually on slope and shaded. Those of Himalayan race white, marbled grey; Indian race: pale cream to warm buff, marked blackish and reddish brown. Incubation by ♀ and ♂ 16-17 days. **459**

Caprimulgus pectoralis *Caprimulgidae*
DUSKY NIGHTJAR 9 ins
Ethiopian: several races cover almost whole region; resident in wooded areas, including plantations of introduced pines and eucalypts in S Africa. ♂: generally warm brown and black, with wine-red wash, also on breast; broad brown collar on hindneck; white spots on first 4 primaries; apical third of 2 outermost tail feathers white; eye brown. ♀: wing spots washed buff, less white on tail. Nocturnal, resting on ground or lengthwise on branch by day. Hawks insects by night from special perch. Musical call, uttered across branch towards dusk or moonlit nights, varies throughout range; one form: *fwey wey wiriu*, third syllable descending and drawn out. Breeds August-November S Africa, laying 2 buffish or pinkish-white eggs, marked rufous or purple with underlying grey, on ground, often shaded by bush. Incubation and fledging much as other *Caprimulgus* species. **460**

Caprimulgus vociferus *Caprimulgidae*
WHIP-POOR-WILL 9-10 ins
Nearctic and Neotropical: breeds SE Canada, from Central Saskatchewan to Nova Scotia, E USA to NE Texas; also mountains S Arizona, New Mexico to Honduras; migratory in N of range, wintering from lowlands of Central S Carolina, Gulf of Florida, to Costa Rica. Habitat woodland near open country. Beautifully mottled and blending plumage characteristic of nightjars: browns, greys, black and buff. Pale stripe from bill over eye bounds black face and throat, which is divided by broader white stripe; short rounded wing-tips barred dark brown and rufous; tail, white-edged in ♂, projects well beyond folded wings. Eye, dark brown, reflects red in light. Insistent onomatopaeic call repeated endlessly by night; uttered with wing-tips below tail, head thrown back at soft preliminary *cluck*. Hunts insects on wing silently by night: many moths, beetles, gnats. Breeds May-June in N of range, laying 2 white or cream eggs, marbled pale brown, grey and lilac, on dead leaves. Incubation by ♀ *c.* 18 days; both parents feed young, who fly *c.* 2½ weeks. **461**

CARACARA,
  CRESTED see **Polyborus plancus**
  RED-THROATED see **Daptrius americanus**

Caracara plancus see **Polyborus plancus**

CARDINAL,
  COMMON see **Pyrrhuloxia cardinalis**
  GREEN see **Gubernatrix cristata**
  RED-CAPPED see under **Paroaria cucullata**
  RED-COWLED see under **Paroaria cucullata**
  RED-CRESTED see **Paroaria cucullata**
  YELLOW see **Gubernatrix cristata**

Carduelis caniceps see under **C. carduelis**

Carduelis cannabina see **Acanthis cannabina**

Carduelis carduelis *Fringillidae*
EURASIAN GOLDFINCH *c.* 4¾ ins
Palaearctic: combined breeding range with Grey-headed *C. caniceps*, (with which it hybridises freely) roughly rectangular between 30° and 60°N, 10°W and 90°E in Asia, with large gap between Caspian and Lake Balkash; also found Canary Is, Azores; introduced New Zealand, USA. Resident and migrant, northern birds winter in S of breeding range. Habitat: edges and clearings of coniferous and broadleaved forests; riverine strips; steppes with trees clumps; almost to tree limit in mountains; all types of cultivated and settled land with trees right into towns. Upperparts tawny brown; wings black with broad golden bar, white tips to flight feathers; black tail also white-tipped; back, white, crimson facial pattern; rump, underparts white. Legs pale flesh, bill pinkish white, eyes dark brown. Juvenile lacks head pattern, plumage streaked generally. Usually feeds low down on variety of seeds, especially thistles, fluttering round heads; on alders in winter; many insects taken in summer. Flocks in autumn. Dancing flight. ♂ displays gold wings to ♀. Call: constant, liquid *tswitt witt witt*;

aggressive *geeze*. Song developed from calls, pleasant, musical: from perch or air. Breeds April to September, solitary or in groups. ♀, attended ♂, builds compact nest of rootlets, grass, wool, plant down, bound cobwebs, softly lined; in end fork of rising or lateral branch, up to 45 ft, on variety of trees and bushes, usually broadleaved. 5 to 6 bluish-white eggs, marked dark chestnut-brown over grey, incubated ♀ 11-13 days; ♀ and ♂ feed young from throat; they fly 13-16 days. 2, occasionally 3 broods. **918**

Carduelis chloris *Fringillidae*
GREENFINCH   *c.* 5¾ ins
Palaearctic: almost all Europe, well into Scandinavia; NW Africa, Azores; Asia Minor, Palestine, N Iran; isolated population Turkestan but replaced E Asia by Oriental *C. sinica;* introduced New Zealand. Resident and migrant, northern birds moving SW in autumn. Habitat open mixed forest and edges, riverine strips with poplar, willows; orchards, plantations, olive and palm groves, cultivated land with hedges, roadsides, parks, gardens, well into European towns. ♂: generally olive green, darker above, yellower on rump, underparts, face, with bright patches on dark wings and forked, dark-tipped tail. ♀ duller, faintly streaked. Juvenile browner, clearly streaked. Legs pale flesh, bill whitish, eyes brown. Hops on ground, perches mainly trees. Flight less undulating than smaller relatives. Huge flocks autumn, winter. often with other seed-eaters. Calls: repeated *chup chup; cheu cheu;* querulous *jeee; tsooet* of alarm. Song, twittering blend of calls, from perch or in bat-like display flight. Takes variety of seeds, small fruit, buds; some insects, spiders, especially for young; regular at bird tables. Breeds early April to September, solitary or in small groups. ♀, attended ♂, builds substantial nest of moss, wool woven round twigs, rootlets; lined finer rootlets, hair, some feathers; in variety of sites 5 to 15 ft up or more, especially in wilder habitats; in thorny or evergreen bushes, ivy, creepers. 4 to 6 off-white to pale blue eggs, streaked and spotted red-brown over violet, indistinguishable from Crossbill, *Loxia curvirostra,* incubated ♀ 12-14 days; ♀ and ♂ feed young from throat; they fly 13-16 days. 2, occasionally 3 broods. **919**

Carduelis flammea see **Acanthis flammea**

Carduelis sinica see under **C. chloris**

Cariama cristata *Cariamidae*
RED-LEGGED SERIEMA   30 ins
Neotropical: E and Central Brazil to Uruguay, Paraguay, N Argentina, E Bolivia. Resident open semi-desert savannah. Upperparts from crown grey-brown; wings dark brown with white band; tail has black and terminal white bands; underparts from cheeks and throat to undertail pale grey, vermiculated dark grey on longer feathers; legs dark red. Hooked bill red with tuft or erect feathers at base, eyes light brown, facial skin bluish. Shy, running very fast, in preference to flying. Yelping contact call of parties intensified by ♂ in courtship when he displays his plumage to ♀. Diet varied: reptiles, including snakes, amphibians, insects; leaves and seeds. Beats large prey on ground to kill and soften it. Builds substantial nest in tree, 5 to 10 ft up; 2 buff eggs, marked red-brown, soon become dull during 25-26 day incubation; both parents tend young in nest until well grown. **241**

CARMINE BEE-EATER see **Merops nubicus**

Carpococcyx renauldi *Cuculidae*
RENAULD'S or
RED-BILLED GROUND CUCKOO   *c.* 24 ins
Oriental: Indochina to E Thailand; resident dense lowland and upland forests with undergrowth and boulders. Upperparts grey, washed green, flecked black; wingtips, tail purplish green; head, neck and breast black, glossed violet; underparts vermiculated greys; long legs, bill red, eyes light yellow, facial skin violet. Runs fast rather than fly. Noisy in dry season; ♂ perches in open, raising and lowering wings, raising head to utter rather harmonious call. Food mainly insects, some small reptiles and mammals. Builds

slight nest of leaves and sticks on ground or up to 12 ft in vegetation; ♀ and ♂ incubate 3 or 4 white eggs. **417**

Carpodacus mexicanus *Fringillidae*
HOUSE FINCH   5½ ins
Nearctic, Neotropical: breeds from N Wyoming, S British Columbia to S Mexico; E to W Kansas, Central Texas; mainly resident but some movement S in winter; introduced S New England, Long Island (NY). Habitat dry open country near water; suited by cultivation and increasing towns, villages. ♂: upperparts dull brown suffused red on crown, back; 'eyebrow', cheeks, rump red; wings, tail brown with pale feather edges; throat, breast red; underparts white, streaked dark brown. ♀, juvenile as ♂ without red; throat, breast as belly. Legs, bill yellowish horn, eyes dark brown. Call harsh chatter; song: 'clear, rolling warble of notes, varying greatly in pitch' (R. H. Pough). Food: seeds of wild plants, also wild and cultivated fruits. Breeds throughout summer; nest of locally available plant fibres, lined soft material, variously sited: holes in trees, buildings, nestboxes; old nests of swallows, orioles; shrubs, vines, cactus clumps, 4 or 5 pale blue eggs, lightly spotted black, incubated ♀. 2, sometimes 3 broods. **920**

CARRION CROW see **Corvus corone**

Casmerodius albus see **Egretta alba**

CASPIAN TERN see **Hydroprogne caspia**

CASSOWARY see **Casuarius casuarius**

Casuarius casuarius *Casuaridae*
AUSTRALIAN CASSOWARY   4½-5½ ft tall
Resident Australia (NE Queensland), New Guinea and adjacent islands in thick scrub and jungle. ♀ larger than ♂; flightless, with coarse black body feathers; bare blue neck and head surmounted by bony casque; red wattles; legs, bill and eyes light brown; innermost of 3 toes with sharp claw. Found singly, in pairs or sometimes small parties, with regular routes through undergrowth and across streams; swims well. Territorial and aggressive during breeding season. Calls deep boom or croak. Diet mainly vegetable: palm nuts, fruits and berries; some insects. Eggs laid July-August Queensland, 3 to 6, light to dark green with coarse granulated shells, in scrape on forest floor. Incubated *c.* 30 days by ♂, who also tends brood for *c.* 4 months. **3**

Catamblyrhynchus diadema *Emberizidae: Thraupinae*
PLUSH-CAPPED FINCH   5½ ins
Neotropical: N Venezuela, Colombia S to N Bolivia and NW Argentina E of Andes; W of Andes S to Lambayeque, Peru. Resident open woodland and scrubby slopes 5,000 to 10,000 ft. Upperparts including wings, tail, dark grey; forecrown deep yellow, feathers plush-like; lores, hindcrown, nape black; cheeks, all underparts chestnut; legs, stubby bill greyish, eyes dark brown. Habits little studied; apparently insectivorous.

CATBIRD see **Dumetella carolinensis**

Catharacta skua see **Stercorarius skua**

Cathartes aura *Cathartidae*
TURKEY VULTURE   25 ins
Nearctic and Neotropical: Canada to Tierra del Fuego and Falkland Islands. Resident South America but migratory farther north. Inhabits open desert, plains, plateaux, forest and jungle. Blackish or blackish brown with silvery wing linings; head and neck bare, bristly; legs pale flesh, bill whitish, cere red, facial skin purplish, eyes grey-brown. Numbers gather at carrion but more social when roosting. Flies and glides buoyantly for long periods. Group 'dances' on ground as display. Makes quiet hisses and grunts. Feeds almost entirely on carrion, locally on eggs, nestlings, rotting fruit. Breeding season variable from March in Florida. No real nest built. Lays 2 creamy

white eggs, with heavy brown markings, in caves, stumps, dense ground cover. ♂ and ♀ incubate for 38-41 days, and feed chicks which fly *c.* 11 weeks. **130**

Catharus fuscater *Muscicapidae : Turdinae*
SLATY-BACKED NIGHTINGALE THRUSH   7 ins
Neotropical: Costa Rica, Panama, NW Venezuela, Colombia; Central Peru to N. Bolivia; resident thick forests, 4,500 to 7,500 ft. Upperparts, including wings, tail and cheeks, dark leaden grey, blacker on crown and nape (dark brownish grey in Peruvian race); throat, breast, flanks lighter grey than back; centre belly white; legs, bill orange, eyes light. Song musical, bell-like. Feeds on ground on invertebrates. **675**

Catharus minimus see under **C. ustulatus**

Catharus ustulatus or Hylocichla ustulata
Muscicapidae : Turdinae
OLIVE-BACKED or SWAINSON'S THRUSH   7 ins
Nearctic: breeds from NW Alaska through most of N and W Canada to New England, mountains W Virginia, N. Michigan, Colorado, S California; winters S America to Argentina. Breeds spruce-fir forests, especially damp areas near water, and in young conifers mixed broad leaved trees; sometimes low scrub; woodland in winter. Upperparts generally olive brown; throat white with black streaks at side; cheeks, upper breast, flanks buffish, spotted black, thinning to white underparts; legs light brown, bill dark, eyes dark brown with buff orbits (helps distinguish from Grey-cheeked, *C. minimus*). Mellow whistles heard at night on migration. Usual calls abrupt *whit*, high-pitched *peep*. Musical, gurgling song, rising in pitch through dozen paired notes, some phrases repeated. Diet: mainly insects, from leaves, ground, e.g. grasshoppers, locusts in field, or in air. Breeds May to July, building neat nest of moss twigs, other plant material, sometimes hard lining, leaf-mould or mud; 3 to 15 ft in small, usually evergreen, tree or shrub. 3 or 4 pale greenish blue eggs, marked light brown; incubation by ♀; both parents feed young.

Catoptrophorus semipalmatus *Scolopacidae*
WILLET   14-17 ins
Nearctic and Neotropical: breeds E coast N America from Nova Scotia to Gulf of Florida, W Indies; inland from S Central Canada to Iowa and Nebraska as summer visitor; winters from Colombia, Venezuela to NE Brazil, Peru; eastern population breeds coastal marshes, beaches, islets, dunes; western by lakes; both winter salt marshes. Spring: upperparts pale grey-brown, darker streaks on head, neck, barred on back; rump white, tail mostly white; broad white bar on wings between black greater coverts and wingtips; underparts white, spotted and barred dark brown; legs blue-grey, bill, eyes dark. Pale grey above and white below in winter. Parties and flocks outside breeding season. Flies with shallow beats, holds wings upward after alighting. Swims easily with half-webbed feet. Spring call *pill will willet;* also loud *kay-ee*, repeated *kip kip, whee wee wee* in flight. Breeds May onwards, sometimes socially. Scrape or quite substantial nest of grass with finer lining, on raised ground if in marsh, holds 3 or 4 brownish or greenish buff eggs, blotched umber and lilac. Incubation by ♀ and ♂, who feign injury and are said to carry young. **283**

CATTLE EGRET see **Bubulcus ibis**

Cecropis daurica see **Hirundo daurica**

Cecropis senegalensis see **Hirundo senegalensis**

CEDAR WAXWING see **Bombycilla cedorum**

CELEBES STARLING see **Scissirostrum dubium**

Celeus elegans *Picidae*
YELLOW-CRESTED or CHESTNUT WOODPECKER 11 ins
Neotropical: Venezuela and Colombia E of Andes S to N Bolivia and Amazonian Brazil; Trinidad; resident forests, mangrove swamps, savannah, sea level to

4,000 ft. Mainly chestnut; crown and crest (raised when excited) buffy white to buff or chestnut according to race; crimson moustachial stripe (not in ♀); rump light buffy yellow or dark buff; inner webs flight feathers barred black and buff; tail black; flanks buffy white; bill ivory white, eyes reddish, facial skin dark grey. Forms small parties; noisy, with loud drumming by ♂ in breeding season. Diet: insects extracted from decayed wood, ants and termites from nests. Breeds April and May Trinidad, excavating hole in dead tree, 3 glossy white eggs incubated by ♀ and ♂, who both tend young.

Centrocercus urophasianus *Tetraonidae*
SAGE GROUSE ♀: 22: ♂: 28 ins
Nearctic: local W North America from S Saskatchewan, W Dakotas and N New Mexico W to Central Washington and E California; moving within area to foothills in summer and desert areas in winter. ♀: mottled yellow-brown, black and white all over from crown to long, pointed tail, except black belly. ♂: similar but has black face and throat split by white half collar and white breast with 2 yellow air sacs and wattles over dark brown eyes; legs greyish, bill dark. Lives in flocks of up to 100, feeding on leaves and shoots of sage in winter, leguminous plants in summer; also berries, seeds and (especially when young) insects; drinks twice a day. Clucking call in flight. In spring up to 400 ♂♂ gather on bare 'strutting ground' when they display, fanning tails, puffing white breasts and inflating sacs, each bout ending in loud *plop*. ♀♀ come to be mated, then lay 6 to 8 olive or greenish white eggs in lined scrape often under sage bush, incubating them for 22 days. Young fly in 1 to 2 weeks. ♂ does not assist at all.

Centropus senegalensis *Cuculidae*
SENEGAL COUCAL 16 ins
Ethiopian: SE Palaearctic (Egypt) and Ethiopian: Senegal and Gambia E to Somalia, S to Angola, Botswana, Transvaal, Rhodesia, Malawi; migratory in part of range. Habitat: bush and grassy open woodland, occasionally forest edge. Upperparts: back and wings chestnut, head and nape blue-black, washed iridescent green; upper tail coverts dark blue green, long tail iridescent green; underparts white; legs lead-grey, bill black, eyes red. Variety *'epomidis'* in W Africa: upper and underparts chestnut brown; head, neck, upper breast black with green iridescence. Remains in thick cover, hopping from bough to bough up bush, then flying heavily to next; largely crepuscular, giving 'water bubbling' call in evenings and night; also calls quiet *tok* at nest. Diet: locusts and other insects, small reptiles, rodents, nestlings. Breeding season variable; makes untidy nest of sticks and other plant material, thickly lined and loosely domed, with entrance at side, usually a few feet off ground. The 4 white eggs become stained during incubation. **418**

Centropus sinensis *Cuculidae*
COMMON COUCAL or CROW PHEASANT 18-21 ins
Oriental: widespread throughout region; resident in savannah grassland and dense secondary forest, cultivated land; up to 4,000 ft. Whole body from head to long tail black, glossed purple head, neck; dark blue on underparts; the whole finely streaked white; legs and deep, curved bill black, eyes crimson. Hunts mud banks of rivers, walking sedately with tail lifted, flying to cover with leisurely flap and glide action. Climbs trees by hops like relatives, often sunning at top after rain. Dull, booming call *boob boob boob boob* repeated and sometimes extended into melodious run up and down scale; also clicking *titektak*. Diet: insects, especially grasshoppers, ants; centipedes; snails; seeds and berries. Breeds February to September in India, ♀ and ♂ building ball or cup nest of grasses, sometimes in grass or in bush or tree. 2 to 5 white eggs incubated by ♀ and ♂, who both tend young. Probably 2 broods in parts of range. **419**

Centropus superciliosus *Cuculidae*
WHITE-BROWED COUCAL 17 ins
SE Palaearctic (S Arabia); Ethiopian: 3 races cover most of the region. Resident in reedbeds, dense riparian cover and tall elephant grass; also gardens and parks in S Africa. Differs from *C. senegalensis* in having crown and mantle dull brown (but black in S race *burchellii*) and distinct white 'eyebrow'; upper tail coverts and bases of tail feathers barred. Behaviour much as *C. senegalensis* with same call 'like water pouring out of bottle', uttered with head thrown back and bill pointed downwards; ♀ often answers ♂; also hoarse *tschak* and hiss of alarm. Diet omnivorous, taking many mice. Breeding season variable; nesting much as *C. senegalensis* but said to interlace twigs round nest and parent carries young between thighs when nest threatened; 2 to 4 white eggs laid. **420**

Centurus carolinus *Picidae*
RED-BELLIED WOODPECKER 8½ ins
Nearctic: Eastern USA, Great Lakes to Florida; resident woodland and its edge; orange groves. ♂: upperparts, including wing coverts and tail, barred black and white; wingtips black with white patch in centre; rump white; 2 black streaks down double-pointed tail; crown, nape red; underparts, including collar, grey-buff, flanks flecked darker. ♀ has forehead grey, flanks unmarked. Legs, bill blackish, eyes dark brown, orbits red. Works up trees jerkily and spirally; sometimes feeds on ground, taking insects and their larvae, especially beetles and bugs; also fruit (bores into oranges), seeds, acorns, occasionally corn. Rattling call, also lower-pitched *churr* and series of flicker-like (*Colaptes*) notes. Breeds May, making hole in tree or telegraph pole with 12 ins shaft; clutch 3 to 6 white eggs incubated by ♀ and ♂, who both tend young. **540**

Centurus rubicapillus see **Melanerpes rubicapillus**

Centurus uropygialis *Picidae*
GILA WOODPECKER 8¼ ins
Nearctic to Neotropical: extreme SW USA and Mexico. Resident saguaro (giant cactus) country, but extending now into cities. Very similar to *C. carolinus* but ♂ has only small red cap and ♀'s head is uniform grey-buff; both have yellow patch on belly. Noisy and conspicuous in desert habitat, with loud, high-pitched *yip* repeated 2 to 6 times rapidly; also 'conversational' rasping *churr*. Drums frequently on tin. Diet: cactus fruits and desert berries; also variety of insects. Breeds April and May, making holes in cacti, cottonwoods, mesquites and sycamores, 15 ft up or more; excavates excess holes, which are used by other species. 3 to 6 white eggs incubated by ♀ and ♂, who also feed young. 2 broods. **541**

Cephalopterus ornatus *Cotingidae*
UMBRELLABIRD 16-19 ins
Neotropical: Guyanas, Venezuela S øf Orinoco, Colombia E of Andes to E Peru, N Bolivia; Amazonian Brazil; forest from sea level to *c.* 4,000 ft, often on islands in larger rivers. (Long-wattled Umbrellabird, *C. penduliger*, sometimes regarded as race of *C. ornatus*, inhabits Pacific slopes Colombia from Cauca S to W Ecuador, ranging higher up mountains.) Uniformly glossy blue-black; erect crest of silky filoplumous feathers with white shafts; short, flat feathered wattle at base of neck. (*C. penduliger* has smaller, rounder crest, but cylindrical feathered lappet up to 18 ins long). ♀: duller, with smaller wattle. Legs slaty grey; bill: upper grey, lower yellowish horn; eyes white or light grey (brown in *C. penduliger*). Crow-like actions but little studied, as haunts treetops, where feeds on fruit. Spreads crest in display to cover crown and 'produces rumbling sound modified trachea and syrinx' (D. W. Snow). **590**

Cephalopterus penduliger see under **C. ornatus**

Cepphus columba *Alcidae*
PIGEON GUILLEMOT 14 ins
W Nearctic and E Palaearctic: rocky coasts and islands from Santa Barbara, California, round N Pacific to Kuriles; movement in winter N to Pribilof and Aleutian Islands. Very similar to Black Guillemot, *C. grylle*, except for black bar partly across white wing patch; underwing usually black. Swims near colonies in mornings, in intricate manoeuvres with calling and display of red gape; swims underwater with wings partly folded. Call a sibilant *see-oo;* also *tsit* reiterated into trill. Food bottom-living fish, crustaceans, molluscs and worms. Breeds from May in small colonies up to 50 pairs, similar sites to Black Guillemot but tunnels in banks Puget Sound. 2 eggs, like Black Guillemot but more heavily marked, incubated by ♀ and ♂ 28 days; young fledge 34-40 days, fed by parents.

Cepphus grylle *Alcidae*
BLACK GUILLEMOT *c.* 13½ ins
Holarctic, discontinuous but wide distribution along temperate, subarctic, arctic coasts, including Baltic; winters mainly offshore. Breeds rocky but not precipitous sea coasts, well up sheltered fjords, sea lochs and in harbours. Summer: uniform glossy blackish brown with broad white wing bar (underwing also mostly white), legs red, bill black (conspicuous red inside), eyes brown. Winter: upperparts barred black and white, giving grey effect; flight feathers, tail blackish-grey; underparts white. Often seen alone at sea or in small parties, diving in concert or displaying as Pigeon Guillemot, *C. columba*. Moves better on land than relatives and often hauls out on rocks; buoyant in water, taking off heavily but flying fast and low. Rather feeble whistle in breeding season, *cf* Pigeon Guillemot. Takes fish from near bottom and marine animals from wrack zone; plankton in winter near sea ice. Breeds socially from early May; 2 white to pale blue-green eggs marked dark brown and grey laid in crevice or under boulders, incubated by ♀ and ♂ 21-24 days; parents feed young *c.* 5 weeks. **344**

Cercomela familiaris *Muscicapidae*: *Turdinae*
FAMILIAR or RED-TAILED CHAT 6 ins
Ethiopian: distributed most of region from Ghana to Ethiopia and southern Africa, absent much of NE; resident rocky, wooded hillsides, scrub, cultivated lands and vicinity of man. Upperparts dark brown, underparts pale brown, lighter on belly; wings dusky, upper tail coverts russet, central tail feathers black, others russet, tipped black; ear coverts rust brown; legs, bill black, eyes brown. Juvenile duller, more spotted. Active, flicks wings sideways and forwards. Call repeated *tjree tjree tjree;* alarm squeaky *whee-chuc-chuc*. Arboreal, but takes insects off ground as well as on wing. Breeding season varies with range; builds large, bulky nest of plant materials and mud, thickly lined wool, hair, feathers; in shallow hole of tree, rock, bank, wall, very like European Robin, *Erithacus rubecula*. 3 or 4 bright greenish blue eggs, marked rufous or chestnut especially at big end. **676**

Cercotrichas galactotes *Muscicapidae*: *Turdinae*
RUFOUS BUSH CHAT 6 ins
Palaearctic, marginally Oriental, Ethiopian: S Iberia, NW Africa eastward between 30° and 40°N to Aral Sea, Lake Balkash: separate sedentary population across Africa between 10° and 20°N, extending to Somalia, Ethiopa. Northern population winters in area of southern birds, also NW Indian subcontinent. Habitat dry scrub and bare ground with scattered bushes; acacia savannah; vineyards, olive groves, roadsides, parks, gardens. Upperparts western race *C. g. galactotes* rufous, brightest on long, graduated tail with black and white tips outer feathers; eastern *syriacus* greyish olive brown except rump, tail; underparts pale buff; white stripe over, dark through eye; legs pale brown, bill mainly dark brown, eyes brown. Partly terrestrial and conspicuous, constantly spreading and moving tail up and down, also droops and flicks wings. Call: *tec tec;* song medley of 'clear, lark-like notes' (H. F. Witherby) delivered from high perch or in butterfly display flight. Food mainly larger insects, spiders, earthworms, usually from bare or shaded ground. Breeds second half May, early June in Mediterranean area; rather untidy nest of local plant debris, with lining finer stems, hair, often piece snake skin; usually in bush, stump, hedge of prickly pear, fairly low. 4 or 6 greyish or greenish grey eggs, densely marked umber and ashy brown. 2 broods in part of range. **677**

Cereopsis novaehollandiae *Anatidae*
CAPE BARREN GOOSE *c.* 32-34 ins
Australasian: breeds islands off W Australia, S Australia and in Bass Strait; occasionally visits nearby mainland in summer. Habitat: beaches, rocky prominences and grassed areas. Ash grey, head paler with white crown; scapulars and wing coverts blotched with dark grey, terminal half of primaries and tips of secondaries black; tail black with grey under coverts. Long legs pink descending to black feet, bill black with greenish yellow cere, eyes dark brown. In small groups; grazes on plants, usually grass, on land at edge of lakes and seashore, only enters sea when pursued. Wary, flies strongly. Call: grunt; ♂ may also trumpet. Breeds May or June onwards in strongly defended territories, usually on W side of island amongst scrub. Nest is heap of plant debris lined with grey down, occasionally built in dense scrub. 3 to 5 white eggs, incubated by both parents; young leave territory *c.* 6 weeks, forming nomadic flocks. **109**

Certhia brachydactyla see under **C. familiaris**

Certhia familiaris *Certhiidae*
TREECREEPER or BROWN CREEPER *c.* 5 ins
Holarctic, Neotropical: main range lies across Eurasia between 50° and 60°N, across N America between 40° and 50°N, but with many extensions and outliers, e.g. S Europe, between Black Sea and Caspian, Himalayas and Chinese Mountains; W coast Pacific to Alaska; through Mexico into Central America. Resident dark spruce, fir forests, lowland to subalpine, also mixed forests and their edges e.g. taiga; to 7,000 ft (Himalayas), 8,500 ft (Guatemala); also in European broad-leaved woods, parks, riversides where Short-toed Tree-creeper, *C. brachydactyla,* does not occur. Upperparts from crown brown, streaked pale buff, rufous on rump; wings with buff bars; whitish 'eyebrow'; underparts from chin pure white; legs pale brown, bill mainly dark brown, eyes brown. Climbs spirally up trunks, along undersides of branches, feet well apart, stiff graduated tail acting as woodpecker's. Short undulating flight from top of one tree to foot of next. Often solitary but with tit flocks autumn, winter. Roosts clefts or characteristically excavates body hole in soft wood or *Sequoia* bark. ♂ chases ♀ in display and feeds her. Calls shrill *tsuu,* often rapidly repeated, softer *tsit;* song thin, high-pitched, recalling Goldcrest, *Regulus regulus,* but louder, with terminal flourish. Food chiefly insects and larvae, spiders and eggs, wood-lice. Breeds early April to early July Britain; ♀ and ♂ squeeze nest into narrow crack, especially behind bark, ivy, sometimes in walls, nestboxes; substantial foundation twigs, wood chips, then cup (often oval) of plant debris, lined bark, feathers, hair, wool; ground level to 30 ft. 5 to 7 white eggs, red-brown markings zoned at big end; incubated mainly ♀ 14-15 days; young, fed ♀ and ♂, fly 14-15 days. Sometimes 2 broods. **813**

Ceryle rudis *Alcedinidae*
PIED KINGFISHER 10 ins
S Palaearctic, Ethiopian: Cyprus (visitor), Asia minor, Iran, Egypt, all sub-Sahara Africa except Somalia; also mainland Oriental region. Common alongside rivers, lakes, sea shore; small groups fishing from perches on bare boughs, wires, boats' masts; often hovers rather clumsily over water, then plunges in. Entirely black and white; mainly black above, streaked and spotted white, especially wings, tail; white below apart from two black bands across chest in ♂, one incomplete in ♀; low crest, long stout bill. Noisy at nesting colony, sharp *keek keek* and repeated jingling call. 3 to 6 white eggs in large chamber end of long tunnel in bank, excavated by ♀ and ♂; both parents feed young and may share incubation. **485**

Cettia cetti *Muscicapidae: Sylviinae*
CETTI'S WARBLER 5½ ins
Palaearctic: patchy distribution E from England (recent colonist), Spain, N Africa across S Europe, Turkey, Central Asia to 80°E. Mainly resident, eastern population winters Iraq to Pakistan; marked population decline in severe winters. Habitat: dense bushes on stream banks, near marshes, reedbeds; occasionally away from water. Uniform dark chestnut upperparts; dull white 'eyebrow'; underparts greyish white, barred brown under tail; broad graduated tail often cocked; legs brown, bill black, paler at base, eyes dark sepia. Very secretive, skulking in thick cover. Song: distinctive loud outburst *chee, chewee, chewee . . .* ; also tremulous *twic,* stuttering alarm note. Feeds on small insects, spiders, snails, earthworms. Breeds from end April onwards; ♀ builds neat cup nest of grass, lined fine grass, hair, in bush near ground. 3 to 5 brick red eggs. Young fed both parents. **732**

Cettia diphone *Muscicapidae: Sylviinae*
CHINESE BUSH WARBLER ♀: 5, ♂: 5¾ ins
E Palaearctic: breeds China from 35°N to S Mongolia, Manchuria, N Korea; also Japan, Taiwan, N Philippines; winters (October to April) SE China. Variety of bushy grassy habitats, always near water. Upperparts grey-brown, redder on crown, tail: dark eye-stripe, buffish 'eyebrow' more conspicuous in worn plumage; underparts dingy white; yellow brown on breast, flanks, under tail coverts; bill brown. ♀ smaller. Very skulking; call distinctive repeated *tyok;* short melodious song delivered from crown of tree or other concealed perch throughout day. Mainly insectivorous. Breeds May to July; building deep cup nest of broad leaved grasses woven around twigs in bush, near ground. 4 or 5 dark pink-red eggs, occasionally speckled darker. Possibly 2 broods.

Cettia squameiceps or Cisticola squameiceps *Muscicapidae: Sylviinae*
SHORT-TAILED BUSH WARBLER 4 ins
E Palaearctic: breeds E Siberia, Korea, E Manchuria, S Sakhalin, Japan; winters Taiwan, SE China to Indochina, Thailand, Burma, Philippines. Habitat: mixed and broadleaved forests, riverine alders with nettle ground layer in E Siberia; lowlands (Hokkaido) to *c.* 4,500 ft (Kyushu) in Japan, thick undergrowth usually by water. Upperparts dark brown; fine streaks on head, white 'eyebrow', black eyestripe; underparts buffish, paler on throat and belly; very short dark tail. Very active but keeps much to cover; in family parties, or singly on migration and in winter. Alarm call: rattling *chmok chmok;* song: high-pitched *si-si-si,* repeated ten times, gradually rising and accelerating in tempo. Food: insects from ground, e.g. small beetles in winter in Burma. Breeds from late May E Siberia; cup nest of dead leaves and broad stems, lined fine grass, in hollow in bank of stream, under roots or fallen tree, at base of bush. 5 to 7 pale pink eggs, densely marked reddish or purplish over lilac. **733**

CETTI'S WARBLER see **Cettia cetti**

CEYLON CRIMSON-BACKED WOODPECKER see **Chrysocolaptes lucidus stricklandi**

CHACHALACA see **Ortalis vetula**

CHACHALACA, RUFOUS-VENTED see **Ortalis ruficauda**

Chaetorhynchus papuensis *Dicruridae*
MOUNTAIN DRONGO 8 ins
Australasian: New Guinea; resident mountain forests, 2,000 to 4,800 ft. Black, head and body glossed blue, including short crest; hidden white at base scapulars; tail nearly square; legs, rather heavy, hooked bill black, eyes dark brown. Sits upright like flycatcher on branch in lower storeys of forest.

CHAFFINCH see **Fringilla coelebs**

CHAFFINCH, BLUE see under **Fringilla coelebs**

Chalcites lucidus *Cuculidae*
SHINING CUCKOO 6½ ins
New Zealand: widespread summer visitor, up to 4,000 ft and including Stewart I, Chatham Is, in habitat of its chief fosterers Grey Warbler, *Gerygone igata,* and endemic Chatham Island *G. albofrontata;* performs remarkable 2,000 mile migration mainly over ocean to Solomon Is, Bismarck Archipelago; sometimes winters North Island. ♂: upperparts from crown metallic green, glinting gold or coppery; flight feathers dark brown; longish tail terminally barred dark brown, outer feathers barred white; cheeks, underparts white, finely barred glossy green, looking black at distance. ♀ similar but crown, nape more purplish bronze, bars on belly more bronze. Legs black, soles of feet yellow, rather broad bill black, eyes dark brown. Juvenile striped on flanks; bars on throat, breast indistinct. Call: clear *tsee-ew* or *tsiu,* heard on night passage, also by day when several birds chase in and out of tree clump. Ventriloquial song rendered in Maori: *kui kui whiti-whiti ora tio-o.* Diet: mainly insects, especially hairy larvae. Courtship feeding when pairing. Egg, greenish or bluish white to dark olive brown, laid in nests of Grey Warbler, other small passerines, including introduced species.

Chalcites xanthorhynchus *Cuculidae*
VIOLET CUCKOO 6½ ins
Oriental: widespread resident, nomad, local migrant W to Assam, inhabiting evergreen forest, also gardens, e.g. in Sarawak, and edges of mangrove swamps. ♂: upperparts and breast glossy violet, underparts heavily barred; legs grey or olive-green, bill yellow, base red, eyes and orbits red. ♀: upperparts bronze green, bill dull yellow. Juvenile: upperparts barred rufous and brown, underparts white, barred brown. Often sits sluggishly in tree and creeps quietly up and down branches, taking off to hawk fly and return. Call: high-pitched *kievik kievik,* also monosyllabic whistles. Diet: flies, ants, beetles and other insects often taken on wing; also fruit. Lays pure white or pink eggs, with zone of reddish spots at big end, in nests of Little Spider-hunter, *Arachnothera longirostris,* and Sunbird, *Aethopyga.*

Chalcomitra senegalensis *Nectariniidae*
SCARLET-CHESTED SUNBIRD 6 ins
Ethiopian: Senegal E to Sudan, down E side Africa to Rhodesia; also Angola, Natal, E Cape (S Africa); resident, some races partly migratory, forest edge, open woodland, savannah, parkland, riverine acacias, cultivated areas, gardens. ♂: satiny dark brown or blackish with metallic green cap and bib, scarlet breast. ♀: upperparts dull dark brown; wings, tail washed bronze, primary wing coverts edged white; underparts heavily mottled. Legs, bill black, eyes dark brown. Juvenile like ♀, with dusky throat. Noisy, especially when in party; best known calls: repeated *tssp teee tee,* sharp *zit* in flight; song, loud trilling warble. Takes flying ants and larger insects than most sunbirds, hawked on wing. Breeding season variable throughout range. Nest-site, sometimes associated with hornets' nest, often used successive years; ♀ builds large oval of various plant materials, usually hanging from fairly low branch. Usually 2 white, cream or bluish white eggs, heavily marked brown or grey, incubated ♀. **820**

Chalcophaps indica *Columbidae*
EMERALD DOVE *c.* 10 ins
Oriental, Australasian: N Indian subcontinent, Assam and Hainan S and E to Philippines, New Guinea and E Australia. Habitat: wooded country. ♂: brownish pink with brilliant bronzed emerald green upperparts, crown and neck grey, prominent white forehead and eyebrows, band of white-fringed feathers across lower back, white-bordered vinous grey patch on shoulder; rump grey, tail brown and grey with broad black cross-band broken in middle. ♀: less white on forehead, white patch on shoulder and white barring on rump less pronounced; central tail feathers redder brown. Legs pinkish grey, bill orange-red or brown with purplish base and ivory tip, eyes dark brown with purplish orbital skin. Race in SE New Guinea across to E Australia differs in ♂ having no white or grey on head and neck, and ♀ having chestnut in place of grey on tail feathers apart from outer two. Single or in pairs, often in clearings or on earth roads, ground feeder taking seeds, grain, fruits and small animals, chiefly termites; flight silent, low and swift. Call: deep soft moaning note repeated at intervals. Breeds all months; fairly compact twig platform usually 5 to 10 ft up in trees or shrubs. 2 creamy buff eggs, incubated *c.* 14 days; young fly *c.* 12 days. **351**

Chamaea fasciata *Muscicapidae: Timaliinae*

WRENTIT 6½ ins

Nearctic: resident most of California W of higher Sierra Nevada and SE deserts, N into Oregon and S to NW Lower California; dense chaparral, evergreen scrub in lower mountains, deciduous thickets along watercourses, damp slopes with mixed shrubs and trees; shrub understorey and clearings in redwood areas. Upperparts from crown to long, rounded tail dark brown; pale edges to flight feathers of short wings; cheeks greyish; underparts buff-brown with long dark streaks; legs, short bill blackish; eyes white. Pairs for life, occupying territory of ¾ to 2½ acres all year, though immatures wander into open woodland. Tends to stay in thick cover, rarely flying more than 20 yds, but hopping rapidly from twig to twig, searching for insects; berries important autumn, winter. Many calls include rasping purr; ♂'s song series of *yips*, speeding up into trill; ♀'s song lacks trill; often answer each other; also both sing slower series: *weeka weeka weeka*. Deep cup nest of plant fibres bound or decorated cobwebs, lichen, usually 1 to 5 ft up in dense canopy near 'edge', e.g. path. 3 to 5 pale greenish blue eggs incubated 16 days; young fly 16 days.

CHANTING GOSHAWK,
DARK see **Melierax metabates**
PALE see **Melierax canorus**

Charadrius alexandrinus *Charadriidae*

KENTISH OR SNOWY PLOVER 6¼ ins

Cosmopolitan: Holarctic, N Temperate, S to Cape of Good Hope, Tasmania and parts of W coast S America; inland in Central Asia, E Africa, W USA; sedentary and migratory apparently throughout range. Habitat: sand and shingle shores and inland equivalents by rivers and lakes in steppes and deserts; also coral limestone coasts in tropics. Resembles Ringed Plover, *C. hiaticula*, but black marks reduced in ♂, not meeting across breast, while ♀ lacks dark mark on forehead. Legs lead grey, bill black, eyes dark brown. Habits much as Ringed Plover but runs even faster. Parties and small flocks in autumn. Usual call *wit wit wit*, run into trill as 'song' during wavering display flight, when body thrown from side to side with wings stretched. Food: insects, their larvae and pupae, also small water animals. Breeds May onwards in N temperate zone; usually bare but sometimes lined and adorned scrape in sand in which 3 stone buff eggs, spotted and scrawled black, are often partly or largely buried. Incubation by ♀ and ♂ *c.* 26½ days; parents tend young who fly in *c.* 6 weeks; possibly two broods at times. **256**

Charadrius cucullatus *Charadriidae*

HOODED DOTTEREL *c.* 8½ ins

Southern Australia and Tasmania; resident on sandy shores and by inland salt lakes. Upperparts dark brown; head and throat black with band round neck enclosing white nape; underparts white, sides of breast with black crescents; white stripe on wings, outer tail coverts white; legs flesh pink, bill orange, tip dark, eyes brown. Behaviour and habits much as Ringed Plover, *C. hiaticula*. Feeds on tidal zone insects and small water animals. Breeds September to January. Scrape in sand close to tideline holds 2 or 3 pale stone eggs, marked purplish black and lavender; incubation and fledging as Ringed Plover. **257**

Charadrius hiaticula *Charadriidae*

RINGED PLOVER *c.* 7½ ins

Palaearctic: temperate to arctic, from Iceland and Ireland to Bering Straits, also Nearctic Greenland and Baffin Island; northern populations migratory. Habitats: sand and shingle shores, low rocky islands, inland up rivers and beside lakes; tundra moorland; mainly sandy and muddy shores and estuaries outside breeding season. Upperparts, including hindcrown, dark brown; forehead white, front of crown black, joining stripe from bill to eye above broad white bar on brown wing; tail brown in centre, black subterminal band edged white; legs orange yellow, bill yellow, tip dark, eyes brown. Immature, resembles Kentish Plover, *C. alexandrinus*, but legs yellow. Characteristic plover actions, running and stopping short to dip quickly at prey; bobs head rapidly when agitated; flies low with syncopated wingbeat. Forms small flocks, often with other waders. Usual call *turrp* and liquid *tooi*, repeated to make 'song' in aerial displays; also elaborate actions on ground. Food as Kentish Plover. Breeds from March in S, much later in far N, making scrape, sometimes lined small pebbles, in sand, shingle, turf, even on rock. Usually 4 stone buff eggs with black speckles and scrawls, incubated by ♀ and ♂ 24-25 days; young tended by parents who often feign injury when endangered, fly *c.* 25 days; 2, perhaps sometimes 3 broods. **258**

Charadrius melanops *Charadriidae*

BLACK-FRONTED DOTTEREL 7 ins

Continental Australia and Tasmania, colonising New Zealand (Hawkes Bay) since *c.* 1960. Resident shingle and mud banks of rivers (as in NZ), lakes and pools. Upperparts brown; forehead, eyestripe, V band across breast black; white 'eyebrows' meet behind crown; wings with black tips and white area shown in flight, scapulars dark chestnut; upper tail coverts rust red, tail dark brown edged white; throat and underparts white; legs orange-pink, bill red, tip black, eyes dark brown with red orbits. Behaviour much as other ringed plovers but flight 'jerky and dipping'. Forms small flocks in winter. Typical calls: high-pitched whistle, soft *tink tink*, clicking *tik tik tik*. Food: water insects, small crustaceans, worms; seeds occasionally. Breeds August onwards S Australia, NZ; April onwards in N. Scrape, sometimes lined pebbles and usually near water, holds 3 stone or greyish-yellow eggs, marked brown and lavender. Incubation (*c.* 18 days) and fledging as other ringed plovers. **259**

Charadrius pecuarius *Charadriidae*

KITTLITZ'S SAND PLOVER *c.* 6½ ins

SE Palaearctic (NE Egypt) and throughout Ethiopian region, including Madagascar; distinct race St Helena. Resident and partial migrant: sand banks of lakes, e.g. Lake Victoria, rivers and coastal beaches; open grassland near water and dry sandy areas at some distance from it. Upperparts brownish black with blackish shoulders and wings; black band behind white forehead, black stripe from bill to eye, white collar joining up over eye with forehead; underparts mainly brown, with rich chestnut lower neck and breast; legs and bill black, eyes brown. Immature no black on head. Usually in small parties, but sometimes up to 100; flies low with feet showing beyond tail. Calls: *pi-peep* in flight, *chirrrt* of alarm. Food: small beetles, other insects and water animals. Breeds throughout year in parts of range. Scrape in sand, not always near water, holds 2 stone buff eggs, heavily marked black and grey-brown, usually buried in sand. Incubation 23-26 days; fledging much as other ringed plovers. **260**

Charadrius tricollaris *Charadriidae*

THREE-BANDED PLOVER *c.* 7 ins

Ethiopian: S from Nigeria and Sudan; distinct race Madagascar. Haunts inland waters, e.g. lakes, lagoons, reservoirs, even fast-flowing rivers with bare shores; also salt marshes. Upperparts rich dark brown; forehead, stripe over eye, cheeks and throat white; two black bars across chest with white between; wingbar and terminal bar on tail white as are underparts; legs dark flesh, bill black, base red, eyes brown with red wattled orbits. Feathers of juvenile's upperparts tipped buff, chest-bands less distinct. Usually in pairs at water's edge, feeding like other ringed plovers. Flight call loud *tiuu-it tiuu-it*; high-pitched *tui tui* of alarm uttered with body leaning forward and bobbing up and down. Food as other ringed plovers. Breeding season variable throughout range. Shallow scrape in sand, sometimes on mound, adorned with pebbles and shells, holds usually 2 eggs resembling Kittlitz's Plover, *C. pecuarius*, but not buried. Incubation and fledging much as relatives. **261**

Charadrius vociferus *Charadriidae*

KILLDEER *c.* 9½ ins

Nearctic and Neotropical: N Canada S throughout N America with populations W Indies, Peru, W Chile; northern birds migrate S, wintering from S British Columbia in W and New York in E to N South America. Habitat: grasslands and cultivated fields, even lawns near houses; winters on grasslands and sea shores. Upperparts dark brown; white stripe from forehead through eye bordered black above and below; white band round chin extends to collar, above two black bands with white between; underparts white; wings blackish with white bar; upper tail coverts and tail chestnut with white-edged black terminal band; legs dull yellow, bill black, eyes brown. Behaves much as Ringed Plover, *C. hiaticula*, but more excitable and noisy, typical call *kill-dee* giving name; prolonged trill of excitement and many other notes recorded. Food almost all animal: insects, spiders, molluscs, crustaceans, worms. Spring displays by pair hovering in air and calling, also on ground. Breeds Texas from March, later farther N. Scrape, lined or with rim ornamented, holds usually 4 light buff eggs, well marked blackish brown. Incubation by ♀ and ♂ *c.* 27-28 days; young tended by both parents; probably two broods in N of range. **262**

CHAT,
CAPE ROBIN see **Cossypha caffra**
CLIFF see **Thamnolaea cinnamomeiventris**
CRIMSON see **Ephthianura tricolor**
FAMILIAR see **Cercomela familiaris**
KAROO see **Erythropygia coryphaeus**
MOCKING see **Thamnolaea cinnamomeiventris**
MOUNTAIN see **Oenanthe monticola**
ORANGE see **Ephthianura aurifrons**
PALM see **Dulus dominicus**
RED-TAILED see **Cercomela familiaris**
RUFOUS BUSH see **Cercotrichas galactotes**
SNOWY-CROWNED ROBIN see **Thamnolaea coronata**
SOOTY see **Myrmecocichla nigra**
WHITE-CROWNED CLIFF see **Thamnolaea coronata**
WHITE-FRONTED see **Ephthianura albifrons**
WHITE-HEADED BLACK see under **Myrmecocichla nigra**
WHITE-THROATED ROBIN see **Cossypha humeralis**
YELLOW-BREASTED see **Icteria virens**

Chauna chavaria *Anhimidae*

NORTHERN OR BLACK-NECKED SCREAMER 34 ins

Neotropical: NW Venezuela and N Colombia; resident in grasslands and marshes. Dark grey with green gloss; crown and crest grey, rest of head white, neck black; under wing coverts white; legs, facial skin red, bill light horn, eyes brown; spur on forward edge of wing. Habits much as other screamers see *Anhima cornuta*: utters sonorous trumpeting call. Diet mainly stems and seeds of water plants, some damage to crops alleged. Builds shallow nest of local plants in marsh; lays 2 white eggs, incubated by ♀ and ♂ *c.* 6 weeks; young leave nest at once and follow parents.

Chelictinia riocourii *Accipitridae*

SWALLOW-TAILED KITE 14½ ins

Ethiopian: Senegal and Gambia E to Somalia, S to N Kenya; breeds deserts or semi-deserts, migrating S to savannah October to February; N and E April to June. Upperparts, including crown, deeply forked tail, most of wings, grey, washed sooty between scapulars (blackish outer margins); primaries pale grey, white inner webs to secondaries; entire underparts from forehead and cheeks white, except for long black patch on under wing coverts; small black patch behind eye; legs yellow, cere and bill grey, eyes red. ♀ slightly larger. Immature much browner. Generally in small parties of 5 to 10, roosting in trees. Spends much of day on wing, hovering *c.* 50 ft up, plunging on prey, chiefly insects, sometimes taken in flight; also small mammals and reptiles: young fed on skinks (W Africa). Silent on migration, noisy at colonies and roosts; rasping *tchee tchi tchi*, rapidly repeated *ti ti ti ti*, softer whistle and feeble mew. Breeds May-June in small colonies, building stick nests usually in acacias 15 to 25 ft up, sometimes close to other species, e.g. Brown Harrier, *Circaetus cinereus*, in Kenya; lays 4 pale sandy eggs, speckled brown. **141**

Chelidoptera tenebrosa *Bucconidae*

SWALLOW-WING   6½ ins
Neotropical; generally distributed S America E of Andes S to N Bolivia and Brazil; forest edge, savannah, clearings, riverside. Generally blackish with long swallow-like wings, white underneath; rump and under tail coverts also white; belly chestnut bordered pale grey; curved, slender bill black. Perches in pairs on stag-headed trees beside rivers, darting out to take flying insects. Breeds, sometimes in groups of 3 or 4 pairs, March to May along Orinoco, August to December Surinam, in long dry season. Excavates slanting tunnel in bank or level ground, laying 2 white eggs in bare chamber. Sometimes sparsely lined (F. Haverschmidt).

CHESTNUT
   CUCKOO see **Piaya cayana**
   QUAIL THRUSH see **Cinclosoma castanotum**
   WOODPECKER see **Celeus elegans**

CHESTNUT-BELLIED
   NUTHATCH see **Sitta canadensis**
   SAND GROUSE see **Pterocles exustus**

CHESTNUT-BREASTED
   FINCH see **Donacola castaneothorax**
   WREN see **Cyphorhinus thoracicus**

CHESTNUT-CAPPED PUFFBIRD see **Bucco macrodactylus**

CHESTNUT-SIDED SHRIKE VIREO see **Cireolanius meliophrys**

CHESTNUT-TAILED
   FOLIAGE GLEANER see under **Automolus leucophthalmus**
   THORNBILL see **Acanthiza uropygialis**

Chibia bracteata see under **Sphecotheres flaviventris**

CHICKADEE BLACK-CAPPED see **Parus atricapillus**

CHICKEN, GREATER PRAIRIE see **Tympanuchus cupido**

CHIFFCHAFF see **Phylloscopus collybita**

CHILEAN
   PLANTCUTTER see **Phytotoma rara**
   TINAMOU see **Nothoprocta perdicaria**

CHINESE BUSH WARBLER see **Cettia diphone**

CHIN-SPOT PUFFBACK see **Batis molitor**

Chionis alba *Chionidae*

YELLOW-BILLED SHEATHBILL   16-17 ins
Antarctic and subantarctic: breeds mainly S Atlantic Ocean, e.g. S Georgia, S Sandwich, S Orkneys, S Shetlands into antarctic archipelago beyond 65°S; partly sedentary even in far south, but wanders in some numbers to Falkland Is and S Patagonia. Pure white; bare pinkish-yellow facial patch with warty caruncles round heavy bill, which has bluish green sheath over base of upper mandible; rest bill yellow or flesh pink, legs blue-grey, eyes dark brown. Small spur at 'wrist' used in fighting. Described as walking like rail, flying like pigeon, behaving like domestic hen; but can run, hop, take off and land from one foot. Reluctant to fly or swim but seen hundreds of miles from land. Very tame and inquisitive. Bowing display; pairs probably for life. Omnivorous: expert scavenger, robbing penguins of food by jumping on chick's back and taking regurgitated krill, also robs nests by cooperative action; eats carrion, faeces, sea-weed (presumably for its animal life), seal afterbirths. Starts building end November; nest of stones, sticks, feathers, debris, in crevice, forming scattered colony often close to penguin rookery; sometimes in petrel burrows. 2 or 3 greyish or off-white eggs, marked dark brown, incubated ♀ and ♂ c. 29 days. Young (often

only one survives) flies 7-8 weeks, tended by both parents. **315**

CHIPPING SPARROW see under **Helmitheros vermivorus**

Chiroxiphia linearis *Pipridae*

LONG-TAILED MANAKIN   ♂: 8 (tail 4) ins
Neotropical: S Mexico to Costa Rica, resident mangroves, woodland edge and secondary growth, sea level to 4,500 ft. ♂: mainly black, back bright light blue, crown red, central tail feathers elongated; legs orange, bill black, eyes dark brown. ♀ almost uniformly dull green, but underparts slightly paler; central tail feathers somewhat elongated. Feeding habits as other manakins. Many notes known, especially call *to-le-do*. Courtship most intense April-May at start of rains: 2 ♂ perform together, 'bouncing' with mewing call and cart-wheeling in turns on low perch; in second form they neatly change places; ♀ may join in (Paul Slud). Breeds May, suspending cup nest of leaves, fronds and moss 7 to 10 ft up in bush. Clutch 2 eggs, incubation and fledging much as other manakins, e.g. *Manacus manacus*. **587**

Chlamydera maculata *Ptilinorhynchidae*

SPOTTED BOWER BIRD   c. 11 ins
Australia: Western race, *C. m. guttata*, Pilbara district, W. Australia, S to c. 30°S, and to Central Australia and N to S Australia; *maculata*, Cloncurry Range, Queensland, E almost to coast, inland S to N Victoria. Habitat: scrubby, relatively low rainfall areas; *guttata* often associated with native fig *Ficus platypoda*. Brownish, mottled with rufous and golden buff, small erectile mantle or neck frill pink (conspicuous when raised, glistens in direct sunlight), tail tipped orange-brown; *guttata* darker and more conspicuously spotted. Legs olive-green, bill black, eyes brown. Juveniles have more heavily marked throat and breast, lack crest. Territorial; small flocks outside breeding season; flight straight with rapid wingbeats. Feeds on fruit, also insects, especially when young. Calls: squeals, clicking and odd sounds; accurate mimic. ♂ builds (April to August) simple double-walled bower never far from water and roughly similar to Satin Bower Bird, *Ptilinorhynchus violaceus*, used for display to ♀ although spectators may also attend; outer part of each wall thin twigs, inner grass stems and long thin leaves (sometimes painted with mixture of saliva and plant material), concealed beneath trees, one end mainly decorated with bleached bones and shells (wide range of bright objects also used), other end large stick platform, whole structure c. 10 to 20 ins high and c. 15 to 30 ins long. Displays start September and breeding c. October, varying in areas of less regular rainfall; shallow twig nest scantily lined leaves and thin twigs, in tree or bush within few 100 yds of bower; 2 grey to greenish eggs, sometimes with darker markings; ♀ incubates. **986**

Chlidonias hybrida *Laridae*

WHISKERED TERN   c. 10 ins
Palaearctic, Ethiopian, Oriental, Australasian: S Europe, Tunisia, SW Asia, Central Middle East across to Turkestan; eastern half of Southern Africa S of L. Victoria, India, E China, Australia and subspecies *C. h. albostriatus* South I., New Zealand. Some birds move S in winter. Habitat: marshy lagoons and swamp pools with plenty of aquatic vegetation; larger, more open waters in winter. Grey with black cap and conspicuous white streak running back from bill to nape of neck, white under tail coverts and edge to slightly forked grey tail. In winter forehead and underparts white; immature similar but crown brownish and mantle mottled. African race, *sclateri*, generally much darker. Legs dark red, bill dark red but blackish in winter, eyes red-brown. Often seen skimming over water like swallow taking insects, also feeds on small fish and other aquatic animals; awkward walker. Usually perched on stone or post sticking out of water. Call: two syllabled rasping sound. Breeds late May onwards in Europe; loosely built heap of weeds floating in shallow water among rushes or other aquatic vegetation to which it may be attached; in colonies in marshes or similar wet places. *Albostriatus*

makes scrape in sand amongst large stones, October onwards. Usually 3 bluish green eggs spotted with blackish brown and ashy grey, chiefly incubated ♀ c. 21 days, both parents tend young. **319**

Chlidonias niger *Laridae*

BLACK TERN   c. 9½ ins
Holarctic: nominate race breeds from SW Europe (local Iberia) into W Asia mainly between 40° and 60°N to about 95°E; winters lakes, rivers and coasts of tropical Africa S to Angola and Tanzania; Nearctic race, *C. n. surinamensis*, breeds from E Alaska S over most of Canada to Pennsylvania across to central California, winters S America down to Chile. Habitat: inland marshes, ponds and lakes when breeding, visiting adjacent grasslands; winters also on coastal and inshore waters. Head and body black, short notched tail, broad wings slate grey above and paler below. Legs dark red-brown, bill black, eyes dark brown. Winter: forehead and forecrown white, rest of crown and nape sooty brown, throat, sides of neck and underparts white, rest of upperparts pale slate grey, primaries and secondaries greyer. Immature: forehead white, crown and nape sooty brown, mantle and back mottled blackish brown, scapulars greyer, wings mostly dark grey; underparts white with dark brown patch on sides of upper breast; legs dark yellowish, bill blackish. Feeds inland mainly on insects on wing or ground, sometimes aquatic animals from water by shallow diving; otherwise picks up small fish and invertebrates from surface of water while hovering briefly. Call: monosyllabic *kik, kik*. Breeds May onwards in loose colonies on marshes or shallow lakes; 3 olive or buff eggs heavily marked with dark brown and ash, in hollow in floating mass of vegetation, old nests of other species or cup of stems lined with finer matter. Both parents incubate c. 21 days and tend young, who fly c. 4 weeks. **320**

Chloephaga hybrida *Anatidae*

KELP GOOSE   30 ins
Neotropical: Lesser Kelp Goose, *C. h. hybrida*, coast of S Chile to Tierra del Fuego; Greater Kelp Goose, *malvinarum*, Falkland Is. Habitat: rocky oceanic shores; often seen hopping from rock to rock feeding on sea-weeds, usually in pairs and fairly tame. ♂: white plumage; bill black, legs lemon-yellow, eyes dark brown. ♀: crown light brown with pale ring round eyes, rest of head and neck blackish brown with fine white lines, mantle and wings dark brown with white coverts and secondaries; metallic green speculum; back, tail, belly white; breast and flanks black barred with white (broader barring in *malvinarum*). Bill yellowish flesh colour, legs deep yellow, eyes dark brown. Nests November on ground among cover lined down and feathers; lays usually 5 or 6 creamy white eggs, incubated c. 30 days. Young tended mainly by ♀. **110**

Chloephaga picta *Anatidae*

MAGELLAN or UPLAND GOOSE   28 ins
Neotropical: Lesser Magellan Goose, *C. p. picta*, Chile and S Argentina including Tierra del Fuego, some movement N in winter; Greater Magellan Goose, *leucoptera*, Falkland Is. Habitat: low ground, on hills and plateaux but seldom near sea, moving in relation to food supplies. ♂: white with black, or black and white, tail; black bars on mantle and flanks; wings white and dark grey with metallic green speculum. ♀: smaller, deep reddish cinnamon barred with black on mantle and lower parts. Legs, ♀ yellow, ♂ black; bill black. 2 phases in ♂: barred form predominating in S, white breasted form elsewhere. *Leucoptera* larger and ♂ always white breasted. Tame unless persecuted; gregarious, feeds on grass. Call: ♂ high soft whistle, ♀ deep harsh cackle. Nests August to November in territories vigorously held by pair; 5 to 7 creamy, glossy eggs in nest on ground down lined amongst bushes and grass. ♀ incubates 30-32 days guarded by ♂, they quickly lead young to water and both tend them. **111**

Chloris chloris see **Carduelis chloris**

Chloroceryle aenea *Alcedinidae*
AMERICAN PYGMY KINGFISHER   5½ ins
Neotropical: Nicaragua and Panama southwards: E
of Andes to S Brazil, E Peru, N Bolivia; W of Andes to
W Ecuador; Trinidad; resident by shaded forest
pools, small streams and ditches, mangrove swamps.
Upperparts dark green, wings and tail spotted buffish
white; throat buff, deepening to russet on white-
centred belly; ♀ has green and white band on breast.
Closely resembles larger (9 ins) Green and Rufous
Kingfisher, *C. indica*, which lacks white on belly. Has
loud rattling call. Feeds on small fish and flying insects
taken from perch. Breeds June to September Trinidad.
Excavates nest hole 12 to 15 ins in sandy bank, or
artificial earth-face often distant from water; clutch
usually 4 glossy white eggs.

Chloroceryle indica see under **C. aenea**

Chlorochrysa phoenicotis *Emberizidae: Thraupinae*
GLISTENING GREEN TANAGER   5¼ ins
Neotropical: headwaters of Rio San Juan, Pacific
Colombia, S to NW Ecuador; creepers on forest trees,
c. 2,500 to *c.* 5,000 ft. Glossy emerald green all over,
except for glossy grey wing coverts, small patch grey
'enamel-like' feathers and orange tuft on side of head.
Diet: fruit, insects. **875**

Chlorodrepanis virens see **Loxops virens**

Chloropsis aurifrons or Aegithina aurifrons
Irenidae
GOLDEN-FRONTED LEAFBIRD   7½ ins
Oriental: Indian subcontinent (from Gulf of Cambay
S and E round coastal ranges of peninsula; Himalayan
foothills from Garhwal E to Nepal, Assam); Ceylon to
Indochina, Sumatra. Resident with local movements
in open broadleaved and deciduous forest and
secondary scrub to *c.* 5,500 ft. Generally leaf-green,
shoulder patches blue; forehead orange, throat dark
blue, broadly bordered black from bill and eye; legs,
bill grey, eyes brown. Pairs or small parties blend with
foliage, which they hunt acrobatically for insects,
spiders, even swinging round twig as on trapeze.
Pollinate blossoms in search for nectar; also take
berries. Aggressive to other species. Strong, rapid
flight. Call (race *aurifrons*) drongo-like *swich-chich-
chich-wee* ending in whistle; *frontalis* has 'voluble
rattle' (Salim Ali); also repeated *tzik* and *chup-chaw*:
accomplished mimic. Breeds January to August in
parts of range, building shallow cup of pine twigs,
grass, leaves, moss, reinforced cobweb, partially
suspended near tip of thin lateral branch; also between
upright twigs; 25 to 40 ft up. 2 or 3 pale or buffish
cream eggs, lightly freckled pale red, incubated
probably by ♀. **643**

Chlorostilbon maugaeus *Trochilidae*
PUERTO RICAN EMERALD HUMMINGBIRD   3½-4 ins
Neotropical: confined to Puerto Rico; resident from
coastal mangrove swamps to forest-covered hilltops,
favouring open areas; also coffee plantations. ♂:
iridescent green with blackish wingtips and forked
tail; legs, bill, eyes dark except pinkish base to lower
mandible. ♀: upperparts green; tail feathers violet
towards ends, outer ones tipped greyish white; cheeks
dusky; underparts whitish with some green on flanks.
See *Aglaiocercus kingi* for general hummingbird habits
and behaviour. **469**

Chordeiles minor *Caprimulgidae*
COMMON NIGHTHAWK   9 ins
Nearctic and Neotropical: breeds throughout N
America from subarctic zone S to W Indies, possibly
NW Colombia; winters S to Argentina (Cordoba,
Buenos Aires) migrating often in parties by day.
Habitat open pine woods to rocky hillsides, right into
city centres; savannah in winter. Rather grey-brown
nightjar type plumage with faint white 'eyebrow',
white throat, rectangular white patches in centre of
blackish flight feathers on pointed wings; black subterminal white patches on dark, slightly forked tail;
underparts strikingly barred grey-brown and white;
no bristles at gape, eyes dark brown. Perches lengthwise on branches, diagonally on wires. Active often

long before dusk, with erratic swooping flight above
trees and house tops: takes insects on wing, small gnats
to large moths. Call: *peent*. Musical hum from feathers,
when ♂, after diving with closed wings, zooms upward again. Breeds from May, laying 2 greyish-white
eggs, marbled, spotted darker grey, on open ground
or on gravelled flat roofs of houses. Sitting ♀ may hiss
at intruder with gape wide open or feign injury.
Incubation 2 weeks; young, fed by both parents, fly
18 days. **462**

Choriotis kori or Ardeotis kori *Otididae*
KORI BUSTARD   Up to 55 ins (♀ smaller)
Ethiopian: E and Southern Africa: resident in open
thorn bush and short grass plains. Upperparts buff
with close black vermiculations; flight feathers black,
barred and mottled white but inner secondaries buff;
upper wing coverts white with black spots near
points, showing as line on closed wing; tail black and
white, barred buff; forehead and crown mottled
black and white, tapering to crest; white 'eyebrow';
chin, throat and loose neck feathers whitish with thin
black bands; underparts white. Legs yellow, bill
horn, eyes yellow. Usually single or in pairs; moves
fast on ground and reluctant to fly, taking off with
kick, then extends neck but folds legs. Sways head and
neck in walk, with tail drooping; but in display ♂ puffs
himself out to appear almost white all over, like Great
Bustard, *Otis tarda*. Mating call, deep repeated *woum*;
usual call nasal *kaa kaa ka*. Eats small vertebrates,
insects, especially locusts; seeds and acacia gum,
hence Afrikaans *Gom Paauw*. Breeding season varies
throughout range according to rains; often nests
sociably. Lays 2 pale greenish-brown eggs, streaked
darker brown, on bare ground; incubated by ♀ *c.*
4 weeks. Young, fed at first by ♀, probably fledge *c.*
5 weeks. **242**

CHOUGH see under **Pyrrhocorax graculus**

CHOUGH,
   ALPINE see **Pyrrhocorax graculus**
   WHITE-WINGED see **Corcorax melanorhamphus**

Chrysococcyx basalis see under **Malurus leucopterus**

Chrysococcyx caprius *Cuculidae*
DIDRIC CUCKOO   20 ins
Ethiopian: whole region, resident open thorn bush,
also plantations of introduced trees and built up areas
in S Africa. ♂: upperparts iridescent bottle green,
glossed bronze, gold and violet; white stripe behind
eye and white on crown; white spots on wing coverts,
secondaries and greenish black tail; underparts white,
flanks barred bronze green, underwing barred black
and white; legs blue-black, bill blackish, eyes and
orbits red. ♀ duller above than ♂ and barring extends
from flanks to breast and neck. Juvenile barred green
all over, bill coral red. Frequently perches lengthwise
on branch. ♂♂ noisy and aggressive in small territories
(sometimes single tree with weaver colony); chase ♀♀
in display with spread tail and quivering wings. ♂'s
plaintive whistling *dee dee deederik*, origin of name; ♀
replies *deea deea deea;* often calls in open and in flight.
Diet mainly insects, clinging woodpecker-like to tree
to search for caterpillars. Lays variable, elongated
blue, greenish or pinkish white egg, plain or spotted
brown and grey, in nests of variety of passerines,
especially weavers, Cape Sparrow, *Passer melanurus*;
Red Bishop, *Euplectes orix*, and Pied Wagtail, *Motacilla
aguimp*. May feed juveniles after they leave foster nest,
pursued by insistent *cheep cheep* calls. **421**

Chrysococcyx
   klass see under **Cinnyris venustus**
   osculans see under **Chthonicola sagittata**

Chrysocolaptes lucidus stricklandi *Picidae*
CEYLON CRIMSON-BACKED WOODPECKER   11½ ins
Endemic subspecies of Golden-backed Woodpecker,
widespread in Oriental region. Upperparts from
crown and crest to rump bright crimson, wings duller;
upper tail coverts, tail black; facial pattern black and
white stripes; underparts buff-white, 'scaled' black,
intense on neck and breast. ♀ has crown and crest

black, speckled white. Legs dull greenish brown, bill
horn brown or grey to whitish tip, eyes yellowish,
outer ring red. Pairs, family parties move from tree to
tree in bounding flight; seldom feeds on ground,
occasionally hawks winged insects; also takes larvae,
nectar from flowers. Discordant trilling laugh, chiefly
in flight. Drums on wood in breeding season, chiefly
December-January. Bores vertically oval hole, 6 to 15
ft up in variety of trees, same chamber used several
years with fresh entrance holes. 1 to 3 white eggs
incubated ♀ 14-15 days; young fly 24-26 days.

Chrysolophus amherstiae *Phasianidae*
LADY AMHERST'S PHEASANT ♀: 26-27 (tail 12-15) ins
                          ♂: 52-68 (tail 34-46) ins
E Palaearctic and Oriental: SE Tibet, SW China,
NE Burma; introduced Britain; resident, unless
driven down by snow, in thickets, especially bamboo,
in rocky mountainous country; also in woods and
scrub. ♂: mantle and scapulars glossy blue-green;
lower back yellow, rump orange; long central tail
feathers white barred black; wings metallic blue;
neck ruff white with blue-black margins; head dark
green with crimson crest; underparts white, to black
under tail coverts; legs, bill bluish grey, eyes yellow,
facial skin white. ♀: like Golden Pheasant *C. pictus* but
more rufous and strongly marked glossy black; tail
feathers rounded; legs, bill blue-grey, eyes brown to
yellow. Flocks of 20-30 through winter, fly more
readily than Golden Pheasant. Display, voice, food
similar to Golden Pheasant, also nesting habits. 6 to 8
buff to cream eggs incubated by ♀, who hardly ever
leaves nest, 23 days. **192**

Chrysolophus pictus *Phasianidae*
GOLDEN PHEASANT   ♀: 25-27 (tail 14-15) ins
                          ♂: 40-44 (tail 32) ins
E Palaearctic: Central China; introduced Britain.
Resident on rocky hills covered with bamboo and
other scrub. ♂: upper back dark green, feathers edged
black; lower back and rump, 'silky', crown and crest
golden yellow; short rounded wings with dark brown
primaries, chestnut and black secondaries, deep blue
tertiaries; long central curved tail feathers black,
spotted cinnamon; tips of tail coverts scarlet; ruff
light orange barred black, underparts scarlet; legs
(with short spurs), bill horn yellow, eyes and facial
skin light yellow. ♀: mixture of browns with glossy
black streaks, spots and bars; legs, bill horn yellow,
eyes brown, facial skin red, grey-green in Amherst
Pheasant. Solitary or in pairs, reluctant to fly.
Courtship: ♂ raises crest and spreads ruff, trails one
wing towards ♀, tail vertically open; then jumps from
side to side of ♀. whistling and clicking. Food: seeds,
leaves, tender shoots, e.g. bamboos; insects. Breeds
probably May-June in wild, nesting on ground,
clutch *c.* 8 pale buff to cream eggs, incubated by ♀ 22
days; ♂ may help with brood as probably monogamous. **193**

Chthonicola sagittata *Muscicapidae: Malurinae*
SPECKLED WARBLER   *c.* 5 ins
Australia: SE Queensland, E New South Wales to
edge of plains, Victoria and perhaps E South Australia; sedentary. Habitat: open forest with some
cover, favours stony hillsides with sparse timber and
scrub. Upperparts dull olive brown broadly streaked
dark brown; primaries brown with whitish edges;
dark tail tipped with white; 'eyebrow' white; underparts white washed olive yellow and strongly streaked
black. Legs dark greyish brown, bill dark brownish,
eyes dark brown. Usually in pairs or small groups;
feeds on insects, sometimes seeds on ground or in low
shrubs, often in association with thornbills and other
small ground birds; takes to low trees when disturbed
or for display. Call: rapid, harsh, rattling sound; quiet
song of few ascending notes in spring; also mimics.
Breeds August onwards; on ground in small depression
below shrub, in, or under, tussock; domed nest with
side entrance, of grass and bark lined lightly softer
plant material, fur and/or feathers; 3, sometimes 4,
glossy reddish brown eggs; parasitised by Black-eared
Cuckoo, *Chrysococcyx osculans*. **758**

CHUKOR see under **Alectoris rufa**

Ciccaba woodfordii *Strigidae*
AFRICAN WOOD OWL 13 ins
Ethiopian: 5 races cover most of region except W Southern Africa; resident in dense forest or riverine bush. Occurs in colour phases of brown from almost black to russet; upperparts spotted white, most pronounced on scapulars, central wing coverts; no ear tufts, facial disc greyish, not very obvious; underparts, including wings and tail, broadly barred black and white, bars closer on belly; legs feathered, feet yellowish, bill and eyes yellow. Immatures paler. Nocturnal, sitting close to tree trunk in daytime. Call: 'cheerful trisyllabic hoot' (O.P.M. Prozesky), rendered 'who are *you?*' Food: nocturnal insects, small mammals. Breeds August onwards in Southern Africa, laying usually single white egg in open hollow in tree. **442**

Cicinnurus regius *Paradisaeidae*
KING BIRD OF PARADISE 5-6½ ins (♂'s tail feathers extra 7 ins)
Australasian: New Guinea and islands to W, Aru Is; resident lowland forests, sea level to 1,700 ft, rarely higher. Smallest member of family; ♂: upperparts, cheeks, chin, crimson, glossed silver; forehead, tail more orange; black spot over eye; central 2 tail feathers wire-like, tipped circular emerald 'blobs'; throat, upper breast, purplish crimson, ringed buff, then emerald green; erectile dark grey 'fans' (up to 2 ins long) at sides of breast, tipped emerald green beyond grey-brown subterminal band; underparts, underwing white; legs violet blue, bill yellow to orange (gape pale green), eyes pale brown. ♀: upperparts dull olive brown; flight feathers and greater coverts darker, edged chestnut; tail olive brown edged pale yellow; cheeks brown, finely streaked, underparts buffish, narrowly barred darker; legs dark blue, bill horn-brown (gape pale green), eyes dark brown. Immature ♂ progresses from ♀-like to ♂ plumage. Keeps to canopy, where ♂'s plumage blends remarkably. Food: tree fruits, even when spiny. ♂ alone in tree hops up and down branch or creeper, reversing body at each hop, occasionally diving straight downwards. Intensive display: 'fans' flexed up sides of neck and pulsated several times, followed by bending wings upward and calling (E. T. Gilliard). Tail wires extended over head and other actions seen in captivity. ♂ calls from display perch repeated, high-pitched *waa waa waa*, and *kii kii kii*, resembling Lesser Bird of Paradise, *Paradisaea minor;* various other sharp and buzzing notes. Breeds March Aru Is; nest found in hole 7 ft up forest tree. 2 creamy white eggs tinged pink, streaked dark brown, incubated captive ♀ 17 days. Young fed ♀ (from throat) leave nest *c.* 14 days, perhaps before fully developed as still beg when month old. **990**

Ciconia alba *Ciconiidae*
WHITE STORK *c.* 40 (body *c.* 21) ins
Palaearctic and Ethiopian, breeds temperate Eurasia from Spain through Asia Minor and Iran to Central Asia and Japan; migrates south to Africa, Arabia, India and NE Asia; small breeding population now in S Africa. Habitat open grasslands and marshes, breeding largely in farms, villages and towns, also damp woodlands. White with black on wings; legs and bill red, eyes grey, bare skin on face black and red. Singly or in small parties, standing or perching, often on one leg; deliberate walk; flies with legs and head held stretched below line of body. Habituated to man when nesting, otherwise shy; large flocks form on migration. Silent apart from hiss, often preceding noisy bill-clattering of mutual display; young more vocal. Main food amphibians, also reptiles, fish, small mammals, insects and other water animals. Breeds from March or April in N temperate, solitary or in small colonies on chimneys and roofs in villages, often on foundation provided, and built up over years with sticks and debris. Generally 3 to 5 chalky white eggs incubated 29-30 days by ♀ (at night) and ♂; young fledge 8-9 weeks but continue to be fed by parents. **68**

Ciconia nigra *Ciconiidae*
BLACK STORK *c.* 38 (body 20) ins
Palaearctic: local from Spain to Mongolia and China; migrates S in autumn, reaching India and southern Africa, where small numbers breed on cliffs; usual habitat mixed forest and wetlands. Mainly black with purple and green gloss, but underparts from breast white; legs scarlet, bill and bare face crimson, all becoming browner in winter, eyes brown. Walks, flies like White Stork but much shyer, often solitary but flocks in winter. Mutual displays but less bill-clattering than White Stork. Various calls, especially guttural *che lee che lee;* young also noisy. Diet mainly fish including eels, and frogs; also reptiles, water animals and occasionally small mammals. Breeds from end April or May in N temperate, always solitary, in tree, sometimes ledge or steep bank; nest of sticks and debris added to each year, holds 3 to 5 white eggs, incubated 6-7 weeks by ♀ (mainly) and ♂. Young, fed by parents, fledge *c.* 10 weeks. **69**

CINCLODES, BAR-WINGED see **Cinclodes fuscus**

Cinclodes fuscus *Furnariidae*
BLACK-FACED SHAKETAIL or
BAR-WINGED CINCLODES 8 (bill ¾) ins
Neotropical: locally distributed from W Venezuela, Colombian Andes S to Cape Horn; southern birds moving N in winter to Uruguay. Habitat: paramo (rocky mountain slopes) up to *c.* 10,000 ft. Thrush-like; upperparts dark earth brown; base of inner flight feathers rufous with black bar; central tail feathers dark brown, outer ones rufous or rufous-tipped; long white 'eyebrow'; underparts whitish, tinged brown, feathers of throat and breast dark-edged; some racial variation in tints; legs, bill dark horn brown; eyes brown. Haunts wet grassland, rocky outcrops and streams, wagging tail like wagtail, other behaviour like dipper *Cinclus*, while Seaside Cinclodes, *C. nigrofumosus*, occupies sea shore like Rock Pipit, *Anthus spinoletta*, even feeding offshore on floating kelp, taking small crustacea and other invertebrates. *Cinclodes* species nest in rock cavities or excavate holes. **562**

Cinclodes nigrofumosus see under **C. fuscus**

CINCLODES, SEASIDE see under **Cinclodes fuscus**

Cinclorhamphus cruralis *Muscicapidae: Malurinae*
BROWN SONGLARK ♀ *c.* 7½, ♂ *c.* 10 ins
Australian mainland apart from Cape York and densely forested areas; spring and summer migrant to S parts of range. ♂: upperparts dark brown with paler streaks; underparts dark brown, darker margins to breast feathers, chin and throat blackish; tail usually held up near vertical. ♀: paler than ♂, throat white, rest of underparts dull white with brown markings. Legs brown, bill black, eyes brown. Frequents open grassland, usually singly or pairs, feeding on ground (insectivorous, also some seeds) or perched post, dead tree or bush. Often flies high; long glides with little wing movement. Call: loud clattering; creaking song, while perched or flying. Breeds September to January, also in winter inland in wet seasons, probably polygamous; nest of coarse grass with softer lining, in depression in ground under or near tuft of grass or shrub; 3 or 4 salmon pink eggs, speckled pinkish red.

Cinclorhamphus mathewsi *Muscicapidae: Malurinae*
RUFOUS SONGLARK ♀ *c.* 7, ♂ *c.* 8 ins
Australia: most of mainland apart from Cape York and densely forested areas in SW and E; visits S part of range in spring and summer. Habitat: lightly wooded grassland. ♂: upperparts dark brown, dull reddish brown margins to feathers; rump and upper tail coverts light rufous; extended 'eyebrow'; chin and throat dull white; underparts whitish pale buff. ♀ smaller. Legs light greyish brown, bill dark brown, eyes brown. Territorial when breeding, feeds on insects, mainly on ground. ♂ calls *wicka-poo, a-wicka-poo* during short flights between trees; when perched utters *witchy-weedle:* virtually silent outside breeding season. Polygamous; builds open cup-shaped nest of coarse grass, lined softly, on ground in slight hollow, usually under tuft of grass or bush; 3 or 4 white eggs with reddish spots. **759**

Cinclosoma castanotum *Muscicapidae: Cinclosomatinae*
CHESTNUT QUAIL THRUSH 9¾ ins
Australasian: inland southern Australia; N to S Northern Territories; absent from SW West Australia; resident mallee, mulga scrub, open forest. Upperparts brown; chestnut on lower back, rump; black, rounded tail tipped white; wings brown, flecked black and white on 'shoulder'; striking head pattern: white streaks separated by black eyestripe and cheek; throat, breast black; flanks, undertail spotted black; rest of underparts white; legs grey, bill black; eyes brown. Walks slowly, deliberately in hunched posture on ground. Runs upright or flies reluctantly with whirring wings if disturbed. Feet used to manipulate insect prey; also eats seeds. Alarm call: low piping whistle. Breeds August to December. Nest in depression on ground, loosely lined bark, leaves; usually under dead bush or grass tussock. 2 white eggs, marked brown, lavender. **717**

Cinclosoma cinnamomeum *Muscicapidae: Cinclosomatinae*
CINNAMON QUAIL THRUSH 8-9 ins
Australasian: southern Australia, farther inland than Chestnut Quail Thrush, *C. castanotum;* N to tropic of Capricorn in W Australia; resident very arid, stony desert. ♂: upperparts, including centre tail, mainly rich chestnut brown; 'shoulder' and outer tail feathers black, tipped white; black around eye; chestnut cheek separates white 'eyebrow' from broad white stripe below eye. Throat, centre breast black; rest underparts white blotched black. ♀ lacks black on head, underparts. Legs grey, bill black, eyes reddish-brown. Behaviour, food and nest similar to Chestnut Quail Thrush. Active around dawn, when ♂ sings monotonous song, 5 plaintive notes, from perch on dead tree; shelters in shade during day. Breeding season: March to April. 2 or 3 pale buff eggs with irregular brown dots, grey under-markings. **718**

Cinclus cinclus *Cinclidae*
DIPPER *c.* 7 ins
Palaearctic: mountainous areas of Europe, Atlas (N Africa), Asia Minor, Central Asia; discontinuous and many races recognised. Mainly sedentary, some downward movement from mountains, and winter dispersal of northern populations. Habitat fast-flowing rivers and streams, usually rocky, in highlands and mountains to 6,800 ft Alps, 17,000 ft E Tibet. Plump, short-tailed, mainly very dark brown, with large white breast patch, edged chestnut in British race; head and nape chocolate becoming slaty on body; legs, bill mainly black-brown, eyes dark brown, orbits white. Blinking action of white eyelid characteristic; oil or preen gland much enlarged as compared terrestrial relatives. Usually seen bobbing on stone or flying bullet-like above watercourses. Also swims, dives expertly, walks on bottom underwater, searching for food: all kinds of small water animals from clear streams, especially larvae under stones. Calls: loud *zit*, sharp *clink clink* in flight; sweet warbling song by ♂ and ♀. Breeds February to June Britain, ♀ and ♂ building large domed nest usually of moss, with grass cup forming lip of entrance, and lined dead leaves. Almost always sited over fast water in steep bank or human artefact, e.g. bridge; under waterfalls. 4 to 6 pointed white eggs, incubated by ♀ *c.* 16 days; young, fed by ♀ and ♂, fly 19-25 days. 2 broods except at higher altitudes. **662**

Cinclus mexicanus *Cinclidae*
AMERICAN DIPPER 8 ins
Nearctic and Neotropical: Aleutian Is. Alaska. S to Guatemala, Panama, E to Black Hills, Dakota; resident similar habitats to *C. cinclus*, though not to such high altitudes; some movement downward in winter. Uniform grey brown with narrow white orbital ring; legs yellowish, bill grey, eyes dark brown. Behaviour and habits as *C. cinclus*. Song melodious alternation of trills and 'rich flute-like notes' (R. H. Pough). Food: aquatic insects, especially caddis fly larvae; small fish. Breeding season May-June; nest, eggs as *C. cinclus* but incubation given as 13, fledging 18 days. **663**

CINNAMON-CRESTED BEE-EATER see
Melittophagus oreobates

CINNAMON QUAIL THRUSH see **Cinclosoma cinnamomeum**

Cinnyris chalybeus *Nectariniidae*
LESSER or SOUTHERN
DOUBLE-COLLARED SUNBIRD   4½ ins
Ethiopian: local in region S of Equator; resident evergreen, *Brachystegia* and dry forests, introduced plantations, gardens. ♂: upperparts, including head, neck, metallic blue or golden green; rump olivaceous; upper tail coverts metallic blue; wings, tail blackish; narrow blue band between green upper and scarlet lower breast; belly grey; pectoral tufts, rest of underparts yellow. ♀: dusky grey above, pale grey belly. Legs, bill black, eyes brown. Juvenile like dark ♀. Swerving, jerky flight; visits variety of flowers for nectar; takes insects and their larvae. Call high-pitched repeated *cheep cheep;* thin, tinkling song often accompanied by display of pectoral tufts. Breeds May to October Tanzania; nest of dry grass, lined plant down, feathers, large entrance hole under 'porch'; suspended from tree or bush at varying heights. Usually 2 eggs uniformly freckled shades of grey, incubated ♀. Probably 2 broods. **821**

Cinnyris talatala *Nectariniidae*
WHITE-BELLIED SUNBIRD   4½ ins
Ethiopian: from Angola and S Tanzania southward; resident open acacia scrub, many other types wooded country, gardens. ♂: upperparts, including head, neck, upper breast, metallic green shot gold and blue; flight feathers dusky grey; tail feathers blue-black edged metallic green; broad metallic violet band across breast, narrow black band below it shading into white underparts; pectoral tufts lemon-yellow. ♀: ashy brown above, paler below, indistinctly streaked. Legs, bill black, eyes dark brown. Juvenile like ♀ but more olive above, yellow below. Usually in pairs; ♂ noisy and conspicuous, calling loud, clear repeated *tzick tzick;* short canary-like melodious song. Food: insects and nectar. Breeding season variable within range, mainly August to December; builds typical pouch nest of plant material suspended from thorn bush a few feet up. 2 grey or greyish white eggs marked slaty or purplish brown, incubated ♀. **822**

Cinnyris venustus *Nectariniidae*
VARIABLE SUNBIRD   4 ins
Ethiopian: much of region, Congo to Sudan and southward to Rhodesia; resident aloes and acacia scrub; woodland and edge; long grass areas with bushes, to higher plateaux Ethiopia, Malawi. ♂ resembles ♂ White-bellied, *C. talatala*, but metallic green of forehead shot blue only; violet band across breast much broader; belly bright yellow in S African race, white and orange red in others; pectoral tufts yellow and orange red. Habits as other sunbirds. Calls short *tssp*, longer churring; soft warbling song. Food: insects, juices from fruits, nectar. Breeds most months, chiefly March to June Kenya; builds oval pouch nest, lightly woven grass, fibres, lined feathers, plant down; hung from bush, creeper, tall plant, varying heights. 2 white or off-white eggs, densely speckled brown and grey in cap, incubated ♀. Occasionally parasitised by Klaas's Cuckoo, *Chrysococcyx klaas.* **823**

Circaetus cinereus *Accipitridae*
BROWN HARRIER or SNAKE EAGLE   *c.* 17 ins
Ethiopian, mainly sedentary, except in Senegal: in wooded e.g. thorn bush areas, but not dense forest; uncommon on open plains: sea level to 8,000 ft. Almost uniform dark slate brown, often with narrow black line above eye; 3 narrow grey bars on whitish-tipped tail, silvery grey lining to flight quills. Legs grey white, bill black, cere pale grey, eyes yellow. Rather sluggish behaviour, spending much time perched or making short flights; sometimes soars high and usually singly in display over breeding area, calling with a loud resonant *kok kok kok kok kaw*, also when perched. Other notes are throaty *hok hok* and deep *kromp kromp*. Food is 70% reptiles, mostly snakes killed on ground; also game birds and poultry. Breeding variable, not con-

fined to dry season. Nest of small sticks, leaf lined, in trees, especially acacia, euphorbia 15 to 40 ft up holds 1 white, usually unmarked egg, incubated about 45 days by ♀ visited by ♂. Chick fledges in 100-109 days, fed by ♀ served by ♂. **142**

Circus aeruginosus approximans see
C. approximans

Circus approximans or C. aeruginosus approximans *Accipitridae*
SWAMP HAWK   22-24 ins (♀ larger)
Australasian: Australia, Tasmania, New Zealand and other island groups; sometimes regarded as race of Marsh Harrier. Resident in swamps, marshes, open grasslands and standing crops. ♂: upperparts dark brown; head, neck, underparts lighter, streaked dark brown; flight feathers blue-grey barred dark brown, tail dark grey, upper coverts white. ♀: dark brown with creamy crown, nape, throat; flight feathers blackish brown, upper wing buff. Legs, cere and bill (tipped dark grey) yellow, eyes yellow brown. Often seen on wing, quartering 10 to 15 ft up, but spends much time perched. Pounces on frogs, small mammals; takes eggs young birds, carrion and fish. Generally silent, but chattering call and scream in breeding season, September to January in Australia. Nest of sticks and local plants in swamps, long tussock grass or crops, holds 3 to 5 pale bluish white eggs, incubated by ♀ 31-34 days. ♂ brings food which ♀ takes in aerial pass; young fly *c.* 6 weeks. **143**

Circus ranivorus *Accipitridae*
AFRICAN MARSH HARRIER   18-20 ins
Ethiopian: Kenya and Uganda to Angola and S Africa; resident in marshes, lake margins, open grasslands and crops, hunts over drier areas. ♂: resembles Swamp Hawk but more variable; head and neck uniform with dark brown upperparts; underparts light and dark brown, similarly barred, pale area on upper wing. ♀ similar to but larger than ♂. Legs yellow, cere and bill blue-grey, eyes yellow. Hunts singly or in pairs, quartering ground, then checking to drop on prey, sometimes snatching it up, more often settling to kill it; takes small mammals, birds, frogs, insects and other predators' leftovers. Apparently silent except at nest. Soaring and diving displays in pairs or by ♂ alone. Breeds May to August in Kenya, building platform of vegetation in reeds, crops or thick cover. 3 to 5 white eggs, sometimes spotted brown, incubated by ♀ *c.* 30 days; she takes food from ♂ by aerial pass; young fly *c.* 6 weeks. **144**

CIRL BUNTING see under **Emberiza cia**

Cissa chinensis *Corvidae*
HUNTING CISSA   Body *c.* 14 (tail *c.* 6½) ins
E Palaearctic, Oriental: resident, lower Himalayas in Garhwal E through Kumaon, Nepal, Sikkim, Bhutan, N Bengal, Assam hills of Brahmaputra R., Manipur, Burma, Thailand, N Vietnam, Cambodia and Malay Peninsula to Sumatra, Borneo and Java, habitat: plains and foothills up to *c.* 5,000 ft in tropical and sub-tropical wet evergreen jungle and mixed, moist deciduous bamboo forest. Mostly blue-green; black stripe from base of bill through eyes to meet across nape; wings chestnut-red with white tips to inner secondaries; long tail with white tips to outer shorter feathers and pale blue subterminal band on longest central tail feather. On death or exposure to sun yellowish tinge to green of head disappears, green plumage turns light blue and chestnut-red on wings becomes grey-brown. Legs and bill orange-crimson or coral red, eyes brownish crimson or dark crimson with orange-crimson or crimson rim. Single or in pairs, sometimes noisy parties, on ground or in thickets, shrubs or trees, often accompanied by laughing thrushes; usually shy and wary; generally heard rather than seen. Call: loud, harsh, repeated *peep-peep* or *kik-wee*, also mimics other birds. Feeds chiefly on large insects and small vertebrates. Breeds April to July; large, shallow nest of twigs, tendrils and bamboo and other leaves, packed with moss and lined with rootlets, in small tree in dense jungle; 4 to 6 eggs, greyish or pale greenish, marked reddish brown. **995**

CISSA, HUNTING see **Cissa chinensis**

Cisticola aridula *Muscicapidae: Sylviinae*
DESERT FANTAIL WARBLER   4½ ins
Ethiopian: whole region, except W Equatorial coast; resident open, dry grassy country. ♂: pale fawn above, streaked black on head, back; mantle duller brown; short, graduated tail black with white tip, subterminal black spots below; underparts paler buffy white. Legs flesh; bill: upper dark, lower pale grey; eyes brown. ♀, non-breeding ♂, have narrow streaking above; paler bill. Inconspicuous, spending most of time near ground; when alarmed ♂ flies erratically, clapping wings and calling. Song: repeated tinkling note delivered from low perch or in cruising display flight. Diet insectivorous. Breeding season varies, usually coinciding with rains; July to September in Sudan, November to March in S. Ball nest, of grass, with side entrance, built in last year's dead grass. Eggs, 3 to 5 (S African races), white to pale blue, often speckled purplish red in zone near large end. **734**

Cisticola exilis *Muscicapidae: Sylviinae*
GOLDEN-HEADED FANTAIL   ♂: 3½ (4½ winter) ins
Oriental, Australasian: Indian subcontinent, China, Indo China, S through Indonesia to Australia; N and E coast continent S to SE South Australia, NE Tasmania; resident low tangled vegetation near water. ♂: upperparts, including short tail, pale golden brown, heavily streaked black on mantle; wings darker; underparts buffy white, ♀, ♂ in winter have black-striped head, long wedge-shaped tail. Legs brown, bill dark brown, eyes pale brown. Behaviour skulking outside breeding season, when ♂♂ perch on top of grass stems, chattering with raised crests. Song drawn out *buzz* followed by *tweet*, delivered from grass or in song flight. Feeds on insects picked off grass stems or hawked. Breeding season varies: wet season in tropics, October to March in SE Australia when vegetation suitable. Domed nest of fine grass, lined plant down, built in low bush or tussock; leaves often stitched into nest. 3 or 4 pale blue eggs, spotted chestnut. ♂♂ probably polygamous. **735**

Cisticola galactotes *Muscicapidae: Sylviinae*
WINDING CISTICOLA or
RUFOUS GRASS WARBLER   5 ins
Ethiopian: several races cover most of region. Resident wetlands, margins of lakes and swamps in tall grass and sedges. Upperparts ashy-grey streaked black; edges flight feathers tawny; rump greyish; tail tawny with black subterminal spots and white edges; crown warm russet, streaked black some races, 'eyebrow' buffish; underparts creamy buff. Non-breeding: upperparts tawny, mantle broadly streaked black. Legs brown, bill dark horn, eyes light brown. Unobtrusive except when breeding: ♂ perches grass stems, uttering single rasping note like clock being wound-up (hence name); flies over territory calling *trit trit*, off-nest ♀ replying *treet treet;* also loud piping call. Insectivorous. Breeding season varies within range; nest elliptical gourd of grass and plant fibres, lined grass, down, ornamented plant and cocoon fluff, 2 to 4 ft up in grasses, sedges, water reeds, sometimes in dry sites. 3 to 5 white or pinky-red eggs, marked shades of brown and red. **736**

CISTICOLA, WINDING see **Cisticola galactotes**

Cisticola subruficapilla *Muscicapidae Sylviinae*
GREY-BACKED WARBLER   4½ ins
Ethiopian: 4 races restricted to S Africa (Cape Province, Orange Free State, Karroo) and SW Africa. Resident dry scrub, heath and bush country, from mountains to coastal dunes and estuaries. Upperparts ashy grey streaked black; flight feathers grey edged brown; tail brown, tipped lighter, with subterminal black spots; crown dark brown streaked black; underparts greyish-white, breast streaked blackish. Call a monotonous pipe *tee tee*. Mainly insectivorous. Breeds August to November; nest ball-shaped, of grass with soft lining, decorated cobwebs, usually low in small bush among grasses. 3 or 4 eggs pale turquoise blue, speckled purplish red. **737**

Cistothorus platensis see under **Telmatodytes palustris**

Cladorhynchus leucocephalus *Recurvirostridae*
BANDED STILT 16 ins
Australasian: southern half of continent; saline lakes, estuaries. Looks much like Black-winged *Himantopus himantopus*; generally white; black wings with white trailing edge; chestnut breast band extends to dark brown patch belly; long legs pink, slender bill black, eyes brown. Immature lacks breast band, wings brown. Usually in pairs or flocks, behaving much as *Himantopus*. Call: barking *chowk* or *chowk-uk*. Breeds colonially July and December on dry salt pans, or sandbanks if water level high; scrape on bare ground holds 2 to 4 off-white or creamy eggs, densely scrawled black or brown over grey; sometimes blotched.

Clamator glandarius *Cuculidae*
GREAT SPOTTED CUCKOO 15-16 (tail 7-8) ins
S Palaearctic and Ethiopian: Iberia, E Mediterranean area to Iraq and SW Iran; N Africa from Morocco to Egypt; very locally, E, W (Senegal, Sierra Leone, Nigeria) and S Africa; northern birds winter tropical S Africa while S African birds move north. Habitat: open, often coniferous forest and its edge, olive groves, savannah. Upperparts dark brown, spotted white; crested crown and sides of head dark grey; throat yellowish white, extending to form partial collar, underparts shading cream to white; long, graduated tail white-edged; legs brownish-grey, bill dark grey-brown, base of lower mandible pale; eyes dark brown, orbits orange. Immature has chestnut patch on wing. Conspicuous in rather fast, undulating flight; perches trees and buildings; hops clumsily on ground. Noisy parties outside breeding season. 'Song' rasping *keeow keeow keeow keeow*; ♀ replies *burroo burroo*; harsh *cark cark* of alarm. Diet: large insects and their larvae. Breeds from end April Iberia, November to January S Africa, parasitising members of crow family *Corvidae*, and starlings *Sturnidae* in S Africa. Several ♀♀ lay in one nest, or one lays 'clutch' in same nest, usually removing fosterer's egg each time. Eggs greenish blue, thickly spotted shades of brown, like those of favourite host Magpie, *Pica pica*. Young do not eject foster brood; sometimes both are reared. **422**

Clangula hyemalis *Anatidae*
LONG-TAILED DUCK or
OLD SQUAW 17 (tail another 5) ins
Holarctic: breeds arctic coasts of Europe, Asia and N America; winters south to Britain, France, Netherlands, Black Sea, Caspian Sea, China, Japan, California, Great Lakes, N Carolina. Habitat: fresh water from small ponds to large rivers and lakes during breeding, otherwise marine with local exceptions. Summer ♂: distinctive long black tail-feathers, also white flanks, brown-black on breast extending up neck to cover head apart from white patch round eye. ♀: mottled brown back, white flanks and dusky crown. In winter white markings more extensive in both sexes. Legs, and bill of ♀, dark grey; ♂ bill pink with dark grey tip, eyes variable, carmine to brown. Not shy, gregarious but rarely with other species; feeds mainly on small water animals, particularly molluscs, diving for as long as 1½ minutes. Rapid flyer; wings appear short with fast low beat. ♂ noisy, emitting loud yodelling note. Nests May and June; 6 to 8 olive-buff eggs in simple hollow amongst heather or rocks near water. ♀ incubates 24 days and tends young who fly after 5 weeks. **112**

CLAPPER RAIL see **Rallus longirostris**

Claravis pretiosa *Columbidae*
BLUE GROUND DOVE *c.* 8½ ins
Neotropical: SE Mexico S to Peru, Bolivia, N Argentina and S Brazil. Habitat: more open woodlands especially clearings, or where little or no undergrowth. ♂: bluish grey, nearly white on forehead and throat, underparts paler; black markings on wing coverts and secondaries give barred effect with wing folded; primaries dark grey, central tail feathers dark bluish grey, outer tail feathers black. ♀: dark brown, belly and flanks greyish, tail coverts and central tail

feathers reddish brown, wing markings purplish red. Legs pink, bill greenish, eyes red or yellowish. Usually in pairs, feeds on ground, taking seeds and similar plant matter; takes off with whistling sound made by wings. Call: low coo; also repeated single hooting note. Builds slight twig platform in trees and shrubs; lays 2 white eggs, incubated *c.* 14 days. **352**

CLARK'S NUTCRACKER see **Nucifraga columbiana**

CLIFF
CHAT see **Thamnolaea cinnamomeiventris**
CHAT, WHITE-CROWNED see **Thamnolaea coronata**

Climacteris picumnus *Climacteridae*
AUSTRALIAN BROWN TREECREEPER *c.* 6 ins
Australasian: mainly SE continental Australia; S Queensland to Victoria, S Australia; resident open forests, cleared land. ♂: upperparts dull brown, richer rump, upper tail coverts; black subterminal bar to tail; buff bar on wing in flight; crown round to breast grey; pale 'eyebrow', cheeks, throat buff; small dark streaks upper breast; underparts buff-brown heavily streaked black and white; under tail coverts white barred blackish brown. ♀ has faint reddish markings upper breast. Legs, bill dull dark grey; eyes blackish brown. Climbs trees, stumps, wooden posts, moving spirally upward like *Certhia* species on large, strong claws; also jumps forward, sideways, backwards and works under nearly horizontal limbs. Wingbeat rapid, then glides. More on ground than relatives, takes household scraps, but most food from bark crevices: insects, spiders. Breeds July to January; nest of fur, hair, small feathers in hollow tree, branch, stump, post usually 3 to 15 but up to 50 ft high. 2 or 3 pinkish white eggs, densely covered pinkish red speckles over purple. 2, even 3 broods in same nest. **814**

Coccothraustes coccothraustes *Fringillidae*
HAWFINCH *c.* 6½ ins
Palaearctic: most of Europe between 40° and 60°N; locally NW Africa; separate populations in Turkestan and across Asia from headwaters of River Ob system E to Pacific and N Japan. Resident and migrant, most northerly birds wintering Mediterranean area, NW Indian sub-continent, China, Japan. Habitat mixed broadleaved forest, lowland and montane; riverine strips, e.g. bordering taiga rivers; parks, orchards, exceptionally conifers. ♂: generally liver brown, darkest on mantle, lightest on breast; nape grey; lores, bib black; blue-black wing has broad white bar, white marks on primaries (4 notched and curled at tips); white tip to short dark tail; under tail coverts white. ♀ somewhat duller and paler. Legs light brown, bill mainly lead blue (summer), pale horn (winter), eyes red brown. Juvenile has yellow throat, underparts spotted and barred. Hops on ground, but usually high in trees. Rapid, undulating flight, often much higher than relatives. Flocks in autumn, usually small. Call: *tzik,* often in flight; also harsh *tzeep*; song rendered *deek waree ree ree* from high perch. Takes kernels of tree fruits, opening stones with very strong mandibles; also variety of seeds, e.g. hornbeam, beech, off tree or ground; buds, hard-bodied insects in spring, summer. Seldom at bird tables but comes to drink. ♂ chases ♀ in courtship, then mutual display and bill-touching. Breeds April to July; solitary or in groups. ♀, attended ♂, builds foundation, small twigs interwoven bark, for shallow cup of rootlets, hair, grass, moss, lichen, usually in fork or near end of lateral branch, 5 to 75 ft, variety of broadleaved trees and shrubs. 3 to 6 bluish-white to brownish green eggs, blotched, scrawled dark purplish-brown, black, grey-brown, incubated ♀ 11-13 days; both parents feed young, who fly 12-14 days. **921**

Cochlearius cochlearius *Ardeidae*
BOATBILL 24 ins
Neotropical: central Mexico to Brazil and N Argentina, resident in freshwater mangrove swamps. Upperparts grey, with black patches on head, back and flanks, crest of short black feathers; underparts brownish; legs greenish brown, broad bill (3 x 2 ins) has grey upper, yellow lower mandible with bare

gular pouch, large eyes dark brown. Rather lethargic (O. L. Austin), skulking in swamps and active chiefly by night. Utters harsh frog-like croak and rattles bill. Diet fish, amphibians, worms, crustaceans, even small mammals, scooped up in shallow water. Breeds alone or in small colonies in mangrove thickets, making shallow stick nest. Both sexes incubate 2 to 4 very pale blue eggs and tend the young. **57**

COCKATIEL see **Nymphicus hollandicus**

COCKATOO, GANG-GANG see **Callocephalon fimbriatum**

COCK OF THE ROCK, PERUVIAN see **Rupicola peruviana**

COCK OF THE WOODS see **Formicarius analis**

COCOA WOODHEWER see **Xiphorhynchus guttatus**

COCRICO see **Ortalis ruficauda**

Coereba flaveola *Emberizidae: Coerebinae*
BANANAQUIT 4½ (bill ½) ins
Neotropical: Central America, W Indies, S of Andes to E Peru, Bolivia, Paraguay, Brazil (Rio Grande do Sul), NE Argentina; W of Andes to Ancash, Peru; second growth scrub, clearings, plantations, parks, gardens; sea level to 4,000 ft, sometimes higher. Variable plumage according to race with melanistic forms on St Vincent, Grenada; basically sooty grey to sooty brown to blackish (e.g. mask) upperparts, rump yellow to olive yellow; long 'eyebrow', wing speculum, under tail coverts white; throat pale grey, underparts lemon yellow; legs, bill blackish, eyes dark brown. Does not flock; both sexes build globular individual roosting nests with entrance near bottom, of grass, plant fibres, rootlets, moss, hung in tree or shrub; if own nest destroyed, may evict other species. Sings most of year: 'thin, high-pitched, of no great charm' (A. F. Skutch); 'rapid wheezy sugary warble' (G. A. C. Herklots). Probes or perforates base of many flowers for nectar; takes insects, spiders off foliage; punctures juicy berries and sucks them; enters houses in W Indies after prey and syrup. Breeds mainly December to February Costa Rica but eggs all months except April (Skutch); ♂ helps ♀ build nest (as above) in which she sleeps before laying 2 or 3 whitish eggs, variably and densely spotted, blotched light brown; ♀ incubates 12-13 days; young, fed ♀ and ♂ by regurgitation, fly 17-19 days. 2 broods at least. **886**

Colaptes auratus *Picidae*
YELLOW-SHAFTED FLICKER 10½ ins
Nearctic: breeds widening band from Alaska to SE Canada and Newfoundland, and S to Gulf of Florida; northern populations migrate SE in autumn. Habitat open wooded country. ♂: upperparts grey-brown with broken black bars and yellow shafts to flight feathers; rump white; two-pointed tail mainly black; crown and back of neck grey with red band at nape; cheeks pinkish buff with black moustache and gorget; underparts creamy, heavily spotted black; underwings and undertail bright yellow. ♀ lacks moustache. Legs grey, bill dark grey, eyes dark brown. More terrestrial than relatives, hopping awkwardly; flight undulating. ♂ chases ♀ in courtship, calling *yucker yucker yucker;* displays plumage if rival appears. Calls: loud repeated *flic*, shrill, descending *kee-oo*. Drums, often on tin roof, and inside nest cavity. Feeds largely on ants; fruits and berries in autumn; migrating parties even explore coastal wrack. Breeds May to August, making hole 3 ins diameter, shaft 1 to 2 ft deep, in woodland or solitary tree, fence post, roof of building; also nest holes of other species in banks; nestboxes. Often uses one for several seasons. 5 to 10 glossy white eggs incubated by ♀ and ♂ *c.* 2½ weeks; both feed young who fly *c.* 3 weeks. **542**

Colaptes chrysoides *Picidae*
GILDED FLICKER 10 ins
SW Nearctic: resident in saguaro desert in extreme SW USA and NW Mexico. Resembles *C. auratus* but ♂ has brown crown and red moustache stripe.

Behaviour, voice and food much as related flickers. Breeds May to August, making hole high in saguaro, cottonwood, willow, laying usually 4 white eggs; details much as *C. auratus* with which some authorities regard it as conspecific. **543**

Colibri coruscans *Trochilidae*
SPARKLING VIOLETEAR   5½ (bill 1) ins
Neotropical: local in Venezuela, Colombia, Ecuador, E Peru and Lima, Bolivia, NW Argentina; resident open mountain slopes, 5,000 to 10,000 ft. Upperparts iridescent green; chin, upper throat, elongated ear coverts and centre of belly iridescent purple blue, lower throat and breast iridescent emerald; flanks, under tail coverts bright green; tail bright blue or green with dusky subterminal bar. Squeaky song remarkably strong for size of bird. Feeding, habits much as other hummingbirds (see *Aglaiocerus kingi*), but records of ♂ sharing incubation of the 2 white eggs. **470**

Colinus virginianus *Phasianidae*
BOBWHITE   8½-10½ ins
Nearctic into Neotropical: resident from SE Canada (Ontario), Maine, S Minnesota, throughout E and Mid-West USA to Mexico, Gulf of Florida, Cuba, W Guatemala; introduced Britain, New Zealand, elsewhere. Distinctive race *ridgwayi* now virtually extinct but *c.* 18 others recognised. Habitat: from scrub and open pinewoods to cultivated and derelict farmland, roadsides to towns and cities. Upperparts and upper breast reddish brown with dark mottling and pale feather edges; erectile crown, flight and tail feathers dark brown; underparts white barred black, flanks to undertail streaked reddish-brown; ♂ has 'eyebrow', face and throat white with black gorget curving up to eye; ♀ buff instead of white. Legs pale yellow, stubby bill and eyes dark. Forms coveys up to 30 in winter, with whirring flight and glide to land. Clear whistle: *bob-white* or *poor-bob-whoit* (last note loud). Food: tree and weed seeds, e.g. chickweed, sorrel; variety of berries, grass, leaves; insects in spring; grit needed for grinding seed. Breeds April onwards, ♀ making grass-lined scrape in grass or scrub, beside wall; ♂ may help. 12 to 20 white eggs incubated by ♀ *c.* 20 days; both parents tend young. 2 or 3 broods. **194**

Colius indicus or Urocolius indicus *Coliidae*
RED-FACED COLY or MOUSEBIRD   11 ins
Ethiopian: Congo River and S Tanzania southward; resident in wooded country, including plantations of introduced trees and built-up areas in S Africa. Upperparts from crest and ear coverts to tail greenish grey; forehead, chin and underparts buffish brown or white; underwing and undertail light chestnut; legs dull red, bill black but cere and base of upper mandible crimson, eyes grey, facial skin red (greenish in juvenile). Gregarious like other colies, but more often on wing, calling clear musical *tiu woo woo*, also from perch. When disturbed, birds crawl mouselike to top of tree before taking off. Diet: mainly fruit. Breeding variable throughout range; makes platform of twigs, moss and wool with cup of grass, usually in thorn bush. Lays 2 to 4 cream or white eggs, usually spotted and scrawled red-brown. Nesting details as *C. macrouros*. **479**

Colius macrouros *Coliidae*
BLUE-NAPED COLY or MOUSEBIRD   13 ins
Ethiopian: Senegal to Somalia, with race *C. m. laeneni* extending N to Air Mts, others S into Tanzania; resident or partial migrant dry, open country and thorn bush; in plantations and gardens, e.g. Khartoum. Upperparts grey, bright blue patch on nape; underparts buff; legs red, bill dark but base of upper mandible and facial skin carmine, eyes dark. Gregarious; flocks of *c.* 30 fly straight and fast between bushes, uttering loud, clear whistle: *pee pee pee*, before or during flight. Omnivorous, but especially fond of fruit, doing some damage to date crops. Breeding variable throughout range; builds platform of twigs or shallow cup of plant fibres, grass-lined. 2 to 4 white eggs, often speckled and scrawled brown incubated by ♀ and ♂ 12 to 14 days; young leave nest after few days but are

tended by ♀ and ♂ until fledged at 17 to 21 days. Off-duty bird often joins flock of own sex, even at height of breeding season.

Colius striatus *Coliidae*
SPECKLED COLY or MOUSEBIRD   11 ins
Ethiopian: some 18 races cover most of region from Nigeria E and S; resident in low scrub and forest edge. Races vary but upperparts generally ash-brown, head and longish crest paler, mantle and rump vermiculated in some races; chin to breast ash-grey, throat blackish, or brownish white, breast barred; sides of face and underparts buff; legs wine-red, upper bill black, lower whitish, eyes variable, facial skin black. Makes shorter flights than *Colius indicus*, flapping and gliding from bush into thick of next one. Alarm call: *tisk tisk tisk;* twittering contact call. Often hangs upside down when feeding on seeds, soft fruits, berries and flowers, doing some damage; also takes nestlings of other birds. Breeds throughout year, making small platform of twigs and stems with nest cup of rootlets and green leaves and laying 2 to 5 cream or chalky white eggs; nesting details as *C. macrouros*. **480**

Coliuspasser
    macrourus see **Euplectes macrourus**
    progne see **Euplectes progne**

COLLARED
    DOVE see **Streptopelia decaocto**
    FLYCATCHER see under **Ficedula hypoleuca**
    HEMIPODE see **Pedionomus torquatus**
    TROGON see **Trogon collaris**

Collocalia esculenta *Apodidae*
WHITE-BREASTED SWIFT   3½ ins
Oriental and Australasian: Indian subcontinent, Andamans, Nicobars and Mergui Archipelago through Malaysia to New Caledonia; resident near caves and habitations, coast to 5,000 ft. Very small with proportionately long pointed wings, tail barely forked; glossy black upperparts; duller below, shading on breast into white underparts. Roost clinging together in clusters. Swallow-like erratic flight, feeding on insects in forest glades, often hawking close to ground. Call: twittering *chit chit* like relatives; no echo location notes. Breeds gregariously, December to April (Indian subcontinent) in variety of sites: caves not used by other species, or near entrance in occupied ones; crevices and holes in rocks and buildings, occasionally hollow trees; colonies in factory sheds in India. Nest cup of various plant materials e.g. moss snatched from branches when hovering, cemented and hinged to wall with saliva; not edible. Lays 2 rather oblong white eggs, incubated by ♀ and ♂, who relieve each other at nest quite violently, sometimes joined by other birds.

COLOURFUL PUFFLEG HUMMINGBIRD see
Eriocnemis mirabilis

Columba albitorques *Columbidae*
WHITE-COLLARED PIGEON   *c.* 12½ ins
Ethiopian: limited to highlands of Central and E Ethiopia and Eritrea. Habitat: rocky mountainous regions and high plateaux with suitable cliffs, rocks or buildings for nesting and roosting. Dark bluish grey with conspicuous white wing patch in flight; striking white collar across nape from ear to ear. Legs red or pinkish, bill black with powdery white cere, eyes dark red. Agile flyer; usually in pairs or small groups but often in larger flocks when coming into roost or visiting crops; walks easily; feeds on ground, usually cultivated, on grain, seeds. Breeds in any month, nesting in holes in cliffs, on ledges in caves, or similar sites on buildings. 2 glossy creamy white eggs, incubated *c.* 16 days; young leave nest *c.* 27 days. **353**

Columba aquatrix *Columbidae*
OLIVE PIGEON   *c.* 15 ins
Ethiopian: E Africa from Ethiopia, Somalia and E Zaïre to Angola and S Africa. Found in heavy woodland, highland forest and juniper forest, usually between 5,000 and 10,000 ft. Large dark pigeon, mainly maroon and bluish grey with white spots on

purple front and wing coverts; ♀ somewhat duller. Forehead and face dark, dull purple; throat paler; crown and nape silver grey. Legs, orbital skin and bill yellow; eyes grey. Wary bird and strong flyer, often making daily migrations from mountain forest, where breeds and roosts, to lowland forest to feed on seeds, berries and fruits. Usually in pairs or small parties, occasionally in large flocks. Call: deep rumbling noise ending in *eoo* or whistling when excited. Breeding season variable, builds scanty platform of twigs in trees or shrubs, usually amongst creeper or similar dense cover, often near edge of trees. 1 white egg, rarely 2; both sexes incubate for *c.* 17 days. **354**

Columba flavirostris *Columbidae*
RED-BILLED PIGEON   *c.* 13 ins
S Nearctic, N Neotropical: races spread across Lower Rio Grande Valley of Texas, Mexico and Central America S to Nicaragua and Costa Rica. Frequents woodland near water in semi-arid or arid regions but may be found in more open country near tree cover. ♂: head, neck, breast and lesser wing coverts dull reddish purple shading to dark bluish grey on outer wing coverts, secondaries, flanks, belly, lower back, rump and under tail-coverts, and dull brownish grey on mantle and scapulars; tail dark grey. Legs dark red, bill pinkish with whitish horn and deep pink base, eyes orange or red with dark red orbital skin. ♀: similar but purplish plumage paler and duller. Flight swift; strong and direct. Feeds on berries, small fruits and acorns. Call: loud, deep-toned cooing. Breeding season variable, March to August in Costa Rica; typical pigeon nest of twigs in tree or shrub, 1 white egg, incubated ♀ and ♂. Usually more than one brood.

Columba guinea *Columbidae*
SPECKLED or CAPE ROCK PIGEON   *c.* 14 ins
Ethiopian: 3 races cover almost whole region except Congo Forests; resident open country and woodlands, cultivated land, usually near rocky outcrops or buildings; common some towns and villages. Head slate grey, neck brown with silvery grey tips to bifurcated feathers; mantle and wings chocolate (reddish purple when plumage fresh), wings spotted white; underparts bluish-grey; legs red, bill black, cere blue-grey, eyes yellow, facial skin red. Southern race *phaenota* smaller and darker. Large numbers at good feeding grounds, but usually solitary, in pairs or small groups. Flight direct and fast, also walks and runs easily. Call: deep guttural *cooo-oo-oo*. Ground feeder on seeds, including grain, may visit trees for fruit. Breeding season depends on region and weather. Builds fairly substantial nest of sticks in cavities at base of leaves of *Borassus* palms, tree-holes, recesses in cliffs or buildings; southern race nests in sea-caves. 2 white eggs, incubated *c.* 15-16 days; young fly 20-23 days (data from captive birds). **355**

Columba livia *Columbidae*
ROCK DOVE   *c.* 13 ins
Palaearctic, Ethiopian, Oriental: Faroes, Shetland and Orkney Is, Scotland and Ireland, particularly N and W coasts and Is, Mediterranean countries, SE Europe, W Asia, Arabia, India, Ceylon, Transcaspia, Turkestan and Africa, N of the Equator. Some local movement in N and S of range. Domestic and feral pigeons, evolved from Rock Dove, are distributed virtually throughout the world, chiefly in large towns. Habitat: cliffs or gorges with caves and fissures for nesting and roosting, rarely seen in trees, may travel some distance for food. Blue-grey; darker on head, breast and belly, iridescent green and purple patch on sides of neck, pale back, whitish rump and two black wing-bars. Legs purplish red, bill black with powdery white cere, eyes orange with blue-grey orbital skin. Variation amongst races e.g. *C. l. intermedia* of Ceylon and India is darker with no white on lower back, *gymnocyclus* of tropical W Africa still darker with red orbital skin. Flight swift, spectacular around cliffs, low over water. Ground feeder taking fallen berries, cultivated grains, seeds and sometimes small animals. Call: similar to crooning *oor-roo-cooo* of domestic and feral pigeons. Social breeder, season usually early summer but prolonged and variable. 2 white eggs laid on slight pad

of twigs, roots and sometimes seaweed on sheltered ledge or in hole; both parents incubate c. 18 days, and feed young on pigeon's milk early on, fly c. 35-37 days. Feral pigeons uses ledges and crevices of buildings. 3 or 4 broods. **356**

Columba oenas *Columbidae*
STOCK DOVE *c.* 13 ins
W Palaearctic: breeds W Europe, N to S Scandinavia, E to Central Asia and S to NW Africa; some winter S to N Sinai. Also found in 'forest islands' of W Siberian steppe. Basically woodland bird but like Wood-pigeon, *C. palumbus*, with which it frequently mingles, has adapted to cultivated country and open suburbs. ♂: darker and bluer grey plumage than larger Wood-pigeon, also no white on neck or wings; blackish tips to secondaries and primaries conspicuous in flight. Legs bright coral red, bill yellowish or dull white with pink base, eyes dark brown. ♀: similar but not so blue-grey, legs and bill usually duskier. Fast flyer; gregarious, feeds on ground taking seeds, grain and small animals. Call: deep *oo-er-oo*. Nests late March to September in holes in old timber, buildings and rocky outcrops, occasionally rabbit burrows or on old nests of other species; may use leaves as well as twigs and straw, but often little or no material. 2 white or creamy white eggs, incubated c. 16-18 days by ♀; both parents feed young with 'pigeon's milk', they fly c. 28 days or earlier. 2 or more broods. **357**

Columba palumbus *Columbidae*
WOODPIGEON *c.* 16 ins
W Palaearctic: breeds Europe up to around 66°N, E to Persia and N India, S to N Africa and W to central Azores. Habitat: adaptable, but usually wooded country of almost any variety, suburbs and towns where sufficient cover. Large rather heavily built pigeon; blue-grey with white patch below glossy purple and green on side of neck and, in flight, broad white band across wing; flanks and belly paler, head and rump slightly bluer than rest of plumage. Legs reddish-purple, bill golden with purplish red base and white cere, eyes yellow with grey orbital skin. Wary, dashes out of cover with clatter of wings; feeds mostly on ground on grain, fruits, nuts etc. and sometimes small animals but in spring and summer also in trees taking young leaves, buds and flowers; gregarious, particularly from autumn to spring. Call: structured cooing of usually 5 notes ending abruptly. Nests spring to autumn, peak mid June to mid September, making twig platform in trees, shrubs or on ledges of buildings; rarely on ground e.g. Orkney. 2 white eggs, incubated 17-19 days by both parents, who tend young, using 'pigeon's milk'; fly 16-35 days. 2 broods. **358**

Columbina passerina *Columbidae*
COMMON GROUND DOVE *c.* 6½ ins
Nearctic, Neotropical: S Carolina and SE Texas S through Mexico, Central America and West Indies to northern S America as far as central Ecuador and N Brazil. Habitat: open country with some tree cover, sandy reefs, open sandy area in forest and savannah–well adapted to cultivated land, villages and towns. ♂: face, sides of neck, breast and underparts dull pink or pinkish grey; nape, crown and hindneck grey, dark spots on lower neck and breast; upperparts grey-brown, wing coverts and outer secondaries pinkish and pale grey with iridescent purplish black or dark blue markings, primaries chestnut with blackish tips; central tail feathers dull dark brown or grey, outer ones black. Some variation with race. ♀: much duller, less grey on head and brownish white in place of pink. Legs dull pink, bill red with blackish tip, eyes vary from dark red to pink. Usually in pairs or small parties, easily approached, mostly on or near ground where feeds chiefly on small seeds. Call: soft low coo with rising inflection, also sharp threatening *wut-wut*. Breeding season prolonged and depends on food supplies; usual pigeon nest but smaller, in tree or shrub, sometimes on ground in tuft of grass. 2 white eggs, incubated 13-14 days; young fly c. 11 days. 2 or more broods. **359**

COLY, RED-FACED see **Urocolius indicus**

COMB DUCK see **Sarkidiornis melanotos**

COMMON
  CARDINAL see **Pyrrhuloxia cardinalis**
  COUCAL see **Centropus sinensis**
  CRANE see **Grus grus**
  CROSSBILL see **Loxia curvirostra**
  CROW see under **Corvus ossifragus**
  EGRET see **Egretta alba**
  GALLINULE see **Gallinula chloropus**
  GO-AWAY-BIRD see **Corythaixodes concolor**
  GOLDENEYE see under **Bucephala islandica**
  GROUND DOVE see **Columbina passerina**
  GUILLEMOT see **Uria aalge**
  GULL see **Larus canus**
  LOON see **Gavia immer**
  MYNAH see **Acridotheres tristis**
  NIGHTHAWK see **Chordeiles minor**
  NODDY see **Anous stolidus**
  POTOO see **Nyctibius griseus**
  PRATINCOLE see **Glareola pratincola**
  RHEA see **Rhea americana**
  SANDPIPER see **Tringa hypoleucos**
  SCOTER see **Melanitta nigra**
  STARLING see **Sturnus vulgaris**
  SWIFT see **Apus apus**
  TAILORBIRD see **Orthotomus sutorius**
  TERN see **Sterna hirundo**
  TIT BABBLER see **Parisoma subcaeruleum**
  WAXBILL see **Estrilda astrild**
  WREN see **Troglodytes troglodytes**

CONDOR,
  ANDEAN see **Vultur gryphus**
  CALIFORNIAN see **Gymnogyps californianus**

Conopophaga lineata *Conopophagidae*
SILVERY-TUFTED or
RUFOUS GNATEATER 5½ (tail nearly 2) ins
Neotropical: E Brazil, Paraguay, NE Argentina; resident bamboo thickets and caatinga (deciduous thorn-clad scrub with cacti and bare areas). Upper-parts, short, rounded wings and tail uniform umber brown; lores and 'eyebrow' blue-grey, with prominent white tuft behind eye; throat, breast cinnamon rufous, white crescent across lower throat, belly white, flanks olivaceous. ♀ has grey tuft behind eye. Legs blue-grey; rather broad, flat hooked bill blackish; eyes light brown. Largely terrestrial or in low shrubs, in pairs. ♂ has simple whistling song ending in lower notes and easily imitated, but accompanied by whirr of wings. Rasping alarm call gives local name *cuspidor* (spitter). Diet: insects and other invertebrates from ground. Builds nest on ground of large dry leaves, lined plant fibres. 2 yellowish eggs, marked with smudged light brown, incubated by ♀ and ♂, who feign injury if disturbed. **571**

Conostoma oemodium *Muscicapidae*:
Paradoxornithinae
GREAT PARROTBILL 12 ins
E Palaearctic, Oriental: Himalayas from Nepal to SE Tibet, W China (NW Yunnan, SW Szechuan), N Burma; secondary growth, rhododendron and bam-boo jungles on hills, 7,000 to 11,000 ft, descending to *c.* 3,000 ft in winter. Upperparts brown; forehead greyish white; underparts pale brown; legs dull green, long powerful bill orange and yellow; eyes pale yellow to orange yellow. Upright carriage. Small parties hop about undergrowth, often with laughing thrushes *Garrulax*, but keeping *c.* 6 ft off ground; also feed on ground, even in snow. Call: clear, musical *wheou wheou* (J. K. Stanford); also grating croaks and *churr* of alarm. Food: insects, especially beetles; seeds, e.g. crab apple, raspberry; green bamboo shoots. Breeds May to July, building compact cup of coarse grass, bamboo leaves, lined fine green grass; in bam-boo clumps. Clutch probably 2 or 3 dull white eggs, sparsely marked pale yellow brown over purple.

Contopus caribaeus see under **C. virens**

Contopus cinereus see under **C. virens**

Contopus virens *Tyrannidae*
EASTERN WOOD PEWEE 6½ ins
Nearctic: breeds Nova Scotia, S Ontario, S Manitoba through Eastern USA to Florida, Gulf Coast, Texas; winters Costa Rica to Colombia and Peru. Habitat: thick woodland to orchards, plantations and parks. Upperparts olive-grey, darker on relatively long wings and deeply notched tail; white margins to wing coverts and inner flight feathers show as bars; underparts buff grey with pale line down centre breast; legs dark grey, bill: upper grey, lower light brown; eyes dark brown. (Very similar but smaller Tropical Pewee, *C. cinereus*, widely distributed in Central and S America, including Trinidad; also W Indies, where sometimes separated as *C. caribaeus*.) Characteristically perches well up tree, sallying out after insects and returning to same branch. Song: clear, plaintive *pee-oo-wee pee-oo*, third phrase *pee-widdi* added in evening; *chip* note when feeding. Breeds from June, building shallow cup of plant materials, lined down and wool, suspended in fork of lateral branch from 6 to 20 ft or more up, hidden from below by lichen covering. 3 or 4 creamy white eggs, marked brown often in zone at big end, incubated by ♀ *c.* 12 days; both parents tend the young who fly *c.* 14 days. 2 broods in S. **577**

COOT see **Fulica atra**

COOT,
  CRESTED see **Fulica cristata**
  RED-KNOBBED see **Fulica cristata**

COPPERSMITH BARBET see **Megalaima haemocephala**

Copsychus sechellarum *Muscicapidae*: *Turdinae*
SEYCHELLES MAGPIE ROBIN *c.* 10 ins
Seychelles (Indian Ocean); confined to island of Frégate, in bushy growth. Black, with blue or green sheen, conspicuous white wing coverts; legs, bill, facial skin black, eyes dark brown. Juvenile black without sheen. Feeds much on ground, even close to buildings, but usually among fallen leaves in bushy under-growth; takes insects, including winged termites, spiders, large millipedes, small lizards. Spreads tail and lowers it before jerking it upward to usual carry-ing position. Display (?threat): fluffing out plumage, trailing wings, tail on ground, bill pointed upward, head turned side to side. Song: 'pleasant series of rising and falling notes with low whistles' (R. Gaymer, M. Penny). Breeds probably March-April, building loose nest of coconut fibres, roots, leaves, feathers, even paper, lined fine grass, at base of coconut palm leaf. Clutch normally single white or pale blue egg.

COQUI FRANCOLIN see **Francolinus coqui**

Coracias abyssinica *Coraciidae*
ABYSSINIAN ROLLER 12 ins to end of normal tail
Ethiopian: Senegal to Ethiopia, E Africa and S Arabia; partially migratory. Habitat: open savannah and semi-desert. Remarkably like *C. garrulus* but brighter and with outermost tail feathers elongated beyond others. Legs light brown, bill black, eyes brown. Juvenile lacks swallow tail but has richer purple-blue flight feathers than *C. garrulus*. Behaviour much as *garrulus*; attacks birds of prey and follows grass fires after disturbed prey. Chuckling and screeching calls but not as harsh as *garrulus*. Breeding season variable, mainly March to June; lays 4 to 6 glossy white eggs in tree hole at varying heights; breeding details as near relatives (see *C. garrulus*). **505**

Coracias bengalensis *Coraciidae*
INDIAN ROLLER 12 ins
Marginally SE Palaearctic (Iran); Oriental; E Arabia, Indian subcontinent, Burma, Thailand; in open country, cultivated land and light deciduous forest; outskirts of towns and villages, gardens. Upperparts chestnut brown; crown blue-green; wings dark and light blue, tail darker with pale subterminal band, central feathers dark green; throat white, breast rufous brown, belly and undertail blue. Often perches, swinging tail up and down, solitarily on wires, posts, trees, whence swoops down to pick up insect and

returns; takes crickets, grasshoppers, beetles; also mice, lizards, frogs. Variety of raucous calls; noisy and demonstrative in courtship when ♂ rockets into air, somersaults and dives down. Breeds March to July in Indian subcontinent. Nest of plant debris and rags in natural hole of tree, or in building, at moderate heights. 4 to 5 pure white eggs incubated by ♀ and ♂ c. 18 days; young fly c. 4 weeks. **506**

Coracias caudata *Coraciidae*
LILAC-BREASTED ROLLER 14½ ins
Ethiopian: E and Southern Africa, except extreme SW; locally migratory. Habitat lowland savannah. Back and scapulars brown, washed green head green; shoulder of wing, outer webs of flight feathers and rump violet; bases of primaries and their coverts pale greenish blue; outer tail feathers elongated and blackish; chin whitish, shading to rich lilac of breast; underparts greenish blue; legs greenish yellow, bill black, eyes brown. Usually singly or in pairs, perched on top of bare tree or on telegraph wires; shelters in heat of day. Aerobatics like other rollers. Calls hoarse and screeching. Takes lizards, insects, following grass fires like *C. abyssinica*. Very shy when breeding, mainly September to December; uses holes in dead trees, palm stumps, anthills. 2 to 3 glossy white eggs incubated by ♀ and ♂ as *C. garrulus*. **507**

Coracias garrulus *Coraciidae*
EUROPEAN ROLLER c. 12 ins
Summer visitor to Palaearctic, breeding from Central Europe to Caspian, also most of Mediterranean area, including NW Africa, and E to River Indus and Turkestan; another extension N of Caspian into Central Asia. Winters almost exclusively on E African savannahs. Breeding habitat open woodland, parklike grassland and steppes with groups of trees; riverine forests with grassy or sandy areas, reaching up to montane zone. Mainly greenish or purplish blue with chestnut mantle, turquoise blue wing patches and black flight feathers; central tail feathers brown washed green, part of others black. Duller all over in winter. Juvenile has head and underparts brownish green. Legs yellowish, bill brownish black, eyes pale brown. Hops on ground, in flight buoyant with crowlike flapping action. Likes exposed perches. Forms parties in winter. Call: harsh *rack kack kackar*, varied in display; also higher-pitched *kaaa*. ♂ rises high in display, then tumbles and somersaults; duets between ♂ and ♀ sitting close together, accompanied by bowing. Takes large insects: locusts, grasshoppers, mantids, caught on wing or pounced upon, also small lizards, scorpions, centipedes; fruit in autumn. Breeds from mid May in Mediterranean area, usually in large tree hole, also old woodpecker holes, cavities and crevices in rocks and walls, old nests of kingfishers and bee-eaters; nestboxes in Slovakia. 4 to 5 glossy white eggs incubated by ♀ and ♂ 18-19 days; both feed young, who fly after 26-28 days. **508**

Coracina novaehollandiae *Campephagidae*
BLACK-FACED CUCKOO SHRIKE 13 ins
Oriental and Australasian: 19 races recognised, from Indian subcontinent and SE China to Timor, Moluccas, Celebes, New Guinea, Australia, Tasmania; occasional in New Zealand. Nomadic in open forests in Australia; in teak, oak and pine forests up to 7,000 ft Burma. Mainly dove grey; forehead, face, throat, primaries black; belly, tip of tail white. Juvenile has dark eyestripe instead of black on head, underparts whitish. Not shy. Characteristic alternate lifting of wings when calling. Harsh grating cry from parties; song: jumble of flute-like notes delivered in flight. Swoops on insect prey from conspicuous perch, also takes insects and worms off ground; some fruit, e.g. figs, and berries. Breeds August to January New South Wales, February to March and again July Queensland; builds nearly flat nest of various plant materials, bound by cobwebs, sometimes decorated bark, usually in fork of lateral branch. 3 olive green to brown eggs, spotted brown over grey at big end. **637**

Coracopsis vasa *Psittacidae*
GREATER VASA PARROT 18-19 ins
Malagasy sub-region: 2 races Madagascar, *C. v. vasa*

in E, *drouhardi* in W; *comorensis* in Comoro Is. Resident in forests of coastal plain, sea level to 3,000 ft, also (*drouhardi*) in open savannah, sub-desert. Almost uniform black-brown, with 'silvery' appearance to edges of wings; legs grey, bill grey to black, eyes brown in white facial skin patch. ♂ slightly bigger than ♀. Noisy, conspicuous, in parties of 10 to 15, often flying over forest, perching in treetops; roosts in hundreds. Calls at night: harsh *car-car*, *ka-kee*, *caaaak*, softer *cree* (A. L. Rand). Feeds with other species on fruit-bearing trees, also on savannah, sandy shores; damages corn crops. Breeds October to December in natural hole c. 10 ft up tree, entered by hollow limb. Clutch probably 3 white eggs.

Coragyps atratus *Cathartidae*
BLACK VULTURE 22 ins
Nearctic and Neotropical: Ohio to Patagonia. Mainly resident in open and wooded country, round towns in subtropics and tropics. Black, including bare head, sometimes with purplish sheen; white patch under spread wing; legs dark brown, bill blackish-brown with pale tip, eyes dark brown. Slow sedate walk but 'sidling half step' with wings raised when hurried. Social for feeding and roosting. Rather laboured flight but steep dives to carrion. Also dives and chases in courtship. Quiet croaking *coo*, and 'snarl' of fear. Eats mainly carrion, also small animals, eggs, rotten fruit. Breeding season variable: from January in Florida. Nesting often colonial, in caves, buildings, tree stumps or on ground; no real nest; 2 pale grey-green eggs marked brown. ♀ and ♂ incubate for 32-39 days, and feed chicks, which fly in 10 or more weeks. **131**

CORAL-BILLED NUTHATCH see **Hypositta coralirostris**

Corcorax melanorhamphus *Grallinidae*
WHITE-WINGED CHOUGH 18 ins
Australasian: eastern areas of continent from N Queensland through Victoria, New South Wales, much of S Australia; mainly resident open grassland with few trees, 'exotic' pine plantations, coastal forest. Black, except for white patch on primaries; long legs black; thin curved bill black; eyes brown in juvenile, orange or red when adult. Lives most of year in small groups of 5 to 10 or more. Display by spreading and moving wings and tail, either as threat or greeting; eye becomes crimson when excited; groups face enemies and hiss. Aggressive call: *cree-ee-ek*; single and double piping and whistles for contact. Forages over ground at ½ mph, turning over stones, litter with bill, eating anything from ants to frogs; scarab larvae from rotten wood; seeds in winter. Breeds September to January in SE, defending group territories c. 100 acres. Group builds nest of mud and plant fibres on lateral branch 25-40 ft up, leave it for week, then one or more ♀♀ return to mate by nest, each laying 3 to 5 creamy white eggs, heavily marked brown and grey. Incubation (c. 20 days) and care of young communal; they leave nest 23-28 days (not more than 4 survive from large 'clutches') but depend on adults for several more weeks. Sometimes 2 broods in large groups. Groups may amalgamate for winter feeding, but retain identity within flock.

CORDON BLEU see **Uraeginthus bengalus**

CORDON BLEU, RED-CHEEKED see **Uraeginthus bengalus**

CORMORANT see **Phalacrocorax carbo**

CORMORANT,
GALAPAGOS see **Nannopterum harrisi**
PIED see **Phalacrocorax varius**

CORN BUNTING see **Emberiza calandra**

CORNCRAKE see **Crex crex**

Corvultur albicollis *Corvidae*
WHITE-NECKED RAVEN c. 20 ins
Ethiopian: Uganda and Kenya S to Cape Province

and S West Africa. Habitat: cliffs and rocky escarpments, travels far for food. Head and neck bronzy brown, broad white collar at base of hindneck, some scattered white feathers across breast (more conspicuous in juvenile); rest black with dull blue and purplish reflections. Legs and heavy bill (smaller in ♀) black with horny white tip, eyes dark brown. Usually in pairs, skilful flyer, bold, always first to dead animal, often scavenges on farms; feeds on carrion, small vertebrates, large insects, fruits and grain. Call: high pitched croak. Breeds August to December; large nest of sticks with lining of grasses, hair and wool, on inaccessible cliff ledge, sometimes in large tree; nest used repeatedly; 5 to 6 blue-green eggs, fairly glossy, marked dark green and brown. **996**

Corvus brachyrhynchos see under **C. ossifragus**

Corvus corax *Corvidae*
RAVEN c. 25 ins
Holarctic, Neotropical, Ethiopian: Europe, America S to Nicaragua, Africa S to 15°N (but Brown-necked race *ruficollis* and Lesser Brown-necked *edithae* S to Kenya); Middle East, Arabia, Asia up to 70°N, but not Japan, E China, SE Asia, Mongolian deserts, Indian subcontinent; Resident sea coasts, bush tundra, rocky moorland, broadleaved and coniferous forests, to warm, cultivated lowlands, bush steppe, deserts. Whole plumage glossy black, robust bill and legs black, eyes dark brown. Solitary, in pairs or flocks, especially at carrion or to roost. Flight appears slow; glides, soars freely, indulges in aerobatics especially in early spring. Calls: deep *pruk pruk*; musical, resonant *kronk* in breeding season. Diet varied, principally carrion, but kills small vertebrates. Breeds late January onwards; solitary, both ♀ and ♂ build substantial nest of sticks, heather stems, seaweed, debris, solidified with grass or moss, lined thickly wool, hair, vegetable bast; on ledge, usually overhung, of cliff, crag, quarry, in trees from 15 to 75 ft; occasionally buildings, even top of steep bank. 4 to 6 light blue or green eggs, liberally marked brown over grey, incubated ♀ c. 21 days; both parents feed young from bill or throat; fledging 35-40 days. **997**

Corvus cornix see under **C. corone**

Corvus corone *Corvidae*
CARRION and HOODED CROW c. 18½ ins
Palaearctic: whole region except northern coastal areas USSR and S Mediterranean area (though breeds Nile delta); Hooded race, *C. c. cornix*, between Rivers Elbe and Yenisea (and Ireland, N Scotland), Carrion, *corone* to W and E; resident and migratory, chiefly Hooded Crows wintering temperate zone. Habitat varied: arable and grassland, moors and hill country; coasts and shores of lakes; suburbs to city centres; generally avoids denser woodland. Carrion Crow uniformly black, glossed green, base of bill fully feathered; Hooded Crow has black head and throat, wings, tail; body grey, but many hybrid forms occur where races meet. Legs, bill black, eyes dark brown. Solitary, pairs, small to large flocks, especially for roosting. Faster wingbeat than Raven, rarely soars. Call: slow, hoarse, often repeated, croaking *kraaarrr*, delivered with jerk of body. Bowing display rather similar to Rook. Almost omnivorous; breaks hard-shelled prey by dropping from height; may kill small birds, rob nests. Breeds March onwards, solitary like Raven; nest of twigs, seaweed, debris, solidified with moss, then usually lined wool, hair, bark strips and bast; in trees at all heights, bushes, cliffs, crags, steep banks; occasionally buildings. 4 to 6 eggs, like Raven's but smaller, glossier, incubated ♀ c. 19 days; both parents feed young from bill or throat; fledging c. 26-35 days. **998**

Corvus frugilegus *Corvidae*
ROOK c. 18 ins
Palaearctic: western range includes Europe, (except Mediterranean area and Scandinavia, where very local in S), N Asia Minor, Iran and large area W Central Asia to Upper Yenisei; eastern range from SE of Lake Baikal to upper River Lena, Manchuria S to most of China; resident and migratory, northern

populations moving into temperate zone where soil seldom freezes; Mediterranean, Iran, NW Indian subcontinent, China. Habitat varied: grassy valleys, small woods, forest edges, parkland, cultivated areas with spinneys, shelterbelts; seldom in mountains. Bare, greyish-white cere round bill; chin, upper throat dark greyish-brown; otherwise black, mostly glossed reddish purple, crown, nape greenish purple; loose flank feathers give baggy appearance round thighs. Juvenile lacks bare cere. Legs, bill black, eyes dark brown. Slow walker; flight steady and direct. Gregarious at all times, large woodland roosts autumn, winter, often with Jackdaws, *C. monedula*. Usual call *kaah,* but wide vocabulary recorded. ♂ droops wings, bows to ♀, fans tail and caws in display on tree or ground; ♀ responds by crouching. Diet: earthworms, insects and larvae, snails; seedlings, fruits, grain; forages by plunging bill deep into soil; carries food in throat pouch. Breeds February onwards colonially into thousands of pairs, usually in small wood or line of tall trees; nest less tidy than Crow, *C. corone,* of sticks, debris, lined grass, leaves, moss. 4 to 6 eggs like Crow's but green rather than blue, markings sometimes more intense. ♀ incubates 16-19 days; both parents feed young, who fledge 29-30 days. **999**

Corvus monedula *Corvidae*
JACKDAW *c.* 13 ins
Palaearctic: Europe, except N Spain, SW France, N Scandinavia and N Russia; Asia Minor E to W edge Himalayas and Mongolia; sedentary and migratory, most of northern breeding birds winter in W and S of range. Habitat: parks and wooded areas with plenty of old timber, also near old buildings, inland and sea cliffs; increasingly in cultivated areas. Generally glossy black, bluish on crown and forehead, tinges of blue elsewhere; nape and side of neck grey, paler in nominate race which breeds S Scandinavia; juveniles lack this grey but are uniform, deep brownish black. Legs and bill black, eyes pearl grey. Quicker and more alert than larger crows, faster wingbeat in flight, also glides about cliff faces or in other upward air currents; gregarious, especially in winter when frequently flocks with Rooks, *C. frugilegus*. Call: short, fairly high *chack*. Omnivorous; forages on grassland, takes insects, other small animals including young birds, eggs, and some plant matter e.g. cereals, fruits and berries; hides food and inedible objects. Breeds April onwards, social; nest varies from mere lining to over 2 cubic yards of material (sticks and any rubbish, lined wool or hair), in cavity in rocks, tree or building, sometimes chimney, also rabbit holes. 4 to 6 light blue-green eggs, spotted and streaked dark brown. ♀ incubates *c.* 19 days; both parents tend young, who fledge 30-35 days. **1000**

Corvus ossifragus *Corvidae*
FISH CROW *c.* 16 ins
Nearctic: Atlantic and Gulf coasts from lower Delaware and Hudson R valleys and S Massachusetts to Florida, Louisiana, E Texas, probably extending N and inland; some movement to S part of range in winter. Habitat: coastal regions, also rivers, swamps and lakes, but never very far from water. Black with steel blue or deep purplish gloss, underparts more greenish; more pointed wings and slimmer than similar Common Crow, *C. brachyrhynchos*. Legs, bill and eyes blackish. Gregarious, often huge roosts, hovers and soars rather like Raven, *C. corax*. Call: terse, nasal *car* or *kark*. Omnivorous: insects, cultivated grains, fruits, marine and aquatic animals from shore, robs nests. Breeds May and June, social; stick nest lined with bark strips, pine needles, moss and grasses, usually in pines or cedars, 20 to 60 ft up; 4 to 6 bluish green eggs, heavily marked with browns. Both parents incubate *c.* 17 days; young fly *c.* 3 weeks. **1001**

Corythaeola cristata *Musophagidae*
GREAT BLUE TOURACO 30 ins
Ethiopian: Equatorial Africa from W coast as far east as W Kenya, especially Congo forests and their extensions, but also other lowland forests including narrow gallery and small patches in otherwise cultivated land. A magnificent bird, running and hopping about in canopy, displaying and calling *kok kok kok,* following by bubbling croaks, then flying off and planing down to half way up another tree before running and hopping to the top. Predominantly blue and apple green, but chestnut belly, black crest and tail band. Large yellow beak slightly hooked and red-tipped. Only touraco without crimson wings. Fruit eater. Flimsy pigeon-like nest in thick medium size tree; 2-3 white eggs, downy active young. **410**

Corythaixodes concolor *Musophagidae*
COMMON GO-AWAY BIRD 20 ins
Ethiopian: most of Southern Africa from about 7°S right down to Cape, and right across to west coast up to mouth of Congo river, wherever habitat suitable. Prefers acacia country but tolerates both drier (SW Africa) and wetter areas (Indian Ocean littoral), but not forest. Grey all over with long grey crest and long tail but black bill. Conspicuous as it flies from tree to tree in small parties, calling loudly with penetrating nasal *g'way gwaaay* from which it gets name. Food mostly fruit, especially figs, but also berries and young shoots. Nest a flimsy pigeon-like affair usually in dense creepers high up in acacia tree, with 2 or 3 white eggs. Nestlings have thick brown down. **411**

Corythaixodes leucogaster *Musophagidae*
WHITE-BELLIED GO-AWAY BIRD 20 ins
Ethiopian: E Africa from Ethiopia and S Sudan to N Tanzania in dry bush country and savannah. Pale grey back, head, crest and chest, but pure white belly. Beak only medium stout, black in ♂, green in ♀ (the only sex difference in any touraco-like bird). Conspicuous, often perching on a tree-top and flying from tree to tree calling loudly its harsh sheep-like bleet just recognisable as *go-awaay* prolonged. Feeding and nesting habits as in other go-away birds. **412**

Corythaixodes personata *Musophagidae*
BARE-FACED GO-AWAY BIRD 20 ins
Ethiopian: two isolated groups, one in Central and SW Ethiopia, the other 700 miles away centred on Tanzania, in same kind of acacia country as *C. concolor,* but not overlapping with it, as ecological niches similar. Ethiopian birds generally grey, especially above, but chest greenish and belly brownish. Southern group have neck and chest white. Both have bare patches of dark skin on face, neck. Feeding, nesting habits as *C. concolor*.

Corythornis cristata *Alcedinidae*
MALACHITE KINGFISHER 5 ins
Ethiopian: all sub-Saharan Africa except Somalia and Gabon area; also S Arabia. Common bushy margins rivers, streams, lakes, swamps, perching on low vegetation whence it dashes off to catch fish, aquatic insects or dragon-flies; very rapid flight, calling *peep, peep.* Mainly ultramarine above, tawny below, but throat white, large crest pale blue, barred black, often raised and lowered when perched; red bill, feet. 3 to 6 round white glossy eggs end of short tunnel road-side or stream bank; parents normally splash in water after feeding young in dirty nest chamber. **486**

Coscoroba coscoroba *Anatidae*
COSCOROBA SWAN 29 ins
Neotropical: breeds S Brazil, Uruguay, Paraguay, Argentina, Chile including Tierra del Fuego, and Falkland Is; winters N to about 25°S. Frequents brackish lakes with dense vegetation and coastal swamps. Smallest swan, all white apart from black tips to primaries. Legs and bill bright rosy pink. Gregarious, feeds by dabbling in shallow water for aquatic and terrestrial plants – also takes seeds, fruits and some animal material. Voice: bugling, ♂ higher-pitched than ♀. Like geese, pairing is fairly permanent; breeding season July to November. Usually solitary or in dispersed groups; pair builds large mound, cup well lined with down, often on old nest. 5 to 9 white eggs, incubated by ♀ for *c.* 35 days; young stay in vicinity of nest for up to 4-5 months. **113**

COSCOROBA SWAN see **Coscoroba coscoroba**

Cosmopsarus regius *Sturnidae*
GOLDEN-BREASTED STARLING *c.* 12 ins
Ethiopian: S Somalia, S Ethiopia, E Kenya, NE Tanzania; resident dry bush country. Upperparts, including earcoverts, wings, dark metallic blue glossed purple; head, neck metallic green; long graduated tail dull metallic gold with blue and violet; underparts rich golden yellow with metallic violet patch on breast. Juvenile duller. Perches in flocks in tree tops, taking off with whistling, chattering cry. Diet: fruits, berries, insects. Breeds March to May in different parts range, lining hole or crack in tree with straw, leaves, roots. 2 to 6 elongated, pale greenish blue eggs, minutely speckled red-brown. **966**

Cossypha caffra *Muscicapidae*: *Turdinae*
CAPE ROBIN 7 ins
Ethiopian: Eastern (S from Sudan) and Southern Africa; resident forest and bush, to high altitudes Tanzania; also cultivated land right into cities. Upperparts olivaceous brown, wing coverts slaty, flight feathers dusky grey, upper tail coverts and outer tail tawny to chestnut, centre feathers blackish; crown grey, 'eyebrow' from bill white; lores to earcoverts black; chin to upper breast tawny; lower breast, flanks grey, belly whitish, under tail coverts buff; legs, bill black, eyes brown. Juvenile mottled. Though accustomed to man, flies to cover if disturbed. Hops on ground, flirting tail. Call soft, up to 6 or 7 notes; alarm *wadeda;* short, very sweet song phrase: *jan-free-derik.* Food mainly insects and berries. Breeding season varies within range; evidently 2 broods Kenya. Nest of moss and rootlets hidden in tree stump, under creepers or moss. 2 or 3 bluish or greenish eggs, densely speckled brown over lilac, often in cap at big end. **678**

Cossypha humeralis *Muscicapidae*: *Turdinae*
WHITE-THROATED ROBIN (CHAT) 6¼ ins
Ethiopian: E Southern Africa, resident dense thorn and riverine scrub. Upperparts, including head, grey; wings blackish, lesser coverts forming conspicuous white bar; upper tail coverts, tail chestnut but central feathers and all tips blackish; white 'eyebrow'; sides of face, neck, breast black; chin and underparts white; under tail coverts chestnut. Solitary or in pairs, sometimes near habitations. Hops on ground. Other habits somewhat as *C. caffra*. **679**

COSTA'S HUMMINGBIRD see **Calypte costae**

Cotinga cayana *Cotingidae*
SPANGLED COTINGA 8½ ins
Neotropical: Guyanas, Venezuela, E Colombia, S to E Peru, N Bolivia and Brazil; resident forests, open woodland, savannah, sea level to 4,000 ft. ♂: crown and back iridescent turquoise blue, feathers with conspicuous black bases; wings and tail black; throat and upper breast reddish purple. ♀: blackish brown above, greyish buff below; feathers have narrow whitish edges. Solitary, feeding on fruit and insects. Builds cup nest high in forest tree, lays 2 white eggs tinged blue. Incubation and care of young by ♀ alone in related species. **591**

COTINGA, SPANGLED see **Cotinga cayana**

Coturnix pectoralis *Phasianidae*
STUBBLE QUAIL 18 ins
Continental non-tropical Australia, Tasmania; nomadic over open grasslands and cultivated areas (stubbles, lucerne). Brown, variegated by lines of white arrowmarks on darker feathers, ♂ has sides of head and throat rufous, separated from crown by white stripe over eye; ♀'s throat and underparts of ♂ and ♀ white; legs flesh-white, bill blackish, eyes red-brown. Usually in coveys, varying in size, at times very large, but seldom seen; calls and small round faeces usual signs of presence. If flushed, rises with loud whirr. Call a loud clear whistle: *two to weep.* Diet mainly seeds and leaves of cultivated cereals and introduced weeds; insects and their grubs. Breeding varies with rainfall, often September to January or February; ♀ makes lined scrape in cover, sometimes standing crops, incubates 7 to 11 buff eggs, marked red-brown all over; precocious young soon fly. **195**

COUCAL,
COMMON see **Centropus sinensis**
SENEGAL see **Centropus senegalensis**
WHITE-BROWED see **Centropus superciliosus**

COUNT RAGGI'S BIRD OF PARADISE see
Paradisaea raggiana

COUROL see **Leptosomus discolor**

COURSER,
TEMMINCK'S see **Cursorius temminckii**
TWO-BANDED see **Hemerodromus africanus**

COWBIRD,
BAY-HEADED see under **Molothrus ater**
BROWN-HEADED see **Molothrus ater**

CRAB PLOVER see **Dromas ardeola**

Cracticus
argenteus see under **C. torquatus**
nigrogularis see under **C. torquatus**

Cracticus torquatus *Cracticidae*

GREY BUTCHERBIRD   11½ ins
Australian: 4 races cover most of continent except
Cape York in NE and large area from Gulf of Carpentaria to W coast and SE into interior, thus isolating the
NW population, formerly regarded as separate species,
Silver-backed Butcherbird *C. argenteus.* Habitat: open
forests and wooded savannah; orchards and gardens
with well spaced trees. ♂: upperparts dove grey; crown
and cheeks, much of wings and tail black; collar,
wing patch, rump, tip of tail white; underparts white
to greyish white. ♀'s crown duller. Legs grey-black,
bill bluish grey, tip black, upper mandible sharply
hooked, eyes red brown. Juvenile brownish where
adult black, confusing with juvenile Pied Butcherbird,
C. nigrogularis. Aggressive and predatory but usually
competes unsuccessfully with *C. nigrogularis* where
both occur. Fluting, warbling song, often in duet,
heard throughout year; some mimicry; strident alarm
calls. Largely insectivorous but also takes small birds,
mice, reptiles, pinned to thorn or wedged in fork as
larder; beetles battered on stones. Breeds July to
January; nest of twigs, lined rootlets, grass, in fork of
tree or bush from ground level to *c.* 30 ft. 3 to 5 variable
grey-green to brownish eggs, spotted red-brown near
big end, incubated ♀, fed by ♂, 23 days. Both parents
feed young, who fly *c.* 4 weeks, but are tended for
several months after this, may stay with parents over
following season. **983**

CRAG MARTIN see **Hirundo rupestris**

CRAKE
BLACK AFRICAN see **Limnocorax flavirostra**
SPOTLESS see **Porzana plumbea**
BLUE see **Anthropoides paradisaea**
BROLGA see **Grus rubicundus**
COMMON see **Grus grus**
CROWNED see **Balearica pavonina**
DEMOISELLE see **Anthropoides virgo**
JAPANESE see **Grus japonensis**
MANCHURIAN see **Grus japonensis**
SANDHILL see under **Grus americana**
SARUS see **Grus antigone**
SIBERIAN WHITE see **Grus leucogeranus**
STANLEY'S see **Anthropoides paradisaea**
WATTLED see **Grus carunculatus**
WHITE-NECKED see **Grus vipio**
WHOOPING see **Grus americana**

Crax daubentoni *Cractaae*

YELLOW-KNOBBED CURASSOW   33 ins
Neotropical: Venezuela and Colombia; resident in
forests and forest edge. ♂: glossy black except for
white underparts, long tail tipped white, crest
feathers curled forward; legs grey, bill black with
yellow knob at base, eyes dark. ♀: barred white on
crest, wing coverts, breast and flanks; no knob on
dusky bill. Runs along branches agilely up to tree-top
to take off in fluttering glide on short, rounded wings.
Strongly territorial in breeding season, then forms

small flocks. Air chambers in neck amplify 'strange
muffled' calls. Diet of buds, tender leaves, fruit, some
small vertebrates and worms. Builds small nest of twigs
and leaves, often over water. 2 or 3 rough-shelled
white eggs incubated *c.* 29 days; young hatch with
developed flight feathers, take wing in 3-4 days, fed by
parents mainly on animal matter. **178**

Creadion carunculatus or Philesturnus caruncul-
atus *Callaeidae*

SADDLEBACK   10 ins
Confined to New Zealand: N Island race now only
Hen I, N Auckland; S Island race on 3 South Cape Is,
SW of Stewart Island; resident lower storeys of forest.
Generally glossy black, with bluish sheen head,
breast; chestnut 'saddle' covers upperparts from back
to upper tail coverts, including wing coverts; flight
feathers dark brown, outer webs glossy black; under
tail coverts chestnut; orange wattles at gape; legs, bill
black, eyes dark brown. N Island race has narrow
yellowish line bordering upper edge saddle; immature
like adult but duller; S Island immature generally olive
brown, pale on underparts, upper and under tail
coverts reddish brown. Makes short flights through
understorey, also hops from branch to branch. Pairs
remain together all year, tearing off bark in search for
insects; also feed on ground, on fruit and berries;
occasionally nectar. Calls: rapid, penetrating *cheep
te te te te; che-che-u-che,* both repeated continually (H.
Guthrie-Smith): softer duets between pair; ♂ has soft
musical song. Breeds October to January, twig nest
with finer lining, in hollow tree or dense epiphytes on
trunk, from near ground to 6 ft. Usually 2 pale grey or
white eggs, marked reddish brown over fainter purple,
incubated ♀ *c.* 21 days S Cape Is); ♂ also broods young
and takes food from ♀ for them; they may remain
some months with parents. **980**

Creagrus furcatus *Laridae*

SWALLOW-TAILED GULL   13 ins
Neotropical: breeds only Galapagos and Malpelo
Island (4°N); disperses to W coast S America:
Ecuador to S Peru. Habitat open sea and rocky islands
where breeds, fishing up to 300 miles away. Upper
mantle and underparts white (breast tinted rosy in
breeding season); back and wing coverts pearly grey;
head slaty grey with narrow black collar; primaries
black, white triangle on spread wing; deeply forked
tail white; legs pink, bill blackish, tip yellow, large
eyes brown, orbits crimson. Head whiter in winter with
greyish rings round eyes and neck. In flight 'pulsating
upward and downward movement of body' (R. C.
Murphy). Largely nocturnal. Travels singly or in
small flocks, soaring high and swooping down spirally.
Food mainly squids; seen chasing surface fish. Pairs
have 9 month breeding cycle, laying single egg,
greenish or bluish white, boldly spotted and blotched
dark brown and mauve, in slight scrape, lined with
small stones on rocky shores. Incubation *c.* 34 days.
Young fly 7-8 weeks but dependent much longer. **321**

Creatophora cinerea *Sturnidae*

WATTLED STARLING   8½ ins
Ethiopian: SW Arabia; Somalia, Ethiopia, W to
Zaire, Angola, S to Cape of Good Hope. Nomadic and
sporadic in open savannah with short grass, and open
bush. Non-breeding ♂: generally grey, rump paler;
head feathered except for black streaks at side throat;
flight and tail feathers black, glossed greenish; white
primary coverts form patch on wing. Head becomes
bare yellow when breeding with black wattles on
crown, forehead, throat. ♀ as non-breeding ♂ but no
white on wing; rump whitish. Legs brown, bill
pinkish, eyes dark brown. Juvenile ♂ as ♀, juvenile ♀
browner. Small parties or large flocks, often with Pied
Starling, *Spreo bicolor;* aerial evolutions like many
relatives. Call: rasping, squeaky whistle; subdued
rasping song; noise of young in colony 'shattering'
(O.P.M. Prozesky). Follows locust swarms, which
control its breeding season; also takes grasshoppers,
crickets, termites, snails, fruit, offal. Colonial up to
thousands of pairs, breeding where locusts have laid
eggs liable to desert site if locusts move. Double or triple
nests common, of thorny twigs in thorn bushes. 3 or 4
pale greenish blue eggs, occasionally speckled. **967**

CREEPER,
BROWN see **Certhia familiaris**
SPOTTED see **Salpornis spilonotus**

CRESTED,
BARBET see **Trachyphonus vaillantii**
BUNTING see **Melophus lathami**
COOT see **Fulica cristata**
DUCK, ANDEAN see **Lophonetta specularoides**
GREBE, GREAT see **Podiceps cristatus**
GUINEAFOWL see **Guttera edouardi**
HONEY BUZZARD see under **Pernis apivorus**
LARK see **Galerida cristata**
LARK, NIGERIAN see **Galerida modesta**
PIGEON see **Ocyphaps lophotes**
SWIFT, INDIAN see **Hemiprocne longipennis**
TERN see under **Sterna bengalensis**
TIT see **Parus cristatus**
TOURACO, PURPLE see **Gallirex
porphyreolophus**

Crex crex *Rallidae*

CORNCRAKE   *c.* 10½ ins
Palaearctic: across temperate zone from Ireland and
France to Near East and W Siberia; summer visitor to
breeding range, wintering Africa, Madagascar,
Arabia. Inhabits grasslands, natural or cultivated,
also drier parts of bogs and marshes. Feathers of
upperparts with black centres and brown margins;
underparts chestnut brown, barred whitish on belly;
grey throat and stripe over eye, chin white; wings
mainly bright chestnut brown; legs pale flesh, bill
pale brown, tip darker, eyes pale brown. Very secretive, flying apparently feebly when flushed, though a
long distance migrant. Walks with bobbing head and
flirting tail, runs swiftly with body horizontal. In
courtship and aggressive displays ♂ fans tail coverts
and fluffs neck feathers. Famous monotonously
repeated *crek crek* call, origin of scientific name and
familial 'crake', delivered by ♂ with head well up and
bill open; other less well known notes. Diet varied:
mainly insects but some other invertebrates and some
plant stems and seeds. Breeds from early May in
Europe in thick cover of grass or other vegetation,
lining scrape, sometimes with 'grass' canopy, and
laying 6 to 14 light greenish grey or buff eggs, marked
red-brown and grey. Incubation by ♀ 14-21 days; ♂
or both parents tend young who fly *c.* 5 weeks, not full
grown for 7 or 8; sometimes two broods. **224**

CRIMSON
CHAT see **Ephthianura tricolor**
FINCH see **Neochmia phaeton**
FINCH, PALE see under **Neochmia phaeton**
ROSELLA see **Platycercus elegans**

CRIMSON-BACKED WOODPECKER CEYLON see
Chrysocolaptes lucidus stricklandi

CRIMSON-CRESTED WOODPECKER see
Phloeoceastes melanoleucos

CRIMSON-HORNED PHEASANT see **Tragopan satyra**

CRIMSON-RUMPED WAXBILL see under **Estrilda
astrild**

CRIMSON-WINGED PARROT see under
Aprosmictes scapularis

Crinifer piscator see under **C. zonurus**

Crinifer zonurus *Musophagidae*

GREY PLANTAIN-EATER   20 ins
Ethiopian: E Africa, especially Uganda. Closely
related *C. piscator* takes over westwards to Guinea
coast with small overlap in Central Africa. Habitat
savannah woodland and cultivated areas, including
suburban gardens. Dark grey with white wing bar;
backward pointing crest; long tail, short wings; bill
greenish yellow, fairly large. Conspicuous, tame and
noisy, running and hopping about in trees, flying up
and dive-bombing its mate, cackling with maniacal
laughter. Fruit eater. Nest of loose sticks in smallish
tree, 2 to 3 white eggs. **413**

Crithagra
   albogularis see **Serinus albogularis**
   flaviventris see **Serinus flaviventris**

Crocethia alba see **Calidris alba**

CROMBEC,
   LONG-BILLED see **Sylvietta rufescens**
   RED-FACED see under **Sylvietta rufescens**

CROSSBILL, COMMON see **Loxia curvirostra**

Crossoptilon crossoptilon *Phasianidae*
ELWES'S or HARMAN'S EARED PHEASANT   28 ins
E Palaearctic: 4 races in China, Tibet, NE India;
inhabits edge between grassy slopes and rhododendron or juniper thickets from *c.* 3,000 to *c.* 14,000 ft.
Upperparts dark ash grey, blackest on neck, palest on
tail coverts, rump; tail metallic blue-black; crown
and nape velvet black, elongated eartufts form white
ring with chin and throat; underparts white to ashy
grey; legs scarlet, bill reddish horn, eyes orange
yellow. Parties of 5 to 10 birds leave cover morning
and evening to feed on seeds, shoots, roots, tubers,
berries and insects; Szechuan (China) birds come
close to houses. Reluctant to fly, scurrying uphill to
cover when surprised. Harsh call like guineafowl
audible for 1 mile. Display like Brown-eared Pheasant,
C. mantchuricum. Breeds probably May onwards Tibet;
nest lined bark, rotten wood, moss, under dead tree;
♀ incubates 4 to 9 greyish green eggs 24 days; monogamous, so ♂ probably helps with brood. **196**

Crossoptilon mantchuricum *Phasianidae*
BROWN-EARED PHEASANT   40 (tail 22) ins
E Palaearctic: W China (NW Shaunsi and Chihli);
sedentary in remains of montane forests up to snow
line. Sexes alike, feathers loose and 'hairy': body and
wings dark brown, becoming black on neck; fluffy tail
white, outer feathers edged purple, central 4 filamentous with black tips; crown velvet black, curved
eartufts and throat white; legs crimson, bill reddish
brown, eyes pale red brown, facial skin red. In flocks
of 10 to 30, running fast if alarmed, taking off uphill
and planing down again; roost in trees. ♂ in courtship
runs round ♀, tail cocked, one wing dropped, wattles
extended, then chases her. Constant cackle when
feeding; repeated *wrack* of alarm; *trip-crra-ah* when
courting. Food dug out with bills: bulbs, roots,
insects; also seeds, leaves and shoots. Breeds May, ♀
lining well-hidden scrape, incubating 5 to 8 pale stone
green eggs 26-27 days; ♂ probably helps with brood.

Crotophaga ani *Cuculidae*
SMOOTH-BILLED ANI   13 ins
S Nearctic and Neotropical: S Florida, W Indies, S to
Argentina on E, and W Ecuador on W of Andes; open
bushy country; round habitations in W Indies.
Generally black, feathers of crown, mantle and breast
with metallic gloss on edges, wings and long tail
purple-black. Legs black, bill black, deep, strongly
keeled or arched on top, shorter than that of *C. major*;
eyes brown. 'Noisy and grotesque in appearance and
movements' (G. A. C. Herklots); weak flyer. Call,
often in flight, shrill *weu-ik weu-ik.* Diet of insects, e.g.
beetles, grasshoppers, bugs; also seeds. Breeds January
to September Trinidad, building in bush or tree, 6 to
20 ft up, deep cup of sticks, tendrils, grass, lined green
leaves which stain blue, chalky covered eggs. Several
♀♀ often lay 10 to 15 eggs in same nest, in layers somewhat separated by leaves; bottom ones usually fail to
hatch; 3 adults may incubate together. **423**

Crotophaga major *Cuculidae*
GREATER ANI   19 (tail 11) ins
Neotropical: Panama S to Argentina on E, Colombia
on W of Andes; swamps, including mangroves.
Generally metallic blue-black, glossed as *C. ani*; legs
black, large black vertically compressed bill with
prominent keel on top, eyes pale green. In pairs or
small parties, with undulating flight of family. Call:
loud harsh *keheeu.* Diet as *C. ani.* Breeds August to
November Trinidad. Nest of twigs, lined leaves, *c.* 10
ft in mangrove over or near water, holds 3 to 10 deep
blue, chalk covered eggs, laid communally. **424**

CROW,
   CARRION see **Corvus corone**
   COMMON see under **Corvus ossifragus**
   FISH see **Corvus ossifragus**
   HOODED see under **Corvus corone**
   KING see under **Dicrurus annectans**

CROW PHEASANT see **Centropus sinensis**

CROW-BILLED DRONGO see **Dicrurus annectans**

CROWNED,
   CRANE see **Balearica pavonina**
   EAGLE see **Stephanoaetus coronatus**
   HORNBILL see **Tockus alboterminatus**
   PLOVER see **Vanellus coronatus**

CUCKOO,
   BLACK-EARED see under **Chthonicola sagittata**
   CHESTNUT see **Piaya cayana**
   DIDRIC see **Chrysococcyx caprius**
   EURASIAN see **Cuculus canorus**
   GREAT SPOTTED see **Clamator glandarius**
   HORSFIELD BRONZE see under **Malurus
      leucopterus**
   KLAAS'S see under **Cinnyris venustus**
   PALLID see **Cuculus pallidus**
   RED-BILLED GROUND see **Carpococcyx renauldi**
   RENAULD'S GROUND see **Carpococcyx renauldi**
   SHINING see **Chalcites lucidus**
   SQUIRREL see **Piaya cayana**
   VIOLET see **Chalcites xanthorhynchus**

CUCKOO DOVE, LARGE BROWN see **Macropygia
phasianella**

CUCKOO ROLLER see **Leptosomus discolor**

CUCKOO SHRIKE,
   BLACK see **Campephaga sulphurata**
   BLACK-FACED see **Coracina novaehollandiae**
   GROUND see **Pteropodocys maxima**

Cuculus canorus *Cuculidae*
COMMON CUCKOO   *c.* 13 ins
Palaearctic, Oriental and Ethiopian: almost throughout Eurasia to Japan, except arctic; Arabia, Indian
sub-continent and SE Asia; NW Africa; most of
Africa S of Sahara, except Congo forests; not Madagascar. Eurasian breeding birds migrate to tropical
Africa, S and SE Asia. African race has complicated
movements. Habitat extremely varied, according to
fosterers. ♂: upperparts and breast blue-grey, pointed
wingtips darker grey; long graduated tail marked and
tipped white; underparts whitish with narrow black
bars; legs yellow, bill: upper dark horn, lower:
greenish; eyes orange yellow. ♀ washed brown across
breast, occasional 'hepatic' with rich chestnut upperparts. Juvenile dark brown above, buffish-white
below, usually barred black all over with white spot
at nape; eyes brown. African race *gularis* has more
yellow on bill, complete bars across tail. Rapid flapping
flight with glide to perch, balancing with wings and
tail; waddles or hops on ground. ♂'s 'song' *coo-coo*,
emphasis on second syllable and with variations. ♀
has water-bubbling call; both utter harsh *kwow wow
wow* and gruff repeated *gror.* Young in nest hisses. ♂
postures to ♀ in display, tail spread and calling
repeatedly. Lays from early May in Britain, parasitising large variety of passerines; each ♀ probably
deposits 6 to 18 eggs. Colour varies from off-white
thickly speckled brown or red to pure buff, in different nests of same fosterer. Incubation by fosterer 12½
days; chick ejects other eggs or young, flies in *c.* 3
weeks fed by foster ♀ and ♂, sometimes by other birds
attracted by red gape and insistent calls. **425**

Cuculus pallidus *Cuculidae*
PALLID CUCKOO   *c.* 13 ins
Australia and Tasmania; open forest, arriving August
in S of range and leaving in February. ♂ generally
light brownish-grey with pale underparts; pale spots
on wing coverts, small white patch on forewing, flight
feathers grey-black barred white; dark, white-edged
feathers on upper tail coverts, pale flecks on long,
graduated tail; underwing grey-brown barred white;

legs olive, bill and eyes dark brown, orbits yellow.
Usually seen singly, behaving much as *C. canorus*, often
perching fence posts. ♂'s series of loud notes, ascending
scale, sometimes varied with harsh calls and uttered at
night, earns name of 'brain fever bird' (shared by
Asian cuckoos). ♀ has hoarse *cheer.* Diet: insects,
especially hairy caterpillars. Lays September onwards
in New South Wales, parasitising over 80 passerines,
especially honey-eaters *Meliphagidae* and other open-
nesting species. Egg flesh pink, sometimes with dark
spots. **426**

Cuncuma vocifer see **Haliaeetus vocifer**

CURASSOW, YELLOW-KNOBBED see **Crax
daubentoni**

CURLEW see **Numenius arquata**

CURLEW,
   BEACH see **Esacus magnirostris**
   DOUBLE-STRIPED STONE see **Burhinus bistriatus**
   HUDSONIAN see **Numenius phaeopus**
   STONE see **Burhinus oedicnemus**

CURLEW SANDPIPER see **Calidris ferruginea**

Cursorius temminckii *Glareolidae*
TEMMINCK'S COURSER   8 ins
Ethiopian: almost throughout region, except NE,
Congo Forests, SW Africa; resident in all types of
short grass country, e.g. airfields, and open bush.
Upperparts dull dark brown; crown chestnut, encircled from nape to eye by black and white stripes;
flight feathers and underwings blue-black; outer tail
feathers white as are throat, belly, under tail coverts;
upper breast light brown, lower dark chestnut; legs
whitish, thin slightly curved bill blackish, eyes brown.
Generally in small flocks, which rise into jerky,
lapwing-like flight with twittering calls. Diet: insects
and their larvae. Breeding season variable throughout
range; lays 2 creamy or pale stone eggs, densely
speckled and scrawled dark brown, on bare ground;
probably incubated by ♀ alone. **309**

CURVE-BILLED THRASHER see **Toxostoma
curvirostre**

Cyanerpes caeruleus *Emberizidae: Coerebinae*
PURPLE or YELLOW-LEGGED
HONEYCREEPER   4½ (bill ¾) ins
Neotropical: Trinidad, Guyanas, Venezuela, Colombia S through E and W Ecuador to SE Peru, Amazonian Brazil, N Bolivia; forest, secondary growth
(Brazilian capoeira), coffee plantations, sea level to *c.*
4,000 ft. ♂ (Trinidad): generally black and purple,
bluer and brighter crown, cheeks, back; eyestripe,
throat, wings, tail black; legs sulphur yellow, bill dark
grey, eyes brown. ♀: rich olive green, throat buff,
underparts variously streaked; under tail coverts
yellowish; creamy patch on dusky underwing; lores
chestnut buff, dappled earcoverts separated from
throat by narrow violet moustachial stripe; legs
greenish yellow. Loose flocks of both sexes roam treetops after varied food: small insects, nectar, fruit,
especially over-ripe oranges; closely related *C. cyaneus*
addicted to arils of *Clusia* seeds. Call: nasal *chaa*;
responds to imitation of Pygmy Owl, *Glaucidium
brasilianum. C. cyaneus* builds very slight hanging nest;
♀ incubates 2 eggs 12-13 days; young, fed mainly ♀,
fly *c.* 14 days. **887**

Cyanocitta stelleri *Corvidae*
STELLER'S JAY   *c.* 12 ins
Nearctic, Neotropical: resident coniferous forests S
Alaska S to Nicaragua and E to central Montana,
Central Colorado, W Texas. Head, neck, mantle and
breast blackish, crest extending back from hind crown,
white stripes down forehead; hind parts pale blue,
wings and tail purplish blue, barred black. Legs, bill
and eyes blackish. Moves by long bounds on ground
and along branches, crest lowered in flight, raised
when calling; gregarious, shy in open woodland but
tamer at camp sites. Call: squawks varying from low
pitched to raucous. Feeds on pine seeds and insects

often taken high-up in trees; also visits picnic and camps for scraps and robs nests; hoards food. Breeds late April onwards; fairly bulky nest of twigs, some roots and dry grass, sometimes cemented with mud, often lined pined needles; usually in conifers 10 to 50 ft up, sometimes in vines and bushes. Lays 3 to 6 light bluish green eggs with small brown, purplish brown or olive markings; ♀ incubates c. 17 days. **1002**

Cyanocorax yncas *Corvidae*
GREEN JAY 12½ ins
Neotropical, marginally Nearctic: SE Texas, Honduras, S to Venezuela N of Orinoco, Colombia, E Ecuador, E and Central Peru, N Bolivia; resident forests with thick undergrowth, thickets, sea level to c. 5,000 ft; flocks after breeding into ranches, towns (USA). Hindcrown, upper mantle white to blue according to race; rest upperparts to centre tail (outer feathers bright yellow) bright green; forehead with upstanding crest, spot above eye, cheek patch, bright blue; side of head, throat, upper breast, black; rest of underparts bright or greenish yellow; legs, bill blackish, eyes dark brown. Jay-like behaviour: skulking when solitary, inquisitive in flocks. Calls include repeated *cheh cheh cheh; cleep cleep;* 'dry throaty rattle' (R. T. Peterson); infrequent soft musical song. Diet: insects, seeds, corn, fruit; robs other birds' nests. Breeds April and May, building nest of thorny twigs, stems, moss, lined fine rootlets, 5 to 15 ft up in bush or small tree in thick cover. 3 to 5 greyish eggs, thickly spotted brown. **1003**

Cyanomitra verticalis *Nectariniidae*
GREEN-HEADED SUNBIRD 6 ins
Ethiopian: W Africa, Congo, Angola; S Sudan through E Africa to N Malawi, NE Zambia; resident evergreen forests, wooded areas, riverine strips, cultivated areas, up to 7,000 ft. Generally olive green with metallic green head, throat; underparts grey, pectoral tufts creamy. ♀ has grey throat. Legs, bill blackish, eyes dark. Juvenile lacks metallic green crown; throat dusky. Attracted to flowering *Erythrina* trees; searches undergrowth as well as treetops for insects. Call double *tee-cheek tee-cheek;* soft warbling song. Breeds April to September (Uganda); builds nest of banana bark, other plant fibres, lined grass; long streamers often hanging from lip of entrance and sides; suspended from bush, often well concealed. 2 pinkish white or buff eggs, marked and marbled shades of brown; incubated ♀. **824**

Cyanopica cyanus *Corvidae*
AZURE-WINGED MAGPIE c. 13½ ins
Palaearctic: 2 populations; SW Europe in open woodland, orchards and groves; SE Asia, S Transbaikalia, Maritime Territory and Ussuri Territory to Korea, Japan and China, in hardwood forests, shrub thickets, parklands and suburbs, favouring river valleys; nomadic outside breeding season. Top of head black with metallic sheen, duller on cheeks; back, shoulders and rump ash grey to buff, lighter on rump, darker on shoulder; throat white; primaries black, margined blue near base and white towards tip; secondaries and long tail feathers blue; underparts whitish to pale buff. Legs and bill black, eyes dark brown. Usually in small flocks, on ground or in bushes. Call: *zhreee,* uttered constantly. Feeds on large insects, other invertebrates, berries and fuits. Breeds May, members of flock nesting near to each other; nest made of rootlets, twigs and moss, lined grass, hair and fur, usually in conifers or thorn bushes, 4 to 8 ft up in branch fork or sometimes in hollow, often near water. 4 to 7 eggs, laid at intervals, incubated ♀, fed by ♂; young leave nest at different times and are mainly tended by ♂. **1004**

Cyanoptila cyanomelana *Muscicapidae*:
Muscicapinae
BLUE AND WHITE or JAPANESE
BLUE FLYCATCHER 6-6½ ins
E Palaearctic: breeds Kuriles and Japan W to Hopei, Manchuria, Korea; winters Hainan, Malaysia, Indonesia (Java). Habitat rocky hillsides (Hopei); along mountain streams in broadleaved and coniferous forest to 5,500 ft; also parks, gardens (Japan). ♂:

upperparts bright cobalt blue, deep purplish on mantle; wings black, edged blue; cheeks to upper breast black; belly, under tail coverts white, axillaries blue. ♀: upperparts olive brown, more russet on rump, tail; chin to breast olive grey or olive yellow; belly white, heavily washed olive or yellowish; under tail coverts white. Legs leaden grey, bill brown, eyes dark brown. Juvenile speckled. Behaves much as *Ficedula* or *Muscicapa* flycatchers. Call low *krrr krrr;* melodious song from high perch ends in grating note. Diet: beetles and other insects. Breeds May to July, building mossy nest like *Muscicapa*, lined moss flower stems, rootlets; in steep woodland bank (Fujiyama), hole in rock face, building. 3 to 5 cream brown eggs, sometimes freckled buff and grey in zone, often parasitised by cuckoos. Incubation and fledging probably as *Muscicapa* species. **776**

Cyanoramphus novaeselandiae *Psittacidae*
RED-CROWNED PARROT ♀: 9-10½, ♂: 10½-12 ins
Confined to main and offshore islands of New Zealand, where several races recognised; resident in mainland forests, flourishing on several islands. ♂: upperparts green, underparts yellowish-green; outer wing violet-blue; crimson markings on head and on each side rump; legs greyish-brown; bill: upper steel blue tipped black, lower blue-grey; eyes orange. ♀ has smaller head and bill, less red on head. Flight rapid and direct, graduated tail spread as bird swoops up to perch with *pretty dick* call; rapid *ki ki ki ki* in flight; other 'conversational' notes. Food: variety of buds, leaves, fruit, seeds; on islands takes *Acaena* seeds, iceplant flowers on ground. Breeds October to March, in hole of tree, rock crevices on islands. 5 to 9 white eggs laid on wood dust, incubated by ♀ 18-20 days (captive); ♀ and ♂ feed young, who fly 5-6 weeks. Yellow-crowned Parakeet, *C. auriceps*, has very similar range, habits and ecology, as does the Orange-fronted, *C. malherbi*, of South Island high level woods; but the Antipodes Island Parakeet, *C. unicolor*, which shares island with Red-Crowned, feeds much on food from penguin colonies and nests on ground. **390**

Cyclarhis gujanensis *Vireonidae*
RUFOUS-BROWED PEPPERSHRIKE 5½ ins
Neotropical: NE Mexico to Peru, Brazil, N Argentina; mainly warm lowland but also highland forests 3,000 to 6,000 ft (Costa Rica); also mangrove, coffee plantations, roadsides, thickets, gardens. Upperparts olive green; flight feathers, tail brown, both edged green; crown brownish grey bordered broad cinnamon-rufous 'eyebrows'; cheeks, hindneck light grey; underparts largely yellow, usually tinged olive above, fading to white; legs flesh, notched upper mandible pale brown or flesh, eyes orange yellow. Bill short, thick, laterally compressed. Sexes separate after breeding. Sings high in trees, repeating same phrase *we don't believe it* or *we've been wishing to meet you* (A. F. Skutch) throughout year when defending territory. Forages low in forest, hunting sometimes in mixed flocks after large caterpillars, pupae. Breeds March to June or July; ♀ and ♂ build deep but thin cup of variable materials bound spider's silk, in fork of vine-clad tree 16 to 30 ft up; in bamboos (Trinidad). 2 or 3 white eggs, variously marked pale reddish brown and chestnut, incubated ♀ and ♂. **904**

Cygnus atratus *Anatidae*
BLACK SWAN 40 ins
Australasian: fairly scarce central, N Australia and Tasmania; introduced New Zealand. Movements influenced by weather; collects near coast during drought and moves inland to exploit any flooded areas, generally frequents large shallow lakes and swamps. Black legs and plumage apart from white primaries and secondaries; bill crimson, eyes dark brown. Wings make distinctive noise in flight; otherwise emits varied high-pitched crooning. Feeds on aquatic vegetation and some pasture plants, particularly in New Zealand, where now locally abundant. Gregarious, often large dense flocks, and non-territorial unlike the white swans; usually nests close together in colonies on islands or edge of rivers and lakes. Both sexes build nest, large steep-sided mound with rough cup lined

with grass, feathers and down, often on old nest. 4 to 7 pale green eggs, incubated c. 36 days by both sexes. Young, sometimes carried on parents' back, fly at 5-6 months. **114**

Cymbilaimus lineatus *Formicariidae*
FASCIATED ANTSHRIKE or
FASCIATED BUSH SHRIKE 7 ins
Neotropical: generally distributed E of Andes to E Peru, N Bolivia, Amazonian Brazil; resident sea level to 4,000 ft in shrubby growth at forest edge. ♂: upperparts, wings and tail black, finely banded white; underparts white, finely banded black; crown blackish with small, backward-pointing crest. ♀: upperparts, wings, tail black finely banded rufous; underparts buff, finely banded black. Powerful bill slightly hooked. Insectivorous. Builds cup nest in vegetation, holding 2 or 3 eggs; incubation probably by ♀ and ♂ c. 2½ weeks; fledging period very short, perhaps 10 days. **566**

Cynanthus latirostris *Trochilidae*
BROAD-BILLED HUMMINGBIRD 3¾ ins
Nearctic to Neotropical: breeds S Arizona to S Mexico, in foothill gullies on or near desert, with rocky outcrops, mesquite and sycamore scrub; northern birds migrate S in autumn. ♂ at distance appears black: generally very dark green with iridescence; throat, cheeks, blue; thin white and black stripes behind eyes; under tail coverts white; legs, eyes dark, long slightly curved bill flaming red. ♀ has white throat, grey underparts, bill red, tipped black. Chattering call exactly like Ruby-throated, *Archilochus colubris*. ♂'s display flight pendulum-like swing in front of ♀, noise of wings 'like *zing* of rifle bullet'. Feeds from flowers, also takes insects on wing or near foliage. Nest like relatives' but usually decorated bark strips; other details much as Ruby-throated; breeds Mexico January to August. **471**

Cyphorinus thoracicus *Troglodytidae*
CHESTNUT-BREASTED WREN 6 ins
Neotropical: Colombia (Central and W Andes), E Ecuador S to Puno, Peru; resident in forest up to 7,500 ft. Upperparts, wings, underparts dark umber brown; cheeks, throat, breast rufous chestnut. Habits generally as other wrens, see *Troglodytes troglodytes*. **666**

Dacelo novaeguineae or D. gigas *Alcedinidae*
KOOKABURRA or LAUGHING JACKASS 18 (bill 2½) ins
E and S Australia; introduced W Australia, Tasmania, New Zealand; resident in open forest land, parks and gardens. Back and wings brown with pale blue spots on shoulder, white patch at base of wing-quills; both conspicuous in flight; tail brown, barred black and tipped white; crown streaked brown, dark stripe through eye; rest of head, neck, underparts buffish white; bill long and heavy, upper black, lower white. Sits motionless on post or stump, breaking into heavy undulating flight. Maintains territory throughout year but some young remain with parents, helping rear brood next year. Loud, raucous laugh origin of name: one bird starts off chorus, usually dawn or sunset. Pounces on small reptiles, crabs, insects, and larvae, sometimes digging them out with bill; also eggs and nestlings, occasionally poultry. Seizes snakes behind head, dropping them from height or battering them against branch. Breeds September to January in native range, using hole in tree trunk or branch or in termites' nest in tree; sometimes excavates hole in bank. 2 to 4 round white eggs, incubated by ♀ and ♂ 25-26 days; young fledge 4-5 weeks. **487**

Dacelo gigas see **D. novaeguineae**

DACNIS, BLACK-FACED see **Dacnis lineata**

Dacnis lineata *Emberizidae: Coerebinae*
BLACK-FACED DACNIS 4¾ ins
Neotropical: S of Andes S to E Peru, N Bolivia, S Amazonian Brazil; W of Andes from Colombia (Magdalena, Cauca valleys) to W Ecuador (Chimbo); open forest, secondary growth (capoeria), orange groves, parks, sea level to c. 4,000 ft. ♂: glossy sky or verditer blue according to race; forehead, upperparts,

including wings, tail, blue black; centre belly, under wing and tail coverts white or golden yellow. ♀: upperparts light olive brown, sometimes tinged blue; wings, tail brown; underparts pale greenish, centre belly white or bright golden yellow. Gregarious outside breeding season. Food: variety of fruits; insects. ♀ builds nest, lays 2 or 3 eggs, incubates them 12-13 days; young, fed ♀ and ♂, fly 13-14 days. **888**

Dapheonositta miranda *Sittidae*
WONDER TREERUNNER or
PINK-FACED NUTHATCH 4¾ ins
Australasian: 3 races New Guinea mountain forests from 6,400 to 13,000 ft. Generally black, faintly scaled by grey wing margins; wings mainly black, with white near base primaries; white area inner web flight feathers shows on spread wing; tail black, outer feathers tipped pinkish white; forehead to chin pink; legs: ♂ blackish green, ♀ yellow; bill black; eyes: ♂ brown, ♀ yellow. ♀ slightly smaller. Immature much duller and greyer, spotted all over, forecrown rusty. Small flocks of 5 to 10 move quickly through forest with short contact calls, behaving much as *Sitta* nuthatches. Feeds chiefly on smaller branches, sometimes on trunks, taking mainly insects and their larvae, spiders. Breeding perhaps May and August.

Daption capensis *Procellariidae*
PINTADO or CAPE PIGEON 16 ins
Southern oceans from Antarctic ice to 25°S with northward movement after breeding, even crossing Equator in Pacific. Contrasting blackish brown to white, dark areas mainly head, neck and wings; legs and bill black, eyes dark brown. Large scavenging flocks round e.g. whaling stations, and parties follow ships. Alights only on cliffs and ledges, where easy to take off. Flocks cackle harshly, but soft cooing calls at nest. Food now largely offal, but naturally squids, fish and crustaceans. Breeds colonially on shores of Antarctica and on outlying islands, often on inaccessible ledge or in niche; one white egg laid in nest of stone chips, incubated c. 40-50 days by ♀ and ♂, who tend chick during its 7 week fledging period. **27**

Daptrius americanus *Falconidae*
RED-THROATED CARACARA 19-22 ins
Neotropical: S Mexico, through South America (E of Andes) to Central Peru and S Brazil. Inhabits primarily humid forest and edges, also drier woodland in Venezuela. Mostly black, with green and blue gloss; white streaks on sides of head and white underparts; legs orange-red, bill yellow, cere grey, facial skin red, eyes red-brown. Often crosses valleys in groups of 3 to 6 to perch in tree tops. Raucous calls give native name Cacáo, also 'forced' laugh and screams; may lean forward, nodding head, when uttering. Apparently flaps wings and calls in display from perch. Lives mainly on wasp grubs, tears open nest and inserts head, or carries part of comb to branch and holds it with foot. Breeds probably in the dry season, building nest of twigs in tree and laying 2 or 3 whitish eggs marked with rich brown.

DARK CHANTING GOSHAWK see **Melierax metabates**

D'ARNAUD'S BARBET see **Trachyphonus darnaudii**

DARTER see **Anhinga anhinga**

Delichon urbica *Hirundinidae*
HOUSE MARTIN 5 ins
Palaearctic: 3 races breed in band across Eurasia between 45° and 70°N; also N Africa, Spain, Asia Minor, and strip from Caspian to N Himalayas; winters mainly eastern Africa, Indian subcontinent, Indo-China. Habitat: open country usually near habitations and water. Upperparts dark metallic blue; rump, underparts white; flight feathers very dark brown; shallow forked tail; legs pinkish, feathered white, bill black, eyes dark brown. Mainly on wing but settles freely on wires, boughs. Inclined to fly higher than Swallow, *Hirundo rustica*, and more regularly social, numbers landing by puddles to collect mud for nest-building. Call: harder, more chirruping than

Swallow; song, less frequently heard, continuous twitter. Takes aerial insects, especially small flies, often over water. Breeds from March (Morocco) onwards; late broods October. Nests colonially, sometimes in hundreds, with mud cups, built by ♀ and ♂ and softly lined feathers, aerial plant fragments, overlapping each other; under eaves, bridges, on inland and sea cliffs. 4 or 5 white eggs incubated ♀ and ♂ c. 14 days. Young, fed ♀ and ♂ and often by young of earlier brood, fly 20 days. 2 or 3 broods. Parents roost in nest. **609**

DEMOISELLE CRANE see **Anthropoides virgo**

Dendragapus obscurus *Tetraonidae*
BLUE GROUSE 18 (♀)-21 (♂) ins
Nearctic: W North America from SE Alaska S to N California on coast; S Sierra Nevada and S New Mexico and E to Black Hills; winter resident in coniferous forest, moving in spring to lower, more open woodlands, sometimes to dry sagebrush. ♂: dark slate-grey, browner on wings, with white throat, white flecks on side of breast and flanks and under tail coverts; tail black with white subterminal band (absent in N Rockies race *richardsonii*); yellow wattles above dark eyes, legs greyish, bill dark. ♀: mottled and barred brown, black and white, with flanks and tail as ♂. Flocks range widely after food sources: conifer buds and needles, herbaceous buds, leaves, flowers and fruits; also grasshoppers. Tree-living in winter, though roosting under snow. Elaborate courtship involving sac inflation, aerial tumbling and fluttering, accompanied by deep hoots. ♀ makes lined scrape in cover of log, rock or tree, lays (from April in S, June or later in N) 7 to 10 buff eggs, speckled brown, and incubates them for c. 3 weeks. Young precocious as other grouse and ♂ plays no part in rearing them. **182**

Dendrocopos major *Picidae*
GREAT SPOTTED WOODPECKER c. 9 ins
Palaearctic: Europe S to NW Africa, Asia E to Japan. Habitat: woodland, usually coniferous. ♂: white patches on shoulder, sides of neck and head, underparts buffish white, nape and under tail coverts crimson; rest black with white bars on wing-quills and white edges to tail. ♀ similar but lacking crimson nape. Juveniles have red crown. Legs greenish grey, bill lead grey, eyes crimson. Powerful bill used to excavate holes for roosting and nesting, to make loud 'drumming' on dead wood or metal, and to seek out wood-boring insect larvae for food; also takes spiders, other small animals, including young birds, and seeds and berries, may visit bird tables. Calls: abrupt penetrating *tchick tchick*, ringing cries in spring. Both sexes bore nest tunnel with large chamber in April; 4 to 7 translucent white eggs, incubated c. 16 days by parents, who both tend young; they fly c. 18-21 days. **544**

Dendrocopos minor *Picidae*
LESSER SPOTTED WOODPECKER c. 5¾ ins
Palaearctic: Europe, NW Africa, Asia Minor and Urals across to Japan. Habitat: open woodlands, exact preference varies e.g. British race, *comminutus*, deciduous while Northern race, *minor*, coniferous. ♂: barred black and white wings and lower back, crown crimson, forehead brownish white; upper back, stripes over eyes and down sides of neck, black; underparts pale, tail black with white edges. ♀: similar but crown brownish white with reddish tips to feathers. Legs greenish grey, bill greyish black, eyes red-brown. Usually high in trees, quieter drummer than Great Spotted Woodpecker, *D. major;* flight slow; feeds on wood-boring insect larvae, also spiders and berries. Call: loud shrill *pee-pee-pee-pee-pee*. Lays May and June 4 to 6 translucent, glossy white eggs in hole bored in decayed wood, lined with a few chips. Both parents incubate c. 14 days and tend young, who fly c. 21 days. **545**

Dendrocopos pubescens see under **D. villosus**

Dendrocopos syriacus *Picidae*
SYRIAN WOODPECKER 9 ins
SE Palaearctic: SE Europe to Palestine and Iran,

replacing Great Spotted Woodpecker, *D. major;* resident in oak forests, up to 6,000 ft in Iran, lowland deciduous woodland, cultivated areas with trees, roadsides, parks and gardens, even in towns. Very similar to *D. major* but distinguished by absence of black bar on cheek. Behaviour much as *D. major.* Ringing call and sharp tik, also 'liquid moorhen-like' note. Drums early spring. Food mainly insects and spiders; also fruits and kernels, e.g. of apricots, almonds, cherries. Excavates hole in oak or other broadleaved tree, often using it for several seasons. 5 to 7 white eggs laid from mid April, incubated by ♀ and ♂ c. 2 weeks; both feed young, who fly c. 3½ weeks. **546**

Dendrocopos villosus *Picidae*
HAIRY WOODPECKER 7½ ins
Nearctic and marginally Neotropical: resident throughout N America from limit of tree growth to Mexico; some movement S in autumn. Resembles *D. major* in black and white pattern but more white on tail and wings heavily spot-barred white; black stripe through not below eye. ♀ lacks red at nape. Race, *D. v. harrisi* of Pacific coast has few spots on upperparts and underparts tinged grey. Larger than Downy Woodpecker, *D. pubescens*, which has much smaller bill and black bars on white outer tail feathers. Wing beats noisy in flight: *prut prut prut*. Families in autumn often joined by other species, especially chickadees (titmice). ♂ chases ♀ in courtship; also mutual bowing. Drums like relatives with bill on dead limb or pole. Food: insects and their larvae dug out from trees; less ready to visit tables than Downy Woodpecker. Breeds April onwards, excavating hole in tree, usually with dead centre and may use same hole several seasons. Lays 3 to 6 white eggs; breeding habits as *D. major.* **547**

Dendrocygna viduata *Anatidae*
WHITE-FACED TREE DUCK 17 ins
Neotropical, Ethiopian: tropical S America to Paraguay and Uruguay; Africa S of Sahara to Angola and Transvaal, Madagascar, Comoro Is. Habitat: flooded ground, swamps, salt-water lagoons, estuaries, pools and rivers. White face, chin and foreneck; nape, sides and back of neck, wings, belly and tail black, upper back and breast chestnut, sides of body barred black and white, back buff and brown. Legs grey, bill blackish grey with pale band near tip, eyes dark. Nocturnal, huge flocks, fairly tame, dives easily, flight strong and slow. Call: liquid chirps and three syllabled *tsi-ri-ri*. Feeds on plants, grazing or gathering under water. Nests throughout year in hollow trees in heavily forested areas, in slight depression on dry ground, lightly lined, or builds elaborate grass nest among reeds. 8 to 12 creamy white eggs with pinkish tinge, incubated 28-30 days by ♀ and ♂. **115**

Dendroica dominica *Parulidae*
YELLOW-THROATED WARBLER 5¼ ins
Nearctic, Neotropical: breeds S New Jersey, Maryland, Ohio, S Michigan, S Wisconsin, SE Nebraska, S to Central Florida, N Bahamas, Gulf Coast, Central Texas; winters from E South Carolina to W Indies; S Texas to Costa Rica. Habitat mature woodland, e.g. sycamore, cypress, pine, in valley bottoms, swamps, riversides; associated with Spanish moss *Tillandsia usneoides* in S USA. ♂: Upperparts chiefly slate grey; white on blackish wings, tail; forehead black, facial pattern black and white; chin to breast yellow; underparts white (northern birds), flanks streaked black. ♀ less black on head. Legs, bill, eyes dark. Both sexes tinged brown in autumn. Haunts treetops, hopping along branches in search of insects, other small animals. Song variable, usually loud and musical: run of clear disyllabic notes down scale, growing fainter, to end on abrupt high note. Breeds April to May; ♀ building nest of bark strips, grass, lined down, feathers, hair; on lateral branch 20 to 100 ft up or in hanging clump of Spanish moss. 3 to 5 pale greenish white eggs, speckled reddish brown over grey at big end, incubated ♀ 11-14 days; young, fed ♀ and ♂, fly 8-14 days. 2 broods S Carolina. The very rare and similar-looking Sutton's Warbler, *D. potomac*, may be hybrid between this and Parula Warbler, *Parula americana.* **891**

Dendroica magnoliae *Parulidae*
MAGNOLIA WARBLER   5 ins
Nearctic: breeds Newfoundland, Central Quebec, Manitoba, SW Mackenzie, S to N Massachusetts, mountains of Virginia, N Michigan, S Saskatchewan, Central Alberta; winters S Mexico to Panama. Habitat open young conifers, e.g. secondary growth spruce, especially round swamps, shallow pools; also forest clearings, woodland roadsides, abandoned tree-clad pastures. ♂: mantle black; wings, tail black with white patches, rump yellow; crown grey, broad white 'eyebrow', black mask; underparts from chin yellow, breast heavily streaked black. ♀ similar but paler, grey instead of black. Legs, bill eyes dark brown. Autumn ♂ and ♀: upperparts olive-green, pale grey collar across yellow underparts; immature similar. Keeps well hidden at low level in cover. Song: short, musical *weeta weeta weetee*. Insectivorous, also worms, plant lice. Breeds May to July, ♀ helped by ♂, building shallow nest of twigs, needles, stems, grass, bound cobwebs and lined black rootlets; in spruce, fir, hemlock, generally 5 to 15 ft up, sometimes higher and over water. Usually 4 white eggs, spotted red-brown, incubated ♀ 11-14 days; young fed ♀ and ♂, fly up to 14 days. **892**

Dendroica petechia *Parulidae*
YELLOW WARBLER   5 ins
Nearctic, Neotropical: breeds from N American tree limit S to N South Carolina, N Alabama, S Missouri, Central W Texas, Mexico, Central America to N Colombia; also Florida Keys, W Indies; winters S Mexico to Peru, E to Guyanas, Brazil. Habitat lowlands with scattered small trees and shrubs, especially riparian willows, alders; also hedgerows, orchards, gardens; in far North and western prairies in small areas scrub. ♂: generally yellow, tinged greenish on back, dusky wings, tail but with prominent yellow spots; throat to belly streaked rufous and rufous on crown some tropical races. ♀ and immature dark greenish yellow above, paler below with few or no streaks; Alaskan immatures greenish but show yellow tail spots. Legs flesh-grey, bill blackish, eyes dark brown. Seldom in treetops, but attacks many garden pests; beetles; grasshoppers, spiders, myriapods on ground. Call, *chip;* song generally introduced *c.* 4 *weets*, with variable cadence at end. Breeds May to July; ♀, helped ♂, builds solid nest of long bark and plant fibres, grass, down, bound cobwebs, silk from tent caterpillars, softly lined; in fork of small tree, bush, or vine tangle, 3 to 5 ft up. 4 or 5 blue-white eggs, thickly speckled patterns of brown and lilac, incubated ♀ 11-14 days; young, fed ♀ and ♂, fly 11-15 days. If cowbird lays in nest, clutch often covered with fresh lining; up to 6 storeys recorded. **893**

Dendroica potomac see under **D. dominica**

Dendroica striata see under **Mniotilta varia**

Dendronanthus indicus *Motacillidae*
FOREST WAGTAIL   8 ins
E Palaearctic; marginally Oriental: E Siberia, Manchuria, Korea, N China, Assam; winters over much of Oriental region. Habitat: montane forest near water; glades, watercourses, openings in evergreen forest. Upperparts shades of grey, darkest head and tail which has white outer edges; wings black with 2 prominent white bars and buff spots when closed; 'eyebrow' white; underparts from chin white with complete and incomplete black bars across upper breast; legs light grey, bill grey, eyes dark brown. Rotates body sideways when standing, tail appearing to wag side to side instead of up and down as other wagtails. Loud chirruping call when flying, running or perched; also faint single note. Diet: small slugs, snails, worms; insects. Breeds May to July according to latitude, building very small neat nest of plant material bound cobwebs on horizontal branch typically over water. Usually 4 greyish-lilac eggs, with smudged purple-brown blotches (E. C. Stuart Baker).

Dendrortyx leucophrys *Phasianidae*
BUFF-CROWNED WOOD PARTRIDGE   12-14 ins
Neotropical: Guatemala, Honduras, Nicaragua (3

races); resident in foothills and highlands from 1,000 to 9,000 ft, in oak, pine and cloud forests, usually in drier secondary growth, scrub or grass understorey. Upperparts from crown rufous, brightest on mantle, becoming olive brown with dusky and buff markings; forehead, face and throat buffish to white; underparts greyish-brown, streaked russet. **197**

DENHAM'S BUSTARD see **Neotis denhami**

DESERT FANTAIL WARBLER see **Cisticola aridula**

DIABLOTIN see **Steatornis caripensis**

DIADEMED SANDPIPER PLOVER see **Phegornis mitchellii**

DIAMOND DOVE see **Geopelia cuneata**

Dicaeum hirundinaceum *Dicaeidae*
MISTLETOE BIRD   *c.* 4 ins
Australasian, Oriental: continental Australia, some Indonesian islands; resident from dense tropical rain forest to arid mulga scrub, following parasitic mistletoes. ♂: upperparts, including head, cheeks, dark satiny blue-black; chin, throat, undertail scarlet; breast off-white, with central broad black streak, shading to white underparts. ♀: upperparts grey-brown with light 'eyebrow', tail black; underparts creamy white, undertail pale scarlet. Legs, bill greyish black, eyes buff-brown. Juvenile like ♀, but bill reddish. Usually in pairs in treetops or among mistletoe *Loranthus* blossoms and berries. Strong, swift flight on narrow wings, both tree to tree and longer distances. Call *wit-a wita* with variations; single sharp flight note; song warbling, sometimes mimicking. Food chiefly mistletoe berries, seeds passing through specialised digestive tract in 25 minutes, causing spread of plant to new host sites. Also other berries, including introduced species; insects, especially for small young. Movements and breeding governed by fruiting of mistletoe, main season September to January, ♀ building pear-shaped nest with slit entrance at side, of plant debris, dried larvae, spider egg-bags, downy plant seeds, bound cobwebs; usually hung from thin branch of leafy tree, up to 50 ft high. Usually 3 white eggs incubated ♀ 12 days; both parents feed young, who fly *c.* 15 days. **815**

Dicrurus adsimilis *Dicruridae*
FORK-TAILED DRONGO   9½ ins
Ethiopian: almost throughout region; resident all types open woodland, including acacia and thorn bush, introduced species, open scrub. Generally black with forked 'fish tail', less marked in ♀; inner webs flight feathers ash-grey; legs, bill black, eyes red. Immature has feathers of mantle, underparts tipped grey. Usually in pairs on prominent perches whence hawking flights after e.g. butterflies; follows forest fires, grazing animals, even perching on them, to catch disturbed insects. Twists and tumbles in fast flight, attacks carnivorous mammals and birds; often associated with helmet shrikes *Prionops* and leads parties of mixed species. Call harsh *wurchee wurchee*, often at night, also 'tin trumpet' note; song chattering and mimicking but with some clear, liquid notes. Breeding season variable within large range; builds flat foundation of plant stems across or wedged in fork of branch, 10 to 20 ft up, lined rootlets, flimsy-looking but well-woven. Usually 3 white or creamy eggs marked pinkish brown; or pale orange, suffused darker and undermarked stone-brown. Both parents believed to incubate eggs and tend young. **979**

Dicrurus annectans *Dicruridae*
CROW-BILLED DRONGO   11 (tail 5) ins
Oriental: breeds Himalayas from Uttar Pradesh and Nepal into Assam, Burma, N Thailand, migrating SE through Malaysia to Indonesia. Habitat: forests, tropical wet evergreen and deciduous, plains to over 2,000 ft; also open forest, bamboo and scrub jungle, tea plantations. Uniformly black with slightly forked tail; glossed green on back, blue elsewhere; bristles jut over powerful dark horn-coloured bill; legs black, eyes reddish. Greater Racket-tailed Drongo, *D.*

paradiseus, very similar except when sporting elongated 'bare' outer tail feathers with 'rackets' at tips. Also indistinguishable in field from Black Drongo or King Crow, *D. macrocercus*, which has relatively longer outer tail feathers. Aggressive like relatives, attacking intruders at nest. Raucous calls; insectivorous diet. Breeds April to May N India, ♀ and ♂ building small, shallow nest of twigs, stems, rootlets, strengthened by cobwebs, between fork of lateral branch usually 30 to 40 ft up and within 10 to 50 yds of forest edge. 3 or 4 salmon pink to creamy eggs, streaked longitudinally red-brown over grey, incubated by ♀. Both parents believed to feed young.

Dicrurus
   macrocercus see under **D. annectans**
   paradiseus see under **D. annectans**

DIDRIC CUCKOO see **Chrysococcyx caprius**

Diglossa caerulescens *Emberizidae: Coerebinae*
BLUISH FLOWERPECKER   5½ ins
Neotropical: Colombian Andes S to N Peru; Cajamarca to NW Bolivia; montane forests. ♂: upperparts dull to greyish blue; lores, forehead narrowly striped black; underparts pale blue or grey. ♀ like ♂ but duller. Bill not as sharply uptilted as most relatives, but has hook on end of upper mandible for getting nectar from tubular corollas: upper mandible hooks tube while sharp lower pierces corolla: several flowers tackled in minute; does not pollinate (A. F. Skutch); also pierces fruit and takes many insects. Song poor, ♀ probably sings too. Builds thick cup nest in low bush for 2 eggs, incubated ♀ probably 14 days. Young, fed ♀ and ♂, fly *c.* 16 days. **889**

DIKKOP, WATER see **Burhinus vermiculatus**

Dinemellia dinemelli *Ploceidae*
WHITE-HEADED BUFFALO WEAVER   9 ins
Ethiopia: NE of region to Kenya, Tanzania; resident acacia woodland, dry thorn bush and scrub. Upperparts, including wings, tail, blackish or dusky brown; head (crown sometimes pale greyish) neck, underparts, base of primaries white (white edges to outer webs secondaries and scapulars, in northern race *ruspolii*); lower rump, upper and under tail coverts, spots on elbow orange red; legs brownish black, bill blackish horn, eyes yellow or brown. Conspicuous in small, scattered flocks, feeding largely on ground; behaviour in trees 'almost parrot-like'; often associates with Superb, *Spreo superbus*, and Hildebrandt's, *S. hildebrandti*, Starlings. Call: harsh, trumpet-like; bubbling twitter. Diet: seeds, fruits; some insects. Breeding season variable within range; nests in scattered colony hung from low boughs thorn trees, several sometimes close together; untidily built of twigs, retort-shaped, entered from below, warmly lined grass, feathers. 3 or 4 greenish white or green eggs, marked shades of brown, black, grey, often in cap at big end. **948**

DIOCH, SUDAN see **Quelea quelea**

Diomedea exulans *Diomedeidae*
WANDERING ALBATROSS   *c.* 4½ ft; wing-span *c.* 11½ ft
Southern oceans, from Tropic of Capricorn to Antarctic, with widespread wandering. Brown immature plumages progress to adult ♂, predominantly white with blackish brown wings; smaller ♀ much browner, with patch on crown; legs in breeding season blue-grey, bill pink to yellow, eyes brown. Usually seen over oceans behind ships in sustained gliding flight. Elaborate courtship on breeding islands, with gobbling, neighing, squealing and bill-clattering; hoarse, croaking call at sea. Diet primarily squids. One white egg, usually speckled red-brown, laid in nest of local plants in colony on bare island, December to January. Incubation 66 days by ♀ and ♂, who attend chick during 7 month fledging, so breeding only every 2 years. **22**

Diomedea immutabilis see under **D. nigripes**

Diomedea irrorata *Diomedeidae*
GALAPAGOS ALBATROSS   *c.* 36 ins; wing span *c.* 8 ft
Breeds Hood I, Galapagos; otherwise ranges throughout Pacific Ocean and southern seas in general. Head and neck white suffused yellow, rest of upperparts and wings sooty brown, mostly barred with wavy blackish and white lines, pale straw-coloured shafts to outer primaries; underparts, wavy grey lines fading into pale throat. ♀ slightly smaller. Large hooked bill shiny yellow, eyes deep brown, legs pale grey. Long take-off, lands clumsily, tottering walk, glides with long narrow wings gracefully and rapidly; generally tame. Call: hoarse croaking. Feeds on squids and fish. Breeds in loose colony April or May onwards. Single large dull whitish egg, finely speckled cinnamon and brown, laid on bare ground where adults may move it considerable distance (M. P. Harris); ♀ incubates *c.* 60 days, both parents brood *c.* 2 weeks then young move to hiding places amongst scrub and boulders, fly *c.* 24 weeks. Most adults breed every year but are subject to mass desertions of eggs (Harris). **23**

Diomedea melanophris *Diomedeidae*   32-38 ins;
BLACK-BROWED ALBATROSS   wing-span up to 8 ft
Southern oceans from Tropic of Capricorn to 60°S, with extensive wandering, occasionally across Equator. White, except for dusky wings, mantle, tail and dark patch round eye; legs pale blue-white, bill mainly yellow, eyes dark brown. Immatures show more black and have dark bills. Approaches ships closer than any other albatross, following them for days. Displays at breeding colonies; when building, ♂ brings material to ♀ with loud braying call. Diet mainly squids, also fish, crustaceans and offal. Breeding season on oceanic islands from October to March or April; single egg, white with pink speckles, laid in nest of mud and plant material, incubated for 56-70 days by ♀; chick, fed by ♀ and ♂, flies in *c.* 5 months. **24**

Diomedea nigripes *Diomedeidae*
BLACK-FOOTED ALBATROSS   28 ins; wing-span 7 ft
Pacific Ocean, ranging from S Bering Sea to coasts of Asia, North America and south to Equator; breeding now confined to Hawaiian Leeward Islands. Very dark grey to tan, with variable white areas on head, underparts and base of primaries; proportion have white rump; legs, bill and eyes dark. May follow ship for hours, taking offal, but main diet squids and fish, caught at night when near surface. Bell-like calls during courtship dances; screeches or groans when fighting over offal at sea. Breeds autumn and winter (corresponding to southern hemisphere seasons) in colonies of few to 25,000 pairs, sometimes with Laysan Albatross *D. immutabilis*. Single white egg in shallow scrape, incubated by ♀ and ♂ for 65 days; chick to sea at *c.* 6 months. **25**

Diophthalma opopsitta see **Opopsitta leadbeateri**

DIPPER see **Cinclus cinclus**

DIPPER, AMERICAN see **Cinclus mexicanus**

Diptrornis fischeri *Muscicapidae*: *Muscicapinae*
WHITE-EYED SLATY FLYCATCHER   6½ ins
Ethiopian: several races, some very local, from SE Sudan to Nyika plateau in Malawi and Zambia. Resident highland forests (gardens in Kenya), their margins, thorn scrub, wooded cultivated areas. Upperparts slate grey; throat, flanks pale grey; breast, under tail coverts white tinged buff; prominent white ring round dark brown eye; legs, bill blackish, rictal bristles prominent. Juvenile spotted white on upperparts; feathers of underparts tipped blackish. Becomes tame in gardens; very active at dusk, picking up insects on ground, especially paths. Also hawks, e.g. ant swarms; occasionally takes berries, young birds. Rather silent: *tsssk* call in evening; hoarse squeal of alarm; song short trilling cadence. Breeding season irregular. Moss nest with leaves, fibres, lined hair, finer fibres, in fork usually at some height in thick foliage or masked by lichens. 2 or 3 pale dull green eggs, heavily marked brown, often in zone. **778**

Dissoura episcopus *Ciconiidae*
WHITE-NECKED or WOOLLY-NECKED STORK   34 ins
Ethiopian and Oriental, with local movements after breeding. Habitat riverbanks and lagoons. Generally iridescent black, violet and blue, with black crown, 'woolly' white neck, white underparts and elongated under tail coverts; legs red, bill black with red tip; eyes brown. Usually in pairs or small parties, retiring to favoured roost tree at dusk. Tumbling courtship display and harsh raucous call. Diet frogs, crustaceans, molluscs and other water animals, also carrion. Breeding season varies with range; from March in Uganda. Solitary or colonial in trees or on cliffs; nest of sticks, lined grasses, holds 2 to 3 white eggs, soon stained. **70**

DIVER,
BLACK-THROATED see **Gavia arctica**
GREAT NORTHERN see **Gavia immer**
RED-THROATED see **Gavia stellata**
WHITE-BILLED see under **Gavia immer**

DIVING PETREL see **Pelecanoides urinatrix**

Dolichonyx oryzivorus *Icteridae*
BOBOLINK   7¾ ins
Nearctic: breeds southern Canada, including Cape Breton I, S to West Virginia, Indiana, N Missouri, New Mexico, NE California; long migration to winter as far S as N Argentina, Paraguay. Habitat large areas tall grass or grain fields; rice plantations on passage. ♂: black with large pale buff patch nape, hindneck, down back; broad wingbar, lower back to upper tail coverts white, some flight feathers pale edged. ♀: upperparts generally streaked dull dark brown and pale buff (feather edges); central pale stripe on dark crown; underparts pale grey brown, flanks streaked. Autumn ♂ resembles ♀: upperparts dark olive green, underparts buffish. Legs light brown, rather broad bill grey, eyes dark brown. Song, on wing or perch, loud, bubbling series of metallic higher and lower notes, pitch rising as song goes on; distinctive flight call *pink*. ♂ spreads rounded tail with pointed feathers in display on ground, partly opens wings, puts head down to show buff nape. Insectivorous spring, summer, turning over stones with bill; seeds in autumn: some damage to grain from migrant flocks. Breeds end May to June, several pairs often near together. ♀ and ♂ build cup nest of grass, stems, rootlets in slight scrape well hidden in grass tussock or field crops. 5 to 7 bluish grey to reddish brown eggs, marked brown over purple, incubated ♀ *c.* 12 days; parents feed young on grasshoppers, crickets; fledging 12-14 days. ♂♂ frequently polygamous.

DOLLAR BIRD see **Eurystomus orientalis**

Domicella domicella *Psittacidae*
PURPLE-CAPPED LORIKEET   12 ins
Australasian: Ceram and Amboyna in Moluccas; resident in lowland forest. Generally rich crimson, darker on back; crown violet, base of neck golden yellow; upper wings olive brown, flight feathers green with yellow patch on inner webs; tail red, tipped brownish; bill orange red. Usually in pairs. Feeds on pollen and nectar from flowers, extracted with brush-tipped tongue. Breeding habits in wild unknown; probably nests in hole of tree, laying 2 white eggs. **391**

Donacola castaneothorax see **Lonchura castaneothorax**

DOTTEREL see **Eudromias morinellus**

DOTTEREL,
BLACK-FRONTED see **Charadrius melanops**
HOODED see **Charadrius cucullatus**

DOUBLE-COLLARED SUNBIRD,
LESSER see **Cinnyris chalybeus**
SOUTHERN see **Cinnyris chalybeus**

DOUBLE-STRIPED STONE CURLEW see **Burhinus bistriatus**

DOVE,
BARBARY see under **Streptopelia decaocto**
BAR-SHOULDERED see **Geopelia humeralis**
BLACK-BILLED BLUE-SPOTTED WOOD see **Turtur abyssinicus**
BLUE-GROUND see **Claravis pretiosa**
BLUE-NAPED FRUIT see **Ptilinopus melanospila**
BLUE-SPOTTED WOOD see under **Turtur abyssinicus**
BROWN see **Macropygia phasianella**
COLLARED see **Streptopelia decaocto**
COMMON GROUND see **Columbina passerina**
DIAMOND see **Geopelia cuneata**
EARED see **Zenaida auriculata**
EMERALD see **Chalcophaps indica**
EMERALD SPOTTED WOOD see **Turtur chalcospilos**
GALAPAGOS see **Zenaida galapagoensis**
LARGE BROWN CUCKOO see **Macropygia phasianella**
LAUGHING see **Streptopelia senegalensis**
LONG-TAILED see **Oena capensis**
MASKED see **Oena capensis**
MOURNING see **Zenaida macroura**
NAMAQUA see **Oena capensis**
NICOBAR see **Caloenas nicobarica**
PEACEFUL see **Geopelia striata**
RED-EYED see **Streptopelia semitorquata**
ROCK see **Columba livia**
RUDDY QUAIL see **Geotrygon montana**
SPOTTED see **Streptopelia chinensis**
STOCK see **Columba oenas**
TURTLE see **Streptopelia turtur**
WONGA see **Leucosarcia melanoleuca**

DOWITCHER,
LONG-BILLED see **Limnodromus scolopaceus**
SHORT-BILLED see under **Limnodromus scolopaceus**

DOWNY WOODPECKER see under **Dendrocopos villosus**

Drepanorhynchus reichenowi or Nectarinia reichenowi *Nectariniidae*
GOLDEN-WINGED SUNBIRD   ♀: 6, ♂: 9 ins
Ethiopian: resident highlands (Kivu Zaire), Mt Elgon (Uganda), Kenya, N Tanzania; forest edge, moorland, mountain scrub, cultivated ground, 5,000 to 11,000 ft. ♂: upperparts metallic bronze and copper, glossed green; broad golden edges to black wings and tail; chin to breast metallic copper and ruby, rest of underparts black. Non-breeding ♂ black except for wings and tail. ♀: olivaceous above, mottled below; flight feathers, relatively short tail edged golden. Legs, long curved bill blackish, eyes dark brown. Juvenile ♂ dull blackish below. Attracted by clumps of orange-flowered salvia *Leonotis elliotii*, *Crotalaria*, other shrubs and plants. ♂ has slow, swerving display flight among bushes. Variety of clear, liquid *tweep* and *tsssp* calls. Food: insects and nectar. Breeds various months in parts of range, January to March N Tanzania, building nest of fine grass stems, lined plant down, with wide entrance, often conspicuously but strongly attached to small bush, 3 to 12 ft up. Usually single whitish egg, heavily marked grey and brown, frequently in cap at big end, incubated ♀. **825**

Dromaius novaehollandiae *Dromaiidae*
EMU   5-6 ft tall
Continental Australia, ranging from dry forest to open plains, replaced in NE by Cassowary, *Casuarius casuarius*. Flightless, brown to brownish black all over; feathers, 'double' due to long aftershafts, vaneless and loose; wing has one digit and terminal claw; no preen gland; legs, bill and eyes light brown; bare neck light blue. Flocks roam plains and may cause damage to crops, leading to ineffective 'Emu war' of 1932; can run up to 30 mph and swim. ♂ utters guttural notes, ♀ has booming call. Diet mainly vegetable, of native fruits; some insects. Breeds April to November; *c.* 9 (7 to 18 recorded) very dark green eggs with granulated surface laid in flat, trampled area under cover and incubated 58-61 days by ♂. Pale grey, striped chicks

leave nest after 2 days and accompany ♂; mature in second year. **4**

Dromas ardeola *Dromadidae*
CRAB PLOVER   *c.* 15 ins
Ethiopian, marginally Palaearctic, Oriental: coasts of Indian Ocean, breeding Port Sudan to Somalia, N coast Kenya, Persian Gulf; visitor S Africa, Madagascar; Pakistan, India, Ceylon, Andamans, Nicobars, open sandy shores and reefs. White except for black mantle and primaries of long, pointed wings; long legs blue grey, stout bill black, eyes dark brown. Immature greyish above. Noisy and gregarious, sometimes forming large blocks. Upright stance often with head sunk between wings; flies with legs, neck stretched. Call: *tchuk tchuk* by nest holes and at night. Diet: crustaceans, especially crabs, molluscs, worms. Breeds from late April Persian Gulf, July to September Kenya, in large colonies, excavating tunnels in sand up to ½ mile from sea; single proportionally very large white egg laid in chamber up to 5 ft from entrance. Incubation period at least 4 weeks; parents bring crabs to young one. **305**

DRONGO,
  BLACK see under **Dicrurus annectans**
  CROW-BILLED see **Dicrurus annectans**
  FORK-TAILED see **Dicrurus adsimilis**
  GREATER RACKET-TAILED see under **Dicrurus annectans**
  MOUNTAIN see **Chaetorhynchus papuensis**
  SPANGLED see under **Sphecotheres flaviventris**

Dryomodus brunneipygia *Muscicapidae: Muscicapinae*
SOUTHERN SCRUB ROBIN   *c.* 8 ins
Australasian: interior S and SW continental Australia; resident lowland scrub; mallee, mulga, pine. Upperparts uniform brown with 2 narrow white bars on closed wing; tail long, graduated at end; underparts ashy, becoming buff on belly; pale 'eyebrow'; legs, bill, eyes dark, white orbits. Usually in pairs and rather tame, answering imitations of its call: *chip-pip-ee*. Feeds on insects from ground and leaf litter. Breeds September to January in different parts of range; very small nest loosely built of bark, twigs, lined grass, rootlets; in slight scrape on ground among scrub, single greenish-grey egg, marked brown often in zone at big end. Building and incubation probably by ♀, as Northern Scrub Robin, *D. superciliaris* (E Northern Territory, N Queensland), which is more rufous on upperparts, and has black and pale blue facial markings. **777**

Dryomodus superciliaris see under **D. brunneipygia**

Dryoscopus cubla *Laniidae*
BLACK PUFF-BACKED SHRIKE   6¼ ins
Ethiopian: Central Kenya, Tanzania, Malawi, SE Zaire, Angola, S Africa to Cape; resident open woodland and bush, riverine forest, sometimes near habitations. ♂: upperparts from crown to mantle, wings and short tail glossy blue-black, tail tipped white; soft downy rump greyish white; inner secondaries, edges wing coverts white; underparts white tinged grey. ♀: white streak from bill halfway over eye; lower back and rump grey. Legs grey, bill black, eyes yellowish orange. Immature has white areas washed buff. Sociable, often joining other species in trees, where hunts larvae; also takes insects on wing; eggs and young birds; occasionally buds. Many calls: hissing *swarr; chak* of alarm followed by *skurr;* whistling *twhew twhew twhew* during prolonged breeding season. Puffed out feathers of back and rump almost surround excited ♂; also buzzes and crackles wings in display, drops vertically with series of whistles and clacks. Nest cup of bark fibres, rootlets, bound cobwebs, well hidden in fork of tree, usually at a height. 2 or 3 white or creamy eggs, marked brown and lilac in zone at big end. **645**

DUCK,
  ANDEAN CRESTED see **Lophonetta specularoides alticola**
  BLUE-BILLED see **Oxyura australis**

  COMB see **Sarkidiornis melanotos**
  FLIGHTLESS STEAMER see **Tachyeres pteneres**
  FLYING STEAMER see under **Tachyeres pteneres**
  LONG-TAILED see **Clangula hyemalis**
  MUSCOVY see **Cairina moschata**
  MUSK see **Biziura lobata**
  TUFTED see **Aythya fuligula**
  WHITE-FACED TREE see **Dendrocygna viduata**

Dulus dominicus *Dulidae*
PALM CHAT   *c.* 7 ins
Neotropical: confined to Hispaniola and Gonave I, W Indies; resident open country with trees, especially royal palms, from low altitudes up to 4,500 ft. Upperparts greyish white to olive brown; short wings greenish; rump dark green; head darker than back; underparts white, striped dark brown; legs blackish, heavy bill horn brown, eyes brown. Juvenile has throat dark brown, rump buffish. Greyer race on Gonave. Usually in flocks, tree-living, active and uttering variety of harsh and musical calls. Resting posture upright, tail pointed down; no 'individual distance' when perched. Diet: berries and blossoms. Breeds March to June, several birds working at once on large communal nest, used outside breeding season and made of dead twigs up to 30 ins long, carried crosswise in bill; usually high in leaf or fruiting fronds of palm; pine tree nests in highlands smaller, housing one or two pairs. Separate entrances lead to nest chambers at end of tunnels; also passages among loose twigs at top of nest. 2 to 4 slightly glossy white eggs, spotted dark grey, often in zone.

Dumetella carolinensis *Mimidae*
CATBIRD   9 ins
Nearctic: breeds Southern Canada S to Central Florida, SE Texas, NE New Mexico, N Utah, NE Oregon, W Washington; winters S to Cuba, Panama. Habitat dense scrub and vine tangles near streams, ponds, swamps, extending into man-modified shrubberies, hedgerows, gardens. Uniformly grey with black crown, blackish central tail feathers, chestnut-brown under tail coverts. Secretive, keeping to cover as a wandering voice with 'catlike, mewing scold' (R. H. Pough); other calls soft cluck, snapping note. Courtship includes song, chasing of ♀ by ♂ and display of under tail coverts. Song short phrase 5 or 6 notes interspersed with mewing and mimicry; sings in moonlight; autumn subsong. Diet: small fruits in season, otherwise mainly insects (some from water), on which young reared. Breeds May to June New England, building rather untidy nest of local plant materials, lined finer fibres. 4 to 6 glossy blue-green eggs incubated mainly by ♀ 12-13 days. Both parents feed young, who fly *c.* 2 weeks. 2 broods. **669**

DUNLIN see **Calidris alpina**

DUNNOCK see **Prunella modularis**

DUSKY
  FLYCATCHER see **Alseonax adustus**
  LORIKEET see **Pseudeos fuscata**
  MOORHEN see under **Gallinula chloropus**
  NIGHTJAR see **Caprimulgus pectoralis**
  WOOD SWALLOW see under **Artamus superciliosus**

EAGLE,
  AFRICAN FISH see **Haliaeetus vocifer**
  BOOTED see **Hieraetus pennatus**
  CROWNED see **Stephanoaetus coronatus**
  GOLDEN see **Aquila chrysaetos**
  HARPY see **Harpia harpyja**
  LONG-CRESTED HAWK see **Lophoaetus occipitalis**
  MARTIAL see **Polemaetus bellicosus**
  MEXICAN see **Polyborus plancus**
  MONKEY-EATING see **Pithecophaga jefferyi**
  SNAKE see **Circaetus cinereus**
  TAWNY see **Aquila rapax**
  VERREAUX'S see **Aquila verreauxi**
  WAHLBERG'S see **Aquila wahlbergi**
  WEDGE-TAILED see **Aquila audax**
  WHISTLING see **Haliastur sphenorus**

WHITE-BREASTED SEA see **Haliaeetus leucogaster**
WHITE-TAILED see **Haliaeetus albicilla**

EAGLE OWL see **Bubo bubo**

EAGLE OWL,
  SPOTTED see **Bubo africanus**
  VERREAUX'S GIANT see **Bubo lacteus**

EARED DOVE see **Zenaida auriculata**

EASTERN
  BLUEBIRD see **Sialia sialis**
  KINGBIRD see **Tyrannus tyrannus**
  MEADOWLARK see **Sturnella magna**
  ROCK NUTHATCH see under **Sitta neumayer**
  ROSELLA see under **Platycercus eximius** and **Psephotus haematodus**
  SPINEBILL see **Acanthorhynchus tenuirostris**
  WHIPBIRD see **Psophodes olivaceus**
  WOOD PEWEE see **Contopus virens**

ECLECTUS PARROT see **Lorius roratus**

EGRET,
  CATTLE see **Bubulcus ibis**
  COMMON see **Egretta alba**
  SNOWY see **Egretta thula**

Egretta alba *or Casmerodius albus Ardeidae*
GREAT WHITE HERON or
COMMON EGRET   35 (body 15) ins
S Palaearctic, Ethiopian, Oriental, Australasian, Nearctic, Neotropical, but very local in this huge area; widespread dispersal after breeding. Pure white, long neck plumes in spring; legs black and yellow, bill black to black and yellow, eyes yellow. Usually gregarious, up to 200 together after breeding, in swamps, shallow lakes, riversides, even bare sea shores; but sometimes solitary. Perches and roosts in trees or on ground. Diet varies seasonally: fish, amphibians, aquatic insects, molluscs, worms; small birds and mammals in dry season. Very silent; low croaking at nest, where young chatter. Breeding season variable; from April onwards in Palaearctic; usually rather diffuse colonies in dense reedbeds, nest a pile of reeds up to 3 ft high; eggs 3 to 5, pale blue, incubated 25-26 days by ♀ and ♂, who tend young during *c.* 6 weeks fledging period. **58**

Egretta sacra *Ardeidae*
REEF HERON   26 ins
Oriental and Australasian: coasts and islands of India, SE Asia, Japan, Polynesia, Australia, Tasmania, New Zealand. Slaty grey, darker above, paler below and tinged brown; narrow white streak on chin and throat; long plumes on lower neck and back during courtship. Legs yellowish-green with lemon-yellow soles, bill brown, eyes yellow, surrounding skin greenish yellow. White plumage phase (not New Zealand) and piebald intermediate occur. Crouching gait with heavy bill and rather short legs; flies usually low over water. Generally hunts alone for tidal fish, molluscs, crustaceans, other marine animals, but parties form at roosts. Guttural croak and bill-snapping during breeding season; alarm note *craw*. Breeds almost throughout year over whole range, sometimes colonially, in scrub jungle, palms, mangroves, vegetation on cliff, caves, crevices, human artefacts; nest of sticks and leaves holds 2 to 3 pale greenish blue eggs, incubated 25-28 days by ♀ and ♂, who tend young for *c.* 5½ week fledging period. **59**

Egretta thula *or Leucophoyx thula Ardeidae*
SNOWY EGRET   22-26 ins
Nearctic and Neotropical: southern USA to Chile and Argentina, in fresh and salt marshes, ponds and ricefields; northern birds move S after breeding. Snow white, with plumes in breeding season; legs black but feet of adults bright yellow, thin bill black with yellow skin at base, eyes pale yellow. Slimmer and more active than other American white herons; flight more graceful than Cattle Egret's, *Bubulcus ibis*; courtship social. Shuffles in water when feeding, to stir up water ani-

mals. Breeding season varies with latitude; colonies usually in mangroves or other swamp trees; nests of sticks. Both sexes incubate 2 to 5 greenish-blue eggs and tend the brood. **60**

EGYPTIAN
GOOSE see **Alopochen aegyptiaca**
PLOVER see **Pluvianus aegyptius**
VULTURE see **Neophron percnopterus**

EIDER, STELLER'S see **Polysticta stelleri**

Elanus caeruleus *Accipitridae*
BLACK-SHOULDERED KITE 12 ins
Cosmopolitan: Palaearctic (SE Iberia, N Africa, Egypt); Oriental (Indian subcontinent, Ceylon, SE Asia); all Ethiopian (not Madagascar); Australasian (regarded by some as separate species *E. notatus:* Celebes, continental Australia, very local New Guinea); Nearctic and Neotropical (regarded by some as separate species *E. leucurus:* SW California, local Central and S America); resident and irregularly migratory or nomadic, on grass savannah, steppes, meadows and cultivated land with trees, often dry or arid, up to 9,000 ft. Upperparts grey, with black shoulders and primaries; underparts white; breast, flanks washed grey; tail short and square; legs, cere yellow, bill black, eyes crimson. Chooses exposed perches, sitting with drooping wingtips and tail moving up and down. Roosts communally up to 120 birds. Flies slowly, hovers like kestrel, often checking several times before dropping on prey, mainly small rodents, reptiles, large insects (sometimes taken in air); follows grass fires and locust swarms; takes offal off Arabian coast. No spectacular displays: pair soars and chases; also short gently fluttering flights. Breeding season varies with range: March to May Europe, September to October S Africa. Pairs build small twig nest, 5 to 60 ft often in isolated tree, which may be used several seasons; rocky ledges in Arabia. 3 to 5 cream or pale buff eggs, marked dark brown, purple and grey, incubated mainly by ♀, fed by ♂, 25-28 days. First ♂, then ♀ takes major share feeding young, who fly 30-40 days. Possibly 2 broods Malaysia, E Africa. **145**

ELEGANT
GRASS PARAKEET see **Neophema elegans**
TERN see **Thalasseus elegans**

ELF OWL see **Micrathene whitneyi**

ELWES'S EARED PHEASANT see **Crossoptilon crossoptilon**

Emberiza
bruniceps see under **E. melanocephalus**
buchanani see under **E. hortulana**

Emberiza calandra *Emberizidae: Emberizinae*
CORN BUNTING *c.* 7 ins
Palaearctic: more or less confined to Europe (including NW Africa) and Near East SW of line from Gulf of Riga to Caspian, with extension through Iran to S of Lake Balkash. Mainly sedentary in open, arid, flat or hilly areas, especially extensive open cornfields, dry steppes with bushes, stony steppes and slopes, even low maquis and coastal scrub. Almost uniformly dull brown streaked black, with dark 'necklace' and paler underparts, belly not streaked; much heavier looking than relatives and lacks white outer feathers on rather short tail. Hops on ground. Short flights often with legs dangling, undulating over longer distances. Perches dumpily isolated bushes, posts, poles, wires. Flocks in autumn, sometimes with other seed-eaters. In display succession of short upward flights by ♂ above ♀, then drops to ground where waves wings, spreads tail. Flight note in flock repeated abrupt *quit;* breeding season call hard *chip,* grating *zeep* when scolding. Song: rapid ticking notes ending in jangle 'like bunch of little keys'. Food mainly vegetable: variety of seeds, wild fruits, grain; also insects, spiders, other invertebrates. Breeds second half May to September; strongly territorial but several pairs close together and some males polygamous. ♀ builds nest of grass, deep cup lined rootlets, bents, hair; usually well hidden in ground cover, crops, rough grass, tangle, but sometimes in bushes up to 6 ft. 3 to 5 off-white to reddish-brown eggs, boldly marked and scrawled blackish-brown, incubated ♀ 12-13 days; ♀, often accompanied ♂, feeds young, who fly 11-14 days. Sometimes 2 broods. **853**

Emberiza cia *Emberizidae: Emberizinae*
ROCK BUNTING *c.* 6¼ ins
Palaearctic: from Iberia, NW Africa across Eurasia to Yellow Sea, roughly between 30° and 50°N; only N of 50° in Siberia or S of 30° in Iran, S China. Sedentary and migratory: vertical movements in mountains; northern birds winter in S of breeding range, e.g. in large flocks with Cirl Buntings, *E. cirlus,* N Africa. Breeds high, open coniferous zone, also subalpine scrub among rocky meadows and scree; villages, vineyards, gardens; up to 6,000 ft Europe; tropical lowlands to 17,500 ft W China. ♂: upperparts brown streaked black, forewing greyish with narrow white bar, rump chestnut, white outer tail feathers; head, breast grey with black stripes above, through, below eye; underparts reddish buff. ♀ duller, head markings less distinct. Legs straw brown, bill dark grey, eyes dark brown. Juvenile like Yellowhammer, *E. citrinella,* but underparts reddish buff. Behaves much as Yellowhammer; terrestrial, perching mainly rocks, bushes. Sharp *zit* call resembles *E. cirlus;* bubbling *tucc* becomes twitter in flight; song shrill *zi zi zi zirr.* Diet: seeds of grain and grasses; also insects, especially grasshoppers. Breeds from early April lowlands to May and June; nest of grass, bark strips, moss, lined fine rootlets, hair; among stones, on steep banks, up to 2 ft in heath or stone wall. 4 to 6 greenish white to violet brown eggs, with zone of scrawls round big end, dark brown over ashy spots. Incubation mainly ♀; period and fledging much as *E. citrinella.* **854**

Emberiza cirlus see under **E. cia**

Emberiza citrinella *Emberizidae: Emberizinae*
YELLOWHAMMER or YELLOW BUNTING *c.* 6½ ins
Palaearctic: combined range of western Yellowhammer and eastern Pine Bunting, *E. leucocephala,* crosses Eurasia between 50° and 60°N, from Britain and Ireland to Sea of Okhotsk, extending to N in Scandinavia, USSR, to S in S Europe, Caucasus with isolated group near headwaters Hoangho. Introduced New Zealand. Yellowhammer mainly sedentary, except northernmost populations; E Asian Pine Buntings winter temperate Asia: Iran to China. Habitat (both species) edges, clearings broadleaved and coniferous forests N to subarctic birch zone and up to subalpine meadows with stunted trees; Yellowhammer also in cultivated land, heaths, commons, but seldom gardens. ♂: upperparts, including wings, chestnut streaked black, rump rufous, outer tail feathers white; head, underparts yellow, varyingly streaked greenish brown, with broad band across breast. Yellow reduced in winter and in ♀, though some as bright as some ♂♂. Legs pale flesh brown, bill: upper dark bluish horn, lower paler; eyes dark brown. Juveniles darker. Spends much time on ground where hops, but perches trees, posts, wires, often flicking tail. Flight finch-like with wing closing, more or less undulating. Flocks autumn with other seed-eaters, roosts socially. Calls: *tink,* single *twick* in flight, *twit-up* in winter flocks; song rendered *little bit of bread and no cheese,* with varying emphasis. ♂ chases ♀ in courtship, also postures before her. Food chiefly vegetable: corn, seeds, fruits, leaves, grass; smaller insects, other invertebrates, including worms. Breeds end March to September; ♂ and ♀ build substantial nest of straw, grass, stalks, lined fine grass, hair, often with 'doorstep' in front; in bank or low in small bush, brambles, other tangle, from ground level to 6 ft in hedge or bush. 3 to 5 whitish, purple white or light red brown eggs, variously scrawled and spotted dark brown or black, incubated ♀ 12-14 days; ♀ and ♂ (from throat at first) feed young, who fly 12-13 days. 2, sometimes 3 brood. **855**

Emberiza flaviventris *Emberizidae: Emberizinae*
GOLDEN-BREASTED BUNTING 6 ins
Ethiopian: Nigeria to Ethiopia, S to S Africa; resident open savannah woodland, stony hillsides with scattered bushes, short grass, gardens. ♂: back rufous grey to blackish, wings with white tipped coverts forming 2 bars, rump grey; white outer feathers to blackish tail; crown, cheeks black with white stripe centre crown and either side eye; chin white, underparts shades of yellow; flanks, under tail coverts pale grey; legs pale brown, bill mainly horn, eyes brown. ♀ similar but duller, with dark streaked crown, greyish breast. Juvenile buffish on head, underparts pale yellow. Often perched on tree, but feeds mainly bare ground, crouching when not walking. Normal call single plaintive *droll-peer,* mate answering soft *sitee; chip* in flight; contact between pair quiet *tsip tsip tsip;* simple varied song: *chwee chi it twee.* Pairs or small parties; takes seeds, insects, mainly from ground. Breeding variable within range; nest frail cup of twigs, grass, fibres, often quite open, a few ft from ground in fork of shrub. 2 or 3 greyish white, greenish or bluish eggs, zoned black and sepia spots, scrawls, incubation and fledging much as *E. citrinella.* Probably 3 or 4 broods Kenya. **856**

Emberiza hortulana *Emberizidae: Emberizinae*
ORTOLAN *c.* 6¼ ins
Palaearctic: most of Europe except NW and N; Asia Minor to Iran and into W Asia roughly between 45° and 55°N as far as Lake Kos Gol; replaced in E by closely related Grey-necked Bunting, *E. buchanani.* Winters W Africa to Somalia, Arabia. Breeds arid country with scattered trees; corn and other arable fields; meadows, cultivated and natural steppes; riparian meadows Siberia; open maquis, mountain slopes up to 6,500 ft Alps, above tree line Greece; winters steppes, savannahs. ♂: upperparts brown streaked black, some white on tail; head, breast greyish olive, narrow yellowish 'spectacles', underparts pinkish buff. ♀ duller, breast streaked; legs, bill brownish red, eyes brown. Rather unobtrusive but habits like other *Emberiza* species; flocks in autumn, often joining Tree Pipits, *Anthus trivialis.* Calls include shrill *tsee-ip,* short *tsip,* piping *tseu* when breeding. Song more musical than Yellowhammer, delivered from elevated perch, sometimes at night. Food seeds and grain; insects (Orthoptera, beetles, moth larvae), snails, young locusts on migration. Breeds from early May Spain, early June Finland; nest of grass, roots, lined fine rootlets, hair; in crop fields, ground cover of *Artemisia,* other tall plants. 4 to 6 bluish white to pinkish or reddish grey eggs, spotted and streaked blackish brown, incubated mainly ♀ 11-14 days; fledging period *c.* 12 days. 2 broods Central Europe. **857**

Emberiza leucocephala *Emberizidae: Emberizinae*
PINE BUNTING *c.* 6½ ins
E Palaearctic: see Yellowhammer, *E. citrinella,* for range, habitats; often considered conspecific. ♂: upperparts much as Yellowhammer; crown white, bordered black; white cheek surrounded by chestnut mask, throat; underparts white, streaked brown breast, flanks; head pattern obscured in winter. ♀ much as Yellowhammer, white replacing yellow. Habits also as Yellowhammer; flocks in autumn; often seen roads, paths Mongolia. Call as Yellowhammer; song like Chaffinch, *Fringilla coelebs.* Food, seeds of grasses, mountain plants; young fed on insects. Breeds end May to July; nest like Yellowhammer, on ground among grass, small bushes, at edge of thicket. 4 to 6 eggs much as Yellowhammer's, incubation and fledging as Yellowhammer. 2 broods. **858**

Emberiza melanocephalus *Emberizidae: Emberizinae*
BLACK-HEADED BUNTING *c.* 6½ ins
Palaearctic: combined range with eastern Red-headed Bunting *E. bruniceps,* now regarded as conspecific: NE Mediterranean area, Georgia, Caucasus, Iran to mountains of Turkestan, all between 30° and 50°N. Both forms winter mainly in plains of NW Indian subcontinent. Breeds sunny lowlands or mountain slopes with dry scrub; bushy steppes, cultivated land with vineyards, orchards, olive groves; riverine strips; winters cultivated land, scrub jungle. ♂: upperparts chestnut, wings, tail (no white outer

feathers) dull brown with pale feather margins; head black, surrounded yellow nape, chin down to underparts; head pattern much obscured winter. ♀: streaked brown above, pale to bright yellow below. Legs dark flesh brown, bill mainly lead blue, eyes brown. Red-headed ♂ has head, throat to upper breast chestnut to golden, greenish mantle, greenish yellow rump; otherwise like Black-headed and ♀ indistinguishable. ♂ flies dangling legs like Corn Bunting, *E. calandra.* Huge flocks winter India, flying into trees when disturbed. Call sharp *zitt;* low *zee* (anxiety); monotonous *chiririri;* musical warbling song. Food summer mainly insects from ground; winter: grain and other seeds. Breeds mid May to end June; nest of grass and dead stems, lined fine bents, hair, well hidden on ground under scrub, among thistles, also up to 3 ft or more in bushes. 4 or 5 light greenish blue eggs, evenly spotted brown over violet, incubated ♀ 14 days; ♀, helped ♂, feeds young. **859**

Emberiza schoeniclus *Emberizidae: Emberizinae*
REED BUNTING   *c.* 6 ins
Palaearctic: virtually all Europe (except Iceland) and large area Central Asia between 30° and 70°N, extending more narrowly to Pacific coast, Sakhalin, Hokkaido, Kuriles, Kamtchatka. Partly sedentary but northern population migrates to S of breeding range, also N Africa, N Indian subcontinent. Variety of wet habitats: marshes, swamps, bogs; lake and river fringes; reedbeds; damp meadows, wet areas in grass steppes, clearings in woodland, N to scrub tundra. In Britain and Ireland also in dry scrub, hedgerows away from water; often winters cultivated land. ♂: upperparts dark and chestnut brown streaked black with white outer tail feathers; head, throat black with white collar, underparts off-white, streaked on flanks; head pattern suffused brown in winter. ♀: brown head with buff 'eyebrow', dark moustachial stripe; underparts buff, streaked dark on flanks. Hops, runs, walks on ground; flight jerky rather than undulating. Flocks winter, often with other species. ♂ chases ♀ in courtship, displays by showing off head and collar, vibrating one or both wings. Calls: sharp *tseep,* metallic *ching, chit* of alarm. Simple but variable song: *tweek tweek tweek tititic,* from stem of plant. Eats seeds of marsh plants and grasses; small insects in summer picked off vegetation or taken in air. Breeds mid April to August; nest of dry grasses, sedge, lined fine bents, hair usually built ♀, well hidden in ground cover, on tussock, stump, sometimes up to 12 ft in bush. 4 to 5 olive brown or buff eggs, boldly marked and scrawled dark brown, incubated ♀ and ♂ 13-14 days; both parents feed young, who fly 10-13 days. Injury feigning common. 2, perhaps sometimes 3 broods. **860**

Emberiza striolata see under **Melophus lathami**

Empidonax alnorum see under **E. traillii**

Empidonax flavirostris *Tyrannidae*
YELLOW-BELLIED FLYCATCHER   5½ ins
Nearctic: breeds from Newfoundland, Central Quebec and Manitoba, S Mackenzie to S New Hampshire, N Pennsylvania, S Wisconsin and Central Alberta; winters from N Mexico to Panama. Habitat: northern forests of conifers and birch with sphagnum ground layer; on migration in alder swamps; upperparts olive-green with dark brown wings and tail, feather edges making white bars on wings; underparts, especially yellower throat, yellower at all seasons than other *Empidonax* species; legs dark, bill dark with pale lower mandible, eyes dark brown with whitish orbits. Song an ascending *pse-ek,* delivered 'like a sneeze' with jerk of head; call leisurely or 'mournful' *che-bunk.* Diet principally insects taken on wing, especially mosquitos in breeding area, flying ants; takes berries when normal food short. Breeds June onwards, making bulky cup of moss and small roots, lined rootlets and grass, on side of mossy mound or in roots of fallen tree. 3 or 4 white eggs, sparsely marked brown, incubated by ♀ *c.* 12 days; both parents feed young who fledge in about same time. **578**

Empidonax minimus *Tyrannidae*
LEAST FLYCATCHER   5¼ ins
Nearctic: breeds Nova Scotia, Ontario, N Alberta, W Central Mackenzie, to N New Jersey, SW N Carolina, Indiana and SW Missouri W to SE Wyoming, E British Columbia; winters NE Mexico to Panama. Wide range of habitats: open country with trees, orchards, gardens, parks but not dense woodland. Upperparts greyer, underparts whiter and lower mandible darker than other *Empidonax* species. Song repeated and distinctive *chebec,* delivered with jerk of head and flirt of tail; call: short *whit.* Jumbled notes in song flight. Diet: small insects taken on wing from variety of perches; also off plants, leaves and the ground. Breeds May onwards, building rather frail-looking cup of plant materials, softly lined, woven into fork of tree usually 6 to 40 ft up. 3 to 6 creamy white eggs, occasionally spotted red-brown, incubated by ♀; young tended by both parents. **579**

Empidonax traillii *Tyrannidae*
TRAILL'S FLYCATCHER   6 ins
Nearctic, marginally Neotropical: breeds over most of Alaska and Canada within tree limit and throughout USA (except SE) into NW Mexico; winters from S Mexico to Venezuela and Ecuador. Northern and eastern populations breed scrub thickets and swamps of alder and willow; Mid-western birds favour dry upland pastures with scrub, as well as orchards, gardens and roadsides. Upperparts olive-brown with darker wings and tail and white wingbars; throat whitest of *Empidonax* species but not separable on plumage in field from slightly smaller Acadian Flycatcher, *E. virescens.* Song of N and E birds emphatic *fee-bee-o,* syllables short, accented, slurred; Mid-western song 'sneezy' *fitz-bew;* alarm call abrupt *wit.* Diet: insectivorous, as relatives. Breeds June onwards, building nest of plant materials, softly lined, usually 2 to 4 ft up in fork of shrub (not suspended) in swamp, occasionally in fern clump; Mid-western nests in dry habitats up to 20 ft in trees. 2 to 4 creamy white eggs, sparsely spotted brown, incubated by ♀ and young tended by both parents. (Two species sometimes split: more northern, *E. alnorum,* Alder Flycatcher 'Fee-bee-o'; most southern, *E. traillii,* Willow Flycatcher 'Fitz-bew'.)

Empidonax virescens see under **E. traillii**

EMU see **Domaius novaehollandiae**

EMERALD
   DOVE see **Chalcophaps indica**
   HUMMINGBIRD, PUERTO RICAN see **Chlorostilbon maugaeus**
   SPOTTED WOOD DOVE see **Turtur chalcospilos**
   TOUCANET see **Aulacorhynchus prasinus**

EMPEROR
   BIRD OF PARADISE see **Paradisaea guilielmi**
   PENGUIN see **Aptenodytes forsteri**

Entomodestes coracinus *Muscicapidae: Turdinae*
BLACK SOLITAIRE   9 ins
Neotropical: Colombia (W Andes) to NW Ecuador; resident canopy of dense humid forest, 3,000 to 7,000 ft. Jet black, except for white areas: cheek patch, axillaries, patch on inner web inner flight feathers, lower part outer tail feathers. Legs and bill noticeably short. Lives in tree tops; has fine song; mainly insectivorous. **680**

Entomyzon cyanotus *Meliphagidae*
BLUE-FACED HONEYEATER   12 ins
Australasian: mainly continental coasts from N Kimberleys, Cape York, S to New South Wales, S Australia; resident open forest country, mainly eucalypts, usually near water. Upperparts to long white-tipped tail golden olive; head to lower neck black with white patches side of head, throat, breast; chin, throat, breast grey, belly white; legs dark grey, bill black, eyes white in blue facial skin. In pairs or small parties, very aggressive to other birds and humans, but can easily be tamed. Acrobatic on blossom when taking nectar; also insects, frequently

from under bark, berries, fruits, doing some damage to orchards. Calls: shrill, whistle, *tweet.* Breeds June to January, even to April; nest of bark strips, lined finer pieces, grass, hair, usually on outer lateral branch, 10 to 30 ft; often takes old nests of babblers, magpie larks, other species. 2 or 3 salmon pink to buff eggs, sparingly marked purplish red, chestnut over pale grey. Sometimes 3 broods. **838**

Eopsaltria australis *Muscicapidae: Muscicapinae*
YELLOW ROBIN   6¾ ins
Australasian: E continental Australia; resident, with some local movements, in forests with thick undergrowth. Upperparts dark grey, upper tail coverts and rump bright yellow-green (yellow in northern race), tail tinged olive; chin greyish white shading into bright yellow underparts; flanks tinged olive. ♀ duller. Legs olive green, bill black, eyes very light brown. Perches on bark of trunk as well as on twigs. Call: loud prolonged piping on one note, beginning very early and continuing to dusk. Food: insects from ground, foliage, occasionally air. Breeds July to January, building nest of bark strips, grasses, bound cobwebs, decorated lichen and trailing bark; in tree fork, 3 to 30 ft. 2 to 4 pale or bluish green eggs, marked reddish brown. **779**

Eopsaltria georgiana or Quoyornis georgianus
Muscicapidae: Muscicapinae
WHITE-BREASTED ROBIN   *c.* 6 ins
Australasian: SW continental Australia; resident dense forests of 'big scrubs'. Upperparts dark grey, becoming dark brown on wings, with white tip to graduated tail; underparts from chin whitish; legs brown, bill dark grey, eyes brown. Usually in pairs, hard to see: clings to bark of tree trunks like nuthatch. Call: loud *kawhow kawhow whowah whow.* Insectivorous. Breeds October, building nest of small twigs, bark strips, leaves, lined small rootlets, grass. 2 olive or bronze-green eggs, darker at big end.

Eos squamata *Psittacidae*
VIOLET-HEADED LORIKEET or
MOLUCCAS RED LORY   11 ins
Australasian: Moluccas to islands of W New Guinea. Predominantly red, with purple collar, underparts; outer flight feathers black with red bases; black tips to inner quills and greater coverts; scapulars partly purple; tail red-purple above, red and golden below. Very little known about habits in wild; species of this genus lay 1 or 2 white eggs in tree holes. **392**

Ephippiorhynchus senegalensis *Ciconiidae*
SADDLEBILL   5½ ft
Ethiopian, except extreme S Africa, in swamps, marshes and on lake shores. Head, neck, upper wing and tail black, iridescent green, violet and blue; otherwise white, including flight feathers; legs red and black, long bill red with black band round middle and yellow frontal 'saddle', eyes bright yellow. Usually solitary, in pairs or family parties; feeds like heron with slow stalk and lightning stab, on water animals of many kinds, including fish, frogs and water beetles; also small mammals and birds. Flies with head and feet held lower than body. Silent except for bill-clattering during display. Breeding season varies with altitude; from June in Uganda; substantial nest of sticks, usually in trees, sometimes cliff ledge, holds 1 to 4 dull white and pitted eggs. **71**

Ephthianura albifrons *Muscicapidae: Malurinae*
WHITE-FRONTED CHAT   *c.* 4½ ins
Australia: S Queensland, New South Wales, Victoria, southern S Australia and S Western Australia as far N as Shark's Bay. Habitat: damp and rough places with low cover e.g. swamps and margins of estuaries and lakes. ♂: head down to upper breast white; broad black band round mid-breast and up nape and hindcrown; back grey, wings brown; tail blackish, outer feathers tipped white; belly white. Legs and bill black, eyes light brown. ♀: no black on head, chest band dark brown and thinner. Usually in pairs or gregarious when not breeding; rapid twisting flight, always on move; feeds on insects. Call: low, metallic *tang.* Breeds July to March, mainly September and Octo-

ber; nest of grass or fine twigs, lined rootlets, hair and fine grasses, in tall grass or low down in shrub, near water; 3, sometimes 4 white eggs, slightly tinged pinkish and marked with reddish or purplish browns; both parents incubate eggs and tend young.

Ephthianura aurifrons *Muscicapidae: Malurinae*
ORANGE CHAT *c.* 4 ins
Australia: W Queensland, W New South Wales, N South Australia, Central Australia, Western Australia S of Pibara district to Morawa and Eucla. Habitat: open country, with some bush cover, or samphire flats. ♂: crown and rump orange-yellow, sides of head yellower, rest of upperparts and wings brown with yellowish green margins to feathers, flight feathers dark grey, tail black; chin and throat black, rest of underparts orange-yellow. ♀: brownish upperparts, rump yellow, 'eyebrow' pale; underparts pale yellowish white. Legs and bill black, eyes dark brownish red. Behaviour and feeding: see Crimson Chat, *E. tricolor*. Call: mellow *cheek-cheek* in flight. Breeds usually September to February; cup-shaped nest of fine twigs, lined rootlets, in small bush *c.* 3 ft up; 3 white eggs, purplish red spots concentrated at larger end; both parents incubate. **760**

Ephthianura tricolor *Muscicapidae: Malurinae*
CRIMSON CHAT *c.* 4 ins
Australia: W of Great Dividing Range, Gulf of Carpentaria S to NW Victoria, N South Australia and Central Australia; Western Australia from Pilbara district S to Moore River; seasonal movements produced by weather. Habitat: open country with some bush cover. ♂: crown and rump scarlet, sides of head brown, back brown with dark streaks, wings brown with brownish white edges to primaries and secondaries; tail dark brown tipped white; throat white, breast scarlet, belly white. ♀: head brown, chest buff, scarlet only on rump. Legs and down-curved bill black, eyes pale buff. Strongly territorial when breeding, otherwise often in small flocks; timid; feeds on insects on ground; swift, twisting flight. Call: metallic *ting*, also various whistles; low chatter used in territorial display. Breeds usually after heavy rainfall, sometimes loose colonies; cup-shaped nest in top of low bush, of fine twigs and grass lined hairs, finer grass and bark fibres; 3, sometimes 4, white eggs with reddish purple spots; both parents build nest, incubate, and tend young.

Epimachus fastosus see under **E. meyeri**

Epimachus meyeri *Paradisaeidae*
SICKLE-BILLED BIRD OF PARADISE ♂: 39 (bill 3½) ins
Australasian: S and E New Guinea; resident tall montane forests 5,400 ft up to 10,000 ft, usually above range of *E. fastosus*. ♂: upperparts black glossed violet; part of back and rump oily green tinged blue; wings and very long graduated tail black; crown velvety with short glossy plumes; chin to upper neck blackish, suffused iridescent bronze-purple; cheeks blue-green; underparts dull olive brown, tinged purple on flanks; large erectile 'fans' on sides upper breast burnished dark brown to black, broadly tipped violet blue; behind these longer set sooty black tufts; similar double set sides lower breast. ♀: upperparts dull rusty to olive brown; crown to hindneck chestnut; base of upper bill, lores, cheeks brownish black, throat blackish brown; underparts buff densely barred black. Legs, bill black (gape yellow), eyes pale blue. Immature ♂ progresses from ♀-like to ♂ plumage. Searches mossy trunks and branches for grasshoppers, other insects; also takes fruits, berries. ♂ displays by expanding breast feathers, then flank plumes, with loud rattling call; turns breast upward, face framed in short feathers of upper breast, wings folded, tail slightly spread, bill closed. Second type makes more use of fans, bill opens to show gape, bird sometimes rotating in jerks (L. S. Crandall). Breeds April (incubated egg found) to mid July (nearly fledged nestling); nest of moss and vine stems attached fork of small tree in understorey, lined rootlets, skeleton leaves. Single egg cinnamon, marked longitudinally brown-grey, reddish brown, small brown and lavender spots, incubated ♀. **991**

Eremialector decoratus *Pteroclididae*
BLACK-FACED SANDGROUSE 10 ins
Ethiopian: 3 races in restricted range, Somalia to Kenya and Central Tanzania. Nomadic in dry bush country, occupying even small open spaces. ♂: upperparts brown, barred black; forehead, base of bill, throat black, white band between forehead and crown, extending over eye as stripe; sides of face, neck, breast dull brown, terminated by black band above white lower breast; belly, flanks black; under tail coverts white; tail pointed not elongated; legs feathered, feet horn, bill dark horn, eyes dark brown. ♀: upperparts with crescents rather than bars, no black on head; neck, upper breast barred and spotted black. Usually in pairs or parties, said to drink regularly in mornings. Calls: whistle of two long and one short note, also repeated *quit quit*. Diet: grass seeds and roots. Breeding season variable; 2 or 3 glossy buff eggs, marked reddish brown and grey, laid on bare ground, incubated by ♀ and ♂ (by night) 23-24 days. **347**

Eremialector quadricinctus *Pteroclididae*
FOUR-BANDED SANDGROUSE *c.* 11½ ins
Ethiopian: broad band from Senegal and Gambia to Lake Chad, Sudan, Ethiopia, NW Kenya and Uganda; W African population moves S in dry season. Habitat: bush or cultivated land in Sudan, Uganda, stony country in Kenya. ♂: upperparts generally brown, chestnut or white and black bars on mantle, rump, tail and wing coverts; crown streaked black, forehead black and white; chestnut, buffish white and black bands across breast; underparts closely barred black and white; underwing grey; tail pointed not elongated. ♀ lacks bands on breast. Legs feathered, feet horn, short bill dark horn, eyes dark brown. Small parties come to drink at dusk with twittering calls. Diet: seeds and roots. Breeds mainly January to March. 2 or 3 clay pink eggs, dotted pale brown and mauve, resemble fallen *Bauhinia* leaves among which often laid. **348**

Eremiornis carteri *Muscicapidae: Malurinae*
SPINIFEX BIRD *c.* 5¾ ins
Australasian: N Australia from Cloncurry, Queensland, to Halls Creek and Fitzroy River, Western Australia, S to Minilya River; also Monte Bello and Barrow Is, Western Australia. Habitat: arid country in spinifex and other low scrub. Upperparts bright brown, crown rufous, long tail darker towards tip; underparts dull white, washed buff towards flanks. Legs light brown, bill and eyes brown. Shy, usually in pairs and on ground; insectivorous. ♂'s call from top of bush likened to French words *je suis, à vous*; ♀ utters grating notes. Nest of finely shredded grass lined fine roots, built by ♀ in bunch of spinifex; 2 pinkish white eggs, well covered with minute pale lilac and purplish to reddish brown markings; both parents tend young.

Eremomela icteropygialis *Muscicapidae: Sylviinae*
YELLOW-BELLIED WARBLER 3½ ins
Ethiopian: from Eritrea westwards S of Sahara, but not reaching S Nigeria or Sierra Leone; southwards through eastern Africa to S Africa, but not in southernmost or eastern coastal areas. Resident dry open bush and true desert. Upperparts, including wings, very short tail, ashy grey; dusky eyestripe but faint pale ring round eye and pale 'eyebrow'; underparts from chin white, shading to pale yellow lower belly; under tail coverts, flanks greyish; legs black, bill blackish, eyes brown. Usually found in pairs or family parties; often with African Penduline Tits, *Anthoscopus caroli*, searching low in trees or bushes, especially *Calotropis* (sodom apple), for insects and their larvae. Calls: 4-syllabled jingle; plaintive *see see;* scolding *chee chiri chee chiri chit*. Breeding season variable within range; nest small, deep, semi-transparent cup of grass, wool, cobwebs, suspended by rim from two twigs or fork of low branch. 2 or 3 white eggs, spotted dark red and sepia over grey. **738**

EREMOMELA, YELLOW-BELLIED see **Eremomela icteropygialis**

Eremophila alpestris *Alaudidae*
SHORE LARK or HORNED LARK *c.* 6½ ins
Holarctic, Neotropical: 40 races; breeds in strip along N Palaearctic coasts from Scandinavia to 160°E in Siberia; also from N African coast, Middle East into mountain ranges of S Asia mainly between 30° and 50°N; almost all N America to 20°N (except NW Alaska, SE USA) with isolated group round Bogota, Colombia; most populations winter lowlands, but northern ones move to southern breeding range. Habitat: rocky alpine meadows up to 17,300 ft in Himalayas; stony steppes; stony areas of lichen tundra; stony deserts; in America, where no competing larks, in variety of open country from arable land to deserts and coastal dunes; grass savannah at *c.* 9,000 ft Colombia; winters coastal shingle and nearby fields. ♂: upperparts brownish; distinctive black and yellow head pattern with short black horns; underparts whitish. ♀ and juvenile have less black. Legs black, bill greyish horn, eyes dark brown. Flocks in winter, sometimes with buntings, usually walking or running over ground. Flight rather undulating. Call: *see-it* like Meadow Pipit, *Anthus pratensis*; song: sweet low warble, song flight not as prominent as most larks. Food: seeds, buds, insects and larvae in summer; also small molluscs, crustaceans in winter. Breeds mid May to July, building simple nest of plant stems, softly lined; pebbles, sheep droppings, plant debris arranged round site on ground. Usually 4 greenish-white eggs, thickly freckled fine yellowish-brown, incubated 10-14 days (N America). Young, fed by ♀ and ♂, leave nest 9-12 days, fly *c.* 7 days later. Usually 2 broods. **601**

Eremophila bilopha *Alaudidae*
TEMMINCK'S HORNED LARK 5¼ ins
Palaearctic: resident but wanders in winter from breeding grounds in S Morocco, E to Algeria, Egypt along coast; N Arabia to Iraq and Syrian Desert. Habitat: deserts and stony wastes but not in mountains so no overlap with *E. alpestris*. Plumage similar to *E. alpestris* but has white not yellow on face. Upperparts uniform sandy, underparts paler; primaries and tail darker; also smaller and less bulky than *E. alpestris*. Call: repeated *see-oo;* song less vigorous than *E. alpestris* but similar and song-flight is performed more often. Feeds on seeds and shoots of small desert plants. Breeding season begins March but mainly April and May; nests of plant stems on ground usually hidden under a clump of vegetation. 2 to 4 brownish speckled eggs. **602**

Eriocnemis mirabilis *Trochilidae*
COLOURFUL PUFFLEG 3¼ (bill ½) ins
Neotropical: only known from subtropical (4,500 to 7,500 ft) zone in W slope of S Western Andes in Cauca, Colombia, where caught and photographed by J. S. Dunning. Resident in forests. ♂: upperparts dark iridescent green; forehead emerald; white patch behind eyes; tail dark bronzy olive above, iridescent brassy olive below; throat and sides of neck iridescent blue green, merging into dark green breast; belly deep iridescent indigo speckled red; under tail coverts mixed iridescent ruby and gold; downy leg 'puffs' white, tipped cinnamon in front, all cinnamon behind. ♀: upperparts and flanks dark green; centre of throat and breast white with green spots; underparts white spotted reddish bronze, most pronounced on under tail coverts; tail mostly bronze green, tipped and edged blue black. Little known of habits as yet; relatives have simple warbling song and lay 1 or 2 white eggs, incubated 14-15 days. Both parents feed young. **472**

Erithacus rubecula *Muscicapidae: Turdinae*
(EUROPEAN) ROBIN 5½ ins
Palaearctic: W Europe, extending into Siberia between 50° and 60°N, and through Asia Minor, Caucasus to S Caspian; very local NW Africa, also Canaries, Azores; northern birds winter temperate W Europe, and Mediterranean E to Iran. Habitat broadleaved and coniferous woodland with thick undergrowth and ground cover; spruce forests with swampy areas in N, montane forests in S of range; parks, gardens, roadsides W Europe, especially

Britain. Upperparts olive brown, separated from orange forehead, throat, breast by grey-blue border; underparts white; legs brown, bill dark olive brown. eyes very dark brown. Juvenile has upperparts mottled buff, underparts mainly buff, 'scaled' brown. Solitary in winter, pairs in summer, strongly territorial. Confident in gardens, comes close in woodland, regarding human as large animal likely to stir prey in litter. Hops on ground, stopping to flick wings and tail, exaggerating this when excited. Usual call repeated, scolding *tic tic;* also soft *tsip:* song shrill but melodious and warbling, phrases lasting up to 3 secs; ♀ also sings. Opposing birds present breasts to each other, swaying body side to side on perch. ♂ feeds ♀ during breeding season, March to July in Britain. Feeds mainly on ground: smaller insects and larvae, spiders, worms, snails; berries and small fruit in autumn; bird tables in gardens. ♀ builds foundation of dead leaves, then mossy cup lined rootlets, hairs; in bank, often ivied, under tussock, in tree holes, stumps, roots; many human artefacts, up to 10 ft high. 5 to 7 white or bluish white eggs, freckled light red usually at big end, incubated by ♀ 12 to 14 days; both parents feed young, who fly 12-15 days. 2, sometimes 3 broods. **681**

Erolia fuscicollis see **Calidris fuscicollis**

Erythropygia coryphaeus *Muscicapidae: Turdinae*
KAROO CHAT   6¼ ins
Ethiopian: SW parts of Southern Africa; resident and numerous in dry, sandy areas. Upperparts sooty brown, tail black with white tips to outer feathers; 'eyebrow' white; centre of chin and throat white with thin black moustachial stripes; underparts uniform brown. Mainly terrestrial, flicking tail when disturbed before flying to cover. Scolds snakes, small carnivores. Mainly insectivorous. Nest of dead sticks, rootlets, lined down, hair, wool, well hidden under dead twigs, low bushes. 2 or 3 greenish-blue eggs, heavily marked reddish-brown. **682**

Erythropygia leucophrys see **E. zambesiana**

Erythropygia zambesiana or E. leucophrys
Muscicapidae: Turdinae
WHITE-BROWED or RED-BACKED SCRUB ROBIN   6 ins
Ethiopian: mainly S of Equator, from Congo to Sudan, then locally down E side to SE coast; resident and local migrant in scrub and secondary forest. Upperparts, including crown, rufous, faintly streaked blackish; flight feathers and wing coverts dusky, white covert tips forming bar on closed wing; rump and tail russet, with narrow blackish subterminal band, white tips; 'eyebrow' white, earcoverts brownish; underparts buffish white, heavily streaked black, throat to chest; legs stone-brown, bill dark brown, eyes brown. Juvenile mottled. Usually solitary or in pairs: can be summoned by imitating bird alarm calls. Flies low for cover if disturbed. Flicks and fans tail when excited. ♂ displays by running along branch, head down, tail cocked, wings drooping. Call *hee-er-wi-er-wi* (R. E. Moreau), scolding alarm; song from tree perch loud, rather monotonous descending notes, repeated. Mainly insectivorous. Breeds chiefly September to February E Africa. Nest deep grass cup, lined rootlets, in tuft or thick herbage on or near ground. 2 or 3 white eggs, marked rusty red over purple. Probably 2 broods. **683**

Esacus magnirostris or Orthorhamphus
magnirostris *Burhinidae*
BEACH CURLEW   21 ins
Oriental, Australasian; race *E. m. recurvirostris* 'Great Stone Curlew': Indian subcontinent, Burma; race *magnirostris:* Andamans, Indonesia, Philippines, New Guinea, northern Australia to coastal New South Wales, Solomon Is. Habitat: reefs, beaches, coastal and riverine mud banks. Resembles *Burhinus* stone curlews (*note:* Australian species is *B. magnirostris* also!) but upperparts unstreaked brown; 'shoulder' dark brown, white and grey wingbars, tip black and white; black band through eye, white above and below; throat, breast grey, belly white; legs greenish-yellow, powerful bill with pronounced gonys yellow, tipped black; eyes yellow. Usually solitary or in pairs, but

parties form in rains in Burma and visit grasslands; usual food small crustaceans and molluscs. Stands still when approached, whereas *Burhinus* crouches, but may bob body like lapwing *Vanellus*. Call: repeated *wer-loo*, often at night; *recurvirostris* utters whistling alarm and chatters when taking wing. Breeds October Australia, laying 1 or 2 creamy white eggs, streaked and blotched olive brown, on bare sand or mud, often close to water.

Estrilda astrild *Estrildidae*
COMMON WAXBILL   4½ ins
Ethiopian: resident in most of region; introduced Portugal, near Obidos. Habitat: wetlands, watersides with trees, tall grass; cultivated land especially when neglected; gardens, villages. ♂: upperparts pale brown, closely barred dusky; lores, eyestripe crimson; cheeks, neck, throat, greyish; centre breast crimson pink; under tail coverts black, rest underparts pale brown, faintly barred buff, tinged pink. ♀ as ♂ but less crimson. Legs, eyes brown, bill red. Immature much as ♀ but bill blackish. (Crimson-rumped Waxbill, *E. rhodopyga*, has similar habitat over much of range.) Very lively, constantly flicking tail side to side. Small parties become large after breeding season, take off calling *chairp chairp chairp*, then reedy twittering flock call; also excited *chee chee churrr chit;* ♂'s song subdued, melodious. Feeds on or near ground, mainly grass seeds. Breeding season variable throughout range; nest pear-shaped, of grass, with entrance at 'stalk'; lined down, feathers; often canopy on top for roosting; in low cover on banks or level grassland. 4 to 8 pink eggs incubated ♀ and ♂. Both feed young from throat. Usual host of Pintailed Whydah, *Vidua macroura*. **937**

Estrilda rhodopyga see under **E. astrild**

Estrilda temporalis *Estrildidae*
SYDNEY WAXBILL or RED-BROWED FINCH   4¾ ins
Australia: eastern coast and ranges from Cape York to SE South Australia; resident scrub or forest edge with dense undergrowth; bushy grassland; watercourses in mountains; gardens, roadsides, into towns. Upperparts, including wings, tail dull yellowish olive; rump crimson; crown, nape grey; face light grey with broad crimson stripe from red bill over eye to back of head; underparts from chin to undertail grey; legs pink, eyes red-brown. Juvenile browner on head, crimson areas duller, bill black. Usually in small groups, larger flocks in winter. Strong flight but prefers to hop on ground. Insistent contact call: piercing *sseee sseee;* twittering song derives from it. Food usually seeds from ground, grassheads, bushes; insects from foliage. Breeding peak October November New South Wales; builds tubular nest of dry and green grass, lined feathers, in dense thorn, sometimes in bunch of foliage, tangle of vines, fork of branch, generally below 6 ft. 4 to 6 white eggs.

Eubucco bourcierii *Capitonidae*
RED-HEADED BARBET   6½ ins
Neotropical: Costa Rica and Panama to Colombia and Ecuador, NE Peru; resident forest undergrowth, clearings, up to c. 7,500 ft in Andes. ♂: upperparts to tail rather dull green; whole head and throat scarlet, shading to orange on breast; narrow blue half collar on hind neck; underparts whitish streaked green; legs dark, stout bill yellow-green, eyes brown. ♀: upperparts green, cheeks blue, throat grey, upper breast orange yellow. Unlike flocking species of barbet, usually solitary and silent. Insectivorous: searches curled up dead leaves; also works vegetation 10 to 30 ft up, sometimes with parties of tanagers. Nests as relatives, in hole; both sexes incubate and tend young. **525**

Eudocimus albus *Threskiornithidae*
WHITE IBIS (AMERICAN)   21-27 ins
Nearctic and Neotropical: from southern USA to NE South America; some post-breeding dispersal. Habitat usually coastal salt, brackish and freshwater lakes. Almost entirely white, sometimes mottled on crown and nape; ends of 4 longest primaries greenish black; legs, slender curved bill and facial skin pinkish, eyes pale blue. Gregarious: concerted flights alternate

flapping and gliding, especially impressive on mass returns to tree roosts. Also feed together, picking up crabs in shallow water, probing mud; and take fish, frogs, snakes. Courtship and threat displays at colonies. Usually silent; harsh triple call in flight or alarm. Lays from March in Florida; colonial, often in large numbers and with other species, in mangroves and other trees. Nest of local material holds usually 3 pale blue or green eggs with brown blotches, incubated c. 21 days by ♀ and ♂. They tend young which fly at c. 5 weeks. **80**

Eudocimus ruber *Threskiornithidae*
SCARLET IBIS   21-27 ins
Neotropical: very local on NE coast South America, perhaps also SE Brazil; seasonal dispersal movements. Habitat tropical coasts: mangrove swamps, estuaries, mudflats. Generally scarlet, except blue-black ends of 4 longest primaries; legs, facial skin scarlet, bill black to brown, eyes dark. Behaviour much as *E. albus*. Usually silent; 'gurgling' alarm call; bill clattering when bickering. Breeds during heavy tropical rains in large colonies like E. albus. Nest of local materials holds usually 2 pale blue or green eggs, blotched brown, incubated c. 21 days by ♀ and ♂, who tend young until they fly at c. 5 weeks. **81**

Eudromias morinellus *Charadriidae*
DOTTEREL   c. 8½ ins
Palaearctic: distribution sporadic from Britain and Central Europe to Siberia; summer visitor to breeding areas; winters S coast Mediterranean, Red Sea and Persian Gulf. Habitat: flattish mountain tops in temperate (but recently colonised lowlying reclaimed land in Netherlands) and subarctic, tundra in arctic; coastal in winter. Upperparts blackish brown; 'eyebrow', throat whitish; brown breast separated by white band from chestnut lower breast and flanks; belly black, undertail white; legs dull yellow, bill black, eyes brown. In winter and juvenile underparts brown with pale band on breast; ♀ brighter than ♂ in summer. Often allows close approach both in passage 'trips' and on breeding area. Stop-go action when feeding like other plovers. Often raises one or both wings, sometimes before flying. Many notes recorded when breeding, but usual call *wit-e-wee wit-e-wee*. Displays complicated, ♀ taking lead. Diet: fly larvae in breeding season; otherwise small animals of tidal zone. Breeds from mid May Scotland. Lined scrape in moss or soil holds usually 3 light buff eggs, heavily marked brownish-black and grey. Incubation usually by ♂, 21½-25½ days; he also tends young, regularly feigning injury when threatened; they fly c. 30 days. **263**

Eudyptes chrysolophus *Spheniscidae*
MACARONI PENGUIN   26-30 ins
Subantarctic seas, with regular northward migrations from breeding colonies on bare islands. Penguin pattern of black and white with orange yellow head plumes extending backwards. Legs and bill orange pink; eyes dark; strong goat-like smell. Gregarious at all times, sometimes forming mixed colonies with Rockhopper Penguin *E. crestatus*. Diet squids and shrimps. Has braying call like its relatives. Nest of small stones, grasses and mud on bare headland or island; eggs 1 to 3, pale blue or chalky white, incubated by ♂ and ♀. ♂ guards while ♀ feeds chicks, but seldom more than one reared. **9**

Eudyptes crestatus see under **E. chrysolophus**

Eudyptes minor *Spheniscidae*
LITTLE BLUE PENGUIN   16 ins
Australasian: three subspecies inhabit southern coasts of continental Australia, Tasmania, New Zealand, Chatham and other islands; offshore outside breeding season. Smallest penguin: slaty blue not black upperparts; chin as well as underparts white; no crest; legs pale flesh pink, soles black; bill black, eyes silver grey. Not gregarious like most penguins and more vocal, with range from catlike mewing to screams, trumpetings and growls when on shore; ducklike quacks at sea. Diet small fishes, swallowed underwater. Breeds from highwater mark to several hundred yards inland,

sometimes climbing several hundred feet to nest usually in cavity, either taken over from petrels or excavated. 2 white eggs incubated mainly by ♂ for c. 40 days; both chicks usually reared by ♂ and ♀, fledging in c. 8 weeks. **10**

Eugenes fulgens see under **Lampornis clemenciae**

Eupetes macrocercus *Muscicapidae : Cinclosomatinae*
MALAY RAIL BABBLER   10-11½ ins
Oriental: Malaysia to Borneo; resident primary forest 2,000 to 4,000 ft. Generally rufous brown, varying in intensity from crown to end of long, graduated tail; broad black mask tapers down neck with white stripe above; small patch bare skin below on neck; belly earthy grey; long legs blue-black, straight bill blackish, eyes dark brown. Juvenile greyer, with white throat. Runs at speed with head raised, tail slightly depressed, over fallen tree trunks and forest debris in hillside ravines. Calls: ticking *tek;* repeated, rattling *chekchekchek.* Food includes cicadas, black beetles, spiders (T. H. Harrisson). Breeding habits apparently unknown.

Euphagus carolinus *Icteridae*
RUSTY BLACKBIRD   9½ ins
Nearctic: breeds from Alaska and northern Canada S to Central Canada and N New England; winters from New Jersey and Ohio River S to Gulf Coast, W to Central Texas. Habitat: wet woodland and thickly wooded swamps, especially with alder and open pools. ♂: uniformly black with green gloss; ♀: slaty grey, little gloss; legs grey, rather slender bill light grey, eyes whitish. Both become 'rusty' in autumn due to brown feather edges, especially on head, breast, upper back. Juvenile is even browner. Large flocks most of year, often with other blackbirds, grackles, keeping up 'constant babble of squeaks, clucks, and whistles' (R. H. Pough), continuing chorus from trees if disturbed. Walks and wades after insects on land and water; also takes seeds, grain, wild fruits. Usual calls: *cack* or lower *cuk;* rather gurgling song of mixed squeaks, musical notes. Breeds May and June, generally solitary; bulky nest of sticks and plant debris with mud cup, lined green grass, up to 20 ft in dense young conifers or shrubs near or over water. 3 to 5 pale blue-green eggs, heavily marked brown over grey.

Euphonia laniirostris see **Tanagra laniirostris**

EUPHONIA, THICK-BILLED see **Tanagra laniirostris**

Euplectes
   hordacea see under **E. orix**
   macrocercus see under **E. macrourus**

Euplectes macrourus or Coliuspasser macrourus *Ploceidae*   ♂ breeding: c. 9; non-breeding: c. 6½ ins
YELLOW-BACKED WIDOW BIRD
Ethiopian: Senegal across to Sudan, S to Angola, Malawi, Mozambique; local resident open grassy plains and swamps. ♂: generally black; mantle, 'shoulders' yellow; flight feathers pale-edged; long graduated tail; under wing coverts buff or buff and black; legs, bill black, eyes dark brown. ♀: brownish, upperparts streaked buff and black (but duller than ♀ Yellow-shouldered, *E. macrocercus*), rump brown; 'eyebrow', cheeks, throat yellowish-buff; feathers of 'shoulder' and 'elbow' edged yellow; underparts buff, faintly streaked yellow; bill horn. Non-breeding ♂ much as ♀, more broadly streaked dull black above; yellow on wings remains. Non-breeding ♀ has underparts suffused yellow. Rare all-black ♂♂ occur. Flits over grass, settling on tallest heads. Large flocks outside breeding season roost in reedbeds. Call: thin *z-e-e-e;* ♂ has short melodious song. Food: grass and other seeds. Breeding variable within range; December to March S Africa; rather unsubstantial ball nest of grasses, with living stems woven in, in short grass areas of swamp. Usually 2 blue or greenish blue eggs, densely marked speckles and scrawls of brown and grey. **949**

Euplectes nigroventris see under **E. orix**

Euplectes orix *Ploceidae*
RED BISHOP   5 ins
Ethiopian: Senegal E to Ethiopia, then S down E side continent to S Africa; breeds tall grass and herbage near water; sugar cane and maize cultivations; wanders to open plains and short grass country after breeding. ♂: generally red (orange-red when old); mantle brownish; crown, cheeks, earcoverts, underparts to belly, black; wings, tail dusky, feathers pale-edged; upper and under tail coverts often as long as tail; legs reddish brown, bill black, eyes brown. ♀: upperparts broadly streaked brownish, buff, black; 'eyebrow' buff; underparts buff to white; breast, flanks streaked dark brown, bill horn. Non-breeding ♂ as ♀ but larger. ♂ hovers over defined territory, puffing out feathers, wings purring; each has 3 or 4 mates whom he may chase in courtship. Courting call: 'sizzling' *zik zik zik;* variety of wheezing and mewing notes. Large roosts in reedbeds. Diet: mainly grass seeds but may attack crops; insects for young. Breeding variable and sporadic; colonies often widely separated and suddenly deserted. ♂ weaves flimsy oval grass nests in bullrushes, reeds *Phragmites* over water; also in corn; ♀ adds lining of grass seed heads; projecting porch. Usually 3 pale turquoise blue eggs incubated ♀ 11-14 days; she feeds young who fly 13-16 days. Very similar and local Zanzibar Red Bishop, *E. nigroventris,* (4 ins) has scarlet crown; Black-winged Red Bishop, *E. hordacea,* (5½ ins) has wings and tail black. **950**

Euplectes progne or Coliuspasser progne *Ploceidae*
LONG-TAILED WIDOW BIRD or   ♀: 6, ♂ breeding:
SAKABULA   19-30, non-breeding 8-9 ins
Ethiopian: Angola, SE Zaire, W and Central Kenya, Zambia, S Africa; local resident open high-level grassland and moorland up to 6,000 ft or more; neighbourhood of swamps, dams, cultivations. ♂: 'one of most striking African birds' (J. G. Williams), jet black including neck ruff; 'shoulders' orange-red, median wing coverts white or buff; central tail feathers up to 2 ft long; legs, black, bill bluish-white, eyes dark brown. ♀: upperparts streaked buff, brown, black; shoulders orange-red, feathers black-centred; underparts pale buff, streaked dusky; under wing coverts black; tail feathers narrow, pointed; bill horn. Non-breeding ♂ much as ♀, more broadly streaked, retains shoulder and wing patches; bill horn. Immature ♂ as ♀. Rather silent; sharp chirping alarm call: *zik;* 'chuckling, swizzling song' (Roberts). Food mainly seeds; also termites. Polygamous ♂ may have 6 to 10 ♀♀, forming flock, sometimes with another ♂; but ♂♂ roost together even in breeding season. Slow, jerky flights of ♂, with tail drooping and spread; may become grounded in wet weather. Visits nests, churring to sitting ♀♀. Breeding depends on rains: October to January or March; ♀ builds rounded, thick-walled grass nest with entrance at side, well hidden in tussock under living stems. 2 to 4 pale greenish white or cream eggs, heavily spotted pale olive-brown and grey, with larger blotches, incubated ♀ 14 days; she also rears young. **951**

Eupodotis australis *Otididae*
AUSTRALIAN BUSTARD   ♀: 35; ♂: 46 ins
Continental Australia, especially N; resident on plains, open scrub and forest. Upperparts generally dark brown with lighter markings; primaries brown, black area of white-tipped feathers on coverts; forehead, crown, elongated neck feathers black; underparts white with blackish band across breast; legs yellow, bill whitish to brown, eyes white. Singly or small groups, stand to watch humans but sometimes squat; walk or run rather than fly, needing long take off. ♂ inflates neck in display, draws head back, spreads ruff, droops wings to ground with tail fanned. Normally silent; deep *hoo* in display. Feeds on grasses and other plants, seeds, leaves and fruits, lizards, insects, especially locusts, small vertebrates. Breeding season July to November depending on rainfall. Lays 1 or 2 glossy, olive-streaked olive-brown eggs in scrape or bare ground on grassy knoll; ♀ incubates c. 4 weeks and feeds chick, which flies in 5-6 weeks. **243**

Eupodotis melanogaster see **Lissotis melanogaster**

Eupodotis senegalensis *Otididae*
WHITE-BELLIED BUSTARD   24 ins
Ethiopian: Sudan W across continent to N Nigeria and Senegal; resident on red sandstone desert, feeding on edge of scrub early and late, then resting in cover. ♂: mantle, breast, wing coverts, scapulars and inner secondaries rich light brown, vermiculated black, with buff white patch on inner primaries; forehead, crown, lower throat black, nape blue ringed black, chin white, neck and breast bluish, underparts buff white, axillaries white. ♀: crown sooty black, nape speckled tawny brown and black, throat white, neck light brown and blue. Legs, bill yellowish white, eyes pale wine red. Shy but reacts to noise with loud *wuk-caire* calls; also snort in breeding season. Stretches neck when running or in short flights. Eats insects, especially locusts, and acacia gum. Breeding season varies throughout range. Lays 2 eggs, olive-brown, spotted red or greenish-buff blotched stone colour, on bare ground. Incubation presumably by ♀, with ♂ in attendance, probably c. 3 weeks. **244**

EURASIAN
   BROWN FLYCATCHER see **Muscicapa latirostris**
   CUCKOO see **Cuculus canorus**
   JAY see **Garrulus glandarius**
   PYGMY OWL see **Glaucidium passerinum**

Eurocephalus anguitimens *Laniidae*
WHITE-CROWNED SHRIKE   9 ins
Ethiopian: S Sudan, Ethiopia to Tanzania; Rhodesia, Botswana, S Africa; Angola. Resident dry thornbush. Dusky brown mantle contrasts with white crown, rump; wings, tail, wide patch behind eye black; underparts white with brown patch side of breast. Immature has brown crown and barred upperparts. Usually perches on upper or outer branches of trees, but hunts insects, other small animals on ground. Noisy parties of 6 to 12 remain within range of each other, fly off calling, with short rapid wingbeats and glides. Call: harsh *kaa kaa kaa.* Breeding season varies with range. Nest small, compact, of plant materials bound cobwebs 'like little flat yellow cheeses stuck on boughs' (R. E. Moreau), also against tree trunks. Clutch probably 2 or 3 white or pale lilac eggs, blotched amber, ochre or violet; but 2 ♀♀ often use same nest. **646**

EUROPEAN
   BEE-EATER see **Merops apiaster**
   GOLDFINCH see **Carduelis carduelis**
   ROBIN see **Erithacus rubecula**
   ROLLER see **Coracias garrulus**
   SPOONBILL see **Platalea leucorodia**

Eurostopodus guttatus *Caprimulgidae*
SPOTTED NIGHTJAR   c. 12 ins
Australasia: continental Australia, Aru Is, New Ireland; resident open woodlands. Upperparts mottled and flecked buff, black and grey, with dark brown wings and barred tail; from bill through eye to back of neck grey; crown brown; throat mottled dark, 2 white patches on upper breast; underparts buff narrowly barred darker. Usually solitary by day on ground, but hawks at dusk in numbers over trees and grassland. Call rendered *caw caw caw gobble gobble gobble,* diminishing in volume. Diet: insects taken on wing. Breeds September to November, laying single yellowish-olive egg, sparsely marked reddish-purple and lavender, on bare ground. Incubation by ♂. **463**

Eurypyga helias *Eurypygidae*
SUN BITTERN   c. 18 ins
Neotropical; 3 races from Central America to S Peru, S Brazil, N Bolivia; W of Andes to W Ecuador. Resident in dense tropical forests along streams and rivers up to at least 3,000 ft. Upperparts narrowly barred grey, brown and olive; underparts paler; wing at rest barred black and white, as is tail, with 2 wide black bands; head blackish with pale bars over and under eye; legs orange, upper bill dark, lower orange, eyes deep red. In display tail raised, wings spread with tips brought forward to frame head and neck, revealing red-orange area with paler penumbra on coverts. This takes place in sunlit glades, with circling,

hopping, raising and lowering of head and erratic leaps. Pairs keep in touch by piping call; hissing and bill-rattling when alarmed. Stalks with body horizontal, neck stretched, along muddy banks or in shallow water, to snatch shrimps, crabs, fish and insects. Breeds local rainy season, making large rounded nest of sticks, leaves, moss and mud 6 to 10 ft in tree or bush. 2 or 3 buffish or clay eggs, spotted grey and brown, incubated by ♀ and ♂ c. 4 weeks. Young fed by parents in nest c. 3 weeks, full grown in 2 months. **240**

Euryceros prevostii see **Aerocharis prevostii**

Eurystomus orientalis *Coraciidae*
BROAD-BILLED ROLLER or DOLLAR BIRD   11 ins
Oriental, E Palaearctic and Australasian: N India to Manchuria and Japan; E to Solomon Is., N and E continental Australia, where summer visitor. Habitat open woodlands with tall trees. Generally brown-grey washed turquoise; wings black-tipped, shoulders greenish blue with prominent light blue-green or silvery 'dollar' spot in middle of each; throat brilliant blue; legs and bill pink, eyes dark brown. Crepuscular; solitary or in pairs, often sitting hunched high in tree; flies high with slow wing action, sometimes somersaulting and swooping but not as spectacularly as other rollers. Call, screeching *kak kak kak*. Takes insects usually at dusk, darting from high perch over treetops: cicadas, moths, beetles. Breeds November to mid January SE Australia, March to May Indian sub-continent, using hole in dead tree, occasionally old Kookaburra, *Dacelo novaeguineae*, nests or termite mounds in trees; takes old magpie nests in China, special nest-boxes on tall chimneys in Japan where 'urbanised'. Lays 2 to 5 white eggs, incubated 18–23 days by both parents, who feed young, fledged 3-4 weeks.

Eutoxeres aquila *Trochilidae*
WHITE-TIPPED SICKLEBILL   5 (bill 1) ins
Neotropical: Costa Rica S to Colombia W of Andes, E of Andes to Ecuador, NE Peru; resident dense forest of tropical zone (sea level to 5,000 ft). Upperparts bronze green, feathers edged tawny brown; crown dark brown; underparts striped buff and black; bronze-green graduated tail with pointed feathers, increasing white tips towards outermost ones; feet variable greyish white, bill mainly black, base of mandible yellow; eyes dark brown. 'Sickle' bill perfectly adapted to probe bent *Heliconia* flowers, clinging with strong feet instead of hovering like other hummingbirds, which it does when 'gleaning' tree trunks for insects. Breeding habits broadly as relatives (see *Aglaiocercus kingi*). **473**

EVENING GROSBEAK see **Hesperiphona vespertina**

FAIRY
    BLUEBIRD see **Irena puella**
    FLYCATCHER see **Stenostira scita**
    PITTA see **Pitta brachyura**
    TERN see **Gygis alba**

Falco area *Falconidae*
SEYCHELLES KESTREL   c. 12 ins
Seychelles (Indian Ocean): confined to main island of Mahé; hunts coastal plateau but found generally. ♂: upperparts dark chestnut, spotted black; upper tail coverts grey, tail grey, barred black, tipped white; primaries dark brown, notched white; head, neck dark grey; throat pale rufous; underparts rufous shading to whitish. ♀ similar but paler. Legs, cere yellow, bill blue-grey, eyes dark brown. Very tame. Soars high in open areas between palms, not known to hover; prey mainly lizards, taking about 2 a day. Call: piercing *cui cui cui*, hence local name *katiti*, at beginning of breeding season (November to March, probably longer); mates on tree or building, now commonest nesting site; also holes in walls, rocks. Clutch apparently 1 or 2 whitish eggs, heavily marked brown, incubated c. 20 days (M. Penny). Rarity believed partly due to competition from introduced Barn Owl, *Tyto alba*.

Falco berigora *Falconidae*
BROWN HAWK or FALCON   15½-18 ins
Australia, Tasmania, New Guinea and Dampier Island: local movements perhaps after food; found from arid interior to moist coastal forests, and in mountains. Generally dark or rufous brown with pale feather edgings on wing and back; darker bars on white-tipped tail; facial pattern dark and pale buff, extending to throat and neck; under tail coverts buff; small variations between races and melanistic form occurs; long legs and cere slaty blue, bill darker, eyes dark brown. Gregarious in winter; spends much time perched, but can fly swiftly and attacks other birds of prey. Feeds mainly on ground-living vertebrates and insects; also carrion. Parrot-like call *karra karra katchy*; also cackles, screams and whistles. Breeding season variable, according to conditions. Usually uses nest of another bird, sometimes on termite mound. Lays 2 to 4 buff eggs, often heavily marked red-brown. Both ♀ and ♂ incubate, period unknown. ♀ remains near nest after hatching, ♂ bringing food. **167**

Falco biarmicus *Falconidae*
LANNER   16-18 ins
Palaearctic and Ethiopian: Mediterranean southward: open country, savannahs and deserts, up to 7,000 ft; seasonal movements within range. ♂: upperparts blue-grey, feathers pale edged and with darker flecks; forehead white and black shading into rufous crown and nape; black moustachial stripe; white tipped tail grey or brownish with darker bars; flight feathers dark brown; underparts pinkish white; legs, cere and eye-ring yellow, bill dark, eyes brown. ♀: larger and browner; immature shades of brown all over with light underparts. Northern races brown and paler than South African *F. b. biarmicus*. Splendid flier, capable of dramatic stoops on prey, which ranges from birds of bustard-size, bats, other mammals, lizards in deserts to locusts. Spectacular display flights and chases, often with screams. Shrill scream, higher-pitched than *F. peregrinus*. Breeding season late winter or early spring in N and S of range, dry season in tropics, but coincides with spring migration over Sahara. Lays 3 or 4 white eggs, speckled all over with shades of brown, in scrape on cliff ledge, in crevice or old nest of other bird in tree. Incubated by ♀ and ♂; period 2½ months from laying to fledging. **168**

Falco cherrug *Falconidae*
SAKER   18 ins
Palaearctic: Central Europe east to Tibet and Manchuria; partly migratory in winter to Mediterranean, NE Africa, Arabia, N India and S China; inhabits plains, steppes and plateaux up to 4,000 ft. Upperparts dark brown edged rufous; tail pale brown with white spots as on wings; crown and nape creamy to buff with black streaks; underparts white spotted dark brown. Immature brown all over. Legs and cere dull yellow, bill dark, eyes brown. Several races show minor differences. Takes off from favourite perch to hunt up to 6 miles away, flying 50 to 100 ft up and frequently hovering like kestrel, dropping on small mammals and lizards; sometimes concentrates on insects; but will stoop after birds up to duck size. Pair reunites for display over nest-site, usually a crag or outcrop but sometimes a tree; no nest is built. Noisy only in breeding season, uttering loud *kek-kek-kek*, hoarse scream and other cries in display. 3 to 6 pale brown, heavily marked eggs laid from March to May and incubated by ♀ and ♂ for 28 days. Fed by both parents, young fly in 40-45 days.

Falco peregrinus *Falconidae*
PEREGRINE   15-19 ins (♀ larger)
World-wide except polar regions and some island groups, but much decreased recently. Resident in open country from sea coast to mountains, also in montane and lowland forests, often coniferous, occasionally in towns. Upperparts blue-grey with black head and moustachial stripe; underparts buffish white, barred black. ♀ usually darker and more heavily barred; juvenile brown above with streaked underparts. Legs and cere yellow, bill dark, eyes brown. Perches for long periods on rock or tree, then takes off into fast winnowing flight, alternating with glides; strikes prey with

headlong stoop or binds to it in air; also seizes it after chase or snatches from perch, taking it to plucking place to eat. Food mainly birds, some mammals, occasionally amphibians. Variety of notes, best known *kek kek kek* of alarm. Aerial displays with dives and 'loops'. Breeds from end March in Holarctic, making scrape on ledge, riverbank, ground, in old nest of other bird, sometimes on building. 3 or 4 eggs, covered rich red-brown, incubated by ♀ and ♂ 28-29 days; both feed young, which fly 5-6 weeks. **169**

Falco sparverius *Falconidae*
AMERICAN KESTREL or
AMERICAN SPARROWHAWK   8½ ins
Nearctic and Neotropical, from Alaska to Tierra del Fuego. Inhabits open deserts, fields, roadsides, woodland edge; also suburban areas and cities. ♂: back rufous with black flecks, crown slate with rufous patch, cheeks black and white, buff collar with black patches; white-tipped tail rufous, with black band; wings grey and black; underparts white to buff. ♀: upper parts deep rufous, barred black, underparts buff with brown flecks; head as ♂. Legs and cere orange-yellow, bill dark, eyes brown. Minor differences between the many races. Perches, often on wires, with constant tail movements; flight buoyant; hovers like Old World Kestrel, *F. tinnunculus*, dropping on prey, which varies throughout huge range from insects in northern summer to scorpions and lizards in Peru; small mammals, birds and amphibians. High-pitched repeated *killy*, also whine and chittering in courtship. Pairs and small groups display before choosing nest-sites, usually hole in tree, building, bank; no nest built. Laying varies with latitude: clutch of 3 to 7 pale pink eggs heavily marked rich brown, incubated mainly by ♀ for 29-30 days. Fed by both parents, young fly in about 30 days. **170**

Falco tinnunculus see under **F. sparverius**

FALCON,
    AFRICAN PYGMY see **Poliohierax semitorquatus**
    BARRED FOREST see **Micrastur ruficollis**
    LAUGHING see **Herpetotherus cachinnans**

FAMILIAR CHAT see **Cercomela familiaris**

FANTAIL,
    GOLDEN-HEADED see **Cisticola exilis**
    GREY see **Rhipidura fuliginosa**
    RUFOUS see **Rhipidura rufifrons**

FANTAIL WARBLER, DESERT see **Cisticola aridula**

FASCIATED ANTSHRIKE see **Cymbilaimus lineatus**

Ferminia cerverai *Troglodytidae*
ZAPATA WREN   6¼ ins
Neotropical: confined to one marsh (c. 5 square miles) on S Cuba, where discovered 1926. Upperparts greyish brown, barred black, spotted on back; cheeks, underparts off-white, barred black on flanks; wings rounded, tail long for a wren; legs grey, sharply pointed bill greyish to yellow, eyes dark brown. Keeps very much to cover, flying only short distances weakly. Warbling, canary-like song. Presumably insectivorous. Said to build domed nest in bush, laying up to 6 white eggs.

FERNBIRD see **Bowdleria punctata**

FERRUGINOUS
    PYGMY OWL see **Glaucidium brasilianum**
    WOOD PARTRIDGE see **Caloperdix oculea**

Ficedula albicollis see under **F. hypoleuca**

Ficedula hypoleuca *Muscicapidae: Muscicapinae*
PIED FLYCATCHER   c. 5 ins
W Palaearctic: main breeding range wedge-shaped from 70°N in Norway and 45°N E France to 55°N 90°E in Siberia; isolated populations Britain, Iberia, NW Africa; replaced with considerable overlap in SE Europe by very similar Collared, *F. albicollis* (also Asia Minor, Caucasus, Iran); winters tropical Africa to

Tanzania. Habitat mixed broadleaved woodland or montane oak and beech (S Europe); mixed conifers Scandinavia, extending to subarctic birch zone; parkland, gardens Central Europe, Britain; winters savannah. ♂: upperparts blackish or black-brown, often suffused grey nape, mantle, rump; broad white wingbar, outer tail feathers white; white blaize or 2 spots on forehead; underparts white; winter: black replaced by brown which is breeding plumage Central Europe. ♀ brown where ♂ blackish, smaller wingbar, usually no white on forehead; wings, tail very dark brown; underparts off white. Legs, bill black, eyes dark brown. Juvenile 'scaly', creamy where ♀ white. ♂ announces presence by aerial sallies, song from favoured perches, may dominate several holes, displaying white breast near them or popping head out. ♂ and ♀ flick wings, tail. Interspecific flights with other small hole-nesters. Call sharp *whit*, lengthened to *whit-tic* when scolding; alarm notes *hweet, zrrr*; simple variable song *tchee tchee tchee tchay tcher*. Food mainly insects, especially moth larvae off leaves when feeding young; some spiders; from foliage, ground, air. Breeds end April to mid July; ♀, accompanied ♂, building nest of oak leaves, grasses, moss, bark, rootlets, lined hair, fine stems; in tree hole typically old woodpecker boring, also in walls, buildings, ground, nestboxes in many areas; ground level to 45 ft. 5 to 9 pale blue eggs, incubated ♀ 12-13 days; ♀, usually helped ♂, who may be polygamous, feeds young; they fly *c.* 16 days. Exceptionally 2 broods. **780**

FIELD WREN,
RUFOUS see **Calamanthus campestris**
STRIATED see under **Calamanthus campestris**

FIGBIRD, YELLOW see **Sphecotheres flaviventris**

FIG PARROT, RED BROWED see **Opopsitta leadbeateri**

FINCH,
ASIAN SPICE see under **Lonchura castaneothorax**
AURORA see **Pytilia phoenicoptera**
CHESTNUT-BREASTED see **Lonchura castaneothorax**
CRIMSON see **Neochmia phaeton**
GOULDIAN see **Poephila gouldiae**
HOUSE see **Carpodacus mexicanus**
MEDIUM GROUND see **Geospiza fortis**
OCHRE-BREASTED BRUSH see **Atlapetes semifurus**
PALE CRIMSON see under **Neochmia phaeton**
PLUM-HEADED see **Aidemosyne modesta**
PLUSH-CAPPED see **Catamblyrhynchus diadema**
QUAIL see **Ortygospiza atricollis**
RED-BROWED see **Estrilda temporalis**
RED-HEADED see **Amadina erythrocephala**
SNOW see **Montifringilla nivalis**
ZEBRA see **Taenopygia castonotis**

FINE SPOTTED WOODPECKER see **Campethera punctuligera**

FINFOOT,
AFRICAN see **Podica senegalensis**
PETERS see **Podica senegalensis**

FIREFINCH,
AFRICAN see **Lagonisticta rubricata**
JAMESON'S see under **Lagonisticta rubricata**

FISCAL
FLYCATCHER see **Melaenornis silens**
SHRIKE see **Lanius collaris**
SHRIKE, LONG-TAILED see **Lanius cabanisi**

FISH
CROW see **Corvus ossifragus**
EAGLE, AFRICAN see **Haliaeetus vocifer**
OWL, MALAYSIAN see **Bubo ketupa**

FLAME-RUMPED TANAGER see under **Ramphocelus icteronotus**

FLAMINGO,
ANDEAN see **Phoenicoparrus andinus**
GREATER see **Phoenicopterus ruber**
LESSER see **phoeniconaias minor**
FLICKER,
GILDED see **Colaptes chrysoides**
YELLOW-SHAFTED see **Colaptes auratus**

FLIGHTLESS STEAMER DUCK see **Tachyeres pteneres**

FLOCK PIGEON see **Phaps histrionica**

Florida caerulea *Ardeidae*
LITTLE BLUE HERON   25-29 ins
Nearctic and Neotropical: southern USA to Peru and Brazil, in freshwater swamps, coastal lagoons and ricefields, also small rocky islands; northern birds move S to Colombia and Venezuela, with late summer dispersal northward as well. Slaty blue back, wings, underparts; dark chestnut brown head and neck; legs black, bill bluish with black tip, eyes yellow. Immatures white with green legs and bluish bills; moulting birds at 1 year blotched dark and white. Wades in stately manner after prey: fish, amphibians, reptiles, crustaceans, insects. Not very noisy but has various strident and harsh calls. Breeding season varies with latitude, from February onwards in W Indies; colonies, often with other species, usually 3 to 10 ft up in bushes over water; slight nest of sticks. Both sexes incubate 2 or 3 or more pale greenish-blue eggs for *c.* 22 days and tend young for probably 35-40 days. **61**

FLOWERPECKER, BLUISH see **Diglossa caerulescens**

FLYCATCHER,
AFRICAN PARADISE see **Tersiphone viridis**
ALDER see under **Empidonax traillii**
AUSTRALIAN BROWN see **Microeca fascinans**
BLACK AND YELLOW SILKY se **Phainoptila melanoxantha**
BLUE AND WHITE see **Cyanoptila cyanomelana**
COLLARED see under **Ficedula hypoleuca**
DUSKY see **Alseonax adustus**
EURASIAN BROWN see **Muscicapa latirostris**
FAIRY see **Stenostira scita**
FISCAL see **Melaenornis silens**
FORK-TAILED see **Muscivora tyrannus**
LEADEN see **Myiagra rubecula**
LEAST see **Empidonax minimus**
PALE see **Bradornis pallidus**
PIED see **Ficedula hypoleuca**
RESTLESS see **Myiagra inquieta**
SATIN see **Myiagra cyanoleuca**
SOCIAL see **Myiozetetes similis**
SOUTH AFRICAN BLACK see **Melaenornis pammelaina**
SPOTTED see **Muscicapa striata**
STREAKED see **Myiodynastes maculatus**
SWAMP see **Alseonax aquaticus**
TRAILL'S see **Empidonax traillii**
VERMILLION-CROWNED see **Myiozetetes similis**
WEST AFRICAN BLACK see under **Melaenornis pammelaina**
WHITE-EYED SLATY see **Dioptrornis fischeri**
WHITE-FLANKED see **Batis molitor**
WILLOW see under **Empidonax traillii**
YELLOW-BELLIED see **Empidonax flaviventris**

FLYING STEAMER DUCK see under **Tachyeres pteneres**

FODY, SEYCHELLES see **Foudia sechellarum**

FOLIAGE GLEANER,
BUFF-THROATED see under **Automolus leucophthalmus**
CHESTNUT-TAILED see under **Automolus leucophthalmus**
WHITE-EYED see **Automolus leucophthalmus**

FOREST
FALCON, BARRED see **Micrastur ruficollis**
ORIOLE, BLACK-HEADED see under **Oriolus larvatus**

WAGTAIL see **Dendromanthus indicus**
WOOD HOOPOE see under **Phoeniculus purpureus**

FORK-TAILED
DRONGO see **Dicrurus adsimilis**
FLYCATCHER see **Muscivora tyrannus**
WOODNYMPH HUMMINGBIRD see **Thalurania furcata**

Formicarius analis *Formicaridae*
COCK OF THE WOODS or   7½ ins
BLACK-FACED ANTTHRUSH
Neotropical: Central America, Trinidad; S America E of Andes to Brazil, N Bolivia, SE Peru; W of Andes in Colombia; resident in forests, sea level to *c.* 5,000 ft. Upperparts uniform olivaceous to red brown; wings dark but inner webs of flight feathers pale orange at base, forming broad bar from below; upper tail coverts usually more red than back; rounded tail blackish; ear coverts of some races chestnut brown; throat blackish; underparts light to dark grey, centre of belly pale buff in some races; under tail coverts light to dark chestnut; legs brownish horn, strong straight bill black, eyes dark brown with conspicuous white ring. Solitary, lives mainly on ground, walking with strutting gait, stopping to deliver call, high note followed by 2 to 5 more in descending scale, with neck feathers ruffled and head held up. Catches insects by flitting over dead leaves, also follows army ants; takes occasional snails, small reptiles. Breeds March onwards, building cup nest of rootlets and leaf stems often in vertical tree hole 2 to 12 ft up; lays 2 smooth white eggs, incubated by ♀ and ♂ *c.* 20 days. Young fed by both parents, fly 18 days. **567**

Foudia madagascarensis see under **F. sechellarum**

Foudia sechellarum *Ploceidae*
SEYCHELLES FODY   *c.* 4½ ins
Seychelles (Indian Ocean): confined to Frégate, Cousin and Cousine Is. Originally forest bird, now widely distributed in palm groves, round habitations, other man-modified habitats. ♂: generally dull olive brown, darker on streaked back and wings; yellow on face merges with rest of plumage; some birds on Cousin show white on wings; bill pink. ♀: dark fawn brown, juvenile similar. Pairs and family parties search palm fronds thoroughly for insects, taking them in air as well; also feed on rotting fruits, copra, human scraps; attacks terns' eggs on Cousin. Larger numbers congregate to drink and bathe. Contact call: *tse tse tse tsea tsea*; alarm *tog tog* (whence probably local name), *tschrr* when more agitated. ♂ and ♀ call alternating *tsip tsip tse tse tse* approaching courtship, when ♂ quivers wings; beats them behind back with bill raised, tail fanned and excited trill; chases ♀. Breeding throughout year, peak in rainy season; territory defended up to 50 yds from nest-site, usually in bushy tree, e.g. *Citrus, c.* 25 ft up, supported by twigs. ♂ begins building bulky domed nest of plant materials, accepted by ♀ who joins in; lining finer materials. 1 or 2 white eggs incubated *c.* 14 days. Both parents feed young from throat on insects; fledging *c.* 14 days. Survives introduction of *F. madagascarensis* by separate ecological needs (J. H. Crook). **952**

FOUR-BANDED SAND GROUSE see **Eremialector quadricinctus**

FOWL,
GREY JUNGLE see under **Gallus gallus**
MALLEE see **Leipoa ocellata**

FOX SPARROW see **Passerella iliaca**

FRANCOLIN,
COQUI see **Francolinus coqui**
JACKSON'S see **Francolinus jacksoni**
SWAINSON'S see **Francolinus swainsoni**

Francolinus coqui *Phasianidae*
COQUI FRANCOLIN   11 ins
Ethiopian: several races, some with very restricted distributions. Nomadic over grasslands and open bush, favouring hillsides. ♂: upperparts grey-brown and chestnut, streaked and barred buff and black; head and neck rufous, throat pale, underparts white barred black; primaries grey. ♀ has black stripe outlining pale throat, upper breast rufous. Legs yellow (♂ spurred), bill blackish brown, eyes red. Usually in coveys of 5 or 6, very reluctant to fly. Call *qui-kit qui-kit* varies in pitch between races. Diet: grass and weed seeds, small insects. Breeds throughout year over whole range; lined scrape in grass or other low cover holds 3 to 8 cream or coffee brown eggs, incubated by ♀; ♂ helps with brood. **198**

Francolinus jacksoni *Phasianidae*
JACKSON'S FRANCOLIN   16 ins
Ethiopia: 3 races in mountains of Kenya. Sedentary in bamboo zone or on steep grassy slopes, 7,500 to 10,000 ft. Upperparts and flight feathers olive brown, mantle greyish; upper back, neck, underparts streaked chocolate and white, throat white; legs (♂ usually double spurred) and bill orange red, dark eyes red-rimmed. Secretive, making rabbit-like runs in vegetation; one race roosts in trees, calling loudly at dusk 'like scythe being sharpened'; low clucking when feeding outside cover early in morning on grass shoots and bulbs, berries, small snails. Breeding season not defined; nest scrape in cover holds 3 or more glossy pale brown eggs. Incubation by ♀; ♂ may help with brood. **199**

Francolinus swainsoni or Pternistis swainsoni *Phasianidae*
SWAINSON'S FRANCOLIN or SPURFOWL   16 ins
Ethiopian: 4 races in southern part of region; nomadic on dry bushveld, usually in neighbourhood of water. Upperparts dark brown with blacker markings and shaft stripes; neck and sides of face mottled black and white; underparts dark brown with black shaft stripes: legs black (♂ spurred), upper bill black, lower reddish, eyes brown, facial skin red. Solitary or family parties; very upright stance, but runs well, weaving through grass. Often in open in afternoons; roosts in trees, whence ♂♂ crow repeated *kwahli* at sunrise and sunset. Digs for mainly vegetable food, often in cultivations near cover, flying up with whirring wings, calling harsh *kek kek kek*. Breeding season variable; nest scrape well lined and hidden under bush or tussocks; 4 to 8 or more cream to deep buff eggs incubated by ♀. **200**

FRANKLIN'S GULL see **Larus pipixcan**

Fratercula arctica *Alcidae*
ATLANTIC PUFFIN   *c.* 12 ins
Holarctic: much as Razorbill, *Alca torda*, but extends to Spitzbergen and Novaya Zemlya, very locally E Greenland and not into Baltic; winters at sea, even crossing Atlantic. Breeds sea cliffs and rocky coasts, offshore islands. Summer: upperparts black, including crown and collar; cheeks, sides of head greyish; underparts white, legs red, deep 'parrot' bill blue, red, yellow, with yellow skin at gape, red-rimmed eyes black-brown. Winter: bill smaller, more yellow, legs yellow. Juvenile has quite small, blackish bill. Social at all times, behaving much as other auks (*Alcidae*) but stands on feet and walks well; whirring flight, landing with feet splayed; uses wings underwater. Call: growling triple *arr* at nest or on sea. Diet: mainly fish, especially sand eels when feeding young, carrying 10 at a time between mandibles. Breeds from early May in sometimes huge colonies, making vestigial nest in burrow, excavated or appropriated, or under boulder. Single white egg, sometimes well marked lilac brown, incubated by ♀ and ♂ 40-43 days; chick, deserted after 40 days, flies in *c.* 7 weeks. **345**

Fregata magnificens *Fregatidae*
MAGNIFICENT FRIGATEBIRD   37-45 ins
Coasts and islands of tropical Atlantic and E Pacific, with some dispersal after breeding. Generally metallic black with 'scaly' wing-coverts due to light margins of

feathers; long, deeply forked tail; ♂ has orange, inflated to red, sac on breast, ♀ has white breast, juvenile, white head; legs: ♂ black, ♀ pink; hooked bill: ♂ leaden blue, ♀ greyish; eyes dark brown. Spends day on wing, or perched in trees or artefact for easy take-off. Seldom enters water but takes food off surface, also chases other birds until they disgorge and preys on young of other sea birds. ♂ inflates sac noisily to attract ♀ to nest site which he chooses. Breeding season variable, begins March-April in W Indies; colonies in trees or on bare ground; nest of sticks and debris holds one chalky white egg, incubated 40-50 days by ♀ and ♂, who tend chick after it is fully feathered at 20 weeks. **53**

FRIARBIRD,
  HELMETED see **Philemon yorki**
  NOISY see **Philemon corniculatus**
  SILVER-CROWNED see under **Philemon yorki**

FRIGATE
  BIRD, MAGNIFICENT, see **Fregata magnificens**
  PETREL see **Pelagodroma marina**

Fringilla coelebs *Fringillidae*
CHAFFINCH   *c.* 6 ins
Palaearctic: most of Europe, tongue extending to R. Yenisei at 90°E, also through Asia Minor to Palestine, Caucasus, N Iran; Canary Is, Azores; introduced New Zealand (now common), S Africa. Resident and migrant, northern populations moving as far as Mediterranean. Habitat variety of coniferous, mixed, broadleaved woodlands from plains to subalpine zone; also cultivated and settled areas, wherever trees present; in Canaries seems to have driven endemic Blue Chaffinch, *F. teydea*, into mountain pine forests. ♂: mantle dark chestnut, rump yellowish green, broad white patch and narrower bar on blackish wing; white outer feathers to dark tail; peaked crown, nape slaty blue; small black patch above bill; cheeks, throat, breast deep pinkish brown to brick red; belly, undertail white. ♀ generally pale yellowish brown with rump, wing, tail as ♂. Legs pale brown, bill varies: ♂ lead-blue summer; otherwise whitish brown; eyes brown. Juvenile as ♀ but ♂ soon shows distinctive traces. Hops or walks on ground; undulating flight. Flocks in autumn with other seed-eaters. Many notes, e.g. *pink; tsup tsup* in flight; *weet* (♂ spring); short rattling song varies geographically. ♂ chases ♀ in courtship, also struts round nest. Diet: seeds (weeds, conifers), beech nuts, small fruit; insects in summer, especially for young; frequent at bird tables. Breeds end March to July. ♀, attended ♂, builds bulbous nest of moss, decorated lichen, bark, woven cobwebs, lined softly, in great variety of sites, mainly bushes, often thorny, evergreen, forks of trees, ivy and creepers. 4 or 5 blue or light brown eggs, with smudgy dark purple-brown spots and streaks, incubated ♀ 12-14 days; both parents feed young, who fly 13-14 days. **922**

Fringilla montifringilla *Fringillidae*
BRAMBLING   *c.* 5¾ ins
Palaearctic: northern replacer of Chaffinch, *F. coelebs*, extending in broad band (roughly either side 60°N) from Scandinavia to Kamtchatka and Sakhalin. Summer visitor, migrating S to temperate and subtropical zones from S Sweden to N Africa, Asia Minor, Iran, Japan. Habitat dry open taiga with clearings; riverine birch and willow; subarctic birchwoods. Shape as Chaffinch, tail more forked. ♂: plum black head, mantle; white rump; wings much as Chaffinch, less white on tail; prominent orange shoulder patch extends over breast; underparts white, flanks spotted black. Head, mantle brownish in winter, resembling ♀. Legs light brown, bill blue-black (summer), yellow (winter), eyes brown. Call rendered *scape*; also *chuc chuc chuc* in flight; short melodious song in spring, also *dwee* followed by rattle. Hops and walks; habits much as Chaffinch. Diet: seeds, berries, beech and hornbeam nuts, huge flocks gathering where these abundant; also moth larvae in summer; bird tables in hard weather. Breeds May to July; ♀ (mainly) builds foundation of grass for cup of moss, decorated birch bark, lichen, lined softly, in fork of birch or conifer, 5

to 18 ft or more. 5 to 7 eggs like Chaffinch but often darker, greener, incubated ♀ *c.* 14 days; both parents feed young, who fly *c.* 14 days. **923**

Fringilla teydea see under **F. coelebs**

FROGMOUTH,
  GOULD'S see **Batrachostomus stellatus**
  OWLET see **Aegotheles cristata**
  TAWNY see **Podargus strigoides**

FRUIT DOVE, BLUE-NAPED see **Ptilinopus melanospila**

FRUITEATER, GREEN AND BLACK see **Pipreola riefferii**

FUKIEN RUFOUS JAY THRUSH see **Garrulax caerulatus**

Fulica atra *Rallidae*
COOT   *c.* 15 ins
Palaearctic (right across Temperate zone and very local Iceland), Oriental (India, Burma, S China, locally Java), Australasian (Continental Australia, Tasmania, locally New Guinea); mainly resident but partly migratory from N of range. Habitat: open waters of lakes, ponds, slow-flowing rivers, usually with riparian cover, but on bare reservoirs and lakes in winter, sometimes estuaries or sea. Almost uniformly black with white wingbar; lobe-footed legs green, bill and frontal shield white, eyes ruby. Juvenile very dark brown with whitish throat and underparts, yellow bill and no shield. Gregarious, though less so when breeding; swims with head bobbing and dives freely; rises off water with pattering feet into heavy-looking flight; may graze some way from water. Aggressive, sitting like Moorhens, *Gallinula chloropus*, to fight. Mutual display. Calls *kowk* and repeated *kow kow kow*; abrupt notes of alarm or aggression. Diet chiefly green water plants and grasses; some water animals and fish eggs. Breeding varies with range; from February in Europe. Builds on platform in open water or in marshes, nest usually large basin of local plants with runway to water. 6 to 10 stone buff eggs, speckled dark brown, incubated by ♀ and ♂ 21-24 days; brood tended by parents, independent *c.* 8 weeks; sometimes 2 broods or more in north of range. **225**

Fulica cristata *Rallidae*
CRESTED or RED-KNOBBED COOT   *c.* 15 ins
SW Palaearctic (Spain, Morocco), Ethiopian (E and S Africa) and Madagascar; resident on lakes and pools with open water and surrounding cover. Plumage resembles Coot, *F. atra*, except for two red knobs at top of frontal shield. Behaviour as Coot; abundant on Rift Valley lakes of Kenya. Call a loud *kronk*, equivalent to *kowk* of Coot; low *kiow kiow* at nest. Diet: water plants and their seeds; small water animals. Breeds April to August in Kenya, July to February in S Africa. Nest generally in water, deep cupped platform of local plants. 3 or 4 stone or buff eggs, minutely speckled purple-brown incubated by sometimes 2 broods or more in north of range. **225**

FULMAR see **Fulmarus glacialis**

Fulmarus glacialis *Procellariidae*
FULMAR   18 ins
Holarctic: temperate to arctic zones, dispersing from breeding stations over the sea. Gull-like white body and grey to grey-brown wings and mantle; a dark phase also occurs; legs pale flesh/blue, bill variable, usually yellowish tip, eyes dark brown. Follows ships at sea, but occupies breeding cliffs much of year, sitting on ledges where displays occur with much gurgling and cackling, or gliding and flapping along cliffs in up-currents. Swims readily, but clumsy on land. Natural diet plankton and small fish, but increasingly offal from ships. Breeds May to September on ledges, steep banks, inland cliffs, buildings, even level ground where abundant; single white egg laid in bare scrape becomes stained during 6-8 week incubation by ♀ and ♂, who tend chick during similar fledging period. **28**

Galachrysia nuchalis *Glareolidae*
WHITE-COLLARED PRATINCOLE   *c.* 10 ins
Ethiopian: throughout region except NE, Congo forests, S to Angola and Zambesi; resident on banks and islands of rivers, often fast-flowing, and lakes. Upperparts and much of underparts sooty brown; white collar from nape to eyes; flight feathers black-brown, with white on basal half secondaries; upper and under tail coverts, base of tail, and belly white; legs red, bill reddish, tip black; eyes brown. W African coastal race *liberiae* has chestnut instead of white collar. Spends much of day squatting or standing on sandbank or rocks, becoming active during rain and at dusk, hawking insects. Call a faint *kip kip* or *killip;* also trilling 'song' on nuptial flight by ♂ and ♀. Food mainly insects. Breeding season variable. Usually colonial, laying on rocks, not even in scrape; or in sand, when eggs half buried. 1 or 2 greyish-white eggs, blotched and scrawled black, brown and dark grey, incubated by ♀ and ♂, period probably as Common Pratincole, *Glareola pratincola*. **310**

GALAH see **Cacatua roseicapilla**

GALAPAGOS
  ALBATROSS see **Diomedea irrorata**
  CORMORANT see **Nannopterum harrisi**
  DOVE see **Zenaida galapagoensis**
  HAWK see **Buteo galapagoensis**
  MOCKINGBIRD see **Nesomimus trifasciatus**

Galbula albirostris *Galbulidae*
YELLOW-BILLED JACAMAR   7½ (bill 1½) ins
Neotropical: Guyanas, Venezuela S of Orinoco, Colombia E of Andes, E Ecuador, E Peru, Amazonian Brazil; resident forest edge and open woodlands. Upperparts to central tail feathers metallic golden green; outer tail feathers rufous; crown metallic to purplish blue; underparts chestnut (♂'s throat white); bill mainly yellow. Insectivorous, catching prey on wing, including large butterflies. Habits much as *G. ruficauda.*

Galbula ruficauda *Galbulidae*
RUFOUS-TAILED JACAMAR   9-11 (bill 2, tail 5) ins
Neotropical: Central America southward: E of Andes to Brazil, Paraguay, NE Argentina; W of Andes to NW Ecuador; Trinidad and Tobago. Resident forest clearings, secondary and scrub woodland, sea level to *c.* 3,000 ft. Upperparts, including head, and upper breast metallic green; throat (♂) white, (♀) buff (partly black in one race); long tail graduated; underparts bright chestnut to buff; bill black. Juvenile duller. Rapid swerving flight. Perches on low branches and bamboos, twisting head to look along back, also opens bill frequently, wiping it on perch. Call: faint *cur-lee* following by chuckles at increasing tempo, ending in harmonious trill; also thin *peep.* Takes insects in aerial sallies: large butterflies and dragon-flies, beaten against perch before swallowing. Breeds March to June, ♂ and ♀ excavating straight-sided tunnel 12 to 18 ins deep in sandy or clay banks; may be straight or curved and used in successive years. 2 to 4 glossy white eggs incubated by ♀ (by night) and ♂ 19-23 days; they feed young who fly 20-26 days. **522**

Galerida cristata *Alaudidae*
CRESTED LARK   6¾ ins
Palaearctic, Ethiopian, marginally Oriental; 27 races. Mainly resident; breeds Europe (not Britain nor all but extreme S Scandinavia) across to Korea, S to Himalayas, Arabia; N African coast, down Nile to Ethiopia, Sudan, and belt across S Sahara to Guinea. Habitat: flat grassy and arid country especially near roads and habitations. Races variable; upperparts including rounded wings, tail, greyish to buffish brown with dark streaks; underparts buffish white streaked with brown; very prominent crest; legs pale flesh, bill dark horn (pale base), eyes black-brown. Call: liquid whistling *whee-wheeoo.* Song like Skylark, *Alauda arvensis*, but less continuous, uttered on ground or in very high song-flight. Less gregarious than *A. arvensis* and runs very swiftly. Feeds mainly on seeds but also takes insects in spring. Breeding season mainly May and June but variable; simple grass nest on ground.

3 to 5 glossy whitish, finely spotted eggs, incubated by ♀ 12-13 days. Young leave nest 9-11 days, flying a week later. 2 (rarely 3) broods. **603**

Galerida magnirostris or Calendula magnirostris *Alaudidae*
THICK-BILLED LARK   7 ins
Ethiopian; 3 races: resident and breeds S Africa north to Transvaal and Drakensburg Mts. Habitat: level ground on sandy soil often by roadsides. Upperparts buffish-brown with broad black streaks, buff 'eye-brow'; underparts buff broadly streaked on chest, breast and flanks; broken black moustachial stripe and another on sides of throat, wings and tail darker, latter with paler outer feathers; legs pale brown, bill dark with horn-coloured lower mandible, eyes brown. Usually seen in pairs. Call double-noted and resembles squeaky hinge; short quavering song uttered while rising in air. Feeds on seeds and insects, especially small beetles. Breeds August to November, making simple grass nest in depression in ground. 2 or 3 dull white heavily speckled eggs. Incubation and fledging much as *G. cristata.* **604**

Galerida modesta *Alaudidae*
NIGERIAN CRESTED LARK   5½ ins
Ethiopian; several races; resident and breeds from Ghana across to W Sudan and extreme NW Uganda, entirely N of Congo forests. Habitat: open cultivated land, grass fields and dusty roadsides. Plumage appears dark: upperparts sandy rufous with black markings, underparts buff with white throat and heavy streaking on breast, dark brown wings and tail with outer-most feathers pale rufous and black diagonal mark on inner web; legs brown, bill black above, light below. Usually in parties of 3 to 6 birds. Song sweet, uttered particularly in hovering song flight. Feeds almost entirely on seeds. Breeds November to March in the middle of dry weather; scanty grass nest on ground. 4 creamy white eggs, densely covered with reddish brown spots. **605**

Galerida theklae *Alaudidae*
THEKLA LARK   6½ ins
Palaearctic and Ethiopian; 8 races; resident and breeds in S and E Iberia, Balearics, coast of N Africa to Nile, Ethiopian mountains, Somaliland, N Kenya. Habitat: dry stony hillsides with low bushy vegetation. Plumage very variable and similar to Crested, *G. cristata,* but shorter bill, greyer under wings and less smudgy breast markings. Best distinguished by its habitat and call which is 2-3, not 4 syllables. Song less mimetic and varied, more often from bushes and trees; more sustained display flight, circling round and hovering. Feeds mainly on seeds and shoots but takes insects in summer. Breeding season mainly March to June; builds small neat grass nest in depression. Usually lays 4 (in Africa 2-3) greyish-white eggs with dense dark spots. Incubation by ♀ 12-13 days. Young fed by both parents, leave nest in 9 days, flying a week later. **606**

Gallicolumba luzonica *Columbidae*
LUZON BLEEDING HEART   *c.* 12½ ins
Philippine Is of Luzon and Polillo. Frequents forests where usually on the ground. Striking red marking on breast ('bleeding heart'); upperparts dark greyish with iridescent fringes to feathers giving amethystine purple appearance, forehead blue-grey. Primaries, second-aries and central tail feathers dark dull brown; 3 dark red-brown bars across closed light blue-grey wing. Throat, breast and underparts white tinged pale pink below, and deeper red surrounding longitudinal patch of blood-red feathers in centre of breast. Legs red, bill blackish, eyes greyish yellow. Ground feeder, taking seeds, berries and probably small animals. Agile walker, preferring if threatened to escape by running after short initial flight; roosts in trees and shrubs. Call: low pitched mournful *coo-coo.* Lays 2 eggs in nest low down in bush, tree or vine. **360**

Gallinago gallinago nigripennis see **Gallinago nigripennis**

Gallinago nigripennis or Gallinago gallinago nigripennis *Scolopacidae*
AFRICAN SNIPE   *c.* 11 (bill 2½) ins
Ethiopian: from Ethiopia down E side to S Africa; by some considered to be race of Common Snipe, *G. gallinago.* Resident, but moves according to local weather; usually breeds moorland 3,000 to 10,000 ft; lower swamps and marshes outside breeding season. Upperparts mottled black, dark brown and buff; wing tips dark with white outer edge; tail, barred black and chestnut, white-edged; head striped buff and black-ish; neck, breast buff brown; flanks barred, underparts white; legs pale green, long bulbous bill red to dark brown; eyes brown. Largely crepuscular, often flushed singly, flying away in zigzags then pitching suddenly; sometimes in parties. Call *scape;* repeated *kip* in breeding season when ♂ 'drums' or 'bleats' in display flight, air passing over wings and through single extended tail feather on either side. Takes small worms and other invertebrates from soft ground. Breeding season variable; from July in Ethiopia. 2 or 3 pale greenish buff eggs, sparsely marked dark brown and grey, incubated in well hidden scrape probably only by ♀ 19-20 days; both parents tend young who fly in *c.* 2 weeks. **284**

Gallinula chloropus *Rallidae*
MOORHEN or COMMON GALLINULE   13-15 ins
Palaearctic (Temperate zone), Ethiopian, Oriental, Hawaii, S Nearctic, Neotropical (except S); closely allied *G. tenebrosa* in Australasia; some migration of northern birds. Found in neighbourhood of fresh water of all kinds, sometimes by minute streams; often in urban parks and gardens in Europe. Upperparts brownish black, underparts dark grey; white stripes on flanks and white under tail coverts; legs green with red 'garter', bill tip yellow, base and frontal shield red, eyes dark red or brown. Juvenile brown with greenish-brown bill and shield. Varies from open to secretive according to range. High-stepping jerky walk with flirting of tail; flies heavily with legs dangling over short distances; swims and dives, often submerging to lie with bill on surface. Fights 'sitting up' on water and striking with feet. Gregarious at times at winter food sources. Chief calls croaking *curruc* and sharp *kik,* often repeated rapidly. Complex display connected with pre-nest platform. Food mainly vegetable: seeds, fruits, shoots; some insects and worms; will attack and kill other birds. Breeding season varies through vast range; March onwards in Holarctic. Nest a basin of local plant material, often on open water, sometimes well hidden. 2 to 11 or more stone-brown, red speckled eggs, incubated ♀ and ♂ 19-22 days; young, tended by ♀ and ♂, fly 6-7 weeks; 2 or 3 broods in north of range. **227**

Gallinula tenebrosa see under **G. chloropus**

GALLINULE,
  AMERICAN PURPLE see **Porphyrula martinica**
  COMMON see **Gallinula chloropus**
  PURPLE see **Porphyrio porphyrio**

Gallirallus australis *Rallidae*
WEKA   21 ins
New Zealand; 4 races: one N Island; two S Island (*G. a. hectori* introduced Chatham Island, thence reintroduced original habitat after becoming extinct there); one Stewart Island (introduced Macquarie Island); haunts drier scrub and forest edge, even urban areas at Gisborne, N Island. Flightless, mainly shades of brown, barred black: N Island *greyi* more grey on underparts, legs brown; S Island *australis* has breast streaked red-brown and black, is dimorphic in part of range with dark, almost black form; Stewart Island *scotti* also dimorphic. Legs and bill reddish, tip dark; eyes light brown. Walks deliberately, flicking tail; can run fast and swim, becoming more active at dusk. Calls shrill, repeated whistle *coo-eet,* one bird often starting off chorus. Omnivorous, taking bright inedible objects, raiding rubbish bins, chicken runs, killing rats; near sea feeds on tide-wrack. Breeds from September to April, nesting on ground in cover; 3 to 6 cream or pinkish eggs, spotted or blotched brown and light purple, incubated 27 days. Usually only raises 1

or 2 young, but has several broods and has bred at 9 months old. **228**

Gallirex porphyreolophus *Musophagidae*
PURPLE CRESTED TOURACO   17 ins
Ethiopian: all along E coast Africa from Mombasa down to Natal, inland to Burundi, Zambia, Rhodesia in gallery forest and more humid savannah woodland, mostly below 4,000 ft. Distinguished from other greenish touracos by blue-grey, violet crest and absence of any white on face. Usual crimson wings conspicuous in flight; bill dark. Behaviour and food as other touracos (see *Corythaeola cristata*), but call longer, up to 25 repeated gobbling barks, *kura kura kura*. Breeds November to January S Africa, laying 2 glossy white eggs in shallow stick nest in tree or creepers. Incubation probably *c.* 12 days and fledging up to 20 days. **414**

Gallus gallus *Phasianidae*   ♀:17, ♂: 26-28
RED JUNGLE FOWL   (tail 11-13) ins
Oriental region: widespread; ancestor of all domestic breeds. Resident in forests, especially sal, *Shorea robusta*, and teak, *Tectona grandis*, up to 6,000 ft in Himalayan foothills; moves locally after rains to bamboo and scrub jungles, near paddyfields, other cultivated land, riverbanks. Hybridises with Grey Junglefowl, *G. sonneratii*, which is confined to Indian subcontinent and Ceylon and very similar in habits. ♂ much as domesticated game cock: red and yellow 'cape' from nape over blackish mantle, also long pointed feathers of lower back over white rump; tail glossy blue black with long curving feathers; wing red, glossy purple, with buff tip; spurred legs and bill greyish, bare face, comb and wattles red, lappets white, eyes light brown. ♀: upperparts dark brown with small black and yellow 'cape'; head and neck chestnut; flanks purplish brown; lower underparts dark grey; bare face and small comb red. Gamebird flight with flaps and final glide. ♂ runs with crouch, neck and tail outstretched; very wild. Usually ♂ and 4 or 5 ♀♀ feeding in open early and late, but up to 50 on stubbles. ♂'s crow ends more abruptly than domestic rooster's; wings rapped against flanks; ♀ clucks; both fly up with cackle. In courtship ♂ fluffs feathers, runs round ♀ with nearer wing trailing and lowered head; then repeats in reverse direction. Takes grain of all kinds, bamboo seeds, shoots of grass and crops, tubers, fruits, berries, insects and their larvae; small reptiles. Breeds mainly March to May, ♀ lining scrape with leaves under cover of bamboos or bush and incubating 5 or 6 pale buff to reddish brown eggs 20-21 days. ♂ probably successively polygamous, may help guard brood of last mate. **201**

Gallus sonneratii see under **G. gallus**

GAMBEL'S QUAIL see under **Lophortyx californicus**

GANG-GANG COCKATOO see **Callocephalon fimbriatum**

GANNET see **Sula bassana**

GANNET,
   AUSTRALIAN see under **Sula bassana**
   CAPE, see under **Sula bassana**
   SOUTH AFRICAN see under **Sula bassana**

GARDENER, QUEENSLAND see **Prionodura newtoniana**

GARDEN WARBLER see **Sylvia borin**

Garrulax caerulatus *Muscicapidae*: *Timaliinae*
FUKIEN RUFOUS JAY THRUSH or
GREY-SIDED LAUGHING THRUSH   11 ins
Oriental: E from Nepal to N Burma, S China, Taiwan. Resident in dense jungle, bamboo thickets. Upperparts rich rufous brown; forehead and around eye black; underparts brown. Calls include loud *O dear dear* and chattering alarm. Breeds April to June (Burma). Nest of bamboo leaves, roots placed in bush or bamboo clump. 2 or 3 pale blue-green eggs. **710**

Garrulus glandarius *Corvidae*
EURASIAN JAY   *c.* 13½ ins
Palaearctic, Oriental: Europe, apart from Scandinavia and N Russia; NW Africa, Asia Minor, E between *c.* 62° and 50°N to Manchuria, Japan, S through E China to N Indo-China. Mainly sedentary, some movement in winter produced by local food shortages; a few populations make definite migrations S and to lower localities in winter. Habitat: woodlands and forests, especially of oak; also orchards and parklands. Forehead and crown greyish white with black streaks, nape and neck light brownish pink; back, breast, flanks and belly similar but darker; throat whitish with black border stripes running back from base of bill; rump and upper tail coverts white; primaries blackish-brown with whitish edges to outer webs, inner webs mottled bluish at base, secondaries black with basal outer web blue and black, alula, primary-coverts and outer greater coverts blue barred black and thinly barred white; tail brown-black, barred blue-grey, legs brown, bill black, eyes bluish white. Secretive, especially when breeding; single or in small groups; inquisitive; weak undulating flight. Call: vociferous; loud, harsh *shaaark, shaaark,* also prolonged *hee-hee-hee*. Feeds on larger insects, sometimes small mammals and frogs, fruits, seeds, especially acorns, cultivated grains; robs nests; in autumn may hoard food, usually acorns, later dug up from under snow. Breeds April and May; nest of sticks and a little earth, lined thin rootlets and grass, well hidden in trees and bushes, occasionally in tree hollows. 5 to 7 eggs, sage green or olive-buff with darker olive spots and usually black hair-line at big end; both parents incubate 16-17 days and tend young, who fledge *c.* 20 days. **1005**

Gavia adamsi see under **G. immer**

Gavia arctica *Gaviidae*
BLACK-THROATED DIVER or
ARCTIC LOON   23-29 (body 14-17) ins
Holarctic: Arctic and temperate zones Eurasia and North America, moving generally southward in autumn to winter in offshore waters; breeds freshwater lakes and pools. Upperparts reticulated black and white in spring with smooth grey head, purple-black throat and streaks on neck; underparts white, which extends to chin in winter, when upperparts very dark brown; legs blackish and flesh, straight bill dark; eyes ruby. Swims low in water with neck straight, taking off clumsily but flies strongly with head held low. Usually in pairs (spring) or solitary (winter) but sometimes in parties. Flight call repeated *kwak kwak kwak*, but eerie wail in spring. Dives expertly for up to minute after fish; also takes crustaceans, molluscs, worms. Breeds May to June often on island or headland with slide into water from simple nest of local plants, in which 2 long, glossy, dark brown black-spotted eggs incubated for 4 weeks by ♀ and ♂. They also tend chicks, which enter water at once, fly in *c.* 9 weeks. **14**

Gavia immer *Gaviidae*
GREAT NORTHERN DIVER or
COMMON LOON   *c.* 27-32 (body 17-20) ins
Nearctic, marginally Palaearctic: breeds almost all N America down to 45°N except arctic coasts where replaced by White-billed, *G. adamsi;* also local Greenland and general Iceland; moves into ice-free seas in winter S to Lower California, Florida, North Sea and British coasts. Upperparts blackish, spotted white all over to give barred impression; head, neck black glossed purple with incomplete collar and throat band of narrow vertical black and white streaks; flight feathers mainly dark brown; tail dark brown tipped white; underparts white streaked black at sides; legs blackish to grey, webs pink-centred; bill blackish; eyes dark red. Winter upperparts generally dark grey with white throat; bill mainly pale grey. Habits as other divers, more reluctant to take wing. 'Running' display by ♂ on water, also gliding flight. Dives up to 3 minutes, taking mainly fish, some crustaceans, worms, molluscs. Repeated flight call as relatives, also celebrated wailing or yodelling cry on water or in flight. Breeds usually larger lakes, generally in open near water, also in vegetation, e.g. reeds; often on

islet; nest varies from wet scrape to substantial pile of local plants, added to during incubation. 2 long, glossy, greenish to dark brown eggs, sparingly spotted blackish brown, incubated ♀ and ♂ 29 days. Usually both parents feed chicks on water, 10-11 weeks. **15**

Gavia stellata *Gaviidae*
RED-THROATED DIVER or
LOON   24-27 (body 14-15) ins
Distribution as *G. arctica*, with a southward migration in the autumn to offshore waters, but breeds smaller waters, often near sea. Upperparts fairly uniform grey-brown in spring ·with dark red throat patch and streaks on neck; underparts white, which extends to chin in winter when upperparts dark brown; legs dark grey, bill paler and noticeably uptilted, eyes red-brown. Swims and takes off as *G. arctica* but flies more readily. In pairs (spring), and solitary (winter). Repeated *kwak kwak kwak* in flight and wails on water in spring. Dives for up to 1½ minutes after small fish. Breeds May to July on islet or bank of small lake or pool, with slide to water from sometimes substantial nest of plant material, holding 2 long, glossy, dark brown black-spotted eggs, incubated for 3½-4 weeks by ♀ and ♂, who also tend active chicks until they fly in *c.* 8 weeks. **16**

Geococcyx californianus *Cuculidae*
ROADRUNNER   20-24 (tail 12) ins
S Nearctic: SW USA to Central Mexico; resident in deserts and open country with scattered cover. Feathers of upperparts have dark brown glossy centres and wide pale edges, giving streaked and mottled effect, continued in miniature up head to long mobile, dark brown crest, and magnified on long feathers of pointed, white-tipped tail; neck and upper breast vertically streaked dark brown on white which extends over underparts; white crescent shows on short, rounded wings in flight; legs grey; bill: upper dark horn, lower yellowish; eyes light green with blue orbits extending back to small area of red skin. Habitually runs although zygodactylous, wings and tail assisting, up to 23 mph; reluctant to fly. Call: 6 to 8 dove-like *coos* descending in pitch; also clatters bill. Diet: lizards, small snakes, insects. Lays, from April and May, 4 to 10 white eggs in nest of sticks low in bush or tree; incubation by ♀ 19 days. Sometimes 2 broods. **427**

Geocolaptes olivaceus *Picidae*
GROUND WOODPECKER   11 ins
Ethiopian: confined to SE and S South Africa; resident on stony hillsides in dry country. Upperparts olive brown, wing coverts spotted white; rump rose red, tail dull brown, barred yellowish white; head and cheeks grey washed light olive; chin and throat off-white; underparts rose pink; legs, bill black, eyes brown. Juvenile duller. Entirely terrestrial, moving by hopping, rarely perching on trees and bushes, but sits upright on rocks, which it climbs like tree. Red rump shows in ponderous flight. Usually in small parties, feeding and roosting among the stones. High-pitched screaming alarm and contact note. Food: ground insects and their larvae. Breeds August to November, excavating hole in bank for clutch of 3 to 5 white eggs. **548**

Geopelia cuneata *Columbidae*
DIAMOND DOVE   *c.* 7¾ ins
N and inland Australia; sometimes invades coastal areas of S Australia. Habitat: open woodland, mulga scrub, gum creeks, and open country with cover and available water. ♂: head, neck and wing coverts dark grey, back and scapulars dark brown, black-edged white spots on wing coverts and scapulars, chin, throat and breast light grey, belly creamy white; long white-edged, brownish grey tail. ♀: grey plumage more suffused with brown, particularly wings. Legs flesh-pink, bill dark; eyes red with orange-red orbital skin, paler in ♀. Usually on ground, feeding on small seeds, young leaves and shoots, or basking in sun; quiet, inconspicuous, in small flocks or couples. Flight very fast, rapid wing-beats punctuated by downward swoops. Call: low sad double *coo*, often· at dawn,

otherwise double note with emphasis on first *coo*. Breeds all months; small twig platform in trees, bushes or similar dense cover, usually low down. 2 white eggs, incubated 12-13 days by both sexes; young fly *c*. 12 days. **361**

Geopelia humeralis *Columbidae*
BAR-SHOULDERED DOVE   *c*. 11 ins
Australasian: N and E Australia, lowlands of New Guinea. Habitat: wooded areas near water, often in coastal mangroves. Upperparts light greyish brown with scaled appearance given by black tips to feathers; wing coverts paler, hind neck and upper mantle light coppery buff, forehead pale bluish grey, rest of head down to breast darker, primaries chestnut with blackish outer webs and tips; longish tail with white tip apart from central feathers; underparts buffish white with pink tinge to lower breast and sides. Legs dull red, bill and orbital skin bluish grey, eyes yellow or greenish. Plumage darker in New Guinea, pinker tinge in Western Australia. Chiefly ground feeder, taking seeds and grain. Call: loud, first 2 notes like ♂ Cuckoo *Cuculus canorus*. Breeding season variable; 2 white eggs on platform of thin twigs and grass low in bushes or trees. **362**

Geopelia striata *Columbidae*
ZEBRA or PEACEFUL DOVE   *c*. 7¾ ins
Oriental, Australasian: S Tenasserim (Burma), S and E to Luzon in Philippines, Lesser Sunda Is, Tenimber and Kei Is, S New Guinea and Australia (mainly wet regions); also introduced Madagascar, St. Helena and Hawaiian Is. Habitat: open country with some tree or bush cover, clearings and edges of forest, cultivated land and gardens. Upperparts dark grey, each feather cross-barred with black; throat light grey, breast light grey streaked with black, rest of underparts creamy white; tail dark grey above, black below, outer feathers tipped white. Legs dull pink, bill grey tipped going bluer towards base, eyes white or pale blue-grey with blue orbital skin. Tame, usually on ground, feeding on small seeds of grass and herbaceous plants, sometimes grain, and some small animals; in pairs or family parties, more gregarious at good feeding places or when not breeding; flies like Diamond Dove *Geopelia cuneata* but more pronounced swooping when wings closed; takes off with distinct whirr. Call: loud melodious *coo*. Breeding depends on weather and food; small frail twig platform, 2 white eggs. Several broods. **363**

Geophaps scripta see **Petrophassa scripta**

Geospiza fortis *Fringillidae*
MEDIUM GROUND FINCH   5½ ins
Confined to Galapagos, resident on ten islands of group, occasional on others, in arid and transitional zones. ♂: black. ♀: upperparts greyish-brown, streaked darker; underparts paler with heavy dark streaks. Plumage is virtually identical *G. magnirostris* and *G. fuliginosa*, specific difference lying in the exact shape of the large, pinkish bill. Legs very dark brown; eyes light brown. Normally tame, like other Galapagos birds. ♂ builds nests, adds to others, even those of different species, and displays by them; his song is simple and not very musical, but serves to attract ♀ to territory. Diet: seeds, fruits, flowers, buds, young leaves; also small insects but large larvae, spiders; feeds much on ground. Breeds rainy season, usually November to February, building bulky domed nest with side entrance, of twigs, grasses, epiphytic lichens or wild cotton; from 3 to 30 ft up in cactus *Opuntia*, acacia, other bush or tree, often at end of branch. Usually 4 greenish-white eggs, speckled brown, incubated ♀ *c*. 12 days, fed by ♂, who also helps her feed young, fledging in *c*. 2 weeks. Several broods. **924**

Geospiza
  fuliginosa see under **G. fortis**
  magnirostris see under **G. fortis**

Geotrygon montana *Columbidae*
RUDDY QUAIL DOVE   *c*. 11 ins
Neotropical: Mexico S to Peru, Bolivia and N Paraguay; resident mainly humid lowland forests.

Plump bird seen low in cover, usually feeding on ground taking seeds, fallen fruit and some small animals. ♂: upperparts, including wings, rich chestnut, mostly with purple-red iridescence, apart from much of wing and head; lower face pinkish white with 2 purplish chestnut, horizontal stripes; breast pinkish brown shading to buff belly, flanks and under tail coverts. Long legs, bill purplish red, eyes yellow or orange brown with purplish red orbital skin. ♀: olive-brown with slight greenish gloss where ♂ chestnut, bronzy buff where ♂ pinkish; legs and orbital skin paler. Call: prolonged booming note. Breeds throughout spring and summer, building twig platform lined with leaves low down in trees and shrubs or even on ground. 2 buff eggs, incubated both sexes *c*. 12 days. **364**

Geronticus calvus *Threskiornithidae*
BALD IBIS   32 ins
Ethiopian: confined to S Africa, but may be conspecific with *G. eremita* the Waldrapp, a decreasing species of S Palaearctic and NE Ethiopian: (formerly Europe) N Africa, Asia Minor, Arabia, Red Sea coast, Ethiopia, Sudan, as plumage and habits almost identical. Resident mountainous country or isolated hills near feeding grounds on grassland. Iridescent dark green, blue and violet with coppery shoulder patch and ruff at back of neck; legs dull red, bare face and upper neck bluish, bony 'crest' and long curved bill red, eyes orange red. Juvenile has mottled dark grey and white feathers on head, bill dark slate grey, red at base. Gregarious; flies gracefully on pointed wings, gliding and soaring near nest sites, where calls loud, high pitched *keeauu klaup klaarp* (Waldrapp has sharp *ka ka* and soft whistle). Food mainly beetles and other insects dug even out of hard ground; also young birds and mammals, frogs, molluscs, worms. Breeds colonially September to December on cliff ledges and caves, making nest of sticks and debris and laying 2 or 3 rough textured, bluish white eggs, marked brown and purple. **82**

Geronticus eremita see under **G. calvus**

Gerygone igata *Muscicapidae: Malurinae*
GREY WARBLER   4½ ins
Australasian: main and some outlying islands New Zealand; resident native primary and secondary forest up to *c*. 4,500 ft, also introduced vegetation from pine plantations to gardens, hedgerows. Upperparts greenish-grey, narrow white streak on wing, white on sides short rounded brown tail shows in flight; throat, breast pale grey; belly, undertail coverts white, variable yellow tinge sides, flanks; legs blackish brown, bill black, eyes very dark brown. Usually in pairs, fluttering on foliage. Song: sweet variable trill, heard at all seasons but peak September-October. Main food insects, spiders, small moths taken on wing. Breeds August to January; ♀ (mainly) builds pear-shaped nest of grass, moss, cobwebs, plant down, lined feathers, entrance near top, suspended firmly from outer branch of tree, 5 to 25 ft up. 3 to 6 pinkish white eggs, evenly spotted red-brown or purple, incubated 17-19 days; both parents feed young, who fly 17-19 days. 2 broods, second parasitised by Shining Cuckoo, *Chalcites lucidus*, summer visitor to NZ. **761**

Gerygone olivacea *Muscicapidae: Malurinae*
WHITE-THROATED WARBLER   *c*. 4½ ins
Australia: N and E from Derby, W Australia, round to Central Victoria; migrant, visits SE Australia in spring and leaves in autumn. Habitat: sapling scrub and open forest. Upperparts pale ashy brown washed olive; wings dark brown; tail dark brown with white band at base and spots at tip; cheeks, chin, throat white (yellow in juveniles); underparts bright yellow. Legs brown, bill black, eyes red. Solitary, secretive, seeks insects amongst outer foliage. Song: distinctive and beautiful warble of descending notes. Breeding season variable, usually August onwards in N, later in S; pear-shaped nest with long tail and hooded entrance near top, attached to leafy branch 3 to 50 ft up, often in eucalypt, of grass, shreds of bark and cobwebs, lined feathers or fur; 3, sometimes 2, white or reddish white eggs marked purplish red. **762**

GIANT
  EAGLE OWL, VERREAUX'S see **Bubo lacteus**
  KINGFISHER see **Megaceryle maxima**
  PETREL see **Macronectes giganteus**

GILA WOODPECKER see **Centurus uropygialis**

GILDED FLICKER see **Colaptes chrysoides**

Glareola nordmanni see under **G. pratincola**

Glareola pratincola *Glareolidae*
COMMON PRATINCOLE   *c*. 10 (2½ tail streamers) ins
Palaearctic, Oriental, Ethiopian; main range from Black Sea to Lake Balkash, extending along Persian Gulf to India, Indo-China, coasts of Yellow Sea; also W Mediterranean, W Africa (River Niger area) and most of E Africa. This includes range of Black-winged Pratincole, often regarded as distinct species *G. nordmanni*. Resident open grasslands and steppes, burnt-over and arable land, often near shallow salt or fresh water. Upperparts almost uniform dark brown, extending over wings to black primaries and narrow white trailing edge; white of rump extends along outer edges of black, forked tail feathers; throat pale fawn with thin black border, underparts white; underwing chestnut, black in *nordmanni*; breast brown; short legs black, bill black, base red, eyes hazel brown. Swallow- or tern-like in air, plover-like on ground, running rapidly with body horizontal. Sometimes wades. Becomes more active towards dusk. Call *kikki kirrick*, sometimes repeated, sometimes shortened. ♂ displays to ♀ on ground. Exaggerated injury-feigning even without eggs or young. Diet: mainly large insects, especially locusts, taken on wing or off ground. Breeds from early May in Spain; often social. Scrape, on bare open ground or partly sheltered by herbage, holds 2 or 3 stone to buff eggs, spotted or marbled black and grey. Incubation by ♀ and ♂ 17-18 days; both tend young, full-grown *c*. 4 weeks. **311**

Glaucidium brasilianum *Strigidae*
FERRUGINOUS PYGMY OWL   6½ ins
Nearctic, Neotropical: S Arizona, S Texas through Central and S America to C Argentina, N Chile; Trinidad. Resident forest and wooded country, including Brazilian cerrado (semi-deciduous plateau woods), plantations, gardens, even towns; riverbottoms in USA. Sepia and rufous colour phases covering most of upperparts; flight feathers obscurely barred, small white spots on wing coverts; tail light chestnut barred umber; light shaft streaks on crown, two distinctive black patches at back of neck, prominent white 'eyebrows'; underparts white, streaked brown; but centre breast, belly unmarked; legs feathered, feet yellow; bill, cere pale greenish yellow; eyes light yellow. Jerks longish tail up and down on perch, but more often heard than seen, uttering series of *chook* calls every second (G. M. Sutton). These can be imitated to call up small birds, and trogons with similar notes; if owl also appears, it is mobbed (G. A. C. Kerklots). Breeds February to April Trinidad in tree hole 15 to 20 ft up; 1 to 5 dull white eggs.

Glaucidium passerinum *Strigidae*
EURASIAN PYGMY OWL   6½ ins
Palaearctic: from Scandinavia and alpine Europe in broad band across Eurasia to Manchuria, between 50° and 60°N. Resident, except for hard weather movements, in dense taiga or montane forests. Upperparts brown spotted white; underparts buff and greyish with dark streaks; tail barred brown and white; legs feathered, claws brown, bill yellowish, eyes yellow. Juvenile darker, few streaks above, underparts spotted brown. Flicks tail when perched, often conspicuously; rounded wings show in flight. Calls: whistling *keeoo*; sharp *kuvitt* like Little Owl *Athene noctua*; monotonous *peeu peeu peeu* in breeding season. Hunts mainly dawn and dusk: voles, mice, lemmings, even hamsters; small birds caught on flight; insects in summer. Breeds from late April, laying 4 to 6 white eggs in tree hole, usually conifer, aspen, sometimes birch. Incubation *c*. 28 days; young fully fledged mid August.

GLAUCOUS GULL see **Larus hyperboreus**

GLEANER,
  BUFF-THROATED FOLIAGE
    see under **Automolus leucophthalmus**
  CHESTNUT-TAILED FOLIAGE see under
    Automolus leucophthalmus
  WHITE-EYED FOLIAGE see **Automolus leucophthalmus**

Gliciphila albifrons or Philidonyris albifrons
Meliphagidae
WHITE-FRONTED HONEYEATER   7 ins
Australasian: temperate continental areas, moving locally in large flocks. Habitat heath and dwarf mallee scrub of interior. Upperparts blackish brown, 'scaly'-looking with pale edged black-centred feathers; outer edges flight feathers washed yellow; white forehead, face, moustachial stripe, ear coverts grey; underparts as upper, but chin, throat darker, belly, undertail coverts paler; legs grey, bill black, white-ringed eye brown with small eye wattle. ♀ brown not black-brown. Closely resembles Yellow-winged, *Meliornis novaehollandiae*. Pairs or small parties active and wary as they search foliage or probe blossoms; flight erratic like *G. melanops*. Variety of calls: *chip chip*, drawn-out *cre-e-ek;* musical canary-like notes. Diet: insects, nectar, especially from *Hakea, Eremophila* in Central Australia. Breeds July or August to January; nest of bark, grasses, lined fur, hair, soft down from *Banksia* cones; usually up to 5 ft top of low bush, sometimes behind bark of tree. 2 or 3 pale pinkish white eggs, heavily marked reddish brown over dull purple. **839**

Gliciphila melanops *Meliphagidae*
TAWNY-CROWNED HONEYEATER   7 ins
Australasia: continental New South Wales, Victoria, S and SW Australia, Kangaroo I, Tasmania; heaths, dwarf scrublands, e.g. mallee, with *Banksias:* avoids dense forest. ♂: crown tawny, shading into dark-streaked brown upperparts; pale edges to wing feathers; white 'eyebrow', black mask extending, with white crescent inset on cheek, round white throat to shade into lightly streaked off-white underparts; undertail coverts white. ♀ duller. Legs horn, bill black, eyes brown. Behaves as relatives; pairs or small parties restlessly searching foliage for insects, nectar, pollen, especially from *Banksia, Grevillea*. Song from prominent perch: long drawn single note, quick double note, repeated 6 to 8 times. ♂ soars upwards and descends calling in display. Breeds June to February or longer; nest deep cup of bark, grass bound cobwebs, decorated spider egg bags, lined plant down; near ground in low bush or tussock. 2 or 3 pink eggs, sparsely marked chestnut at big end. **840**

GLISTENING GREEN TANAGER see under
Chlorochrysa phoenicotis

Glossopsitta pusilla *Psittacidae*
LITTLE LORIKEET   6½ ins
Australasian: coastal areas of SE Queensland, Victoria, New South Wales, SE South Australia; Tasmania; open riverine and montane forests; nomadic after food. Shades of green with bronze-brown patch covering base of neck, mantle, scapulars; red mask; undertail dusky yellow; legs greenish-grey, bill black eyes yellow. Family parties make flocks, attracted by flowering of eucalypts. Call a noisy high-pitched screech, also chatters while feeding, often with other species; flies either twisting and turning with whirring wings or direct over long distances. Food: nectar of eucalypts, other flowering plants; some fruits. Breeds August to January in hole of tree or branch, usually of living eucalypt near water. 3 or 4 white eggs laid on wood dust, incubated by ♀ c. 18 days (captive); ♀ feeds young who fly c. 30 days. **393**

GLOSSY
  IBIS see **Plegadis falcinellus**
  STARLING, BLUE-EARED see **Lamprocolius chalybeus**
  STARLING, BURCHELL'S see **Lamprotornis australis**
  SWIFTLET, see **Collocalia esculenta**

Glyphorhynchus spirurus *Dendrocolaptidae*
WEDGE-BILLED WOODCREEPER   5½ (bill ½) ins
Neotropical: Central America to S America E of Andes; N Bolivia and Brazil; resident in forests and more open woodland, sea level to c. 7,000 ft. Upperparts rufous brown, becoming chestnut on rump; band across inner webs of flight feathers pale cinnamon; throat and 'eyebrow' buff; underparts dark brown with white arrow-shaped spots or shaftstreaks on breast; strong bill slightly upturned. Song, 'fine rapid, ascending trill' (A. F. Skutch). Behaves like treecreeper, spiralling up trunk then flying down to base of another tree; supports itself on stiff tail feathers and extracts small insects, their larvae and eggs from bark with bill. Breeds tree holes and crevices at varying heights, usually low, laying 2 or 3 white eggs in pad on rootlets and plant stems; incubation by ♀ and ♂. **559**

GNATCATCHER,
  BLUE-GREY see **Polioptila caerulea**
  RUFOUS see **Conopophaga lineata**
  SILVERY-TUFTED see **Conopophaga lineata**

GNATWREN, LONG-BILLED see **Ramphocaenus melanurus**

GO-AWAY-BIRD,
  BARE-FACED see **Corythaixodes personata**
  COMMON see **Corythaixodes concolor**
  WHITE-BELLIED see **Corythaixodes leucogaster**

GODWIT,
  BLACK-TAILED see **Limosa limosa**
  HUDSONIAN see under **Limosa limosa**

GOLDCREST see **Regulus regulus**

GOLD-CROWNED KINGLET see **Regulus satrapa**

GOLDEN
  BOWER BIRD see **Prionodura newtoniana**
  EAGLE see **Aquila chrysaetos**
  ORIOLE see **Oriolus oriolus**
  PHEASANT see **Chrysolophus pictus**
  PIPIT see **Tmetothylacus tenellus**
  PLOVER see **Pluvialis apricaria**
  PLOVER, LESSER see **Pluvias dominica**
  PLOVER, PACIFIC see **Pluvialis dominica**
  WHISTLER see **Pachycephala pectoralis**

GOLDEN-BREASTED
  BUNTING see **Emberiza flaviventris**
  STARLING see **Cosmopsarus regius**

GOLDEN-CROWNED TANAGER see **Iridosornis rufivertex**

GOLDENEYE,
  BARROW'S see **Bucephala islandica**
  COMMON see under **Bucephala islandica**

GOLDEN-FRONTED
  LEAFBIRD see **Chloropsis aurifrons**
  REDSTART see **Myioborus ornatus**

GOLDEN-HEADED FANTAIL see **Cisticola exilis**

GOLDEN-RUMPED TINKER BIRD see **Pogoniulus bilineatus**

GOLDEN-TAILED WOODPECKER see **Campethera abingoni**

GOLDEN-WINGED
  SPARROW see **Arremon schlegeli**
  SUNBIRD see **Drepanorhynchus reichenowi**

GOLDFINCH,
  AMERICAN see **Spinus tristis**
  EUROPEAN see **Carduelis carduelis**
  GREY-HEADED see under **Carduelis carduelis**

GOLDIE'S LORIKEET see **Psitteuteles goldiei**

GOLIATH HERON see **Ardea goliath**

GOOSE,
  BARNACLE see **Branta leucopsis**
  CANADA see **Branta canadensis**
  CAPE BARREN see **Cereopsis novaehollandiae**
  EGYPTIAN see **Alopochen aegyptiaca**
  GREY LAG see **Anser anser**
  HAWAIIAN see **Branta sandvicensis**
  KELP see **Chloephaga hybrida**
  KNOB-BILLED see **Sarkidiornis melanotos**
  MAGELLAN see **Chloephaga picta**
  MAGPIE see **Anseranas semipalmata**
  PYGMY see **Nettapus auritus**
  SNOW see **Anser caerulescens**
  SPURWING see **Plectopterus gambensis**

GOSHAWK,
  DARK CHANTING see **Melierax metabates**
  PALE CHANTING see **Melierax canorus**

GOULDIAN FINCH see **Poephila gouldiae**

GOULD'S FROGMOUTH see **Batrachostomus stellatus**

GRACKLE see **Gracula religiosa**

GRACKLE,
  GREATER ANTILLEAN see **Quiscalus niger**
  PURPLE see **Quiscalus quiscala**

Gracula religiosa *Sturnidae*
INDIAN HILL MYNAH or GRACKLE   c. 11½ ins
Oriental: most of region except Philippines, number of sub-species with some variation in plumage and size e.g. *G. r. indica*, SW peninsular India, c. 10 ins and more extensive wattles. Habitat: tropical moist deciduous and semi-evergreen forest, foothills, hill tracts and plains up to 5,000 ft on continent. Black, glossed purple and greenish; bright orange-yellow patch of bare skin and fleshy wattles on sides of head and nape; broad white band on primaries. Legs yellow, bill orange, eyes dark brown. Sociable and noisy, small parties outside breeding season, usually in tree tops; in flight wings touch above and below, make humming noise. Call: wide range of whistles, wails, screeches and gurgles; good mimic in captivity, therefore captured in great numbers. Feeds on fruits and berries, also flower buds, nectar and insects. Usually breeds April to July; loose nest of fine twigs, grass, feathers and rubbish in hole c. 30 to 50 ft up in tree, often at forest edge or isolated clump; sometimes different pairs build one nest above the other; 2 or 3 blue or greenish blue eggs, lightly marked with reddish brown. **968**

Grallaricula ferrugineipectus *Formicariidae*
RUSTY-BREASTED ANTPITTA   4¾ ins
Neotropical: NW Venezuela, Colombia, N Peru; resident in undergrowth of humid forests, 4,500 to 7,000 ft. Upperparts olive brown (rufous brown in one race); underparts ochreaceous with white crescent across lower throat and white centre to belly. Although relatives terrestrial, only lands to seize prey from perch 3 ft up; also takes insects in air. 'Waggles small tail and flashes wings.' (C. P. Schwartz). ♂'s song phrases 16 to 18 notes in three sections. Breeds rainy season, building platform of twigs with cup of leaf stems, 2 to 4 ft up in bush or tree. 2 pale greenish or greyish eggs marked shades of brown; incubation 16-17 days; young fledge 13 days. **568**

Grallina cyanoleuca *Grallinidae*
MAGPIE LARK   10-12 ins
Australian: throughout continent; not Tasmania; habitats various, in neighbourhood of water. ♂: upperparts, including head, throat, black; black eye-stripe crosses white face; much of wings, base and tip tail, underparts, white; ♀ has forehead and throat white, no white above eyes. Legs black, bill whitish grey, eyes pale yellow. Holds 15 to 20 acre territory most of year, but large flocks form autumn and roost communally. Flies strongly but spends most time on ground e.g. by farm ponds, on roads, feeding on insects; takes freshwater snails (thus heping to control liver fluke); also cattle ticks (I. C. R. Rowley). Song

duet: 2 notes from one bird followed at once by 3 from mate. Breeds September to January, often several pairs same tree, or with other black and white species; builds bowl-shaped nest, of (usually) black mud, lined grass, feathers, on bare lateral branch 30 to 40 ft up and generally over water. 3 or 4 pinkish to red-buff eggs, marked purplish-red often in zone, incubated ♀ and ♂. Both parents feed young, independent month after fledging. Several broods. **981**

GRASS
PARAKEET, ELEGANT see **Neophema elegans**
PARROT, ELEGANT see **Neophema elegans**
WARBLER, RUFOUS see **Cisticola galactotes**
WREN, BLACK see **Amytornis housei**

GRASSHOPPER
WARBLER see **Locustella naevia**
WARBLER, GRAY'S see **Locustella fasciolata**

GRAUER'S BROADBILL see **Pseudocalyptomena graueri**

GRAY'S GRASSHOPPER WARBLER see **Locustella fasciolata**

GREAT
ARGUS PHEASANT see **Argusianus argus**
BLUE TOURACO see **Corythaeola cristata**
BUSTARD see **Otis tarda**
GREY OWL see **Strix nebulosa**
GREY SHRIKE see **Lanius excubitor**
HORNED OWL see **Bubo virginianus**
NORTHERN DIVER see **Gavia immer**
PARROTBILL see **Conostoma oemodium**
PIED-BILLED GREBE see **Podilymbus gigas**
POTOO see **Nyctibius grandis**
REED WARBLER see **Acrocephalus arundinaceus**
SHEARWATER see **Puffinus gravis**
SKUA see **Stercorarius skua**
SPOTTED CUCKOO see **Clamator glandarius**
SPOTTED WOODPECKER see **Dendrocopos major**
TIT see **Parus major**
WHITE HERON see **Egretta alba**

GREAT-CRESTED GREBE see **Podiceps cristatus**

GREATER
ANI see **Crotophaga major**
ANTILLEAN GRACKLE see **Quiscalus niger**
BIRD OF PARADISE see **Paradisaea apoda**
FLAMINGO see **Phoenicopterus ruber**
PRAIRIE CHICKEN see **Tympanuchas cupido**
RACKET-TAILED DRONGO see under **Dicrurus annectans**
VASA PARROT see **Coracopsis vasa**
YELLOW-BELLIED TROGON see **Trogon viridis**

GREBE,
GREAT-CRESTED see **Podiceps cristatus**
GREAT PIED-BILLED see **Podilymbus gigas**
HORNED see **Podiceps auritus**
LITTLE see **Tachybaptus ruficollis**
PIED-BILLED see **Podilymbus podiceps**
SLAVONIAN see **Podiceps auritus**
WESTERN, see **Aechmophorus occidentalis**

GREEN AND BLACK FRUITEATER see **Pipreola riefferii**

GREEN AND RUFOUS KINGFISHER see under **Chloroceryle aenea**

GREEN
BEE-EATER, LITTLE see **Merops orientalis**
BROADBILL see **Calyptomena viridis**
CARDINAL see **Gubernatrix cristata**
JAY see **Cyanocorax yncas**
PIGEON see **Treron australis**
PIGEON, PINTAILED see under **Treron sphenura**
TANAGER, GLISTENING see **Chlorochrysa phoenicotis**
WHITE-EYE see under **Zosterops pallida**
WOOD HOOPOE see **Phoeniculus purpureus**

WOOD PARTRIDGE see **Rollulus roulroul**
WOODPECKER see under **Picus canus**

GREENBUL, ZANZIBAR SOMBRE see **Andopadus importunus**

GREENFINCH see **Carduelis chloris**

GREENFINCH, ORIENTAL see under **Carduelis chloris**

GREEN-HEADED SUNBIRD see **Cyanomitra verticalis**

GREENLET, TAWNY-CROWNED see **Hylophilus ochraceiceps**

GREENSHANK see under **Tringa erythropus**

GREY
BUTCHERBIRD see **Cracticus torquatus**
FANTAIL see **Rhipidura fuliginosa**
HERON see **Ardea cinerea**
HORNBILL see **Tockus nasutus**
HYPOCOLIUS see **Hypocolius ampelinus**
JUNGLE FOWL see under **Gallus gallus**
LAG GOOSE see **Anser anser**
OWL, GREAT see **Strix nebulosa**
PARROT, AFRICAN see **Psittacus erithacus**
PARTRIDGE see **Perdix perdix**
PHALAROPE see **Phalaropus fulicarius**
PLANTAIN-EATER see **Crinifer zonurus**
PLOVER see **Pluvialis squatarola**
SHRIKE, GREAT see **Lanius excubitor**
SHRIKE, LESSER see **Lanius minor**
WAGTAIL see **Motacilla cinerea**
WARBLER see **Gerygone igata**

GREY-BACKED
CAMAROPTERA see **Camaroptera brevicaudata**
SHRIKE see **Lanius tephronotus**
WARBLER see **Cisticola subruficapilla**

GREY-BREASTED WHITE-EYE see **Zosterops lateralis**

GREY-CHEEKED
NUNLET see **Nonnula ruficapilla**
THRUSH see **under Catharus minimus**

GREY-HEADED
GOLDFINCH see under **Carduelis carduelis**
GULL see **Larus cirrocephalus**
KINGFISHER see **Halcyon leucocephala**
WHISTLER see under **Pachycephala pectoralis**
WOODPECKER see **Picus canus**

GREY-NECKED
BUNTING see under **Emberiza hortulana**
ROCKFOWL see **Picathartes gymnocephalus**

GREY-SIDED LAUGHING THRUSH see **Garrulux caerulatus**

GREY-TAILED TATTLER see **Tringa brevipes**

GRIFFON VULTURE see **Gyps fulvus**

GROSBEAK,
EVENING see **Hesperiphona vespertina**
ROSE-BREASTED see **Pheuticus melanocephalus**

GROUND
CUCKOO, RED-BILLED see **Carpococcyx renauldi**
CUCKOO, RENAUD'S see **Carpococcyx renauldi**
CUCKOO SHRIKE see **Pteropodocys maxima**
DOVE, BLUE see **Claravis pretiosa**
DOVE, COMMON see **Columbina passerina**
FINCH, MEDIUM see **Geospiza fortis**
HORNBILL see **Bucorvus leadbeateri**
HORNBILL, ABYSSINIAN see **Bucorvus abyssinicus**
PARROT see **Pezoporus wallicus**
ROLLER, LONG-TAILED see **Uratelornis chimaera**

WOODPECKER see **Geocolaptes olivaceus**

GROUSE,
BLACK see **Lyrurus tetrix**
BLACK-FACED SAND see **Eremialector decoratus**
BLUE see **Dendragapus obscurus**
CHESTNUT-BELLIED SAND see **Pterocles exustus**
FOUR-BANDED SAND see **Eremialector quadricinctus**
RED see **Lagopus lagopus**
SAGE see **Centrocercus urophasianus**
SHARP-TAILED see **Pediocetes phasianellus**
WILLOW see **Lagopus lagopus**

Grus americana *Gruidae*
WHOOPING CRANE   48-54 ins
Nearctic: now breeds only Wood Buffalo Park, Great Slave Lake, Mackenzie, Canada; winters Arkansas Refuge, Texas; one of world's rarest birds. Habitat: very wet muskeg or wooded bog; coastal marshland in winter, stopping at lakes and swamps on migration. Wingspan *c.* 7½ ft; almost uniformly white except for black primaries and greater coverts, bare red crown and cheeks; legs black, bill horn grey, eyes pale yellow. Brownish-buff juvenile resembles much commoner juvenile Sandhill Crane, *G. canadensis*. Territorial summer and winter, pair requiring *c.* 400 acres. Elaborate courtship dance started by ♂♂, joined by ♀♀; jumping, bowing, wing-flapping; starts in winter, intensifies before spring migration mid-April. Return migration September-October. Piercing 'whooping' cry, hence name. May feed communally in winter on plant material, amphibians, crustaceans, other invertebrates; probably molluscs, frogs in summer. Probably pairs for life, nesting from early May, collecting pile of vegetation on wet ground but above water level. 2 buff or olive eggs, marked brown, incubated 34-35 days. Usually one young in wild, flies September, remains with parents over winter.

Grus antigone *Gruidae*
SARUS CRANE   60 ins
Oriental, Australasian: Indian subcontinent and SE Asia, with recent extension to NE Australia. Resident on grassy plains and in clearings, sometimes small, surrounded by forest. More or less uniform pale grey with white plumes on wings and white crown; head and upper neck bare red skin; legs pink, bill grey with darker tip, eyes yellow. Pairs for life, birds feeding and flying close together; sometimes join in parties up to 60. Striking display dances with wing spreading and leaping, uttering trumpeting calls, also heard in flight, with raucous note before and after take-off. Duets between members of pair. Diet: grain, berries, roots, insects, small vertebrates, especially fish; accompanies cattle to catch what they disturb, e.g. frogs. Breeds during rains, mainly July to October. Nest a mass of local plants on swampy ground. Usually 2 pinkish-white eggs, sometimes marked brown, incubated mainly by ♀, guarded by ♂, *c.* 30 days; both parents tend young. **217**

Grus canadensis see under **G. americana**

Grus carunculatus or Bugeranus carunculatus *Gruidae*
WATTLED CRANE   50 ins
Ethiopian: Abyssinia and Zaire southward to Cape, migrant locally. Inhabits open swamps and marshes. Back, wing coverts and long ornamented plumes grey; flight feathers blackish; crown slate; neck white, underparts black; two white partly feathered wattles hang from chin; legs black, stout bill reddish-brown, eyes orange yellow, facial skin red and warty. ♀ has more white on crown. Usually in small parties, even in breeding season, sometimes consorting with antelopes. Communal and pair dances. Guttural but quite melodious *hornk;* 'jabbers' while feeding, mainly on insects and small vertebrates, including fish. Protracted breeding season, possibly double brooded. Nests in swamp or on island, sometimes built up of vegetation, sometimes on flattened area. Lays 1 or 2 sandy or cream eggs, heavily marked brown and lilac. Incubation by ♀ and ♂, who also tend the young. **218**

Grus grus *Gruidae*

COMMON CRANE   *c.* 44 (body 23) ins
Palaearctic: from Baltic across Eurasia to E Siberia and E China; isolated pockets round Mediterranean; winters in subtropical S Asia, N and E Africa north of Equator. Inhabits very wet areas, often in or near wooded country, sometimes close to cultivation, also shallow lagoons in S Europe; wet and dry open country in winter. Body lead grey, primaries, most of head and neck blackish, but sides of head and neck white and red patch on crown; legs black, bill greenish-horn, base reddish, eyes red. Shy and terrestrial; walks with long strides, runs, swims if necessary. Gregarious outside breeding season, migrating flocks flying in Vs, neck and legs stretched. Call a loud *grooh;* many other notes in breeding season. Display dances by parties of all sizes, even in winter quarters. Forages on surface and by probing in earth for variety of small marsh or fresh water animals; rodents, young birds, also insects; probably partly vegetarian. Breeding season from mid-April onwards according to latitude. Usually nests on mound of local plants in very swampy ground, surrounded by grasses, reeds or bog vegetation. 2 glossy brownish eggs, marked rich brown. ♀ and ♂ incubated *c.* 29 days. ♀ has chief share in tending precocious young: fully fledged at 10 weeks. **219**

Grus japonensis *Gruidae*

JAPANESE OR MANCHURIAN CRANE   *c.* 42 ins
E Palaearctic: SE Siberia (Lake Khanka), Manchuria (now very rare), Japan (Kuccharo Marsh, Hokkaido); moves southward in autumn from breeding habitat of marshes and lakesides. Pure white with black secondaries and pale grey stripes down neck from partly grey-black head; rest of head bare red skin with coarse black filoplumes; legs black, bill greenish horn, eyes dark brown. Secretive in tall marsh vegetation in summer. Display dances after reciprocal calling *koroo* between members of pair; also loud sonorous call in early morning and variety of other notes recorded. Diet: mainly water plants and grasses, water animals, especially loach, in summer; occasionally attacks crops. Lays from March, building layered nest of alder branches and reeds on *yachimanako* (floating island) in lake. 2 creamy eggs, sparsely marked reddish and grey incubated by ♀ (night) and ♂ (day) 32-34 days; parents feed the young at first with flying insects. **220**

Grus leucogeranus *Gruidae*

SIBERIAN WHITE CRANE   48 ins
E Palaearctic: confined to valleys of lower Ob, Yana to Indigirka and upper Lena in Siberia as summer visitor to tundra marshes; winter visitor to swamps and floodlands in S Caspian, India S of Himalayas, lower Yangtse river, China. Snow-white with black wing-tips, hidden when at rest; legs rusty red, bill tip slate grey becoming reddish to merge with bare red face; eyes yellow. Winters in parties of 3 or 4 up to *c.* 70. Wades and rests in shallow water, often feeding with head submerged on bulbs and corms of aquatic plants; also shoots and seeds. Displays in pairs or communally like other cranes. Call *koonk koonk* in flight. Breeds in subarctic summer, building mound nest of local plants. Lays 2 olive-grey eggs; incubation and fledging much as Common Crane, *Grus grus.* **221**

Grus rubicundus *Gruidae*

BROLGA OR NATIVE COMPANION   45-50 ins
Continental Australia (except SW); resident or nomadic over plains and swampy areas. Almost uniform light blue-grey, paler on neck; head bare red and grey skin with black bib; legs light brown, bill dark horn, eyes yellow. Usually in pairs or flocks, which display with remarkable dances like other cranes. Graceful in flight, sometimes soaring to great heights. Deep trumpeting call. Eats small vertebrates, insects, some plants and roots. Breeding season September to March or wet season in N, spring in S. Nest a substantial platform of vegetation, often forming small island in swamp. 2 glossy white eggs, marked reddish-purple, incubated by ♀ and ♂ *c.* 32 days; both parents tend young. **222**

Grus vipio *Gruidae*

WHITE-NECKED CRANE   50 ins
E Palaearctic: eastern half S Siberia; NE Mongolia, China; summer visitor to marshy areas of steppes; winters in Japan and Korea. Rather like Sarus, *G. antigone,* but lower neck darker, contrasting with white stripes from head down front and back; wing-tips black, tail and undertail coverts dark grey, breast and belly slate black; legs pink, bill greenish, eyes brownish yellow. Behaviour much as other cranes; winters in parties of 3 or 4 to *c.* 40 birds. ♂ very attentive to ♀ in spring with leaping dances and mutual calling: trumpeting *kruw-koro kruw koro* to ♀'s *kuck kuck.* Digs up roots and bulbs of aquatic plants, sometimes raids bean crops; aggressive when feeding. Lays from April in Siberia, building nest of local plants in marshy area. 2 pale buff or greenish eggs, marked heavily brown and grey, incubated mainly by ♀ for 30-33 days; both parents tend the young.

GUACHARO see **Steatornis caripensis**

GUAM RAIL see **Rallus owstoni**

GUANAY see **Phalacrocorax bougainvillii**

GUAN, RED-TAILED see **Ortalis ruficauda**

Gubernatrix cristata *Emberizidae: Pyrrhuloxiinae*

GREEN OR YELLOW CARDINAL   8 ins
Neotropical: SE Brazil, E Argentina; scrub country and woodland. ♂: back olive, streaked black; wings dusky brown, edged olive, lesser coverts bright yellow; central 4 tail feathers dusky brown, rest mainly yellow; crown and showy crest black; 'eyebrow', wide moustachial stripe yellow, throat black; rest of underparts olive yellow, centre belly brighter. ♀ has 'eyebrow', moustachial stripe white, ear coverts, upper breast greyish. Legs, bill grey, eyes brown. Food: seeds, some insects, especially when rearing young. Builds cup nest in bush, laying 4 green eggs, spotted purplish black; breeding details much as Cardinal, *Pyrrhuloxia cardinalis.* **868**

GUILLEMOT,
    BLACK see **Cepphus grylle**
    COMMON see **Uria aalge**
    PIGEON see **Cepphus columba**

GUINEAFOWL,
    CRESTED see **Guttera edouardi**
    HELMETED see under **Numida meleagris**
    TUFTED see **Numida meleagris**
    VULTURINE see **Acryllium vulturinum**

GULL,
    BLACK-HEADED see **Larus ridibundus**
    BONAPARTE'S see **Larus philadelphia**
    CALIFORNIA see **Larus californicus**
    COMMON see **Larus canus**
    FRANKLIN'S see **Larus pipixcan**
    GLAUCOUS see **Larus hyperboreus**
    GREY-HEADED see **Larus cirrocephalus**
    HARTLAUB'S see **Larus novaehollandiae**
    HEERMANN'S see **Larus heermanni**
    HERRING see **Larus argentatus**
    LESSER BLACK-BACKED see under **Larus argentatus**
    LITTLE see **Larus minutus**
    PACIFIC see **Larus pacificus**
    PATAGONIAN BLACK-HEADED see under **Larus ridibundus**
    RED-BILLED see **Larus scopulinus**
    RING-BILLED see under **Larus californicus**
    SABINE'S see **Xema sabini**
    SILVER see **Larus novaehollandiae**
    SWALLOW-TAILED see **Creagrus furcatus**

GURNEY'S PITTA see **Pitta gurneyi**

Guttera edouardi *Numididae*

CRESTED GUINEAFOWL   *c.* 20 ins
Ethiopian: 10 races throughout region, some very local in distribution; resident in primary forest and thick bush; deciduous woods and streambanks in dry season. Grey-black all over, polkadotted bluish-white; black crest and collar round bare neck; legs black, bill greyish, eyes brown, bare skin of face blue, throat crimson. Small flocks rarely venture out of cover, then retire into trees with raucous calls. But bird standing upright with neck stretched utters deep *tok a tok tok tok.* Diet: insects, especially termites, molluscs; seeds, roots and shoots; parties forage among dead leaves. Breeds probably throughout year over wide range; several pairs may nest near together, lining scrapes under bushes or fallen trees. ♀ incubates 8 to 10 or more pale buff eggs, speckled darker brown.

Gygis alba or Anous alba *Laridae*

FAIRY OR WHITE TERN   *c.* 12 ins
S Hemisphere: central Atlantic, Indian and Pacific Oceans; breeds on islands, Fernando Noronha, S Trinidad, Ascension and St Helena, then disperses to tropical offshore and pelagic waters far from breeding grounds. Ivory white, forked tail, long translucent wings with dusky shafts. Immature: mantle flecked brownish, black spot behind eyes, darker shafts to wings and tail. Legs black, bill black, looks uptilted, eyes black with black orbital ring. Flight swift and erratic; fairly tame; shallow swoops to take fish and some crustacea from surface, often catches small flying fish. Call: soft buzzing notes. Breeds usually between May and January; single greyish white to buff or greyish pink egg, marked with black or reddish brown, placed in slight depression along branch of tree, often high-up, or occasionally on rock. Both sexes incubate 30-36 days by sitting behind egg and covering it with fluffed out breast feathers. Chick has sharp claws to remain on swaying branch; it can fly *c.* 50 days but may not leave site finally until 100 or more days old. **322**

Gymnogyps californianus *Cathartidae*

CALIFORNIA CONDOR   *c.* 50 ins
Nearctic: confined to southern coastal mountains California, one of world's rarest birds. Breeds rocky gorges and canyons. Wingspan 9 to 10 ft. Generally dull black with whitish ruff and secondaries grey-edged; underwing coverts white; bare head orange to greyish yellow, shading to light grey on neck; purple patch side of neck; small red wattle below crop; legs whitish grey, bill grey, eyes dark brown. Immature has downy grey back, grey head, attains full plumage 5 to 7 years. Magnificent soaring flight, but spends much time perched, preening and sunning. Roosts up to 20 birds together. Silent. Food mainly carrion, travelling up to 50 miles to find it; also small ground squirrels. Breeds early February to May, on bare rock in cave or crevice, sometimes with narrow access. Single white egg incubated ♀ and ♂ at least 6 weeks. Chick fed by ♀ and ♂ until year old, remains on nest ledge 10 weeks, often much longer; only one brood every 2 years.

Gymnomystax mexicanus *Icteridae*

ORIOLE BLACKBIRD   12 ins
Neotropical: Guyanas, N Venezuela, E Colombia, E Ecuador, E Peru, parts Brazil; resident savannah, campos, gardens. Golden yellow; back, wings, tail black; large conical bill blackish also bare facial skin round dark brown eyes. Plumage shows convergence with Old World Golden Oriole, *Oriolus.* **909**

Gymnorhina dorsalis see under **G. tibicen**

Gymnorhina tibicen *Cracticidae*

AUSTRALIAN MAGPIE   17½ ins
Australasian: 9 races: S New Guinea E to Oriomo River; throughout continent except SW where replaced by Western Magpie, *G. dorsalis;* range of White-backed form *G. t. hypoleuca* includes S end Great Dividing Range, and 100 mile coastal belt through southern New South Wales, Victoria, S Australia; also Tasmania; both forms introduced New Zealand. Habitat: open woodland and pastures,

cultivated land and suburban areas with trees. ♂ *tibicen*: upperparts, including head, flight feathers, tail tip, and underparts, black; nape, rump, upper tail, shoulders, underwing white; legs black, bill blue grey tipped black; eyes orange brown. ♀ has lower nape and rump greyish, shorter bill than ♂. Juvenile mottled grey or buff on darker plumage, bill dark. ♂ *hypoleuca* has pure white back, grey in ♀ and juvenile; intergrades occur. Group territories (10 to 30 acres) occupied by up to 7 birds, usually dominant polygamous ♂ and mates or two 'socially equal' pairs. Flocks of non-territorial immatures move about nomadically. Steady flapping flight; aggressive to other birds and humans. Song: 'wonderful modulated whistle' (A. R. Wallace) from single birds and groups throughout year; thin contact and harsh aggressive calls. Diet: soil invertebrates, frogs, reptiles, small birds; grain; carrion. Breeds August to October; ♀ selects site and builds nest of twigs, lined softly, 20 to 50 ft up in outer canopy of eucalypt; also in bushes and human artefacts. Usually 3 or 4 variable but often blue-green eggs, densely spotted brown, incubated ♀, sometimes fed ♂, 20-21 days. Mainly ♀ feeds young, who fly *c.* 4 weeks, but are dependent up to 2 months. **984**

Gypaetus barbatus *Accipitridae*
LAMMERGEIER 40-45 ins
Palaearctic (S Europe, Middle East, N Africa) Ethiopian, Oriental (Afghanistan, India, Tibet). Sedentary with large territory, in high mountain ranges, foraging over steppes and plains; sometimes commensal. Upperparts, wings and tail blackish grey with white feather shafts, crown and face dirty white with mask of black 'hairs', which forms 'beard', underparts reddish buff; legs grey-black, bill dark horn, eyes yellow, red rimmed. Immature dark brown. Spends much of day away from settlements soaring and gliding up to 80 mph or perching on crags. Not aggressive. Usually silent, weak screams or whistles in display. Feeds on offal and carrion, drops bones to break them, scooping marrow with gouge-shaped tongue. Breeding season varies with distribution. Eggs laid January and February in North, June in South Africa, in cave or overhung ledge on crag or gorge, 1,000 to 14,000 ft up, in nest of dead sticks with motley lining. Usually 2 pale rufous eggs, mottled with brown and purple, incubated by ♀ or ♀ and ♂ *c.* 7½ weeks; both feed young, which fledge in *c.* 110 days. **146**

Gypohierax angolensis *Accipitridae*
PALM-NUT VULTURE 25 ins
Ethiopian region, coinciding with distribution of oil palm *Elaeis guineensis*. White, except for black on back, rounded wings and tail, which has white terminal band. Slight crest. Legs flesh to yellow; bill yellow, cere grey; skin pink round yellow legs. Immature plumage brown. Usual habitat along rivers, streams and by lakes, but also in savannah, even breeding far from oil palms. Tame and confiding towards man. Feeds from sunrise onwards on husks of oil palm nuts, *Raphia* fruits, crabs, molluscs, occasionally fish, snails, locusts. Call: growling *pruk-kurr,* high-pitched *tcheeu, karrr* when threatening; and quacks at roost. Sedentary, pair remaining near site, over which they roll and dive in display. Breeding season varies throughout range; nest of sticks usually in tree, 30 to 200 ft up. Single white egg, heavily marked dark brown and lilac, incubated by ♀ for *c.* 44 days; chick fledges in about three months. **147**

Gypopsitta vulturina *Psittacidae*
VULTURINE PARROT 9 ins
Neotropical: Brazil E of Amazon; resident in forest. Back green, scapulars orange; golden yellow collar bordered black round bare head with orange and black skin; tail blue, inner webs of outer feathers yellow; underparts greenish blue, under wing coverts and axillaries crimson. Habits in wild little known.

Gyps africanus *or Pseudogyps africanus Accipitridae*
AFRICAN WHITE-BACKED VULTURE 32 ins
Ethiopian: Senegal and Sudan south to Transvaal; on open plains, savannah and riverine strips. Upperparts brown, tail black, primaries blackish; underparts tawny brown; back and rump white; head and

neck blackish, down covered; pale under wing coverts distinguish from Ruppell's Vulture, *Gyps ruppellii;* legs black-brown; bill dark; eyes dark brown. Spends much time on wing once suitable thermals arise; also perches in parties, waiting for prey, to which it follows smaller scavengers. Display: slow circling over breeding site. Squeals at carcases; croaks at nest. Feeds exclusively on carrion. Breeds usually in dry season, singly or in loose colonies in trees, especially fever thorn; rather small flattish nest of sticks holds single white egg, sometimes blotched red, incubated by ♀ with ♂ often nearby. ♂ brings food to ♀; later both feed chick; whole breeding cycle 7-8 months. **148**

Gyps bengalensis *or Pseudogyps bengalensis Accipitridae*
INDIAN WHITE-BACKED VULTURE 35 ins
Oriental: Indian subcontinent to Burma and Indo-China. Generally sedentary: local movements e.g. to Afghanistan in summer. Found in cultivated, wooded country, not dense forests; often commensal. Generally blackish, rather glossy on back with white patch on lower back; secondaries look pale grey; white bar on underwing in flight; legs black; bill dark horn, eyes yellow-brown, bare head with dark grey neck. A late riser, soaring in suitable currents up to 9,000 ft; spends much time perched near food sources. Slow circling displays by pair close together. Variety of grunts, hisses and squeals. Lives exclusively on carrion. Lays one egg, faintly or boldly marked red and lavender-grey, in India mainly November to early January. Colonies in big trees in villages or along rivers, usually 40 to 60 ft up; nest of sticks, variously lined and built co-operatively by ♀ and ♂. Single egg, faintly or boldly marked red and lavender-grey, incubated 45-52 days by ♀ and ♂; chick fledges *c.* 3 months. **149**

Gyps fulvus *Accipitridae*
GRIFFON VULTURE 38-41 ins
Palaearctic (Europe, Middle East, NW Africa) and Oriental; winters NE Africa and N India. Lives in mountainous country, foraging in plains. Generally golden and sandy brown, much darker on flight feathers with pale under wing coverts; white 'woolly' ruff at base of down-covered head and neck; immature ruff brown; legs grey, bill horn, cere slate-grey, eyes golden to brown. Gregarious behaviour, taking off from roost when currents sufficient to sustain soaring flight, but perches about 16 hours a day. Slow circling display flight by pair over nest-site. Rather silent, but has variety of greeting grunts, anxiety whistles and threat hisses. Lives exclusively on carrion, fought over until dominance order worked out. Lays November to February; colonial, 50 to 60 pairs on crags; nest in overhung or crevice site, flattish, of sticks with lining, sometimes green built by ♀ and ♂, who incubate single white egg, occasionally flecked red-brown, for *c.* 52 days. Fledging period 110-115 days.

Gyps ruppellii see under **G. africanus**

HADADA IBIS see **Hagedashia hagedash**

Haematopus bachmani see under **H. moquini**

Haematopus moquini *Haematopodidae*
AFRICAN BLACK OYSTERCATCHER *c.* 20 ins
Ethiopian: confined to W, S and SE coasts of Southern Africa, though black forms occur in W Nearctic and New Zealand and have been given distinct specific status as *H. bachmani* and *H. unicolor.* Their habits are all very similar. Resident on sandy beaches, rocky coasts, lagoons and estuaries. Glossy black all over; legs pink, bill vermilion, eyes red with orange orbits. Immature duller, with mottled underparts. Habits much as Oystercatcher, *H. ostralegus* with similar calls, feeding and nesting habits, but eggs usually only 1 or 2; breeding season Cape Province, November to May. **253**

Haematopus ostralegus *Haematopodidae*
OYSTERCATCHER *c.* 17 ins
Range almost cosmopolitan but discontinuous and confusion exists on status of black oystercatchers (see African Black Oystercatcher *H. moquini*). Palaearctic

(coasts of Europe, large inland area Central Asia, local to Siberian and Korean coasts); Australasian (Continental Australia, Tasmania, South Island NZ); Nearctic (W coast and extreme SE North America); Neotropical coasts (except extreme S), but American birds often separated as *H. palliatus.* Partly sedentary but extreme N and S populations migrate, northern birds reaching S Africa. Haunts rocky, shingly and sandy coasts and similar habitats inland, also valley fields, moorland, even open woodland; muddy shores and estuaries outside breeding season. Upperparts glossy black with broad white wingbar; underparts, rump white, tail with black terminal band; whitish half-collar on non-breeding birds. Legs pink, bill orange red, eyes dark red with orange orbits. Scorns concealment, flying with fast, shallow beats or running along shore; swims and dives if attacked. Huge flocks form in winter. Usual *kleep* call reiterated at speed by piping parties, heads down, bills open, to end in trill; also sharp *pic pic* of alarm or aggression. Mutual displays by pair. Breeds from early April in N temperate, making scrape, often ornamentally lined, on shingle, sand, rocks, grass and moorland. 2 to 4 light buff eggs, spotted and scrawled black-brown, incubated by ♀ and ♂ 24-27 days. Young, tended by ♀ and ♂, leave nest 1-2 days, fly *c.* 5 weeks. **254**

Haematopus unicolor see under **H. moquini**

Hagedashia hagedash *Threskiornithidae*
HADADA IBIS 30 ins
Ethiopian, except SW quarter. Resident along wooded riversides and on coastal swamps and shores. Generally olive-grey, paler on head, neck and underparts; iridescent green shows on back and rounded wings in good light; flight feathers, rump and tail iridescent blue-black; legs and bill crimson to black, eyes whitish. Juvenile duller, with shorter bill. Usually in pairs or small flocks but forming large roosts. Flight powerful with bill pointing downward; legs do not project beyond tail. Well known alarm call *haha hahaha,* also 'loud mournful note'. Feeds along banks and on shore on large insects, snails and worms. Breeding season varies with latitude; nest usually on bough over river, also in creepers or trees on cliff: small platform of sticks lined with grass. Usually 3 grey-green or buff eggs with brownish markings, incubated for *c.* 4 weeks; young fly *c.* 5 weeks. **83**

HAIRY WOODPECKER see **Dendrocopus villosus**

Halcyon leucocephala *Alcedinidae*
GREY-HEADED KINGFISHER 8 ins
Ethiopian: most of sub-Saharan Africa except Congolese rain forest area; also S Arabia. Some birds winter southern Africa, move N to breed in Malawi, Zambia, S Zaire. Found woodland savannah, dry bush, feeding entirely on land, pouncing down from look-out perch on tree, wire on to insects, small reptiles in grass. Call a weak, chattering *ji ji ji.* Head, nape ashy brown or grey; back black, rump, tail, flight feathers bright greenish blue; throat, breast white; flanks, belly, under wing, tail coverts dark chestnut; bill, feet red. 3-5 white, round glossy eggs in short tunnel in bank. **488**

Halcyon sancta *Alcedinidae*
SACRED KINGFISHER 9 ins
Australasian: New Guinea, New Hebrides, New Caledonia, most of continental Australia, Tasmania, New Zealand; summer visitor to southern part of range wintering SE Asia; in open forest usually near river, lake or estuary; cultivated land and gardens in NZ. Upperparts greenish blue but inner webs of flight feathers and tail brown; black band from bill round neck; throat white; collar and underparts buffish white; legs brown, bill black, eyes brown. Juveniles darker below. Feeds from water or land, plunging or flopping in after fish, chasing lizards and frogs; also crustaceans, land and water insects, worms; sometimes mice, small birds. Loud *kee kee kee* is territorial call; loud repeated *krech* ending in scream during display, also used when alarmed. Breeds October to January in Australia and NZ, in hollow limb of tree, termites's nest, burrow excavated in bank 4 to 9 ins

with nest chamber 6 to 8 ins wide. 4 to 6 glossy white eggs incubated by ♀ and ♂ *c.* 18 days; both feed young, who fly *c.* 24 days. **489**

Halcyon senegalensis *Alcedinidae*
WOODLAND or ANGOLA KINGFISHER   8 ins
Ethiopian: most of tropical Africa but absent Somalia, eastern parts Kenya, Tanzania, and Congolese rain forest zone; also found eastern S Africa. Replaced by very similar Mangrove Kingfisher, *H. senegaloides*, down E coast. Similar habitat, behaviour to preceding species but appearance less striking, voice more. Generally pale blue, to grey on head, white on belly; wing tips coverts black; legs black; upper bill red, lower black. Makes single sharp high-pitched note, followed by descending trill endlessly repeated in breeding season, usually coinciding with early rains. Nests principally natural tree-holes (has taken nest-box); mainly ♀ incubates 3 to 5 white eggs *c.* 13 days. Young, fed by both parents, fledge 18-22 days. **490**

Halcyon senegaloides see under **H. senegalensis**

Halcyon smyrnensis *Alcedinidae*
WHITE-BREASTED KINGFISHER   10 ins
SE Palaearctic (Asia Minor, Iran) and almost whole mainland of Oriental region; locally migratory. Habitat: woodland and cultivated land both near and distant from water; flooded paddyfields, ponds, sea shores. Head, neck, flanks, undertail dark chocolate brown; rump, most of wings, tail, turquoise blue; purple blue on wing coverts; flight feathers dark brown; legs and heavy pointed bill red, eyes dark brown. Solitary or in pairs, feeding in forest on lizards, grasshoppers, other insects, worms, occasionally mice and birds; crabs from shore and paddyfields, fish from water; has territory and favourite hunting perches. 'Song' long-drawn, tremulous whistling *kililili* repeated again and again from treetop, each phrase ending in snipe-like *peent;* loud cackling flight call. Distinctive wing pattern plays part in display. Breeds January to August in Indian sub-continent, ♀ and ♂ excavating tunnel up to 3 ft in bank; both incubate 4-7 round white eggs and feed young. **491**

Haliaeetus albicilla *Accipitridae*
WHITE-TAILED EAGLE   27-36 ins (♀ larger than ♂)
Holarctic: from Norway and Mediterranean to Siberia, Japan, Kuriles, Greenland and Iceland. Migrates southward to Oriental region, occasionally Africa, some populations sedentary. Habitat: sea coasts, large river valleys and lakes; in Asia up to 7,000 feet. Generally dark brown all over; wing-tips grey; wedge-shaped tail white (brown when immature); legs yellow; bill and cere pale yellow, eyes yellow. Flies low to hunt, snatching fish from surface or diving. Displays throughout year, fierce fights known. Roosts on trees or crags. Feeds on fish, sometimes stranded water birds, fair sized mammals or carrion. Variety of barking calls with head thrown up or back, ♀ deeper than ♂. Lays from February in S and to April or May in N of range. Builds nest of sticks and debris on crag or tree with 1 to 3, usually 2, dull white eggs, incubated by ♀, but ♂ often at nest, for 37-40 days. Young fed by ♀ and ♂ for about 70 days. **150**

Haliaeetus leucogaster *Accipitridae*
WHITE BREASTED SEA EAGLE   25-27 ins
Oriental and Australasian: India to South China, New Guinea, Bismarck Archipelago, Australia and Tasmania. Habitat: sea coasts and up large rivers, especially in open country. All white except for grey-brown back, upper wing and upper tail coverts; legs yellowish white; cere bluish grey, eyes hazel brown. Immature, shades of brown all over. Slim and graceful for an eagle, spends much time soaring or perched on rocks and trees; pairs often seen together with regular roost. Soaring increases in display period. Feeds chiefly on fish and sea snakes, also takes young water birds, mammals and carrion, and robs nests in heronries. Loud, nasal *ahahah* call, duck-like quack, and duets with heads pointing upward. Breeding season prolonged and varies with latitude; nest of sticks 50 to 100 feet up on high tree or rock with 2 or 3 pure white, coarse textured eggs, usually incubated by ♀

for 40 or more days, relief periods by ♂. Chicks fledge 65-70 days but are dependent for 6 months. **151**

Haliaeetus vocifer or Cuncuma vocifer *Accipitridae*
AFRICAN FISH EAGLE   30 ins
Mainly Ethiopian; migrates locally. Haunts vicinity of rivers, lakes and swamps up to 4,000 ft. Head, upper breast, mantle and tail white, rump and much of wings black, rest of body rich chestnut. Immature shows much more brown. Legs yellowish to flesh, bill and claws black, cere yellow, eyes hazel brown. Usually seen perched on tall tree above water, gregarious when food plentiful. Hunts in early morning for fish, alive or dead, water birds, even flamingos, and some carrion. Evening display. Calls with clear, yelping *weech-hye-hye-hya* from perch or wing, *quok* of alarm; very noisy, throwing head upward and backward. Breeding season varies throughout range, usually at onset of dry season. Several eyries of sticks with lining of plant material in tall trees or crags, sometimes in bushes or on ground. Usually 2 white slightly glossy eggs incubated 44-45 days usually by ♀. Chicks fledge in 65-75 days and are fed by both parents. **152**

Haliastur sphenorus *Accipitridae*
WHISTLING EAGLE or KITE   20-22 ins
Continental Australia, not Tasmania, East New Guinea, New Caledonia. Usually vicinity of water but also open, dry country. Nomadic rather than migratory. Generally rich brown with pale margins to feathers of back and wing-coverts, wing-tips black, tail tipped grey; legs yellow, bill yellow to grey, eyes dark brown. Immature darker than adult. Wings held level with body in flight, like kite, easy and buoyant. Usually found in pairs or small parties. Nuptial displays in flocks. Feeds on rabbits, small mammals, reptiles, fish, insects, carrion. Call a loud whistling *chew-ew-ew* during day and dusk. Peak of laying July to October; nest of sticks usually in outstanding tree along river, holds 2 or 3 bluish white eggs marked brown and purple. Incubated probably by ♀ for *c.* 4 weeks; chicks fledge in at least 40 days. **153**

HAMERKOP see **Scopus umbretta**

HARLEQUIN DUCK see **Histrionicus histrionicus**

HARMAN'S EARED PHEASANT see **Crossoptilon crossoptilon**

Harpia harpyja *Accipitridae*
HARPY EAGLE   34-37 ins
Neotropical: S Mexico to E Bolivia, S Brazil, N Argentina; inhabits lowland tropical forest. Upperparts marbled slaty-black, head ash-grey with divided blackish crest; tail grey barred black; underparts white with black upper breast; thighs barred black; legs pale yellow, bill and lores blackish, eyes light brown. Remarkably inconspicuous in spite of size; soaring in display not recorded. Loud wailing call at nest. Lives mainly on tree-living mammals: monkeys, sloths, opossums, also agoutis from ground. Probably lays April in Brazil. Builds at great height in trees e.g. silk cotton *Ceiba pentandra* large nest of sticks lined with greenery. Lays probably 2 eggs, pure white before staining. Incubation and fledging periods not known but breeds every other year.

HARPY EAGLE see **Harpia harpyja**

HARRIER,
    AFRICAN MARSH see **Circus ranivorus**
    BROWN see **Circaetus cinereus**
    SWAMP see **Circus approximans**

HARRIER HAWK, AFRICAN see **Polyboroides typus**

HARTLAUB'S
    BUSTARD see **Lissotis hartlaubii**
    GULL see **Larus novaehollandiae**
    TOURACO see under **Tauraco livingstonii**

HAWAIIAN GOOSE see **Branta sandvicensis**

HAWFINCH see **Coccthraustes coccothraustes**

HAWK,
    AFRICAN HARRIER see **Polyboroides typus**
    BROWN see **Falco berigora**
    GALAPAGOS see **Buteo galapagoensis**
    RED-SHOULDERED see **Buteo lineatus**
    SAVANNAH see **Heterospizias meridionalis**

HAWK,
    EAGLE, LONG-CRESTED see **Lophoaetus occipitalis**
    OWL see **Surnia ulula**

HAZELHEN see **Tetrastes bonasus**

HEDGE ACCENTOR see **Prunella modularis**

HEERMANN'S GULL see **Larus heermanni**

HELMETBIRD see **Aerocharis prevostii**

HELMET
    FRIARBIRD see **Philemon yorki**
    SHRIKE, STRAIGHT-CRESTED see **Prionops plumata**
    SHRIKE, WHITE see **Prionops plumata**

HELMETED
    GUINEAFOWL see under **Numida meleagris**
    HONEYEATER see **Meliphaga cassidix**

Helmitheros vermivorus *Parulidae*
WORM-EATING WARBLER   5½ ins
Nearctic: S New England, W New York, N Indiana, S Iowa S to Virginia, N Georgia, S Missouri; winters Bahamas, W Indies, Central America from Chiapos to Panama. Habitat secondary woodland of youngish trees with thick understorey; also scrub-clad hillsides above swamps or streams. Upperparts, including wings, tail, olive-green; buff head with 4 black stripes; underparts pale buff; legs light brown, bill yellowish horn, eyes dark brown. Juveniles browner; immature like adult with rusty brown on wings. Usually seen on ground among dead leaves, walking slowly, bobbing head, carrying tail high, looking for small invertebrates; also climbs tree trunks like Black and White Warbler, *Mniotilta varia*. Call: sharp *dzt;* song rapid trill, loud and rich, fluctuating in volume; resembles Chipping Sparrow, *Spizella passerina;* twittering flight song. Breeds May to July, ♀ accompanied ♂, building nest of dead leaves, grass, rootlets, lined moss-stalks, hair, fine bents: on ground usually sheltered by small bush, or on slope in drift of leaves. 3 to 6 white eggs, variably marked brown, incubated ♀ *c.* 13 days; ♀ and ♂ feed young; injury-feigning common at nest. **894**

Hemerodromus africanus or Rhinoptilus africanus *Glareolidae*
TWO-BANDED COURSER   9 ins
Ethiopian: several races covering most of region. Resident rocky thorn scrub, sandy plains and salt deserts. Upperparts tawny (grey-brown in race *gracilis* of Kenya and Tanzania) mottled black and buff crescents; outer primaries black, secondaries and inner primaries tawny; upper tail coverts white above mottled tail; streaks on face and neck; underparts from throat buff with two narrow black bands across chest; underwings and axillaries white; legs white, bill black, eyes brown. Usually in pairs or small parties, very reluctant to fly, but utters plover-like *pee-wee* when flushed; longer, whickering call on night flights. Diet: insects, especially beetles and flies. Breeding season November in Tanzania. One egg, creamy buff scrawled dark brown with grey spots, laid in scrape fully in open; incubation probably by ♀ alone. **312**

Hemiprocne longipennis *Hemiprocnidae*
INDIAN CRESTED SWIFT   8 ins
Oriental: widespread throughout region; resident in

wooded country from coastal mangrove swamps, rubber estates, residential areas and forests up to 4,000 ft in Malaysia. Upperparts green, including crown and pointed vertical crest on forehead; bronze wash on neck; flight feathers and long, needle-like tail dark green (ear coverts chestnut in ♂); rump, throat, breast, flanks grey; belly, undertail white. Perches bare treetops, sitting upright with crest erect, frequently opening and closing tail feathers. Small flocks collect for 'joy flights' (T. H. Harrisson), also sweep low to surface of water to sip and up again; take insects by aerial sallies from perch on forest edge or by river; odd birds quarter air in regular sweeps (Lord Medway); c. 6 attacked swarm of bees over forest (B. E. Smythies). Calls: double *whit-tuck whit-tuck,* loud parrot-like *kia kia kia* or *kip kee keep* from perch or in flight. Breeds December to July, varying throughout range, fashioning minute shallow half-saucer of bark and feathers cemented by saliva and attached to side of horizontal, often dead branch, resembling knot. Single greyish-white egg fits 'like acorn in cup' (Smythies), incubated by ♀ and ♂ sitting across branch, which takes weight, and covering egg with feathers.

HEN, SWAMP see under **Porphyrio porphyrio**

HERMIT
   HUMMINGBIRD, LONG-TAILED see **Phaethornis superciliosus**
   THRUSH see under **Hylocichla ustulatus**

HERON
   BOATBILL see **Cochlearius cochlearius**
   GOLIATH see **Ardea goliath**
   GREAT WHITE see **Casmerodius albus**
   GREY see **Ardea cinerea**
   LITTLE BLUE see **Florida caerulea**
   LOUISIANA see **Hydranassa tricolor**
   NIGHT see **Nycticorax nycticorax**
   REEF see **Egretta sacra**
   WHITE-FACED see **Notophoyx novaehollandiae**
   YELLOW-CROWNED NIGHT see **Nyctanassa violacea**

Herpetotheres cachinnans *Falconidae*
LAUGHING FALCON   18-22 ins
Neotropical: Mexico S to E Bolivia, N Argentine, Paraguay, S Brazil; in broken humid forest or drier wooded country. Upperparts dark brown; head, neck and underparts buff, with black shaft-streaks on crown and black mask extending round neck; tail barred black and white; legs and cere dull yellow, bill black, eyes dark brown. Small rough scales on legs probably protective adaptation against venomous bites. Spends much time sitting upright on perch, seldom flying or soaring, but when hunting sometimes moves neck through 180°, then pounces with thud on prey, usually snakes, but also lizards. Two-note call gives Costa Rican name *Guaco;* may be repeated fifty times; apparent duets by pair. Breeding season first half April in Mexico. Nests in cavity in tree top or where limb broken off, sometimes in old nest of other species. Lays single whitish egg, heavily marked with rich brown. Details of incubation and fledging not known; ♂ brings food to ♀ and chick.

HERRING GULL see **Larus argentatus**

Hesperiphona vespertina *Fringillidae*
EVENING GROSBEAK   8 ins
Nearctic, Neotropical: breeds from Central British Columbia, N Michigan southward in mountains to S Mexico; locally E to Gulf of St Lawrence; winter range much wider: E to New England, S to Maryland, Kentucky, Missouri, lowlands in western states. Summer habitat northern conifer zone. ♂: basically yellow, but tail, primaries and some wing coverts black, inner secondaries and coverts white; hind crown, nape, cheeks, upper mantle, chin to centre breast dark brown. ♀: yellow and brown areas much paler; white wing bar primaries, more white secondaries, white on tail, including tip. Legs brown, very large bill chalky white (winter), pale green (summer), eyes dark brown. Flocks in winter; characteristic undulating flight. Calls: chirp like House Sparrow, *Passer*

domesticus, also chattering; song: series of short, abrupt musical warbles, ending in shrill whistle. Food: buds, fruit, seeds, e.g. box elder, ash-leaved maple; seeds, insects in summer; attracted to bird tables, especially by sunflower seeds, salt, sometimes to new localities. Breeds May-June in small groups; nest foundation small twigs, cup lined fine rootlets, usually in dense needle cluster near end of lateral branch of conifer, 20 to 60 ft up. 3 or 4 blue green eggs, lightly marked grey, olive, dark brown, incubated ♀. **925**

Heterospizias meridionalis *Accipitridae*
SAVANNAH HAWK   20-25 ins
Neotropical: E Panama to Ecuador, E Peru, Bolivia and Central Argentina; inhabits grassland with scattered marshes or tree-lined ponds. Generally rufous brown with darker mantle and wing-coverts; tail black with white tip and broad bar, wing-tips black, whitish areas round black bill; legs and cere yellow, eyes orange. Immature has buffish white underparts and is generally mottled or barred dark brown. Long-legged, with upright stance, appearing sluggish but able to move rapidly. Hunts marshland vertebrates and many insects, follows grass fires. Soars and plays with nest material in air. High-pitched call ending in wail, also snarling *wiek* on wing. Breeding season probably variable; eggs laid March, April in Trinidad, usually in isolated tree. Nest of thin sticks lined with grasses; 1 or 2 bluish eggs sometimes with reddish spots. Details of incubation and fledging uncertain. **154**

Hieraetus pennatus *Accipitridae*
BOOTED EAGLE   18-21 ins
Palaearctic and Oriental: Spain, North Africa: S Asia E to Central China: some migrate to Africa and Indian subcontinent in winter. Inhabits woodland both deciduous and coniferous from sea level up to 10,000 ft. Two phases: normal pale adult has dark brown mantle and wings (with lighter bars) and barred tail; head, neck, underparts light tawny brown to white, uppertail coverts light buff. Dark phase almost uniform dark-brown with paler areas on head and upper tail coverts. Legs feathered, feet and cere yellow, bill dark, eyes brown. High pitched double whistle: *ki-kiee* and scream *kleeek.* Dashing, swift flight, often among tree-tops; roosts on trees and rocks; pair usually close together and perform spectacular diving and swooping displays. Hunts, over open country as well as woodland, birds up to partridge size, small mammals and reptiles. Lays from March to May according to range usually in tree, sometimes on rock; nest of sticks lined with greenery, holds 2 white eggs, marked brown. Incubated by ♀ for at least a month. Young, fed by both parents, fledge in about 2 months. **155**

HILDEBRANDT'S STARLING see under **Spreo superbus**

HILL MYNAH, INDIAN see **Gracula religiosa**

Himantopus himantopus *Recurvirostridae*
BLACK-WINGED or
BLACK-NECKED STILT   *c.* 15 (bill *c.* 2½) ins
Cosmopolitan: breeds between 50°N and S in five main areas; SE Palaearctic and Oriental (Central Europe and Egypt to Indo-China); Australasian, including New Zealand; Ethiopian (band S of Sahara to S Africa); S Nearctic and Neotropical (S USA to NW South America; subtropical S America); also local S Mediterranean area; partly resident or locally migratory. Habitat: vegetated shores of shallow fresh and brackish pools, salt marshes, wet hay and rice fields; coastal lagoons chiefly in winter. Winter ♂ white except for glossy black mantle and wings; back of crown and nape dusky in summer; ♀ as winter ♂ but wings black-brown; very long legs pink, straight bill black, eyes crimson. Juvenile brown on head, nape and wings. Some races e.g. American, Australian, have black from head down nape and are sometimes regarded as distinct species: *H. mexicana, H. leucocephalus;* a black subspecies *H. h. novaeseelandiae* is local in South Island, New Zealand. Usually in parties or small flocks; flies with legs projecting 6½ to 7 ins

beyond tail, sometimes used to navigate. Long strides when walking, with neck partly withdrawn. Sharp repeated *kik kik kik* call on breeding grounds. Mutual dancing displays. Takes variety of small water animals by deep wading. Breeds socially from end April in Spain; lined scrape, open on mud or hidden in local, e.g. salt marsh, plants, holds 3 or 4 pale stone eggs, spotted or blotched dark brown and grey. Incubation by ♀ and ♂ 25-26 days; both tend brood for 30-31 days. **301**

Himantopus
   leucocephalus see under **H. himantopus**
   mexicana see under **H. himantopus**

Hippolais polyglotta *Muscicapidae: Sylviinae*
MELODIOUS WARBLER   5 ins
Palaearctic: breeds France, Iberia, Italy, Sicily and N African coast from Morocco to Tunis; winters tropical W Africa. Habitat: riverine woodland, gardens, roadsides with broadleaved trees, scrub often in marshy areas; in winter gardens and cultivations. Upperparts uniform brownish olive, pale yellow 'eyebrow' and eyering; underparts pale yellow, wings and tail darker. Legs grey, bill (quite heavy) dark brown, eyes dark brown. Appears to flutter like young bird when flying; active and restless. Call: sparrow-like chatter; song rich, musical and varied, often imitative. Has parachuting song flight. Food: insects, also berries in autumn. Breeds mid May onwards; builds neat compact grass nest in bushes, especially oleanders. 4 or 5 dull rose-pink eggs with black spots and streaks, incubated ♀ 12 days. Young, fed by both parents, fledge 12 days. Sometimes 2 broods. **739**

Hirundo abyssinica or Cecropis abyssinica
Hirundinidae
STRIPED SWALLOW   7 ins
Ethiopian: 5 races; resident in semi-arid belt from Sierra Leone to Ethiopia then S to Cape; some local migration. Habitat: anywhere outside forest, often near houses and bridges. Head and rump deep tawny; mantle blue-black; underparts white, profusely streaked with black; wings and tail blue-black, latter with white spots and elongated outer feathers; under wing coverts tawny. ♀ has shorter tail. Young duller. Legs brown, bill black, eyes brown. Quite tame and has typical 'flutter and sail' flight. Voice 2 or 3 tinny mewing chirps and some nasal squeaks; song, pleasant series of organ-like notes. Food: aerial insects. Breeding season variable within range; colonial, builds retort-shaped mud nest with long entrance in caves and under roofs. Usually 3 pure white eggs. **610**

Hirundo albigularis *Hirundinidae*
WHITE-THROATED SWALLOW   6½ ins
Ethiopian; breeds from Rhodesia and Angola S to Cape; winter area not known but recorded Zambia and Angola. Habitat: open country often near water and/or human habitation. Upperparts similar to *H. rustica* with prominent chestnut forehead, throat white, blue-black band across chest often broken in centre, rest underparts greyish-white; wings dark, tail with white patches on inner webs and outer feathers slightly elongated. ♀ has shorter tail. Feet and bill black, eyes brown. Very fast flier. Normally occurs singly or in pairs. Call and song a soft twittering. Food aerial insects. Breeds mainly November to January, building open cup nest of mud, softly lined, plastered to wall or cliff or under eaves of verandah. 3 or 4 eggs, pinkish-white with reddish and slate spots; incubation and fledging much as *H. rustica.* **611**

Hirundo cucullata or Cecropis cucullata *Hirundinidae*
LARGER STRIPED SWALLOW   7½ ins
Ethiopian; breeds Cape Province, Natal and Transvaal; winters Angola, Tanzania, Zambia and S Zaire. Habitat: open country, usually near human habitations. Top of head and nape chestnut with narrow glossy blue-black streaks; mantle and wings glossy steel blue, rump tawny; sides of face, ear coverts and underparts whitish streaked dusky; tail has white spots. Legs dusky brown, bill black, eyes brown. Call: sparrow-like *chissik* or *chi-chi-chi;* constant twittering when in flock; also short, cheerful song.

Food: aerial insects. Breeds in southern summer. Mud nest large and building takes a long time, but same nest often used in successive years; retort-shaped with tubular entrance passage; in buildings and caves, rocks, culverts, drainpipes. 3 or 4 white eggs. **612**

Hirundo daurica or Cecropis daurica *Hirundinidae*
RED-RUMPED SWALLOW   7 ins
Palaearctic, Oriental, (Ethiopian): 12 races breed S Europe, N Africa, Asia Minor, S Iran to Himalayas, Indian subcontinent, Ceylon; also S Siberia, Korea, parts of Japan. Five races resident and breeding across S Sahara to Ethiopia, then S to Malawi, often considered separate *H. rufula;* and scattered populations SE Asia (e.g. Indo-China, Philippines, Lesser Sunda Is) as *H. striolata*. Habits of all three much the same. Southern races *daurica* resident, northern ones winter in southern breeding areas. Habitat from tropical savannah to temperate mountains, up to 15,500 ft Himalayas, also rocky limestone country, sea coasts, towns (e.g. Morocco, Israel). Upperparts blue-black, except for chestnut forehead, nape, rump; underparts buff, streaked darker; wings and deeply forked tail metallic blue; legs brown-black, bill black, eyes dark brown. Deliberate flight, also soars like House Martin, *Delichon urbica,* but not as gregarious. Distinctive 'wailing' flight-call rendered *quitsch;* nasal song similar to but not as pleasing as *H. rustica*. Food: aerial insects. Breeds early May to July in Europe, suspending distinctive spouted mud nest, softly lined, from roof of cave, cleft, inside various buildings. 3 to 5 pure white eggs; 2 broods. **613**

Hirundo dimidiata *Hirundinidae*
PEARL-BREASTED SWALLOW   5½ ins
Ethiopian: 2 races; resident, *dimidiata* in Rhodesia and Damaraland to Cape; *marwitzi,* Angola and Zambia to SW Tanzania. Habitat: open woodland and cultivated country. Upperparts including sides of face, breast, wings and tail, glossy steel blue; underparts white, greyer on chest; no white in tail. ♀ has shorter outer tail feathers. Young have greenish wash above. Legs and bill black, eyes brown. Song characteristic *chip-cheree-chip-chip* usually from perch. Food: aerial insects. Breeds mainly September to January, bowl-shaped mud nest built largely by ♂ plastered to wall and usually supported on ledge; also deep in wells. 3 pure white eggs. **614**

Hirundo fuligula or Ptyonoprogne fuligula
Hirundinidae
AFRICAN ROCK MARTIN   4¾ ins
Ethiopian: 7 races; resident (some local migration) in all Africa S of Sahara. Habitat: precipitous cliffs and, increasingly, in towns, never far from water. Dark sooty brown except chin to chest and under wing coverts, which are pale russet; tail slightly forked with conspicuous white spots in flight; legs dusky brown, bill black, eyes brown. Flies weakly and does not stray far from habitat except when congregating round grass fire. Call: low twitter or high-pitched *twee;* song: high-pitched *cheep-cheep-cheep-churr* repeated several times, in flight. Food: aerial insects. Breeding season variable within range; builds mud and grass cup on ledge or half-cup against wall, if possible in overhung angle. Usually 3 white eggs, freely spotted with brown. **615**

Hirundo rufula see under **H. daurica**

Hirundo rupestris or Ptyonoprogne rupestris
Hirundinidae
CRAG MARTIN   5¾ ins
Palaearctic: 2 races; *H.r. rupestris* breeds S Europe N to Pyrenees, Alps, Greece, Mediterranean islands, Morocco, Algeria, Asia Minor and across to all but easternmost China; winters in southern breeding range S to Sudan, Ethiopia, and S India. Race *theresae* apparently resident high in Atlas Mts. Habitat: mountain gorges, inland and coastal cliffs. Rather bulky, with broad triangular wings; upperparts brown, underparts buffish with streaked throat, no breast band; white circles on tail. Feeds on aerial insects off cliff faces and repeats same path along face several times. Call and song a weak twittering. Long

breeding season; builds half-cup mud nest softly lined in cleft rocks, caves, ruined or sometimes occupied buildings, in small colonies, often with other swallows and swifts. 3 or 4 white eggs, finely spotted brown; incubated 14 days. Young fledge 25-26 days. **616**

Hirundo rustica *Hirundinidae*
(BARN) SWALLOW   7½ ins
Holarctic, marginally Oriental: 7 (or 8) races; breeds in whole Palaearctic between 30°N and 70°N, extending to SE China and Taiwan; all N America (except some SE States and nothern half of Canada). Old World races winter Africa S of 12°N, Indian subcontinent and to N Australia; New World races from Panama to Central Chile and N Argentina. Habitat: open cultivated country with farms and buildings, usually near water. Upperparts metallic blue; forehead chestnut; chin and throat dark chestnut; lower throat has dark blue band, rest of underparts creamy to rufous-buff; tail deeply forked, with white spots. ♀ has shorter tail and less metallic throat band. Juvenile duller, short-tailed. Legs and bill black, eyes dark brown. Not very gregarious in summer but collects in autumn flocks and huge roosts in reed-beds, other vegetation. Call: characteristic *tswit-tswit;* song: warbling twitter with short trill. Food: insects from air and water surface. Breeds mid May to September, ♀ and ♂ building open mud and straw nest, lined feathers, on ledge usually in building of some kind; natural sites in caves or on cliffs now very rare. Usually 4 or 5 white eggs, marked reddish spots over ashy grey. Incubation mainly by ♀ 14-15 days. Young, fed by both parents, fledge *c.* 21 days. 2 (sometimes 3) broods. **617**

Hirundo senegalensis or Cecropis senegalensis *Hirundinidae*
MOSQUE SWALLOW   9 ins
Ethiopian: 3 races; resident from Senegal to Kordofan (Sudan) to 8°N, coastal Ghana and Congo E to Ethiopia then S to Zambia, Malawi and Mozambique; considerable local movements in small parties. Habitat: commonest in large timber woodland, also by houses. Plumage like *H. daurica* but no chestnut on nape; upperparts blue-black with chestnut rump; underparts, including tail coverts, pale rufous; legs and bill black, eyes brown. Rather lethargic and has the 'flutter and sail' flight as *H. abyssinica*. Calls: single note like tin trumpet and guttural croak; song a low twitter. Food: aerial insects. Breeding season variable within range; occupies hole in tree, filling it to correct size with mud, or builds large retort-shaped mud nest under cliff or bridge, or (if in house) rim of mud on board. 3 or 4 pure white eggs. **618**

Hirundo smithii *Hirundinidae*
WIRE-TAILED SWALLOW   6 ins
Ethiopian, Oriental: 2 races; resident, *H. s. smithii* in W Ghana to Benguela, and E Ethiopia to Zambia and Natal outside rain-forest areas; *filifera* in Afghanistan, most of Indian subcontinent, N Thailand, Laos, S Annam. Habitat: towns and villages, open country. Head chestnut, rest of upperparts glossy violet-blue, lores brown; underparts white; tail with white patches and very narrow, elongated outer feathers. ♀ has much shorter tail. Young much duller. Legs and bill black, eyes brown. Rather solitary. Call: low twitter seldom heard. Food: aerial insects. Breeding season variable within range; builds open or half-cup nest of mud, lined feathers, placed very close to overhang and not supported below. Usually 3 eggs, white with rather heavy reddish or brown spots. Incubation by ♀ 14 days. Young, fed by both parents, fly 18 to 21 days. **619**

Hirundo striolata see under **H. daurica**

HISPANIOLA PARROT see **Amazonia ventralis**

Histrionicus histrionicus *Anatidae*
HARLEQUIN DUCK   16 ins
Holarctic: Atlantic race, *H. h. histrionicus,* breeds Iceland, Greenland, N Labrador, wintering S to Long Island, NY; Pacific, *pacificus,* breeds E Siberia and N America from S Alaska to mountains of California and Colorado; winters S to California and Japan. Habitat:

swift rivers and streams; winter: coastal, off rough, rocky shores. ♂: striking white markings bordered by black on blue-grey head and body; stripe on crown and flanks chestnut red; speculum metallic purple; longish tail dark brown. ♀: grey-brown with white patches on head, larger one on cheek, two smaller ones in front of and behind eyes. Legs pale bluish, short bill lead-blue, nail whitish, eyes reddish-brown; all duller on ♀. Usually in small parties, swimming buoyantly, sometimes in formation and not associating with other species. Walks easily, flies swiftly in small compact flocks, often swinging from side to side. ♂ has soft whistle, ♀ croaks. Day feeder, using short dive, sometimes from wing, taking small water animals. Breeds May to July, often socially, on small islands in shelter of rocks or vegetation. 5 to 8 creamy or light buff eggs laid in nest of down and plant debris; incubated by ♀ *c.* 28 days; she tends young, who fly *c.* 40 days. **116**

HOATZIN see **Opisthocomus hoatzin**

HONEY BUZZARD see **Pernis apivorus**

HONEY BUZZARD, CRESTED see under **Pernis apivorus**

HONEYCREEPER,
  PURPLE see **Cyanerpes caeruleus**
  YELLOW-LEGGED see **Cyanerpes caeruleus**

HONEYEATER,
  BLACK see **Myzomela nigra**
  BLUE-FACED see **Entomyzon cyanotus**
  HELMETED see **Meliphaga cassidix**
  SPINY-CHEEKED see **Acanthagenys rufogularis**
  STRIPED see **Plectorhyncha lanceolata**
  TAWNY-CROWNED see **Gliciphila melanops**
  WHITE-BEARDED see **Meliornis novaehollandiae**
  WHITE-CHEEKED see **Meliornis niger**
  WHITE-EARED see **Meliphaga leucotis**
  WHITE-FRONTED see **Gliciphila albifrons**
  YELLOW-FACED see **Meliphaga chrysops**
  YELLOW-TUFTED see **Meliphaga melanops**
  YELLOW-WINGED see **Meliornis novaehollandiae**

HONEYGUIDE, LESSER see **Indicator minor**

HOODED
  CROW see **Corvus corone**
  DOTTEREL see **Charadrius cucullatus**
  MERGANSER see **Mergus cucullatus**
  ROBIN see **Petroica cucullata**
  WHEATEAR see **Oenanthe monacha**

HOOPOE see **Upupa epops**

HOOPOE,
  FOREST WOOD see under **Phoeniculus purpureus**
  GREEN WOOD see **Phoeniculus purpureus**
  WHITE-HEADED WOOD see under **Phoeniculus purpureus**

Hoplopterus
  armatus see **Vanellus armatus**
  spinosus see **Vanellus spinosus**

HORNBILL,
  ABYSSINIAN GROUND see **Bucorvus abyssinicus**
  ASIAN WHITE-CRESTED see **Berenicornis comatus**
  CROWNED see **Tockus alboterminatus**
  GREY see **Tockus nasutus**
  GROUND see **Bucorvus leadbeateri**
  INDIAN PIED see **Anthracocerus malabaricus**
  PAPUAN see **Aceros plicatus**
  RED-BILLED see **Tockus erythrorhynchus**
  VAN DER DECKEN'S see **Tockus deckeni**
  YELLOW-BILLED see **Tockus flavirostris**

HORNED
  GREBE see **Podiceps auritus**
  LARK see **Eremophila alpestris**

Hydranassa tricolor *Ardeidae*
LOUISIANA or TRICOLOURED HERON   24-28 ins
Nearctic and Neotropical: breeds from New Jersey and California S to central Argentina and NW Peru; wanders northward late summer. Habitat coastal mangrove swamps, mudflats and marshes. Upperparts slate grey with white to rufous line down neck to white belly and rump; purplish crest with white nuptial plumes, buff on back; immature more rufous; legs variable, yellow to orange, bill blackish, eyes orange. Slender-looking active heron, often wading deeply after fish, sometimes leaping out of water; also takes amphibians, reptiles and water animals, e.g. prawns. Utters variety of harsh croaks and deep groans, 'rasping *raah*' when bickering. Breeding season variable, May to August W Indies. Colonies, often with other species, in trees, especially mangroves a few ft above water, or on ground. Nest, slight platform of sticks, holds 3 to 7 pale blue green eggs, incubated by ♀ and ♂ for at least 3 weeks; they also tend the young. **62**

Hydrobates pelagicus *Hydrobatidae*
STORM PETREL   6 ins
N Atlantic (E side W to Iceland) and Mediterranean, dispersing after breeding; sometimes driven inland by storms. Sooty grey with squared tail and white rump; narrow pale wingbar in fresh plumage and white underwing; legs and bill black; eyes very dark brown. Fluttering zigzag flight and short glides behind ships, occasionally pattering over water or settling to swim buoyantly. Displays at colonies by night when visiting birds call and those on nests reply with long series of purring notes ending in sharp *chikka*. Food mainly plankton but will take scraps from ships' kitchens. Breeds May to September in excavated burrow, pile of stones or stone walls, on bare islands and headlands. One white, brown zoned, egg laid in vestigial nest and incubated 5½ weeks by ♀ and ♂, who tend chick for 8-9 weeks.

Hydroprogne caspia *Laridae*
CASPIAN TERN   *c.* 21 ins
Holarctic, Ethiopian, Oriental and Australasian: locally, N America, Europe, Africa and Asia through to New Zealand and Australia; tends to move to S of range in winter. Habitat: shallow, coastal waters, also inland lakes and larger rivers. Underparts white, crown black (streaked white outside breeding season), back and wings grey, rump and tail paler, often white; legs black, large bill red, eyes dark brown. Immature: underparts mottled, bill duller and more orange. Single or small groups, can soar to great heights; fishes by flying close to surface with bill down and plunging into water, also feeds on surface like gulls and may take small birds, eggs, and rob other birds. Call: deep, harsh *kaah* or *kaak-kaa*. Breeds sandy or rocky islands in colonies, groups or isolated, mid May onwards; 2 or 3 pinkish buff eggs spotted with dark brown in scrape on ground usually with light lining of plant debris, occasionally nests on mat of floating vegetation near shores of shallow lakes. Incubates *c.* 21 days, young fly *c.* 4½ weeks. **323**

Hylocichla mustelina *Muscicapidae: Turdinae*
WOOD THRUSH   8 ins
Nearctic: breeds from Central New Hampshire, SE Ontario, Central Wisconsin, SE Dakota, S to N Florida, Louisiana, E Texas; winters from S Mexico to W Panama. Habitat deciduous woodland with thick undergrowth, especially by streams, lakes, swamps; also parks and gardens with shady trees. Upperparts chestnut brown, head brightest; cheeks whitish, mottled chestnut; underparts white, spotted black from gorget to lower belly; legs pale flesh, bill brown, eyes dark brown, orbits white. Lives mainly on forest floor, scratching dead leaves and debris for insects and other small invertebrates; also takes small fruits. Call low *tuc tuc;* alarm rapid, repeated *pit.* Fluty rippling song like Hermit Thrush, *Catharus guttatus,* divided into short phrases and .pauses, with final high-pitched trill audible close up. Breeds May to June New England, making compact nest local plant materials with cup of mud or hardened leaf-mould, lined rootlets. 3 or 4 greenish blue eggs incubated by ♀ *c.* 2 weeks; both parents feed young, who fledge rapidly *c.* 10 days. Sometimes 2 broods. **684**

Hylocichla ustulata see **Catharus ustulatus**

Hylomanes momotula *Momotidae*
TODY MOTMOT   6½-7 (bill 1) ins
Neotropical: S Mexico to NW Colombia but not continuous distribution; resident in undergrowth of humid forests sea level to *c.* 4,500 ft. Smallest motmot: upperparts, including short tail, dull green; crown dull chestnut, 'eyebrow' blue, ear coverts black, bordered white; throat and centre of belly dull white; rest of underparts pale olive brown. 'Elusive and little known' (A. F. Skutch). Flies out from perch to take insects in air or fruit from twigs; also takes eggs of other birds. Nesting habits much as relatives, see *Momotus momota.*

Hylophilus ochraceiceps *Vireonidae*
TAWNY-CROWNED GREENLET   4½ ins
Neotropical: Central America, Guyanas, adjacent Venezuela S into E Brazil; western race Venezuela (Amazonas), Colombia, E and NW Ecuador S to N Bolivia, W Amazonian Brazil; forest and woodland, sea level to 4,500 ft. Upperparts dark olive green to olive (tail dull rufous eastern race); crown bright orange, tinged olive towards nape (forehead, lores orange, crown olive, eastern race); throat grey, breast olivaceous to yellowish olive, belly grey (throat, breast buffish, underparts whitish eastern race). Legs brown, bill horn brown, eyes dark brown. **905**

Hypocolius ampelinus *Bombycillidae*
GREY HYPOCOLIUS   9 ins
S Palaearctic: restricted to parts of SW Asia, especially Iraq, migrating irregularly to NW Indian subcontinent. Habitat: scrub in semi-desert and cultivated land, palm groves, gardens. Generally pale grey, tinged blue on back, buffish on forehead, underparts; primaries black, tipped white; long tail broadly tipped black; black mask extending to thin erectile band round back of neck. ♀: duller, grey instead of black on head. Juvenile buff brown, without black except on tail. Legs light brown, rather strong bill black, eyes dark brown. Behaviour like waxwings *Bombycilla,* gregarious after breeding, not very active, but flight swift and direct into cover where parties remain silent. Call: squeaking note. Diet: fruits and berries, some insects. Breeds June, building large, rather untidy nest of twigs, softly lined, usually well hidden in leaves of palm tree. 4 or 5 pale grey eggs, marked blackish, sometimes very heavily.

HYPOCOLIUS, GREY see **Hypocolius ampelinus**

Hypositta coralirostris *Sittidae*
MADAGASCAR or
CORAL-BILLED NUTHATCH   *c.* 5 ins
Madagascar: forests of humid east, nearly sea level to *c.* 5,500 ft. Upperparts dull greenish blue, flight feathers dark brown, edged blue green; tail dark brown, washed bluish; forehead and crown greenish brown; underparts tawny yellow, washed greenish; legs blackish, bill coral-red tipped black, eyes deep red. Behaves like treecreepers *Certhia,* hunting upper trunks and larger branches of forest trees, then flying down to next one. Often 2 or 3 in mixed flocks of other birds. Presumably mainly insectivorous. Breeds probably August and September.

Hypsipetes flavala or Microscelis flavalus
Pycnonotidae
BROWN-EARED or ASHY BULBUL   8 ins
E Palaearctic-Oriental: Himalayas E to Yunnan, S through Burma, Thailand, Malaysia; resident primary and secondary forest. Upperparts, including crest, dark brown, shading to yellowish green on wings and dark-tipped tail; throat white, breast grey; under tail coverts bright yellow; legs blackish to flesh, bill black, eyes dark red, pale brown or greyish olive. Noisy parties work lower canopy, undergrowth, bamboo thickets. Puffs out white feathers of throat in display. Variety of calls, variously described, for different races. Breeds May in Burma, building flimsy cup of bamboo leaves suspended between stems, e.g. dead bracken, up to 15 ft. 3 to 5 eggs, pinkish grey, marked red, black and purple, incubated mainly by ♀, fed by ♂, who also helps with brood, fed at first on insects, then berries. **639**

Ibidorhyncha struthersii *Recurvirostridae*
IBISBILL   *c.* 16 ins
E Palaearctic, Oriental: W Turkestan through Himalayas and N Assam to Szechuan and Inner Mongolia; high plateaux usually between 6,000 and 10,000 ft; some movement to lower foothills in winter. Breeds along rocky and clear mountain streams, often where gradient has decreased in fairly wide valley. Front of head, throat, breast band, black; rest of upperparts mostly grey-brown; basal markings on rump black; tail ash grey with thin wavy blackish barring; white wing patch partly concealed; cheeks, neck, upper breast blue-grey, rest of underparts white; long legs blood red, long down-curved bill bright red, eyes dark red. Smooth flight; usually in pairs. Good swimmer; often feeds by wading breast-high and ducking head and neck under water, using bill to seek out small crustacea, insects, other water animals from under stones. Calls: in flight ringing whistle, quickly repeated; shrill mournful cry when disturbed. Wary when breeding, March onwards; scrape in ground, sometimes pebbled-lined, usually on crest of small ridge in or on edge of shingle bed, boulders on small island in stream or on bank. 3 or 4 stone grey eggs, sometimes tinged greenish or brownish, with sepia, pale bluish-grey or reddish markings. Incubating ♀ or ♂ blends perfectly with surrounding water-smoothed boulders.

IBIS,
  BALD see **Geronticus calvus**
  BLACK see **Pseudibis papillosa**
  GLOSSY see **Plegadis falcinellus**
  HADADA see **Hagedashia hagedash**
  SACRED see **Threskiornis aethiopicus**
  SCARLET see **Eudocimus ruber**
  STRAW-NECKED see **Threskiornis spinicollis**
  WATTLED see **Bostrychia carunculata**
  WHITE (AMERICAN) see **Eudocimus albus**
  WHITE (AUSTRALIAN) see under **Threskiornis spinicollis**

Ibis
  ibis see **Mycteria ibis**
  leucocephalus see **Mycteria leucocephalus**

Icterus galbula *Icteridae*
BALTIMORE ORIOLE   7½ ins
Nearctic: breeds southern Canada, including Nova Scotia, S to N Georgia, Central Louisiana, S Texas; W to Central Montana, E Colorado; winters S Mexico to Colombia. Habitat edge mature broad-leaved woodland especially by streams; also road-sides, parks, gardens. ♂: head, gorget, mantle, most of wings, base and centre tail glossy black; shoulder patch, lower back, rump, underparts from breast orange; wings white bar and edges; tips outer tail feathers orange yellow. ♀: variable, sometimes like 'faded' ♂, black flecked orange brown; or olive yellow above with yellow underparts, rump, tail. Immature much as ♀ but upperparts uniform olive yellow. Legs light grey, bill grey, eyes brown. (Usually enough orange to distinguish from Orchard Oriole, *I. spurius*, with black and maroon ♂, predominantly green ♀). ♂ displays to ♀ on branch, exposing plumage features and singing: mixture of whistled 2-note phrases and softer single notes, individual to each ♂; some song from ♀, and ♂ sings after moult. Call mellow single or double whistle; rattle of alarm. Food mainly insects, some fruit. Breeds May-June; ♀, ♂ nearby, builds bag-nest *c.* 6 ins deep, narrow at tip, usually of light-coloured plant fibres, bark, hair, twine, suspended from end twigs of drooping branch; returns annually to same site. 4 to 6 pale grey eggs, marked and scrawled black and brown at big end, incubated mainly ♀: 12-14 days; ♀ and ♂ feed young, who fly *c.* 2 weeks. **910**

Icteria virens *Parulidae*
YELLOW-BREASTED CHAT   7½ ins
Nearctic, marginally Neotropical: breeds Connecticut, S Ontario, Iowa, Montana, S British Columbia S to N Florida, Gulf Coast, E Mexico; winters N Mexico S to Costa Rica. Habitat dense bush and vine tangles with scattered trees, probably originally by streams, pools, now in young growth on burnt or cut-over land, abandoned fields. Upperparts from crown dark olive green, tinged brown flight feathers, tail; broad white 'eyebrow' and short white stripe from gape enclose blue-black mask round white-ringed eye; underparts from chin to belly yellow, under tail coverts white; legs, powerful bill black, eyes dark brown. Hard to see as keeps to canopy or dense thicket, occasionally flying up to 'sing' in air, flapping slowly or hovering with legs dangling. Calls, emphatic *chuck* or *chuck-uck;* song: disjointed phrases, often widely spaced; whistles, mews, squeaks, scolding and trumpeting sounds, singly or repeated. Insectivorous but takes much fruit. Breeds May to July, building bulky nest of dead leaves, grass, bark, lined fine grass, 3 to 5 ft up in bushes, vine tangle. 4 white eggs, evenly spotted brown; incubation (♀) and fledging periods *c.* 2 weeks. If parasitised by Cowbird, *Molothrus ater*, often destroys own clutch with intruders egg. **895**

Icterus spurius see under **I. galbula**

INCA TERN see **Larosterna inca**

INDIAN
  CRESTED SWIFT see **Hemiprocne longipennis**
  HILL MYNAH see **Gracula religiosa**
  PEAFOWL see **Pavo cristatus**
  PIED HORNBILL see **Anthracocerus malabaricus**

RING-NECKED PARAKEET see **Psittacula krameri**
ROLLER see **Coracias benghalensis**
WHITE-BACKED VULTURE see **Gyps bengalensis**
WHITE-EYE see **Zosterops palpebrosa**

Indicator indicator *Indicatoridae*
GREATER or
BLACK-THROATED HONEYGUIDE   8 ins
Ethiopian: whole region except W African rain-forests and Kalahari, in wide variety of habitats. Greyish brown above, off-white below, bright pink bill; ♂ has black throat patch; white outer tail feathers conspicuous in flight. Feeds on wax, grubs, honey from bees' nests to which it attracts humans, honeybadgers (ratels) by excited chattering. Parasitises hole-nesting barbets, woodpeckers, bee-eaters, laying similar white eggs in their nests.

Indicator minor *Indicatoridae*
LESSER HONEYGUIDE   5½ ins
Ethiopian: same range, habitats as preceeding species, but not in fact a guide to honey though does eat bees' wax, grubs as well as other insects, caterpillars. Dull olive above, pale grey to white below, white outer tail feathers. Perches inconspicuously on branch, calling monotonously *pew pew pew*. Also parasitises small hole-nesting barbets, kingfishers etc. **533**

Irediparra gallinacea *Jacanidae*
LOTUS BIRD or AUSTRALIAN JACANA   *c.* 12 ins
Oriental, Australasian: Borneo, Moluccas, Celebes, New Guinea, Continental Australia; resident in swamps and ponds. Upperparts brown glossed green; nape, back of neck, breast and flanks black; throat and upper breast white framed golden yellow, which extends to head; downward dark stripe from eye; underparts white but under wing coverts black; legs green, bill, dark tipped, with light base merging into red frontal comb, eyes light brown. Behaviour much as relatives but flight weaker. Call of alarm sharp and 'trumpet-like'. Food: water animals and plants. Breeds September to February in Australia; April in Borneo. Nest a pile of green water plants, half submerged or on platform out from shore. Usually 4 glossy, yellowish olive eggs marked with blotches and interlacing dark brown lines. Incubation and fledging much as African Jacana, *Actophilornis africana*. **249**

Irena puella *Irenidae*
FAIRY BLUEBIRD   11 ins
Oriental: widespread in region; resident evergreen forest. Rather thrush-like in shape but more slender; ♂: upperparts from crown to upper tail coverts purplish blue; flight feathers, tail, underparts and face black; legs, bill blackish, eyes red. ♀: dull blue-green; primaries and tail dark brown, black patch round eye. Juvenile ♂ as ♀, but feathers of upperparts fringed blue. Usually in flocks, occasionally solitary or pairs, constantly on move from tree to tree. Drinks and bathes midday. Call: repeated *be quick;* also sharp, loud whistle, sometimes followed by bubbling call. Diet: exclusively fruit, especially figs, gathering with other species at ripe tree. Breeds March to May (Burma), building rather flimsy cup of twigs, rootlets, moss, lined moss roots, in bush or sapling. 2 pale to reddish grey or buff eggs, marked brown, purple and grey. **644**

Iridoprocne bicolor see **Tachycineta bicolor**

Iridosornis rufivertex *Emberizidae: Thraupinae*
GOLDEN-CROWNED TANAGER   7 ins
Neotropical: very local Venezuela, most of Colombia, E and W Ecuador; forests of temperate zone (7,500 ft upwards). Upperparts glossy purplish blue, underparts similar but darker, under tail coverts chestnut (blue in one race); head black, centre crown golden yellow. **876**

Ispidina picta *Alcedinidae*
AFRICAN PYGMY KINGFISHER   4 ins
Ethiopian: whole of sub-Saharan Africa except Somalia, SW Africa. Habitat: forest, bush, savannah, not necessarily near water as mainly land feeder, on grass crickets etc, but small fish also taken. Perches on

low bush, pounces down into grass. Flies off with very rapid flight, calling squeakily. Mainly ultramarine above, tawny below, throat white; distinguished from very similar Malachite Kingfisher, *Corythornis cristata*, by lack of crest. 3 to 5 white eggs in short tunnel in bank. **492**

JABIRU see **Jabiru mycteria**

Jabiru mycteria *Ciconiidae*
JABIRU   4½ ft
Neotropical, from Central America to E Peru, Paraguay, Uruguay and N Argentina. Sedentary; habitat in Brazil open wet grasslands with ponds by rivers. White, with bare head and neck black, to red at base. Legs and very heavy bill black, eyes brown. Several hops to take off, then flight light and graceful, often soars to great height. Feeds singly, catching snakes in grassland, also fish, molluscs, especially *Ampullaria*, and crustaceans. Breeds usually on limbs of tall trees or rock, building large flat nest of sticks with thick lining of grass; 2 to 4 grey or yellowish white eggs incubated by ♀ and ♂; *c.* 4 months from incubation to fledging. **72**

JACAMAR,
  RUFOUS-TAILED see **Galbula ruficauda**
  THREE-TOED see **Jacamaralcyon tridactyla**
  YELLOW-BILLED see **Galbula albirostris**

Jacamaralcyon tridactyla *Galbulidae*
THREE-TOED JACAMAR   6¼ (bill 1½) ins
Neotropical: SE Brazil from Minas Gerais to Parana; resident in forest. Upperparts blackish glossed green; head chestnut brown streaked buff; underparts white, flanks greyish; hind toe absent; long bill black. Insectivorous, taking flying insects in aerial sallies. Excavates nest hole like relatives (see *Galbula ruficauda*).

JACANA,
  AFRICAN see **Actophilornis africanus**
  AUSTRALIAN see **Irediparra gallinacea**
  LESSER see **Microparra capensis**
  WATTLED see **Jacana spinosa**

Jacana jacana see **J. spinosa**

Jacana spinosa or J. jacana *Jacanidae*
WATTLED or SOUTH AMERICAN JACANA   10 ins
Neotropical: resident from Mexico southward; widespread E of Andes to Bolivia and N Argentina; W of Andes to Colombia, W Ecuador, NW Peru; W Indies: marshes, swampy riversides and lakes. Head, neck, mantle black, rest of plumage dark chestnut except for yellow-green, dark-tipped flight feathers; legs dusky green, bill yellow, frontal shield and wattles red or yellow, eyes brown. Juvenile greyish-brown above, whitish below, with white 'eye-brow'. Habits much as other jacanas; cackling call. Food: water plants and invertebrate animals taken from their leaves. Breeds June to February, sex roles reversed, larger ♀ often polyandrous. Shallow untidy nest among water plants, holds 3 to 5 buff-brown eggs, heavily scrawled black, incubated by ♂ 22-24 days. Probably at least 2 broods. **250**

JACKASS, LAUGHING see **Dacelo nouaeguineae**

JACKASS PENGUIN see **Spheniscus demersus**

JACKDAW see **Corvus monedula**

JACK SNIPE see **Lymnocryptes minimus**

JACKSON'S FRANCOLIN see **Francolinus jacksoni**

JACKY WINTER see **Microeca fascinans**

JAMESON'S FIREFINCH see under **Lagonisticta rubricata**

JAPANESE CRANE see **Grus japonensis**

JAVAN BROWN WOOD OWL see **Strix leptogrammica**

JAVA SPARROW see **Padda oryzivora**

JAY,
  EURASIAN see **Garrulus glandarius**
  GREEN see **Cyanocorax yncas**
  MEXICAN see **Aphelocoma ultramarina**
  SCRUB see **Aphelocoma coerulescens**
  SIBERIAN see **Perisoreus infaustus**
  STELLER'S see **Cyanocitta stelleri**

JAY THRUSH, FUKIEN RUFOUS see **Garrulax caerulatus**

JUNGLE
  FOWL see **Megapodius freycinet**
  FOWL, GREY see under **Gallus gallus**
  FOWL, RED see **Gallus gallus**
  NIGHTJAR see **Caprimulgus indicus**

Jynx torquilla *Picidae*
WRYNECK   *c*. 6½ ins
Palaearctic: main range across Eurasia from S Scandinavia, Britain (now very rare) and N Iberia between 50° and 60°N in W Asia to Pacific between 40° and 60°; also NW Africa, Crimea, Caucasus, mountains of Central Asia; northern populations winter S Asia and Africa N of Equator. Habitat: broadleaved forests, especially oak, larch woods, tree groups on steppes, riverine woodland, cultivated areas, roadsides, parks, gardens. Grey-brown: upperparts mottled, streaked and vermiculated various patterns; underparts pale brown or buff, barred on breast, flecked on belly, greyish tail with several darker bars; legs and bill pale brownish-horn, eyes hazel brown. Perches like passerine as well as clinging to trunks like woodpecker, sometimes with help of tail. Often on ground, hopping with tail raised, and perches on bushes. Flight rather laboured. Small parties form on migration. Spring call shrill, ringing *quee quee quee* . . . resembling calls of small falcons and Lesser Spotted Woodpecker, *Dendrocopos minor*; also repeated *tuk* of alarm; hisses and contorts neck if disturbed on nest. Mutual display; ♂ and ♀ face each other, shake heads and expose pink gape. Feeds largely on ants picked off from grass or tree crevices with rapid action of long vermiform tongue; also takes eggs and nestlings from nestboxes. Breeds mid April onwards, using, but not excavating, holes in trees, banks, ground, sometimes in walls, posts, nestboxes. 7 to 10 white eggs incubated by ♀ and ♂ 12-14 days; both feed young, who fly 19-21 days. Sometimes 2 broods. **549**

KAGU see **Rhynochetos jubatus**

KAKA see **Nestor meridionalis**

KAKAPO see **Strigops habroptilus**

Kakatoe roseicapilla see **Cacatua roseicapilla**

KALEEJ PHEASANT see **Lophura lophura**

KAROO CHAT see **Erythropygia coryphaeus**

KEEL-BILLED TOUCAN see **Ramphastos sulfuratus**

KELP GOOSE see **Chloephaga hybrida**

KENTISH PLOVER see **Charadrius alexandrinus**

KESTREL,
  AMERICAN see **Falco sparverius**
  OLD WORLD see under **Falco sparverius**
  SEYCHELLES see **Falco area**

KIKUYU WHITE-EYE see **Zosterops kikuyensis**

KILLDEER see **Charadrius vociferus**

KING
  BIRD OF PARADISE see **Cicinnurus regius**
  CROW see under **Dicrurus annectans**
  PARROT see **Aprosmictus scapularis**
  SHAG see **Phalacrocorax atriceps**

VULTURE, ASIA see **Sarcogyps calvus**
VULTURE, AMERICA see **Sarcorhamphus papa**

KINGBIRD,
  EASTERN see **Tyrannus tyrannus**
  OLIVE-BACKED see **Tyrannus melancholicus**
  TROPICAL see **Tyrannus melancholicus**
  WESTERN see **Tyrannus verticalis**

KINGFISHER see **Alcedo atthis**

KINGFISHER,
  AMERICAN PYGMY see **Chloroceryle aenea**
  ANGOLA see **Halcyon senegalensis**
  BELTED see **Megaceryle alcyon**
  GIANT see **Megaceryle maxima**
  GREEN AND RUFOUS see **Chloroceryle aenea**
  GREY-HEADED see **Halcyon leucocephala**
  MALACHITE see **Corythornis cristata**
  MANGROVE see under **Halcyon senegalensis**
  PIED see **Ceryle rudis**
  PYGMY see **Ispidina picta**
  SACRED see **Halcyon sancta**
  WHITE-BREASTED see **Halcyon smyrnensis**
  WOODLAND see **Halcyon senegalensis**

KINGLET,
  GOLD-CROWNED see **Regulus satrapa**
  RUBY-CROWNED see **Regulus calendula**

KINKIMAVO see **Tylas eduardi**

KITE,
  BLACK see **Milvus migrans**
  BLACK-SHOULDERED see **Elanus caeruleus**
  SWALLOW-TAILED see **Chelictinia riocourii**
  YELLOW-BILLED see **Milvus migrans aegyptius**

KITTIWAKE see **Rissa tridactyla**

KITTLITZ'S
  MURRELET see **Brachyramphus brevirostris**
  SAND PLOVER see **Charadrius pecuarius**

KIWI, BROWN see **Apteryx australis**

KLAA'S CUCKOO see under **Cinnyris venustus**

KNOB-BILLED GOOSE see **Sarkidiornis melanotos**

KNOT see **Calidris canutus**

KNYSNA SCRUB WARBLER see **Bradypterus sylvaticus**

KOKAKO see **Callaeas cinerea**

KOOKABURRA see **Dacelo novaeguineae**

KORI BUSTARD see **Choriotis kori**

KURRICHANE THRUSH see **Turdus libonyanus**

LADY AMHERST'S PHEASANT see **Chrysolophus amherstiae**

LA FRESNAYE'S VANGA see **Xenopirostris xenopirostris**

Lagonisticta jamesoni see under **L. rubricata**

Lagonisticta rubricata *Estrildidae*
AFRICAN FIREFINCH   4½ ins
Ethiopian: Angola, W Africa E to Eritrea, Ethiopia, S through E Africa, Malawi, Zambia, E Rhodesia to S Africa; resident forest edge or riverine bush; thorn scrub with tall grass; neglected cultivation. ♂: generally claret red; crown, nape underlying grey; back, wings earth brown; belly, tail, under tail coverts black; white spots side breast. ♀ has brown crown; underparts pale claret, washed pale brown. Legs, eyes brown, bill blue-black. Very similar Jameson's Firefinch, *L. jamesoni*, is paler, favours more arid habitat. Pairs or small parties, keeping to thick undergrowth, fly low from bush to bush. Attracted by imitating alarm notes

of other species. Call: clear metallic trill, usually followed by *wink wink wink*; repeated *chit* of alarm; low chirping song. Diet: small seeds; insects. Breeding season varies within range; builds flimsy grass nest with large side entrance, thinly lined feathers. 3 to 6 white eggs, incubated ♀; ♀ and ♂ feed young. **938**

Lagopus lagopus *Tetraonidae*
WILLOW and RED GROUSE   15-16 ins
Willow Grouse, *L.l. lagopus*, Holarctic temperate and subarctic from Scandinavia through N Eurasia to Alaska and parts N Canada; Red Grouse, *L.l. scoticus*, in Britain and Ireland, introduced Belgium. Resident on moorland and heaths with willow, birch and juniper scrub. Willow Grouse: dark rufous brown in spring with darker outer tail feathers, white wings and under tail coverts; becomes white in winter except for tail (thus very like ♀ Rock Ptarmigan, *L. mutus*); legs feathered white, bill black, eyes hazel with red wattles above. Red Grouse ♂: dark rufous brown all year with darker tail and wings, ♀ yellower on body in spring. Packs in autumn, flying up to 1 mile when disturbed; later pairs form and ♂ prominent in territory, calling *go-bak go-bak*. Burrows in snow for food and cover in winter. Diet heather, other shoots, berries and seeds; also insects, especially when young. Breeds from March in Britain, later in N; ♀ lines scrape in heath-type vegetation or tussocks, laying from 6 to 11 yellowish eggs, blotched smeary red-brown, incubates them for 23-26 days with ♂ near; he helps guard precocious brood, which fly 12-13 days. **183**

Lagopus leucurus *Tetraonidae*
WHITE-TAILED PTARMIGAN   12½ ins
Nearctic: Alpine zone from Cascade Mountains, and Rockies of New Mexico N to Central Alaska and NW Mackenzie. All white in winter; upperparts, including centre of tail and breast mottled yellow-brown, black and white in summer; belly, most of wings and outer tail feathers white; legs feathered white, bill black, red wattles over dark brown eyes. Found on high windswept ridges, in flocks of up to 100, feeding on dwarf willow and sheltering in snowbanks, but may come down to conifer forest to take needles, buds, flowers and fruits of low-growing plants in summer, also some insects. Cackling alarm call when flushed; also hoots and clucking notes, especially from ♂, who stays near ♀ when she lays (from mid June in S) usually 6 to 8 buff eggs marked in shades of brown in lined scrape, incubating them for *c*. 3 weeks. ♂ assists her look after precocious brood. **184**

Lagopus mutus *Tetraonidae*
ROCK PTARMIGAN   14 ins
Holarctic: temperate alpine and arctic zones; very local Europe, widespread Asia, Alaska, also arctic Canada and Greenland. Sedentary on shrub, moss and lichen tundra, also among rocks close to snow line in summer. ♂: body, head and centre of tail mottled grey brown in spring, outer tail feathers black, wings white; ♀ browner. Both greyer in autumn and white in winter when ♂ has black stripe through eye. Legs feathered white, bill black, eyes brown with red wattles above. Families form packs late autumn, which often crouch rather than fly and burrow in snow for cover and food. Curious snoring call when alerted; ♂ in spring has 'coughing' song during display by jumping, descending with spread wings. Diet of leaves, seeds, berries of many alpine-arctic plants. Breeds from May in Britain, ♀ lining scrape made by ♂, usually in open or among stones, laying 5 to 9 buff eggs, marked yellow-brown and incubating them 21½-26 days, with ♂ near. Both attend brood, which flies *c*. 10 days. Injury-feigning characteristic with eggs or young. **185**

Lalage sueurii *Campephagidae*
WHITE-WINGED TRILLER   7 ins
Oriental, Australasian; Java and adjacent islands E to Celebes; continental Australia; summer visitor to open woodland and scrub in Australia. ♂: crown, mantle, flight and tail feathers glossy black; lower back, rump grey; large shoulder patches, webs secondaries, all underparts white. ♀: brown above, with pale 'eyebrow'; underparts whitish, washed brown on breast. Two moults annually: in April ♂ becomes brown on

head and mantle. Legs, gill, eyes dark. Melodious song, with *joey joey* call as it flies between trees. Takes insects, especially cicadas, and larvae from foliage. Breeds September to January Australia; ♀ and ♂ building small open nest of plant material, bound cobwebs, decorated bark, spider's egg bags, typically in fork of lateral branch. One to 3 eggs, light or bright bluish-green, heavily marked red-brown. Incubation by ♀ and ♂ *c.* 14 days; both parents feed young, who fly *c.* 12 days.

LAMMERGEIER see **Gypaetus barbatus**

Lampornis clemenciae *Trochilidae*

BLUE-THROATED SYLPH or HUMMINGBIRD 5 ins

Nearctic to Neotropical: mountains of W Texas, S New Mexico and S Arizona to S Mexico; northern birds move S in autumn. Confined to dense riverine vegetation in mountainous canyons, 5,000 to 7,600 ft. ♂: generally dark green; white stripe behind eye, iridescent light blue gorget; flight feathers dark brown washed green; under tail coverts white, heavily flecked green; slightly forked tail blue-black with conspicuous white area on each extremity. ♀ similar but with white throat. Legs, bill, eyes dark. Closely resembles Rivoli's Hummingbird, *Eugenes fulgens*, but both sexes constantly fan tail, to show its more extensive white. Call, excited piercing *seep* uttered in flight and when perched, bird hunching restlessly from side to side. (J. T. Marshall). Feeds principally at flowers, chasing other species away; takes insects off sycamore leaves. Nest relatively large cup of plant materials bound with spider's web, attached to flower stalk or other slender support on stream bank. Incubation of 2 eggs and feeding as other hummingbirds (see *Aglaiocercus kingi*).

Lamprocolius chalybeus *Sturnidae*

BLUE-EARED GLOSSY STARLING 8½-9 ins

Ethiopian: Ethiopia across continent to W Africa, southward to NE South Africa. Some local movements from acacia bush and open woodlands, even entering towns. Very similar to Cape Glossy Starling, *L. nitens*; generally iridescent blue-green; earcoverts, belly violet blue, lores black; 'shoulders' magenta and bronze or violet blue according to race; black terminal spots on wing coverts; legs, bill black, eyes orange. Juvenile sooty black below, washed greenish all over; eyes dark grey. Large flocks form after breeding, flying up noisily from ground, where hops. Roosts trees, reedbeds with 'deafening chatter'. Call: loud nasal *squeare squeare*, followed by rattling whistle, becoming 'hysterical whistle' of alarm; also chirps and warblings. Food: fruit, berries, insects. Breeds September to January Rhodesia, in holes in trees, posts, other artefacts; sometimes takes over old nest at top of thorn tree; holes lined grass, feathers, sometimes snakeskin, 3 to 20 ft up or more. 3 or 4 pale blue eggs, sparingly speckled or marked umber over lilac. **969**

Lamprotornis australis *Sturnidae*

BURCHELL'S GLOSSY STARLING 12-14 ins

Ethiopian: much of Southern Africa, including Botswana, to S Angola, Ngamiland; resident dry open bush with tall trees. Upperparts metallic green with purple sheen, black subterminal spots on feathers; 'shoulder' bronze; long, graduated, wedge-shaped tail purple over dark barring; earcoverts, cheeks dark purple; hindneck, rump, belly purple; head, nape, chin to upper breast green, glossed purple; legs, bill black, eyes brown. Immature duller, browner below. Singly, pairs, large flocks, usually near water. Rather laboured flapping flight, but aerial manoeuvres before roosting in reedbeds. Walks on ground. Loud, harsh calls but not unmusical song. Diet: insects, fruit. Breeds November, December and March SW Africa, 6 ft upwards in tree holes, lined green grass. 3 or 4 sky blue eggs, speckled reddish-purple, often concentrated big end. Presumably 2 broods some areas. **970**

Laniarius aethiopicus *Laniidae*

BOUBOU 9 ins

Ethiopian: almost throughout region, from highland forest to scrub in dry watercourses, also bush, coastal scrub, gardens. Upperparts and cheeks glossy blue-black; middle and some secondary wing coverts white; underparts white tinged pinkish; legs bluish slate, bill black, eye reddish brown. Immature duller. Pairs skulk in thick cover, betraying presence by clear bell-like calls. In duet ♂ gives three calls, answered so quickly by ♀'s 'groaning *huee*' that only one bird seems to be involved; at least seven combinations identified; also harsh alarm calls: *churr* and *tchak*. Varied shrike diet includes many young birds. Breeding season varies with range. Nest of tendrils, dry stems, rootlets, softly lined, in bush or fork of branch often quite open. 2 rather glossy blue-green or greenish buff eggs, spotted and speckled brown over lilac and grey. **647**

Lanioturdus torquatus *Laniidae*

WHITE-TAILED SHRIKE 5½ ins

Ethiopian: NW Southern Africa; resident open thorn bush, edges of mixed woodland. Upperparts grey; rather pointed wings black with prominent white bar when closed and flight feathers tipped white; short tail with 2 black subterminal spots; head black and white; underparts, chin to undertail white with broad black breast band and grey flanks. Pairs or small parties forage restlessly for insects, mainly on ground, sometimes up to 70 ft, creeping about foliage. Short, slow flights. Call: loud, clear *huo huo huo*, recorded duetting; alarm: *squee squee*; various other churring, croaking notes. Breeds January-February, building cup nest of grass, bark strips, bound cobwebs, lined fine grass, fairly high in tree fork. 2 dull white to blue-grey eggs, zoned dark and light brown markings.

Lanius cabanisi *Laniidae*

LONG-TAILED FISCAL SHRIKE 12 ins

Ethiopian: resident southern Somalia S to E Tanzania as far as Dar es Salaam; inland to Kenya: Kilosa and Nairobi. Habitat grasslands with scattered bushes, low open coastal scrub. Upperparts black, shading to grey on rump; very long tail black; white wingbar; underparts white; legs, bill dark grey, eyes reddish. Often in small parties perched together in same bush, raising, lowering and swinging tails like pendulum (J. G. Williams); also bickers noisily, but has clear whistle as well as harsh calls, commonest *chit-er-row*. Food as relatives. Breeding season protracted in Kenya. Large nest of grass, rootlets, finer lining, low in thick bush, often thorny. 3 or 4 buff or cream eggs, spotted and speckled brown over lavender. **648**

Lanius collaris *Laniidae*

FISCAL SHRIKE 9 ins

Ethiopian: widely distributed in region from Eritrea, Sudan S to S Africa (Transvaal); westwards S of Sahara to Sierra Leone, SW to Angola; some local migration. Variety of habitats, including lightly wooded country, cultivated areas, near houses. ♂: upperparts, including most of head, glossy back, white scapulars forming broad V on back; rump, upper tail coverts grey; wings black, white bases to primaries; tail black with white outermost and white tipped central feathers; underparts white, axillaries black and white; legs, bill black, eyes brown. ♀ has chestnut flanks. Immature ash-brown above, greyish brown below, finely barred. Usually perches telegraph poles, other vantage points, whence attacks large insects, especially Orthoptera, mice, small birds, impaling them on thorny larder, often sisal bush. Call: *cheee cheee cheee*; other harsh notes and a pleasing song. Breeds all through year Kenya, seasonally elsewhere. Neat nest of grass, rootlets, cotton, lined fine fibres, grass, hair, in fork of bush or tree. Usually 3 creamy or pinkish eggs, spotted sepia, brown, chestnut over lilac. Sometimes 2 broods. **649**

Lanius collurio *Laniidae*

RED-BACKED SHRIKE 6¾ ins

Palaearctic: from N Iberia, Mediterranean area to beyond 60°N in Scandinavia and Russia: E through Asia Minor, Crimea, Iran, Palestine to W Siberia, Turkestan, Outer Mongolia, NW Manchuria, W China. European birds migrate to Southern Africa; Black Sea, and Caspian birds to E Africa; Asian birds to India, SW Arabia, NE Africa. Habitat open scrub, e.g. heathland, commons in England, thickets, cultivated land with bushes; similarly in winter up to 6,000 ft Tanzania. ♂: back and most of wings chestnut, flight feathers darker, crown, nape, rump blue-grey; tail black, edged white; mask black; underparts pinkish buff. Legs grey-black, bill black, eyes dark brown. ♀, juvenile duller, russet brown above, buffish below, with crescentic 'scaly' markings. Legs brownish-grey, bill brownish horn. Sometimes perches openly, sometimes skulks; frequent movements and spreading of tail; undulating flight with glide to new perch. Hawks flying insects, catches small birds, mammals, frogs, lizards, worms, impaling some on thorny larder. Usual call: *chack chack*, but many others recorded; also infrequent warbling, mimicking song. Breeds mid-May to July; ♂ mainly builds substantial nest of moss, grass, stalks, wool, feathers, softly lined, usually in thorny bush or creeper, e.g. brambles, sometimes small trees, from 6 ins to 7½ ft up. 3 to 6 very variable eggs, white, pink, buffish or green, markings of red, brown over grey usually in zone, incubated ♀ 13-16 days; both parents feed young, who fly *c.* 14 days. Parasitised by Cuckoo, *Cuculus canorus*, in Europe. **650**

Lanius cristatus *Laniidae*

BROWN SHRIKE 7½ ins

E Palaearctic: from Central Siberia, NE up Olenek River to Kamtchatka; also N Mongolia, China, Korea, Manchuria, Japan. The several races winter China, Thailand, Indian subcontinent, Ceylon, Malaysia, Philippines, Borneo. Habitat open country with bushes, riverine woods, orchards, parks. ♂: upperparts greyish-brown; head russet brown; forehead, 'eye-brow' white; wings grey-brown; tail yellowish-brown; underparts ochre; legs blackish, bill mainly black, eyes dark brown, orbit pale blue. ♀, juvenile much as *Lanius collurio*, with which sometimes considered conspecific, linked by red-tailed races. Habits much as *L. collurio*. Call: scolding *chr-r-r-r*; subsong in winter quarters. Food mainly insects, birds, small mammals. Large nest of grass, twigs, lined seed down, wool, scraps, usually low in thorny bush. 4 to 6 eggs cream to pink, marked chestnut over grey; incubation and fledging as *L. collurio*.

Lanius excubitor *Laniidae*

GREAT GREY SHRIKE 9½ ins

Holarctic, Oriental, marginally Ethiopian: Iberia through Europe E to Central Russia, Siberia and Kamtchatka; S to Iran, Arabia, Indian subcontinent; N Africa to *c.* 10°N; Alaska SE through Yukon to Hudson Bay, Quebec, Newfoundland; Eurasian birds winter Mediterranean area, Asia Minor; Siberian birds in Mongolia, N Manchuria; American birds to Kansas, California, New Mexico, Texas. Habitat: woodland edge, open country with bushes, marsh and scrub tundra to savannah and desert. ♂: upperparts grey; wings, tail black with white markings; white border above black mask (distinguishes from Lesser Grey Shrike, *L. minor*, but absent in juvenile); underparts white, sometimes tinged pink; rump white. ♀ slightly duller, with crescentic marks on underparts; juvenile brownish-grey above, underparts more marked. Legs black, bill mainly black-brown, eyes dark brown. Prominent perch from which to hunt or defend territory against other birds, even large hawks. Constant tail movements. Short low flights between perches with final glide upwards; longer flights undulating; hovers when hunting. Prey: largely insects, small birds, mammals, reptiles and frogs; sometimes stored in larder. Call: *truu*; harsh *sheck sheck* of alarm; song, sometimes in winter, medley of warblings, call notes, mimicry. Breeds from April to June; ♀ and ♂ build bulky nest of twigs, grass, moss, lined finer materials, up to 40 ft in fork of tree of bush. 5 to 7 eggs in N, fewer in S, greyish white to buff, marked olive brown over grey, incubated ♀ 14-16 days. Both parents feed young, who fly 18-20 days. Sometimes 2 broods in S. **651**

Lanius minor *Laniidae*

LESSER GREY SHRIKE 8 ins

Palaearctic: from France E across Europe to Asia Minor, NW Iran; separate race from S Urals to Turkestan, Altai, Afghanistan; both races winter E and S Africa. Habitat; grassland and edges of cultivation with bushes, trees; roadsides, groves, gardens; passage and winter in scrub and thorn bush. Very similar to

L. excubitor: upperparts including rump grey; wings, tail black and white; black mask meets over forehead but no white stripe above; underparts buff tinged pink. Juvenile buffish grey and scaly above. Legs brown-black, bill black, eyes dark brown. Habits much as other *Lanius* shrikes; aggressive against other species. Glides more than *Lanius collurio*; uses larder less for prey, chiefly insects; sometimes fruit. Call, probably alarm, harsh *sheck sheck*; jumbly, sometimes mimicking song. Breeds mid May onwards; ♀ and ♂ build nest of twigs, various plant stems, lined soft materials, usually 10 to 30 ft in broadleaved tree with good visibility. 5 to 7 bluish-green eggs, marked olive- and pale greenish-brown in zone, incubated mainly ♀ 15-16 days; both parents feed young, who fly 14-15 days. **652**

Lanius schach *Laniidae*
BLACK-HEADED OF LONG-TAILED SHRIKE   9-10 ins
Oriental, Australasian: widespread in S and SE Asia to New Guinea; Indian subcontinent N to Himalayas; northern birds move S in winter. Habitat: cultivated and open country with bushes and scrub, from lowlands to 5,500 ft (Burma). Head, neck, mantle cinereous grey; wings black but major coverts rufous; rump, upper tail coverts red, tail brown; black mask across forehead, 'eyebrow' white; underparts whitish; legs, bill black, eyes dark brown. Habits much as other *Lanius* shrikes. Usual call harsh *garlik garlik*, followed by yapping *yaon yaon*; alarm like distant Corncrake, *Crex crex*; prolonged musical song in breeding season. Prey: insects, eggs, nestlings, small reptiles. Breeds March to July in different parts of range; nest of twigs, stems, wool, cotton, woven into fork 10 to 15 ft up in tree. 4 to 6 greenish-white eggs, marked olive-green, brown and black. Incubation and fledging much as relatives. **653**

Lanius senator *Laniidae*
WOODCHAT SHRIKE   6¾ ins
Palaearctic: Iberia, S France, Italy, Adriatic coast, Greece, Turkey, N Arabia, Iran; winters S Arabia and Africa S of Sahara but N of Equator. Habitat: open ground with scattered trees, shrubs: olive groves, orchards, gardens, woodland clearings and edge; sometimes thick woodland. ♂: mantle and wings black with large white patch; rump white; tail black, edged white; crown, nape chestnut; black mask meets over forehead; underparts from chin white. ♀ duller; juvenile like *L. collurio* but greyer, scapulars paler. Legs slate-black, bill mainly bluish-black, eyes dark brown. Habits much as *L. collurio* but perches higher and sits more within canopy of trees than other shrikes. Calls include harsh, chattering *kiwick kiwick*; song superior to other European shrikes, sustained warbling but with harsh and mimicking notes. Prey: insects and their larvae, worms, small birds and nestlings. Breeds late April onwards, substantial nest of weed stems, especially *Gnaphalium*, lined softly; usually over 10 ft up on lateral branch, sometimes in bush. 5 or 6 pale green eggs, marked grey-brown over ashy, usually in zone, incubated ♀ *c.* 16 days; both parents feed young, who fly 19-20 days. Occasionally 2 broods. **654**

Lanius tephronotus *Laniidae*
TIBETAN OF GREY-BACKED SHRIKE   10 ins
E Palaearctic: Kashmir, Tibet, Yunnan (Likiang Range); winters to SE Asia. Habitat: open scrub at high altitudes; plains and cultivated land in winter. Upperparts from crown dark lead-grey; rump, upper tail coverts rufous; tail chestnut brown; wings blackish, feathers pale edged; black mask extends through ear coverts; underparts pale, becoming rufous lower belly. Legs, bill blackish, eyes dark brown. Habits as other *Lanius* shrikes. Harsh grating call. Food mainly insects: crickets, grasshoppers; also lizards, nestlings; uses larder. Breeds June-July, building untidy cup of wool, twigs, grass, rags, feathers, lined fine grass; usually 6 to 10 ft in thorn bush or small tree. 4 to 6 pale green eggs, blotched and spotted grey-brown; incubation and fledging much as other *Lanius* species.

LANNER see **Falco biarmicus**

LAPLAND BUNTING see **Calcarius lapponicus**

LAPWING see **Vanellus vanellus**

LARGER STRIPED SWALLOW see **Hirundo cucullata**

LARK,
  BIFASCIATED see **Alaemon alaudipes**
  BUSH see **Mirafra africana**
  CRESTED see **Galerida cristata**
  HORNED see **Eremophila alpestris**
  MAGPIE see **Grallina cyanoleuca**
  NIGERIAN CRESTED see **Galerida modesta**
  RUFOUS-NAPED see **Mirafra africana**
  SHORE see **Eremophila alpestris**
  SHORT-TOED see **Calandrella cinerea**
  TEMMINCK'S HORNED see **Eremophila bilopha**
  THEKLA see **Galerida theklae**
  THICK-BILLED see **Galerida magnirostris**
  WOOD see **Lullula arborea**

LARK QUAIL see **Ortyxeles meiffrenii**

Larosterna inca *Laridae*
INCA TERN   *c.* 16 ins
Neotropical: fairly sedentary, breeds coasts of Peru and Chile. Habitat: Humboldt current region, especially guano islands and rocky sections of shore line. Dark bluish grey, lighter on throat and under tail coverts, white moustachial streak from bill below eyes ending in long curling white feathers on cheeks; primaries and outer tail coverts brownish black, four outer primaries edged white, secondaries mostly broadly tipped white. Legs crimson, bill strong, somewhat curved, blood-red. Immature: browner and head paler, moustachial streak greyish, legs and bill reddish brown. In flight rapid wing-beats giving fluttering effect. Catches small fish by plunging into water at angle, also scavenges off other predators; plaintive call. Breeds throughout year on islands, in burrows, crevices amongst rocks or under tangled vegetation; 2 brown eggs, spotted and blotched with darker brown and grey. **324**

Larus argentatus *Laridae*
HERRING GULL   *c.* 22 ins
Holarctic: breeds SE Alaska, Canada, Atlantic coast USA down to Long I, Britain and Ireland; NW France, Netherlands, Scandinavia; fairly sedentary, some movement S in winter with younger birds reaching subtropics. (Closely related Lesser Black-backed Gull, *L. fuscus*, breeds SE Iceland, Britain and Ireland, Portugal, Brittany (France), Netherlands, Scandinavia, N USSR, W Asia S to Caspian Sea across to L. Baikal; also Mediterranean; migratory, wintering Mediterranean, Persian Gulf, Arabian Sea, Red Sea and coast and inland lakes tropical Africa.) Variation with race; head, hindneck, throat and breast white (streaked brown in winter), mantle, back and scapulars pale blue-grey, rest of body and tail white; wings grey with narrow white border on hind edge, black and white tips. Legs pinkish or yellow, bill deep yellow, vermilion spot on gonys and white tip; eyes pale yellow, orbital ring orange. Immature: light brown mottled with dark brown, wings darker and belly paler, generally paler with age; bill brownish. (*Fuscus*: mantle from blackish to slate-grey, head and neck dusky streaking in winter, legs yellow.) Gregarious, follows ships within continental shelf. Call: often dry *kak-kak-kak* or loud trumpeting *kyow-kyow-kyow*. Scavenger, takes fish and other small aquatic animals, robs nests, breaks open molluscs by dropping on hard surface. Breeds late April onwards, usually in colonies; nest rough pile of seaweed, grass and litter, sometimes only lined scrape, sited among littoral vegetation or rocks, also dunes, cliff ledges and roof tops; 2 or 3 eggs varying from pale blue and shades of green to dark brown, spotted and streaked very dark brown. Both parents incubate 28-33 days and tend young, who fly *c.* 6 weeks. **325**

Larus californicus *Laridae*
CALIFORNIA GULL   *c.* 21 ins
Nearctic: breeds eastern N Dakota and S Mackenzie S to Wyoming, N Utah and E California; winters coast Texas, and S British Columbia inland to N Utah and S to SW Mexico. Habitat: inland lakes and marshes and adjacent uplands, favours Pacific coast in winter. Looks similar to Herring Gull, *L. argentatus*, but larger white patches at wing tips, mantle greyer, black along with red tip to yellow bill; legs greenish grey-yellow. In large flocks at good feeding places, takes fish and other aquatic animals, insects from freshly cultivated land, sometimes other terrestrial animals, also scavenges amongst garbage. Call: dry *kak-kak-kak*. Breeds in colonies often with Ring-billed Gull, *L. delawarensis*, on islands in lakes or marshes usually near water's edge; 3 olive or buff to buff-brown eggs, spotted with brown, in variably lined scrape on ground or more substantial nest of weeds and other plant debris. Incubation and care of young by both sexes. **326**

Larus canus *Laridae*
COMMON GULL   *c.* 17 ins
Holarctic; breeds N America: N Mackenzie and NW Alaska S to N Saskatchewan and central British Columbia; Europe and Asia; Iceland (rare), Faeroes, N Scandinavia and N USSR S to Baltic and Caspian Sea, Mongolia and Kamtchatka; winters S as far as S California, Mediterranean and S China coasts. Habitat: coastal and inland waters, bogs and marshes. Head, neck, body and tail white, lower mantle, back, scapulars and most of wings pale blue-grey; white tips to secondaries, wing tips black with terminal white fringe. Legs greenish, bill yellow-green, eyes brown to whitish with red orbital ring. Winter: head and neck streaked dark grey. Immature: mottled brown on crown, hindneck, back and wings; black band on tail. Habits similar to other gulls e.g. Herring Gull, *L. argentatus*. Call: like Herring Gull but shriller and shorter. Feeds inland on insects, worms, seeds; on coast as other gulls. Breeds late April to mid June in colonies or solitary pairs on rocky knolls and ledges, or among vegetation, also water's edge among boulders or rushes, bogs and moorland; nest varies from lined scrape to platform of plant debris; 2 or 3 pale blue or green to dark olive eggs, blotched and streaked brown often mainly at big end. Both parents incubate 22-25 days and tend young, who leave nest 3-5 days and fly *c.* 5 weeks. **327**

Larus cirrocephalus *Laridae*
GREY-HEADED GULL   *c.* 16 ins
Neotropical (*L.c. cirrocephalus*): breeds inland eastern S America; winters coasts Peru, Argentina and S Brazil. Ethiopian (*poiocephalus*): breeds Gambia and Ethiopia S to S Africa; winters coasts W Africa from Gambia to Walvisch Bay and eastern Africa (including Madagascar) to Port Elizabeth. Habitat: lakes and coast. Head and throat pale grey, mantle grey; neck, tail and underparts white. Legs and bill red, eyes pale yellow. Winter: head and throat white with pale grey half-hood. Immature: upperparts and tip of tail ash-brown, head white with dark patches; legs yellowish brown, bill yellowish. Usually solitary or small parties, flocks at good feeding and roosting places; feeds on small fish, molluscs and insects; cackling cry. Usually breeds June onwards making nest among rushes of roots and mud covered with grass and rushes, or floating nest of old weeds, also nests on rocky islets using scarcely any material; 2 or 3 olive brown eggs, blotched darker brown with grey undermarkings. Incubation (Africa) *c.* 21 days. **328**

Larus delawarensis see under **L. californicus**

Larus fuscus see under **L. argentatus**

Larus heermanni *Laridae*
HEERMANN'S GULL   *c.* 18 ins
Neotropical: Pacific coast N America; breeds NW Mexico and Baja California then spreads N as far as Vancouver Is and S to Guatemala; keeps to coastline. Head and upper neck white, greyish brown in winter, mantle slate coloured; lower neck, underparts and upper tail coverts pale grey, tail dull black tipped white, wing quills mostly white tipped, underwing greyish brown; legs black, bill red. Immature: deep brown, wings and tail darker, buff edges to tail, legs and bill blackish. Usually feeds over kelp beds just

offshore, taking chiefly small fish and shrimps, sometimes robs fish from Brown Pelicans, *Pelecanus occidentalis*, as they surface, and eggs of other birds. Call: high-pitched *whee-ee*, often series of muffled cackling notes in winter. Nests April to June on coastal islands in large colonies; 2 or 3 light grey, cream or bluish eggs with lavender, brown or dark olive markings, in depression in sand or among small rocks, sometimes lightly lined with sticks or grass; occasionally more of a nest among grass or seaweeds.

Larus hyperboreus *Laridae*
GLAUCOUS GULL   *c.* 28 ins
Holarctic: islands and coast of Arctic Ocean; S to Newfoundland, James Bay, N Mackenzie and Pribilof Is. in N America, wintering edge of open water S to Long I. (NY), Great Lakes and California; in Palae-arctic ranges from Franz Josef Land S to Iceland and N coast USSR, wintering S to Mediterranean, Caspian Sea and Japan. Outside breeding season frequents sea-coast, sometimes harbours, inland lakes and rivers. Mantle, back, and scapulars pale grey, primaries and secondaries pale grey tipped white; winter, white head, neck and throat streaked pale brown, more so in ♀. Immature: creamish buff mottled pale brown, primaries brown. Legs flesh colour, thick bill yellow with pale tip and vermilion gonys (angle), eyes and orbital ring yellow. Heavy, powerful flight, usually solitary; feeds on carrion, fish, crabs, sometimes seaweed, robs and kills other birds, their young and eggs. Call: hoarse long croaks. Breeds colonies, sometimes small, late May onwards on high cliff ledges, also coastal dunes and small islets in lakes. 3 greyish brown eggs marked with dark brown, incubated *c.* 28 days by both parents; both also tend young.

Larus maculipennis see under **L. ridibundus**

Larus minutus *Laridae*
LITTLE GULL   *c.* 11 ins.
Palaearctic: breeds locally N Netherlands, Baltic countries, USSR from White Sea, L. Onega and L. Ladoga across to Okhotsk Sea, S to N Transcaucasia and L. Zaisan; winters coasts Europe and E Asia S to Mediterranean, Black and Caspian Seas, and Yang-tse-Kiang. Habitat: swampy grasslands, marshes and marshy lakes in breeding season, otherwise moves to coast, inshore waters, estuaries and large lakes inland. Hood black, upperwing grey, underwing blackish (paler when immature), tail and body white, scapulars and back pale grey; in winter pale grey on mantle, hindneck and sides of upper breast, hood reduced to dark grey cap. Legs red, browner winter and immatures, bill red-brown, blackish winter and immatures, eyes dark brown. Solitary or small flocks, flight similar to terns', snatches food (fish and other small aquatic animals) from surface water and takes insects on wing. Call: *kek-kek-kek*. Breeds late May to mid June usually in colonies; loosely built nest of aquatic plant debris in tussock or amongst reeds. Usually 3 eggs, yellowish buff to olive brown marked dark brown and ash-grey; both sexes incubate. **329**

Larus novaehollandiae *Laridae*
SILVER GULL   *c.* 16 ins
Australasian, Ethiopian: coasts Australia, Tasmania, New Caledonia; replaced New Zealand, Chatham and Auckland Is by Red-billed Gull *L. scopulinus*; also coast S Africa from Namaqualand to Natal, where named Hartlaub's Gull. Habitat: coastlines, estuaries and sometimes inland waters. White with pale grey back; outer primaries mainly black with large white spot near tip, most of other primaries white with black band near tip. Legs and bill red, eyes white, narrow orbital ring orange-red. Immature: similar, but mantle mottled brown, brown markings on wing and narrow subterminal brown band on tail; legs greyish, bill brownish, eyes and orbital ring dark. Feeds chiefly on fish; also takes other aquatic animals, flying ants and other insects on the wing; visits freshly cultivated land and scavenges near towns and ports. Call: strident, repeated *ki-och*. Breeds April to December in colonies or isolated pairs, on offshore islands, also islands in estuaries and salt lakes; 2 or 3 usually brownish olive eggs, blotched and marked with brown and black, in

nest or nearby plant debris, lined finer grass stems. Both parents incubate *c.* 24 days; young leave nest *c.* 4 weeks and disperse *c.* 2 weeks later. Generally 2 broods.

Larus pacificus *Laridae*
PACIFIC GULL   *c.* 25 ins
Australasian: Australian waters from Sharks Bay, Western Australia, to Tasmania and S New South Wales; breeds throughout range, sedentary when adult. Habitat: coastal waters, estuaries and shores, often harbours and offshore islands. Head, neck and underparts white; wings black above, white below; tail has black subterminal band. Legs yellow, heavy bill orange-yellow with plum-red tip, eyes white with yellow ring. Immature brownish, becoming mottled with age, legs and bill greyish. Call: deep, harsh *kiaw*. Feeds on carrion, fish, crabs and other aquatic invertebrates, seabird eggs and young. Breeds August to January in colonies or isolated pairs, on rocky headlands, along coastline or on lower sandy sites and edges of lagoons; 2 or 3 deep grey-brown eggs, blotched darker brown, in substantial nest of long grass stems and other plant debris. **330**

Larus philadelphia *Laridae*
BONAPARTE'S GULL   *c.* 14 ins
Nearctic: breeds interior Alaska and W Canada, winters coasts Mexico, USA, and occasionally Peru, Hawaiian Is, Bermuda, Britain. Habitat: coastal bays, harbours, estuaries and sometimes fresh waters; lakes and rivers of spruce forest belt for breeding. Head bluish black, narrow white ring round eye with gap at front, mantle pearl grey, outer primaries largely white with black tips; underparts, rump and tail white. Legs orange-red, small bill black, sometimes reddish at base, eyes brown with black orbital ring. Winter: head white with dusky cheek patch. Immature: similar cheek patches; crown, nape, scapulars and back greyish brown; forehead, neck and underparts white; tail white with subterminal dusky band, bill dusky, legs pale brownish. Flight tern-like; gregarious, less noisy than other gulls; feeds on small fish, crustaceans and marine worms, picked from surface while fluttering over water, also swims on surface to feed, can catch prey on wing and relies on insects when breeding inland. Call: rough *cherr*. Nests June and July, building loose twig and stick platform, lined dried moss, grass and lichens, on horizontal branches of low coniferous trees; 2 to 4 brownish yellow to dark olive-buff eggs with brown markings, incubated mainly by ♀; young leave nest within 5-6 days.

Larus pipixcan *Laridae*
FRANKLIN'S GULL   *c.* 13½ ins
Nearctic: breeds S Manitoba and S Alberta S to SW Minnesota, S Dakota and Utah; winters Gulf coast Texas S to W coast S America as far as Chile. Habitat: marshes or along shallow lake shores, visiting cultivated land during day. Head black, back and wings grey, wing tips black bordered white; in winter black on head reduced to dusky area across back, immature similar but browner with no black on wing tips. Legs and bill red, eyes dark. Graceful and agile flyer; feeds on aquatic and terrestrial insects, especially latter when breeding, sometimes taken on wing. Call: shrill, clear *po-lee*, also cluckings and mews. Breeds early summer onwards in colonies among reeds in shallow water; 3 pale buffish eggs with darker brown markings in well finished cup in large floating mass of old stalks attached to surrounding plants. Adults may tend each others' young. **331**

Larus ridibundus *Laridae*
BLACK-HEADED GULL   *c.* 15 ins
Palaearctic: breeds Britain, Ireland and W Europe to Turkestan and E Asia; winters coasts Europe, N Africa and Asia S to Gambia, Red Sea, Persian Gulf, India, Philippines, China and Japan. Other similar species, e.g. Patagonian Black-headed Gull *L. maculipennis* southern S America N to Brazil and Chile. Habitat: coastal and inland, favouring sandy and muddy shores, estuaries, harbours, semi-tidal rivers, lakes and reservoirs, feeding over farmland and, in winter, in cities, especially in Britain. Hood coffee brown,

reduced to few dusky markings in winter, neck and body white, lower mantle, back and wings blue-grey; white band on front edge of wing broadens to include most of outer 5 primaries, inner margin and tips of outer primaries unbroken black. Legs and bill deep red, eyes brown. Immature: mantle uneven brown, some brownish grey on wing coverts and back of head, subterminal blackish brown band on tail. Flight buoyant for gull, tramples in shallow water or wet mud to bring up food; small crustaceans, molluscs, worms and fish; also picked from surface of water; will take insects on wing. Call: harsh *kwup*, strident *kwarr* and almost dove-like sounds. Breeds April to July in colonies on coastal sandhills, saltmarshes, *Spartina* beds, shingle and sandbanks; inland on lakesides and islands, bogs and swamps; nest loosely built of plant debris, either on vegetation or in scrape on ground; 2 or 3 eggs, pale blue or greenish to dark umber, blotched dark brown and underlying grey. Both parents incubate *c.* 22-24 days and tend young, who fly 5-6 weeks. **332**

Larus scopulinus *Laridae*
RED-BILLED GULL   *c.* 14½ ins
Australasian: New Zealand, coast and offshore islands, also larger lakes inland. Head, neck, underparts and tail white, mantle, back and wing coverts uniform pale grey; primaries black with white tips and bases, 2 outer ones broad subterminal white bands; ♂ larger than ♀. Legs and bill scarlet, eyes silvery white with red eyelids. Immature: mantle suffused pale buff, dark brownish band on wing; legs purplish brown, bill brownish black, eyes brown. Sub-antarctic race slightly darker with stouter bill. Feeds on small fish, insects, earthworms and sometimes berries, also scavenges. Call: strident, tremulous scream. Breeds October onwards in dense colonies on rock stacks and cliffs, also sandbanks and flats near mouths of rivers; sub-antarctic race nests in caves and cavities. 2, sometimes 3, brownish ochre eggs with darker spots and blotches, in well formed nest of grass and other plant debris; both parents incubate *c.* 21 days.

Lathamus discolor *Psittacidae*
SWIFT PARROT   9½ ins
Australasian: Tasmania, islands of Bass Strait; migrates in numbers to SE Australia after breeding and moves locally after food. Habitat: wet and dry sclerophyll forest, savannah, orchards. Upperparts rich green, crown dark blue, red mask, yellow lores; shoulder patches, innermost coverts, underwing coverts red, undertail coverts dull red; wings blue; narrow pointed tail pale blue washed red; legs brown, bill brownish-horn, eyes pale yellow. Rapid weaving, whirring flight, darting out and back to feeding trees, where creeps through foliage; rests on topmost dead branches; seldom on ground except to drink. Call: excited chittering whistle, distinctive clinking flight notes. Food: nectar from eucalypts and other flowering trees; fruits, seeds; also insects and larvae, attacking psyllid lerps on eucalypts. Breeds September to February, 20 to 60 ft up in tree hole. 3 to 5 white eggs laid on decayed wood, incubated by ♀ 20 days, ♂ bear; young fly probably after 6 weeks. **394**

LEATHERHEAD see **Philemon corniculatus**

Legatus leucophaius see under **Cacicus cela**

Leiothrix argentauris *Muscicapidae* : *Timaliinae*
SILVER EARED MESIA   7 ins
Oriental: E from Nepal across Indo-China, SW China
to Sumatra. Breeds in broadleaved mountain forests,
also secondary growth in cleared areas, moving to
lower altitudes in winter, flocking with other species.
♂: mantle olive with red wingbar, yellow patch on
brown folded wing; crown black; throat scarlet,
blending with orange-yellow underparts; rump, undertail crimson. ♀ lacks red throat, rump; duller yellow
below. Legs yellow-brown, bill yellow, eyes red. Forms
flocks of up to 10, feeding on insects or fruit near ground.
Bold behaviour, but flies weakly. Voice: low clear
song; also noisy call *quir quir quir*. Breeds April to
August. ♀ and ♂ build cup nest of bamboo leaves, moss,
lined roots. 3 or 4 eggs indistinguishable from those of
Pekin Robin, *L. lutea*. **711**

Leiothrix lutea *Muscicapidae* : *Timaliinae*
PEKIN ROBIN   5 ins
E Palaearctic, Oriental: from S Himalayas across N
Indo-China, China N to Yangtze Valley. Breeds
mountain forest, moving lower in winter; most abundant below 2,000 ft in S China. Head olive green;
mantle, flanks greyer; rump more olive flecked white;
black centre to forked olive tail; crimson, yellow patches
on folded wing; throat orange-yellow merging into
orange breast; rest of underparts white; legs yellow,
bill red; eyes red-brown. Gregarious, flocking with
other species outside breeding season. Song of ♂
accompanied by wing flapping display; characteristic
call, loud *tee tee tee tee*. Diet includes seeds, insects.
Breeds April to June. Nest built near ground, suspended from vertical or lateral branch; deep cup of
leaves, grass, moss, lined fine grass. 3 to 5 pale green-
white eggs, blotched grey-brown at blunt end. **712**

Leipoa ocellata *Megapodiidae*
MALLEE FOWL   22-27 ins
S and W Australia; sedentary in arid country inland.
Back brown with black and white crossbars to feathers
giving 'ocellated' effect; tail tipped white, crown
black, neck slate-grey; throat pale brown, underparts
white with black central stripe; legs blue-grey, bill
slate-black, facial skin black and white, eyes hazel. Shy
disposition and seldom seen, but calls represented by
onomatopoeic native names *gnow* and *lowan*. Diet of
green buds in spring, later seeds, e.g. of acacias; young
feed on insects. ♂ and ♀ begin collecting material
April or May and excavate hole 15 ft across, 3 or 4 ft
deep, which they fill with dry leaves to 1 ft above
ground level, then cover with loose sand. ♀ lays 5 to 35
eggs, delicate pink when fresh, at long intervals in
central cavity; ♂ keeps mound at 92 °F, regulating heat,
which is derived at first from fermentation of leaves,
later from sun; process occupies him for 11 months.
Young dig their way out of mound, run in a few hours,
fly in a day and look after themselves entirely. **175**

Leptolophus hollandicus see **Nymphicus
hollandicus**

Leptopoecile sophiae *Muscicapidae* : *Sylviinae*
SEVERTGOV'S TIT WARBLER   3½ ins
Palaearctic: 4 races; resident in highlands of Sinkiang,
Kashmir, Tibet just reaching NW India and SE USSR;
moves lower down in winter. Habitat: scrub and juniper thickets from 8,000 ft to alpine zone. ♂: forehead
and 'eyebrow' whitish ochre, crown and nape reddish
brown, crest violet; mantle brownish grey; rump and
tail glossy violet blue; chin to breast reddish brown
with violet lustre, belly light ochre with golden gloss
on sides; wings olive with greyish and rufous edgings.
♀ and juvenile much duller. Legs brownish black, bill
black (paler tip), eyes red. Very active in undergrowth
but flight weak; joins flocks in autumn. Call, a thin
squeak. Food mainly insects though some seeds in
winter. Breeds mainly in May; ♂ brings material and
♀ builds nest (mainly moss, fluff, feathers) in thicket,
especially rhododendron, 2-3 ft up. 4 to 6 white eggs
with purplish-black spots, incubated by ♀ and ♂. **740**

Leptoptilus crumeniferus *Ciconiidae*
MARABOU   60 ins
Ethiopian region, except extreme S, migratory in N
of range and in S Africa. Slate-grey upperparts with
green iridescence; underparts white; head, neck and
breast with air-filled sac bare, crimson to black, with
white ruff at base; legs grey, heavy bill greyish-white,
eyes light brown. Largely commensal, but often near
lake or river; follows locusts and attracted to carrion
in open country. Vulture-like, soaring high up to
watch for feeding opportunities, to descend at speed
with rush of air through wings. Generally silent, except
for croaks and grunts at nests and bill-rattling in
mutual display. Scavenger, associating with and
driving away vultures; frogs and locusts also important
in diet and destroys *Quelea* nests. Breeding variable
throughout range; colonial in trees, cliffs, even on
buildings in towns; in W Africa often with pelicans;
rather small nest of sticks holds 2 to 3 granulated white
eggs; incubation and fledging periods apparently not
known. **73**

Leptosomus discolor *Leptosomatidae*
CUCKOO ROLLER or COUROL   *c.* 17 ins
Malagasy: confined to Madagascar and Comoro Is;
resident forest and scrub. ♂: upperparts blackish,
heavily glossed purple and green; crown and hindcrown blackish, forming slight crest; head, cheeks,
naps, underparts to breast grey, becoming paler on
underwing (tips black), under tail coverts; feathers
between base of hooked serrated black bill and dark
brown eye 'brushed' forward over upper mandible;
legs orange. ♀ and immature: upperparts dark brown
glossed green; chestnut-tipped wing coverts form patch
on closed wing; breast and face, including frontal tuft,
chestnut narrowly barred black; rest underparts buff
to pale buff spotted dark brown. 2 powderdown
patches on rump give 'bloom' to plumage. Singly or in
pairs; normally flies direct with slow wingbeats but ♂
has undulating display flight, calling repeated *quiyu
quiyu qui*; also from conspicuous bare perch, puffing out
throat. Soft whistling and bubbling calls between pair.
Food off upper branches: locusts, stick insects, beetles,
hairy larvae; chameleons; prey beaten against perch
before swallowing. Nests in hollow tree, perhaps also
hole in bank, laying 2 creamy buff eggs in bare
chamber. Young fed as adults.

Lerwa lerwa *Phasianidae*
SNOW PARTRIDGE   *c.* 15 ins
E Palaearctic, marginally Oriental: Himalayas between *c.* 10,000 and 17,000 ft, from NW Pakistan
through Nepal, Sikkim, Bhutan to Tibet and W China;
may descend below 7,500 ft in severe winters. Habitat:
alpine pastures, open hillsides with some vegetation
above tree line and up to snow line. Upperparts
narrowly barred black and white; underparts mostly
rich chestnut with pale broad streaks, especially belly
and flanks. Legs and bill bright red, eyes brownish red
or blood red. Gregarious, small family parties or
groups up to *c.* 20, tame when not persecuted; covey
scatters when alarmed with great whirring and clapping of wings; flight fast and strong. Call: low alarm
whistle, shriller when strongly threatened; ♂ utters 2
to 4 subdued clucks, rising in intensity, followed by
quickly repeated high-pitched challenge. Food: lichen,
moss, seeds and plant shoots; probably some insects.
Breeds May to July; 3 to 6 pale buff to dirty grey-buff
eggs finely marked with red, in scrape in ground
under cover of rock or bush, sometimes lined with
leaves and moss.

LESSER
  BIRD OF PARADISE see under **Paradisaea
    guilielmi**
  BLACK-BACKED GULL see under **Larus
    argentatus**
  CRESTED TERN see **Sterna bengalensis**
  DOUBLE-COLLARED SUNBIRD see **Cinnyris
    chalybeus**
  FLAMINGO see **Phoeniconaias minor**
  GOLDEN PLOVER see **Pluvialis dominica**
  GREY SHRIKE see **Lanius minor**
  HONEYGUIDE see **Indicator minor**
  JACANA see **Microparra capensis**

SPOTTED WOODPECKER see **Dendrocopos minor**

Leucophoyx thula see **Egretta thula**

Leucopsar rothschildi *Sturnidae*
ROTHSCHILD'S STARLING or MYNAH   *c.* 10 ins
Oriental: confined to Bali, where local and rare in
remaining forests; *c.* 180 birds in captivity 1969. White
plumage, tips of flight and tail feathers black; long
white crest. Legs bluish grey, strong bill blue-grey and
yellow, bare facial skin blue, eyes dark brown. Little
known of habits in wild but aggressive in captivity
against both its own and other species. Has bred in
large communal aviaries and special compartments
with varying success. Most successful period May-June
in US zoos. Has built in nestboxes, hollow trunks and
rock crevice, using twigs, straws, grass and feathers.
3 or 4 eggs usual clutch, but one pair raised 9 young
from 2 broods. **971**

Leucosarcia melanoleuca *Columbidae*
WONGA DOVE   *c.* 15 ins
E Australia, E coast from N Queensland to Melbourne,
Victoria. Habitat: rain forest, also sheltered gullies in
heathlands and more open woodland. ♂: upperparts
dark slate-grey, forehead and chin white; throat slate-
grey, rest of underparts mottled black on white, broad
white band from sides of neck to white of upper breast.
♀: smaller, slightly less bluish. Legs pinkish red, bill
purplish pink or purplish red at base, darker at tip,
eyes dark brown or red, orbital skin pink with blue
grey outer edge. Wary, good walker, feeding on seeds
on ground; when flushed rises with loud wing flap but
lands quietly on branch, remaining motionless and
well camouflaged. Territorial, usually in pairs, but
more gregarious at good feeding or watering places.
Call: repeated loud and high pitched series of *coos*.
Usually breeds October to January; twig platform
fairly high up in trees or shrubs. 2 white eggs incubated
♀ and ♂. Possibly two broods. **365**

LEVAILLANT'S BARBET see **Trachyphonus
vaillantii**

LIGHT-MANTLED SOOTY ALBATROSS see
Phoebetria palpebrata

LILAC-BREASTED ROLLER see **Coracias candata**

LILY TROTTER see **Actophilornis africanus**

Limicola falcinellus *Scolopacidae*
BROAD-BILLED SANDPIPER   *c.* 6½ ins
Palaearctic: subarctic zone in Scandinavia, very
locally across N Russia and Siberia; summer visitor,
wintering muddy shores E Mediterranean, Black and
Caspian Seas, into Oriental region, Micronesia, even
Australia. Breeds wet meadows, bogs, tundra, often in
wooded areas, cf. Jack Snipe, *Lymnocryptesminimus*.
Summer: upperparts dark pattern like Jack Snipe;
head striped; wings dark brown; tail centrally brown,
edges white; throat, neck, breast streaked brown;
underparts white; legs dark, variable, flattened bill
blackish, base yellow, eyes dark brown. Much greyer
in winter with white throat and eye-stripe. Juvenile
has buff underparts. Apparently nowhere common,
usually solitary on migration and in winter. Rather
skulking, crouching when disturbed. Call a trill like
Temminck's Stint, *Calidris temminckii*, with rather
harsh trilling song in display flight. Diet: insects, earthworms, small freshwater and marine animals. Breeds
from first week June, making well hidden scrape in
moss and tall cover. 4 whitish eggs, heavily spotted red-
brown, incubated by ♀ and ♂; period and fledging
unknown. **285**

Limnocorax flavirostra *Rallidae*
AFRICAN BLACK CRAKE   *c.* 9 ins
Ethiopian; resident in swamps and lakesides. Blackish-
slate all over; legs orange-red, bill greenish-yellow,
eyes red. Immature has olive-brown upperparts. Flirts
tail like Moorhen, *Gallinula chloropus*, as it walks in open
or traverses water-lily leaves; also climbs plant stems;
runs fast but flies reluctantly like its relatives. Calls in
duet deep *churr* and high-pitched trill; also clucking

notes. Food: worms and water insects. Breeds throughout year with two peaks suggesting two broods. Large loose nest of grass, sometimes lined green leaves, in riparian cover. 2 to 6 pale stone or buff eggs, marked reddish brown and purple, incubated by ♀ and ♂ for c. 2 weeks; both parents tend the brood. **229**

Limnodromus griseus see under **L. scolopaceus**

Limnodromus scolopaceus *Scolopacidae*
LONG-BILLED DOWITCHER   *c.* 12 (bill 2½) ins
E Palaearctic and Nearctic: NE Siberia, N Alaska to Yukon; winters S California to Guatemala, mainly by fresh waters, estuaries and reed-fringed bays. Breeds 'muskegs': wooded swamps with quaking vegetation. Very difficult to tell from Short-billed Dowitcher, *L. griseus*, of which long considered to be western race. Summer: upperparts mottled dark brown and buff like snipe; wing tips very dark brown with white bar and trailing edge; lower back, rump white, tail barred; crown dark brown and stripe through eye on whitish cheek; breast and underparts chestnut, much richer colour than *griseus*, and more heavily barred and flecked; legs greenish black, bill blackish brown, eyes dark brown. Winter: upperparts much duller, underparts from face and throat mainly white; distinguished from *griseus* by paler, finely barred tail. Single or repeated 'thin piping note'; *griseus* has 'low mellow three-note whistle', also song flight with quivering wings. Looks compact, walking and flying with head drawn in and bill pointing downwards. Probes mud or sand deeply for worms, leeches, small molluscs; also takes insects and larvae, some seeds and roots. Breeds from June, making sparsely lined scrape, often partly sheltered by dwarf birch. 4 eggs in shades of buff, marked dark brown and grey, incubated by ♀ and ♂ c. 3 weeks. ♂ sometimes cares for the brood. **286**

Limosa haemastica see under **L. limosa**

Limosa limosa *Scolopacidae*
BLACK-TAILED GODWIT   15-17 (bill 3¾-4¾) ins
Palaearctic, including Iceland; otherwise mainly N temperate from Britain across Eurasia to Kamtchatka; replaced in Nearctic by Hudsonian Godwit, *L. haemastica*, regarded by some as conspecific. Winters from Britain S to subtropics, tropics and beyond: Africa, Oriental region to Australia, Tasmania, on muddy freshwaters, estuaries and sea shores. Breeds meadows, often grazed, swampy heaths and moors, lakesides, forest clearings. Summer: crown and upperparts dark brown with pale feather edges; face to breast light chestnut, barred lower down; black wing tips and trailing edge below broad white bar; dark rump, tail white with broad black terminal band; underparts white, sparsely barred; very long legs blackish-green, long almost straight bill flesh pink, tip brown, eyes dark brown. Winter: grey-brown above, face, breast lighter, underparts light grey. Stately walk with head well up, flies with neck slightly bent and legs well beyond tail. Call: *wicker wicker wicker*; *kwee-yet* like Lapwing, *Vanellus vanellus*, on breeding ground; sings in display flight, which goes up to 200 ft. Also courtship on ground. Probes for small animals in soil or mud, and wades deeply; also takes insects and molluscs from plant stems. Breeds from end March in S of range; scrape, sometimes well lined and with stems interlaced over it, in thick cover, holds 4 blue green to dark brown eggs, spotted and blotched darker brown and grey; incubated by ♀ and ♂ 22-24 days; both tend young, who fly 4-5 weeks. **287**

LIMPKIN see **Aramus guarauna**

LINNET see **Acanthis cannabina**

Lissotis hartlaubii *Otididae*
HARTLAUB'S BUSTARD   24 ins
Ethiopian: Sudan, Somalia, E Africa; resident in open country at varying elevations. ♂: similar to Black-bellied Bustard, *L. melanogaster*, but lower back and rump black and back of neck grey. ♀: generally darker above, neck spotted and streaked light fawn with whitish streak in front; black crescents on breast; lower

back and rump not entirely black. Legs yellowish brown, bill yellow, eyes very light brown. Shy and difficult to tell from Black-bellied Bustard, so little known of habits, which may be assumed to be similar. Feeds on beetles, locusts and other insects. Breeding season probably May and June in Somalia. Lays probably 2 eggs, sandy brown, marked brown and grey, on bare ground. Incubation and parental care as other bustards.

Lissotis melanogaster or Eupodotis melanogaster *Otididae*
BLACK-BELLIED BUSTARD   26 ins
Ethiopian: across Africa from about Lat. 16°N to Zambia and Angola in suitable habitat, which is open grassland or cultivated areas for feeding, with cover nearby. Local movements in search of food. ♂: mantle and scapulars tawny with black shaft-stripes; rump and tail vermiculated black and fawn; upper wing coverts mainly white, flight feathers black and white; head, cheeks, nape buff with short crest, throat silver grey; white line down side of neck leads to white patch on side of breast, while black of underparts extends in thin black line up centre of neck to throat. ♀: neck buff, barred blackish, upper wing coverts light fawn, belly white and no black line down neck. Legs yellowish brown, bill yellow, eyes light brown. White on wings very conspicuous in flight. Usually in pairs in moist areas, squatting when danger threatens and hard to flush. Like other small bustards ♂ makes display flights, dropping to ground with wings held high. Rather silent, with soft whistle and barking *or-buk or-buk* in breeding season, which varies throughout range. Feeds mainly on insects, especially locusts and grasshoppers. Lays 1 or 2 glossy, buff eggs, boldly marked chestnut brown and grey, on bare ground. Incubation and parental care as other smaller bustards. **245**

LITTLE
   BEE-EATER see **Melittophagus pusillus**
   BLUE HERON see **Florida caerulea**
   BLUE PENGUIN see **Eudyptes minor**
   BUSTARD see **Otis tetrax**
   GREBE see **Tachybaptus ruficollis**
   GREEN BEE-EATER see **Merops orientalis**
   GULL see **Larus minutus**
   LORIKEET see **Glossopsitta pusilla**
   OWL see **Athene noctua**
   SPIDERHUNTER see **Arachnothera longirostris**
   STINT see under **Calidris temminckii**
   TERN see **Sterna albifrons**
   WATTLEBIRD see **Anthochaera chrysoptera**

LIVINGSTONE'S TOURACO see **Tauraco livingstonii**

Lobibyx novaehollandiae *Charadriidae*
AUSTRALIAN SPUR-WINGED PLOVER   15 ins
SE Australia and Tasmania; colonised South Island, New Zealand since *c.* 1940. Resident on edge of swamps, lagoons and streams; on crop fields and shores in NZ. Upperparts brown, crown and shoulders black; underparts and rump white, black tip to tail; bony yellow spur at 'wrist' of wing which is white below with dark trailing edge; legs reddish, bill and facial wattles yellow, eyes yellow. Described as more like small heron than plover, flying low with slow beats of rounded wings. Walks sedately but can run fast; shy and hard to approach. Alarm or aggressive call grating rattle *kerrick kerrick*. Food mainly animal: insects and small crustaceans, some plant material. Breeds July to January, making scrape often on dry or stony ground but not far from water. 4 light olive eggs, marked brownish black and dull grey; incubation and fledging probably as Lapwing, *Vanellus vanellus*. **264**

Lobipes lobatus see **Phalaropus lobatus**

Lochmias nematura *Furnariidae*
SHARP-TAILED STREAMCREEPER   6¼ ins
Neotropical: locally distributed from E Panama throughout S America to NE Argentina; mountain watercourses from 5,000 to 8,500 ft. Fairly uniform dark umber or chestnut brown according to race; rather short black tail; underparts spotted white; one race has white 'eyebrow'; bill rather slender, slightly

curved. Unobtrusive; haunts sewage effluents in Brazil, searching for insects.

Locustella fasciolata *Muscicapidae: Sylviinae*
GRAY'S GRASSHOPPER WARBLER   7 ins
Palaearctic: breeds in narrow belt of NE Asia from River Ob to Japan (Hokkaido) and Sakhalin; winters Philippines, Moluccas, Sundas and W New Guinea. Habitat: grassy thickets often near streams and in clearings. Upperparts dark brown, olive tinge on head and russet on tail coverts; 'eyebrow' ashy-grey; underparts whitish, breast and neck scaly grey, flanks olive-brown; wings and tail reddish brown, latter rounded. Juvenile darker. Legs flesh brown, bill dark brown, eyes nut brown. Very secretive, moving about in grass cover; very difficult to flush from nest. Call: distinctive *tokkok-trook*. Song brief, loud and flutelike, of 10 notes (2 slow ones in middle). ♂ starts to sing on ground, runs up twig, then down again; often sings at night. Food insects. Breeds mainly June; builds quite large deep nest of fallen leaves and grass on damp ground in dense vegetation. 4 dirty white eggs with few large dark spots over dense but faint lilac spots. **741**

Locustella naevia *Muscicapidae: Sylviinae*
GRASSHOPPER WARBLER   5 ins
Palaearctic: several races; breeds in band between 40°N and 60°N from W Europe to 95°E; winters S Europe, N Africa and in Asia from Caspian Sea to W India. Habitat: rank grass with scattered bushes or young trees, marshy or dry. Upperparts yellowish olive brown, each feather with dark centre; underparts white or buffish, sometimes with spots and streaks on throat and flanks; wings dark, tail reddish brown and rounded. Legs pale yellowish brown, bill dark brown, eyes brown. Very secretive. Displaying ♂ walks along stems with tail spread and flapping wings. Call: hard *tchick*; song, rapid, uniform, ventriloquial, high pitched trill like angler's reel. Often at night. Food: insects and larvae. Breeds May to July; builds grass nest, typically hidden in tussock of grass, rushes or other thick low cover, sometimes a foot up, entrance often by run. Usually 6 creamy eggs with dense brownish red spots and generally a dark hairstreak; incubation both sexes 14 days. Young, fed by ♂ and ♀, fledge 10-12 days. 2 broods in S of range. **742**

LOGRUNNER, NORTHERN see **Orthonyx spaldingi**

Lonchura castaneothorax or Donacola castaneothorax *Estrildidae*
CHESTNUT-BREASTED FINCH   4½ ins
Australasian: tropical continental N Australia to New South Wales; New Guinea; introduced other islands. Resident reedbeds, grasslands in coastal districts, swamps with wild rice *Oryza sativa*, cultivated areas. Meets competition from introduced Asian Spice Finch, *L. punctulata*. ♂: upperparts dark cinnamon, wings greyish-brown; rump, upper tail coverts, central tail feathers yellowish, rest of tail darker; crown, hind-neck greyish-brown; lores, cheeks, throat black; breast pale chestnut with black band and borders; underparts white streaked cinnamon and black at sides; flanks, under tail coverts black. ♀ very similar, slightly paler. Legs grey, bill bluish-grey, eyes brown. Immature generally shades of brown. Single birds have undulating flight, large flocks (sometimes of juveniles) fly rapidly with quick turns. Call: single *tit*; song, high-pitched, lasts 12 seconds; duets and trios between birds. Feeds largely grass seeds, perching on stalks to hold several together with feet; flocks damage crops autumn, winter; takes termites on wing in spring. Complex and variable mutual courtship display with bodily contact. Breeds colonially second half wet season in N, ♀ and ♂ building small domed nest of green grass, usually woven round living stems, softly lined; sometimes 1 to 3 ft up in shrub, bamboos. 5 or 6 white eggs incubated ♀ and ♂ 12-13 days; both feed young from throat; fledging *c.* 3 weeks. 2 or 3 broods. **939**

Lonchura punctulata see under **L. castaneothorax**

LONG-BILLED
   DOWITCHER see **Limnodromus scolopaceus**

Lophoaetus occipitalis *Accipitridae*
LONG-CRESTED HAWK EAGLE   22½ ins
Ethiopian: Senegal to Ethiopia, and S to Cape of Good Hope; resident well wooded and cultivated areas, moister savannahs and riverine tree belts, but not dense rain forest. Very dark brown or black, except for white patches above and below 'wrist' of wing; white bars on tail, white under wing coverts spotted black; shanks greyish brown, feet and cere yellow, bill-tip dark, eyes golden or reddish brown. Immature more mottled. Pair usually near together, rests in dense tree during heat of day; hunts from conspicuous perch, taking principally small mammals, also reptiles, large insects (*Orthoptera*). Noisy display flight, uttering loud, ringing *keee-ee-ay*; also repeated *kik kik kik kik keee*. Breeds probably annually, March onwards in N, August to December in S of range; pair builds stick nest 20 to 60 ft up, often in wild fig or introduced eucalypt; usually 2 dull white eggs, clouded brown, grey, lilac, sometimes spotted brown, incubated by ♀, fed by ♂; she sits tight, sometimes on empty nest. First ♂, then ♀ brings food to young (usually only one survives), who fledges *c.* 55 days. **156**

Lopholaimus antarcticus *Columbidae*
TOPKNOT PIGEON   *c.* 17½ ins
Australia E coast from Cape York to NW Victoria. Habitat: rain forest and adjacent ridges or eucalyptus forest, seen in open country flying between patches of suitable forest. ♂: grey, much paler below; feathers have silky-white down-like bases; wings and back pale slate grey, lighter on lower back, rump and upper tail coverts, primaries black; long black tail with band of silver and grey at base. Distinctive double crest: one on forehead grey, other on crown chestnut, bordered black. Thick bill rose-red with greenish lead base, legs purplish red, eyes orange with red orbital skin. ♀: similar but smaller, eyes yellower. Gregarious, sometimes large numbers at good feeding places; roosts tall trees on high ridges, descending into forest in daytime to feed on fruits and berries off branches. Call: low *coo*. Large nest of sticks high up in tall trees; single white egg. **366**

Lophonetta specularoides *Anatidae*
ANDEAN and PATAGONIAN
CRESTED DUCK   24 ins
Neotropical: Andean race, *L.s. alticola*, in high valleys and plateaux Andes of S Peru, Bolivia, N Chile and Argentina; Patagonian Crested Duck, *specularoides*, breeds on inland freshwaters S Chile N to Santiago, Patagonia and W Argentina N to Mendoza, Tierra del Fuego and Falkland Is; winters near seashore and salt water. Habitat (*alticola*): mountain lakes between 10,000 and 15,000 ft or higher. Forehead, face and neck pale grey-brown; crest, hind crown and band behind eyes darker; mantle, breast and flanks mottled grey-brown and brown; back, rump. upper tail coverts and belly mottled dark and pale brown; tail and under tail coverts black, wings earthy brown with pink speculum. Patagonian race similar, but smaller, greyer and more spotted underparts. Legs and bill dark grey, eyes orange-yellow. Isolated pairs or families; pair strongly territorial, even attacking other species. Call: deep repeated quack, ♀ long series of short grumbling notes. Feeds on shores, flats and in shallow water, taking small animals and some plant matter. Breeding season variable, usually September to November; lays 5 to 9 cream eggs in holes or in dense grass lined with down, young immediately led to water. **117**

Lophortyx californicus *Phasianidae*
CALIFORNIA QUAIL   10½ ins
Nearctic: originally W coast N America from Oregon to Lower California; now introduced more widely in Canada and USA, also Chile, Hawaii, New Zealand; local movements seasonally in native range. Habitats with low trees and shrubs, open spaces with low cover: from oak woods and chaparral-sagebrush to city parks and gardens, up to 5,000 ft in S of range in summer. ♂: complex plumage pattern with dark brown upperparts, black cheeks and throat bordered white; breast and 'scaly' nape grey-blue; flanks barred black and white, belly scaled black on white with chestnut patch; curved head plume shared with Gambel's Quail, *L. gambelii*. ♀ has similar but much duller pattern, with dark-spotted white face and throat. Legs, bill and eyes dark. Gregarious up to 50 birds, except when courting and nesting. Covey runs if approached, splits up in flight if pursued. Roosts in trees. Assembly call: *come right* or *come right here*; ♂ crows loud *kah-ah* in spring. Food mainly vegetable, soft leaves and buds in spring; seeds, fruits rest of year; some insects, spiders and snails, especially during first week of life. Breeds in spring, lining scrape with grass or leaves, usually hidden by shrubs, log or other cover. 10 to 17 buffish eggs, marked dull brown, incubated by ♀ and ♂ 21-23 days. **202**

Lophortyx gambelii see under **L. californicus**

Lophura leucomelana see **L. lophura**

Lophura lophura or Lophura leucomelana *Phasianidae*
KALEEJ PHEASANT   20-27 ins
Oriental: several races widespread over region; hybridises with and sometimes regarded as one species with Silver Pheasant, *L. nycthemerus*. Resident in denser forests than Red Jungle Fowl, *Gallus gallus*, especially in gullies with watercourses or near cultivation. ♂: races differ considerably; black-breasted *L.l. lathami* predominantly dark purple on head and body, dark green on curved tail with white-scaled rump; crest and wingtips dark brown; spurred legs grey-brown, bill light yellow, facial skin red, eyes reddish. ♀: brown above, chestnut brown below, scaled and feathershafted white; crown and crest chestnut brown. Secretive, chiefly revealed by harsh crow of ♂, who drums by vibrating wings against body; guttural cooing and rapidly repeated *whoop keet keet* of alarm; low clucking notes. Food: young leaves and stems, grain and bamboo seeds, fallen figs; some insects and their larvae, especially termites, leaping after them in air. Breeding peaks March to May, July to August. 6 to 9 white or buff to reddish buff eggs laid in scrape on ground and incubated by ♀ 20-21 days. ♂, successively polygamous, may help last mate with young; 2 broods.

Lophura nycthemerus see under **L. lophura**

Lorius roratus or L. pectoralis *Psittacidae*
ECLECTUS PARROT   20 ins
Oriental (Lesser Sunda Islands), Australasian: Moluccas, New Guinea and offshore islands, Bismarck and Solomons, extreme N Queensland; feeds humid scrub, nests and roosts rain forest. Discovered 1913, outstanding example of sexual dimorphism; ♂: generally dark green, red on flanks and underwings; wings edged blue; legs flesh-grey, bill: upper red, lower dark; eyes yellow. ♀: generally red, purplish blue hindneck, belly; wings edged blue; undertail and terminal band yellow; blue round eye; legs pale flesh-grey, bill dark brown, eyes yellow. Noisy and conspicuous even in tree tops, small flocks revealed by clicking note of ♀♀ and falling seeds. Flies high above canopy with raucous *kurrah* or *kar kar kar* and slow flapping action. ♀ also has mellow whistle. Food: various nuts and seeds; large flocks collect for eucalypt nectar. Breeds October to December in tree hole up to 70 ft to edge of forest, by clearing or near water. 2 white eggs incubated by ♀ *c.* 30 days. ♂ feeds ♀ who feeds young; they leave nest 8-9 weeks, full grown 3-3½ months.

Loxia curvirostra *Fringillidae*
COMMON or RED CROSSBILL   6 ins
Holarctic, Oriental, Neotropical: from Iberia across Eurasia roughly between 40° and 60°N to near Pacific at 130°E, but many scattered populations in mountains, e.g. N Africa, Tibet-China, Japan, and tropically in S Annam, Philippines (N Luzon). In America breeds right down W coast from Alaska to Panama and E along 50°N to Newfoundland, with outliers N Georgia, S Honduras, N Nicaragua; altogether 21 races recognised. Type habitat spruce *Picea* forests, lowland and montane; often in pines; in spruce, larch and fir up to 13,500 ft in Asia. Resident but liable to mass eruptions away from breeding areas, from which outlying groups probably established. ♂: variable brick red shading to dark brown on wings (with pale bar), short forked tail and cheeks; palest on underparts. ♀ yellowish green, streaked on upperparts, brightest on rump, breast. Juvenile browner, heavily striated. Immature ♂ orange-red. Legs, cross-tipped bill, eyes dark brown. Seldom on ground except to drink. Rapid undulating flight with loud *chup chup* calls, which change slightly when party lands on tree to feed, working cones in parrotlike postures. Song rendered *tik tik tik tukai tukai tukai*, interspersed with long drawn *tukao*. Flocks break up after noisy 'parties', flapping and gliding flights by ♂♂. Diet primarily conifer seeds, extracted by tongue after scale levered or split by mandibles; also takes pips from fleshy fruits, some seeds and variety of insects. Breeds variably, January to July. ♀, partly assisted ♂, makes foundation of twigs for cup of grass, wool, moss, hair, lichen, softly lined; usually near end of lateral branch or at very top of conifer, sometimes near trunk, 20 to 60 ft up. 3 or 4 eggs indistinguishable from Greenfinch, *Carduelis chloris*, incubated ♀ 13-16 days; both parents feed young from throat, they fly 18-22 days. **926**

Loxops parva see under **L. virens**

Loxops virens or Chlorodrepanis virens *Drepanidae*
AMAKIHI c. 4½ (bill c. ½) ins
Confined Hawaiian Islands, separate races on 6 main islands, as opposed to *L. parva*, confined to Kauai. Resident native forest above c. 1,500 ft Hawaiian race *virens*, ♂: upperparts yellowish olive, tinged orange especially on rump; flight and tail feathers brownish, edged olive; lores and line over forehead blackish; underparts olive-yellow. ♀ duller, upperparts tinged ashy, underparts paler. Legs and curved bill blackish, eyes very dark brown. Juvenile much as ♀. Forms small parties outside breeding season. Strong on wings and legs, dashing into cover at speed. ♂'s song 'slow, level trill' (P. H. Baldwin), also component in more complex song used in fighting and defence of territories, held October to June, after which song not heard. Searches for insects in trees, probing bark (especially strong-billed Kauai race *L.v. stejneri*), opening folded leaves, taking scale insects sometimes in quantity; attacks blossoms of koa and ohia *Metrosideros* trees, pierces corollas of lobelias to get at nectar, insects; also takes berries. Breeds probably March onwards, building open cup nest in dense twigs of small ohia tree several feet up, of sticks, grass, spider egg-cases, lined rootlets, plant fibres, lichen. 2 or 3 creamy white eggs freckled pale lilac and smoke grey in cap at big end, incubated ♀, but both parents probably feed young.

Lullula arborea *Alaudidae*
WOOD LARK 6 ins
Palaearctic; 2 races; *L.a. arborea* breeds Britain, Scandinavia to 60°N, east to Urals south to Spain and N Italy; winters S England and Europe to N Africa. *L.a. pallida* breeds N Africa, Mediterranean Islands, Asia Minor to Iran; recorded wintering in Egypt. Habitat: wood edges, hillsides with few trees, heaths, other bare areas, winters in fields. Upperparts brown with darker streaks; short crest, prominent buffish 'eyebrow'; black and white 'flash' (alula) shows on closed wing; underparts white to buffish with dark spots on breast; short tail; legs brownish flesh; bill, upper: dark brown, lower: paler; eyes umber. Call liquid *titloo-eet*; song musical and mellow with characteristic *lu-lu-lu* phrase, usually from tree and often at night. Nomadic in winter, usually in family parties. Feeds mainly on small insects. Breeding season end March to July; quite substantial grass nest on ground in a depression. 3 or 4 greyish-white, finely freckled, eggs. Incubation 13-15 days by ♀, ♂ in attendance. Young leave nest 11-12 days before flying a week later. Usually 2 broods. **607**

Luscinia calliope *Muscicapidae: Turdinae*
SIBERIAN RUBYTHROAT 5½ ins
E Palaearctic: large area Central Asia between 50° and 65°N, extending W of River Ob at 60°; E to Kamtchatka, Sakhalin, Hokkaido; isolated population mountains NW China; winters S Asia E to Philippines. Habitat typically taiga: dark coniferous or mixed forests with fallen trees, mosses, lichens, especially damp valleys. Upperparts dark brown; white 'brow' stripe cuts eye; thin white and black moustachial stripes; chin, throat ruby red; upper breast greyish, underparts shading to whitish. ♀ has throat white, head stripes fainter. Legs, bill brown, eyes dark brown. Juvenile mottled. Skulks in cover both summer and winter, though occasionally seen gardens in Burma (B. E. Smythies). Call ventriloquial *twee twee*, rattling churr of alarm; loud, often nocturnal song of nightingale type, but less sustained, often starts with mimicry. Food: insects, earthworms, snails. Nesting habits much as Bluethroat, *L. svecica*; open cup-shaped nest of local plant materials, on ground among grasses and tall herbs or low bushes. 4 to 6 greenish-grey eggs, marked red-brown at big end; incubation and fledging probably much as *L. svecica*. **685**

Luscinia luscinia *Muscicapidae: Turdinae*
THRUSH NIGHTINGALE 6½ ins
Palaearctic: across Eurasia from Denmark, S Sweden into headwaters of Ob system between 50° and 60°N, extending southward E and W of Black Sea; winters Ethiopian region mainly S of Equator in E Africa. Habitat rather open riverine or lakeside forest with thick undergrowth and ground cover especially of nettles *Urtica*; wooded steppes, shrub-clad swamps in cultivated land; occasionally parks, gardens. Upperparts uniform olivaceous brown; upper tail coverts, tail slightly rufous; underparts pale greyish brown, lightly spotted on breast, whitish on throat, belly; legs pale brown, bill mainly dark brown, eyes dark brown. Juvenile mottled above, 'scaly' below. Resembles Robin, *Erithacus rubecula*, but more skulking, though carriage more upright. Takes long hops on ground where spends much time. Call *whit*, sharper than Nightingale, *L. megarhynchos*, and song more powerful, with 'marvellously pure bell-like notes' (B. W. Tucker) replacing the flutelike *piuu*. Food small insects, worms, snails taken from litter layer; berries, small fruits in season. Breeds from early May to June, ♀ building foundation dead leaves, cup of grasses, stalks, lined finer material; usually on ground among nettles. 4 or 5 pale whitish eggs, covered with dense olive brown markings, incubated by ♀ 13 days; both parents feed young, who leave nest c. 11 days, fully fledged 3 weeks. **686**

Luscinia megarhynchos see under **L. luscinia**

Luscinia svecica *Muscicapidae: Turdinae*
BLUETHROAT 5½ ins
Palaearctic, marginally Nearctic: most of N Eurasia from Rhine and Danube to Bering Straits, with isolated groups N Alaska: also very local Iberia, France and Caucasus to S Caspian; winters N Africa, S Asia. Habitat dense scrub on borders lakes and rivers, extending into marginal aquatic zone; also marshy grassland with scattered bushes; willow and birch swamps on tundra; subalpine scrub round marshy meadows to 9,600 ft; winters mainly in dense riparian cover. ♂: upperparts dark brown with pale 'eyebrow'; rufous base to tail; blue gorget separated from white underparts by narrow black, white and chestnut bands. Red spot on gorget of northern and eastern races, white spot on southern race, virtually unspotted race *magna* from SE. ♀ has whitish gorget bordered streaky dark brown; underparts pale brown. ♂ autumn resembles ♀ with traces blue and chestnut. Legs yellow-brown, bill, eyes dark brown. Juvenile like Robin, *Erithacus rubecula*. Secretive, Robin-like when in open but carriage more upright; flirts and spreads tail. Call *tacc tacc* and plaintive *hweet*; song rich, nightingale-like but imitative, with metallic *ting ting ting*. Food small insects, worms, snails from thick cover and ground; berries in autumn. Breeds from mid June Scandinavia, early May in S. ♀ builds nest of dry grass with finer lining, well hidden in bank, under tussocks, dead reeds, low vegetation. 4 to 7 greenish to reddish-cream eggs, spotted red-brown in zone, incubated by ♀ 13-14 days; both parents feed young, who leave nest c. 14 days. **687**

LUZON BLEEDING HEART see **Gallicolumba luzonica**

Lybius leucomelas or Tricholaema leucomelas *Capitonidae*
PIED BARBET 6½ ins
Ethiopian: throughout southern Africa, in woodland of all types, especially thorn bush. Upperparts black, spotted white and yellow, flight and tail feathers blackish, edged yellow-white; forehead red; black mask and gorget; 'eyebrow', underparts whitish; legs and powerful bill black, eyes dark brown. Active, flight fast and direct, usually singly or in pairs. Often calls nasal *tnhar tnhar* from treetop; hollow, hoopoe-like *poop poop* in breeding season, which varies over range. Food mainly berries and fruit. Nests in hole of tree-trunk or bough, occasionally old tubular swallows' nests; lays 3 or 4 white eggs in bare chamber. **526**

Lybius torquatus *Capitonidae*
BLACK-COLLARED BARBET 6 ins
Ethiopian: most of Africa S of Equator, in coastal forest, savannah or park-like country with large fruiting trees, especially figs. Most races have conspicuous crimson face, throat, breast; black crown, nape, chest-band; stippled black and grey upperparts; yellow belly, edges of secondaries. Crimson replaced by pink in Malawi race, by white-spotted black in Tanzania, Mozambique. Call a loud repeated whistle, *kor kooroo*. Food mainly fruit, some insects. 3 white eggs laid in tree-hole, sometimes old woodpecker's. Often parasitised by Lesser Honeyguide, *Indicator minor*. **527**

Lymnocryptes minimus *Scolopacidae*
JACK SNIPE c. 7½ (bill 1½) ins
N Palaearctic: temperate and subarctic zones from Scandinavia and Baltic to NE Siberia; winters from temperate Eurasia S to Africa, India, Ceylon, in marshes, often by small stream or spring. Breeds usually large swamps with sedge and cotton grass. Upperparts and rather rounded wings mottled dark brown with greenish sheen, pale feather edges making two light bars on back; crown very dark brown, face striped, breast brown; underparts white; legs greenish-grey, bill yellowish flesh to grey, eyes dark brown. Usually solitary, springing up to pitch again not far off. Spring call hollow sound resembling distant horse cantering, uttered in display flight or on ground as bird planes down with whir rather like African and Common Snipe, *Gallinago nigripennis* and *G. gallinago*; then 'bounces' in air as if on invisible string. Probes in mud for small molluscs, insects; also some seeds. Breeds from early June; scrape, sometimes lined, in moss or hummock, hold 4 cream to olive brown eggs, marked rich dark browns, incubated by ♀ c. 24 days.

LYREBIRD,
PRINCE ALBERT'S see under **Menura novaehollandiae**
SUPERB see **Menura novaehollandiae**

Lyrurus tetrix *Tetraonidae*
BLACK GROUSE 16-17 (♀) – 20-22 (♂) ins
Palaearctic: N Temperate from Britain across Eurasia to NE Siberia and E China; resident in swampy heaths, moors and bogs, usually along forest edge, sea level to 6,000 ft. ♂: glossy blue-black, including lyre-shaped tail, with white wing bar and under tail coverts; brownish eclipse plumage in autumn. ♀: mottled brown and black with white wing-bar and forked tail. Legs feathered, toes and eyes brown, with red wattles above, bill brown-black. Families pack in autumn up to several hundred birds, sometimes ♂♂ together. Perches freely in trees, roosting in them or on ground. Typical gamebird flight of wing-beats and glides. Usually silent away from 'lek' (forest clearing or grassy area of open ground) where ♂♂, watched by ♀♀, congregate in spring and autumn to display like turkeys, with jumping runs, 'rookooing' calls but few actual fights. Diet exclusively vegetable from ground or trees: shoots, especially conifers, leaves, flowers and berries; also gleans crop fields. ♂♂ polygamous, take no part in rearing brood. ♀ lines scrape in fairly thick cover, laying 6 to 10 yellowish-white sparsely marked eggs which she incubates 24-29 days; young can fly 15-20 days. **186**

Macgregoria pulchra *Paradisaeidae*
MOLUCCAN BIRD OF PARADISE ♂: 13-15 ins
Australasian: resident mountains W and SE New Guinea, 8,900 to 12,800 ft in montane Podocarpus (pine) forests. ♂: generally velvet black; black-tipped primaries pale cinnamon; orange wattles round eyes and over earcoverts, narrow in front of eyes, broad and lappet-like above and behind. ♀ similar but smaller. Juvenile dusky black. Legs bluish-grey, bill black, eyes red or reddish brown. In pairs or small parties. Display (A. L. Rand): 2 or more birds chase each other through forest near tree limit, hopping along branches and flying, sometimes gliding, over gaps, air whistling through extended primaries, also calling *chic chic chic chic*. Food: tree fruits. Strong pair bond; breeding probably begins August when ♀, accompanied by ♂, builds bulky nest of plant stems and moss, lined finer stems, leaves c. 50 ft up in large pine. Probably single egg, earthy pink spotted brown, incubated ♀ in short spells. Both parents feed young one, ♂ perhaps taking major share.

MACARONI PENGUIN see **Eudyptes chrysolophus**

MACAW,
BLUE AND YELLOW see **Ara ararauna**
HYACINTHINE see **Anodorhynchus hyacinthinus**

Machaeropterus regulus *Pipridae*
STRIPED MANAKIN
3½ ins
Neotropical: Venezuela, Colombia, E Ecuador, NE Peru, W and Central Brazil; resident in forests from sea level to 4,000 ft. ♂: upperparts green, including sides of head and neck; inner flight feathers with white inner webs; tail, short, greyish-brown, feathers broad and stiff; crown and nape crimson; throat dull white; underparts pinkish chestnut, striped white and suffused scarlet on breast; legs, bill greyish, eyes red. ♀: upperparts olive-green; underparts whitish with brownish breast band. Display by ♂ includes 'sharp, buzzing sound' with bill wide open, followed by rapidly revolving both over and under slender twig, holding on by feet (A. F. Skutch). Breeding habits resemble *Manacus manacus*. **588**

Macrodipteryx vexillarius or Semeiophorus vexillarius *Caprimulgidae*
PENNANT-WINGED
11 ins
NIGHTJAR
(excluding 'pennants')
Ethiopian: breeds from 4°S except extreme S Africa; southern populations migrate N over Equator after breeding. Habitat varied, including thick bush, nesting on rocky timbered ground. ♂ (non-breeding) and ♀: dark brown, upperparts mottled buff; dark rufous collar on hind neck; primaries blackish, barred rufous, secondaries tipped white; small white patches on breast; throat and breast mottled brown and grey; belly whitish, sparsely barred black. In breeding season ♂'s two inner primaries elongated, one with white base, lighter inner and dark outer web. Rests lengthwise on branch. Often flies by day. Sailing courtship flight by ♂ with fluttering pennants and bat-like twittering pipe; also call rendered *kuwhoop kuwhoop kuwhoop . . churr*. ♂ may break off pennants after courtship. Food: insects hawked on wing. Drinks at dusk before hunting. Breeds August to January or longer, according to area, laying 2 rich pink or pinkish brown eggs, marbled and blotched red, brown and purple in bare place on ground.

Macronectes giganteus *Procellariidae*
GIANT PETREL
32-38 ins
Southern oceans from 30° to 65°S, moving northward after breeding almost to Equator, found increasingly offshore near human food sources. Generally dull brown, paler on face and neck and becoming mottled through pigment fading; legs brown to black, heavy bill (larger in ♂) horn to greenish, eyes brown-flecked or grey white. Immature more uniform dark brown; white plumage phase occurs. Less agile on wing than albatrosses but better on land than relatives and may feed there. Mutual displays with mewing calls at breeding sites; also hoarse croaking. Scavenging flocks at ports, but natural diet squids and crustaceans, also carrion, penguin eggs and chicks. One white egg laid August to October in vestigial to substantial nest mound on high ground of bare islands; incubated at least 6 weeks by ♀ and ♂, who eventually leave chick to fledge in 102-117 days. **29**

Macronyx ameliae *Motacillidae*
ROSY-BREASTED LONGCLAW
8 ins
Ethiopian: Kenya, Tanzania, S to Natal; resident grassy plains, often edges of marshes. ♂: upperparts black, feathers tawny-edged; underparts rich salmon pink with black band across breast, curving upward to gape. ♀: underparts buffish-brown, pink paler, confined mainly to belly; black streaks not band across breast. Legs brown (hind claw very long and curved), bill, eyes dark. Shy, but conspicuous when soaring, uttering plaintive song, then hovering, legs hanging downwards, before landing. Runs fast; does not perch in trees. Call: sharp *chuit chuit*. Eats mainly insects, with small molluscs, seeds. Breeding season varies with range; builds grass nest, lined rootlets, in or under tussock, often on wet ground. 3 or 4 very pale green eggs, mottled brown and lilac. **628**

Macronyx capensis *Motacillidae*
ORANGE-THROATED LONGCLAW
8 ins
Ethiopian: resident E Southern Africa, reaching to coast in S. Habitat: open grassland, often near permanent water source or beside sea. ♂: upperparts

dull brown; wing edged bright orange yellow, flight feathers edged pale yellow; outer tail feathers tipped white; yellow crown heavily streaked blackish-brown, 'eyebrow' orange; chin, throat bright orange, bordered black; underparts ochre to orange, flanks brown. ♀ paler on chin and throat. Legs (long hind claw) pale brown, bill darker, eyes brown. Ground-living but conspicuous, usually in pairs. Flies heavily with whirring wings when flushed, soon landing, often uttering mewing call. Sings on wing lively *chwirri chwirri chwirri chwee*. Insectivorous. Breeding as genus. **629**

Macronyx croceus *Motacillidae*
YELLOW-THROATED LONGCLAW
8 ins
Ethiopian: Senegal and Angola to Natal, not Congo forests; resident open, e.g. *Brachystegia*, woodlands, bush-clad grassland; swamps, cultivated land, near coast in S Africa. Closely resembles *M. capensis* but edge of wing, 'eyebrow', chin and throat bright not orange yellow; edges of flight and tail feathers yellower; underparts rich yellow, buff on flanks slightly streaked darker brown. Legs etc as relatives, hind toe nearly 2 ins. This species, in which sexes alike, show most striking resemblance to Nearctic meadow-larks *Sturnella*. Few 'lark-like flaps' when flushed; also slow flapping courtship flight with spread tail and song. Ordinary call repeated whistling *tuewhee*. Insectivorous. Breeding varies with range; builds well-hidden nest of grass and rootlets under tuft or in tall grass. 3 whitish or pale green eggs, spotted brown over purple-grey mottling, often at big end. **630**

Macropygia phasianella *Columbidae*
c. 14 ins
LARGE BROWN CUCKOO DOVE or BROWN PIGEON
Australasian, Oriental: races distributed across E Australia, Kangean I., Java, Sumatra, Lombok, Klagger I., Sumbawa, Flores, Engaro, Mentawi Is, Simalur I., Batan Is, Botel Tobago, Calayan I., N Borneo and Philippines. Habitat: forests; prefers glades and small openings. ♂: Australian form: head, neck and breast reddish brown, tinged pink on upper breast, shading to golden brown on lower breast; throat and underparts (neck downwards) speckled blackish grey; mantle and hindneck purple and green gloss; long tail. ♀: smaller, with rich rufous crown, lacks pink tinge and speckling more prominent. Legs and bill black or dark brown, eyes white or bluish, often with red outer ring. Most other races richer red-brown colour with more or less conspicuous blackish and rufous speckling on neck and underparts of ♀. Call: loud three syllable coo. Long tail used as support while feeding in trees or shrubs on fruits and berries; also feeds on ground. Breeds November to January in Australia; scanty twig platform usually low down in trees or shrubs, single creamy white egg. **367**

MADAGASCAR NUTHATCH see **Hypositta coralirostris**

MAGELLAN GOOSE see **Chloephaga picta**

MAGELLANIC PLOVER see **Pluvianellus socialis**

MAGNIFICENT FRIGATE BIRD see **Fregata magnificens**

MAGNOLIA WARBLER see **Dendroica magnoliae**

MAGPIE see **Pica pica**

MAGPIE,
AUSTRALIAN see **Gymnorhina tibicen**
AZURE-WINGED see **Cyanopica cyanus**
WESTERN see under **Gymnorhina tibicen**

MAGPIE GOOSE see **Anseranas semipalmata**

MAGPIE LARK see **Grallina cyanoleuca**

MAGPIE ROBIN, SEYCHELLES see **Copsychus sechellarum**

MALACHITE
KINGFISHER see **Corythornis cristata**

SUNBIRD see **Nectarinia famosa**

Malaconotus zeylonus *Laniidae*
BOKMAKIERIE SHRIKE
9 ins
Ethiopian: SW Southern Africa; resident open savannah and bush, plantations of introduced trees, gardens. Upperparts green; flight feathers dusky, green-edged; central tail feathers blackish, tinged green and faintly barred, outer feathers black with broad yellow tips; crown, hindneck, cheeks, earcoverts ashy grey; 'eyebrow' yellow, lores and line down side neck black, linking with broad band across bright yellow underparts; flanks washed grey. Legs lead-grey, bill black, eyes brown. Usually in pairs, often on ground near trees, hunting insects. Low flight, when black and yellow tail conspicuous. Birds duet in sight of each other on high perches; renderings: *bokmakierie, ko-koveet*; alarm calls: *tok tok tok*; *kwirr kirr kirr*. Breeds July to October, Cape, mainly September to December, Transvaal, ♀ and ♂ building large compact nest of twigs, grass, roots, lined fibres, rootlets; usually in thick bush a few feet up. Usually 3 or 4 greenish blue eggs, which are spotted and speckled reddish brown, incubated mainly ♀ c. 12 days; young fly c. 15 days. **655**

Malacoptila panamensis *Bucconidae*
7 ins
WHITE-WHISKERED PUFFBIRD or SOFTWING
Neotropical: S Mexico through Central America to Colombia and W Ecuador; resident at intermediate levels in lowland rain forest up to 4,500 ft. Stout, large-headed, short-tailed, ♂: upperparts from head to tail rich chestnut brown or bright cinnamon, spotted and streaked tawny and buff; throat, breast and flanks cinnamon or tawny buff (feathers edged darker), underparts shade to whitish; white tufts on cheeks 'like walrus tusks' (A. F. Skutch), smaller one on forehead. ♀: less rufous, more olive and grey. Legs pale grey, bill: upper blackish, lower bluish horn; large eyes dull red. Solitary, pairs or family parties, usually 15 to 20 ft up, flying from burrows straight to trees and often staying immobile until darts from perch to seize prey with loud clack of bill; mainly large insects and their larvae; moths, Orthoptera, also spiders, lizards. Sometimes forages in clearings early, late or in wet weather. Jerks tail when alarmed. Usually silent but utters soft, variable *peep* whistle and *tzee* call; ♂ has low twittering song. Breeds March to July Costa Rica (A. F. Skutch), ♀ and ♂ excavating 1½ to 2 ft descending tunnel in slightly sloping ground; ring of sticks and leaf fragments masks entrance; nest chamber lined leaves. ♂ takes major share incubating usually 2 blunt white eggs for at least 14 days, and broods young for first 6 days of 20 day fledging period. ♀ brings food at first to entrance and young scramble up to it; when brooding at night ceases, they screen themselves with leaves. **524**

MALAYSIAN
BROWN WOOD OWL see **Strix leptogrammica**
FISH OWL see **Bubo ketupu**
RAIL BABBLER see **Eupectes macrocerus**

MALEO see **Macrocephalon maleo**

MALLARD see **Anas platyrhynchos**

MALLEE FOWL see **Leipoa ocellata**

Malurus assimilis *Muscicapidae: Malurinae*
PURPLE-BACKED WREN
c. 5¼ ins
Australia: E of continent (W of Great Dividing Range) N to Gulf of Carpentaria and S to NW Victoria, through central and South Australia to Western Australia (apart from southern part); frequents dry scrubland. ♂: crown and sides of head purplish blue; cobalt round eye and ear coverts; mantle and upper back purplish blue; throat, chest, collar and lower back black, belly white; wings brown with chestnut shoulder patches; tail dull blue tipped white save 2 central feathers. ♀ as ♀ Variegated Wren, *M. lamberti*. Legs brown, bill black, eyes brown. Behaviour and feeding like Blue Wren, *M. cyaneus*. Breeds September to December; domed nest of grass and plant stalks

with side entrance, in bush; 3 or 4 white eggs, spotted pinkish red. **763**

Malurus callainus *Muscicapidae : Malurinae*
TURQUOISE WREN   *c.* 5 ins
Australia: Eyre Peninsula, S Australia, N to Macdonnel Range, Central Australia, and interior New South Wales; recently Great Victoria Desert, *c.* 70 miles W of S Australian border. Habitat: low scrub and saltbush areas, favours gorges. Like Black-backed Wren, *M. melanotus*, but lightly coloured (turquoise) blue plumage in ♂; differentiated from Banded Blue Wren, *M. splendens*, by broad black band across lower back and no violet tone. Legs brown to black, bill black, eyes brown. ♀ as Black-backed Wren. Behaviour and feeding and calls similar to Blue Wren, *M. cyaneus*, but shyer. Nest and nest-site like Black-backed Wren; 3 or 4 white eggs, slight pinkish tinge, finely freckled with reddish brown. **764**

Malurus cyaneus *Muscicapidae : Malurinae*
BLUE WREN   *c.* 6½ ins
Australia: Eyre Peninsula (S Australia), Victoria N to Dawson River (Queensland), up to 300 miles inland; also Tasmania and Bass Strait islands. Habitat: open forests and scrubland, also shrubby gardens and parks. ♂: crown, cheeks and upper back pale blue; nape, hind neck, lower back, upright tail and throat black; chest blue-black; rest underparts white; wings grey-brown; legs and bill black, eyes dark brown. ♀: upperparts and tail brown; 'eyebrow' orange-brown; underparts creamy white; legs and bill orange-brown. Non-breeding ♂, as ♀ but bill black, tail blue and lores pale flesh; older dominant ♂♂ keep full plumage throughout year. Small parties with one dominant ♂ in full plumage (if he dies, replaced by supporting ♂, who rapidly develops full plumage); moves by rapid hops; feeds on ground and amongst low cover; weak flyer. Call: loud, rapid sequence of notes finishing with trill. Food: insects, sometimes small seeds. Breeding pair assisted by additional ♂♂ and later young from earlier broods. Dominant ♀ lays 3 or 4 white to reddish white eggs, marked reddish brown; others help with nest building, incubation (*c.* 14 days) and rearing young; domed nest of grass, bark fibre and cobwebs with side entrance, lined wool or feathers, *c.* 3 ft up in bush or tussock. Young fledge *c.* 12 days but spend another week in dense cover and fed by group for further 4 weeks. Sometimes parasitised by cuckoos. **765**

Malurus cyanotus *Muscicapidae : Malurinae*
BLUE AND WHITE WREN   *c.* 4¾ ins
Australia (distribution includes race *M.c. leuconotus*, sometimes given specific status as White-backed Wren): Central Queensland to NW Victoria, N South Australia, S Northern Territory and Western Australia (N to Pilbara, S to Perth); frequents dry scrubby areas. ♂: blue with silky white shoulder patches. ♀: upperparts brown; underparts white; tail grey with bluish tinge. Legs pale brown; bill, ♂ black, ♀ brown; eyes brown. Secretive, chiefly insectivorous. Call: sustained reeling, thus local name *Wee-rirr-eer-ri*. Breeds in parties of up to 10 with single full plumaged ♂; domed nest, high side entrance, of grass lined feathers, wool or plant down, in low bush; 3 or 4 white eggs, marked with purplish or reddish brown. **766**

Malurus elegans see under **M. lamberti**

Malurus lamberti *Muscicapidae : Malurinae*
VARIEGATED WREN   *c.* 5½ ins
Australia: western range, Kimberley Division S to *c.* 30°S, E to central Australia; eastern range, coastal regions S Queensland and New South Wales S to *c.* 35°S. Habitat: mallee, mulga, saltbush and scrubby sandy plains. ♂: head and upper back shining blue, cheeks paler blue; collar, chin to breast, lower back and rump black; shoulder patches chestnut; wings brown, pale edged; long graduated tail dull blue; belly and under tail coverts pale buffy-white. Legs brown, bill black, eyes dark brown. ♀: tail much as ♂, otherwise grey-brown above, head olive-grey, underparts pale, chestnut patch round eye. (Similar Redwinged Wren, *M. elegans*, differentiated by lighter blue

on head and upper back.) Secretive, in pairs or family parties; insectivorous. Call: few brief rattling notes, generally silent. Breeds September to December, pair often assisted by additional ♂: domed nest, side entrance near top, of grasses and plant stalks, lined plant down, usually in bush. 3, sometimes 4 eggs, white with purplish red spots and specks, incubated *c.* 15 days; young fledge *c.* 13 days. Often 2 broods. **767**

Malurus leucopterus *Muscicapidae : Malurinae*
BLACK AND WHITE WREN   *c.* 4¾ ins
Only Dirk Hartog and Barrow Is., Western Australia. Habitat: dwarf scrub and spinifex on fairly open flats. Similar to closely related Blue and White Wren, *M. cyanotus*, but blue in latter replaced by blue-black; subordinate ♂♂ in breeding group may not attain full plumage. Secretive, in pairs or family parties. Call: similar but weaker than Blue and White Wren. Breeds June to September; domed nest, high side entrance, of fine grass bound spiders' webs and cocoons, lined finer grass and webs, usually in low bush or tuft of spinifex about a foot up; 3 or 4 white eggs, spotted with reddish brown. Parasitised by Horsfield Bronze Cuckoo, *Chrysococcyx basalis*.

Malurus melanocephalus *Muscicapidae : Malurinae*
RED-BACKED WREN   *c.* 5 ins
Australia: Kimberley Division, Western Australia, across to N Queensland and E Australia, S to Hunter River, New South Wales. Habitat: low scrub and long grass, usually damp areas. ♂: head, neck, underparts and tail velvety-black; back red; flight feathers brown. Legs brown, bill black, eyes brown. ♀: upperparts greyish brown, wings, tail and underparts pale; bill brown. Tame, usually in pairs or small parties; insectivorous; reeling song similar to other wrens. Breeds August to February; domed nest of grass and bark shreds, side entrance near top, lining of finer grasses, plant down; in tussock of grass often near, sometimes over, water; 3 or 4 white eggs, spotted with reddish brown. **768**

Malurus melanotus *Muscicapidae : Malurinae*
BLACK-BACKED WREN   *c.* 5½ ins
Australia: central Queensland to NW Victoria and nearby mallee areas S Australia. ♂: forehead, crown, back and underparts bright blue; broad black band across nape and hindneck narrowing round breast and forward over eyes; rump black; wings dark brown; tail blue. Legs dark brown, bill black, eyes brown. ♀: upperparts brownish grey; underparts pale; tail blue; bill and around eyes chestnut. Usually in pairs or small parties, in low bushes, scrub and thickets; reeling song like Blue Wren, *M. cyaneus*. Feeds on insects. Breeds September to December; domed nest, entrance near top, of grass and bark fibres lined feathers, fine grasses or wool, in bush; 3 to 4 white eggs with fine red freckles. **769**

Malurus splendens see under **M. callainus**

Manacus manacus *Pipridae*
WHITE BEARDED or BLACK
AND WHITE MANAKIN   3¾-4¼ ins
Neotropical: generally distributed E of Andes to NE Peru, NE Bolivia, Paraguay, NE Argentina; Brazil; W of Andes in Colombia; Trinidad; resident in forest and secondary woodland undergrowth. ♂: upperparts including crown, wings, tail, black; sides of head, throat, 'beard', breast and collar on hindneck (extending some races to upper back) white; rump dark grey, underparts pale grey; Colombian race has upper mantle, throat, breast yellowish white; rump and belly olive-grey. Legs pale orange; bill: upper: dusky grey, lower: leaden; eyes dark brown. ♀ generally olive green, greyish on throat; underparts greenish yellow. Each ♂ displays on dancing ground, cleared space of *c.* 3 × 2 ft, with 2 or more saplings between which he flies with 'beard' puffed out, making snapping, clicking and whirring sounds with wings: shafts of secondaries are thickened and outer primaries thin, stiff and curved. ♀ joins in 'dance' and eventually mates on main perch. Display continues throughout year at varying intensity, ♂♂ mating with several ♀♀. Ordinary call by ♂ and ♀ trilling *peerr*. Diet: mainly

small fruits taken on wing, and some insects. Breeds Trinidad January to September with peak in June. ♀ builds shallow woven cup of plant fibres and stems, suspended below fork of lateral branch, usually 1 to 5 ft up, often over water and trailing materials. 2 creamy white eggs, heavily streaked umber brown and grey with zone at big end, incubated by ♀ 18-19 days; fed by her, young fledge *c.* 2 weeks. **589**

MANAKIN,
   LONG-TAILED see **Chiroxiphia linearis**
   STRIPED see **Machaeropterus regulus**
   WHITE-BEARDED see **Manacus manacus**

MANCHURIAN CRANE see **Grus japonensis**

MANDARIN see **Aix galericulata**

MANGROVE KINGFISHER see under **Halcyon senegalensis**

MANX SHEARWATER see **Puffinus puffinus**

MANY-BANDED ARAÇARI see **Pteroglossus pluricinctus**

MARABOU see **Leptoptilus crumeniferus**

MARBLED
   MURRELET see under **Brachyrhamphus brevirostris**
   TEAL see **Marmaronetta augustirostris**

Margarornis squamiger *Furnariidae*
PEARLED TREERUNNER   6¼ ins
Neotropical: NW Venezuela and Colombia S to Peru and Bolivia; resident in forests. Upperparts chestnut, tinged olive on crown and hindneck in one race; inner flight feathers and tail chestnut, tail feathers ending in bare spines; stripe over eye yellowish white; feathers of underparts sulphur yellow or white according to race, broadly edged black, giving the 'pearled' appearance; legs grey, bill light horn, eyes brown. Insectivorous but little known of habits. **563**

Marmaronetta angustirostris or Anas angustirostris *Anatidae*
MARBLED TEAL   *c.* 16 ins.
Palaearctic: parts of Mediterranean (S Portugal, S Spain, S France, Persia) extending W to Canary Is; E through Near East to S Russia, Transcaspia and NW India; winters in warmer parts of range. Habitat: fresh or brackish water and marshes with plenty of cover, in winter prefers more open water. ♂ and ♀ similar: mottled greyish brown and creamy white; crown, upperparts and sides darker, eye stripe blackish brown. Legs olive-brown, long narrow bill blackish with white subterminal line in ♂, eyes brown. Very shy, in small groups or alone, flies low and well. Call: ♂ weak nasal squeak, ♀ almost inaudible quack. Feeds on aquatic plant matter. Nests May to early June in sheltered clumps of reeds or grass, sometimes away from water. 9 to 13 creamy white eggs, incubated *c.* 25 days. **118**

MARSH
   HARRIER, AFRICAN see **Circus ranivorus**
   OWL, AFRICAN see **Asio capensis**
   SANDPIPER see **Tringa stagnatilis**
   TIT see **Parus palustris**
   WARBLER see **Acrocephalus palustris**
   WREN, LONG-BILLED see **Telmatodytes palustris**
   WREN, SHORT-BILLED see under **Telmatodytes palustris**

MARTIAL EAGLE see **Polemaetus bellicosus**

MARTIN,
   AFRICAN RIVER see **Pseudochelidon eurystomina**
   AFRICAN ROCK see **Hirundo fuligula**
   AFRICAN SAND see **Riparia paludicola**
   CRAG see **Hirundo rupestris**
   HOUSE see **Delichon urbica**

Megacephalon maleo *Megapodiidae*
MALEO   *c.* 20 ins
Confined to Celebes, resident in forests, coming to shore in breeding season. Blackish brown glossed green, tail black; underparts white tinged pink; head naked with prominent black casque; legs bluish-black, partly webbed feet yellow, bill black to brown, eyes brown. Little known of habits, but eats fruit said to make eggs unpalatable. Breeding season April to August, when pinkish eggs laid singly in pits dug obliquely 3 ft into sand; incubation by heat from surface and birds do not visit pits again. Clutch size unknown, but 7 to 8 eggs laid in same area. Young, as of other megapodes, independent from hatching. **176**

Megaceryle alcyon *Alcedinidae*
BELTED KINGFISHER   11-14 ins
Nearctic: breeds from Alaska SE into E and Mid-USA, S to Gulf of Florida, also down W coast; northern populations winter Central and S America; along streams and by ponds; also coastal bays, especially in winter. Big, rough-crested head, upperparts, including tail and breast band, blue-grey, spotted white on back, wings, tail; broad white collar from throat; primaries black with white streaks when open and 2 white bars on secondaries; flanks shaded grey-blue, undertail black, barred white; ♀ has chestnut band on lower breast; legs dark red, bill horny-grey, eyes light brown. Flies with deep, irregular wingbeats 'as though changing step' (R. T. Peterson). Loud rattling call. Dives for fish from perch or after hovering. Breeds May to June, excavating hole in river bank up to 6 ft. 5 to 8 white eggs incubated by ♀ and ♂ *c.* 21 days; both parents feed young who fly after 3-4 weeks.

Megaceryle maxima *Alcedinidae*
GIANT KINGFISHER   16 ins
Ethiopian: whole of sub-Saharan Africa except Somalia, along mountain forest streams, wooded rivers, lake edges. Local, uncommon, shy. Very imposing bird with large crested head, enormous bill. Both sexes dark slate-grey above with white spots, streaks, bars; below ♂ has chestnut breast but mainly white abdomen, ♀ has chestnut abdomen but breast is white with black spots. May be seen perched on commanding bough, flying up river, or flying high above trees calling harshly, a sharp *kakh* or sometimes excited raucous cackle. Usually 3 white glossy eggs end of long tunnel. **493**

Megalaima haemocephala *Capitonidae*
COPPERSMITH BARBET   6½ ins
Oriental: widespread throughout region to Philippines; open wooded country, teak forests of Burma, up to 6,000 ft; roadside groves, habitations, even large towns in plains. Heavily built: upperparts, including short tail, blue green, crown red; nape, eye, moustachial stripe black; patches above and below eye, and throat, yellow; crimson breast patch; underparts yellowish white streaked green; legs coral-red, bill dark horn brown, eyes brown, orbits red. Solitary, pairs, parties of dozen, sometimes more on fruiting tree, with other species. Rapid, straight flapping flight. Suns itself on bare branches. Call: loud, mellow persistently repeated (up to *c.* 120 in minute) *tonk* or

took, like tap of metal hammer on metal, hence 'Coppersmith'. Bill shut; bare skin either side throat inflates and collapses at each note, body jerks, head turns side to side. Food: fruit of banyan, peepul, other wild figs; berries; moths, termites caught in clumsy sallies. Breeds mainly February to May, excavating hole *c.* 16 ins in rotten, often thin trunk or branch. 2 to 4 dull white eggs laid on bare wood, incubated ♀ and ♂; both also tend young.

Megapodius freycinet or M. reinwardt
Megapodiidae
SCRUB FOWL   *c.* 20 ins
Australasian: NW Australia, New Guinea E to Fiji, Philippines, Celebes; Oriental: NE Borneo and Nicobars; inhabits inland forests, breeding in jungle strips along creeks and round islands. Plumage variable over several subspecies: back and wings chestnut brown; head, neck and underparts grey, flanks and under tail coverts chestnut; face sparsely feathered, crest dark brown, legs orange, bill reddish brown, facial skin scarlet, eyes dark brown. Secretive, not flying unless pressed. Call described as: *cha-wong cha-wa cha-cha-cha cha-rook-ka*. Food scratched from ground: plant shoots, seeds, berries, some insects. Breeding from September and October to December in NE Australia. Typically, several pairs scratch together mound of plant debris and soil, 10 to 15 ft high and 15 to 35 ft across; *c.* 15 eggs, pinkish when fresh, are laid by each ♀ individually in 3 ft tunnels in mound, which has temperature of 95-102°F. Incubation of each egg *c.* 6 weeks; young independent at once. **177**

Megapodius reinwardt see **M. freycinet**

Melaenornis edolioides see under **M. pammelaina**

Melaenornis pammelaina *Muscicapidae*: *Muscicapinae*
SOUTH AFRICAN BLACK FLYCATCHER   8 ins
Ethiopian: local from Kenya (Ndoto Mtns) to S Africa (Natal, Transvaal) and across to W African coast S of Congo; resident woodlands, e.g. *Brachystegia* edge with acacia savannah; cultivated land with trees. Entirely black, glossed blue; legs dull black, bill black, eyes dark brown. Juvenile spotted tawny. Drongos, *Dicrurus* species, with which it often associates, have forked tails; Black Cuckoo Shrike, *Campephaga sulfurata*, has yellow wattles. (The primarily W African Black Flycatcher, *M. edolioides*, blackish-slate without gloss, also occurs in woodlands and cultivated areas.) This species partly crepuscular and not very conspicuous. Generally silent, but early morning song, bill pointed upwards, piping *twee twee twee eeee*. Usually sails down from perch to take insects on ground, where it hops about, e.g. on burnt areas, after ants, termites; also follows fires and may hawk aerially. Breeding September to December in N of range, using abandoned cup nest of thrush, chat or similar bird, re-lining it with fibres, rootlets; or in hole in rotten wood when lays foundation of twigs. 2 or 3 whitish eggs, marked lilac-brown. **781**

Melaenornis silens or Sigelus silens *Muscicapidae*: *Muscicapinae*
FISCAL FLYCATCHER   7½ ins
Ethiopian: S and SE southern Africa; resident savannah and low open bush, cultivated land and gardens. ♂: upperparts, head to rump, mainly glossy black; white spots on flight feathers; secondaries also edged white (show as white windows in flight); tail feathers black, all outer ones with white bases; underparts white, chest, flanks tinged grey. ♀: brownish or sooty black above, without gloss; underparts off-white; legs, bill black, eyes brown. Juvenile spotted above, mottled below. Usually in pairs; uses prominent perch for aerial sallies after insects or downward pounce to ground. Call: *zirrr*; alarm *skisk*; rather feeble protracted song, often several birds together, flitting about with tails fanned. Breeds August to January; large nest of twigs, plant debris, lined rootlets, plant down, in forked branch or base of aloe leaf *c.* 20 ft up. 3 pale greenish blue eggs, covered small red speckles, incubated 13-15 days. **782**

Melanerpes formicivorus *Picidae*
ACORN WOODPECKER   9-9½ ins
Nearctic, Neotropical: Pacific coast USA from SW Oregon through Central America to Andes of Colombia; resident (N of range) oak woods and coniferous forests with scattered oaks. Back, wings, tail glossy black; rump and broad wing patch white; forehead yellowish white, extending in front of eye to breast band; scarlet crown and nape, separated from forehead in ♀ by black band; area round eye, chin, throat black; lower breast, sides streaked black, belly white; legs, bill blackish, eyes whitish. In small communities of up to 6, based on storage tree which they perforate (50,000 holes in one yellow pine) and stud with acorns, filling excess holes with pebbles, and interrupting efforts with chases and display flights (W. E. Ritter). Many parrot-like calls, especially *jacob jacob jacob*. Nest-hole in tree apparently also excavated communally, used afterwards by many other birds. 4 to 6 white eggs.

Melanerpes pucherani *Picidae*
BLACK-CHEEKED WOODPECKER   7½ ins
Neotropical: Central American S to Colombia and W Ecuador; resident in primary forest and clearings. Upperparts, including inner flight feathers, black barred white; forehead yellow, crown and nape crimson (mid-crown black in ♀); cheeks, side of neck, wing coverts black; central tail feathers barred white on inner webs; throat dull white, breast pale olive grey; underparts barred buff and black, centre of belly crimson; legs, bill greyish brown, eyes dark brown. Habits much as *M. rubricapillus*, but does not drum so much. Begins excavating nest-hole in tree or sometimes fence post February in Panama, laying from March. **550**

Melanerpes rubricapillus or Centurus rubricapillus *Picidae*
WAGLER'S or RED-CROWNED
WOODPECKER   6½-7½ ins
Neotropical: Panama and Costa Rica S to Venezuela and Colombia; Tobago; resident in scrub, cactus, palm and bamboo groves, plantations, gardens. Upperparts, including flight feathers and central tail feathers, barred black and white; rump white; forehead white or yellow, crown and nape crimson (nape only in ♀); face and underparts smoky grey or olive brown (racial variation); centre of belly crimson-orange; legs horn-grey, bill black, facial skin grey, eyes lightish brown. Call: repeated *churr churr churr*; drums in March in Panama, in shorter bursts than *Centurus carolinus*. ♂ follows ♀ in display, then holds wings at 45°, calling *wick wick*. He also excavates hole in tree in which ♀ lays 2 white eggs. Both incubate, ♂ at night, and feed young, fledged by end May or June. **551**

Melanitta nigra *Anatidae*
BLACK OR COMMON SCOTER   19 (body 12½) ins
Holarctic: European race, *nigra*, breeds NW Palaearctic wintering S on coasts of W Europe, Mediterranean, Black and Caspian Seas; American Black Scoter, *americana*, breeds NE Asia and northern N America, wintering S to China, Japan, California, N Carolina and Great Lakes. Habitat: lakes, usually in mountain country during breeding season; otherwise marine. ♂: black apart from orange-yellow patch on bill. ♀ and immature: dark brown with whitish brown side of head, dark crown and bill. Legs: ♂ blackish, ♀ browner, eyes brown. Takes off slowly, often flies low; formation varies from lines to denser flocks. ♂ gives plaintive piping, ♀ hoarser *kr-r-r*. Feeds on small aquatic animals, mainly molluscs, but more varied on fresh water. Nests early June, laying 5 to 7 creamy buff eggs in hollow lined with grasses, some lichens, moss and down, amongst cover, typically heather, a few metres from water. ♀ incubates *c.* 27 days and tends young, who fly after 6-7 weeks. **119**

Melanodryas cucullata see **Petroica cucullata**

Meleagris gallopavo *Meleagridae*
WILD TURKEY   ♀ 36, ♂ 48 ins
Nearctic, marginally Neotropical: from Pennsylvania and Oklahoma in USA to S Mexico; formerly much

more widespread but 7 races still extant; reintroduced some areas. Resident open woodlands, thickets, clearings and prairie 'oases'. Wild ancestor of farmyard turkey; very dark bronzed brown with black crescented feather tips on body, wing coverts; white bars on flight feathers; dark bars on tail with black then buff terminal bands; bare, warty head and neck red, blue, even white; ♂ has appendage (caruncle) over bill, black bristles on breast; legs light brown, bill dark horn, eyes dark. Weak flier, though roosts in trees, feeds on ground on variety of fruits, grain, seeds, some insects; drinks twice daily. ♂ gobbles early in morning to summon his several ♀♀. Display by fanning tail, distending caruncle, puffing and gobbling. ♀ makes leaf-lined nest on ground, lays April or May, 8 to 15 buff eggs, spotted darker brown, and incubates them 28 days, then tends brood. Sexes separate after mating. **211**

Melierax canorus or M. poliopterus *Accipitridae*
PALE CHANTING GOSHAWK 19 ins
Ethiopian: East and Southern Africa; rather open, semi-desert country. Upperparts rather pale grey, darker on lower back, white upper tail coverts; primaries black, tail barred black and white with grey central feathers; underparts closely barred grey and white; legs red, bill dark, cere orange, eyes red. Immature mottled in shades of brown with white on underparts. Flies with rapid wing beats and short glides, perches upright, showing red legs. Generally silent but utters melodious whistles, especially in breeding season, when ♂ 'sings' from tree-top, and pair soars at about 300 ft. Feeds principally on lizards and insects in long grass, also mammals up to hare size, and flies down quail. Breeding season seems to coincide with second half of dry season. Builds slight nest of sticks and debris usually 10 to 30 ft in acacia or euphorbia trees, for 1 or 2 pale bluish or greenish white eggs. Apparently only ♀ incubates, other details not recorded. **157**

Melierax metabates *Accipitridae*
DARK CHANTING GOSHAWK 19 ins
Ethiopian: W and Central Africa, SW Arabia. Lives generally in thicker vegetation than *M. canorus*. Similar to but much darker grey than *M. canorus*, with underparts very closely vermiculated, legs and cere deeper red. Immature darker brown than *M. canorus*. More tree living than *M. canorus*, hunting doves, but taking mainly small vertebrates and insects from ground. Similar melodious whistles to *M. canorus*, perhaps higher-pitched. Breeding similar to *M. canorus*, young probably fed mainly by ♀.

Melierax poliopterus see **M. canorus**

Meliornis niger *Meliphagidae*
WHITE-CHEEKED HONEYEATER 7 ins
Australasian: continental from Herberton Range (N Queensland) to Victoria, S and SW Australia as far as Perth; very local in open wooded country, heaths. Generally black; head, back, especially underparts streaked white; white 'eyebrow', broad white cheek patch; wings black with conspicuous wax-yellow patch; tail black; legs, bill black, eyes brown. Usually in flocks; resembles *M. novaehollandiae* in habits, but ♂ towers above nest-site, dropping with closed wings, making final glide to perch. Squeaky whistling call *chip choo chippy choo*. Food; insects, nectar, pollen, fruits. Breeds July to December; nest of bark strips, grasses, lined soft plant down, e.g. from *Banksia* cones; usually close to ground in grass tussock. Usually 2 salmon pink eggs, zoned reddish brown markings over purplish grey. **841**

Meliornis novaehollandiae *Meliphagidae*
WHITE-BEARDED or YELLOW-WINGED HONEYEATER 7 ins
Australasian: continental from S Queensland, New South Wales, Victoria to S and SW Australia; Tasmania; Bass Strait Is. Habitat coastal heathlands, open woodland when eucalypts in flower, gardens, usually near water. Generally black, white streaks head, back, especially underparts; conspicuous wax-yellow patch on wings; tail black, tipped white; white

stripes on throat give 'beard' effect; legs, bill black, eyes white which, with white-tipped tail, distinguish from *M. niger*. Noisy, restless, in pairs or parties, with sharp shrill calls and chattering alarm. Diet: insects (some caught on wing); pollen, nectar, fruit. Breeds June to January, throughout year if weather suitable; nest of bark, grass, twigs, lined plant down, e.g. from dead cones *Banksia*, generally in *Banksia* or other thick bush. 2 or 3 pinkish buff eggs, becoming darker at big end where dark chestnut and grey markings concentrate, incubated by ♀ 15 days; fledging period *c.* 16 days.

Meliphaga cassidix *Meliphagidae*
HELMETED HONEYEATER 8½ ins
Australasian: S Victoria (Dandenong and Gippsland Ranges); confined to swamp gum *Eucalyptus ovata* areas, in lower cover spring, summer, mature woodland autumn, winter. Forehead, crown, nape bright olive yellow; broad black mask; upperparts generally olive-brown tinged olive-yellow on wings, white-tipped tail; cheeks, throat, ear tufts bright yellow; underparts yellow tinged grey, shading to pale yellow; legs grey, bill black, eyes brown. Rather larger and darker than *M. melanops*, with erectile crest and crown more clearly demarcated. Small parties form after breeding, very aggressive among themselves and against other species. Calls: *tooey-t tooey-t*; repeated *churl churl*; trilling note. Diet mainly insects from leaves, crevices or taken on wing. Breeds August to December; nest of bark, fine grass, leaves, lined soft bark and down; usually suspended from branch of small bush or tree. Usually 2 pale flesh-coloured eggs, with rounded reddish-brown spots over purplish grey, concentrated at big end.

Meliphaga chrysops *Meliphagidae*
YELLOW-FACED HONEYEATER *c.* 6 ins
Australasian: continental from Cairns (N Queensland) to S Australia, making definite spring and autumn movements. Habitat open forest and scrub of coastal districts and Dividing Range; orchards, gardens. Upperparts olive tinged grey-brown; wings, tail brown, tinged olive; yellow 'wedge' under eye, moustachial and eyestripes black; underparts dull grey-white, flanks brown; legs slate blue, bill black, eyes grey blue. Lively parties feed among blossoms and leaves. Autumn call *chip*, harsh *kheer* in spring; series of *chickip* calls becomes song. Diet: insects, nectar from eucalypts, native and introduced fruits. Breeds July to January; nest neat cup of moss, bark bound cobwebs, lined grass rootlets; usually suspended from thin 'weeping' branch of bush or tree, 4 to 12 ft. 2 or 3 pinkish buff eggs, spotted and streaked rich reddish chestnut over purplish grey at big end. **842**

Meliphaga leucotis *Meliphagidae*
WHITE-EARED HONEYEATER 8½ ins
Australasian: continental S Queensland to Victoria, S Australia, parts W Australia; Kangaroo I. Habitat: heath, scrub, open eucalypt forest; heaths and adjoining scrub (New South Wales); gardens. Upperparts olive green; wings, tail brown, tinged yellowish olive outer margins wings, outer webs tail feathers; crown dark grey; cheeks, throat, breast black, ear coverts white; underparts olive tinged yellow; legs dark grey, bill black, eyes light brown. Call loud, clear *come-up come-up do-it-well do-it-well*; also short double *chop chop*. Food: insects, nectar. Breeds July to December; nest of thin bark strips, grasses, bound cobwebs, lined hair, fur, other soft materials; in low bush or tree up to 10 ft or more. 2 or 3 pale flesh pink or white eggs, sparsely marked pinkish and reddish brown, especially towards big end. **843**

Meliphaga melanops *Meliphagidae*
YELLOW-TUFTED HONEYEATER 7¾ ins
Australasian: continental S Queensland to Victoria, SE of S Australia; coastal scrub to inland tall eucalypt forest, usually near water. Very like *M. cassidix* but upperparts more 'scaly', underparts greener; yellow tuft at lower end black mask, but yellow area below mask smaller. Legs grey, bill black, eyes dark brown. Habits much as *M. cassidix*; usually in flocks after breeding, inquisitive and sociable; fond of bathing.

Feeding or flight call *cheop cheop*; also harsh forms of *cassidix* calls and tuneful trilling. Takes insects on wing and from under bark; nectar from eucalypts; native fruits, berries. Breeds June to December; nest of bark strips, grasses bound cobwebs, decorated spider egg bags, lined fur, hair, plant down; generally suspended from branch or low shrub, sometimes in grass tussock. 2 or 3 pinkish buff eggs well marked dark reddish brown over purplish grey. Injury feigning by adult at nest. **844**

Melittophagus bullockoides *Meropidae*
WHITE-FRONTED BEE-EATER 9 ins
Ethiopian: most of southern Africa from Angola, central Kenya down to Transvaal, Zululand in bush, dry ravines, river and lake margins, not forest. Conspicuous scarlet throat; chest, belly, nape, brown; back, wings, tail green; tail coverts above and below deep blue; off-white crown, forehead, band below black stripe through eye. Square tail, long curved bill. Hawks insects from perch on bush, often over water or from its surface. Voice less musical than most bee-eaters, rather shrill, nasal *waar*. Nest in groups, 2-4 glossy white round eggs in long tunnel in bank. **498**

Melittophagus bulocki *Meropidae*
RED-THROATED BEE-EATER 9 ins
Ethiopian: replaces preceding species to N; resident coast-to-coast belt Senegal, Zaire to Ethiopia, Uganda, in dry open country. Very similar in habits, plumage to *M. bullockoides*, lacking only its white head, which is wholly blue-green; rare variant has daffodil-yellow throat. Typical bee-eater call, soft liquid *quilp quilp*. Breeds in large colonies, excavating holes in late November soft soil in Nigeria; activities resumed late January with courtship chases, cleaning of holes. 2 to 4 white eggs laid synchronously in colony, incubated 20-21 days. Young attended by parents and 'helpers' for *c.* 6 weeks, being 'weaned' from unspecialised insect diet to nearly 90% Hymenoptera. **499**

Melittophagus gularis *Meropidae*
BLACK BEE-EATER 8 ins
Ethiopian: W African forest zone, just into W Uganda. Very beautiful forest species, black, scarlet, Cambridge blue. Above, mainly black; throat scarlet; breast black spotted chestnut, blue; belly blue; tail square, black above, blue below. Feeding, breeding as other bee-eaters (see *M. bulocki*).

Melittophagus oreobates *Meropidae*
CINNAMON-CHESTED BEE-EATER 8 ins
Ethiopian: most of eastern Africa, i.e. NE Zaire, S Sudan, SW Ethiopia, all Uganda, W and central Kenya, N and W Tanzania, in highland forest. All green above except black bands, white tips on secondaries, tail feathers; yellow throat, wide black band upper breast, then rich cinnamon below; black stripe through eye, white patch below. Square tail, long curved bill. Hawks insects from tree perch as other bee-eaters, nesting habits also similar (see *M. bulocki*); voice sharper *tsee-ip*. **500**

Melittophagus pusillus *Meropidae*
LITTLE BEE-EATER 6 ins
Ethiopian: very common in low country, wet or dry, throughout tropical Africa. Distinctly smaller than *M. oreobates*, but voice, plumage almost identical, lacking only white neck patches, tips to wing, tail feathers. Not a forest species, not gregarious. Perches on grass stem, low bush, whence hawks insects like flycatcher. Tunnel-nester, 2-4 white eggs. **501**

Mellisuga helenae *Trochilidae*
BEE HUMMINGBIRD ♀: 2¾, ♂: 2½ ins
Neotropical: confined to Cuba and Isle of Pines, in woodland, shrubberies and gardens, occasionally more open country. ♂ (smallest bird in world): upperparts bluish, more intense on black-tipped tail; forehead, gorget and lateral plumes iridescent red; underparts greyish white. ♀: upperparts green, underparts whitish with white tips to outer tail feathers. Legs, bill, eyes dark. Call or song high-pitched squeaking, stimulated by other ♂♂; very small wings give bee-like hum in flight. Hovers in front of flowers with tail

cocked. Other habits as family; see under *Aglaiocercus kingi*.

MELODIUS WARBLER see **Hippolais polyglotta**

Melophus lathami *Emberizidae: Emberizinae*
CRESTED BUNTING   6 ins
Oriental, E Palaearctic: Outer Himalayas, Yunnan, Burma. Mainly resident rocky, cultivated slopes with patches of low scrub, up to 5,000 ft Kashmir, hard weather movements to lowlands. ♂: glossy black, including pointed crest, with wings, rump, tail chestnut. ♀ paler, tail tinged cinnamon and confusion possible with Striolated Bunting, *Emberiza striolata*. Perches and sings from bush tops. Singly, pairs, scattered parties. Call: *tweet twe twe too;* song rendered *which which which whee whee which* (India). Feeds mainly on grass seeds, but sometimes hawks flies, flying ants in parties; searches burnt areas. Breeds April-May, ♀ and ♂ build grass nest, lined fine material, in bank, wall, sheltered by stone, clod, bush. 3 or 4 pale greenish to stone brown eggs, marked red, brown, purple, incubated ♀ and ♂; both also tend young.

Melopsittacus undulatus *Psittacidae*
BUDGERIGAR   7½ ins
Australasian: most of continental Australia, but only coastal in S; on grassland, its edges with savannah and scrub; riverine trees, acacia clumps, saltbush *Atriplex* plains; seasonal movements according to food and water supplies. Green, upperparts barred black and yellow; wings edged white; front of head and throat yellow, some feathers tipped blue, and black spots across throat; central tail feathers greenish-blue, outer feathers green with yellow band; legs greyish blue, bill olive-grey, cere blue (brown in breeding ♀), eyes white. Small parties to flocks of thousands in interior; feeds and drinks early, rests in shade, feeds again late. Birds in large flocks drink floating on water with wings extended above. Scratches with foot over wing. Calls: quiet two-syllabled screech, warbling contact note, conversational chatter. Food: grass seeds, especially spinifex *Triodia* and Mitchell grass *Astrebla*; also ripening corn; flies up trees when disturbed. Breeds August to January in S, June to September in N or any time following rains. Social, several using holes in same tree, usually near water; also stumps, fence posts, fallen logs. 4 to 8 white eggs laid on decayed wood, incubated by ♀ 18 days; young fly *c.* 30 days, ♂♂ mature in 2 months; often 2 broods. **395**

Melospiza melodia *Emberizidae: Emberizinae*
SONG SPARROW   6¼ ins
Nearctic marginally Neotropical: from S Alaska, Hudson Bay, Newfoundland S to N Carolina, N Georgia, Missouri, N Dakota, Central Mexico; winters from S Canada to S Florida and Gulf Coast. Common habitat denominator bush cover, not far from water: alder swamps, lakesides, felled woodland, abandoned farms, gardens. Races vary somewhat in colour but upperparts generally rich brown streaked black with pale edges to wing coverts; crown chestnut, face striped black (through eye, moustachial) and whitish; underparts white; breast, flanks strongly streaked very dark brown with central spot; legs light brown, bill light horn, eyes dark brown. Shorter-tailed juvenile lacks centre breast spot. Long, rounded tail moved up and down in flight. Usual call loud *tchunk;* sings from elevated perch even in winter: 7 to 11 lively and varied notes, rendered by Thoreau: *Maids, maids, maids, hang up your tea-kettle-ettle-ettle.* Food about ⅔ vegetable (seeds), ⅓ invertebrates, accounting for more than ½ diet in summer. ♂ strongly territorial, retaining same one for several years (life span may be 7), dominating ♀ by 'pouncing' attack (M. M. Nice). Breeding March onwards (general laying date Ohio 25th April—Nice), ♀ building nest of grass, leaves, lined hair, early ones usually well-hidden under dead grass and herbs, later up to 4 ft in bush or young conifer. 3 to 5 greenish white eggs, often heavily marked brown, incubated ♀ 12-13 days; both parents feed young, who leave nest 10 days, independent 28-30 days. Second laying may follow 6-19 days after first brood leaves nest. Some bigamy. Frequent parasitism by Cowbird, *Molothrus ater*. **861**

Menura alberti see under **M. novaehollandiae**

Menura novaehollandiae *Menuridae*
SUPERB LYREBIRD   38 ins
Australasian: S Queensland to Victoria; resident in forests and scrubland. Upperparts dark brown, rufous on wings; underparts pale grey brown; strong legs and pointed bill grey, eyes brown with pale orbits. ♂'s lyre tail formed by outer pair of feathers, nearly 2 ft long, curved and light brown with crescentic golden bars and black tips; next 6 pairs are 'strings', brown above, white below, lacking barbules; central pair 'feelers', long and narrow, lack outer web, cross near insertion and curve out to opposite tips of lyre. Very shy, ♂ particularly hard to approach. Builds up to 12 'dancing mounds' over *c.* ½ mile, raking them up from damp soil; visits them in turn to display, uttering remarkable series of mimicking calls and own notes with lyre display of tail as brief climax; gives few high-pitched notes, folds tail and moves off. Own calls include resounding *choo choo choo* at dawn; ♀ also can mimic up to 20 different sounds, including human and mechanical noises. Progress mainly by flying leaps, but ascends high in trees to roost. Scratches litter or breaks up rotten logs for insects, worms, crustaceans, molluscs. Builds late in May to early June bulky domed nest of sticks, fronds, moss bark, lined rootlets, bark fibres, finally own down; on or near ground, on rock ledge, between 2 trees, in stumps or fern clump. Single (largest passerine) egg laid July: purplish-brown, marked shades of grey and blackish brown, sometimes zoned; left for week, then incubated by ♀ 35-40 days. She tends young for *c.* 6 weeks, polygamous ♂ playing no part. Prince Albert's Lyrebird, *M. alberti*, of the subtropical rain forests of SE Queensland and NE New South Wales does not build display mounds but has broadly similar habits. **597**

MERGANSER, HOODED see **Mergus cucullatus**

Mergus albellus *Anatidae*
SMEW   ♀ 15, ♂ 16 ins
Palaearctic: breeds NW Europe across to N Asia and down to Rumania in E Europe; winters S over Europe to Mediterranean, Iran and across to N India, China and Japan. While breeding frequents lakes and backwaters, otherwise any fresh waters, sometimes floodlands, estuaries and occasionally marine in sheltered bays. ♂: white with black markings, grey sides and dark patch running round eye and forward to bill; crest erected in display. ♀ and immatures: greyer with chestnut crown and face showing up white cheeks and throat. Legs and short bill grey, eyes: ♂ red, ♀ reddish brown. Virtually silent; usually in small groups, often with Goldeneye, *Bucephala clangula*, and other ducks; takes off readily and flies rapidly. Dives, suddenly, for up to a minute in pursuit of small water animals, chiefly fish. Nests May and June in tree cavities near water, lined with some down, moss and a few feathers, laying 6 to 9 creamy or pale buff eggs; incubated by ♀ *c.* 28 days; young tended by ♀ alone. **120**

Mergus cucullatus *Anatidae*
HOODED MERGANSER   18 (body 12) ins
Nearctic: breeds S of Central Canada; winters Great Lakes, Atlantic States, S of New York, Gulf States and Pacific States. Habitat: quiet lakes and pools surrounded by woods, woodland swamps and slow streams; larger ponds and swifter streams when not breeding. ♂: black and white with brown-grey flanks and fan-shaped white, black-bordered crest on head. ♀: grey body, dark brown upperparts and head with buff crest; throat pale. Legs yellowish brown, ♀ more dusky; bill black, edged orange in ♀, eyes: ♂ yellow, ♀ hazel. Often on wing, rapid flight with quick wing-beats, usually in small parties, diurnal, rarely with other species; feeds on small animals, chiefly fish, in shallow water using short dives. Almost silent apart from courtship when ♂ emits guttural purring. Nests late April to early June in holes in trees in flooded areas near great rivers, on shores of lakes or in swamps, using little down, some feathers and chips of wood. 9 to 12 glossy pure-white eggs, incubated by ♀ *c.* 31 days; young are also tended by ♀ and fly after 6 weeks. **121**

Merops apiaster *Meropidae*
EUROPEAN BEE-EATER 11 (central tail feathers 5) ins
W Palaearctic, Ethiopian: breeds May, June S Europe, N Africa, SW Asia eastwards to W Siberia, Kashmir, then migrates S to whole of Africa, Arabia, NW Indian subcontinent. Some birds breed S Africa October to December, then migrate N. Found most types open country, not rain forest or high mountains. General colour chestnut and blue with yellow throat; forehead white; crown, mantle, wing coverts chestnut; scapulars, rump golden yellow; flight feathers blue-green; tail green; breast, abdomen blue-green. Gregarious in small parties, nesting colonies. Perches on bare boughs, telegraph wires, whence hawks for bees, other insects. Flight graceful, swallow-like; voice a musical *quilp*; 5-6 white eggs end of tunnel in sandy bank; incubation by ♀ and ♂ 20 days; both feed young, who fly 20-25 days. **502**

Merops orientalis *Meropidae*
LITTLE GREEN
BEE-EATER 11 (central tail feathers 6) ins
SE Palaearctic, Ethiopian, Oriental: several races, widely distributed all across from Senegal to Ethiopia, Egypt, Arabia, India, Indo-China. Mostly resident, but Egyptian race migrates up Nile valley after breeding early spring. Avoids forest, tolerates very arid conditions. Mainly golden green with black stripe through eye, across lower throat; flight feathers brown, central tail feathers greatly elongated to narrow black filaments. Tame, gregarious, hawks insects from low perch or picks them from flowers. Call a repeated soft *chee*. Usual bee-eater nesting habits: incubation of 3 to 7 white eggs by ♀ and ♂ *c.* 20 days; fledging period 20-25 days. **503**

Merops ornatus *Meropidae*
RAINBOW BIRD   9 ins
Australasian: Celebes, New Guinea and continental Australia, to most of which summer visitor, September-October to February-March. Habitat: open savannah woodlands, sandy plains of alluvial land, fields and roadsides. Generally bright light green; crown, nape golden brown; flight feathers dusky; rump sky blue; black tail has 2 elongated (shorter in ♀) spine-like central feathers, ending in blobs; black mask above thin blue stripe; black band divides golden-yellow chin, upper throat from pale underparts; underwing orange-brown; legs grey, bill blackish, eyes red. Immature duller, browner, lacking blue cheek stripe, black throat band, long tail feathers. Spends much time on bare perch or in air, sallying after and hawking aerial instincts. Call in flight repeated, whirring *peer peer peer*; impressive in volume from migrating flocks. Breeds from October in Australia, ♀ and ♂ excavating 1 to 3 ft sloping tunnel in sandy bank, leading to nest chamber for 5 to 7 glossy white eggs; incubation and fledging much as relatives. **504**

Merops rubicoides *Meropidae*
SOUTHERN CARMINE BEE-EATER   *c.* 14 ins
Ethiopian: replaces *M. rubicus* to S; resident coast-to-coast belt Angola to Mozambique, Natal, thence migrates N to Zaire, Tanzania. Differs from *M. rubicus* only in throat being carmine too.

Merops rubicus *Meropidae*
CARMINE BEE-EATER 14 (central tail feathers 7) ins
Ethiopian: resident coast-to-coast belt Senegal, Somalia; in non-breeding season migrates S to NE Zaire, Tanzania; common Kenya coast in winter. A low country bird of coastal bush, savannah, arid bush, also swamps, river margins. Very beautiful: blue-green head, throat: sky-blue tail coverts, otherwise all carmine. Besides trees, wires, often perches backs cattle, storks, whence catches insects they disturb; also frequents grass fires same reason. Call loud metallic *tuk tuk*. Always gregarious; nests as other bee-eaters (see *M. apiaster*).

MESIA, SILVER-EARED see **Leiothrix argentauris**

MESITE, BROWN see **Mesitornis unicolor**

Mesitornis unicolor or Mesoenas unicolor
Mesitornithidae
BROWN MESITE   12-13 ins
E Madagascar; sedentary in rain forest with thin shrub cover. Upperparts, including crown and long, full tail, brown with bluish shaftstreaks; short wings blackish brown; white stripe from bill through eyes meet at nape; underparts lighter brown; legs and straight bill leaden grey, eyes light yellow. Terrestrial, poor flier or even unable to fly, reaching nests by hopping up branches. Feeds on insects and fruit. Lays from November, building slender platform of twigs, lined leaves and grass, in fork of sloping tree, 3 to 6 ft up. Single whitish egg, zoned deep chocolate and grey, incubated probably by ♀ alone; young one precocious, soon leaving nest.

Mesoenas unicolor see **Mesitornis unicolor**

MEXICAN
    EAGLE see **Polyborus plancus**
    JAY see **Aphelocoma ultramarina**

MEYER'S PARROT see **Poicephalus meyeri**

Micrastur ruficollis *Falconidae*
BARRED FOREST FALCON   13-15 ins
Neotropical: SE Mexico, Costa Rica, Panama to E Peru, N Argentine, Paraguay, E and S Brazil; resident in forest. Rufous phase: upperparts rufous brown, darker on crown and rather short wings; throat and breast rufous, underparts evenly banded black and white; long tail black with 3 or 4 narrow white bands. Grey phase: upperparts grey, washed brown on wings and sides of breast. Legs, cere, facial skin yellow, bill black, dull yellow at base, eyes (♂) light orange (♀) yellow. Intermediate and dark grey forms occur. Immatures very variable. Crepuscular; perches low down and concealed by cover, through which it zig-zags in flight. Hunts by dashing on party of small birds, often when they are following army ants; also takes small lizards, occasionally mice. Barking call, like small dog, uttered once or repeatedly; also fowl-like cackle. Breeding habits as yet unknown. **171**

Micrathene whitneyi *Strigidae*
ELF OWL   5½-6 ins
Nearctic: SW USA to Mexico, where some northern birds winter. Resident *Saguaro* cactus deserts, woodlands of all kinds: mesquite, oak (canyons 3,000 to 5,700 ft), pine and oak. Usual mottled owl pattern of browns, greys, black and white, with white stripes on wings and mantle; facial disc with white 'eyebrows'; underparts striped reddish-brown; very short tail barred; feet light grey, bill dark, eyes yellow. Daytime roost in holes of giant cacti. Call of 6 high, cackling notes; duet between ♂ and ♀ of 'yips, whines and barks as of young puppy' (J. T. Marshall); also challenges Acorn Woodpeckers, *Melanerpes formicivorus*. Feeds on insects taken in air, off foliage or ground. Breeds April to June in woodpecker holes in cacti, oaks, sycamores, pines, laying 3 white eggs. As parent brings food to young both birds rock bodies. **443**

Microeca fascinans *Muscicapidae : Muscicapinae*
AUSTRALIAN BROWN FLYCATCHER
or JACKY WINTER   c. 5½ ins
Australasian: continental Australia; originally forest, now adapted to parks, orchards, gardens. Upperparts grey-brown; central feathers of tail dark brown, outer ones whitish; underparts pale grey to white; legs, bill, eyes dark. Confiding; constantly on move with tail swinging from side to side. Call: *you did you did you did*. Takes insects on wing or on ground. Breeds August to December; nest of bark, lichens, lined fine grass, horsehair, fastened by cobwebs usually in fork of lateral dead branch of tree up to 70 ft. Usually 2 greenish blue eggs, marked purplish brown over lilac, often in zone. **783**

Micropalma himantopus *Scolopacidae*
STILT SANDPIPER   8½ (bill 1½) ins
Nearctic: N Manitoba and Hudson Bay across Mackenzie to NE Alaska; winters S America to Central Argentina and Chile on fresh and salt

marshes, mud flats. Breeds tundra, crosses prairies on passage. Summer: upperparts mottled dark brown and pale grey, extending over wings to very dark tips; rump white, tail grey-brown; crown and cheek patch russet; underparts barred buff and dark brown; legs yellowish-green, bill brownish, tip black, eyes dark brown. Winter: upperparts fairly uniform brown; stripe over eye and underparts mainly white. Behaves much as other waders, e.g. flocks and aerial evolutions. Wades in muddy pools, plunging head below surface, also scything movements like Avocet, *Recurvirostra avosetta*, taking small water animals. Breeds from June, making scrape on tundra moss for 4 greenish-buff eggs, spotted dark brown all over, incubated ♀ and ♂. **288**

Microparra capensis *Jacanidae*
LESSER JACANA   6½ ins
Ethiopian: mainly E half of region, Mali and S Sudan to Cape; habitat much as African Jacana, *Actophilornis africana*; grassy swamps in Zambia. Crown, rump, tail and flanks chestnut, rest of upperparts golden buff glossed green; sides of neck golden; underparts whitish, under wing coverts black; legs greenish brown, bill brownish olive, eyes brown. Looks and behaves much as young African Jacana, with mouse-like action over floating vegetation. Flies more readily and strongly, but little known of habits. Call a sharp *kruk*. Food: water insects and plant seeds. Breeding season shows two peaks, suggesting two broods. Small floating nest of water plant stems and debris holds 2 to 4 eggs, resembling African Jacana's but smaller; incubation by ♀ and ♂ 22-24 days; both parents tend young. **251**

Microscelis flavalus see **Hypsipetes flavala**

MIGRATORY NIGHTJAR see **Caprimulgus indicus**

Milvus migrans *Accipitridae*
BLACK KITE   22-23 ins
Palaearctic (N temperate), Ethiopian (including Madagascar), Oriental and Australasian; northern populations migrate in winter. Found in wooded, often cultivated country, frequently near water, also in dry areas (Africa), and in towns and villages (especially Asia) as scavenger. Upperparts very dark brown, underparts rufous brown; head paler; long tail hardly forked; young birds generally paler. Legs and cere orange, bill dark, eyes greyish. Social, often in flocks at tree roosts. Flight light and buoyant, will follow ships after garbage. Display flight may involve pair interlocking claws and falling almost to earth. Alarm call repeated *kiki*; gull-like squeal in breeding season. Takes prey from ground or water: great variety of vertebrates, including fish, insects, carrion and garbage. Breeds from end April in S Europe; sociable or solitary, building nest of sticks and debris usually in trees, on buildings and sometimes bushes on cliffs. 2 to 3 white eggs, sparsely marked red-brown incubated by ♀ and ♂ c. 4 weeks; both feed young, fly 6 weeks.

Milvus migrans aegyptius *Accipitridae*
YELLOW-BILLED KITE   22½ ins
SE Palaearctic (Egypt, Red Sea coasts) and Ethiopian (S Arabia, Somalia, coast of Kenya); migrating N to S in winter. Very like nominate race, but head and hind neck browner, ear coverts darker, more rufous underparts and tail, with 7 to 8 rather distinct blackish bars; bill yellow in adult, black in immature. **158**

Mimocichla plumbea *Muscicapidae : Turdinae*
RED-LEGGED THRUSH   10-11 ins
Neotropical: W Indies (N Bahamas, Cuba, Hispaniola, Puerto Rico, Dominica, smaller islands) much racial variation. Resident lowland and mountain forests; plantations, gardens. Predominantly slate grey, wings striped black and white, long graduated tail black with white-tipped outer feathers; mask black, chin streaked black and white, breast grey (Hispaniola, Puerto Rico) shading to white (belly ochre, Cuba); legs red, bill orange, eyes dark brown, orbits red. Occupies thrush niche in gardens, feeding mainly on insects, other small invertebrates. Alarm call *wet wet*; song sustained but rather weak. Builds bulky cup nest in bush or tree, laying 3 to 5 whitish to pale green eggs, spotted dark brown. **688**

Mimus polyglottos *Mimidae*
MOCKINGBIRD   10½ ins
Nearctic, Neotropical: breeds mainly from Maryland, Ohio, S Iowa, S Wyoming, Central California S to West Indies, Gulf Coast, S Mexico. Habitat originally forest edge and clearings; adapted to man-modified shrubberies, gardens. Generally grey; wings blackish with 2 white bars and patch near 'wrist'; long graduated tail dark with white outer feathers; legs, bill greyish; eyes light yellow. Aggressive and conspicuous, attacking intruders, including dogs, in territory. Display by ♂ involves raising wings to show white; ♂ and ♀ also dance opposite each other. Several harsh calls; song medley of notes repeated usually 3 times, including mimicked phrases. Sings from open perch throughout year and on moonlit nights. Diet: fruit, berries, seeds in season; otherwise insects. Breeds May-June, ♀ and ♂ rapidly building large nest of plant materials and debris, lined finer fibres, 3 to 20 ft up in low tree or shrub. 3 to 6 greenish to buff eggs, blotched and spotted brown, incubated mainly by ♀ 12-14 days; both ♀ and ♂ feed young, who fly from 10 days. 2 or more broods. **670**

Mirafra africana *Alaudidae*
RUFOUS-NAPED (BUSH) LARK   6-7 ins
Ethiopian: 19 races; resident and breeds Africa S of Sahara especially E and S, (rare W of Cameroun). Habitat: cultivated, grassy country and open bush from coastal plains to mountain grassland. Fairly stocky with fairly long bill. Upperparts buff to tawny with black streaks, fewer on rump; short crest; broad whitish 'eyebrow'; underparts tawny with black streaks on chest and breast; wings brown with greyish tips; tail rather short, dusky with paler edges. Legs, bill flesh colour, eyes and culmen brown. Call: mournful, clear whistle *chiwicki-chiwi*. Song varied and sweet, often in hovering song flight. Has conspicuous flapping/gliding courtship flight. Runs at 5 mph. Food: insects and seeds. Breeding season mainly November to June but depends on timing of rains. Nest of dried grass usually in tussock; lays 2-3 brownish white eggs with darker markings. **608**

MISTLE THRUSH see **Turdus viscivorus**

MISTLETOE BIRD see **Dicaeum hirundinaceum**

MITCHELL'S SANDPIPER PLOVER see **Phegornis mitchelli**

Mniotilta varia *Parulidae*
BLACK AND WHITE WARBLER   5½ ins
Nearctic, Neotropical: breeds Newfoundland, N Ontario, Central Manitoba, Central W Mackenzie S to N Georgia, Central Alabama, E Texas; W to S Dakota, Kansas; winters Florida, N Mexico S to Guadeloupe, Venezuela, Ecuador. Habitat broad-leaved and mixed woodlands, especially shrubby secondary growth from swamps to upland; scarcer in northern conifer forests. ♂ generally streaked or barred black and white all over, except white underparts; striped crown distinguishes from Blackpoll Warbler, *Dendroica striata*. ♀ white from chin to under tail coverts, tinged brown where ♂ black. Legs, bill, eyes dark. Juvenile much browner. Runs up tree trunks, over and under branches like treecreeper *Certhia*. Song: 2 main forms: c. 8 high screeping notes 'thin and wiry'; second less frequent, more elaborate; calls: weak *tsip*, louder *chick*; hisses when alarmed. Insectivorous, takes eggs and pupae from bark. Breeds April to July, ♀ (mainly) builds partly domed nest of dead leaves, bark, grass, rootlets, lined hairs, in ground at base of tree, bush, plants, stump, under log. Usually 5 white or creamy eggs, heavily marked shades of brown, lavender, tending to zone, incubated ♀, who often feigns injury, 11-14 days; both parents feed young, who fly c. 12 days. **896**

MOCKINGBIRD see **Mimus polyglottos**

MOCKINGBIRD, GALAPAGOS see **Nesominus trifasciatus**

MOCKING CHAT see **Thamnolaea cinnamomeiventris**

Molothrus ater *Icteridae*
BROWN-HEADED COWBIRD　　　　　　　8 ins
Nearctic, marginally Neotropical: breeds much of southern Canada S to Central Virginia, Tennessee, Louisiana, S Mexico; winters Maryland, Ohio Valley, Texas, Central California, S to S Mexico. Habitat grasslands, cultivated areas; woodland edge, scrub, gardens. ♂ very dark glossy blue-black except glossy dark coffee-brown head, neck, purplish in autumn. ♀: generally grey-brown, pale on faintly streaked underparts, darker on wings. Legs, bill grey, eyes dark brown. Juvenile dark olive brown, scaled pale buff above, off-white streaked brown below. Keeps territory during laying period, otherwise in flocks. Call squeaky 3-note whistle; rattle of alarm; song, squeaky but musical, accompanies display when ♂ puffs out feathers, spreads tail, droops wings, stretching neck upward. Originally followed bison herds, now follows cattle, taking disturbed insects and ticks off them; also grass seeds, especially yellow foxtail *Setaria glauca*, weeds, grain. Lays May-June: parasitic on many, usually smaller passerines, laying 4 or 5 white eggs, evenly marked brown, on successive days in different nests. Watches host building, deposits egg after host has laid. Incubation by host 11-12 days; young fledge 9-10 days. Bayheaded Cowbird, *M. badius*, not parasitic but often takes nests of other species; sometimes ♀ and ♂ build their own. **911**

Molothrus badius see under **M. ater**

MOLUCCAN BIRD OF PARADISE see **Macgregoria pulchra**

MOLUCCAS RED LORY see **Eos squamata**

Momotus momota *Momotidae*
BLUE-CROWNED MOTMOT　　　　　　15-16 ins
Neotropical: Central and much of northern S America, both sides of Andes; Trinidad and Tobago; resident edges of rain forest, secondary growth, Brazilian cerrado (tall plateau scrub), plantations. Upperparts iridescent green to blue-green, including long tail; vanes of 2 longest feathers break off to leave spoon-shaped tips; crown, throat light blue with black spots on top and black mask; blue-edged black spot on breast; throat and underparts cinnamon or green according to race; short legs, strong bill dark, eyes red. Sits upright, high in foliage, dropping to ground to feed. Tail moves like pendulum when excited or may be held to one side; two birds may perch alongside or facing each other. Makes short flights between trees. Display involves leaf-carrying. Duetting call booming *bou*, answered *hou* by mate; hence Trinidadian name *bouhoutou*; also deep-carrying *coot*, clack or yap of alarm. Diet mainly fruit, also larger insects, beaten against perch before swallowing. Follows army ants to glean disturbed insects and lizards. Pairs probably for life, breeding May Trinidad; for up to 10 weeks ♀ and ♂ excavate long tunnel (up to 7 ft) often with one or more sharp turns. 3 glossy white eggs incubated by ♀ and ♂ c. 21 days. Parents bring insects at first, later fruit to young, who fly c. 30 days. **496**

MONARCH, BLACK-FACED see **Monarcha melanopsis**

Monarcha melanopsis *Muscicapidae: Muscicapinae*
BLACK-FACED MONARCH　　　　　　c. 6 ins
Australasian: E continental Australia from Cape York to E Victoria; New Guinea, Timor; summer visitor to brushes and dense scrub New South Wales. Generally grey with black frontal patch, throat separated by grey band from chestnut underparts; whitish patch round reddish brown eye; legs, bill dark. Searches leaves, branches and makes aerial sallies after variety of insects. Call loud whistling *why-yew witch-yew*. Breeds November to January, building cup nest of green moss, lined fine rootlets, in thin vertical or lateral fork of branch, up to 30 ft high. 2 or 3 white eggs, marked reddish and lavender. **793**

Monasa flavirostris *Bucconidae*
YELLOW-BILLED NUNBIRD　　　　　　10½ ins
Neotropical: Colombia, along base of E Andes to E Peru; W Amazonian Brazil; resident in lowland forests, especially along edges. Generally black, but upper and under wing coverts largely white; slender curved bill yellowish. Habits little studied, but takes insects on wing in circular flights, sweeping back up to perch; also small lizards, frogs, centipedes, scorpions from ground. Apparently social, with communal displays. Believed to excavate nesting burrow in bank, as does White-fronted Nunbird, *M. morphoeus*; fledging period probably c. 30 days (A. F. Skutch).

Monasa morphoeus see under **M. flavirostris**

MONKEY-EATING EAGLE see **Pithecophaga jefferyi**

Monticola angolensis *Muscicapidae: Turdinae*
MOTTLED or ANGOLA ROCK THRUSH　　　　9 ins
Ethiopian: S Congo area and Angola in band eastward largely between 10° and 15°S, to Tanzania, Malawi, Mozambique; resident low hills in open woodland and bush. ♂ upperparts mottled pale blue-grey and black; upper tail coverts and tail bright tawny, central feathers brown; cheeks, throat pale blue-grey; underparts tawny, brightest on breast; lower belly white. ♀: upperparts buff and black; cheeks, throat, mottled black buff; underparts tawny brown shading paler; legs, eyes dark brown, bill dark horn. Juvenile more spotted and mottled. Shy and solitary; perches trees rather than rocks. Call fluted 2-note whistle, second note higher; chattering alarm. Mainly insectivorous. Breeds chiefly September to December, making simple twig nest, sometimes more substantial, in shallow tree hole. 3 or 4 turquoise blue eggs with small brown spots. **689**

Monticola cinclorhynchus *Muscicapidae: Turdinae*
BLUE-HEADED or WHITE-THROATED
ROCK THRUSH　　　　　　　　　7 ins
E Palaearctic: northern race *M.c. gularis* breeds Siberia (Amur basin to River Argun), Manchuria, N Korea, N Hopei: nominate race, Afghanistan, Himalayan foothills to Assam; *gularis* winters SE Asia, N Vietnam, Burma; *cinclorhynchus*, S India, Bangladesh, Burma. Nominate ♂: upperparts from crown blue to blackish; conspicuous white patch on wing; underparts, rump chestnut. ♂ *gularis* has triangular white patch on throat, less white on wings; wings, tail browner. ♀: upperparts brown, underparts whitish, brown feather margins giving scaly effect. Legs light brown, bill blackish brown, eyes deep brown. Solitary or in pairs on lightly forested hillsides of pine and oak, 4,000 to 9,000 ft; winters broadleaved forests, bamboo thickets, plantations and villages. Drops from perch to take prey, either swallowing it on spot or returning; also searches litter; takes frogs, lizards. Song loud, clear, of 3 notes. Breeds April to July; ♀ and ♂ build untidy nest of local plant material in hollow in bank, rock ledge, tree roots. 3 to 5 creamy white to buff eggs, densely freckled red. ♀ and ♂ incubate, and tend young. 2 broods. **690**

Monticola saxatilis *Muscicapidae: Turdinae*
ROCK THRUSH　　　　　　　　　7½ ins
Palaearctic: Iberia (very local NW Africa), S Europe, Asia Minor into mountains SW Asia, broadly between 30° and 50°N; isolated population W of Yellow Sea; winters tropical Africa. Habitat rocky, boulder-strewn hillsides with scattered low vegetation, up to 11,500 ft Afghanistan; also quarries and buildings in hills; winters savannah, steppes. ♂: upperparts including head, throat, blue, shading to white back, rump; wings blackish; underparts and short tail mainly orange. ♀: upperparts mottled dark brown, underparts rufous buff, 'scaled' darker. ♂ winter has feathers upperparts brown-tipped, whitish on underparts. Legs brown, bill, eyes dark brown. Juvenile resembles ♀. Mainly terrestrial, standing upright or crouching, taking long hops. Perches, swinging tail, on rocks, trees, wires. Flies low. Call soft *chee chee*; song loud, fluty, from perch or in display flight: upward flutter, gentle descent; ♂ also struts before ♀, drooping wings.

Food mainly large insects, other invertebrates including worms, small lizards. Breeds May onwards; ♀, accompanied ♂, makes neat nest grasses, moss, finely lined; in hole or crevice of rock, wall, even tree. 4 or 5 pale blue eggs, sometimes faintly spotted reddish, incubated mainly by ♀ 14-15 days; both parents feed young, who fly 14-16 days. Sometimes 2 broods. **691**

Monticola solitarius *Muscicapidae: Turdinae*
BLUE ROCK THRUSH　　　　　　　8 ins
Palaearctic: narrow zone from Iberia, NW Africa between 30° and 45°N, through Mediterranean area (where sedentary), Iran, Himalayas to Korea, Taiwan, Japan; winters N Africa, Asia to Ceylon, Borneo, Celebes. Habitat much as *M. saxatilis*, up to 12,500 ft NW Himalayas; in towns S Europe, coastal in Japan; winters rocky steppes, savannahs. ♂ of European race *solitarius* all blue with darker wings, tail; other races have varying amounts of chestnut on belly, most pronounced in *philippensis*, breeding Japan. ♀ resembles ♀ *M. saxatilis* but much darker. Legs, bill bluish, eyes very dark brown. Perches rocks, buildings, frequently trees in Asia. Calls *tchee*, *weet-weet* and high-pitched *tsee*; fluty song resembles Blackbird, *Turdus merula*. Food mainly from ground; insects, other invertebrates, small snakes and lizards; marine animals Japan; berries and fruit. Breeds April to May S Europe. Nest, site and breeding details as *M. saxatilis*. 3 to 6 glossy, pale blue eggs, sometimes speckled red-brown. **692**

Montifringilla nivalis *Ploceidae*
SNOW FINCH　　　　　　　　　c. 7 ins
Palaearctic: interrupted distribution in mountain ranges from Pyrenees to Altai, Tibet, including Alps, Balkans, Caucasus; resident rugged, rocky slopes and screes, mountain-top tundra, glacier edges, up to 22,000 ft Alps, 16,000 ft Tibet; partly commensal, descending to high habitations in winter. ♂: upperparts chocolate brown, rather 'scaly'; wings mainly white with black primaries; central tail black but sides white; head grey, shading to white underparts; black bib. ♀ shows less white on wings, tail; head brown. Juvenile similar, duller. Legs black, bill mainly black summer, yellow winter, eyes dark brown. Hops or walks quickly; stance upright, tail frequently flicked; perches rocks, buildings, not trees. Flocks in winter; tame round alpine buildings. Call: penetrating, wheezy *tsweek*, becoming *tswaa* in flight. Short monotonous song from perch or in fluttering flight, ending in spiral descent with spread wings and tail. Feeds entirely on ground: insects, especially beetles and spiders in summer; seeds from herbs and conifers; human leavings. Breeds from end April in Alps, building untidy nest of plant stems, debris, in clefts, stone walls, under eaves. 4 or 5 pure white eggs incubated mainly ♀ c. 18 days; young fed by both parents. Sometimes 2 broods. **953**

MOORHEN see **Gallinula chloropus**

MOORHEN, DUSKY see under **Gallinula chloropus**

MOREPORK see **Ninox novaeseelandiae**

MOSQUE SWALLOW see **Hirundo senegalensis**

Motacilla aguimp *Motacillidae*
AFRICAN PIED WAGTAIL　　　　　　8 ins
Ethiopian: widely distributed throughout region; resident, now largely associated with habitations; but also sandy river banks, even rocky streams, coastal lagoons. Upperparts black with white 'eyebrow' and triangular white patch at side of neck; upper wing coverts white, also spots on edge flight feathers; outermost tail feathers white; underparts white with black breast band. Juvenile ashy grey instead of black. Legs, bill, eyes dark. Confiding, usually in pairs, but communal roosts in reedbeds. Call canary-like *tssp*; subdued but pleasant song, uttered more often than by *M. alba*: in flight, on perch, when running. Diet almost entirely insects. Breeds almost throughout year, building cup nest of leaves and dry grass, lined hair, rootlets: in artificial sites on buildings, also steep riverbanks. 2 or 3 pale brown, grey or green eggs, speckled darker brown; incubation and fledging much as *M.*

alba; likewise parasitised by cuckoos. 2, perhaps 3 broods. **631**

Motacilla alba *Motacillidae*
WHITE WAGTAIL or PIED WAGTAIL   *c.* 7 ins
Palaearctic, Oriental, marginally Nearctic: almost all Eurasia (including Iceland, Japan) except SE Asia; very locally NW Africa, E Greenland, recently NW Alaska; winters over wide area to Nigeria, Kenya, Indian subcontinent. Borneo, Philippines. Habitats varied, usually near water, e.g. riverbanks; also steppes tundra, alpine meadows; cultivated land, farms, gardens. White race, *M.a alba* has crown, wings, tail (except white outer feathers) black; mantle, rump clear grey; face, forehead white; wings blackish-brown with double white bar; belly white. Pied race *M.a. yarrellii* ♂ has black mantle and rump, ♀ dark grey. Throat both races white in winter. Juveniles predominantly grey to grey-brown upperparts. Legs, bill black, eyes black-brown. Runs fast with bobbing tail, taking off into undulating flight or agile sally after insects, which form main diet. Perches above ground freely, roosting in hundreds in trees, also in reedbeds and buildings. Wades in shallows. Call *tschizzick* with variants; *chick* of alarm. Simple twittering song, also heard from migrants. Breeds end March to August Britain, building cup nest of varied plant materials, lined wool, hair, some feathers; in recess, natural or artificial, on building, steep bank, or flat on ground like *M. flava*. 5 to 6 off-white eggs speckled grey incubated mainly by ♀ 13-14 days; young fed ♀ and ♂, fly 14-16 days. 2, sometimes 3, broods. **632**

Motacilla cinerea *Motacillidae*
GREY WAGTAIL   *c.* 7 ins
Palaearctic: most of W Europe (locally NW Africa) through Balkans, Asia Minor into mountains of Asia, E to Sakhalin, Japan, Kamtchatka; partly resident in W, otherwise migrates to N Africa, S and SE Asia as far as New Guinea. Habitat by fast-flowing rivers and streams to 6,500 ft Alps, 13,000 ft Kashmir; sometimes by still waters and buildings in Europe in winter. ♂: spring: upperparts blue grey, rump yellow-green, wings, tail (white outer feathers) black; pale 'eyebrow' and moustachial stripe; throat black, underparts yellow. ♀ has throat white; juvenile resembles her. Winter: underparts from throat pale yellow. Legs brownish-flesh, bill mainly grey black, eyes black-brown. Running gait, undulating flight like other wagtails, usually seen close to water, bobbing tail vigorously when perched. Generally solitary or in pairs, but communal roosts reported. Call note *tzitzti* more sibilant than *M. alba*; also tremulous *tchipp*. ♂ sings infrequently, often with slow display flight. Takes mainly water insects, also small crustaceans, fish fry; marine molluscs, sandhoppers on coast. Breeds end March to July Britain, building solid nest of plant materials, lined hair, on ledge or in recess, natural or artificial. 4 to 6 pale buff eggs, marbled grey-brown, incubated mainly by ♀ 13-14 days; young, fed by ♀ and ♂, fly *c.* 12 days. 2 broods. **633**

Motacilla flava *Motacillidae*
YELLOW WAGTAIL   *c.* 6½ ins
Palaearctic: almost whole region except N Siberia, NW Britain, Ireland, Iceland, but including Nearctic coast of Alaska; winters tropical Asia, Africa, mainly S of Lat 25°N. Breeds marshy grassland verging on reed-beds; heaths, moors, dunes, bush and grass steppes, tundra; cultivated land; river valleys, lake shores in winter. ♂♂ all races: mantle olive-green, wings, tail blackish brown with 2 pale wingbars and white outer tail feathers. ♀♀ duller, browner above with pale 'eyebrows', underparts pale yellow; juvenile as ♀ but bib of dark spots. Legs black, bill mainly grey-black, eyes black-brown. Great variety in heads of yellow-breasted ♂♂: crowns range from black *M.f. feldegg* to bright yellow *flavissima*, white-headed *leucocephala*. Split by some authorities into several species but now usually regarded as one. Most pipit-like of wagtails, though perches off ground readily. Flocks of several races form on migration. Call: shrill *tsweep*; pleasant song seldom heard but uttered in ♂'s courtship, which includes flight with feathers puffed, spread tail hanging, wings shivering. Food mainly insects off

ground or taken on wing, often when disturbed by grazing animals. Breeds end April to July Britain, building nest of local plant material, lined hair, wool, well-hidden on ground in variety of cover. 5 to 6 eggs very like *M. cinerea*, incubated by ♀ 12-13 days; young, fed by ♀ and ♂, fly *c.* 13 days. 2 broods in S of range. **634**

MOTMOT,
    BLUE-CROWNED see **Momotus momota**
    RUFOUS see **Baryphthengus ruficapillus**
    TODY see **Hylomanes momotula**

MOTTLED ROCK THRUSH see **Monticola angolensis**

MOUNTAIN
    CHAT see **Oenanthe monticola**
    DRONGO see **Chaetorhynchus papuensis**

MOURNING DOVE see **Zenaida macroura**

MOUSEBIRD,
    BLUE-NAPED see **Colius macrouros**
    SPECKLED see **Colius striatus**

MURRE see **Uria aalge**

MURRELET,
    KITTLITZ's see **Brachyramphus brevirostris**
    MARBLED see under **Brachyrhamphus brevirostris**

Muscicapa adusta see **Alseonax adustus**

Muscicapa latirostris *Muscicapidae*: *Muscicapinae*
ASIAN BROWN FLYCATCHER   *c.* 4¾ ins
E Palaearctic, marginally Oriental: summer visitor southern E Siberia, Manchuria, Sakhalin, S Kuriles, Korea; also parts N Indian subcontinent; winters Oriental region from Indian subcontinent to Indonesia, Philippines. Habitat mainly broadleaved woodland with or without dense undergrowth; sometimes with conifers; parkland (Japan): winters high in forest canopy. Resembles ♀ Pied Flycatcher, *Ficedula hypoleuca*, without wing bar and with conspicuous white ring round eye; underparts not streaked; legs black, noticeably broad bill mainly black, eyes dark brown. Habits much as Spotted Flycatcher, *M. striata*, but feeds more on ground. Song agreeable and melodious. Probably entirely insectivorous, including beetles; grasshoppers evidently from ground. Breeds first half May Japan, to June Siberia; breeding details similar to Spotted Flycatcher, building neat, lichen-covered nest on lateral tree bough close to trunk. 4 or 5 light grey green or cream eggs, sometimes washed light red, incubated ♀ only. **684**

Muscicapa striata *Muscicapidae*: *Muscicapinae*
SPOTTED FLYCATCHER   *c.* 5½ ins
W Palaearctic: summer visitor almost all Europe (including Britain, Ireland, NW Africa and excepting parts N Scandinavia, N Russia) extending wedge-shaped into W Asia beyond Lake Baikal to upper reaches Amur River at 50°N; winters Ethiopian region, NW India. Upperparts mouse-grey, underparts off-white; dark streaks forehead, breast; pale feather edges show on closed wings; legs black, bill mainly blackish, eyes dark brown. Juvenile 'scaly'. Solitary, pairs, family parties. Upright posture on exposed perch: branch, post, gable; head sunk, tail hanging vertically; then sallies after insects with audible snap, sometimes prolonged chase. Flicks wings, tail. Hops on ground. ♂ holds head up, bill vertical, in display, while flirting tail. Call shrill *tzee*, lengthened to *tzee-tuc-tuc* of alarm, especially with young. Quiet song *sip sip sree, sreeti sree sip*, sometimes with warble. Food principally small insects taken on wing; berries in autumn. Breeds second half May to August Britain; nest, built mainly by ♀, of moss, bark and other fibres, wool, bound cobwebs, decorated lichens; lined rootlets, hair, feathers; on small ledge, in open cavity, tree fork, snag-end, ivy, other creepers; rock-faces, walls, buildings; sometimes old nests bigger birds, near end of leafy bough; open nestboxes; 1½ to

30 ft. 4 to 6 greenish blue or grey eggs blotched rich chestnut, occasionally immaculate; incubated by ♀ and ♂ 12-14 days; both ♀ and ♂ feed young, who fly 12-15 days. Often 2 broods. **785**

Muscivora tyrannus *Tyrannidae*
FORK-TAILED   ♀: 11 (tail 6¾-7¾),
FLYCATCHER   ♂: 16 (tail 9-12) ins
Neotropical: northern race *M.t. monachus* breeds S Mexico to N South America; southern *tyrannus* in Uruguay, Paraguay, Argentina, wintering N as far as Curacao, Trinidad; northern birds also move south after breeding. Habitat semi-arid pastures, savannah, woodland, habitations. ♂: upperparts grey; rump, very long, much forked and graduated tail, most of head, black; semi-hidden crest yellow; underparts white. ♀ has shorter tail. Southern birds on territories call *cric cric cric* towards sunset, collect for communal display involving ♂'s straight upward flight and zigzag descent with scissoring of tail feathers; after which roosts in thick cover (C. S. Andrade). Also assemble before migration. Aggressive like Kingbird, *Tyrannus tyrannus*. Diet mainly insects taken in flight. Southern race breeds October to February, building cup nest of plant material fairly low in trees and bushes. ♀ lays and incubates 3 or 4 white eggs, marked brown mainly at big end. Both parents feed young, rearing 2 broods. **580**

MUSCOVY DUCK see **Cairina moschata**

MUSK DUCK see **Biziura lobata**

Musophaga rossae *Musophagidae*
ROSS'S TOURACO   20 ins
Ethiopian: Equatorial Africa as far E as W Kenya and Tanzania, in great arc round Congo forests (not in them) from NE to SW, with small isolated population in Cameroun. Further W replaced by *M. violacea* all along Guinea coast and hinterland. In gallery and scattered patches of forest, savannah woodland, cultivated areas with trees. Uniform steely blue-black except for crimson crest and wings, very noticeable in flight. Bright yellow beak and orbits. Very loud splendid ringing call as birds run about and display in the branches. Eats fruit. Flimsy pigeon-like nest in small tree, 2-3 white eggs. **415**

Musophaga violacea see under **M. rossae**

MUTTON BIRD see **Puffinus tenuirostris**

Mycteria americana *Ciconiidae*
WOOD STORK   *c.* 40 ins
Nearctic and Neotropical: from Florida through Greater Antilles to E Peru, Paraguay, Uruguay and Argentina; post-breeding dispersal northward. Habitat: swamps, ponds, and coastal lagoons. White with black flight feathers and tail; head and neck bare, slate grey; legs black, feet pinkish yellow, heavy slightly curved bill black or variable, eyes grey-brown. Flies swiftly with head and neck stretched; normally gregarious, and soaring parties take place mid-morning and early afternoon. Walk rather stately. Mutual displays at nest. Usually silent but has 'fizzing' note at nest, and bill clattering. Diet fish, especially minnows, reptiles and amphibians. Breeding season varies with range; colonial in trees, e.g. mangroves; nest of sticks holds 2 to 5 creamy white granulated eggs, incubated 28-32 days by ♀ and ♂, who tend brood until they become independent at *c.* 11 weeks. **74**

Mycteria ibis or *Ibis ibis* *Ciconiidae*
YELLOW-BILLED STORK   3½ ft
Ethiopian and Madagascar; some migration, e.g. to Ghana in November for breeding. Habitat river and coastal sandbanks, large shallow lakes. White, partly tinged crimson, with black flight feathers and tail, and red head; immature largely silvery-grey; legs pink with black toes, bill yellow with darker tip, eyes brown. 'Goose-stepping' gait; flies with neck and legs stretched and dives from height, driving air noisily through wings. Silent, but has squeaky, nasal call; bill-clattering in mutual display. Diet fish, frogs, reptiles and small water animals, often hunted with

head underwater and wings open. Breeding season variable through range; colonial, in trees or bushes on ledges; flat nest of sticks with grass lining holds 2 to 3 dull or greenish white eggs. **75**

Mycteria leucocephalus or Ibis leucocephalus
Ciconiidae
PAINTED STORK   40 ins
Oriental; India through Burma to Indo-China and SW China; coastal mud-flats, jheels (lakes), flooded paddyfields and marshes. White with black and white bars on wings and innermost secondaries pink; legs red-brown, bill orange, eyes surrounded by bare yellow and red skin. Juvenile largely brown. Normally small parties or pairs but huge numbers at heronries. Often walks through water with bill submerged and open, probing mud, then waggling one leg and flicking wing to drive prey towards bill. Stands hunchbacked; flight accompanied by slight opening and closing of bill, soars with other species. Silent except for bill-clattering and 'low moan' of greeting. Food mainly fish, also reptiles, frogs, crustaceans, insects. Breeding depends on monsoons; colonial, often with other species; nest of sticks with finer lining usually in trees in or over water. 2 to 5 white eggs, sometimes marked brown, incubated by ♀ and ♂, who also feed young. **76**

Myiagra cyanoleuca *Muscicapidae: Muscicapinae*
SATIN FLYCATCHER   6½ ins
Australasian: summer visitor (September) eastern continental Australia and Tasmania, migrating N in autumn as far as New Guinea and neighbouring islands. Breeds areas with tall trees. ♂: whole upperparts dark glossy green with very pale brown outer edge to tail; throat black; underparts white. ♀: upperparts brown, faintly tinged bluish; crown, nape dull blue-black; throat, breast rust red, sharply demarcated from white underparts; legs, bill, eyes dark. Feathers of crown kept raised but not as crest; constant movement of tail. Usually in pairs. Call: piping whistle *chee-ee chee-ee*; short rasping note. Food: insects, chiefly taken on wing. Breeds November to January; nest of bark strips, bound and decorated cobwebs, lichens, lined rootlets, hair; usually in fork of dead lateral bough protected by live one. 2 or 3 dull to faint bluish or greenish white eggs, spotted brown and lavender, usually in zone. **794**

Myiagra inquieta or Seisura inquieta
Muscicapidae: Muscicapinae
RESTLESS FLYCATCHER   8 ins
Australasian: continental Australia round N and E coastal regions, except Cape York, to Kangaroo Island, inland to limit of savannah; separate population SW Australia. Sedentary open woodland, scrubs, cultivated land, orchards, often near stream, pool, small swamp. Upperparts from forehead black glossed dark blue, most vividly on head, dullest on flight feathers; underparts white (♀ has upper breast tinged buff and is generally duller); legs black, rather flattened, tapering bill with fringe of bristles black; eyes brown. Peaked head feathers make crest when excited. Constant 'nervous' movements. Display or aggressive posture perched upright with bill pointing vertically to emphasise white breast. Call 2-syllabled whistle; harsh, rising alarm note. Food mainly insects on ground, some from air: flies, butterflies, caterpillars; hunts from dead branch; more often hovers few ft above ground, making prolonged quiet whirring. Breeding season protracted; builds fairly open nest in fork of lateral, often eucalypt, 3 to 60 ft up; cup of bark, grass, bound cobwebs, lined hair, fur, decorated lichen. 3 or 4 white eggs, zone of reddish brown and lilac spots, 2 broods. **795**

Myiagra rubecula *Muscicapidae: Muscicapinae*
LEADEN FLYCATCHER   6 ins
Australasian: summer visitor continental Australia, from NW and Northern Territory, Cape York to Victoria; New Guinea; arrives New South Wales September. Habitat mainly coastal wooded areas with tall trees. ♂: similar to but rather duller than Satin Flycatcher with smaller black throat patch. ♀: red on throat less vivid than Satin Flycatcher, demarcation

between it and white underparts less defined. Call: harsh, grating, frog-like; hence local name 'frog bird'. Food: insects caught on wing or on foliage in tree tops. Breeds October to January; nest and site similar to Satin flycatcher, *M. cyanoleuca*. Usually 3 white or faintly bluish white eggs, spotted at centre or big end brown and lavender. **796**

Myioborus miniatus *Parulidae*
SLATE-THROATED REDSTART   5 ins
Neotropical: Central America, NW Guyanas, Venezuela, Colombia S through NW Brazil, Ecuador to Bolivia (La Paz, Cochabamba); edge of cloud level forests, secondary growth, *c.* 3,000 to 7,000 ft. Upperparts and crown slaty grey; tail blackish, outer feathers and under tail coverts white; cheeks grey, throat blackish; underparts bright yellow or orange red, tinged ochre upper breast. Remains single (race *M.m. hellmayri* Guatemala) or mated (race *aurantiacus* Costa Rica) outside breeding season, joining flocks of other species. Song (throughout year) rising sequence of *chees*; call, weak *chip*. Takes insects in aerial sallies, often fanning tail; also searches lower vegetation, tree trunks; takes white 'protein bodies' from petioles of *Cecropia*. Breeds from March (Costa Rica) to May; ♀ (mainly) builds domed nest of straws, grass, rootlets, lined finer fibres, rootlets, generally in earth bank or on steep slope, among epiphytes on fallen log, or hidden by ferns. 2 or 3 white eggs, heavily speckled reddish brown, incubated ♀ 13-15 days; young leave nest 12-14 days, but ♀ and ♂ continue feeding them for several weeks. Injury feigning common at nest. **897**

Myioborus ornatus *Parulidae*
GOLDEN-FRONTED REDSTART   5 ins
Neotropical: NW Venezuela, Colombia in E Andes; separate race Central and W Andes; forests. Upperparts dark olive-grey, tail blackish, outer feathers, under tail coverts white; crown lemon yellow; chin, checks white or all orange-yellow in western race; nape, sides of neck black; underparts lemon or orange yellow; legs greyish, bill dark grey, eyes brown. Habits, food, breeding much as *M. miniatus*. **898**

Myiodynastes masculatus *Tyrannidae*
STREAKED FLYCATCHER   8½ ins
Neotropical: Central America, Trinidad and Tobago, generally distributed S America W of Andes to NW Peru, E of Andes to La Pampa, Argentina; southern populations migratory. Habitat mangrove swamps, forest edge and clearings, plantations and open woodlands, cerrado (low deciduous woodland); sea level to *c.* 5,000 ft. Upperparts dark brown streaked buff; rump and tail mainly chestnut, wings brown; concealed crest orange; whitish forehead joins yellow 'eyebrow'; broad blackish eye stripe; chin, throat white, feathers dark-shafted; upper breast and flanks yellowish white streaked dark brown; underparts less streaked, undertail coverts pale yellow; bill; upper black, lower much paler; eyes brown. Migratory race blackish above, streaked buffy white; underparts white, heavily streaked black. Usual call, loud harsh scream. Insectivorous diet. Breeds May to July Trinidad, building open nest of twigs and grass 20 to 40 ft or more up, either in hollow or bromeliad clump. 3 pale creamy white eggs, heavily marked pale reddish brown and lavender, incubated by ♀; young fed by both parents. **581**

Myiopsitta monacha *Psittacidae*
QUAKER PARAKEET   *c.* 11 (tail 5) ins
Neotropical: Bolivia, E through Paraguay, Uruguay, to Argentina (Rio Negro); open woodland, palm groves, cultivated land. Generally bright grass green; flight feathers blue; outermost feathers of long, pointed tail may have yellow inner webs; forehead, throat, breast pale grey; legs leaden grey, bill mainly white tinged brown, eyes black. 'Bristles up' head and neck feathers in aggression. Gregarious, flocks attacking cornfields, orchards; natural food: fruits, seeds, especially thistles. Breeds communally, from November, up to 12 pairs in same structure, large ball-shaped nest of thorny twigs, unlined; each pair has entrance and nest chamber, where 4 to 6 dull white eggs incubated probably only by ♀. Brazilian Teal,

Amazonetta brasiliensis, may take over nest, the only one built by a parrot not in hole.

Myiozetetes similis *Tyrannidae*
VERMILION-CROWNED or SOCIAL FLYCATCHER 7 ins
Neotropical: Central America, S America E of Andes to Bolivia, Paraguay, NE Argentina; W of Andes to Tumbes, Peru; resident open woodland and clearings, often near water; sea level *c.* 5,000 ft. Upperparts greyish brown, crown and cheeks darker than back; buff margins to inner webs flight feathers; tail brown; concealed crest vermilion; broad white stripe over eye to nape; throat white; underparts yellow; legs, short bill dark, eyes dark brown. Habits much as other tyrannid flycatchers, e.g. *Tyrannus* species. **582**

MYNAH,
   COMMON see **Acridotheres tristis**
   INDIAN HILL see **Gracula religiosa**
   ROTHSCHILD's see **Leucopsar rothschildi**

Myrmecocichla nigra *Muscicapidae: Turdinae*
SOOTY CHAT   7 ins
Ethiopian: large area W and centre of region: Cameroon, Angola to Zambia, Sudan, E Africa; resident open short grass country or light bush, often among termite hills. ♂: glossy black all over; white shoulder patch less extensive and tail shorter than White-headed Black Chat, *Thamnolaea arnotti*. ♀ umber or sooty brown. Legs, bill orange, eyes light. Juvenile ♂ black no gloss, juvenile ♀ darker than adult. Terrestrial, hopping with tail cocked and often spread. Whistling calls; thrush-like song often from termite mound, ♂ swaying body up and down. Breeds January to March, August to October Uganda, building grass nest, lined flowers, down, soft stems, in hole in old termite hill, sand bank, stump; also excavates 3 ft tunnel if necessary and roosts in it. 4 or 5 white or bluish-white eggs with occasional black spots. 2 broods.

Myzomela nigra *Meliphagidae*
BLACK HONEYEATER   4¼ ins
Australasian: temperate inland zone of continent, making erratic movements governed by temperature; habitat open woodlands in dry, hot areas, ♂: generally brownish black with dull black extension down centre breast into white underparts; legs, bill black, eyes dark brown. ♂: upperparts brown, 'scaly' on wings due to pale feather edges; white 'eyebrow'; underparts whitish with brown band on throat. Immature similar. Nomadic flocks search flowering trees and shrubs, often work country after bush fire for insects. Quick flight, with sudden zigzag movements. Call long monotonous whistle; short twittering song. Diet chiefly insects, nectar from emu bush, mistletoe berries. Breeds September to December, ♀ building shallow open nest of dead twigs, grass, bound cobwebs, lined fine grass, vegetable down; usually in fork of lateral branch of dead bush, up to 60 ft. Usually 2 yellowish buff eggs, indistinctly zoned umber and grey at big end, incubated mainly by ♀ *c.* 18 days; ♀ and ♂ feed young, who fly *c.* 2½ weeks. **845**

NAMAQUA DOVE see **Oena capensis**

Nannopterum harrisi *Phalacrocoracidae*
GALAPAGOS CORMORANT   36-38 ins
Confined to Galapagos, breeding Albemarle and Narborough islands. Flightless giant, brown all over, with small, rounded wings; hairlike plumage has faint green gloss and white filoplumes on head and neck; legs black, bill: upper mandible blackish, lower, horn brown; eyes emerald. Swims efficiently and gracefully with body low but head held up; dives with forward leap after squids and fish, including eels. Waddles or jumps ashore, and holds out wings to dry like relatives. Croaks and hisses, while young beg with loud cries. Breeds in small groups on bare rocks, building large nests of local debris; both sexes incubate 2 or 3 chalky blue-green eggs and tend the young, of which usually only one survives. **46**

NARROW-BILLED PRION see under **Pachyptila desolata**

NATIVE COMPANION see **Grus rubicundus**

Nectarinia famosa *Nectariniidae*
MALACHITE SUNBIRD ♀: 5, ♂ (with tail): 9 ins
Ethiopian: Eritrea, Ethiopia, Sudan, S to S Africa. Resident and locally migratory E Africa forest edge and glades, bushy grassland, highland scrub, moorland and bamboo zones from 5,500 to 9,500 ft; to sea level S Africa, where found open country, gardens. ♂: upperparts, including head, neck metallic green tinged golden; upper tail coverts metallic emerald green; flight feathers, tail black, edged green and blue, central feathers elongated; underparts deep metallic blue (or golden green); bright yellow pectoral tufts. Non-breeding plumage resembles ♀ but black flight and tail feathers (with central elongation) retained, also metallic wings and upper tail coverts. ♀: upperparts olivaceous brown; pale 'eyebrow'; tail blackish, slightly metallic, outermost feathers edged white, all (except non-elongated central pair) tipped white; underparts dusky yellow, mottled darker. Bill, legs black, eyes brown. In pairs or small parties among flowers, e.g. thistles, heaths, *Leonotis;* main food insects; nectar, e.g. from *Protea* S Africa. Fond of bathing and drinking in dew. ♂ fluffs pectoral tufts in display after settling near ♀ from 'butterfly' flight. Aggressive to other sunbirds and larger species. Call on wing harsh, shrill; ♀ also has harsh *tsi-tsee;* ♂'s song jingling succession of *chees*. Breeds most often rainy season, ♀ building bulky nest of beard moss, grass, bound cobwebs, decorated lichens, lined down, fur, feathers; suspended from outside bush 4 to 6 ft up, among large herbs, or over water. 2, sometimes 3, pale cream eggs, streaked and spotted grey and greyish brown, incubated ♀ 14 days. Young, fed by ♀ and ♂, roost in nest for some time after fledging. Sometimes parasitised by cuckoos. **826**

Nectarinia killimensis *Nectariniidae*
BRONZY SUNBIRD ♀: 5½, ♂ (with tail): 9 ins
Ethiopian: NE Zaire, Angola, Uganda, Kenya, Tanzania, Malawi, Zambia, E Rhodesia; partially migratory, especially southern race *N.k. arturi*. Widespread open woodland, open grassland (*arturi*), scrub, gardens, up to 6,000 ft. ♂: mainly dull metallic green (especially head, neck) or bronzy gold, except for purplish black wings, tail (central feathers much elongated and narrowly edged bronze gold), underparts. ♀ resembles ♀ Malachite Sunbird, *N. famosa*, but bill more curved, central tail feathers slightly elongated, tail tinged purple not blue, chin whitish, streaked underparts much brighter yellow. Juvenile like ♀ but ♂ has throat feathers black, tipped white. Legs, bill, eyes dark. Habits as other sunbirds; main food insects but attracted to *Erythrina, Leonitis, Crotalaria*, southern race to *Loranthus* Buffalo Bean flowers. Call loud shrill *pee-yoo pee-yoo;* also doubles piping. Breeding varies within range, September to April S Africa; nest of grasses, other plant material, bound cobwebs, often projecting 'porch', attached twig tip few feet up. Usually 1 egg, pale bluish cream heavily marked sepia, ashy brown, incubated ♀. **827**

Nectarinia pulchella *Nectariniidae*
BEAUTIFUL SUNBIRD ♀: 4½, ♂: 6 ins
Ethiopian: local E from Senegal, Sierra Leone to Sudan, Eritrea, Ethiopia, Somalia S to S Tanzania; not coastal. Resident bush country, savannah, woodland; acacias and *Delonix elata*, especially when flowering; also cultivated land, gardens. ♂: generally shining metallic green with scarlet breast patch bordered yellow each side; central tail feathers elongated; belly black in race *melanogaster* E of Rift Valley. Non-breeding ♂ upperparts dull grey-brown, underparts whitish but retains metallic rump, wing coverts, long tail feathers. ♀: ashy grey with whitish 'eyebrow'; tail white-edged and tipped; underparts yellowish white, faintly streaked on breast. Legs, bill, eyes dark. Call sharp clear *tsp;* ♂ has soft warbling song. Habits and food as rest of family. Breeds June to November in different parts of range, building elongated but compact nest of grass, bark fibres, leaves, bound cobwebs, entrance near top; suspended from twig on tree or bush. Usually 2 glossy white eggs, densely mottled grey and brown; incubated ♀. **828**

Nectarinia tacazze *Nectariniidae*
TACAZZE SUNBIRD ♀: 5½, ♂ (with tail): 9 ins
Ethiopian: Eritrea, Ethiopia, S Sudan, E Uganda, Kenya, N Tanzania; resident highlands over 7,000 ft: forests with marshy glades, gardens, vicinity of houses; probably locally migratory. ♂: generally black-looking but upperparts and breast show as brilliant metallic violet certain lights, glossed copper on head; wings, tail (with elongated central feathers), lower underparts dull black. Non-breeding ♂ resembles ♀ with retention of wing and tail plumage. ♀ as ♀ Malachite Sunbird, *N. famosa,* but underparts darker, tail longer. Can withstand cold weather. Often with other sunbirds. Call loud single or double *tsssp;* ♂'s song sustained warbling, usually high in tree. Food: insects, nectar from 'red hot poker' and garden blossoms. Breeding season varies within range; builds pear-shaped nest of plant fibres, lichens, bound cobwebs, decorated bark, suspended by webs from branch or twig. Usually single pale buff egg, heavily marked and scrawled buff and sepia; incubated ♀. **829**

Nectarinia violacea *Nectariniidae*
ORANGE-BREASTED SUNBIRD ♀: 5, ♂: 6½ ins
Ethiopia: southernmost coastal S Africa; mountain slopes and plateaux with heaths, proteas. ♂: head, upper mantle, throat metallic green; back, upper tail coverts olive green; wings (flight feathers yellow-edged), tail (central feathers elongated) blackish; upper breast metallic violet; underparts orange, tinged brown on breast; pectoral tufts yellow. ♀: olive green; tail dusky; underparts paler green. Legs, bill black, eyes brown. Tame, conspicuous, usually in pairs, ♂ giving harsh *tsearp* call from bush tops. Also *teer-turp* repeated twice; short high-pitched song. Sometimes hawks insects, not affected by moderately bad weather; also takes spiders; nectar of *Erica, Protea,* other flowers. Breeds mainly May to August, but recorded all months; nest of twigs, *Protea* down, grass, lined vegetable down, usually 9 ins to 3 ft small bush, sometimes top of tall tree. Single or 2 whitish eggs, heavily freckled grey-brown, especially at big end, incubated ♀ 15 days; ♀, helped ♂, feeds young, who fledge 15 days.

NENE see **Branta sandvicensis**

Neochmia albiventer see under **N. phaeton**

Neochmia phaeton *Estrildidae*
CRIMSON FINCH *c.* 5 ins
Australasian: tropical N Australia, except Cape York Peninsula where replaced by Pale Crimson Finch, *N. albiventer*, sometimes regarded as conspecific; race *N.p. evangelina* S New Guinea. Resident riparian grasslands, cane grass and pandanus palms; settlements in N Australia; pineapple plantations Queensland; vicinity of surface water. ♂: brown above, wings and tail, ashy on head, all washed red; face, throat crimson; upper tail coverts, underparts white; sides of breast spotted white; belly, under tail coverts black. ♀ duller, lacks crimson and black on underparts which are light brown; face, throat light crimson. Legs flesh yellow, bill mainly red, eyes yellowish brown. Immature generally dull greyish brown, bill black. Pairs or flocks of 18 to 20. Flies or hops between rank grass tussocks, climbing up and down stalks to take seeds; also termites, spiders; dew off leaves. Flicking tail movements; aggressive to neighbours. Penetrating multiple call; low song ends 3 melodious notes. ♂ has song flight and carries grass when courting; elaborate ceremonies at nest site. Breeds January to April in N, several pairs near together; bulky bottle nest of grass, bark, leaves, lined feathers and fur; in tall grass, bush, 10 to 50 ft up on butts of pandanus leaves; on and inside buildings. 5 to 8 white eggs incubated ♀ and ♂, who tend young for 3 weeks. **940**

Neodrepanis coruscans *Philepittidae*
FALSE SUNBIRD *c.* 4 ins
Confined to wet forests of Madagascar. Upperparts iridescent blue; wings dull yellow and blackish; underparts dull yellow marked blackish; light blue wattle round brown eye; legs, curved bill horn brown. ♀ lacks wattle, dark green above, yellowish below. Formerly considered to be a sunbird (*Nectariniidae*), as it visits flowers with long corollas to feed; usually searches twigs for insects. Quiet, solitary or in small parties. Call: soft hissing.

Neophemia elegans *Psittacidae*
ELEGANT GRASS PARAKEET 9 ins
Two areas of continental Australia: SW Victoria, W New South Wales, SE South Australia; SW West Australia; nomadic in mallee scrub, open savannah, sandy coasts, saltbush plains, cultivated land; forest/cultivation edge in W Australia. Generally olive yellow with dark blue wings and forehead; tail blue with yellow edges; lores yellow; legs grey, bill greyish-horn, eyes brown. ♀ duller; juvenile has no blue forehead. In pairs or flocks, which make brief excursions from trees, sometimes zig-zag flights at great height. Calls: *tsit* in flight, 'wren-like' (*Malurus*) twittering and warbling. Food: seeds of grass, clover, other herbs; berries and fruits. ♂ jerks head in courtship to regurgitate food. Breeds August to October usually in tree hole at some height. 4 or 5 white eggs incubated by ♀ *c.* 18 days; she feeds young, who fly *c.* 30 days and join parents. **396**

Neophron percnopterus *Accipitridae*
EGYPTIAN VULTURE 26 ins
S Palaearctic (Europe, N Africa, Middle East), W Oriental (Indian subcontinent). Migrates in north of range, perhaps following domestic animals. Found in open places, deserts and cultivated land, largely commensal, up to at least 10,000 ft. White, tinged cream, except for predominantly black flight feathers, large wedge-shaped tail; legs yellow, bill dark brown, eyes red in head of yellow-orange skin. Immature dark brown. Scavenges in settlements, collecting in numbers and perching on buildings, trees, even ground. Spends much time soaring and swooping in display flights with vigorous dives at partner. Hisses, mews and growls in anger or alarm. An 'opportunist at carcases' (L. H. Brown), raids flamingo and other colonies, known to break ostrich eggs by hurling stones at them from bill. Follows plough to catch insects, molluscs and crustaceans. Breeding season varies throughout the range. ♀ and ♂ build slight nest of sticks and rags in hole on crags, buildings and masonry, occasionally trees. Usually 2 dirty white eggs, often blotched brown and grey, incubated by ♀ and ♂ for about 42 days. Chicks fledge *c.* 3 months. **159**

Neotis denhami *Otididae*
DENHAM'S BUSTARD 44 ins
Ethiopian: the three races *N.d. denhami*, Jackson's, *jacksoni*, and Stanley's, *stanleyi*, cover most of region except SW, on open plains where partly migratory. ♂: back of neck chestnut, mantle to upper tail coverts brown, finely vermiculated black, contrasting upper wing coverts blackish with large white spots, outer primaries black, inner with white bands; tail blackish with broad white bands; crown black with broken central white stripe, cheeks, front of neck, breast slate grey; throat and underparts white. ♀ has front of neck and breast vermiculated buff and black. Legs green, bill light yellow, tip dark, eyes yellow brown. Usually in pairs on ground, only making short flights. ♂'s spectacular display like Kori, *Choriotis kori.* Call guttural *khha-khha*. Follows burning grass after insects, the main food, with some plants and berries. Breeding season varies throughout range. Lays 1 or 2 light brown eggs, streaked darker brown, incubated by very light-sitting ♀ *c.* 4 weeks. Young fly after 5-6 weeks.

Nesillas sechellensis see **Bebrornis sechellensis**

Nesomimus trifasciatus *Mimidae*
GALAPAGOS MOCKINGBIRD 10-11 ins
Confined to Galapagos, where up to 11 forms on different islands have been given species status. Hood Island form *macdonaldi:* upperparts grey-brown; wings, tail black; white margins to wing coverts show as 3 faint bars; black markings on face; throat, underparts generally buffish white, diffusely spotted blackish; under wing coverts white, feathers with dark brown centres; legs, bill blackish, eyes brown. Longer shank and compressed bill distinguish from

Mimus. Frequently runs rather than fly, using wings as balancers. Extremely adaptable: on close terms with man, especially on Hood. Call note *peent*: sweet song. Food mainly insects, probing bill in crevices of rocks; also takes seabird eggs if cracked, young of other birds, carrion, fruit, faeces; has even drunk disinfectant (J. B. Nelson). Feeds in competitive groups each with strict pecking order. Breeds mainly rainy season, choosing one of several rough nests, of twigs, moss, lined grass, rootlets, in fork of shrub. 3 or 4 light green eggs, marked reddish brown; incubation and fledging as *Mimus*. **671**

Nestor meridionalis *Psittacidae*

KAKA   17-19 ins

Australasian: confined to New Zealand with races *septentrionalis* in North, *meridionalis* in South and Stewart Islands; on many coastal islands; habitat native forest, occasionally penetrating towns after nectar of tree blossoms. Predominantly olive-brown, dull green and red; greyish white crown, tawny orange patch below eye; rump and belly crimson; under wing scarlet; legs dark grey, bill (♂'s upper mandible larger and more curved than ♀'s) dark brown to steel grey, cere brown, eyes dark. Southern race brighter, ♂ with collar of gold-tipped crimson feathers; mottled in northern race. Partly nocturnal, small flocks flying above forest by day and night, with harsh *ka-aa* and musical whistles. Food: nectar, leaves and fruit of forest trees; also insects, attacking dead wood to extract larvae. Breeds October to February, using same hole in large hollow tree (entrance 10 to 30 ft up) for many years. 4 to 5 white eggs laid on powdered wood, incubated *c.* 21 days; young fly 10 weeks. **397**

Netta erythrophthalma *Anatidae*

AFRICAN or RED-EYED POCHARD   20 ins

Ethiopian race *N.e. brunnea*: Angola and Ethiopia to Cape; Neotropical race *erythrophthalma*: widely but patchily distributed, Venezuela, Colombia, Ecuador, Peru W of Andes, Chile (Arica) E Brazil, NW Argentina. Gregarious, common diving duck, abundant on most lakes, subject to seasonal movements. ♂: dark blackish and brown, sides of head and neck dark chestnut with violet tinge. ♀: brown with patches at base of bill, on throat and side of neck. Broad white wing-bar noticeable in flight. S American race slightly smaller and darker. Legs dark grey, bill grey; eyes: ♂ red, ♀ dark brown. Feeds on aquatic plant matter and some small animals. Call: low nasal *par-ah-ah,* occasionally deep quacking when flying. Breeding season variable; usual duck's nest of reeds and other plant debris lined with down, in reed beds or rushes usually in very wet places or even several feet of water. 5 to 8 or more white or creamy white eggs, incubated by ♀. **122**

Nettapus auritus *Anatidae*

PYGMY GOOSE   13 ins

Ethiopian: Gambia and Ethiopia to S Africa, also Madagascar. Habitat: weed-covered bays, small lakes and sluggish rivers. ♂: back iridescent bottle green, flanks, breast and base of neck chestnut, underparts white. Striking four-coloured head and neck: crown bottle green, back half of neck and head emerald green, thin black stripes demarking colour patches; face, throat and lower neck white. ♀: duller with less striking head, black speckling replacing greens and black. Legs grey; bill, ♂ orange-red, ♀ grey; eyes brown to red. Behaviour atypical of geese: quick twisting flight, perches in trees; in pairs or gregarious; good diver and can hide underwater with only bill showing. Call: ♂ soft whistle, ♀ weak quack. Feeds on floating vegetation, often water lily seeds. Breeds any month; down-lined nest in tree hole, cliff or ant hill; sometimes uses old tree nests of other species. 7 to 10 ivory white eggs. **123**

NEUMAYER'S ROCK NUTHATCH see **Sitta neumayer**

NEWTON'S BOWER BIRD see **Prionodura newtoniana**

NEW ZEALAND PIPIT see **Anthus novaeseelandiae**

NICOBAR DOVE see **Caloenas nicobarica**

NIGERIAN CRESTED LARK see **Galerida modesta**

NIGHT
    HERON see **Nycticorax nycticorax**
    HERON, YELLOW-CROWNED see **Nyctanassa violacea**

NIGHTHAWK,
    COMMON see **Chordeiles minor**
    WEST INDIAN see **Chordeiles gundlachii**

NIGHTINGALE see under **Luscinia luscinia**

NIGHTINGALE, THRUSH see **Luscinia luscinia**

NIGHTINGALE THRUSH, SLATY-BACKED see **Catharus fuscater**

NIGHTJAR,
    DUSKY see **Caprimulgus pectoralis**
    JUNGLE see **Caprimulgus indicus**
    MIGRATORY see **Caprimulgus indicus**
    PENNANT-WINGED see **Macrodipteryx vexillarius**
    SOUTH AFRICAN see **Caprimulgus pectoralis**
    SPOTTED see **Eurostopdus guttatus**

Nilaus afer *Laniidae*

NORTHERN BRUBRU   5 ins

Ethiopian: several races cover most of region; replaced Tanzania southward to Zululand by Black-browed, *N. nigritemporalis,* sometimes considered conspecific. Habitat: open bush, forest edge. ♂; upperparts black, but broad broken dorsal streak, edges wing coverts, inner secondaries brownish white; likewise outer edges tail feathers; forehead and prolonged 'eyebrow' white; underparts white, sides of breast, flanks chestnut. ♀: black replaced by shades of dark brown, blackish streaks throat and neck. Legs bluish grey, bill mainly black; eyes dark brown. Juvenile mottled or barred brown, blackish brown and white. Singly or in pairs, sometimes in mixed parties, often searching leaves for insects and silent except when ♂ utters clear whistle, answered at once by ♀'s lower note. Breeding season varies with range; neat cup nest of plant material bound cobwebs, usually in fork of thorn tree 20 to 30 ft up. 2 greyish or whitish eggs, marked black or very dark brown over grey.

Nilaus nigritemporalis see under **N. afer**

Ninox novaeseelandiae *Strigidae*

MOREPORK, SPOTTED or BOOBOOK OWL   11½ ins

Australasian: New Guinea, continental Australia and Tasmania, New Zealand and islands, Norfolk and Lord Howe Is. Resident in forests and settled areas. Upperparts brown, flecked buff on head and neck, otherwise white; forehead and face white with black rictal bristles; flight feathers spotted white and buff on upper, barred on lower surface; tail dark brown with faint paler bars; underparts mottled brown and white, washed orange brown; under tail coverts barred brown and white; feathered shanks yellow brown to buff, toes yellow, bill variable, mainly brown, eyes golden. Calls 'more pork' (more accurately *quor-coo*), sometimes repeating 'pork' several times; also hunting scream and vibrant *cree cree* in breeding season. Hawks for insects at dusk: wetas, moths, beetles, also spiders (NZ) sometimes lizards, rodents, small birds. Catches insects in flight with talons, transfers to bill. Breeds October to January, making scrape in hole of tree or recess in dense vegetation, sometimes in open on tree-fork. Usually 2 white eggs incubated by ♀ 30-32 days; she broods small young, taking food for them from ♂, who later feeds them direct; fledging *c.* 5 weeks. **444**

NODDY, COMMON see **Anous stolidus**

NOISY
    FRIARBIRD see **Philemon corniculatus**
    PITTA see under **Pitta brachyura**
    SCRUB BIRD see under **Atrichornis rufescens**

Nonnula ruficapilla *Bucconidae*

GREY-CHEEKED NUNLET   6 ins

Neotropical: E Panama to N Colombia, E Peru and W Brazil; resident open forest, secondary growth and thickets. Upperparts brown, crown rufous or reddish brown; cheeks, sides of neck, breast grey; underparts cinnamon rufous to cinnamon buff, shading to white on belly; legs, strong curved bill and eyes dark. Forms small flocks. Often in company with other forest species, feeding on insects and other small invertebrates taken from leaves.

NORTHERN
    DIVER, GREAT see **Gavia immer**
    LOGRUNNER see **Orthonyx spaldingi**
    SCREAMER see **Chauna chavaria**
    SCRUB ROBIN see under **Dryomodus bruneipygia**

Nothoprocta perdicaria *Tinamidae*

CHILEAN TINAMOU   12 ins

Resident, with local movements, in S Bolivia, W Paraguay and W Argentina, inhabiting open and dense thorny scrub. Upperparts sandy brown barred black, white margins along sides giving streaked effect; throat white, barred black lower down, underparts buff-grey to white; primaries black, notched buff on outer webs; legs, bill and eyes brown. Apparently pairs for life; runs and flies with diffidence, preferring to stand motionless or crouch when alarmed. Call a melodious, usually polysyllabic whistle, especially frequent in breeding season. Diet principally animal, from ground layer. Polygamous, one or more ♀♀ laying up to 10 or 12 richly marked, glossy eggs in scrape covered with feathers when unattended. Incubation *c.* 3 weeks by ♂; precocious chicks, buff with stripes, run soon after hatching and fly when half-grown. **6**

Notophoyx novaehollandiae *or* Ardea novae-hollandiae *Ardeidae*

WHITE-FACED HERON   26 ins

Australia, Tasmania, Celebes, Molucca; breeding New Zealand since 1940; some movement after nesting and has colonised small offshore islands. Bluish-grey with white on forehead, chin and round eye; pale grey nuptial plumes on back; underparts light grey but chestnut brown on breast; black wing-quills show in flight; legs greenish yellow, bill black, eyes yellow. Haunts swamps, lakesides, streams, singly, in pairs or small flocks after breeding. May rest, neck hunched, on post when not foraging in open for fish, reptiles, amphibians and small water animals. Flight call guttural *graaw,* other notes at nest. Breeds September to January in Australia, in colonies often with other species; the nest is a variable platform of sticks in tree over or near water, which holds from 3 to 5 pale bluish green eggs, incubated for 25 days by ♀ and ♂, who also tend the young during a fledging period of 6 weeks. **65**

Notornis mantelli *Rallidae*

TAKAHE   25 ins

Confined to South Island of New Zealand, in *Danthonia* tussock-grass alluvial flats at 2,500 to 4,000 ft in mountains; sedentary but moves into nearby *Nothofagus* beech woods in winter. Head, neck, breast and flanks iridescent blue, rest of upperparts suffused green; flightless wings blue (greater coverts) and green (lesser coverts) with spur at 'wrist'; underparts blue-black, under tail coverts white; legs, frontal shield and base of huge bill scarlet, tip pink; eyes dark. Immature brown, without gloss. Very secretive, 'lost' for 50 years, 1898-1948; green droppings often best evidence of presence. Pair bond persists and pairs remain on territories; present population *c.* 170 pairs. Aggressive posture with wings raised, neck ruffed. Presents under tail coverts in mutual display; ♂ fans tail when mating. Repeated *oomf* alarm call; *coo-eet* in duets. Main food succulent bases of *Danthonia* grasses; also seeds and flowers; rarely insects, except for chicks; *Hypoleis* ferns in beech woods. Breeds October to March, building canopied nest between tussocks, stems laid down and nipped off; usually two runways and latrine 2 yards off. 1 or 2 dull cream eggs, blotched

Nucifraga columbiana *Corvidae*
CLARK'S NUTCRACKER   *c.* 12½ ins
Nearctic: mountainous areas S Alaska, SW Alberta and W South Dakota to N Lower California and New Mexico; nests at 6,000 to 8,000 ft, otherwise 3,000 to 12,000 ft, may move S in winter. Habitat: timberline down to lower limit of coniferous forest. Grey, paler on forehead with nasal tufts, long, pointed black wings with white patch on secondaries; tail white, central feathers black. Legs, bill and eyes blackish. Usually in small parties, on wing or in forest treetops; may descend mountains rapidly checking at times by opening wings, producing loud roar. Call: chiefly long, grating, fairly high-pitched *kr-a-a-a*. Feeds on pine seeds, acorns, cedar and juniper berries and other fruits, insects, especially in summer, and carrion; will rob other birds' nests and visit camp sites for scraps. Breeds February onwards in conifers with thick foliage, often on S side 15 to 50 ft up; twig nest thickly (1½ ins) lined with grass, bark shreds and pine needles; 2 to 6, usually 3, pale green eggs with small brown and lavender spots. Both parents incubate very tightly *c.* 17 days and tend young, fledge *c.* 3 weeks. The thick nest lining and close incubation are presumably adaptations to the early breeding season. **1006**

Numenius arquata *Scolopacidae*
CURLEW   22-25 (bill *c.* 5) ins
Palaearctic: Faeroes, Ireland and Britain across Eurasia to Central Asia; summer visitor, either moving locally or S to Ethiopian and Oriental regions to winter on muddy coasts or inland marshes. Breeds typically moorland, heaths and grassland, damp or dry, also dunes, cultivated land. Upperparts light brown streaked darker, finer markings on head, neck, breast; wing tips blackish brown; white rump shades into barred tail; throat, flanks, underparts white with sparse dark streaks; legs greenish grey, bill dark brown, base pink; eyes brown. Single birds to large flocks in winter on shore or inland. Flight rather slow and gull-like, legs reach beyond tail like many waders. Sedate walk with body horizontal, also when perching on rock or post. Usual calls origins of names *Cur-lew* and *Whaup* (Scots); wonderful bubbling 'song' on wing. Probes small animals from soil or mud; takes larger crustaceans, molluscs, even frogs from surface; also seeds and berries. Breeds from second half April, making large lined scrape, usually quite open, in heather, grass or rushes. 4 glossy greenish brown eggs, marked rather lightly brown and grey, incubated by ♀ and ♂ 28-30 days; both tend young for 5-6 weeks. **289**

Numenius phaeopus *Scolopacidae*
WHIMBREL   15-16 (bill 3½) ins
Holarctic: discontinuous mainly in subarctic zone: Iceland, Scotland and N Europe, NE Siberia, Alaska, Hudson Bay; winters far S to Tierra del Fuego, S Africa, Tasmania, New Zealand, on sandy and muddy shores. Breeds barer ground than Curlew, *N. arquata*: moorland and marshy tundra. Similar to but darker than Curlew, crown black-brown divided by pale stripe, legs greenish grey, bill dark horn, base pink, eyes dark brown. Less wary than Curlew but similar in habits. Call of 'seven whistles' repeated *titti*, also used on breeding ground as Curlew-like bubbling in display flight. Food as Curlew but more animals picked from vegetation, less from probing. Breeds from late May in S of range, making lined scrape, open or partly sheltered. 4 olive green to light brown eggs, heavily marked dark brown, incubated by ♀ and ♂ *c.* 24 days; both tend young for *c.* 4 weeks. **290**

Numida meleagris *Numididae*
TUFTED GUINEAFOWL   20-22 ins
SW Palaearctic: relict population Central Morocco; 15 races cover Ethiopian region, including *N.m. mitrata* sometimes regarded as separate species, Helmeted Guineafowl. Habitat: dry thorn bush, open woodland, grassland, cultivated areas. Generally black, polka-dotted white all over, outer web secondaries speckled or barred; mainly bare head and neck usually cobalt blue; bony crest yellow, tipped maroon; tuft of white bristles (not in *mitrata*) over nostrils, red and blue wattles at base of horn-coloured bill; legs, eyes very dark brown. Ancestor of domesticated stock. In large flocks, going to roost noisily in trees, but generally walks rather than fly. Regular drinking in evening. Diet varied: insects, worms, molluscs; roots, bulbs, seeds; attacks corn crops. Repeated cackling call *kamacki kamacki*; low whistle; some racial variation. Long breeding season; 2 ♀♀ often share scrape in ground, laying 10 to 20 or more creamy or yellowish buff eggs with deep pore marks, speckled brown and white. **210**

Numida mitrata see under **N. meleagris**

NUNBIRD,
　　WHITE-FRONTED see under **Monasa flavirostris**
　　YELLOW-BILLED see **Monasa flavirostris**

NUNLET, GREY-CHEEKED see **Nonnula ruficapilla**

NUTCRACKER, CLARK'S see **Nucifraga columbiana**

NUTHATCH see **Sitta europaea**

NUTHATCH,
　　CORAL-BILLED see **Hypositta coralirostris**
　　EASTERN ROCK see under **Sitta neumayer**
　　MADAGASCAR see **Hypositta coralirostris**
　　NEUMAYER'S ROCK see **Sitta neumayer**
　　PINK-FACED see **Daphoenositta miranda**
　　RED-BREASTED see **Sitta canadensis**

Nyctaea scandiaca *Strigidae*
SNOWY OWL   21-24 ins, ♀ much larger than ♂
Holarctic: subarctic and arctic coastal areas, almost all above 60°N and beyond 80°N in Greenland; rare or absent where no lemmings. Mainly resident, but disperses S when food scarce. Habitat: dry tundra with rocky ridges, ice-free nunataks (hillocks) in land-ice, rocky islands, alpine zone in Scandinavia; moors, coastal marshes in winter. ♂: pure white or creamy, with few brown spots and flecks especially on wings; facial disc incomplete, ear tufts vestigial; legs feathered, claws and bill blackish brown, eyes golden. ♀: upperparts and much of underparts white, barred brown; rest of plumage white. Hunts by day, flight like big hawk, often striking down prey like falcon: mainly lemmings, other rodents, snow hares; birds up to ptarmigan and duck. Perches on ground or rock, occasionally in tree, often sits down. Arched defence posture. Rather silent; low *krow-ow* of excitement, also wild *rik rik rik* bill clicked in anger. Breeds from end April N Europe, making scrape among moss and stones on ridge or hillock with wide view. 4 to 10 white eggs incubated by ♀ 33 days; ♂ stays near and both feed young, who leave nest 2½-3½ weeks, fly 5-6 weeks. **445**

Nyctanassa violaceus *Ardeidae*
YELLOW-CROWNED NIGHT HERON   22-28 ins
Nearctic and Neotropical: from Mid-USA to N Peru, Colombia and E Brazil; disperses northward after breeding. Habitat mainly coastal, mudflats, swamps, to dry rocky islands; inland in USA. Generally blue or darker grey, but crown white tinged yellow, with white plumes and white cheek on otherwise black head; juvenile spotted olive brown. Legs dull orange, bill mainly blackish, eyes orange to scarlet. More erect stance than Black-crowned Night Heron, *Nycticorax nycticorax*; folded neck projects forward in flight. Most skulking American heron, tends to feed singly or in very small groups, mainly on crustaceans. Calls similar to Black-crowned but higher pitched. Lays from March to May in Florida; nests, in large or small colonies, usually in trees, well built of sticks, hold 2 to 6 pale blue green eggs, incubated by ♀ and ♂, who also tend young; whole cycle takes *c.* 2 months. **63**

Nyctibius grandis *Nyctibiidae*
GREAT POTOO   19½ ins
Neotropical: resident Panama to Peru and Brazil in open forest or forest edge, cultivated land with trees; savannah. Generally white or greyish white, marbled black and rufous and looking grey in distance; black on inner webs of flight feathers; 8 or 9 bars on tail; gape flesh-coloured, eyes bright brown. Nocturnal, solitary, tree-living, sitting cross-wise in upright attitude on branch. Scratches head over wing. Active especially on moonlit nights, sallying out from and returning to same perch after flying insects; flight silent. Churring call rhythmic *oorrr ooorr ooo*; also barking *wow*. Breeds July Brazil, laying single white egg, sparsely marked lilac and brown, in crevice of tree stump, usually near ground but sometimes high up. ♀ and ♂ incubate in relaxed position but, if approached, stretch out and 'freeze' with bill pointed upward. Also threaten by opening eyes wide, fluffing and spreading plumage, snapping bill and stretching gape. Young one, fed by ♀ and ♂, adopts 'freezing' posture while in nest. **456**

Nyctibius griseus *Nyctibiidae*
COMMON POTOO   15 (tail 8) ins
Neotropical: Mexico to Argentina; Trinidad and several W Indies. Resident in similar habitats to *N. grandis*. Greyish brown, mottled and vermiculated cinnamon, grey and black; broad black streaks on crown, narrower on back, scapulars, underparts; black spots across breast; wings and tail barred; bill notched; eyes bright yellow. Grey plumage phase very like *N. grandis*. Habits much as *N. grandis* but distinctive call 'six sad notes' in descending scale: *poor me all a-lone* and final sigh. Food: insects of several orders e.g. bugs, grasshoppers, beetles. Breeds April and August Trinidad; November to December Brazil. Breeding much as *N. grandis*; favourite site Trinidad is top of broken-off bamboo culm, 40 to 50 ft up. Fledging period 44 days. **457**

Nycticorax nycticorax *Ardeidae*
BLACK-CROWNED NIGHT HERON   24 (body 12) ins
Holarctic temperate zones, Oriental to Japan and Philippines, Neotropical to Argentina, Hawaii; northern populations migrate after breeding. Crepuscular, nesting and roosting in wooded swamps and riverbanks, even in gardens and villages in Asia; feeds in open marshes and rivers mainly on small fish, amphibians and variety of small water animals. Glossy greenish black head and back, with white nuptial plumes; underparts greyish white, extending round neck; tail and rounded wings grey; legs pale yellow (pink in spring), bill greenish black, eyes crimson; juvenile distinct in spotted brown bittern-like plumage. Hoarse raven-like *quock* uttered on wing; also calls at nest and in greeting. Breeding season variable over huge range. Complicated displays associated with ♂ attracting ♀ to nest-site in colony, usually with other species, in bushes and trees at varying heights, sometimes in reeds or other ground cover. Nest of radiating sticks holds 3 to 5 light bluish-green eggs, incubated 21 days by ♀ and ♂; young fed by parents in nest 3-4 weeks, fledge *c.* 6 weeks; occasionally 2 broods. **64**

Nymphicus hollandicus or Leptolophus hollandicus *Psittacidae*
COCKATIEL or QUARRION   12 ins
Australasian: continental Australia away from coasts; savannah scrub, riverine trees, country roadsides; nomadic food movements in N, seasonal migrations in S. ♂: generally grey; forehead, sides of head, tapering crest yellow; orange spot below eye; white patch across wing coverts; tail dark grey to blackish underneath; legs grey, bill dark grey, eyes dark brown. ♀ and juvenile duller, undertail barred yellow. Even, easy flight; parties often follow boomerang-like trajectory out and back, usually to dead limb and often perching lengthwise. Flocks up to hundreds near water. Pleasant, warbling call *queel queel* in flight, also chattering conversationally. Food: seeds of grasses and herbs, ripening wheat and grain from stubbles; mistletow berries, acacia seeds. Breeds August to December or any time following rains, in large hollow of live or dead tree, preferably eucalypt near water. 4 to 7 white eggs laid on decayed wood, incubated by ♀ and ♂ 21-23 days; young fly *c.* 4 weeks. **398**

brown and mauve, incubated by ♀ and ♂ *c.* 28 days; both parents tend young. **230**

Oceanites oceanicus *Hydrobatidae*
WILSON'S PETREL   *c.* 7 ins
Southern oceans, breeding many Antarctic island groups and migrating northward into N Atlantic, Indian Ocean and Pacific as far as N Peru. Sooty black, square-tailed and white rumped like Storm Petrel, *Hydrobates pelagicus*, but long legs with yellow-webbed feet extend ½ inch beyond tail in flight; bill black, eyes deep brown. Flies more gracefully than Storm Petrel and may plane over surface in series of 'hops' (V. C. Wynne-Edwards); becomes very excited towards sunset (Murphy). Chattering calls at burrows variously described; gentle peeps when taking food off water, mainly *Euphausia* (krill) in Antarctic; also molluscs, small fish, offal, algae. Lays one white egg from mid December to end January in cavity under rocks or excavated (*c.* 15 ins) burrow in turf, on bare cliffs, slopes or hill tops of oceanic islands. Incubation *c.* 43 days by ♀ and ♂, who feed chick until it fledges in up to 7½ weeks.

OCHRE-BREASTED BRUSH FINCH see **Atlapetes semirufus**

Ocyphaps lophotes *Columbidae*
CRESTED PIGEON   *c.* 13 ins
Australasian: Australia, apart from heavy rainfall regions and E of Great Dividing Range in E Australia. Habitat: lightly timbered country and cultivated land where cover available, common farms; seldom far from water. Mostly grey with grey-brown back and rump; black crest, pale brown wings with black bars and metallic green-purple speculum; longish dark tail with white tip. Legs pinkish red, short bill black, eyes orange with pinkish red orbital skin. In pairs or flocks, up to 1000+ at times, often hurrying across ground with crests bobbing. Flight swift, rapid wing-beats punctuated with gliding. Ground feeder taking mainly seeds, but also young shoots and leaves. Roosts in small densely foliated trees. Call: soft plaintive *coo*, also startled *wok*. Mainly breeds spring and summer; 2 white eggs in twig platform in low trees or bushes, incubated *c.* 19 days. **368**

Oena capensis *Columbidae*
NAMAQUA, LONG-TAILED or MASKED DOVE   10 ins
Ethiopian: Senegal, Sudan and Red Sea coast to SW Arabia and S Africa. Local movements related to food supplies and breeding areas. Frequents dry open country with some cover; adapted to cultivated areas, open suburbs and villages. Very small dove with long almost completely black tail; ♂ has black mask (lacking in ♀) covering face, front of throat and chest; crown, back of head and wing shoulders grey; mantle brown, sides of neck, breast and belly white; Madagascan race slightly darker and greyer. Purplish red legs and bill, orange at tip, eyes brown. Usually in family parties; feeds on small seeds on the ground in open spaces, walking about quickly; flies fast and straight; raises and fans out tail briefly on landing. Silent apart from occasional deep *coo*. Breeding season depends on region and weather but usually March onwards. 2 dull cream eggs are laid on a tiny platform of rootlets and grass in low cover; young fly *c.* 16 days. **369**

Oenanthe hispanica *Muscicapidae*: *Turdinae*
BLACK-EARED WHEATEAR   5¾ ins
Palaearctic: Mediterranean area except Egypt, Libya; E through Asia Minor to Iran; winters S of Sahara to 10°N. Habitat: rocky lowland plains, dry hills, grassland, Mediterranean heaths with spiny oaks up to *c.* 2,000 ft; semi-desert steppes in winter. ♂ western race variable, creamy buff to whitish with black mask (sometimes also throat), wings, tip and centre of white tail; eastern race has more black on face, throat. ♀ resembles Wheatear, *O. oenanthe*, but wings blacker. Legs, bill black, eyes brown. Juvenile spotted. Behaviour much as Wheatear, also song; rasping alarm note. Food mainly insects from ground or low bushes, e.g. ants, larvae; also some seeds. Breeds early May to June and July; ♀ builds well-hidden nest among stones or in rock cleft, also in low cover, e.g. heather, gorse. 4 or 5 blue-green eggs, spotted red-brown in zone, incubated by ♀ as Wheatear; both parents feed young. Probably 2 broods. **694**

Oenanthe monacha *Muscicapidae*: *Turdinae*
HOODED WHEATEAR   6¾ ins
SE Palaearctic, Ethiopian, Oriental: Egypt, Sudan, Palestine, Iraq, Arabia, NW Indian subcontinent; resident bare wadis and ravines in desert and bush. ♂ mainly black, with white rump, tail (except black central feathers and outer tips), crown, nape and underparts. ♀: upperparts fawn, lower back, tail isabelline (dark central feathers and outer tips); throat, breast pale buff, underparts almost white. Legs, bill, eyes dark brown. Buoyant, butterfly-like flight. Song sweet, sustained warble. Habits little known; probably breeds May; general resemblance to Wheatear, *O. oenanthe*. **695**

Oenanthe monticola *Muscicapidae*: *Turdinae*
MOUNTAIN CHAT   7 ins
Ethiopian: NW and S southern Africa; resident dry rocky and stony areas, not always in hills; penetrates built-up areas. ♂ variable: shoulder patch, rump, outer tail feathers white; rest of plumage may be black, grey or blackish, grey, except for blackish flight feathers. ♀: sooty black or brown; upper and under tail coverts white; tail feathers, except central ones, mainly white, blackish tips. Legs, bill, eyes brown. Juvenile resembles ♀. In pairs or small parties. Perches prominently; flicks wings and jerks tail on alighting. Call 'short, cheerful whistle' (O. P. M. Prozesky); chattering alarm; song clear and ringing, delivered from perch or on wing in soaring flight, which ends in sudden drop and rapid flight near ground. **696**

Oenanthe oenanthe *Muscicapidae*: *Turdinae*
WHEATEAR   5¾-6 ins
Holarctic: almost whole Palearctic except extreme N Siberia and Pacific coast, but including Iceland, parts NW Africa; Nearctic: much of Alaska; coasts Greenland, Baffin Land, Labrador; winters tropical Africa, S Arabia. Variety of open habitats from sand dunes, heaths, steppes, shrub and rocky tundra, rocky hillsides, meadows and scree to snow zone; waste land and ruins in cultivated areas and towns; dry savannah, steppes in winter. ♂: upperparts from crown grey; wings black; rump, upper tail white, bordered black; white stripe over black mask; throat white, breast buff shading to pale belly. ♂ N African race *O.o. seebohmi* has black throat. ♀ brown above, buff below, dark brown where ♂ black; he resembles her in winter, as does juvenile. Mainly terrestrial, hopping or flitting near ground between elevated perches, where pauses in upright stance, moving and spreading tail Perches on trees, especially N Europe; shelters in holes. Calls *chac chac* or *weet chac chac*. Warbling song delivered from perch or in display flight, when ♂ flutters few feet up after parading before ♀. Food small insects, spiders, centipedes; also some grass and other seeds. Breeds second half April to July Britain. Nest mainly by ♀ of local plant materials fur-lined: up to 2 ft in hole in ground, in boulders, stone walls, rock clefts. 5 or 6 pale blue eggs incubated mainly by ♀ *c.* 14 days; both parents feed young, who fly *c.* 15 days. Sometimes 2 broods. **697**

OILBIRD see **Steatornis caripensis**

OLD SQUAW see **Clangula hyemalis**

OLD WORLD
  KESTREL see under **Falco sparverius**
  WHITE PELICAN see **Pelecanus onocrotalus**

OLIVE
  PIGEON see **Columba arquatrix**
  THRUSH see **Turdus olivaceus**
  WARBLER see **Peucedramus taeniatus**

OLIVE-BACKED
  KINGBIRD see **Tyrannus melancholicus**
  ORIOLE see **Oriolus sagittatus**
  THRUSH see **Catharus ustulatus**

Onychognathus morio see under **O. nabouroup**

Onychognathus nabouroup *Sturnidae*
PALE-WINGED STARLING   10 ins
Ethiopian: S Africa (Karoo, Orange Free State) W and N to Angola; resident hills and gorges in desert country. Generally glossy blue-black, greenish sheen on head; base of primaries light chestnut (appears as whitish window on wing in flight); legs, bill black, eyes golden yellow. Small parties to flocks, even when breeding, fly often at height to drink morning and early evening. Varied calls: *chor chor* when perched; *churr churr*, similar to calls of Redwinged Starling, *O. morio*. Diet: berries, fruit, insects. Breeds December to April SW Africa; nest of grass, softly lined, in cleft of cliff and rocks, usually inaccessible. 3 or 4 pale greenish blue eggs, sparsely flecked rusty red. **972**

OPEN-BILLED STORK, ASIAN see **Anastomus oscitans**

Opisthocomus hoatzin *Opisthocomidae*
HOATZIN   22-26 ins
Neotropical: S America E of mountains; sedentary in dense riverine forests of Amazon system. Upperparts predominantly dark brown, flecked white on neck, nape and mantle; wing coverts white margins, reddish patch on outer primaries; tail tipped yellow; underparts reddish-yellow to reddish; prominent stiff red-brown crest; legs dark horn, thick bill (upper mandible articulated) horn, facial skin blue, eyes red. Neck very long and digests food in huge crop. Emits strong musky smell. Flies reluctantly, climbs among branches using wings, cannot grip with feet. Feeds morning, evening and at night on leaves, flowers, fruit of 3 or 4 tree species, e.g. *Montrichardia*, *Avicennia*. Calls 'hoarse, nasal and frog-like' and shrill nasal *shay*. Breeds throughout year, apparently double brooded and possibly polygamous, in colonies in trees 6 to 16 ft above water. Flat nest of loosely arranged twigs holds 2 to 4 buff eggs with pink spots, incubated for *c.* 4 weeks. Chicks, fed from parents' crop, are based on nest for some weeks, but scramble about branches, using unique wing claws as well as feet and bill; they can swim well if necessary. **212**

Opopsitta leadbeateri or Diophthalma opopsitta *Psittacidae*
RED-BROWED FIG PARROT or LORILET   5¼ ins
Australasian: New Guinea lowlands and offshore islands; Aru Is, three coastal areas NE Queensland, each with own race; large areas of scrub and riverine forest up to 5,000 ft. Generally green with blue and red on wing (underwing very dark), blue on forehead and cheek, red patch through eye; flanks yellowish; legs grey, bill grey, cere blue, eyes pale. ♀ has eye patch bluish-green. Very rapid flight, just over canopy; movements to feeding areas vary with weather. Parties sun and preen mutually on dead tops of trees after rain. Calls: insect-like *zit zit*: sharp, clear-cut *brik brik brik*; softly after feeding, louder in flight. Roosts in forests, feeds forest edge on figs, other rotting fruit from treetops, nectar. Breeds September to November using tree hole 30-40 ft up and laying 2 white eggs; other details unknown. **399**

ORANGE CHAT see **Ephthianura aurifrons**

ORANGE-BILLED SPARROW see under **Arremon schlegeli**

ORANGE-BREASTED SUNBIRD see **Nectarinia violacea**

ORANGE-CHEEKED PARROT see under **Gypopsitta vulturina**

ORANGE-CROWNED WARBLER see **Vermivora celata**

ORANGE-THROATED LONGCLAW see **Macronyx capensis**

ORCHARD ORIOLE see under **Icterus galbula**

Oreoica gutturalis *Muscicapidae: Pachycephalinae*
AUSTRALIAN CRESTED BELLBIRD 9 ins
Australian: generally distributed, mainly inland, in dry mulga scrub, mallee woodlands. Upperparts khaki brown, including wings (grey edges to secondaries), tail; nape to hindcrown light grey, rising to thin black crest on forecrown, whence black stripe down through eye becomes broad black gorget round white face, throat; underparts white tinged light buff; legs blackish, rather short bill black. ♀ brown where ♂ black and white, throat pale. Juvenile much as ♀. Singly or in pairs. Call: *chuc a chuc chuc;* song rendered *Dick, Dick, the devil,* repeated; bell-like note at end, ventriloquial; ♀ may follow up with single note or repeat last 3. Food: insects and grass-feeding larvae on ground, where hops with upright posture. Breeds generally September to December, ♀ and ♂ building cup nest of bark, twigs, leaves, even cloth, lined grasses, bark rootlets, in thick fork or hollowed stump 2 to c. 10 ft up; rim often 'decorated' semi-paralysed larvae. Usually 3 white eggs, marked sepia and black, incubated ♀ and ♂; both also tend young.

ORIENTAL GREENFINCH see under **Carduelis chloris**

ORIOLE,
 AFRICAN BLACK-HEADED see **Oriolus larvatus**
 BALTIMORE see **Icterus galbula**
 BLACK-HEADED FOREST see under **Oriolus larvatus**
 BLACK-WINGED see under **Oriolus larvatus**
 GOLDEN see **Oriolus oriolus**
 OLIVE-BACKED see **Oriolus sagittatus**
 ORCHARD see under **Icterus galbula**
 WESTERN BLACK-HEADED see under **Oriolus larvatus**

ORIOLE BLACKBIRD see **Gymnomystax mexicanus**

Oriolus brachyrhynchus see under **O. larvatus**

Oriolus larvatus *Oriolidae*
AFRICAN BLACK-HEADED ORIOLE 9 ins
Ethiopian: Sudan, Ethiopia, E Africa, SE Congo, Angola, S Africa; local migrant forests, inland and coastal scrub and bush, other wooded areas including parks, gardens. Upperparts greenish yellow; head, nape, upper breast black; wing coverts black, tipped white, edged yellow-green; flight feathers blackish, edged white; central tail feathers greenish-yellow, rest black, tipped golden yellow; hindneck, underparts golden yellow; legs grey-blue, bill pinkish brown, eyes red. Immature's head, nape flecked yellow, earcoverts blackish, chin to upper breast streaked black, bill blackish. Black-headed Forest Oriole, *O. monacha* (Eritrea, Ethiopia), Western Black-headed Oriole, *O. brachyrhynchus* (Sierra Leone to Uganda), Black-winged Oriole, *O. nigripennis* (Sierra Leone to Sudan, Uganda, N Angola) all very similar in plumage and what is known of habits. Usually in pairs but flocks when fruit ripe; haunts canopy, sitting motionless for long periods. Call: 2 or 3-syllabled *we-er-ou* (A. W. Vincent); harsh repeated *kweer* of alarm; some mimicry. Diet: caterpillars; seeds and fruit, doing some damage to crops. Breeding season varies within range; builds basket nest of grass, moss or tendrils, blended with surroundings and suspended from slender fork at end of lateral branch, usually high up tree. 2 to 4 white, cream or pink eggs, spotted reddish-brown or sepia over lavender, generally in zone. Incubation and fledging much as Golden Oriole, *O. oriolus.* **976**

Oriolus
 monacha see under **O. larvatus**
 nigripennis see under **O. larvatus**

Oriolus oriolus *Oriolidae*
GOLDEN ORIOLE c. 9½ ins
Palaearctic, Oriental: from extreme NW Africa and Iberia throughout continental Europe to 60°N and E to headwaters of R Yenisei at about 90°E; southwards limits N Mediterranean area, Asia Minor, Iran to Indian subcontinent, with apparent gap from between Caspian and Lake Balkash S to Persian Gulf. Only

Asian population resident, rest winter tropical Africa. Habitat: open broadleaved woodland and riverine strips; parks, orchards, tree clumps in cultivated areas, tropical gardens; up to 4,300 ft Alps, 7,000 ft Himalayan valleys; winters forest canopy. ♂: brilliant yellow head and body; yellow primary coverts make patch on black wing when closed; tail black, outer feathers tipped yellow. ♀: upperparts golden green to greenish yellow; wings brown, tail as ♂ but browner; lores greyish black; underparts greyish-white to yellowish, streaked dark brown; underwing, under tail coverts yellow. Legs dark grey, bill dark pink, eyes dark red. Juvenile much as ♀ but ♂ brighter. Normally arboreal, hopping when on ground; very secretive in canopy, heard more often than seen. Undulating, rather laboured flight, sweeping upward to perch. Bathes freely. Spring call, musical fluting *ori-ole;* various harsh, cat-like notes, rattling *chrrr* of alarm. ♂ pursues ♀ closely in courtship chases. Diet: insects from canopy in spring: beetles, flies, bees and larvae; spiders, small molluscs; fruit and berries in autumn. Breeds from end April; hammock-like nest, built mainly ♀ of grass, fibres, wool, bark, paper, lined grassheads and woven round fork or between twigs, usually at some height up tree. 3 to 5 glossy white eggs, spotted black mainly at big end, incubated ♀ and ♂ 14-15 days. Young, fed ♀ and ♂, fly 14-15 days. **977**

Oriolus sagittatus *Oriolidae*
OLIVE-BACKED ORIOLE 11 ins
Australasian: mainly coastal from W Australia (Kimberley area) across N, down E coasts and as far W as Adelaide; inland some parts New South Wales. Regular migrant some areas, nomadic in others, dependent on fruiting of trees. Habitat: rain forests in N; riverine woodland with open country; occasionally mallee scrub New South Wales. Upperparts dusky green, streaked black; flight feathers and upper surface tail dark grey; upper wing coverts tinged buff; underparts white streaked black; undertail dark grey, feathers tipped white; legs blackish blue, bill orange brown, eyes orange. Tree-living in thick cover like other orioles; swift, silent undulating flight in open. Call: monotonous whistle of 3 notes; squeaks and chattering while feeding on fruit, e.g. wild figs, camphor laurel; takes insects in areas where fruit not available. Breeds November to January SE Australia; deep cup nest of bark, leaves, cocoons, lichens, lined fine grass; suspended at end of drooping branch of eucalypt or casuarina tree, usually near edge of dense forest. 3 or 4 creamy eggs, spotted brown, chestnut over grey; incubation and fledging much as relatives. **978**

ORPHEAN WARBLER see **Sylvia hortensis**

Ortalis ruficauda *Cracidae*
COCRICO, RED-TAILED GUAN or
RUFOUS-VENTED CHACALACA 18-21 ins
Neotropical: N Colombia, Venezuela to Orinoco, Tobago; resident in secondary forest and scrub. Upperparts and breast olive green, lower back browner; underparts grey-brown, flanks rufous; forehead, crown and head grey; tail coverts rufous, tail bronze-green, tipped white, wings tipped chestnut; legs and bill dark blue, facial skin red, eyes dark blue. Lives mainly in trees, small flocks moving from branch to branch, then gliding for c. 100 yards. Dust bathes in clearings. Territorial confrontations as breeding season approaches. 'Sings' in mornings; native name Guacharaca onomatopoeic; ♂'s voice lower owing to looped windpipe; sound 'resounds through forest for up to 2 hours' (Helen Lapham); also cluckings and other notes. Diet of fruit, including palm nuts, and leaves. Breeds from April (rainy season) to July; colonial, partly polygamous. Builds nest of sticks and dry grass, apparently from ground to 50-80 ft in trees. 2 to 4 whitish eggs incubated by ♀ with ♂ near, c. 24-26 days. Young soon leave nest. **179**

Ortalis vetula *Cracidae*
PLAIN CHACALACA 20-24 ins
S Nearctic (Texas) to Neotropical (Nicaragua); resident in scrubby woodland and its edge, also cultivated land. Upperparts dark olive-brown with green-

ish gloss, tail tipped white; underparts brown; legs and bill black, ♂'s facial skin red in spring, eyes dark brown. Dust bathes in open; when surprised, flies into cover, running along branches, waving wings. Loud, raucous *cha-cha-la-ca* gives name, often in concerted chorus from tree-tops. Courtship on ground, ♂ strutting in front of ♀ with head erect and low-pitched calls due to curved windpipe. Diet of plant stems, fallen fruit, insects and worms; sometimes leaves from trees. Breeds from March and April, building loose nest of twigs and leaves up to 10 ft in trees or bushes. 3 or 4 granulated white eggs incubated c. 3 weeks; young leave nest after a day and soon fly. **180**

Orthonyx spaldingi *Muscicapidae: Cinclosomatinae*
NORTHERN LOGRUNNER 9 ins
Australasian: rain forest along coastal range of N Queensland, Cairns to Rockingham Bay. Almost black above, including wings, short tail; flanks, mantle washed olive brown; pale orbits, underparts white; throat, breast chestnut in ♀; legs grey, bill black, eyes brown. Forms small flocks, runs, walks on ground. Loud calls include series of notes *chow chilla chow chow;* occasionally mimics other species. Feeds, using splayed spiny tail quills as prop, scratching ground with alternate feet. Diet mainly insects, some berries. Breeds May to August. Builds domed nest with side entrance, of leaves, moss on ground, in vines, ferns or tree stump up to 10 ft. 2 white eggs. **719**

Orthorhamphus magnirostris see **Esacus magnirostris**

Orthostomus sutorius *Muscicapidae: Sylviinae*
COMMON TAILORBIRD 5 ins
Oriental: widespread throughout region, including Ceylon, S China; resident undergrowth of forests, scrub jungle, gardens, even in towns; up to 5,000 ft Himalayas. Upperparts from neck to long, graduated tail olive to yellowish green; wings light brown edged greenish; tail feathers (2 central ones elongated) tipped whitish; forehead, crown rufous; narrow eyestripe on whitish face; underparts to under tail coverts white, tinged buff; legs pinkish flesh, thin pointed bill dark grey, eyes light brown to red. Active, searching creepers, other plants for insects, their eggs and larvae; also takes some nectar. Long tail flicked over back in flight (B. E. Smythies). Loud call: *chw-ee chw-ee* or *chip chip*, repeated 25 times in 10 seconds. Breeds April onwards, usually within 6 ft of ground in low bush or hanging branch; soft cup of plant down, lined hairs, grasses, built in cradle formed by one (folded), 2 or more large leaves sewn together with threads of spider's web, cocoon silk, wool, cotton. Bill pierces hole in leaf, pulls thread through; leaves kept together by friction with threads; each stitch separate. 3 or 4 pointed eggs, shades from white to pale blue, sparsely freckled brown and black, mainly at big end, incubated ♀ and ♂; both also tend young.

ORTOLAN see **Emberiza hortulana**

Ortygospiza atricollis *Estrildidae*
QUAIL FINCH 4 ins
Ethiopian: from Senegal, Gambia across to E Africa; also Eritrea, Ethiopia; S through N Malawi, Zambia, Rhodesia to S Africa; resident open grassland, especially round shallow pools and swamps. ♂: upperparts mottled grey and brown; narrow white edges to brown flight feathers, white tip to short blackish tail; forehead, cheeks, throat black; chin, circle round eyes white; underparts barred black and white with chestnut band lower breast; belly white, under tail coverts brown and black. ♀ paler, brown for black on head. Legs light brown, bill red, eyes brown. Immature much as ♀ but bill blackish. Ground-living in small flocks after breeding; flies up steeply, wings whirring like quail, then drops to cover again. Incessant bell-like call *tirrilink tirrilink* on wing; subdued warbling song on ground. ♂ towers in courtship flight, then falls 'like stone' with clicking noise. Diet: mainly grass seeds; attacks crops. Breeding season varies within range; builds rough pear-shaped nest of grass, often with 'porch', lined finer stems, feathers; near ground in tussock. 2 to 4 white eggs.

Ortyxelos meiffrenii *Turnicidae*
LARK QUAIL or QUAIL PLOVER *c.* 5 ins
Ethiopian: ranges in broad band S of Equator from Senegal, Ghana, N Nigeria to Ethiopia, Sudan, N Kenya and N Uganda. Habitat: arid scrub with burr-bearing heskanit grass. *Cenchrus catharticus*, probably its main food. Upperparts tawny, vermiculated and streaked black and white; flight feathers black with broad white tips, tawny band on primaries; 'shoulder' and outer coverts white; breast tawny; underparts white; legs pale flesh, bill yellowish, culmen blue, eyes brown. Lark-like on wing when whites show up, flies strongly but jerkily; runs and squats on ground. Call: soft, low whistle. Breeds December and January, laying 2 creamy or stone coloured eggs, marked black, brown and grey, in lightly lined scrape on bare ground.

OSPREY see **Pandion haliaetus**

OSTRICH see **Struthio camelus**

Otis tarda *Otididae*
GREAT BUSTARD ♀: 30-33; ♂: *c.* 40 ins
Palaearctic: reduced and interrupted range through temperate zone from Portugal and Morocco, Central Europe, Asia Minor to Central and E China. Mainly resident, some movement S of northern and eastern birds in winter, e.g. to Mediterranean, Japan and India. Inhabits steppe grasslands and arid hills, also cultivated land, especially large cornfields in Europe. ♂: upperparts sandy, barred black, wings mainly white with black primaries; head and neck grey-mauve, with bristly white 'moustaches'; breast and base of neck chestnut marked black; underparts white. ♀: smaller, slimmer, no moustache or chestnut on breast; young ♂ like ♀. Legs brown, bill yellowish, tip darker, eyes hazel. Shy, taking cover when alarmed or to flight, when white on wings shows up, with rapid beats. Normal walk deliberate. Parties and flocks, mainly ♀♀ form after breeding, and non-breeding ♂♂ remain gregarious. Remarkable ♂ display by turning over wing coverts and tail feathers to show white, head sunk, throat sac distended. Rather silent: bark of aggression and *kraang* of anxiety; young whistle when alarmed. Eats leaves, buds and seeds, and animals, especially beetles and voles. Breeding season from end April in S Europe, later in N. ♀ flattens area in cover, lays 2 to 4 greenish or olive-brown eggs, streaked liver brown, incubating them 25-28 days. Young fed insects by ♀ at first, fledge in about 5 weeks. ♂ does not assist. **246**

Otis tetrax *Otididae*
LITTLE BUSTARD *c.* 17 ins
Palaearctic: temperate zone from Iberia, N Africa, France to S Russia and W Asia; sedentary and migratory, eastern population moving south in winter. Inhabits stony hill country, steppes and deserts, heaths, cultivations especially in Europe. ♂: crown and upperparts mottled sandy-brown with fine black vermiculations; most of wing white with partly black primaries: (summer) cheeks and throat slate-blue bordered white V; rest of neck black with white band; underparts white. ♂ (winter), ♀ and young have front of neck and breast buffish, streaked black, legs greyish yellow, bill black and grey, eyes pale yellow. Shy, taking to flight with rattling call and becoming almost whiter from below; flies with rapid wingbeats and hiss, action like partridge. Will also crouch and run when disturbed. Flocks in autumn. Calls *dahg* when alarmed; ♂ utters abrupt *ptrrr* in display, when, tail fanned and wings drooped, he jerks head, leaps and stamps in descent. Food vegetable and animal, especially locusts and grasshoppers. Breeding season from end April in SW Europe. ♀ makes scrape in cover, lays 3-4 greenish to olive brown eggs, streaked brown, and incubates them *c.* 3 weeks with ♂ in attendance. ♀ feeds young at first. Possibly double-brooded. **247**

Otus asio *Strigidae*
SCREECH OWL 6½-10 ins
Nearctic, marginally Neotropical: SE Alaska and Canada to Florida Keys and Central Mexico. Resident, with some winter dispersal, in woodlands,

wooded canyons, orchards, gardens. Variable: 'red' phase has upperparts rufous brown with pale bars on wings and back; prominent 'horns' and crown black-streaked, facial disc and throat roughly fringed black; underparts pale, flecked rufous and black; legs feathered, bill dark horn, eyes yellow. In 'grey' and 'brown' phases these colours replace rufous brown. Nocturnal; mournful wailing hoot usually runs down scale; also series of short calls. Diet: mice, meadow voles, small birds; insects, including cutworms, locusts. Breeds April-May, in tree cavities or old woodpecker holes, buildings, nestboxes, laying 4 to 8 white eggs. **446**

Otus gurneyi *Strigidae*
GREAT SCOPS OWL 12 ins
Confined to Philippines: Mindanao and Marieduque, considered to be rare but numbers unknown. Generally rufous; wings darker, mottled brown, striped blackish; buff edges to scapulars show as stripe down back; tail tawny rufous; as are forehead, prominent ear tufts; crown darker; facial disc bright rufous; chin, throat (with white patch) tawny; underparts striped dark brown; legs fully feathered, feet pale grey; bill greyish white; eyes brown. Habits apparently not studied.

Otus insularis *Strigidae*
BARE-LEGGED SCOPS OWL *c.* 7½ ins
Seychelles (Indian Ocean); confined to main island of Mahè, in mountain forests. Generally russet brown with black shaft streaks, most prominent on underparts; legs long, eyes yellow. Calls: *toc toc* (?♂), 'repeated sawing noise' (?♀) (R. Gaymer, M. Penny). Food includes lizards, grasshoppers, but little known of habits. Decrease attributed partly to competition from introduced Barn Owl, *Tyto alba*.

Otus leucotis *Strigidae*
WHITE-FACED OWL 10 ins
Ethiopian: 2 races cover most of region except Congo Forests, extreme S Africa. Resident in woodland, thorn bush, long grass, especially in hot, low-lying areas. Upperparts, wings and tail finely vermiculated brownish grey, narrowly barred darker grey; mantle streaked black and large white markings outer edges of scapulars; crown to nape black, forehead grey; face white, disc fringed black, 'horns' tipped black; underparts less closely vermiculated, black streaks most pronounced; under wing coverts white; bill bluish, with bristles, eyes orange. Juvenile lacks black on head. Nocturnal, roosting in trees along watercourses, but but sometimes hunts by day, especially after grass fires, for insects and mice. ♂'s call: *cuc-coo;* ♀ replies with stammering *wh-h-h-roo;* bill clicked in anger. Breeding season variable, usually uses old nests of other birds, occasionally shallow hole or fork in tree, laying 2 to 4 white eggs. Incubation and fledging probably as *O. scops.* **447**

Otus scops *Strigidae*
SCOPS OWL *c.* 7½ ins
All Old World regions: from N Mediterranean area and NW Africa E to Central Asia, SE to Indian sub-continent and Ceylon. SE Asia to Celebes, Moluccas, N to Luzon, Manchuria, Japan. Separate range includes S Arabia, most of Ethiopian region except Congo Forests, SW Africa. Resident except in Palaearctic whence migrates to tropical Africa and Asia. Habitat: arid and lightly forested areas, riverine forests, open oak woods, orchards, cultivated land with trees, towns and suburbs. Variable: upperparts generally brownish grey to rufous brown with black shaft streaks, white streaks and fine vermiculation; head and 'horns' appear speckled; partial facial disc finely barred, dark fringed; underparts vermiculated with black vertical streaks; legs feathered, feet grey, bill bluish-black, eyes lemon yellow. Much greyer plumage phase occurs. Mainly nocturnal, sitting upright by day against trunk, in bushes or creepers: very hard to see. Generally solitary; parties in winter areas. ♂'s 'song': monotonous but musical, whistling *kiu* repeated at 2 second intervals, from dusk through night; ♀'s reply higher-pitched, 2 or 3 syllables. Takes mainly large insects: moths, beetles, locusts; lizards, small

mammals and birds. Breeds from end April, in hollow trees, cavities and crevices in rocks, old woodpecker holes, occasionally old nests. ♀ lays 4 or 5 white eggs, incubating them 24-25 days. ♂ brings food to her for young, who leave nest 3 weeks, before fully fledged. **448**

OVENBIRD see **Seiurus auricapillus**

OWL,
  AFRICAN MARSH see **Asio capensis**
  AFRICAN WOOD see **Ciccaba woodfordii**
  BARN see **Tyto alba**
  BARRED see **Strix varia**
  BOOBOOK see **Ninox novaeseelandiae**
  BOREAL see **Aegolius funereus**
  BURROWING see **Speotyto cunicularia**
  EAGLE see **Bubo bubo**
  ELF see **Micrathene whitneyi**
  EURASIAN PYGMY see **Glaucidium passerinum**
  FERRUGINOUS PYGMY see **Glaucidium brasilianum**
  GREAT GREY see **Strix nebulosa**
  GREAT HORNED see **Bubo virginianus**
  HAWK see **Surnia ulula**
  JAVAN BROWN WOOD see **Strix leptogrammica**
  LITTLE see **Athene noctua**
  LONG-EARED see **Asio otus**
  MALAYSIAN BROWN WOOD see **Strix leptogrammica**
  MALAYSIAN FISH see **Bubo ketupu**
  RICHARDSON's see **Aegolius funereus**
  SAW-WHET see **Aegolius acadicus**
  SCOPS see **Otus scops**
  SCREECH see **Otus asio**
  SEYCHELLES see **Otus insularis**
  SHORT-EARED see **Asio flammeus**
  SNOWY see **Nyctaea scandiaca**
  SOOTY see **Tyto novaeseelandiae**
  SPOTTED EAGLE see **Bubo africanus**
  TAWNY see **Strix aluco**
  TENGMALM's see **Aegolius funereus**
  VERREAUX's GIANT EAGLE see **Bubo lacteus**
  WHITE-FACED see **Otus leucotis**

OWLET FROGMOUTH see **Aegotheles cristata**

OXPECKER,
  RED-BILLED see **Buphagus erythrorhynchus**
  YELLOW-BILLED see **Buphagus africanus**

Oxyruncus cristatus *Tyrannidae*
SHARPBILL 6½-7 ins
Neotropical: Costa Rica and Panama S through E South America to Paraguay; resident in tree tops of humid tropical forests, up to 4,000 ft in Amazonian Brazil. Upperparts predominantly olive green, very dark brown on relatively long wings and tail and a crown which is crested, yellow and scarlet, bordered black; underparts pale yellow to white, heavily spotted dark brown; rather short, strong-toed legs pale, strong pointed bill dark, eyes light brown. Said to be solitary and strong flier with diet of fruit. Nest and breeding habits unknown. **583**

Oxyura australis *Anatidae*
BLUE-BILLED DUCK *c.* 16 ins
Australasian: southern Australia in deep, densely vegetated swamps; gathers in large flocks in winter on extensive open fresh waters. ♂: head and neck glossy black; foreneck, upper breast, flanks and back chestnut; rest of underparts brown flecked black; tail black; wings dark brown. Eclipse throughout winter much greyer. ♀: upperparts blackish brown, chin and throat brown speckled black; foreneck, breast, belly mottled light brown and black. Legs, ♂ grey, ♀ grey-brown; bill, ♂ blue, ♀ grey-brown; eyes brown. Shy, swims swiftly and low in water, almost helpless on land; seldom flies but after laborious take-off moves swiftly. Call: virtually silent, ♂ low rattling note in display, ♀ weak quack of alarm. Dabbles on surface or dives deeply for small aquatic animals, chiefly insects, and plant matter. Builds nest September to November in dense vegetation, occasionally on ground, of plant debris on trampled down platform of herbage, often

covered by dome of reeds. Usually 5 or 6 light green eggs, incubated *c.* 26-28 days; young leave nest after day and feed themselves, guarded by ♀. **124**

OYSTERCATCHER see **Haematopus ostralegus**

OYSTERCATCHER, AFRICAN BLACK see **Haematopus moquini**

Pachycephala pectoralis *Muscicapidae: Pachycephalinae*
GOLDEN WHISTLER *c.* 7 ins
Oriental, Australasian: 3 main areas of distribution, each with many island races: Indonesia E from Java to Celebes, Moluccas; Bismarck Arch. to Fiji; mainly coastal E, S and SW continental Australia with Tasmania. Replaced in New Guinea and much of N Australia by Grey-headed, *P. simplex.* Nomadic in winter in open forests; closed canopy in summer, from mallee scrub of S Australia, eucalypts of SE to dense rain forests. ♂: upperparts generally olive green with yellow band on neck; flight feathers black, tinged orange-green secondaries; tail black; head black, chin, throat white, banded black on breast; underparts yellow. ♀: upperparts generally greyish brown, tinged olive, wings, tail coverts; throat mottled greyish-white, breast grey, underparts whitish. Legs slate grey, bill black, eyes red. Juvenile rufous, flight feathers grey; resembles ♀ at 1 year old, ♂ plumage not full until *c.* 3 years old; absent altogether some races. Great variation in ♂'s head plumage and bill within each population group: black breast bar from broad to nearly absent; bill short stubby (Tasmania), powerful, shrike-like (Tannibar Is.). Dipping flight from tree to tree; ♂ unwilling to expose himself above, often visible from ground. Song loud, slurred, liquid whistles, accelerating to whip-crack; may be set off by human voice. Searches foliage for insects, especially beetles, larvae; some berries. Breeding season varies within range; ♀ and ♂ build nest of fine twigs, bark, lined rootlets, grass, deep in bush or small tree up to 15 ft. 2 or 3 smooth creamy or buff eggs, freckled brown and grey, incubated by ♀ and ♂, both feed young. **800**

Pachycephala simplex see under **P. pectoralis**

Pachyptila belcheri see under **P. desolata**

Pachyptila desolata *Procellariidae*
ANTARCTIC PRION 10½ ins
Subantarctic and antarctic zones; breeds islands and antarctic coast, most southerly birds moving N after nesting. Upperparts mainly grey-blue, darker on crown and blackish behind and below eyes; dark areas show in flight as inverted W across wings; tail feathers broadly tipped black; underparts light pearly grey. Bill: upper mandible steel grey, side of lower mandible bluish; distinguished from other prions by moderate width of bill (i.e. about half its length), while lamellae or thin plates not usually visible when bill closed; they are much better developed on Broad-billed *P. vittata* and Narrow-billed *P. belcheri.* Flies singly, in groups or flocks, turning rapidly side to side, showing now lighter now darker. Comes ashore to burrows mainly by night, crooning and moaning above them and from inside. Plankton 'krill' scooped up by bill from surface and just below as bird 'hydroplanes' with wings raised, breast touching water and feet propelling it; can also dive well; does not follow ships. Breeds southern summer in large colonies in clefts or burrows, to which it can dig in snow, and caves. Laying of single white egg follows temporary exodus of ♀♀, ♂♂ guarding nests. Incubation ♀ and ♂ 45 days; young, fed ♀ and ♂ from throat, leave nest *c.* 50 days. **30**

Pachyptila vittata see under **P. desolata**

Pachyrhamphus marginatus *Cotingidae*
BLACK-CAPPED BEARD 5 ins
Neotropical: Guyanas, N Venezuela, E Colombia, E Ecuador, E Peru to N Bolivia; Amazonia and other provinces Brazil; resident forests, forest edge, clearings, sea level to 4,500 ft. ♂: upperparts grey (mixed black on mantle), tail black, tipped white; crown

black, feathers tipped iridescent blue; underparts pale grey. ♀: crown rufous to blackish; upperparts, including cheeks and breast, olive; wings with tawny margins; central tail feathers olive-brown, outer black, all tipped fawn; underparts mainly pale yellow. Legs brown, bill dark horn, eyes dark brown. Insectivorous: grasshoppers, small beetles, lepidopterous larvae. Closely related White-winged Becard. *P. polychopterus,* of wider distribution (Guatemala to Argentina, Trinidad and Tobago) breeds during rainy seasons, ♀ making untidy domed nest of grasses, ♂ standing by, at end of high lateral branch, often near wasp nest; clutch 2 white eggs, heavily marked dark brown. **592**

Pachyrhamphus polychopterus see under **P. marginata**

PACIFIC
GOLDEN PLOVER see **Pluvialis dominica**
GULL see **Larus pacificus**

Padda oryzivora *Estrildidae*
JAVA SPARROW 5-5½ ins
Oriental (Ethiopian): Indonesia; introduced Malaysia, Borneo, St Helena, Seychelles, Tanzania (Zanzibar area); round habitations where introduced; mangroves in Malaysia; rice fields. Generally grey; crown, throat, band behind ear coverts, upper tail coverts, tail black; cheeks, under tail coverts white; lower flanks, belly wine red. Legs brown, large bill pink, eyes dark brown. Juvenile much browner. White form occurs commonly. Rather sedentary. Call: sharp *chyup;* soft metallic whistling song ending in trill. Diet: seeds, rice, cultivated grain. Breeds colonially: domed nest of grass in tree, bush, under eaves of building. 4 to 7 white eggs. **941**

PAGODA STARLING see **Temenuchus pagodarum**

Pagodroma nivea *Procellariidae*
SNOW PETREL 12 ins
Southern oceans from Antarctic to 50°S, moving north after breeding. Almost entirely white except for black spot by eye; legs dark blue-grey, bill black, eyes brown. Juveniles show grey vermiculations on back. Found in highly co-ordinated flocks, active far into night, but scatter for breeding. Unable to stand or walk. Loud caws on breeding areas, also 'linnet-like twittering' and 'half-whistling, half-shrieking call'. Food mainly crustaceans, but also some fish and even carrion. One white egg laid end November or December in cavity or niche in rocks, sometimes more than 50 miles from sea in scattered colonies on hill tops. Incubation and fledging duties shared by ♀ and ♂.

PAINTED
BUNTING see **Passerina ciris**
QUAIL see **Turnix varia**
SNIPE see **Rostratula benghalensis**
STORK see **Ibis leucocephalus**

PALAWAN PEACOCK PHEASANT see **Polyplectron emphanum**

PALE
CHANTING GOSHAWK see **Melierax canorus**
CRIMSON FINCH see **Neochmia phaeton**
FLYCATCHER see **Bradornis pallidus**
WHITE-EYE see **Zosterops pallidus**

PALE-WINGED STARLING see **Onychognathus nabouroup**

PALLAS'S SANDGROUSE see **Syrrhaptes paradoxus**

PALLID CUCKOO see **Cuculus pallidus**

PALM CHAT see **Dulus dominicus**

PALM-NUT VULTURE see **Gypohierax angolensis**

Pandion haliaetus *Accipitridae*
OSPREY 20-23 ins
Almost throughout northern hemisphere, migrating

south in autumn; also breeds Australasia and South Africa. Vicinity of rivers, lakes or sea coasts. Upperparts mainly dark brown, underparts white with brown band across breast; head and neck mainly white with brown stripe through eye; outer primaries blackish, tail brown; legs greenish white, bill dark with blue cere, eyes yellow. Spends much time perched then flies over water, splash-diving with feet forward to grip fish. Usual call a triple whistle, also alarm and nesting calls. Diet mainly fish, occasionally birds. Breeding season variable, from April in North temperate zone. Nesting colonial or solitary, on tree, crag, rock, ruin, artificial substrate, even ground. Builds large structure of sticks and debris, with finer lining; usually 3 eggs, white heavily marked brown and grey. Incubated mainly by ♀ 32-38 days. ♂ feeds young via ♀, fledged at 52-54 days. **160**

Panurus biarmicus *Muscicapidae: Paradoxornithinae*
BEARDED TIT or REEDLING 6½ (tail 3) ins
Palaearctic: main range N and S of Black Sea E to headwaters River Ob; small separate populations W to England, Iberia; larger area Manchuria, possibly elsewhere E Asia. Mainly resident extensive reed beds in freshwater or brackish marshes; disperses in winter, suffering heavy mortality in severe weather. ♂: head lavender grey with broad tapering black 'moustaches'; rest of upperparts tawny; long graduated tail edged white; wings striped white, tawny, black; underparts white, flanks more buff; under tail coverts black. ♀ has tawny head, lacks black 'moustaches', under tail. Juvenile similar but more black on wings, tail. Legs black; bill yellow; eyes pale yellow. Moves jerkily up and down reeds, often straddling two stems. Flies with whirring wings, 'loose' tail jerked rhythmically. Distinctive call: nasal *ping ping;* also twittering flight call in winter flocks of 40 to 50. Diet: mainly insects picked off reed stems; eats seeds of reed mace, reeds in winter. Breeds end April to July; ♂ takes larger share building nest of dead reeds, sedges, lined reed 'flowers', low in swampy vegetation. 5 to 7 white eggs, with numerous spots, streaks, scrawls liver brown, incubated ♀ and ♂ 12-13 days; both parents feed young, who leave nest 9-12 days. 2, sometimes 3 broods. **721**

PAPUAN HORNBILL see **Aceros plicatus**

Paradisaea apoda *Paradisaeidae*
GREATER BIRD
OF PARADISE ♂: 17-18 (normal tail 6-7) ins
Australasian: S New Guinea, Arus Is, introduced Little Tobago (Caribbean); resident inland tropical forest on plains and hills up to 3,000 ft. ♂: upperparts, including wings, tail, maroon; central tail feathers wire-like, blackish brown, up to 30 ins long; head, neck orange-yellow; forehead, lores, chin, black glossed green; throat to upper neck iridescent oil-green; upper breast brownish black to dark maroon according to race; underparts maroon; huge tufts lacy plumes on each side breast up to 23 ins long, basal ⅔ yellow to orange, outer ⅓ pale cinnamon; legs pale brown, bill light grey-blue, pale tipped, eyes lemon yellow. ♀: generally maroon, darker head and round neck; upper breast, underparts paler; legs pale brown, bill bluish grey, eyes lemon yellow. Immature ♂ progresses from ♀-like plumage over 5 years. Active, noisy, ♂ calling *wawk wawk wawk, wok wok wok wok* (A. R. Wallace). Feeds chiefly tree fruits, probably also insects. Display: dancing parties 12 to 20 ♂♂ in large tree with spreading branches fly excitedly with elevated plumes, expanded to form 'two magnificent golden fans' while head is bent, wings raised over back, tail bent forward under perch. When ♀ appears, ♂♂ freeze on perches, arranged in hierarchy, dominant ♂ in centre (E. T. Gilliard). Breeds December to January Aru Is, nest of sticks lined rootlets in tree. 2 brownish eggs marked longitudinally red- and blackish-brown, incubated by ♀, who also raises young as no pair bond formed.

Paradisaea guilielmi *Paradisaeidae*
EMPEROR BIRD OF PARADISE ♂: 12½-13 ins
Australasian: mountains of Huon Peninsula, New Guinea; resident mountain forests *c.* 2,200 to 4,000 ft, occasionally higher. ♂: upperparts, including lesser

wing coverts, sides of breast, glossy straw yellow; central tail feathers wire-like, up to 27½ ins long; crown, cheeks, throat to upper breast metallic oil-green; otherwise deep maroon tinged grey with light patch each side lower breast; huge tufts each side breast up to 14½ ins long, basal half usually ivory white tinged yellow, outer half lacy, tends to decompose; legs flesh brown, bill blue grey, eyes reddish brown, ♀ resembles ♂ without ornamental plumes; eyes yellow. Immature ♂ progresses from ♀-like to ♂ plumage. Call (captive): soft clear *poop poop poop;* loud piercing cry. Display (captive): preliminary bobbing, wing-flicking, then after loud call ♂ turns under perch, body remaining close to it, wings, tail widely spread, 'wires' reaching far above; lacy plumes erected to make complete circle round inverted belly; plumes waved as body moved side to side; sustained several minutes. Food chiefly fruits of forest trees. Single or 2 creamy to rose-cinnamon eggs, streaked brown and grey, incubated ♀. Hybrids known in wild with *Paradisaea raggiana* and Lesser Bird of Paradise, *P. minor*.

Paradisaea minor see under **P. guilielmi**

Paradisaea raggiana *Paradisaeidae*
COUNT RAGGI'S BIRD
OF PARADISE ♂: 13-14 (normal tail 6-7) ins
Australasian: S New Guinea; resident forest and forest edge, often near ravines, sea level to 5,000 ft; tree clumps in rocky grasslands; native gardens. ♂: back yellow to brown, according to race; wings, tail, pale to dark wine brown; central tail feathers wire-like up to 19 ins long; head, neck orange yellow; fore-head, lores, chin, black glossed green; collar, greater wing coverts yellow; cheeks, gorget oil-green; upper breast blackish; underparts pale to dark wine-brown; lacy tufts on side breast up to 21 ins long, basal ⅔ red to apricot outer ⅓ pale rosy cinnamon; legs grey-brown, bill blue grey, eyes yellow. ♀: upperparts including wings maroon to yellow; tail maroon; forehead, 'face' blackish brown; hind crown to neck dull yellow; gorget blackish brown to black, some-times traces yellow; underparts greyish wine-brown; legs light brown, bill chalky blue, eyes bright yellow. Immature ♂ progresses from ♀-like to ♂ plumage 5 years. ♀♀ and immature ♂♂ feed on fruits in parties 15 to 20 ft up, usually middle and upper branches. ♂ near display area calls high-pitched *kiing*, followed by resonant *kiii kiii kiii*, becoming louder, ending explos-ive *waw woow*. ♂♂, probably in parties 3 to 6, occupy own spaces on sloping limbs in tree clump. ♂ bends forward nearly to perch, raises wings upward and for-ward to meet 'back to back' even over top of head. Wings clapped rapidly, flank plumes raised nearly straight up and expanded. Dominance hierarchy as *P. apoda*. Nest of vines, dead leaves, lined leaf fibres *c.* 15 ft in fork of slender sapling on forest edge (E.T. Gilliard). Single or 2 pinkish cream eggs, marked longitudinally reddish brown over violet, incubated (captive) ♀ 13-15 days; young, fed ♀ with insects from throat, fledged *c.* 28 days. **992**

PARADISE
FLYCATCHER, AFRICAN see **Terpsiphone viridis**
FLYCATCHER, SEYCHELLES see **Terpsiphone corvina**
WHYDAH, BROAD-TAILED see under **Steganura paradisaea**
WHYDAH, SHARP-TAILED see **Steganura paradisaea**

PARAKEET
INDIAN RING-NECKED see **Psittacula krameri**
PILEATED see **Purpureicephalus spurius**
QUAKER see **Myiopsitta monacha**
RAINBOW see **Trichoglossus haematodus**
RED-CROWNED see **Cyanoramphus novaeselandiae**
ROSE-RINGED see **Psittacula krameri**

PARDALOTE,
BLACK-HEADED see **Pardalotus melanocephalus**
SPOTTED see **Pardalotus punctatus**

Pardalotus melanocephalus *Dicaeidae*
BLACK-HEADED PARDALOTE *c.* 4 ins
Australasian: Mid-Western continental Australia to N Queensland, and S to New South Wales; resident forests. Upperparts predominantly greenish brown, becoming yellowish upper tail coverts; crown, wings black (with white or pale feather edges and red at alula); lower tail black, tipped white; eyestripe black between white 'eyebrow' and cheek; underparts from chin whitish, suffused more or less yellow; legs grey; short, broad bill dark; eyes brown. Behaviour much as relatives. Food insects and their larvae. Breeds June to January in different parts of range, building domed nest of bark in chamber at end of hollowed-out tunnel, generally in bank or hole left by stump, 1½ to 2 ft long. Usually 4 white eggs. **816**

Pardalotus punctatus *Dicaeidae*
SPOTTED PARDALOTE *c.* 3½ ins
Australasian: E continental Australia, (except Cape York), Victoria, S to W Australia; Tasmania. Resi-dent forests, upland birds probably moving to coast in winter. ♂: upperparts blackish (crown) to greyish brown (back), heavily spotted white; base upper tail chestnut brown to crimson; prominent white 'eye-brow', cheeks vermiculated grey, throat, base of undertail yellow; rest underparts buff-brown. ♀: generally darker, spots on head bright yellow; under-parts buff-white. Legs flesh brown, bill black, eyes grey. Juvenile like ♀ but duller. Usually in pairs or flocks on outer foliage eucalyptus, searching leaves slowly for insects and their larvae; after covering one tree, birds flit one by one to next, calling incessantly, but territorial when breeding. Call loud, monotonous, ventriloquial: *slee-p* (high-pitched) *ba-bee* (much lower); also soft *pee-too*. ♂ takes pair-forming initiative in breeding season (August to January in different parts of range), may choose site, often used several years, of tunnel excavated by ♀ and ♂ for 1½ to 2 ft in stream bank or cliff, rarely tree; domed nest of bark, grass in chamber at end. Usually 4 white eggs incu-bated by ♀ and ♂ 14-16 days. **817**

Pardalotus striatus *Dicaeidae*
YELLOW-TIPPED PARDALOTE 3½-4 ins
Australasian: Tasmania, wintering S continental Australia, where occasionally breeds. Habitat forest treetops. Upperparts olive-grey to brownish lower back; tail black, slightly tipped white; wings black, small yellow spot near shoulder, narrow white bar; 'eyebrow' yellow to white; ear coverts black streaked white; cheeks white; chin, throat yellow; underparts buff and white; legs blackish-brown, bill black, eyes brownish olive. Very like *P. melanocephalus* but crown streaked white, cheeks vermiculated grey, flanks paler. Usually in pairs, behaving much as *P. punctatus*. Calls: *pick-it-up; chip chip*: soft *cheeoo;* long trill. Takes great variety insects captured in eucalypt leaves; some spiders. Breeds August to December Tasmania, building domed nest of bark, grass, sometimes feathers, in small hollow, hole of tree, even up to 50 ft or more; occasionally tunnels hole in bank of creek like *P. punctatus*. Usually 4 white eggs. **818**

Parisoma subcaeruleum *Muscicapidae: Timaliinae*
COMMON TIT BABBLER 5¾ ins
Ethiopian: southern third Africa; resident in light thorn bush and acacia scrub, especially along water-courses. Upperparts bluish grey, darker around eye; throat white, streaked black; breast and flanks pearl grey; rest underparts white; brick red under tail coverts contrast with black tail, tipped white; bill and legs black, eyes blackish brown. Searches foliage actively for small insects, spiders; also eats fruit. Rattling call: *cherik tik tik;* warbling song includes mimicry. Breeding season very variable: September to February, later in SE. Neat, thin-walled nest cup of fibres, covered with spider's silk, in fork near ground. 2 or 3, usually white eggs, blotched darker. **713**

Paroaria coronata see **P. cucullata**

Paroaria cucullata or P. coronata *Emberizidae: Pyrrhuloxiinae*
RED-CRESTED CARDINAL 7½ ins
Neotropical: S Brazil, Uruguay, Paraguay, SE Bolivia, Argentina to Buenos Aires, La Pampa; resident wet scrub, bushy woodland. Upperparts grey, tail black; crested head, throat to centre upper breast scarlet; underparts white; legs grey, bill horn brown, eyes dark brown. Hardy in captivity. Loud song with repetitive phrases, warbling and harsher notes. Food: seeds; insects, especially for young. Breeding much as Cardinal, *Pyrrhuloxia cardinalis*; solid nest of plant material fairly low in bush; 3 or 4 whitish eggs, spotted greyish green, heavily marked olive-buff and brown. Closely related to Red-capped, *P. gularis*, of E Brazil and Red-cowled, *P. dominicana*, of northern S America. **869**

Paroaria
dominicana see under **P. cucullata**
gularis see under **P. cucullata**

PARROT,
AFRICAN GREY see **Psittacus erithacus**
BLUE-CHEEKED AMAZON see **Amazonia brasiliensis**
BLUE-HEADED AMAZON see **Amazonia brasiliensis**
BROWN see **Poicephalus meyeri**
CRIMSON-WINGED see under **Aprosmictus scapularis**
ECLECTUS see **Lorius roratus**
ELEGANT GRASS see **Neophema elegans**
GREATER VASA see **Coracopsis vasa**
GROUND see **Pezoporus wallicus**
HISPANIOLA see **Amazonia ventralis**
KING see **Aprosmictus scapularis**
MEYER'S see **Poicephalus meyeri**
ORANGE-CHEEKED see under **Gypopsitta vulturina**
RED-BACKED see **Psephotus haematonotus**
RED-BILLED see **Pionus sordidus**
RED-BROWED FIG see **Opopsitta leadbeateri**
RING-NECKED see **Barnardius barnardi**
SWIFT see **Lathamus discolor**
VULTURINE see **Gypositta vulturina**

PARROTBILL, GREAT see **Conostoma oemodium**

PARTRIDGE,
BARBARY see under **Alectoris rufa**
BUFF-CROWNED WOOD see **Dendrortyx leucophrys**
FERRUGINOUS WOOD see **Caloperdix oculea**
GREEN WOOD see **Rollulus roulroul**
GREY see **Perdix perdix**
RED-LEGGED see **Alectoris rufa**
SNOW see **Lerwa lerwa**

Parula americana see under **Dendroica dominica**

PARULA WARBLER see under **Dendroica dominica**

Parus atricapillus *Paridae*
BLACK-CAPPED CHICKADEE 5¼ ins
Nearctic: breeds from Newfoundland, Central Quebec, Ontario, Mackenzie, Alaska S to N New Jersey, mountains N Carolina, Indiana, S Missouri, N New Mexico, NW California; winters to Maryland, Central Texas. Resident or summer visitor woodland, orchards, tree lines. Closely resembles Willow Tit, *P. montanus*, and Marsh Tit, *P. palustris*. Crown glossy black, large black gorget gradually merging into white breast, pale, striated appearance of closed wing. Behaviour as other *Parus* tits; joins foraging flocks of several species. Call rapid *chick-a-dee, dee* repeated up to 10 times; also softly whistled *dee-dee*, both very different from Willow Tit notes. Food chiefly insects, especially larvae in summer; wild berries, fruits, seeds; frequently at bird tables. Breeds end April onwards New England; nest of moss, lined plant down, fur, feathers, in hole excavated in rotten pine, birch, 1 to 10 ft up; natural holes and nestboxes up to 50 ft. 6 to 8 or more white eggs, lightly speckled red-brown; incubation and fledging as relatives. **802**

Parus caeruleus *Paridae*
BLUE TIT *c.* 4½ ins
W Palaearctic: Europe, except N Scandinavia and including NW Africa, Canaries (only tit), Asia Minor, to Caucasus, Iran; replaced in E by very similar but White-headed Azure Tit, *P. cyaneus*, with which hybridises. Resident rather open broadleaved forests, lowland, riverine, montane; also conifers where few or no competitors; cork oak woods, olive groves, palm oases; cultivated land, parks, gardens well into cities; also reed beds in winter. General impression blue, from cobalt crown, wings (white bar), tail, yellowish green mantle; forehead, border of crown, cheeks, nape patch white; black eyestripe, back of head, bib; underparts sulphur yellow; legs dark slate blue, bill mainly black, eyes dark brown. Juvenile suffused yellow. Active, acrobatic like other *Parus* tits; short flights direct, longer ones undulating. Most of year works woods in parties with other tits; creeps along trunks, often feeds in litter. Roosts in cavities. Calls: *tsee tsee tee tsit;* sibilant hiss; churring scold. Song rapid liquid trill. ♂ and ♀ raise crests, shiver wings in display; also slow butterfly flight by ♂, who feeds ♀ courtship onwards. Food: minute insects, their pupae, larvae, eggs; spiders; mainly from twigs and shrubs; also buds, flowers, soft fruits, some seeds; common at bird tables. Breeds end March to July Britain, ♀ and ♂ building nest of moss, grass, plant fibres, lined hair, wool, feathers; in hole of tree, stump, wall, occasionally behind bark, in old nests bigger birds; nestboxes, many artefacts readily taken. 7 to 16 or more white eggs, lightly freckled red-brown, incubated by ♀ *c.* 14 days; ♀ and ♂ feed young, who fly *c.* 19 days. **803**

Parus cristatus *Paridae*
CRESTED TIT *c.* 4½ ins
W Palaearctic: Europe, except NE, SE, Ireland, most of Britain (distinct race N Scotland), Mediterranean area; but extending to W Siberia between 50° and 60°N. Resident almost exclusively coniferous forest, especially pines, spruces, lowland to subalpine zones. Upperparts brown, wings, tail darker; pointed crest whitish with black feather centres; cheeks off-white with black crescents, separated by black gorget, continued as narrow collar; underparts whitish, suffused buff on flanks; legs olive grey, bill black, eyes red-brown. Behaves much as Blue Tit but feeds more on tree trunks. Calls: distinctive purring trill also thin *zee zee zee.* Trill becomes song as ♂ flutters round tree-tops or chases ♀, whom he feeds with crest erect and raised wings as she quivers on branch. Food: insects and their larvae, also conifer seeds (which it hides) and berries. Breeds mid April to mid June; ♀ excavates or enlarges hole, builds nest of moss, lined thickly felted hair, fur, feathers, in dead wood, usually conifer, occasionally mouse hole, old nest, nestbox; ground level to 10 ft. 5 to 8 or more white eggs, spotted dark red often in zone, incubated by ♀ 13-15 days; young, fed mainly by ♀, fly 16-20 days. Exceptionally 2 broods. **804**

Parus
cyaneus see under **P. caeruleus**
leucomelas see under **P. niger**

Parus major *Paridae*
GREAT TIT *c.* 5½ ins
Palaearctic, Oriental: Europe except NE, Asia S of 60°N, except some southern areas but including much of Indonesia; in this huge range potentially distinct species occur. Resident broadleaved woodland of many types: oaks, olive groves, tropical forests, mangroves, bamboos, also pines in Asia; up to 13,700 ft Yunnan; and cultivated lands, parks, gardens. Upperparts yellowish green to blue grey with white bar, pale feather edges on wings; white outer tail feathers; crown, nape glossy blue-black extending round white cheeks to join gorget and central stripe (broader and expanding on belly in ♂) down sulphur yellow underparts; legs lead blue, bill mainly black, eyes brown-black. Juvenile suffused yellowish. Behaves as other *Parus* tits but perhaps more aggressive and frequently hammers nut on branch with powerful bill. Feeds much on beech mast on ground when available; common at bird tables. Roosts in cavities. Call ringing *tink tink tink* only best known of extensive vocabulary; song *tee-cher tee-cher tee-cher,* amphasis on first syllable. ♂ postures to ♀ and chases her. Mainly insectivorous, especially moth larvae in spring; spiders, small molluscs, worms; fruit, nuts, peas, buds. Breeds end March to July in Britain; ♀ and ♂ build foundation, often substantial, of moss and grass, usually lined hair, in hole of tree or stump up to 15 ft or higher, sometimes in rock crevices, walls, behind bark, old nests; nest-boxes and many artefacts. 5 to 12 white eggs, marked red brown, incubated by ♀ 12-16 days; young, fed by ♀ and ♂, fly *c.* 19 days. Occasionally 2 broods. **805**

Parus montanus *Paridae*
WILLOW TIT *c.* 4½ ins
Palaearctic: broad band across Eurasia, mainly between 50° and 65°N from Britain to E Siberia, Kamtchatka, Sakhalin, Japan. Very similar to Marsh Tit, *P. palustris,* and Black-capped Chickadee, *P. atricapillus,* for long regarded as conspecific; *P. songarus* of Central Asian mountains also closely related. Resident damp coniferous forests, dominated by spruce and, higher up, *Abies* firs; also subarctic birch zone and montane shrubs up to 7,300 ft; broadleaved woodlands, dry and damp, in W Europe, Britain. Very like juvenile Marsh Tit with dark smoky brown not glossy black crown; looks generally more unkempt than Marsh Tit; light patch on secondaries also guide. Usually solitary or in pairs, seldom joining other tits or visiting bird tables; often dives deeply into cover from which it calls distinctive *zit zit zit,* harsh 'squeezed-out' *chichit-tchay-tchay.* Ordinary song repeated *piu,* but has rich warbling song, not carrying far, resembling *Carduelis* finch. Food mainly insects and their larvae, spiders; also seeds which it may hide. Breeds early May to mid June Britain, ♀ building rather slight pad of moss, grass, lined fur, hair, feathers, plant debris; hole excavated (oval entrance) in rotten branch, stem of bush, occasionally bank; has taken nestbox when material to be 'excavated' provided. 6 to 9 white eggs, marked red-brown, incubated by ♀ *c.* 13 days; young, fed by ♀ and ♂, fly *c.* 18 days. **806**

Parus niger *Paridae*
SOUTHERN BLACK TIT 6 ins
Ethiopian: parts Zambia, Malawi, Portuguese E Africa, eastern S Africa. Replaced to N by Black Tit, *P. leucomelas,* with all-glossy plumage except for large pale wing patch and very similar habits. Resident thick dry bush and scrub. ♂: generally glossy blue-black; conspicuous white shoulder patch; edges flight feathers, outer webs outer tail feathers and tips of all, white; breast to belly rather slaty; lower belly, under tail coverts black and white. ♀: duller, paler above, dark grey below. Legs, bill black, eyes brown. Juvenile like ♀ but white on wings tinged cream. Pairs or small parties always on move and calling, like other *Parus* tits; ♂ often calls from exposed perch shrill harsh *twiddy,* followed by *zeet zeet zeet;* also loud buzzing *zeu zeu zeu twit.* Mainly insectivorous. Breeding season varies within range, September to January; nest of plant materials softly lined, in hole of tree. 3 or 4 creamy white eggs, well spotted bright red-brown; apart from small clutch, breeding details much as other *Parus* tits. **807**

Parus palustris *Paridae*
MARSH TIT *c.* 4½ ins
Palaearctic: Europe except peripheral areas; Caucasus; separate population E Asia westward along 50°N to 85°E, Sakhalin, Hokkaido, Korea. Resident mixed broadleaved woodland usually with dense undergrowth, riverine forests, orchards, parks, gardens, up to 4,300 ft (Alps). Upperparts, including wings, tail, brown; crown glossy black, cheeks white; underparts dull white, flanks suffused buff; legs blue-grey, bill black, eyes dark brown. Habits as other tits but spends more time in undergrowth, woodland glades. Usual calls *pitchu* or *pitchit-chuu;* thin *tzee tzee tzee;* nasal repeated *tchaa,* less emphatic than Willow Tit, *P. montanus: chickabeebee* may be lengthened form of this; usual songs repeated *tschuppi* and *pitchaweeo.* Food mainly insects, also seeds from thistles to beech, often stored individually, berries; regular at bird tables. Breeds early April to end June Britain; ♀ builds foundation of moss with felted cup of hair, fur, plant down; in cavity or crack of tree, wall, often with very small hole. 6 to 8 or more white eggs, lightly spotted red-brown, incubated by ♀ *c.* 13 days; ♀ and ♂ feed young, who fly 16-18 days. **808**

Parus songarus see under **P. montanus**

Passer domesticus *Ploceidae*
HOUSE OR ENGLISH SPARROW *c.* 5¾ ins
Cosmopolitan commensal: 'natural' range obscured by introductions but probably almost all Europe, parts N Africa, including Nile Valley, SW Asia, Indian sub-continent, Ceylon, Burma and across Central Asia to Manchuria, mainly between 50° and 60°N. Hybridises with Spanish Sparrow, *P. hispaniolensis,* in parts Mediterranean area. Introduced N America, where widespread from S Canada to S Mexico; W Indies, especially Cuba; temperate and subtropical S America; SE South Africa and some Mascarene Is; SE Australia, Tasmania; New Zealand. Mainly resident in cultivated areas, villages, towns, cities; Kashmir and Himalayan populations winter S Iran, NW India. ♂: upperparts rich brown streaked black; flight and tail feathers dark or blackish brown, pale-edged; narrow white bar on closed wing; crown grey bordered rich brown; cheek pattern grey and white; glossy black gorget in greyish-white underparts. ♀ generally duller, head dull grey brown; juvenile similar. Legs pale brown, bill black (summer ♂), horn-brown, base yellow (♀, winter ♂), eyes light brown. Gregarious at all times; equally at home on ground where hops with flirting tail or aloft; swift, rather whirring flight. Displays include 'sparrows' wedding' when several ♂♂ pursue ♀. Single ♂ puffs breast, droops wings towards ♀, who solicits mating with twittering. Builds winter roosting nests. Calls include *cheep, chissick,* metallic *teu teu;* chirping sometimes develops into song. Omnivorous, but takes much grain, seeds, also fruit, buds; attacks flowerheads; insects fed to young; human scraps. Breeds mainly March to September in Europe; colonial, scattered or close together. ♀ and ♂ build untidy but roughly globular nest of grass, straws, debris, lined feathers, with entrance at side, but in cavities often reduced to lined cup; in trees up to 60 ft, bushes, bottoms of large nests, mud cups of House Martin, *Delichon urbica,* nests; creepers on walls, buildings of all kinds. 3 to 6 off-white to bluish white eggs, variably marked grey, dark grey, brown, incubated mainly ♀ 9-18 days; young, fed by ♀ and ♂ from bill or crop, fly 11-18 days. Up to 4 broods. **954**

Passer hispaniolensis see under **P. domestica**

Passer melanurus *Ploceidae*
CAPE SPARROW 6 ins
Ethiopian: S and NW Southern Africa; local resident, now largely commensal with man, in native and introduced trees, especially in drier built-up areas; sometimes in quite arid conditions. ♂: upperparts uniform chestnut; flight and tail feathers blackish, edged buff; white-tipped median coverts form bar on closed wing; head, face, gorget black; broad white line from eye down neck; hindneck earth brown; underparts whitish, flanks grey; legs, eyes brown, bill black. ♀ similar but generally paler; head greyish, 'eyebrow' white. Juvenile resembles ♀. Tame and confiding, forms large flocks after breeding, builds special roosting nests. Calls harsh *chissip;* strident *chirrr chirrr* of alarm; jerky repetitive song: *chip chollop tlip tlop.* Diet: seeds, grain, soft shoots, damaging to gardens; insects fed to young. Breeds mainly September or October to March, building large untidy nests of grass, stems, debris, lined feathers; elongated entrance at side; usually in trees, so competition with introduced House Sparrow, *P. domesticus,* reduced, but also in creepers, under eaves, in old nests swallows, other weavers. 3 to 6 whitish or greenish eggs, speckled or heavily marked dark brown over grey, incubated mainly ♀, 12-14 days; young, fed both parents, fly 16-25 days. Several broods. **955**

Passer montanus *Ploceidae*
TREE SPARROW 5½ ins
Palaearctic, Oriental: most of Europe except N

Scandinavia, Adriatic coast and Balkans; Asia between 65° and 30°N, not Indian subcontinent, but extending into SE mainland and Indonesia; Japan, Taiwan. Introduced N America, some islands SE Asia, Australia, New Zealand but without devastating success of House Sparrow, *P. domesticus*. Mainly sedentary, but dispersals, perhaps regular movements, from Central and N Europe. Habitat: open country with scattered trees and small woods, cultivated areas, orchards; villages and towns, especially SE Asia, Japan. Plumage much as House Sparrow but sexes alike with chocolate crown and nape, crescentic black patch on white cheek. Legs pale brown, bill dark (summer), blackish brown to yellow at base (winter, juvenile), eyes dark brown. Less obtrusive than House Sparrow even where common; associates in winter with other sparrows, finches, buntings, also large flocks on own. Calls resemble House Sparrow's but *chip* sharper and hard-sounding *tec tec* in flight distinctive; repeated chirping song. ♂ postures to ♀ in display, raising and lowering chocolate crown feathers. Takes seeds, corn, insects (e.g. beetles, larvae, aphids) and spiders; less frequent at bird tables than House Sparrow. Breeds April to September in Britain; usually colonial; ♀ and ♂ build neater version of House Sparrow nest with definite flask shape when in open in tree up to 25 ft; very commonly in tree holes, buildings, rock clefts, where reduced to cup; takes nestboxes readily; often in bottom of large nests, e.g. herons, hawks. 4 to 6 off-white eggs variably marked dark brown or grey, incubated ♀ and ♂ 12-14 days; young, fed by ♀ and ♂, fly 12-14 days. 2, sometimes 3 broods. **956**

Passerella iliaca *Emberizidae: Emberizinae*
FOX SPARROW   7¼ ins
Nearctic: from Pribilof Is, N Alaska, SW over forested Canada to Colorado, Nevada, S California; winters from Maryland, S Indiana, S Missouri, New Mexico, British Columbia, to Central Florida, Gulf Coast, Central Texas, Lower California. Habitat dense, often coniferous thickets, also riparian alders, willows, burnt-over land, meadow/woodland edges. Races vary in grey and brown tones; upperparts generally rich brown streaked grey; pale edges to coverts form narrow wingbars; rump, tail orange-brown; crown chestnut streaked darker; pale 'eyebrow', white moustachial stripe with brown above, below; large central spot on white, brown-streaked underparts. Western race especially dark. Legs light brown, bill yellowish, eyes dark brown. Rather wary and secretive but sings from exposed perch, even in winter, richest phrasing of any 'sparrow', short but clear and melodious, rising in pitch, then final cadence; call, drawn-out *stssp*. Food mainly from ground; kicks litter with both feet to expose small animals. Breeds June in N; large nest of grass, moss, roots, lined feathers, fur, holds 4 pale greenish eggs, thickly spotted reddish brown. **862**

Passerina amoena *Emberizidae: Pyrrhuloxiinae*
LAZULI BUNTING   5¼ ins
Nearctic: breeds S British Columbia, S Alberta, SE Saskatchewan, NW Dakota to NW Lower California, N New Mexico, W Texas; winters lower California, mainland Mexico. Variety of scrub habitats from coastal sage-brush of California, thickets of willow, rose, poison oak, dogwood, with open grassy spaces or areas of *Artemisia*, mustard; also newly colonised burnt-over land; occasionally up to 8,000 ft. ♂: upperparts, including head to breast, light blue (head, rump brilliant in good light, otherwise appear blackish), upper back streaked brownish; broad and narrow white wingbars; breast orange brown shading paler on flanks, underparts white. First year ♂ blue only on head. ♀: generally unstreaked brown above, paler below; wings, rump, tail tinged bluish; light wingbars. Legs dark, bill grey, eyes brown. As habitats ephemeral, tends to be nomadic, especially when population high. Call: soft *tsip*; harsher *zid'l* from night migrants; loud song 8 to 14 notes, in groups of 2 to 4 with abrupt changes in pitch. When feeding, bends slender stems to get at seeds in autumn; summer diet: grasshoppers, bugs, beetles, cicadas and larvae from herb and shrub layers. Breeds June, July; nest of green or dry grass,

stems, finer fibres, usually low in bush or hidden on ground below one. 3 or 4 bluish green eggs, occasionally dark speckled, incubated ♀ 12 days; ♀ and ♂ feed young. Sometimes 2 broods. **870**

Passerina ciris *Emberizidae: Pyrrhuloxiinae*
PAINTED BUNTING   5¼ ins
Nearctic: SE North Carolina, N Mississippi, S Kansas S to N Florida, S Louisiana, SE New Mexico; winters Central Florida, Central Mexico to Panama. Variety of scrub habitats: woodland edge, riverine strips, into well-wooded towns S USA. ♂: mantle yellow-green; wings dusky, glossed green; tail purplish brown; head, neck, cheeks, stripe down to side breast dark violet blue; rest of plumage bright red, also orbits. ♀ has upperparts green, wings, tail darker; underparts yellowish to amber on belly. ♂ darker autumn, young ♂ like ♀ with some blue on head. Legs dark brown, bill grey or light horn, eyes dark brown. Very shy, keeps much to cover except when ♂ sings from tree or bush top loud, clear *pew-eata pew-eata I eaty you too;* call: sharp 2- or 3-note chirp. Diet mainly seeds, e.g. foxtail grass; also insects, e.g. cotton worms, boll weevils. Breeds May to July, ♀ building deep, thin-walled cup of grass, stems, bark strips, dead leaves, lined hair, rootlets; usually in fork, well hidden in bush or tree. 3 or 4 white eggs, marked reddish brown, incubated ♀ *c.* 12 days; ♀ and ♂ feed young. Often 2 broods. **871**

Passerina leclancheri *Emberizidae: Pyrrhuloxiinae*
RAINBOW BUNTING   5 ins
Neotropical: SW Mexico; dry lowlands with scattered bushes and scrub. ♂: upperparts (except for greenish crown and tinge shoulders) bright blue, darker on wings, tail; underparts, including ring round eye, yellow. ♀: olive-green, tinged blue on tail; underparts yellow. Legs brown, bill horn brown, eyes brown. Searches litter of underbrush for seeds and insects. Simple song from bush-top (W. Beebe). Breeding much as other *Passerina* species. **872**

PASTOR, ROSY see **Sturnus roseus**

PATAGONIAN
    BLACK-HEADED GULL see under **Larus
       ridibundus**
    CRESTED DUCK see **Lophonetta specularoides**

Pavo cristatus *Phasianidae*   ♀: 38, ♂: 40-46
INDIAN PEAFOWL   (80-92 with train) ins
Oriental: Indian subcontinent and Ceylon; introduced Andaman Is. Resident lowland forests or well-wooded country up to *c.* 5,000 ft in Outer Himalayas and Peninsular Hills; moist and dry deciduous forest near streams; also semi-tame in villages and cultivated areas. ♂: brilliant iridescent blue neck and breast; lower back light bronze-green, scalloped black; rump black; 'train' of upper tail coverts metallic bronze green with purplish and black centred, coppery 'eyes'; scapulars and wing coverts closely barred black and buff; primaries and their coverts chestnut; face white and black, fan-shaped crest of spatulate wiry feathers. ♀: head (crested as ♂) and nape rufous brown, upperparts brown, mottled paler; primaries brown; lower neck metallic green, breast buff glossed green, belly buffy white. Legs, bill horn-grey, eyes dark brown. Immature ♂ as ♀, but primaries chestnut. Small parties of ♂ and 3 to 5 ♀♀ when nesting, but sexes segregate after breeding. Feeds and drinks in open early and late, prefaced by crowing *may-awe*, also stimulated by thunder. Scream: *ka-an ka-an* repeated 6 to 8 times with head movements; alarm *tok tok* by ♀ with neck fluffed. ♂ displays by raising train and quivering drooped wings, strutting, prancing, shivering train and presenting back view; ♀ occasionally responds. Rests during day in thickets. Runs to escape, seldom taking wing, when rockets upwards with loud flaps, to fly quite dexterously. Roosts in tall trees. Diet: seeds, grain, lentils, ground nuts, shoots, berries, figs; invertebrates, small reptiles; can be pest near villages. Breeds June to September in N, April-May in S, January to March Ceylon. Usually hides nest in thorny undergrowth, but sometimes semi-feral

birds use ruins and house tops. 4 to 8 pale cream to buff eggs, finely pitted, incubated by ♀ *c.* 28 days; she tends brood. ♂ successively polygamous. **203**

PEACEFUL DOVE see **Geopelia striata**

PEACOCK PHEASANT, PALAWAN see **Polyplectron emphanum**

PEAFOWL,
    AFRICAN see **Afropavo congensis**
    INDIAN see **Pavo cristatus**

PEARL-BREASTED SWALLOW see **Hirundo dimidiata**

PEARLED TREERUNNER see **Margarornis squamiger**

Pedioecetes phasianellus *Tetraonidae*
SHARP-TAILED GROUSE   19 ins
Nearctic: N America from Central Alaska to Mid-West USA, and W to Baffin Bay. Local resident in prairies and brushlands, resorting to forests in winter, when northern birds move S. Mottled yellow-brown, black and white all over, darker on wings, much lighter on underparts; sharp pointed tail; black and white stripes on cheeks, tufted crest; legs feathered, bill and eyes dark. Lives in flocks, which fly with flaps and glides when disturbed from feeding on buds and shoots, especially of northern trees; also buds and berries of junipers. Complicated courtship dances on 'leks' (see *Lyrurus tetrix*) by up to 50 ♂♂, in rounded postures, uttering booming calls from inflated sacs. Flight call: *whucker whucker whucker.* ♀ lays from April in Colorado to early May in Canada 7 to 15 fawn-brown eggs, usually marked red-brown and lilac, in lined scrape well hidden in local cover; she incubates them for *c.* 3 weeks; young fully grown in 6 weeks to 2 months. **187**

Pedionomus torquatus *Pedionomidae*
PLAINS WANDERER or
COLLARED HEMIPODE   ♀ 4, ♂ 5 ins
SE Australia; open grasslands and plains, making local movements within range. Reddish-brown, buff and black upperparts, underparts paler; collar of black spots on white; ♀ has chestnut breast; legs yellow, slender pointed bill and eyes brown; tail very short, wings short and rounded. Prefers to run or stand still rather than fly and has upright posture unlike true hemipodes, surveying surroundings above vegetation. Probably partly nocturnal. Diet: seeds and other vegetable matter; insects. Breeds September to January, making scrape in ground; 4 pale yellow or green eggs, spotted grey and olive, incubated by ♂; role of sexes reversed as in hemipodes (*Turnicidae*, Family 40).

PEKIN ROBIN see **Leiothrix lutea**

Pelagodroma marina *Hydrobatidae*
WHITE-FACED STORM or FRIGATE PETREL   8 ins
Southern oceans and N Atlantic; distinct race on Galapagos Islands in Pacific; northward migration after breeding. Upperparts brownish: crown, nape and cheeks smoky; tail and wings blackish brown; underparts from chin white; legs and bill black, eyes brown; rump white in one race. Only storm petrel regularly seen in coastal waters. Like relatives visits colonies at dusk, dancing over nest-holes; flight very erratic. Calls in burrows 'twittering', 'squeaky' and 'groaning'; low notes on wing. Food mainly small crustaceans, e.g. *Euphausia*, from plankton. Breeding season varies widely according to range, from March-April in N Atlantic, early November New Zealand; colonies on bare or scrub-covered islands. One white egg zoned with violet undermarks laid in burrow *c.* 2 ft long. Incubation mainly by ♀ for 53-56 days; chick, fed by ♀ and ♂, fledges in 52-67 days. **36**

Pelecanoides urinatrix *Pelecanoididae*
DIVING PETREL   7½-8 ins
Subantarctic and South Temperate oceans, breeding usually remote islands and migrating over sea after-

wards. The race illustrated, *exsul,* sometimes regarded as separate species breeding Kerguelen, Crozet Is and elsewhere; range of *urinatrix* circumpolar, including Falkland Is, Tristan da Cunha, islands off New Zealand. Upperparts from crown to tail black except for white edges to new secondaries; cheeks grey; underparts white, tinged smoky under wings; race *exsul* has black bill proportionately broader at base, usually shows grey speckling on breast; legs blue, eyes dark brown. Silent at sea, but variety of wailing, mewing, cooing, chattering calls over breeding station, off which (in New Zealand area) parties collect from April onwards, nocturnally clearing out or excavating burrows in turf of island. Single white egg laid in chamber at end of burrow August, incubated ♀ and ♂ *c.* 5 weeks; chick, fed by ♀ and ♂ on paste of small crustaceans (main food of adult with small fish), fledges *c.* 7 weeks. Moult, during which birds briefly flightless, takes place at sea. **37**

Pelecanus conspicillatus *Pelecanidae*
AUSTRALIAN PELICAN *c.* 48 ins
Two races in continental Australia, Tasmania, New Guinea and Amboina; accidental New Zealand. Sedentary on mudflats, islands, estuaries, shores and islands of inland lakes. Mainly white, with black on wings and tail; legs grey-blue, bill yellow orange, eyes brown. Found in flocks, fishing in shallows or resting on shore; swims and flies well but waddles on land. Food principally fresh and saltwater crustaceans. Mainly silent but utters hoarse croak; young in nest chatter. Breeds colonially from September to March on flat ground, making scrape, surrounded by local plant material, for 2 to 3 dirty white eggs, coated with lime and stained during 4-5 week incubation by ♀; young, fed by ♀ and ♂, fledge in *c.* 2 months. **39**

Pelecanus occidentalis *Pelecanidae*
BROWN PELICAN 42-48 ins
Three races in S Nearctic and N Neotropical, including West Indies and Galapagos; N American birds winter Florida, California and farther S. Habitat coasts and lagoons with shallow shores and mangrove swamps. Dark grey-brown body with silvery upperparts; crown straw-coloured, turning white on face and neck which in summer has nape and sides brown; legs black, bill mainly grey with brown pouch, eyes light yellow. Gregarious: noted for formation flying, with heads tucked into bodies; also soars to great heights and has various displays at nest-site. Diet of fish caught by shallow plunges with wings half open. Mainly silent but young have piercing scream. Breeding season variable; builds stick nest colonially on ground or in trees, laying 2 to 3 eggs, chalky white at first. Incubation *c.* 30 days by ♀ and ♂; young fly *c.* 9 weeks, mature in 3-4 years. **40**

Pelecanus onocrotalus *Pelecanidae*
OLD WORLD WHITE PELICAN 54-72 ins
SE Palaearctic, Ethiopian and very local Oriental region; northernmost Palaearctic birds move S in autumn. Habitat margins of shallow rivers, lakes, deltas and coasts. Predominantly white, tinged pink and with crest in spring; wingtips and trailing edges black, yellow patch on breast; legs pink to orange; bill blue and pink, pouch pink or yellow, eyes dark. Manifests social behaviour by formation flying and communal fishing, driving shoreward in crescent, splashing wings and feet, to scoop up prey in shallows; also crash dives; principal food fish. Displays at colonies, with guttural calls. Breeding season varies with range; colonies on shore or in marsh, with nests of trampled local vegetation for the 1 to 2 chalky white eggs, incubated *c.* 30 days by ♀ and ♂, who feed young for *c.* 60 days. **41**

PELICAN,
AUSTRALIAN see **Pelecanus conspicillatus**
BROWN see **Pelecanus occidentalis**
OLD WORLD WHITE see **Pelecanus onocrotalus**

PENDULINE
TIT see **Remiz pendulinus**
TIT, AFRICAN see under **Eremomela icteropygialis**

PENGUIN,
ADELIE see **Pygoscelis adeliae**
EMPEROR see **Aptenodytes forsteri**
JACKASS see **Spheniscus demersus**
LITTLE BLUE see **Eudyptes minor**
MACARONI see **Eudyptes chrysolophus**
PERUVIAN see **Spheniscus humboldti**

PENNANT-WINGED NIGHTJAR see **Macrodipteryx vexillarius**

PEPPERSHRIKE, RUFOUS-BROWED see **Cyclarhis gujanensis**

Perdix perdix *Phasianidae*
COMMON or GREY PARTRIDGE *c.* 12 ins
W Palaearctic: from Scandinavia, Ireland and Spain across Europe, Asia Minor to Central Asia; introduced N America. Sedentary, typically on farm land in Europe; also rough grasslands, heaths, steppes, semi-desert, shingle and dunes. Upperparts brown with black and white streaks; crown, neck and breast grey, inverted chocolate 'horseshoe' on lower breast (fainter on ♀); flanks grey, barred chestnut; face and throat orange brown; legs grey, bill greenish horn, eyes brown, facial skin red. Spends winter in coveys of varying size, breaking up into pairs after communal displays. Walks with neck withdrawn, runs to take off into skimming flight, swerving easily; roosts on ground. Call (♂ especially) *kirric kirric;* cackling in flight. Feeds on wide range of plants; insects, especially ants, important for young. Breeds late March onwards in Europe, lining scrape in thick cover, ♀ incubating 9 to 20 olive brown eggs 23-25 days; ♂ and ♀ tend brood, which flies at 16 days. **205**

PEREGRINE see **Falco peregrinus**

Perisoreus infaustus *Corvidae*
SIBERIAN JAY *c.* 12 ins
Palaearctic: mid Scandinavia E to N Kamchatka down to N Japan; sedentary, some movement for food in hard winters. Habitat: deep in forest, rarely at margins. Upperparts olive brown with blackish brown cap and brownish cheeks; rump and long, rounded tail rufous, central tail feathers grey; wing coverts bright rufous with brown edges; throat light grey; underparts greyish brown. Legs black, short bill black and slightly curved at tip of upper mandible, eyes dark brown. Tame; tail spread out like fan in flight which is easy and quiet; generally lively and restless. Call: *kuk-kuk* or *kei-kei.* Food, similar to Eurasian Jay, *Garrulus glandarius,* includes seeds of conifers and berries (may hoard these in tree hollows). Pairs for life; breeds April and May; solid nest of twigs and plant stalks, lined lichens and feathers, 5 to 20 ft up tree in denser parts of coniferous forests. 3 or 4 eggs, greenish white or dingy greyish white, marked grey and violet-grey streaks, incubated 16-17 days; young fledge *c.* 5 weeks.

Pernis apivorus *Accipitridae*
HONEY BUZZARD *c.* 20-23 ins
W Palaearctic; summer visitor Britain, Iberia, S Scandinavia E to River Ob (W Siberia), extending SE to Caucasus, N Iran; winters tropical Africa. Closely related *P. ptilorhynchus* in E Asia, *P. celebensis* Indonesia, Philippines. Habitat wooded areas, broadleaved (especially beech) and coniferous, with glades and meadows; not cultivated land. Upperparts dark brown, sometimes marked white; crown, sides of head usually grey; underparts very variable from white to dark brown, usually white barred and marked brown; tail barred, with broad subterminal band; legs, eyes, lower part of cere yellow, rest of cere and bill blackish. Broad-winged flight with soaring and hovering, developing into diving and wing-clapping displays by ♂. Rather squeaky high-pitched flight call; several other notes described. Walks and runs with ease, feeding on ground nests of bumble bees and wasps (honey, insects and larvae) scratched out with strong feet, bird sometimes disappearing in hole; insects taken in bill and tails snipped off before eating; attacks tree nests in tropics; also other insects, worms, frogs, lizards, occasionally small mammals and birds; berries.

Breeds from end May in Europe, building nest of sticks, lined greenery, often in side branch or on old nest of other bird, 30 to 75 ft up. Usually 2 whitish eggs, richly marked red-brown to chocolate and incubated by ♀ and ♂ 30-35 days; young, fed by both parents, fly 40-44 days.

Pernis
celebensis see under **P. apivorus**
ptilorhynchus see **P. apivorus**

PERUVIAN
COCK OF THE ROCK see **Rupicola peruviana**
PENGUIN see **Spheniscus humboldti**

PETCHARY, BLACK-BANDED see under **Cacicus cela**

PETERS FINFOOT see **Podica senegalensis**

PETREL,
BERMUDA see **Pterodroma cahow**
CAPPED see under **Pterodroma cahow**
DIVING see **Pelecanoides urinatrix**
FRIGATE see **Pelegodroma marina**
GIANT see **Macronectes giganteus**
SNOW see **Pagodroma nivea**
STORM see **Hydrobates pelagicus**
WHITE-FACED see **Pelagodroma marina**

Petroica cucullata or Melanodryas cucullata
Muscicapidae: Muscicapinae
HOODED ROBIN 6½ ins
Australasian: continental Australia except extreme N; mainly sedentary but some local movements. Habitat dry savannah and mulga scrub; edges of open forest. ♂: upperparts mainly black, hood extending down breast; white stripe from breast over shoulder; white patch on blackish wings, underparts white. ♀: upperparts brownish grey, underparts paler; lacks white on shoulder but small white markings tip of tail; legs, bill bluish, eyes dark brown. Rather unobtrusive inspite of ♂'s plumage. Call rather high-pitched and feeble, with trill on descending scale; also single unmusical note; often calls at night. Takes insects and spiders, mainly from ground. Breeds August to December, building nest of bark, grasses, bound cobwebs, in fork of lateral branch usually near ground but up to 20 ft. Usually 2 pale olive to apple green eggs, mottled rich brown, especially at big end. **786**

Petroica goodenovii *Muscicapidae: Muscicapinae*
RED-CAPPED ROBIN 5 ins
Australasian: almost all continental Australia except humid forests and deserts; resident open forests inland, with varying tree preferences in different areas. ♂: upperparts, including head, dull black to blackish brown, white markings wings, tail; throat black, sometimes tinged red; large 'cap' and breast scarlet; underparts white. ♀: dull brown above; pale buff wing markings; cap dull reddish brown; underparts white. Legs, bill black, eyes dark brown. Behaviour much as Scarlet Robin, *P. multicolor.* Call like ticking of clock; 'delicate little song' (H. J. Frith). Food mainly insects taken in flight, off trees, on ground. Breeds July to December E Australia, making nest of bark fibres, grass, bound cobwebs, lined fur, feathers, decorated lichen to blend with site in fork, upper side lateral branch, twig junctions; from 6 to 20 ft up. Usually 2 bluish white to grey-green eggs, spotted brown at big end, incubated ♀, fed by ♂, *c.* 12 days; both parents feed young. **787**

Petroica multicolor *Muscicapidae: Muscicapinae*
SCARLET ROBIN 5 ins
Australasian: E continental Australia from Darling Downs (Queensland), through New South Wales, Victoria to Flinders Ranges (S Australia); also York and Eyre's Peninsulas; Kangaroo Is, Tasmania, Bass Strait Is; separate races SW Australia, Norfolk, other SW Pacific Is. Habitat: open forests in summer, denser cover in winter. ♂: upperparts, including head, throat, black; prominent white forehead, wings, and tail feathers; breast scarlet; underparts white. ♀: upperparts brown; buff on forehead, wings, tail;

throat greyish white, breast strongly tinged scarlet, underparts dull white to pale brown. Legs, bill black; eyes hazel. Juvenile mottled brown. Moves quietly in pairs, foraging from low vantage points, still except for occasional tail flick, then darts to ground after insects, their larvae, worms. Call low trilling whistle mainly in spring; sharp double calls and clicking notes. Breeds July to December, ♀ building nest like Red-capped Robin, *P. goodenovii*, but thicker, from 2 to 40 ft in fork, on lateral branch, behind bark, in hollow, outside decorated appropriately. Usually 3 pale green or bluish to dull brownish white eggs, densely spotted brown over purplish grey, incubated by ♀, fed by ♂, 15 days; both parents feed young, who fly 16-18 days. **788**

Petroica rodinogaster *Muscicapidae : Musiciapinae*
PINK ROBIN   *c.* 4 ins
Australasia: S Victoria, Tasmania; winters farther N, e.g. New South Wales. Breeds damp fern gullies of wet sclerophyll forests. ♂: upperparts slaty black, tail blackish brown; small white spot on forehead; underparts rose pink, under tail coverts white. ♀: olive-brown above, tail brown, wings marked rich buff; underparts pale brown. Legs, bill black-brown, eyes blackish. Juvenile mottled. Very quiet, unobtrusive, flits from tree to tree, occasionally dropping to ground after small insects. Call quiet *tic tic;* song pleasant quiet warble; virtually silent in winter. Breeds October to January Tasmania, building small cup of moss, lichen, bound cobwebs, lined fine rootlets: in low bush or tree in gully. 3 or 4 greenish white eggs, minutely spotted brown, umber, purple in zone at big end. **789**

Petronia petronia *Ploceidae*
ROCK SPARROW   5½ ins
Palaearctic: from Canary Is, Mediterranean area, Asia Minor, Palestine to mountains and deserts of SW Asia, Tibet, China between 30° and 50° N; sedentary, forming large flocks in winter, usually near breeding sites. Habitat: warm, dry rocky slopes with grass or low scrub, olive groves, higher cultivated areas, buildings of all kinds; often commensal with man, even into towns. Upperparts dull brown with feathers paler-edged on back and wing coverts; white tips to tail feathers; pale 'eyebrow' and stripe over brown crown; ear coverts dull brown, face paler, underparts pale, faintly 'scaly'; narrow yellow breast band; legs, stout bill light brown, eyes brown. Juvenile lacks yellow on breast. Winter flocks perform evolutions before going to roost. ♂ has rolling, gliding display flight with pipit-like descent; usually near nest-site. Calls: *tut*, grating *chwee*, finch-like *pey-ee*. Food mainly from ground, probably much as House Sparrow, *Passer domesticus.* Breeds end April onwards (France) usually in colonies in rock clefts, hollow trees, old nest holes of other birds, human artefacts, including wells in deserts; untidy sparrow-like nest of plant debris and feathers. 3 to 6 off-white eggs, streaked or blotched darkly, incubated ♀, fed by ♂. Both parents feed young on insects, fledging *c.* 3 weeks. 2 broods. **957**

Petrophassa albipennis *Columbidae*
WHITE-QUILLED ROCK PIGEON   *c.* 12 ins
Kimberley Division of Western Australia, adjacent areas of Northern Territory. Habitat: sandstone cliffs and scattered rocks with water nearby, rarely seen in trees. Plump, generally dark brown, except black-tipped white primaries and primary coverts; head, neck, mantle and breast paler and with dark spots. Legs brown-black, bill blackish, eyes brown. In pairs or small flocks, shy and difficult to flush; ground feeder taking chiefly seeds. Breeding season variable; 2 cream eggs in slight hollow lined with soft dead grass, in ground near tuft of spinifex or stone. **370**

Petrophassa scripta or Geophaps scripta *Columbidae*
SQUATTER PIGEON   *c.* 12½ ins
Australasian: inland NE and E Australia. Habitat: open country with water available. Upperparts, short wings and black-edged tail grey-brown with pale tinge, face and throat distinctive black and white markings, lower breast and belly bluish grey with white sides; glossy green and purple patch on closed wing. Legs dull purple, bill black, eyes dark brown

with pale blue orbital skin, yellow or pink at corners. Stays on ground unless threatened, when rises with loud whirring of wings, scattering to seek cover in grass; also crouches to hide, hence name. Feeds mainly on grass seed. Call: frequent low crooning notes between paired birds. Breeds usually from September to January subject to weather and food supplies; 2 cream eggs in shallow scrape in ground, lightly lined with plant debris, incubated *c.* 17 days. **371**

Peucedramus taeniatus *Parulidae*
OLIVE WARBLER   5 ins
Nearctic, Neotropical: mainly resident, from S New Mexico and White Mountains, Arizona, to Guatemala; northern birds move S in winter. Habitat open coniferous forest 8,500 to 12,000 ft. ♂: back grey to darker tail with pale feather edges; wings dark grey, with whitish edges to flight feathers and 2 white bars on coverts; head, neck to upper back and throat buff-brown with thick black mask; underparts white, greyish on sides, flanks. ♀ has greyish crown, faint mask, pale yellow face, throat; less white on wings, tail. Immature ♂ may breed in similar plumage. Often associates with flocks of Western Bluebirds, *Sialia mexicana*, after breeding; feeds from ground to canopy, slowly searching branches for insects. Usual call *peta* recalls Western Bluebird; song: series of loud, liquid notes on descending scale (R. H. Pough). Breeds June (Arizona), building nest of various plant materials, lined down, usually hidden in foliage or mistletoe near end of lateral tree branch, 30 to 80 ft in conifer. 3 or 4 grey or bluish white eggs, thickly freckled blackish.

PEWEE,
EASTERN WOOD see **Contopus virens**
TROPICAL see under **Contopus virens**

Pezoporus wallicus *Psittacidae*
GROUND PARROT   13 ins
Australasian: N Tasmania; very locally coasts of Victoria, New South Wales, southern W Australia; flat ground or hilltops on coastal heaths with scattered *Banksia* or grasstrees (blackboys); also estuarine flats, swamps, grasslands; resident or moving locally. Green upperparts, including long, graduated tail, barred and mottled brown and yellow; pale stripe on wing; underparts heavily barred yellow; undertail brown; red frontal patch; legs flesh brown, bill horn-brown, eyes pale brown or yellow. When flushed, short, swift zigzag flight, flapping and gliding, pitching after 50 or 100 yds; longer flights undulating. Runs well, climbs reeds, but cannot perch effectively. Usually single or in pairs, emits strong scent. Calls at dusk 30-40 minutes: 3 or 4 bell-like notes sometimes followed by sharper notes. Food: seeds of grasses and herbs, fallen fruits; forces seedheads to ground or passes bill along them. Breeds September-December, lining hollow in grass, sometimes in centre of tussock, concealed by outer stems. 3 or 4 white eggs incubated *c.* 21 days; young leave nest *c.* 28 days, still unable to fly. **400**

Phaethon lepturus *Phaethonidae*
YELLOW-BILLED
TROPICBIRD   30-32 (body 15-16) ins
Tropical oceans, dispersing after breeding to open sea and coastal waters. Glossy white (but race *fulvus* in Indian Ocean suffused peach or even salmon pink); broad black stripe through eye links with black on mantle and wings; black on tail of 12 feathers, central pair much elongated; legs bluish, toes black, bill orange red, eyes brown. Usually alone at sea, resting on water with tail raised; clumsy on land but graceful in flight. Most active at island colonies early morning and evening. Dives after food: squids, fish, marine crustaceans, especially crabs (see also under *Pterodroma cahow*, Bermuda Cahow). Harsh tern-like scream of alarm or in flight; softer calls at nest. Breeding season varies with range; at 5 to 10 month intervals on Ascension Island. One egg, pinkish ground richly marked in purple and brown, laid in hole, crevice or burrow of other species, on bare island or sea cliff; incubated 28 days by ♀ and ♂; they feed chick, which fledges fully in 70-85 days. **38**

Phaethornis superciliosus *Trochilidae*
LONG-TAILED HERMIT   *c.* 6 (bill 1½) ins
Neotropical: S Mexico, Central America, Guyanas, Venezuela S of Orinoco, N and E Colombia, W and E Ecuador, E Peru, N Bolivia, Amazonian Brazil; resident in forests from sea level to *c.* 6,000 ft. Upperparts greyish brown, outer flight feathers with pale buff or whitish tips; rump and upper tail coverts tinged orange, elongated central tail feathers white; much of head dark brown with lighter stripes; underparts grey tinged buff, under tail coverts pale buff to white, with darker markings. Legs, long curved bill, eyes dark. ♂♂ gather, up to 100 in *c.* 250 yds, and display by wagging tails, singing squeaky song, thus attracting ♀♀; display areas may persist for years. Hovers in front of food plants, e.g. wild plantain, introduced banana flowers, to which long bill gives access. Builds typical hummingbird nest usually up to 9 ft, often beneath curled palm frond. ♀ lays 2 white eggs, incubates them *c.* 17 days, feeds young by regurgitation until they fly *c.* 3½ weeks. **474**

PHAINOPEPLA see **Phainopepla nitens**

Phainopepla nitens *Bombycillidae*
PHAINOPEPLA   7½ ins
Nearctic; marginally Neotropical: breeds from Central California, S Utah and mid W Texas to Central Mexico; winters from S California, S Arizona southward. Habitat: riparian trees, often mesquites in desert country. ♂: generally glossy black from tall-crested crown to long tail; large white patch on black-tipped wings; white crescents lower breast; ♀: mainly brownish-grey with black in crest; wing patch pale grey; under tail coverts white-edged. Juvenile much as ♀. Legs, bill black, eyes light red. Flocks up to 50 wander after breeding, searching for berry-bearing trees, especially parasitic mistletoes; also take insects high in air. Slow wing-beats and fluttering flight. Call: repeated whistling *quirt;* song rather uneven between pleasant and squeaky notes. Breeds July (California), making shallow nest of twigs, fibres, down, bound cobwebs, usually in fork of bush or tree up to 20 ft, in thicket or open woodland; sometimes hidden by mistletoe or other growth. Usually 3 greenish white eggs, speckled black and brown. Both parents tend young. **661**

Phainoptila melanoxantha *Bombycillidae*
BLACK AND YELLOW SILKY FLYCATCHER   7½ ins
Neotropical: Costa Rica and W Panama; resident mountain forests from *c.* 5,000 ft to timberline. ♂: upperparts from crown deep black, glossed bluish green; chin, throat, thighs, wings, tail dull sooty black; rump lemon yellow tinged olive; sides, flanks yellow; lower breast, belly grey; upper breast, under tail coverts yellowish olive. ♀: crown black, glossed bluish green; hindneck slate grey, upperparts olive green, mixed yellow on rump; cheeks olive grey, chin, throat paler; underparts as ♂. Legs dark brown, bill blackish, eyes brown. Presumably mainly insectivorous but habits not studied.

Phalacrocorax africanus *Phalacrocoracidae*
LONG-TAILED SHAG   22-24 ins
Ethiopian, marginally Palaearctic; across Africa W to R. Gambia; also Madagascar, Egypt; local movements according to season. Uniform velvety black with relatively long tail; wing coverts and scapulars hoary grey, crest and white plumes in breeding season; immatures brownish-white underparts; legs purplish black, bill dark. Gregarious in large or small flocks, on lakes and rivers whose bends they follow in flight. Roosts communally, preferably in trees. Swims and dives after fish and amphibians, e.g. *Xenopus*. Silent, except for hiss on nest; young cackle. Breeding season varies; builds nest of local plants in colonies on ground, islands or low trees, often with other species. Both sexes incubate 2 to 4 chalky blue eggs and tend the young. **47**

Phalacrocorax atriceps *Phalacrocoracidae*
BLUE-EYED SHAG   28-33 ins
One of group of closely related species in southern oceans, also occurring inland in South America,

breeding S Chile and Argentina; in winter northward movement to Uruguay, but generally sedentary. Upperparts black glossed green, blue and violet; underparts white, also wingbar and patch on back; closed wing looks scaly; crest 2½ ins. Legs pinkish brown, bill olive or horn brown with yellow pouch; nasal caruncles (warts) on *P.a. georgianus*. Eyelid blue, not eye which is brown. Habituated to man on S Georgia and other islands, but feeds naturally on shrimps and fish, e.g. *Notothemia*. Mutual courtship includes curtseying, 'graceful minuet' and neck-twisting (Murphy). Rather silent, with quiet call at nest. Lays from end October in south of range to end February in north, 1 to 3 chalky, greenish white eggs in pile of various materials, on cliff ledge, stack or rocky island, also by lakes inland. Both sexes incubate eggs and tend young. **48**

Phalacrocorax bougainvilli *Phalacrocoracidae*
GUANAY 30 ins
Neotropical: confined to coasts of Chile and Peru, with local movements after breeding, e.g. to Colombia, and mass migrations after food failures. Main supplier (85%) of guano, derived from diet of anchovies, which are dependent on cold Humboldt Current. Upperparts glossy greenish black; underparts, chin and base of neck white; plumes at back of head and scattered filoplumes; legs flesh-pink, bill horny or brownish black with accretions, facial skin red, orbital ring green, eyes dark brown. Most aerial cormorant, capable of sustained flight on long wings, diving on surface organisms in flocks, one colony taking 1,000 tons in day. Upright stance on colonies, where 'mumbles and grunts' (Murphy). Breeding season practically continuous but peak December-January. Some colonies estimated 8,000 years old. Both sexes incubate usually 3 chalky nile-blue eggs in nest of debris and may brood young together. **49**

Phalacrocorax carbo *Phalacrocoracidae*
CORMORANT *c.* 36 (body *c.* 22) ins
Holarctic, Oriental, Australasian, Ethiopian; almost cosmopolitan but discontinuous: mainly coastal W Europe (including Iceland), but inland from lower Danube River across Eurasia, mainly between 40° and 50°N, to Manchuria and Japan; Indian subcontinent and Ceylon, S China, then gap to E and SW continental Australia, Tasmania, New Zealand; NW and SW African coasts, mainly inland down E side, Ethiopia to S Africa; N American footholds Gulf of St Lawrence, W Greenland. Resident and migratory, depending on access to food fish; habitat from rocky coasts with sheltered bays and estuaries to lakes, pools, marshes, river valleys; sea level to mountains in tropics. Upperparts bronze-brown, feathers edged black; otherwise glossy blue-black, except for white chin, extending to throat in African race *lugubris*, white thigh patch, and 'frosted' plumes on neck (briefly in spring). Legs black, hooked bill grey, base and throat sac yellowish; cinnamon skin under blue eyes. Juvenile dark brown, underparts becoming white, mottled brown. Flight rapid, regular, neck, feet stretched, low over water; sometimes soars and slides. Rather upright posture on rock or tree, often holding wings half open. Waddles on land; swims low, either submerging quietly or diving with jump; uses feet underwater on dives of *c.* 1 minute. Food almost entirely fish from near bottom; some crustaceans. Mutual display initiated by ♀. Silent except when nesting when various guttural croaks and softer calls uttered. Breeds colonially March onwards in Europe; on rocky ledges or slopes; in trees, often dead, from 6 to 30 ft up. ♀ and ♂ build nest of twigs, seaweed, dry stalks, debris, lined finer material. 3 or 4 pale blue eggs with chalky white deposit incubated ♀ and ♂ 27–29 days. Both feed young, who fly *c.* 7 weeks. Possibly 2 broods some areas. **50**

Phalacrocorax varius *Phalacrocoracidae*
PIED CORMORANT 32 ins
Continental Australia, Tasmania, New Zealand and Lord Howe Island. Sedentary, on coastal islands, also swamps, lakes and estuaries. Upperparts black, glossed dark green, wings bronze-grey glossed green and feathers bordered black; underparts from chin white; legs black, bill dark horn but variable, pouch yellow, eyes sea-green surrounded blue skin, with yellow spot in front. Often associates with other cormorants, and feeds mainly on estuarine fishes. Calls deep croak and monotonous wheeze. Two peaks of breeding, September to December and March to July, apparently involving different birds; colonies on trees, e.g. mangroves, bushes, ground or cliffs; nests of sticks lined feathers and leaves. Both sexes incubate 3 to 5 chalky bluish white eggs and tend the young. **51**

Phalaenoptilus nuttalli *Caprimulgidae*
POOR WILL 7½ ins
Nearctic, marginally Neotropical: breeds NW North Dakota, SE British Columbia, S to Central Mexico and from W Iowa, E Kansas, Central Texas W to Pacific; winters from S Texas, S California to Central Mexico; dry open country with scattered scrub; sometimes open forest. ♂: upperparts pale grey-brown patterned with dark cross markings; flight feathers, tail barred dark and light brown, and white-tipped; crown greyish; dark mask; white throat bordered dark brown below; underparts mottled. ♀ shows less white on tail; juvenile's pattern less defined, throat buffish. Legs, bristle-fringed bill dark grey, eyes dark brown. Famous as only bird of which individuals have been proved to hibernate, clinging to crevice in rock face. Roosts during day under cover on ground or on tree branch. Flight mothlike, wavering, as it hunts flying insects, sometimes watching them from ground and making quick sally. Call 'harsh and melancholy' (R. H. Pough) *poor-will-ee*. Breeds May to July, laying 2 white eggs (pinkish when fresh) on bare ground, rocks or near grass tuft or low shrub.

PHALAROPE,
GREY see **Phalaropus fulicarius**
RED see **Phalaropus fulicarius**
RED-NECKED see **Phalaropus lobatus**

Phalaropus fulicarius *Phalaropodidae*
GREY OR RED PHALAROPE *c.* 8 ins
Holarctic; discontinuous circumpolar range, mainly in arctic zone, as far S as Iceland (very local) and Hudson Bay; winters mainly in plankton-rich seas off coasts of N Chile and W Africa. Breeds shores of freshwater pools in moss or grass tundra, sometimes by sea. Summer: upperparts dark brown with light streaks; wings brown with white bar, dark grey tips and trailing edge; rump and tail dark grey edged white; white patch round eye and cheek; underparts chestnut brown; legs horn, bill yellow, tip black, eyes brown; ♀ brighter than ♂. Winter: upperparts grey; black stripe through eye, rest of head and underparts white; bill dull yellow. Singly, in parties or flocks on passage. Swims habitually like small, bouyant gull. Call, short *twit*, becomes twittering from flock. ♀ dominates courtship. Takes water insects and larvae (mosquitoes), small crustaceans (gammarids), picked off water after being disturbed by rotation and leg movements; also feeds on land. Breeds second half June in S of range, ♀ choosing scrape among debris and littoral vegetation. 4 buff eggs, often heavily marked dark brown and chestnut, incubated by ♂ at least 19 days. He tends young, sometimes helped by ♀, 16-20 days. **303**

Phalaropus lobatus or Lobipes lobatus
Phalaropodidae
RED-NECKED PHALAROPE *c.* 6½ ins
Holarctic: broader band than Grey Phalarope, extending farther S, to Scotland and Ireland, Aleutian Islands; winters Arabian Sea, probably also N of New Guinea and off Peru. Breeds neighbourhood of bog pools and on tundra from sea level to subalpine zone. Summer: upperparts, wings and tail much as Grey Phalarope, *P. fulicarius;* head, nape, sides of breast and flanks grey; white throat patch extends over neck, bordered below and behind by broad orange band; underparts white, legs blue-grey, thin bill blackish, eyes very dark brown; ♀ brighter than ♂. Winter very like Grey Phalarope but back darker and needle-like bill distinctive. Remarkably tame and resembles Grey Phalarope generally in habits. Complicated courtship on water with ♀♀ taking lead and pursuing ♂♂. Call *twit* lower-pitched than Grey Phalarope, repeated by ♀ in ceremonial flight. Food as Grey Phalarope, probably more flying insects. Breeds singly, socially from end May; scrape well hidden close to water holes. 4 pale green to buff eggs, heavily marked dark brown. Incubation by ♂ 20 days; he tends young 2½-3 weeks. **304**

Phaps histrionica *Columbidae*
FLOCK PIGEON *c.* 11½ ins
N Australia S to Minilya R. in W Australia, north-eastern S Australia and north-western New South Wales; occasionally visits coastal areas. Habitat: open country, grassland or semi-desert, sometimes with scattered cover. ♂: strikingly marked, black and white about head contrasting with rufous back, bluish grey underparts and white lower throat; upperparts light reddish brown, wing quills bluish grey with coverts edged white, metallic blue speculum on inner quills, outer feathers of short tail bluish grey spotted white. ♀: duller with only faint indications of ♂'s markings. Legs pink-grey, bill blackish, eyes dark brown. Flight strong, often fairly high. Nomadic usually in large flocks; ground feeder, taking seeds and young leaves. Call: soft double *coo* when breeding. Food supplies control breeding; 2 creamy white eggs in scrape or depression in ground sheltered by clump of grass or bush. **372**

Pharomachrus mocinno *Trogonidae*
QUETZAL 14 (add 24 for ♂'s tail plumes) ins
Neotropical: S Mexico to Costa Rica and Panama; resident rain forest of oaks, alders, laurels up to 9,000 ft in S, 7,000 ft in N of range. ♂: upperparts, including head, narrow ridged crest, neck and upper breast intense iridescent green; lower breast, belly, under tail coverts crimson; golden green wing coverts hide black flight feathers; upper tail coverts golden green glossed blue or violet, two central feathers elongated to form train; outer tail feathers white; legs blackish, bill yellow, eyes black. ♀: upperparts as ♂, but head smoky grey; breast and much of belly dark grey; lower belly and under tail coverts paler than ♂; longest upper tail coverts only slightly exceed tail; outer tail feathers narrowly barred black; bill, eyes black. Upright perching posture, fanning tail when alarmed; ♂ drops backward off perch to save train. Undulating flight, calling *wac wac;* varied vocabulary of musical calls. ♂ circles above ♀ in display; also flies erratically, vibrating plumes. Diet: small fruit off trees taken in flight; small reptiles, insects, especially beetles, small snails. Breeds April onwards, taking over or ♀ and ♂ excavating hole in decayed tree with shaft up to 12 ins; entrance 14 to 60 ft up; used for second brood if still serviceable. 2 light blue eggs laid on bare chamber. Incubated ♀ and ♂ 17-18 days; ♂ sits facing hole with train bent over head and projecting up to 12 ins. Parents tend young *c.* 31 days; 2 broods. **481**

Phasianus colchicus *Phasianidae*
RING-NECKED PHEASANT ♀, 21-25 (tail 8-10), ♂: 30-35 (tail up to 20) ins
S Palaearctic, NE Oriental: wild (40 subspecies) from SE Russia, Asia Minor E to Mongolia, SW China, Korea, Japan, Taiwan, Burma; introduced Europe, N America, New Zealand. Native habitat dense reedbeds, deciduous woodland with thick cover interspersed by cultivations; introduced into farmland, thickets, even moorland edge. ♂: variable, but usually burnished copper with pale U's on back, black crescents breast and flanks, bars on long tail; metallic dark green head with eartufts sometimes separated by white collar; wings mottled brown. ♀: brown with buff Us and black crescents like ♂. Legs horn-grey, bill pale horn-green, facial skin red round hazel eyes. Probably skulking in native habitats except for wing-rattling display of ♂ with loud *kok kok* crows; *kuttuk kuttuk* when flushed, many other notes. Food varied throughout range, mixed vegetable (shoots, seeds, berries) and invertebrates, occasionally small vertebrates. Breeds March onwards in Europe, polygamous; ♀ lines scrape in thick cover, lays 8 to 15 olive brown eggs, incubates them 22-27 days; precocious young fly 12-14 days; ♂ seldom helps. **204**

Phegornis mitchellii *Charadriidae*
MITCHELL'S or
DIADEMED SANDPIPER PLOVER   7 ins
Neotropical: puna (rocky Andean slopes) zone of Peru from Lima, Junins, to Argentina (Chubut), Chile (Churico); mountain bogs, lake and riversides, 10,000 to 16,000 ft in N of range, wintering 6,500 to 10,000 ft. Upperparts orange rufous to brown; head, neck dark grey, divided from crown by white bar; white spot below eye; underparts vermiculated grey and white; white breast patch; ♀ duller; legs orange, slightly curved bill black, eyes dark brown. Very little studied. Clear, penetrating and low, plaintive whistles on breeding ground. Feeds on insects from water or riparian plants. Breeds October, laying 2 olive-buff eggs, well marked black and dark brown, in sparsely lined scrape on river shingle or sand, incubated ♀ and ♂; both also tend the young.

Pheucticus ludovicianus see **P. melanocephalus**

Pheucticus melanocephalus or P. ludovicianus
Fringillidae
ROSE-BREASTED GROSBEAK   8 ins
Nearctic: breeds from Central Canada SE to N USA: Central New Jersey, mountains of Georgia, Central Ohio, S Missouri, Central Kansas; winters from S Mexico to Venezuela, Ecuador. Habitat essentially edge between tall forest and secondary or shrub growth, e.g. by rivers, streams, pools, marshes; also in cultivated areas, parks, residential suburbs. ♂: upperparts, including whole head, throat, wings, tail, glossy black, but white on wing (2 bars, patch on outer edge), rump, tail (especially underneath); upper breast, under wing coverts rosy red, underparts white. ♀: striped (especially crown), streaked, barred dark brown, buff and white (underparts). Legs blackish, bill white (♂), yellow horn (♀), eyes very dark brown. Immature ♂ much as ♀ but traces red on buff breast band. Song: melodious warble of 12 to 24 rapidly uttered whistling notes; call: sharp 'almost metallic' *clink*. Food: wild seeds, fruits; insects important in summer, including 'potato bug' (Colorado beetle); feeds both treetops and near ground, actions 'almost parrotlike'. Several ♂♂ chase ♀ in courtship. Breeds mainly June; frail nest of twigs, stems, lined grass, rootlets, 6 to 15 ft in fork or on lateral branch of tree. 3 to 5 greenish blue eggs, spotted brown over purple at big end, incubated ♀ and ♂ (who may sing softly on nest) *c.* 14 days; both parents feed young. **927**

Philemon argenticeps see under **P. yorki**

Philemon corniculatus *Meliphagidae*
NOISY FRIARBIRD OR LEATHERHEAD   12¾ ins
Australasian: tropical and temperate continental areas from Cape York to Lakes Entrance; seasonally nomadic. Habitat open forest scrub, cultivated land, gardens. Upperparts grey brown, darker on tail; bare head black and pink with white ruff upper back; 'bearded' silvery chin, throat with black lines; underparts cream; white tips under tail feathers; legs dark grey, bill black with knob at base, eyes red. Noisy and aggressive, feeding on trees in canopy and secondary layers, but may sit quietly, and less active than other friarbirds. Gurgling calls rendered as *poor soldier*, *Pimlico, four-o-clock;* often in chorus from dead tree. Diet: insects (catching termites, beetles in flight),

nectar, native and cultivated fruits, doing damage to orchards. Breeds August to December or January; nest deep cup of bark, grasses bound cobwebs, cocoons, neatly lined dry grass; suspended from hanging branch, often over water, up to 50 ft or more. 2 to 4 pinkish buff eggs, marked chestnut over dull purplish grey. **846**

Philemon yorki *Meliphagidae*
HELMETED FRIARBIRD   13 ins
Australasian: continental N, E Queensland, Thursday I. Habitat open forest country, often swampy. Upperparts brown; head silvery whitish with light brown streaks; underparts silvery brown; bare face and 'helmet' or casque on forehead black; legs, bill black, eyes brown. Differs from Silver-crowned Friarbird, *P. argenticeps*, in smoother back of head and rise of helmet, which is rounded knob in *argenticeps*. Aggressive to other birds as it searches flowering trees, but shyer with humans than other friarbirds. Very noisy: call repeated *poor devil poor devil*. Diet: insects, nectar, native fruits and berries. Breeds August to January; nest of bark strips, grass, rootlets, woven together, lined fine grasses, rootlets; usually suspended from fork of tree up to 40 ft or more. 3 or 4 pinkish white eggs, spotted and boldly marked reddish brown over dull purple. **847**

Philepitta castanea *Philepittidae*
VELVET ASITY   *c.* 6 ins
Madagascar: confined to East; resident wooded mountain slopes, sea level to 5,500 ft. Plump; ♂: velvety black with slight purple sheen; small yellow patch at 'wrist'; blue wattle curves from flange at base bill (blackish, broad at base, becoming narrower and curved) over and round red eye; legs black. Immature ♂ without wattle has yellowish fringes to feathers. ♀ mainly olive green above, underparts yellowish or greenish white, edged olive. Rather inactive, perching in low bushes but not on ground; occasionally in treetops to sun itself; also in secondary growth. Makes short flights. Usually singly or small parties; sometimes with flocks of mixed species. Reported to have whistling, thrushlike song (A. L. Rand). Food mainly small berries from low bushes. Lays from end August, building pear-shaped rather compressed nest, top woven into supporting twigs, 'porch' over side entrance, of mosses, plant fibres, dead leaves, lined broad dead leaves; *c.* 6 ft in sapling over rocky watercourse. Clutch probably 3 pure white eggs (Rand).

Philesturnus carunculatus see **Creadion carunculatus**

Philetarius socius *Ploceidae*
SOCIABLE WEAVER   5½ ins
Ethiopian: resident dry areas of W and Central Southern Africa. Crown to nape earth brown; sides of neck, mantle, scapulars, flanks 'scaly' due to blackish feathers with buff margins; rest of upperparts earth brown; flight feathers with broad buff margins; outer tail feathers blackish, tipped brown; lores, chin black; underparts stone-brown; legs light brown, bill horn, eyes dark brown. Crown of immature spotted blackish; lores, chin buffish white. Found in flocks of few to several hundred, quarrelsome, feeding on ground: grass seeds, insects; independent of water. Call: nasal *klok klok*. Breeding season variable. Nests communally, roof of strong twigs on branch of isolated tree covers nest chambers of finer stems, sharp ends aligned along entrance tunnel, above which rounded chamber occupied by pair throughout year. Some sites occupied for 100 years. Flocks leave daily to feed in open country. 3-4 dull white eggs, thickly marked pale olive and slate grey. **958**

Philidonyris albifrons see **Gliciphila albifrons**

Philohela minor *Scolopacidae*
AMERICAN WOODCOCK   10-12 ins
Nearctic: SE Canada mainly down E side USA to N Florida, S Louisiana; winters from New Jersey, Ohio to Florida, Texas. Habitat: damp woodlands and scrub, meadows. Upperparts as Eurasian Woodcock, *Scolopax rusticola*, with 4 dark brown bars on crown

and nape; dark brown wing tips; fanned tail rufous, with black and white border; underparts almost uniform warm brown extending to under wing coverts; legs flesh-brown, long bill horn brown, tip dark, eyes black-brown. Crepuscular, behaving much as Eurasian relative but display quite distinct. ♂ calls low, nasal *peent*, ascends with trilling noise of wings to *c.* 200 ft, utters bubbling warble, 'volplanes' down to pitch abruptly near ♀. Food probed with bill from soft ground. Breeds April onwards in N of range; scrape, lined leaves, under thin cover holds 3 or 4 buff eggs, marked yellow-brown; incubation by ♀ *c.* 21 days; young fly from 4 weeks (W. Sheldon). **291**

Philomachus pugnax *Scolopacidae*
RUFF   ♀: 8½-10; ♂: *c.* 11-12 ins
Palaearctic: broad zone NE from Scandinavia, Britain, Netherlands (isolated areas W France, Hungary) through temperate to arctic zone in N Siberia; winters close to breeding areas and S to S Africa and Oriental region, round shallow lakes and pools, muddy shores and estuaries. Breeds grassy marshes and wet meadows in SW to lightly wooded or bare tundra. Spring ♂ unique with ruff and eartufts in several colours (black, white, purple, red-brown, barred buff) above bare yellow wattled face; upperparts heavily mottled dark and light brown; narrow white wing bar; tail dark with oval white patches at side; underparts white, legs variable shades yellow, bill black-brown, eyes dark brown. ♀ and winter ♂ mottled dark brown above, throat to belly buffish brown, underparts white. Holds itself straighter than Redshank, *Tringa totanus*, often stretching neck upward. Parties or flocks on passage and in winter. In spring renowned displays of ♂♂ on 'hills' in breeding area, with mainly mock fights watched by ♀♀. Diet: variety of insects taken off vegetation; also worms, snails, small crustaceans. Breeds from first week May in S of range, making usually very well hidden, lined scrape in grass tuft, often not far from 'hill'. 4 pale grey to greenish eggs, heavily marked dark brown and ash grey, incubated by ♀ 21 days; she tends young for *c.* 4 weeks; ♂♂ promiscuous, take no part in nesting. **292**

Phlegopsis nigromaculata *Formicariidae*
BLACK-SPOTTED BARE-EYE   7 ins
Neotropical: E Colombia to N Bolivia; Amazonian Brazil; resident in forest undergrowth. Upperparts olive brown spotted black; flight feathers and tail rufous chestnut; head, neck, breast and upper belly black; lower belly olive brown; legs, bill dark grey, eyes dark brown. Insectivorous. **569**

Phloeoceastes melanoleucos *Picidae*
BLACK AND WHITE or
CRIMSON-CRESTED WOODPECKER   14 (bill 2) ins
Neotropical: Central America, Trinidad, S America E of Andes to N Argentina; resident forests, swampy woods, plantations, grassland with scattered trees (campo), sea level to 5,000 ft. ♂: predominantly black; crest, crown, cheeks crimson; white patch base of bill; small black and white patch ear coverts; white lines down sides of neck join in patch upper back; underparts barred buffy white and black; base of flight feathers and under wing coverts white. ♀ has centre of crown black; white stripe down neck begins at bill. Legs yellowish grey, bill greyish horn to ivory, eyes yellow, facial skin yellowish to blue-grey. Behaviour and habits in general as other woodpeckers. Breeds April Trinidad, excavating hole in dead stump or tree and laying 2 glossy white eggs.

Phoebetria palpebrata *Diomedeidae*
LIGHT-MANTLED SOOTY
ALBATROSS   25-30 ins; wing-span *c.* 6 ft
Two subspecies in southern oceans from Antarctic to 40°S. Brown, dark on wings and wedge-shaped tail, very dark on head, with white on eyelids; legs flesh-white, bill mainly black, eyes dark hazel. Immatures similar. Will follow ships but more suspiciously than other albatrosses, and takes offal, quarrelling over it with 'hollow, ghostly trumpetings' (Murphy). Normal diet squids and fish near surface. Distinctive *pee-oo* call at breeding places, which are occupied from October

to May, not gregariously, though sometimes in small groups on cliff ledges and terraces, where one whitish egg laid in pile of mud and plant material, incubated for *c.* 60 days by ♀ and ♂; they also tend chick during fledging of *c.* 3½ months. **26**

Phoeniconaias minor *Phoenicopteridae*
LESSER FLAMINGO 40 ins
Ethiopian (E and S Africa, Madagascar) and Oriental (NW India); on brackish lakes inland and coastal lagoons; may wander outside breeding season and nest outside usual range. Pinker than Greater Flamingo, *Phoenicopterus ruber*, with black flight feathers and upper wing blotched darker on lighter crimson; legs red, bill red, tip black, eyes light yellow. World population estimated 4½ m. of which 1 m. pairs may nest on single E African lake, with huge flocks outside breeding season manoeuvring in mass formation for evening take-off to feed; also communal displays. Voice in flight a goose-like honking. 'Organic soup' filtered through platelets on insides of both mandibles from surface of water, usually without submerging head, which is swished from side to side. Relatively few but huge breeding colonies known, with first eggs laid March or early April in E Africa, in cone-shaped mud nest with hollow on top. 1 to 3 chalky white eggs incubated by ♀ and ♂ for *c.* 4 weeks; chick, fed by parents for some weeks, flies at 65-70 days. Each population believed to breed once in 3 years. **89**

Phoenicoparrus andinus *Phoenicopteridae*
ANDEAN FLAMINGO *c.* 48 ins
Neotropical: confined to puna zone of SW Peru, plateaus of W Bolivia, extreme N Chile and NW Argentina; brackish lakes up to 12,500 ft for breeding, migrating to lowland marshes. White plumage tinged pink, becoming carmine at base of neck and upper breast; wings carmine and black; legs (hind toe absent) yellow, bill yellow, tip black, eyes pale yellow. Behaviour little studied, but believed to resemble other flamingoes and to be highly social. Feeding methods like Lesser Flamingo, *Phoeniconaias minor*. Eight breeding colonies known; details of nesting, incubation and fledging apparently like Lesser Flamingo. **90**

Phoenicopterus ruber *Phoenicopteridae*
GREATER FLAMINGO Nearly 60 ins (♂ larger than ♀)
S Palaearctic, Oriental, Ethiopian (E coast Africa), Neotropical (very local W Indies, NE South America, Galapagos); coastal areas, but inland in Caspian region; post-breeding dispersal over SW Asia. Habitat saline lagoons. Generally pinkish-white but American, *Ph. r. ruber*, bright rose pink all over, confined to upper wing in other races; flight feathers black; legs deep pink, bill tip black, rest and facial skin pink, eyes yellow. Gregarious with mass displays in breeding areas. Flies in undulating lines, long neck and feet extended, with goose-like honking. On ground flocks gabble and have variety of other notes. Fewer platelets on inside of bill than Lesser Flamingo, *Phoeniconaias minor*, and takes greater range of food: small molluscs and crustaceans as well as minute plants, much of it from bottom of lake. Breeding season variable throughout range; colonies of closely packed cone-shaped mud nests with hollows on top, built by ♀ assisted by ♂. Both incubate 1 or 2 white eggs for 28-32 days, then feed chick at first until it joins kindred flock, to fledge at *c.* 11 weeks. **91**

Phoeniculus bollei see under **P. purpureus**

Phoeniculus purpureus *Phoeniculidae*
GREEN WOOD HOOPOE 15-16 ins
Ethiopian: most of sub-Saharan Africa outside the W African forest zone, where replaced by Forest Wood Hoopoe, *Scoptelus castaneiceps*. Different races of this and other closely allied species of wood hoopoes and scimitar-bills frequent several types of woodland, including orchard bush, gallery forest, acacia woodland and highland forest (the White-headed, *P. bollei*). All are slim, long-tailed arboreal birds with slender down-curving bills; their general colour is black glossed green or violet. *P. purpureus* has white wing-bar, white-tipped tail feathers, red bill, feet. All nest in tree-holes, climb about like woodpeckers, often hang upsidedown like tits seeking insect food. Most are sociable, noisy birds; *P. purpureus's* alternative name *kakelaar* accurately describes its harsh chattering call. It lays 3 to 5 pale blue eggs in a hole, generally of a live tree. **510**

Phoenicurus ochruros see under **P. phoenicurus**

Phoenicurus phoenicurus *Muscicapidae: Turdinae*
REDSTART 5½ ins
Palaearctic: almost all continental Europe, including Britain; Asia Minor, Caucasus, Iran; very local NW Africa; E into Siberia between 50° and 60°N as far as Lake Baikal; winters S of Sahara to Equator. Habitat open canopy broadleaved and pine woods sometimes with thick undergrowth, up to subalpine tree limit and arctic birch zone; also gardens, parks, orchards, roadsides; scrub and savannah in winter. ♂: upperparts grey, wings very dark brown, tail orange-chestnut; forehead white, face, throat black; breast, flanks orange shading to white belly; obscured in winter by white feather edges and mottled underparts. ♀: upperparts light grey-brown, tail as ♂; underparts pale buff. Legs, bill black, eyes dark brown. Juvenile like Robin, *Erithacus rubecula*, but tail chestnut. All plumages of Black Redstart, *Ph. ochruros*, greyer. Bright quivering tail conspicuous as bird flits about trees, sallying into air after insects. Much more in open on migration. Call *hweet* becomes scolding *hwee-tucc-tucc;* song brief tuneful warble; sometimes mimics. Food: great variety small insects and other invertebrates off trees, bushes, ground; berries in autumn. Breeds end April to July Britain; ♀ builds nest of grass, moss, other plant material, softly lined: in holes in trees, rocks, buildings, walls, behind bark, in nestboxes and old nests; in tunnel under ground vegetation. 5 to 7 blue eggs, sometimes tinged greenish or faintly spotted reddish, incubated by ♀ 13-14 days; both parents feed young, who fly 14-16 days. Occasionally 2 broods. **698**

Phylloscopus collybita *Muscicapidae: Sylviinae*
CHIFFCHAFF 4¼ ins
Palaearctic: from Canaries, extreme NW Africa, Ireland and Britain over Europe (except parts Iberia; Greece and islands; much of Scandinavia) in broad band across Asia between 50° and 70°N to taper off about 150°E; separate area Asia Minor, Caucasus, N Iran; winters Mediterranean area, N Africa and across Arabia to parts of N and Central Indian subcontinent. Habitat: small woods, overgrown hedgerows, riparian scrub, montane broadleaved and coniferous forests to *c.* 6,000 ft Alps and 6,500 ft Altai; also parks and gardens with rhododendrons especially N Britain. Upperparts brownish olive green; 'eyebrow' pale yellow; wings, tail dark brown, feathers edged olive green; underparts whitish; throat, breast, flanks streaked yellowish buff; under wing coverts lemon yellow. Juvenile browner. Races vary as to amount of yellow and green and confusion exists with Plain Willow Warbler, *P. neglectus*, of SW Asian montane forests. Legs dark brown, bill blackish brown, eyes dark brown. Small parties outside breeding season, sometimes with other species. Restless and active, searching foliage for insects and hawking them in air. Call and alarm note soft, plaintive *hooet*, higher pitched and less dissyllabic than Willow Warbler, *P. trochilus;* song: repetition of two notes which give English name in irregular sequences, sometimes with grating churr interposed. Courting ♂ follows ♀ with quivering wings and sibilant variant of song, or floats on slowly flapping wings. Breeds from late April, ♀ building rounded nest of leaves and rather coarse stems with side entrance, lined feathers, usually from few inches to 3 ft above ground in brambles, dead sticks overgrown with vegetation, low bushes, often evergreen, and lower branches of trees. Usually 6 white eggs, evenly spotted purplish brown, incubated ♀ *c.* 13 days. Young, fed mainly ♀, fly *c.* 14 days. Often 2 broods in S. **743**

Phylloscopus neglectus see under **P. collybita**

Phylloscopus sibilatrix *Muscicapidae: Sylviinae*
WOOD WARBLER 5 ins
Palaearctic: mainly European, between 45° and 63°N with extensions or discrete areas Pyrenees, Italy, Yugoslavia, Crimea, E coast Black Sea and to Urals; winters Central Africa. Habitat: broadleaved woods, especially oak, birch, beech, with sparse undergrowth; also subalpine spruce and mixed montane forest; winters in forest and savannah. Upperparts green; wings, tail dark brown, feathers yellow-edged; 'eyebrow' sulphur yellow; chin, upper breast pale sulphur yellow, under wing coverts yellow, rest underparts pure white. Winter and juvenile duller and browner. Legs pale yellowish brown; bill: upper, blackish brown, lower, yellowish flesh; eyes brown-black. More arboreal than relatives, like them searching leaves for insects and sallying into air; also takes berries in autumn. Stance often horizontal, wings drooping. ♂'s display flight like dragonfly, descending in spirals; also slow butterfly action; much posturing and quivering on perch. Call: plaintive, piping *pu-u*. Songs: single note repeated with increasing speed to loud trill; sustained *pu-u*, stronger than call, repeated 7 to 14 times; sometimes uttered on wing. Breeds mid May onwards, ♀ building domed nest of grass, fibres, moss, with quite large side entrance, usually in slight depression on ground; lined fine grass, hairs, not feathers; concealment varies in dead leaves, bracken, grass tussocks, often on bank. 5 to 7 white eggs, thickly speckled purplish brown over grey, incubated ♀ *c.* 13 days. Young, fed ♀ and ♂, fly 11-12 days. **744**

Phylloscopus trochilus *Muscicapidae: Sylviinae*
WILLOW WARBLER 4¼ ins
Palaearctic: 3 races in broad band across Eurasia from Britain and Ireland mainly between 50° and 70°N, extending farther S in Western Europe to about 170°E; these E Siberian birds migrate *c.* 7,500 miles to winter in tropical or S Africa with rest of species; in savannah and forest up to 9,000 ft. Breeds open woodland to bushy scrub, usually with scattered trees; also riverine mixed forest of taiga, bush tundra, steppes with open birch woods. Upperparts olive green, yellower on rump; wings, tail dark brown, feathers edged olive green; 'eyebrow' yellow; underparts whitish with yellow streaks mainly on breast; under wing coverts yellow; legs pale to dark brown, bill brown, eyes hazel. Juvenile has yellower underparts, but adult very hard to distinguish from Chiffchaff, *P. collybita*, except by voice or in hand. Less restless than Chiffchaff; displays with slow wing flaps while perched. Call: plaintive dissyllabic *hoo-eet;* song: liquid rippling phrase down scale with flourish at end. Food mainly small insects, berries in autumn. Breeds end April onwards, ♀ building domed nest of grass, moss, fibres, with side entrance to fine grass cup lined feathers; usually very well hidden in ground vegetation, occasionally up to 5 ft on 'platform'. 6 to 7 pale pink eggs, spotted light red or heavily marked dark red-brown, incubated ♀ *c.* 13 days. Young, fed ♀ and ♂, fly 13-14 days. **745**

Phytotoma rara *Phytotomidae*
CHILEAN OR RUFOUS-TAILED PLANTCUTTER 8 ins
Neotropical: Chile (Atacama to Aysen), Argentina (Neuquen to Rio Negro); resident with local seasonal movements: open scrub, orchards, gardens; mountain valleys up to 6,500 ft in spring. ♂: upperparts olive brown, streaked black; wings black, some coverts edged white; central tail feathers dusky, others with outer web and tip black, inner webs chestnut or rufous; crown chestnut, cheeks black, moustachial stripe and lower ear coverts white; underparts rufous. ♀: upperparts olive brown; streaked black; narrow pale double bar on wings; tail as ♂; throat buff, underparts buff streaked black. Legs short; bill stout, conical, serrated; eyes orange yellow. Sometimes in small parties; flies sluggishly. ♂ has 'unmusical, rasping trill' (J. D. Goodall) from exposed perch. Food: buds, shoots, young leaves, fruit; considered pest by farmers. Breeds October to December; nest foundation of twigs, cup lined small twigs, rootlets; in fork of lateral branch on thorny bush, shrub, fruit tree. 2 to 4 greenish blue eggs, spotted dark brown or black.

Piaya cayana *Cuculidae*
SQUIRREL or
CHESTNUT CUCKOO $15\frac{1}{2}$-$17\frac{1}{2}$ (tail 9-10) ins
Neotropical: Mexico S to N Argentina on E and NW
Peru on W of Andes; resident in forest, savannah,
cerrado (plateau scrub), 'cocoa woodland' (Trinidad).
Upperparts chestnut brown; very long tail maroon
above, black below, strongly graduated, each feather
broadly tipped white; throat and neck pale cinnamon;
underparts grey darkening to black on belly and under
tail coverts; legs dark grey, bill yellow-green, eyes
crimson, orbits red or yellow. 'Squirrel-like in movements' (G. A. C. Herklots), restless and inquisitive.
Calls: loud *tic tic tic* and sharp *wick-kerr*. Diet insectivorous. Breeds July Trinidad, building nest of sticks
in thick bush *c.* 20 ft up, laying 2 white eggs, tinged
yellow. **428**

Pica pica *Corvidae*
(BLACK-BILLED) MAGPIE   body *c.* 9, tail *c.* 9 ins
Holarctic: across Eurasia to E China (apart from
Tibet); Morocco, Algiers and Tunisia; Kamchatka,
S Alaska, SW Canada and Central USA; sedentary,
some local movement. Habitat: woodland, low bushes
and scrub; cultivated land, usually with plentiful
cover, but more open regions where less persecuted.
Head to upper breast and mantle, and inner scapulars,
black glossed blue-purple; rump white to brown, rest
of scapulars and breast, flanks and belly white; wings
partly black, variously glossed, inner webs primaries
mostly white; long wedge-shaped tail black below,
bronze green above with subterminal band of red-
purple merging into blue-purple and green-purple at
tips. Legs and bill black, eyes dark brown. Flight
slowish with fairly rapid wing-beats; solitary, pairs,
small, sometimes large parties; may perch on back of
sheep and search for insects in fleece. Call: fast, harsh
chattering. Food similar to Crow, *Corvus corone,*
chiefly insects, greater tendency to rob nests; usually
feeds on ground; hoards food and bright objects.
Breeds March onwards, solitary; nest of twigs and
mud lined inner layer fine roots and grass, usually
covered by canopy of thorny twigs with side entrance;
in trees near top, thick bushes or sometimes ground
vegetation; 5 to 7 greenish or yellowish eggs, densely
mottled brown and grey, incubated by the ♀ 17-18
days. Both parents tend the young, who fly 22-27
days. **1007**

Picathartes gymnocephalus *Muscicapidae:
Timaliinae*
GREY-NECKED ROCKFOWL   14 ins
Ethiopian: Sierra Leone, Ghana, Togo; resident
humid montane forests with ground layer of mossy
boulders. Upperparts slaty grey and soft; flight and
tail feathers brown; 2 black patches at back of head;
rest of head bare, bright yellow; neck and underparts
silky white; powerful legs and feet light grey; big
bill blackish, large eyes dark brown. Mainly ground-
living, taking long, graceful hops over rocky terrain,
flying little on rounded wings. Inquisitive about man.
Low croaking call, but generally quiet. Food: insects
(follows ant columns), snails, crustaceans, small frogs
from forest streams. Breeds socially March to September (Ghana), several pairs sticking mud nests, lined
plant fibres and feathers, to usually overhung rock
face, 5 to 15 ft up. 2 creamy-white eggs, heavily
marked brown. White-necked, *P. oreas,* confined to
Cameroon, has bare skin of head blue and red; habits
believed to be similar. Probably 2 broods.

Picathartes oreas see under **P. gymnocephalus**

PICULET, SCALED see **Picumnus squamulatus**

Picumnus squamulatus *Picidae*
SCALED PICULET $3\frac{1}{2}$ ins
Neotropical: N Venezuela and Colombia; resident in
forests sea level to *c.* 6,000 ft. Upperparts olive brown,
feathers edged blackish, margins of inner flight feathers
yellowish; underparts off-white, black margins to
feathers giving scaled appearance. Usually solitary;
perches crosswise on branches; soft tail feathers give
no support on tree trunks. Usual undulating woodpecker flight but rather weak. Forages through creep-

ers and along forest edge after small insects, extracted
also from rotten wood. Can only excavate nest hole in
rotten wood, but general breeding habits as larger
woodpeckers e.g. *Celeus elegans.* **552**

Picus canus *Picidae*
GREY-HEADED WOODPECKER   10 ins
Palaearctic and Oriental: across Eurasia from S
Scandinavia and France, mainly between 50° and
60°N, to Sakhalin, Hokkaido (Japan) and SE Asia to
Sumatra, with extension W in Himalays; resident.
Where Green Woodpecker, *P. viridis,* also occurs,
found in denser forests with conifers; otherwise in
mixed and broadleaved woodland up to 9,500 ft in
Asia; also groups of trees in cultivated land, parks,
gardens and orchards. ♂: upperparts light green,
yellower on rump, flight feathers and tail brown with
light bars; forehead red, black streak from bill to eye,
also moustachial stripe; throat white; rest of head and
underparts grey; ♀ has no red, but black spots on
crown. Legs and bill greyish; eyes light yellow. Call
like 'yaffling' laugh of *P. viridis* but slower and falls
away at end; also drums on dead limbs. Feeds largely
on ants on ground, except when in competition with
P. viridis; also insects and their larvae mainly from
bark and wood of decaying trees. Breeds from end
April in Europe, excavating hole in broadleaved tree.
5 to 7 white eggs incubated by ♀ and ♂ *c.* $2\frac{1}{2}$ weeks;
both feed young, who fly *c.* $3\frac{1}{2}$ weeks. **553**

Picus viridis see under **P. canus**

PIED
    BARBET see **Lybius leucomelas**
    BUTCHERBIRD see under **Cracticus
        torquatus**
    CORMORANT see **Phalacrocorax varius**
    CURRAWONG see **Strepera graculina**
    FLYCATCHER see **Ficedula hypoleuca**
    HORNBILL, INDIAN see **Anthracocerus
        malabaricus**
    KINGFISHER see **Ceryle rudis**
    STARLING see under **Creatophora cinerea**
    WAGTAIL see **Motacilla alba**
    WAGTAIL, AFRICAN see **Motacilla aguimp**

PIED-BILLED
    GREBE see **Podilymbus podiceps**
    GREBE, GREAT see **Podilymbus gigas**

PIGEON,
    BROWN see **Macropygia phasianella**
    CAPE see **Daption capensis**
    CRESTED see **Ocyphaps lophotes**
    FLOCK see **Phaps histrionica**
    GREEN see **Treron australis**
    OLIVE see **Columba arquatrix**
    PINTAILED GREEN see **Treron sphenura**
    RED-BILLED see **Columba flavirostris**
    SPECKLED see **Columba guinea**
    SQUATTER see **Petrophassa scripta**
    WHITE-COLLARED see **Columba albitorquis**
    WHITE-QUILLED ROCK see **Petrophassa
        albipennis**

PIGEON GUILLEMOT see **Cepphus columba**

PILEATED PARAKEET see **Purpureicephalus
spurius**

PILOT BIRD see **Pycnoptilus floccosus**

PINE BUNTING see **Emberiza leucocephala**

PINK ROBIN see **Petroica rodinogaster**

PINK-FACED NUTHATCH see **Daphoenositta
miranda**

PINTADO see **Daption capensis**

PINTAIL see **Anas acuta**

PINTAILED
    GREEN PIGEON see under **Treron sphenura**

WHYDAH see **Vidua macroura**

Pionus sordidus *Psittacidae*
RED-BILLED PARROT   11 ins
Neotropical: tropical and subtropical zones, N Venezuela, Colombia, E and W Ecuador, E Peru, N
Bolivia; resident in forests, often montane. Back dull
green, feathers sandy-edged in some races; under tail
coverts and inner webs outer tail feathers red; crown
dusky green; throat and upper breast blue, underparts
pale green to olive-brown; legs, bill red. Probably
c. 4 white eggs in dead tree. **401**

Pipilo erythrophthalmus *Emberizidae: Emberizinae*
RUFOUS-SIDED TOWHEE   8 ins
Nearctic: marginally Neotropical; western race
breeds Canada southward through USA to N. Mexico;
eastern, southern races to Florida, with gap in mid
West. But winters almost whole USA to Mexico.
Habitat woodland edge and clearings with heavy
undergrowth; abandoned farmland, scrub, gardens.
♂: upperparts, including head, breast, black (spotted
white in western race); white wingbars and outer
edge primaries; white outer tips of long rounded
tail; lower breast, belly white, flanks rufous, under
tail coverts orange-buff. ♀ brown where ♂ black, but
tail blackish. Legs light grey, bill slate grey, eyes red
(white in southern race). Juvenile rich brown above,
buff below, streaked darker brown. Noisy and conspicuous though lives close to ground; wings rustle in
flight. Call 2-note *to-whee;* song rendered *Drink your
teeee.* Scratches litter with both feet to attack insects
in humus; also some fruits, berries in season. Breeds
from early May New England, ♀ building nest of
coarse stems, leaves, bark, lined fine bents, rootlets,
hair, usually well hidden in ground cover; shrub,
tussock stump, dead sticks; sometimes up to 5 ft in
bush. 4 to 6 white eggs finely spotted red-brown,
incubated mainly ♀; young fledge 10-12 days. **863**

PIPIT,
    AUSTRALIAN see **Anthus novaeseelandiae**
    GOLDEN see **Tmetothylacus tenellus**
    MEADOW see **Anthus pratensis**
    NEW ZEALAND see **Anthus novaeseelandiae**
    PLAIN-BACKED see **Anthus leucophrys**
    RED-THROATED see **Anthus cervinus**
    RICHARD'S see **Anthus novaeseelandiae**
    SANDY PLAIN-BACKED see under **Anthus
        leucophrys**
    TREE see **Anthus trivialis**

Pipreola riefferii *Cotingidae*
GREEN AND BLACK FRUITEATER   8 ins
Neotropical: N and W Venezuela, Colombia, E and W
Ecuador, Peru; resident in forests and secondary
growth from *c.* 4,000 to *c.* 8,000 ft. ♂; upperparts,
including tail, grass green, inner flight feathers with
narrow terminal white band; crown and sides of head
greenish to iridescent black; throat and upper breast
dark to blackish green, bordered narrow yellow line;
underparts yellow mixed with green; legs and bill
yellow to orange yellow. ♀: head and breast green like
back. Keeps to understorey but ventures into open
spaces after berries. Surprisingly high-pitched staccato
chatter (A. H. Miller). Long or discontinuous breeding season; nest *c.* 5 ft up in tree, bush, vine, of green
moss blending with trunks, lined rootlets. Clutch 2
eggs, cream with mid brown spots mainly in zone. **593**

Piranga rubra *Emberizidae: Thraupinae*
SUMMER TANAGER $7\frac{1}{2}$ ins
Nearctic, marginally Neotropical: breeds Delaware,
Central Ohio, SE Wisconsin, SE Nebraska, Central
New Mexico, SE California, S to S Florida, Gulf
Coast, N Mexico; winters Central Mexico, S to
Guyanas, Peru. Habitat dry open woodlands of pine,
oak, hickory, including secondary growth; outskirts
of towns. ♂: uniformly rosy red all over. ♀: upperparts
olive green, brightest on wings; underparts yellow,
brightest under tail. Juvenile autumn like ♀ but more
orange, ♂ in first spring often mixed red and green.
Legs dark grey, bill yellow, eyes dark brown. Arboreal
like all tanagers, roosting trees, bushes and singing rich
melodious phrases, resembling American Robin,

Turdus migratorius, from high perch; Call: rapid *chick tucky tuck*. Feeds largely on insects, catching bees, wasps, beetles on wing, also tearing open small wasp nests (A. F. Skutch); some seeds in autumn. Breeds May-June, ♀ builds shallow nest of stems, bark strips, leaves, lined fine grasses, near end of lateral branch 10 to 15 ft up. 3 or 4 pale bluish or greenish eggs, marked brown, incubated ♀ 12-14 days; ♀ and ♂ tend young. **877**

Pithecophaga jefferyi *Accipitridae*
MONKEY-EATING EAGLE   *c.* 36 ins
Oriental: Mindanao and perhaps Luzon in Philippines; recently extinct Leyte and Samar Is; owing to persecution, killed for specimens or collected for zoos, down to estimated 50 pairs. Habitat: heavy forest, *c.* 500 to 4,000 ft. Upperparts dark grey-brown, pale edges to feathers of wings and mantle; elongated erectile feathers on crown and nape buff with dark shaft streaks; underparts white with rufous streaks on thighs; sides of throat and lesser under wing coverts, chin streaked with black; tail brown with 4 or 5 darker bars. Legs dull yellow, bill greenish blue, eyes blue-grey. Usually seen flying silently amongst trees, occasionally soars over forest; feeds on flying lemurs, monkeys, squirrels and birds. Call: long, mellow whistle. Observed pair laid mid November; large nest of branches and sticks lined twigs, often leafy, high in tree; site used year after year and clearly indicated by heaps of bones below; 1, sometimes 2, eggs incubated mostly by ♀ for *c.* 60 days. Young fully feathered 9 weeks and fledge *c.* 15 weeks; ♂ brings food for ♀ and young.

Pithys albifrons *Formicariidae*
WHITE-PLUMED ANTBIRD   4¼ ins
Neotropical: Guyana, S and NW Venezuela, E Colombia S to E Peru and Amazonian Brazil; resident forest and savannah, sea level to 4,000 ft. Back and wings grey; collar at nape, rump, tail and underparts chestnut; white plumes on forehead sweep back to form 'horns', those on chin form 'beard'; head dark grey, white stripe behind eye; legs reddish, bill dark grey, eyes brown. Mainly terrestrial, seldom higher than 15 ft, in parties of up to 25, feeding largely on ants and termites and following army ants to pick up disturbed insects and spiders. **570**

Pitta angolensis see under **P. brachyura**

Pitta brachyura *Pittidae*
BLUE-WINGED or FAIRY PITTA   7 ins
E Palaearctic and Oriental, widespread Indian subcontinent, SE Asia, extending to Korea and Japan, northern populations migratory; can be treated as one species with African Pitta, *P. angolensis*, breeding from Congo and Central Tanzania to Transvaal, and Noisy Pitta or Dragoon Bird, *P. versicolor*, of E Australia from Cape York to N New South Wales. Habitat generally dense primary or secondary forest and scrub; also mangrove swamps, plantations and gardens. A brilliant member of a brilliantly coloured family: upperparts green, rump and much of wing cobalt blue, latter with black, white and green bars; short tail barred black and blue terminally; crown brown with black central streak meeting broad mask at back of neck; throat white; underparts fawn shading to crimson; legs horn-grey to flesh, bill dark horn, eyes dark brown. Feeds on ground, scratching insects and spiders from leaves; also takes hornets; in Australia fond of slugs and snails, smashing shells like thrush on stone or stump; small shrimps also recorded (Asia). Runs very fast but takes wing readily with whirring quail-like flight, perching high in trees.

Bobs and flirts short tail like dipper. Aggressive crouch with feathers fluffed out, wings spread, bill pointed upwards. Noisy before rain, whistling *walk to work* (Australia) and other calls. Breeding season varies throughout wide range; builds large untidy oval ball-like nest of bamboo leaves, moss, grass, roots, sticks, with finer lining; entrance at side; on bank of forest stream, between buttress roots of trees, in thorny bushes (Africa). 2 to 5 white or creamy eggs, heavily marked red and purple, incubated by ♀ and ♂, who both feed the young. **572**

Pitta guajana *Pittidae*
BANDED or BLUE-TAILED PITTA   8 ins
Oriental: Malaysia to Borneo; resident in dry lowland jungle Malaysia, but between 2,000 and 4,000 ft Borneo; often near habitations. Upperparts dark brown, including wing with conspicuous narrow white bar; tail dark blue; head black with yellow stripe over eye broadening at back of neck; throat white surrounded bright light yellow; underparts yellow closely barred black, with blue patch on belly (absent on duller ♀); legs brown, bill black, eyes brown. Habits as family; hops fast, settles low bushes. Food: ants, cockroaches and soft-bodied insects. **573**

Pitta gurneyi *Pittidae*
GURNEY'S PITTA   9 ins
Oriental: Burma and Thailand; resident evergreen forest, particularly in valleys and with sparse undergrowth. ♂: upperparts brown; hind crown iridescent light blue, broad black mask; throat white, bordered buff below; centre underparts black, flanks yellow, partly barred blackish brown; under tail coverts pale blue. ♀: crown and nape yellow; underparts yellow barred black. Legs flesh pink, bill dark brown, eyes brown. Reluctant to fly, hops away when approached. Alarm note *kirrr,* also sharp double note uttered with flapping wings and jerking tail; noisy morning and evening. Habits much as other pittas; breeds October Thailand; clutch 4 eggs. **574**

Pitta versicolor see under **P. brachyura**

Pityriasis gymnocephala *Laniidae*
BORNEO BRISTLEHEAD or
BALD-HEADED WOOD SHRIKE   10 ins
Oriental: confined to Borneo; resident lowland peat swamp and forest up to 4,000 ft. ♂: generally slaty grey; crown golden, rest of partly bare head, neck, throat to upper breast red, with grey bristle patch on ear coverts; lower belly red; legs yellow; massive hooked bill black; eyes brown. ♀ has red spots on flanks. Usually in small parties, moving slowly through middle canopy and not easily alarmed; sometimes break into chorus, 'rolling note' followed by nasal whining; also crow-like harsh calls. Food mainly insects, perhaps especially beetles, and their larvae; spiders. Little known of nesting; egg white, spotted brown and slaty grey, mainly at big end.

Platalea leucorodia *Threskiornithidae*
EURASIAN SPOONBILL   34 (body 15) ins
Palaearctic, Oriental and NE Ethiopian; breeds N temperate Eurasia E to China and S to India; winters tropical Africa, SE Asia. Habitat open marshes, mud-flats, estuaries, breeding in thick cover. White, with

nuptial crest, orange patch on throat and yellow at base of neck in summer; juveniles have black wing-tips and short ibis-like bill. Legs black, spatulate bill black with yellow tip, eyes red, facial skin black and yellow. Often at rest on one leg on ground but perches in trees. Parties fly in line with regular flaps, sometimes gliding. Can swim short distances. Silent, apart from 'low grunting sound'; young squeak or wheeze. Feeds mainly at dusk, sweeping end of bill under water to pick up variety of water animals from fish and amphibians to insects, also plant stems and fruits. Breeding season variable, from April in Europe; forms dense colonies of own species in reed beds, bare islets, bushes and trees; nest of sticks, debris or reeds holds usually 3 or 4 eggs, dull white with brown markings. Parents incubate them for *c.* 3 weeks, then feed young which leave nest *c.* 4 weeks, fly *c.* 7 weeks. **84**

Platycercus elegans *Psittacidae*
CRIMSON ROSELLA   13½ ins
Australasian: confined to strip of continental Australia from NE Queensland to near Adelaide; resident mainly montane sclerophyll and rain forests up to 6,000 ft, savannah woodlands and clearings; suburban gardens, city parks. Generally rich crimson, back feathers black-centred; wings, under wing coverts blue; median upper coverts black; tail green, washed blue; cheeks violet-blue; legs grey, bill greyish-horn, eyes brown. Juvenile dull green with red on crown, breast, under tail coverts. Undulating flap-glide flight, frequently spreads tail on alighting. Pairs or small flocks, with juveniles staying together. Often with Eastern Rosella. *P. eximius*, but species separate if disturbed. Rests in shade, chattering softly, stripping twigs and leaves. Calls: repeated three-note whistle; screech of alarm. Food: grass and other seeds from ground, e.g. thistles; blossoms and fruits of eucalypts, acacias, other native and introduced trees; acorns; nectar; insects and their larvae; may damage orchards. Breeds September to January in tree hole at varying heights. 5 to 8 white eggs laid on decayed wood, incubated by ♀, who leaves nest to feed and be fed by ♂, *c.* 3 weeks; fledge *c.* 5 weeks. **402**

Platycercus eximius see under **P. elegans** and **Psephotus haematodus**

Plectopterus gambensis *Anatidae*
SPUR-WINGED GOOSE   30-36 ins
Ethiopian: 2 races spread across middle half of Africa; Spur-winged Goose, *gambensis*, from Gambia, Sudan and Ethiopia down to Zambesi; Black Spur-winged Goose, *niger*, S of Zambesi into S Africa. Habitat: lakes and swamps. ♂: large black and white goose; upperparts iridescent bronze and green, wing shoulder mostly white and tipped with spur, underparts, face and throat white. ♀: duller, lacking ♂'s small red patch on side of neck; spur and white shoulder patch smaller. Southern race smaller with black flanks and less white on face. Dull purplish red legs, bill and frontal knob; eyes brown; bare skin on face and neck grey, on top of ♂'s head dull red. Often perches in trees; shy; gregarious, often in large numbers, spends day on open water or in swamps; visits (flocks in strings) morning and evening feeding places on cultivated areas or grassland where young stems taken along with other plant matter such as fruits and nuts. Call: high pitched whistle. Breeds all months, making large nest of reeds and roots well formed into cup, usually in grass or reed beds but sometimes in ant hills or old tree-nests; 7 to 12 shining ivory-white eggs. **125**

Plectorhyncha lanceolata *Meliphagidae*
STRIPED HONEYEATER   8½ ins
Australasian: E continental from mid-Queensland to S Australia; nomadic in autumn. Habitat scrub of native pine *Callitris,* she-oak *Casuarina,* mallee. Upperparts from crown grey, streaked (lanceolated) with black-centred feathers becoming dark brown wings, white-tipped tail; narrow pale 'eyebrow'; chin, throat white; underparts off-white indistinctly streaked dark brown on belly; legs slate blue, bill bluish horn, eyes brown. Pairs or small parties work blossom and foliage like relatives. Song: *chirp chirp cherry cherry chirp;* loud whistling calls like Olive-backed Oriole, *Oriolus*

sagittatus. Diet: insects, nectar, especially from *Nicotina*, fruits, sometimes damaging orchards. Breeds August to December; purse shaped nest of grasses, rootlets woven with plant down, wool, occasionally Emu feathers, lined fine grass, hair feathers; usually suspended near end 'weeping' branch of *Callitris* or other tree, up to 30 ft. 3 or 4 very pale pinkish white eggs, minutely speckled reddish-brown over purplish grey, concentrated at big end. **848**

Plectrophenax nivalis *Emberizidae: Emberizinae*
SNOW BUNTING   *c.* 6½ ins
Holarctic: right round N Eurasian and American coasts and on arctic island groups, most northerly breeding passerine; southernmost groups: Scotland, Labrador, Aleutian Is, Kamtchatka; sedentary or migratory S to 35°N. Habitat rocky lichen tundra, rocky coasts, mountain tops, nunataks in land ice; also villages, encampments, even towns in Greenland; winters open coasts, salt marshes, cultivated land, hilltops (Scotland). ♂: pure white except for black back, primaries, central tail feathers, but most of year obscured rusty brown on head, breast; back brown mottled black but wings stay mainly white. ♀ much as winter ♂, less white on wings and tail. Legs black, bill black (summer), brownish yellow (winter), eyes brown. Juvenile similar. Normally runs, but can hop. Perches rocks, low buildings, fences, also trees in USSR. Swift undulating flight. Flocks in winter, birds 'leapfrogging' each other as they feed on seeds, grain; young fed insects; also takes seeds, buds. Usual calls musical *tirrirririripp*; high-pitched *tweet*; *tuu* of anxiety; short loud song typically *turee turee turee turi-wee*. ♂'s song flight 20-30 ft up with stretched wings, tail, fluttering beats; also has erratic darting flight and displays to ♀ on ground. Breeds end May to July; ♂ accompanied ♀, builds foundation dark moss, cup of grass, lined fine stems, few to many feathers; generally 6 ins to 2 ft or more in scree, below boulders, rock crevice, wall or other artefact, even nestboxes. 4 to 6 off-white, bluish or greenish eggs, boldly marked red and dark brown over violet, incubated ♀ 12-13 days; both parents feed young, who leave nest 10-12 days. Often 2 broods in S of range. **864**

Plegadis falcinellus *Threskiornithidae*
GLOSSY IBIS   *c.* 22 (body 12) ins
S Palaearctic (temperate Eurasia), Ethiopian (including Madagascar), Oriental, Australasian, SE Nearctic, Neotropical (W Indies); winters tropical Africa, Asia. Habitat marshes, lagoons and flooded land; also mudflats and shore. Rich purple-brown, darker on wings and tail, glossed green and purple; duller in winter. Legs pale greenish-brown, bill dark grey-brown, eyes dark brown, facial skin purplish black. Gregarious, usually in parties, flying with rapid wing action or gliding, in compact groups or undulating lines, sometimes plunging downwards *en masse*. Wades, swims if necessary, probes mud for leeches and wide range of water animals. Generally silent but utters guttural croak and grunts. Breeding season varies in enormous range: colonies, often large and with other species, in reed beds, bushes, or trees over water. Nest of sticks, lined with greenery, holds usually 3 or 4 deep green to blue eggs, incubated by ♀ and ♂ *c.* 3 weeks. Chicks fed by parents in nest for *c.* 2 weeks, then leave and are fed communally. **85**

Plocepasser mahali *Ploceidae*
STRIPE-BREASTED or
WHITE-BROWED SPARROW WEAVER   6 ins
Ethiopian: Ethiopia, S Sudan, S Somalia, E Africa S to S Africa; Angola; local resident dry bush, acacia and other thorn and mopane scrub; short grass plains, cultivated areas, villages. Upperparts including ear-coverts light brown; wings, tail dusky; flight feathers pale-edged; white tips to upper tail coverts show as band on closed wing; rump, upper tail coverts white; head, lores, moustachial stripe blackish; conspicuous white 'eyebrow'; underparts whitish; legs light brown, bill blackish grey, eyes brown. Pairs or small parties, usually near breeding colony. Call: harsh *chick chick;* 'pleasant, loud, challenging song' (O. P. M. Prozesky), often continued after sunset; chittering at colonies. Takes insects, mainly from ground; probably independent of water. Breeding season variable; forms large colonies usually on one side of group of trees; untidy retort-shaped nest, with entrance below, protected by prickly stalks, lined grass tops, feathers, often second hole at side to roosting chamber. 2 or 3 cream or pinkish white eggs, freckled red over grey, often in zone. **959**

Ploceus cucullatus *Ploceidae*
SPOTTED-BACKED or
BLACK-HEADED WEAVER   7 ins
Ethiopian: most of region except SW Africa and Cape; resident tall forest, especially near water; cultivated areas and near habitations. ♂: upperparts mottled black and yellow; rump, upper tail coverts grey mottled yellow; flight feathers blackish, edged pale yellow; tail olive-grey; forehead yellow tinged orange; crown, nape yellow finely mottled black; cheeks, chin, centre throat black; underparts yellow; legs flesh; bill black, eyes red. ♀: upperparts dull brown, mottled on back; wings, tail as ♂; forehead, nape, cheeks yellow-green finely streaked darker; underparts yellow shading to white; side breast, flanks greyish-brown; bill horn. Non-breeding ♂ somewhat as ♀, but upperparts brown or ash grey, streaked darker; underparts yellow to buffish. Immature similar but browner above. Gregarious, feeding on seeds, cultivated grain, but also flower juices. Alarm call, sharp *zip;* repeated *chuck chuck* when carrying nest material. Flocks, normally noisy, may become silent and fly away from colony, circling about before returning, comparable to 'dreads' at tern colonies. Breeding season variable within range; ♂ builds suspended kidney-shaped nest from drooping and stripped twigs of thorn, introduced eucalypt, often over water. ♀ then takes over and lines with soft material and polygamous ♂ may leave after mating. Usually 3 greenish blue eggs, variably speckled reddish or brown, incubated ♀, who also rears young. **960**

Ploceus manyar *Ploceidae*
STRIATED WEAVER   4½ ins
Oriental: Pakistan, India, Ceylon, Burma (except S), Annam, Thailand, Indonesia (Java, Bali, Bawean); resident tall grassland, reedy margins of ponds and lakes; large flocks roost swampy reed beds. ♂: upperparts tawny brown, streaked darker; flight feathers, tail dark brown; crown to nape yellow; face, chin very dark brown; underparts tawny, boldly streaked black on breast. ♀, non-breeding ♂ have brown heads. Call: *chit chit chit*; attractive song in courtship chase and invitation to nest; continual chittering while building. Diet mainly seeds, grain; raids paddy fields. Breeding between February and September dependent on SW monsoon and paddy cultivation. Large colonies in marshy reedbeds, *kaing* grass (Burma), rushes; ♂ builds several nests, retort-shaped, woven into living stems, with short entrance hole below; 'cock nests' plastered mud and dung along inner edge, breeding nest softly lined. 2 to 4 pure white eggs, incubated ♀; ♂ has several mates. **961**

PLOVER,

Pluvialis apricaria *Charadriidae*
GOLDEN PLOVER   *c.* 11 ins
NW Palaearctic: temperate and subarctic (2 races) from Iceland to NW Siberia; southerly migration or local movements after breeding. Habitats: rough grassland and grass moors; dry or wet heather moors, disintegrating bogs, tundra; grassland and coastal flats in winter. Upperparts spangled black and gold; in summer northern race *P.a. altifrons* shows white band between them and black underparts; difference much less clear cut in southern *apricaria*. Flight feathers blackish, under tail coverts partly white, tail barred black and gold. Underparts pale in winter and races indistinguishable; legs greenish grey, bill black, eyes dark brown. Winter flocks often with Lapwings, *Vanellus vanellus*, splitting off into fast flapping flight with simultaneous twisting of bodies from light to dark characteristic of waders. On ground runs a few paces, stops, bending to probe for food, variety of invertebrate animals from soil and grass layers. Usual call *tlui*; also musical trilling; in spring ♂♂ perform in air with wailing 'song' *terr pee-oo terr pee-oo*; also communal displays and scrape-forming on ground. Breeds from end March Britain, much later in far N, sometimes socially. Lined scrape, often on slight mound, sometimes partly sheltered, holds 3 or 4 buff eggs, boldly marked dark red-brown often in zone. Incubation by ♀ and ♂ 27-28 days; parents tend young, injury-feigning when threatened, fledging *c.* 4 weeks. **265**

Pluvialis dominica *Charadriidae*
LESSER or PACIFIC GOLDEN PLOVER   9½ ins
E Palaearctic and Nearctic: Asian race *fulva* in arctic zone Siberia, W Alaska; American *dominica* in arctic Canada; summer visitors, wintering far S in Oriental, Australasian, Neotropical regions. Breeds arctic tundra; in winter on grasslands, sand and mud flats. Summer plumage like small, darker Golden Plover, *P. apricaria* of northern race, with golden spangled upperparts, white band round forehead to shoulders, black underparts, but axillaries and underwing grey, not white. Winter upperparts duller, underparts pale. Legs greyish black, bill black, eyes brown. Habits like Golden Plover; flight calls *tuu* and quavering *quee-i-i-a* from passage flocks in N America; many other notes recorded. Food in summer insects, small molluscs, crustaceans, spiders, worms, *Vaccinium* and *Empetrum* berries, marine invertebrates on migration and in winter. Breeds in S from early, in N from late June. Sparsely lined scrape, often on bare ridge, holds usually 4 light buff eggs, heavily marked dark brown; incubation as *P. apricaria*; young fledge *c.* 30 days. **266**

Pluvialis squatarola *Charadriidae*
GREY or BLACK-BELLIED PLOVER   *c.* 11 ins
Holarctic: subarctic and arctic; N coastal areas Siberia, Alaska, Canada and some islands; summer visitor, wintering all round world from S America to Australia. Breeds dry tundra; stones, moss, lichens; winters along estuaries and saltings, inland by pools and lakes. Summer plumage: upperparts spangled silver-grey and black with white border from forehead to scapulars; underparts black, under tail coverts white; flight feathers and axillaries blackish, tail barred black and white. Winter upperparts brownish-grey, underparts white or pale ash-brown. Legs ash-grey, bill and eyes black. Resembles Golden Plover, *P. apricaria*, but more on shore in winter, mixing with other waders. Territorial ♂♂ display fly spring; usual call high-pitched *tlee-oo-ee*; harsh alarm note; triple whistle in spring. Food: insects and variety of small marine animals. Breeds from end May Alaska. Lined scrape in moss or peat holds usually 4 light buff eggs, marked dark brown often in zone. Incubation by ♀ and ♂ 23 days; both parents tend young. **267**

Pluvianellus socialis *Charadriidae*
MAGELLANIC PLOVER   8 ins
Neotropical: Chile (Magallanes) and N Tierra del Fuego; winters Argentina N to Chubut; seaside lagoons with bare shores. Upperparts from crown bluish grey, paler on forehead; main flight feathers dark brownish grey with white bar across secondaries; underparts from throat white with brownish breast band; upper tail coverts white with black central streak; tail brownish black, edged white; under tail coverts curl round tail; short legs pink; straight, pointed bill mainly black, large eyes crimson. Runs with speed; 'headlong, twisting' flight. Food: minute water animals, e.g. crustaceans. Breeds November (Tierra del Fuego), laying 1 or 2 smoke grey eggs, spotted and scrawled dark brown, in scrape on bare ground or among shingle on shore.

Pluvianus aegyptius *Glareolidae*
EGYPTIAN PLOVER   8 ins
SE Palaearctic (Egypt); Ethiopian: Senegal across to Eritrea, S to Uganda, Angola; banks of lakes and rivers, sometimes in villages. Crown, neck, mask, upper back with elongated feathers, and breast band all black, washed bottle-green; wings grey, flight feathers black and white; lower back and tail grey, tipped black and white; throat and 'eyebrow' white; breast and underparts creamy buff; legs blue-grey, short bill black, eyes brown. Juvenile lacks green wash and is more tawny. Unafraid of man and reputed to enter crocodile's mouth. Flight jerky like Common Sandpiper, *Tringa hypoleucos*. Calls *chee chee chee* on wing, and repeated *creek creek*. Feeds on insects and small molluscs. Breeding season varies throughout range; 2 or 3 eggs, cream speckled and scrawled dark brown and black, are partly or wholly buried in sand, bird sitting over them; chicks also buried in sand, moistened with regurgitated water, and shaded by parents. **313**

POCHARD,
   AFRICAN see **Netta erythrophthalma**
   RED-EYED see **Netta erythrophthalma**

Podargus strigoides *Podargidae*
TAWNY FROGMOUTH   *c.* 19 ins
Australia and Tasmania: resident in forests, spreading to suburban areas. Upperparts dark grey-brown, mottled lighter, with bars on tail and wings; faint pale stripe over eye; underparts pale, flecked darker; bristles round light brown bill, eyes orange red. Found singly or in pairs. Nocturnal, spending day asleep in frozen upright position on end of snag. Call, repeated booming or grunting *oom*. Aggressive display by opening huge pale gape, fluffing feathers, extending wings and clapping them. Feeds by pouncing from perch on ground-living animals from insects to mice. Breeds August to December, builds platform of sticks in tree up to 40 ft. 2 to 4 rounded whitish eggs incubated by ♀ *c.* 30 days; both parents feed young, who fly *c.* 35 days. **455**

Podica senegalensis *Heliornithidae*
AFRICAN or PETER'S FINFOOT   24 ins
Ethiopian: throughout region except NE and SW; sedentary by slow-flowing rivers, pools, streams in forest, among mangroves on estuaries. ♂: upperparts brown, washed blue or peacock green and spotted white; stiff-shafted tail dark brown; crown and nape blackish with white stripe down each side, throat and breast blue-grey, belly whitish or dark grey; legs bright red, bill red, tip horn-brown, eyes dark brown. ♀: brighter, with whitish throat and breast and yellow eyes. Juveniles paler than ♀. Shy, scuttling to cover when disturbed; normally swims low in water, but nimble on land, climbing tree trunks then dropping into water; no evidence of diving unless alarmed. Various calls from croaks and growls to booming note. Searches floating water plants for dragonfly larvae, but takes many small water animals. Breeds throughout year near Equator, September to November in S; nest on horizontal branch, fallen tree or flood debris holds usually 2 glossy pale buff or cream eggs, heavily streaked dark brown and lilac; incubation probably by ♀ and ♂.

Podiceps auritus *Podicipedidae*
SLAVONIAN or HORNED GREBE   12½-15 (body 8) ins
Holarctic: temperate to subarctic zones of Eurasia and North America, migrating south in autumn to edge of subtropical; winters mainly offshore. In spring dark brown above with orange 'ear' tufts, flanks chestnut, underparts white, as in winter when uniform dark brown above; legs and bill black, eyes scarlet. Swims buoyantly and dives frequently after small aquatic animals, and flies readily after long take-off. Mutual displays at breeding colonies; usually solitary in winter. Call: rippling trill in spring; also harsh notes. Breeds May to July, building floating nest in aquatic vegetation, e.g. sedges; eggs 3 to 5, white and pointed, soon stained and covered when not attended. Incubation 3-3½ weeks by ♀ and ♂, who also care for striped young, independent in *c.* 30 days. **18**

Podiceps cristatus *Podicipedidae*
GREAT CRESTED GREBE   19 (of which body 12) ins
Temperate Palaearctic, Ethiopian and S Australasian, northern birds moving south in autumn to winter offshore or on large lakes. In spring upperparts dark with short 'horns' and chestnut tippets; underparts whitish as in winter, when dark brown above with white cheeks; legs greenish, bill mainly pink; eyes crimson. White wing bar shows in flight. Swims low with straight neck, diving for *c.* ½ min after small fish; also insects, crustaceans, some plant stems. Classic mutual displays of which head waggling most spectacular, accompanied by barks, groans and other calls; persistent *pee-ah* hunger cry of chicks. Breeding season varies with range: March to September in Palaearctic. Floating nest in reed bed or other cover holds 3 to 6 chalky white, soon stained eggs, incubated *c.* 4 weeks by ♀ and ♂; they care for striped chicks, often splitting brood, for up to 2½ months. **19**

Podiceps ruficollis see **Tachybaptus ruficollis**

Podilymbus gigas *Podicipedidae*
GREAT PIED-BILLED GREBE   18 ins
Neotropical: confined to Lake Atitlan, Guatemala, at 5,000 ft. Resembles Pied-billed Grebe, *P. podiceps*, but twice the size: mainly dark brown with streaked flanks and white under tail; throat very dark brown in spring, streaked white in winter; legs slaty, bill heavy, white in spring with black central band, otherwise brownish; eyes brown. Apparently almost flightless, spending day out in open water or in thick cover. Little known of habits and believed that young preyed on by introduced fish. Numbers probably less than 100 birds. Breeding much as *P. podiceps*; clutch 4 or 5 white eggs.

Podilymbus podiceps *Podicipedidae*
PIED-BILLED GREBE   13 ins
Nearctic, Neotropical: breeds from Nova Scotia, S Ontario, Central Manitoba, S Mackenzie, Central British Columbia throughout Americas to S Argentina; winters from New York southward on Atlantic, from S British Columbia on Pacific coast. Habitat: small pools to large lakes, marshes with channels; also coasts and estuaries in winter. Generally grey brown, darker on upperparts; face, neck pale buff; chin patch black in summer, white in winter; underparts barred dull brown and whitish; under tail coverts white; legs blackish, blunt compressed bill white with median black band, eyes dark brown, orbits white. Juvenile has brown and white head pattern, no band on dusky bill, resembling winter adult. Skulking, often submerging except for bill. Early spring migrant, remaining until ponds freeze in autumn. Spring call: series of loud, ringing *cow-cow-cow* notes; also wailing and grunting. Diet: variety of water animals: fish, frogs and tadpoles, snails, insects. Breeds May onwards, building mound nest of water plants, floating sometimes in feet of water but anchored to growing stems and usually well hidden. 5 to 7 blue or greeny white eggs soon stain-brown; incubation by ♀ and ♂ 23-24 days. **20**

Poephila gouldiae *Estrildidae*
GOULDIAN FINCH   *c.* 5 ins
Australia: tropical northern areas; some southward

movement to breed. Habitat: riparian grasslands with tall trees; edges of mangrove swamps and thickets. ♂: upperparts bright green; flight feathers mostly brown; rump blue; tail with elongated central feathers black; head, cheeks, throat black bordered blue; narrow yellow band on nape; breast light purple; underparts yellow, under tail coverts white. Red-headed phase occurs (about 1:3 to black) and rare yellow-headed. ♀ duller especially on back. Legs yellow, bill greyish-white tipped red, eyes very dark brown. Immature generally ashy grey and brown; legs, eyes brown, bill black and white. Pairs or flocks, fond of sunbathing. Flight call: *twit twit twit*, also 'drawn-out mournful note' and social call of 7 syllables; high pitched whispering song inaudible at distance. Ritualised but variable courtship: ♂ presents plumage to ♀, sings. Mating always in nest. Bill-wiping and body shaking displacement activities. Rarely feeds ground, climbing grass and reed stems after seeds; takes more insects than relatives, especially for young, hawking in air; also spiders from webs. Drinks by suction like pigeon. Breeds socially January to April, even June; small thin-walled nest, sometimes none at all, usually in tree hole or termite mound, sometimes in bush or tall grass. 4 to 8 white eggs become discoloured by same-sized pieces charcoal carried into nest; incubation ♀ and ♂ 12-13 days; both feed young, who fly *c.* 3 weeks and mature very quickly, ♂♂ breeding when 8 weeks old. 2 or 3 broods. **942**

Pogoniulus bilineatus *Capitonidae*
GOLDEN-RUMPED TINKER BIRD   4 ins
Ethiopian: Uganda, Kenya S to Natal, in forest areas. Glossy black above, golden yellow rump; pale grey, greenish yellow below; white stripes above, below eye; stout bill able to excavate nesting hole in tree, where 2 to 4 white eggs are laid. The several species of tinker birds are small barbets feeding in thick foliage on fruit, insects. Get their name from resonant bell-like *tink*, endlessly repeated. **528**

Pogoniulus chrysoconus *Capitonidae*
YELLOW-FRONTED TINKERBIRD   3½ ins
Ethiopian: most of sub-Saharan African except Congolese rain-forests and Somalia. Also a forest species, but not exclusively so, and occurring woodland, dry bush. Resembles a pallid version of *P. bilineatus* with conspicuous yellow forehead. Same food, call, nesting habits. **529**

Poicephalus meyeri *Psittacidae*
BROWN or MEYER'S PARROT   9 ins
Ethiopian: 6 races cover almost whole region; savannahs with acacias, baobabs, usually near water; local movements after breeding. Upperparts sooty brown, including wingtips and tail; forehead, scapulars, under wing coverts yellow; lower back turquoise blue; tail coverts yellow-green; chin to breast brown; lower breast and flanks blue or greenish-blue, mottled brown; lower belly greenish-blue, thighs yellow; legs and bill blackish, eyes brown. Juvenile much less yellow. Gregarious in family parties after breeding. Swift flight but waddling walk. Drinks dawn and dusk; roosts tree holes. Flight call high-pitched *chee chee chee*; disyllabic conversational notes. Food: fruits, berries. Breeding season varies with range. 2 to 4 white eggs laid in tree hole (sometimes old barbet's nest) or in dense creepers. **403**

Polemaetus bellicosus *Accipitridae*
MARTIAL EAGLE   30-34 ins
Ethiopian, from Senegal and Somalia south to Cape; resident, making local movements. Inhabits savannah and thornbush, also open plains and semi-desert. ♂ upperparts brownish grey with crest, pale margins to fresh plumage, indistinct bars on wings; underparts white with dark brown spots and bars on thighs; feet and cere blue-grey, bill black, eyes yellow. ♀ larger and more heavily spotted; immature shows white spots and bars on upperparts. Largest African eagle, spends much time on wing, often at great height. Avoids settlements and roosts in trees. Hunts by slanting swoop at speed, taking birds up to bustard size, hyraxes and small antelopes. Not noisy but has clear display call and rather feeble whistle near nest.

Breeding season varies, not connected with dry or wet seasons. Builds in tree, up to 80 ft, huge nest of sticks lined with greenery, for single white egg with brown markings. ♀ usually incubates *c.* 45 days. Chick fed by both parents, flies *c.* 100 days. **161**

Polihierax semitorquatus *Falconidae*
AFRICAN PYGMY FALCON $7\frac{1}{2}$ ins
Ethiopian: Somalia and Sudan S to Orange River; sedentary in desert and thornbush. Upperparts blue grey with white collar, face and forehead; upper tail coverts white, tail and flight feathers black with white spots and bars; underparts white; ♀ has chestnut back. Legs red, bill dark, cere orange or red, eyes brown. Generally silent but has shrill rising call of repeated notes. Roosts in nests of weavers and other birds. Like shrike with hawks' bill, perches on vantage point and flicks tail (also bobs head), then sallies after flying insects; also takes reptiles and small birds. Breeding season variable. Uses nests of other species: weavers, buffalo-weavers and starlings, usually taking over when they are empty. Lays 2 or 3 dull white eggs, apparently incubated by ♀, details unknown. **172**

Polioptila caerulea *Muscicapidae: Polioptilinae*
BLUE-GREY GNATCATCHER $4\frac{1}{2}$ ins
Nearctic: breeds from S Mexico N to Great Lakes, N California; winters southern USA, Mexico, Guatemala, Cuba, Bahamas. Habitat: canopy of broad-leaved woodland; also scrubby thickets in W Indies. ♂: upperparts blue grey, flight feathers edged white; forehead narrowly bordered black; orbits, underparts white; long tail black with white outer feathers. ♀ lacks black on head. Legs, bill black; eyes dark brown. Feeds among outer branches, catching insects in flight; tail often cocked. ♂ has quiet, warbling song; twanging *ting* call also characteristic. Breeding season April onwards; ♀ and ♂ build nest of tendrils, bark, grass, covered with lichens, cobwebs, placed on lateral branch or in fork from 10 to 60 ft up. 4 or 5, bluish white eggs, heavily speckled reddish brown, incubated ♀ and ♂ 13 days; both parents feed young, who leave nest 10-12 days. **722**

Polyboroides typus *Accipitridae*
AFRICAN HARRIER HAWK or
GYMNOGENE 24-27 ins
Ethiopian: Ethiopia and Central Sudan S to Zambesi and W to Gambia; resident in forests with cultivated patches, wetter savannahs, watercourses in drier country. Upperparts grey with black flight feathers and spots on wing coverts; underparts and tail barred black and white; legs, cere and facial skin yellow, bill dark grey, eyes dark brown. Buoyant, erratic flight; spends much time in cover though has soaring and undulating display flights. Adopts extraordinary positions when probing for food; can hang head-downwards, and tarsal joint bends both ways. Call a tremulous whistle but normally silent. Food: eggs and young birds, other small vertebrates. Lays from January in N to September in S of range, building small nest of sticks, lined with leaves, in tree from 30 to 150 ft up. Usually 2 eggs, buffish with rich brown markings, incubated mainly by ♀ *c.* 5 weeks; young, fed by ♀ and ♂, fly *c.* 60 days. **162**

Polyborus cheriway see **P. plancus**

Polyborus plancus, P. cheriway or Caracara plancus *Falconidae*
CRESTED CARACARA or MEXICAN EAGLE 20-24 ins
Nearctic and Neotropical: 4 races from Southern USA (Florida, Texas, Arizona) to Tierra del Fuego, including Cuba, Isle of Pines, Falkland Islands. Resident in open or sparsely wooded country, well watered or arid. Crown (with short crest), lower back black; throat and cheeks white; broad collar and upper breast white, barred black; primaries mostly buff, rest of wing dark; tail barred buff-white with black terminal band; belly and thighs black; under wing coverts very dark brown; long legs yellow, bill whitish with blue base, facial skin red, eyes brown. Walks, runs, scratches ground almost like poultry, searching cowpats for beetles, picking up caterpillars. Attends carrion with vultures, kills injured birds and mammals up to sheep, also fish, turtles. Alarm call *trak trak trak;* cackles from perch with head thrown back: *kwik kwik kwik kwik kwerr*, origin of Caracara. Direct raven-like flight, seldom soaring; roosts in trees. Aerial fights between ♂♂ herald breeding season; lays Florida January or February; November in Argentina. Large nest of sticks in tree, tall cactus, palmetto, holds 2 or 3 white to buff eggs, heavily marked red-brown. Incubation by ♀ and ♂ *c.* 28 days; both parents feed young, who fledge 2-3 months. **173**

Polyplectron emphanum *Phasianidae*
PALAWAN PEACOCK ♀: 16 (tail 6-7) ins
PHEASANT ♂: 20 (tail 9-10) ins
Oriental: island of Palawan (N of Borneo), resident in dense, humid forests on lower slopes of hills. ♂: basically dark brown to black, but exposed feathers of mantle, wing coverts, tertiaries sheeny blue and green, as are ruff, nape and pointed crest; greater tail coverts long and broad, blackish brown spotted pale buff with large blue-green 'eyes'; tail feathers form similar outer fan; legs and bill black, eyes brown, facial skin red. ♀: generally brown, upperparts richer than underparts and freckled buff; black patches and tawny bars on wings; tail with black subterminal band; face and throat pale grey-brown, flat dark brown crest; legs, bill dark grey, eyes brown. Secretive, in pairs or family parties, but noisy: both sexes cackle; ♂ utters double whistle from tree; *hahahha* of alarm. In display ♂ fans coverts and tail, trails one wing at ♀. Diet omnivorous, but young at first need insects. Nests on ground, ♀ laying and incubating 2 rosy to buff-white eggs for 18 days; monogamous, so ♂ probably helps with brood. **206**

Polysticta stelleri or Somateria stelleri *Anatidae*
STELLER'S EIDER 18 ins
NE Palaearctic: breeds arctic Siberia, New Siberian Is and Alaska; winters on coasts of N Scandinavia and N Pacific. Frequents tundra lochs and pools during breeding; in winter prefers roughest, deepest and rockiest coastlines. ♂: upperparts pale with black on back extending forward round base of neck and up throat to bill; pale green marks on head and nape, underside and breast, used in display, reddish brown; long curved scapulars black and white. ♀: dark brown with blue speculum bordered by white. Both sexes have small rounded crest; legs and bill bluish grey, duller in ♀, eyes dark brown. Usually shy and wild; often seen in dense flocks, sometimes swimming in single file. Takes off more swiftly than other eiders; flight fast, wings making whistling noise. Feeds by day almost entirely on animal matter, diving and upending in shallows. Nests mid June to early July among mosses and grass on tundra or occasionally among rocks on coast, making hollow lined grass, moss and lichens, mixed down and feathers, and laying 7 or 8 dull yellowish olive eggs; ♀ incubates and tends young. The illustration also shows ♂ and ♀ Common Eiders, *Somateria mollissima*. **126**

Pomatorhinus erythrogenys *Muscicapidae: Timaliinae*
RUSTY-CHEEKED SCIMITAR BABBLER 10-11 ins
Oriental: Himalayas from Bangladesh across N Indo-China and S China to 30°N; Taiwan. Breeds dense forest and forest fringes, most abundant above 2,000 ft, moves to lower altitudes in winter. Generally brown above; mantle, wings, forehead, vent chestnut; nape greyer; underparts greyish-white; throat finely streaked brown; breast boldly spotted/streaked black; flanks grey; legs brown, long curved bill black, eye, pale yellow. Gregarious; feeds on ground, scratching leaf litter with both feet. Call: whistling *keerr-r*, answered by other birds. Distinctive song, series of guttural whistles. Diet includes insects, seeds. Breeds March to June. Domed nest has side entrance built grass, leaves, on ground or in low vegetation. Usually 3 or 4 glossy white eggs. **714**

Pomatostomus superciliosus *Muscicapidae: Timaliinae*
WHITE-BROWED BABBLER $7\text{-}8\frac{3}{4}$ ins
Australasian: interior southern Australia, N to Tropic of Capricorn in W Australia; local resident in open forest, mallee, arid scrub. Upperparts, including broad white-tipped tail, brown; underparts white, browner ventrally; broad white 'eyebrow' from bill to well behind eye; legs grey; long curved bill black; eyes brown. Sociable: small flocks of 6 to 12 occupy territory, feed, roost communally; also mutual preening. Many calls include reedy *churrr*, strident alarm call. Diet mainly insects. Breeds July to December. Flock builds co-operatively bulky domed stick nest, lined fine grass, bark, in outer branches of tree. Flock roosts in nest until complete (2 or 3 months) when single ♀ lays and incubates 3 brown-streaked eggs. Fledglings communally fed. **715**

POORWILL see **Phalaenoptilus nuttallii**

Porphyrio melanotus see under **P. porphyrio**

Porphyrio porphyrio *Rallidae*
(OLD WORLD) PURPLE GALLINULE 19-20 ins
SW Palaearctic (very local Mediterranean and Near East), Ethiopian, Oriental, Australasian; resident in swamps, reed and papyrus beds and other thick riparian cover, coming into open to feed. Upperparts uniform dark purple (Palaearctic) or dark green (other regions), underparts dark purplish-blue; legs, bill and frontal shield red, dark eyes red-rimmed. Australasian form, sometimes regarded as distinct species *P. melanotos,* (Swamp Hen or Pukeko) has white under tail coverts and frequently produces albinistic birds. Juveniles grey and with pale underparts in some races. Varies from shy to bold in different parts of huge range. Flirts tail and flies heavily like Moorhen, *Gallinula chloropus.* Climbs over vegetation and sometimes holds food parrot-like in one foot. Variety of calls include piercing shriek, booming, sighing, bleating and *ayik* of anxiety. Diet varied: seeds and flowers of water plants; sometimes damages crops, from bananas to rice; also insects and water animals including fish, and birds' eggs. Breeding season variable; makes substantial nest of local plant stems, clearing space around it. 2 to 10 eggs, buff with dark red spots, incubated by ♀ and ♂ *c.* 3 weeks; both parents tend the young. **231**

Porphyrula martinica *Rallidae*
AMERICAN PURPLE GALLINULE 13 ins
Nearctic and Neotropical: SE USA and W Indies to Uruguay and N Argentina; some southward movement in autumn. Habitat: freshwater swamps, marshes, ricefields. Upperparts brown, glossed bronze-green on back, washed blue on part of wings; head, neck, underparts deep purple; under tail coverts white; legs yellow, bill red, tipped yellow; frontal shield bluish-white, eyes red. Immature much duller. Can run fast over water lilies on long-toed feet, but normally stalks rather deliberately. Climbs to perch in shrubs. Swims well, usually in cover, but flies apparently feebly like relatives, legs dangling. Cackling *kek kek kek* in flight; also guttural calls. Food small water animals; seeds and other parts of plants. Breeds May onwards in USA, building basket nest of rushes and grasses in tuft or attached to rushes in water for 3 to 12 (according to latitude) pale buff eggs, spotted chestnut brown. Incubation and fledging much as Moorhen, *Gallinula chloropus.* **232**

Porzana carolina *Rallidae*
SORA RAIL *c.* 8 ins
Nearctic: N Canada to Central USA in marshes of grass and sedge, river and lakesides with *Typha* (reedmace or cat-tail) and *Zizania* (wild rice); winters from Southern USA to Venezuela and Peru in marshes and ricefields. Crown, upperparts and tail olive-brown, feathers with pale margins and black centres; forehead, cheeks and breast grey, face and centre of throat black, sides of breast and flanks barred brown and white, belly pale grey; legs green, bill yellow, eyes red; ♀ shows less black on face. Very secretive, swims and dives well, flies with apparently weak, fluttering action, legs dangling. Spring call plaintive *ker-wee;* also 'whinny' of 15 clear whistles. Diet: small water animals, seeds in autumn, especially wild rice. Breeds May and June in swamps, bogs and wet meadows, building substantial nest of local plants,

sometimes with canopy and runway. 8 to 12 brown-buff eggs, spotted red-brown, incubated by ♀ and ♂ c. 2 weeks; both tend young. **233**

Porzana plumbea *Rallidae*
SPOTLESS CRAKE or PUTOTO 8 ins
Australasian and Oriental: E and S Continental Australia, Tasmania, New Zealand, Tonga and Chatham Islands; Malaysia, Philippines. Resident in fresh and saltwater swamps and streambanks; in forest on some New Zealand islands. Upperparts dark slate merging to chocolate brown on back and wings; chin paler grey; underparts leaden grey, under tail coverts black, barred white; legs reddish, bill black, eyes red. Flies only short distance, runs fast, swims well, diving to escape enemies; usually found singly or in pairs. Three distinct calls: 'squeak' by ♂ and ♀, crooning or purring by ♀, repeated *crak crak crak* of ♂. Food small water animals; green shoots. Breeds September or October to January in Australasia. Nest of dry stems of water plants hidden in tussock holds 2 to 5 or more cream or pale blue eggs, marked light brown; incubation by ♀ and ♂ c. 2½ weeks; both tend young. **234**

POTOO,
COMMON see **Nyctibius griseus**
GREAT see **Nyctibius grandis**

PRAIRIE CHICKEN, GREATER see **Tympanuchus cupido**

PRATINCOLE,
AUSTRALIAN see **Stiltia isabella**
BLACK-WINGED see under **Glareola pratincola**
COMMON see **Glareola pratincola**
WHITE-COLLARED see **Galachrysia nuchalis**

PRINCESS STEPHANIE'S BIRD OF PARADISE see **Astrapia stephaniae**

PRION,
ANTARCTIC see **Pachyptila desolata**
BROAD-BILLED see under **Pachyptila desolata**
NARROW-BILLED see under **Pachyptila desolata**

Prionodura newtoniana *Ptilonorhynchidae*
GOLDEN or NEWTON'S BOWER BIRD
or QUEENSLAND GARDENER c. 9½ ins
Australia: 2 separate populations in dense, tangled, mountainous rain-forest in Queensland; Atherton Tableland and Bellenden Ker Range, 1,500 to 5,000 ft; Mount Cook, c. 125 miles N of Endeavour River. ♂: brownish with olive-green tint; small crest towards back of head, patch on hind neck; breast, belly pale golden-yellow; tail, apart from 2 inner feathers and distal ends of adjacent ones, pale yellow. ♀: upperparts olive-brown; underparts ashy grey. Legs, ♂ slate-blue, ♀ black, bill dark brown, eyes pale yellowish, ♀ browner. Large bower, added to each season by ♂, becoming U-shaped thick-walled structure like 2 pyramids one much larger than other, supported by 2 saplings a yard apart with low perch (display-stick) kept clear; inner wall of larger pyramid and vicinity of display-stick decorated with pale moss, lichens and flowers during breeding season; main bower may have smaller structures nearby. Call: near bower, frog-like croak; mimics. Feeds on fruits and some insects. Breeds at start of rainy season; shallow cup-shaped nest of leaves, ferns and mosses, lined thin twigs, near ground in protected position; 2 lustrous white eggs. **987**

Prionops plumata *Laniidae*
WHITE or STRAIGHT-CRESTED
HELMET SHRIKE 9 (tail c. 4) ins
Ethiopian: widely distributed in region S to Angola, Rhodesia, Mozambique; resident open acacia and *Brachystegia* woodland and bush. Upperparts black glossed green; black wings show long white bar when closed; black tail white-edged; crown and short forward-pointing crest grey to white according to race; small grey or blackish bar behind earcoverts; under-parts white; legs orange to orange-red; bill black; eyes and eye wattle yellow. Juvenile has head brown-

ish or ashy. Flocks of up to 12 travel silently through woodland, breaking into chatter when they stop to feed; often in parties of other species. Flute-like notes as well as chattering call, also bill-snapping. Food mainly insects. Breeding season varies within range; compact nest of grass and plant fibres, covered with cobwebs and lined bark, well hidden on lateral branch or in fork at some height. 3 or 4 pinkish-white, bluish-green or pale stone eggs, spotted rufous and purplish brown over blue or pale purple usually in zone. Several birds may share duties at one nest. **656**

Procnias
alba see under **P. nudicollis**
avetana see under **P. nudicollis**

Procnias nudicollis *Cotingidae*
BARE-THROATED BELLBIRD 10½ ins
Neotropical: SE Brazil, Paraguay, NE Argentina; resident in forest canopy. ♂: all white (one of few tropical birds so coloured) except for bare greenish skin round eye and throat, covered with black bristles. ♀: upperparts, wings and tail olive green; head black, throat and upper breast olive green, with pale streaks; underparts yellowish white, streaked olive, thus closely resembling ♀ White Bellbird, *P. alba*, the ♂ of which has throat feathered, and cylindrical, sparsely feathered wattle hanging from forehead. Nests of related species flimsy platforms of sticks, 15 to 20 ft up in cacao trees. ♂ apparently takes no part in nesting, but mates with ♀ after elaborate courtship. Bearded Bellbird, *P. avetana*, lays one pale brown egg, marked dark brown; incubation 23 days, fledging 33 days. **594**

Progne subis *Hirundinidae*
PURPLE MARTIN 7 ins
Nearctic, marginally Neotropical: 2 races; *P.s. subis* breeds S Canada down W coast to Central Mexico and along Gulf coast to Florida, winters Venezuela to S and E Brazil; *hesperia* breeds Baja California, W Arizona lowlands and coastal W Sonora (Mexico); winter range unknown but migrates through Central America. Habitat now mostly suburban gardens and farmland. ♂: metallic blue all over, shading to brown on wings and tail. ♀: dark brown above, pale brown below shading to white on belly. ♂ in first year like ♀ but greyer. Very tame. Huge roosts after breeding. Calls: low mellow chirp, continuous twitter in nest; guttural alarm. Feeds on aerial insects but also snails (probably for calcium). Arrives early but breeding starts April, mainly in 'apartment boxes' but naturally in holes in cliffs or trees; nest usually of grass and feathers with low mud wall near entrance. Green leaves often found, possibly increasing humidity. 3 to 5 pure white eggs, incubated mainly ♀ 13 days. Young fledge 24-28 days. **620**

Promerops cafer *Meliphagidae* ♀: 9 to 11 ins
CAPE SUGARBIRD ♂: 17 (tail up to 12) ins
Ethiopian: southernmost S Africa; replaced by smaller *P. gurneyi* in mountains of eastern S Africa, Rhodesia. Mainly resident on hillsides with proteas; some movement in summer after food. ♂: upperparts dusky brown, streaked olive; rump greenish yellow; wings dusky, pale edged; very long tail dusky; forehead, crown buff, finely streaked brown; throat whitish, thin black moustachial stripe; rufous on breast; belly, flanks whitish, streaked dark brown; under tail coverts bright yellow; legs, bill black, eyes brown. ♀ similar but much shorter tail. Juvenile as ♀ but browner above, less streaked below. In pairs in winter when breeds, otherwise small parties. On territory ♂ often perches on bush top to call, sing, chase other ♂♂; also aerial dance in courtship, wings clapped loudly, tail feathers writhe over back. Normal flight straight, swift, tail stretched behind. Call: *chick*; song: 'creaking and clanging'. Diet mainly insects, hawked in air; some protea honey. Breeding peak April to June; ♀ builds cup nest of twigs, rush stems, lined protea fluff. 2 light buff to reddish brown eggs, marked dark purple, fine brown spots, scrawls, incubated ♀ 17 days. Young, mainly fed ♀ on insects, spiders, some honey, fly 18-20 days, tended further 3 weeks. 2 broods (G. J. Broekhuysen). **849**

Promerops gurneyi see under **P. cafer**

Prosthemadera novaeseelandiae *Meliphagidae*
TUI or PARSON BIRD ♀: 11½, ♂: 12½ ins
Confined to New Zealand and neighbouring islands; separate race, *P.n. chathamensis*, Chatham I group; resident primary and secondary forest, manuka scrub with tall trees, occasionally in introduced vegetation; up to 3,500 ft. ♂: generally iridescent metallic green, with bluish purple gloss; back, scapulars dark brown glossed bronze; sides, belly reddish brown; under tail coverts metallic green; double tuft of white curly feathers at throat, lacy white filamentous collar, small white wing-bar. ♀ has smaller throat tufts, paler belly. Immature mainly slaty black. Chatham race larger with longer throat plumes, bluer breast. Legs, bill blackish brown; eyes very dark. Active and noisy in flight, also aerobatic, diving with closed wings. Diet: insects, fruits, nectar from many native species; also introduced plants. Alarm call: high-pitched *k-e-e-e*, also jackdaw-like *chack*; beautiful, variable song resembles Bellbird, *Anthornis melanura*; intersperses more harsh sounds, though 'richer notes more fluid and resonant' (R. A. Falla). Breeds mainly November to January; bulky twig nest lined fine plant material, sometimes feathers, in outer fork of tree 10 to 50 ft up. 2 to 4 white or pale pink eggs, marked reddish brown mainly at big end, incubated ♀ 14 days, ♂ singing nearby. Young, fed first by ♀, later with ♂'s help, on insects and berries (G. T. H. Moon), fly c. 21 days. **850**

Prunella collaris *Prunellidae*
ALPINE ACCENTOR c. 7 ins
Palaearctic: interrupted distribution from Iberia, NW Africa, through southern Europe and mountain ranges of S and E Asia to Japan. Breeds rocky and alpine meadows from c. 5,000 ft to snowline; some-times in low shrub vegetation; some movement down-wards in winter. Upperparts rather rich brown with pale feather edges; head, neck, breast grey; whitish gorget spotted black; flanks streaked chestnut; 2 white wing-bars due to spots on coverts; legs pinkish brown, bill brownish-black and yellow, eyes red-brown. Runs and walks on ground, perches bushes where available; short undulating flights. Family parties and small flocks after breeding. Call: rippling, rather lark-like *chirrup*; song 'decidedly lark-like' (B. W. Tucker) from ground, perch or in song-flight. Food: variety of insects and their larvae in summer; spiders, snails, seeds (grasses) and berries. Breeds late May to July, building well-hidden cup nest of grass, rootlets, green moss, lichens, lined feathers, hairs, in cleft or rocky recess, below shrub, grass tuft, occasionally among young trees. 3 or 4 pale blue eggs incubated ♀ and ♂ c. 15 days. Young, fed from crop by ♀ and ♂, leave nest before fledged and keep with parents for some time. 2 broods.

Prunella modularis *Prunellidae*
DUNNOCK or HEDGE ACCENTOR c. 5¾ ins
Palaearctic: most of Europe to 70°N in Scandinavia, absent much of Balkans, S Russia but separate population E Asia Minor, Caucasus, N Iran; Crimea. Winters southward to N Africa, Egypt, Palestine. Original habitat young coniferous forest or low-growing subalpine *Pinus montana* to 7,000 ft; scrub and heath; mixed woods and clearings, but in W Europe in man-modified hedgerows, gardens, parks. Generally warm brown streaked blackish; head, breast, throat grey; crown and ear coverts browner; narrow buffish wingbar; legs pinkish-brown, bill mainly black-brown, eyes bright brown. Juvenile more spotted, with brown head. Unobtrusive 'little brown bird', keeping much to cover but foraging in open for seeds (winter), insects and their larvae (summer); hops, or walks with crouching gait. Sometimes perches prominently, flicking wings. Flies low and straight. Rather solitary. Usual call shrill piping *tseep*, often repeated and pro-longed in alarm. Song high-pitched warble lasting 4-5 secs. Breeds March to August Britain, ♀ building compact mossy nest on foundation of twigs with wool and hair lining in bush, hedge, low growth, e.g. brambles, dead sticks, creepers. 4 or 5 deep blue eggs incubated by ♀ 11-13 days; young, fed by ♀ and ♂, fly c. 12 days. 2, sometimes 3 broods. Favourite host

of Cuckoo, *Cuculus canorus*. Japanese *Prunella rubida* very closely allied. **674**

PRZEVALSKI'S ROSEFINCH see **Urocynchramus pylzowi**

Psephotus haematodus *Psittacidae*
RED-BACKED PARROT   11 ins
Australasian: Victoria and parts of adjacent Australian states; resident in savannahs, also roadsides, farm areas, parks and gardens. ♂: upperparts from forehead to wings bluish green, but crown and upper breast deep green; under wing coverts and edges of primaries blue; rump red, tail green and blue above; shoulders, lower breast yellow; belly, under tail white; legs blue, bill black, eyes brown. ♀: upperparts pale olive; rump and tail green; shoulders, edges of primaries pale blue; neck, breast scaly, dull olive; underparts white; bill grey. From pairs to flocks of 500, often with Eastern Rosella, *Platycercus eximius*, and may interbreed. Flight fast and direct. Rests during heat of day, preening mutually, or may feed, fluttering between shady patches. Pleasant, thin whistle and warbling call. Food: seeds of grasses and herbs in short-grass country, also green leaves and fallen fruit. Breeds August to January in hole often in dead tree and near water. 4 to 7 white eggs laid on decayed wood and incubated 20 days by ♀; young fledge *c.* 30 days. **404**

Pseudeos fuscata *Psittacidae*
DUSKY LORIKEET   11 ins
Australasian: New Guinea and some offshore islands; resident in savannah and forest up to at least 5,000 ft. Variable: generally dusky brown; yellow orange patch on crown and band on nape; feathers of mantle fringed red, grey, olive; rump yellowish white, upper tail coverts black, tail greyish or olive-purple; wings tinged purple, olive and chestnut; under wing coverts partly red; belly, thighs orange-red with bands across throat and breast; under tail coverts purple blue, undertail red to olive; legs dark grey, bill red or yellow, eyes red. Flocks feed tops of flowering trees; daily movements with *Trichoglossus* species from feeding trees to roost, reported in thousands.

Pseudibis papillosa *Threskiornithidae*
BLACK IBIS   30 ins
Oriental: India, SE to Borneo as straggler. Habitat marshes and muddy stream banks and paddyfields. Glossy black, with bare head, red warty patch on crown of Indian race. Conspicuous white wing spot; legs coral red, bill bluish, eyes brown to red. Less gregarious than Sacred Ibis, *Threskiornis aethiopicus*; solitary, pairs or family parties. Perches freely in trees, wades or works water's edge for fish, amphibians, worms and insects. 'Weird and characteristic cry' (Smythies) on taking wing, with loud and peculiar calls in breeding season, which is March to October in N India. Nest of sticks in tall trees holds 2 to 4 sea-green eggs, sometimes with brown markings. Incubation and fledging periods not recorded. **86**

Pseudocalyptomena graueri *Eurylaimidae*
GRAUER'S or
AFRICAN GREEN BROADBILL   *c.* 5½ ins
Ethiopian: only known from two areas, in Kivu (SE Zaire) and Kigui (SW Uganda); forest at *c.* 6,500 ft. Generally bright grass green, wings relatively short, tail short, rounded; forehead greenish buff, streaked brown; cheeks spotted blackish; earcoverts, throat, breast, under tail coverts pale blue; legs light grey green, bill black, no rictal bristles; eyes very dark brown. Juvenile duller, under tail coverts green. Groups of 2 or 3 *c.* 8 ft up in undergrowth, seen to search spurge *Neoboutonia* tree. Slow, gliding flight. Calls: repeated soft *cree cree*, high-pitched *prrrp*. Food includes insects (beetles) and larvae; snails; seeds, buds, fruits. Few birds seen mostly shot; nothing known about breeding.

Pseudochelidon eurystomina *Hirundinidae*
AFRICAN RIVER MARTIN
Ethiopian: confined to Lower Congo and Ubangi Rivers and Gabon; riparian, coastal after breeding. Distinct from other hirundines; often given mono-

typic subfamily, *Pseudochelidoninae*: all black, glossed green on upperparts, purple on head, neck; purplish below; projecting points on central feathers of square tail; legs pinkish; bill scarlet, tipped yellow; eyes red. Gregarious and nomadic, on breeding area only when river low. Takes insects on wing; lands on bare ground. Continuous chatter at breeding colony, changing to rasping *cheer-cheer cheer* on rising (J. P. Chapin); also chipping note in flight. Breeds February to April in large colonies, excavating burrows in flattish sandbanks; nest chamber sparsely lined dead leaves, other plant debris. Usually 3 white eggs.

Pseudogyps
  africanus see **Gyps africanus**
  bengalensis see **Gyps bengalensis**

Psittacula krameri *Psittacidae*
ROSE-RINGED or
INDIAN RING-NECKED PARAKEET   16½ ins
Oriental and Ethiopian: two races cover most of Indian subcontinent, Sikkim, Burma, Ceylon, SE China; introduced Egypt, Oman; two races from Senegal and Nigeria to Sudan, Uganda, Eritrea, Somalia, N Ethiopia; Oriental races resident light secondary jungle, orchards, cultivations, towns, also plains and uplands in Burma; African races resident thorn scrub and semi-arid plains. Main African race *P.k. krameri*: ♂ yellow-green with long pointed tail; throat black, narrow orange-red half collar each side neck, nape with blue bloom; legs olive yellow, bill crimson, eyes pale yellow, orbit orange; ♀ lacks throat patch, collar and bloom on nape; juvenile similar but yellower. Oriental *borealis* ♂ bluer on head and wider, more distinct rosy half collar; ♀ has indistinct emerald collar. Flocks fly over high and fast, screaming *kee-ak*: tens in Africa, hundreds in India, where roosts with crows and mynahs. African diet: fruit, oil palm nuts, seeds, crops; in India larger numbers very destructive on crops, gnawing half-ripe fruit, nibbling grain; often gleaning in railway yards. Displaying ♂ sidles up to feed ♀; struts, postures. Breeds Africa October to January, India January to April; tree holes, some excavated by ♀ and ♂, sometimes old nests of barbets, woodpeckers; also in rocks and walls in India, 10 to 30 ft up. 4 to 6 white eggs incubated by ♀; 4 weeks from egg-laying to young flying. **405**

Psittacus erithacus *Psittacidae*
AFRICAN GREY PARROT   14-15 ins
Ethiopian: Gulf of Guinea to Kenya, Tanzania, N Angola; Principe and Fernando Po Is. Resident in forests. Generally grey with bright scarlet tail and under tail coverts; legs, bill black, eyes pale yellow. Very old birds show scarlet intermixed with grey. Flocks fly over high and fast, squawking and whistling, out to feed in clearings, back at dusk or later to communal roosts. Quiet while feeding: high in trees on seeds and fruit, especially oil palm nuts, but also raids maize crops. Breeds July to December over tropical Africa, laying 2 to 4 smooth or pitted white eggs in high tree hole; incubation by ♀, fed by ♂ 28-29 days. ♀ feeds young for first week, then ♂ helps; fledging period 3-4 months. **406**

Psitteuteles goldiei *Psittacidae*
GOLDIE'S LORIKEET
Australasian: Central New Guinea; montane forests from 4,500 to 7,000 ft. Upperparts dark green streaked pale on hind neck; forehead, crown red, nape blue, extending to eyes; tail olive green, side of head purple-pink sometimes streaked black; underparts and under wing coverts pale green, streaked darker; under wing greyish black with central yellow area; under tail yellowish olive; legs slaty grey, bill black, eyes brown. Apparently does not form flocks, lives in upper parts of trees. **407**

Psophia leucoptera *Psophiidae*
PALE-WINGED TRUMPETER   18-22 ins
Neotropical: Amazonian Brazil to E Peru, N and E Bolivia; resident in forests. Generally black, feathers of head and neck velvety, metallic purple at base of neck; feathers of lower mantle with broad yellowish margins; wing coverts edged bronze-green, inner

flight feathers white or buffish; legs dark horn, bill yellowish, eyes dark. Spends day on ground in flocks of 100 or more, running fast and flying weakly, but roosts in trees. Bathes in shallow water. Crane-like dances in courtship. Group of ♂♂ utter prolonged booming calls with back feathers raised, bill opening and closing. Diet: fruit and berries; various insects e.g. ants, tabanid flies. Breeds March to April, making simple nest in tree-hole or on ground, usually at foot of tree. Clutch 6 to 10 dirty white eggs, incubated by ♀; young leave nest soon after hatching. **238**

Psophodes olivaceus *Muscicapidae: Cinclosomatinae*
EASTERN WHIPBIRD   10 ins
Australasian: E continental Australia from N Queensland through New South Wales to SE Victoria. Resident in rain forest and moist gullies. Upperparts dark olive green; head, including prominent crest, centre throat, breast black; white patch over cheek and side throat; underparts grey-brown, washed olive, flecked white ventrally; legs red-brown; bill black; eye brown. Mainly terrestrial but secretive, hopping actively in undergrowth. Distinctive call of ♂, long whistle increasing in volume to whip-crack, answered by ♀, *choo-choo*. Also harsh scolding alarm call. Food includes terrestrial insects, earthworms. Breeds October to January. Bulky cup nest of loose twigs, lined rootlets, built in dense undergrowth. 2, occasionally 3, pale blue eggs blotched red-brown over grey. **720**

PTARMIGAN,
  ROCK see **Lagopus mutus**
  WHITE-TAILED see **Lagopus leucurus**

Pternistis swainsonii see **Francolinus swainsonii**

Pterocles exustus *Pteroclididae*
CHESTNUT-BELLIED SANDGROUSE   12½ ins
E Palaearctic (Egypt) and Ethiopian: across Africa N of Equator; in open desert. ♂: dull brown, sides of head, throat and wing coverts yellow-buff, coverts mottled chocolate and buff; flight feathers and underwing blackish brown, inner primaries with broad white edges; narrow black band across breast; belly and lower flanks dark chestnut, elongated needle tail. ♀: mostly light brown, barred or spotted dark brown except for yellowish side of head and buff area between spotted breast and finely barred belly. Legs feathered, feet dark brown, small bill blackish, eyes dark brown. Gregarious, huge flocks gather in morning and evening, circle high over water, land quickly and fly off after a few seconds drinking, with distended crops. Call in flock musical guttural chuckling. Main food plant seeds. Breeding season varies with range. 2 or 3 stone or greyish eggs, streaked olive or reddish brown and spotted violet, laid on bare ground. **349**

Pterodroma cahow *Procellariidae*
BERMUDA CAHOW   14-18 ins
Considered by some authorities to be subspecies of Capped Petrel, *P. hasitata*. Confined in modern times to Bermuda in N Atlantic, where population of 20-30 pairs survives, after re-discovery in 1945, under rigid protection. Dark grey-brown upperparts and almost black wedge-shaped tail, but pale tail coverts; underparts and forehead white; legs pale pink, bill black, eyes brown. Nocturnal, so escaped notice for many years after near-extinction. Takes surface organisms, which may be cause of high pesticide residues and recent lack of breeding success. Other danger from Yellow-billed Tropicbird, *Phaethon lepturus*, killing chicks in nesting crevices. Ingenious baffle devised by R. Thorsell now prevents tropicbirds entering. One white egg laid early January originally in excavated burrow, but now, owing to denudation of islands, usually in rocky crevice in offshore islet. Incubation 51-54 days by ♀ and ♂, chick fully fledged 90-100 days. **31**

Pterodroma hasitata see under **P. cahow**

Pteroglossus pluricinctus *Ramphastidae*
MANY-BANDED ARAÇARI   13½ (bill 4¾) ins
Neotropical: Venezuela N and S of Orinoco, adjacent Brazil, Colombia E of Andes S to NE Peru; resident

forests, sea level to *c.* 4,000 ft. Upperparts, including wings, tail, slaty green; rump crimson; head, nape, throat black; underparts crimson mixed black, crossed by 2 black bands. Bill: upper white; culmen and lower mandible black; base outlined white. Call: weak, rather high-pitched. Roosts in old woodpecker holes, other cavities, sometimes 5 or 6 birds close together, tails folded over heads. Food: fruit, insects (especially to young), reptiles, small birds. Nests natural tree holes, usually high up; 2 to 4 white eggs laid on bare floor of nest chamber, incubated ♀ and ♂. Both feed young, who fly probably 6½ weeks, but return to roost with parents for a time. **536**

Pteropodocys maxima *Campephagidae*
GROUND CUCKOO SHRIKE 13 ins
Australia (except NW): very open wooded country, usually in interior. Upperparts, head and throat to upper breast grey; flight and tail feathers black (tail slightly forked, edged whitish); rump, underparts pale grey, barred narrow black crescents; bill to ear-coverts black; legs, bill blackish, eyes dark brown. Usually in pairs or small parties, moving rapidly over ground with undulating flight to nearest trees when disturbed. Call: plaintive rippling on wing; prolonged harsh cry (N. W. Cayley). Food: insects and their larvae. Breeds August to December, building rather flat nest of rootlets, grass and plant stems, wool, bound cobwebs, lined fine grass, generally in fork of lateral branch to 70 ft up tree. Usually 3 dull green eggs, with 'fleecy' olive-brown markings.

Ptilinopus melanospila *Columbidae*
BLUE-NAPED FRUIT DOVE *c.* 11½ ins
Oriental, marginally Australasian: islands from Java E to Celebes then N to Palawan and Mindanao, not Borneo. Habitat: woodland, forest edge or suitable cover in more open country. ♂: plump, head pale silver grey with large black patch on hind crown and nape, median yellow stripe down chin and throat, lower belly yellow; long tail coverts bright purplish red while shorter ones yellow or orange with red tips, rest of plumage deep green often tinged golden bronze, going bluish green in old feathers. Legs purplish red, bill yellow but variable e.g. blackish with pale greenish tip, eyes yellow buff with greyish or greenish orbital skin. ♀: lacks contrasting head markings and is mostly green. Call: single *coo* often repeated. Feeds on berries and fruits from branches. **373**

Ptilinorhynchus violaceus *Ptilinorhynchidae*
SATIN BOWER BIRD *c.* 12½ ins
Australasian: Atherton Tableland, Queensland, S to Otway Ranges, Victoria, but very rare between area above Townsville to Bunya Mts. Habitat: wet sclerophyll forests and moist gullies, moves to more open country in winter; in S more open forest where sufficient undergrowth, even gardens. Fully mature ♂ black with refractive edges to feathers giving glossy lilac blue effect in sunlight. Legs dull greenish yellow, partly feathered bill dull blue with bright greenish yellow tip, eyes intense blue, shade variable. ♀: upperparts greyish green; underparts, yellowish green feathers edged blackish brown; immature similar. Northern race, *minor*, smaller. Noisy nomadic flocks form in late summer, wandering in some areas as far as 100 miles from breeding range; June to August ♂ builds bower for displaying; 2 parallel walls of arched dry twigs, display area at one entrance strewn with bright objects, usually blue, greenish-yellow, brown and grey. Bower usually in undergrowth and on old site; avenue 4 or 5 ins wide, often runs N and S, walls 10 to 14 ins high, 3 to 4 ins thick, inner twigs painted or plastered with mixture of saliva and often charcoal; less substantial bowers built by immature ♂♂; neighbours attach each others' bowers and steal display objects. Call: low, melancholy whistle *whee-ooo*. Feeds on fruit and sometimes insects. Breeds November and December; ♀ builds shallow twig nest lined with leaves, in topmost branches of tree or in bunch of mistletoe; 2 (sometimes 1) cream or buff eggs with darker markings, incubated ♀ 19-23 days. **988**

Ptyonoprogne
  fuligula see **Hirundo fuligula**

---

rupestris see **Hirundo rupestris**

PUERTO RICAN EMERALD HUMMINGBIRD see **Chlorostilbon maugaeus**

PUERTO RICO TODY see **Todus mexicanus**

PUFF-BACKED SHRIKE, BLACK see **Dryoscopus cubla**

PUFFBACK, CHIN-SPOT see **Batis molitor**

PUFFBIRD,
  CHESTNUT-CAPPED see **Bucco macrodactylus**
  WHITE-WHISKERED see **Malacoptila panamensis**

Puffinus gravis *Procellariidae*
GREAT SHEARWATER 17-20 ins
Breeds only Tristan da Cunha group in S Atlantic and Falkland Islands, but wanders widely into northern hemisphere, even to arctic circle. Upperparts dark brown with conspicuous cap against white neck and throat; underparts white with patch across base of tail; legs grey and pink, bill black and horn, eyes brown. Usually seen in flight, gliding over waves and flapping when calm in parties or flocks, sometimes very large at human food sources. Uses wings when diving after squids and fish; also takes offal when available. Voice harsh and raucous, with croaks when visiting breeding station. Lays one white egg in second week November in burrow among rank grass on oceanic island. Incubation *c.* 55 days by ♀ and ♂, who tend chick intermittently until independent at *c.* 105 days. **32**

Puffinus pacificus *Procellariidae*
WEDGE-TAILED SHEARWATER 18 ins
Breeds on small oceanic islands in S Pacific and Indian Oceans, its home for rest of year. Two plumage phases occur, one brown all over, other with white breast. Tail long and wedge-shaped; legs pale brown; narrow vertically compressed bill dark brown; eyes brown. Usual shearwater behaviour pattern of off-shore gatherings during day in breeding season and nocturnal visits to colony, when calls described as 'like growls and snarls of fighting cats'. Diet small fish and squids. Long breeding season; eggs laid early December and last young fledge in June. One white egg in vestigial nest in burrow and incubated by ♀ and ♂ in turns; they feed chick during its prolonged fledging period. **33**

Puffinus puffinus *Procellariidae*
MANX SHEARWATER 14 ins
Three subspecies in N Atlantic and Mediterranean; another, *P.p. opisthomelas*, (sometimes divided into several races of very limited range) in N Pacific; movement south from NE Atlantic breeding stations in autumn. Atlantic subspecies *puffinus* contrasting black above and white below, but *mauretanicus* (breeds Balearics) is more or less uniformly sooty brown while *yelkouan* (E Mediterranean) is intermediate; Pacific race, *opisthomelas*, has sooty under tail coverts and sooty wash almost across breast; legs pink and black, bill dull black. Flies with bursts of wingbeats, followed by gliding, wings tipping from side to side to 'shear' water. Rafts of birds on sea during day in breeding season, diving when approached; do not follow ships, but feed principally on small fish and squids, making enormous journeys to find them. Colonies visited at night when wild rookooing calls answered by birds inside burrows. Breeds May to October (earlier in Mediterranean) on turf-capped and rocky islands, headlands, and hill tops up to 2,500 ft. One white egg laid in scrape at end of excavated tunnel in earth, or among stones, perhaps several feet long. Incubation 7½ weeks by ♀ and ♂, who feed chick for 8½ weeks, then leave it to fledge. **34**

Puffinus tenuirostris *Procellariidae*
MUTTONBIRD or
SHORT-TAILED SHEARWATER 16 ins
Southeast Australia, with centre Bass Strait; north-ward on migration into Pacific as far as Bering Strait,

---

W North and Central American coasts. All brown, legs purplish black, bill leaden grey; eyes brown. Darker and lighter colour phases occur. As with other shear-waters, large gatherings form on sea in evenings near breeding colonies; birds first return to excavate or renovate burrows, then leave for several weeks before actually nesting. Main diet marine crustacea, trans-muted to oil, basis of Muttonbird 'industry'. Usual 'unearthly' calls of visiting birds, but depart silently in morning. Gregarious on nesting islands, laying one white egg in late November at end of burrow but sometimes in cover on ground if numbers very great. Incubation *c.* 53 days by ♀ and ♂, who tend chick but eventually leave it to fledge in *c.* 94 days. **35**

PUFFLEG, COLOURFUL see **Eriocnemis mirabilis**

PUKEKO see under **Porphyrio porphyrio**

PURPLE
  CRESTED TOURACO see **Gallirex porphyreolophus**
  GALLINULE see **Porphyrio porphyrio**
  GALLINULE AMERICAN see **Porphyrula martinica**
  GRACKLE see **Quiscalus quiscala**
  HONEYCREEPER see **Cyanerpes caeruleus**
  MARTIN see **Progne subis**
  SANDPIPER see **Calidris maritima**

PURPLE-BACKED WREN see **Malurus assimilis**

PURPLE-CAPPED LORIKEET see **Domicella domicella**

Purpureicephalus spurius *Psittacidae*
PILEATED PARAKEET 15 ins
Australasian: confined to SW West Australia; in wet sclerophyll forest and scrub. ♂: back and wings rich green; forehead, crown, nape crimson; cheeks, rump, upper tail coverts yellow-green; breast, belly deep violet-blue; flanks, under tail coverts red, mixed green; under wing coverts blue; outer primaries ultramarine; central tail feathers deep green, outer feathers blue, white edged; legs light brown, bill bluish grey, eyes dark brown. ♀ duller than ♂, more green on flanks and under tail coverts; juvenile dark green crown; generally duller. In pairs or small flocks, flying fast for short distances but with sweeping wing beats in display. Calls: harsh repeated *chelyup*: staccato *shrek shrek shrek* in flight. Food: principally eucalypt but many other seeds; also removes seeds from fruits; local damage to grain and orchards. Breeds August-November, in tree hole like relatives. 4 to 7 white eggs incubated by ♀, fed by ♂, *c.* 3 weeks; ♀ feeds young at first, later ♂ also; fly *c.* 5 weeks.

PUTOTO see **Porzana plumbea**

Pycnonotus barbatus *Pycnonotidae*
WHITE-VENTED or BLACK-EYED BULBUL 8 ins
S Palaearctic: NW Africa, Egypt, Palestine, Red Sea coast; Ethiopian: most of region except SW. Resident open wooded country, including gardens; bush and quite arid areas. Upperparts and throat to breast grey-brown; crown, face, chin blackish, contrasting with rest of plumage; underparts light brown to whitish, under tail coverts lemon yellow; legs, bill, wattle round eye black; eyes dark brown. Race *P.b. schoanus* (Somalia) has white patch side of neck, breast feathers edged whitish. Juvenile duller. Generally in pairs; confiding with humans. Collects in parties to chatter at snakes or small carnivores. Call (S Africa); *come back to Pretoria;* also repeated *chit chit*. Insects taken off foliage; diet about equally of fruit. Breeds January onwards in N, building neat cup of grasses, leaves, often suspended in fork of twig. 2 or 3 white or pinkish eggs, heavily speckled reddish brown over lilac. **640**

Pycnonotus cafer *Pycnonotidae*
RED-VENTED BULBUL 8 ins
Oriental: Indian subcontinent, Ceylon, Burma; intro-duced Singapore; and, in Australasia, Fiji, Melbourne

area, Auckland NZ; resident scrub jungle, forest clearings, habitations, gardens, up to 8,000 ft. Upperparts dark greenish black; crested head, breast black, shading to grey belly, under tail coverts bright red; cheeks, rump white, blackish tail white-tipped. Legs dark brown, bill blackish, eyes very dark brown. Hybridises freely with White-cheeked, *P. leucogenys*. Lively and familiar garden bird, with several calls and inconsiderable song. ♂ fluffs feathers in display, spreads under tail coverts; ♀ responds by lowering head, moving bill side to side. Hunts insects on wing in evenings; collects in flocks to feed on e.g. banyan fruits; also takes peas, seeds, buds. Breeds March to July, ♀ and ♂ building cup nest in low bush, tree stump, building, of plant materials, lined rootlets, horsehair. 2 to 4 pinkish white eggs, marked purple and red, incubated by ♀ and ♂, who both tend young. Probably 2 broods. **641**

Pycnonotus
   capensis see under **P. nigricans**
   leucogenys see under **P. cafer**

Pycnonotus nigricans *Pycnonotidae*
RED-EYED BULBUL   8 ins
Ethiopian: W Southern Africa, but not S coastal belt; resident riverine forest, bush country not far from water. Upperparts sooty brown; head and throat blackish, contrasting with light brown underparts; lower belly whitish; under tail coverts yellow; legs, bill black, eyes reddish brown, facial wattle red. Juvenile pale brown above. Lively and noisy, often on exposed perch, raising crown feathers to form crest. Gregarious at times. Call, liquid whistling *piet pop le wiet;* melodious warbling song, similar to voice of Cape Bulbul, *P. capensis*. Diet: insects and fruits; visits wells to drink. Breeds November to March; nest of twigs, grass, lined rootlets, 3 to 12 ft in small tree or bush, often thorny. 3 pinkish white eggs, marked red to purple over grey, incubated ♀ 11-12 days; young, fed ♀ and ♂, fly 13 days. **642**

Pycnoptilus floccosus *Muscicapidae : Malurinae*
PILOT BIRD   *c.* 6½ ins
Australia: Blue Mts and Port Hacking, New South Wales, S to Dandenong Ranges, Victoria; may be some winter movement to lower altitudes. Habitat: moist gullies and wet forests. Upperparts brown with rufous wash to hind parts and wings, particularly upper tail coverts; head, neck and mantle more sooty; throat and breast rufous-ochre with brown mottling; belly white with less distinct mottling. Legs black, bill brown, eyes red. Usually on ground amongst tangled vegetation or fallen timber and ferns. Believed to guide Superb Lyrebird, *Menura novaehollandiae,* to food, thus name; reverse probably true: feeds on forest floor with White-browed Scrub Wren, *Sericornis frontalis*, from material scratched up by Lyrebirds. Call: loud, melodius, resembles words *guinea-a-week;* mimicked by Superb Lyrebird. Food: insects, earth worms and some small berries. Breeds August to January; untidy domed nest with side entrance, on or near ground amongst forest litter and undergrowth, of bark strips, leaves, tree fern roots and some grass thus blending with surroundings; lined feathers and fine bark fibres; 2 smoky-brown to dusky-grey eggs, darker at larger end. **770**

PYGMY
   FALCON, AFRICAN see **Polihierax
      semitorquatus**
   GOOSE see **Nettapus auritus**
   KINGFISHER see **Ispidina picta**
   KINGFISHER, AMERICAN see **Chloroceryle aena**
   OWL, EURASIAN see **Glaucidium passerinum**
   OWL, FERRUGINOUS see **Glaucidium brasilianum**

Pygoscelis adeliae *Spheniscidae*
ADELIE PENGUIN   *c.* 30 ins
Antarctic, with seasonal migrations of 1½ to 60 miles to and from breeding stations at foot of ice-cliff slopes, up to 1,000 ft high. Typical penguin pattern; feet pinky grey, bill grey black; eyes dark. Birds returning to breed walk at *c.* 3 mph, but can outstrip man when running or tobogganing. Some evidence

of 'play' when riding ice floes, among which it feeds on shrimps *Euphausia*. Arrives traditional colonies by established routes in October. Mutual display by head lifting before laying in November: eggs 1 or 2 white, incubated on pile of small stones for *c.* 36 days by ♂, then ♀. Chicks fed by ♂ and ♀, join creche in *c.* 4 weeks. **11**

Pyrrhocorax graculus *Corvidae*
ALPINE CHOUGH   *c.* 15½ ins
Palaearctic: mountain regions of S Europe, Morocco, Caucasus, N Iran, central Asia, Altai, Tibet and Himalayas. Resident alpine zones up to and above snow line, may move to lower levels in winter; commensal with man in Alps. Black with greenish tinge. Legs yellowish red, bill yellow, eyes dark brown. (Chough, *P. pyrrhocorax*, similar, but longer bill bright red). Gregarious when not breeding, soars and glides in air currents over mountain slopes and cliffs, often perches on large isolated rocks. Call: melodious rattling and chirring. Feeds on large insects and other invertebrates from surface soil; scavenges; also takes berries. Fairly protracted breeding season from May and June, colonial; nest of fir twigs, heather, rootlets and grass, lined grass, wool and feathers, on foundation of sticks in clefts and cavities in steep rock faces, also stone walls and under roofs; 2 to 5 eggs, variable colour but usually pale yellowish green or brown with brownish markings, sometimes scanty. **1008**

Pyrrhocorax pyrrhocorax see under **P. graculus**

Pyrrhula
   cineracea see under **P. pyrrhula**
   murina see under **P. pyrrhula**

Pyrrhula pyrrhula *Fringillidae*
BULLFINCH   *c.* 5¾ ins
Palaearctic: from N Iberia, Britain and Ireland in broad band (roughly between 50° and 65°N) across Eurasia to Kamtchatka, Sakhalin, Japan; isolated population N Asia Minor, Caucasus, N Iran; Azores where sometimes separated as *P. murina*. Asian population grey-breasted '*P. cineracea*'. Resident and migrant, eastern birds wintering Manchuria, China, Japan; western eruptive, mostly to Mediterranean. Habitat primarily coniferous forest with dense undergrowth, mixed birch, poplar in taiga, with beech between 5,000 and 7,500 ft in mountains; cultivated areas, parks, gardens in W Europe. ♂: upperparts grey; crown, wings (with pale bar), tail black; rump white; underparts from bill rosy red (♀ pinkish grey), lower belly, under tail coverts white. Legs, eyes brown, stubby bill black. Juvenile like ♀ without black cap. Usually in pairs but parties, small flocks in winter. Seldom on ground where hops. Short undulating flight between cover. ♂ displays breast to ♀ in courtship. Call: piping *teu* or *teu teu* on wing or perched; sometimes three varying notes but no real song. Seeds of ash *Fraxinus* preferred food of British birds (Ian Newton) but great variety seeds, fruit, buds taken; young fed on insect larvae. Breeds mid April to September; ♀, attended ♂, builds foundation small twigs for cup of fine black or brown rootlets and hair; in thick or thorny bush, often evergreen, ivied trunks, epicormic shoots, 3 to 6 ft or higher. 4 to 6 greenish blue eggs, streaked dark purple-brown in zone at big end, incubated ♀ 12-14 days; both parents feed young from throat; they fly 15-17 days. 2 broods. **928**

Pyrrhuloxia cardinalis or Richmondena cardinalis
Emberizidae : Pyrrhuloxiinae
CARDINAL   8¼ ins
Nearctic, marginally Neotropical: breeds New England, S Ontario, N. Illinois, SE Dakota, S to Florida, Gulf Coast; also Central Texas, S Arizona to S Mexico; introduced Bermuda, SW California, Hawaii; sedentary. Habitat dense scrub with open areas adjacent: woodland edges, riverine strips, swamps; parks, gardens. ♂ uniformly red except for black face, bib. ♀: upperparts greenish brown, underparts pinkish brown; red on wings, tail, crest; some black on face, bib. Legs brown, big conical bill pinkish, eyes brown. Juvenile like dark ♀. Sallies from cover to feed on wild seeds, fruits, some insects; comes readily to bird tables

providing large seeds, even becoming established in their vicinity. Call: sharp click; song: repetition of short, whistled phrases, changing in pitch and variously rendered; ♀ also sings. Breeds April to August Tennessee, throughout year farther S, building nest of twigs, stems, leaves, fibres, lined rootlets, grass, hair, 5 to 10 ft up in bush or tangle of vines, brambles; piles of brush. 3 or 4 white or greenish eggs, finely spotted red-brown, lavender, incubated ♀ 12-13 days with ♂ attentive, feeding her away from nest. ♀ and ♂ feed young, who leave nest 9-10 days, tended by ♂ *c.* 3 weeks while ♀ starts second nest. 2, sometimes 3, 4 broods. **873**

Pytilia phoenicoptera *Estrildidae*
RED-WINGED PYTILIA or AURORA FINCH   4½-4¾ ins
Ethiopian: Ethiopia, S Sudan W to Cameroun, S to Uganda; partly migratory. Habitat: bush and tall grassland, into cultivated areas, villages, even towns. ♂: generally grey-brown; outer edges flight feathers, upper wing coverts, upper tail coverts, much of tail crimson; cheeks, chin to upper breast grey: underparts barred white. ♀ browner all over and more heavily barred. Legs brownish flesh, bill greenish-black, eyes red. Juvenile even browner than ♀, crimson duller, bill brown. Haunts dense cover, but pairs may feed in open with other waxbills, on seeds and insects. Occasional chirping call. Breeds October-November N Nigeria, building globular loosely made grass nest, lined feathers, usually in thick cover of tree or bush. 4 rather large white eggs. **943**

PYTILIA, RED-WINGED see **Pytilia phoenicoptera**

QUAIL,
   CALIFORNIA see **Lophortyx californicus**
   GAMBEL's see under **Lophortyx californicus**
   LARK see **Ortyxelos meiffrenii**
   PAINTED see **Turnix varia**
   STUBBLE see **Coturnix pectoralis**

QUAIL
   DOVE, RUDDY see **Geotrygon montana**
   FINCH, see **Ortygospiza atricollis**
   THRUSH, CHESTNUT see **Cinclosoma
      castanotum**
   THRUSH, CINNAMON see **Cinclosoma
      cinnamomeum**

QUAKER PARAKEET see **Myiopsitta monacha**

QUARRION see **Nymphicus hollandicus**

QUEENSLAND GARDENER see **Prionodura
newtoniana**

Quelea quelea *Ploceidae*
RED-BILLED QUELEA or SUDAN DIOCH   5 ins
Ethiopian: narrow band from W coast S of Sahara to Sudan, Ethiopia, then S down E side continent, spreading W into Angola and into northern S Africa, making seasonal migrations. Habitat dry thorn bush, scrub, acacia savannah, thence descending on cultivated areas. ♂: upperparts streaked black and buff; flight and tail feathers yellow-edged; head markings variable: forehead, cheeks, throat either blackish or brownish black, or buffish tawny; chin, throat, earcoverts sometimes whitish; underparts whitish or buffish white, with rosy or tawny breast shading to belly; often breast, flanks mottled dark brown; legs orange or pale pink, bill red, eyes brown. ♀: crown brownish or greyish brown finely streaked dusky; 'eyebrow', earcoverts dusky: throat white or buffish-white. Non-breeding ♂ and juvenile resemble ♀. Enormous flocks roost swamps, reed beds by lake or river. Probably prefers wild grass seeds but attracted to rice, millet and guinea corn in millions, subjected to expensive but ineffectual control measures. Call: soft *tek tek;* shrill *chak-chak* of alarm; metallic tinkling song in breeding colonies, where also much chattering. Monogamous: ♂ courts by raising and quivering wings, tilting body side to side, bill pointed upwards; but pair bond depends on nest. Dry season affects ♀♀ more than ♂♂, but survivors soon build up population, establishing colonies in wet season away from winter-

ing areas; usually breeds December to April S Africa. Large colonies (estimated 10 million nests Lake Chad area) crowd thorn trees over several acres, but others scattered. ♂ builds purse-shaped nest of green grass with large side entrance. 2 or 3 pale greenish blue eggs incubated ♀ 12 days; young, fed by ♀ and ♂, fly 13 days. Only one brood at each site. Vultures, hawks, carnivores, even leopards, feed on fallen young in huge colonies. **962**

Quiscalus niger *Icteridae*
GREATER ANTILLEAN GRACKLE   10-12 ins
Neotropical: Greater Antilles (W Indies); resident open settled and cultivated areas; large roosts in towns. ♂: black, glossed violet or steel blue; long tail wedge-shaped; legs, bill black, eyes light yellow. ♀ similar but duller. Harsh calls *chak chak, chin chin chi-lin*; also high-pitched *whee-see-ee* and bell-like note. Food various; specialised jaw muscles and slight keel within upper bill adapted for opening nuts; also takes fish, robs other nests. Gregarious at all times, breeding in colonies; large cup nest of sticks, soft plant materials high in trees, palms; occasionally in cat-tail (reed mace) swamps. 3 to 5 pale blue or clay-coloured eggs, spotted and scrawled dark brown; incubation and fledging as *Q. quiscala*. **912**

Quiscalus quiscala *Icteridae*
PURPLE GRACKLE   12 ins
Nearctic; breeds from Central Canada (S Mackenzie) SE over N America to S Florida, Gulf Coast, SE Texas; winters S from Maryland, Ohio Valley, Kansas. Habitat originally open woodland near water, adapted to cultivated land, pastures, parks, right into cities. ♂: very dark all over, glossed from green to blue or purple in different plumage phases. ♀ smaller, duller, glossy only head, neck breast. Legs, bill dark grey, eyes yellow. Juvenile uniform dull brown, eyes brown. Gregarious at all times, huge roosts city parks; often joins Red-winged Blackbird, *Agelaius phoeniceus*, and Starlings, *Sturnus vulgaris*. Call harsh *cack*; song: ascending squeaky, metallic notes 'like rusty iron gate'. ♂ displays plumage to ♀, depresses central tail feathers to emphasise keel effect. Food various: digs out insect grubs; wild fruits, nuts; waste, sometimes good grain; also fish taken in water, shellfish, small reptiles, mammals, birds and eggs; dunks dry bread. Breeds April onwards; colonies 25 pairs or more; bulky nest of twigs, stalks, grass, often cemented mud, lined fine grass; almost from ground level to 50 ft in tree, often evergreen, also bushes, holes in trees and buildings, other birds' nests, often near water or in clump on farmland. 5 pale blue eggs, spotted and scrawled brown or black, incubated *c.* 2 weeks; young fly *c.* 18 days. **913**

Rallina tricolor *Rallidae*
RED-NECKED RAIL or TRICOLOURED RAIL   11½ ins
Australasian: coast of N Queensland, New Guinea, Aru Islands. Migratory, arriving Queensland beginning of wet season to haunt dense tropical scrub along creeks and on slopes of rocky ridges. Back, wings and

tail dull brown; head, neck, mantle and breast rufous; belly brown mottled black; legs and rather long bill greenish, eyes dark. Very shy, usually found single or in pairs. Calls a repeated *kare*, also sharp *tok tok tok*. Feeds on insects and freshwater animals. Breeds January to April in Queensland, lining scrape on ground, often at base of tree, with dead leaves. 4 or 5 white eggs, marked red-brown and purple, incubated by ♀ and ♂ *c.* 2½ weeks; both probably also tend young. **235**

Rallus longirostris *Rallidae*
CLAPPER RAIL   14-16 (bill 2) ins
Nearctic and Neotropical: down E and W coasts USA, to W Indies, Central America, S Brazil and NW Peru; northern birds move S in winter. Race illustrated is western *R.l. levipes*. Habitat: salt marshes, mangrove swamps. Upperparts predominantly grey or grey brown, as on wings, shading from head (throat whitish, short white 'eyebrow') to buff breast and flanks; white belly barred grey-brown from legs to under tail coverts; legs yellowish, bill orange, tip dark; eyes light brown. Behaves much as relatives but swims frequently. Call a clattering *kek kek kek*, ending lower and slower. Breeds April to December Trinidad, building nest of local plants, hidden in tall grass or attached to rushes or to mangrove roots in swamps. Lays 3 to 13 eggs according to latitude, buff spotted brown and grey; often 2 broods. **236**

Rallus owstoni *Rallidae*
GUAM RAIL   11 ins
Confined to Guam in Marianas Islands, Micronesia; sedentary in long grass and ferns on damp ground at woodland edges. Upperparts brown; underparts and part of wings barred black and white; throat and stripe over eye grey, eyestripe brown; legs grey, bill dark brown, eyes red. Relatively tame, appearing on roads where killed by cars (J. A. Tubb). Has rattling chuckling call (Tubb); young call *tsip*. 'Leathery land slug' identified in food (J. T. Marshall). Breeds probably throughout year but no details available. **237**

Ramphocaenus melanurus *Muscicapidae*: *Polioptilinae*
LONG-BILLED GNAT WREN   5-5½ (bill 1) ins
Neotropical: tropical SE Mexico S to N Brazil, N Peru; also Trinidad. Resident dense forest undergrowth, dry forest. Crown, nape dull reddish brown; mantle grey brown; sides of head to flanks cinnamon; underparts buffy white to pale cinnamon; throat mottled black; narrow tail black, tipped white; legs pale lead-grey; very long bill brownish-white, eyes dark, orbits greyish. Often found among branches of fallen tree or in tangle of creepers. Call: distinctive soft trilled whistle. Insectivorous. Breeds April to June (Trinidad), building deep cup nest of grass, leaves, moss, lined dark plant fibres, in upright fork of bush or sapling *c.* 1½ ft up. 2 dull white eggs, spotted and speckled shades of brown, sometimes in zone. **723**

Ramphocelus icteronotus *Emberizidae*: *Thraupinae*
YELLOW-RUMPED TANAGER   8 ins
Neotropical: Panama, Colombia to NW Ecuador; damp clearings in forest, sea level to 5,000 ft or more. ♂: generally velvety black; lower back, rump, upper tail coverts lemon yellow. ♀: upperparts, including head, wings, tail, brownish black; rump, underparts bright yellow. Closely resembles and hybridises with Flame-rumped Tanager, *R. flammigerus*. Roosts trees, bushes. Food: fruit, insects. Breeds often in groups, ♀ building low, open nest. Usually 2 eggs, incubated ♀ 12 to 14 days, ♂ sometimes presenting food to eggs and both parents feeding young, who fly 10-13 days. **878**

Ramphocelus nigrogularis *Emberizidae*: *Thraupinae*
MASKED CRIMSON TANAGER   8 ins
Neotropical: SE Colombia from Caqueta S to E Peru and W into Amazonian Brazil; forests, especially secondary growth near watercourses, sea level to *c.* 4,000 ft. ♂: crimson, with throat, mask, mantle, wings, tail, centre belly black; base of lower mandible

silvery. ♀ similar but duller. Arboreal, roosting trees, bushes. Diet: fruit, insects. Breeds often in groups, details much as *R. icteronotus*. **879**

Recurvirostra avosetta *Recurvirostridae*
AVOCET   *c.* 17 (bill *c.* 3¼) ins
Mainly Palaearctic, with centre in Turkestan, extending E to Manchuria, S to Persian Gulf (isolated area Pakistan), W to scattered localities W Europe, especially North Sea coasts, Iberia; isolated areas Tunisia, Nile Delta, Lake Victoria, S Africa; local movements after breeding or to Ethiopian region, especially Rift Valley lakes; also other salt or alkaline lakes, estuaries. Breeds sand or mud shores of shallow salt and brackish waters, inland or coastal. White, patterned black on head and nape, scapulars, wing coverts and primaries; long legs blue-grey, uptilted, finely pointed bill black, eyes red-brown. Immatures black-brown and generally washed pale buff. Usually in parties or flocks at all seasons. Flies with neck partly retracted, legs well beyond tail, glides to land. Rests often on one leg or 'sits; walks quickly with body horizontal and neck curved. Call *klooet*, repeated rapidly in alarm. Mutual and social displays on ground. Diet: mainly small crustaceans and insects swept up when wading by scything action of bill; also swims and upends. Breeds from second half April Europe; sparsely lined scrape in open usually on low mound close to water holds 4 eggs very like lightly marked Lapwings, *Vanellus vanellus*. Incubation by ♀ and ♂ 21-22 days; they tend young at least 6 weeks. **302**

Regulus calendula *Muscicapidae: Sylviinae*
RUBY-CROWNED KINGLET   4 ins
Nearctic; marginally Neotropical: Alaska and arctic Canada S down Rockies and along Canada-USA border, expanding in E from Washington DC to just N of Newfoundland; one race on Guadeloupe I, Mexico; winters from N of $40°$N S to Guatemala. Breeding habitat: coniferous forest, often open stands; also spruce bogs, mixed woods; winters all types woodlands. Upperparts uniform olive grey; wings, tail dusky, narrowly edged yellowish-olive; 2 whitish wingbars; no 'eyebrow' but whitish orbits; ♂ has small scarlet patch on crown, usually concealed; underparts greyish-white; legs, bill blackish, eye very dark brown. Characteristic wing-flicking. Not very gregarious outside breeding season; but may associate other species. Defends territory vigorously, ♂ displaying scarlet crown. Calls: sharp, grating *kerr*, scolding chatter; song, heard on passage, remarkably loud, starts 4 to 8 high-pitched notes, then 5 to 10 octave lower, ending with repeated ascending groups of 3 short notes. Food: mainly insects, especially ants, aphids; seeds and berries in winter. Breeds May onwards, building mossy ball nest, lined feathers and suspended near tip of conifer branch. 5 to 11 creamy white eggs, speckled reddish-brown over lavender, incubated ♀ *c.* 16 days; young, fed ♀ and ♂, fly 18-20 days. **746**

Regulus regulus *Muscicapidae: Sylviinae*
GOLDCREST $3\frac{1}{2}$ ins
Palaearctic, marginally Oriental: very disrupted range, from Azores, N Iberia, Britain and Ireland over much of Europe NE to River Petchora; possibly separate population headwater of Rivers Ob and Yenisei; also from E coast Black Sea and N Iran to mountains of Turkestan, Himalayas, Tibet; separate population Amurland, Sakhalin, Japan. Resident conifer and mixed forests, occasionally pure broad-leaved, up to 5,000 ft Japanese Alps, over 14,000 ft E Tibet; some migration of northern populations in winter. Upperparts yellowish green; wings dark brown with some greenish edges and 2 white wingbars, one more prominent; tail dark brown, feathers edged green; forehead dusky brown, lemon yellow (to orange in ♂) crown stripe framed in black; whitish line round eye; throat pale brown, underparts whitish, tinged yellowish brown. Juvenile has upperparts all greyish brown tinged green and mottled black, especially sides of crown. Legs brown, bill black brown, eyes dark brown. Flits restlessly, generally high in trees, often in parties of titmice. ♂ shows crest mainly in display. Call: very thin, needling *zeeo zeeo zeeo;* song: thin and high-pitched repetition of almost dissyllabic note with terminal flourish. Food mainly insects at all stages. Breeds from early April to July, ♀ and ♂ building moss basket nest suspended usually from conifer branch near tip, held together with cobwebs, lined small dark feathers; also in ivy, other creepers, various bushes, 5 to 40 ft up. 7 or 8 buffish white eggs finely marked light brown usually in zone, incubated ♀ *c.* 16 days. Young, fed ♀ and ♂, fly 18-20 days. 2 broods. **747**

Regulus satrapa *Muscicapidae: Sylviinae*
GOLDEN-CROWNED KINGLET $3\frac{1}{2}$-4 ins
Nearctic: range as Ruby-Crowned, *R. calendula*, but not so far N, only just reaching Alaska; winters from Nova Scotia and British Columbia S through USA and Mexico to Guatemala. Breeding habitat: spruce forest, often in secondary growth mixed with birch, firs; on passage in broadleaved woods, thickets and weedy tangles; in winter usually in conifers, consorting with own species, chickadees, creepers, woodpeckers. Sometimes snared on burdock burs. Upperparts sombre olive-grey; wings, with 2 yellowish bars, and tail, dusky, edged yellowish; ♂ has orange crown (♀ yellow) with conspicuous black borders and white 'eyebrow'; hindneck grey; cheeks, underparts dull greyish to buffy olive; legs, bill, eyes all dark. Juvenile has no crown patch at first. Calls: single to several high-pitched notes like those of Treecreeper, *Certhia familiaris:* song 4 to 8 high notes, then rapidly descending series. Food: insects at all stages from egg. Breeds June onwards; nest globular, of moss and *Usnea*

lichen, bound cobwebs, lined feathers, fur, woven top and bottom in twigs of conifer branch, 30 to 60 ft up, occasionally lower. 8 to 10 creamy eggs, speckled red-brown over lavender, incubated ♀ *c.* 16 days; young, fed ♀ and ♂, fly 18-20 days. **748**

Remiz pendulinus *Paridae*
PENDULINE TIT $4\frac{1}{2}$ ins
Palaearctic: Central Europe across Eurasia mainly between $40°$ and $50°$N with some southward extensions, e.g. S France, Italy, Iberia. Mainly resident, some dispersion: reed marshes and dense scrub by rivers, freshwater and brackish lakes with variety of trees; also wooded steppes; reed beds in winter. ♂: upperparts rusty brown; head (with broad black mask), rump grey; wings, tail blackish with pale feather edges; throat white, underparts very pale buff, streaked rust on flanks; legs, bill blackish, eyes dark brown. Some races, e.g. *R.p. macronyx*, have black heads and throats; others, e.g. *coronatus*, have pale crown with mask merging back of head. ♀, much duller; juvenile lacks mask. Feeds in summer often high in trees, taking minute insects from extremities of twigs; also searches willows, reeds, reed mace; small seeds in winter from shore vegetation and withered flowerheads. Usual call soft plaintive *seeou*, also *tseep tseep tseep* from family parties. Breeds May onwards, ♂ starts by weaving basic loop of plant fibres, ♀ joins in to build fleecy, bottle-shaped nest of down, hung from tips of willow, tamarisk, other twigs overhanging water, 5 to 20, even 60 ft up, completed *c.* 2 weeks. 6 to 8 rather pointed white eggs incubated ♀ *c.* 13 days; she mainly tends young, who fly 16-18 days. **809**

Rhamphastos sulfuratus *Ramphastidae*
KEEL-BILLED TOUCAN   18-20 (bill $5\frac{1}{2}$) ins
Netropical: Mexico to Venezuela, N Colombia; resident in lowland rain forest up to 2,600 ft. Predominantly black; crown and mantle dark maroon; upper tail coverts white; throat, upper breast deep yellow; under tail coverts crimson; legs blackish; bill variable: upper mandible pea green with wedge-shaped orange patch at cutting edge, tip crimson; lower, pea green at base, light blue, tip crimson; eyes brown. Loosely gregarious, small flocks, mixed with other species, straggling through forest in undulating flight. Sometimes playful 'fencing' with bills. Display not spectacular but courtship-type feeding noted. Bathes in water collected in tree crotches. Call: monotonous croaking repeated for several minutes with head jerking and swaying of body, other birds joining in. In captivity roosts with bill laid along back, tail folded forward over it, to become 'featureless ball of feathers' (A. F. Skutch). When feeding, tears piece off fruit, juggles it with tips of bill, throws head back to let it drop into gullet; similarly drinks by dipping bill into water and tilting it up; also takes cicadas and other large insects. Nests in tree holes, sometimes enlarging old woodpecker borings; height very variable; some lining of green leaves. 2 to 4 white eggs incubated by ♀ and ♂ *c.* 16 days; both parents feed young, born with 'heel' pads on tarsus; bill develops over several months; fledging 6-7 weeks.

Rhea americana *Rheidae*
COMMON RHEA   60 ins tall
Resident South America from NE Brazil to Central Argentina in well vegetated country rather than open grassland. Both sexes rather drab brown all over, ♂ with black base to neck; no tail feathers; legs and bill light brown, eyes dark. Wings longer than Ostrich's but useless; runs very fast with neck almost horizontal. Flocks of 20 to 30 break up in breeding season when ♂♂ fight each other and display to ♀♀, running, jerking neck and wings and roaring, noise accentuated by inflated oesophagus. Repertory of other calls. Food mainly vegetable; some insects and small vertebrates. Nest scrape in concealed site made and lined by ♂; several ♀♀ lay 12 to 30 eggs, golden yellow at first, in

same nest, where incubated by ♂ for c. 6 weeks. ♂ tends brood, who grow big as adults in 4 months, mature at 2 years. **2**

RHEA, COMMON see **Rhea americana**

Rhinoptilus africanus see **Hemerodromus africanus**

Rhipidura fuliginosa *Muscicapidae: Muscicapinae*
GREY FANTAIL   6½ (tail 3-3½) ins
Australasian: all round continental Australia; Tasmania; New Zealand, New Caledonia, New Hebrides; disperses after breeding into interior Australia. Habitat forest edge and scattered trees in grassland, along streams; less often in thick forest; common cultivated areas, parks, gardens in NZ. Upperparts greyish or olive brown; 2 small white bars on wing; outer feathers of tail have white inner webs, central pair dark; white 'eyebrow' and ear coverts; throat white, narrow black band at base; underparts yellowish buff. Black form in South Island, NZ, sooty black above, chocolate brown below, sometimes small white patch behind eye. Legs dark brown, bill, eyes black. Immature duller. Wags small body side to side, tail upward and downward, fanning it; but closed when pursuing insects on wing. Follows flocks, even humans, who disturb prey. Highly territorial when breeding. Call sharp *cheet;* rasping twittering gives Maori name *piwaka-waka*. Breeds August to January, building 'tailed' nest of assorted plant materials, bound cobwebs, lined hair, in fork among twigs at end of branch, often over stream, lake, 6 to 20 ft up. 2 to 4 creamy eggs, spotted grey, brown, mainly at big end, incubated ♀ and ♂ 15 days; both feed young, who fly c. 15 days. 2 to 5 broods (New Zealand). **790**

Rhipidura rufifrons *Muscicapidae: Muscicapinae*
RUFOUS FANTAIL   6½ ins
Australasian: islands to Guam, including Celebes, Solomons; continental Australia from extreme NW eastward to Gulf of Carpentaria; Cape York to Otway Ranges, Victoria; southern populations migratory. Habitat humid forests, migrating through dry ones. Upperparts brown tinged rufous, becoming orange-rufous lower back, tail, of which terminal half blackish brown; throat white, lower throat black, breast feathers black edged white, rest of underparts white; legs, bill, eyes brown. Acrobatic in flight though not as masterly as Grey Fantail, *R. fuliginosa*; flies directly through dense undergrowth; tail kept fanned. Takes insects off foliage at lower levels of forest, also on wing and feeds more on ground than Grey Fantail. Breeds November to January New South Wales, building nest similar to but rather coarser than Grey Fantail, usually in thin lateral fork 3 to 30 ft up in understorey. Usually 2 stone to buff eggs, minutely spotted yellow or reddish brown at big end; incubation and fledging as *R. fuliginosa*. **791**

Rhynochetus jubatus *Rhynochetidae*
KAGU   22 ins
Australasian: confined to remoter mountain forests of New Caledonia. Upperparts of loose plumage ashy grey, tinged brownish on back and coverts of broad, rounded wings which are barred black, white and chestnut; ragged erectile crest pale grey, underparts pale buffish grey; scattered powderdown; legs, bill orange-red, eyes red. Little studied in wild. Cannot fly well; runs fast for short distances, wings partly spread. Normally on ground but can perch 3 or 4 ft up. In display pair stand erect facing each other, crests raised, wings spread; ♂ attacks ♀'s feet. Also whirling antics, holding tip of tail or wing in bill. Loud rattling call heard at night; probably nocturnal in wild. Food: molluscs, especially snail *Placostylus bavayi*, shell broken by blow of bill; worms, insects to locust size. Breeds probably August to January in wild; ♀ and ♂ in captivity build nest of stocks and leaves. Single buff egg, marked brown over grey, incubated ♀ and ♂ 36 days. Chick leaves nest after 3 days, feeds itself in 4 weeks. **239**

Rhyticeros plicatus see **Aceros plicatus**

RICHARDSON'S OWL see **Aegolius funereus**

RICHARD'S PIPIT see **Anthus novaeseelandiae**

Richmondena cardinalis see **Pyrrhuloxia cardinalis**

RIFLEMAN see **Acanthisitta chloris**

RING-BILLED GULL see under **Larus californicus**

RING-NECKED
  PARAKEET, INDIAN see **Psittacula krameri**
  PARROT, see **Barnardius barnardi**
  PHEASANT see **Phasianus colchicus**

RINGED
  PLOVER see **Charadrius hiaticula**
  TEAL see **Calonetta leucophrys**

Riparia paludicola *Hirundinidae*
AFRICAN SAND MARTIN   4½ ins
Palaearctic (marginally), Ethiopian, Oriental: 7 races; breeds W Morocco, all Africa south of French Sudan and Ethiopia (not Zaire), Madagascar, Indian subcontinent S to Bombay; Laos, Thailand, Philippines, Taiwan. Many races partially migratory within Africa. Habitat: open country, especially by streams and rivers. Upperparts mouse brown, chin to upper belly mouse brown, rest underparts white (sometimes all mouse brown); tail slightly forked; legs brownish-black, bill black, eyes brown. Often congregates in large flocks. Call a dry *svee-svee;* twittering warble in breeding season. Feeds on aerial insects preferably over water. Breeding season variable and often prolonged, especially in N. Nests colonially in holes in sandbanks (c. 2 ft deep). 3 or 4 white eggs. **621**

Rissa tridactyla *Laridae*
KITTIWAKE   c. 16 ins
Holarctic: *R. t. tridactyla*, Gulf of St Lawrence, coasts of Labrador, arctic Canada, Greenland, arctic Europe, Britain and Ireland, N France; *pollicaris*, coasts Bering Sea and N Pacific. Habitat: only truly oceanic gull, outside breeding season disperses to open sea 60°N to Tropic of Cancer. Differs from Common Gull, *Larus canus*, in lacking white patches on black wing tips. Legs brownish black, bill greenish yellow, eyes dark brown with orange-red orbital ring. Immature (tarrock): some blackish mottling above eyes and round ears, broad black collar on hindneck, black terminal band on tail, back mottled with black, diagonal blackish bar on wings. Often follows ships, picks food up from surface in flight, settles and dives, or plunges in from flight like terns; also feeds on flats at low tide; takes small fish and marine invertebrates. Breeds May to July in noisy colonies on cliffs or walls of sea caves, occasionally on building (Britain); makes neat nest on ledge, of seaweed, sometimes grass and moss, with deepish cup; 1 to 3 pale blue-grey to light brown eggs, marked darker brown and underlying ashy. Both parents incubate c. 21-24 days; young fly 4-5 weeks. **333**

RIVER MARTIN, ALPINE see **Pseudochelidon eurystomina**

RIVOLI'S HUMMINGBIRD see under **Lampornis clemenciae**

ROADRUNNER see **Geococcyx californianus**

ROATOLO see **Mesitornis unicolor**

ROBIN,
  AMERICAN see **Turdus migratorius**
  EUROPEAN see **Erithacus rubecula**
  HOODED see **Petroica cucullata**
  NORTHERN SCRUB see under **Dryomodus brunneipygia**
  PEKIN see **Leiothrix lutea**
  PINK see **Petroica rodinogaster**
  RED-BACKED see **Erythropygia zambesiana**
  RED-CAPPED see **Petroica goodenovii**
  SCARLET see **Petroica multicolor**
  SOUTHERN SCRUB see **Dryomodus brunneipygia**
  WHITE-BREASTED see **Eopsaltria georgiana**
  WHITE-BROWED see **Erythropygia zambesiana**
  YELLOW see **Eopsaltria australis**

ROBIN CHAT,
  CAPE see **Cossypha caffra**
  SNOWY-CROWNED see **Thamnolaea coronata**
  WHITE-THROATED see **Cossypha humeralis**

ROCK
  BUNTING see **Emberiza cia**
  DOVE see **Columba livia**
  MARTIN, AFRICAN see **Hirundo fuligula**
  NUTHATCH, EASTERN see under **Sitta neumayer**
  PIGEON, WHITE-QUILLED see **Petrophassa albipennis**
  PTARMIGAN see **Lagopus mutus**
  SANDPIPER see under **Calidris maritima**
  SPARROW see **Petronia petronia**
  THRUSH see **Monticola saxatilis**
  THRUSH, SWINHOE'S see **Monticola gularis**
  THRUSH, WHITE-THROATED see **Monticola gularis**

ROCKFOWL,
  GREY-NECKED see **Picathartes gymnocephalus**
  WHITE-NECKED see under **Picathartes gymnocephalus**

ROCKHOPPER see under **Eudyptes chrysolophus**

ROCKWREN see **Xenicus gilviventris**

ROLLER,
  ABYSSINIAN see **Coracias abyssinica**
  CUCKOO see **Leptosomus discolor**
  EUROPEAN see **Coracias garrulus**
  INDIAN see **Coracias bengalensis**
  LILAC-BREASTED see **Coracias caudata**
  LONG-TAILED GROUND see **Uratelornis chimaera**

Rollulus roulroul *Phasianidae*
GREEN WOOD PARTRIDGE   10 ins
Oriental: Malaysia, Indonesia, Borneo; sedentary in dense evergreen forest up to 4,000 ft, favouring drier and sometimes open spots, also bamboos. ♂: upperparts bright green; head, neck and underparts blue-black; graduated crest scarlet; wings dark brown with orange primaries; tail terminally black; legs red, bill black and red, eyes hazel, facial skin scarlet. ♀: lacks crest, underparts green, wings chestnut, bill black. Moves actively in small coveys, keeping to cover; later pairs keep together. Call a soft mellow whistle. Diet: seeds, fruit, plant stems; insects scratched or dug up. Builds domed nest of dead leaves and stems with side entrance; lays 4 to 6 creamy white eggs incubated by ♀; ♂ and ♀ feed brood 5-6 days; they stay with parents c.3 months. **207**

ROOK see **Corvus frugilegus**

ROSE-BREASTED GROSBEAK see **Pheucticus melanocephalus**

ROSE-COLOURED STARLING see **Sturnus roseus**

ROSE-RINGED PARAKEET see **Psittacula krameri**

ROSEATE
  SPOONBILL see **Ajaia ajaja**
  TERN see **Sterna dougallii**

ROSEFINCH,
  LONG-TAILED see **Uragus sibiricus**
  PRZEVALSKI'S see **Urocynchramus pylzowi**

ROSELLA,
  CRIMSON see **Platycercus elegans**
  EASTERN see under **Platycercus eximius** and **Psephotus haematodus**

ROSS'S TOURACO see **Musophaga rossae**

Rostratula benghalensis *Rostratulidae*
PAINTED SNIPE   ♀: 10, ♂: 9½ ins
S and E Palaearctic (Asia Minor, Iran, S China, Japan), Ethiopian and Madagascar, Oriental (not Borneo, Celebes), Australasian (not New Guinea, New Zealand). Nomadic, haunting swamps, ponds and ricefields, coastal *Salicornia* marshes, sea level to 7,000 ft. Sex roles reversed. ♀: upperparts rich bronze-green with dark vermiculations and yellow V on back; wings spotted and barred buff; sides of head and neck chestnut brown with white 'spectacles' round eyes and black bank across breast; stripe from white underparts curls up round wing. ♂: olive-brown above glossed green with buff central stripe from bill over crown; white 'spectacles', back and wings much as ♀; throat white, mottled olive brown neck and breast crossed by black band; underparts as ♀. Legs slatey-blue, long bill purplish brown, eyes, set for binocular vision, dark brown. Secretive, most active dawn and dusk; runs and stands with lowered head, flies like rail rather than snipe. 'Song' *koht khot koht;* alarm call *kek.* Whistle from ♂, more powerful noises from ♀ in spectacular courtship: wings extended like Sun Bittern, *Eurypyga helias,* tail fanned; also as threat. Diet: large insects, e.g. crickets, molluscs and worms; some grasses. Breeding season variable, makes scrape in bush or sedge cover, laying 4 pale yellow eggs, heavily marked black and purple, incubated by ♂ *c.* 20 days; he also tends brood, feigning injury if disturbed. **252**

ROSY PASTOR see **Sturnus roseus**

ROSY-BREASTED LONGCLAW see **Macronyx ameliae**

ROTHSCHILD'S
  MYNAH see **Leucopsar rothschildi**
  STARLING see **Leucopsar rothschildi**

ROYAL TERN see under **Thalasseus elegans**

RUBY-CROWNED KINGLET see **Regulus calendula**

RUBY-THROATED HUMMINGBIRD see **Archilochus colubris**

RUBYTHROAT, SIBERIAN see **Luscinia calliope**

RUDDY QUAIL DOVE see **Geotrygon montana**

RUFF see **Philomachus pugnax**

RUFOUS
  BUSH CHAT see **Cercotrichas galactotes**
  FANTAIL see **Rhipidura rufifrons**
  FIELD WREN see **Calamanthus campestris**
  GNATEATER see **Conopophaga lineata**
  GRASS WARBLER see **Cisticola galactotes**
  HUMMINGBIRD see **Selasphorus rufus**
  JAY THRUSH, FUKEIN see **Garrulax caerulatus**
  MOTMOT see **Baryphthengus ruficapillus**
  SCRUB BIRD see **Atrichornis rufescens**
  SONGLARK see **Cinclorhamphus mathewsi**

RUFOUS-BROWED PEPPERSHRIKE see **Cyclarhis gujanensis**

RUFOUS-CROWNED WARBLER see **Basileuterus rufifrons**

RUFOUS-NAPED LARK see **Mirafra africana**

RUFOUS-SIDED TOWHEE see **Pipilo erythrophthalmus**

RUFOUS-TAILED
  JACAMAR see **Galbula ruficauda**
  PLANTCUTTER see **Phytotoma rara**

RUFOUS-VENTED CHACHALACA see **Ortalis ruficauda**

Rupicola peruviana *Cotingidae*
PERUVIAN or
ANDEAN COCK OF THE ROCK   11 ins
Neotropical: NW Venezuela, Colombian Andes to E and W Ecuador, E and S Peru, N Bolivia; resident steep ravines above watercourses, 4,000 to 7,500 ft. ♂: generally brilliant orange, surmounted by narrow, bushy crest from base of bill to top of nape; wings and tail black, inner flight feathers pearly grey. Legs yellow, small bill, almost hidden by fringe of crest, orange yellow; eyes yellow, rimmed black and yellow. ♀: generally, including small crest and tail, orange brown to dull red; inner flight feathers greyish brown. Ground living, unlike most of family, with strong legs. ♂♂ have social displays, rather like leks of grouse; each clearing small area and performing rather static dances, holding a posture for several minutes. ♀♀ gather and watch. Also nests socially, ♀ building shallow mud cup, strengthened with leaves and twigs and attached to rock face; several quite close together, 2 eggs incubated by ♀ only. **595**

RUPPELL'S VULTURE see under **Gyps africanus**

RUSTY BLACKBIRD see **Euphagus carolinus**

RUSTY-BREASTED ANT PITTA see **Grallaricula ferrugineipectus**

RUSTY-CHEEKED SCIMITAR BABBLER see **Pomatorhinus erythrogenys**

Rynchops nigra *Rynchopidae*
BLACK SKIMMER   16-20 ins
Nearctic and Neotropical: from New Jersey on Atlantic coast to Buenos Aires, from Mexico on Pacific to Magallanes, Chile; has bred Lake Titicaca in Andes; winters from Mexico S to Straits of Magellan. Habitat: beaches, saltings and estuaries; grassland in S America in winter. Upperparts from crown to base of forked tail black, with white trailing edges to wings; forks of tail, underparts from forehead white, legs red, bill black, red based, lower mandible longer and larger than upper; eyes dark brown. Spends much of day resting on sandbanks and beaches, feeding mostly dawn and dusk over calm, shallow water. Skims surface, wings above body, lower bill entering water; when it strikes fish, upper bill closes; prey flipped out, swallowed, and flight proceeds without pause. Call compared to dog's bark: resonant *auw.* Breeds May onwards in USA in scattered colonies, up to 4,000 pairs, often with terns. 2 to 5 light buff eggs, marked all over black, purple and grey, incubated mainly by ♀ in scrape in sand. Mandibles of chick equal length on hatching, lower develops when nearly full grown. **342**

SABINE'S GULL see **Xema sabini**

SABREWING HUMMINGBIRD, LAZULINE see **Campylopterus falcatus**

SACRED
  IBIS see **Threskiornis aethiopicus**
  KINGFISHER see **Halcyon sancta**

SADDLEBACK see **Creadion carunculatus**

SADDLEBILL see **Ephippiorhynchus senegalensis**

SAGE GROUSE see **Centrocercus urophasianus**

Sagittarius serpentarius *Sagittariidae*
SECRETARY BIRD   *c.* 48 ins
Ethiopian; sedentary. Open plains, also savannah, bushveld and cultivated land. Upperparts bluish grey with long black crest; underparts greyish white; rump black, upper tail coverts white; graduated tail with long central feathers, grey, black and white; legs flesh, bill dark grey, cere bluish, facial skin pink, eyes hazel. Walks deliberately with constant head movements; broad winged in flight with projecting legs and tail. Quick stamping steps startle prey (ground animals, including snakes) which is seized by quick thrust of head, or stamped upon if large. Roosts in

trees. Territorial when breeding, with soaring displays. Normally silent, growls in display and at nest. Breeding season variable, lays May to June in Kenya; up to 40 ft in tree or bush. Lays 2 or 3 white eggs, streaked brown, in flat nest of sticks with finer lining. Incubated by ♀ *c.* 45 days. Chicks fed by both parents, fly in 65-80 days. **174**

SAKABULA see **Euplectes progne**

SAKER see **Falco cherrug**

Salpornis spilonotus *Sittidae*
SPOTTED CREEPER   6 ins
Oriental (Indian subcontinent), Ethiopian: most of region S to Zambia, Rhodesia, N South Africa; Himalayan foothills, in Africa savannah, acacia, *Brachystegia* woodland. Generally brown: upperparts, wings liberally spotted white, and wings tipped white; soft-feathered blackish tail barred white; black eye-stripe, broad white 'eyebrow'; underparts washed buff, also spotted white and blackish; legs lead grey; slender curved bill dusky, base lower mandible whitish, eyes brown. Habits like treecreepers, *Certhia* species, climbing trunks to probe bark, flying on to base of next tree; but can also move head downwards; often with other species. Longer flights undulating. Calls: shrill, whistling *sweepy swip swip;* single *tseee;* harsh *kek kek kek.* Food: insects from bark: caterpillars, beetles, ants. Breeding season variable within African range; March and April Asia; small cup of plant material, adorned lichens, cocoons, larval faeces, woven to lateral branch, often at fork or near trunk, 25 ft or more up. 2 or 3 pale turquoise blue eggs, zoned black spots, brown and lavender markings, incubated ♀, ♂ singing nearby. Both parents brood young.

Saltator atripennis *Emberizidae: Pyrrhuloxiinae*
BLACK-WINGED SALTATOR   8½ ins
Neotropical: Colombian Andes, W Ecuador; open woodlands, pastures, thickets, *c.* 2,500 to 7,500 ft. Upperparts bright olive green; wings, tail black; head, neck black (crown grey in one race), long 'eyebrow', ear coverts, throat white; underparts light grey, under tail coverts cinnamon buff. Voice rather weak. Diet: berries, fruit, some flowers and seeds. Breeding: ♀, accompanied ♂, builds bulky open nest near ground in bush. Usually 2 eggs, incubated ♀ 13-14 days, ♂ in attendance; both parents tend young, who leave nest but are fed for several weeks. 2 or more broods. **874**

SALTATOR, BLACK-WINGED see **Saltator atripennis**

SANDERLING see **Calidris alba**

SAND
  MARTIN, AFRICAN see **Riparia paludicola**
  PLOVER, KITTLITZ's see **Charadrius pecuarius**

SANDGROUSE,
  BLACK-FACED see **Eremialector decoratus**
  CHESTNUT-BELLIED see **Pterocles exustus**
  FOUR-BANDED see **Eremialector quadricinctus**
  PALLAS's see **Syrrhaptes paradoxus**

SANDHILL CRANE see under **Grus americana**

SANDPIPER,
  BROAD-BILLED see **Limicola falcinellus**
  BUFF-BREASTED see **Tryngites subruficollis**
  COMMON see **Tringa hypoleucos**
  CURLEW see **Calidris ferruginea**
  MARSH see **Tringa stagnatilis**
  PURPLE see **Calidris maritima**
  RED-BACKED see **Calidris alpina**
  ROCK see under **Calidris maritima**
  SPOTTED see under **Tringa hypoleucos**
  STILT see **Micropalma himantopus**
  WHITE-RUMPED see **Calidris fuscicollis**
  WOOD see **Tringa glareola**

SANDPIPER PLOVER
  DIADEMED see **Phegornis mitchelli**
  MITCHELL's see **Phegornis mitchelli**

Sarcogyps calvus or Torgos calvus *Accipitridae*
ASIAN KING VULTURE   32 ins
Oriental region: Indian subcontinent to Laos; S Yunnan. Resident in forests, sometimes dense and humid, as well as cultivated land. Generally black, with white patches above thigh and thin white line on spread wing. Ruff black, bare head and neck red to orange; legs red, bill dark horn, cere orange, eyes brown. Immature brown. Slimmer and longer winged than *Gyps bengalensis*. Rather solitary but up to 10 may gather at carcase. Soars much of day, and flies over grass fires after small carcasses. Spectacular aerial display flights with loud roaring calls; also squeaks, hisses and grunts. Feeds on carrion. Peak of laying in India February to March, in trees from 3 to 100 ft, sometimes with other vultures. ♀ and ♂ build nest of sticks and leafy branches, incubating 1 greenish white, rarely marked egg for about 45 days and then tending chick. **163**

Sarcorhamphus papa *Cathartidae*
SOUTH AMERICAN KING VULTURE   *c.* 31 ins
Neotropical: Central America southward, to Argentina E of Andes and N Peru to W of them. Primary habitat rain forest, but hunts savannah and grassy areas up to 4,000 ft, coastal marshes El Salvador. Body plumage, under wing coverts creamy white; rump, tail, most of wings black; bare head and neck variable orange, red, blue, with bristly feathers on crown; legs greyish white, strongly hooked bill reddish-orange with black base, caruncles and cere orange; eyes white in reddish orbits. Immature sooty black, acquiring white with age. Rather laboured flapping flight followed by glide. Circling, wing flapping and whistling in courtship. Does not approach habitations. Not very gregarious, 3 or 4 together in air, but up to 50 at carcass, where dominates other vultures; also kills new born calves, small reptiles. Breeds from March Panama, nesting in hollow stump near ground, laying 1 to 3 white eggs, incubated ♀ and ♂ 56-58 days (captive). Young may stay with parents up to 2 years. **132**

Sarkidiornis melanotos *Anatidae*
COMB DUCK or
KNOB-BILLED GOOSE   ♀: *c.* 24, ♂: 30 ins
Ethiopian, Oriental, Neotropical: Africa from Gambia and Sudan S to Cape and Madagascar; India, Ceylon, Burma and SE China; S American race from Venezuela to S Brazil, Paraguay and N Argentina. Habitat: large open waters or rivers. ♂: black with iridescent green and bronze upperparts and white underparts; head and neck white with black spots. ♀: smaller and duller. S American race similar but both sexes have darker flanks. Legs grey-black, bill black with flat knob in ♂, eyes brown. Essentially tree duck, usually in flocks; flies powerfully in V formation, with rushing sound, may travel inland to feed on cultivated areas, roosts in trees at night. Call: short hoarse whistle; loud trumpet-like calls when disturbed near nest. Feeds on aquatic plants and insects, grass and crops. Breeds all months, making large nest of reeds and rushes lined with feathers, on ground in long grass, in reeds or hollows of trees. Polygamous. Lays 4 to 8 shining yellowish white eggs. **127**

Saxicola torquata *Muscicapidae*: *Turdinae*
STONECHAT   5 ins
Palaearctic, Oriental, Ethiopian: most of Europe (very local NW Africa) SW of line Denmark to Crimea; Asia Minor, Caucasus connected by mountains with vast area Asia to China. Korea, Sakhalin, Japan; much of E Africa, extending W to Zaire, in small isolated mountain areas; Madagascar. Mainly sedentary, part N population moves south in winter. Habitat: variety open country, flat or hilly, with bushes, scattered trees; heaths, moors, rough grassland, subalpine meadows and scrub; to 15,300 ft W China; also cultivated land, roadsides; heath, scrub and wasteland in winter. ♂: upperparts black-brown; white wing patch and rump (more pronounced some races), dark brown tail; head, throat black, partial white collar runs into chestnut breast which shades to whitish belly; duller autumn due to brown feather margins. ♀ has upperparts mottled dark brown; face, throat brown. Legs, bill black, eyes dark brown. Juvenile resembles ♀. Flits between exposed perches, often calling and flirting tail, then drops to ground after prey. Calls: hard *tsak tsak,* becoming *hwee-tsak-tsak* of alarm; song variable but musical, sometimes delivered in display flight when ♂ rises up to 100 ft and 'dances in air'. Food mainly ground-living insects, worms, snails; small seeds and fruits. Breeds second half March to August Britain; ♀ building nest of grass and moss, lined softly with hair, fur, feathers; usually well hidden in low vegetation, sometimes 2 ft up in thick bush. 5 or 6 pale blue eggs spotted red-brown in zone, incubated by ♀ 14-15 days; both parents feed young, who fly 12-16 days. 2, sometimes 3 broods. **699**

Scenopoeetes dentirostris *Ptilinorhynchidae*
TOOTH-BILLED CATBIRD or
STAGEMAKER   *c.* 10½ ins
Australasian: tropical NE Queensland between Cooktown and Mount Spec; wet montane forest a few miles inland. Upperparts, including wings, tail, brown; underparts fawn mottled brown; yellowish base to throat feathers visible when singing; legs, bill, eyes reddish brown. Toothed bill used by ♂ to saw through leaf petioles for daily decoration of 'stage' (display ground); leaves strewn pale side uppermost contrast with dark forest floor. Stage usually oval or circular, between 3 and 8 ft diameter, only seen August to December. ♂ perches on 'singing stick', uttering constant penetrating stream of melody; own notes, mainly *chuck chuck,* and mimicked calls. Food: fruit, some insects, large ground molluscs. Breeds November to January; flimsy, saucer-shaped nest of thin sticks lined finer twigs, in thick foliage 20 to 100 ft up; 2 creamy to creamy brown eggs. Young fed mainly on insects.

Scissirostrum dubium *Sturnidae*
CELEBES STARLING   *c.* 9 ins
Australasian, Oriental: confined to Celebes Is, where abundant in variety of habitats. Generally slaty mouse grey; wings, tail black, coverts edged grey; rump, upper tail coverts, flanks black with long, stiff, wax-like red appendages; lores (with bristles), orbits blackish; under wing coverts slaty grey, under tail coverts smoky black; legs, bill orange, eyes red. Juvenile browner, tips of specialised feathers less waxy. Gregarious, forming large breeding colonies in dead trees. Behaves like woodpecker, using stiff tail feathers to support itself against tree trunks, both for digging out larvae and excavating nest hole. Nostrils in bony grooves open almost directly upwards, presumably as protection against 'sawdust'. Also takes grain and fruit. Breeding season irregular.

Scolopax rusticola *Scolopacidae*
EURASIAN WOODCOCK   *c.* 13½ (bill *c.* 3) ins
Palaearctic: broad band mainly between 50° and 60°N, covering W Europe except Mediterranean area, and extending across Eurasia to Sakhalin and Japan; isolated areas Atlantic Islands, Corsica, Caucasus, Himalayas. Northern populations move south and some winter N Africa, Middle East, India, Ceylon, S China, usually near water and in thick cover. Breeds broadleaved and mixed forests, also open conifers, wet woodlands, scrub, even moorland edge. Upperparts, including rounded wings, complex pattern of browns, buff and black with bars on nape, dark streaks on face; tail with dark subterminal band; underparts fairly evenly barred light and dark brown; legs and long bill dull flesh, large eyes, set far back in head, black-brown. Crepuscular in habits, so usually seen when flushed, flying off rather noisily through trees, or in 'roding' display over wood early or late, when ♂ calls high-pitched *chissick* and deep croak; also courts on ground. Probes in damp earth for small animals, especially earthworms. Breeds from end March in S of range; scrape, lined dead leaves usually partly sheltered by bracken, brambles, other lightish cover, on dry ground. 4 rather round buff eggs, spotted and streaked chestnut and lilac; incubated by ♀ 20-21 days; she tends young *c.* 2½ weeks, sometimes flying with them between legs if disturbed. **293**

Scopus umbretta *Scopidae*
HAMERKOP   22-24 ins (♀ smaller than ♂)
Ethiopian: S Sudan to Cape, and west to Senegal (3 races); resident in open areas near water. All brown with 'hammer head' silhouette; legs and bill black, eyes brown. Generally seen singly or in pairs, but semi-nocturnal with owl-like flight, neck partly extended, giving curious small-bodied appearance. Courtship display elaborate, accompanied by yapping cackle; calls in flight thin and squeaking; also grunts. Feeds by shuffling in water to disturb aquatic animals, especially frogs; also scavenges roads for carrion; young fed largely on tadpoles. Breeds almost throughout year, building enormous domed nest largely of sticks in tree-fork 15 to 40 ft up, with mud-plastered entrance; 3 to 6 white eggs incubated by ♀ and ♂ for *c.* 30 days; young fly in *c.* 7 weeks. **66**

SCRUB ROBIN, WHITE-BROWED see **Erythropygia zambesiana**

SCRUB WARBLER, KNYSNA see **Bradypterus sylvaticus**

SCRUB WREN,
   SPOTTED see **Sericornis maculatus**
   WHITE-BROWED see **Sericornis frontalis**

Scytalopus magellanicus *Rhinocryptidae*
ANDEAN TAPACULO   4½-5 ins
Neotropical: NW Venezuela, Colombia (Santa Maria Mtns, Andes) S to N Bolivia; W Argentina (Mendoza) and Chile (Atacoma) to Tierra del Fuego, Cape Horn, Falkland Is; resident in forests, especially in ravines, up to 13,000 ft. Small short-tailed wren-like bird whose plumage varies from very dark uniform slaty grey to pale silvery with cinnamon flanks and rump barred dark grey; some races have pale grey 'eyebrow'; southern races sometimes show silvery crown spot. Immature: upperparts cinnamon brown; wings marked black and buff; rump, tail barred yellowish. Like all family, very poor flier, creeping over forest floor, skulking in thick cover. Call rendered *choo-rin choo-rin* (race *S.m. fuscus* N Chile) distinct from *pa-tras pa-tras* (race *magellanicus* S Chile); startling *ha-hu ha-hu* when disturbed. Diet mainly insects and their larvae; spiders. Breeds October-November Chile; *magellanicus* builds rather large nest of roots, fibres, moss, lined fine grass, hair, in crevice among rocks, behind bark, under tree roots; *fuscus* makes 2 ft tunnel with tiny entrance in thick vegetation of steep bank. 2 to 4 round glossy white eggs incubated ♀ and ♂; if flushed, bird leaves nest on foot.

SCYTHEBILL, BLACK-BILLED see
Campylorhamphus falcularius

SEA EAGLE, WHITE-BREASTED see **Haliaeetus leucogaster**

SEASIDE CINCLODES see under **Cinclodes fuscus**

SECRETARY BIRD see **Sagittarius serpentarius**

SEDGE
   WARBLER see **Acrocephalus schoenobaenus**
   WARBLER, AFRICAN see **Bradypterus baboecala**

SEEDEATER,
   VARIABLE see **Sporoptila americana**
   WHITE-THROATED see **Serinus albogularis**

SEEDSNIPE, WHITE-BELLIED see **Attagis malouinus**

Seisura inquieta see **Myiagra inquieta**

Seiurus auricapillus *Parulidae*
OVENBIRD   6 ins
Nearctic: breeds Newfoundland, Central Quebec, N Ontario, SW Mackenzie S to E North Carolina, Georgia, Arkansas, Colorado. S Alberta; winters from S Carolina and Gulf Coast to Lesser Antilles; through Mexico to Colombia. Habitat: floor of mature dry woodlands with not too dense undergrowth; also swampy forest with heavier cover. Upperparts olive brown, darker on wings; rufous crown stripe bordered black; white and faint black moustachial stripes; throat white; underparts white spotted black on breast, flanks; colours deeper and richer in autumn. ♀ has paler crown stripe. Legs light brown, bill horn brown, eyes dark brown, orbits white. Does not wag tail but raises it slightly and droops wings as steps over leaves. Usual song repeated *teacher teacher;* flight song May to September, often nocturnal and up to 100 ft above trees, jumble of notes, warbling and twitterings. Food: invertebrate animals from litter. Breeds May to July, ♀ and ♂ building domed nest of leaves, fibres, lined grass, hair; rather open sites but sunk in ground and hard to see. 4 or 5 white eggs, spotted brown, incubated ♀ *c.* 12 days; both parents feed young, who fly *c.* 12 days. Sometimes 2 broods. **899**

Selasphorus rufus *Trochilidae*
RUFOUS HUMMINGBIRD   3½ ins
Nearctic: breeds Alaska to NW California; winters chiefly S Mexico. Habitats various: forest edge to gardens. ♂: upperparts from nape to dark-tipped tail rufous; forehead, wing coverts glossy green, flight feathers dark brown; gorget orange, upper breast white shading into rufous, then white lower belly. Legs, bill, eyes dark. ♀ indistinguishable from ♀ *S. sasin*. ♂'s display rapid dive in oval flight path close to ♀, producing loud whine as descent checked; normally subdued hum in flight. Other details much as *S. sasin*, but nests low down, in vines, bushes, hanging branches. **475**

Selasphorus sasin *Trochilidae*
ALLEN'S HUMMINGBIRD   3½ ins
Nearctic: breeds humid coastal areas of SW Oregon through California, including islands; winters chiefly N Lower California. Habitat: moist canyon bottoms and scrubby conifer forest edge; also scrub and gardens of coast, overlapping in central California with *Calypte anna*. ♂: upperparts (head, back, wing coverts) iridescent green; flanks, rump, black-tipped tail reddish brown; gorget coppery or scarlet; white triangle on breast. ♀ has throat white spotted dark and tinged scarlet, underparts white, tail rufous, black and white, but cannot be told in field from *S. rufus*. Legs, bill, eyes dark. ♂'s display in two parts: shallow swoops along broad U 20 to 30 ft across and 19 to 15 ft high, bobbing tail violently at bottom to give interrupted buzz; then final faster, smooth swoop from 100 ft with veering recovery and brief 'ripping' sound, probably mechanical. Torpid at night like *Calypte anna*. Squeaks, calls *chick* when feeding, rattling noise when ♂ chases ♀; also sharp *bzee* by ♂ (and ♂ *S. rufus*). Food as *Calypte anna*. Breeds May to June, ♀ building deep cup of plant materials, bound spider web, lined feathers, in twigs or vines on densely canopied trees or shrubs from 3 to 80 ft up. 2 white eggs incubated by ♀ 17 days; ♀ fledges young 22 days. 2 broods. **476**

Semeiphorus vexillarius see **Macrodipteryx vexillarius**

SENEGAL COUCAL see **Centropus senegalensis**

Sericornis frontalis *Muscicapidae*: *Malurinae*
WHITE-BROWED SCRUB WREN   *c.* 4¾ ins
Australia: S Queensland to Victoria and SE South Australia, also Kent Group in Bass Strait. Habitat: areas of thick undergrowth with high rainfall. ♂: upperparts dark brown tinged olive, upper tail coverts rufous; white 'eyebrow', lores black; subterminal black band across tail; throat yellowish white streaked blackish; underparts pale dull yellow, flanks brown. ♀: less dusky brown, less streaked throat, less distinct tail bar. Legs brown, bill black, eyes pale buff. Tame, active, usually on or near ground; insectivorous. Call: sharp whistles. Breeds usually September to January; domed nest with side entrance, of bark fibres, leaves and fine grass, on or near ground in thick undergrowth; 3 greyish-white eggs, marked purplish brown. **771**

Sericornis maculatus *Muscicapidae*: *Malurinae*
SPOTTED SCRUB WREN   *c.* 5 ins
Australia: SW Australia, Wooramel River to Eucla and some islands. Habitat: thickets on dunes, denser undergrowth in damp areas inland and dried up watercourses. ♂: upperparts brownish grey, white 'eyebrow', black subterminal band across tail, black and white patch on wing coverts; breast and throat white streaked black, belly yellow (white in E race, *S.m. mellori*). ♀: weaker streaks on breast and fainter tail band. Legs brown, bill dark brown, eyes yellowish-white. Shy, rarely flies but moves quickly through thick low cover or along ground where feeds on insects. Call: sharp, rapid, repeated *tsi-tsi-tsi*. Usually breeds September to January, sometimes early as July; oval, domed nest with covered side entrance, of grasses, occasionally seaweeds, often inner wall of leaves; some feathers or fur added to lining during incubation; well hidden among coarse grass or overhanging twining plants, generally on creek banks or

other moist places. Incubates *c.* 23 days, 3 or 4 fleshy-white eggs with brownish purple spots and short streaks; young fledge *c.* 15 days.

SERIN see **Serinus serinus**

Serinus alario or Alario alario *Fringillidae*
BLACK-HEADED CANARY   5 ins
Ethiopian: W Southern Africa; resident drier grassland and bush. ♂: upperparts to tail light chestnut, flight feathers blackish; head, chin to centre breast black; sides neck, underparts white, ♀: light brown, streaked darker, above; shoulder patch light chestnut; underparts buff, shading to whitish belly. Legs slate, bill mainly grey, eyes brown. Usually seen singly, in pairs or small flocks, feeding mainly on seeds off ground. Call: gentle *tweeet;* quiet melodious song. Breeds August to April; cup nest of twigs lined plant down, a few feet up in tree or bush. 3 to 5 greenish white eggs, speckled red to dark brown. **929**

Serinus albogularis or Crithagra albogularis *Fringillidae*
WHITE-THROATED SEEDEATER or CANARY 6 ins
Ethiopian: SW Southern Africa; resident dry scrub, especially dry water courses, hillsides. Upperparts ash brown, faintly streaked dusky; rump yellowish; flight, tail feathers dusky, pale edged; chin, throat white, streaked ash brown; cheeks, remaining underparts uniform ash brown, belly whitish. Legs blackish, stout bill horn brown, eyes brown. Immature browner above, faintly streaked below. Singly or in pairs; small flocks in winter, sometimes with Bully Canary, *S. sulphuratus;* hops on ground; flight rapid, direct. Call: low-pitched *squee-yik;* song strong and melodious. Breeds summer, ♀ and ♂ building nest lined protea down, sited in dry cones of these flowers or in trees and bushes up to 50 ft high. 3 to 5 white eggs, sometimes speckled purplish or dark brown, incubated 12-13 days. Young fly 15½ to 17 days.

Serinus flaviventris or Crithagra flaviventris *Fringillidae*
YELLOW CANARY   6 ins
Ethiopian: W Southern Africa; resident open woodland, usually near water fresh or salt. ♂: upperparts olive green, streaked darker, contrasting rump bright yellow; flight and tail feathers dusky, pale edged; forehead, cheeks, 'eyebrow' bright yellow, moustachial and eye stripes olive green; underparts canary yellow. ♀: upperparts, including head, greyish olive, 'eyebrow' buff white; underparts off-white, breast, flanks tinged yellow, breast heavily streaked darker brown. Legs blackish, bill horn brown, eyes hazel. Immature as ♀ but duller. Flocks in winter. Hops on ground, often flying into trees in alarm, then down again to resume feeding on seeds, also takes termites. Calls: high-pitched *tirriyip* or *tiyee;* song, powerful and sustained, series of distinct phrases. Breeds July to November Cape, midsummer to March farther N, building neat cup nest 1 to 10 ft up in bush or tree. 3 or 4 greenish white eggs, often boldly marked dark brown or black at big end, incubated ♀ 12 days. **930**

Serinus serinus *Fringillidae*
SERIN   4½ ins
W Palaearctic: continental W Europe (recently extreme S Sweden, England), NW Africa, Asia Minor, Palestine; resident and migrant, most northerly birds winter Mediterranean area. Habitat forest edges and tree clumps; orchards, vineyards, roadsides, parks, gardens; subalpine conifers in Spain; up to 8,000 ft High Atlas. ♂: upperparts streaked greenish brown, bright yellow on rump, crown, nape, extending over chin, throat, breast; rest underparts white, flanks streaked. ♀ duller, more streaked, less yellow. Juvenile still duller, browner, more streaked. Legs dark brown, short bill horn brown, eyes dark brown. Feeds partly on ground where hops. Dancing flight like redpolls, *Acanthis* species, Goldfinch, *Carduelis carduelis*. Often in small flocks. Flight call *tirilillit* with variants; *tsooet* of anxiety; sparrow-like chirps; rather sibilant jangling song. Fluttering, bat-like display flight like Greenfinch *Carduelis chloris*. Eats variety of seeds from wild and garden plants, also from trees, e.g. alder, birch. Breeds

February to August, solitary or in groups. ♀, attended ♂, builds nest of grass, weeds, moss, rootlets, lichens, bound cobwebs, lined softly; usually in fork or flat towards end of lateral branch of variety of trees, 5 to 30 ft up. 3 to 5 pale blue eggs, spotted and streaked purple, red-brown at big end, incubated ♀ *c.* 13 days; ♀ and ♂ feed young from throat 14-16 days. Frequently 2 broods. **931**

Serinus sulphuratus see under **S. albogularis**

Setophaga ruticilla *Parulidae*
AMERICAN REDSTART   5½ ins
Nearctic: breeds most of Canada E of Rockies and eastern USA to N Carolina, N Georgia, S Alabama; winters W Indies, Central Mexico to Ecuador, Guyanas. Habitat rather open broad-leaved woodland, secondary growth near swamps, roadsides, residential areas of towns. ♂: upperparts, including head, breast, glossy black; broad orange base to dark brown flight and outer tail feathers; central tail all brown; sides breast bright salmon-orange narrowing on flanks. Little change autumn but young ♂ resembles ♀, greyish olive green where ♂ black, yellow where orange. Legs, bill, eyes dark. Extremely active; droops wings, fans tail, sallies into air after insects, catching several in darting, syncopated flight; also feeds on ground. Song distinctive, high-pitched, sibilant but very variable; one ♂ may use several versions. Breeds May and June; nest of bark shreds, grass, bound cobwebs, plant fibres, and lined with fine grass, rootlets and hair, in upright fork of tree or bush, 5 to 25 ft up. Usually 4 whitish eggs, marked brown and grey, incubated ♀ *c.* 12 days; young leave the nest 12-14 days, with the ♂ continuing to feed them. **900**

SEVERTGOV'S TIT WARBLER see **Leptopoecile sophiae**

SEYCHELLES
  BRUSH WARBLER see **Bebrornis sechellensis**
  FODY see **Foudia sechellarum**
  KESTREL see **Falco area**
  MAGPIE ROBIN see **Copsychus sechellarum**
  OWL see **Otus insularis**
  PARADISE FLYCATCHER see **Tersiphone corvina**

SHAG,
  BLUE-EYED see **Phalacrocorax atriceps**
  KING see **Phalacrocorax atriceps**
  LONG-TAILED see **Phalacrocorax africanus**

SHARP-TAILED
  GROUSE see **Pedioecetes phasianellus**
  PARADISE WHYDAH see **Steganura paradisaea**
  STREAMCREEPER see **Lochmias nematura**

SHARPBILL see **Oxyruncus cristatus**

SHEARWATER,
  GREAT see **Puffinus gravis**
  MANX see **Puffinus puffinus**
  SHORT-TAILED see **Puffinus tenuirostris**
  WEDGE-TAILED see **Puffinus pacificus**

SHEATHBILL, YELLOW-BILLED see **Chionis alba**

SHELDUCK see **Tadorna tadorna**

SHINING CUCKOO see **Chalcites lucidus**

SHOEBILL see **Balaeniceps rex**

SHORE LARK see **Eremophila alpestris**

SHORT-BILLED
  DOWITCHER see under **Limnodromus scolopaceus**
  MARSH WREN see under **Telmatodytes curvirostris**

SHORT-EARED OWL see **Asio flammeus**

SHORT-TAILED
  BUSH WARBLER see **Cisticola squameiceps**
  SHEARWATER see **Puffinus tenuirostris**

SHORT-TOED
  LARK see **Calandrella cinerea**
  TREECREEPER see under **Certhia familiaris**

SHOVELER see **Anas clypeata**

SHRIKE,
  BALD-HEADED WOOD see **Pityriasis gymnocephala**
  BLACKCAP BUSH see **Tchagra minuta**
  BLACK CUCKOO see **Campephaga sulphurata**
  BLACK-FACED CUCKOO see **Coracina novaehollandiae**
  BLACK-HEADED see **Lanius schach**
  BLACK-HEADED BUSH see **Tchagra senegala**
  BLACK PUFF-BACKED see **Dryoscopus cubla**
  BROWN-HEADED see **Tchagra australis**
  BUSH see **Cymbilaimus lineatus**
  FISCAL see **Lanius collaris**
  GREAT GREY see **Lanius excubitor**
  GREY-BACKED see **Lanius tephronotus**
  GROUND CUCKOO see **Pteropodocys maxima**
  LESSER GREY see **Lanius minor**
  LONG-TAILED see **Lanius schach**
  LONG-TAILED FISCAL see **Lanius cabanisi**
  RED-BACKED see **Lanius collurio**
  RED-TAILED see **Lanius cristatus**
  STRAIGHT-CRESTED HELMET see **Prionops plumata**
  WHITE-CROWNED see **Eurocephalus anguitimens**
  WHITE HELMET see **Prionops plumata**
  WHITE-TAILED see **Lanioturdus torquatus**

SHRIKE VIREO, CHESTNUT-SIDED see **Vireolanius meliophrys**

Sialia mexicana see under **Peucedramus taeniatus**

Sialia sialis *Muscicapidae: Turdinae*
EASTERN BLUEBIRD   7 ins
Nearctic to Neotropical: breeds from E Canada S to S Florida, Gulf Coast, Honduras; W to E Montana, E Colorado, W Central Texas, S Arizona, W Mexico (Sinaloa); winters from S New England and S Michigan southward. Habitat open country with scattered trees, forest clearings; orchards, gardens. ♂: upperparts, including head, chin and black-tipped wings, bright blue; throat, breast reddish brown; lower belly, under tail coverts white. ♀: brownish above, except part wings, tail; duller below with white throat. Legs dark brown, bill grey, eyes dark brown, orbits white. Juvenile brown, spotted white, above; underparts white, mottled grey. ♂ prominent on territory; courtship flight up to 100 ft, then sails downward. Call liquid *cher-wee* from perch or in flight; song rapid series of notes similar to call, often 2 variations sung alternatively. Diet ⅔ insects, ⅓ fruits (bayberry, poison ivy, sumac); takes grasshoppers, crickets, beetles, larvae mainly from ground. Breeds May to June onwards New England, building cup of grass, plant stems in tree holes, old woodpecker borings, nestboxes, 2 to 30 ft up. 4 to 6 pale blue eggs incubated by ♀; ♂ and ♀ feed young, who fly 15-19 days. ♂ often takes over first brood while ♀ nests again. **700**

SIBERIAN
  JAY see **Perisoreus infaustus**
  RUBYTHROAT see **Luscinia calliope**
  TATTLER see **Tringa brevipes**
  WHITE CRANE see **Grus leucogeranus**

SICKLE-BILLED BIRD OF PARADISE see **Epimachus meyeri**

SICKLEBILL, WHITE-TIPPED see **Eutoxeres aquila**

SILKY FLYCATCHER, BLACK AND YELLOW see **Phainoptila melanoxantha**

SILVER
  GULL see **Larus novaehollandiae**
  PHEASANT see under **Lophura lophura**

SILVER-BACKED BUTCHERBIRD see under **Cracticus torquatus**

SILVER-CROWNED FRIARBIRD see under **Philemon yorki**

SILVER-EARED MESIA see **Leiothrix argentauris**

SILVEREYE see **Zosterops lateralis**

SILVERY TUFTED GNATEATER see **Conopophaga lineata**

Sitta canadensis *Sittidae*
RED-BREASTED NUTHATCH   4½ ins
Nearctic: breeds from Newfoundland, S Quebec, N Manitoba, Central Yukon, SE Alaska, S to Massachusetts, mountains SW North Carolina, Michigan, Colorado, S California; winters S to N Florida, Gulf Coast, N Mexico; mainly resident northern conifer forests but disperses southwards when cone crop fails. ♂: upperparts dark grey from blackish crown to tail; broad white 'eyebrows' meet over bill; black eyestripe; cheeks, chin white shading into chestnut brown underparts. ♀ (and juvenile) slate grey head markings; paler below. Legs dark, bill horn-brown, eyes dark brown. Usually seen actively searching treetop needles. Call abrupt nasal *ank*; song rapid series of tinny rather short notes. Takes conifer seeds in winter; insects from bark of broadleaved trees; also bird table items which may be hidden in holes or crevices. Breeds May to June, lining excavated hole in tree with plant debris, fur, feathers; almost any height; also old woodpecker borings, natural holes, nestboxes. 5 or 6 white eggs, heavily marked red-brown; incubation and fledging much as nuthatch, *S. europaea*. **810**

Sitta cinnamoventris see under **S. europaea**

Sitta europaea *Sittidae*
NUTHATCH   *c.* 5½ ins
Palaearctic, Oriental: most of Europe (includes S Britain, very local NW Africa) S of 60°N; Asia Minor, Caucasus, Iran; eastward between 50° and 60°N to spread widely E Siberia, Sakhalin, Japan, Taiwan, S into S China, SE Asia, Indian subcontinent. Oriental populations sometimes separated as *S. cinnamoventris*. Replaced in Himalayas by very similar *S. himalayensis*. Siberian birds may disperse S or W. Resident variety of woodland, broadleaved in Europe, from oaks, beeches in N to olives in S; mixed montane forests; conifers in Asia (Siberian taiga, dry pines in S up to 9,200 ft); also tropical forests, savannah, cultivated land, parks, gardens. Upperparts blue-grey from crown to tail, side feathers black at base, white on outer ones; black eyestripe; cheeks, throat white, underparts buff or white, becoming chestnut on flanks; legs yellow brown, bill mainly dark slate, eyes dark grey-brown. Superficially woodpecker-like with short instead of stiff tail, but moves effectively all ways on trunks, occasionally walls; perches across branches. Hops on ground. May associate with other species. Roosts tree holes. ♂ displays plumage, including white tail spots, to ♀, also floats down beside her and feeds her. Calls many; *chwit chwit*, shrill repeated *zit, sirrr* of excitement. 3 songs: repeated clear, piping *twee*; rapid trilling; loud ringing *pee pee pee*. Insectivorous, with spiders, some snails; nuts of many kinds autumn, often stuck in crevices and hammered, also stored. Breeds early April to mid June Britain; ♀ and ♂ reduce entrance to cavity with mud 'plaster'; inside loose nest of bark, dead leaves, no separate lining; usually in knot hole, old woodpecker boring; sometimes wall, nestbox; 3 to 60 ft. 6 to 9 white eggs, usually heavily marked dark red over grey, incubated ♀ 14-15 days; young, fed ♀ and ♂, fly 23-25 days. **811**

Sitta himalayensis see under **S. europaea**

Sitta neumayer *Sittidae*
NEUMAYER'S or ROCK NUTHATCH   5½ ins
Palaearctic: restricted range from Adriatic through Balkans, S Asia Minor, Near East, Caucasus, Iran, where overlaps with very similar Eastern Rock Nuthatch, *S. tephronota*. Resident sunny rocky limestone slopes and steep faces with dry scrub; lowland to over 3,000 ft. Paler version of *S. europaea*, underparts browner, no white in tail, eyestripe fainter. Vocabulary like *S. europaea* but includes 'rich fluty cadences' and jay-like screams; song: rising and falling scale of shrill pipit-like notes. Food mainly insects, spiders caught in crevices or under stones, even on branches of roadside trees visited winter. Breeds March to April (Greece), making bottle-shaped nest of wet mud and sandy loam, fitted into or hidden in cleft, attached to overhang; thick lining of feathers, hair, plant fragments. Clutch-size, incubation and fledging much as *S. europaea*, but eggs more heavily marked. **812**

Sitta tephronota see under **S. neumayer**

SKIMMER, AMERICAN see **Rynchops nigra**

SKUA,
    GREAT see **Stercorarius skua**
    LONG-TAILED see **Stercorarius longicauda**

SKYLARK see **Alauda arvensis**

SLAVONIAN GREBE see **Podiceps auritus**

SLATE-THROATED REDSTART see **Myioborus miniatus**

SLATY FLYCATCHER, WHITE-EYED see **Dioptrornis fischeri**

SLATY-BACKED NIGHTINGALE THRUSH see **Catharus fuscater**

SMEW see **Mergus albellus**

Smicrornis brevirostris *Muscicapidae: Malurinae*
BROWN WEEBILL   *c.* 3½ ins
Australia: central Queensland to Victoria, S Australia and SW Australia, N to mid Western Australia. Habitat: tree foliage of open forest, particularly eucalypts. Head grey-brown, back and scapulars olive, rump yellowish olive; wings brown, edged olive; tail brown with black subterminal bar and white spot near tip of outer feathers; throat and breast grey, rest of underparts pale yellow. Legs and short bill brown, eyes yellowish white. Usually in pairs or small flocks; moves constantly among small twigs and leaves of outer branches, sometimes hovers; feeds on insects. Call: brisk whistle of several notes. Small spherical nest with hooded entrance high in side, suspended in drooping branch, well hidden; of fine grasses, bound spider's webs and decorated cocoons, sometimes lined feathers and down; 3, sometimes 2, cream to buff eggs with brownish spots. Incubates *c.* 19 days; young fledge 15-20 days. **772**

Smithornis capensis *Eurylaimidae*
AFRICAN BROADBILL
Ethiopian: several races cover region, mainly S of Equator and except SW. Resident in forest up to 6,000 ft, bamboo thickets, dense riverine scrub. ♂: upperparts olivaceous grey to brown; feathers of mantle and back have basal two-thirds white and some black markings at ends; crown black; underparts white, streaked black; legs brown; bill: upper black, lower white; eyes yellow. ♀: has crown grey with blackish streaks. Notable for circular moth-like hovering flight over a few feet, with wings vibrating and apparently producing horn-like sound; white patch on back shows up. Otherwise rather lethargic, remaining on perch except when hunting beetles and other insects on wing; ants, grasshoppers, spiders on ground. ♀ has mewing *twee-uu* call. Breeding season variable throughout range; builds untidy domed nest of plant materials, cemented by spider's webs and slung by handle of moss and roots from horizontal twig a few feet up; often with trail of hanging fibres;

entrance at side with slight porch. Clutch usually 3 white eggs. **557**

SMOOTH-BILLED ANI see **Crotophaga ani**

SNAKE EAGLE see **Circaetus cinereus**

SNIPE,
    AFRICAN see **Gallinago nigripennis**
    JACK see **Lymnocryptes minimus**
    PAINTED see **Rostratula benghalensis**

SNOW
    BUNTING see **Plectrophenax nivalis**
    FINCH see **Montifringilla nivalis**
    GOOSE see **Anser caerulescens**
    PARTRIDGE see **Lerwa lerwa**
    PETREL see **Pagodroma nivea**

SNOWY
    EGRET see **Egretta thula**
    OWL see **Nyctaea scandiaca**
    PLOVER see **Charadrius alexandrinus**

SNOWY-CROWNED ROBIN CHAT see **Thamnolaea coronata**

SOCIAL
    FLYCATCHER see **Myiozetetes similis**
    WEAVER see **Philetairus socius**

SOFTWING see **Malacoptila panamensis**

SOLITAIRE, BLACK see **Entomodestes coracinus**

Somateria stelleri see **Polysticta stelleri**

Somateria mollissima see under **Polysticta stelleri**

SOMBRE
    BULBUL see **Andropadus importunus**
    GREENBUL, ZANZIBAR see **Andropadus importunus**

SONG
    SPARROW see **Melospiza melodia**
    THRUSH see under **Turdus iliacus**

SONGLARK,
    BROWN see **Cinclorhamphus cruralis**
    RUFOUS see **Cinclorhamphus mathewsi**

SOOTY
    ALBATROSS, LIGHT-MANTLED see **Phoebetria palpebrata**
    CHAT see **Myrmecocichla nigra**
    OWL see **Tyto tenebricosa**
    TERN see **Sterna fuscata**

SORA RAIL see **Porzana carolina**

SOUTH AFRICAN
    BLACK FLYCATCHER see **Melaenornis pammelaina**
    GANNET see under **Sula bassana**
    NIGHTJAR see **Caprimulgus pectoralis**

SOUTH AMERICAN KING VULTURE see **Sarcorhamphus papa**

SOUTHERN
    BLACK TIT see **Parus niger**
    DOUBLE-COLLARED SUNBIRD see **Cinnyris chalybeus**
    SCRUB ROBIN see **Dryomodus brunneipygia**

SPANGLED
    COTINGA see **Cotinga cayana**
    DRONGO see under **Sphecotheres flaviventris**

SPANISH SPARROW see under **Passer domesticus**

SPARKLING VIOLETEAR HUMMINGBIRD see **Colibri coruscans**

SPARROW,
    AMERICAN TREE see **Spizella arborea**
    CAPE see **Passer melanurus**
    CHIPPING see under **Helmitheros vermivorus**
    FOX see **Passerella iliaca**
    GOLDEN-WINGED see **Arremon schlegeli**
    HOUSE see **Passer domesticus**
    JAVA see **Padda oryzivora**
    ORANGE-BILLED see under **Arremon schlegeli**
    ROCK see **Petronia petronia**
    SONG see **Melospiza melodia**
    SPANISH see under **Passer domesticus**
    TREE see **Passer montanus**
    WHITE-FRONTED see **Zonotrichia albicollis**

SPARROWHAWK see **Accipiter nisus**

SPARROWHAWK, AMERICAN see **Falco sparverius**

SPARROW WEAVER,
    STRIPE-BREASTED see **Plocepasser mahali**
    WHITE-BROWED see **Plocepasser mahali**

SPECKLED
    MOUSEBIRD see **Colius striatus**
    PIGEON see **Columba guinea**
    WARBLER see **Chthonicola sagittata**

SPECKLE-FRONTED WEAVER see **Sporopipes frontalis**

Speotyto cunicularia *Strigidae*
BURROWING OWL   9 ins
Nearctic and Neotropical: W North America S to N Tierra del Fuego; not W Indies; northern population moves S in winter. Habitat: prairies, plains and fields. Upperparts brown, profusely polkadotted white, with streaks on crown; white and black 'eyebrows'; white throat with black collar; breast much as back; belly pale, streaked darker; claws pale horn, bill horn, eyes yellow. Largely diurnal, sitting in daytime on ground or fence post; bobs up and down by bending long legs. Hovers when hunting, mainly at dusk; for insects, especially locusts, crickets and grasshoppers; also small mammals. Call a tremulous chuckling or chattering; mellow dove-like *coo-co-hoo* at night. Breeds April to May in old prairie dog and other burrows, or excavating 5 or 10 ft, at end of which 6 to 12 white eggs laid on grass lining and incubated by ♀ and ♂ *c.* 4 weeks; both parents feed young. Sometimes several pairs in same set of burrows; one often stands at entrance, disappearing when approached. **449**

Sphecotheres flaviventris *Oriolidae*
YELLOW FIGBIRD   10 ins
Australia: N and S coastal areas; resident rainforests, open woodlands, valley scrub, sometimes entering towns. ♂: upperparts olive green; flight feathers black, edged green; longish tail black, outer feathers white; head, nape, ear coverts glossy black; underparts from chin bright yellow; lower belly, under tail coverts white. ♀: upperparts brown, streaked darker; rump, tail greenish; whitish underparts heavily spotted black. Legs brown; strong, slightly hooked bill blackish; eyes dark brown in bare red facial skin, duller in ♀. Parties and flocks up to 30, may associate with other species at fruiting trees, where flutters noisily, plucking fruit or berries; but hard to see when perched. Also takes insects on wing. Breeds October to January, building saucer nest of twigs, tendrils, usually at end of drooping branch, up to 50 ft. Usually 3 greenish eggs, spotted red-brown or purple-red. Spangled Drongo, *Chibia bracteata*, and Helmeted Friarbird, *Philemon yorki*, often nest in same tree.

Spheniscus demersus *Spheniscidae*
JACKASS PENGUIN   25 ins
Resident in South African coasts, breeding on bare islands and found otherwise in offshore waters. The plumage departs from usual penguin pattern, white on breast extending to side of head, with narrow black horseshoe on breast. Legs and bill blackish, eyes dark with flesh-pink patch round them. Gregarious at all times. The Jackass's breeding colonies have been

exploited for their store of guano, end product of a diet estimated at one-third pilchards, with other small fish, squids and crustaceans making up balance. Breeding takes place mainly from November to March; 2 to 4 greenish eggs are laid in nest of local plant material and stones in a burrow or cavity and incubated by ♀ and ♂ in turns for *c.* 4 weeks. Both parents feed the chicks, which fledge in *c.* 3 months. **12**

Spheniscus humboldti *Spheniscidae*
PERUVIAN PENGUIN 27 ins
Resident in area of Humboldt Current off W coast South America, breeding on bare islands, otherwise offshore. Rather like Jackass, *S. demersus,* with black horseshoe on white breast; legs black, bill black and white with pink at gape, eyes dark, ringed with pink skin. Loud donkey-like braying call, especially at colonies. Fairly gregarious, and breeding stations exploited for guano, as feeds on anchovies and other small fish of Humboldt Current. Mutual displays at colonies and breeding goes on throughout year; 2 white eggs laid in burrows, caves or crevices, but in open where island denuded of guano layer, incubated by ♂ and ♀, who both tend the young. **13**

Sphyrapicus varius *Picidae*
YELLOW-BELLIED SAPSUCKER 8 ins
Nearctic and marginally Neotropical: breeds over most of Canada, with extension S down W coast, also in Mid-West to Mexico, and to New England; Canadian population migrates S as far as Panama in autumn. Habitat: woodlands and orchards. Upperparts barred black and white, including wingtips; white patch sandwiched between black on wing coverts; black and white head pattern with red forehead and red throat surrounded by black; underparts pale yellow, flanks flecked dark brown. ♀ has white throat. Red-headed and breasted race in W North America. Works quickly from one tree to another, drilling parallel rows of small holes and returning to take sap (even when frozen) and small insects, especially bark beetles. Does not drum rapidly but taps distinctive rhythm: several rapid thumps followed by several slow ones, on tree limbs, metal, wires. Call: nasal, mewing *churrr,* slurred downwards. Breeds May and June, ♀ and ♂ excavating hole in tree with shaft 6 ins to 1½ ft deep. 4 to 7 glossy white eggs incubated by ♀ and ♂ 14 days; young, fed by both parents on insects, fly *c.* 25 days. **554**

SPICE FINCH, ASIAN see under **Lonchura castaneothorax**

SPIDERHUNTER,
LITTLE see **Arachnothera longirostris**
STREAKED see **Arachnothera magna**

SPINEBILL, EASTERN see **Acanthorhynchus tenuirostris**

SPINIFEX BIRD see **Eremiornis carteri**

SPINY-CHEEKED HONEYEATER see **Acanthagenys rufogularis**

Spinus tristis *Fringillidae*
AMERICAN GOLDFINCH 5 ins
Nearctic: breeds from Newfoundland across southern Canada, then S to N Georgia, Central Arkansas, S Colorado, Central Nevada, N Lower California; winters S to Gulf Coast, S Mexico. Habitat open country with weeds, scattered trees, bushes. ♂: bright yellow with black cap, wings (white patch at base, white bar and feather edges to secondaries) notched tail (white feather edges); upper tail coverts white. ♀: upperparts suffused brown, no cap; underparts pale yellow, shading to white. Winter ♂ much as ♀ but more buff-brown and wings remain black, shoulder patch yellow. Immature even browner. Legs, bill flesh-coloured, eyes very dark brown. Large flocks in winter, sometimes with other finches; undulating flight. Calls: *per-chic-o-ree; zwe-zweee;* song: series of trills and twitters, with *swee* notes. Food: weed seeds, insects, buds in spring, birch, alder, conifer seeds in winter. Breeds late in season; nest of grass, plant stems,

bark, lined down, in upright fork of tree or bush, few to 20 ft up. 5 very pale blue eggs incubated ♀ **932**

Spizella arborea *Emberizidae: Emberizinae*
AMERICAN TREE SPARROW 6¼ ins
Nearctic: Alaska, N Canada, S to Newfoundland; winters SE Canada, S Minnesota, S British Columbia to S Carolina, Central Arkansas, New Mexico, NE California. Habitat tree limit in far N: alders, willows, forest edges; weedy fields and thickets in winter. Upperparts rich brown streaked black with chestnut patch between 2 narrow white wingbars; flight feathers, tail blackish, pale edged; crown, eyestripe chestnut, rest of head greyish with small dark moustachial stripe shading into underparts; dark central breast spot, flanks tinged chestnut. Legs blackish, bill: upper grey, lower yellow; eyes dark brown. Juvenile duller, streaked dusky above and below. Call, thin *tseet;* double whistle in flock, combined in mass twittering. Sweet, rather metallic, canary-like song may be heard winter areas. Food: grass, weed seeds winter, jumping up to reach intact heads. Breeds June; nest often of green stems, bark, lined hair or feathers, on or near ground sheltered low vegetation. 4 or 5 greenish white eggs, evenly speckled reddish brown, incubated ♀ 12-13 days. Young leave nest 9-10 days but are fed by ♀ and ♂ 2 more weeks. **865**

Spizella passerina see under **Helmitheros vermivorus**

SPOONBILL,
EUROPEAN see **Platalea leucorodia**
ROSEATE see **Ajaia ajaja**

Sporophila americana *Fringillidae*
VARIABLE SEEDEATER 4½ ins
Neotropical: Central America, Guyanas, NE Venezuela, parts Colombia, W Ecuador, W Peru, Amazonian Brazil; Tobago and Chacachacare I. Habitat forest edge, grassland, fields, gardens; sea level to 4,500 ft. ♂: upperparts, including head, cheeks, wings (white spots coverts, white bar flight feathers), tail, black; rump, upper tail coverts grey; underparts, including incomplete collar, white, but variable black breast band and upper throat sometimes black; flanks grey in some races; underwings, under tail black. ♀: upperparts shades of olive; underparts paler; centre belly, under tail coverts pale buff; axillaries, under wing coverts whitish. Legs, bill black, eyes brown. Sweet warbling song. Food mainly seeds. Breeds February to June Tobago; cup nest of weed stems, lined fine grass, in fork of bush or tree. 2 pale creamy eggs, marked shades of chestnut and blackish brown, incubated ♀. **933**

Sporopipes frontalis *Ploceidae*
SPECKLE-FRONTED WEAVER 4½-5 ins
Ethiopian: Senegal across continent to Red Sea, Sudan, E Africa; resident dry thorn scrub, woodland, edges of cultivation. Upperparts to rump dusky light brown; wings, tail dusky, feathers edged buff-white; forehead, crown, moustachial stripe black, speckled white; nape, neck rufous; cheeks, breast greyish; rest underparts white; legs pinkish brown, bill pale brown; eyes brown. Large flocks form after breeding, often found near water. Hops on ground. Several may take over old nest as communal roost. Diet: small seeds. Call: liquid *tsssk;* twittering, finch-like song. Breeds October to February, solitary or small groups, building large domed grass nest, usually hung from end of branch, 10 to 15 ft up. Up to 4 greyish-green or dull grey eggs, often densely marked with dark longitudinal streaks.

SPOT-BREASTED WREN see *Thryothurus maculipectus*

SPOTLESS CRAKE see **Porzana plumbea**

SPOTTED
BOWER BIRD see **Chlamydera maculata**
CREEPER see **Salpornis spilonotus**
CUCKOO, GREAT see **Clamator glandarius**
DOVE see **Streptopelia chinensis**
EAGLE OWL see **Bubo africanus**

FLYCATCHER see **Muscicapa striata**
NIGHTJAR see **Eurostopodus guttatus**
OWL see **Ninox novaeseelandiae**
PARDALOTE see **Pardalotus punctatus**
REDSHANK see **Tringa erythropus**
SANDPIPER see under **Tringa hypoleucos**
SCRUB WREN see **Sericornis maculatus**
THICK-KNEE see **Burhinus capensis**
WOOD DOVE, EMERALD see **Turtur chalcospilos**
WOODPECKER, FINE see **Campethera punctuligera**
WOODPECKER, GREAT see **Dendrocopos major**
WOODPECKER, LESSER see **Dendrocopos minor**
WREN see **Campylorhunchus griseus**

SPOTTED-BACKED WEAVER see **Ploceus cucullatus**

Spreo
bicolor see under **Creatophora cinera**
hildebrandti see under **S. Superbus**

Spreo superbus *Sturnidae*
SUPERB STARLING 7 ins
Ethiopian: Somalia, Ethiopia, Sudan, E Africa; resident and partial migrant thorn bush and acacia country; vicinity of habitations. Generally metallic blue green, head blackish; wings green with velvety black spots on coverts; breast divided from chestnut underparts by thin white band; under tail coverts, axillaries, underwing white; legs, bill slaty grey, eyes pale yellow. Juvenile has head, neck, upperparts dull black. Hildebrandt's Starling, *S. hildebrandti,* has no white breast stripe, eyes orange red and different gloss. Gregarious, tame with man, feeds on ground in parties on insects, berries, man-provided scraps. Courtship: jumps about on ground, wings trailing, neck stretched. Call: chattering; loud whining alarm note; song, varied whistling; imitates other species. Breeding season varies within range; nest of twigs, grass, lined feathers, low in thorny tree or bush, often in tree or cliff holes. Usually 4 blue green eggs. **973**

SPUR-WINGED PLOVER, AUSTRALIAN see **Lobibyx novaehollandiae**

SPURFOWL, SWAINSON's see **Francolinus swainsonii**

SPURWING
GOOSE see **Plectopterus gambensis**
PLOVER see **Vanellus spinosus**

SQUATTER PIGEON see **Petrophassa scripta**

SQUIRREL CUCKOO see **Piaya cayana**

STANLEY'S CRANE see **Anthropoides paradisaea**

STARLING,
BLUE-EARED GLOSSY see **Lamprocolius chalybeus**
BURCHELL's GLOSSY see **Lamprotornis australis**
CELEBES see **Scissirostrum dubium**
COMMON see **Sturnus vulgaris**
GOLDEN-BREASTED see **Cosmopsarus regius**
HILDEBRANDT's see under **Spreo superbus**
PAGODA see **Temenuchus pagodarum**
PALE-WINGED see **Onychognathus nabouroup**
PIED see under **Creatophora cinerea**
RED-WINGED see under **Onychognathus nabouroup**
ROSE-COLOURED see **Sturnus roseus**
ROTHSCHILD's see **Leucopsar rothschildi**
SUPERB see **Spreo superbus**
WATTLED see **Creatophora cinerea**

STEAMER DUCK,
FLIGHTLESS see **Tachyeres pteneres**
FLYING see under **Tachyeres pteneres**

Steatornis caripensis *Steatornithidae*
OILBIRD, GUACHARO or DIABLOTIN 17 ins
Neotropical: Guyana, Venezuela, Colombia or Ecuador and Peru; Trinidad; resident in mountainous

forest country with suitable caves; sea coast in Trinidad. Rich brown, barred black and with very scattered white spots, especially on wing coverts; upperparts partly chestnut; most of wing dusky with white leading edge; narrow white and brown bars on tail, outer feathers white-spotted; underparts cinnamon buff; legs whitish-pink, hooked bill dark horn, bristles 2 ins long, eyes reflect ruby, facial skin grey. Gregarious, nocturnal, cave-dwelling, spending day crouched on ledges, flying out at dusk to feed on fruits of trees, especially *Lauraceae*. Fruit taken by bill, stored in stomach (or crop) where digested during day; seeds defaecated on to floor of cave, forming deep humus. Screaming and snarling calls, also echo-locating clicks in caves. Occasionally calls outside; probably uses both large eyes and sense of smell to find trees with ripe fruit. Breeds throughout year, making nest in cave of regurgitated fruit and excreta, with shallow saucer; used year after year. 2 to 4 white pointed eggs become stained during 33 day incubation by ♀ and ♂, who feed young. They become very fat before fledging in *c.* 120 days, when taken to be used for their oil. **454**

Steganura orientalis see under **S. paradisaea**

Steganura paradisaea *Estrildidae*
SHARP-TAILED PARADISE
WHYDAH   ♀: 5, ♂ (with tail): 15-16 ins
Ethiopian: resident locally over most of region in open dry thorn bush and woodland savannah. ♂: upperparts including wings, broad pointed tail, black; central tail feathers have bare elongated shafts; broad light brown collar on hindneck; underparts chestnut to tawny with black bib and under tail coverts. Non-breeding ♂: upperparts tawny streaked black; head mottled black and buff with creamy central stripe; wings, short tail blackish; underparts tawny to white, sides spotted black. ♀ like non-breeding ♂ but duller, with buff 'eyebrow'. Legs, eyes brown, bill black. Juvenile generally brownish, bill horn brown. (Only fairly recently separated from Broad-tailed, *S. orientalis*, which has elongated central tail feathers broad to tips.) Small flocks feed grass seeds on ground. Rather silent; ♂'s call sharp *chip;* short, sparrow-like song. ♂ in display ascends vertically, cruises with central tail feathers raised almost at 90° to body; also hovers over ♀♀, raising wings slowly and rhythmically. Perches prominently. Breeding season depends on hosts, usually melba finches, *Pytilia* species; eggs white, rather larger than host's. Polygamous. **944**

STELLER'S
EIDER see **Polysticta stelleri**
JAY see **Cyanocitta stelleri**

Stenostira scita *Muscicapidae: Muscicapinae*
FAIRY FLYCATCHER   4½ ins
Ethiopian: SW southern Africa, but not S coastal belt; local migrant to acacia savannah and riverine forest, also introduced trees near houses, reed beds. Upperparts dark grey; white wing coverts and inner secondaries make conspicuous white line on black wing when closed; tail black, all feathers except central ones with white tips, outermost ones mainly white; cheeks, ear coverts black; chin, throat white tinged pink; breast, flanks grey; belly white with pink centre; legs, bill black, eyes dark brown. Juveniles paler, browner. Usually singly or in pairs, slender, graceful, with relatively long tail; searches low vegetation and trees for insects. Bobs and fans tail when excited. Chirping call: *cheep cheep;* prolonged chattering; sunbird-like *kisskisskiss.* Breeds October to December; ♀ builds neat nest twigs, grass, rootlets, bound and decorated cobwebs, lichen, softly lined. 2 or 3 cream-coloured eggs, tinged green and minutely speckled brown. **797**

Stephanibyx coronatus see **Vanellus coronatus**

Stephanoetus coronatus *Accipitridae*
CROWNED EAGLE   32-36 ins
Ethiopian; chiefly in forests, also riverine strips, open woodland and rocky hills up to 10,000 ft. Normally sedentary. Upperparts blue black, but head shades of dark brown with prominent black and white double crest; underparts barred black, white and brown; 2

black bars on upper wing, underside grey with dark bars and chestnut coverts; legs feathered, feet and cere yellow, bill dark, eyes olive-brown. Immature much lighter, with white head and underparts. Noisier than most eagles; high pitched repeated *kewee* by displaying ♂, ♀ mellower repeated *koi;* both call repeated *quee* at nest. Hunts over large area, almost entirely after mammals, especially hyraxes and small antelopes, dropping on them from perch; but chases monkeys in tree tops. After long period of display flights and building most clutches laid July to October in large nest of sticks lined with greenery. 1 or 2 white eggs marked red-brown incubated mainly by ♀ for 7 weeks. If two hatch one eaglet kills other; fed by both parents, it flies in 103-115 days. **164**

Stercorarius longicauda *Stercorariidae*   *c.* 20-22
LONG-TAILED SKUA   (central tail feathers 5-8) ins
Holarctic: rather narrow band along arctic coasts of Eurasia and N America with extensions S to Kamchatka and Hudson Bay; winters at sea in S Hemisphere. Breeds moss, lichen, less often shrub tundra; also Norwegian fjells. Upperparts uniform dark brown; crown, pointed wing tips, tail blackish brown; sides of neck light yellow; pale area on underwing; underparts from throat white; legs slate grey to black, bill black, eyes dark brown. 'Dark phase' plumage very rare. Juvenile, short-tailed, mottled and barred whitish. Most slender and graceful of skuas, flying and hovering rather like tern, also soars. Playful chases of other birds but less piratical than relatives. Often in parties on migration and even when breeding. Attacks intruders but seldom strikes. Calls: shrill *kree kree* and rattling *k-r-r-r.* Food mainly lemmings, also other rodents, insects, crustaceans, young birds (Alaska), eggs. Breeds from second week June, but may miss season if no lemmings. Sometimes social; scrape in open, often on low mound, holds 2 greenish to olive eggs, sparsely spotted towards big end. Incubation by ♀ and ♂ 23 days; they continue to tend young after full-grown at *c.* 3 weeks. **316**

Stercorarius skua or Catharacta skua *Stercorariidae*
GREAT SKUA   *c.* 23 ins
Unique distribution; Palaearctic: Iceland, Faeroes, N Scotland and islands; Neotropical: extreme S Argentina and Falkland Islands; Australasian: extreme S New Zealand and outlying islands; islands of southern oceans and Antarctica, penetrating farther than any other bird. Palaearctic birds move S and, like relatives, winter at sea. Several races recognised in S Hemisphere and have been given specific status by some authors. Breeds rocky coasts, often snow or ice-bound, up to 3,500 ft in antarctic; moorland in Palaearctic. Nearly uniform dark brown, upperparts streaked tawny brown; darker patch at 'wrist' of wing; light area base of primaries shows up in flight; legs and bill blackish, eyes dark brown. Looks like lumpy, short-tailed gull. 'Clubs' form on traditional sites near breeding ground, also to bathe and preen in fresh water. Enormous numbers at whaling stations. Pirate and scavenger, forcing other seabirds to disgorge food or killing them and their young, e.g. lurks edge of penguin colonies; also fish, other marine animals, carrion and garbage. Calls deep *hah-hah-hah* or *tuk tuk* when attacking intruders. Displays on ground with wings raised and *a-er a-er a-er* call. Breeding peak December in S American populations; June in Palaearctic. Loosely social; scrape, sometimes well lined, on moor or bare ground, holds 2 olive-grey to red-brown eggs, usually marked dark brown. Incubation by ♀ and ♂ 27-30 days; ♂ feeds young, ♀ broods them at first; full grown 6-7 weeks. Often 3 adults at nest (New Zealand). **317**

Sterna albifrons *Laridae*
LITTLE TERN   *c.* 10 ins
Semi-cosmopolitan: Portugal, Britain and Ireland, S Baltic E to L. Zaisan, Turkestan and Persian Gulf, wintering S to coast E Africa; other populations in Nigeria, NE Africa and India across to E China, Japan, Philippines, N and E Australia; Massachusetts USA, across to Central California S to Venezuela, British Honduras and S Mexico. Habitat: sea coast with sandy beaches, low-lying flat rocky coasts, coral lime-

stone terraces or reef walls, also estuaries and broad rivers with extensive sandbanks; winters mainly on shallow tropical coasts. Crown and nape black, extends in stripe over eyes to upper base of bill leaving white forehead, rest of upperparts mostly blue-grey, outer primaries blackish grey on outer web, tail and underparts white; in winter lores also white, crown mottled, central tail feathers grey. Immature: crown buffy white, streaked black; upperparts grey, mottled sandy buff. Legs orange-yellow, duller in winter, bill yellow with black tip, mostly blackish in immature, eyes dark brown. Very active and noisy, dives vertically for small fish and crustacea. Call: shrill *kip-kip-kip.* Breeds May onwards, solitary pairs or small colonies, on sand or shingle beaches, river sand bars inland or similar artificial sites; 2 or 3 pale stone, green or blue eggs, spotted light brown with ashy undermarkings. Both parents incubate 19-22 days and tend young who leave bare nest scrape within day and fly *c.* 4 weeks. **334**

Sterna bengalensis *Laridae*
LESSER CRESTED TERN   *c.* 15½ ins
Ethiopian, Oriental, Australasian: breeds coasts Red Sea, E Africa, Persian Gulf, India, Malay Archipelago and N Australia; mainly tropical and sub-tropical waters but winters S Mediterranean. Upperparts and tail grey; black crown and nape can be raised as crest, white on forehead of variable extent; underparts white. Legs black, bill orange-yellow, eyes brown. Winter: white on forehead more extensive, crown streaked white, wings darker. Immature: blackish bar along wing shoulder and bill greenish yellow. Crested Tern, *S. bergii*, larger and differentiated by lemon-yellow bill. Often with other terns, resting on water; plunges after small fish in both shallow and open sea, also feeds on surface and mudflats; loud, harsh alarm cry. Breeds spring onwards N Australia, June to August N and W of range; colonies usually on sand spit; single light stone egg, blotched and spotted with dark purple or black with lavender or grey undermarking; in scrape on bare ground, incubated *c.* 3 weeks.

Sterna bergii see under **S. bengalensis**

Sterna dougallii *Laridae*
ROSEATE TERN   *c.* 15 ins
Cosmopolitan: N America (some colonies as far S as Venezuela), Europe through Asia, W Red Sea, E Africa, E China, Malay Peninsula to Australia; winters down coasts of Africa to Cape, Indian Ocean, W Pacific down to Australia, and Gulf Coast to Brazil. Habitat: maritime, particularly rocky coastal areas. Similar to Common and Arctic Terns, *S. hirundo* and *S. paradisaea*, but whiter, often rosy tinge to breast; outer tail feathers are white and much longer than in other terns. Immature: head may appear completely black. Legs red, bill black, vermilion at base during breeding, eyes dark brown. Flight buoyant, shallower wing-beats, but habits and feeding similar to Common Tern. Call: rasping, long *aaak,* and plaintive *chuick.* Usually breeds June onwards in colonies frequently with *S. hirundo;* makes bare scrape often in cover or among boulders, on rocky islets and pebbly or sandy shores. Lays 1 or 2 cream or buff eggs, light or reddish brown streaks and freckles with ashy undermarkings; both parents incubate 21-26 days and tend young, who fly *c.* 4 weeks. **335**

Sterna fuscata *Laridae*
SOOTY TERN OR WIDEAWAKE   *c.* 18 ins
S Hemisphere: tropical and sub-tropical pelagic waters; *S. f. fuscata* breeds islets off S coast USA, Bahamas, W Indies, Fernando Noronha, Ascension and St Helena, occasionally wanders as far N as Maine USA, Britain and W Europe; other races spread round world, for example: *serrata*, coasts of N Australia and New Caledonia; *oahuensis*, Hawaiian Is and S through Oceania. Upperparts brownish black, underparts white; broad white band on forehead; deeply forked tail; immature wholly dark, paler on belly and speckled buff on upperparts. Legs and bill black, eyes brown. Usually in small parties but huge flocks gather over tuna schools which drive prey to surface; feeds

by hovering and swooping to surface to snatch small fish and squid, also catches flying fish in air; rarely dives. Most of year spent on wing. Call: squeaky, rendered *wideawake*, hence alternative common name, carries far over water. Breeds, at less than annual intervals some stations, in immense closely-packed colonies; single white to pinky white egg, speckled and blotched with violet or brown, on bare soil or sometimes in shallow depression; both sexes incubate *c.* 24 days, young fly *c.* 6 weeks. **336**

Sterna hirundo *Laridae*
COMMON TERN   *c.* 14 ins
Holarctic: breeds coast and lakes Europe, Azores, Madeira, Canary Is, Sardinia, Tunisia, W Asia, Cyprus, Asia Minor, Syria, Iraq, Persia E to Ladakh and Tibet; E Labrador, central Ontario, N Manitoba, S Mackenzie S to W Indies down Atlantic E coast, only to S Alberta, N Dakota, S Wisconsin and N Pennsylvania inland; winters down W coast Africa to Cape, Madagascar, coasts of Arabian Sea, Florida and W Mexico S to Magellan Strait, ranges across Pacific, occasionally visiting E Australia. Habitat: sea coasts, inshore waters, inland lakes and rivers. Pale grey back, wings, blackish tips to primaries; tail and underparts white, crown black; similar to Arctic Tern, *S. paradisaea,* but distinguished by black tip to scarlet bill. Winter plumage and immature: forehead and forecrown white, rest of crown streaked blackish, bill darker; juvenile similar but forehead buff and brownish bars on back. Legs red, paler in winter, eyes dark brown. Light, buoyant, graceful flight; often hovers briefly when fishing, dropping with partly closed wings, which usually remain visible when bird enters water; awkward walker. Gregarious; feeds on aquatic animals, chiefly fish. Call: threatening, harsh piercing *kee-ar-r-r-r;* also rapid series of short, high pitched *kik-kik-kik* notes. Breeds in colonies, sometimes huge, late May to early June, on open sites; pebbly or sandy beaches or flat rocks on islands and peninsulas. Usually 3 eggs, pale brown spotted dark brown and ash-grey; in hollow in sand but variable e.g. sometimes substantial grass cup; both sexes, mainly ♀, incubate *c.* 25 days, young brooded by ♀ leave nest *c.* 3 days and fly *c.* 4 weeks. **337**

Sterna paradisaea *Laridae*
ARCTIC TERN   *c.* 15 ins
Holarctic: islands and coasts Arctic Ocean S to British Columbia, Hudson Bay, Massachusetts, Britain and Ireland, N Netherlands, Baltic and central Siberia. Long migration, e.g. nestling ringed White Sea (NW Russia) recovered Fremantle (W Australia), to winter oceans of S Hemisphere, principally southern zone of pack ice S to *c.* 70°S. Habitat: breeds marshes chiefly in low-lying tundra, sea coasts with salt marshes or rocky coasts with low islets; pelagic waters when migrating and wintering. Similar to Common Tern, *S. hirundo,* but bill entirely blood-red when breeding (otherwise black) and immature yellow with black tip instead of brownish; also legs shorter. Underparts greyish, white near black cap. Feeds on insects, fish and crustacea, mainly latter when at sea. Call: harsh *kee-yaah* when annoyed, also rising squeaky *kee-kee-kee.* Usually breeds in colonies, late May onwards, laying commonly 2 brownish, pale blue or greenish eggs marked with brown and ash-grey in hollow made by ♀, sometimes lined with grass, shells or pebbles, or depression in stony lichen-covered ground or amongst dense cover of moss; site varies from rocky and sandy coastal islands, beaches and dunes, to islands in freshwater lakes in far north. Both sexes incubate *c.* 22 days and tend young who fly *c.* 3 weeks. **338**

Sterna sandvicensis *Laridae*
SANDWICH OR CABOT'S TERN   *c.* 16 ins
Holarctic: breeds coasts Baltic, N Sea, S France, Tunisia, Black and Caspian Seas; winters coasts W and S Africa, Red and Arabian Seas, Persian Gulf and NW India. American race, Cabot's Tern, *S.s. acuflavida,* Atlantic and Gulf coasts from Virginia to British Honduras, Bahamas and West Indies; winters S to Columbia and Brazil, and on Pacific coasts S Mexico and Guatemala. Breeds low-lying sandy or

pebbly coasts and islands, locally some inland lakes, otherwise maritime. Upperparts pale silvery grey including long narrow wings; neck, upper tail coverts and deeply forked tail white; forehead, crown and nape jet black; underparts white. In winter forehead white, rest of black cap mottled with white. Legs black, bill black with yellowish tip, eyes brown. Flight fast but heavier than smaller terns, plunges into water from considerable height in straight slant, often submerging; feeds on small aquatic animals, chiefly fish, shrimps and marine worms. Call: loud grating *kirrick.* Breeds early May onwards in colonies on low-lying islands, sometimes rocky, dunes and sandy or pebbly beaches; 1 or 2 brownish white eggs, usually blotched with blackish or reddish brown and ash grey; in scrape sometimes lined with marram grass. Both sexes incubate *c.* 22 days, young, fed ♀ and ♂, assemble on shore 7-15 days and fly *c.* 5 weeks.

Sterna sumatrana *Laridae*
BLACK-NAPED TERN   *c.* 13 ins
Ethiopian, Oriental, Australasian: breeds coral islands from Madagascar, Seychelles to Chagos Is., Andaman Is., Malay Archipelago, S China, Philippines, Liu Kiu to Samoa, down to inshore islands of Great Barrier Reef; sedentary, keeping to tropical lagoons and coastal waters. Head white with black crescent on nape extending to front of eyes, mantle light grey, upperparts and wings grey-white, long, deeply forked tail paler, leading primary medium grey with dark grey outer web; rosy tinge on white underparts. Legs black, bill greyish black, eyes dark brown. Immature: grey-brown mottling on nape and mantle, legs and bill yellowish. Usually in calmer waters of lagoons or shallow coral pools, often with other terns, diving or hovering above surface, taking small fish; emits barking note. Breeds spring and early summer in dense colonies; 2 creamy white eggs with blotches of brown and grey undermarkings, in scrape, lined with small particles such as fragmented coral, in shingle and crevices near water; incubation and fledging much as other *Sterna* species. **339**

STILT,
     BANDED see **Cladorhynchus leucocephala**
     BLACK-WINGED see **Himantopus himantopus**

STILT SANDPIPER see **Micropalma himantopus**

Stiltia isabella *Glareolidae*
AUSTRALIAN or
LONG-LEGGED PRATINCOLE   *c.* 9½ ins
Australasian (N and E Australia, New Guinea) summer visitor, wintering Oriental (Java to Borneo); habitat dry, bare inland plains. Upperparts rufous brown, wings brown, black-tipped; upper tail coverts white, short tail black, white edged; throat grey-white, breast brown, belly and flanks rich dark brown, rest of underparts white, underwings black; long legs brown, slightly curved bill black, base red, eyes brown. Usually in flocks. Runs rapidly; characteristic zigzag swallow-like flight and habits much as Common Pratincole, *Glareola pratincola.* Takes insects on wing or ground. Breeds September to February, laying 2 pale stone eggs, marked dark brown and grey, in slight scrape on bare ground. **314**

STINT,
     LITTLE see under **Calidris temminckii**
     TEMMINCK'S see **Calidris temminckii**

STOCK DOVE see **Columba oenas**

STONE CURLEW see **Burhinus oedicnemus**

STONE CURLEW, DOUBLE STRIPED see **Burhinus bistriatus**

STONECHAT see **Saxicola torquata**

STORK,
     ASIAN OPEN-BILLED see **Anastomus oscitans**
     BLACK see **Ciconia nigra**
     JABIRU see **Jabiru mycteria**
     PAINTED see **Mycteria leucocephalus**

     WHITE see **Ciconia alba**
     WHITE-NECKED see **Dissoura episcopus**
     WOOD see **Mycteria americana**
     WOOLLY-NECKED see **Dissoura episcopus**
     YELLOW-BILLED see **Mycteria ibis**

STORM PETREL see **Hydrobates pelagicus**

STORM PETREL, WHITE-FACED see **Pelagodroma marina**

STRAIGHT-CRESTED HELMET SHRIKE see **Prionops plumata**

STRAW-NECKED IBIS see **Threskiornis spinicollis**

STREAK-BREASTED TREEHUNTER see under **Thripadectes virgaticeps**

STREAK-CAPPED TREEHUNTER see **Thripadectes virgaticeps**

STREAKED
     FLYCATCHER see **Myiodynastes maculatus**
     SPIDERHUNTER see **Arachnothera magna**

STREAMCREEPER, SHARP-TAILED see **Lochmias nematura**

STREAMER-TAILED HUMMINGBIRD see **Trochilus polytmus**

Strepera graculina *Cracticidae*
PIED CURRAWONG   20 ins
Australasian: E of continent from Cape York to S Australia, predominantly coastal; Lord Howe I. Breeds mainly mountainous, forest country, descending to plains, tablelands in winter, where some now resident; inland along watercourses. Generally black, with white at base primaries, rump, base and tips tail feathers, under tail coverts; legs, bill black, eyes yellow. Juvenile brownish. Large flocks (up to 1,000) autumn and winter, roost communally. Active and noisy, flying high overhead and landing heavily in trees. Hops on ground; clings to tree trunk and probes bark with strong bill. Call: loud, ringing *curra-wong,* often in flight. Omnivorous: mainly insects and larvae; valuable predator on stick insects which deplete eucalypts (J. L. Readshaw), but damages fruit in summer; berries in winter; young birds, carrion. Breeds August onwards, building nest of sticks, lined rootlets, bark, grass, usually 20 to 60 ft up in fork of eucalypt. 3 light brown eggs, marked darker brown. **985**

Streptopelia chinensis *Columbidae*
SPOTTED DOVE   *c.* 12½ ins
Oriental: Indian subcontinent, Ceylon, Indo-Malaysian region and S China. Habitat: woodland, forest edge and cultivated country with cover. Head bluish-grey tinged with pink, chin pale, back and sides of neck bifurcated feathers black at base and white at tip changing to pinkish buff at back; upperparts dull brown, wing edge slate blue; underparts deep wine pink at throat, shading to grey lower belly; long brown-grey tail with broad white terminal border. Legs purplish red, bill dark brown, eyes orange with mauve orbital skin. Indian form, *S. c. suratensis,* smaller, head less grey, breast paler and more mauve, belly white, back and wing coverts spotted white. Walks and runs well, usually in pairs or small parties on ground in open areas such as roads, stubble fields or even courtyards; feeds on seeds and grain. Rises almost vertically with wing clatter but flight often short. Call: soft *kroo-kroo-kroo,* local variations. Breeding season variable and prolonged, commonly April to July in N India; flimsy twig and grass-stem platform, fairly low down in trees or bushes, sometimes on ledge of building. 2 white eggs, incubated *c.* 13 days. **374**

Streptopelia decaocto *Columbidae*
COLLARED DOVE   *c.* 12½ ins
Palaearctic, NW Oriental: Indian subcontinent, Middle East, Europe, E Arabia (coast of Oman

peninsula), Chinese Turkestan, N and Central China, and Korea; NW range across Europe to Iceland only recent. Habitat: arid country near cultivation but has spread through adaptation to heavily cultivated areas, towns, villages etc. Upperparts pale grey-brown, head paler and greyer; narrow white-edged black half-collar on back of neck. Underparts soft grey with pinkish flush, particularly on breast; distal half of long tail white when viewed from below, basal half and primaries blackish. Generally greyer than similar domesticated Barbary Dove, *S. risoria*. Legs purplish red, bill black, eyes red with grey orbital skin. Gregarious when not breeding, feeds on ground on young shoots, berries, split grain and poultry feed. Calls: loud tri-syllabic *coo*; 'hysterical' squawk. Breeding season variable, March to September in Europe; builds rough twig platform, lined with some plant debris, in tree, shrub or on ledge of building. 2 white eggs, incubated *c.* 14 days by parents who both tend young; fly *c.* 18-20 days. 2 or more broods. **375**

Streptopelia risoria see under **S. decaocto**

Streptopelia semitorquata *Columbidae*
RED-EYED DOVE   *c.* 13 ins
Ethiopian: widespread throughout region. Frequents woodland and forest in well-watered regions, sometimes reed beds, often cultivated land during day. Upperparts dark grey-brown, wing edge and rump dark grey-blue; under wing coverts, flanks and sides of rump bluish grey. Nape, neck, throat to belly mauve-pink; black, grey edged, half collar on sides of neck; tail, basal half blackish, rest grey. Legs purplish red, bill blackish, eyes red or orange with red orbital skin. Tame; single, in pairs or small flocks but may aggregate in larger numbers at good feeding places; flies out of trees with wings clattering. Takes berries from trees but usually feeds on ground on seeds, cultivated grains and small animals. Call: loud musical coo. Breeding related to food supplies; makes platform of twigs and grass stems in tree or shrub, often high up; lays 2 (occasionally 1) pale cream eggs, incubated *c.* 13 days. **376**

Streptopelia senegalensis *Columbidae*
LAUGHING DOVE   *c.* 10½ ins
Ethiopian, SW Palaearctic, Oriental: Africa, Arabia, Indian subcontinent, Afghanistan and Turkestan, locally Middle East, and introduced W Australia; some seasonal movement. Habitat: arid scrub or thorn bush country near water, adapted to towns, villages and cultivated land. ♂: head, neck and chest lilac, shading to creamy white lower belly and white under tail coverts; mantle, scapulars and inner coverts tawny, outer coverts blue-grey; secondaries darker, primaries dark brownish grey, edged whitish; black patches bordered with glossy brown on undersides of neck; longish graduated grey-brown tail with white edges. ♀: mantle duller and less red. Legs purplish red, bill blackish, eyes dark brown. Races from N and W of range vary, e.g., *S.s. cambayensis*, Indian subcontinent and E Arabia, smaller and duller, with more white underneath. Tame, small flocks; ground feeder, taking seeds and cultivated grain, also plucks seeds from growing weeds. Flight usually slow unless threatened. Call: distinctive soft coo of usually 5 syllables. Builds scanty twig nest in open bush or on overhanging branch, sometimes in roof of hut; 2 white glossy eggs; both parents incubate, and tend young. **377**

Streptopelia turtur *Columbidae*
TURTLE DOVE   *c.* 10½ ins
W Palaearctic: breeds Europe, Canary Is, Madeira, N Africa, SW Asia from Kirghiz Steppes and Turkistan S to Iraq, Persia, Afghanistan, Fayum and locally Nile Delta; winters in N Africa. Habitat: usually low country, in open woodland, copses, parkland, shrubberies, outer suburbs and any area with suitable cover of bushes or large hedges; SW range fairly dry regions where some cover and water available. Top of head, back of neck and outer wing coverts grey, black silver-tipped neck patch, throat and underparts pale vinous, belly and under tail coverts

white; rufous black-spotted inner coverts and scapulars; flight feathers blackish grey; mantle, back and rump brown, long graduated tail black with broad white edges. Southern races brighter. Legs purplish red, bill blackish, eyes golden with reddish purple orbital skin. Rapid flight, more gregarious when not breeding, similar habits to Woodpigeon, *Columba palumbus*, feeding on seeds, young shoots and sometimes small molluscs in open fields and cultivated land. Call: deep purring coo. Breeds mid May onwards, earlier in S, sometimes fairly social; slight platform of twigs in tall bushes, hedges and trees, in Turkestan often inside deserted buildings, 2 white eggs, incubated *c.* 13 days by both sexes; both also tend young who fly *c.* 15 days. 2 broods. **378**

STRIATED
    FIELD WREN see under **Calamanthus campestris**
    WEAVER see **Ploceus manyar**

Strigops habroptilus *Psittacidae*
KAKAPO   23-26 ins
New Zealand; now confined to Fiordland (S Island) and perhaps Stewart I. Resident mainly *Nothofagus* beech rain forest into subalpine and alpine zones. Upperparts moss-green with bluish sheen; underparts greenish yellow; owl-like facial disc yellowish brown, faintly streaked; throat yellowish white; flight feathers, tail barred brown, dull yellow; back mottled brown with pale yellow feathershafts, similarly below; legs brownish grey, bill yellowish white to brown, cere pale brown, bristles at base; eyes dark brown. ♂ generally larger. Flightless, walking through beaten tracks in vegetation, also clambers up trunks and branches, gliding for *c.* 100 yds. Nocturnal, roosting in crevices or excavated holes. Bittern-like boom in breeding season (December to February), also 'hisses, croaks, screams and mewings' (G. R. Williams). Food: fruits of shrubs, leaves and roots of grasses; blades chewed and left hanging on plant. Lays 2 to 4 white eggs in bare scrub and among tree roots, in crevice, burrow excavated up to 9 ft, incubation probably by ♀. possibly 2 broods sometimes. **408**

STRIOLATED BUNTING see under **Melophus lathami**

STRIPE-BREASTED SPARROW WEAVER see **Plocepasser mahali**

STRIPED
    HONEYEATER see **Plectorhyncha lanceolata**
    MANAKIN see **Machaeropterus regulus**
    SWALLOW see **Hirundo abyssinica**
    SWALLOW, LARGER see **Hirundo cucullata**

Strix aluco *Strigidae*
TAWNY OWL   *c.* 15 ins
Palaearctic and Oriental: most of Europe between 40° and 60°N, extending into NW Africa, Iran and almost to Persian Gulf, W Siberia; separate population in Himalayas and Burma-Chinese mountains. Resident in light deciduous and mixed forests, open parkland, gardens and habitations; coniferous forests in Asia, up to ravines at 9,000 ft in Burma. Upperparts generally rufous brown, mottled and streaked dark brown, with whitish patches on shoulders and wing coverts; complete greyish-brown facial disc in rounded head, no tufts; underparts buff, streaked and faintly barred darker, as are wings and tail; legs feathered, claws off-white, tipped black, bill pale greenish-yellow, eyes bluish-black with purplish orbits. Grey phase common in some areas of Europe. Nocturnal but will sun itself in captivity; roosts in foliage or buildings. Arched defence posture. Wing claps by ♂ in courtship. Hunting call sharp *kievick*; 'song' rolling *hoo hoo hoo, c.* 5 seconds pause: faint *oo*, then quavering *hoooo*. . . . ; occasionally by day. Pounces from tree on variety of small mammals, especially mice and voles; frogs, crabs, fish, large insects, snails and earthworms. Occasionally hovers. Breeds from end February in Britain, usually in hole of tree, rock, building, especially chimneys (and chimney type nestboxes); frequently in old nests up to 20 ft; on ground among

roots or in short burrows. 2 to 5 white eggs incubated by ♀ 28-30 days. ♂ brings food to young, who fledge *c.* 5 weeks, but may leave nest earlier. **450**

Strix leptogrammica *Strigidae*
BROWN WOOD OWL   *c.* 20 ins
Oriental: several races Indian subcontinent, Ceylon, Burma, SE Asia; resident in forest, especially primary relicts, up to 12,000 ft. Upperparts dark brown, with pale stripes and dark-light barring on wings; 'eyebrows', part of facial disc and 'collar' light chestnut; breast dark brown; underparts and under tail coverts buffish, closely barred darker; legs pale blue, bill black-horn, with bristles; eyes dark brown. Nocturnal, very shy in daylight. Usually in pairs. Calls vary somewhat with race but basically mellow double hoot; squawks, shrieks, chuckles and bill-snapping also recorded. Takes reptiles, rodents, birds, probably fish; also grubs (T. H. Harrisson). Breeds Indian subcontinent January to March, making vestigial nest in hollow tree fork, shelving cliff ledge, bare ground at foot of tree or rock. Usually 2 white eggs, from which single young is reared by both parents, who defend it fiercely.

Strix nebulosa *Strigidae*
GREAT GREY OWL   24-33 (tail 12) ins
Holarctic: across Eurasia from N Scandinavia and Poland between 50° and 70°N to Pacific from Sakhalin N to Gulf Anadyr, where almost linked to American range running through Alaska and Central Canada to NW USA. Resident, with occasional dispersal in food shortage, dense lichen-clad taiga; in N America, mixed forest of spruce and poplars, also coniferous forests of pines and firs. Upperparts: mottled dark grey-brown and light; large facial disc with concentric fine barrings and black chin spot, no ear tufts; throat whitish, underparts narrowly barred and both streaked vertically dark grey-brown; wings and long tail barred; feathered legs finely barred, bill light horn, eyes yellow. Nocturnal; call a deep booming series of *whoos*, each lower in pitch. Takes mainly small to medium-sized mammals: lemmings, mice, squirrels, from trees or ground. Breeds May to June USA; usually takes over large old nest of other bird in conifer, sometimes on rock faces. Variable clutch, 1 to 9 white eggs, incubated by ♀ *c.* 30 days. Young leave nest *c.* 3 weeks, well before fledging (H. Mikkola). **451**

Strix varia *Strigidae*
BARRED OWL   18-24 ins
Nearctic: roughly S from 54°N in Canada to Gulf of Florida and Honduras; northern birds moving S in hard winters. Otherwise resident in woodlands, often swampy. Upperparts mottled brown, blackish and white with dark and light bars on wings and tail; barring of large round head, including upper breast, and facial disc in concentric rings; underparts buff with dark vertical streaks; legs feathered, bill yellow-horn, eyes brown. Nocturnal; emphatic hoot usually of 8 syllables in groups of 4, with terminal *aw: who cooks for you; who cooks for you-all?* (J. B. May). Mutual courtship includes nodding and bowing with variety of calls. Takes mainly rats, mice, frogs. Lays from January to April in N America, according to latitude, 2 to 4 white eggs in tree cavity or large old nest of other bird; incubation and fledging much as *S. aluco.* **452**

Struthidea cinerea *Grallinidae*
APOSTLEBIRD   13 ins
Australasian: Central Northern Territory E and S through Queensland and New South Wales W of Great Dividing Range; marginally S Australia, rare Victoria. Resident open wooded country, often near watercourses. Generally grey, wings brown; tail black glossed green; feathers of head, neck, throat with lighter tips; legs and stubby bill black, eyes dark grey with creamy outer ring. Juvenile more uniform on head, eyes brown. In groups of 4 to 20 with dominant pair; gatherings of several hundred inland due to food or water: drinks several times daily and often bathes. Group territory maintained when breeding (August to December) with regular roosts in trees. Call, probably alarm: *ch-kew ch-kew;* also squeaking

notes when breeding. Diet: mainly seeds, feeding along roads, round farms. Several birds build nest of fresh mud (sometimes Emu dung) and grass, lined finer grass, on lateral branch shrub or tree, 8 to 50 ft. Clutch 2 to 5 off-white eggs, marked blackish, slate grey; sometimes two ♀♀ lay same nest; incubated 19 days. Young, fed by group, dominated by ♀ and ♂, leave nest 23 days, fly a week later. Sometimes 2 broods same season, perhaps laid by different ♀♀.

Struthio camelus *Struthionidae*
OSTRICH   6-7 ft tall
Formerly found in Syria and Arabia, wild Ostriches are now confined to Africa. Five subspecies are known, distinguished partly by colour of bare skin on head, neck and thighs. Once extensively farmed for their plumes (hence small feral population in South Australia). The ♂ is black with white wings and tail; ♀ and juvenile have pale brown bodies. Legs, feet and bill are horn-coloured; eyes brown with prominent eyelashes. Ostriches resemble large grazing mammals with which they consort on savannahs and open bush country, feeding on vegetation, but swallowing a variety of objects to help grind their food in the gizzard. Main call a hollow boom, resembling distant lion's roar without terminal grunt. Breeding season varies with latitude; eggs are laid in a scrape made by polygamous ♂ on the ground. Usually 3 ♀♀ lay 6 to 8 yellowish white eggs in common nest and ♂ incubates them by night, ♀♀ partly by day for 5-6 weeks. The chicks can run fast at a month old. **1**

STUBBLE QUAIL see **Coturnix pectoralis**

Sturnella magna *Icteridae*
EASTERN MEADOWLARK $10\frac{3}{4}$ ins
Nearctic, marginally Neotropical: breeds southern Canada through E USA to Florida, Gulf Coast, N Mexico; most birds leave N of range (to S New Jersey, Ohio Valley, Kansas) in winter. Habitat open grassland with scattered trees or other perches. ♂: upperparts streaked and barred (wings, tail) dark and light brown; prominent white outer tail feathers; head greyish, striped blackish with short yellow 'eyebrow', broad white moustachial stripe; broad black band divides yellow chin from underparts, which become off-white on streaked flanks, under tail coverts. ♀ smaller, paler, narrower breast band. Legs pale horn, pointed bill light grey, eyes dark brown. Winter, juvenile browner: black areas masked, white areas buffish. Remarkable plumage convergence with Yellow-throated Longclaw, *Macronyx croceus*, of similar ecology in Africa. Constantly jerks tail open in walking; flies, beating short wings vigorously, then gliding. Sings from exposed perch 3 to 5 clear, high, long drawn-out whistled notes: *tsee-you tsee-ear,* often slurred. Chattering calls. Food: insects, especially beetles, grasshoppers, in summer; seeds in winter. Breeds May to June; ♀♀ choosing ♂♂, but sometimes polygamous; loosely built partially domed nest of grass and plant stems in scrape in thick, often uniform cover. Usually 5 white eggs, spotted brown over purple, incubated ♀: 13-15 days; young leave nest before fully fledged, 11-12 days. **914**

Sturnella neglecta *Icteridae*
WESTERN MEADOWLARK $9\frac{1}{2}$ ins
Nearctic, marginally Neotropical; breeds from SW Canada through western USA to N Mexico; E to Minnesota, S Wisconsin, N Illinois, Oklahoma, Central Texas; leaves area N of Nebraska, Utah in winter. Does not hybridise with *S. magna* where ranges overlap, even nesting same fields. Habitat as *S. magna*, plumage very similar but slightly paler; yellow on chin extends on to cheeks near base of bill; flanks spotted rather than streaked black. Distinctive song, deep rich melody of 6 or 7 notes of clear bubbling quality; also sharp call *chuck*. Habits, food, breeding as *S. magna* but chooses rather drier nest sites. Often 2 broods.

Sturnus roseus *Sturnidae*
ROSY PASTOR or
ROSE-COLOURED STARLING   *c.* 9 ins
Palaearctic: SE Europe W to Hungary, S to Turkey

and Syria, E to Iran, Turkestan, Aral-Caspian region and Altai, NE to S Russia; winters India. Habitat: rocky or broken ground and old buildings while breeding, otherwise any open country particularly where grassy and cultivated; also low thorn jungle in semi-desert. ♂: crest on crown and nape, head, upper mantle, upper breast black glossed reddish purple, body rose pink; under tail coverts black glossed blue-purple, tail black glossed blue-purple and green, primaries and most coverts glossed blue-purple and green, lesser coverts blacker. ♀: shorter crest, generally less glossy. Legs horny brown, bill brown, yellow at gape and basal half lower mandible, eyes brown. Behaviour, feeding and calls similar to Common Starling, *S. vulgaris*; huge flocks at good feeding places, e.g. fields of ripening grain or locust swarms; visits flowering trees for nectar. Breeding season variable, usually May or June onwards, colonial; site may be used by large numbers then suddenly deserted again; nest in holes in rocky hillside, walls or ruins; untidy heap of twigs, grass, straw, lined roots, feathers; sometimes little material used. 3 to 5 very pale bluish or bluish white eggs, incubated ♀ *c.* 12 days. Both parents tend young, who fly 14-19 days.

Sturnus vulgaris *Sturnidae*
COMMON STARLING   *c.* $8\frac{1}{2}$ ins
Palaearctic, marginally Oriental: SE Iceland, W Europe, apart from Iberia and S France, E to mid Lapland across to L. Baikal, SE to Iran across to Kashmir, and (apart from Transcaspia) to L. Baikal; Karachi (Pakistan) introduced N America (now widespread), S Africa, Australia, New Zealand. Some sedentary populations in W and S Europe where other populations winter; also migrates to Mediterranean countries and SW Asia. Habitat: varied; open lightly wooded country, grassy plains and meadows with nearby tree cover, cultivated areas, farms, villages, towns. Blackish, feathers of upperparts tipped buff, underparts tipped white especially in winter; crown, nape, cheeks, chin and throat glossed green, upper breast, sides of head and mantle glossed reddish purple; scapulars, back, rump and upper tail coverts glossed green and purple, lower breast glossed bronze-green; tail and wings black-brown with blue-green gloss on secondaries and coverts; darker and glossier in summer. ♀ more spotted and less glossy. Legs reddish brown, bill greyish or greenish brown in winter, lemon-yellow in summer, eyes dark brown, thin, paler ring in ♀. Large flocks in winter, huge roosts. Usually feeds on ground in small flocks, walks quickly and jerkily. Call: grating *tcherrr;* song lively medley of warbling, chirruping, gurgling and clicking, often includes imitations of other birds and noises. Feeds on insects and other terrestrial invertebrates, sometimes small vertebrates and vegetable matter. Breeds March onwards, solitary or social; nest of straw and grass, lined with feathers and other softer material, in cavity, in walls, roofs, cliffs, trees and sometimes in ground or in pile of stones in treeless areas; 4 to 7 pale blue eggs; ♂ and ♀ incubate *c.* 12-13 days and both tend young, who fly 22-27 days; sometimes 2 broods in favourable early season. **974**

SUBALPINE WARBLER see **Sylvia cantillans**

SUDAN DIOCH see **Quelea quelea**

SUGARBIRD, CAPE see **Promerops cafer**

Sula bassana *Sulidae*
GANNET   36 (body 23) ins
N Atlantic, breeding rocky islands, stacks and sea cliffs, clockwise from Newfoundland to Channel Islands though some authorities regard S African *S. capensis* and Australian *S. serrator* as conspecific; young birds migrate to W African coasts, but instinct declines with age. Predominantly white, with black wingtips and buff suffusion of head; speckled brown juvenile becomes whiter annually; legs brown-black, bill bluish white, eyes pale grey. Gregarious: adults spend most of year at or near breeding station, flying out over sea alone or in small parties, and diving for fish from height with neat splash; also use shallow oblique dive when scavenging harbours or behind

ships. Complicated displays at colonies designed to reduce mutual aggression; growling call when landing, different 'snoring' note when leaving, otherwise silent. Breeds May to August on cliff ledges and tops of stacks; nest of seaweed and debris for usually one chalky white, soon stained egg, incubated $6\frac{1}{2}$ weeks by ♀ and ♂, who feed chick for *c.* 2 months. **42**

Sula capensis see under **S. bassana**

Sula leucogaster *Sulidae*
BROWN BOOBY   28-30 ins
Pacific (2 races), S Atlantic and Indian Oceans, dispersing after breeding on offshore and oceanic islands. Dark chocolate brown with white breast, belly, under wings; legs pale yellow to green; bill and naked face yellowish or bluish; eyes pale grey. Colombian *S.l. etesiaca* ♂ grey-headed. Noted for ability to make rapid dives, though less spectacular than other gannets in flight. Takes off from tree perches, even roosting in palms. Mutual displays at colonies where adults quack and hiss. Diet of squids, prawns, flying fish to flatfish. Breeding continuous some areas, 8 month cycle on Ascension Island; colonies on bare ground or in scrub, nests from unlined scrapes to collections of debris and stones; usually 2 chalky, bluish white eggs, incubated by ♀ and ♂ for 40-43 days; they usually only rear one chick, able to fly in *c.* 15 weeks. **43**

Sula nebouxii *Sulidae*
BLUE-FOOTED BOOBY   26 ins
Pacific coast of Central America, breeds bare or xerophilous islands Gulf of California to N Peru. Generally cinnamon above and white below; head hoary, large white patches at junction of neck and back and on rump and upper tail-coverts, primaries blackish brown; legs bright blue, bill dull greenish blue, eyes yellow, ♀ with black blotches; ♀♀ larger than ♂♂. Fishes by diving in small parties, probably taking larger species than anchovies, but not a significant contributor to guano industry. Adapted to bare rocks, cannot perch like Red-footed Booby. Courtship includes 'goose-stepping' by ♂ with tail raised and beseeching whistle; also presents feather; ♀ has 'strident, raucous trumpeting' as have young ♂♂. Breeding season varies, nests more scattered than other gannets, circle of debris with 1 to 3 pale chalky blue eggs incubated by ♀ and ♂, who also tend young to fledging, the whole cycle taking about 3-4 months (October to January) in Peru. **44**

Sula serrator see under **S. bassana**

Sula sula *Sulidae*
RED-FOOTED BOOBY   27-29 ins
Southern oceans: Atlantic, Pacific and Indian, dispersing after breeding on tree-clad oceanic and offshore islands. Generally white, tinged buff-brown, with blackish primaries, long tail pale grey-brown and grey under wings; legs red, bill light blue, brown tip, facial skin variable to blue, eyes chestnut. May breed in brown 'intermediate' plumage with white rump and tail. Only regularly tree-perching and nesting gannet, partly nocturnal. Flies in flocks of 40 to 80 and catches (especially) flying fish by diving from height and chasing underwater; also takes squids. Adults croak when returning with fish; young chatter and squawk; also harsh cries of annoyance. Breeding season varies; colonial nests of sticks in low tree growth, sometimes cliff ledges. Both sexes incubate the 1 or 2 chalky, pale blue eggs for *c.* 44 days; chicks can fly in *c.* 15 weeks. **45**

SUMMER TANAGER see **Piranga rubra**

SUN BITTERN see **Eurypyga helias**

SUNBIRD,
  BEAUTIFUL see **Nectarinia pulchella**
  BRONZY see **Nectarinia killimensis**
  GOLDEN WINGED see **Drepanorhynchus reichenowi**
  GREEN-HEADED see **Cyanomitra verticalis**
  MALACHITE see **Nectarinia famosa**

SUNBIRD,
   ORANGE-BREASTED see **Nectarinia violacea**
   SCARLET-CHESTED see **Chalcomitra senegalensis**
   SOUTHERN DOUBLE-COLLARED see **Cinnyris chalybeus**
   TACAZZE see **Nectarinia tacazze**
   VARIABLE see **Cinnyris venustus**
   WHITE-BELLIED see **Cinnyris talatala**

SUPERB
   LYREBIRD see **Menura novaehollandiae**
   STARLING see **Spreo superbus**

SURFBIRD see **Aphriza virgata**

Surnia ulula *Strigidae*
HAWK OWL   14-15 ins
Holarctic: across Eurasia from Scandinavia to Pacific between 50° and 70°N, almost continuous with American range from Alaska SE to Atlantic coast of Canada; isolated groups in Central Asian mountains. Resident, with rare dispersals S in food shortages, in fairly dense taiga (larch rather than spruce), also open conifers and mixed larch woodland. Palaearctic race *S. u. ulula*: upperparts mottled and barred blackish brown and white, crown blackish, finely spotted white; long tail brown, faintly barred white; incomplete facial disc greyish, bordered black; underparts white narrowly barred blackish; legs feathered, claws blackish-brown, bill yellowish, eyes bright yellow. American race *caparoch* has broader bars on underparts. Largely diurnal, perching in open on pole or tree-top, often with body inclined forward, raising and lowering tail, then pitching downward into noiseless hunting flight after rodents (mice, voles, lemmings), squirrels and birds to grouse size. Call chattering and hawk-like; screams at nest. Breeds from end March in holes of dead or dying trees, sometimes made by woodpeckers, old nests of other birds, occasionally cliff ledges. 3 to 9 glossy white eggs incubated mainly by ♀ *c*. 4 weeks; both parents feed young. **453**

SUTTON'S WARBLER see under **Dendroica dominica**

SWAINSON'S
   FRANCOLIN see **Francolinus swainsonii**
   SPURFOWL see **Francolinus swainsonii**
   THRUSH see **Catharus ustulatus**

SWALLOW see **Hirundo rustica**

SWALLOW,
   BARN see **Hirundo rustica**
   DUSKY WOOD see under **Artamus superciliosus**
   LARGER STRIPED see **Hirundo cucullata**
   MASKED WOOD see under **Artamus superciliosus**
   MOSQUE see **Hirundo senegalensis**
   PEARL-BREASTED see **Hirundo dimidiata**
   RED-RUMPED see **Hirundo daurica**
   STRIPED see **Hirundo abyssinica**
   TREE see **Tachycineta bicolor**
   WHITE-BREASTED WOOD see **Artamus leucorhynchus**
   WHITE-BROWED WOOD see **Artamus superciliosus**
   WHITE-THROATED see **Hirundo albigularis**
   WIRE-TAILED see **Hirundo smithii**

SWALLOW TANAGER see **Tersina viridis**

SWALLOW-TAILED
   GULL see **Creagrus furcatus**
   KITE see **Chelictinia riocourii**

SWALLOW-WING see **Chelidoptera tenebrosa**

SWAMP
   FLYCATCHER see **Alseonax aquaticus**
   HARRIER see **Circus approximans**
   HEN see under **Porphyrio porphyrio**

SWAN,
   BLACK see **Cygnus atratus**
   COSCOROBA see **Coscoroba coscoroba**

SWIFT,
   ALPINE see **Apus melba**
   COMMON see **Apus apus**
   INDIAN CRESTED see **Hemiprocne longipennis**

SWIFT PARROT see **Lathamus discolor**

SWIFTLET,
   GLOSSY see **Collocalia esculenta**
   WHITE-BREASTED see **Collocalia esculenta**

SWINHOE'S ROCK THRUSH see **Monticola gularis**

SYDNEY WAXBILL see **Estrilda temporalis**

SYLPH,
   BLUE-THROATED see **Lampornis clemenciae**
   LONG-TAILED see **Aglaiocercus kingi**

Sylvia atricapilla *Muscicapidae: Sylviinae*
BLACKCAP   5½ ins
Palaearctic: breeds Europe between 35° and 65°N to 50°E, then W Siberia to 85°E between 50° and 60°N; winters S Europe, N Africa, Canaries, tropical Africa, varying year to year. Migratory divide SE: SW at 12°E. ♂: crown jet black, nape grey, mantle, rump greyish olive-brown; chin, throat, breast pale grey; belly white, flanks greyish; wings and tail dark grey with paler edges. ♀ and juvenile crown bright to dull red-brown, remainder like ♂ but browner. Legs dark slate, bill slaty black to brownish black, eyes brown. Numerous, extravagant displays, head and back feathers raised, wings drooped or flapped. ♂♂ often assemble excitedly during incubation. Call: typical *tacc-tacc*; song clear rich warble, and rather stereotyped (see Garden Warbler, *S. borin*). Food: insects, and more fruit than most warblers. Breeds late April onwards; builds neat nest dry stems, rimmed cobwebs, wool, lined finer grass, rootlets, hair; suspended from fork of small bush, dead stems among nettles, other low cover. Usually 5 eggs, very variable buffish with brown spots and marbling, incubated ♀ and ♂ 10-12 days. Young, fed by both parents, fledge 10-13 days but leave earlier if disturbed. 2 broods. **749**

Sylvia borin *Muscicapidae: Sylviinae*
GARDEN WARBLER   5½ ins
Palaearctic: breeds in Europe between 40° and 65°N to 50°E; then between 50° and 60°N to 95°E; winters eastern Africa south to Cape with dividing line in Europe, some migrating SW, others SE. Habitat: open deciduous and mixed woodland with abundant undergrowth, also low scrub, young conifers in N; winters forests, gardens and thorn bush savannah. Uniform and nondescript; upperparts brown, tinged olive, underparts white, buffer on breast and flanks; wings and tail dark brown. Legs greyish brown, bill dark brown, eyes greyish brown. Displays very pronounced, ♂ spreading tail and fluttering wings very rapidly. Calls: typical *tacc-tacc* and low grating churr; song even, flowing musical warble similar but more subdued and sustained than Blackcap, *S. atricapilla*. Food: insects, also fruit and berries in late autumn. Breeds May and June; builds fairly substantial grass nest, lined rootlets, hair in bushes, brambles, saplings, other low cover. 4 or 5 eggs, pale buff with olive and brown spots, incubated ♀ *c*. 12 days. Young, fed by both parents, leave nest 9–10 days before able to fly. Sometimes 2 broods in S. **750**

Sylvia cantillans *Muscicapidae: Sylviinae*
SUBALPINE WARBLER   4¾ ins
Palaearctic: 3 races; breeds Mediterranean area and islands; probably all migratory, wintering in zone along S Sahara from Senegal to E Chad. Migrates through Egypt in spring but never in autumn. Habitat: thickets, bushes, open woodland, especially damper areas. ♂: upperparts ash grey, white moustachial streak; chin to breast pale pink to pinkish chestnut with white tips; belly white; wings dark with pale fringes; tail quite long, dark with white border.

♀ browner on upperparts, paler on underparts, less prominent moustachial stripe. Juvenile browner still. Legs yellow-brown, bill bluish-slate, eyes brown-buff, orbital ring terracotta (dark gold when juvenile). Calls: typical *tacc-tacc*; alarm *chat-chat-chat-chat*; song like Whitethroat, *S. communis*, but more sustained and has some prolonged musical notes. Food: insects. Breeds mid April to early June, builds neat slight nest of grasses and thistledown in low bushes. 3 or 4 eggs, greenish or greyish white with fine dark spots, incubated probably only ♀ 12-13 days. Young, fed by both parents, fledge 11-12 days. 2 broods. **751**

Sylvia communis *Muscicapidae: Sylviinae*
WHITETHROAT   5½ ins
Palaearctic: breeds in broad belt 35° to 65°N from W Europe to 95°E (belt thinner in E); winters in extensive areas of savannah in Africa, S of Sahara and Arabia; one race in India and SW Asia. Habitat: open country with bushes, brambles; woodland edge, riparian vegetation, heaths, subalpine bush zones. ♂: head slate grey; upperparts brown; underparts white with buffish pink on upper breast, flanks darker; wings dark with rufous edges; tail dark with white edges. ♀ similar but crown brown, and duller outer tail feathers. Legs pale brown, bill greyish horn, eyes yellowish brown. Pronounced courtship displays; conspicuous dancing song flight. Assemblies *cf* Blackcap, *S. atricapilla*, in breeding season. Calls: typical *tacc-tacc* and hoarse *charr*; song short rapid warble with many harsh grating notes. Food: insects but also berries in autumn. Breeds May onwards. ♂ builds nest before ♀'s arrival; she may use this or build another: substantial cup lined with (usually black) hair and decorated with wool, in low bushes, long grass, rushes, heather, other thick cover. 4 to 6 eggs very variable, greenish with 'dirty' yellow markings, overlaid dark spots, often in zone. Incubation mainly ♀ 11-13 days. Young, fed by both parents, fledge 10-12 days. 2 broods.

Sylvia hortensis *Muscicapidae: Sylviinae*
ORPHEAN WARBLER   6 ins
Palaearctic: 4 races; breeds round Mediterranean, then Turkey eastward between Caspian Sea and Persian Gulf in broadening range to 75°E; winters in narrow band across Africa on southern edge of Sahara; one race in S India. Habitat: wooded areas (especially cork-oak), orchards, gardens. ♂: head dull blackish, merging to grey-brown mantle and rump; underparts greyish white (white throat) with pinkish tinge on breast in breeding season; wings and tail dark, latter with white outer feathers. ♀: browner, no pinkish tinge but has dark crown. Juvenile more uniform upperparts. Legs dark, bill dark, eyes pale straw. Keeps high in trees unlike most *Sylvia* species. Call: typical *tac-tac*, also loud rattling alarm. Song like Song Thrush, *Turdus philomelos*, each phrase repeated 4-5 times. Food: insects, occasionally berries. Breeds early May onwards S Europe, building nest of grasses, roots, mixed flowerheads, plant down, lined rootlets, usually among lateral branches of tree 5 to 8 ft up, sometimes much lower or higher. 4 to 6 eggs, pale greenish white with ashy spots and brownish streaks, incubated ♀ and ♂; fledging period *c*. 14 days. **752**

Sylvia melanocephala *Muscicapidae: Sylviinae*
SARDINIAN WARBLER   5¼ ins
Palaearctic: breeds Mediterranean area E through Asia Minor between Persian Gulf and Aral Sea to 95°E. Mainly resident. Habitat: usually dry thickets and bushes; winters more in open woodland. ♂: head and nape glossy black extending just below eye; mantle and rump dark grey; underparts white, less pure on belly, flanks grey; wings brown-black; graduated tail black with white edges. ♀: head ash-grey, upperparts brown, greyer on rump, underparts white with darker sides. Juvenile duller. Legs flesh brown, bill black, eyes bright brown, orbital ring and eyelids pink. Has dancing song-flight. Call: hard distinctive stuttering like machine gun. Song like Whitethroat, *S. communis*, but more musical and sustained and interspersed with alarm note. Food: insects, with grapes, figs and seeds in autumn and

winter. Breeds mid April onwards; builds neat substantial nest of grass 2 to 4 ft up in bushes. 3 or 4 very variable eggs, incubated ♀ and ♂ 13-14 days. Young, fed mainly by ♀, fledge 11 days. 2 broods. **753**

Sylvia nisoria *Muscicapidae : Sylviinae*
BARRED WARBLER 6 ins
Palaearctic: breeds in block from Lombardy to W Mongolia and Finland to Bosphorus, also between Black and Caspian Seas, Kirghiz Steppes and N Afghanistan; winters E Africa and S Arabia. Habitat: bushy places and thickets, especially thorns, often in damper areas. ♂: upperparts greyish brown, underparts white with dark grey crescentic bars; wings dark grey brown with 2 paler bars; tail long and dark grey with white outer feathers and tips. ♀ similar but browner and bars less distinct. Juvenile no bars. Legs brownish grey, bill dark horn, eyes: adult bright yellow, juvenile at first dark brown. Very skulking. Seems to form associations with Red-backed Shrike, *Lanius collurio*. Calls: typical *Sylvia tacc* and loud harsh chatter, also included in song which is similar to Garden Warbler *S. borin*. Food: mainly insects. Breeds late May to June; builds rather untidy grass nest, lined hair, rootlets, fairly high in fork of bush, occasionally tree. 5 greyish white eggs with fine speckles, incubated ♀ and ♂ 14-15 days. Young fledge 14-16 days. **754**

Sylvietta rufescens *Muscicapidae: Sylviinae*
LONG-BILLED CROMBEC 4½ ins
Ethiopian: from E and SE Zaire, Zambia, Malawi to S Africa. Resident open savannah, dry thorn bush and scrub in hilly country. Upperparts, including wings, very short tail, greyish; cheeks, ear coverts, underparts buffish brown; light buff 'eyebrow', dusky eyestripe; legs yellowish brown; long decurved bill (distinguishing from very similar Red-faced, *S. whytii*) dusky brown, eyes pale brown. Pairs or small family parties, often mixed with other species, restlessly search foliage and twigs for insects like *Phylloscopus* warblers. Alarm call 3 shrill notes, emphasis on first; simple song *richi-tiddlit*. Breeds September to April; rather large, deep purse-shaped nest, higher side suspended from twig, of fine grass, lined grass, rootlets. 2 white eggs, marked red or brown. **755**

Sylvietta whytii see under **S. rufescens**

SYRIAN WOODPECKER see **Dendrocopos syriacus**

Syrrhaptes paradoxus
Pteroclididae c. 13-16 (of which tail
PALLAS'S SANDGROUSE c. 2½-3½) ins
Palaearctic: SE Russia into Turkestan and Mongolia, periodically erupting westward, actually breeding Britain 1888-9. Habitat: sandy and saline steppes and semi-desert. ♂: generally sandy-looking, upperparts densely marked black crescents; head sandy buff and grey, which extends over breast to narrow band of black bars; lower belly black; flight feathers of rounded wings mainly pale grey; tail barred grey and sandy, with 2 central feathers elongated to fine points, others white-tipped. ♀: duller, spots extend up nape over crown, black crescentic border to pale throat; wings, tail not so tapering. Legs feathered, claws black; very short bill grey-blue; eyes dark brown. Very hard to see when crouching; rises heavily, but flight fast with rapid beats and humming sound. Waddles with very short steps. Flocks regularly visit drinking places, where both sips, and gulps like pigeon. Double or triple flight call rendered: *chack chack* or *kockerik kockerik*; soft *kok kok* on ground. Diet: variety of seeds and young shoots. Breeds April to June Asia, making bare or sparsely lined scrape in open. Usually 3 elliptical stone to yellow brown eggs, marked purplish brown over grey, incubated ♀ and ♂, 3½ weeks. Young feed on seeds. 2 or 3 broods.

TACAZZE SUNBIRD see **Nectarinia tacazze**

Tachybaptus ruficollis or Podiceps ruficollis
Podicipedidae
LITTLE GREBE or DABCHICK 10½ ins
Widespread in S Palaearctic, Oriental and Ethiopian regions, with closely allied species in Australasia. Breeding plumage rich dark brown above with dark red cheeks and yellow-green skin at gape; underparts lighter; becomes lighter all over in winter. Legs and bill mainly black; eyes red-brown. Often resident in breeding habitat of lakes, ponds, swamps and slow-flowing rivers, though many move to coast and northern birds migrate south in autumn. Forms parties then, but often solitary or in pairs, keeping to cover in breeding season. Swims buoyantly and dives freely after small fish, water insects, molluscs and crustaceans, but reluctant to take wing. Loud trilling call in spring; alarm note a sharp *wit wit*. Breeding season varies with latitude, April to September in Palaearctic. Floating nest, well-hidden in aquatic vegetation, holds 4 to 6 white eggs, soon stained by weeds when covered when left, incubated for 3½ weeks by ♀ and ♂; both care for young, who fledge in about 6 weeks; 2, sometimes 3, broods a year. **21**

Tachycineta bicolor or Iridoprocne bicolor
Hirundinidae
TREE SWALLOW 5 ins
Nearctic: breeds in broad band across N America extending to California and Central Alaska in W; winters all across southern USA S to Panama, also Cuba. Habitat: mostly open wooded country near water and habitations. Upperparts glossed steel-blue and bronze-green; underparts white. Very hardy and tame. After breeding congregates in huge flocks. Display flight: sexes chase erratically then ♂ grasps ♀'s breast and they tumble near to the ground. Call: continuous twitter; song: separate liquid notes *weet-twit-weet*, especially early in morning. Food mainly aerial insects but also some vegetable matter. Breeding season March onwards; ♀ builds nest of grass and feathers (usually white) in old treeholes and nest-boxes. 4 to 6 (rarely up to 10) white unglossed eggs; incubated by ♀ fed by ♂, 13-16 days. Young, fed by both parents, fledge 16-24 days. 2 broods. **622**

Tachyeres patachonicus see under **T. pteneres**

Tachyeres pteneres *Anatidae* c. 29-33 ins
MAGELLANIC FLIGHTLESS STEAMER DUCK
Neotropical: coast S America from Corral, Chile, to Cape Horn and Staten I.; breeds Chiloe I. southwards ♂: crown bluish grey, rest of head and neck pale grey mottled white, white stripe behind eyes, throat marked reddish brown; breast and remaining upperparts mottled grey; underparts mostly white. ♀: darker grey on head and neck, larger and darker reddish patch on throat; tail feathers less curled. Legs yellow, bill orange-yellow, duller in ♀, with black nail; eyes dark brown. Cannot fly but uses short wings when diving and for moving over the surface fast, up to 12 miles per hour; flapping and running, throwing up much spray. Visits freshwater springs on islands to drink. Tame; usually in pairs or small flocks, larger in winter and often in association with Flying Steamer Ducks, *T. patachonicus;* feeds gregariously at high tide on marine invertebrates, especially molluscs, from shellfish banks or among kelp beds; parties split up and rest on rocks as they become exposed, fiercely defend their perches. Call: shrill repeated *qu-i-e-u-ll* followed by *kek-kek-kek-kek*. Nests under thick vegetation on islands, islets and isolated points; c. 5 to 8 creamy white eggs in down lining, ♀ alone incubates sitting very tight. **128**

Tadorna tadorna *Anatidae*
SHELDUCK 24 (body 16) ins
Palaearctic: breeds coasts of W Europe, locally shores of Mediterranean, Black and Caspian Seas, saline lakes of Central Asia to E Siberia, Mongolia and Tibet; winters from southern part of breeding range to N Africa, Arabia, India, S China and Japan, following relatively local post-breeding 'moult migration' and then moving on. Habitat: low lying sandy or muddy coasts and estuaries, coastal sand-dunes and inland lakes and swamps. ♂: striking plumage of black and chestnut markings on white; head and neck black with metallic-green sheen; broad chestnut band round body, black scapulars, primaries and tips of tail feathers, dusky broad strip along centry of belly. ♀:

a little duller with no red knob at base of bill. Legs pink, bill red, eyes brown. Usually silent; but calls repeated *ak-ak-ak*. Gregarious; often rests at sea, buoyant in water; slow wing-beat but takes off easily; feeds in shallow water on small animals, sometimes taking plant matter. Breeding season depends on locality but in Europe lays 8 to 15 eggs in May, in nest of almost pure down plus some marram grass or similar material in rabbit-hole or under dense cover. ♀ incubates c. 28 days; both parents tend young who fly c. 45 days. Broods may combine with one ♀ or ♂♀ in attendance. **129**

Taenopygia castanotis *Estrildidae*
ZEBRA FINCH 4½ ins
Australasian: continent and Lesser Sunda Is. Nomadic in grasslands near water; spinifex plains with scrub patches, e.g. mulga; cleared and cultivated lands; parks, orchards, gardens; displaced some areas by introduced Spice Finch, *Lonchura punctulata*. ♂: back brownish-grey; wings blackish-brown; upper tail coverts black, barred white; tail brownish-black; head, nape blue-grey; black and white stripes on face, earcoverts chestnut; breast grey, narrowly barred black; flanks chestnut spotted white; underparts from chin off-white. ♀ duller. Legs orange-yellow; large bill, eyes red. Immature much as ♀, bill black. Pairs or flocks from 50 to 100. Variety of calls: *tia* from flocks in flight; *tet tet* of contact; aggressive *wssst*. Perches on ground, picking up or jumping to take grass and other seeds; hawks insects or takes them off leaves. Drinks like pigeon. Mutual display dance with bill wiping, tail twisting towards other bird; ♂ shows off plumage; probably pairs for life. Makes small roosting nests. Breeding influenced by rainfall: October to April in N; social but each pair has own bush, building bottle nest of grass, soft stalks, lined feathers, generally low in thorny shrub, including introduced species vines; holes in trees, buildings, old nests, even rabbit, kingfisher burrows. 3 to 7 faint bluish-white eggs, incubated ♀ and ♂ 12½-16 days. Both feed young, who leave nest within 3 weeks, but led back at night by parents. 2 broods. **945**

TAILORBIRD, COMMON see **Orthostomus sutorius**

TAKAHE see **Notornis mantelli**

TANAGER,
 BAY-HEADED see **Tangara gyrola**
 BLACK AND GREEN see **Tangara nigroviridis**
 BLACK-HEADED see **Tangara cyanoptera**
 BLUE-GREY see **Thraupis episcopus**
 FLAME-RUMPED see under **Ramphocelus icteronotus**
 GLISTENING GREEN see **Chlorochrysa phoenicotis**
 GOLDEN-CROWNED see **Iridosornis rufivertex**
 MASKED CRIMSON see **Ramphocelus nigrogularis**
 SUMMER see **Piranga rubra**
 SWALLOW see **Tersina viridis**
 YELLOW-RUMPED see **Ramphocelus icteronotus**

Tanagra laniirostris or Euphonia laniirostris
Emberizidae : Thraupinae
THICK-BILLED EUPHONIA 5 ins
Neotropical: Costa Rica, Panama, N Venezuela, Colombia, Ecuador, Peru: Bolivia, adjacent parts Brazil; open woodland sea level to c. 4,500 ft. ♂: upperparts, including cheeks, neck, wings, tail, steely blue; inner web outer 2 pairs tail feathers largely white in one race; sides of head and nape purplish; forehead, entire underparts shades of yellow. ♀: olive green above, olive yellow below, brightest on centre belly; white spots on lores. ♂ sometimes breeds incomplete plumage. Food: principally fruit, berries, especially mistletoe. Nest mainly built ♀, domed, with side entrance, on ground. 3 to 5 eggs incubated ♀ 13-14 days; ♀ and ♂ tend young in nest 3 weeks or longer. **880**

Tangara cyanoptera *Emberizidae : Thraupinae*
BLACK-HEADED TANAGER 5 ins
Neotropical: NW Guyanas, Venezuela, NE Colombia, Brazil (N Roraima); forests from sea level to c. 7,000 ft.

♂: generally glossy 'opalescent silvery greenish straw colour' (Meyer de Schauensee); head, wings, tail black, flight and tail feathers edged dark blue. ♀: upperparts yellowish green, wings, tail feathers edged green; head, nape greyish blue; throat, breast greyish, streaked bluish; belly yellow, tinged green. Arboreal, roosts trees, bushes. Diet: fruit, insects. Courtship feeding recorded; ♀ and ♂ build nest. Usually 2 eggs incubated ♀ 13-15 days; ♀ and ♂ feed young, who fly 14-16 days. 2 or 3 broods. **881**

Tangara gyrola *Emberizidae: Thraupinae*
BLUE-RUMPED GREEN or
BAY-HEADED TANAGER   5½ ins
Neotropical: Costa Rica, Panama, Trinidad, Guyanas, Venezuela, Colombia S to Amazonian Brazil, E Peru, N Bolivia, W Ecuador; forest and its edge, cocoa plantations, scrub; sea level to *c.* 7,000 ft. Plumage variable throughout range, but distinguished by bright green upperparts, reddish chestnut head, green or bright blue underparts; some races have blue rump, yellow or rufous shoulders, yellow band on nape; northern races greenest, southern and western bluest; bill grey, eyes brown. Pairs wander at all seasons through rain forest. Inquisitive, can be 'called up' by imitating Pygmy Owl, *Glaucidium brasilianum* (G. A. C. Herklots). Song: 'whining tang' (A. F. Skutch). Food: fruit of melastomes, pokeweed *Phytolacca rivinoides, Cecropia;* insects from crevices, moss. Breeds March to May Trinidad, longer season Costa Rica; ♀ builds shallow nest of dark roots, moss, lined fine fibres, in tree 9 to 25 ft or higher. 2 oval, creamy eggs, spotted brown, incubated ♀ 13-15 days; ♀ and ♂ tend young 14-16 days. 2 or 3 broods. **882**

Tangara nigroviridis *Emberizidae: Thraupinae*
BLACK AND GREEN TANAGER   5½ ins
Neotropical: N Venezuelan mountains from Miranda W to Colombia; E and NW Ecuador S to NW Bolivia; resident open forest country from sea level to *c.* 8,000 ft. Mantle streaked black and green; crown and lower back silvery blue or green in different lights; wings, tail black, feathers edged dark blue; throat blue; mask, underparts black, densely spotted silvery green or blue. Habits, breeding much as other *Tangara* species. **883**

TAPACULO, ANDEAN see **Scytalopus magellanicus**

Tarsiger cyanurus *Muscicapidae: Turdinae*
RED-FLANKED BLUETAIL   5½ ins
Palaearctic: mainly Siberia between 50° and 65°N, extending W to Kola Peninsula N Russia; E to Kamtchatka (isolated), Sakhalin, Japan; discrete Himalayan, W Chinese population sometimes regarded as distinct *T. rufilatus;* winters mainly Ryukyu Is, Taiwan. Habitat swampy taiga of spruce and silver fir; subalpine conifers, birch, rhododendrons up to 10,500 ft in Himalaya; mountain birds mainly sedentary. ♂: upperparts rich bright blue from forehead to tail; throat white, flanks rufous, underparts pale grey. ♀: upperparts olive brown but tail blue; breast band light brown, flanks paler than ♂. Legs, eyes dark brown, bill dark grey. Quivers tail like Redstart, *P. phoenicurus*, as it moves quietly about vegetation. Call: *tic tic;* song repetitive. Food mainly insects off lower vegetation and ground, sometimes from air. Breeding much as *Luscinia* species; nest of moss, lined hair, well hidden in recess in ground among moss, leaves, tree roots, stumps. 3 to 5 white eggs, sparsely spotted red-brown at big end. **701**

Tarsiger rufilatus see under **T. cyanurus**

TATTLER,
  GREY-TAILED see **Tringa brevipes**
  SIBERIAN see **Tringa brevipes**
  WANDERING see under **Tringa brevipes**

Tauraco
  hartlaubi see under **T. livingstonii**
  leucolophus see under **T. livingstonii**

Tauraco livingstonii *Musophagidae*
LIVINGSTONE'S TOURACO   16 ins
Ethiopian: there are about a dozen different kinds of

small greenish touracos in Southern Africa, living either in different habitats or different regions, whose precise classification is arguable. All have crimson wings conspicuous in flight and crests of various lengths and colours. Most have some red about head and green body colour shades into blue to varying extents, especially in long tail. All run and hop about in branches of tall trees almost like squirrels, feed on fruit, have rather guttural croaking calls, make flimsy pigeon-like nests with 2-3 white eggs. *T. livingstonii* is forest species of SE, from S Tanzania to Mozambique, Rhodesia and Zululand; has tall green crest, red bill. *T. schuettii* (Black-billed Touraco) differs only in black bill, short rounded crest, lives alongside *Corythaeola cristata* (the Great Blue) in Zaire. *T. hartlaubi* (Hartlaub's) inhabits mountain forests Kenya, N Tanzania; much bluer, has red orbit, white patch in front. *T. leucolophus* (White-crested) is dry country bird found N of Congo forests and Lake Victoria, with distinctive white head, crest. *T. schalowi* (Schallow's) replaces Livingstone's westwards across to Angola; has even longer crest, otherwise similar. **416**

Tauraco
  schalowi see under **T. livingstonii**
  schuettii see under **T. livingstonii**

TAWNY
  EAGLE see **Aquila rapax**
  FROGMOUTH see **Podargus strigoides**
  OWL see **Strix aluco**

TAWNY-CROWNED
  GREENLET see **Hylophilus ochraceiceps**
  HONEYEATER see **Gliciphila melanops**

TAWNY-SHOULDERED BLACKBIRD see under **Agelaius xanthamus**

Tchagra australis *Laniidae*
BROWN-HEADED BUSH SHRIKE   8 (tail 3) ins
Ethiopian: local over much of the region from Somalia S to Transvaal, W to Guinea; resident long grass areas with scattered trees and bushes in swamps and forest edges. Upperparts from crown earth-brown; wings mainly chestnut; rump, upper tail coverts olive-brown; tail (except brown central feathers) black, tipped white; crown bordered black above white 'eyebrow' and black eye-stripe; underparts white or creamy, washed grey and olive-brown on flanks; legs pale blue, bill black, eyes dark brown with greyish inner rim. Usually hides away but ♂ has display flight, rising with whirring wings, then planing down like pipit, uttering descending scale of musical notes; also claps wings on short flights between bushes. Piping call and *churr* of alarm. Mainly insectivorous. Breeding season varies within range; shallow cup nest of rootlets, plant fibres, usually in low bush among long grass. 2 or 3 white eggs, streaked and spotted purplish brown over lilac, incubated ♀ *c.* 12 days; young fledge *c.* 15 days.

Tchagra minuta or Bocagia minuta *Laniidae*
BLACKCAP BUSH SHRIKE   7 ins
Ethiopian: W Africa to Ethiopia, Sudan, E Africa S to Malawi, Zambia, Rhodesia; through Zaire S to Angola; Local migrant swamps, grasslands; on higher and drier ground in bracken and low bushes. ♂: upperparts tawny with black markings mantle and scapulars; wings chestnut; tail black, tipped buffish; crown glossy black; underparts deep buff, throat white; legs blue-grey, bill black, eyes pink. ♀ has white stripe from bill over eye. Juvenile has crown tawny, streaked black; bill horn. Frequently climbs stems of elephant grass, chattering when alarmed. *Chup* call of ♂ answered by ♀'s harsh bleating cry; also whistling song. Short courtship flight; suddenly checks, then mounts with rapidly fluttering wings. Hunts insects mainly on ground. Breeding season varies within range. Neat nest of stems, rootlets, often decorated snakeskins, in fork of bush, woven in upright plant stems, sometimes on stump, 2-3 ft up. 2 or 3 glossy white eggs, streaked reddish or purple brown.

Tchagra senegala *Laniidae*
BLACK-HEADED BUSH SHRIKE   8 (tail *c.* 4) ins
Ethiopian, SW Palaearctic: throughout Africa S of Sahara except Gabon, W Congo, extending to coasts Morocco, Algeria; Red Sea coast, S Arabia, Aden. Resident both desert and riverine scrub, open woodlands, mixed grassland and bush, neglected cultivations, gardens. Plumage much as *T. australis* except for black crown. Display flight also as *T. australis:* may rise to 200 ft. Clear piping call and churring alarm. Mainly insectivorous, especially beetles; also mice, rats, young birds. Breeding season varies widely within vast range; rather flat cup nest of weed stems and grass, lined rootlets, usually in low tree or bush, a few feet up. 2 or 3 usually white eggs, well marked with spots, streaks and bunting-like scrawls in shades of brown and grey, incubated ♀ *c.* 12 days, young fledge 15 days. **657**

TEAL,
  BRAZILIAN see **Amazonetta brasiliensis**
  MARBLED see **Marmaronetta angustirostris**
  RINGED see **Calonetta leucophrys**

Telmatodytes palustris *Troglodytidae*
LONG-BILLED MARSH WREN   5 ins
Nearctic: breeds Canada from S New Brunswick to Central British Columbia, S to Florida, Gulf Coast, Texas, New Mexico, N Lower California; winters from S New Jersey, Utah, Washington to S Florida, Central Mexico; large areas of tall aquatic vegetation in fresh or salt marshes. Upperparts generally dark brown; back striped black and white; flight feathers, tail barred darker and lighter; crown very dark brown, prominent white 'eyebrow', dark eyestripe; underparts pale buff to white; legs, bill brown, eyes dark brown. Bill noticeably larger than Short-billed Marsh Wren, *Cistothorus platensis*, found in rather drier habitats. Habits generally as other wrens; ♂♂ polygamous, build 'cock's nests', aggressive on territory, attacking other species and their nests. Call: low *tsuck;* grating alarm notes run into chatter. Song of ♂ loud, rapid rattling notes, ending in weak whistle, delivered reed perch or in fluttering flight. Breeds May onwards, weaving domed nest into stems of *Typha*, bulrushes, other tall plants, 1 to 3 ft up; exterior wet leaves, finer material within, lined feathers. 5 to 6 pale chocolate eggs, heavily spotted dark chocolate, incubated by ♀. 2 broods. **667**

Temenuchus pagodarum *Sturnidae*
PAGODA STARLING   *c.* 8½ ins
Mainly Oriental: E Afghanistan and India from Himalayan foothills to Ceylon; some seasonal movement, leaves colder N parts in winter. Habitat: open, deciduous forest and scrub jungle, cultivated areas and vicinity of habitations. Forehead, crown, nape and long pointed crest (shorter in ♀) glossy black, rest of upperparts grey, wings blackish, tail brown with white edging and tip; underparts reddish fawn. Legs lemon-yellow, bill greenish lead, distal half lemon-yellow, eyes bluish white or yellowish cream. Sociable, usually in family parties, large roosts in leafy trees and shrubs, also reed beds. Call: creaking and chattering; rambling, warbling song by ♂ during breeding; reasonable mimic. Feeds on fruit, berries and nectar, grasshoppers and other insects; typically follows cattle which disturb prey. Breeds February to September, peaks vary with area and climate; ♂ and ♀ build nest of grass, leaves, feathers and rubbish stuffed into hole in tree or wall, colonial where suitable holes close together; 3 or 4 pale blue eggs, both parents incubate and tend young. Sometimes 2 or even 3 broods. **975**

TEMMINCK'S
  COURSER see **Cursorius temminckii**
  HORNED LARK see **Eremophila bilopha**
  STINT see **Calidris temminckii**

TENGMALM'S OWL see **Aegolius funereus**

Terathopius ecaudatus *Accipitridae*
BATELEUR   24 ins
Ethiopian; wanders to Arabia. Resident on open

savannah, plains and thornbush, breeding from sea level to 7,000 ft. ♂ general appearance black with chestnut back, tail and under tail coverts; upper wing brown, broad white bar across flight feathers; ♀ similar with more brown on wing; legs, face and cere bright red; bill dark tipped, eyes brown. Juveniles brown all over. Soars most of day, showing very short fanned tail and very long wings, and moving at 35 to 50 mph; also rolls in air with loud wing noises. Has variety of barks and screams with subdued notes on perch. Scavenger and carrion feeder, taking some snakes, small mammals and birds alive. Solitary, building, often close to roads or river, nest of sticks lined with greenery, at 20 to 60 ft in tree, often acacia. Lays 1 chalky white egg, incubated by ♀ for 42-43 days. Chick fed by ♀ and ♂, fledges 90-125 days. Second ♂ often associates with pair during breeding but does not visit nest. **165**

TERN,
ARCTIC see **Sterna paradisaea**
BLACK see **Chlidonias niger**
BLACK-NAPED see **Sterna sumatrana**
CABOT'S see **Sterna sandvicensis**
CASPIAN see **Hydroprogne caspia**
COMMON see **Sterna hirundo**
CRESTED see under **Sterna bengalensis**
ELEGANT see **Thalasseus elegans**
FAIRY see **Gygis alba**
INCA see **Larosterna inca**
LESSER CRESTED see **Sterna bengalensis**
LITTLE see **Sterna albifrons**
ROSEATE see **Sterna dougallii**
ROYAL see under **Thalasseus elegans**
SANDWICH see **Sterna sandvicensis**
SOOTY see **Sterna fuscata**
WHISKERED see **Chlidonias hybrida**
WHITE see **Gygis alba**

Terpsiphone corvina *Muscicapidae: Muscicapinae*
SEYCHELLES PARADISE
FLYCATCHER   ♀: *c.* 8; ♂: (with tail) up to 20 ins
Seychelles (Indian Ocean): confined to island of La Digue, in dense *Calophyllum* woodland on lowland plateau. ♂: shining blue-black, crested and very long tailed, 2 central feathers up to 12 ins. ♀: upperparts, including wings, tail, chestnut; underparts pale cream; head blue-black. Legs, bill, facial skin blue. Hunts insects (flies, lacewings) in flight and sallying up from perch; also takes larvae, spiders. Call: repeated short whistles in flight. Breeds throughout year (W. Fraser), building base of cobwebs and palm 'matting', oval cup bound cobwebs to supporting twigs, lined thin palm strands; on drooping branches of native trees. Clutch normally single white or pale blue egg, marked red brown mainly at big end, incubated ♀ 17-18 days; the young are fed mainly by ♀ early stages, and they fledge *c.* 2 weeks (W. Fraser). **798**

Terpsiphone viridis *Muscicapidae: Muscicapinae*
AFRICAN PARADISE
FLYCATCHER   ♀: 8; ♂: (with tail) 12-14 ins
Ethiopian: almost whole region, including SW Arabia, except extreme W and SW; not Madagascar; locally migratory. Habitats varied: high forest with openings, riverine strips, rubber plantations (Cameroon), semi-arid areas (Nigeria), acacia and thorn bush, cultivated areas, gardens. ♂: crested head, neck, breast either metallic blue-green or glossy blue-grey; rest of upperparts and tail rich chestnut, central feathers elongated, flight feathers dusky, edged chestnut. Underparts mainly grey; under tail and under wing coverts white. In white phase (common E Kenya) back, wings, tail white. ♀: less glossy on slightly crested head; chin, throat dark grey; tail feathers slightly elongated. Legs slate, bill blackish, facial skin round brown eye cobalt blue. Immature like ♀ but paler. Habits as other flycatchers, taking much food on wing and attacking birds of prey. Call soft *zik zik zik;* harsh alarm note; 'fine, clear, violent, rippling song' (K. Hyatt). Breeds perhaps throughout year some areas, building nest of plant materials, bound cobwebs, decorated lichens, cocoons, usually in low fork of branch, often over water. 2 or 3 white or creamy eggs,

with zone of reddish and purplish grey spots, incubated ♀ (at night) and ♂. 2 broods. **799**

Tersina viridis *Emberizidae: Tersininae*
SWALLOW TANAGER   5¾ ins
Neotropical: E Panama S to Peru, Bolivia, Paraguay, NE Argentina, Brazil to Rio Grande do Sul; W of Andes to NW Ecuador; Trinidad; forests from sea level to *c.* 5,000 ft. ♂: turquoise blue, wings, tail black, feathers fringed turquoise; face, forehead, throat black; underparts white, flanks narrowly barred black on turquoise. ♀: upperparts, including neck, upper breast, grass green; inner webs wing and tail feathers dark brown; underparts yellow streaked brown; flanks narrowly barred green. Legs grey, very broad bill black, eyes chestnut. Territorial when breeding, otherwise in flocks of own species. Calls varied, unmusical; ♂'s song poorly developed. Insects taken swallow-like on wing; fruits plucked by perching, rotated in open bill until pulp scraped off and stored in throat sac; seeds dropped. Breeds onset rainy season, ♀ and ♂ excavating tunnel 15 ins into earth bank; cup of rootlets in chamber; also takes over other birds' holes and uses artefacts, e.g. in wall. 3 pointed glossy white eggs, tinged creamy, incubated ♀ *c.* 15 days; she mainly tends young, who fly *c.* 3½ weeks. **885**

Tetrao urogallus *Tetraonidae*
CAPERCAILLIE   ♀: 23-25; ♂: 33-35 ins
Palaearctic: local Scotland (reintroduced) and temperate W Europe across USSR but not so far E as Black Grouse; sedentary in coniferous and mixed forest, including taiga. ♂: vermiculated dark slate-grey; wing coverts dark brown, throat and sides of head black, breast glossy blue-green, black tail, tail coverts and belly flecked white. ♀: barred and mottled buff, black and white, rufous patch on breast, rounded tail. Legs feathered, toes grey brown, bill pale horn, eyes brown, red wattles above. Surprisingly deft in game-bird type flight through trees, perching on them freely; also burrows in snow to roost in north; walks and runs well. Turkey-like display posture of ♂ with remarkable 'song' of rapid clicks accompanied by wing swishing and ending in *plop*. Food as Black Grouse, *Lyrurus tetrix*. Breeds from April in Scotland, several ♀♀ lining scrapes, often at base of tree, near ♂'s display area. ♀ incubates 5 to 8 pale yellow eggs, sparsely blotched light brown, 27-29 days; young fly 15-20 days. **188**

Tetrapterus paradisaea see **Anthropoides paradisaea**

Tetrastes bonasus *Tetraonidae*
HAZELHEN   14 ins
Palaearctic: mainly N Temperate from SE France and Scandinavia across Asia to Japan (Hokkaido); sedentary in thick coniferous and mixed forests. Generally mottled brown above; underparts white, barred chestnut; tail grey with black and white terminal bands. ♂ has black throat, bordered white and tufted crest. Legs feathered, feet greyish-brown, bill black, eyes brown. In pairs on territories much of year, but small flocks in cold winters. Flushes at close range usually into tree, perching more than other grouse. Burrows in snow in winter. Intense courtship and territorial activity by ♂, who gives drawn-out whistle followed by chirp; ♀ replies quiet *tih.* Diet of buds, leaves, catkins and berries. Breeds from May onwards, ♀ lining scrape in dry area and laying 4 to 15 buff eggs, marked brown, which she incubates *c.* 3 weeks. Young eat insects at first, then vegetarian; fly in *c.* 14 days before full-grown. **189**

Thalasseus elegans *Laridae*
ELEGANT TERN   *c.* 16½ ins
Neotropical; breeds islands and locally coasts Gulf of California and NW Mexico; winters Pacific coast S to Chile, irregular visitor California. Crown and nape black, feathers elongated (crown streaked white in winter), mantle and upper wing grey, deeply forked tail whitish; neck, underparts, rump and edge of wing white; breast tinged rosy in breeding season. (Royal Tern, *T. maximus,* similar, but mantle and wings paler and tail greyer). Legs black, bill orange-red and

slenderer than Royal Tern. Often seen resting on sandy beaches between ocean and estuaries or bays in which it dives for fish, in small parties with other species or large unmixed flocks. Call: loud *kree-ee-ee,* repeated twice. Nests April to May in colonies, often in association with Royal Tern; single egg of variable colour, usually light beige heavily marked with black or very dark brown, in shallow depression in bare, sun-baked ground. **340**

Thalasseus maximus see under **T. elegans**

Thalurania furcata *Trochilidae*
FORK-TAILED WOODNYMPH   4¼ (bill nearly 1) ins
Neotropical: Central America, then generally distributed E of Andes through Amazonian Brazil to Peru, Bolivia, E Argentina; W of Andes in Colombia, W Ecuador; resident forests, streambanks, clearings from sea level to *c.* 5,000 ft. ♂: upperparts from crown and including gorget iridescent green to purple; flight feathers bronze green; underparts iridescent purple or green according to race; forked tail blue-black; legs, bill, eyes dark. ♀: upperparts glossy green, coppery on crown; underparts grey, or with green spots lower belly; slightly forked tail dark steely blue, outermost feathers white-tipped. Habits as hummingbirds in general; see under *Aglaiocercus kingi.* **477**

Thamnolaea arnottii see under **Myrmecocichla nigra**

Thamnolaea cinnamomeiventris *Muscicapidae: Turdinae*
MOCKING or CLIFF CHAT   9 ins
Ethiopian: most of region except parts of NE and SW; resident cliffs, boulder-covered hillsides, also habitations. ♂: head, breast, wings, tail glossy black; shoulder white; rump, underparts rich chestnut. Sometimes white line divides black and chestnut on breast. ♀ grey where ♂ black, no white shoulder patch. Legs, bill black, eyes brown. Pairs or family parties. Flies low with glides, raising wings, tail slowly several times on alighting; often takes long downward jumps with closed wings, opening them as it lands. Call clear double whistle; harsh *kret kret kret* of alarm followed by whistle; loud warbling song, mimics other species. Mainly insectivorous. Breeding season varies within range; nest cup of plant material with finer lining in cave, cleft, under boulders, hole in wall, even old nest of swallow. 3 cream or pale bluish-green eggs, marked pale chestnut over mauve. **702**

Thamnolaea coronata *Muscicapidae: Turdinae*
SNOWY-CROWNED ROBIN or
WHITE-CROWNED CLIFF CHAT   *c.* 7 ins
Ethiopian: Togoland, N Nigeria, N Cameroon, Sudan; resident rocky gorges and cliffs; race *T.c. kordofanensis* in granite hills and kopjes of Sudan. ♂ similar to Mocking Chat, *T. cinnamomeiventris,* but whole crown white or mixed black and white; no white upper breast (though present in very local race *kordofanensis*). ♀: mantle brown, head and cheeks greyish-brown; chin to breast brown washed chestnut; normally no white on shoulder; wing coverts edged grey. Habits much as Mocking Chat. Breeds May to July Darfur, Sudan, but details apparently unknown. **703**

THEKLA LARK see **Galerida theklae**

THICK-BILLED
EUPHONIA see **Tanagra laniirostris**
LARK see **Galerida magnirostris**

THICK-KNEE, SPOTTED see **Burhinus capensis**

THORNBILL,
CHESTNUT-TAILED see **Acanthiza uropygialis**
YELLOW-TAILED see **Acanthiza chrysorrhoa**

THRASHER,
BROWN see **Toxostoma rufum**
CURVE-BILLED see **Toxostoma curvirostre**

Thraupis episcopus or T. virens *Emberizidae*: *Thraupinae*
BLUE-GREY TANAGER					7 ins
Neotropical: Central America, S to NW Peru and E of Andes to N Bolivia, Amazonian Brazil; Trinidad, Tobago; open woodlands, bushy savannah, clearings, plantations, parks, gardens, sea level to *c.* 7,000 ft. Generally pale blue, darkest on back, wings, tail; shoulder purplish blue, violet or white in different races; sometimes white wingbar. ♀ and juvenile duller, greener. Legs blackish, bill greyish, eyes brown. Conspicuous, in pairs or small parties, arboreal like relatives. Flight intention call protracted, unmusical *s-e-e-e-p*. Takes fruits, e.g. *Cassia*, and seeds from bean plants; also catches insects. Breeds January to July Trinidad, ♀ and ♂ building nest of grass, stems, leaves, moss, ornamented down; usually well hidden near end of lateral branch 10 to 30 ft up in, e.g. mango tree. 2 or 3 cream to greyish green eggs, profusely marked shades of brown, often with cap of fine hair-lines, incubation ♀, ♂ nearby, 12-14 days; ♀ and ♂ feed young, who fly 14-20 days; sometimes dispossesses smaller species, hatching and rearing both broods (A. F. Skutch). Several broods in some areas and seasons. **884**

THREE-BANDED PLOVER see **Charadrius tricollaris**

Threskiornis aethiopicus *Threskiornithidae*
SACRED IBIS					30 ins
Ethiopian (including Madagascar), SE Palaearctic (S Iraq but not now Egypt), and Oriental; closely allied species in Australasia. Seasonal movements in Africa, coinciding with rains. Habitat rivers and lakesides. White, with bare black head and neck, flight feathers tipped iridescent green, innermost secondaries and scapulars have fluffy plumes of violet-blue; juvenile has feathered head and lacks plumes. Legs and bill black, eyes dark brown. Solitary or small parties when not breeding. Flies in formation, flapping and gliding, neck outstretched. Silent except for occasional harsh croak. Thrusts bill into soft mud when feeding on worms, molluscs and crustaceans; also takes locusts, scavenges and even kills young cormorants. Breeding variable throughout range: colonies, often with other species, in trees, rocky islets or ground in swamps. Stick nest lined with grass and reeds holds 2 or 3 chalky greenish or bluish white eggs, usually marked red-brown; incubation and fledging periods not known. **87**

Threskiornis molucca see under **T. spinicollis**

Threskiornis spinicollis *Threskiornithidae*
STRAW-NECKED IBIS				*c.* 29 ins
Continental Australia, occasionally New Guinea. Tasmania. Nomadic over swamps, rivers and lakesides, farm land. Upperparts dark grey with green and purple gloss, neck below bare black head dark grey and white ending in straw-coloured tuft on breast; underparts and tail white; legs red to black, bill black, eyes brown. Usually gregarious. Takes variety of small water animals from shallow water and will follow plough to take insects and their larvae, nicknamed 'Farmer's Friend.' Flies in lines or Vs with neck and legs extended. Breeding season September to December, in colonies often large and with White Ibis, *T. molucca*, in patches of reeds or bushes in swamps. Platform of local vegetation holds 3 to 5 dull white eggs. **88**

Thripadectes rufobrunneus see under **T. virgaticeps**

Thripadectes virgaticeps *Furnariidae*
STREAK-CAPPED TREEHUNTER			8½ ins
Neotropical: N and NW Venezuela, Colombia to E and W Ecuador; resident humid forests, 2,000 to *c.* 7,000 ft. Back reddish brown, rump, upper tail coverts and tail rufous chestnut; crown and nape olive brown, feathers with dusky edges and white shaftstreaks; throat cinnamon rufous, feathers edged dusky; underparts cinnamon brown, suffused olive on breast; legs and powerful bill grey, eyes brown. Closely related Streak-breasted Treehunter, *T. rufobrunneus*, found

similar habitats, 4,500 to 7,500 ft in Central America. Solitary, with harsh monosyllabic notes. Searches for insects, spiders, frogs, small reptiles in moss, dead leaves and bromeliad clumps on branches, tearing them open with strong bill. Breeds February to August Central America, excavating 2 ft tunnel in bank, building nest of rootlets for 2 white eggs, probably incubated by ♀ and ♂, who both certainly feed young. **564**

Thripias namaquus *Picidae*
BEARDED WOODPECKER				9 ins
Ethiopian: a northern race from Chad to Ethiopia, Somalia, N Uganda, Kenya; southern race from Angola across to S Uganda, Kenya coast down to northern S Africa, in bush veld, open acacia woodland, also mountain forest. Southern race predominantly dull olive green with off-white barring both above and below; northern race much darker, blackish rather than olive green; both races have conspicuous crimson crown, nape in ♂, black in ♀, sides of head broad black and white stripes, throat white. Undulating flight, yaffling call like European Green Woodpecker, *Picus viridis*. **555**

THRUSH,
ANGOLA ROCK see **Monticola angolensis**
BLACK-FACED ANT see **Formicarius analis**
BLUE ROCK see **Monticola solitarius**
FUKIEN RUFOUS JAY see **Garrulax caerulatus**
GREY-CHEEKED see under **Catharus ustulatus**
GREY-SIDED LAUGHING see **Garrulax caerulatus**
HERMIT see under **Catharus ustulatus**
KURRICHANE see **Turdus libonyanus**
MISTLE see **Turdus viscivorus**
MOTTLED ROCK see **Monticola angolensis**
OLIVE see **Turdus olivaceus**
OLIVE-BACKED see **Catharus ustulatus**
RED-LEGGED see **Mimocichla plumbea**
ROCK see **Monticola saxatilis**
SLATY-BACKED NIGHTINGALE see **Catharus fuscater**
SONG see under **Turdus iliacus**
SWAINSON'S see **Catharus ustulatus**
SWINHOE'S ROCK see **Monticola gularis**
WHITE'S see under **Turdus viscivorus**
WHITE-THROATED ROCK see **Monticola gularis**
WOOD see **Hylocichla mustelina**

THRUSH NIGHTINGALE see **Luscinia luscinia**

Thryothorus maculipectus *Troglodytidae*
SPOT-BREASTED WREN				5½ ins
Neotropical: Mexico, Costa Rica, S to Colombia, W Ecuador, NW Peru; resident forests 4,000 to 7,500 ft. Upperparts light reddish to olive-brown; crown brighter; tail barred grey and black; cheeks white; also underparts, heavily spotted and barred black; belly unspotted in one local race. Habits generally as other wrens; see *Troglodytes troglodytes*.

Tichodroma muraria *Sittidae*
WALLCREEPER				*c.* 6½ (bill 1) ins
Palaearctic: discontinuous distribution in mountains from N Iberia, Atlas, Alps, other European ranges, to Asia Minor, Caucasus, Iran via Himalayas E to NW China. Mainly resident but some vertical migration and wandering; habitat steep overhung cliffs, with deep crevices, often near glaciers or snow line, to 7,500 ft (Alps), 3,000 to 16,000 ft (Himalayas); in winter often on buildings. Generally grey, very rounded wings, tail brown-black with large crimson patches on wings, white spots on primaries and corners of tail; throat, breast black in summer, otherwise white; legs, bill black, eyes brown-black. Flitting, butterfly-like flight distinctive, in between climbing about rock faces, buildings, continually flicking wings; regular on ground, seldom on trees. Usually solitary as in rock roost. In display ♂ flutters or climbs round ♀, extending or withdrawing head, dipping tail. Call clear piping *da du dia doi*; song, both sexes, of short melodious phrases. Food: insects, spiders, centipedes from crevices, under stones or surface soil in shade of E or N facing cliffs. Breeds mid May to June; ♀, helped ♂, uses moss, grass, rootlets, lined wool, hair,

odd feathers, for well-hidden nest in narrow cleft or hole of cliff, exceptionally in wall. Usually 4 white eggs, sparsely freckled red-brown at big end, incubated ♀; young, fed ♀ and ♂ from bill, fly *c.* 3 weeks.

TINAMOU,
CHILEAN see **Nothoprocta perdicaria**
WHITE-THROATED see **Tinamus guttatus**

Tinamus guttatus *Tinamidae*
WHITE-THROATED TINAMOU			13 ins
Neotropical: SW Venezuela and SE Colombia to NW Bolivia; both sides Amazon in Brazil; resident in forests. Upperparts dark chestnut-brown, barred black on lower back; inner flight feathers spotted buff; underparts light brown, darker on breast, throat whitish; under tail coverts chestnut. Legs, bill, eyes dark brown. Habits much as *Nothoprocta* but better in water and roosts in trees. ♂ covers eggs in nest with leaves and incubates them for *c.* 20 days, leading young from nest and tending them. **7**

TINKER BIRD,
GOLDEN-RUMPED see **Pogoniulus bilineatus**
YELLOW-FRONTED see **Pogoniulus chrysoconus**

TIT,
AFRICAN PENDULINE see under **Eremomela icteropygialis**
AZURE see under **Parus caeruleus**
BEARDED, COMMON see **Panurus biarmicus**
BLACK see under **Parus niger**
BLUE see **Parus caeruleus**
CRESTED see **Parus cristatus**
GREAT see **Parus major**
LONG-TAILED see **Aegithalos caudatus**
MARSH see **Parus palustris**
PENDULINE see **Remiz pendulinus**
SOUTHERN BLACK see **Parus niger**
WILLOW see **Parus montanus**
WREN see **Chaemia fasciata**

TIT BABBLER, COMMON see **Parisoma subcaeruleum**

TIT WARBLER, SEVERTGOV'S see **Leptopoecile sophiae**

TITYRA, BLACK-TAILED see **Tityra cayana**

Tityra cayana *Cotingidae*
BLACK-TAILED TITYRA				8¼ ins
Neotropical: Guyanas, Venezuela and Colombia E of Andes S to N and E Bolivia, E and S Brazil, Paraguay, NE Argentina; resident open woodlands, burned areas from sea level to *c.* 4,000 ft. Generally pale grey to greyish white; crown, cheeks, wings and tail black; strong hooked bill dark grey, pinkish at base, eyes brown, bare skin round eye and base of bill reddish pink. ♀ has dark back grey, back and breast streaked black; in southern race crown and cheeks grey, streaked black; underparts also streaked black. Often perches on top of dead trees in burned areas; roosts and nests in tree holes, driving out other species by filling up hole with twigs and leaves. Small flocks forage communally for fruits and berries, also insects taken in flight or picked off leaves. Clutch probably 2 buff eggs, incubated by ♀ and ♂ on guard; he helps feed young, who fly *c.* 3 weeks. 2 broods apparently normal. Related species nest in old woodpecker holes 40 to 100 ft up; ♀ incubates eggs *c.* 21 days, broods young but both parents feed them; fledge 25 days. **596**

Tmetothylacus tenellus *Motacillidae*
GOLDEN PIPIT					6 ins
Ethiopian: S Sudan, E Ethiopia, Somalia, S to Tanzania; resident in dry bush country. ♂: upperparts pale olive-green, dark-centred feathers giving mottled appearance; wings, tail, underparts (with black breast band) canary yellow. Brown when on ground, becomes bright yellow on wing. ♀: upperparts dusky brown, yellow edges to flight feathers, outer tail; underparts buff-brown; centre belly, under wing coverts yellow; juvenile similar. Legs, bill greyish; eyes dark; long hind claw. Habits between pipits and

wagtails. Usually singly, family parties, small flocks. Perches freely above ground, wagging tail. ♂ has thin whistling call; repeated to form song in display flight, descending from tree with wings in V over back. Insectivorous. Breeds May to July; nest of grass, lined rootlets, just off ground in tussock. 2 to 4 rosy or greenish white eggs, heavily mottled clay-brown. **635**

Tockus alboterminatus *Bucerotidae*
CROWNED HORNBILL 20 ins
Ethiopian: E Africa from Somalia down to Mozambique, W to SE Congo, Zambia. Genus contains some dozen species of similar appearance, habits with overlapping ranges throughout drier parts of region. All are slim long-tailed mainly black and white birds with large down-curving often coloured bills, feeding on fruit, insects, eggs and young of small birds. *T. alboterminatus* brownish black above, white chest, belly, small white streaks head, neck; dull red bill; no spots on wings; white-tipped outer tail feathers. Flight slow, flopping, dipping and rising, some gliding. Loud-voiced, usually repeated piping whistles, *wek wek wek* or similar. Hole-nester, entrance reduced small slit by mud-plastering, through which incarcerated female fed by male; after her exit young re-plaster. Eggs 2-3, dirty white. **517**

Tockus deckeni *Bucerotidae*
VAN DER DECKEN'S HORNBILL 17-20 ins
Ethiopian: Central Ethiopia, S Somalia, down through Kenya to N Tanzania in dry bush, open acacia woodland. ♂'s bill bright red with terminal half yellowish, ♀'s all black. Paler head than *T. alboterminatus*, outer tail feathers all white. **518**

Tockus erythrorhynchus *Bucerotidae*
RED-BILLED HORNBILL 17-18 ins
Ethiopian: almost whole African tropics except western rain-forest areas of Congo, N Angola, wherever dry bush, open woodland. Closely resembles *T. deckeni*, distinguished by white spots on wing coverts, all-red bill. **519**

Tockus flavirostris *Bucerotidae*
YELLOW-BILLED HORNBILL 17-20 ins
Ethiopian: Ethiopia, Somalia down to N Tanzania, across to NE Uganda. Differs from *T. erythrorhynchus* only in deep orange-yellow bill, less white in outer tail feathers. **520**

Tockus nasutus *Bucerotidae*
GREY HORNBILL 18-20 ins
Ethiopian: dry-country areas throughout the whole region. Easily distinguishable from other *Tockus* species by generally pale tawny brown coloration, with grey head, neck, prominent white 'eyebrow', pale stripe down back. Bill black in ♂, red, yellow in ♀. Restricted to drier country than others. **521**

Todus mexicanus *Todidae*
PUERTO RICO TODY 4-4½ ins
Neotropical: Puerto Rico; resident lowlands and foothills, scrub areas along streams; secondary woodland, citrus and coffee plantations; city areas; also in dense rain forests of higher hills. Upperparts vivid green from forehead to tail; underparts white with red throat patch, flanks and undertail coverts yellow; legs brown; long bill: upper dark, lower bright red; eyes light yellow. Fearless of man. Sits on low twig, bill pointing at 45°, flies out to snap insects or flutters round leaves picking them off. Most in evidence warm mornings after rain. Call harsh *pree* or *pree-ah*, loud for size of bird, uttered with legs stretched on perch. Whirring rattle of attenuated outer primaries during display. Diet: flies, beetles, small Homoptera, moths, earwigs, small lizards. Breeds May or June, excavating tunnel 8 to 10 ft up in bank, 1 to 1½ ft deep, chiselled with bill, scraped out with feet; bare nest chamber at end. 2 to 6 glossy white eggs incubated by ♀ and ♂; fledged by early July. **494**

TODY, PUERTO RICO see **Todus mexicanus**

TODY MOTMOT see **Hylomanes momotula**

TOPKNOT see **Lopholaimus antarcticus**

Torgus calvus see **Sarcogyps calvus**

TOUCAN, KEEL-BILLED see **Ramphastos sulfuratus**

TOUCANET,
 BLUE-THROATED see **Aulacorhynchus caeruleogularis**
 EMERALD see **Aulacorhynchus prasinus**

TOURACO,
 BLACK-BILLED see under **Tauraco livingstonii**
 GREAT BLUE see **Corythaeola cristata**
 HARTLAUB's see under **Tauraco livingstonii**
 LIVINGSTONE's see **Tauraco livingstonii**
 PURPLE-CRESTED see **Gallirex porphyreolophus**
 ROSS's see **Musophaga rossae**
 SCHALLOW's see under **Tauraco livingstonii**
 WHITE-CRESTED see under **Tauraco livingstonii**

TOWHEE, RUFOUS-SIDED see **Pipilo erythrophthalmus**

Toxostoma curvirostre *Mimidae*
CURVE-BILLED THRASHER 11 ins
Nearctic, Neotropical: S Texas, S New Mexico, S Arizona to S Mexico; resident semi-arid country with scattered cactus and mesquite. Upperparts grey with 2 white bars on wings and white tip to long graduated blackish tail; throat white, underparts mottled buff; legs greyish, curved bill light brown, eyes bright red. Call sharp 2 or 3 note whistle; trills and chatters like wren. Song 'clear, melodious carol' (R. H. Pough) with little repetition. Feeds regularly on ground, scattering loose leaves, debris, searching for insects and their larvae; also takes fruit. Breeds end May and June; nest of twigs, lined rootlets and plant fibres, 3 to 10 ft in cactus clump, especially cholla, or thorny bush. 4 pale blue-green eggs, minutely speckled brown, incubated mainly by ♀, but both parents feed young. 2 or 3 broods. **672**

Toxostoma rufum *Mimidae*
BROWN THRASHER 11½ ins
Nearctic: breeds N Maine, SE Ontario, N Michigan, S Alberta S to S Florida Gulf Coast, E Louisiana; winters from N Carolina, SE Missouri to S Florida, Central Texas; woodland edge and clearings, secondary growth, scrubby pastures, gardens. Upperparts rufous brown from crown to long graduated tail; 2 white wingbars; cheeks buff, throat white, underparts buff streaked brown, under tail coverts whitish; legs light brown, bill light grey, eyes yellow. Calls: hissing note, clicking noise, 3-note whistle. Song, from conspicuous perch (otherwise not often visible) loud, rich, of short phrases often doubled and reminiscent of Song Thrush, *Turdus philomelos;* some mimicry. Food mostly from ground, digging with bill for insects and scattering leaves and debris; berries, fruit, corn form one-third diet. Breeds May-June onwards New England, building nest of 4 layers: twigs, leaves, smaller stems, lining of rootlets; from ground level to 5 ft in dense, often thorny shrub. 4 or 5 pale blue eggs, with small brown spots, incubated mainly by ♀ *c.* 13 days; both parents feed young, who fly *c.* 12 days, and rear 2 broods. **673**

Trachyphonus darnaudii *Capitonidae*
D'ARNAUD'S BARBET 6 ins
Ethiopian: from Sudan across to the Horn of Africa, S to Tanzania, in dry bush country and semi-desert. This and next two species generally similar, mainly black or brown above with prominent yellow or white spots, mainly yellow below with black spots; some red on head, above or under tail. D'Arnaud's lacks red on head, is least colourful. All are ground-living barbets, feeding mainly on termites, other insects, though D'Arnaud's eats fruit too. Short bubbling song, *woo-ter-ti-took* repeated in chorus during bobbing, tail-flirting display. Most are tunnel-nesters, D'Arnaud's lays 2 to 4 white eggs end of J-shaped vertical tunnel in flat ground. **530**

Trachyphonus erythrocephalus *Capitonidae*
RED AND YELLOW BARBET 9 ins
Ethiopian: same range, habitat, habits as preceding species, similar plumage but more colourful, with large white spots above, much red on head face. Louder, more musical call; nesting tunnel in bank. **531**

Trachyphonus vaillantii *Capitonidae*
CRESTED or LEVAILLANT'S BARBET 8½ ins
Ethiopian: Angola, Tanzania S to eastern S Africa in bush, woodland of drier kinds. More colourful than *Lybius* barbets, black rather than brown on back, nape, crown; black crest; crimson streaks in yellow underparts, crimson upper tail coverts. Nests in tree-hole, not ground-tunnel; 3 dull white eggs. Voice a nightjar-like churring and 'xylophonic clinking'. **532**

TRAGOPAN, SATYR see **Tragopan satyra**

Tragopan satyra *Phasianidae*
SATYR TRAGOPAN or CRIMSON
HORNED PHEASANT ♀: 23; ♂: 27 ins
E Palaearctic, Oriental: Central and E Himalayas; resident high forests up to 12,000 ft, moving downhill in winter to 6,000 ft. ♂: rich orange crimson, back and rump olive brown polkadotted black-bordered white spots; scapulars crimson, rest of wing dark brown mottled buff; head, crest and loop round throat black; crimson streak either side of crest; legs pink, bill black, eyes brown, horns and lappets blue and scarlet. ♀: upperparts rufous to yellow-brown, barred and blotched black and buff; pale stripes on crown; scapulars tinged crimson; chin and throat white; underparts paler than back; tail rufous brown barred black; legs whitish, bill horn, eyes brown. Shy and tree-living, one or two birds often feed with other species in glades of forest on buds, leaves, berries, seeds and insects. Call a bleating goat-like *kya kya ky;* ♂ also calls loudly from branch. Display: stately walk; one-sided trailing of wing; sudden rush with spread wings to stop fluffed out, wings moving up and down, head shaken to show extended horn and lappets. Breeds May, June, building stick nest with grass lining in tree or on ground. ♀ incubates 2 to 4 reddish buff eggs, freckled darker for *c.* 28 days. ♂ assists with brood. **208**

TRAILL'S FLYCATCHER see **Empidonax traillii**

TREE
 DUCK, WHITE-FACED see **Dendrocygna viduata**
 PIPIT see **Anthus trivialis**
 SPARROW see **Passer montanus**
 SPARROW, AMERICAN see **Spizella arborea**
 SWALLOW see **Tachycineta bicolor**

TREECREEPER see **Certhia familiaris**

TREECREEPER,
 AUSTRALIAN BROWN see **Climacteris picumnus**
 SHORT-TOED see under **Certhia familiaris**

TREEHUNTER,
 STREAK-BREASTED see under **Thripadectes virgaticeps**
 STREAK-CAPPED see **Thripadectes virgaticeps**

TREERUNNER,
 PEARLED see **Margarornis squamiger**
 WONDER see **Daphoenositta miranda**

Treron apicauda see under **T. sphenura**

Treron sphenura *Columbidae*
WEDGE-TAILED GREEN PIGEON *c.* 13 ins
Oriental: N India from Kashmir and Assam E and S to Burma, Yunnan, Annam, Tonkin, Hainan I., Malay Peninsula, Sumatra, Java and Lombok. Habitat: more open forest and woodland in mountains and foothills, usually between 2,000 and 8,000 feet; higher parts of range usually vacated in winter. ♂: generally yellowish green with long tapering tail, crown tinged orange-rufous; variable patch of maroon on back and scapulars, chin and throat yellow, breast

pale orange-pink. ♀: similar but lacking rufous and maroon patches. Legs red, bill light blue going greyer at tip; eyes, inner ring blue, outer ring red, with light blue orbital skin. Agile climber, feeds chiefly on fruits and berries from branch, often in small parties with Pintailed Green Pigeon, *T. apicauda* (differentiated by larger size, tail and two conspicuous yellow bars on black wings). Flight swift, noisy and rather undulating. Call: series of rich mellow whistles, terminating abruptly. Breeds April onwards; twig platform in trees, often on large bough close to trunk, usually 20 to 50 feet up. 2 white eggs, incubated *c.* 14 days; young fly *c.* 12 days.

Trichoglossus haematodus or T. moluccanus
Psittacidae
RAINBOW PARAKEET   12 ins
Oriental (Lesser Sunda Is) and Australasian: New Guinea, Bismarck and Solomon Is, New Caledonia, continental Australia from N Queensland E and S to near Adelaide; savannah and montane forest, up to 6,000 ft in New Guinea, where also on forest edges, by watercourses and clearings; nomadic in Australia, following food sources. Upperparts (neck to tail) and lower underparts green; head mauve-blue to yellow band at nape; breast, flanks orange-red; belly dark violet-blue; under wing coverts yellow and orange; under tail dusky yellow; legs greenish-grey, bill coral, eyes red. In pairs, small parties and flocks (from January or February in Australia); swift, wheeling flight, often with other lorikeets, very noisy and chattering. Flocks break up into pairs with fights between ♂♂ and ♀♀. Food: nectar especially from eucalypts; seeding heads of grass-trees, fruit, unripe green; birds turn upside down to reach flowers. Breeds August-November in Australia, in tree hole, usually in eucalypt, sometimes cavity in building. 2 white eggs incubated by ♀ 26 days, ♂ near. Fledging period *c.* 8 weeks; often 2 broods. **409**

Trichoglossus moluccanus see **T. haematodus**

Tricholaema leucomelas see **Lybius leucomelas**

TRICOLOURED RAIL see **Rallina tricolor**

Trigonoceps occipitalis *Accipitridae*
WHITE-HEADED VULTURE   32 ins
Ethiopian: Eritrea to Orange River. Inhabits mainly deserts, open plains and thorn scrub. Upperparts including ruff dark brown and black band across breast; thick white down on head gives triangular outline. Legs flesh pink, bill pink with black tip, cere bluish green, eyes brown. Immature darker all over. Rather solitary, roosting alone or in pairs, but up to 10 at water. Usually silent, 'shrill chittering' at carcase. Feeds on large and small carrion, also kills young birds and even small antelopes. Breeding season varies according to latitude. Builds large flat nest of sticks, lined hair and grass, usually in solitary acacia or baobab tree about 20 ft high. Lays 1 white egg sometimes marked brown and grey, incubated at least 6 weeks mainly or entirely by ♀. **166**

TRILLER, WHITE-WINGED see **Lalage sueurii**

Tringa brevipes *Scolopacidae*
GREY-TAILED or
SIBERIAN TATTLER   10 (bill 1½) ins
E Palaearctic: alpine zone of NE Siberia. (Verkhoyansk Mountains), wintering S to SE Australia, Tasmania, New Zealand on shores of all types, mangrove swamps, estuaries. Breeds alpine tundra. Upperparts almost uniform slate-grey, barred white on tail; white 'eyebrow', dark stripe through eye; underparts white, streaked and barred in summer; legs yellowish, bill dark with long nasal groove, eyes dark brown. Habits as other *Tringa* species but usually solitary in winter; sometimes joins other waders. Calls: high-pitched double whistle: *too-weet*, repeated trill; less noisy than Wandering Tattler, *T. incana*, of Nearctic, with which sometimes considered to be conspecific. Nesting habits as other *Tringa* species. **294**

Tringa erythropus *Scolopacidae*
SPOTTED REDSHANK   *c.* 12 ins
Palaearctic: narrow range through subarctic and arctic zones from N Scandinavia to NE Siberia; winters temperate and subtropical zones N of Equator, e.g. Mediterranean area and Oriental region, by muddy fresh waters, estuaries and sea shores. Breeds marshes and swamps near limit of tree growth, extending into shrub tundra. Summer: black almost all over, relieved by white crescents and bars on back, wings and, less noticeably, underparts; rump white, tail barred black and white; legs dark red, bill dark brown, base red, eyes brown. Winter: upperparts generally grey; underparts from face and neck pale grey to white; legs duller. Juvenile mottled and barred brown and white. Resembles Redshank, *T. totanus*, in many respects, associating with it and Greenshank, *T. nebularia*. Call sharp *tchooet*, lengthened or repeated on passage, more complicated song on breeding ground. Diet: mainly small insects caught in water when wading or swimming, with side to side motion of bill; also crustaceans, snails, worms, even small frogs and fish. Breeds from end May; scrape, lined leaves or needles, in cover often near pine trees, holds 4 buff to pale green eggs, heavily marked dark brown and ash-grey. Incubation mainly by ♂, probably *c.* 2½ weeks; he also tends brood. **295**

Tringa glareola *Scolopacidae*
WOOD SANDPIPER   *c.* 8 ins
Palaearctic: broad band through temperate to arctic zones, from Scotland (recently colonised) across Eurasia above 50°N to Okhotsk Sea; isolated area Transcaucasia; winters in Ethiopian, Oriental, Australasian regions by lakes, slow-flowing rivers, sheltered lagoons, salt marshes. Breeds swamps, bogs, most numerous where taiga meets birch-willow area. Summer: upperparts mottled dark brown and white; pale stripes meet in V over bill on streaked head; breast, flanks barred; rump white, tail barred; wing tips dark; no white bar; underparts white; legs olive-green, bill dark, base olive, eyes black-brown. Winter: upperparts more uniform grey brown. Often solitary or small parties, larger flocks on passage, but not gregarious in winter. Flies up with *tchiff tchiff tchiff* call. Various renderings of song uttered in tremulous, undulating display flight by both ♂ and ♀. Diet: mainly small water and marsh insects, probed for or picked up in shallows or mud; also worms and molluscs in winter. Breeds from end May; usually lined scrape in cover, sometimes old nest of other bird in tree. 4 variable cream to pale green eggs, heavily marked dark brown and grey, incubation by ♀ and ♂ 22-23 days; first both, then ♂ tends young *c.* 4 weeks. **296**

Tringa hypoleucos or Actitis hypoleucos *Scolopacidae*
COMMON SANDPIPER   *c.* 7¾ ins
Palaearctic: almost whole region between 40° and 65°N; also isolated area highlands of E Africa. (Some regard Spotted Sandpiper, *Tringa macularia*, which breeds throughout temperate Nearctic, as conspecific.) Winters occasionally N temperate but mainly in tropical regions of S Hemisphere. Breeds neighbourhood of clear fresh or sheltered salt water, e.g. Scottish sea lochs, in wooded, cultivated ground or moorland edge. Summer: upperparts dark brown with blackish mottling; narrow white bar on dark-tipped wing; rump and tail brown with white and barred edges; throat and underparts white with brownish patches sides of breast; legs greenish-grey, bill dark brown, eyes brown. Winter: upperparts more uniform. Bobbing action at water's edge, curiously jerky flight low over water and repeated *twee wee wee* calls. Usually solitary or in pairs, but small parties on passage. Song rendered *kittywiper* repeated as ♂ flies past ♀ on winnowing wings; then often chases her; also wing-raising display on ground. Diet: mainly littoral insects, snails and crustaceans picked off shore; some seeds and other plant material. Breeds from late April in S of range; sometimes substantially lined scrape, in open or very well hidden, often under trees or shrubs, holds 4 pinkish buff eggs, spotted red-brown; incubated by ♀ and ♂ 21-23 days; both tend young *c.* 4 weeks. **297**

Tringa
incana see under **T. brevipes**
macularia see under **T. hypoleucos**
nebularia see under **T. erythropus**

Tringa stagnatilis *Scolopacidae*
MARSH SANDPIPER   *c.* 9 ins
Palaearctic: restricted and discontinuous band along 50°N from Austria through USSR N of Caspian and Aral Seas to E Siberia; winters mainly E Africa round shallow lakes, e.g. in Rift Valley. Breeds marshy shores of steppe pools and salt lakes. Summer: upperparts boldly mottled black and light brown, extending over head and dark-tipped wings; prominent white rump and barred tail; throat white with dark brown spots, becoming flecks on flanks; underparts white; slender legs dark olive, thin bill dark brown, base green; eyes dark brown. Winter: upperparts more or less dull brown; face, throat, breast white. Slim active wader, usually single or small parties in winter. Calls variously described: *kee-oo* on passage; trilling song in display flight. Diet: water and marsh insects, snails, crustaceans, taken by wading off muddy shore. Breeds from early May Central Europe. 4 cream to buff eggs, marked rich brown and grey, in scrape on ground, incubated by ♀ and ♂. **298**

Tringa totanus *Scolopacidae*
REDSHANK   *c.* 11 ins
Palaearctic: broad band from Britain and Ireland across region to S China and Siberia; also Iceland (distinct race), N Scandinavia, locally SW Europe; moves in winter to coasts or migrates across Equator to S Africa, Indonesia, Philippines. Breeds dunes, saltings, lowland grass fields to moorland, and up to 15,000 ft on steppes and subalpine Himalayas. Upperparts generally grey-brown, obscurely mottled black; broad white trailing edge to dark-tipped wings; rump white, tail barred black and white; throat, neck, breast streaked brown down to pale underparts and barred flanks; legs orange red, bill red, tip dark, eyes brown. Winter: upperparts greyer; juvenile has pale orange legs. Noisiest of shore birds at all times; found singly, pairs or large flocks. Usual calls *tuuu* and *tu tu tu*, but many other notes; songs: repeated musical *tu* and, by ♂ and ♀, *taweeo taweeo taweeo*, uttered in rushing and gliding display flight. Picks variety of small animals off herbage, from shallow water or by probing. Breeds from early April in S; lined scrape in open, partly sheltered or very well hidden. 4 buff eggs, spotted or streaked red-brown, incubated by ♀ and ♂ 23-24 days; first pair, then ♂ tends young *c.* 3½ weeks. **299**

Tringytes subruficollis *Scolopacidae*
BUFF-BREASTED SANDPIPER   7¼-8 ins (♀ smaller)
Nearctic: arctic coasts from N Alaska to N Mackenzie; winters S to Argentina and Uruguay, on dry open pampas. Breeds dry tundra; on passage on grasslands and freshwater margins. Summer: upperparts mottled dark brown and buff; wings (white underwings) and tail (white edged) grey-brown; head, neck and underparts uniform buff with dark spots on crown; legs dull orange, bill black, eyes dark brown. Upright stance, more like plover than sandpiper; flies with neck drawn in; flocks perform evolutions low over ground, not rising or falling much. Rather silent; distinctive spring call *chik*, like two stones knocked together. Repeated *tink* in display, involving movements of wings and apparently confined to ♂♂. Diet on passage almost exclusively larvae and pupae of flies. Breeds from early June; sparsely lined scrape in peat or moss holds 4 greenish blue to buff eggs, heavily marked purple-black, rich brown and violet; incubated by ♀. **300**

Trochilus polytmus *Trochilidae*
STREAMERTAIL   4¼ ins: streamers 10 ins
Neotropical: confined to Jamaica, from semi-arid lowlands to humid forests in mountains; also man-modified habitats. ♂: generally bright green; crown black with two tufts at nape; flight feathers dark brown; tail blue-black with seasonal elongation of two black streamers. ♀ lacks streamers, has bronzed crown, mostly white underparts and outer tail feathers tipped white. ♂'s bill ranges from red to black from W to E,

♀'s duller. Call: loud repeated *tee tee tee*; ♂'s streamers whir in flight. Diet: nectar and small insects taken on wing. Builds nest of local plant materials on sometimes sloping twig of tree or shrub; ♀ incubates 2 white eggs as other hummingbirds. **478**

Troglodytes troglodytes *Troglodytidae*
COMMON or WINTER WREN   *c.* 3¾ ins
Holarctic: most of W Europe, including NW Africa; Asia Minor, Himalayas to E China, Japan, Sakhalin; Kurile and Aleutian Is.; broad band N America either side Lat. 50°N, with tongues S in Rockies, Mid West E Coast mountains. Resident primarily coniferous and broadleaved forests with thick undergrowth, especially along watercourses; in man-modified shrubberies, gardens in Europe; coastal in Scotland, Iceland, Aleutian Is. Generally russet brown, more buff below; upperparts including wings, short tail closely barred darker brown; pale 'eyebrow'. Legs brownish flesh; bill: upper black-brown, lower pale horn; eyes dark brown. Juvenile more mottled, less barred. Extremely active, moving in and out of thick low vegetation and making short whirring flights. Bobs up and down when perched. Hops or runs on ground. Clicking *tic tic tic* call, often repeated quickly or churred. Remarkably loud shrill song with final trill, lasting *c.* 5 secs. Diet mainly insects, spiders, other invertebrates, prised out of shelter. Breeds March to August Britain; ball nest with entrance near top, of variety of local plant materials, one of several made by ♂, chosen and lined feathers by ♀: in banks, creepers, bushes, rocks, much reduced when in walls or other crevices; in old nests of other birds. 5 to 6 white eggs, freckled red-brown often in zone, incubated by ♀ 14-15 days; ♀, sometimes with ♂, feeds young, who fly 16-17 days. 2 broods. **668**

TROGON,
   BAR-TAILED see **Trogon collaris**
   BLACK-THROATED see **Trogon rufus**
   COLLARED see **Trogon collaris**
   GREATER YELLOW-BELLIED see **Trogon viridis**
   RED-BELLIED see **Trogon collaris**
   WHITE-TAILED see **Trogon viridis**

Trogon collaris *Trogonidae*
COLLARED, RED-BELLIED or
BAR-TAILED TROGON   10½ ins
Neotropical: Central America S to N Bolivia, Brazil; W of Andes to Colombia, NW Ecuador; Trinidad and Tobago; resident in forests from sea level to *c.* 7,000 ft. ♂: upperparts and breast iridescent green; wing coverts vermiculated black and white; flight feathers dusky black with white bases showing as bar on underwing; central tail feathers glossy blue-green, tipped black; outer tail feathers barred black and white, tipped white; white bar across breast, belly crimson; legs dark, bill dull yellow, eyes dark brown. ♀: upperparts and breast sandy brown; white round eye; breast band white; belly light crimson; central tail feathers rufous, outer feathers tipped white with black subterminal bar. Upright posture on perch in forest, where revealed by various whistling, hooting and cawing calls. Diet: insects and their larvae, spiders, small lizards and tree frogs; berries and small fruit. Breeds April to July Trinidad; ♀ and ♂ excavating hole in decayed tree or old termite nest; 2 white or greenish white eggs incubated by ♀ and ♂ 17-19 days; both feed young, who fledge *c.* 2½ weeks. **482**

Trogon rufus *Trogonidae*
BLACK-THROATED TROGON   10½ ins
Neotropical: S Honduras to NE Argentina E of Andes; W of Andes to Colombia, Ecuador; resident forests up to 4,000 ft, 2,500 ft in Central America. ♂: upperparts coppery green, throat black, breast bluish-green, belly orange yellow; flight feathers black, white edged, wing coverts vermiculated black and white; central tail feathers bronzed green or gold according to race and black-tipped, outer feathers barred black and white; legs blackish, bill yellow, eyes dark brown, orbits pale blue. ♀ like ♂ *T. collaris,* but belly yellow, outer tail feathers barred black and white, white tipped; white crescents at eyes; legs dark, bill grey. Upright posture with tail straight downward like relatives; darts to pick insects off leaves while hover-

ing; also berries, small fruit. Calls: weak, mellow *cow cow cow*, churring and rattling *krrr-re-eck*, also clear modulated notes. Breeds April in Central America, excavating hole 4 to 12 ft up in slender decayed tree. 2 white eggs incubated *c.* 18 days; parents feed young on insects; fledge 14-15 days. **483**

Trogon strigilatus see **T. viridis**

Trogon viridis or T. strigilatus *Trogonidae*
GREATER YELLOW-BELLIED or
WHITE-TAILED TROGON   11½ ins
Neotropical: Panama S to NW Bolivia and Brazil; W of Andes to Colombia, Ecuador; Trinidad; resident forests and scrubby savannah up to *c.* 7,000 ft. ♂: upperparts bronze green, rump purplish blue; flight feathers blackish, show white bar below; central tail feathers greenish blue, broadly tipped black; outer feathers black, tipped white; crown, breast, purplish blue, throat black; belly orange yellow; legs, eyes dark, orbits pale blue, bill pale greenish or bluish grey. ♀: upperparts, breast and flanks dark grey; wing coverts black, finely barred white; outer tail feathers tipped and barred white; belly orange yellow. Behaves as relatives. Call loud *tok toktok tok tok tok toktok;* also squeaky double note; answers to rather similar call of Pygmy Owl, *Glaucidium brasilianum.* Diet: insects and spiders; berries and small fruit. Breeds April to July Trinidad, in holes of dead trees. 2 rough, glossy, greenish white eggs incubated by ♀ and ♂ 17-19 days; parents feed young, who fledge *c.* 3 weeks.

TROPICAL
   KINGBIRD see **Tyrannus melancholicus**
   PEWEE see under **Contopus virens**

TROPIC BIRD,
   YELLOW-BILLED see **Phaethon lepturus**
   WHITE-TAILED see **Phaethon lepturus**

TRUMPETER, WHITE-WINGED see **Psophia leucoptera**

TUFTED
   DUCK see **Aythya fuligula**
   GUINEAFOWL see **Numida meleagris**

TUI see **Prosthemadura novaeseelandiae**

Turdoides jardinei *Muscicapidae* : *Timaliinae*
ARROW-MARKED BABBLER   9½ ins
Ethiopian: most of region: N to 5°S in Zaire,2 S in Kenya; forest edges, thorn scrub, rank grass, especially along watercourses. Ash-brown above, black centres to head feathers; flight feathers, tail bronze black; underparts paler grey; throat, upper breast flecked white; underwing tawny; legs, bill black; eyes orange. Small noisy flocks feed on ground, flying low between bushes. Many harsh scolding calls include rook-like *kaa, kaa.* Diet mainly insects. Breeding season very variable, almost whole year in N of range. Roots, grass-stems used to build large nest in thick bush, tree or driftwood along stream bed. 3 turquoise eggs. **716**

Turdus iliacus *Muscicapidae* : *Turdinae*
REDWING   8¼ ins
Palaearctic: Eurasia between 60° and 70°N to *c.* 160°E; southern range in Europe moving towards 50°N, increasing Britain; also France, Iceland; winters W, S Europe, N Africa, SW Asia. Habitat open woodland of taiga, mixed birch, willow, alder; subarctic birch zone and riverine trees; parks and gardens in Scotland; winters often cultivated land with woods and hedges. Upperparts dark brown (Song Thrush, *T. philomelos*, much lighter) with pronounced pale 'eyebrow', fainter moustachial stripe; underparts pale buff shading to white, thickly streaked dark brown; flanks and under wing coverts chestnut-red (orange in Song Thrush), rest of underwing white. Legs yellow-brown, bill black-brown and yellow, eyes dark brown. Gregarious in winter, often social when breeding. Hops or runs in bursts, then stands upright. Call in flight soft, penetrating *seeip; chittuck* or *chic* of alarm; short song phrase of 3 or 4 notes, heard some-

times from mass twittering of flock in early spring. Takes variety of insects in summer, berries in autumn and winter, also worms, molluscs from ground. Breeds late April to early August; ♀, sometimes accompanied ♂, builds nest of grass, twigs, moss, wool, with mud cup and fine inner lining; in conifer, birch, shrubs, tree roots, steep banks, buildings, up to 25 ft. 5 or 6 eggs very like small Blackbird's, *T. merula;* incubated by ♀ and ♂ *c.* 13 days; both feed young, who fly 14 days. 2 broods. **704**

Turdus libonyanus *Muscicapidae* : *Turdinae*
KURRICHANE THRUSH   9 ins
Ethiopia: E and S Africa S of Equator: Tanzania, E Zaire to Natal; resident acacia savannahs, open woodland, rocky hills, usually near watercourses; sometimes in gardens. Upperparts, including wings, tail, brownish slate-grey; chin and throat white with conspicuous black moustachial stripes; upper breast grey buff; underparts light tawny brown shading to whitish; legs yellowish, bill orange red, eyes brown. Juvenile has black spots on underparts. Usually feeds on ground under trees, scratching out insects, also takes fruits. Call musical, whistling *tchi chee;* squeak of alarm; quiet song in breeding season, broadly August to January throughout range. Large nest, decorated leaves and lichens on mud base, lined finer plant materials, in fork of tree or stump. Usually 3 dark bluish eggs, densely speckled brown over pale lilac. **705**

Turdus merula *Muscicapidae* : *Turdinae*
BLACKBIRD   10 ins
Palaearctic, marginally Oriental: almost all Europe (including NW Africa) S of 60°N (N of it in Scandinavia) with narrow extension E through Asia Minor, Caucasus, mountains of S Asia, to S China; northern populations winter southward to N Africa. Introduced New Zealand. Habitat variety of wooded country with dense undergrowth or mossy ground layer: broad-leaved and mixed woods in plains to subalpine conifers towards tree limit; parks, gardens, vineyards, palm oases; cultivated land to cities in Europe; similar lowland habitats in winter. ♂: jet black with orange-yellow bill and orbits; partial albinos common. ♀: generally dark brown, throat pale, light brown breast spotted darker. Legs dark brown, bill from black to orange, less bright in ♀; eyes dark brown. Juvenile mottled rufous. Spends much time on ground, running or hopping, but often skulks, though song perches usually exposed. Flight direct except in ♂'s butterfly display. Variety of ritual postures and complicated manoeuvres on territorial boundaries, sometimes fierce fights. Call *tchook tchook;* high pitched *tsee,* scolding *tchic tchic.* Song mellow, fluting with rather feeble ending, but some performers superb. Takes great variety of insects, other invertebrates, especially worms; fruit and berries of many kinds. Breeds end February to August Britain; ♀, sometimes helped ♂, builds substantial nest of local plant material and debris, with mud cup, fine lining; in trees, bushes, e.g. brambles, woodland banks, great variety of sites on cultivated land and human artefacts, ground level to 12 ft or more. 3 to 5 greenish blue eggs, more or less heavily freckled brown or red-brown, often at big end, incubated by ♀ 12-15 days; both parents feed young, who fly 12-15 days. 2, 3 even more broods. **706**

Turdus migratorius *Muscicapidae* : *Turdinae*
AMERICAN ROBIN   10 ins
Nearctic and Neotropical: breeds from NW Alaska through much of Canada to W South Carolina, Central Alabama, Arkansas, Mexico, to Guatemala; winters as far N as S Maine, S Ontario, Nebraska, Wyoming, S British Columbia. Habitat open areas with scattered trees, forest edges and clearings; orchards and gardens, reaching high densities in residential areas like Blackbird, *T. merula,* its Old World counterpart (despite name). ♂: upperparts generally grey, becoming blackish on head (white patch round eye), parts of wings (flight feathers pale edged) and longish tail; throat white streaked black; underparts chestnut red, under tail coverts white. ♀ duller and paler. Legs greyish, bill yellow, eyes dark brown. Juvenile greyish above, buff below, mottled

and spotted. Large flocks on migration and in winter roosts, usually in swamp; birds feed in small parties during day on great variety of fruit and berries (palmetto in winter); also take earthworms, insects and their larvae from ground. Fights between ♂♂ for territory in spring and against image in windows, shiny surfaces. Variety of calls, including high-pitched hiss. Loud song, strongest before dawn, of 2 and 3 note phrases with pauses, each phrase varying in pitch. Breeds May to August, building bulky nest of plant stems and debris, with mud cup and fine inner lining; first nests often in evergreen or conifer, second brood nests in deciduous cover. 3 to 5 blue-green eggs incubated by ♀ *c.* 13 days; both parents feed young, who fledge *c.* 14 days. 2 broods. **707**

Turdus olivaceus *Muscicapidae: Turdinae*
OLIVE THRUSH 9½ ins
Ethiopian: several races, some very local, cover most of eastern and southern Africa. Habitat evergreen and deciduous forest, open hillsides by streams, montane heaths up to 10,000 ft Kilimanjaro; cultivated land, urban gardens. Upperparts, including cheeks, wings, tail, dark olive slate; chin, throat whitish, streaked dark brown; underparts dusky olive shading to orange-rufous on belly, flanks; under tail coverts whitish, marked dusky; legs yellow-brown, stout bill orange-yellow, eyes brown. Juvenile streaked above, spotted below. Fast, direct flight. Dominates other garden birds. In display ♂ puffs out feathers, spreads tail, shuffles round ♀ with wings trailing. Call *tsit* on take-off; low *tschuk tschuk* of alarm; simple, variable song. Scratches leaves and debris for insects and other invertebrates, including snails, cracked open against stone. Thrush habit of running forward, stopping with head cocked one side, darts forward again usually to pull out worm; also takes fruit. Breeding season varies within range; builds grassy cup, often on stout foundation of earth and plant materials, close to tree trunk in forest, on stump or in thick bush. 3 to 5 bluish green eggs, spotted fine brown or blotched rufous over purple. **708**

Turdus philomelos see under **T. iliacus**

Turdus viscivorus *Muscicapidae: Turdinae*
MISTLE THRUSH 10½ ins
Palaearctic: Europe, including NW Africa, but except N Scandinavia, most of S Russia; extending E between 50° and 60°N to meet narrow band through Asia Minor, Caucasus, mountains SW Asia; northern birds migrate to temperate and Mediterranean areas. Habitat subalpine coniferous forest (not dense spruce), also montane oak, beech, up to 11,500 ft Himalayas; lowland mixed woods, cultivated land, parks, gardens, into cities. Upperparts grey brown with pale outer tail feathers; ear coverts finely mottled; whitish underparts heavily spotted black-brown, underwing whitish; legs yellowish brown, bill dark horn and yellow; eyes brown. Juvenile 'scaly', sometimes confused with White's Thrush, *Zoothera dauma*. Upstanding carriage on ground, where spends much time. Flies with wing closures, rather undulating. Parties form autumn, causing confusion with gregarious Fieldfare, *T. pilaris*. Display by rather leisurely chases from perch to perch. Usual call, emphasised when excited, rattling chatter; also repeated *tuc tuc tuc;* song, from exposed perch, loud, less fluty than Blackbird, *T. merula*. Takes fruits and berries when available, also molluscs, earthworms, variety of insects; sometimes young birds. Breeds second half February to June Britain; ♀ building substantial foundation of moss, lichens, grasses, wool with earth cup and fine lining, often green grass; from ground level to 50 ft, typically in fork of tree or on lateral bough, conifer or broadleaved; also bushes, low rock faces, buildings. 3 to 5 creamy buff or pale blue green eggs, marked red-brown over grey or violet; incubated by ♀ 13-14 days; both parents feed young, who fly 14-16 days. 2 broods. **709**

TURKEY VULTURE see **Cathartes aura**

TURKEY, WILD see **Meleagris gallopavo**

Turnix varia *Turnicidae*
PAINTED BUTTONQUAIL *c.* 8 ins
Continental Australia and Tasmania; resident open forest, heathlands, tall scrub. Upperparts very dark brown with pale feather margins, mantle greenish, nape chestnut, both spotted white; crown brown, broad white 'eyebrow', throat and underparts grey, sides of breast greenish; legs orange, bill dark, eyes red-brown; ♀ brighter than ♂. Partly nocturnal, pairs or family parties scratch for grass seeds, grain, shoots, small insects; they drink with 'bibbling' action of mandible and dust frequently; if flushed, only fly short distance. ♀ conducts courtship and utters loud booming call by means of specialised vocal organ. Breeding season September to February in E Australia. Both sexes build nest in sheltered scrape on ground, but ♂ incubates the 4 buffish or white eggs, thickly marked brown and grey, 12-13 days, ♂ tends the brood, who have 3 moults in 10 weeks. **213**

TURNSTONE see **Arenaria interpres**

TURQUOISE WREN see **Malurus callainus**

TURTLE DOVE see **Streptopelia turtur**

Turtur abyssinicus *Columbidae*
BLACK-BILLED BLUE-SPOTTED
WOOD DOVE *c.* 7 ins
Ethiopian: Senegal across to Ethiopia and N Uganda. Habitat: dry scrub and open woodland. Plump; upperparts light brown, forehead pale grey, 2 broad black bands over rump, iridescent dark blue blotches on secondaries; underparts brownish pink, flanks pale chestnut, under tail coverts white. Legs purple, bill black or dark, eyes dark brown. (Blue-spotted Wood Dove, *Turtur afer*, almost identical but range only overlaps in S Ethiopia; slightly darker, larger greener wing patches and red base to bill.) Tame, usually in pairs; ground feeder, taking seeds and similar plant matter; flies rapidly but rarely any distance. Call: prolonged soft cooing. Breeding season variable; lays 2 dark cream eggs on small platform of twigs, sometimes on old nest of other species, in tree or shrub. **379**

Turtur afer see under **T. abyssinicus**

Turtur chalcospilos *Columbidae*
EMERALD SPOTTED WOOD DOVE 7 ins
Ethiopian: N Somalia, Ethiopia, Katanga and Angola S to Natal and Cape. Habitat: dry bush-veld and open woodland, also cultivated areas. Plump; head grey, forehead paler, narrow black line from gape to eye; upperparts light brown, 2 shining emerald green, sometimes bluish, patches on closed wing, 2 dark bands across lower back; underparts light mauve-pink with pale chin. Wing mainly chestnut but blackish primaries and outer secondaries, tail brownish with black tip. Legs purplish red, bill black with reddish purple base, eyes dark brown. Single or in pairs; feeds on ground taking small grain, seeds and some small animals. Flight usually short, rapid, often zigzag; raises tail briefly on landing. Call: prolonged melancholy cooing, running up and down scale. Breeds any month, building usual twig platform in tree or bush, rarely more than 2 or 3 yards from ground; lays 2 pale cream eggs incubated ♀ and ♂. Both parents feed young, who fly 16 days. **380**

TWO-BANDED COURSER see **Hemerodromus africanus**

Tylas eduardi *Oriolidae*
KINKIMAVO 9 ins
Madagascar: race *T.e. eduardi* in forests of humid east, occasionally secondary growth, sea level to *c.* 5,500 ft; *albigularis* in central western savannah. Upperparts olive-brown, crown encircled black and white; underparts, including underwing, under tail coverts deep ochre; flight feathers greyish, tail dusky: *albigularis* greyer above, whiter below. Legs, bill black, eyes yellow. Moves rather slowly along larger branches of forest mid-storey, gleaning medium-sized insects; often in mixed flocks, e.g. with Helmetbird, *Aerocharis prevostii*. Breeds August to September.

Tympanuchus cupido *Tetraonidae*
GREATER PRAIRIE CHICKEN 18 ins
Nearctic: now very local in Central to S USA, migratory in north of range. Habitat originally tall-grass prairie, now also open and scrubby grasslands and cropfields. Barred white on shades of brown, with blackish rounded tail, dark brown head and crest; ♂ has long feathers on sides of neck, orange yellow wattles above eye and air sacs; legs feathered, feet greyish, bill and eyes dark. Lives in open in winter, burrowing in snow to roost. Spring displays by ♂♂ at 'leks' (see *Lyrurus tetrix*): short run with neck feathers raised and sacs distended, giving booming sound, then cackles and leaps in air. Breeds May to June, ♀ lining scrape in thick vegetation for 11, 12 or more olive eggs speckled brown, which she incubates for 23-24 days then takes chicks away; on wing in July. **190**

Tyrannus melancholicus *Tyrannidae*
OLIVE-BACKED OR TROPICAL KINGBIRD 9 ins
Nearctic and Neotropical: breeds S Texas, S Arizona through Mexico and Central America to S America W of Andes to Peru; E of Andes to Rio Negro, Argentina; Trinidad and Tobago, Grenada. Resident chaparral desert, savannah, parkland, cultivated land and gardens, borders of lakes and rivers, sea level to 8,000 ft. Upperparts greyish green; wings, forked tail blackish brown with light edges to wing coverts, inner flight and tail feathers; head and neck grey with concealed orange crest, black mask; throat and breast greyish white; underparts lemon yellow; legs, bill black, eyes dark brown. Behaviour and diet as other kingbirds; flies nearly vertically down to perch; most active in evenings. Tremulous call *pip-pree;* also staccato high-pitched ascending notes. Breeds throughout year, building bulky cup nest like other kingbirds, usually at end of lateral branch up to 40 ft in tree. 2 to 4 creamy white eggs, boldly marked reddish brown and violet grey, often in zone, incubated by ♀ *c.* 14 days; young, fed by both parents, fly *c.* 14 days. **584**

Tyrannus tyrannus *Tyrannidae*
EASTERN KINGBIRD 8½ ins
Nearctic: breeds from S Canada throughout USA (except SW) to S Florida, Gulf Coast, Texas, N New Mexico; winters from Costa Rica E to Guyanas and S through W Brazil to S Bolivia, Peru, NW Argentina. Habitat open country with trees, woodland with occasional higher trees, gardens and parks; winters on campo (open grassland with trees), savannahs. Upperparts dark grey, with white edges to coverts making narrow bars on wings; long tail, often fanned, black broadly tipped white; thin orange crest normally housed in crown; underparts from throat white; legs, bill blackish, eyes dark brown. Rapid aerobatics with quick wingbeats give quivering effect. Attacks large birds crossing territory, even landing on their backs. Spreads wings and tail in display flight. Usual call *tzi tzee;* also high-pitched strident note extended into squeaky chattering; full song reserved for dawn chorus. Watches for insects from elevated perch, taking great variety on wing, off leaves, surface of water, sometimes ground; berries and seeds in autumn. Lays second half May after ♀ and ♂ have built bulky nest of sticks and grass with finer lining, usually 20 to 25 ft up on lateral branch, but occasionally up to 80 ft and down to stumps, fence posts, low shrubs near water. 3 to 5 creamy white eggs, marked brown and grey, incubated by ♀ *c.* 13 days; young, fed by parents, fly *c.* 2 weeks. **585**

Tyrannus verticalis *Tyrannidae*
WESTERN KINGBIRD 9 ins
Nearctic, marginally Neotropical: breeds from British Columbia and Manitoba S through western half USA to N Texas and N New Mexico; winters from NW Mexico to El Salvador; occurs on autumn passage E coast USA. Habitat open country with trees, fences and wires; frequent round ranches and into towns. Upperparts grey; flight feathers dark grey to black; long tail black with white outer feathers; thin concealed orange crest; throat white, breast pale grey, underparts lemon yellow; legs, bill horn grey, eyes brown. Calls: high-pitched squeaks, chattering and

twittering, less shrill than *T. tyrannus*. Diet almost entirely of insects, especially grasshoppers. Breeds sometimes socially, several pairs in one grove, building cup nest of soft materials, typically on lateral branch 15 to 30 ft up, but may use artifact sites if no trees. 4 creamy white eggs, marked brown and grey, incubated and young tended as *T. tyrannus*. **586**

Tyto alba *Tytonidae*
BARN OWL *c.* 13½ ins
Cosmopolitan; Palaearctic: Europe E to Black Sea, N Africa, Arabia; Oriental: Indian subcontinent, much of SE Asia, Java and islands; Australasian: continental Australia, Tasmania, E New Guinea and islands; Nearctic: S of 50°N; Neotropical: except extreme S. Resident and migratory, also dispersal of young. Habitat varied: usually lightly wooded, mainly arid and rocky, frequently in or close to habitations. Race *T. a. alba*: upperparts orange buff, finely mottled grey and white; heart-shaped facial disc and underparts white; race *guttata* greyer on back, underparts buff spotted black, as in several other of over 30 races; Asian *stertens* has grey upperparts. Long legs feathered white, feet dark brown; bill yellowish to flesh-white; eyes black. Nocturnal, spending day perched upright in cavity, but sometimes hunting in daylight and often in evening when feeding young; quarters ground with light, wavering flight. Wing-clapping by ♂ in display. Crouches with wings spread horizontally in defence. Call a loud shriek often given in flight; hissing and snoring noises, especially by young; *kee-yak* like Tawny Owl, *Strix aluco*; snaps bill when angry like other owls. Food predominantly mice and other small rodents; some small birds, insects. Breeds almost the year round, making scrape, surrounded by pellets, in large cavity in tree, rocks or building, sometimes in old nest, e.g. of Hamerkop, *Scopus umbretta*, in Africa. 4 to 7 rather pointed white eggs incubated by ♀ 32-34 days; both parents feed young, who fly 9-12 weeks; often 2 broods. **429**

Tyto tenebricosa *Tytonidae*
SOOTY OWL 15 ins (♀ larger than ♂)
Australasian: New Guinea; two areas E continental Australia; Victoria (round Melbourne) to SE Queensland; N Queensland (including Atherton Tableland); rather wet, densely forested country. Upperparts: brownish black, streaked and flecked white; underparts sooty, mottled white and closely barred; rounded facial disc greyish-white; black round eyes and rim; tail very short; legs grey, feathers pale; bill brown; very large eyes brown. Habits much as Barn Owl, *T. alba*, roosting by day usually in hollow tree, sometimes in thick vegetation. Call: whistling screech, other screaming notes. Breeds October to December in southern range, laying 2 white eggs in tree holes. **430**

Upupa epops *Upupidae*
HOOPOE 11 (bill 2-2½) ins
Palaearctic up to between 50° and 60°N; almost all Oriental region except SE islands; Ethiopian except Congo Forest; W Madagascar. Northern populations winter S Asia and Africa S of Equator in open bush, low scrub, cultivated areas. Darker African race, with broader black and white bands, sometimes regarded as separate species *U. africana*. Breeding habitat: dry open park-like country, forest clearings, grassy and wooded steppes, palm groves; gardens, orchards and vineyards. Head, with fanned black-tipped crest, upper back and breast variable pinkish-brown; scapulars and back banded cream and black; rounded wings black banded white; rump white, upper tail coverts black with some white; tail black with broad white band; flanks and belly whitish, streaked dark brown; legs slate grey, fine curved bill blackish to greyish, eyes brown. Rises from ground into fluttering flight, looking predominantly black and white. But walks and runs swiftly, probing ground for large insects and their larvae, especially mole crickets; also lizards and various invertebrates. Crest usually flat but extended when alarmed. Fond of dust baths but not known to drink. Small parties on migration. 'Song': soft *hoop hoop hoop*; also chatters when excited and has cat-like *kiaow* call. Breeds from April in Europe, August in S Africa; in holes in trees, rock faces, walls

of stone and earth, even occupied buildings, piles of stones, drainage holes, anthills. 5 to 8 off-white or yellowish olive eggs incubated by ♀ and ♂ 16-19 days; both feed young, who fly 20-27 days; sometimes 2 broods. **509**

UMBRELLABIRD see **Cephalopterus ornatus**

UMBRELLABIRD, LONG-WATTLED see under
Cephalopterus ornatus

Upupa africana see under **U. epops**

Uraeginthus bengalus *Estrildidae*
RED-CHEEKED CORDON BLEU *c.* 5 ins
Ethiopian: resident W Africa E to Eritrea, Ethiopia, Somalia, S to E Congo, Uganda, Kenya, N Tanzania, in thorn bush and acacia savannah, forest edge, neglected cultivations; gardens and habitations. ♂: upperparts light brown; rump, tail, underparts azure blue; crimson cheek patch; belly brown some races; under tail coverts white. ♀, immature duller, lack cheek patch. Legs, eyes brown, bill pearly pink. Tame and confiding, like many of its relatives visits bird tables. Pairs or family parties. Call: weak, squeaky; 3-note song *ts ts tseeee* repeated continuously. Food: seeds, largely taken from ground. Breeding season varies within range; nest spherical or oval, sometimes with outer network of stems, rootlets, of fine green grass, lined feathers, in bush, tree, thatched roof, old nests of weavers; some races, e.g. *U.b. schoanus* of Central Ethiopia, build near hornets' nests. 4 or 5 white eggs. **946**

Uragus sibiricus *Fringillidae*
LONG-TAILED ROSEFINCH 10-11 (tail 3½) ins
E Palaearctic: E Kazakhstan and S Siberia to Sakhalin, Kuriles, N China, N Japan, Manchuria, Mongolia; nomadic in autumn and winter. Habitat: dense riparian scrub, wooded hillsides, boggy forests of pine, birch, alder, willows; sea buckthorn thickets; to 5,500 ft in Altai. ♂: generally pink with dark feathershafts on back; wing coverts mostly blackish-brown with broad white tips; flight feathers blackish, white-tipped; central tail feathers mainly black, outer ones mainly white; forehead, throat, cheeks silvery pink. ♀: yellowish-grey where ♂ pink, except rump, upper tail coverts. Immature similar but duller. Small flocks of juveniles form after breeding. Flight fluttering, wingbeats producing peculiar trill. ♂♂ flit about during courtship with soaring song flight, gliding down to ♀. Call: melodious 3-note whistle; song 'ripples like brook of spring water' (M. D. Zverev). Food mainly seeds, pecked at while swinging on plant. Breeding season from first half May (race *U.s. ussuriensis*); nest of dry grass, stalks, plant fibres, softly lined, placed *c.* 6 ft up, close to trunk of small tree, bush. 3 to 6 rich blue-green eggs marked brown incubated by ♀ and ♂, who also feed young. **934**

Uratelornis chimaera *Coraciidae: Brachypteracinae*
LONG-TAILED GROUND ROLLER *c.* 18 ins
Confined to SW Madagascar; resident sandy bush and desert country. Upperparts light buffish brown with dark feather shafts and pale edges; flight feathers of rather short, rounded wings dark brown, wing coverts pale blue grey; outer feathers of very long, graduated tail white; white gorget framed by black and rufous streaks and black breast band; underparts pale buff; long legs light brown, heavy bill horn brown, large eyes light brown. Runs to cover when alarmed, standing still with tail raised. Normally on ground but perches scattered bushes. Reputed to 'hibernate' in dry season. ♀ and ♂ excavate slightly ascending tunnel *c.* 4 ft long with chamber at end. 3 or 4 eggs incubated by ♀, fed by ♂.

Uria aalge *Alcidae*
COMMON GUILLEMOT or MURRE *c.* 16½ ins
Holarctic: similar to but much less extensive than Black Guillemot, *Cepphus grylle*, mainly NE Atlantic coasts Norway to Portugal, Iceland, Newfoundland area, and both sides Pacific to N California and Kuriles; isolated stations elsewhere; replaced to N by Brünnich's Guillemot, *U. lomvia*; winters at sea.

Breeds sea cliffs and offshore stacks. Summer: northern race *U. a. aalge* very similar to Razorbill, *Alca torda*, except for straight pointed bill; southern *albionis* has upperparts brown not black. Both show 'bridled' form with narrow white ring round eye tailing off into line along side of head; bridled proportion generally increases in colonies S to N. Legs yellowish to black, bill black (yellow inside), eyes black-brown. Throat and cheeks white in winter. Social at all times, with mutual and communal head-twisting displays. Rests on shanks on ledges, but can stand if necessary. Behaviour much as Razorbill. Usual call, from ledges or sea, growling *arrr*, with various elaborations. Takes mainly fish, marine worms, small crustaceans; fish carried more or less lengthwise in bill. Breeds from end April in S, in colonies on cliff ledges, sometimes top of stack or rocky island. One egg, immensely variable from white, blue, green, brown to (rare) red, with dark brown blotches, scrawls and spots, laid on bare ledge, tapering shape causing it to rotate and not roll over in wind. Incubation by ♀ and ♂ 28-30 days, fledging as Razorbill. **346**

Uroaetus audax see **Aquila audax**

Urocynchramus pylzowi *Fringillidae*
PRZEVALSKI'S ROSEFINCH *c.* 8 (tail 3½) ins
E Palaearctic: W China and Mongolia; thick low scrub, e.g. dwarf willows, rhododendrons, *Potentilla tenuifolia*, usually near water; vertical migration downhill in winter. ♂: upperparts from crown sandy brown, streaked black; flight feathers blackish brown edged warm buff or tawny; pale buff bar on brown coverts; central feathers of long, graduated tail blackish brown, edged white, outer ones crimson-rose; lores, 'eyebrow', cheeks, underparts rosy red shading to white on belly. ♀'s underparts white, faintly tinged rose on breast; throat, breast, flanks streaked black; outer tail feathers dull rosy white. Legs black, bill black and yellow, eyes dark brown. Presumably mainly seed-eating. Breeds alpine areas May, details unknown.

VAN DER DECKEN'S HORNBILL see **Tockus deckeni**

Vanellus armatus *or Hoplopterus armatus*
Charadriidae
BLACKSMITH PLOVER *c.* 12 ins
Ethiopian: S from Kenya and Angola; resident in open country usually near fresh or brackish water. Forehead, crown, back of neck and upper tail coverts white; upper wing coverts and scapulars pale grey; cheeks, throat, nape, breast black; underparts white, also tail, but with broad terminal black band; black spur on wing; legs and bill black, eyes red. Juvenile similar but browner. Usually in pairs or small parties, sometimes larger flocks in good feeding areas, e.g. in evening on grassland where cattle have grazed; also recently burnt areas. Call: loud *klink klink klink*, like blacksmith hitting anvil. Food: insects and their larvae, small molluscs, worms. Breeds April to August in Kenya; from September in Cape Colony. Lined scrape among debris, often near water, holds 2 to 4 buffish brown eggs, marked dark brown and grey. Incubation and fledging much as other plovers (see *V. vanellus*). **268**

Vanellus coronatus *or Stephanibyx coronatus*
Charadriidae
CROWNED PLOVER *c.* 12 ins
Ethiopian: E and S of region; resident, with local movements, on grassland in plains, sparsely wooded areas, even semi-desert, up to several thousand feet. Upperparts fawn brown, crown encircled by white above black stripe; black line between fawn breast and white underparts; flight feathers mainly black, white patch at base of wing; under wing and tail coverts and rump white; black subterminal band to tail; legs red, bill red, tip dark, eyes orange-yellow. Juvenile has buff edges to feathers of upperparts. Usually in pairs or small parties, building up to large flocks after breeding. Walks and runs with body horizontal, but stance upright. Plover-like dip forward to catch prey, mainly insects, especially beetles, grasshoppers and locusts, which it gleans from freshly burnt areas. Flight call *kree kree kree kreeip*; *kie-wiet* of

alarm. Communal dances at dusk and in night. Breeding mainly from July to December. Lined scrape holds usually 2 or 3 buffish brown eggs, marked dark brown and grey; incubation and fledging probably as other *Vanellus* plovers. **269**

Vanellus senegallus or Afribyx senegallus
Charadriidae
WATTLED PLOVER   14½ ins
Ethiopian: most of region except Congo forests and extreme SW; local movements seasonally. Mainly swamps but lowland grassland and cultivated areas near water. ♂: upperparts olivaceous brown; crown black but centre and forehead white; neck streaked black; outer wing coverts, inner secondaries white, other flight feathers black, wing spur small; white tail has subterminal black bar; chin, throat black; breast, upper belly pale grey brown, divided from rest of white underparts by blackish band; underwing white; legs, bill (black-tipped), eyes yellow, broad dark red and yellow wattles. ♀ has much less black on throat. Gregarious and tame; noisy in breeding season with shrill *peep peep*, intensified as alarm note (said to be sure indicator of water); also *choo-ee* call. Food: insects and grass seeds. Breeds March-April in N of range, September to December in S, making vestigial scrape, often on mound. 3 to 4 buff or olive brown eggs, marked black, sepia grey. Incubation and fledging as *V. vanellus*; sometimes 2 broods in S. **270**

Vanellus spinosus or Hoplopterus spinosus
Charadriidae
SPURWING PLOVER   10½ ins
SE Palaearctic (Greece, Turkey, Asia Minor, Middle East); Ethiopian N of Equator (has bred S Africa); some local migration by night. Habitats: alluvial and cultivated country near fresh water, e.g. Nile Valley, becoming habituated to man; marshes by sea in recent colonisation of Greece. Predominantly black and white with brown back and upper wing coverts; crown and crest black; cheeks, sides and back of neck and rump white; tail and tips of sharply spurred wings black; chin to belly black, underwing and tail coverts white; legs and bill black, eyes carmine. Juvenile duller. Noisy and aggressive, attacking intruders near nest. Hunched posture and slow flight. Often seen with crocodiles. Monotonous, plaintive call by night, also *did ye do it* in flight and sharp *trak trak trak* of alarm. Food mostly taken at waterside: beetles and other insects. Breeds mainly April-August. Scrape, often lined, on sand or mud flats, rocky islets in rivers. 3 or 4 greyish-buff eggs, marked dark brown and lilac, incubated by ♀ and ♂; details as *V. vanellus*. May have 2 broods. **271**

Vanellus tectus or Sarciphorus tectus *Charadriidae*
BLACKHEAD PLOVER   10 ins
Ethiopian: across region from Senegal, widening to include Red Sea coast, Uganda, Kenya; local migrations. Habitat dry plains and open areas in bush. Upperparts pale brown; outer wing coverts white, flight feathers dark; white tail has subterminal black bar; crown black with short, pointed crest; forehead white, extending over eye round nape; chin white, surrounded black from eye to longish plumes of breast; rest of underparts white; legs carmine, small red wattle in front of orange-brown eye. Small flocks; tame, but will mob passing birds of prey, though rather slow in flight. Shrill whistling call as birds rise in alarm; also loud hollow cry. Feeds largely by night on insects and molluscs. Breeding season variable throughout range; makes scrape on open ground, lined grass, often edged fine gravel. 2 or 3 clay or buff eggs, spotted and blotched black and purple. Incubation and fledging much as *V. vanellus*. **272**

Vanellus tricolor or Zonifer tricolor *Charadriidae*
BANDED PLOVER   *c*. 10½ ins
Continental Australia (except tropical N), Tasmania; nomadic according to local conditions. Habitat short grassland usually near water; cultivated land; mud flats, sometimes arid plains. Upperparts light brown; head and neck blackish with white stripe behind eye; throat whitish, black band from below eye downwards across breast; primaries black, outer secondaries

black and white; tail white with terminal black band; underparts white; rather short legs purplish red, bill yellow, tip black; bulbous red wattles above it; eyes yellow. Habits much as other *Vanellus* plovers. Call: melodious *a chee chee chee*. Food: insects, flushed by shuffling with foot, and their larvae; seeds of grasses. Breeds July to November, often socially. Scrape on bare ground, sometimes in cattle dung, holds usually 4 light brown eggs, marked dark brown and grey; incubation by ♀ and ♂ *c*. 28 days: feigns injury or mobs intruders near nest or brood. **273**

Vanellus vanellus *Charadriidae*
LAPWING   *c*. 12 ins
Palaearctic: broad band (S Scandinavia to Mediterranean) across temperate zone from Atlantic to Pacific; partial migrant southward from breeding areas to N Africa, Middle East, Oriental region, Japan. Habitats: open country from coastal saltings to moorlands at 3,000 ft; arable fields, wet meadows, shingle and sand dunes; winters on grassland (often when flooded) and flat coastal areas. ♂: upperparts, including crown and curved crest, metallic green; broad black band across breast; chin, cheeks, underparts white; also tail, with black terminal band; under tail coverts rufous buff. ♀: crest shorter and suffusion of buff on cheeks and back in winter, also in juvenile. Legs brownish flesh, bill black, eyes dark brown. In winter flocks feed scattered, coalesce to rest, breaking up into pairs early spring when ♂♂ give tumbling flight displays, 'singing' *peerweet weet weet . . . weet weet;* usual call *pee-weet* gives alternative name. ♂ also shows rufous under tail in scrape-forming action. Food much as Golden Plover, *Pluvialis apricaria*, 90% animal matter. Breeds, often socially, from mid March Britain. Lined scrape, sometimes quite substantial nest of dead stems, on hummock or flat in variety of situations, holds usually 4 light brown eggs, marked dark brown; incubation by ♀ and ♂ 24-31 days; both parents tend young who fly 4½-5 weeks. **274**

VANGA, LAFRESNAYE'S see **Xenopirostris xenopirostris**

VARIABLE
    SEEDEATER see **Sporophila americana**
    SUNBIRD see **Cinnyris venustus**

VARIEGATED WREN see **Malurus lamberti**

VASA PARROT, GREATER see **Coracopsis vasa**

VELVET ASITY see **Philepitta castanea**

VERDIN see **Auriparus flavus**

VERMILION-CROWNED FLYCATCHER see **Myiozetetes similis**

Vermivora celata *Parulidae*
ORANGE-CROWNED WARBLER   5 ins
Nearctic: breeds from near tree limit Alaska, NW Canada, S to S Manitoba, New Mexico, N Lower California; winters from S USA to Guatemala. Habitat open woodlands with heavy undergrowth, young secondary growth, riparian thickets and, in far N, stream bottoms with dwarf trees; chaparral scrub in California; winters live-oak woods (Florida), woodland edge, parks, gardens. Upperparts olive green, feathers grey-tipped except on rump; round orange crown patch usually concealed; underparts yellow, lightly streaked. Duskier in autumn and immature with less difference between upper and underparts. Legs brown, bill dark, eyes dark brown. Western race ('Lutescent Warbler') much yellower. Song: varied, musical trill, rising in pitch after slow beginning, then dying away; call: sharp *chip*. Insectivorous, feeding different levels of vegetation. Breeds from early April in S to June in N of range; nest of coarse grass, bark fibres, softly lined, generally well hidden on ground. Usually 5 white eggs, finely spotted red-brown, incubated ♀ *c*. 12 days; young fly after same period. **901**

EAGLE see **Aquila verreauxii**
GIANT EAGLE OWL see **Bubo lacteus**

Vidua macroura *Estrildidae*
PINTAILED WHYDAH   ♀: 4½; ♂ (with tail): 12-13 ins
Ethiopian: almost throughout region; resident grasslands, open bush and scrub; cultivated areas; near habitations. ♂: crown, back, shoulders, flight feathers, tail with enormously elongated 4 central feathers, black; rest of plumage white. ♀: brown, streaked darker like sparrow, with buff stripe over crown. Non-breeding ♂ like ♀ but more white on wings. Legs black, bill red, eyes dark brown. Immature earth-brown, streaked above, buff below, bill reddish-black. In small parties, ♂♂ outnumbered by ♀♀, immatures; large flocks after breeding, roosting in trees. Jerky, erratic flight, ♂ wiggling tail; in display dances or hovers over ♀, chases other ♂♂; repeats *tseet tseet tsip* in courtship flight, quivering wings; also shrill, sustained twittering song; repeated *chitt* of alarm. Food mainly grass and other small seeds. Breeding season depends on hosts: Waxbill, *Estrilda astrild* and *Cisticola* species, sometimes laying first egg, white or pale cream, in nest; young reared with host's brood. Probably polygamous. **947**

VIOLET CUCKOO see **Chalcites xanthorhynchus**

VIOLETEAR HUMMINGBIRD, SPARKLING see **Colibri coruscans**

VIOLET-HEADED LORIKEET see **Eos squamata**

VIREO,
    CHESTNUT-SIDED SHRIKE see **Vireolanius meliophrys**
    WHITE-EYED see **Vireo griseus**

Vireo griseus *Vireonidae*
WHITE-EYED VIREO   5 ins
Nearctic, marginally Neotropical: breeds E USA from Massachusetts, Ohio, S Wisconsin, SE Nebraska, to S Florida, Gulf Coast, N Mexico; winters from SE USA to Honduras. Habitat woodland edge, dense broadleaved thickets with brambles, vines, often near water, secondary growth on hillsides, hedgerows. Upperparts greenish yellow, wing feathers dusky with pale edges and two distinct white bars, tail feathers dusky edged yellow; narrow yellow 'spectacles'; chin white shading to yellow on flanks, belly; legs brown, bill dark brown, eyes white. Immature shows yellow 'spectacles' round brown eyes. Inquisitive, can be called up by 'squeaking', otherwise hard to see. Calls: harsh mew, short tick, single loud whistle; song series of 5 to 7 distinct notes very variable but constantly repeated. Mainly insectivorous but takes fruit autumn and winter: sumac, grapes, wax myrtle. Breeds end May-June; rather cone-shaped, ragged-looking nest of leaves, moss, wasp nest 'paper', sticks woven with plant fibres and suspended but well hidden 3 to 6 ft up in thick vegetation. 4 white eggs, scattered brown dots at big end. **906**

Vireolanius melitophrys *Vireonidae*
CHESTNUT-SIDED SHRIKE VIREO   *c*. 7 ins
Neotropical: S Mexico to Guatemala; resident mainly oak forests 4,000 to 10,000 ft. Upperparts including wings, tail, olive green; crown, hindneck slate-grey bordered broad dull yellow 'eyebrows'; black band from lores to earcoverts, black moustachial stripe; underparts white, with chestnut breast band extending to sides and flanks. Hunts, often in pairs, high in trees, moving cautiously, sometimes hanging upside down to seize insect; larger prey held beneath one foot and tackled with strong bill. Calls include low, nasal rattle, penetrating screech. Breeding habits unknown (A. F. Skutch).

Vultur gryphus *Cathartidae*
ANDEAN CONDOR   48-52 ins
Neotropical: Andes from Venezuela to Cape Horn; commonest Central Peru to Aysén (Chile); resident mountains, above 10,000 ft N of Peru, to sea level farther S. Largest flying bird, wingspan 9-10 ft.

Generally glossy black; whitish patch upper wing coverts; white ruff; bare head and neck usually red, sometimes black; ♂ has fleshy dark red or black crest; legs grey, bill horn white, eyes brown. Main food carrion: located by eyesight from height; first bird to carcase may be followed by 10 to 20 others, planing down in spirals, final approach on foot; also takes coastal refuse in S of range, dead birds on Peruvian guano islands. Lays September-October in large nest of sticks and debris in mountain cave or cleft. Single (occasionally 2) white egg, incubated ♀ and ♂ 54-58 days; chick takes 16 months to fledge, fed ♀ and ♂, so breeding only in alternate years.

VULTURE
AFRICAN WHITE-BACK see **Gyps africanus**
ASIAN KING see **Sarcogyps calvus**
BLACK see **Coragyps atratus**
EGYPTIAN see **Neophron percnopterus**
GRIFFON see **Gyps fulvus**
INDIAN WHITE-BACKED see **Gyps bengalensis**
PALM-NUT see **Gypohierax angolensis**
RUPPELL's see under **Gyps africanus**
SOUTH AMERICAN KING see **Sarcorhamphus papa**
TURKEY see **Cathartes aura**
WHITE-BACKED see **Gyps africanus**
WHITE-HEADED see **Trigonoceps occipitalis**

VULTURINE
GUINEAFOWL see **Acryllium vulturinum**
PARROT see **Gypositta vulturina**

WAGTAIL,
AFRICAN PIED see **Motacilla aguimp**
FOREST see **Dendromanthus indicus**
GREY see **Motacilla cinerea**
PIED see **Motacilla alba**
WHITE see **Motacilla alba**
YELLOW see **Motacilla flava**

WAHLBERG's EAGLE see **Aquila wahlbergi**

WALDRAPP see under **Geronticus calvus**

WALLCREEPER see **Tichodroma muraria**

WANDERING
ALBATROSS see **Diomedea exulans**
TATTLER see under **Tringa brevipes**

WARBLER,
AFRICAN SEDGE see **Bradypterus baboecala**
BARRED see **Sylvia nisoria**
BLACK AND WHITE see **Mniotilta varia**
BLACKPOLL see under **Mniotilta varia**
CANADA see **Wilsonia canadensis**
CETTI's see **Cettia cetti**
CHINESE BUSH see **Cettia diphone**
CLAMOROUS see **Acrocephalus stentoreus**
DESERT FANTAIL see **Cisticola aridula**
GARDEN see **Sylvia borin**
GRASSHOPPER see **Locustella naevia**
GRAY's GRASSHOPPER see **Locustella fasciolata**
GREAT REED see **Acrocephalus arundinaceus**
GREY see **Gerygone igata**
GREY-BACKED see **Cisticola subruficapilla**
KNYSNA see **Bradypterus sylvaticus**
MAGNOLIA see **Dendroica magnoliae**
MARSH see **Acrocephalus palustris**
MELODIOUS see **Hippolais polyglotta**
OLIVE see **Peucedramus taeniatus**
ORANGE-CROWNED see **Vermivora celata**
ORPHEAN see **Sylvia hortensis**
PARULA see under **Dendroica dominica**
PLAIN WILLOW see under **Phylloscopus collybita**
REED see under **Acrocephalus palustris**
RUFOUS-CROWNED see **Basileuterus rufifrons**
RUFOUS GRASS see **Cisticola galactotes**
SARDINIAN see **Sylvia melanocephala**
SEDGE see **Acrocephalus schoenbaenus**
SEVERTGOV's TIT see **Leptopoecile sophiae**
SHORT-TAILED BUSH see **Cisticola squameiceps**
SPECKLED see **Chthonicola sagittata**
SUBALPINE see **Sylvia cantillans**

SUTTON's see under **Dendroica dominica**
WHITE-THROATED see **Gerygone olivacea**
WILLOW see **Phylloscopus trochilis**
WILSON's see **Wilsonia pusilla**
WOOD see **Phylloscopus sibilatrix**
WORM-EATING see **Helmitheros vermivorus**
YELLOW see **Dendroica patechia**
YELLOW-THROATED see **Dendroica dominica**

WATER DIKKOP see **Burhinus vermiculatus**

WATTLEBIRD, LITTLE see **Anthochaera chrysoptera**

WATTLED
CRANE see **Grus carunculatus**
IBIS see **Bostrychia carunculata**
JACANA see **Jacana jacana**
PLOVER see **Vanellus senegallus**
STARLING see **Creatophora cinerea**

WAXBILL,
COMMON see **Estrilda astrild**
CRIMSON-RUMPED see under **Estrilda astrild**
SYDNEY see **Estrilda temporalis**

WAXWING,
BOHEMIAN see **Bombycilla garrulus**
CEDAR see **Bombycilla cedrorum**

WEAVER,
BLACK-HEADED see **Ploceus cucullatus**
SOCIAL see **Philetarius socius**
SPECKLED-FRONTED see **Sporopipes frontalis**
SPOTTED-BACKED see **Ploceus cucullatus**
STRIATED see **Ploceus manyar**
STRIPE-BREASTED SPARROW see **Plocepasser mahali**
WHITE-BROWED SPARROW see **Plocepasser mahali**
WHITE-HEADED BUFFALO see **Dinemellia dinemelli**

WEDGE-BILLED WOODCREEPER see **Glyphorhynchus spirurus**

WEDGE-TAILED
EAGLE see **Aquila audax**
GREEN PIGEON see **Treron sphenura**
SHEARWATER see **Puffinus pacificus**

WEEBILL, BROWN see **Smicrornis brevirostris**

WEKA see **Gallirallus australis**

WEST AFRICAN BLACK FLYCATCHER see under **Melaenornis pammelaina**

WEST INDIAN NIGHTHAWK see **Chordeiles gundlachii**

WESTERN
BLACK-HEADED ORIOLE see under **Oriolus larvatus**
BLUEBIRD see under **Peucedramus taeniatus**
GREBE see **Aechmophorus occidentalis**
KINGBIRD see **Tyrannus verticalis**
MAGPIE see under **Gymnorhina tibicen**
MEADOWLARK see **Sturnella neglecta**

WHALE HEAD see **Balaeniceps rex**

WHEATEAR see **Oenanthe oenanthe**

WHEATEAR,
BLACK-EARED see **Oenanthe hispanica**
HOODED see **Oenanthe monacha**

WHIMBREL see **Numenius phaeopus**

WHIPBIRD, EASTERN see **Psophodes olivaceus**

WHIP-POOR-WILL see **Caprimulgus vociferus**

WHISKERED TERN see **Chlidonias hybrida**

WHISTLER,
GOLDEN see **Pachycephala pectoralis**
GREY-HEADED see under **Pachycephala pectoralis**

WHISTLING EAGLE see **Haliastur sphenorus**

WHITE
BELLBIRD see under **Procnias nudicollis**
CRANE, SIBERIAN see **Grus leucogeranus**
HELMET SHRIKE see **Prionops plumata**
HERON, GREAT see **Egretta alba**
IBIS (AMERICAN) see **Eudocimus albus**
IBIS (AUSTRALIAN) see under **Threskiornis spinicollis**
PELICAN see **Pelecanus onocrotalus**
STORK see **Ciconia alba**
TERN see **Gygis alba**
WAGTAIL see **Motacilla alba**

WHITE-BACKED
VULTURE, AFRICAN see **Gyps africanus**
VULTURE, INDIAN see **Gyps bengalensis**

WHITE-BEARDED
HONEYEATER see **Meliornis novaehollandiae**
MANAKIN see **Manacus manacus**

WHITE-BELLIED
BUSTARD see **Eupodotis senegalensis**
GO-AWAY-BIRD see **Corythaixoides leucogaster**
SEEDSNIPE see **Attagis malouinus**
SUNBIRD see **Cinnyris talatala**

WHITE-BILLED DIVER see under **Gavia immer**

WHITE-BREASTED
KINGFISHER see **Halcyon smyrnensis**
ROBIN see **Eopsaltria georgiana**
SEA EAGLE see **Haliaeetus leucogaster**
SWIFTLET see **Collocalia esculenta**
WOOD SWALLOW see **Artamus leucorhynchus**

WHITE-BROWED
BABBLER see **Pomatostomos superciliosus**
COUCAL see **Centropus superciliosus**
SCRUB ROBIN see **Erythropygia zambesiana**
SCRUB WREN see **Sericornis frontalis**
SPARROW WEAVER see **Plocepasser mahli**
WOOD SWALLOW see **Artamus superciliosus**

WHITE-CHEEKED
BULBUL see under **Pycnonotus cafer**
HONEYEATER see **Meliornis niger**

WHITE-COLLARED
PIGEON see **Columba albitorquis**
PRATINCOLE see **Galachrysia nuchalis**

WHITE-CRESTED
HORNBILL, ASIAN see **Berenicornis comatus**
TOURACO see under **Tauraco livingstonii**

WHITE-CROWNED
CLIFF CHAT see **Thamnolaea coronata**
SHRIKE see **Eurocephalus anguitimens**
SPARROW see **Zonotrichia leucophrys**

WHITE-EARED HONEYEATER see **Meliphaga leucotis**

WHITE-EYE,
GREEN see under **Zosterops pallida**
GREY-BREASTED see **Zosterops lateralis**
INDIAN see **Zosterops palpebrosa**
KIKUYU see **Zosterops kikuyensis**
PALE see **Zosterops pallidus**
YELLOW see **Zosterops senegalensis**

WHITE-EYED
FOLIAGE GLEANER see **Automolus leucophthalmus**
SLATY FLYCATCHER see **Dioptrornis fischeri**
VIREO see **Vireo griseus**

WHITE-FACED
  HERON see **Notophoyx novaehollandiae**
  OWL see **Otus leucotis**
  STORM PETREL see **Pelagodroma marina**
  TREE DUCK see **Dendrocygna viduata**

WHITE-FLANKED FLYCATCHER see **Batis molitor**

WHITE-FRONTED
  BEE-EATER see **Melittophagus bullockoides**
  CHAT see **Ephthianura albifrons**
  HONEYEATER see **Gliciphila albifrons**
  NUNBIRD see under **Monasa flavirostris**

WHITE-HEADED
  BLACK CHAT see under **Myrmecocichla nigra**
  BUFFALO WEAVER see **Dinemellia dinemelli**
  VULTURE see **Trigonoceps occipitalis**
  WOOD HOOPOE see under **Phoeniculus purpureus**

WHITE-NECKED
  CRANE see **Grus vipio**
  RAVEN see **Corvultur albicollis**
  STORK see **Dissoura episcopus**
  ROCKFOWL see under **Picathartes gymnocephalus**

WHITE-PLUMED ANTBIRD see **Pithys albifrons**

WHITE-QUILLED ROCK PIGEON see **Petrophassa albipennis**

WHITE-RUMPED SANDPIPER see **Calidris fuscicollis**

WHITE-TAILED
  EAGLE see **Haliaeetus albicilla**
  PTARMIGAN see **Lagopus leucurus**
  SHRIKE see **Lanioturdus torquatus**
  TROGON see **Trogon viridis**
  TROPIC BIRD see **Phaethon lepturus**

WHITE-THROATED
  BEE-EATER see **Aerops albicollis**
  ROBIN CHAT see **Cossypha humeralis**
  ROCK-THRUSH see **Monticola gularis**
  SEEDEATER see **Serinus albogularis**
  SPARROW see **Zonotrichia albicollis**
  SWALLOW see **Hirundo albigularis**
  TINAMOU see **Tinamus guttatus**
  WARBLER see **Gerygone olivacea**

WHITE-TIPPED SICKLEBILL see **Eutoxeres aquila**

WHITE-VENTED BULBUL see **Pycnonotus barbatus**

WHITE-WHISKERED PUFFBIRD see **Malacoptila panamensis**

WHITE-WINGED
  BECARD see under **Pachyramphus marginatus**
  CHOUGH see **Corcorax melanorhamphus**
  TRILLER see **Lalage sueurii**
  TRUMPETER see **Psophia leucoptera**

WHITE'S THRUSH see under **Turdus viscivorus**

WHITETHROAT see **Sylvia communis**

WHITETHROAT, LESSER see **Sylvia curruca**

WHOOPING CRANE see **Grus americana**

WHYDAH,
  BROAD-TAILED PARADISE see under **Steganura paradisaea**
  PINTAILED see **Vidua macroura**
  SHARP-TAILED PARADISE see **Steganura paradisaea**

WIDOW BIRD,
  LONG-TAILED see **Euplectes progne**
  YELLOW-BACKED see **Euplectes macrourus**

YELLOW-SHOULDERED see under **Euplectes macrourus**

WILD TURKEY see **Meleagris gallopavo**

WILLET see **Catoptrophorus semipalmatus**

WILLOW
  GROUSE see **Lagopus lagopus**
  TIT see **Parus montanus**
  WARBLER see **Phylloscopus trochilus**
  WARBLER, PLAIN see under **Phylloscopus collybita**

Wilsonia canadensis *Parulidae*
CANADA WARBLER   5½ ins
Nearctic: breeds limited area Canada W to Central Manitoba, S Alberta and in USA to N Connecticut, mountains N Georgia, Central Minnesota; winters Guatemala to Ecuador, Peru. Habitat broadleaved and mixed forests with thick undergrowth, borders of swamps, riparian scrub; scrub and young secondary growth on migration. ♂: upperparts grey, forehead usually black, crown spotted black; line of bill to eye and orbit yellow; lores black, stripe running into distinctive 'necklace' of black spots on yellow underparts; under tail coverts white. Back washed greenish in autumn, breast spots tipped yellow. ♀ duller, only traces of necklace; upperparts greener in autumn. Legs flesh, bill dark, eyes dark brown. Active fly catcher, feeding mainly near ground but sallying into air after insects, clicking bill. Song loud, rich irregular, notes often slurred; call *chip*, common to many relatives. Breeds May and June; nest of dead leaves, bark, grass, lined finer materials, rootlets, hair, on or near ground in moss, stump, tree roots, under laurels, ferns, generally damp area, sometimes over water. 4 white eggs, evenly speckled brown, incubated ♀ *c.* 12 days; young fly after same period. **902**

Wilsonia pusilla *Parulidae*
WILSON'S WARBLER   5 ins
Nearctic: breeds Alaska, most of Canada to NE USA; also western USA to Central W Texas, S California; winters New Mexico to Panama. Habitat: low scrub in open wet areas: by streams and pools, bogs, bushy swamps especially with alders, willows. ♂: upperparts bright olive green; crown glossy black; forehead, cheeks, 'eyebrow', underparts bright yellow. ♀ usually lacks black cap; crown feathers both sexes narrowly tipped olive in autumn. Legs flesh, bill: upper brownish black, lower flesh pink, eyes very dark brown. Immature's 'black' eyes show up against yellow forehead. Very active but most feeding within 10 ft of ground; gleans insects off leaves, also makes aerial sallies. Twitches tail spasmodically. Song: weak, rapid, chattering series of *chip* notes; calls: 'quiet lisp' and harsher *chut*. Breeds early June in NE USA; nest almost ball of leaves, moss, grass, rootlets, lined finer grass, hair, on wet ground in moss or sedge tussock, sometimes few feet up in dense vegetation. Usually 4 white eggs, marked shades of brown, incubated ♀ *c.* 12 days; young fly after same period. **903**

WILSON'S WARBLER see **Wilsonia pusilla**

WINDING CISTICOLA see **Cisticola galactotes**

WINTER WREN see **Troglodytes troglodytes**

WIRE-TAILED SWALLOW see **Hirundo smithii**

WONDER TREERUNNER see **Daphoenositta miranda**

WONGA DOVE see **Leucosarcia melanoleuca**

WOOD
  DOVE, BLACK-BILLED BLUE-SPOTTED see **Turtur abyssinicus**
  DOVE, BLUE-SPOTTED see under **Turtur abyssinicus**
  DOVE, EMERALD SPOTTED see **Turtur chalcospilos**

HOOPOE, FOREST see under **Phoeniculus purpureus**
HOOPOE, GREEN see **Phoeniculus purpureus**
HOOPOE, WHITE-HEADED see under **Phoeniculus purpureus**
LARK see **Lullula arborea**
OWL, AFRICAN see **Ciccaba woodfordii**
OWL, JAVAN BROWN see **Strix leptogrammica**
OWL, MALAYSIAN BROWN see **Strix leptogrammica**
PARTRIDGE, BUFF-CROWNED see **Dendrortyx leucophrys**
PARTRIDGE, FERRUGINOUS see **Caloperdix oculea**
PARTRIDGE, GREEN see **Rollulus roulroul**
PEWEE, EASTERN see **Contopus virens**
SANDPIPER see **Tringa glareola**
SHRIKE, BALD-HEADED see **Pityriasis gymnocephala**
STORK see **Mycteria americana**
SWALLOW, DUSKY see under **Artamus superciliosus**
SWALLOW, MASKED see under **Artamus superciliosus**
SWALLOW, WHITE-BROWED see **Artamus superciliosus**
SWALLOW, WHITE-BREASTED see **Artamus leucorhynchus**
THRUSH see **Hylocichla mustelina**
WARBLER see **Phylloscopus sibilatrix**

WOODCHAT see **Lanius senator**

WOODCOCK see **Scolopax rusticola**

WOODCOCK, AMERICAN see **Philohela minor**

WOODCREEPER,
  BUFF-THROATED see **Xiphorhynchus guttatus**
  WEDGE-BILLED see **Glyphorhynchus spirurus**

WOODHEWER, COCOA see **Xiphorhynchus guttatus**

WOODLAND KINGFISHER see **Halcyon senegalensis**

WOODNYMPH HUMMINGBIRD, FORK-TAILED see **Thalurania furcata**

WOODPECKER,
  ACORN see **Melanerpes formicivorus**
  BEARDED see **Thripias namaquus**
  BENNETT'S see **Campethera bennettii**
  BLACK AND WHITE see **Phloeoceastes melanoleucos**
  BLACK-CHEEKED see **Melanerpes pucherani**
  CEYLON CRIMSON-BACKED see **Chrysocolaptes lucidus**
  CHESTNUT see **Celeus elegans**
  CRIMSON-CRESTED see **Phloeoceastes melanoleucos**
  DOWNY see under **Dendrocopos villosus**
  FINE SPOTTED see **Campethera punctuligera**
  GILA see **Centurus uropygialis**
  GOLDEN-TAILED see **Campethera abingoni**
  GREAT SPOTTED see **Dendrocopos major**
  GREEN see under **Picus canus**
  GREY-HEADED see **Picus canus**
  GROUND see **Geocolaptes olivaceus**
  HAIRY see **Dendrocopos villosus**
  LESSER SPOTTED see **Dendrocopos minor**
  RED-BELLIED see **Centurus carolinus**
  RED-CROWNED see **Melanerpes rubricapillus**
  SYRIAN see **Dendrocopos syriacus**
  YELLOW-CRESTED see **Celeus elegans**

WOODPIGEON see **Columba palumbus**

WOOLLY-NECKED STORK see **Dissoura episcopus**

WORM-EATING WARBLER see **Helmitheros vermivorus**

WREN,
BANDED BLUE see under **Malurus callainus**
BICOLOURED see **Campylorhynchus griseus**
BLACK-AND-WHITE see **Malurus leucopterus**
BLACK-BACKED see **Malurus melanotus**
BLACK GRASS see **Amytornis housei**
BLUE see **Malurus cyaneus**
CACTUS see **Campylorhynchus bruneicapillas**
CHESTNUT-BREASTED see **Cyphorhinus thoracicus**
COMMON see **Troglodytes troglodytes**
LONG-BILLED MARSH see **Telmatodytes palustris**
PURPLE-BACKED see **Malurus assimilis**
RED-BACKED see **Malurus melanocephalus**
RED-WINGED see under **Malurus lamberti**
RUFOUS FIELD see **Calamanthus campestris**
SHORT-BILLED MARSH see under **Telmatodytes palustris**
SPOT-BREASTED see **Thryothurus maculipectus**
SPOTTED see **Campylorhynchus griseus**
SPOTTED SCRUB see **Sericornis maculatus**
STRIATED FIELD see under **Calamanthus campestris**
TURQUOISE see **Malurus callainus**
VARIEGATED see **Malurus lamberti**
WHITE-BROWED SCRUB see **Sericornis frontalis**
WINTER see **Troglodytes troglodytes**
ZAPATA see **Ferminia cerverai**

WREN TIT see **Chaemia fasciata**

WREN-THRUSH see **Zeledonia coronata**

WRYBILL PLOVER see **Anarhynchus frontalis**

WRYNECK see **Jynx torquilla**

Xema sabini *Laridae*
SABINE'S GULL   *c.* 13½ ins
Holarctic: breeds Arctic Ocean, islands and coast S to SW Alaska and N Hudson Bay in West; Spitsbergen, Franz Joseph Land, and N Siberia from Taimyr Peninsula to Bering Strait; winters temperate pelagic waters, moving in Pacific to coast of Peru. Hood dark grey with black border where it joins white neck; lower mantle, back and scapulars pale slate-grey, rump, underparts and forked tail white; wing, primary region up to wrist black, conspicuous white triangle on secondaries, rest pale slate-grey. In winter forehead and crown white, nape and hind neck mottled brown-black, lower neck white tinged with ash-grey. Legs greyish, stout bill black with yellow tip, eyes dark brown with vermilion orbital skin. Immature: mottled brown upperparts, broad brown-black terminal band to white tail, dusky tip to bill. Usually solitary or in small parties; picks up food by skimming surface of sea or running over ground; takes insects, their larvae, earthworms, crustacea and other aquatic animals. Call: short, harsh grating note, also squeaking. Breeds from late May, in colonies or isolated, on islets in low, marshy tundra, often near ice and Arctic Terns, *Sterna paradisaea*, whose eggs it may rob; 3 brown to olive-buff eggs spotted with darker olive-brown in hollow with little grass lining; both sexes incubate *c.* 24 days. **341**

Xenicus gilviventris *Xenicidae*
ROCK WREN   3¾ ins
Confined to South Island, New Zealand; resident high level scrub, screes, moraines and bare slopes of mountains. Upperparts rather dull brownish green; thin pale yellow stripe in black patch at 'wrist' on wing; very short tail; 'eyebrow' creamy white; underparts grey-brown, tinged yellow on flanks. ♀ browner above than ♂. Legs, with large feet, long hind toe, blackish; thin pointed bill dark grey; eyes dark brown. Bobs and bows on alighting; flies few yards between rocks when feeding. Diet: insects, spiders; fruit of alpine plants. Call: 3 penetrating notes, emphasis on first; also thin piping note. Breeds September to November, building substantial domed nest of plant debris, lined feathers, in rock crevice. 2 or 3 white eggs. Both parents feed young on insects: grasshoppers, moths, beetles (M. F. Soper). **576**

Xenopirostris xenopirostris *Vangidae*
LAFRESNAYE'S VANGA   *c.* 10 ins
Confined to Madagascar: resident forest canopy, scrub areas of sandy subdesert. Upperparts to tail grey; 'untidy' crown; face, bib black; underparts from throat, nape white; legs slaty grey; heavy, compressed and hooked bill, with uptilted lower mandible, grey; eyes reddish. Solitary, pairs, family parties, sometimes with other forest species. Usually perched in tree or bush, sometimes conspicuously on top, where utters sudden, sharp whistle, repeated at intervals (A. L. Rand). Diet: insects (ants, beetles, grasshoppers). Breeds December, building substantial nest in tree or bush, laying 3 or 4 whitish eggs, marked brown. **658**

Xenops minutus *Furnariidae*
PLAIN XENOPS   5 ins
Neotropical: Mexico to S America E of Andes: Bolivia, S Brazil, Paraguay, NE Argentina; W of Andes to W Ecuador; resident forests sea level to 5,000 ft; also secondary woodland, plantations, gardens. Upperparts uniform umber brown; primaries black with buffy yellow bar, secondaries dark brown and basally cinnamon; tertiaries mostly cinnamon; central tail feathers light cinnamon, next two pairs black, outermost black only at base; pale stripe over and behind eye, ear coverts brown, black-edged, with white stripe below; underparts olive brown; legs grey, stout upturned bill pale horn, eyes brown. Extracts insects and their larvae, especially ants, from inside slender decaying twigs, vines, leaf stalks, hammering them open with bill, then inserted and pushed upward. Solitary, roosting in tree hole. Both sexes have fine, sharp, rapid trilling song, repeated at daybreak; sharp call in flight, also to attract mate. Breeds December to May Central America, in tree or branch hole, 5 to 30 ft up, excavating like small woodpecker and lining chamber with bast fibres. Both parents incubate 2 glossy white eggs 15-17 days, feed young until they fledge 13-14 days. Probably 2 broods. **565**

XENOPS, PLAIN see **Xenops minutus**

Xiphorhynchus guttatus *Dendrocolaptidae*
BUFF-THROATED WOODCREEPER or COCOA WOODHEWER   9½ (bill 1)-11 (bill 1½) ins
Neotropical: Central America (Guatemala to Panama); Trinidad and Tobago; S America E of Andes to N Bolivia, Amazonian and coastal Brazil; W of Andes in Colombia; resident in forests, plantations, mangrove swamps. Generally brown to russet brown; wings, rump and tail rufous chestnut, blackish shafts extending as spines; crown blackish with many buff spots; hindneck (and mantle in some races) streaked buff; throat buff, upper breast streaked buff; underparts olive grey in race *X.g. susurrans;* powerful bill pale horn to black, nearly straight, eyes brown. 'Walks' or runs up tree or branch, often in spiral, probing for insects, their larvae and eggs in crevices and prising off bark; holds itself against trunk like woodpecker. Feeds on ground upon insects disturbed by army ants. Distinctive call: *c.* 5 notes up, followed by 10 down scale; also short *kee-you* and loud musical whistle. Breeds April to August Trinidad, building nest of stems, leaves and plant down in natural or old woodpecker's hole in tree. 2 white eggs incubated by ♀ and ♂ for perhaps *c.* 2 weeks; young tended for perhaps 2½ weeks by both parents. **560**

YELLOW
CANARY see **Serinus flaviventris**
CARDINAL see **Gubernatrix cristata**
FIGBIRD see **Sphecotheres flaviventris**
ROBIN see **Eopsaltria australis**
WAGTAIL see **Motacilla flava**
WARBLER see **Dendroica patechia**
WHITE-EYE see **Zosterops senegalensis**

YELLOW-BACKED WIDOW BIRD see **Euplectes macrourus**

YELLOW-BELLIED
EREMOMELA see **Eremomela icteropygialis**

FLYCATCHER see **Empidonax flaviventris**
SAPSUCKER see **Sphyrapicus varius**
TROGON, GREATER see **Trogon viridis**

YELLOW-BILLED
HORNBILL see **Tockus flavirostris**
JACAMAR see **Galbula albirostris**
KITE see **Milvus migrans aegyptius**
NUNBIRD see **Monasa flavirostris**
OXPECKER see **Buphagus africanus**
SHEATHBILL see **Chionis alba**
STORK see **Mycteria ibis**
TROPIC BIRD see **Phaethon lepturus**

YELLOW-BREASTED CHAT see **Icteria virens**

YELLOW-COLLARED LOVEBIRD see **Agapornis personata**

YELLOW-CRESTED WOODPECKER see **Celeus elegans**

YELLOW-CROWNED NIGHT HERON see **Nyctanassa violacea**

YELLOW-FACED HONEYEATER see **Meliphaga chrysops**

YELLOW-FRONTED TINKER BIRD see **Pogoniulus chrysoconus**

YELLOW-KNOBBED CURASSOW see **Crax daubentoni**

YELLOW-LEGGED HONEYCREEPER see **Cyanerpes caeruleus**

YELLOW-RUMPED
CACIQUE see **Cacicus cela**
TANAGER see **Ramphocelus icteronotus**

YELLOW-SHAFTED FLICKER see **Colaptes auratus**

YELLOW-SHOULDERED
BLACKBIRD see **Agelaius xanthomus**
WIDOW BIRD see under **Euplectes macrourus**

YELLOW-TAILED THORNBILL see **Acanthiza chrysorrhoa**

YELLOW-THROATED
LONGCLAW see **Macronyx croceus**
WARBLER see **Dendroica dominica**

YELLOW-TIPPED PARDALOTE see **Pardalotus striatus**

YELLOW-TUFTED HONEYEATER see **Meliphaga melanops**

YELLOW-WINGED HONEYEATER see **Meliornis novaehollandiae**

YELLOWHAMMER see **Emberiza citrinella**

ZANZIBAR
SOMBRE GREENBUL see **Andropadus importunus**
RED BISHOP see under **Euplectes orix**

ZAPATA WREN see **Ferminia cerverai**

ZEBRA FINCH see **Taenopygia castanotis**

Zeledonia coronata *Muscicapidae*: *Turdinae*
WREN-THRUSH   *c.* 5½ ins
Neotropical: Costa Rica to W Panama; resident humid forest with dense undergrowth from 5,000 ft, commonest 7,000 to 10,000 ft. Crown tawny, edged dull black; forehead, lores slate grey; hindneck dusky olive; upperparts to upper tail coverts dark brownish olive; wings, tail feathers brown; cheeks, chin, underparts slate grey; flanks, under tail coverts dark olive; legs, bill brown to blackish; eyes dark brown. Creeps about fallen trunks, branches, searching for insects and

larvae. Call: same note repeated 6 to 8 times at equal intervals.

Zenaida auriculata *Columbidae*
EARED DOVE   *c.* 9½ ins
Neotropical: races distributed across Is of S Caribbean, southern Lesser Antilles, and S America down to 40° S. Habitat: arid or semi-arid open country with some bush or tree cover, and cultivated land. Looks much like Mourning Dove, *Zenaida macroura*, but shorter, less graduated tail (lacks white in West Indian race) and stronger bill; lower facial markings dark iridescent blue rather than dull black. Legs purplish red, bill blackish, eyes dark brown with dark grey orbital skin. Largely terrestrial, often in flocks at good feeding and roosting places. Diet: seeds, cultivated grain and some small animals. Call: loud first *coo*, second hoarse, followed by 2 or 3 softer *coos;* varies with race. Occasionally nests in large colonies e.g. NE Brazil, usually singly or in clusters, building typical twig platform in trees and shrubs or scanty nest on ground amongst trees. 2 white eggs, incubated *c.* 14 days. **381**

Zenaida galapagoensis *Columbidae*
GALAPAGOS DOVE   *c.* 12½ ins
Galapagos Is: dry rocky low country, particularly with trees, some bushes or tree cacti. Thickly set and upright in stance with longish down curved bill. ♂: head, neck and breast dull wine-red to purplish pink, shading to buffish belly and pale grey on under tail coverts; upperparts earthy brown with black and white markings on wing coverts and scapulars; 2 black stripes sandwiching white patch on side of head. ♀: duller and paler, breast washed with brown which predominates on head. Legs red, eyes brown with light blue orbital skin. Still tame despite persecution, spends much time on ground flicking soil back and sideways looking for seeds to eat; agile runner and walker but worse flyer than most other doves. Calls: ♂, soft deep *bob-bob-bob-rururur-bububurr;* ♀, *burrr.* Nests March to September, early peak, using a few twigs in hollows and crevices in rocks or on ground in sheltered depression. 2 white eggs, incubated *c.* 13 days; young fly *c.* 17 days. **382**

Zenaida macroura *Columbidae*
MOURNING DOVE   *c.* 12 ins
Nearctic, N Neotropical: breeds British Columbia, Manitoba, S Ontario and Nova Scotia S to Mexico, Bahamas, Cuba and Hispaniola; leaves more northern parts in winter. Habitat: open woodland, cultivated country with some cover, arid areas and semi-desert where water available. Light brown upperparts shading to bluish grey on centre of crown, nape and outer wing; black markings on wing coverts and scapulars; upper throat pale, most of head reddish buff with black streaks behind and below eye. Deep vinous pink breast, rest of underparts buff; flanks blue-grey; long white-edged graduated tail. Legs purplish red, thin bill blackish with reddish gape edge, eyes dark brown, narrow orbital skin greenish blue or light blue. Flight swift, wings make whistling sound; usually in pairs or small parties, larger flocks at good feeding places or roosts; ground feeder, taking seeds, cultivated grain and some small animals. Call: faint disyllabic *coo* followed by 2 or 3 louder *coos*. Breeding season variable; builds twig platform, often on old nest of another species, occasionally on ground or ledge of building. 2 white eggs, incubated 14-16 days, young fly 13-15 days. 2 or 3 broods. **383**

Zonifer tricolor see **Vanellus tricolor**

Zonotrichia albicollis *Emberizidae: Emberizinae*
WHITE-THROATED SPARROW   6¾ ins
Nearctic: breeds Canada, N USA E of Rockies, to New England, mountains NE Pennsylvania, Central Wisconsin, S Montana; winters Massachusetts, S Pennsylvania, Ohio Valley, Missouri, S to Florida, Gulf Coast, NE Mexico. Habitat dense cover: forest

clearings, edges, scrubby pastures; winter flocks in similar areas. Upperparts usual 'sparrow' pattern with 2 white wingbars; head striped white and black with yellow lores; white throat bordered dark moustachial stripes; cheeks, breast greyish shading to white underparts, buff on flanks. Autumn ♂ has head pattern obscured light brown streaks. ♀ has brown crown, throat, flanks, streaked dark brown. Call: *sst* song, described as 'melancholy', rendered *Old Sam Peabody, Peabody, Peabody, Peabody*. Feeds chiefly on ground, scratching invertebrates from litter; also wild fruits. Breeds May, June; ♀ building nest of grass, moss, rootlets, lined fine bents, hair in hollow on ground, mossy hummock over-hung by vegetation, occasionally up to 2 ft in conifer. 4 or 5 pale greenish eggs, heavily marked brown, incubated ♀; ♀ and ♂ feed young, who fly 12-14 days. **866**

Zonotrichia leucophrys *Emberizidae: Emberizinae*
WHITE-CROWNED SPARROW   7 ins
Nearctic: breeds NW North America (including Greenland) SE to S Quebec, S to New Mexico, S California; winters from Mississippi, S Missouri, S Colorado, Oregon to Central Mexico. Habitat extensive scrub close to open grassy areas; riparian dwarf willow thickets in N, also windswept coastal areas; similarly in winter. ♂ very like White-throated, *Z. albicollis*, but mantle greyer, black and white head pattern shows broad white crown stripe bordered black; white throat merges into off-white underparts. Minor differences between races. Legs light brown, bill pink or yellowish, eyes dark brown. Juvenile has buff crown, ear coverts. Partial expansion of crown when excited shows white feathers as low crest. Posture more erect than *Z. albicollis*. Flocks in winter, feeding mainly off ground, in autumn with other species on weed seeds. Call: *chick;* sweet plaintive song of 5 or 6 notes. Breeds from end May, building bulky cup nest of twigs, grass, bark, lined rootlets, hair, on ground under bush or close to it in bush. 4 pale greenish eggs, thickly spotted 2 shades brown; incubation and fledging much as *Z. albicollis*. **867**

Zoothera dauma see under **Turdus viscivorus**

Zosterops kikuyuensis *Zosteropidae*
KIKUYU WHITE-EYE   5 ins
Ethiopian: 3 races in NW Uganda, Kenya, Tanzania; resident highland forests, bamboo thickets, gardens. Upperparts bright green; broad yellow area forehead; white eye-ring large and conspicuous; underparts: throat yellow, centre breast, flanks yellowish-green; legs, bill dark, eyes brown. Race *Z.k. mbuluensis* (S Kenya, N Tanzania) lighter green above; *chyulunsis* (SE Kenya) underparts rich canary yellow. Immature darker, duller. Habits much as *Z. senegalensis;* gregarious outside breeding season; Chyulu birds among giant lobelias in clearings. High-pitched piping call in flock; song, soft clear warble. Mainly insectivorous. Breeding season variable; ♀ and ♂ build deep cup nest beard moss or lichen, usually slung lateral fork of small tree or bush. Usually 2 elongated pale blue eggs, incubated ♀ and ♂ 11-12 days; both parents feed young, who fly 10-13 days. Probably 2 broods. **830**

Zosterops lateralis *Zosteropidae*
GREY-BREASTED WHITE-EYE or
SILVEREYE   4¾ ins
Australasia: E and SE continental Australia; Tasmania; colonised New Zealand 1856, several offshore islands subsequently. Habitat: forest; sub-alpine scrub up to *c.* 3,500 ft (NZ); settled countryside with trees. Upperparts bright yellowish green; flight, tail feathers brown, outer webs yellowish green; upper back, scapulars tinged grey; underparts pale greyish white but variable; sides, flanks chestnut brown; under wing coverts white; eye ring white, lores black. Legs pale brown, bill brown, eyes light brown. ♀ more cinnamon brown; immature lacks eye ring. Conspicuous winter flocks (in which pairs remain mated) come readily to

human food (NZ). Territorial chases and various aggressive displays, including wing-fluttering, bill clattering. Flock calls chirping *cli cli cli* or plaintive *creee;* alarm at nest *swang:* many other notes and 3 types song (one by both sexes) identified (C. A. Fleming). Food mainly insects, fruits, nectar from native and introduced flowers. Breeds August to February (NZ); ♀ and ♂ build nest of grasses, other plant fibres, bound cobwebs, attached to foliage of outer canopy like hammock, 3 to 30 ft; also on ferns, bamboos. 3 or 4 pale blue eggs incubated by ♀ and ♂ 11-12 days; both feed young, who fly 9-12 days. 2, sometimes 3 broods. **831**

Zosterops pallida *Zosteropidae*
PALE WHITE-EYE   4½ ins
Ethiopian: Ethiopia, Pare Mtns (NE Tanzania), Mt Kulal (N Kenya), SW and S Africa; resident various woodland types; introduced plantations, gardens (S Africa). Upperparts, sides of neck, face moss green; forehead yellow; white eye ring, lores black; underparts: throat, under tail coverts yellow; breast, belly whitish; flanks pale buff. Legs greyish, bill black, eyes brown. Immature duller. Pairs and small parties rove canopy like other species, following each other from tree to tree. Call: soft, low-pitched *peep peep;* song subdued warble, including mimicry, ending loud *too chee titti chee chee,* repeated. Mainly insectivorous. Breeds April to December (Ethiopia); ♀ and ♂ build very deep cup fine grasses in bush or tree. 2 pale blue eggs incubated ♀ and ♂ 11-12 days; both parents feed young, who fly 10 to 13 days. Hybridises with Green White-eye, *Z. virens,* and may therefore be conspecific. **832**

Zosterops palpebrosa *Zosteropidae*
INDIAN WHITE-EYE   4 ins
SE Palaearctic, Oriental: E Afghanistan, Indian subcontinent, Thailand, Malaysia, SW China, Indochina, Indonesia to Flores; hill forests (to 5,000 ft Burma), cultivated land, gardens, mangroves. Upperparts yellow brown, wings, tail darker; eye white ringed, lores dark brown; underparts: throat, breast yellow, belly white, under tail coverts yellow. Legs olive grey, sharp bill black, eyes yellow brown. Behaves as relatives. Flock call querulous *chee chee chee* or *tseer tseer;* short song by ♂ begins almost inaudibly, ends almost harshly, repeated without variation. Feeds in trees on insects (weevils, ants, their eggs and larvae), buds, seeds, fruits. Breeds mid April to mid July Burma; ♀ and ♂ build nest fine grass bound cob-webs, suspended in fork of twigs on shrub or tree, 2 or 4 pale blue eggs incubated ♀ and ♂ 11-12 days; both parents feed young, who fly *c.* 12 days. 2 broods. **833**

Zosterops senegalensis *Zosteropidqe*
YELLOW WHITE-EYE   4 ins
Ethiopian: Senegal to Eritrea, S through E and Central Africa to Portuguese East Africa, S and SW Africa; resident open thorn bush, *Brachystegia,* acacia, savannah woodland, cultivated areas, gardens. Upperparts powdery yellow green, forehead, yellow; narrow white ring round eye, black confined to edge of mandible and below eye; underparts canary yellow. Legs greyish, small bill black, eyes brown. Immature darker. Pairs, parties search bushes, dense foliaged trees for insects, frequently with other species, e.g. sunbirds; fond of bathing. Flock call weak, piping in flight, twittering when feeding; also 'short tinny note'; ♂ has soft warbling song. Food almost entirely insects, especially small larvae; small fruits in season. Breeding varies within range; June (N Nigeria), April to June (Uganda); ♀ and ♂ build nest of grasses, tendrils, decorated lichen, lined hair, in upright fork or suspended from lateral. 2 or 3 clear blue or white eggs, incubated ♀ and ♂ 11-12 days; both parents feed young, who fly 10-13 days.

Zosterops virens see under **Z. pallida**